THE SCRIBNER QUARTO OF MODERN LITERATURE

THE SCRIBNER QUARTO OF MODERN LITERATURE

Edited by
A. WALTON LITZ

CHARLES SCRIBNER'S SONS
NEW YORK

Library of Congress Cataloging in Publication Data
Main entry under title:

The Scribner quarto of modern literature.

Includes index.
1. American literature—20th century. 2. English literature—20th century. I. Litz, A. Walton.
PS535.5.S36 820'.8'0091 77-13423
ISBN 0-684-15336-X

1 3 5 7 9 11 13 15 17 19 Q/C 20 18 16 14 12 10 8 6 4 2

Printed in the United States of America

Cover Photo by Tom Pix from Peter Arnold

Acknowledgments

SHORT STORIES

"The Eyes" by Edith Wharton from *The Edith Wharton Reader* is reprinted by permission of Charles Scribner's Sons. Copyright 1910 Charles Scribner's Sons.

E. M. Forster, "The Other Side of the Hedge." From *The Collected Tales of E. M. Forster.* Published 1947 by Alfred A. Knopf, Inc. Reprinted by permission.

James Joyce, "Two Gallants." From *Dubliners* by James Joyce. Originally published by B. W. Huebsch, Inc. in 1916. Copyright © 1967 by the Estate of James Joyce. All rights reserved. Reprinted by permission of The Viking Press.

D. H. Lawrence, "The Rocking-Horse Winner." From *The Complete Short Stories of D. H. Lawrence,* Vol. III. Copyright 1933 by The Estate of D. H. Lawrence, © 1961 by Angelo Ravagli & C. M. Weekley, Executors of The Estate of Frieda Lawrence Ravagli. Reprinted by permission of The Viking Press.

Willa Cather, "Neighbour Rosicky." Copyright 1932 by Willa Cather and renewed 1960 by the Executors of the Estate of Willa Cather. Reprinted from *Obscure Destinies,* by Willa Cather, by permission of Alfred A. Knopf, Inc.

Sherwood Anderson, "A Death in the Woods." Reprinted by permission of Harold Ober Associates Incorporated. Copyright © 1926 by The American Mercury, Inc. Renewed 1953 by Eleanor Copenhaver Anderson.

Ernest Hemingway, "Big Two-Hearted River" (copyright 1925 Charles Scribner's Sons) is reprinted by permission of Charles Scribner's Sons from *In Our Time* by Ernest Hemingway.

F. Scott Fitzgerald, "Babylon Revisited" (copyright 1931 The Curtis Publishing Company) is reprinted by permission of Charles Scribner's Sons from *Taps at Reveille* by F. Scott Fitzgerald.

William Faulkner, "Dry September." Copyright 1930 and renewed 1958 by William Faulkner. Reprinted from *Collected Stories of William Faulkner* by permission of Random House, Inc.

Katherine Anne Porter, "Flowering Judas." Copyright, 1930, 1958, by Katherine Anne Porter. Reprinted from her volume *Flowering Judas and Other Stories* by permission of Harcourt Brace Jovanovich, Inc.

Eudora Welty, "Why I Live at the P.O." Copyright, 1941, 1949 by Eudora Welty. Reprinted from her volume *A Curtain of Green and Other Stories* by permission of Harcourt Brace Jovanovich, Inc.

Graham Greene, "The Basement Room." From *Twenty-one Stories* by Graham Greene. Copyright 1947, © renewed 1975 by Graham Greene. Reprinted by permission of The Viking Press.

(*continued on page 591*)

PREFACE

My primary aim in planning *The Scribner Quarto of Modern Literature* was to include as much important literature as possible within a manageable volume. The richness and variety of the works included (three novels, five plays, twenty short stories, and a broad representation of poetry and literary criticism) should make the *Quarto* a suitable text for a wide range of courses in modern literature. In choosing the works, I was guided first by a concern for their literary quality, and only secondarily by a desire to provide an historical survey of the various genres. However, the Short Story and Poetry sections were planned along historical lines, as their Introductions indicate, and reflect my view of the history of modern literature (problems of space and copyright made it impossible to establish any true historical structure in the Novel and Drama sections). The Critical Essays in the last section were chosen because they raise large issues of interpretation and literary value that are directly relevant to the preceding poetry, drama, and fiction. Most of the essays focus on problems of language and the relationship between literature and society as found in the major genres. Many of the essays are by writers included elsewhere in the volume, or comment upon works found in the earlier sections.

The selections begin at the turn of the century and extend to the present decade. Two poets from an earlier period—Gerard Manley Hopkins and Emily Dickinson—are included because their works were not available until well into this century, when they had a profound impact on the development of modern poetry. Although my major emphasis has been upon the established writers who were the makers of modern literature in the first half of the century, more recent writers are well represented. An attempt has been made to keep a balance between British and American authors, but where a subject or form was dominated by one country—as in the case of American writers of short fiction—I have not hesitated to reflect that emphasis.

I wish to thank Peter Givler and Helen McInnis, of Charles Scribner's Sons, whose advice made this a better book; and Lawrence Davidow, who helped in many ways and was responsible for the excellent Glossary of Critical Terms.

A.W.L.

CONTENTS

DRAMA 293

POETRY 421

THE SHORT STORY

The modern short story had its distant origin in the art of the traditional story-teller, who held his audience with a tale that could be recited at one sitting or with a cycle of short tales; and much of its power still derives from a close association with the oral tradition. Even the most experimental of contemporary short story writers, such as Donald Barthelme, runs a great risk when he strays too far from the ancient elements of the tale: suspense, concentration, and consistency of tone. The short story as a self-conscious art form, however, did not appear until the early nineteenth century, just as the novel did not evolve out of other long fictions until the beginning of the eighteenth century; and like the novel, the short story was the product of a special convergence of social and artistic forces. One factor that accelerated the writing of short stories in the early nineteenth century was the rise and proliferation of the literary magazines, which could only handle the novel in serial form and therefore created a demand for the short, self-contained story. But another and deeper force that shaped the genre was Romantic poetry with its emphasis on intensity, the lyric moment, and unity of atmosphere and effect. In the criticism and practice of Edgar Allan Poe, the first master of the short story, a Romantic aesthetic is used to justify the length and structure of the tale. The short story turned out to be an ideal form for handling fantasy or the grotesque, since it emphasized "poetic" qualities which could express the inner life, and for that reason it may have flourished more readily in Europe and the United States than in England. Romance and fantasy have always found a more secure home outside of England. The strong tradition of the English novel of manners tended to produce miniature novels, novellas, rather than the classic short story. By contrast, the American scene, with its "thinness" of inherited manners and social forms, and the American Puritan imagination, with its penchant for symbolism and the grotesque, were ideally suited for the short story. Poe, Hawthorne, Melville, and Henry James made major contributions to the genre, along with a host of lesser American writers, and the selections which follow show that the dominance of American short story writers has continued into the twentieth century. Frank O'Connor was simply stating an historical fact when he declared, in 1963, that "the Americans have handled the short story so wonderfully that one can say that it is a national art form." Even such a personal and idiosyncratic English writer as D. H. Lawrence went to school to the nineteenth-century American masters of the shorter form.

By the turn of the century the economic forces that had produced the classic short story had greatly intensified. Magazines were multiplying to satisfy a mass audience, which was later the audience of radio and television and the motion pictures. The demand for short stories sharply increased, especially for those that could be easily written to a formula. In 1891 William Dean Howells speculated on the reasons for the remarkable success of the short story in America:

> I am not sure that the Americans have not brought the short story nearer perfection in the all-round sense than almost any other people, and for reasons very simple and near at hand. It might be argued from the national hurry and impatience that it was a literary form peculiarly adapted to the American temperament, but I suspect that its extraordinary development among us is owing much more to more tangible facts. The success of American magazines, which is nothing less than prodigious, is only commensurate with their excellence. . . . The serial novels they must have, of course; but rather more of course they must have short stories, and by operation of the law of supply and demand, the short stories, abundant in quantity and excellent in quality, are forthcoming because they are wanted.

Howell's diagnosis of the literary marketplace was shrewd and accurate, but his nineteenth-century faith in "supply and demand" made him far too sanguine about the impact on quality. As the demand for short stories grew, the literary equivalent of "Gresham's Law" came into effect: stories which were merely technically competent drove out the unusual or distinguished ones. Formula books on "How to Write the Short Story" became commonplace, and the genre was in danger of being reduced to lifeless rules concerning plot, character, and subject-matter. Edgar Allan Poe had spoken of the "unity of effect or impression" that sets the short story apart from the novel and had placed the short story just below the lyric poem in his hierarchy of literary forms. He had set down certain characteristics of length and structure that would promote the subordination of every detail to a single design. But Poe's "rules" were practical and flexible, based on his own experience as a craftsman, and he would surely have been delighted by the wide range in techniques and length found in the following selections. The line between a long "short story" and a short novel or novella is not easily drawn, and part of the power of the short story has been its ability to assimilate many characteristics of the novel while maintaining a certain purity of form. The mechanical "rules" established for the short story in the early years of this century threatened this essential openness and flexibility, and the short story was not liberated from the formal prison created by its own popularity until a new combination of forces, both social and artistic, revivified the genre.

One of these forces was the new interest in regional experience, both in England and America, which enlarged the subject-matter of the short story. In England the modern short story has been marked by a wider interest in provincial settings and in the behavior of lower- and middle-class characters. In America, the expanding frontier at the end of the nineteenth century opened up new areas of experience and new dialects suitable to express them, and such regional writers as Sarah Orne Jewett, Hamlin Garland, and Mark Twain rushed to mine this new territory. Typical of these regional writers was Kate Chopin, who found in the manners and history of her adopted Louisiana powerful images for portraying some of the deepest themes in the American imagination. She managed to combine the fresh charm of "local color" with sophisticated methods learned from Flaubert and Maupassant. In this century Willa Cather, Sherwood Anderson, Eudora Welty, and Flannery O'Connor have all demonstrated the possibilities inherent in a cosmopolitan treatment of provincial settings. In Anderson's "Death in the Woods," for example, the overtones of myth and ritual "lift" the local scene to a universal level of experience. Southern writers have been so prominent in the rise of the modern American short story precisely because of their obsessive interest in exploring the universal implications of local experience. William Faulkner is the best example of a regional writer who discovers strength rather than weakness in his deliberately restricted subject-matter. His legendary Yoknapatawpha County, based on his observations of the northern Mississippi country in which he spent most of his life, is such a powerful enlargement of a regional scene that it becomes in the reader's mind a self-sufficient world, reflecting in mythic form the major obsessions of American history.

Another factor in the rejuvenation of the short story was the "new journalism" which reacted against the ornate rhetoric of nineteenth-century journalism by stressing simplicity, concision, and the use of natural speech in reporting actual events. Stephen Crane's life as a journalist supplied the realistic, solid foundation for "The Open Boat," and when one compares the story with Crane's newspaper account of the same event the impact of the "new journalism" is obvious. The same influence can be traced in Hemingway's early stories, such as "Big Two-Hearted River," where one aim is accuracy and simplicity in the reporting of natural fact. The late nineteenth-century passion for realism which marked both fiction and the drama had often been impeded by the inherited literary language, with its stock metaphors and elaborate syntax. The "new journalism" helped the writer of short stories to clear his palette and to work in the primary colors of directly perceived facts and events.

But if the modern short story had been confined merely to realistic reportage, few of the stories in this section would have been written. The great achievement of the modern short story has been the merging of a cleaner, more realistic descriptive language with sophisticated patterns of suggestion and symbolism. This ambition of writing a tightly organized story in which every detail of narrative and dialogue works simultaneously on the levels of "realism" and "symbolism" may be traced to the exemplary stories of Flaubert, Maupassant, Chekhov, and James, and no writer put their lessons to better advantage than the young James Joyce. Joyce's "Two Gallants" may seem at first reading to be merely an Irish landscape, a depressing and realistic account of the meaningless lives of three young Dubliners. But gradually we discover patterns of symbolism which link the exploited servant girl with the plight of Ireland, and the unfeeling Corley with the militarism and male chauvinism that Joyce found implicit in the romantic code of "gallantry" and "honor." At its deepest reaches, through symbol and suggestion, "Two Gallants" speaks of the moral, political, and religious paralysis that afflicts all of Ireland.

Often the symbolism of the modern short story may seem a bit too overt or intrusive: the ritual circling of the dogs in "Death in the Woods" as they return to their primeval roles; the combination of religious and erotic symbolism in "Flowering Judas," where Porter can be seen deliberately manipulating her literary and Christian references; the Gothic imagery of Flannery O'Connor. But more often these elements are absorbed into the realistic surface of dialogue and action. The short story has enormous possibilities, and the form can encompass both the fantasy of Barthelme and the novelistic impulses of E. M. Forster or Graham Greene. But like all genres it is focused on a "normative" form, against which we measure all variations, and that normative form—which replaced the formula stories of a half-century and more ago—is best found in the structure of "Big Two-Hearted River" or "Babylon Revisited" or "Revelation," where the wider meanings are allowed to rise naturally from the realistic narrative. The trout under the bridge in "Big Two-Hearted River," holding themselves tightly against the strong current, are both part of the natural landscape and a powerful emblem for Nick's sought-after equilibrium of mind and spirit. (For Hemingway's view of his art, see the passages from *Death in the Afternoon* reprinted in the Essay section.)

Another leading characteristic of the modern short story, displayed by most of the stories in this section, is a preoccupation with ways of seeing and ways of telling, with the process of perception as well as the end-product. The poet J. V. Cunningham once defined the aim of literary study as learning "not what to say / But how the saying must be said," and many short stories talk continuously through their narrative forms about our difficulties in "reading" the world around us. Henry James's "The Real Thing" is primarily a witty fable about the difficulties the artist has in transforming "the real thing" into his imagined model, but it also traces the spiritual growth of the narrator as he learns the profound connections (and conflicts) between aesthetics and the moral act of "being ourselves." "Death in the Woods" is as much a story about how the narrator reconstructs and understands his earlier experience as it is a story about that experience. "The Open Boat" seeks to involve us in the act of being "interpreters," while "See the Moon?" tells us that what we see is determined by the forms we use to report what we have seen. In their richness and variety, both of subject and narrative method, the following short stories outline the major contours of modern English and American literature.

The Real Thing

Henry James (1843–1916)

Born in New York in 1843, Henry James was the son of a famous American philosopher-theologian, Henry Sr., and the younger brother of an even more famous philosopher-psychologist, William. He received an international education in America and Europe and after a brief period of study at the Harvard Law School (1862–63) began to write reviews and stories for the American magazines. In 1869 he made the first of a series of extensive visits to Europe, and in 1876 he settled in London where he published some of his finest international fictions, including *Daisy Miller* (1878) and *The Portrait of a Lady* (1881). During the 1880s James wrote three major novels, *The Bostonians* (1886), *The Princess Casamassima* (1886), and *The Tragic Muse* (1890). In the early 1890s he tried, unsuccessfully, to become a man of the theater, but after the failure of his play *Guy Domville* in 1895 he devoted his full energy once again to fiction. The three novels which are the foundation of James's greatness—*The Ambassadors, The Wings of the Dove,* and *The Golden Bowl*—were written between 1900 and 1904.

In 1904 James returned to the United States for the first time in over twenty years and recorded his impressions in a work of social criticism, *The American Scene.* Between 1907 and 1909 Charles Scribner's Sons published the "New York Edition" of his novels and tales, which included critical prefaces by James. During his last years James devoted most of his effort to autobiographical volumes, *A Small Boy and Others, Notes of a Son and Brother,* and *The Middle Years.* He became a British subject in 1915, the year before his death.

Throughout his career James was a prolific writer of short stories; of the twenty-four volumes in the "New York Edition," nine were devoted to stories and novellas. "The Real Thing" first appeared in 1893.

I

When the porter's wife, who used to answer the house-bell, announced "A gentleman and a lady, sir," I had, as I often had in those days—the wish being father to the thought—an immediate vision of sitters. Sitters my visitors in this case proved to be; but not in the sense I should have preferred. There was nothing at first however to indicate that they mightn't have come for a portrait. The gentleman, a man of fifty, very high and very straight, with a moustache slightly grizzled and a dark grey walking-coat admirably fitted, both of which I noted professionally—I don't mean as a barber or yet a tailor—would have struck me as a celebrity if celebrities often were striking. It was a truth of which I had for some time been conscious that a figure with a good deal of frontage was, as one might say, almost never a public institution. A glance at the lady helped to remind me of this paradoxical law: she also looked too distinguished to be a "personality." Moreover one would scarcely come across two variations together.

Neither of the pair immediately spoke—they only prolonged the preliminary gaze suggesting that each wished to give the other a chance. They were visibly shy; they stood there letting me take them in—which, as I afterwards perceived, was the most practical thing they could have done. In this way their embarrassment served their cause. I had seen people painfully reluctant to mention that they desired anything so gross as to be represented on canvas; but the scruples of my new friends appeared almost insurmountable. Yet the gentleman might have said "I should like a portrait of my wife," and the lady might have said "I should like a portrait of my husband." Perhaps they weren't husband and wife—this naturally would make the matter more delicate. Perhaps they wished to be done together—in which case they ought to have brought a third person to break the news.

"We come from Mr. Rivet," the lady finally said with a dim smile that had the effect of a moist sponge passed over a "sunk" piece of painting, as well as of a vague allusion to vanished beauty. She was as tall and straight, in her degree, as her companion, and with ten years less to carry. She looked as sad as a woman could look whose face was not charged with expression; that is her tinted oval mask showed waste as an exposed surface shows friction. The hand of time had played over her freely, but to an effect of elimination. She was slim and stiff, and so well-dressed, in dark blue cloth, with lappets and pockets and buttons, that it was clear she employed the same tailor as her husband. The couple had an indefinable air of prosperous thrift—they evidently got a good deal of luxury for their money. If I was to be one of their luxuries it would behove me to consider my terms.

"Ah Claude Rivet recommended me?" I echoed; and I added that it was very kind of him, though I could reflect that, as he only painted landscape, this wasn't a sacrifice.

The lady looked very hard at the gentleman, and the gentleman looked round the room. Then staring at the floor a moment and stroking his moustache, he rested his pleasant eyes on me with the remark; "He said you were the right one."

"I try to be, when people want to sit."

"Yes, we should like to," said the lady anxiously.

"Do you mean together?"

My visitors exchanged a glance. "If you could do anything with me I suppose it would be double," the gentleman stammered.

"Oh yes, there's naturally a higher charge for two figures than for one."

"We should like to make it pay," the husband confessed.

"That's very good of you," I returned, appreciating so unwonted a sympathy—for I supposed he meant pay the artist.

A sense of strangeness seemed to dawn on the lady. "We mean for the illustrations—Mr. Rivet said you might put one in."

"Put in—an illustration?" I was equally confused.

"Sketch her off, you know," said the gentleman, colouring.

It was only then that I understood the service Claude Rivet had rendered me; he had told them how I worked in black-and-white, for magazines, for story-books, for sketches of contemporary life, and consequently had copious employment for models. These things were true, but it was not less true—I may confess it now; whether because the aspiration was to lead to everything or to nothing I leave the reader to guess—that I couldn't get the honours, to say nothing of the emoluments, of a great painter of portraits out of my head. My "illustrations" were my pot-boilers; I looked to a different branch of art—far and away the most interesting it had always seemed to me—to perpetuate my fame. There was no shame in looking to it also to make my fortune; but that fortune was by so much further from being made from the moment my visitors wished to be "done" for nothing. I was disappointed; for in the pictorial sense I had immediately *seen* them. I had seized their type—I had already settled what I would do with it. Something that wouldn't absolutely have pleased them, I afterwards reflected.

"Ah you're—you're—a—?" I began as soon as I had mastered my surprise. I couldn't bring out the dingy word "models": it seemed so little to fit the case.

"We haven't had much practice," said the lady.

"We've got to *do* something, and we've thought that an artist in your line might perhaps make something of us," her husband threw off. He further mentioned that they didn't know many artists and that they had gone first, on the off-chance—he painted views of course, but sometimes put in figures; perhaps I remembered—to Mr. Rivet, whom they had met a few years before at a place in Norfolk where he was sketching.

"We used to sketch a little ourselves," the lady hinted.

"It's very awkward, but we absolutely *must* do something," her husband went on.

"Of course we're not so *very* young," she admitted with a wan smile.

With the remark that I might as well know something more about them the husband had handed me a card extracted from a neat new pocket-book—their appurtenances were all of the freshest—and inscribed with the words "Major Monarch." Impressive as these words were they didn't carry my knowledge much further; but my visitor presently added: "I've left the army and we've had the misfortune to lose our money. In fact our means are dreadfully small."

"It's awfully trying—a regular strain," said Mrs. Monarch.

They evidently wished to be discreet—to take care not to swagger because they were gentlefolk. I felt them willing to recognize this as something of a drawback, at the same time that I guessed at an underlying sense—their consolation in adversity—that they *had* their points. They certainly had; but these advantages struck me as preponderantly social; such for instance as would help to make a drawing-room look well. However, a drawing-room was always, or ought to be, a picture.

In consequence of his wife's allusion to their age Major Monarch observed: "Naturally it's more for the figure that we thought of going in. We can still hold ourselves up." On the instant I saw that the figure was indeed their strong point. His "naturally" didn't sound vain, but it lighted up the question "*She* has the best one," he continued, nodding at his wife with a pleasant after-dinner absence of circumlocution. I could only reply, as if we were in fact sitting over our wine, that this didn't prevent his own from being very good; which led him in turn to make answer: "We thought that if you ever have to do people like us we might be something like it. *She* particularly—for a lady in a book, you know."

I was so amused by them that, to get more of it, I did my best to take their point of view; and though it was an embarrassment to find myself appraising physically, as if they were animals on hire or useful blacks, a pair whom I should have expected to meet only in one of the relations in which criticism is tacit, I looked at Mrs. Monarch judicially enough to be able to exclaim after a moment with conviction: "Oh yes, a lady in a book!" She was singularly like a bad illustration.

"We'll stand up, if you like," said the Major; and he raised himself before me with a really grand air.

I could take his measure at a glance—he was six feet two and a perfect gentleman. It would have paid any club in process of formation and in want of a stamp to engage him at a salary to stand in the principal window. What struck me at once was that in coming to me they had rather missed their vocation; they could surely have been turned to better account for advertising purposes. I couldn't of course see the thing in detail, but I could see them make somebody's fortune—I don't mean their own. There was something in them for a waistcoat-maker, an hotel-keeper or a soap-vendor. I could imagine "We always use it" pinned on their bosoms with the greatest effect; I had a vision of the brilliancy with which they would launch a table d'hôte.

Mrs. Monarch sat still, not from pride but from shyness, and presently her husband said to her: "Get up, my dear, and show how smart you are." She obeyed, but she had no need to get up to show it. She walked to the end of the studio and then came back blushing, her fluttered eyes on the partner of her appeal. I was reminded of an incident I had accidentally had a glimpse of in Paris—being with a friend there, a dramatist about to produce a play, when an actress came to him to ask to be entrusted with a part. She went through her paces before him, walked up and down as Mrs. Monarch was doing. Mrs. Monarch did it quite as well, but I abstained from applauding. It was very odd to see such people apply for such poor pay. She looked as if she had ten thousand a year. Her husband had used the word that described her: she was in the London current jargon essentially and typically "smart." Her figure was, in the same order of ideas, conspicuously and irreproachably "good." For a woman of her age her waist was surprisingly small; her elbow moreover had the orthodox crook. She held her head at the conventional angle, but why did she come to *me?* She ought to have tried on jackets at a big shop. I feared my visitors were not only destitute but "artistic"—which would be a great complication. When she sat down again I thanked her, observing what a draughtsman most valued in his model was the faculty of keeping quiet.

"Oh *she* can keep quiet," said Major Monarch. Then he added jocosely: "I've always kept her quiet."

"I'm not a nasty fidget, am I?" It was going to wring tears from me, I felt, the way she hid her head, ostrich-like, in the other broad bosom.

The owner of this expanse addressed his answer to me. "Perhaps it isn't out of place to mention—because we ought to be quite business-like, oughtn't we?—that when I married her she was known as the Beautiful Statue."

"Oh dear!" said Mrs. Monarch ruefully.

"Of course I should want a certain amount of expression," I rejoined.

"Of *course!*"—and I had never heard such unanimity.

"And then I suppose you know that you'll get awfully tired."

"Oh we *never* get tired!" they eagerly cried.

"Have you had any kind of practice?"

They hesitated—they looked at each other. "We've been photographed—*immensely,*" said Mrs. Monarch.

"She means the fellows have asked us themselves," added the Major.

"I see—because you're so good-looking."

"I don't know what they thought, but they were always after us."

"We always got our photographs for nothing," smiled Mrs. Monarch.

"We might have brought some, my dear," her husband remarked.

"I'm not sure we have any left. We've given quantities away," she explained to me.

"With our autographs and that sort of thing," said the Major.

"Are they to be got in the shops?" I enquired as a harmless pleasantry.

"Oh yes, *hers*—they used to be."

"Not now," said Mrs. Monarch with her eyes on the floor.

II

I could fancy the "sort of thing" they put on the presentation copies of their photographs, and I was sure they wrote a beautiful hand. It was odd how quickly I was sure of everything that concerned them. If they were now so poor as to have to earn shillings and pence they could never have had much of a margin. Their good looks had been their capital, and they had good-humouredly made the most of the career that this resource marked out for them. It was in their faces, the blankness, the deep intellectual repose of the twenty years of country-house visiting that had given them pleasant intonations. I could see the sunny drawing-rooms, sprinkled with periodicals she didn't read, in which Mrs. Monarch had continuously sat; I could see the wet shrubberies in which she had walked, equipped to admiration for either exercise. I could see the rich covers the Major had helped to shoot and the wonderful garments in which, late at night, he repaired to the smoking-room to talk about them. I could imagine their leggings and waterproofs, their knowing tweeds and rugs, their rolls of sticks and cases of tackle and neat umbrellas; and I could evoke the exact appearance of their servants and the compact variety of their luggage on the platforms of country stations.

They gave small tips, but they were liked; they didn't do anything themselves, but they were welcome. They looked so well everywhere; they gratified the general relish for stature, complexion and "form." They knew it without fatuity or vulgarity, and they respected themselves in consequence. They weren't superficial; they were thorough and kept themselves up—it had been their line. People with such a taste for activity had to have some line. I could feel how even in a dull house they could have been counted on for the joy of life. At present something had happened—it didn't matter what, their little income had grown less, it had grown least—and they had to do something for pocket-money. Their friends could like them, I made out, without liking to support them. There was something about them that represented credit—their clothes, their manners, their type; but if credit is a large empty pocket in which an occasional chink reverberates, the chink at least must be audible. What they wanted of me was to help to make it so. Fortunately they had no children—I soon divined that. They would also perhaps wish our relations to be kept secret: this was why it was "for the figure"—the reproduction of the face would betray them.

I liked them—I felt, quite as their friends must have done—they were so simple; and I had no objection to them if they would suit. But somehow with all their perfections I didn't easily believe in them. After all they were amateurs, and the ruling passion of my life was the detestation of the amateur. Combined with this was another perversity—an innate preference for the represented subject over the real one: the defect of the real one was so apt to be a lack of representation. I liked things that appeared; then one was sure. Whether they *were* or not was a subordinate and almost always a profitless question. There were other considerations, the first of which was that I already had two or three recruits in use, notably a young person with big feet, in alpaca, from Kilburn, who for a couple of years had come to me regularly for my illustrations and with whom I was still—perhaps ignobly—satisfied. I frankly explained to my visitors how the case stood, but they had taken more precautions than I supposed. They had reasoned out their opportunity, for Claude Rivet had told them of the projected *édition de luxe* of one of the writers of our day—the rarest of the novelists—who, long neglected by the multitudinous vulgar and dearly prized by the attentive (need I mention Philip Vincent?), had had the happy fortune of seeing, late in life, the dawn and then the full light of a higher criticism; an estimate in which on the part of the public there was something really of expiation. The edition preparing, planned by a publisher of taste, was practically an act of high reparation; the wood-cuts with which it was to be enriched were the homage of English art to one of the most independent representatives of English letters. Major and Mrs. Monarch confessed to me they had hoped I might be able to work *them* into my branch of the enterprise. They knew I was to do the first of the books, "Rutland Ramsay," but I had to make clear to them that my participation in the rest of the affair—this first book was to be a test—must depend on the satisfaction I should give. If this should be limited my employers would drop me with scarce common forms. It was therefore a crisis for me, and naturally I was making special preparations, looking about for new people, should they be necessary, and securing the best types. I admitted however that I should like to settle down to two or three good models who would do for everything.

"Should we have often to—a—put on special clothes?" Mrs. Monarch timidly demanded.

"Dear yes—that's half the business."

"And should we be expected to supply our own costumes?"

"Oh no; I've got a lot of things. A painter's models put on—or put off—anything he likes."

"And you mean—a—the same?"

"The same?"

Mrs. Monarch looked at her husband again.

"Oh she was just wondering," he explained, "if the costumes are in *general* use." I had to confess that they were, and I mentioned further that some of them—I had a lot of genuine greasy last-century things—had served their time, a hundred years ago, on living world-stained men and women; on figures not perhaps so far removed, in that vanished world, from *their* type, the Monarchs', *quoi!* of a breeched and bewigged age. "We'll put on anything that *fits,*" said the Major.

"Oh I arrange that—they fit in the pictures."

"I'm afraid I should do better for the modern books. I'd come as you like," said Mrs. Monarch.

"She has got a lot of clothes at home: they might do for contemporary life," her husband continued.

"Oh I can fancy scenes in which you'd be quite natural." And indeed I could see the slipshod rearrangements of stale properties—the stories I tried to produce pictures for without the exasperation of reading them—whose sandy tracts the good lady might help to people. But I had to return to the fact that for this sort of work—the daily mechanical grind—I was already equipped: the people I was working with were fully adequate.

"We only thought we might be more like *some* characters," said Mrs. Monarch mildly, getting up.

Her husband also rose; he stood looking at me with a dim wistfulness that was touching in so fine a man. "Wouldn't it be rather a pull sometimes to have—a—to have—?" He hung fire; he wanted me to help him by phrasing what he meant. But I couldn't—I didn't know. So he brought it out awkwardly: "The *real* thing; a gentleman, you know, or a lady." I was quite ready to give a general assent—I admitted that there was a great deal in that. This encouraged Major Monarch to say, following up his appeal with an unacted gulp: "It's awfully hard—we've tried everything." The gulp was communicative; it proved too much for his wife. Before I knew it Mrs. Monarch had dropped again upon a divan and burst into tears. Her husband sat down beside her, holding one of her hands; whereupon she quickly dried her eyes with the other, while I felt embarrassed as she looked up at me. "There isn't a confounded job I haven't applied for—waited for—prayed for. You can fancy we'd be pretty bad first. Secretaryships and that sort of thing? You might as well ask for a peerage. I'd be *anything*—I'm strong; a messenger or a coal-heaver. I'd put on a gold-laced cap and open carriage-doors in front of the haberdasher's; I'd hang about a station to carry portmanteaux; I'd be a postman. But they won't *look* at you; there are thousands as good as yourself already on the ground. *Gentlemen,* poor beggars, who've drunk their wine, who've kept their hunters!"

I was as reassuring as I knew how to be, and my visitors were presently on their feet again while, for the experiment, we agreed on an hour. We were discussing it when the door opened and Miss Churm came in with a wet umbrella. Miss Churm had to take the omnibus to Maida Vale and then walk half a mile. She looked a trifle blowsy and slightly splashed. I scarcely ever saw her come in without thinking afresh how odd it was that, being so little in herself, she should yet be so much in others. She was a meagre little Miss Churm, but was such an ample heroine of romance. She was only a freckled cockney, but she could represent everything, from a fine lady to a shepherdess; she had the faculty as she might have had a fine voice or long hair. She couldn't spell and she loved beer, but she had two or three "points," and practice, and a knack, and mother-wit, and a whimsical sensibility, and a love of the theatre, and seven sisters, and not an ounce of respect, especially for the "h." The first thing my visitors saw was that her umbrella was wet, and in their spotless perfection they visibly winced at it. The rain had come on since their arrival.

"I'm all in a soak; there *was* a mess of people in the 'bus. I wish you lived near a stytion," said Miss Churm. I requested her to get ready as quickly as possible, and she passed into the room in which she always changed her dress. But before going out she asked me what she was to get into this time.

"It's the Russian princess, don't you know?" I answered; "the one with the 'golden eyes,' in black velvet, for the long thing in the *Cheapside.*"

"Golden eyes? I *say!*" cried Miss Churm, while my companions watched her with intensity as she withdrew. She always arranged herself, when she was late, before I could turn round; and I kept my visitors a little on purpose, so that they might get an idea, from seeing her, what would be expected of themselves. I mentioned that she was quite my notion of an excellent model—she was really very clever.

"Do you think she looks like a Russian princess?" Major Monarch asked with lurking alarm.

"When I make her, yes."

"Oh if you have to *make* her—!" he reasoned, not without point.

"That's the most you can ask. There are so many who are not makeable."

"Well now, *here's* a lady"—and with a persuasive smile he passed his arm into his wife's—"who's already made!"

"Oh I'm not a Russian princess," Mrs. Monarch protested a little coldly. I could see she had known some and didn't like them. There at once was a complication of a kind I never had to fear with Miss Churm.

This young lady came back in black velvet—the gown was rather rusty and very low on her lean shoulders—and with a Japanese fan in her red hands. I reminded her that in the scene I was doing she had to look over some one's head. "I forget whose it is; but it doesn't matter. Just look over a head."

"I'd rather look over a stove," said Miss Churm; and she took her station near the fire. She fell into position, settled herself into a tall attitude, gave a certain backward inclination to her head and a certain forward droop to her fan, and looked, at least to my prejudiced sense, distinguished and charming, foreign and dangerous. We left her looking so while I went downstairs with Major and Mrs. Monarch.

"I believe I could come about as near it as that," said Mrs. Monarch.

"Oh you think she's shabby, but you must allow for the alchemy of art."

However, they went off with an evident increase of comfort founded on their demonstrable advantage in being the real thing. I could fancy them shuddering over Miss Churm. She was very droll about them when I went back, for I told her what they wanted.

"Well, if *she* can sit I'll tyke to bookkeeping," said my model.

"She's very ladylike," I replied as an innocent form of aggravation.

"So much the worse for *you*. That means she can't turn round."

"She'll do for the fashionable novels."

"Oh yes, she'll *do* for them!" my model humorously declared. "Ain't they bad enough without her?" I had often sociably denounced them to Miss Churm.

III

It was for the elucidation of a mystery in one of these works that I first tried Mrs. Monarch. Her husband came with her, to be useful if necessary—it was sufficiently clear that as a general thing he would prefer to come with her. At first I wondered if this were for "propriety's" sake—if he were going to be jealous and meddling. The idea was too tiresome, and if it had been confirmed it would speedily have brought our acquaintance to a close. But I soon saw there was nothing in it and that if he accompanied Mrs. Monarch it was—in addition to the chance of being wanted—simply because he had nothing else to do. When they were separate his occupation was gone and they never *had* been separate. I judged rightly that in their awkward situation their close union was their main comfort and that this union had no weak spot. It was a real marriage, an encouragement to the hesitating, a nut for pessimists to crack. Their address was humble—I remember afterwards thinking it had been the only thing about them that was really professional—and I could fancy the lamentable lodgings in which the Major would have been left alone. He could sit there more or less grimly with his wife—he couldn't sit there anyhow without her.

He had too much tact to try and make himself agreeable when he couldn't be useful; so when I was too absorbed in my work to talk he simply sat and waited. But I liked to hear him talk—it made my work, when not interrupting it, less mechanical, less special. To listen to him was to combine the excitement of going out with the economy of staying at home. There was only one hindrance—that I seemed not to know any of the people this brilliant couple had known. I think he wondered extremely, during the term of our intercourse, whom the deuce I *did* know. He hadn't a stray sixpence of an idea to fumble for, so we didn't spin it very fine; we confined ourselves to questions of leather and even of liquor—saddlers and breeches-makers and how to get excellent claret cheap—and matters like "good trains" and the habits of small game. His lore on these last subjects was astonishing—he managed to interweave the station-master with the ornithologist. When he couldn't talk about greater things he could talk cheerfully about smaller, and since I couldn't accompany him into reminiscences of the fashionable world he could lower the conversation without a visible effort to my level.

So earnest a desire to please was touching in a man who could so easily have knocked one down. He looked after the fire and had an opinion on the draught of the stove without my asking him, and I could see that he thought many of my arrangements not half knowing. I remember telling him that if I were only rich I'd offer him a salary to come and teach me how to live. Sometimes he gave a random sigh of which the essence might have been: "Give me even such a bare old barrack as *this,* and I'd do something with it!" When I wanted to use him he came alone; which was an illustration of the superior courage of women. His wife could bear her solitary second floor, and she was in general more discreet; showing by various small reserves that she was alive to the propriety of keeping our relations markedly professional—not letting them slide into sociability. She wished it to remain clear that she and the Major were employed, not cultivated, and if she approved of me as a superior, who could be kept in his place, she never thought me quite good enough for an equal.

She sat with great intensity, giving the whole of her mind to it, and was capable of remaining for an hour almost as motionless as before a photographer's lens. I could see she had been photographed often, but somehow the very habit that made her good for that purpose unfitted her for mine. At first I was extremely pleased with her ladylike air, and it was a satisfaction, on coming to follow her lines, to see how good they were and how far they could lead the pencil. But after a little skirmishing I began to find her too insurmountably stiff; do what I would with it my drawing looked like a photograph or a copy of a photograph. Her figure had no variety of expression—she herself had no sense of variety. You may say that this was my business and was only a question of placing her. Yet I placed her in every conceivable position and she managed to obliterate their differences. She was always a lady certainly, and into the bargain was always the same lady. She was the real thing, but always the same thing. There were moments when I rather writhed under the serenity of her confidence that she *was* the real thing. All her dealings with me and all her husband's were an implication that this was lucky for *me.* Meanwhile I found myself trying to invent types that approached her own, instead of making her own transform itself—in the clever way that was not impossible for instance to poor Miss Churm. Arrange as I would and take the precautions I would, she always came out, in my pictures, too tall—landing me in the dilemma of having represented a fascinating woman as seven feet high, which (out of respect perhaps to my own very much scantier inches) was far from my idea of such a personage.

The case was worse with the Major—nothing I could do would keep *him* down, so that he became useful only for the representation of brawny giants. I adored variety and range, I cherished human accidents, the illustrative note; I wanted to characterise closely, and the thing in the world I most hated was the danger of being ridden by a type. I had quarrelled with some of my friends about it; I had parted company with them for maintaining that one *had* to be, and that if the type was beautiful—witness Raphael and Leonardo—the servitude was only a gain. I was neither Leonardo nor Raphael—I might only be a presumptuous young modern searcher; but I held that everything was to be sacrificed sooner than character. When they claimed that the obsessional form could easily *be* character I retorted, perhaps superficially, "Whose?" It couldn't be everybody's—it might end in being nobody's.

After I had drawn Mrs. Monarch a dozen times I felt surer even than before that the value of such a model as Miss Churm resided precisely in the fact that she had no positive stamp, combined of course with the other fact that what she did have was a curious and inexplicable talent for imitation. Her usual appearance was like a curtain which she could draw up at request for a capital performance. This performance was simply suggestive; but it was a word to the wise—it was vivid and pretty. Sometimes even I thought it, though she was plain herself, too insipidly pretty; I made it a reproach to her that the figures drawn from her were monotonously (*bêtement,* as we used to say) graceful. Nothing made her more angry: it was so much her pride to feel she could sit for characters that had nothing in common with each other. She would accuse me at such moments of taking away her "reputytion."

It suffered a certain shrinkage, this queer quantity, from the repeated visits of my new friends. Miss Churm was greatly in demand, never in want of employment, so I had no scruple in putting her off occasionally, to try them more at my ease. It was certainly amusing at first to do the real thing—it was amusing to do Major Monarch's trousers. They *were* the real thing, even if he did come out colossal. It was amusing to do his wife's back hair—it was so mathematically neat—and the particular "smart" tension of her tight stays. She lent herself especially to positions in which the face was somewhat averted or blurred; she abounded in ladylike back views and *profils perdus.* When she stood erect she took naturally one of the attitudes in which court-painters represent queens and princesses; so that I found myself wondering whether, to draw out this accomplishment, I couldn't get the editor of the *Cheapside* to publish a really royal romance, "A Tale of Buckingham Palace." Sometimes however the real thing and the make-believe came into contact; by which I mean that Miss Churm, keeping an appointment or coming to make one on days when I had much work in hand, encountered her invidious rivals. The encounter was not on their part, for they noticed her no more than if she had been the housemaid; not from intentional loftiness, but simply because as yet, professionally, they didn't know how to fraternise, as I could imagine they would have liked—or at least that the Major would. They couldn't talk about the omnibus—they always walked; and they didn't know what else to try—she wasn't interested in good trains or cheap claret. Besides, they must have felt—in the air—that she was amused at them, secretly derisive of their ever knowing how. She wasn't a person to conceal the limits of her faith if she had had a chance to show them. On the other hand Mrs. Monarch didn't think her tidy; for why else did she take pains to say to me—it was going out of the way, for Mrs. Monarch—that she didn't like dirty women?

One day when my young lady happened to be present with my other sitters—she even dropped in, when it was convenient, for a chat—I asked her to be so good as to lend a hand in getting tea, a service with which she was familiar and which was one of a class that, living as I did in a small way, with slender domestic resources, I often appealed to my models to render. They liked to lay hands on my property, to break the sitting, and sometimes the china—it made them feel Bohemian. The next time I saw Miss Churm after this incident she surprised me greatly by making a scene about it—she accused me of having wished to humiliate her. She hadn't resented the outrage at the time, but had seemed obliging and amused, enjoying the comedy of asking Mrs. Monarch, who sat vague and silent, whether she would have cream and sugar, and putting an exaggerated simper into the question. She had tried intonations—as if she too wished to pass for the real thing—till I was afraid my other visitors would take offence.

Oh they were determined not to do this, and their touching patience was the measure of their great need. They would sit by the hour, uncomplaining, till I was ready to use them; they would come back on the chance of being wanted and would walk away cheerfully if it failed. I used to go to the door with them to see in what magnificent order they retreated. I tried to find other employment for them—I introduced them to several artists. But they didn't "take," for reasons I could appreciate, and I became rather anxiously aware that after such disappointments they fell back upon me with a heavier weight. They did me the honour to think me most *their* form. They weren't romantic enough for the painters, and in those days there were few serious workers in black-and-white. Besides, they had an eye to the great job I had mentioned to them—they had secretly set their hearts on supplying the right essence for my pictorial vindication of our fine novelist. They knew that for this undertaking I should want no costume-effects, none of the frippery of past ages—that it was a case in which everything would be contemporary and satirical and presumably genteel. If I could work them into it their future would be assured, for the labour would of course be long and the occupation steady.

One day Mrs. Monarch came without her husband—she explained his absence by his having had to go to the City. While she sat there in her usual relaxed majesty there came at the door a knock which I immediately recognised as the subdued appeal of a model out of work. It was followed by the entrance of a young man whom I at once saw to be a foreigner and who proved in fact an Italian acquainted with no English word but my name, which he uttered in a way that made it seem to include all others. I hadn't then visited his country, nor was I proficient in his tongue; but as he was not so meanly constituted—what Italian is?—as to depend only on that member for expression he conveyed to me, in familiar but graceful mimicry, that he was in search of exactly the employment in which the lady before me was engaged. I was not struck with him at first, and while I continued to draw I dropped few signs of interest or encouragement. He stood his ground however—not importunately, but with a dumb dog-like fidelity in his eyes that amounted to innocent impudence, the manner of a devoted servant—he might have been in the house for years—unjustly suspected. Suddenly it struck me that this very attitude and expression made a picture; whereupon I told him to sit down and wait till I should be free. There was another picture in the way he obeyed me, and I observed as I worked that there were others still in the way he looked wonderingly, with his head thrown back, about the high studio. He might have been crossing himself in Saint Peter's. Before I finished I said to myself "The fellow's a bankrupt orange-monger, but a treasure."

When Mrs. Monarch withdrew he passed across the room like a flash to open the door for her, standing there with the rapt pure gaze of the young Dante spell-bound by the young Beatrice. As I never insisted, in such situations, on the blankness of the British domestic, I reflected that he had the making of a servant—and I needed one, but couldn't pay him to be only that—as well as of a model; in short I resolved to adopt my bright adventurer if he would agree to officiate in the double capacity. He jumped at my offer, and in the event my rashness—for I had really known nothing about him—wasn't brought home to me. He proved a sympathetic though a desultory ministrant, and had in a wonderful degree the *sentiment de la pose.* It was uncultivated, instinctive, a part of the happy instinct that had guided him to my door and helped him to spell out my name on the card nailed to it. He had had no other introduction to me than a guess, from the shape of my high north window, seen outside, that my place was a studio and that as a studio it would contain an artist. He had wandered to England in search of fortune, like other itinerants, and had embarked, with a partner and a small green hand-cart, on the sale of penny ices. The ices had melted away and the partner had dissolved in their train. My young man wore tight yellow trousers with reddish stripes and his name was Oronte. He was sallow but fair, and when I put him into some old clothes of my own he looked like an Englishman. He was as good as Miss Churm, who could look, when requested, like an Italian.

IV

I thought Mrs. Monarch's face slightly convulsed when, on her coming back with her husband, she found Oronte installed. It was strange to have to recognise in a scrap of a lazzarone a competitor to her magnificent Major. It was she who scented danger first, for the Major was anecdotically unconscious. But Oronte gave us tea, with a hundred eager confusions—he had never been concerned in so queer a process—and I think she thought better of me for having at last an "establishment." They saw a couple of drawings that I had made of the establishment, and Mrs. Monarch hinted that it never would have struck her he had sat for them. "Now the drawings you make from *us,* they look exactly like us," she reminded me, smiling in triumph; and I recognised that this was indeed just their defect. When I drew the Monarchs I couldn't anyhow get away from them—get into the character I wanted to represent; and I hadn't the least desire my model should be discoverable in my picture. Miss Churm never was, and Mrs. Monarch thought I hid her, very properly, because she was vulgar; whereas if she was lost it was only as the dead who go to heaven are lost—in the gain of an angel the more.

By this time I had got a certain start with "Rutland Ramsay," the first novel in the great projected series; that is I had produced a dozen drawings, several with the help of the Major and his wife, and I had sent them in for approval. My understanding with the publishers, as I have already hinted, had been that I was to be left to do my work, in this particular case, as I liked, with the whole book committed to me; but my connexion with the rest of the series was only contingent. There were moments when, frankly, it *was* a comfort to have the real thing under one's hand; for there were characters in "Rutland Ramsay" that were very much like it. There were people presumably as erect as the Major and women of as good a fashion as Mrs. Monarch. There was a great deal of country-house life—treated, it is true, in a fine fanciful ironical generalised way—and there was a considerable implication of knickerbockers and kilts. There were certain things I had to settle at the outset; such things for instance as the exact appearance of the hero and the particular bloom and figure of the heroine. The author of course gave me a lead, but there was a margin for interpretation. I took the Monarchs into my confidence, I told them frankly what I was about, I mentioned my embarrassments and alternatives. "Oh take *him!*" Mrs. Monarch murmured sweetly, looking at her husband; and "What could you want better than my wife?" the Major enquired with the comfortable candour that now prevailed between us.

I wasn't obliged to answer these remarks—I was only obliged to place my sitters. I wasn't easy in mind, and I postponed a little timidly perhaps the solving of my question. The book was a large canvas, the other figures were numerous, and I worked off at first some of the episodes in which the hero and the heroine were not concerned. When once I had set *them* up I should have to stick to them—I couldn't make my young man seven feet high in one place and five feet nine in another. I inclined on the whole to the latter measurement, though the Major more than once reminded me that *he* looked about as young as any one. It was indeed quite possible to arrange him, for the figure, so that it would have been difficult to detect his age. After the spontaneous Oronte had been with me a month, and after I had given him to understand several times over that his native exuberance would presently constitute an insurmountable barrier to our further intercourse, I waked to a sense of his heroic capacity. He was only five feet seven, but the remaining inches were latent. I tried him almost secretly at first, for I was really rather afraid of the judgement my other models would pass on such a choice. If they regarded Miss Churm as little better than a snare what would they think of the representation by a person so little the real thing as an Italian street-vendor of a protagonist formed by a public school?

If I went a little in fear of them it wasn't because they bullied me, because they had got an oppressive foothold, but because in their really pathetic decorum and mysteriously permanent newness they counted on me so intensely. I was therefore very glad when Jack Hawley came home: he was always of such good counsel. He painted badly himself, but there was no one like him for putting his finger on the place. He had been absent from England for a year; he had been somewhere—I don't remember where—to get a fresh eye. I was in a good deal of dread of any such organ, but we were old friends; he had been away for months and a sense of emptiness was creeping into my life. I hadn't dodged a missile for a year.

He came back with a fresh eye, but with the same old black velvet blouse, and the first evening he spent in my studio we smoked cigarettes till the small hours. He had done no work himself, he had only got the eye; so the field was clear for the production of my little things. He wanted to see what I had produced for the *Cheapside,* but he was disappointed in the exhibition. That at least seemed the meaning of two or three comprehensive groans which, as he lounged on my big divan, his leg folded under him, looking at my latest drawings, issued from his lips with the smoke of the cigarette.

"What's the matter with you?" I asked.

"What's the matter with *you?"*

"Nothing save that I'm mystified."

"You are indeed. You're quite off the hinge. What's the meaning of this new fad?" And he tossed me, with visible irreverence, a drawing in which I happened to have depicted both my elegant models. I asked if he didn't think it good, and he replied that it struck him as execrable, given the sort of thing I had always represented myself to him as wishing to arrive at; but I let that pass—I was so anxious to see exactly what he meant. The two figures in the picture looked colossal, but I supposed this was *not* what he meant, inasmuch as, for aught he knew to the contrary, I might have been trying for some such effect. I maintained that I was working exactly in the same way as when he last had done me the honour to tell me I might do something some day. "Well, there's a screw loose somewhere," he answered; "wait a bit and I'll discover it." I depended upon him to do so: where else was the fresh eye? But he produced at last nothing more luminous than "I don't know—I don't like your types." This was lame for a critic who had never consented to discuss with me anything but the question of execution, the direction of strokes and the mystery of values.

"In the drawings you've been looking at I think my types are very handsome."

"Oh they won't do!"

"I've been working with new models."

"I see you have. *They* won't do."

"Are you very sure of that?"

"Absolutely—they're stupid."

"You mean *I* am—for I ought to get round that."

"You *can't*—with such people. Who are they?"

I told him, so far as was necessary, and he concluded heartlessly: *"Ce sont des gens qu'il faut mettre à la porte."*

"You've never seen them; they're awfully good"—I flew to their defence.

"Not seen them? Why all this recent work of yours drops to pieces with them. It's all I want to see of them."

"No one else has said anything against it—the *Cheapside* people are pleased."

"Every one else is an ass, and the *Cheapside* people the biggest asses of all. Come, don't pretend at this time of day to have pretty illusions about the public, especially about publishers and editors. It's not for *such* animals you work—it's for those who know, *coloro che sanno;* so keep straight for *me* if you can't keep straight for yourself. There was a certain sort of thing you used to try for—and a very good thing it was. But this twaddle isn't *in* it." When I talked with Hawley later about "Rutland Ramsay" and its possible successors he declared that I must get back into my boat again or I should go to the bottom. His voice in short was the voice of warning.

I noted the warning, but I didn't turn my friends out of doors. They bored me a good deal; but the very fact that they bored me admonished me not to sacrifice them—if there was anything to be done with them—simply to irritation. As I looked back at this phase they seem to me to have pervaded my life not a little. I have a vision of them as most of the time in my studio, seated against the wall on an old velvet bench to be out of the way, and resembling the while a pair of patient courtiers in a royal ante-chamber. I'm convinced that during the coldest weeks of the winter they held their ground because it saved them fire. Their newness was losing its gloss, and it was impossible not to feel them objects of charity. Whenever Miss Churm arrived they went away, and after I was fairly launched in "Rutland Ramsay" Miss Churm arrived pretty often. They managed to express to me tacitly that they supposed I wanted her for the low life of the book, and I let them suppose it, since they had attempted to study the work—it was lying about the studio—without discovering that it dealt only with the highest circles. They had dipped into the most brilliant of our novelists without deciphering many passages. I still took an hour from them, now and again, in spite of Jack Hawley's warning: it would be time enough to dismiss them, if dismissal should be necessary, when the rigour of the season was over. Hawley had made their acquaintance—he had met them at my fireside—and thought them a ridiculous pair. Learning that he was a painter they tried to approach him, to show him too that they were the real thing; but he looked at them, across the big room, as if they were miles away: they were a compendium of everything he most objected to in the social system of his country. Such people as that, all convention and patent-leather, with ejaculations that stopped conversation, had no business in a studio. A studio was a place to learn to see, and how could you see through a pair of feather-beds?

The main inconvenience I suffered at their hands was that at first I was shy of letting it break upon them that my artful little servant had begun to sit to me for "Rutland Ramsay." They knew I had been odd enough —they were prepared by this time to allow oddity to artists—to pick a foreign vagabond out of the streets when I might have had a person with whiskers and credentials; but it was some time before they learned how high I rated his accomplishments. They found him in an attitude more than once, but they never doubted I was doing him as an organ-grinder. There were several things they never guessed, and one of them was that for a striking scene in the novel, in which a footman briefly figured, it occurred to me to make use of Major Monarch as the menial. I kept putting this off, I didn't like to ask him to don the livery—besides the difficulty of finding a livery to fit him. At last, one day late in the winter, when I was at work on the despised Oronte, who caught one's idea on the wing, and was in the glow of feeling myself go very straight, they came in, the Major and his wife, with their society laugh about nothing (there was less and less to laugh at); came in like country-callers—they always reminded me of that—who have walked across the park after church and are presently persuaded to stay to luncheon. Luncheon was over, but they could stay to tea—I knew they wanted it. The fit was on me, however, and I couldn't let my ardour cool and my work wait, with the fading daylight, while my model prepared it. So I asked Mrs. Monarch if she would mind laying it out—a request which for an instant brought all the blood to her face. Her eyes were on her husband's for a second, and some mute telegraphy passed between them. Their folly was over the next instant; his cheerful shrewdness put an end to it. So far from pitying their wounded pride, I must add, I was moved to give it as complete a lesson as I could. They bustled about together and got out the cups and saucers and made the kettle boil. I know they felt as if they were waiting on my servant, and when the tea was prepared I said: "He'll have a cup, please—he's tired." Mrs. Monarch brought him one where he stood, and he took it from her as if he had been a gentleman at a party squeezing a crush-hat with an elbow.

Then it came over me that she had made a great effort for me—made it with a kind of nobleness—and that I owed her a compensation. Each time I saw her after this I wondered what the compensation could be. I couldn't go on doing the wrong thing to oblige them. Oh it *was* the wrong thing, the stamp of the work for which they sat—Hawley was not the only person to say it now. I sent in a large number of the drawings I had made for "Rutland Ramsey," and I received a warning that was more to the point than Hawley's. The artistic adviser of the house for which I was working was of opinion that many of my illustrations were not what had been looked for. Most of these illustrations were the subjects in which the Monarchs had figured. Without going into the question of what *had* been looked for, I had to face the fact that at this rate I shouldn't get the other books to do. I hurled myself in despair on Miss Churm—I put her through all her paces. I not only adopted Oronte publicly as my hero, but one morning when the Major looked in to see if I didn't require him to finish a *Cheapside* figure for which he had begun to sit the week before, I told him I had changed my mind—I'd do the drawing from my man. At this my visitor turned pale and stood looking at me. "Is *he* your idea of an English gentleman?" he asked.

I was disappointed, I was nervous, I wanted to get on with my work; so I replied with irritation: "Oh my dear Major—I can't be ruined for *you!*"

It was a horrid speech, but he stood another moment—after which, without a word, he quitted the studio. I drew a long breath, for I said to myself that I shouldn't see him again. I hadn't told him definitely that I was in danger of having my work rejected, but I was vexed at his not having felt the catastrophe in the air, read with me the moral of our fruitless collaboration, the lesson that in the deceptive atmosphere of art even the highest respectability may fail of being plastic.

I didn't owe my friends money, but I did see them again. They reappeared together three days later, and, given all the other facts, there was something tragic in that one. It was a clear proof they could find nothing else in life to do. They had threshed the matter out in a dismal conference—they had digested the bad news that they were not in for the series. If they weren't useful to me even for the *Cheapside* their function seemed difficult to determine, and I could only judge at first that they had come, forgivingly, decorously, to take a last leave. This made me rejoice in secret that I had little leisure for a scene; for I had placed both my other models in position together and I was pegging away at a drawing from which I hoped to derive glory. It had been suggested by the passage in which Rutland Ramsay, drawing up a chair to Artemisia's piano-stool, says extraordinary things to her while she ostensibly fingers out a difficult piece of music. I had done Miss Churm at the piano before—it was an attitude in which she knew how to take on an absolutely poetic grace. I wished the two figures to "compose" together with intensity, and my little Italian had entered perfectly into my conception. The pair were vividly before me, the piano had been pulled out; it was a charming show of blended youth and murmured love, which I had only to catch and keep. My visitors stood and looked at it, and I was friendly to them over my shoulder.

They made no response, but I was used to silent company and went on with my work, only a little disconcerted—even though exhilarated by the sense that *this* was at least the ideal thing—at not having got rid of them after all. Presently I heard Mrs. Monarch's sweet voice beside or rather above me: "I wish her hair were a little better done." I looked up and she was staring with a strange fixedness at Miss Churm, whose back was turned to her. "Do you mind my just touching it?" she went on—a question which made me spring up for an instant as with the instinctive fear that she might do the young lady a harm. But she quieted me with a glance I shall never forget—I confess I should like to have been able to paint *that*—and went for a moment to my model. She spoke to her softly, laying a hand on her shoulder and bending over her; and as the girl, understanding, gratefully assented, she disposed her rough curls, with a few quick passes, in such a way as to make Miss Churm's head twice as charming. It was one of the most heroic personal services I've ever seen rendered. Then Mrs. Monarch turned away with a low sigh and, looking about her as if for something to do, stooped to the floor with a noble humility and picked up a dirty rag that had dropped out of my paint-box.

The Major meanwhile had also been looking for something to do, and, wandering to the other end of the studio, saw before him my breakfast-things neglected, unremoved, "I say, can't I be useful *here?*" he called out to me with an irrepressible quaver. I assented with a laugh that I fear was awkward, and for the next ten minutes, while I worked, I heard the light clatter of china and the tinkle of spoons and glass. Mrs. Monarch assisted her husband—they washed up my crockery, they put it away. They wandered off into my little scullery, and I afterwards found that they had cleaned my knives and that my slender stock of plate had an unprecedented surface. When it came over me, the latent eloquence of what they were doing, I confess that my drawing was blurred for a moment—the picture swam. They had accepted their failure, but they couldn't accept their fate. They had bowed their heads in bewilderment to the perverse and cruel law in virtue of which the real thing could be so much less precious than the unreal; but they didn't want to starve. If my servants were my models, then my models might be my servants. They would reverse the parts—the others would sit for the ladies and gentlemen and *they* would do the work. They would still be in the studio—it was an intense dumb appeal to me not to turn them out. "Take us on," they wanted to say—"we'll do anything."

My pencil dropped from my hand; my sitting was spoiled and I got rid of my sitters, who were also evidently rather mystified and awestruck. Then, alone with the Major and his wife I had a most uncomfortable moment. He put their prayer into a single sentence: "I say, you know—just let *us* do for you, can't you?" I couldn't—it was dreadful to see them emptying my slops; but I pretended I could, to oblige them, for about a week. Then I gave them a sum of money to go away, and I never saw them again. I obtained the remaining books, but my friend Hawley repeats that Major and Mrs. Monarch did me a permanent harm, got me into false ways. If it be true I'm content to have paid the price—for the memory.

Désirée's Baby

Kate Chopin (1851–1904)

The daughter of a French mother and an Irish father, Kate Chopin (née Kate O'Flaherty) was reared in St. Louis. At the age of nineteen she married a New Orleans banker and soon became an intense student of Creole manners and Southern history. Her first novel, *At Fault* (1890), was followed by two collections of stories, *Bayou Folk* (1894, which includes "Désirée's Baby") and *A Night in Acadie* (1897). Although the Chopin family often lived abroad, Kate Chopin's attention was always fixed on the Louisiana scene; in her handling of regional details and the theme of historical guilt, she foreshadowed in some ways the work of William Faulkner.

After the death of her husband Kate Chopin returned to St. Louis. Her last work, *The Awakening* (1899), is (for its time) an unusually frank and powerful treatment of sexual problems.

As the day was pleasant, Madame Valmondé drove over to L'Abri to see Désirée and the baby.

It made her laugh to think of Désirée with a baby. Why, it seemed but yesterday that Désirée was little more than a baby herself; when Monsieur in riding through the gateway of Valmondé had found her lying asleep in the shadow of the big stone pillar.

The little one awoke in his arms and began to cry for "Dada." That was as much as she could do or say. Some people thought she might have strayed there of her own accord, for she was of the toddling age. The prevailing belief was that she had been purposely left by a party of Texans, whose canvas-covered wagon, late in the day, had crossed the ferry that Coton Maïs kept, just below the plantation. In time Madame Valmondé abandoned every speculation but the one that Désirée had been sent to her by a beneficent Providence to be the child of her affection, seeing that she was without child of the flesh. For the girl grew to be beautiful and gentle, affectionate and sincere,—the idol of Valmondé.

It was no wonder, when she stood one day against the stone pillar in whose shadow she had lain asleep, eighteen years before, that Armand Aubigny riding by and seeing her there, had fallen in love with her. That was the way all the Aubignys fell in love, as if struck by a pistol shot. The wonder was that he had not loved her before; for he had known her since his father brought him home from Paris, a boy of eight, after his mother died there. The passion that awoke in him that day, when he saw her at the gate, swept along like an avalanche, or like a prairie fire, or like anything that drives headlong over all obstacles.

Monsieur Valmondé grew practical and wanted things well considered: that is, the girl's obscure origin. Armand looked into her eyes and did not care. He was reminded that she was nameless. What did it matter about a name when he could give her one of the oldest and proudest in Louisiana? He ordered the *corbeille* from Paris, and contained himself with what patience he could until it arrived; then they were married.

Madame Valmondé had not seen Désirée and the baby for four weeks. When she reached L'Abri she shuddered at the first sight of it, as she always did. It was a sad looking place, which for many years had not known the gentle presence of a mistress, old Monsieur

Aubigny having married and buried his wife in France, and she having loved her own land too well ever to leave it. The roof came down steep and black like a cowl, reaching out beyond the wide galleries that encircled the yellow stuccoed house. Big, solemn oaks grew close to it, and their thick-leaved, far-reaching branches shadowed it like a pall. Young Aubigny's rule was a strict one, too, and under it his negroes had forgotten how to be gay, as they had been during the old master's easy-going and indulgent lifetime.

The young mother was recovering slowly, and lay full length, in her soft white muslins and laces, upon a couch. The baby was beside her, upon her arm, where he had fallen asleep, at her breast. The yellow nurse woman sat beside a window fanning herself.

Madame Valmondé bent her portly figure over Désirée and kissed her, holding her an instant tenderly in her arms. Then she turned to the child.

"This is not the baby!" she exclaimed, in startled tones. French was the language spoken at Valmondé in those days.

"I knew you would be astonished," laughed Désirée, "at the way he has grown. The little *cochon de lait!* Look at his legs, mamma, and his hands and fingernails,—real fingernails. Zandrine had to cut them this morning. Isn't it true, Zandrine?"

The woman bowed her turbaned head majestically, "Mais si, Madame."

"And the way he cries," went on Désirée, "is deafening. Armand heard him the other day as far away as La Blanche's cabin."

Madame Valmondé had never removed her eyes from the child. She lifted it and walked with it over to the window that was lightest. She scanned the baby narrowly, then looked as searchingly at Zandrine, whose face was turned to gaze across the fields.

"Yes, the child has grown, has changed;" said Madame Valmondé, slowly, as she replaced it beside its mother. "What does Armand say?"

Désirée's face became suffused with a glow that was happiness itself.

"Oh, Armand is the proudest father in the parish, I believe, chiefly because it is a boy, to bear his name; though he says not,—that he would have loved a girl as well. But I know it isn't true. I know he says that to please me. And mamma," she added, drawing Madame Valmondé's head down to her, and speaking in a whisper, "he hasn't punished one of them—not one of them—since baby is born. Even Négrillon, who pretended to have burnt his leg that he might rest from work—he only laughed, and said Négrillon was a great scamp. Oh, mamma, I'm so happy! it frightens me."

What Désirée said was true. Marriage, and later the birth of his son, had softened Armand Aubigny's imperious and exacting nature greatly. This was what made the gentle Désirée so happy, for she loved him desperately. When he frowned she trembled, but loved him. When he smiled, she asked no greater blessing of God. But Armand's dark, handsome face had not often been disfigured by frowns since the day he fell in love with her.

When the baby was about three months old, Désirée awoke one day to the conviction that there was something in the air menacing her peace. It was at first too subtle to grasp. It had only been a disquieting suggestion; an air of mystery among the blacks; unexpected visits from far-off neighbors who could hardly account for their coming. Then a strange, an awful change in her husband's manner, which she dared not ask him to explain. When he spoke to her, it was with averted eyes, from which the old love-light seemed to have gone out. He absented himself from home; and when there, avoided her presence and that of her child, without excuse. And the very spirit of Satan seemed suddenly to take hold of him in his dealings with the slaves. Désirée was miserable enough to die.

She sat in her room, one hot afternoon, in her *peignoir,* listlessly drawing through her fingers the strands of her long, silky brown hair that hung about her shoulders. The baby, half naked, lay asleep upon her own great mahogany bed, that was like a sumptuous throne, with its satin-lined half-canopy. One of La Blanche's little quadroon boys—half naked too—stood fanning the child slowly with a fan of peacock feathers. Désirée's eyes had been fixed absently and sadly upon the baby, while she was striving to penetrate the threatening mist that she felt closing about her. She looked from her child to the boy who stood beside him, and back again; over and over. "Ah!" It was a cry that she could not help; which she was not conscious of having uttered. The blood turned like ice in her veins, and a clammy moisture gathered upon her face.

She tried to speak to the little quadroon boy; but no sound would come, at first. When he heard his name uttered, he looked up, and his mistress was pointing to the door. He laid aside the great, soft fan, and obediently stole away, over the polished floor, on his bare tiptoes.

She stayed motionless, with gaze riveted upon her child, and her face the picture of fright.

Presently her husband entered the room, and without noticing her, went to a table and began to search among some papers which covered it.

"Armand," she called to him, in a voice which must have stabbed him, if he was human. But he did not notice. "Armand," she said again. Then she rose and tottered towards him. "Armand," she panted once more, clutching his arm, "look at our child. What does it mean? tell me."

He coldly but gently loosened her fingers from about his arm and thrust the hand away from him. "Tell me what it means!" she cried despairingly.

"It means," he answered lightly, "that the child is not white; it means that you are not white."

A quick conception of all that this accusation meant for her nerved her with unwonted courage to deny it. "It is a lie; it is not true, I am white! Look at my hair, it is brown; and my eyes are gray, Armand, you know they are gray. And my skin is fair," seizing his wrist. "Look at my hand; whiter than yours, Armand," she laughed hysterically.

"As white as La Blanche's," he returned cruelly; and went away leaving her alone with their child.

When she could hold a pen in her hand, she sent a despairing letter to Madame Valmondé.

"My mother, they tell me I am not white. Armand has told me I am not white. For God's sake tell them it is not true. You must know it is not true. I shall die. I must die. I cannot be so unhappy, and live."

The answer that came was as brief:

"My own Désirée: Come home to Valmondé; back to your mother who loves you. Come with your child."

When the letter reached Désirée she went with it to her husband's study, and laid it open upon the desk before which he sat. She was like a stone image: silent, white, motionless after she placed it there.

In silence he ran his cold eyes over the written words. He said nothing. "Shall I go, Armand?" she asked in tones sharp with agonized suspense.

"Yes, go."

"Do you want me to go?"

"Yes, I want you to go."

He thought Almighty God had dealt cruelly and unjustly with him; and felt, somehow, that he was paying Him back in kind when he stabbed thus into his wife's soul. Moreover he no longer loved her, because of the unconscious injury she had brought upon his home and his name.

She turned away like one stunned by a blow, and walked slowly towards the door, hoping he would call her back.

"Good-by, Armand," she moaned.

He did not answer her. That was his last blow at fate.

Désirée went in search of her child. Zandrine was pacing the sombre gallery with it. She took the little one from the nurse's arms with no word of explanation, and descending the steps, walked away, under the live-oak branches.

It was an October afternoon; the sun was just sinking. Out in the still fields the negroes were picking cotton.

Désirée had not changed the thin white garment nor the slippers which she wore. Her hair was uncovered and the sun's rays brought a golden gleam from its brown meshes. She did not take the broad, beaten road which led to the far-off plantation of Valmondé. She walked across a deserted field, where the stubble bruised her tender feet, so delicately shod, and tore her thin gown to shreds.

She disappeared among the reeds and willows that grew thick along the banks of the deep, sluggish bayou; and she did not come back again.

Some weeks later there was a curious scene enacted at L'Abri. In the centre of the smoothly swept back yard was a great bonfire. Armand Aubigny sat in the wide hallway that commanded a view of the spectacle; and it was he who dealt out to a half dozen negroes the material which kept this fire ablaze.

A graceful cradle of willow, with all its dainty furbishing, was laid upon the pyre, which had already been fed with the richness of a priceless *layette.* Then there were silk gowns, and velvet and satin ones added to these; laces, too, and embroideries; bonnets and gloves; for the *corbeille* had been of rare quality.

The last thing to go was a tiny bundle of letters; innocent little scribblings that Désirée had sent to him during the days of their espousal. There was the remnant of one back in the drawer from which he took them. But it was not Désirée's; it was part of an old letter from his mother to his father. He read it. She was thanking God for the blessing of her husband's love:—

"But, above all," she wrote, "night and day, I thank the good God for having so arranged our lives that our dear Armand will never know that his mother, who adores him, belongs to the race that is cursed with the brand of slavery."

The Open Boat

Stephen Crane (1871–1900)

Stephen Crane was born in Newark, New Jersey, the son of a Methodist minister. After his father's death in 1880 the family moved to Asbury Park, New Jersey; Crane was educated at private schools and later attended Lafayette College and Syracuse University (1890–91). His first novel, *Maggie: A Girl of the Streets,* was written in 1891 but did not appear until 1893. In 1892 Crane became a free-lance reporter, and for the remainder of his brief life he worked continuously as a journalist, finding inspiration for his fiction in the clean style of the "new journalism." *The Red Badge of Courage* was published in 1895, and although Crane had never seen a military action at that time (he later covered the Spanish-American War), his treatment of the Civil War has the authority of an eye-witness account.

"The Open Boat," based on an experience Crane himself underwent in January 1897 and later reported for the *New York Press,* is his finest achievement. Joseph Conrad said of the story that "by the deep and simple humanity of its presentation it seems somehow to illustrate the essentials of life itself, like a symbolic tale."

In 1899 Crane settled in England and soon became acquainted with Conrad, H. G. Wells, Ford Madox Ford, and Henry James. Seriously ill with tuberculosis, he travelled to Germany for treatment and died there at the age of twenty-eight.

A Tale Intended to be after the Fact: Being the Experience of Four Men from the Sunk Steamer Commodore

I

None of them knew the color of the sky. Their eyes glanced level, and were fastened upon the waves that swept toward them. These waves were of the hue of slate, save for the tops, which were of foaming white, and all of the men knew the colors of the sea. The horizon narrowed and widened, and dipped and rose, and at all times its edge was jagged with waves that seemed thrust up in points like rocks.

Many a man ought to have a bathtub larger than the boat which here rode upon the sea. These waves were most wrongfully and barbarously abrupt and tall, and each froth-top was a problem in small-boat navigation.

The cook squatted in the bottom, and looked with both eyes at the six inches of gunwale which separated him from the ocean. His sleeves were rolled over his fat forearms, and the two flaps of his unbuttoned vest dangled as he bent to bail out the boat. Often he said, "Gawd! that was a narrow clip." As he remarked it he invariably gazed eastward over the broken sea.

The oiler, steering with one of the two oars in the boat, sometimes raised himself suddenly to keep clear of water that swirled in over the stern. It was a thin little oar, and it seemed often ready to snap.

The correspondent, pulling at the other oar, watched the waves and wondered why he was there.

The injured captain, lying in the bow, was at this time buried in that profound dejection and indifference which comes, temporarily at least, to even the bravest and most enduring when, willy-nilly, the firm fails, the army loses, the ship goes down. The mind of the master of a vessel is rooted deep in the timbers of her, though he command for a day or a decade; and this captain had on him the stern impression of a scene in the grays of dawn of seven turned faces, and later a stump of a topmast with a white ball on it, that slashed to and fro at the waves, went low and lower, and down. Thereafter there was something strange in his voice. Although steady, it was deep with mourning, and of a quality beyond oration or tears.

"Keep'er a little more south, Billie," said he.

"A little more south, sir," said the oiler in the stern.

A seat in this boat was not unlike a seat upon a bucking broncho, and by the same token a broncho is not much smaller. The craft pranced and reared and plunged like an animal. As each wave came, and she rose for it, she seemed like a horse making at a fence outrageously high. The manner of her scramble over these walls of water is a mystic thing, and, moreover, at the top of them were ordinarily these problems in white water, the foam racing down from the summit of each wave requiring a new leap, and a leap from the air. Then, after scornfully bumping a crest, she would slide and race and splash down a long incline, and arrive bobbing and nodding in front of the next menace.

A singular disadvantage of the sea lies in the fact that after successfully surmounting one wave you discover that there is another behind it just as important and just as nervously anxious to do something effective in the way of swamping boats. In a ten-foot dinghy one can get an idea of the resources of the sea in the line of waves that is not probable to the average experience, which is never at sea in a dinghy. As each slaty wall of water approached, it shut all else from the view of the men in the boat, and it was not difficult to imagine that this particular wave was the final outburst of the ocean, the last effort of the grim water. There was a terrible grace in the move of the waves, and they came in silence, save for the snarling of the crests.

In the wan light the faces of the men must have been gray. Their eyes must have glinted in strange ways as they gazed steadily astern. Viewed from a balcony, the whole thing would doubtless have been weirdly picturesque. But the men in the boat had no time to see it, and if they had had leisure, there were other things to occupy their minds. The sun swung steadily up the sky, and they knew it was broad day because the color of the sea changed from slate to emerald-green streaked with amber lights, and the foam was like tumbling snow. The process of the breaking day was unknown to them. They were aware only of this effect upon the color of the waves that rolled toward them.

In disjointed sentences the cook and the correspondent argued as to the difference between a lifesaving station and a house of refuge. The cook had said: "There's a house of refuge just north of the Mosquito Inlet Light, and as soon as they see us they'll come off in their boat and pick us up."

"As soon as who see us?" said the correspondent.

"The crew," said the cook.

"Houses of refuge don't have crews," said the correspondent. "As I understand them, they are only places where clothes and grub are stored for the benefit of shipwrecked people. They don't carry crews."

"Oh, yes, they do," said the cook.

"No, they don't," said the correspondent.

"Well, we're not there yet, anyhow," said the oiler, in the stern.

"Well," said the cook, "perhaps it's not a house of refuge that I'm thinking of as being near Mosquito Inlet Light; perhaps it's a lifesaving station."

"We're not there yet," said the oiler in the stern.

II

As the boat bounced from the top of each wave the wind tore through the hair of the hatless men, and as the craft plopped her stern down again the spray slashed past them. The crest of each of these waves was a hill, from the top of which the men surveyed for a moment a broad tumultuous expanse, shining and wind-riven. It was probably splendid, it was probably glorious, this play of the free sea, wild with lights of emerald and white and amber.

"Bully good thing it's an onshore wind," said the cook. "If not, where would we be? Wouldn't have a show."

"That's right," said the correspondent.

The busy oiler nodded his assent.

Then the captain, in the bow, chuckled in a way that expressed humor, contempt, tragedy, all in one. "Do you think we've got much of a show now, boys?" said he.

Whereupon the three were silent, save for a trifle of hemming and hawing. To express any particular optimism at this time they felt to be childish and stupid, but they all doubtless possessed this sense of the situation in their minds. A young man thinks doggedly at such times. On the other hand, the ethics of their condition was decidedly against any open suggestion of hopelessness. So they were silent.

"Oh, well," said the captain, soothing his children, "we'll get ashore all right."

But there was that in his tone which made them think; so the oiler quoth, "Yes! if this wind holds."

The cook was bailing. "Yes! if we don't catch hell in the surf."

Canton-flannel gulls flew near and far. Sometimes they sat down on the sea, near patches of brown seaweed that rolled over the waves with a movement like carpets on a line in a gale. The birds sat comfortably in groups, and they were envied by some in the dinghy, for the wrath of the sea was no more to them than it was to a covey of prairie chickens a thousand miles inland. Often they came very close and stared at the men with black bead-like eyes. At these times they were uncanny and sinister in their unblinking scrutiny, and the men hooted angrily at them, telling them to be gone. One came, and evidently decided to alight on the top of the captain's head. The bird flew parallel to the boat and did not circle, but made short sidelong jumps in the air in chicken fashion. His black eyes were wistfully fixed upon the captain's head. "Ugly brute," said the oiler to the bird. "You look as if you were made with a jackknife." The cook and the correspondent swore darkly at the creature. The captain naturally wished to knock it away with the end of the heavy painter, but he did not dare do it, because anything resembling an emphatic gesture would have capsized this freighted boat; and so, with his open hand, the captain gently and carefully waved the gull away. After it had been discouraged from the pursuit the captain breathed easier on account of his hair, and others breathed easier because the bird struck their minds at this time as being somehow gruesome and ominous.

In the meantime the oiler and the correspondent rowed. And also they rowed. They sat together in the same seat, and each rowed an oar. Then the oiler took both oars; then the correspondent took both oars; then the oiler; then the correspondent. They rowed and they rowed. The very ticklish part of the business was when the time came for the reclining one in the stern to take his turn at the oars. By the very last star of truth, it is easier to steal eggs from under a hen than it was to change seats in the dinghy. First the man in the stern slid his hand along the thwart and moved with care, as if he were of Sèvres. Then the man in the rowing-seat slid his hand along the other thwart. It was all done with the most extraordinary care. As the two sidled past each other, the whole party kept watchful eyes on the coming wave, and the captain cried: "Look out, now! Steady, there!"

The brown mats of seaweed that appeared from time to time were like islands, bits of earth. They were traveling, apparently, neither one way nor the other. They were, to all intents, stationary. They informed the men in the boat that it was making progress slowly toward the land.

The captain, rearing cautiously in the bow after the dinghy soared on a great swell, said that he had seen the lighthouse at Mosquito Inlet. Presently the cook remarked that he had seen it. The correspondent was at the oars then, and for some reason he too wished to look at the lighthouse; but his back was toward the far shore, and the waves were important, and for some time he could not seize an opportunity to turn his head. But at last there came a wave more gentle than the others, and when at the crest of it he swiftly scoured the western horizon.

"See it?" said the captain.

"No," said the correspondent, slowly; "I didn't see anything."

"Look again," said the captain. He pointed. "It's exactly in that direction."

At the top of another wave the correspondent did as he was bid, and this time his eyes chanced on a small, still thing on the edge of the swaying horizon. It was precisely like the point of a pin. It took an anxious eye to find a lighthouse so tiny.

"Think we'll make it, Captain?"

"If this wind holds and the boat don't swamp, we can't do much else," said the captain.

The little boat, lifted by each towering sea and splashed viciously by the crests, made progress that in the absence of seaweed was not apparent to those in her. She seemed just a wee thing wallowing, miraculously top up, at the mercy of five oceans. Occasionally a great spread of water, like white flames, swarmed into her.

"Bail her, cook," said the captain, serenely.

"All right, Captain," said the cheerful cook.

III

It would be difficult to describe the subtle brotherhood of men that was here established on the seas. No one said that it was so. No one mentioned it. But it dwelt in the boat, and each man felt it warm him. They were a captain, an oiler, a cook, and a correspondent, and they were friends—friends in a more curiously ironbound degree than may be common. The hurt captain, lying against the water jar in the bow, spoke always in a low voice and calmly; but he could never command a more ready and swiftly obedient crew than the motley three of the dinghy. It was more than a mere recognition of what was best for the common safety. There was surely in it a quality that was personal and heartfelt. And after this devotion to the commander of the boat, there was this comradeship, that the correspondent, for instance, who had been taught to be cynical of men, knew even at the time was the best experience of his life. But no one said that it was so. No one mentioned it.

"I wish we had a sail," remarked the captain. "We might try my overcoat on the end of an oar, and give you two boys a chance to rest." So the cook and the correspondent held the mast and spread wide the overcoat; the oiler steered; and the little boat made good way with her new rig. Sometimes the oiler had to scull sharply to keep a sea from breaking into the boat, but otherwise sailing was a success.

Meanwhile the lighthouse had been growing slowly larger. It had now almost assumed color, and appeared like a little gray shadow on the sky. The man at the oars could not be prevented from turning his head rather often to try for a glimpse of this little gray shadow.

At last, from the top of each wave, the men in the tossing boat could see land. Even as the lighthouse was an upright shadow on the sky, this land seemed but a long black shadow on the sea. It certainly was thinner than paper. "We must be about opposite New Smyrna," said the cook, who had coasted this shore often in schooners. "Captain, by the way, I believe they abandoned that lifesaving station there about a year ago."

"Did they?" said the captain.

The wind slowly died away. The cook and the correspondent were not now obliged to slave in order to hold high the oar. But the waves continued their old impetuous swooping at the dinghy, and the little craft, no longer under way, struggled woundily over them. The oiler or the correspondent took the oars again.

Shipwrecks are *apropos* of nothing. If men could only train for them and have them occur when the men had reached pink condition, there would be less drowning at sea. Of the four in the dinghy none had slept any time worth mentioning for two days and two nights previous to embarking in the dinghy, and in the excitement of clambering about the deck of a foundering ship they had also forgotten to eat heartily.

For these reasons, and for others, neither the oiler nor the correspondent was fond of rowing at this time. The correspondent wondered ingenuously how in the name of all that was sane could there be people who thought it amusing to row a boat. It was not an amusement; it was a diabolical punishment, and even a genius of mental aberrations could never conclude that it was anything but a horror to the muscles and a crime against the back. He mentioned to the boat in general how the amusement of rowing struck him, and the weary-faced oiler smiled in full sympathy. Previously to the foundering, by the way, the oiler had worked a double watch in the engine room of the ship.

"Take her easy now, boys," said the captain. "Don't spend yourselves. If we have to run a surf you'll need all your strength, because we'll sure have to swim for it. Take your time."

Slowly the land arose from the sea. From a black line it became a line of black and a line of white—trees and sand. Finally the captain said that he could make out a house on the shore. "That's the house of refuge, sure," said the cook. "They'll see us before long, and come out after us."

The distant lighthouse reared high. "The keeper ought to be able to make us out now, if he's looking through a glass," said the captain. "He'll notify the lifesaving people."

"None of those other boats could have got ashore to give word of this wreck," said the oiler, in a low voice, "else the lifeboat would be out hunting us."

Slowly and beautifully the land loomed out of the sea. The wind came again. It had veered from the northeast to the southeast. Finally a new sound struck the ears of the men in the boat. It was the low thunder of the surf on the shore. "We'll never be able to make the lighthouse now," said the captain. "Swing her head a little more north, Billie."

"A little more north, sir," said the oiler.

Whereupon the little boat turned her nose once more down the wind, and all but the oarsman watched the shore grow. Under the influence of this expansion doubt and direful apprehension were leaving the minds of the men. The management of the boat was still most absorbing, but it could not prevent a quiet cheerfulness. In an hour, perhaps, they would be ashore.

Their backbones had become thoroughly used to balancing in the boat, and they now rode this wild colt of a dinghy like circus men. The correspondent thought that he had been drenched to the skin, but happening to feel in the top pocket of his coat, he found therein eight cigars. Four of them were soaked with seawater; four were perfectly scatheless. After a search, somebody produced three dry matches; and thereupon the four waifs rode impudently in their little boat and, with an assurance of an impending rescue shining in their eyes, puffed at the big cigars, and judged well and ill of all men. Everybody took a drink of water.

IV

"Cook," remarked the captain, "there don't seem to be any signs of life about your house of refuge."

"No," replied the cook. "Funny they don't see us!"

A broad stretch of lowly coast lay before the eyes of the men. It was of low dunes topped with dark vegetation. The roar of the surf was plain, and sometimes they could see the white lip of a wave as it spun up the beach. A tiny house was blocked out black upon the sky. Southward, the slim lighthouse lifted its little gray length.

Tide, wind, and waves were swinging the dinghy northward. "Funny they don't see us," said the men.

The surf's roar was here dulled, but its tone was nevertheless thunderous and mighty. As the boat swam over the great rollers the men sat listening to this roar. "We'll swamp sure," said everybody.

It is fair to say here that there was not a lifesaving station within twenty miles in either direction; but the men did not know this fact, and in consequence they made dark and opprobrious remarks concerning the eyesight of the nation's lifesavers. Four scowling men sat in the dinghy and surpassed records in the invention of epithets.

"Funny they don't see us."

The light-heartedness of a former time had completely faded. To their sharpened minds it was easy to conjure pictures of all kinds of incompetency and blindness and, indeed, cowardice. There was the shore of the populous land, and it was bitter and bitter to them that from it came no sign.

"Well," said the captain, ultimately, "I suppose we'll have to make a try for ourselves. If we stay out here too long, we'll none of us have strength left to swim after the boat swamps."

And so the oiler, who was at the oars, turned the boat straight for the shore. There was a sudden tightening of muscles. There was some thinking.

"If we don't all get ashore," said the captain—"if we don't all get ashore, I suppose you fellows know where to send news of my finish?"

They then briefly exchanged some addresses and admonitions. As for the reflections of the men, there was a great deal of rage in them. Perchance they might be formulated thus: "If I am going to be drowned—if I am going to be drowned—if I am going to be drowned, why, in the name of the seven mad gods who rule the sea, was I allowed to come thus far and contemplate sand and trees? Was I brought here merely to have my nose dragged away as I was about to nibble the sacred cheese of life? It is preposterous. If this old ninny-woman, Fate, cannot do better than this, she should be deprived of the management of men's fortunes. She is an old hen who knows not her intention. If she has decided to drown me, why did she not do it in the beginning and save me all this trouble? The whole affair is absurd. . . . But no; she cannot mean to drown me. She dare not drown me. She cannot drown me. Not after all this work." Afterward the man might have had an impulse to shake his fist at the clouds. "Just you drown me, now, and then hear what I call you!"

The billows that came at this time were more formidable. They seemed always just about to break and roll over the little boat in a turmoil of foam. There was a preparatory and long growl in the speech of them. No mind unused to the sea would have concluded that the dinghy could ascend these sheer heights in time. The shore was still afar. The oiler was a wily surfman. "Boys," he said swiftly, "she won't live three minutes more, and we're too far out to swim. Shall I take her to sea again, Captain?"

"Yes; go ahead!" said the captain.

This oiler, by a series of quick miracles and fast and steady oarsmanship, turned the boat in the middle of the surf and took her safely to sea again.

There was a considerable silence as the boat bumped over the furrowed sea to deeper water. Then somebody in gloom spoke: "Well, anyhow, they must have seen us from the shore by now."

The gulls went in slanting flight up the wind toward the gray, desolate east. A squall, marked by dingy clouds and clouds brickred, like smoke from a burning building, appeared from the southeast.

"What do you think of those lifesaving people? Ain't they peaches?"

"Funny they haven't seen us."

"Maybe they think we're out here for sport! Maybe they think we're fishin'. Maybe they think we're damned fools."

It was a long afternoon. A changed tide tried to force them southward, but wind and wave said northward. Far ahead, where coastline, sea, and sky formed their mighty angle, there were little dots which seemed to indicate a city on the shore.

"St. Augustine?"

The captain shook his head. "Too near Mosquito Inlet."

And the oiler rowed, and then the correspondent rowed; then the oiler rowed. It was a weary business. The human back can become the seat of more aches and pains than are registered in books for the composite anatomy of a regiment. It is a limited area, but it can become the theater of innumerable muscular conflicts, tangles, wrenches, knots, and other comforts.

"Did you ever like to row, Billie?" asked the correspondent.

"No," said the oiler; "hang it!"

When one exchanged the rowing-seat for a place in the bottom of the boat, he suffered a bodily depression that caused him to be careless of everything save an obligation to wiggle one finger. There was cold seawater swashing to and fro in the boat, and he lay in it. His head, pillowed on a thwart, was within an inch of the swirl of a wave-crest, and sometimes a particularly obstreperous sea came inboard and drenched him once more. But these matters did not annoy him. It is almost certain that if the boat had capsized he would have tumbled comfortably out upon the ocean as if he felt sure that it was a great soft mattress.

"Look! There's a man on the shore!"

"Where?"

"There! See 'im? See 'im?"

"Yes, sure! He's walking along."

"Now he's stopped. Look! He's facing us!"

"He's waving at us!"

"So he is! By thunder!"

"Ah, now we're all right! Now we're all right! There'll be a boat out here for us in half an hour."

"He's going on. He's running. He's going up to that house there."

The remote beach seemed lower than the sea, and it required a searching glance to discern the little black figure. The captain saw a floating stick, and they rowed to it. A bath towel was by some weird chance in the boat, and, tying this on the stick, the captain waved it. The oarsman did not dare turn his head, so he was obliged to ask questions.

"What's he doing now?"

"He's standing still again. He's looking, I think. . . . There he goes again—toward the house. . . . Now he's stopped again."

"Is he waving at us?"

"No, not now; he was, though."

"Look! There comes another man!"

"He's running."

"Look at him go, would you!"

"Why, he's on a bicycle. Now he's met the other man. They're both waving at us. Look!"

"There comes something up the beach."

"What the devil is that thing?"

"Why, it looks like a boat."

"Why, certainly, it's a boat."

"No; it's on wheels."

"Yes, so it is. Well, that must be the lifeboat. They drag them along shore on a wagon."

"That's the lifeboat, sure."

"No, by God, it's—it's an omnibus."

"I tell you it's a lifeboat."

"It is not! It's an omnibus. I can see it plain. See? One of these big hotel omnibuses."

"By thunder, you're right. It's an omnibus, sure as fate. What do you suppose they are doing with an omnibus? Maybe they are going around collecting the life-crew, hey?"

"That's it, likely. Look! There's a fellow waving a little black flag. He's standing on the steps of the omnibus. There come those other two fellows. Now they're all talking together. Look at the fellow with the flag. Maybe he ain't waving it!"

"That ain't a flag, is it? That's his coat. Why, certainly, that's his coat."

"So it is; it's his coat. He's taken it off and is waving it around his head. But would you look at him swing it!"

"Oh, say, there isn't any lifesaving station there. That's just a winter-resort hotel omnibus that has brought over some of the boarders to see us drown."

"What's that idiot with the coat mean? What's he signaling, anyhow?"

"It looks as if he were trying to tell us to go north. There must be a lifesaving station up there."

"No; he thinks we're fishing. Just giving us a merry hand. See? Ah, there, Willie!"

"Well, I wish I could make something out of those signals. What do you suppose he means?"

"He don't mean anything; he's just playing."

"Well, if he'd just signal us to try the surf again, or to go to sea and wait, or go north, or go south, or go to hell, there would be some reason in it. But look at him! He just stands there and keeps his coat revolving like a wheel. The ass!"

"There come more people."

"Now there's quite a mob. Look! Isn't that a boat?"

"Where? Oh, I see where you mean. No, that's no boat."

"That fellow is still waving his coat."

"He must think we like to see him do that. Why don't he quit it? It don't mean anything."

"I don't know. I think he is trying to make us go north. It must be that there's a lifesaving station there somewhere."

"Say, he ain't tired yet. Look at 'im wave!"

"Wonder how long he can keep that up. He's been revolving his coat ever since he caught sight of us. He's an idiot. Why aren't they getting men to bring a boat out? A fishing boat—one of those big yawls—could come out here all right. Why don't he do something?"

"Oh, it's all right now."

"They'll have a boat out here for us in less than no time, now that they've seen us."

A faint yellow tone came into the sky over the low land. The shadows on the sea slowly deepened. The wind bore coldness with it, and the men began to shiver.

"Holy smoke!" said one, allowing his voice to express his impious mood, "if we keep on monkeying out here! If we've got to flounder out here all night!"

"Oh, we'll never have to stay here all night! Don't you worry. They've seen us now, and it won't be long before they'll come chasing out after us."

The shore grew dusky. The man waving a coat blended gradually into this gloom, and it swallowed in the same manner the omnibus and the group of people. The spray, when it dashed uproariously over the side, made the voyagers shrink and swear like men who were being branded.

"I'd like to catch the chump who waved the coat. I feel like socking him one, just for luck."

"Why? What did he do?"

"Oh, nothing, but then he seemed so damned cheerful."

In the meantime the oiler rowed, and then the correspondent rowed, and then the oiler rowed. Gray-faced and bowed forward, they mechanically, turn by turn, plied the leaden oars. The form of the lighthouse had vanished from the southern horizon, but finally a pale star appeared, just lifting from the sea. The streaked saffron in the west passed before the all-merging darkness, and the sea to the east was black. The land had vanished, and was expressed only by the low and drear thunder of the surf.

"If I am going to be drowned—if I am going to be drowned—if I am going to be drowned, why, in the name of the seven mad gods who rule the sea, was I allowed to come thus far and contemplate sand and trees? Was I brought here merely to have my nose dragged away as I was about to nibble the sacred cheese of life?"

The patient captain, drooped over the water jar, was sometimes obliged to speak to the oarsman.

"Keep her head up! Keep her head up!"

"Keep her head up, sir." The voices were weary and low.

This was surely a quiet evening. All save the oarsman lay heavily and listlessly in the boat's bottom. As for him, his eyes were just capable of noting the tall black waves that swept forward in a most sinister silence, save for an occasional subdued growl of a crest.

The cook's head was on a thwart, and he looked without interest at the water under his nose. He was deep in other scenes. Finally he spoke. "Billie," he murmured, dreamfully, "what kind of pie do you like best?"

V

"Pie!" said the oiler and the correspondent, agitatedly. "Don't talk about those things, blast you!"

"Well," said the cook, "I was just thinking about ham sandwiches, and—"

A night on the sea in an open boat is a long night. As darkness settled finally, the shine of the light, lifting from the sea in the south, changed to full gold. On the northern horizon a new light appeared, a small bluish gleam on the edge of the waters. These two lights were the furniture of the world. Otherwise there was nothing but waves.

Two men huddled in the stern, and distances were so magnificent in the dinghy that the rower was enabled to keep his feet partly warm by thrusting them under his companions. Their legs indeed extended far under the rowing-seat until they touched the feet of the captain forward. Sometimes, despite the efforts of the tired oarsman, a wave came piling into the boat, an icy wave of the night, and the chilling water soaked them anew. They would twist their bodies for a moment and groan, and sleep the dead sleep once more, while the water in the boat gurgled about them as the craft rocked.

The plan of the oiler and the correspondent was for one to row until he lost the ability, and then arouse the other from his seawater couch in the bottom of the boat.

The oiler plied the oars until his head drooped forward and the overpowering sleep blinded him; and he rowed yet afterward. Then he touched a man in the bottom of the boat, and called his name. "Will you spell me for a little while?" he said meekly.

"Sure, Billie," said the correspondent, awaking and dragging himself to a sitting position. They exchanged places carefully, and the oiler, cuddling down in the seawater at the cook's side, seemed to go to sleep instantly.

The particular violence of the sea had ceased. The waves came without snarling. The obligation of the man at the oars was to keep the boat headed so that the tilt of the rollers would not capsize her, and to preserve her from filling when the crests rushed past. The black waves were silent and hard to be seen in the darkness. Often one was almost upon the boat before the oarsman was aware.

In a low voice the correspondent addressed the captain. He was not sure that the captain was awake, although this iron man seemed to be always awake. "Captain, shall I keep her making for that light north, sir?"

The same steady voice answered him. "Yes. Keep it about two points off the port bow."

The cook had tied a lifebelt around himself in order to get even the warmth which this clumsy cork contrivance could donate, and he seemed almost stove-like when a rower, whose teeth invariably chattered wildly as soon as he ceased his labor, dropped down to sleep.

The correspondent, as he rowed, looked down at the two men sleeping underfoot. The cook's arm was around the oiler's shoulders, and, with their fragmentary clothing and haggard faces, they were the babes of the sea—a grotesque rendering of the old babes in the wood.

Later he must have grown stupid at his work, for suddenly there was a growling of water, and a crest came with a roar and a swash into the boat, and it was a wonder that it did not set the cook afloat in his lifebelt. The cook continued to sleep, but the oiler sat up, blinking his eyes and shaking with the new cold.

"Oh, I'm awful sorry, Billie," said the correspondent, contritely.

"That's all right, old boy," said the oiler, and lay down again and was asleep.

Presently it seemed that even the captain dozed, and the correspondent thought that he was the one man afloat on all the oceans. The wind had a voice as it came over the waves, and it was sadder than the end.

There was a long, loud swishing astern of the boat, and a gleaming trail of phosphorescence, like blue flame, was furrowed on the black waters. It might have been made by a monstrous knife.

Then there came a stillness, while the correspondent breathed with open mouth and looked at the sea.

Suddenly there was another swish and another long flash of bluish light, and this time it was alongside the boat, and might almost have been reached with an oar. The correspondent saw an enormous fin speed like a shadow through the water, hurling the crystalline spray and leaving the long glowing trail.

The correspondent looked over his shoulder at the captain. His face was hidden, and he seemed to be asleep. He looked at the babes of the sea. They certainly were asleep. So, being bereft of sympathy, he leaned a little way to one side and swore softly into the sea.

But the thing did not then leave the vicinity of the boat. Ahead or astern, on one side or the other, at intervals long or short, fled the long sparkling streak, and there was to be heard the *whirroo* of the dark fin. The speed and power of the thing was greatly to be admired. It cut the water like a gigantic and keen projectile.

The presence of this biding thing did not affect the man with the same horror that it would if he had been a picnicker. He simply looked at the sea dully and swore in an undertone.

Nevertheless, it is true that he did not wish to be alone with the thing. He wished one of his companions to awake by chance and keep him company with it. But the captain hung motionless over the water jar, and the oiler and the cook in the bottom of the boat were plunged in slumber.

VI

"If I am going to be drowned—if I am going to be drowned—if I am going to be drowned, why, in the name of the seven mad gods who rule the sea, was I allowed to come thus far and contemplate sand and trees?"

During this dismal night, it may be remarked that a man would conclude that it was really the intention of the seven mad gods to drown him, despite the abominable injustice of it. For it was certainly an abominable injustice to drown a man who had worked so hard, so hard. The man felt it would be a crime most unnatural. Other people had drowned at sea since galleys swarmed with painted sails, but still—

When it occurs to a man that nature does not regard him as important, and that she feels she would not maim the universe by disposing of him, he at first wishes to throw bricks at the temple, and he hates deeply the fact that there are no bricks and no temples. Any visible expression of nature would surely be pelleted with his jeers.

Then, if there be no tangible thing to hoot, he feels, perhaps, the desire to confront a personification and indulge in pleas, bowed to one knee, and with hands supplicant, saying, "Yes, but I love myself."

A high cold star on a winter's night is the word he feels that she says to him. Thereafter he knows the pathos of his situation.

The men in the dinghy had not discussed these matters, but each had, no doubt, reflected upon them in silence and according to his mind. There was seldom any expression upon their faces save the general one of complete weariness. Speech was devoted to the business of the boat.

To chime the notes of his emotion, a verse mysteriously entered the correspondent's head. He had even forgotten that he had forgotten this verse, but it suddenly was in his mind.

A soldier of the Legion lay dying in Algiers;
There was lack of woman's nursing, there was
  dearth of woman's tears;
But a comrade stood beside him, and he took that
  comrade's hand,

And he said, "I never more shall see my own, my
native land."

In his childhood the correspondent had been made acquainted with the fact that a soldier of the Legion lay dying in Algiers, but he had never regarded the fact as important. Myriads of his school-fellows had informed him of the soldier's plight, but the dinning had naturally ended by making him perfectly indifferent. He had never considered it his affair that a soldier of the Legion lay dying in Algiers, nor had it appeared to him as a matter for sorrow. It was less to him than the breaking of a pencil's point.

Now, however, it quaintly came to him as a human, living thing. It was no longer merely a picture of a few throes in the breast of a poet, meanwhile drinking tea and warming his feet at the grate; it was an actuality—stern, mournful, and fine.

The correspondent plainly saw the soldier. He lay on the sand with his feet out straight and still. While his pale left hand was upon his chest in an attempt to thwart the going of his life, the blood came between his fingers. In the far Algerian distance, a city of low square forms was set against a sky that was faint with the last sunset hues. The correspondent, plying the oars and dreaming of the slow and slower movements of the lips of the soldier, was moved by a profound and perfectly impersonal comprehension. He was sorry for the soldier of the Legion who lay dying in Algiers.

The thing which had followed the boat and waited had evidently grown bored at the delay. There was no longer to be heard the slash of the cut-water, and there was no longer the flame of the long trail. The light in the north still glimmered, but it was apparently no nearer to the boat. Sometimes the boom of the surf rang in the correspondent's ears, and he turned the craft seaward then and rowed harder. Southward, some one had evidently built a watch fire on the beach. It was too low and too far to be seen, but it made a shimmering, roseate reflection upon the bluff in back of it, and this could be discerned from the boat. The wind came stronger, and sometimes a wave suddenly raged out like a mountain cat, and there was to be seen the sheen and sparkle of a broken crest.

The captain, in the bow, moved on his water jar and sat erect. "Pretty long night," he observed to the correspondent. He looked at the shore. "Those lifesaving people take their time."

"Did you see that shark playing around?"

"Yes, I saw him. He was a big fellow, all right."

"Wish I had known you were awake."

Later the correspondent spoke into the bottom of the boat. "Billie!" There was a slow and gradual disentanglement. "Billie, will you spell me?"

"Sure," said the oiler.

As soon as the correspondent touched the cold, comfortable seawater in the bottom of the boat and had huddled close to the cook's lifebelt he was deep in sleep, despite the fact that his teeth played all the popular airs. This sleep was so good to him that it was but a moment before he heard a voice call his name in a tone that demonstrated the last stages of exhaustion. "Will you spell me?"

"Sure, Billie."

The light in the north had mysteriously vanished, but the correspondent took his course from the wide-awake captain.

Later in the night they took the boat farther out to sea, and the captain directed the cook to take one oar at the stern and keep the boat facing the seas. He was to call out if he should hear the thunder of the surf. This plan enabled the oiler and the correspondent to get respite together. "We'll give those boys a chance to get into shape again," said the captain. They curled down and, after a few preliminary chatterings and trembles, slept once more the dead sleep. Neither knew they had bequeathed to the cook the company of another shark, or perhaps the same shark.

As the boat caroused on the waves, spray occasionally bumped over the side and gave them a fresh soaking, but this had no power to break their repose. The ominous slash of the wind and the water affected them as it would have affected mummies.

"Boys," said the cook, with the notes of every reluctance in his voice, "she's drifted in pretty close. I guess one of you had better take her to sea again." The correspondent, aroused, heard the crash of the toppled crests.

As he was rowing, the captain gave him some whiskey-and-water, and this steadied the chills out of him. "If I ever get ashore and anybody shows me even a photograph of an oar—"

At last there was a short conversation.

"Billie! . . . Billie, will you spell me?"

"Sure," said the oiler.

VII

When the correspondent again opened his eyes, the sea and the sky were each of the gray hue of the dawning. Later, carmine and gold was painted upon the waters. The morning appeared finally, in its splendor, with a sky of pure blue, and the sunlight flamed on the tips of the waves.

On the distanct dunes were set many little black cottages, and a tall white windmill reared above them. No man, nor dog, nor bicycle appeared on the beach. The cottages might have formed a deserted village.

The voyagers scanned the shore. A conference was held in the boat. "Well," said the captain, "if no help is coming, we might better try a run through the surf right away. If we stay out here much longer we will be too weak to do anything for ourselves at all." The others silently acquiesced in this reasoning. The boat was headed for the beach. The correspondent wondered if none ever ascended the tall wind-tower, and if then they never looked seaward. This tower was a giant, standing with its back to the plight of the ants. It represented in a degree, to the correspondent, the serenity of nature amid the struggles of the individual—nature in the wind, and nature in the vision of men. She did not seem cruel to him then, nor beneficent, nor treacherous, nor wise. But she was indifferent, flatly indifferent. It is, perhaps, plausible that a man in this situation, impressed with the unconcern of the universe, should see the innumerable flaws of his life, and have them taste wickedly in his mind, and wish for another chance. A distinction between right and wrong seems absurdly clear to him, then, in this new ignorance of the grave-edge, and he understands that if he were given another opportunity he would mend his conduct and his words, and be better and brighter during an introduction or at a tea.

"Now, boys," said the captain, "she is going to swamp sure. All we can do is to work her in as far as possible, and then when she swamps, pile out and scramble for the beach. Keep cool now, and don't jump until she swamps sure."

The oiler took the oars. Over his shoulders he scanned the surf. "Captain," he said, "I think I'd better bring her about and keep her head-on to the seas and back her in."

"All right, Billie," said the captain. "Back her in." The oiler swung the boat then, and, seated in the stern, the cook and the correspondent were obliged to look over their shoulders to contemplate the lonely and indifferent shore.

The monstrous inshore rollers heaved the boat high until the men were again enabled to see the white sheets of water scudding up the slanted beach. "We won't get in very close," said the captain. Each time a man could wrest his attention from the rollers, he turned his glance toward the shore, and in the expression of the eyes during this contemplation there was a singular quality. The correspondent, observing the others, knew that they were not afraid, but the full meaning of their glances was shrouded.

As for himself, he was too tired to grapple fundamentally with the fact. He tried to coerce his mind into thinking of it, but the mind was dominated at this time by the muscles, and the muscles said they did not care. It merely occurred to him that if he should drown it would be a shame.

There were no hurried words, no pallor, no plain agitation. The men simply looked at the shore. "Now, remember to get well clear of the boat when you jump," said the captain.

Seaward the crest of a roller suddenly fell with a thunderous crash, and the long white comber came roaring down upon the boat.

"Steady now," said the captain. The men were silent. They turned their eyes from the shore to the comber and waited. The boat slid up the incline, leaped at the furious top, bounced over it, and swung down the long back of the wave. Some water had been shipped, and the cook bailed it out.

But the next crest crashed also. The tumbling, boiling flood of white water caught the boat and whirled it almost perpendicular. Water swarmed in from all sides. The correspondent had his hands on the gunwale at this time, and when the water entered at that place he swiftly withdrew his fingers, as if he objected to wetting them.

The little boat, drunken with this weight of water, reeled and snuggled deeper into the sea.

"Bail her out, cook! Bail her out!" said the captain.

"All right, Captain," said the cook.

"Now boys, the next one will do for us sure," said the oiler. "Mind to jump clear of the boat."

The third wave moved forward, huge, furious, implacable. It fairly swallowed the dinghy, and almost simultaneously the men tumbled into the sea. A piece of lifebelt had lain in the bottom of the boat, and as the correspondent went overboard he held this to his chest with his left hand.

The January water was icy, and he reflected immediately that it was colder than he had expected to find it off the coast of Florida. This appeared to his dazed mind as a fact important enough to be noted at the time. The coldness of the water was sad; it was tragic. This fact was somehow mixed and confused with his opinion of his own situation, so that it seemed almost a proper reason for tears. The water was cold.

When he came to the surface he was conscious of little but the noisy water. Afterward he saw his companions in the sea. The oiler was ahead in the race. He was swimming strongly and rapidly. Off to the correspondent's left, the cook's great white and corked back bulged out of the water; and in the rear the captain was hanging with his one good hand to the keel of the overturned dinghy.

There is a certain immovable quality to a shore, and

the correspondent wondered at it amid the confusion of the sea.

It seemed also very attractive; but the correspondent knew that it was a long journey, and he paddled leisurely. The piece of life preserver lay under him, and sometimes he whirled down the incline of a wave as if he were on a hand-sled.

But finally he arrived at a place in the sea where travel was beset with difficulty. He did not pause swimming to inquire what manner of current had caught him, but there his progress ceased. The shore was set before him like a bit of scenery on a stage, and he looked at it and understood with his eyes each detail of it.

As the cook passed, much farther to the left, the captain was calling to him, "Turn over on your back, cook! Turn over on your back and use the oar."

"All right, sir." The cook turned on his back, and, paddling with an oar, went ahead as if he were a canoe.

Presently the boat also passed to the left of the correspondent, with the captain clinging with one hand to the keel. He would have appeared like a man raising himself to look over a board fence if it were not for the extraordinary gymnastics of the boat. The correspondent marveled that the captain could still hold to it.

They passed on nearer to shore—the oiler, the cook, the captain—and following them went the water jar, bouncing gaily over the seas.

The correspondent remained in the grip of this strange new enemy—a current. The shore, with its white slope of sand and its green bluff topped with little silent cottages, was spread like a picture before him. It was very near to him then, but he was impressed as one who, in a gallery, looks at a scene from Brittany or Algiers.

He thought: "I am going to drown? Can it be possible? Can it be possible? Can it be possible?" Perhaps an individual must consider his own death to be the final phenomenon of nature.

But later a wave perhaps whirled him out of this small deadly current, for he found suddenly that he could again make progress toward the shore. Later still he was aware that the captain, clinging with one hand to the keel of the dinghy, had his face turned away from the shore and toward him, and was calling his name. "Come to the boat! Come to the boat!"

In his struggle to reach the captain and the boat, he reflected that when one gets properly wearied drowning must really be a comfortable arrangement—a cessation of hostilities accompanied by a large degree of relief; and he was glad of it, for the main thing in his mind for some moments had been horror of the temporary agony. He did not wish to be hurt.

Presently he saw a man running along the shore. He was undressing with the most remarkable speed. Coat, trousers, shirt, everything flew magically off him.

"Come to the boat!" called the captain.

"All right, Captain." As the correspondent paddled, he saw the captain let himself down to bottom and leave the boat. Then the correspondent performed his one little marvel of the voyage. A large wave caught him and flung him with ease and supreme speed completely over the boat and far beyond it. It struck him even then as an event in gymnastics and a true miracle of the sea. An overturned boat in the surf is not a plaything to a swimming man.

The correspondent arrived in water that reached only to his waist, but his condition did not enable him to stand for more than a moment. Each wave knocked him into a heap, and the undertow pulled at him.

Then he saw the man who had been running and undressing, and undressing and running, come bounding into the water. He dragged ashore the cook, and then waded toward the captain; but the captain waved him away and sent him to the correspondent. He was naked—naked as a tree in winter; but a halo was about his head, and he shone like a saint. He gave a strong pull, and a long drag, and a bully heave at the correspondent's hand. The correspondent, schooled in the minor formulae, said, "Thanks, old man." But suddenly the man cried, "What's that?" He pointed a swift finger. The correspondent said, "Go."

In the shallows, face downward, lay the oiler. His forehead touched sand that was periodically, between each wave, clear of the sea.

The correspondent did not know all that transpired afterward. When he achieved safe ground he fell, striking the sand with each particular part of his body. It was as if he had dropped from a roof, but the thud was grateful to him.

It seems that instantly the beach was populated with men with blankets, clothes, and flasks, and women with coffeepots and all the remedies sacred to their minds. The welcome of the land to the men from the sea was warm and generous; but a still and dripping shape was carried slowly up the beach, and the land's welcome for it could only be the different and sinister hospitality of the grave.

When it came night, the white waves paced to and fro in the moonlight, and the wind brought the sound of the great sea's voice to the men on the shore, and they felt that they could then be interpreters.

The Eyes

Edith Wharton (1862–1937)

Edith Wharton was born into the fashionable New York society that Henry James knew as a young man, and its gradual vulgarization in the years after the Civil War became one of her leading themes. In 1885 she married a wealthy Boston banker. The marriage was an emotional disaster, and it was not until the turn of the century that Edith Wharton was able to free her artistic energies. Her novel *The House of Mirth* appeared in 1905, followed by *Ethan Frome* (1911), *The Custom of the Country* (1913), and *The Age of Innocence* (1920).

Like her good friend Henry James, Mrs. Wharton spent much of her early life in Europe, and in 1910 she took up residence in France. Between 1899 and 1936 she produced eleven volumes of short stories, many of them reminiscent of James's in their treatments of the international theme and the supernatural. "The Eyes" was published in *Tales of Men and Ghosts* (1910).

I

We had been put in the mood for ghosts, that evening, after an excellent dinner at our old friend Culwin's, by a tale of Fred Murchard's—the narrative of a strange personal visitation.

Seen through the haze of our cigars, and by the drowsy gleam of a coal fire, Culwin's library, with its oak walls and dark old bindings, made a good setting for such evocations; and ghostly experiences at first hand being, after Murchard's opening, the only kind acceptable to us, we proceeded to take stock of our group and tax each member for a contribution. There were eight of us, and seven contrived, in a manner more or less adequate, to fulfil the condition imposed. It surprised us all to find that we could muster such a show of supernatural impressions, for none of us, excepting Murchard himself and young Phil Frenham—whose story was the slightest of the lot—had the habit of sending our souls into the invisible. So that, on the whole, we had every reason to be proud of our seven "exhibits," and none of us would have dreamed of expecting an eighth from our host.

Our old friend, Mr. Andrew Culwin, who had sat back in his arm-chair, listening and blinking through the smoke circles with the cheerful tolerance of a wise old idol, was not the kind of man likely to be favoured with such contacts, though he had imagination enough to enjoy, without envying, the superior privileges of his guests. By age and by education he belonged to the stout Positivist tradition, and his habit of thought had been formed in the days of the epic struggle between physics and metaphysics. But he had been, then and always, essentially a spectator, a humorous detached observer of the immense muddled variety show of life, slipping out of his seat now and then for a brief dip into the convivialities at the back of the house, but never, as far as one knew, showing the least desire to jump on the stage and do a "turn."

Among his contemporaries there lingered a vague tradition of his having, at a remote period, and in a romantic clime, been wounded in a duel; but this legend no more tallied with what we younger men knew of his character than my mother's assertion that he had once been "a charming little man with nice eyes" corresponded to any possible reconstitution of his physiognomy.

"He never can have looked like anything but a bundle of sticks,'' Murchard had once said of him. "Or a phosphorescent log, rather,'' some one else amended; and we recognised the happiness of this description of his small squat trunk, with the red blink of the eyes in a face like mottled bark. He had always been possessed of a leisure which he had nursed and protected, instead of squandering it in vain activities. His carefully guarded hours had been devoted to the cultivation of a fine intelligence and a few judiciously chosen habits; and none of the disturbances common to human experience seemed to have crossed his sky. Nevertheless, his dispassionate survey of the universe had not raised his opinion of that costly experiment, and his study of the human race seemed to have resulted in the conclusion that all men were superfluous, and women necessary only because some one had to do the cooking. On the importance of this point his convictions were absolute, and gastronomy was the only science which he revered as a dogma. It must be owned that his little dinners were a strong argument in favour of this view, besides being a reason—though not the main one—for the fidelity of his friends.

Mentally he exercised a hospitality less seductive but no less stimulating. His mind was like a forum, or some open meeting-place for the exchange of ideas: somewhat cold and draughty, but light, spacious and orderly—a kind of academic grove from which all the leaves have fallen. In this privileged area a dozen of us were wont to stretch our muscles and expand our lungs; and, as if to prolong as much as possible the tradition of what we felt to be a vanishing institution, one or two neophytes were now and then added to our band.

Young Phil Frenham was the last, and the most interesting, of these recruits, and a good example of Murchard's somewhat morbid assertion that our old friend "liked 'em juicy.'' It was indeed a fact that Culwin, for all his dryness, specially tasted the lyric qualities in youth. As he was far too good an Epicurean to nip the flowers of soul which he gathered for his garden, his friendship was not a disintegrating influence: on the contrary, it forced the young idea to robuster bloom. And in Phil Frenham he had a good subject for experimentation. The boy was really intelligent, and the soundness of his nature was like the pure paste under a fine glaze. Culwin had fished him out of a fog of family dulness, and pulled him up to a peak in Darien; and the adventure hadn't hurt him a bit. Indeed, the skill with which Culwin had contrived to stimulate his curiosities without robbing them of their bloom of awe seemed to me a sufficient answer to Murchard's ogreish metaphor. There was nothing hectic in Frenham's efflorescence, and his old friend had not laid even a finger-tip on the sacred stupidities. One wanted no better proof of that than the fact that Frenham still reverenced them in Culwin.

"There's a side of him you fellows don't see. *I* believe that story about the duel!'' he declared; and it was of the very essence of this belief that it should impel him—just as our little party was dispersing—to turn back to our host with the joking demand: "And now you've got to tell us about *your* ghost!''

The outer door had closed on Murchard and the others; only Frenham and I remained; and the devoted servant who presided over Culwin's destinies, having brought a fresh supply of soda-water, had been laconically ordered to bed.

Culwin's sociability was a night-blooming flower, and we knew that he expected the nucleus of his group to tighten around him after midnight. But Frenham's appeal seemed to disconcert him comically, and he rose from the chair in which he had just reseated himself after his farewells in the hall.

"*My* ghost? Do you suppose I'm fool enough to go to the expense of keeping one of my own, when there are so many charming ones in my friends' closets?—Take another cigar,'' he said, revolving toward me with a laugh.

Frenham laughed too, pulling up his slender height before the chimney-piece as he turned to face his short bristling friend.

"Oh,'' he said, "you'd never be content to share if you met one you really liked.''

Culwin had dropped back into his arm-chair, his shock head embedded in the hollow of worn leather, his little eyes glimmering over a fresh cigar.

"Liked—*liked?* Good Lord!'' he growled.

"Ah, you *have,* then!'' Frenham pounced on him in the same instant, with a side-glance of victory at me; but Culwin cowered gnomelike among his cushions, dissembling himself in a protective cloud of smoke.

"What's the use of denying it? You've seen everything, so of course you've seen a ghost!'' his young friend persisted, talking intrepidly into the cloud. "Or, if you haven't seen one, it's only because you've seen two!''

The form of the challenge seemed to strike our host. He shot his head out of the mist with a queer tortoise-like motion he sometimes had, and blinked approvingly at Frenham.

"That's it,'' he flung at us on a shrill jerk of laughter; "it's only because I've seen two!''

The words were so unexpected that they dropped down and down into a deep silence, while we continued to stare at each other over Culwin's head, and Culwin stared at his ghosts. At length Frenham, without speaking, threw himself into the chair on the other side of the hearth, and leaned forward with his listening smile . . .

II

"Oh, of course they're not show ghosts—a collector wouldn't think anything of them . . . Don't let me raise your hopes . . . their one merit is their numerical strength: the exceptional fact of their being *two.* But, as against this, I'm bound to admit that at any moment I could probably have exorcised them both by asking my doctor for a prescription, or my oculist for a pair of spectacles. Only, as I never could make up my mind whether to go to the doctor or the oculist—whether I was afflicted by an optical or a digestive delusion—I left them to pursue their interesting double life, though at times they made mine exceedingly uncomfortable . . .

"Yes—uncomfortable; and you know how I hate to be uncomfortable! But it was part of my stupid pride, when the thing began, not to admit that I could be disturbed by the trifling matter of seeing two——

"And then I'd no reason, really, to suppose I was ill. As far as I knew I was simply bored—horribly bored. But it was part of my boredom—I remember—that I was feeling so uncommonly well, and didn't know how on earth to work off my surplus energy. I had come back from a long journey—down in South America and Mexico—and had settled down for the winter near New York, with an old aunt who had known Washington Irving and corresponded with N. P. Willis. She lived, not far from Irvington, in a damp Gothic villa, overhung by Norway spruces, and looking exactly like a memorial emblem done in hair. Her personal appearance was in keeping with this image, and her own hair—of which there was little left—might have been sacrificed to the manufacture of the emblem.

"I had just reached the end of an agitated year, with considerable arrears to make up in money and emotion; and theoretically it seemed as though my aunt's mild hospitality would be as beneficial to my nerves as to my purse. But the deuce of it was that as soon as I felt myself safe and sheltered my energy began to revive; and how was I to work it off inside of a memorial emblem? I had, at that time, the illusion that sustained intellectual effort could engage a man's whole activity; and I decided to write a great book—I forget about what. My aunt, impressed by my plan, gave up to me her Gothic library, filled with classics bound in black cloth and daguerreotypes of faded celebrities; and I sat down at my desk to win myself a place among their number. And to facilitate my task she lent me a cousin to copy my manuscript.

"The cousin was a nice girl, and I had an idea that a nice girl was just what I needed to restore my faith in human nature, and principally in myself. She was neither beautiful nor intelligent—poor Alice Nowell!—but it interested me to see any woman content to be so uninteresting, and I wanted to find out the secret of her content. In doing this I handled it rather rashly, and put it out of joint—oh, just for a moment! There's no fatuity in telling you this, for the poor girl had never seen any one but cousins . . .

"Well, I was sorry for what I'd done, of course, and confoundedly bothered as to how I should put it straight. She was staying in the house, and one evening, after my aunt had gone to bed, she came down to the library to fetch a book she'd mislaid, like any artless heroine on the shelves behind us. She was pink-nosed and flustered, and it suddenly occurred to me that her hair, though it was fairly thick and pretty, would look exactly like my aunt's when she grew older. I was glad I had noticed this, for it made it easier for me to decide to do what was right; and when I had found the book she hadn't lost I told her I was leaving for Europe that week.

"Europe was terribly far off in those days, and Alice knew at once what I meant. She didn't take it in the least as I'd expected—it would have been easier if she had. She held her book very tight, and turned away a moment to wind up the lamp on my desk—it had a ground glass shade with vine leaves, and glass drops around the edge, I remember. Then she came back, held out her hand, and said: 'Good-bye.' And as she said it she looked straight at me and kissed me. I had never felt anything as fresh and shy and brave as her kiss. It was worse than any reproach, and it made me ashamed to deserve a reproach from her. I said to myself: 'I'll marry her, and when my aunt dies she'll leave us this house, and I'll sit here at the desk and go on with my book; and Alice will sit over there with her embroidery and look at me as she's looking now. And life will go on like that for any number of years.' The prospect frightened me a little, but at the time it didn't frighten me as much as doing anything to hurt her; and ten minutes later she had my seal ring on her finger, and my promise that when I went abroad she should go with me.

"You'll wonder why I'm enlarging this incident. It's because the evening on which it took place was the very evening on which I first saw the queer sight I've spoken of. Being at that time an ardent believer in a necessary sequence between cause and effect I naturally tried to trace some kind of link between what had just happened to me in my aunt's library, and what was to happen a few hours later on the same night; and so the coincidence between the two events always remained in my mind.

"I went up to bed with rather a heavy heart, for I was bowed under the weight of the first good action I had ever consciously committed; and young as I was, I saw the gravity of my situation. Don't imagine from this that I had hitherto been an instrument of destruction. I had been merely a harmless young man, who had followed his bent and declined all collaboration with Providence. Now I had suddenly undertaken to promote the moral order of the world, and I felt a good deal like the trustful spectator who has given his gold watch to the conjurer, and doesn't know in what shape he'll get it back when the trick is over . . . Still, a glow of self-righteousness tempered my fears, and I said to myself as I undressed that when I'd got used to being good it probably wouldn't make me as nervous as it did at the start. And by the time I was in bed, and had blown out my candle, I felt that I really *was* getting used to it, and that, as far as I'd got, it was not unlike sinking down into one of my aunt's very softest wool mattresses.

"I closed my eyes on this image, and when I opened them it must have been a good deal later, for my room had grown cold, and intensely still. I was waked by the queer feeling we all know—the feeling that there was something in the room that hadn't been there when I fell asleep. I sat up and strained my eyes into the darkness. The room was pitch black, and at first I saw nothing; but gradually a vague glimmer at the foot of the bed turned into two eyes staring back at me. I couldn't distinguish the features attached to them, but as I looked the eyes grew more and more distinct: they gave out a light of their own.

"The sensation of being thus gazed at was far from pleasant, and you might suppose that my first impulse would have been to jump out of bed and hurl myself on the invisible figure attached to the eyes. But it wasn't—my impulse was simply to lie still . . . I can't say whether this was due to an immediate sense of the uncanny nature of the apparition—to the certainty that if I did jump out of bed I should hurl myself on nothing—or merely to the benumbing effect of the eyes themselves. They were the very worst eyes I've ever seen: a man's eyes—but what a man! My first thought was that he must be frightfully old. The orbits were sunk, and the thick red-lined lids hung over the eyeballs like blinds of which the cords are broken. One lid drooped a little lower than the other, with the effect of a crooked leer; and between these folds of flesh, with their scant bristle of lashes, the eyes themselves, small glassy disks with an agate-like rim, looked like sea-pebbles in the grip of a star-fish.

"But the age of the eyes was not the most unpleasant thing about them. What turned me sick was their expression of vicious security. I don't know how else to describe the fact that they seemed to belong to a man who had done a lot of harm in his life, but had always kept just inside the danger lines. They were not the eyes of a coward, but of some one much too clever to take risks; and my gorge rose at their look of base astuteness. Yet even that wasn't the worst; for as we continued to scan each other I saw in them a tinge of derision, and felt myself to be its object.

"At that I was seized by an impulse of rage that jerked me to my feet and pitched me straight at the unseen figure. But of course there wasn't any figure there, and my fists struck at emptiness. Ashamed and cold, I groped about for a match and lit the candles. The room looked just as usual—as I had known it would; and I crawled back to bed, and blew out the lights.

"As soon as the room was dark again the eyes reappeared; and I now applied myself to explaining them on scientific principles. At first I thought the illusion might have been caused by the glow of the last embers in the chimney; but the fireplace was on the other side of my bed, and so placed that the fire could not be reflected in my toilet glass, which was the only mirror in the room. Then it struck me that I might have been tricked by the reflection of the embers in some polished bit of wood or metal; and though I couldn't discover any object of the sort in my line of vision, I got up again, groped my way to the hearth, and covered what was left of the fire. But as soon as I was back in bed the eyes were back at its foot.

"They were an hallucination, then: that was plain. But the fact that they were not due to any external dupery didn't make them a bit pleasanter. For if they were a projection of my inner consciousness, what the deuce was the matter with that organ? I had gone deeply enough into the mystery of morbid pathological states to picture the conditions under which an exploring mind might lay itself open to such a midnight admonition; but I couldn't fit it to my present case. I had never felt more normal, mentally and physically; and the only unusual fact in my situation—that of having assured the happiness of an amiable girl—did not seem of a kind to summon unclean spirits about my pillow. But there were the eyes still looking at me . . .

"I shut mine, and tried to evoke a vision of Alice Nowell's. They were not remarkable eyes, but they were as wholesome as fresh water, and if she had had more imagination—or longer lashes—their expression might have been interesting. As it was, they did not prove very efficacious, and in a few moments I perceived that they had mysteriously changed into the eyes at the foot of the bed. It exasperated me more to feel these glaring at me through my shut lids than to see them, and I opened my eyes again and looked straight into their hateful stare . . .

"And so it went on all night. I can't tell you what that night was like, nor how long it lasted. Have you ever lain in bed, hopelessly wide awake, and tried to keep your eyes shut, knowing that if you opened 'em you'd see something you dreaded and loathed? It sounds easy, but it's devilish hard. Those eyes hung there and drew me. I had the *vertige de l'abîme,* and their red lids were the edge of my abyss . . . I had known nervous hours before: hours when I'd felt the wind of danger in my neck; but never this kind of strain. It wasn't that the eyes were awful; they hadn't the majesty of the powers of darkness. But they had—how shall I say?—a physical effect that was the equivalent of a bad smell: their look left a smear like a snail's. And I didn't see what business they had with me, anyhow—and I stared and stared, trying to find out . . .

"I don't know what effect they were trying to produce; but the effect they *did* produce was that of making me pack my portmanteau and bolt to town early the next morning. I left a note for my aunt, explaining that I was ill and had gone to see my doctor; and as a matter of fact I did feel uncommonly ill—the night seemed to have pumped all the blood out of me. But when I reached town I didn't go to the doctor's. I went to a friend's rooms, and threw myself on a bed, and slept for ten heavenly hours. When I woke it was the middle of the night, and I turned cold at the thought of what might be waiting for me. I sat up, shaking, and stared into the darkness; but there wasn't a break in its blessed surface, and when I saw that the eyes were not there I dropped back into another long sleep.

"I had left no word for Alice when I fled, because I meant to go back the next morning. But the next morning I was too exhausted to stir. As the day went on the exhaustion increased, instead of wearing off like the fatigue left by an ordinary night of insomnia: the effect of the eyes seemed to be cumulative, and the thought of seeing them again grew intolerable. For two days I fought my dread; and on the third evening I pulled myself together and decided to go back the next morning. I felt a good deal happier as soon as I'd decided, for I knew that my abrupt disappearance, and the strangeness of my not writing, must have been very distressing to poor Alice. I went to bed with an easy mind, and fell asleep at once; but in the middle of the night I woke, and there were the eyes . . .

"Well, I simply couldn't face them; and instead of going back to my aunt's I bundled a few things into a trunk and jumped aboard the first steamer for England. I was so dead tired when I got on board that I crawled straight into my berth, and slept most of the way over; and I can't tell you the bliss it was to wake from those long dreamless stretches and look fearlessly into the dark, *knowing* that I shouldn't see the eyes . . .

"I stayed abroad for a year, and then I stayed for another; and during that time I never had a glimpse of them. That was enough reason for prolonging my stay if I'd been on a desert island. Another was, of course, that I had perfectly come to see, on the voyage over, the complete impossibility of my marrying Alice Nowell. The fact that I had been so slow in making this discovery annoyed me, and made me want to avoid explanations. The bliss of escaping at one stroke from the eyes, and from this other embarrassment, gave my freedom an extraordinary zest; and the longer I savoured it the better I liked its taste.

"The eyes had burned such a hole in my consciousness that for a long time I went on puzzling over the nature of the apparition, and wondering if it would ever come back. But as time passed I lost this dread, and retained only the precision of the image. Then that faded in its turn.

"The second year found me settled in Rome, where I was planning, I believe, to write another great book—a definitive work on Etruscan influences in Italian art. At any rate, I'd found some pretext of the kind for taking a sunny apartment in the Piazza di Spagna and dabbling about in the Forum; and there, one morning, a charming youth came to me. As he stood there in the warm light, slender and smooth and hyacinthine, he might have stepped from a ruined altar—one to Antinous, say; but he'd come instead from New York, with a letter (of all people) from Alice Nowell. The letter—the first I'd had from her since our break—was simply a line introducing her young cousin, Gilbert Noyes, and appealing to me to befriend him. It appeared, poor lad, that he 'had talent,' and 'wanted to write'; and, an obdurate family having insisted that his calligraphy should take the form of double entry, Alice had intervened to win him six months' respite, during which he was to travel abroad on a meagre pittance, and somehow prove his ability to increase it by his pen. The quaint conditions of the test struck me first: it seemed about as conclusive as a mediæval 'ordeal.' Then I was touched by her having sent him to me. I had always wanted to do her some service, to justify myself in my own eyes rather than hers; and here was a beautiful occasion.

"I imagine it's safe to lay down the general principle that predestined geniuses don't, as a rule, appear before one in the spring sunshine of the Forum looking like one of its banished gods. At any rate, poor Noyes wasn't a predestined genius. But he *was* beautiful to see, and charming as a comrade. It was only when he began to talk literature that my heart failed me. I knew all the symptoms so well—the things he had 'in him,' and the things outside him that impinged! There's the real test, after all. It was always—punctually, inevitably, with the inexorableness of a mechanical law—it was *always* the wrong thing that struck him. I grew to find a certain fascination in deciding in advance exactly which wrong thing he'd select; and I acquired an astonishing skill at the game . . .

"The worst of it was that his *bêtise* wasn't of the too obvious sort. Ladies who met him at picnics thought him intellectual; and even at dinners he passed for clever. I, who had him under the microscope, fancied now and then that he might develop some kind of a slim talent, something that he could make 'do' and be happy on; and wasn't that, after all, what I was concerned with? He was so charming—he continued to be so charming—that he called forth all my charity in support of this argument; and for the first few months I really believed there was a chance for him . . .

"Those months were delightful. Noyes was constantly with me, and the more I saw of him the better I liked him. His stupidity was a natural grace—it was as beautiful, really, as his eyelashes. And he was so gay, so affectionate, and so happy with me, that telling him the truth would have been about as pleasant as slitting the throat of some gentle animal. At first I used to wonder what had put into that radiant head the detestable delusion that it held a brain. Then I began to see that it was simply protective mimicry—an instinctive ruse to get away from family life and an office desk. Not that Gilbert didn't—dear lad!—believe in himself. There wasn't a trace of hypocrisy in him. He was sure that his 'call' was irresistible, while to me it was the saving grace of his situation that it *wasn't,* and that a little money, a little leisure, a little pleasure would have turned him into an inoffensive idler. Unluckily, however, there was no hope of money, and with the alternative of the office desk before him he couldn't postpone his attempt at literature. The stuff he turned out was deplorable, and I see now that I knew it from the first. Still, the absurdity of deciding a man's whole future on a first trial seemed to justify me in withholding my verdict, and perhaps even in encouraging him a little, on the ground that the human plant generally needs warmth to flower.

"At any rate, I proceeded on that principle, and carried it to the point of getting his term of probation extended. When I left Rome he went with me, and we idled away a delicious summer between Capri and Venice. I said to myself: 'If he has anything in him, it will come out now,' and it *did.* He was never more enchanting and enchanted. There were moments of our pilgrimage when beauty born of murmuring sound seemed actually to pass into his face—but only to issue forth in a flood of the palest ink . . .

"Well, the time came to turn off the tap; and I knew there was no hand but mine to do it. We were back in Rome, and I had taken him to stay with me, not wanting him to be alone in his *pension* when he had to face the necessity of renouncing his ambition. I hadn't, of course, relied solely on my own judgment in deciding to advise him to drop literature. I had sent his stuff to various people—editors and critics—and they had always sent it back with the same chilling lack of comment. Really there was nothing on earth to say——

"I confess I never felt more shabbily than I did on the day when I decided to have it out with Gilbert. It was well enough to tell myself that it was my duty to knock the poor boy's hopes into splinters—but I'd like to know what act of gratuitous cruelty hasn't been justified on that plea? I've always shrunk from usurping the functions of Providence, and when I have to exercise them I decidedly prefer that it shouldn't be on an errand of destruction. Besides, in the last issue, who was I to decide, even after a year's trial, if poor Gilbert had it in him or not?

"The more I looked at the part I'd resolved to play, the less I liked it; and I liked it still less when Gilbert sat opposite me, with his head thrown back in the lamplight, just as Phil's is now . . . I'd been going over his last manuscript, and he knew it, and he knew that his future hung on my verdict—we'd tacitly agreed to that. The manuscript lay between us, on my table—a novel, his first novel, if you please!—and he reached over and laid his hand on it, and looked up at me with all his life in the look.

"I stood up and cleared my throat, trying to keep my eyes away from his face and on the manuscript.

" 'The fact is, my dear Gilbert,' I began——

"I saw him turn pale, but he was up and facing me in an instant.

" 'Oh, look here, don't take on so, my dear fellow! I'm not so awfully cut up as all that!' His hands were on my shoulders, and he was laughing down on me from his full height, with a kind of mortally-stricken gaiety that drove the knife into my side.

"He was too beautifully brave for me to keep up any humbug about my duty. And it came over me suddenly how I should hurt others in hurting him: myself first, since sending him home meant losing him; but more particularly poor Alice Nowell, to whom I had so longed to prove my good faith and my desire to serve her. It really seemed like failing her twice to fail Gilbert——

"But my intuition was like one of those lightning flashes that encircle the whole horizon, and in the same instant I saw what I might be letting myself in for if I didn't tell the truth. I said to myself: 'I shall have him for life'—and I'd never yet seen any one, man or woman, whom I was quite sure of wanting on those terms. Well, this impulse of egotism decided me. I was ashamed of it, and to get away from it I took a leap that landed me straight in Gilbert's arms.

" 'The thing's all right, and you're all wrong!' I shouted up at him; and as he hugged me, and I laughed and shook in his clutch, I had for a minute the sense of self-complacency that is supposed to attend the footsteps of the just. Hang it all, making people happy *has* its charms——

"Gilbert, of course, was for celebrating his emancipation in some spectacular manner; but I sent him away alone to explode his emotions, and went to bed to sleep off mine. As I undressed I began to wonder what their after-taste would be—so many of the finest don't keep! Still, I wasn't sorry, and I meant to empty the bottle, even if it *did* turn a trifle flat.

"After I got into bed I lay for a long time smiling at the memory of his eyes—his blissful eyes . . . Then I fell asleep, and when I woke the room was deathly cold, and sat up with a jerk—and there were the *other eyes* . . .

"It was three years since I'd seen them, but I'd thought of them so often that I fancied they could never take me unawares again. Now, with their red sneer on me, I knew that I had never really believed they would come back, and that I was as defenceless as ever against them . . . As before, it was the insane irrelevance of their coming that made it so horrible. What the deuce were they after, to leap out at me at such a time? I had lived more or less carelessly in the years since I'd seen them, though my worst indiscretions were not dark enough to invite the searchings of their infernal glare; but at this particular moment I was really in what might have been called a state of grace; and I can't tell you how the fact added to their horror . . .

"But it's not enough to say they were as bad as before: they were worse. Worse by just so much as I'd learned of life in the interval; by all the damnable implications my wider experience read into them. I saw now what I hadn't seen before: that they were eyes which had grown hideous gradually, which had built up their baseness coral-wise, bit by bit, out of a series of small turpitudes slowly accumulated through the industrious years. Yes—it came to me that what made them so bad was that they'd grown bad so slowly . . .

"There they hung in the darkness, their swollen lids dropped across the little watery bulbs rolling loose in the orbits, and the puff of flesh making a muddy shadow underneath—and as their stare moved with my movements, there came over me a sense of their tacit complicity, of a deep hidden understanding between us that was worse than the first shock of their strangeness. Not that I understood them; but that they made it so clear that some day I should . . . Yes, that was the worst part of it, decidedly; and it was the feeling that became stronger each time they came back . . .

"For they got into the damnable habit of coming back. They reminded me of vampires with a taste for young flesh, they seemed so to gloat over the taste of a good conscience. Every night for a month they came to claim their morsel of mine: since I'd made Gilbert happy they simply wouldn't loosen their fangs. The coincidence almost made me hate him, poor lad, fortuitous as I felt it to be. I puzzled over it a good deal, but couldn't find any hint of an explanation except in the chance of his association with Alice Nowell. But then the eyes had let up on me the moment I had abandoned her, so they could hardly be the emissaries of a woman scorned, even if one could have pictured poor Alice charging such spirits to avenge her. That set me thinking, and I began to wonder if they would let up on me if I abandoned Gilbert. The temptation was insidious, and I had to stiffen myself against it; but really, dear boy! he was too charming to be sacrificed to such demons. And so, after all, I never found out what they wanted . . ."

III

The fire crumbled, sending up a flash which threw into relief the narrator's gnarled face under its grey-black stubble. Pressed into the hollow of the chairback, it stood out an instant like an intaglio of yellowish red-veined stone, with spots of enamel for the eyes; then the fire sank and it became once more a dim Rembrandtish blur.

Phil Frenham, sitting in a low chair on the opposite side of the hearth, one long arm propped on the table behind him, one hand supporting his thrown-back head, and his eyes fixed on his old friend's face, had not moved since the tale began. He continued to maintain his silent immobility after Culwin had ceased to speak, and it was I who, with a vague sense of disappointment at the sudden drop of the story, finally asked: "But how long did you keep on seeing them?"

Culwin, so sunk into his chair that he seemed like a heap of his own empty clothes, stirred a little, as if in surprise at my question. He appeared to have half-forgotten what he had been telling us.

"How long? Oh, off and on all that winter. It was infernal. I never got used to them. I grew really ill."

Frenham shifted his attitude, and as he did so his elbow struck against a small mirror in a bronze frame standing on the table behind him. He turned and changed its angle slightly; then he resumed his former attitude, his dark head thrown back on his lifted palm, his eyes intent on Culwin's face. Something in his silent gaze embarrassed me, and as if to divert attention from it I pressed on with another question:

"And you never tried sacrificing Noyes?"

"Oh, no. That fact is I didn't have to. He did it for me, poor boy!"

"Did it for you? How do you mean?"

"He wore me out—wore everybody out. He kept on pouring out his lamentable twaddle, and hawking it up and down the place till he became a thing of terror. I tried to wean him from writing—oh, ever so gently, you understand, by throwing him with agreeable people, giving him a chance to make himself felt, to come to a sense of what he *really* had to give. I'd foreseen this solution from the beginning—felt sure that, once the first ardour of authorship was quenched, he'd drop into his place as a charming parasitic thing, the kind of chronic Cherubino for whom, in old societies, there's always a seat at table, and a shelter behind the ladies' skirts. I saw him take his place as 'the poet': the poet who doesn't write. One knows the type in every drawing-room. Living in that way doesn't cost much—I'd worked it all out in my mind, and felt sure that, with a little help, he could manage it for the next few years; and meanwhile he'd be sure to marry. I saw him married to a widow, rather older, with a good cook and a well-run house. And I actually had my eye on the widow . . . Meanwhile I did everything to help the transition—lent him money to ease his conscience, introduced him to pretty women to make him forget his vows. But nothing would do him: he had but one idea in his beautiful obstinate head. He wanted the laurel and not the rose, and he kept on repeating Gautier's axiom, and battering and filing at his limp prose till he'd spread it out over Lord knows how many hundred pages. Now and then he would send a barrelful to a publisher, and of course it would always come back.

"At first it didn't matter—he thought he was 'misunderstood.' He took the attitudes of genius, and whenever an opus came home he wrote another to keep it company. Then he had a reaction of despair, and accused me of deceiving him, and Lord knows what. I got angry at that, and told him it was he who had deceived himself. He'd come to me determined to write, and I'd done my best to help him. That was the extent of my offence, and I'd done it for his cousin's sake not his.

"That seemed to strike home, and he didn't answer for a minute. Then he said: 'My time's up and my money's up. What do you think I'd better do?'

" 'I think you'd better not be an ass,' I said.

" 'What do you mean by being an ass?' he asked.

"I took a letter from my desk and held it out to him.

" 'I mean refusing this offer of Mrs. Ellinger's: to be her secretary at a salary of five thousand dollars. There may be a lot more in it than that.'

"He flung out his hand with a violence that struck the letter from mine. 'Oh, I know well enough what's in it!' he said, red to the roots of his hair.

" 'And what's the answer, if you know?' I asked.

"He made none at the minute, but turned away slowly to the door. There, with his hand on the threshold, he stopped to say, almost under his breath: 'Then you really think my stuff's no good?'

"I was tired and exasperated, and I laughed. I don't defend my laugh—it was in wretched taste. But I must plead in extenuation that the boy was a fool, and that I'd done my best for him—I really had.

"He went out of the room, shutting the door quietly after him. That afternoon I left for Frascati, where I'd promised to spend the Sunday with some friends. I was glad to escape from Gilbert, and by the same token, as I learned that night, I had also escaped from the eyes. I dropped into the same lethargic sleep that had come to me before when I left off seeing them; and when I woke the next morning, in my peaceful room above the ilexes, I felt the utter weariness and deep relief that always followed on that sleep. I put in two blessed nights at Frascati, and when I got back to my rooms in Rome I found that Gilbert had gone . . . Oh, nothing tragic had happened—the episode never rose to *that.* He'd simply packed his manuscripts and left for America—for his family and the Wall Street desk. He left a decent enough note to tell me of his decision, and behaved altogether, in the circumstances, as little like a fool as it's possible for a fool to behave . . ."

IV

Culwin paused again, and Frenham still sat motionless, the dusky contour of his young head reflected in the mirror at his back.

"And what became of Noyes afterward?" I finally asked, still disquieted by a sense of incompleteness, by the need of some connecting thread between the parallel lines of the tale.

Culwin twitched his shoulders. "Oh, nothing became of him—because he became nothing. There could be no question of 'becoming' about it. He vegetated in an office, I believe, and finally got a clerkship in a consulate, and married drearily in China. I saw him once in Hong Kong, years afterward. He was fat and hadn't shaved. I was told he drank. He didn't recognise me."

"And the eyes?" I asked, after another pause which Frenham's continued silence made oppressive.

Culwin, stroking his chin, blinked at me meditatively through the shadows. "I never saw them after my last talk with Gilbert. Put two and two together if you can. For my part, I haven't found the link."

He rose, his hands in his pockets, and walked stiffly over to the table on which reviving drinks had been set out.

"You must be parched after this dry tale. Here, help yourself, my dear fellow. Here, Phil——" He turned back to the hearth.

Frenham made no response to his host's hospitable summons. He still sat in his low chair without moving, but as Culwin advanced toward him, their eyes met in a long look; after which the young man, turning suddenly, flung his arms across the table behind him, and dropped his face upon them.

Culwin, at the unexpected gesture, stopped short, a flush on his face.

"Phil—what the deuce? Why, have the eyes scared *you?* My dear boy—my dear fellow—I never had such a tribute to my literary ability, never!"

He broke into a chuckle at the thought, and halted on the hearth-rug, his hands still in his pockets, gazing down at the youth's bowed head. Then, as Frenham still made no answer, he moved a step or two nearer.

"Cheer up, my dear Phil! It's years since I've seen them—apparently I've done nothing lately bad enough to call them out of chaos. Unless my present evocation of them has made *you* see them; which would be their worst stroke yet!"

His bantering appeal quivered off into an uneasy laugh, and he moved still nearer, bending over Frenham, and laying his gouty hands on the lad's shoulders.

"Phil, my dear boy, really—what's the matter? Why don't you answer? *Have* you seen the eyes?"

Frenham's face was still hidden, and from where I stood behind Culwin I saw the latter, as if under the rebuff of this unaccountable attitude, draw back slowly from his friend. As he did so, the light of the lamp on the table fell full on his congested face, and I caught its reflection in the mirror behind Frenham's head.

Culwin saw the reflection also. He paused, his face level with the mirror, as if scarcely recognising the countenance in it as his own. But as he looked his expression gradually changed, and for an appreciable space of time he and the image in the glass confronted each other with a glare of slowly gathering hate. Then Culwin let go of Frenham's shoulders, and drew back a step . . .

Frenham, his face still hidden, did not stir.

The Other Side of the Hedge

E. M. Forster (1879–1970)

Edward Morgan Forster, the son of an architect, was born in London. His father died when he was young, and he was reared by his mother and paternal aunts. He was sent as a day boy to Tonbridge School, Kent, and afterwards to King's College, Cambridge. After leaving Cambridge Forster soon took up residence in Italy where he drafted his first two novels, *Where Angels Fear to Tread* (1905) and *A Room with a View* (1908). These novels have an Italian background, but in *The Longest Journey* (published in 1907, the year he returned to England) Forster dealt with his English experiences at Tonbridge and Cambridge. His first important success, *Howard's End,* appeared in 1910, providing a compelling image of contemporary threats to the nineteenth-century liberal imagination.

Forster had been writing short stories for some years, and *The Celestial Omnibus* (1911) collected the best of his early work, including "The Other Side of the Hedge." During the first World War Forster spent three years in Alexandria, while in 1912 and 1921 he visited India. These experiences led to his most famous novel, *A Passage to India* (1924), where the liberal imagination is found to be almost incapable of handling an alien culture. After *A Passage to India* Forster published no more major fiction; an early novel with a homosexual theme, *Maurice,* appeared posthumously in 1971. In 1927 Forster delivered the Clark Lectures at King's College, Cambridge, on the subject of the art of fiction. They were published the same year as *Aspects of the Novel* (a selection from this appears in the Essay section). In 1946 King's made Forster an honorary fellow, and he spent his remaining years in Cambridge. The work of his later years was composed mainly of lectures and essays.

My pedometer told me that I was twenty-five; and, though it is a shocking thing to stop walking, I was so tired that I sat down on a milestone to rest. People outstripped me, jeering as they did so, but I was too apathetic to feel resentful, and even when Miss Eliza Dimbleby, the great educationist, swept past, exhorting me to persevere, I only smiled and raised my hat.

At first I thought I was going to be like my brother, whom I had had to leave by the roadside a year or two round the corner. He had wasted his breath on singing, and his strength on helping others. But I had travelled more wisely, and now it was only the monotony of the highway that oppressed me—dust under foot and brown crackling hedges on either side, ever since I could remember.

And I had already dropped several things—indeed, the road behind was strewn with the things we all had dropped; and the white dust was settling down on them, so that already they looked no better than stones. My muscles were so weary that I could not even bear the weight of those things I still carried. I slid off the milestone into the road, and lay there prostrate, with my face to the great parched hedge, praying that I might give up.

A little puff of air revived me. It seemed to come from the hedge; and, when I opened my eyes, there was a glint of light through the tangle of boughs and dead leaves. The hedge could not be as thick as usual. In my weak, morbid state, I longed to force my way in, and see what was on the other side. No one was in sight, or I should not have dared to try. For we of the road do not admit in conversation that there is another side at all.

I yielded to the temptation, saying to myself that I

would come back in a minute. The thorns scratched my face, and I had to use my arms as a shield, depending on my feet alone to push me forward. Halfway through I would have gone back, for in the passage all the things I was carrying were scraped off me, and my clothes were torn. But I was so wedged that return was impossible, and I had to wriggle blindly forward, expecting every moment that my strength would fail me, and that I should perish in the undergrowth.

Suddenly cold water closed round my head, and I seemed sinking down for ever. I had fallen out of the hedge into a deep pool. I rose to the surface at last, crying for help, and I heard someone on the opposite bank laugh and say: "Another!" And then I was twitched out and laid panting on the dry ground.

Even when the water was out of my eyes, I was still dazed, for I had never been in so large a space, nor seen such grass and sunshine. The blue sky was no longer a strip, and beneath it the earth had risen grandly into hills—clean, bare buttresses, with beech trees in their folds, and meadows and clear pools at their feet. But the hills were not high, and there was in the landscape a sense of human occupation—so that one might have called it a park, or garden, if the words did not imply a certain triviality and constraint.

As soon as I got my breath, I turned to my rescuer and said:

"Where does this place lead to?"

"Nowhere, thank the Lord!" said he, and laughed. He was a man of fifty or sixty—just the kind of age we mistrust on the road—but there was no anxiety in his manner, and his voice was that of a boy of eighteen.

"But it must lead somewhere!" I cried, too much surprised at his answer to thank him for saving my life.

"He wants to know where it leads!" he shouted to some men on the hill side, and they laughed back, and waved their caps.

I noticed then that the pool into which I had fallen was really a moat which bent round to the left and to the right, and that the hedge followed it continually. The hedge was green on this side—its roots showed through the clear water, and fish swam about in them—and it was wreathed over with dog-roses and Traveller's Joy. But it was a barrier, and in a moment I lost all pleasure in the grass, the sky, the trees, the happy men and women, and realized that the place was but a prison, for all its beauty and extent.

We moved away from the boundary, and then followed a path almost parallel to it, across the meadows. I found it difficult walking, for I was always trying to out-distance my companion, and there was no advantage in doing this if the place led nowhere. I had never kept step with anyone since I left my brother.

I amused him by stopping suddenly and saying disconsolately, "This is perfectly terrible. One cannot advance: one cannot progress. Now we of the road——"

"Yes. I know."

"I was going to say, we advance continually."

"I know."

"We are always learning, expanding, developing. Why, even in my short life I have seen a great deal of advance—the Transvaal War, the Fiscal Question, Christian Science, Radium. Here for example—"

I took out my pedometer, but it still marked twenty-five, not a degree more.

"Oh, it's stopped! I meant to show you. It should have registered all the time I was walking with you. But it makes me only twenty-five."

"Many things don't work in here," he said. "One day a man brought in a Lee-Metford, and that wouldn't work."

"The laws of science are universal in their application. It must be the water in the moat that has injured the machinery. In normal conditions everything works. Science and the spirit of emulation—those are the forces that have made us what we are."

I had to break off and acknowledge the pleasant greetings of people whom we passed. Some of them were singing, some talking, some engaged in gardening, hay-making, or other rudimentary industries. They all seemed happy; and I might have been happy too, if I could have forgotten that the place led nowhere.

I was startled by a young man who came sprinting across our path, took a little fence in fine style, and went tearing over a ploughed field till he plunged into a lake, across which he began to swim. Here was true energy, and I exclaimed: "A cross-country race! Where are the others?"

"There are no others," my companion replied; and, later on, when we passed some long grass from which came the voice of a girl singing exquisitely to herself, he said again: "There are no others." I was bewildered at the waste in production, and murmured to myself, "What does it all mean?"

He said: "It means nothing but itself"—and he repeated the words slowly, as if I were a child.

"I understand," I said quietly, "but I do not agree. Every achievement is worthless unless it is a link in the chain of development. And I must not trespass on your kindness any longer. I must get back somehow to the road, and have my pedometer mended."

"First, you must see the gates," he replied, "for we have gates, though we never use them."

I yielded politely, and before long we reached the moat again, at a point where it was spanned by a bridge. Over the bridge was a big gate, as white as ivory, which was fitted into a gap in the boundary hedge. The gate opened outwards, and I exclaimed in amazement, for from it ran a road—just such a road as I had left—dusty under foot, with brown crackling hedges on either side as far as the eye could reach.

"That's my road!" I cried.

He shut the gate and said: "But not your part of the road. It is through this gate that humanity went out countless ages ago, when it was first seized with the desire to walk."

I denied this, observing that the part of the road I myself had left was not more than two miles off. But with the obstinacy of his years he repeated: "It is the same road. This is the beginning, and though it seems to run straight away from us, it doubles so often, that it is never far from our boundary and sometimes touches it." He stooped down by the moat, and traced on its moist margin an absurd figure like a maze. As we walked back through the meadows, I tried to convince him of his mistake.

"The road sometimes doubles, to be sure, but that is part of our discipline. Who can doubt that its general tendency is onward? To what goal we know not—it may be to some mountain where we shall touch the sky, it may be over precipices into the sea. But that it goes forward—who can doubt that? It is the thought of that that makes us strive to excel, each in his own way, and gives us an impetus which is lacking with you. Now that man who passed us—it's true that he ran well, and jumped well, and swam well; but we have men who can run better, and men who can jump better, and who can swim better. Specialization has produced results which would surprise you. Similarly, that girl——"

Here I interrupted myself to exclaim: "Good gracious me! I could have sworn it was Miss Eliza Dimbleby over there, with her feet in the fountain!"

He believed that it was.

"Impossible! I left her on the road, and she is due to lecture this evening at Tunbridge Wells. Why, her train leaves Cannon Street in—of course my watch has stopped like everything else. She is the last person to be here."

"People always are astonished at meeting each other. All kinds come through the hedge, and come at all times—when they are drawing ahead in the race, when they are lagging behind, when they are left for dead. I often stand near the boundary listening to the sounds of the road—you know what they are—and wonder if anyone will turn aside. It is my great happiness to help someone out of the moat, as I helped you. For our country fills up slowly, though it was meant for all mankind."

"Mankind have other aims," I said gently, for I thought him well-meaning; "and I must join them." I bade him good evening, for the sun was declining, and I wished to be on the road by nightfall. To my alarm, he caught hold of me, crying: "You are not to go yet!" I tried to shake him off, for we had no interests in common, and his civility was becoming irksome to me. But for all my struggles the tiresome old man would not let go; and, as wrestling is not my speciality, I was obliged to follow him.

It was true that I could have never found alone the place where I came in, and I hoped that, when I had seen the other sights about which he was worrying, he would take me back to it. But I was determined not to sleep in the country, for I mistrusted it, and the people too, for all their friendliness. Hungry though I was, I would not join them in their evening meals of milk and fruit, and, when they gave me flowers, I flung them away as soon as I could do so unobserved. Already they were lying down for the night like cattle—some out on the bare hillside, others in groups under the beeches. In the light of an orange sunset I hurried on with my unwelcome guide, dead tired, faint for want of food, but murmuring indomitably: "Give me life, with its struggles and victories, with its failures and hatreds, with its deep moral meaning and its unknown goal!"

At last we came to a place where the encircling moat was spanned by another bridge, and where another gate interrupted the line of the boundary hedge. It was different from the first gate; for it was half transparent like horn, and opened inwards. But through it, in the waning light, I saw again just such a road as I had left—monotonous, dusty, with brown crackling hedges on either side, as far as the eye could reach.

I was strangely disquieted at the sight, which seemed to deprive me of all self-control. A man was passing us, returning for the night to the hills, with a scythe over his shoulder and a can of some liquid in his hand. I forgot the destiny of our race. I forgot the road that lay before my eyes, and I sprang at him, wrenched the can out of his hand, and began to drink.

It was nothing stronger than beer, but in my exhausted state it overcame me in a moment. As in a dream, I saw the old man shut the gate, and heard him say: "This is where your road ends, and through this gate humanity—all that is left of it—will come in to us."

Though my senses were sinking into oblivion, they seemed to expand ere they reached it. They perceived the magic song of nightingales, and the odour of invisible hay, and stars piercing the fading sky. The man whose beer I had stolen lowered me down gently to sleep off its effects, and, as he did so, I saw that he was my brother.

Two Gallants

James Joyce (1882–1941)

James Joyce was born in Dublin, the eldest son of a popular, reckless tax collector and a sensitive mother who was a devout Roman Catholic. At the age of six he was sent to Clongowes Wood College, a fashionable Jesuit boarding school, and remained there until 1891 when the declining family fortune obliged his withdrawal. His father, John Stanislaus Joyce, was an ardent supporter of Charles Stewart Parnell, the leader of the Irish "Home Rule" movement, and the fall of Parnell in 1890–91 had a profound impact on both father and son. The nine-year-old James wrote a poem attacking Parnell's opponents, which was printed by his father; no copy has survived.

In 1893 Joyce entered Belvedere College, a Jesuit grammar school, and from 1898 to 1902 he attended University College, Dublin. Gradually, as his religious faith gave way to doubt and active opposition, Joyce saw himself as a priest of the imagination, destined to surmount the confines of "Home, Fatherland, and Church." In the autumn of 1902 Joyce left Dublin for Paris but returned the next year to be with his dying mother. In June 1904 he met Nora Barnacle (their second meeting was on June 16th, the day celebrated in *Ulysses*), and by October he had persuaded her to leave Ireland. They travelled first to Pola and then to Trieste, where they remained until 1915. The Joyce family, which by then included two children, moved to Zurich for the remainder of the war years, and in 1920 they moved to Paris. Joyce stayed in France until the German invasion of 1940; he then took his family back to Zurich, where he died a year later.

Joyce's early publications include a suite of poems, *Chamber Music* (1907), and fifteen short stories written in 1904–07 but not published until 1914: *Dubliners.* In these stories Joyce sought, in a style of "scrupulous meanness," to portray Dublin as the center of Irish "paralysis." Also in 1904 he began an autobiographical novel, *Stephen Hero,* which after radical revision appeared in 1914 as *A Portrait of the Artist as a Young Man.* The two works which occupied the rest of Joyce's artistic life were *Ulysses* (1922), which bears the dateline "Trieste-Zurich-Paris, 1914–1921," and *Finnegans Wake,* upon which Joyce labored from 1923 until its publication in 1939. *Ulysses* is an epic account of one day in the life of Dublin, in which the events of 16 June 1904 correspond, both ironically and heroically, to Homer's *Odyssey. Finnegans Wake* tells of the night-time life of a Dublin family, and in its dense pages Joyce dissolves and reforms the English language so as to express the dislocations of time and space which mark our dreams. If the personages of *Ulysses* are typical and sometimes mythical, those of *Finnegans Wake* are archetypes of all human experience.

The grey warm evening of August had descended upon the city and a mild warm air, a memory of summer, circulated in the streets. The streets, shuttered for the repose of Sunday, swarmed with a gaily coloured crowd. Like illumined pearls the lamps shone from the summits of their tall poles upon the living texture below which, changing shape and hue unceasingly, sent up into the warm grey evening air an unchanging unceasing murmur.

Two young men came down the hill of Rutland Square. One of them was just bringing a long monologue to a close. The other, who walked on the verge of the path and was at times obliged to step on to the road, owing to his companion's rudeness, wore an amused listening face. He was squat and ruddy. A yachting cap was shoved far back from his forehead and the narrative to which he listened made constant waves of expression break forth over his face from the corners of his nose and eyes and mouth. Little jets of wheezing laughter followed one another out of his convulsed body. His eyes, twinkling with cunning enjoyment, glanced at every moment towards his companion's face. Once or twice he rearranged the light waterproof which he had slung over one shoulder in toreador fashion. His breeches, his white rubber shoes and his jauntily slung waterproof expressed youth. But his figure fell into rotundity at the waist, his hair was scant and grey and his face, when the waves of expression had passed over it, had a ravaged look.

When he was quite sure that the narrative had ended he laughed noiselessly for fully half a minute. Then he said:

—Well! . . . That takes the biscuit!

His voice seemed winnowed of vigour; and to enforce his words he added with humour:

—That takes the solitary, unique, and, if I may so call it, *recherché* biscuit!

He became serious and silent when he had said this. His tongue was tired for he had been talking all the afternoon in a public-house in Dorset Street. Most people considered Lenehan a leech but, in spite of this reputation, his adroitness and eloquence had always prevented his friends from forming any general policy against him. He had a brave manner of coming up to a party of them in a bar and of holding himself nimbly at the borders of the company until he was included in a round. He was a sporting vagrant armed with a vast stock of stories, limericks and riddles. He was insensitive to all kinds of discourtesy. No one knew how he achieved the stern task of living, but his name was vaguely associated with racing tissues.

—And where did you pick her up, Corley? he asked.

Corley ran his tongue swiftly along his upper lip.

—One night, man, he said, I was going along Dame Street and I spotted a fine tart under Waterhouse's clock and said good-night, you know. So we went for a walk round by the canal and she told me she was a slavey in a house in Baggot Street. I put my arm round her and squeezed her a bit that night. Then next Sunday, man, I met her by appointment. We went out to Donnybrook and I brought her into a field there. She told me she used to go with a dairyman. . . . It was fine, man. Cigarettes every night she'd bring me and paying the tram out and back. And one night she brought me two bloody fine cigars—O, the real cheese, you know, that the old fellow used to smoke. . . . I was afraid, man, she'd get in the family way. But she's up to the dodge.

—Maybe she thinks you'll marry her, said Lenehan.

—I told her I was out of a job, said Corley. I told her I was in Pim's. She doesn't know my name. I was too hairy to tell her that. But she thinks I'm a bit of class, you know.

Lenehan laughed again, noiselessly.

—Of all the good ones ever I heard, he said, that emphatically takes the biscuit.

Corley's stride acknowledged the compliment. The swing of his burly body made his friend execute a few light skips from the path to the roadway and back again. Corley was the son of an inspector of police and he had inherited his father's frame and gait. He walked with his hands by his sides, holding himself erect and swaying his head from side to side. His head was large, globular and oily; it sweated in all weathers; and his large round hat, set upon it sideways, looked like a bulb which had grown out of another. He always stared straight before him as if he were on parade and, when he wished to gaze after some one in the street, it was necessary for him to move his body from the hips. At present he was about town. Whenever any job was vacant a friend was always ready to give him the hard word. He was often to be seen walking with policemen in plain clothes, talking earnestly. He knew the inner side of all affairs and was fond of delivering final judgments. He spoke without listening to the speech of his companions. His conversation was mainly about himself: what he had said to such a person and what such a person had said to him and what he had said to settle the matter. When he reported these dialogues he aspirated the first letter of his name after the manner of Florentines.

Lenehan offered his friend a cigarette. As the two young men walked on through the crowd Corley occasionally turned to smile at some of the passing girls but Lenehan's gaze was fixed on the large faint moon circled with a double halo. He watched earnestly the passing of the grey web of twilight across its face. At length he said:

—Well . . . tell me, Corley, I suppose you'll be able to pull it off all right, eh?

Corley closed one eye expressively as an answer.

—Is she game for that? asked Lenehan dubiously. You can never know women.

—She's all right, said Corley. I know the way to get around her, man. She's a bit gone on me.

—You're what I call a gay Lothario, said Lenehan. And the proper kind of a Lothario, too!

A shade of mockery relieved the servility of his manner. To save himself he had the habit of leaving his flattery open to the interpretation of raillery. But Corley had not a subtle mind.

—There's nothing to touch a good slavey, he affirmed. Take my tip for it.

—By one who has tried them all, said Lenehan.

—First I used to go with girls, you know, said Corley, unbosoming; girls off the South Circular. I used to take them out, man, on the tram somewhere and pay the tram or take them to a band or a play at the theatre or buy them chocolate and sweets or something that way. I used to spend money on them right enough, he added, in a convincing tone, as if he were conscious of being disbelieved.

But Lenehan could well believe it; he nodded gravely.

—I know that game, he said, and it's a mug's game.

—And damn the thing I ever got out of it, said Corley.

—Ditto here, said Lenehan.

—Only off of one of them, said Corley.

He moistened his upper lip by running his tongue along it. The recollection brightened his eyes. He too gazed at the pale disc of the moon, now nearly veiled, and seemed to meditate.

—She was . . . a bit of all right, he said regretfully.

He was silent again. Then he added:

—She's on the turf now. I saw her driving down Earl Street one night with two fellows with her on a car.

—I suppose that's your doing, said Lenehan.

—There was others at her before me, said Corley philosophically.

This time Lenehan was inclined to disbelieve. He shook his head to and fro and smiled.

—You know you can't kid me, Corley, he said.

—Honest to God! said Corley. Didn't she tell me herself?

Lenehan made a tragic gesture.

—Base betrayer! he said.

As they passed along the railings of Trinity College, Lenehan skipped out into the road and peered up at the clock.

—Twenty after, he said.

—Time enough, said Corley. She'll be there all right. I always let her wait a bit.

Lenehan laughed quietly.

—Ecod! Corley, you know how to take them, he said.

—I'm up to all their little tricks, Corley confessed.

—But tell me, said Lenehan again, are you sure you can bring it off all right? You know it's a ticklish job. They're damn close on that point. Eh? . . . What?

His bright, small eyes searched his companion's face for reassurance. Corley swung his head to and fro as if to toss aside an insistent insect, and his brows gathered.

—I'll pull it off, he said. Leave it to me, can't you?

Lenehan said no more. He did not wish to ruffle his friend's temper, to be sent to the devil and told that his advice was not wanted. A little tact was necessary. But Corley's brow was soon smooth again. His thoughts were running another way.

—She's a fine decent tart, he said, with appreciation; that's what she is.

They walked along Nassau Street and then turned into Kildare Street. Not far from the porch of the club a harpist stood in the roadway, playing to a little ring of listeners. He plucked at the wires heedlessly, glancing quickly from time to time at the face of each newcomer and from time to time, wearily also, at the sky. His harp too, heedless that her coverings had fallen about her knees, seemed weary alike of the eyes of strangers and of her master's hands. One hand played in the bass the melody of *Silent, O Moyle,* while the other hand careered in the treble after each group of notes. The notes of the air throbbed deep and full.

The two young men walked up the street without speaking, the mournful music following them. When they reached Stephen's Green they crossed the road. Here the noise of trams, the lights and the crowd released them from their silence.

—There she is! said Corley.

At the corner of Hume Street a young woman was standing. She wore a blue dress and a white sailor hat. She stood on the curbstone, swinging a sunshade in one hand. Lenehan grew lively.

—Let's have a squint at her, Corley, he said.

Corley glanced sideways at his friend and an unpleasant grin appeared on his face.

—Are you trying to get inside me? he asked.

—Damn it! said Lenehan boldly, I don't want an introduction. All I want is to have a look at her. I'm not going to eat her.

—O . . . A look at her? said Corley, more amiably. Well . . . I'll tell you what. I'll go over and talk to her and you can pass by.

—Right! said Lenehan.

Corley had already thrown one leg over the chains when Lenehan called out:

—And after? Where will we meet?

—Half ten, answered Corley, bringing over his other leg.

—Where?

—Corner of Merrion Street. We'll be coming back.

—Work it all right now, said Lenehan in farewell.

Corley did not answer. He sauntered across the road swaying his head from side to side. His bulk, his easy pace, and the solid sound of his boots had something of the conqueror in them. He approached the young woman and, without saluting, began at once to converse with her. She swung her sunshade more quickly and executed half turns on her heels. Once or twice when he spoke to her at close quarters she laughed and bent her head.

Lenehan observed them for a few minutes. Then he walked rapidly along beside the chains to some distance and crossed the road obliquely. As he approached Hume Street corner he found the air heavily scented and his eyes made a swift anxious scrutiny of the young woman's appearance. She had her Sunday finery on. Her blue serge skirt was held at the waist by a belt of black leather. The great silver buckle of her belt seemed to depress the centre of her body, catching the light stuff of her white blouse like a clip. She wore a short black jacket with mother-of-pearl buttons and a ragged black boa. The ends of her tulle collarette had been carefully disordered and a big bunch of red flowers was pinned in her bosom stems upwards. Lenehan's eyes noted approvingly her stout short muscular body. Frank rude health glowed in her face, on her fat red cheeks and in her unabashed blue eyes. Her features were blunt. She had broad nostrils, a straggling mouth which lay open in a contented leer, and two projecting front teeth. As he passed Lenehan took off his cap and, after about ten seconds, Corley returned a salute to the air. This he did by raising his hand vaguely and pensively changing the angle of position of his hat.

Lenehan walked as far as the Shelbourne Hotel where he halted and waited. After waiting for a little time he saw them coming towards him and, when they turned to the right, he followed them, stepping lightly in his white shoes, down one side of Merrion Square. As he walked on slowly, timing his pace to theirs, he watched Corley's head which turned at every moment towards the young woman's face like a big ball revolving on a pivot. He kept the pair in view until he had seen them climbing the stairs of the Donnybrook tram; then he turned about and went back the way he had come.

Now that he was alone his face looked older. His gaiety seemed to forsake him, and, as he came by the railings of the Duke's Lawn, he allowed his hand to run along them. The air which the harpist had played began to control his movements. His softly padded feet played the melody while his fingers swept a scale of variations idly along the railings after each group of notes.

He walked listlessly round Stephen's Green and then down Grafton Street. Though his eyes took note of many elements of the crowd through which he passed they did so morosely. He found trivial all that was meant to charm him and did not answer the glances which invited him to be bold. He knew that he would have to speak a great deal, to invent and to amuse, and his brain and throat were too dry for such a task. The problem of how he could pass the hours till he met Corley again troubled him a little. He could think of no way of passing them but to keep on walking. He turned to the left when he came to the corner of Rutland Square and felt more at ease in the dark quiet street, the sombre look of which suited his mood. He paused at last before the window of a poor-looking shop over which the words *Refreshment Bar* were printed in white letters. On the glass of the window were two flying inscriptions: *Ginger Beer* and *Ginger Ale*. A cut ham was exposed on a great blue dish while near it on a plate lay a segment of very light plum-pudding. He eyed this food earnestly for some time and then, after glancing warily up and down the street, went into the shop quickly.

He was hungry for, except some biscuits which he had asked two grudging curates to bring him, he had eaten nothing since breakfast-time. He sat down at an uncovered wooden table opposite two work-girls and a mechanic. A slatternly girl waited on him.

—How much is a plate of peas?" he asked.

—Three halfpence, sir, said the girl.

—Bring me a plate of peas, he said, and a bottle of ginger beer.

He spoke roughly in order to belie his air of gentility for his entry had been followed by a pause of talk. His face was heated. To appear natural he pushed his cap back on his head and planted his elbows on the table. The mechanic and the two work-girls examined him point by point before resuming their conversation in a subdued voice. The girl brought him a plate of hot grocer's peas, seasoned with pepper and vinegar, a fork and his ginger beer. He ate his food greedily and found it so good that he made a note of the shop mentally. When he had eaten all the peas he sipped his ginger beer and sat for some time thinking of Corley's adventure. In his imagination he beheld the pair of lovers walking along some dark road; he heard Corley's voice in deep energetic gallantries and saw again the leer of the young woman's mouth. This vision made him feel keenly his own poverty of purse and spirit. He was tired of knocking about, of pulling the devil by the tail, of shifts and intrigues. He would be thirty-one in November. Would he never get a good job? Would he never have a home of his own? He thought how pleasant it would be to have a warm fire to sit by and a good dinner to sit down to. He had walked the streets long enough with friends and with girls. He knew what those friends were worth: he knew the girls too. Experience had embittered his heart against the world. But all hope had not left him. He felt better after having eaten than he had felt before, less weary of his life, less vanquished in spirit. He might yet be able to settle down in some snug corner and live happily if he could only come across some good simple-minded girl with a little of the ready.

He paid twopence halfpenny to the slatternly girl and went out of the shop to begin his wandering again. He went into Capel Street and walked along towards the City Hall. Then he turned into Dame Street. At the corner of George's Street he met two friends of his and stopped to converse with them. He was glad that he could rest from all his walking. His friends asked him had he seen Corley and what was the latest. He replied that he had spent the day with Corley. His friends talked very little. They looked vacantly after some figures in the crowd and sometimes made a critical remark. One said that he had seen Mac an hour before in Westmoreland Street. At this Lenehan said that he had been with Mac the night before in Egan's. The young man who had seen Mac in Westmoreland Street asked was it true that Mac had won a bit over a billiard match. Lenehan did not know: he said that Holohan had stood them drinks in Egan's.

He left his friends at a quarter to ten and went up George's Street. He turned to the left at the City Markets and walked on into Grafton Street. The crowd of girls and young men had thinned and on his way up the street he heard many groups and couples bidding one another goodnight. He went as far as the clock of the College of Surgeons: it was on the stroke of ten. He set off briskly along the northern side of the Green, hurrying for fear Corley should return too soon. When he reached the corner of Merrion Street he took his stand in the shadow of a lamp and brought out one of the cigarettes which he had reserved and lit it. He leaned against the lamp-post and kept his gaze fixed on the part from which he expected to see Corley and the young woman return.

His mind became active again. He wondered had Corley managed it successfully. He wondered if he had asked her yet or if he would leave it to the last. He suffered all the pangs and thrills of his friend's situation as well as those of his own. But the memory of Corley's slowly revolving head calmed him somewhat: he was sure Corley would pull it off all right. All at once the idea struck him that perhaps Corley had seen her home by another way and given him the slip. His eyes searched the street: there was no sign of them. Yet it was surely half-an-hour since he had seen the clock of the College of Surgeons. Would Corley do a thing like that? He lit his last cigarette and began to smoke it nervously. He strained his eyes as each tram stopped at the far corner of the square. They must have gone home by another way. The paper of his cigarette broke and he flung it into the road with a curse.

Suddenly he saw them coming towards him. He started with delight and, keeping close to his lamp-post, tried to read the result in their walk. They were walking quickly, the young woman taking quick short steps, while Corley kept beside her with his long stride. They did not seem to be speaking. An intimation of the result pricked him like the point of a sharp instrument. He knew Corley would fail; he knew it was no go.

They turned down Baggot Street and he followed them at once, taking the other footpath. When they stopped he stopped too. They talked for a few moments and then the young woman went down the steps into the area of a house. Corley remained standing at the edge of the path, a little distance from the front steps. Some minutes passed. Then the hall-door was opened slowly and cautiously. A woman came running down the front steps and coughed. Corley turned and went towards her. His broad figure hid hers from view for a few seconds and then she reappeared running up the steps. The door closed on her and Corley began to walk swiftly towards Stephen's Green.

Lenehan hurried on in the same direction. Some drops of light rain fell. He took them as a warning and, glancing back towards the house which the young woman had entered to see that he was not observed, he ran eagerly across the road. Anxiety and his swift run made him pant. He called out:

—Hallo, Corley!

Corley turned his head to see who had called him, and then continued walking as before. Lenehan ran after him, settling the waterproof on his shoulders with one hand.

—Hallo, Corley! he cried again.

He came level with his friend and looked keenly in his face. He could see nothing there.

—Well? he said. Did it come off?

They had reached the corner of Ely Place. Still without answering Corley swerved to the left and went up the side street. His features were composed in stern calm. Lenehan kept up with his friend, breathing uneasily. He was baffled and a note of menace pierced through his voice.

—Can't you tell us? he said. Did you try her?

Corley halted at the first lamp and stared grimly before him. Then with a grave gesture he extended a hand towards the light and, smiling, opened it slowly to the gaze of his disciple. A small gold coin shone in the palm.

The Rocking-Horse Winner

D.H. Lawrence (1885–1930)

David Herbert Lawrence was born in a colliery village in Nottinghamshire, England, the son of a coal miner and a school teacher who, it was thought, had married "beneath her." After leaving Nottingham High School at the age of sixteen, Lawrence held several jobs before entering University College, Nottingham, where he received a teaching certificate after two years. He took up a teaching position at Croyden, near London, and began to write verse and fiction. His first novel, *The White Peacock* (1911), was followed by his semi-autobiographical novel, *Sons and Lovers* (1913), and *The Prussian Officer and Other Stories* (1914). In April 1912 Lawrence met Frieda Weekley (born Frieda von Richthofen), the German wife of a university professor at Nottingham; they fell in love and soon left together for Germany, returning to England in 1913. Lawrence and Frieda were married in 1914 after she obtained a divorce. Their intense, nomadic relationship was to form one of the unifying designs in Lawrence's life and art.

The years of the first World War were difficult ones for Lawrence. He was looked upon with suspicion because of his German wife and bohemian ways, and he in turn felt a deep disgust for the war. It was, however, a period of great productivity. His first volume of verse, *Love Poems and Others* (1913), was followed by three more collections, *Amores* (1916), *Look! We Have Come Through* (1917), and *New Poems* (1918), while his major novels, *The Rainbow* and *Women in Love,* were completed in 1915–16 (published in 1916 and 1920). After the war Lawrence's restless imagination led him to the Mediterranean countries, Ceylon, Australia, New Mexico, and Mexico, the settings for such works as *Kangaroo* (1923) and *The Plumed Serpent* (1926). Lawrence's production of poetry and fiction remained prodigious, but his health—always delicate—began to fail. After returning to Europe in 1925 he spent much of his time painting, studying Etruscan art, and writing and rewriting his last novel, *Lady Chatterley's Lover,* which was privately printed in Florence in 1928 and published in an expurgated edition in 1932 (the full text did not escape the English censor until 1960). In June 1928 Lawrence left Florence in failing health; he died in the south of France, of tuberculosis, on March 2, 1930.

During the period 1918–30 Lawrence published five volumes of verse, the most important being *Birds, Beasts and Flowers* (1923). His *Collected Poems* appeared in 1928. Three collections of short stories also appeared: *England, My England* (1922), *The Ladybird* (1923), and *The Woman Who Rode Away* (1928). "The Rocking-Horse Winner," written in 1926, was published in the posthumous volume *The Lovely Lady* (1933).

There was a woman who was beautiful, who started with all the advantages, yet she had no luck. She married for love, and the love turned to dust. She had bonny children, yet she felt they had been thrust upon her, and she could not love them. They looked at her coldly, as if they were finding fault with her. And hurriedly she felt she must cover up some fault in herself. Yet what it was that she must cover up she never knew. Nevertheless, when her children were present, she always felt the centre of her heart go hard. This troubled her, and in her manner she was all the more gentle and anxious for her children, as if she loved them very much. Only she herself knew that at the centre of her heart was a hard little place that could not feel love, no, not for anybody. Everybody else said of her: "She is such a good mother. She adores her children." Only she herself, and her children themselves, knew it was not so. They read it in each other's eyes.

There were a boy and two little girls. They lived in a pleasant house, with a garden, and they had discreet servants, and felt themselves superior to anyone in the neighbourhood.

Although they lived in style, they felt always an anxiety in the house. There was never enough money. The mother had a small income, and the father had a small income, but not nearly enough for the social position which they had to keep up. The father went into town to some office. But though he had good prospects, these prospects never materialised. There was always the grinding sense of the shortage of money, though the style was always kept up.

At last the mother said: "I will see if *I* can't make something." But she did not know where to begin. She racked her brains, and tried this thing and the other, but could not find anything successful. The failure made deep lines come into her face. Her children were growing up, they would have to go to school. There must be more money, there must be more money. The father, who was always very handsome and expensive in his tastes, seemed as if he never *would* be able to do anything worth doing. And the mother, who had a great belief in herself, did not succeed any better, and her tastes were just as expensive.

And so the house came to be haunted by the unspoken phrase: *There must be more money! There must be more money!* The children could hear it all the time, though nobody said it aloud. They heard it at Christmas, when the expensive and splendid toys filled the nursery. Behind the shining modern rocking-horse, behind the smart doll's house, a voice would start whispering: "There *must* be more money! There *must* be more money!" And the children would stop playing, to listen for a moment. They would look into each other's eyes, to see if they had all heard. And each one saw in the eyes of the other two that they too had heard. "There *must* be more money! There *must* be more money!"

It came whispering from the springs of the still-swaying rocking-horse, and even the horse, bending his wooden, champing head, heard it. The big doll, sitting so pink and smirking in her new pram, could hear it quite plainly, and seemed to be smirking all the more self-consciously because of it. The foolish puppy, too, that took the place of the teddy-bear, he was looking so extraordinarily foolish for no other reason but that he heard the secret whisper all over the house: "There *must* be more money!"

Yet nobody ever said it aloud. The whisper was everywhere, and therefore no one spoke it. Just as no one ever says: "We are breathing!" in spite of the fact that breath is coming and going all the time.

"Mother," said the boy Paul one day, "why don't we keep a car of our own? Why do we always use uncle's, or else a taxi?"

"Because we're the the poor members of the family," said the mother.

"But why *are* we, mother?"

"Well—I suppose," she said slowly and bitterly, "it's because your father has no luck."

The boy was silent for some time.

"Is luck money, mother?" he asked, rather timidly.

"No, Paul. Not quite. It's what causes you to have money."

"Oh!" said Paul vaguely. "I thought when Uncle Oscar said *filthy lucker,* it meant money."

"Filthy lucre does mean money," said the mother. "But it's lucre, not luck."

"Oh!" said the boy. "Then what *is* luck, mother?"

"It's what causes you to have money. If you're lucky you have money. That's why it's better to be born lucky than rich. If you're rich, you may lose your money. But if you're lucky, you will always get more money."

"Oh! Will you? And is father not lucky?"

"Very unlucky, I should say," she said bitterly.

The boy watched her with unsure eyes.

"Why?" he asked.

"I don't know. Nobody ever knows why one person is lucky and another unlucky."

"Don't they? Nobody at all? Does *nobody* know?"

"Perhaps God. But He never tells."

"He ought to, then. And aren't you lucky either, mother?"

"I can't be, if I married an unlucky husband."

"But by yourself, aren't you?"

"I used to think I was, before I married. Now I think I am very unlucky indeed."

"Why?"

"Well—never mind! Perhaps I'm not really," she said.

The child looked at her to see if she meant it. But he saw, by the lines of her mouth, that she was only trying to hide something from him.

"Well, anyhow," he said stoutly, "I'm a lucky person."

"Why?" said his mother, with a sudden laugh.

He stared at her. He didn't even know why he had said it.

"God told me," he asserted brazening it out.

"I hope He did, dear!" she said, again with a laugh, but rather bitter.

"He did, mother!"

"Excellent!" said the mother, using one of her husband's exclamations.

The boy saw she did not believe him; or rather, that she paid no attention to his assertion. This angered him somewhere, and made him want to compel her attention.

He went off by himself, vaguely, in a childish way, seeking for the clue to 'luck'. Absorbed, taking no heed of other people, he went about with a sort of stealth, seeking inwardly for luck. He wanted luck, he wanted it, he wanted it. When the two girls were playing dolls in the nursery, he would sit on his big rocking-horse, charging madly into space, with a frenzy that made the little girls peer at him uneasily. Wildly the horse careered, the waving dark hair of the boy tossed, his eyes had a strange glare in them. The little girls dared not speak to him.

When he had ridden to the end of his mad little journey, he climbed down and stood in front of his rocking-horse, staring fixedly into its lowered face. Its red mouth was slightly open, its big eye was wide and glassy-bright.

"Now!" he would silently command the snorting steed. "Now, take me to where there is luck! Now take me!"

And he would slash the horse on the neck with the little whip he had asked Uncle Oscar for. He *knew* the horse could take him to where there was luck, if only he forced it. So he would mount again and start on his furious ride, hoping at last to get there. He knew he could get there.

"You'll break your horse, Paul!" said the nurse.

"He's always riding like that! I wish he'd leave off!" said his elder sister Joan.

But he only glared down on them in silence. Nurse gave him up. She could make nothing of him. Anyhow, he was growing beyond her.

One day his mother and his Uncle Oscar came in when he was on one of his furious rides. He did not speak to them.

"Hallo, you young jockey! Riding a winner?" said his uncle.

"Aren't you growing too big for a rocking-horse? You're not a very little boy any longer, you know," said his mother.

But Paul only gave a blue glare from his big, rather close-set eyes. He would speak to nobody when he was in full tilt. His mother watched him with an anxious expression on her face.

At last he suddenly stopped forcing his horse into the mechanical gallop and slid down.

"Well, I got there!" he announced fiercely, his blue eyes still flaring, and his sturdy long legs straddling apart.

"Where did you get to?" asked his mother.

"Where I wanted to go," he flared back at her.

"That's right, son!" said Uncle Oscar. "Don't you stop till you get there. What's the horse's name?"

"He doesn't have a name," said the boy.

"Gets on without all right?" asked the uncle.

"Well, he has different names. He was called Sansovino last week."

"Sansovino, eh? Won the Ascot. How did you know this name?"

"He always talks about horse-races with Bassett," said Joan.

The uncle was delighted to find that his small nephew was posted with all the racing news. Bassett, the young gardener, who had been wounded in the left foot in the war and had got his present job through Oscar Cresswell, whose batman he had been, was a perfect blade of the 'turf'. He lived in the racing events, and the small boy lived with him.

Oscar Cresswell got it all from Bassett.

"Master Paul comes and asks me, so I can't do more than tell him, sir," said Bassett, his face terribly serious, as if he were speaking of religious matters.

"And does he ever put anything on a horse he fancies?"

"Well—I don't want to give away—he's a young sport, a fine sport, sir. Would you mind asking him himself? He sort of takes a pleasure in it, and perhaps he'd feel I was giving him away, sir, if you don't mind."

Bassett was serious as a church.

The uncle went back to his nephew and took him off for a ride in the car.

"Say, Paul, old man, do you ever put anything on a horse?" the uncle asked.

The boy watched the handsome man closely.

"Why, do you think I oughtn't to?" he parried.

"Not a bit of it! I thought perhaps you might give me a tip for the Lincoln."

The car sped on into the country, going down to Uncle Oscar's place in Hampshire.

"Honour bright?" said the nephew.

"Honour bright, son!" said the uncle.

"Well, then, Daffodil."

"Daffodil! I doubt it, sonny. What about Mirza?"

"I only know the winner," said the boy. "That's Daffodil."

"Daffodil, eh?"

There was a pause. Daffodil was an obscure horse comparatively.

"Uncle!"

"Yes, son?"

"You won't let it go any further, will you? I promised Bassett."

"Bassett be damned, old man! What's he got to do with it?"

"We're partners. We've been partners from the first. Uncle, he lent me my first five shillings, which I lost. I promised him, honour bright, it was only between me and him; only you gave me that ten-shilling note I started winning with, so I thought you were lucky. You won't let it go any further, will you?"

The boy gazed at his uncle from those big, hot, blue eyes, set rather close together. The uncle stirred and laughed uneasily.

"Right you are, son! I'll keep your tip private. Daffodil, eh? How much are you putting on him?"

"All except twenty pounds," said the boy. "I keep that in reserve."

The uncle thought it a good joke.

"You keep twenty pounds in reserve, do you, you young romancer? What are you betting, then?"

"I'm betting three hundred," said the boy gravely. "But it's between you and me, Uncle Oscar! Honour bright?"

The uncle burst into a roar of laughter.

"It's between you and me all right, you young Nat Gould," he said, laughing. "But where's your three hundred?"

"Bassett keeps it for me. We're partners."

"You are, are you! And what is Bassett putting on Daffodil?"

"He won't go quite as high as I do, I expect. Perhaps he'll go a hundred and fifty."

"What, pennies?" laughed the uncle.

"Pounds," said the child, with a surprised look at his uncle. "Bassett keeps a bigger reserve than I do."

Between wonder and amusement Uncle Oscar was silent. He pursued the matter no further, but he determined to take his nephew with him to the Lincoln races.

"Now, son," he said, "I'm putting twenty on Mirza, and I'll put five on for you on any horse you fancy. What's your pick?"

"Daffodil, uncle."

"No, not the fiver on Daffodil!"

"I should if it was my own fiver," said the child.

"Good! Good! Right you are! A fiver for me and a fiver for you on Daffodil."

The child had never been to a race-meeting before, and his eyes were blue fire. He pursed his mouth tight and watched. A Frenchman just in front had put his money on Lancelot. Wild with excitement, he flayed his arms up and down, yelling *"Lancelot! Lancelot!"* in his French accent.

Daffodil came in first, Lancelot second, Mirza third. The child, flushed and with eyes blazing, was curiously serene. His uncle brought him four five-pound notes, four to one.

"What am I to do with these?" he cried, waving them before the boy's eyes.

"I suppose we'll talk to Bassett," said the boy. "I expect I have fifteen hundred now; and twenty in reserve; and this twenty."

His uncle studied him for some moments.

"Look here, son!" he said. "You're not serious about Bassett and that fifteen hundred, are you?"

"Yes, I am. But it's between you and me, uncle. Honour bright?"

"Honour bright all right, son! But I must talk to Bassett."

"If you'd like to be a partner, uncle, with Bassett and me, we could all be partners. Only, you'd have to promise, honour bright, uncle, not to let it go beyond us three. Bassett and I are lucky, and you must be lucky, because it was your ten shillings I started winning with. . . ."

Uncle Oscar took both Bassett and Paul into Richmond Park for an afternoon, and there they talked.

"It's like this, you see, sir," Bassett said. "Master Paul would get me talking about racing events, spinning yarns, you know, sir. And he was always keen on knowing if I'd made or if I'd lost. It's about a year since, now, that I put five shillings on Blush of Dawn for him: and we lost. Then the luck turned, with that ten shillings he had from you: that we put on Singhalese. And since that time, it's been pretty steady, all things considering. What do you say, Master Paul?"

"We're all right when we're sure," said Paul. "It's when we're not quite sure that we go down."

"Oh, but we're careful then," said Bassett.

"But when are you *sure?"* smiled Uncle Oscar.

"It's Master Paul, sir," said Bassett in a secret, religious voice. "It's as if he had it from heaven. Like Daffodil, now, for the Lincoln. That was as sure as eggs."

"Did you put anything on Daffodil?" asked Oscar Cresswell.

"Yes, sir. I made my bit."

"And my nephew?"

Bassett was obstinately silent, looking at Paul.

"I made twelve hundred, didn't I, Bassett? I told uncle I was putting three hundred on Daffodil."

"That's right," said Bassett, nodding.

"But where's the money?" asked the uncle.

"I keep it safe locked up, sir. Master Paul he can have it any minute he likes to ask for it."

"What, fifteen hundred pounds?"

"And twenty! And *forty,* that is, with the twenty he made on the course."

"It's amazing!" said the uncle.

"If Master Paul offers you to be partners, sir, I would, if I were you: if you'll excuse me," said Bassett.

Oscar Cresswell thought about it.

"I'll see the money," he said.

They drove home again, and, sure enough, Bassett came round to the garden-house with fifteen hundred pounds in notes. The twenty pounds reserve was left with Joe Glee, in the Turf Commission deposit.

"You see, it's all right, uncle, when I'm *sure!* Then we go strong, for all we're worth. Don't we, Bassett?"

"We do that, Master Paul."

"And when are you sure?" said the uncle, laughing.

"Oh, well, sometimes I'm *absolutely* sure, like about Daffodil," said the boy; "and sometimes I have an idea; and sometimes I haven't even an idea, have I, Bassett? Then we're careful, because we mostly go down."

"You do, do you! And when you're sure, like about Daffodil, what makes you sure, sonny?"

"Oh, well, I don't know," said the boy uneasily. "I'm sure, you know, uncle; that's all."

"It's as if he had it from heaven, sir," Bassett reiterated.

"I should say so!" said the uncle.

But he became a partner. And when the Leger was coming on Paul was 'sure' about Lively Spark, which was a quite inconsiderable horse. The boy insisted on putting a thousand on the horse, Bassett went for five hundred, and Oscar Cresswell two hundred. Lively Spark came in first, and the betting had been ten to one against him. Paul had made ten thousand.

"You see," he said, "I was absolutely sure of him."

Even Oscar Cresswell had cleared two thousand.

"Look here, son," he said, "this sort of thing makes me nervous."

"It needn't, uncle! Perhaps I shan't be sure again for a long time."

"But what are you going to do with your money?" asked the uncle.

"Of course," said the boy, "I started it for mother. She said she had no luck, because father is unlucky, so I thought if *I* was lucky, it might stop whispering."

"What might stop whispering?"

"Our house. I *hate* our house for whispering."

"What does it whisper?"

"Why—why"—the boy fidgeted—"why, I don't know. But it's always short of money, you know, uncle."

"I know it, son, I know it."

"You know people send mother writs, don't you, uncle?"

"I'm afraid I do," said the uncle.

"And then the house whispers, like people laughing at you behind your back. It's awful, that is! I thought if I was lucky——"

"You might stop it," added the uncle.

The boy watched him with big blue eyes, that had an uncanny cold fire in them, and he said never a word.

"Well, then!" said the uncle. "What are we doing?"

"I shouldn't like mother to know I was lucky," said the boy.

"Why not, son?"

"She'd stop me."

"I don't think she would."

"Oh!"—and the boy writhed in an odd way—"I *don't* want her to know, uncle."

"All right, son! We'll manage it without her knowing."

They managed it very easily. Paul, at the other's suggestion, handed over five thousand pounds to his uncle, who deposited it with the family lawyer, who was then to inform Paul's mother that a relative had put five thousand pounds into his hands, which sum was to be paid out a thousand pounds at a time, on the mother's birthday, for the next five years.

"So she'll have a birthday present of a thousand pounds for five successive years," said Uncle Oscar. "I hope it won't make it all the harder for her later."

Paul's mother had her birthday in November. The house had been 'whispering' worse than ever lately, and, even in spite of his luck, Paul could not bear up against it. He was very anxious to see the effect of the birthday letter, telling his mother about the thousand pounds.

When there were no visitors, Paul now took his meals with his parents, as he was beyond the nursery control. His mother went into town nearly every day. She had discovered that she had an odd knack of sketching furs and dress materials, so she worked secretly in the studio of a friend who was the chief 'artist' for the leading drapers. She drew the figures of ladies in furs and ladies in silk and sequins for the newspaper advertisements. This young woman artist earned several thousand pounds a year, but Paul's mother only made several hundreds, and she was again dissatisfied. She so wanted to be first in something, and she did not succeed, even in making sketches for drapery advertisements.

She was down to breakfast on the morning of her birthday. Paul watched her face as she read her letters. He knew the lawyer's letter. As his mother read it, her face hardened and became more expressionless. Then a cold, determined look came on her mouth. She hid the letter under the pile of others, and said not a word about it.

"Didn't you have anything nice in the post for your birthday, mother?" said Paul.

"Quite moderately nice," she said, her voice cold and absent.

She went away to town without saying more.

But in the afternoon Uncle Oscar appeared. He said Paul's mother had had a long interview with the lawyer, asking if the whole five thousand could not be advanced at once, as she was in debt.

"What do you think, uncle?" said the boy.

"I leave it to you, son."

"Oh, let her have it, then! We can get some more with the other," said the boy.

"A bird in the hand is worth two in the bush, laddie!" said Uncle Oscar.

"But I'm sure to *know* for the Grand National; or the Lincolnshire; or else the Derby. I'm sure to know for *one* of them," said Paul.

So Uncle Oscar signed the agreement, and Paul's mother touched the whole five thousand. Then something very curious happened. The voices in the house suddenly went mad, like a chorus of frogs on a spring evening. There were certain new furnishings, and Paul had a tutor. He was *really* going to Eton, his father's school, in the following autumn. There were flowers in the winter, and a blossoming of the luxury Paul's mother had been used to. And yet the voices in the house, behind the sprays of mimosa and almond-blossom, and from under the piles of iridescent cushions, simply trilled and screamed in a sort of ecstasy: "There *must* be more money! Oh-h-h; there *must* be more money. Oh, now, now-w! Now-w-w—there *must* be more money!—more than ever! More than ever!"

It frightened Paul terribly. He studied away at his Latin and Greek with his tutor. But his intense hours were spent with Bassett. The Grand National had gone by: he had not 'known', and had lost a hundred pounds. Summer was at hand. He was in agony for the Lincoln. But even for the Lincoln he didn't 'know', and he lost fifty pounds. He became wild-eyed and strange, as if something were going to explode in him.

"Let it alone, son! Don't you bother about it!" urged Uncle Oscar. But it was as if the boy couldn't really hear what his uncle was saying.

"I've got to know for the Derby! I've got to know for the Derby!" the child reiterated, his big blue eyes blazing with a sort of madness.

His mother noticed how overwrought he was.

"You'd better go to the seaside. Wouldn't you like to go now to the seaside, instead of waiting? I think you'd better," she said, looking down at him anxiously, her heart curiously heavy because of him.

But the child lifted his uncanny blue eyes.

"I couldn't possibly go before the Derby, mother!" he said. "I couldn't possibly!"

"Why not?" she said, her voice becoming heavy when she was opposed. "Why not? You can still go from the seaside to see the Derby with your Uncle Oscar, if that's what you wish. No need for you to wait here. Besides, I think you care too much about these races. It's a bad sign. My family has been a gambling family, and you won't know till you grow up how much damage it has done. But it has done damage. I shall have to send Bassett away, and ask Uncle Oscar not to talk racing to you, unless you promise to be reasonable about it: go away to the seaside and forget it. You're all nerves!"

"I'll do what you like, mother, so long as you don't send me away till after the Derby," the boy said.

"Send you away from where? Just from this house?"

"Yes," he said, gazing at her.

"Why, you curious child, what makes you care about this house so much, suddenly? I never knew you loved it."

He gazed at her without speaking. He had a secret within a secret, something he had not divulged, even to Bassett or to his Uncle Oscar.

But his mother, after standing undecided and a little bit sullen for some moments, said:

"Very well, then! Don't go to the seaside till after the Derby, if you don't wish it. But promise me you won't let your nerves go to pieces. Promise you won't think so much about horse-racing and *events,* as you call them!"

"Oh no," said the boy casually. "I won't think much about them, mother. You needn't worry. I wouldn't worry, mother, if I were you."

"If you were me and I were you," said his mother, "I wonder what we *should* do!"

"But you know you needn't worry, mother, don't you?" the boy repeated.

"I should be awfully glad to know it," she said wearily.

"Oh, well, you *can,* you know. I mean, you *ought* to know you needn't worry," he insisted.

"Ought I? Then I'll see about it," she said.

Paul's secret of secrets was his wooden horse, that which had no name. Since he was emancipated from a nurse and a nursery-governess, he had had his rocking-horse removed to his own bedroom at the top of the house.

"Surely you're too big for a rocking-horse!" his mother had remonstrated.

"Well, you see, mother, till I can have a *real* horse, I like to have *some* sort of animal about," had been his quaint answer.

"Do you feel he keeps you company?" she laughed.

"Oh yes! He's very good, he always keeps me company, when I'm there," said Paul.

So the horse, rather shabby, stood in an arrested prance in the boy's bedroom.

The Derby was drawing near, and the boy grew more and more tense. He hardly heard what was spoken to him, he was very frail, and his eyes were really uncanny. His mother had sudden strange seizures of uneasiness about him. Sometimes, for half an hour, she would feel a sudden anxiety about him that was almost anguish. She wanted to rush to him at once, and know he was safe.

Two nights before the Derby, she was at a big party in town, when one of her rushes of anxiety about her boy, her first-born, gripped her heart till she could hardly speak. She fought with the feeling, might and main, for she believed in common sense. But it was too strong. She had to leave the dance and go downstairs to telephone to the country. The children's nursery-governess was terribly surprised and startled at being rung up in the night.

"Are the children all right, Miss Wilmot?"

"Oh yes, they are quite all right."

"Master Paul? Is he all right?"

"He went to bed as right as a trivet. Shall I run up and look at him?"

"No," said Paul's mother reluctantly. "No! Don't trouble. It's all right. Don't sit up. We shall be home fairly soon." She did not want her son's privacy intruded upon.

"Very good," said the governess.

It was about one o'clock when Paul's mother and father drove up to their house. All was still. Paul's mother went to her room and slipped off her white fur cloak. She had told her maid not to wait up for her. She heard her husband downstairs, mixing a whisky and soda.

And then, because of the strange anxiety at her heart, she stole upstairs to her son's room. Noiselessly she went along the upper corridor. Was there a faint noise? What was it?

She stood, with arrested muscles, outside his door, listening. There was a strange, heavy, and yet not loud noise. Her heart stood still. It was a soundless noise, yet rushing and powerful. Something huge, in violent, hushed motion. What was it? What in God's name was it? She ought to know. She felt that she knew the noise. She knew what it was.

Yet she could not place it. She couldn't say what it was. And on and on it went, like a madness.

Softly, frozen with anxiety and fear, she turned the door-handle.

The room was dark. Yet in the space near the window, she heard and saw something plunging to and fro. She gazed in fear and amazement.

Then suddenly she switched on the light, and saw her son, in his green pyjamas, madly surging on the rocking-horse. The blaze of light suddenly lit him up, as he urged the wooden horse, and lit her up, as she stood, blonde, in her dress of pale green and crystal, in the doorway.

"Paul!" she cried. "Whatever are you doing?"

"It's Malabar!" he screamed in a powerful, strange voice. "It's Malabar!"

His eyes blazed at her for one strange and senseless second, as he ceased urging his wooden horse. Then he fell with a crash to the ground, and she, all her tormented motherhood flooding upon her, rushed to gather him up.

But he was unconscious, and unconscious he remained, with some brain-fever. He talked and tossed, and his mother sat stonily by his side.

"Malabar! It's Malabar! Bassett, Bassett, I *know!* It's Malabar!"

So the child cried, trying to get up and urge the rocking-horse that gave him his inspiration.

"What does he mean by Malabar?" asked the heart-frozen mother.

"I don't know," said the father stonily.

"What does he mean by Malabar?" she asked her brother Oscar.

"It's one of the horses running for the Derby," was the answer.

And, in spite of himself, Oscar Cresswell spoke to Bassett, and himself put a thousand on Malabar: at fourteen to one.

The third day of the illness was critical: they were waiting for a change. The boy, with his rather long, curly hair, was tossing ceaselessly on the pillow. He neither slept nor regained consciousness, and his eyes were like blue stones. His mother sat, feeling her heart had gone, turned actually into a stone.

In the evening, Oscar Cresswell did not come, but Bassett sent a message, saying could he come up for one moment, just one moment? Paul's mother was very angry at the intrusion, but on second thoughts she agreed. The boy was the same. Perhaps Bassett might bring him to consciousness.

The gardener, a shortish fellow with a little brown moustache and sharp little brown eyes, tiptoed into the room, touched his imaginary cap to Paul's mother, and stole to the bedside, staring with glittering, smallish eyes at the tossing, dying child.

"Master Paul!" he whispered. "Master Paul! Malabar came in first all right, a clean win. I did as you told me. You've made over seventy thousand pounds, you have; you've got over eighty thousand. Malabar came in all right, Master Paul."

"Malabar! Malabar! Did I say Malabar, mother? Did I say Malabar? Do you think I'm lucky, mother? I knew Malabar, didn't I? Over eighty thousand pounds! I call that lucky, don't you, mother? Over eighty thousand pounds! I knew, didn't I know I knew? Malabar came in all right. If I ride my horse till I'm sure, then I tell you, Bassett, you can go as high as you like. Did you go for all you were worth, Bassett?"

"I went a thousand on it, Master Paul."

"I never told you, mother, that if I can ride my horse, and *get there,* then I'm absolutely sure—oh, absolutely! Mother, did I ever tell you? I *am* lucky!"

"No, you never did," said his mother.

But the boy died in the night.

And even as he lay dead, his mother heard her brother's voice saying to her: "My God, Hester, you're eighty-odd thousand to the good, and a poor devil of a son to the bad. But, poor devil, poor devil, he's best gone out of a life where he rides his rocking-horse to find a winner."

Neighbour Rosicky

Willa Cather (1876–1947)

Willa Cather was born in Virginia but moved at an early age to Nebraska, where her experiences with the pioneering settlers of that region became (as she later acknowledged) the most important part of her life as a writer. Educated at home before high school, she graduated from the University of Nebraska in 1895, worked as a journalist and teacher in Pittsburgh, served as editor of *McClure's* magazine in New York, and—after 1911—travelled widely in the United States and Europe. Her first collection of stories, *The Troll Garden* (1905), was followed in 1913 by her first major novel, *O Pioneers! The Song of the Lark* (1915) and *My Antonia* (1918) were among the works which established her reputation as a major novelist. In 1922 Willa Cather won the Pulitzer Prize for her war novel, *One of Ours.*

After *A Lost Lady* (1923), Willa Cather turned from Midwest settings to the Southwest. *The Professor's House* (1925), her most autobiographical novel, was followed by *Death Comes for the Archbishop* (1927), a fictional retelling of the life of Archbishop Lamy in nineteenth-century New Mexico. Willa Cather was a master of short fiction, often using her stories as testing-grounds for the themes and techniques of her novels. "Neighbour Rosicky" was published in *Obscure Destinies* (1932).

I

When Doctor Burleigh told neighbour Rosicky he had a bad heart, Rosicky protested.

"So? No, I guess my heart was always pretty good. I got a little asthma, maybe. Just a awful short breath when I was pitchin' hay last summer, dat's all."

"Well now, Rosicky, if you know more about it than I do, what did you come to me for? It's your heart that makes you short of breath, I tell you. You're sixty-five years old, and you've always worked hard, and your heart's tired. You've got to be careful from now on, and you can't do heavy work any more. You've got five boys at home to do it for you."

The old farmer looked up at the Doctor with a gleam of amusement in his queer triangular-shaped eyes. His eyes were large and lively, but the lids were caught up in the middle in a curious way, so that they formed a triangle. He did not look like a sick man. His brown face was creased but not wrinkled, he had a ruddy colour in his smooth-shaven cheeks and in his lips, under his long brown moustache. His hair was thin and ragged around his ears, but very little grey. His forehead, naturally high and crossed by deep parallel lines, now ran all the way up to his pointed crown. Rosicky's face had the habit of looking interested,—suggested a contented disposition and a reflective quality that was gay rather than grave. This gave him a certain detachment, the easy manner of an onlooker and observer.

"Well, I guess you ain't got no pills fur a bad heart, Doctor Ed. I guess the only thing is fur me to git me a new one."

Doctor Burleigh swung round in his desk-chair and frowned at the old farmer. "I think if I were you I'd take a little care of the old one, Rosicky."

Rosicky shrugged. "Maybe I don't know how. I expect you mean fur me not to drink my coffee no more."

"I wouldn't, in your place. But you'll do as you choose about that. I've never yet been able to separate a Bohemian from his coffee or his pipe. I've quit trying. But the sure thing is you've got to cut out farm work. You can feed the stock and do chores about the barn, but you can't do anything in the fields that makes you short of breath."

"How about shelling corn?"

"Of course not!"

Rosicky considered with puckered brows.

"I can't make my heart go no longer'n it wants to, can I, Doctor Ed?"

"I think it's good for five or six years yet, maybe more, if you'll take the strain off it. Sit around the house and help Mary. If I had a good wife like yours, I'd want to stay around the house."

His patient chuckled. "It ain't no place fur a man. I don't like no old man hanging round the kitchen too much. An' my wife, she's a awful hard worker her own self."

"That's it; you can help her a little. My Lord, Rosicky, you are one of the few men I know who has a family he can get some comfort out of; happy dispositions, never quarrel among themselves, and they treat you right. I want to see you live a few years and enjoy them."

"Oh, they're good kids, all right," Rosicky assented.

The Doctor wrote him a prescription and asked him how his oldest son, Rudolph, who had married in the spring, was getting on. Rudolph had struck out for himself, on rented land. "And how's Polly? I was afraid Mary mightn't like an American daughter-in-law, but it seems to be working out all right."

"Yes, she's a fine girl. Dat widder woman brings her daughters up very nice. Polly got lots of spunk, an' she got some style, too. Da's nice, for young folks to have some style." Rosicky inclined his head gallantly. His voice and his twinkly smile were an affectionate compliment to his daughter-in-law.

"It looks like a storm, and you'd better be getting home before it comes. In town in the car?" Doctor Burleigh rose.

"No, I'm in de wagon. When you got five boys, you ain't got much chance to ride round in de Ford. I ain't much for cars, noway."

"Well, it's a good road out to your place; but I don't want you bumping around in a wagon much. And never again on a hay-rake, remember!"

Rosicky placed the Doctor's fee delicately behind the desk-telephone, looking the other way, as if this were an absent-minded gesture. He put on his plush cap and his corduroy jacket with a sheepskin collar, and went out.

The Doctor picked up his stethoscope and frowned at it as if he were seriously annoyed with the instrument. He wished it had been telling tales about some other man's heart, some old man who didn't look the Doctor in the eye so knowingly, or hold out such a warm brown hand when he said good-bye. Doctor Burleigh had been a poor boy in the country before he went away to medical school; he had known Rosicky almost ever since he could remember, and he had a deep affection for Mrs. Rosicky.

Only last winter he had had such a good breakfast at Rosicky's, and that when he needed it. He had been out all night on a long, hard confinement case at Tom Marshall's,—a big rich farm where there was plenty of stock and plenty of feed and a great deal of expensive farm machinery of the newest model, and no comfort whatever. The woman had too many children and too much work, and she was no manager. When the baby was born at last, and handed over to the assisting neighbour woman, and the mother was properly attended to, Burleigh refused any breakfast in that slovenly house, and drove his buggy—the snow was too deep for a car—eight miles to Anton Rosicky's place. He didn't know another farm-house where a man could get such a warm welcome, and such good strong coffee with rich cream. No wonder the old chap didn't want to give up his coffee!

He had driven in just when the boys had come back from the barn and were washing up for breakfast. The long table, covered with a bright oilcloth, was set out with dishes waiting for them, and the warm kitchen was full of the smell of coffee and hot biscuit and sausage. Five big handsome boys, running from twenty to twelve, all with what Burleigh called natural good manners,—they hadn't a bit of the painful self-consciousness he himself had to struggle with when he was a lad. One ran to put his horse away, another helped him off with his fur coat and hung it up, and Josephine, the youngest child and the only daughter, quickly set another place under her mother's direction.

With Mary, to feed creatures was the natural expression of affection,—her chickens, the calves, her big hungry boys. It was a rare pleasure to feed a young man whom she seldom saw and of whom she was as proud as if he belonged to her. Some country housekeepers would have stopped to spread a white cloth over the oilcloth, to change the thick cups and plates for their best china, and the wooden-handled knives for plated ones. But not Mary.

"You must take us as you find us, Doctor Ed. I'd be glad to put out my good things for you if you was expected, but I'm glad to get you any way at all."

He knew she was glad,—she threw back her head and spoke out as if she were announcing him to the whole prairie. Rosicky hadn't said anything at all; he merely smiled his twinkling smile, put some more coal on the fire, and went into his own room to pour the Doctor a little drink in a medicine glass. When they were all seated, he watched his wife's face from his end of the table and spoke to her in Czech. Then, with the instinct of politeness which seldom failed him, he turned to the Doctor and said slyly; "I was just tellin' her not to ask you no questions about Mrs. Marshall till you eat some breakfast. My wife, she's terrible fur to ask questions."

The boys laughed, and so did Mary. She watched the Doctor devour her biscuit and sausage, too much excited to eat anything herself. She drank her coffee and sat taking in everything about her visitor. She had known him when he was a poor country boy, and was boastfully proud of his success, always saying: "What do people go to Omaha for, to see a doctor, when we got the best one in the State right here?" If Mary liked people at all, she felt physical pleasure in the sight of them, personal exultation in any good fortune that came to them. Burleigh didn't know many women like that, but he knew she was like that.

When his hunger was satisfied, he did, of course, have to tell them about Mrs. Marshall, and he noticed what a friendly interest the boys took in the matter.

Rudolph, the oldest one (he was still living at home then), said: "The last time I was over there, she was lifting them big heavy milkcans, and I knew she oughtn't to be doing it."

"Yes, Rudolph told me about that when he come home, and I said it wasn't right," Mary put in warmly. "It was all right for me to do them things up to the last, for I was terrible strong, but that woman's weakly. And do you think she'll be able to nurse it, Ed?" She sometimes forgot to give him the title she was so proud of. "And to think of your being up all night and then not able to get a decent breakfast! I don't know what's the matter with such people."

"Why, Mother," said one of the boys, "if Doctor Ed had got breakfast there, we wouldn't have him here. So you ought to be glad."

"He knows I'm glad to have him, John, any time. But I'm sorry for that poor woman, how bad she'll feel the Doctor had to go away in the cold without his breakfast."

"I wish I'd been in practice when these were getting born." The doctor looked down the row of close-clipped heads. "I missed some good breakfasts by not being."

The boys began to laugh at their mother because she flushed so red, but she stood her ground and threw up her head. "I don't care, you wouldn't have got away from this house without breakfast. No doctor ever did. I'd have had something ready fixed that Anton could warm up for you."

The boys laughed harder than ever, and exclaimed at her: "I'll bet you would!" "She would, that!"

"Father, did you get breakfast for the doctor when we were born?"

"Yes, and he used to bring me my breakfast, too, mighty nice. I was always awful hungry!" Mary admitted with a guilty laugh.

While the boys were getting the Doctor's horse, he went to the window to examine the house plants. "What do you do to your geraniums to keep them blooming all winter, Mary? I never pass this house that from the road I don't see your windows full of flowers."

She snapped off a dark red one, and a ruffled new green leaf, and put them in his buttonhole. "There, that looks better. You look too solemn for a young man, Ed. Why don't you git married? I'm worried about you. Settin' at breakfast, I looked at you real hard, and I seen you've got some grey hairs already."

"Oh, yes! They're coming. Maybe they'd come faster if I married."

"Don't talk so. You'll ruin your health eating at the hotel. I could send your wife a nice loaf of nut bread, if you only had one. I don't like to see a young man getting grey. I'll tell you something, Ed; you make some strong black tea and keep it handy in a bowl, and every morning just brush it into your hair, an' it'll keep the grey from showin' much. That's the way I do!"

Sometimes the Doctor heard the gossipers in the drug-store wondering why Rosicky didn't get on faster. He was industrious, and so were his boys, but they were rather free and easy, weren't pushers, and they didn't always show good judgment. They were comfortable, they were out of debt, but they didn't get much ahead. Maybe, Doctor Burleigh reflected, people as generous and warm-hearted and affectionate as the Rosickys never got ahead much; maybe you couldn't enjoy your life and put it into the bank, too.

II

When Rosicky left Doctor Burleigh's office he went into the farm-implement store to light his pipe and put on his glasses and read over the list Mary had given him. Then he went into the general merchandise place next door and stood about until the pretty girl with the plucked eyebrows, who always waited on him, was free. Those eyebrows, two thin India-ink strokes, amused him, because he remembered how they used to be. Rosicky always prolonged his shopping by a little joking; the girl knew the old fellow admired her, and she liked to chaff with him.

"Seems to me about every other week you buy ticking, Mr. Rosicky, and always the best quality," she remarked as she measured off the heavy bolt with red stripes.

"You see, my wife is always makin' goose-fedder pillows, an' de thin stuff don't hold in dem little down-fedders."

"You must have lots of pillows at your house."

"Sure. She makes quilts of dem, too. We sleeps easy. Now she's makin' a fedder quilt for my son's wife. You know Polly, that married my Rudolph. How much my bill, Miss Pearl?"

"Eight eight-five."

"Chust make it nine, and put in some candy fur de women."

"As usual. I never did see a man buy so much candy for his wife. First thing you know, she'll be getting too fat."

"I'd like dat. I ain't much fur all dem slim women like what de style is now."

"That's one for me, I suppose, Mr. Bohunk!" Pearl sniffed and elevated her India-ink strokes.

When Rosicky went out to his wagon, it was beginning to snow,—the first snow of the season, and he was glad to see it. He rattled out of town and along the highway through a wonderfully rich stretch of country, the finest farms in the country. He admired this High Prairie, as it was called, and always liked to drive through it. His own place lay in a rougher territory, where there was some clay in the soil and it was not so productive. When he bought his land, he hadn't the money to buy on High Prairie; so he told his boys, when they grumbled, that if their land hadn't some clay in it, they wouldn't own it at all. All the same, he enjoyed looking at these fine farms, as he enjoyed looking at a prize bull.

After he had gone eight miles, he came to the graveyard, which lay just at the edge of his own hay-land. There he stopped his horses and sat still on his wagon seat, looking about at the snowfall. Over yonder on the hill he could see his own house, crouching low, with the clump of orchard behind and the windmill before, and all down the gentle hill-slope the rows of pale gold cornstalks stood out against the white field. The snow was falling over the cornfield and the pasture and the hay-land, steadily, with very little wind,—a nice dry snow. The graveyard had only a light wire fence about it and was all overgrown with long red grass. The fine snow, settling into this red grass and upon the few little evergreens and the headstones, looked very pretty.

It was a nice graveyard, Rosicky reflected, sort of snug and homelike, not cramped or mournful,—a big sweep all around it. A man could lie down in the long grass and see the complete arch of the sky over him, hear the wagons go by; in summer the mowing-machine rattled right up to the wire fence. And it was so near home. Over there across the cornstalks his own roof and windmill looked so good to him that he promised himself to mind the Doctor and take care of himself. He was awful fond of his place, he admitted. He wasn't anxious to leave it. And it was a comfort to think that he would never have to go farther than the edge of his own hayfield. The snow, falling over his barnyard and the graveyard, seemed to draw things together like. And they were all old neighbours in the graveyard, most of them friends; there was nothing to feel awkward or embarrassed about. Embarrassment was the most disagreeable feeling Rosicky knew. He didn't often have it,—only with certain people whom he didn't understand at all.

Well, it was a nice snowstorm; a fine sight to see the snow falling so quietly and graciously over so much open country. On his cap and shoulders, on the horses' backs and manes, light, delicate, mysterious it fell; and with it a dry cool fragrance was released into the air. It meant rest for vegetation and men and beasts, for the ground itself; a season of long nights for sleep, leisurely breakfasts, peace by the fire. This and much more went through Rosicky's mind, but he merely told himself that winter was coming, clucked to his horses, and drove on.

When he reached home, John, the youngest boy, ran out to put away his team for him, and he met Mary coming up from the outside cellar with her apron full of carrots. They went into the house together. On the table, covered with oilcloth figured with clusters of blue grapes, a place was set, and he smelled hot coffee-cake of some kind. Anton never lunched in town; he thought that extravagant, and anyhow he didn't like the food. So Mary always had something ready for him when he got home.

After he was settled in his chair, stirring his coffee in a big cup, Mary took out of the oven a pan of *kolache* stuffed with apricots, examined them anxiously to see whether they had got too dry, put them beside his plate, and then sat down opposite him.

Rosicky asked her in Czech if she wasn't going to have any coffee.

She replied in English, as being somehow the right language for transacting business: "Now what did Doctor Ed say, Anton? You tell me just what."

"He said I was to tell you some compliments, but I forgot 'em." Rosicky's eyes twinkled.

"About you, I mean. What did he say about your asthma?"

"He says I ain't got no asthma." Rosicky took one of the little rolls in his broad brown fingers. The thickened nail of his right thumb told the story of his past.

"Well, what is the matter? And don't try to put me off."

"He don't say nothing much, only I'm a little older, and my heart ain't so good like it used to be."

Mary started and brushed her hair back from her temples with both hands as if she were a little out of her mind. From the way she glared, she might have been in a rage with him.

"He says there's something the matter with your heart? Doctor Ed says so?"

"Now don't yell at me like I was a hog in de garden, Mary. You know I always did like to hear a woman talk soft. He didn't say anything de matter wid my heart, only it ain't so young like it used to be, an' he tell me not to pitch hay or run de corn-sheller."

Mary wanted to jump up, but she sat still. She admired the way he never under any circumstances raised his voice or spoke roughly. He was city-bred, and she was country-bred; she often said she wanted her boys to have their papa's nice ways.

"You never have no pain there, do you? It's your breathing and your stomach that's been wrong. I wouldn't believe nobody but Doctor Ed about it. I guess I'll go see him myself. Didn't he give you no advice?"

"Chust to take it easy like, an' stay round de house dis winter. I guess you got some carpenter work for me to do. I kin make some new shelves for you, and I want dis long time to build a closet in de boys' room and make dem two little fellers keep dere clo'es hung up."

Rosicky drank his coffee from time to time, while he considered. His moustache was of the soft long variety and came down over his mouth like the teeth of a buggy-rake over a bundle of hay. Each time he put down his cup, he ran his blue handkerchief over his lips. When he took a drink of water, he managed very neatly with the back of his hand.

Mary sat watching him intently, trying to find any change in his face. It is hard to see anyone who has become like your own body to you. Yes, his hair had got thin, and his high forehead had deep lines running from left to right. But his neck, always clean shaved except in the busiest seasons, was not loose or baggy. It was burned a dark reddish brown, and there were deep creases in it, but it looked firm and full of blood. His cheeks had a good colour. On either side of his mouth there was a half-moon down the length of his cheek, not wrinkles, but two lines that had come there from his habitual expression. He was shorter and broader than when she married him; his back had grown broad and curved, a good deal like the shell of an old turtle, and his arms and legs were short.

He was fifteen years older than Mary, but she had hardly ever thought about it before. He was her man, and the kind of man she liked. She was rough, and he was gentle,—city-bred, as she always said. They had been shipmates on a rough voyage and had stood by each other in trying times. Life had gone well with them because, at bottom, they had the same ideas about life. They agreed, without discussion, as to what was most important and what was secondary. They didn't often exchange opinions, even in Czech,—it was as if they had thought the same thought together. A good deal had to be sacrificed and thrown overboard in a hard life like theirs, and they had never disagreed as to the things that could go. It had been a hard life, and a soft life, too. There wasn't anything brutal in the short, broad-backed man with the three-cornered eyes and the forehead that went on to the top of his skull. He was a city man, a gentle man, and though he had married a rough farm girl, he had never touched her without gentleness.

They had been at one accord not to hurry through life, not to be always skimping and saving. They saw their neighbours buy more land and feed more stock than they did, without discontent. Once when the creamery agent came to the Rosickys to persuade them to sell him their cream, he told them how much money the Fasslers, their nearest neighbours, had made on their cream last year.

"Yes," said Mary, "and look at them Fassler children! Pale, pinched little things, they look like skimmed milk. I'd rather put some colour into my children's faces than put money into the bank."

The agent shrugged and turned to Anton.

"I guess we'll do like she says," said Rosicky.

III

Mary very soon got into town to see Doctor Ed, and then she had a talk with her boys and set a guard over Rosicky. Even John, the youngest, had his father on his mind. If Rosicky went to throw hay down from the loft, one of the boys ran up the ladder and took the fork from him. He sometimes complained that though he was getting to be an old man, he wasn't an old woman yet.

That winter he stayed in the house in the afternoons and carpentered, or sat in the chair between the window full of plants and the wooden bench where the two pails of drinking-water stood. This spot was called "Father's corner," though it was not a corner at all. He had a shelf there, where he kept his Bohemian papers and his pipes and tobacco, and his shears and needles and thread and tailor's thimble. Having been a tailor in his youth, he couldn't bear to see a woman patching at his clothes, or at the boys'. He liked tailoring, and always patched all the overalls and jackets and work shirts. Occasionally he made over a pair of pants one of the older boys had outgrown, for the little fellow.

While he sewed, he let his mind run back over his life. He had a good deal to remember, really; life in three countries. The only part of his youth he didn't like to remember was the two years he had spent in London, in Cheapside, working for a German tailor who was wretchedly poor. Those days, when he was nearly always hungry, when his clothes were dropping off him for dirt, and the sound of a strange language kept him in continual bewilderment, had left a sore spot in his mind that wouldn't bear touching.

He was twenty when he landed at Castle Garden in New York, and he had a protector who got him work in a tailor shop in Vesey Street, down near the Washington Market. He looked upon that part of his life as very happy. He became a good workman, he was industrious, and his wages were increased from time to time. He minded his own business and envied nobody's good fortune. He went to night school and learned to read English. He often did overtime work and was well paid for it, but somehow he never saved anything. He couldn't refuse a loan to a friend, and he was self-indulgent. He liked a good dinner, and a little went for beer, a little for tobacco; a good deal went to the girls. He often stood through an opera on Saturday nights; he could get standing-room for a dollar. Those were the great days of opera in New York, and it gave a fellow something to think about for the rest of the week. Rosicky had a quick ear, and a childish love of all the stage splendour; the scenery, the costumes, the ballet. He usually went with a chum, and after the performance they had beer and maybe some oysters somewhere. It was a fine life; for the first five years or so it satisfied him completely. He was never hungry or cold or dirty, and everything amused him: a fire, a dog fight, a parade, a storm, a ferry ride. He thought New York the finest, richest, friendliest city in the world.

Moreover, he had what he called a happy home life. Very near the tailor shop was a small furniture-factory, where an old Austrian, Loeffler, employed a few skilled men and made unusual furniture, most of it to order, for the rich German housewives up-town. The top floor of Loeffler's five-storey factory was a loft, where he kept his choice lumber and stored the odd pieces of furniture left on his hands. One of the young workmen he employed was a Czech, and he and Rosicky became fast friends. They persuaded Loeffler to let them have a sleeping-room in one corner of the loft. They bought good beds and bedding and had their pick of the furniture kept up there. The loft was low-pitched, but light and airy, full of windows, and good-smelling by reason of the fine lumber put up there to season. Old Loeffler used to go down to the docks and buy wood from South America and the East from the sea captains. The young men were as foolish about their house as a bridal pair. Zichec, the young cabinet-maker, devised every sort of convenience, and Rosicky kept their clothes in order. At night and on Sundays, when the quiver of machinery underneath was still, it was the quietest place in the world, and on summer nights all the sea winds blew in. Zichec often practised on his flute in the evening. They were both fond of music and went to the opera together. Rosicky thought he wanted to live like that for ever.

But as the years passed, all alike, he began to get a little restless. When spring came round, he would begin to feel fretted, and he got to drinking. He was likely to drink too much of a Saturday night. On Sunday he was languid and heavy, getting over his spree. On Monday he plunged into work again. So he never had time to figure out what ailed him, though he knew something did. When the grass turned green in Park Place, and the lilac hedge at the back of Trinity churchyard put out its blossoms, he was tormented by a longing to run away. That was why he drank too much; to get a temporary illusion of freedom and wide horizons.

Rosicky, the old Rosicky, could remember as if it were yesterday the day when the young Rosicky found out what was the matter with him. It was on a Fourth of July afternoon, and he was sitting in Park Place in the sun. The lower part of New York was empty. Wall Street, Liberty Street, Broadway, all empty. So much stone and asphalt with nothing going on, so many empty windows. The emptiness was intense, like the stillness in a great factory when the machinery stops and the belts and bands cease running. It was too great a change, it took all the strength out of one. Those blank buildings, without the stream of life pouring through them, were like empty jails. It struck young Rosicky that this was the trouble with big cities; they built you in from the earth itself, cemented you away from any contact with the ground. You lived in an unnatural world, like the fish in an aquarium, who were probably much more comfortable than they ever were in the sea.

On that very day he began to think seriously about the articles he had read in the Bohemian papers, describing prosperous Czech farming communities in the West. He believed he would like to go out there as a farm hand; it was hardly possible that he could ever have land of his own. His people had always been workmen; his father and grandfather had worked in shops. His mother's parents had lived in the country, but they rented their farm and had a hard time to get along. Nobody in his family had ever owned any land,—that belonged to a different station of life altogether. Anton's mother died when he was little, and he was sent into the country to her parents. He stayed with them until he was twelve, and formed those ties with the earth and the farm animals and growing things which are never made at all unless they are made early. After his grandfather died, he went back to live with his father and stepmother, but she was very hard on him, and his father helped him to get passage to London.

After that Fourth of July day in Park Place, the desire to return to the country never left him. To work on another man's farm would be all he asked; to see the sun rise and set and to plant things and watch them grow. He was a very simple man. He was like a tree that has not many roots, but one tap-root that goes down deep. He subscribed for a Bohemian paper printed in Chicago, then for one printed in Omaha. His mind got farther and farther west. He began to save a little money to buy his liberty. When he was thirty-five, there was a great meeting in New York of Bohemian athletic societies, and Rosicky left the tailor shop and went home with the Omaha delegates to try his fortune in another part of the world.

IV

Perhaps the fact that his own youth was well over before he began to have a family was one reason why Rosicky was so fond of his boys. He had almost a grandfather's indulgence for them. He had never had to worry about any of them—except, just now, a little about Rudolph.

On Saturday night the boys always piled into the Ford, took little Josephine, and went to town to the moving-picture show. One Saturday morning they were talking at the breakfast table about starting early that evening, so that they would have an hour or so to see the Christmas things in the stores before the show began. Rosicky looked down the table.

"I hope you boys ain't disappointed, but I want you to let me have de car tonight. Maybe some of you can go in with de neighbours."

Their faces fell. They worked hard all week, and they were still like children. A new jack-knife or a box of candy pleased the older ones as much as the little fellow.

"If you and Mother are going to town," Frank said, "maybe you could take a couple of us along with you, anyway."

"No, I want to take de car down to Rudolph's, and let him an' Polly go in to de show. She don't git into town enough, an' I'm afraid she's gettin' lonesome, an' he can't afford no car yet."

That settled it. The boys were a good deal dashed. Their father took another piece of apple-cake and went on: "Maybe next Saturday night de two little fellers can go along wid dem."

"Oh, is Rudolph going to have the car every Saturday night?"

Rosicky did not reply at once; then he began to speak seriously: "Listen, boys; Polly ain't lookin' so good. I don't like to see nobody lookin' sad. It comes hard fur a town girl to be a farmer's wife. I don't want no trouble to start in Rudolph's family. When it starts, it ain't so easy to stop. An American girl don't git used to our ways all at once. I like to tell Polly she and Rudolph can have the car every Saturday night till after New Year's, if it's all right with you boys."

"Sure it's all right, Papa," Mary cut in. "And it's good you thought about that. Town girls is used to more than country girls. I lay awake nights, scared she'll make Rudolph discontented with the farm."

The boys put as good a face on it as they could. They surely looked forward to their Saturday nights in town. That evening Rosicky drove the car the half-mile down to Rudolph's new, bare little house.

Polly was in a short-sleeved gingham dress, clearing away the supper dishes. She was a trim, slim little thing, with blue eyes and shingled yellow hair, and her eyebrows were reduced to a mere brush-stroke, like Miss Pearl's.

"Good evening, Mr. Rosicky. Rudolph's at the barn, I guess." She never called him father, or Mary mother. She was sensitive about having married a foreigner. She never in the world would have done it if Rudolph hadn't been such a handsome, persuasive fellow and such a gallant lover. He had graduated in her class in the high school in town, and their friendship began in the ninth grade.

Rosicky went in, though he wasn't exactly asked. "My boys ain't goin' to town tonight, an' I brought de car over fur you two to go in to de picture show."

Polly, carrying dishes to the sink, looked over her shoulder at him. "Thank you. But I'm late with my work tonight, and pretty tired. Maybe Rudolph would like to go in with you."

"Oh, I don't go to de shows! I'm too old-fashioned. You won't feel so tired after you ride in de air a ways. It's a nice clear night, an' it ain't cold. You go an' fix yourself up, Polly, an' I'll wash de dishes an' leave everything nice fur you."

Polly blushed and tossed her bob. "I couldn't let you do that, Mr. Rosicky. I wouldn't think of it."

Rosicky said nothing. He found a bib apron on a nail behind the kitchen door. He slipped it over his head and then took Polly by her two elbows and pushed her gently toward the door of her own room. "I washed up de kitchen many times for my wife, when de babies was sick or somethin'. You go an' make yourself look nice. I like you to look prettier'n any of dem town girls when you go in. De young folks must have some fun, an' I'm goin' to look out fur you, Polly."

That kind, reassuring grip on her elbows, the old man's funny bright eyes, made Polly want to drop her head on his shoulder for a second. She restrained herself, but she lingered in his grasp at the door of her room, murmuring tearfully: "You always lived in the city when you were young, didn't you? Don't you ever get lonesome out here?"

As she turned round to him, her hand fell naturally into his, and he stood holding it and smiling into her face with his peculiar, knowing, indulgent smile without a shadow of reproach in it. "Dem big cities is all right fur de rich, but dey is terrible hard fur de poor."

"I don't know. Sometimes I think I'd like to take a chance. You lived in New York, didn't you?"

"An' London. Da's bigger still. I learned my trade dere. Here's Rudolph comin', you better hurry."

"Will you tell me about London some time?"

"Maybe. Only I ain't no talker, Polly. Run an' dress yourself up."

The bedroom door closed behind her, and Rudolph came in from the outside, looking anxious. He had seen the car and was sorry any of his family should come just then. Supper hadn't been a very pleasant occasion. Halting in the doorway, he saw his father in a kitchen apron, carrying dishes to the sink. He flushed crimson and something flashed in his eye. Rosicky held up a warning finger.

"I brought de car over fur you an' Polly to go to de picture show, an' I made her let me finish here so you won't be late. You go put on a clean shirt, quick!"

"But don't the boys want the car, Father?"

"Not tonight dey don't." Rosicky fumbled under his apron and found his pants pocket. He took out a silver dollar and said in a hurried whisper: "You go an' buy dat girl some ice cream an' candy tonight, like you was courtin'. She's awful good friends wid me."

Rudolph was very short of cash, but he took the money as if it hurt him. There had been a crop failure all over the county. He had more than once been sorry he'd married this year.

In a few minutes the young people came out, looking clean and a little stiff. Rosicky hurried them off, and then he took his own time with the dishes. He scoured the pots and pans and put away the milk and swept the kitchen. He put some coal in the stove and shut off the draughts, so the place would be warm for them when they got home late at night. Then he sat down and had a pipe and listened to the clock tick.

Generally speaking, marrying an American girl was certainly a risk. A Czech should marry a Czech. It was lucky that Polly was the daughter of a poor widow woman; Rudolph was proud, and if she had a prosperous family to throw up at him, they could never make it go. Polly was one of four sisters, and they all worked; one was book-keeper in the bank, one taught music, and Polly and her younger sister had been clerks, like Miss Pearl. All four of them were musical, had pretty voices, and sang in the Methodist choir, which the eldest sister directed.

Polly missed the sociability of a store position. She missed the choir, and the company of her sisters. She didn't dislike housework, but she disliked so much of it. Rosicky was a little anxious about this pair. He was afraid Polly would grow so discontented that Rudy would quit the farm and take a factory job in Omaha. He had worked for a winter up there, two years ago, to get money to marry on. He had done very well, and they would always take him back at the stockyards. But to Rosicky that meant the end of everything for his son. To be a landless man was to be a wage-earner, a slave, all your life; to have nothing, to be nothing.

Rosicky thought he would come over and do a little carpentering for Polly after the New Year. He guessed she needed jollying. Rudolph was a serious sort of chap, serious in love and serious about his work.

Rosicky shook out his pipe and walked home across the fields. Ahead of him the lamplight shone from his kitchen windows. Suppose he were still in a tailor shop on Vesey Street, with a bunch of pale, narrow-chested sons working on machines, all coming home tired and sullen to eat supper in a kitchen that was a parlour also; with another crowded, angry family quarrelling just across the dumb-waiter shaft, and squeaking pulleys at the windows where dirty washings hung on dirty lines above a court full of old brooms and mops and ash-cans. . . .

He stopped by the windmill to look up at the frosty winter stars and draw a long breath before he went inside. That kitchen with the shining windows was dear to him; but the sleeping fields and bright stars and the noble darkness were dearer still.

V

On the day before Christmas the weather set in very cold; no snow, but a bitter, biting wind that whistled and sang over the flat land and lashed one's face like fine wires. There was baking going on in the Rosicky kitchen all day, and Rosicky sat inside, making over a coat that Albert had outgrown into an overcoat for John. Mary had a big red geranium in bloom for Christmas, and a row of Jerusalem cherry trees, full of berries. It was the first year she had ever grown these; Doctor Ed brought her the seeds from Omaha when he went to some medical convention. They reminded Rosicky of plants he had seen in England; and all afternoon, as he stitched, he sat thinking about those two years in London, which his mind usually shrank from even after all this while.

He was a lad of eighteen when he dropped down into London, with no money and no connexions except the address of a cousin who was supposed to be working at a confectioner's. When he went to the pastry shop, however, he found that the cousin had gone to America. Anton tramped the streets for several days, sleeping in doorways and on the Embankment, until he was in utter despair. He knew no English, and the sound of the strange language all about him confused him. By chance he met a poor German tailor who had learned his trade in Vienna, and could speak a little Czech. This tailor, Lifschnitz, kept a repair shop in a Cheapside basement, underneath a cobbler. He didn't much need an apprentice, but he was sorry for the boy and took him in for no wages but his keep and what he could pick up. The pickings were supposed to be coppers given you when you took work home to a customer. But most of the customers called for their clothes themselves, and the coppers that came Anton's way were very few. He had, however, a place to sleep. The tailor's family lived upstairs in three rooms; a kitchen, a bed-room, where Lifschnitz and his wife and five children slept, and a living-room. Two corners of this living-room were curtained off for lodgers; in one Rosicky slept on an old horsehair sofa, with a feather quilt to wrap himself in. The other corner was rented to a wretched, dirty boy, who was studying the violin. He actually practised there. Rosicky was dirty, too. There was no way to be anything else. Mrs. Lifschnitz got the water she cooked and washed with from a pump in a brick court, four flights down. There were bugs in the place, and multitudes of fleas, though the poor woman did the best she could. Rosicky knew she often went empty to give another potato or a spoonful of dripping to the two hungry, sad-eyed boys who lodged with her. He used to think he would never get out of there, never get a clean shirt to his back again. What would he do, he wondered, when his clothes actually dropped to pieces and the worn cloth wouldn't hold patches any longer?

It was still early when the old farmer put aside his sewing and his recollections. The sky had been a dark grey all day, with not a gleam of sun, and the light failed at four o'clock. He went to shave and change his shirt while the turkey was roasting. Rudolph and Polly were coming over for supper.

After supper they sat round in the kitchen, and the younger boys were saying how sorry they were it hadn't snowed. Everybody was sorry. They wanted a deep snow that would lie long and keep the wheat warm, and leave the ground soaked when it melted.

"Yes, sir!" Rudolph broke out fiercely; "if we have another dry year like last year, there's going to be hard times in this country."

Rosicky filled his pipe. "You boys don't know what hard times is. You don't owe nobody, you got plenty to eat an' keep warm, an' plenty water to keep clean. When you got them, you can't have it very hard."

Rudolph frowned, opened and shut his big right hand, and dropped it clenched upon his knee. "I've got to have a good deal more than that, Father, or I'll quit this farming gamble. I can always make good wages rail-roading, or at the packing house, and be sure of my money."

"Maybe so," his father answered dryly.

Mary, who had just come in from the pantry and was wiping her hands on the roller towel, thought Rudy and his father were getting too serious. She brought her darning-basket and sat down in the middle of the group.

"I ain't much afraid of hard times, Rudy," she said heartily. "We've had a plenty, but we've always come through. Your father wouldn't never take nothing very hard, not even hard times. I got a mind to tell you a story on him. Maybe you boys can't hardly remember the year we had that terrible hot wind, that burned everything up on the Fourth of July? All the corn an' the gardens. An' that was in the days when we didn't have alfalfa yet,—I guess it wasn't invented.

"Well, that very day your father was out cultivatin' corn, and I was here in the kitchen makin' plum preserves. We had bushels of plums that year. I noticed it was terrible hot, but it's always hot in the kitchen when you're preservin', an' I was too busy with my plums to mind. Anton come in from the field about three o'clock, an' I asked him what was the matter.

" 'Nothin',' he says, 'but it's pretty hot, an' I think I won't work no more today.' He stood round for a few minutes, an' then he says: 'Ain't you near through? I want you should git up a nice supper for us tonight. It's Fourth of July.'

"I told him to git along, that I was right in the middle of preservin', but the plums would taste good on hot biscuit. 'I'm goin' to have fried chicken, too,' he says, and he went off an' killed a couple. You three oldest boys was little fellers, playin' round outside, real hot an' sweaty, an' your father took you to the horse tank down by the windmill an' took off your clothes an' put you in. Them two box-elder trees was little then, but they made shade over the tank. Then he took off all his own clothes, an' got in with you. While he was playin' in the water with you, the Methodist preacher drove into our place to say how all the neighbours was goin' to meet at the schoolhouse that night, to pray for rain. He drove right to the windmill, of course, and there was your father and you three with no clothes on. I was in the kitchen door, an' I had to laugh, for the preacher acted like he ain't never seen a naked man before. He surely was embarrassed, an' your father couldn't git to his clothes; they was all hangin' up on the windmill to let the sweat dry out of 'em. So he laid in the tank where he was, an' put one of you boys on top of him to cover him up a little, an' talked to the preacher.

"When you got through playin' in the water, he put clean clothes on you and a clean shirt on himself, an' by that time I'd begun to get supper. He says: 'It's too hot in here to eat comfortable. Let's have a picnic in the orchard. We'll eat our supper behind the mulberry hedge, under them linden trees.'

"So he carried our supper down, an' a bottle of my wild-grape wine, an' everything tasted good, I can tell you. The wind got cooler as the sun was goin' down, and it turned out pleasant, only I noticed how the leaves was curled up on the linden trees. That made me think, an' I asked your father if that hot wind all day hadn't been terrible hard on the gardens an' the corn.

" 'Corn,' he says, 'there ain't no corn.'

" 'What you talkin' about?' I said. 'Ain't we got forty acres?'

" 'We ain't got an ear,' he says, 'nor nobody else ain't got none. All the corn in this country was cooked by three o'clock today, like you'd roasted it in an oven.'

" 'You mean you won't get no crop at all?' I asked him. I couldn't believe it, after he'd worked so hard.

" 'No crop this year,' he says. 'That's why we're havin' a picnic. We might as well enjoy what we got.'

"An' that's how your father behaved, when all the neighbours was so discouraged they couldn't look you in the face. An' we enjoyed ourselves that year, poor as we was, an' our neighbours wasn't a bit better off for bein' miserable. Some of 'em grieved till they got poor digestions and couldn't relish what they did have."

The younger boys said they thought their father had the best of it. But Rudolf was thinking that, all the same, the neighbours had managed to get ahead more, in the fifteen years since that time. There must be something wrong about his father's way of doing things. He wished he knew what was going on in the back of Polly's mind. He knew she liked his father, but he knew, too, that she was afraid of something. When his mother sent over coffee-cake or prune tarts or a loaf of fresh bread, Polly seemed to regard them with a certain suspicion. When she observed to him that his brothers had nice manners, her tone implied that it was remarkable they should have. With his mother she was stiff and on her guard. Mary's hearty frankness and gusts of good humour irritated her. Polly was afraid of being unusual or conspicuous in any way, of being "ordinary," as she said!

When Mary had finished her story, Rosicky laid aside his pipe.

"You boys like me to tell you about some of dem hard times I been through in London?" Warmly encouraged, he sat rubbing his forehead along the deep creases. It was bothersome to tell a long story in English (he nearly always talked to the boys in Czech), but he wanted Polly to hear this one.

"Well, you know about dat tailor shop I worked in in London? I had one Christmas dere I ain't never forgot. Times was awful bad before Christmas; de boss ain't got much work, an' have it awful hard to pay his rent. It ain't so much fun, bein' poor in a big city like London, I'll say! All de windows is full of good t'ings to eat, an' all de pushcarts in de streets is full, an' you smell 'em all de time, an' you ain't got no money,—not a damn bit. I didn't mind de cold so much, though I didn't have no overcoat, chust a short jacket I'd outgrowed so it wouldn't meet on me, an' my hands was chapped raw. But I always had a good appetite, like you all know, an' de sight of dem pork pies in de windows was awful fur me!

"Day before Christmas was terrible foggy dat year, an' dat fog gits into your bones and makes you all damp like. Mrs. Lifschnitz didn't give us nothin' but a little bread an' drippin' for supper, because she was savin' to try for to give us a good dinner on Christmas Day. After supper de boss say I can go an' enjoy myself, so I went into de streets to listen to de Christmas singers. Dey sing old songs an' make very nice music, an' I run round after dem a good ways, till I got awful hungry. I t'ink maybe if I go home, I can sleep till morning n' forgit my belly.

"I went into my corner real quiet, and roll up in my fedder quilt. But I ain't got my head down, till I smell somet'ing good. Seem like it git stronger an' stronger, an' I can't git to sleep noway. I can't understand dat smell. Dere was a gas light in a hall across de court, dat always shine in at my window a little. I got up an' look round. I got a little wooden box in my corner fur a stool, 'cause I ain't got no chair. I picks up dat box, and under it dere is a roast goose on a platter! I can't believe my eyes. I carry it to de window where de light comes in, an' touch it and smell it to find out, an' den I taste it to be sure. I say, I will eat chust one little bite of dat goose, so I can go to sleep, and tomorrow I won't eat none at all. But I tell you, boys, when I stop, one half of dat goose was gone!"

The narrator bowed his head, and the boys shouted. But little Josephine slipped behind his chair and kissed him on the neck beneath his ear.

"Poor little Papa, I don't want him to be hungry!"

"Da's long ago, child. I ain't never been hungry since I had your mudder to cook fur me."

"Go on and tell us the rest, please," said Polly.

"Well, when I come to realize what I done, of course, I felt terrible. I felt better in de stomach, but very bad in de heart. I set on my bed wid dat platter on my knees, an' it all come to me; how hard dat poor woman save to buy dat goose, and how she get some neighbour to cook it dat got more fire, an' how she put it in my corner to keep it away from dem hungry children. Dey was a old carpet hung up to shut my corner off, an' de children wasn't allowed to go in dere. An' I know she put it in my corner because she trust me more'n she did de violin boy. I can't stand it to face her after I spoil de Christmas. So I put on my shoes and go out into de city. I tell myself I better throw myself in de river; but I guess I ain't dat kind of a boy.

"It was after twelve o'clock, an' terrible cold, an' I start out to walk about London all night. I walk along de river awhile, but dey was lots of drunks all along; men, and women too. I chust move along to keep away from de police. I git onto de Strand, an' den over to New Oxford Street, where dere was a big German restaurant on de ground floor, wid big windows all fixed up fine, an' I could see de people havin' parties inside. While I was lookin' in, two men and two ladies come out, laughin' and talkin' and feelin' happy about all dey been eatin' an' drinkin', and dey was speakin' Czech,—not like de Austrians, but like de home folks talk it.

"I guess I went crazy, an I done what I ain't never done before nor since. I went right up to dem gay people an' begun to beg dem: 'Fellow-countrymen, for God's sake give me money enough to buy a goose!'

"Dey laugh, of course, but de ladies speak awful kind to me, an' dey take me back into de restaurant and give me hot coffee and cakes, an' make me tell all about how I happened to come to London, an' what I was doin' dere. Dey take my name and where I work down on paper, an' both of dem ladies give me ten shillings.

"De big market at Covent Garden ain't very far away, an' by dat time it was open. I go dere an' buy a big goose an' some pork pies, an' potatoes and onions, an' cakes an' oranges fur de children,—all I could carry! When I git home, everybody is still asleep. I pile all I bought on de kitchen table, an' go in an' lay down on my bed, an' I ain't waken up till I hear dat woman scream when she come out into her kitchen. My goodness, but she was surprise! She laugh an' cry at de same time, an' hug me and waken all de children. She ain't stop fur no breakfast; she git de Christmas dinner ready dat morning, and we all sit down an' eat all we can hold. I ain't never seen dat violin boy have all he can hold before.

"Two three days after dat, de two men come to hunt me up, an' dey ask my boss, and he give me a good report an' tell dem I was a steady boy all right. One of dem Bohemians was very smart an' run a Bohemian newspaper in New York, an' de odder was a rich man, in de importing business, an' dey been travelling togedder. Dey told me how t'ings was easier in New York, an' offered to pay my passage when dey was goin' home soon on a boat. My boss say to me: 'You go. You ain't got no chance here, an' I like to see you git ahead, fur you always been a good boy to my woman, and fur dat fine Christmas dinner you give us all.' An' da's how I got to New York."

That night when Rudolph and Polly, arm in arm, were running home across the fields with the bitter wind at their backs, his heart leaped for joy when she said she thought they might have his family come over for supper on New Year's Eve. "Let's get up a nice supper, and not let your mother help at all; make her be company for once."

"That would be lovely of you, Polly," he said humbly. He was a very simple, modest boy, and he, too, felt vaguely that Polly and her sisters were more experienced and worldly than his people.

VI

The winter turned out badly for farmers. It was bitterly cold, and after the first light snows before Christmas there was no snow at all,—and no rain. March was as bitter as February. On those days when the wind fairly punished the country, Rosicky sat by his window. In the fall he and the boys had put in a big wheat planting, and now the seed had frozen in the ground. All that land would have to be ploughed up and planted over again, planted in corn. It had happened before, but he was younger then, and he never worried about what had to be. He was sure of himself and of Mary; he knew they could bear what they had to bear, that they would always pull through somehow. But he was not so sure about the young ones, and he felt troubled because Rudolph and Polly were having such a hard start.

Sitting beside his flowering window while the panes rattled and the wind blew in under the door, Rosicky gave himself to reflection as he had not done since those Sundays in the loft of the furniture-factory in New York, long ago. Then he was trying to find what he wanted in life for himself; now he was trying to find what he wanted for his boys, and why it was he so hungered to feel sure they would be here, working this very land, after he was gone.

They would have to work hard on the farm, and probably they would never do much more than make a living. But if he could think of them as staying here on the land, he wouldn't have to fear any great unkindness for them. Hardships, certainly; it was a hardship to have the wheat freeze in the ground when seed was so high; and to have to sell your stock because you had no feed. But there would be other years when everything came along right, and you caught up. And what you had was your own. You didn't have to choose between bosses and strikers, and go wrong either way. You didn't have to do with dishonest and cruel people. They were the only things in his experience he had found terrifying and horrible; the look in the eyes of a dishonest and crafty man, of a scheming and rapacious woman.

In the country, if you had a mean neighbour, you could keep off his land and make him keep off yours. But in the city, all the foulness and misery and brutality of your neighbours was part of your life. The worst things he had come upon in his journey through the world were human,—depraved and poisonous specimens of man. To this day he could recall certain terrible faces in the London streets. There were mean people everywhere, to be sure, even in their own country town here. But they weren't tempered, hardened, sharpened, like the treacherous people in cities who live by grinding or cheating or poisoning their fellowmen. He had helped to bury two of his fellow-workmen in the tailoring trade, and he was distrustful of the organized industries that see one out of the world in big cities. Here, if you were sick, you had Doctor Ed to look after you; and if you died, fat Mr. Haycock, the kindest man in the world, buried you.

It seemed to Rosicky that for good, honest boys like

his, the worst they could do on the farm was better than the best they would be likely to do in the city. If he'd had a mean boy, now, one who was crooked and sharp and tried to put anything over on his brothers, then town would be the place for him. But he had no such boy. As for Rudolph, the discontented one, he would give the shirt off his back to anyone who touched his heart. What Rosicky really hoped for his boys was that they could get through the world without ever knowing much about the cruelty of human beings. "Their mother and me ain't prepared them for that," he sometimes said to himself.

These thoughts brought him back to a grateful consideration of his own case. What an escape he had had, to be sure! He, too, in his time, had had to take money for repair work from the hand of a hungry child who let it go so wistfully; because it was money due his boss. And now, in all these years, he had never had to take a cent from anyone in bitter need,—never had to look at the face of a woman become like a wolf's from struggle and famine. When he thought of these things, Rosicky would put on his cap and jacket and slip down to the barn and give his work-horses a little extra oats, letting them eat it out of his hand in their slobbery fashion. It was his way of expressing what he felt, and made him chuckle with pleasure.

The spring came warm, with blue skies,—but dry, dry as a bone. The boys began ploughing up the wheat-fields to plant them over in corn. Rosicky would stand at the fence corner and watch them, and the earth was so dry it blew up in the clouds of brown dust that hid the horses and the sulky plough and the driver. It was a bad outlook.

The big alfalfa-field that lay between the home place and Rudolph's came up green, but Rosicky was worried because during that open windy winter a great many Russian thistle plants had blown in there and lodged. He kept asking the boys to rake them out; he was afraid their seed would root and "take the alfalfa." Rudolph said that was nonsense. The boys were working so hard planting corn, their father felt he couldn't insist about the thistles, but he set great store by that big alfalfa-field. It was a feed you could depend on,—and there was some deeper reason, vague, but strong. The peculiar green of that clover woke early memories in old Rosicky, went back to something in his childhood in the old world. When he was a little boy, he had played in fields of that strong blue-green colour.

One morning, when Rudolph had gone to town in the car, leaving a work-team idle in his barn, Rosicky went over to his son's place, put the horses to the buggy-rake, and set about quietly raking up those thistles. He behaved with guilty caution, and rather enjoyed stealing a march on Doctor Ed, who was just then taking his first vacation in seven years of practice and was attending a clinic in Chicago. Rosicky got the thistles raked up, but did not stop to burn them. That would take some time, and his breath was pretty short, so he thought he had better get the horses back to the barn.

He got them into the barn and to their stalls, but the pain had come on so sharp in his chest that he didn't try to take the harness off. He started for the house, bending lower with every step. The cramp in his chest was shutting him up like a jack-knife. When he reached the windmill, he swayed and caught at the ladder. He saw Polly coming down the hill, running with the swiftness of a slim greyhound. In a flash she had her shoulder under his armpit.

"Lean on me, Father, hard! Don't be afraid. We can get to the house all right."

Somehow they did, though Rosicky became blind with pain; he could keep on his legs, but he couldn't steer his course. The next thing he was conscious of was lying on Polly's bed, and Polly bending over him wringing out bath towels in hot water and putting them on his chest. She stopped only to throw coal into the stove, and she kept the tea-kettle and the black pot going. She put these hot applications on him for nearly an hour, she told him afterwards, and all that time he was drawn up stiff and blue, with the sweat pouring off him.

As the pain gradually loosed its grip, the stiffness went out of his jaws, the black circles round his eyes disappeared, and a little of his natural colour came back. When his daughter-in-law buttoned his shirt over his chest at last, he sighed.

"Da's fine, de way I feel now, Polly. It was a awful bad spell, an' I was so sorry it all come on you like it did."

Polly was flushed and excited. "Is the pain really gone? Can I leave you long enough to telephone over to your place?"

Rosicky's eyelids fluttered. "Don't telephone, Polly. It ain't no use to scare my wife. It's nice and quiet here, an' if I ain't too much trouble to you, just let me lay still till I feel like myself. I ain't got no pain now. It's nice here."

Polly bent over him and wiped the moisture from his face. "Oh, I'm so glad it's over!" she broke out impulsively. "It just broke my heart to see you suffer so, Father."

Rosicky motioned her to sit down on the chair where the tea-kettle had been, and looked up at her with that lively affectionate gleam in his eyes. "You was awful good to me, I won't never forgit dat. I hate it to be sick on you like dis. Down at de barn I say to myself, dat young girl ain't had much experience in sickness, I don't want to scare her, an' maybe she's got a baby comin' or somet'ing."

Polly took his hand. He was looking at her so intently and affectionately and confidingly; his eyes seemed to caress her face, to regard it with pleasure. She frowned with her funny streaks of eyebrows, and then smiled back at him.

"I guess maybe there is something of that kind going to happen. But I haven't told anyone yet, not my mother or Rudolph. You'll be the first to know."

His hand pressed hers. She noticed that it was warm again. The twinkle in his yellow-brown eyes seemed to come nearer.

"I like mighty well to see dat little child, Polly," was all he said. Then he closed his eyes and lay half-smiling. But Polly sat still, thinking hard. She had a sudden feeling that nobody in the world, not her mother, not Rudolph, or anyone, really loved her as much as old Rosicky did. It perplexed her. She sat frowning and trying to puzzle it out. It was as if Rosicky had a special gift for loving people, something that was like an ear for music or an eye for colour. It was quiet, unobtrusive; it was merely there. You saw it in his eyes,—perhaps that was why they were merry. You felt it in his hands, too. After he dropped off to sleep, she sat holding his warm, broad, flexible brown hand. She had never seen another in the least like it. She wondered if it wasn't a kind of gypsy hand, it was so alive and quick and light in its communications,—very strange in a farmer. Nearly all the farmers she knew had huge lumps of fists, like mauls, or they were knotty and bony and uncomfortable-looking, with stiff fingers. But Rosicky's was like quick-silver, flexible, muscular, about the colour of a pale cigar, with deep, deep creases across the palm. It wasn't nervous, it wasn't a stupid lump; it was a warm brown human hand, with some cleverness in it, a great deal of generosity, and something else which Polly could only call "gypsy-like,"—something nimble and lively and sure, in the way that animals are.

Polly remembered that hour long afterwards; it had been like an awakening to her. It seemed to her that she had never learned so much about life from anything as from old Rosicky's hand. It brought her to herself; it communicated some direct and untranslatable message.

When she heard Rudolph coming in the car, she ran out to meet him.

"Oh, Rudy, your father's been awful sick! He raked up those thistles he's been worrying about, and afterwards he could hardly get to the house. He suffered so I was afraid he was going to die."

Rudolph jumped to the ground. "Where is he now?"

"On the bed. He's asleep. I was terribly scared, because, you know, I'm so fond of your father." She slipped her arm through his and they went into the house. That afternoon they took Rosicky home and put him to bed, though he protested that he was quite well again.

The next morning he got up and dressed and sat down to breakfast with his family. He told Mary that his coffee tasted better than usual to him, and he warned the boys not to bear any tales to Doctor Ed when he got home. After breakfast he sat down by his window to do some patching and asked Mary to thread several needles for him before she went to feed her chickens,—her eyes were better than his, and her hands steadier. He lit his pipe and took up John's overalls. Mary had been watching him anxiously all morning, and as she went out of the door with her bucket of scraps, she saw that he was smiling. He was thinking, indeed, about Polly, and how he might never have known what a tender heart she had if he hadn't got sick over there. Girls nowadays didn't wear their heart on their sleeve. But now he knew Polly would make a fine woman after the foolishness wore off. Either a woman had that sweetness at her heart or she hadn't. You couldn't always tell by the look of them; but if they had that, everything came out right in the end.

After he had taken a few stitches, the cramp began in his chest, like yesterday. He put his pipe cautiously down on the window-sill and bent over to ease the pull. No use,—he had better try to get to his bed if he could. He rose and groped his way across the familiar floor, which was rising and falling like the deck of a ship. At the door he fell. When Mary came in, she found him lying there, and the moment she touched him she knew that he was gone.

Doctor Ed was away when Rosicky died, and for the first few weeks after he got home he was hard driven. Every day he said to himself that he must get out to see that family that had lost their father. One soft, warm moonlight night in early summer he started for the farm. His mind was on other things, and not until his road ran by the graveyard did he realize that Rosicky wasn't over there on the hill where the red lamplight shone, but here, in the moonlight. He stopped his car, shut off the engine, and sat there for a while.

A sudden hush had fallen on his soul. Everything here seemed strangely moving and significant, though signifying what, he did not know. Close by the wire fence stood Rosicky's mowing-machine, where one of the boys had been cutting hay that afternoon; his own work-horses had been going up and down there. The new-cut hay perfumed all the night air. The moonlight silvered the long, billowy grass that grew over the graves and hid the fence; the few little evergreens stood out black in it, like shadows in a pool. The sky was very blue and soft, the stars rather faint because the moon was full.

For the first time it struck Doctor Ed that this was really a beautiful graveyard. He thought of city cemeteries; acres of shrubbery and heavy stone, so arranged and lonely and unlike anything in the living world. Cities of the dead, indeed; cities of the forgotten, of the "put away." But this was open and free, this little square of long grass which the wind for ever stirred. Nothing but the sky overhead, and the many-coloured fields running on until they met that sky. The horses worked here in summer; the neighbours passed on their way to town; and over yonder, in the cornfield, Rosicky's own cattle would be eating fodder as winter came on. Nothing could be more undeathlike than this place; nothing could be more right for a man who had helped to do the work of great cities and had always longed for the open country and had got to it at last. Rosicky's life seemed to him complete and beautiful.

Death in the Woods

Sherwood Anderson (1876–1941)

Born and reared in Ohio, Sherwood Anderson knew firsthand the manners and morals of small-town life. After serving in the Spanish-American War, Anderson became a successful advertising man and manager of a paint factory, but his intense, private ambition was to be a writer. In 1912 the conflict between Anderson's public and private lives induced a nervous breakdown, after which he abandoned his career and marriage to start afresh as a writer in Chicago. The publication in 1919 of *Winesburg, Ohio,* a series of sketches about the frustrations and provinciality of small-town America, brought Anderson considerable fame. Three other collections of short stories quickly followed: *The Triumph of the Egg* (1921), *Horses and Men* (1923), and *Death in the Woods* (1933; the title story dates from 1926).

Anderson turned his hand to novels and drama but without the success he had attained in the shorter form. His stories, with their economical handling of complex psychological patterns, had a marked influence on the early writings of Hemingway and Faulkner, who were also indebted to Anderson for his friendship and generous support.

She was an old woman and lived on a farm near the town in which I lived. All country and small-town people have seen such old women, but no one knows much about them. Such an old woman comes into town driving an old worn-out horse or she comes afoot carrying a basket. She may own a few hens and have eggs to sell. She brings them in a basket and takes them to a grocer. There she trades them in. She gets some salt pork and some beans. Then she gets a pound or two of sugar and some flour.

Afterwards she goes to the butcher's and asks for some dog-meat. She may spend ten or fifteen cents, but when she does she asks for something. Formerly the butchers gave liver to anyone who wanted to carry it away. In our family we were always having it. Once one of my brothers got a whole cow's liver at the slaughterhouse near the fair grounds in our town. We had it until we were sick of it. It never cost a cent. I have hated the thought of it ever since.

The old farm woman got some liver and a soup-bone. She never visited with anyone, and as soon as she got what she wanted she lit out for home. It made quite a load for such an old body. No one gave her a lift. People drive right down a road and never notice an old woman like that.

There was such an old woman who used to come into town past our house one summer and fall when I was a young boy and was sick with what was called inflammatory rheumatism. She went home later carrying a heavy pack on her back. Two or three large gaunt-looking dogs followed at her heels.

The old woman was nothing special. She was one of the nameless ones that hardly anyone knows, but she got into my thoughts. I have just suddenly now, after all these years, remembered her and what happened. It is a story. Her name was Grimes, and she lived with her husband and son in a small unpainted house on the bank of a small creek four miles from town.

The husband and son were a tough lot. Although the son was but twenty-one, he had already served a term in jail. It was whispered about that the woman's husband stole horses and ran them off to some other county. Now and then, when a horse turned up missing, the man had also disappeared. No one ever caught him. Once, when I was loafing at Tom Whitehead's livery-barn, the man came there and sat on the bench in front. Two or three other men were there, but no one spoke to him. He sat for a few minutes and then got up and went away. When he was leaving he turned around and stared at the men. There was a look of defiance in his eyes. "Well, I have tried to be friendly. You don't want to talk to me. It has been so wherever I have gone in this town. If, some day, one of your fine horses turns up missing, well, then what?" He did not say anything actually. "I'd like to bust one of you in the jaw," was about what his eyes said. I remember how the look in his eyes made me shiver.

The old man belonged to a family that had had money once. His name was Jake Grimes. It all comes back clearly now. His father, John Grimes, had owned a sawmill when the country was new, and had made money. Then he got to drinking and running after women. When he died there wasn't much left.

Jake blew in the rest. Pretty soon there wasn't any more lumber to cut and his land was nearly all gone.

He got his wife off a German farmer, for whom he went to work one June day in the wheat harvest. She was a young thing then and scared to death. You see, the farmer was up to something with the girl—she was, I think, a bound girl and his wife had her suspicions. She took it out on the girl when the man wasn't around. Then, when the wife had to go off to town for supplies, the farmer got after her. She told young Jake that nothing really ever happened, but he didn't know whether to believe it or not.

He got her pretty easy himself, the first time he was out with her. He wouldn't have married her if the German farmer hadn't tried to tell him where to get off. He got her to go riding with him in his buggy one night when he was threshing on the place, and then he came for her the next Sunday night.

She managed to get out of the house without her employer's seeing, but when she was getting into the buggy he showed up. It was almost dark, and he just popped up suddenly at the horse's head. He grabbed the horse by the bridle and Jake got out his buggy-whip.

They had it out all right! The German was a tough one. Maybe he didn't care whether his wife knew or not. Jake hit him over the face and shoulders with the buggy-whip, but the horse got to acting up and he had to get out.

Then the two men went for it. The girl didn't see it. The horse started to run away and went nearly a mile down the road before the girl got him stopped. Then she managed to tie him to a tree beside the road. (I wonder how I know all this. It must have stuck in my mind from small-town tales when I was a boy.) Jake found her there after he got through with the German. She was huddled up in the buggy seat, crying, scared to death. She told Jake a lot of stuff, how the German had tried to get her, how he chased her once into the barn, how another time, when they happened to be alone in the house together, he tore her dress open clear down the front. The German, she said, might have got her that time if he hadn't heard his old woman drive in at the gate. She had been off to town for supplies. Well, she would be putting the horse in the barn. The German managed to sneak off to the fields without his wife seeing. He told the girl he would kill her if she told. What could she do? She told a lie about ripping her dress in the barn when she was feeding the stock. I remember now that she was a bound girl and did not know where her father and mother were. Maybe she did not have any father. You know what I mean.

Such bound children were often enough cruelly treated. They were children who had no parents, slaves really. There were very few orphan homes then. They were legally bound into some home. It was a matter of pure luck how it came out.

II

She married Jake and had a son and daughter, but the daughter died.

Then she settled down to feed stock. That was her job. At the German's place she had cooked the food for the German and his wife. The wife was a strong woman with big hips and worked most of the time in the fields with her husband. She fed them and fed the cows in the barn, fed the pigs, the horses and the chickens. Every moment of every day, as a young girl, was spent feeding something.

The she married Jake Grimes and he had to be fed. She was a slight thing, and when she had been married for three or four years, and after the two children were born, her slender shoulders became stooped.

Jake always had a lot of big dogs around the house, that stood near the unused sawmill near the creek. He was always trading horses when he wasn't stealing something and had a lot of poor bony ones about. Also he kept three or four pigs and a cow. They were all pastured in the few acres left of the Grimes place and Jake did little enough work.

He went into debt for a threshing outfit and ran it for several years, but it did not pay. People did not trust him. They were afraid he would steal the grain at night. He had to go a long way off to get work and it cost too much to get there. In the winter he hunted and cut a little firewood, to be sold in some nearby town. When the son grew up he was just like the father. They got drunk together. If there wasn't anything to eat in the house when they came home the old man gave his old woman a cut over the head. She had a few chickens of her own and had to kill one of them in a hurry. When they were all killed she wouldn't have any eggs to sell when she went to town, and then what would she do?

She had to scheme all her life about getting things fed, getting the pigs fed so they would grow fat and could be butchered in the fall. When they were butchered her husband took most of the meat off to town and sold it. If he did not do it first the boy did. They fought sometimes and when they fought the old woman stood aside trembling.

She had got the habit of silence anyway—that was fixed. Sometimes, when she began to look old—she wasn't forty yet—and when the husband and son were both off, trading horses or drinking or hunting or stealing, she went around the house and the barnyard muttering to herself.

How was she going to get everything fed?—that was her problem. The dogs had to be fed. There wasn't enough hay in the barn for the horses and the cow. If she didn't feed the chickens how could they lay eggs? Without eggs to sell how could she get things in town, things she had to have to keep the life of the farm going? Thank heaven, she did not have to feed her husband—in a certain way. That hadn't lasted long after their marriage and after the babies came. Where he went on his long trips she did not know. Sometimes he was gone from home for weeks, and after the boy grew up they went off together.

They left everything at home for her to manage and she had no money. She knew no one. No one ever talked to her in town. When it was winter she had to gather sticks of wood for her fire, had to try to keep the stock fed with very little grain.

The stock in the barn cried to her hungrily, the dogs followed her about. In the winter the hens laid few enough eggs. They huddled in the corners of the barn and she kept watching them. If a hen lays an egg in the barn in the winter and you do not find it, it freezes and breaks.

One day in winter the old woman went off to town with a few eggs and the dogs followed her. She did not get started until nearly three o'clock and the snow was heavy. She hadn't been feeling well for several days and so she went muttering along, scantily clad, her shoulders stooped. She had an old grain bag in which she carried her eggs, tucked away down in the bottom. There weren't many of them, but in winter the price of eggs is up. She would get a little meat in exchange for the eggs, some salt pork, a little sugar, and some coffee perhaps. It might be the butcher would give her a piece of liver.

When she had got to town and was trading in her eggs the dogs lay by the door outside. She did pretty well, got the things she needed, more than she had hoped. Then she went to the butcher and he gave her some liver and some dog-meat.

It was the first time anyone had spoken to her in a friendly way for a long time. The butcher was alone in his shop when she came in and was annoyed by the thought of such a sick-looking old woman out on such a day. It was bitter cold and the snow, that had let up during the afternoon, was falling again. The butcher said something about her husband and her son, swore at them, and the old woman stared at him, a look of mild surprise in her eyes as he talked. He said that if either the husband or the son were going to get any of the liver or the heavy bones with scraps of meat hanging to them that he had put into the grain bag, he'd see him starve first.

Starve, eh? Well, things had to be fed. Men had to be fed, and the horses that weren't any good but maybe could be traded off, and the poor thin cow that hadn't given any milk for three months.

Horses, cows, pigs, dogs, men.

III

The old woman had to get back before darkness came if she could. The dogs followed at her heels, sniffing at the heavy grain bag she had fastened on her back. When she got to the edge of town she stopped by a fence and tied the bag on her back with a piece of rope she had carried in her dress-pocket for just that purpose. That was an easier way to carry it. Her arms ached. It was hard when she had to crawl over fences and once she fell over and landed in the snow. The dogs went frisking about. She had to struggle to get to her feet again, but she made it. The point of climbing over the fences was that there was a short cut over a hill and through a woods. She might have gone around by the road, but it was a mile farther that way. She was afraid she couldn't make it. And then, besides, the stock had to be fed. There was a little hay left and a little corn. Perhaps her husband and son would bring some home when they came. They had driven off in the only buggy the Grimes family had, a rickety thing, a rickety horse hitched to the buggy, two other rickety horses led by halters. They were going to trade horses, get a little money if they could. They might come home drunk. It would be well to have something in the house when they came back.

The son had an affair on with a woman at the county seat, fifteen miles away. She was a rough enough woman, a tough one. Once, in the summer, the son had brought her to the house. Both she and the son had been drinking. Jake Grimes was away and the son and his woman ordered the old woman about like a servant. She didn't mind much; she was used to it. Whatever happened she never said anything. That was her way of getting along. She had managed that way when she was a young girl at the German's and ever since she had married Jake. That time her son brought his woman to the house they stayed all night, sleeping together just as though they were married. It hadn't shocked the old woman, not much. She had got past being shocked early in life.

With the pack on her back she went painfully along across an open field, wading in the deep snow, and got into the woods.

There was a path, but it was hard to follow. Just beyond the top of the hill, where the woods was thickest, there was a small clearing. Had someone once thought of building a house there? The clearing was as large as a building lot in town, large enough for a house and a garden. The path ran along the side of the clearing, and when she got there the old woman sat down to rest at the foot of a tree.

It was a foolish thing to do. When she got herself placed, the pack against the tree's trunk, it was nice, but what about getting up again? She worried about that for a moment and then quietly closed her eyes.

She must have slept for a time. When you are about so cold you can't get any colder. The afternoon grew a little warmer and the snow came thicker than ever. Then after a time the weather cleared. The moon even came out.

There were four Grimes dogs that had followed Mrs. Grimes into town, all tall gaunt fellows. Such men as Jack Grimes and his son always keep just such dogs. They kick and abuse them, but they stay. The Grimes dogs, in order to keep from starving, had to do a lot of foraging for themselves, and they had been at it while the old woman slept with her back to the tree at the side of the clearing. They had been chasing rabbits in the woods and in adjoining fields and in their ranging had picked up three other farm dogs.

After a time all the dogs came back to the clearing. They were excited about something. Such nights, cold and clear and with a moon, do things to dogs. It may be that some old instinct, come down from the time when they were wolves and ranged the woods in packs on winter nights, comes back into them.

The dogs in the clearing, before the old woman, had caught two or three rabbits and their immediate hunger had been satisfied. They began to play, running in circles in the clearing. Round and round they ran, each dog's nose at the tail of the next dog. In the clearing, under the snow-laden trees and under the wintry moon they made a strange picture, running thus silently, in a circle their running had beaten in the soft snow. The dogs made no sound. They ran around and around in the circle.

It may have been that the old woman saw them doing that before she died. She may have awakened once or twice and looked at the strange sight with dim old eyes.

She wouldn't be very cold now, just drowsy. Life hangs on a long time. Perhaps the old woman was out of her head. She may have dreamed of her girlhood, at the German's, and before that, when she was a child and before her mother lit out and left her.

Her dreams couldn't have been very pleasant. Not many pleasant things had happened to her. Now and then one of the Grimes dogs left the running circle and came to stand before her. The dog thrust his face close to her face. His red tongue was hanging out.

The running of the dogs may have been a kind of death ceremony. It may have been that the primitive instinct of the wolf, having been aroused in the dogs by the night and the running, made them somehow afraid.

"Now we are no longer wolves. We are dogs, the servants of men. Keep alive, man! When man dies we become wolves again."

When one of the dogs came to where the old woman sat with her back against the tree and thrust his nose close to her face he seemed satisfied and went back to run with the pack. All the Grimes dogs did it at some time during the evening, before she died. I knew all about it afterward, when I grew to be a man, because once in a woods in Illinois, on another winter night, I saw a pack of dogs act just like that. The dogs were waiting for me to die as they had waited for the old woman that night when I was a child, but when it happened to me I was a young man and had no intention whatever of dying.

The old woman died softly and quietly. When she was dead and when one of the Grimes dogs had come to her and had found her dead all the dogs stopped running.

They gathered about her.

Well, she was dead now. She had fed the Grimes dogs when she was alive, what about now?

There was the pack on her back, the grain bag containing the piece of salt pork, the liver the butcher had given her, the dog-meat, the soup bones. The butcher in town, having been suddenly overcome with a feeling of pity, had loaded her grain bag heavily. It had been a big haul for the old woman.

It was a big haul for the dogs now.

IV

One of the Grimes dogs sprang suddenly out from among the others and began worrying the pack on the old woman's back. Had the dogs really been wolves that one would have been the leader of the pack. What he did, all the others did.

All of them sank their teeth into the grain bag the old woman had fastened with ropes to her back.

They dragged the old woman's body out into the open clearing. The worn-out dress was quickly torn from her shoulders. When she was found, a day or two later, the dress had been torn from her body clear to the hips, but the dogs had not touched her body. They had got the meat out of the grain bag, that was all. Her body was frozen stiff when it was found, and the shoulders were so narrow and the body so slight that in death it looked like the body of some charming young girl.

Such things happened in towns of the Middle West, on farms near town, when I was a boy. A hunter out after rabbits found the old woman's body and did not touch it. Something, the beaten round path in the little snow-covered clearing, the silence of the place, the place where the dogs had worried the body trying to pull the grain bag away or tear it open—something startled the man and he hurried off to town.

I was in Main Street with one of my brothers who was town newsboy and who was taking the afternoon papers to the stores. It was almost night.

The hunter came into a grocery and told his story. Then he went to a hardware shop and into a drugstore. Men began to gather on the sidewalks. Then they started out along the road to the place in the woods.

My brother should have gone on about his business of distributing papers but he didn't. Everyone was going to the woods. The undertaker went and the town marshal. Several men got on a dray and rode out to where the path left the road and went into the woods, but the horses weren't very sharply shod and slid about on the slippery roads. They made no better time than those of us who walked.

The town marshal was a large man whose leg had been injured in the Civil War. He carried a heavy cane and limped rapidly along the road. My brother and I followed at his heels, and as we went other men and boys joined the crowd.

It had grown dark by the time we got to where the old woman had left the road but the moon had come out. The marshal was thinking there might have been a murder. He kept asking the hunter questions. The hunter went along with his gun across his shoulders, a dog following at his heels. It isn't often a rabbit hunter has a chance to be so conspicuous. He was taking full advantage of it, leading the procession with the town marshal. "I didn't see any wounds. She was a beautiful young girl. Her face was buried in the now. No, I didn't know her." As a matter of fact, the hunter had not looked closely at the body. He had been frightened. She might have been murdered and someone might spring out from behind a tree and murder him. In a woods, in the late afternoon, when the trees are all bare and there is white snow on the ground, when all is silent, something creepy steals over the mind and body. If something strange or uncanny has happened in the nieghborhood all you think about is getting away from there as fast as you can.

The crowd of men and boys had got to where the old woman had crossed the field and went, following the marshal and the hunter, up the slight incline and into the woods.

My brother and I were silent. He had his bundle of papers in a bag slung across his shoulder. When he got back to town he would have to go on distributing his papers before he went home to supper. If I went along, as he had no doubt already determined I should, we would both be late. Either mother or our older sister would have to warm our supper.

Well, we would have something to tell. A boy did not get such a chance very often. It was lucky we just happened to go into the grocery when the hunter came in. The hunter was a country fellow. Neither of us had ever seen him before.

Now the crowd of men and boys had got to the clearing. Darkness comes quickly on such winter nights, but the full moon made everything clear. My brother and I stood near the tree, beneath which the old woman had died.

She did not look old, lying there in that light, frozen and still. One of the men turned her over in the snow and I saw everything. My body trembled with some strange mystical feeling and so did my brother's. It might have been the cold.

Neither of us had ever seen a woman's body before. It may have been the snow, clinging to the frozen flesh, that made it look so white and lovely, so like marble. No woman had come with the party from town; but one of the men, he was the town blacksmith, took off his overcoat and spread it over her. Then he gathered her into his arms and started off to town, all the others following silently. At that time no one knew who she was.

V

I had seen everything, had seen the oval in the snow, like a miniature race track, where the dogs had run, had seen how the men were mystified, had seen the white bare young-looking shoulders, had heard the whispered comments of the men.

The men were simply mystified. They took the body to the undertaker's, and when the blacksmith, the hunter, the marshal and several others had got inside they closed the door. If father had been there perhaps he could have got in, but we boys couldn't.

I went with my brother to distribute the rest of his papers and when we got home it was my brother who told the story.

I kept silent and went to bed early. It may have been I was not satisfied with the way he told it.

Later, in the town, I must have heard other fragments of the old woman's story. She was recognized the next day and there was an investigation.

The husband and son were found somewhere and brought to town and there was an attempt to connect them with the woman's death, but it did not work. They had perfect enough alibis.

However, the town was against them. They had to get out. Where they went I never heard.

I remember only the picture there in the forest, the men standing about, the naked girlish-looking figure, face down in the snow, the tracks made by the running dogs and the clear cold winter sky above. White fragments of clouds were drifting across the sky. They went racing across the little open space among the trees.

The scene in the forest had become for me, without my knowing it, the foundation for the real story I am now trying to tell. The fragments, you see, had to be picked up slowly, long afterwards.

Things happened. When I was a young man I worked on the farm of a German. The hired-girl was afraid of her employer. The farmer's wife hated her.

I saw things at that place. Once later, I had a half-uncanny, mystical adventure with dogs in an Illinois forest on a clear, moonlit winter night. When I was a schoolboy, and on a summer day, I went with a boy friend out along a creek some miles from town and came to the house where the old woman had lived. No one had lived in the house since her death. The doors were broken from the hinges; the window lights were all broken. As the boy and I stood in the road outside, two dogs, just roving farm dogs no doubt, came running around the corner of the house. The dogs were tall, gaunt fellows and came down to the fence and glared through at us, standing in the road.

The whole thing, the story of the old woman's death, was to me as I grew older like music heard from far off. The notes had to be picked up slowly one at a time. Something had to be understood.

The woman who died was one destined to feed animal life. Anyway, that is all she ever did. She was feeding animal life before she was born, as a child, as a young woman working on the farm of the German, after she married, when she grew old and when she died. She fed animal life in cows, in chickens, in pigs, in horses, in dogs, in men. Her daughter had died in childhood and with her one son she had no articulate relations. On the night when she died she was hurrying homeward, bearing on her body food for animal life.

She died in the clearing in the woods and even after her death continued feeding animal life.

You see it is likely that, when my brother told the story, that night when we got home and my mother and sister sat listening, I did not think he got the point. He was too young and so was I. A thing so complete has its own beauty.

I shall not try to emphasize the point. I am only explaining why I was dissatisfied then and have been ever since. I speak of that only that you may understand why I have been impelled to try to tell the simple story over again.

Big Two-Hearted River

Ernest Hemingway (1899–1961)

Born and reared in Oak Park, Illinois, a suburb of Chicago, Hemingway graduated from high school in 1917 and worked for a brief period as a reporter for the Kansas City *Star*. When the United States entered World War I he volunteered for the ambulance service and was severely wounded at the Italian front. After the armistice he became a foreign correspondent for the Toronto *Star* and soon settled into the life of an expatriate writer in Paris. His first important volume of short stories, *In Our Time* (1925), is characterized by the austerity and precision found in "Big Two-Hearted River." Hemingway's first novel, *The Sun Also Rises* (1926), based on his experiences in Paris and Spain, was followed in 1929 by his great novel of the first World War, *A Farewell to Arms.* Between 1923 and 1933 Hemingway wrote most of his important short stories. *The Fifth Column and the First Forty-nine Stories* (1938) collects the stories of *In Our Time, Men Without Women* (1927), and *Winner Take Nothing* (1933), along with a few later stories and a play about the Spanish Civil War.

The 1930s was a difficult decade for Hemingway: essentially an aloof stylist, he did not adjust easily to the climate of political activism and social commitment. However, his experience as a reporter and partisan in the Spanish Civil War did produce a highly successful novel, *For Whom the Bell Tolls* (1940). During the later days of World War II Hemingway was a reporter and participant on the Western front, but the novel based partly on this experience, *Across the River and Into the Trees* (1950), lacks the clean objectivity of *A Farewell to Arms* and the healthy romanticism of *For Whom the Bell Tolls.* In *The Old Man and the Sea* (1952), however, Hemingway produced a fable which combines his famous gift for realistic description with a new-found interest in overt symbolism. He was awarded the Nobel Prize for Literature in 1954, but the success of *The Old Man and the Sea* was not repeated. His last years were marked by a steady physical and mental disintegration, and he committed suicide in 1961.

PART I

The train went on up the track out of sight, around one of the hills of burnt timber. Nick sat down on the bundle of canvas and bedding the baggage man had pitched out of the door of the baggage car. There was no town, nothing but the rails and the burned-over country. The thirteen saloons that had lined the one street of Seney had not left a trace. The foundations of the Mansion House hotel stuck up above the ground. The stone was chipped and split by the fire. It was all that was left of the town of Seney. Even the surface had been burned off the ground.

Nick looked at the burned-over stretch of hillside, where he had expected to find the scattered houses of the town and then walked down the railroad track to the bridge over the river. The river was there. It swirled against the log spiles of the bridge. Nick looked down into the clear, brown water, colored from the pebbly bottom, and watched the trout keeping themselves steady in the current with wavering fins. As he watched them they changed their positions by quick angles, only to hold steady in the fast water again. Nick watched them a long time.

He watched them holding themselves with their noses into the current, many trout in deep, fast moving water, slightly distorted as he watched far down through the glassy convex surface of the pool, its surface pushing and swelling smooth against the resistance of the log-driven piles of the bridge. At the bottom of the pool were the big trout. Nick did not see them at first. Then he saw them at the bottom of the pool, big trout looking to hold themselves on the gravel bottom in a varying mist of gravel and sand, raised in spurts by the current.

Nick looked down into the pool from the bridge. It was a hot day. A kingfisher flew up the stream. It was a long time since Nick had looked into a stream and seen trout. They were very satisfactory. As the shadow of the kingfisher moved up the stream, a big trout shot upstream in a long angle, only his shadow marking the angle, then lost his shadow as he came through the surface of the water, caught the sun, and then, as he went back into the stream under the surface, his shadow seemed to float down the stream with the current, unresisting, to his post under the bridge where he tightened facing up into the current.

Nick's heart tightened as the trout moved. He felt all the old feeling.

He turned and looked down the stream. It stretched away, pebbly-bottomed with shallows and big boulders and a deep pool as it curved away around the foot of a bluff.

Nick walked back up the ties to where his pack lay in the cinders beside the railway track. He was happy. He adjusted the pack harness around the bundle, pulling straps tight, slung the pack on his back, got his arms through the shoulder straps and took some of the pull off his shoulders by leaning his forehead against the wide band of the tump-line. Still, it was too heavy. It was much too heavy. He had his leather rod-case in his hand and leaning forward to keep the weight of the pack high on his shoulders he walked along the road that paralleled the railway track, leaving the burned town behind in the heat, and then turned off around a hill with a high, fire-scarred hill on either side onto a road that went back into the country. He walked along the road feeling the ache from the pull of the heavy pack. The road climbed steadily. It was hard work walking up-hill. His muscles ached and the day was hot, but Nick felt happy. He felt he had left everything behind, the need for thinking, the need to write, other needs. It was all back of him.

From the time he had gotten down off the train and the baggage man had thrown his pack out of the open car door things had been different. Seney was burned, the country was burned over and changed, but it did not matter. It could not all be burned. He knew that. He hiked along the road, sweating in the sun, climbing to cross the range of hills that separated the railway from the pine plains.

The road ran on, dipping occasionally, but always climbing. Nick went on up. Finally the road after going parallel to the burnt hillside reached the top. Nick leaned back against a stump and slipped out of the pack harness. Ahead of him, as far as he could see, was the pine plain. The burned country stopped off at the left with the range of hills. On ahead islands of dark pine trees rose out of the plain. Far off to the left was the line of the river. Nick followed it with his eye and caught glints of the water in the sun.

There was nothing but the pine plain ahead of him, until the far blue hills that marked the Lake Superior height of land. He could hardly see them, faint and far away in the heat-light over the plain. If he looked too steadily they were gone. But if he only half-looked they were there, the far-off hills of the height of land.

Nick sat down against the charred stump and smoked a cigarette. His pack balanced on the top of the stump, harness holding ready, a hollow molded in it from his back. Nick sat smoking, looking out over the country. He did not need to get his map out. He knew where he was from the position of the river.

As he smoked, his legs stretched out in front of him, he noticed a grasshopper walk along the ground and up onto his woolen sock. The grasshopper was black. As he had walked along the road, climbing, he had started many grasshoppers from the dust. They were all black. They were not the big grasshoppers with yellow and black or red and black wings whirring out from their black wing sheathing as they fly up. These were just ordinary hoppers, but all a sooty black in color. Nick had wondered about them as he walked, without really thinking about them. Now, as he watched the black hopper that was nibbling at the wool of his sock with its fourway lip, he realized that they had all turned black from living in the burned-over land. He realized that the fire must have come the year before, but the grasshoppers were all black now. He wondered how long they would stay that way.

Carefully he reached his hand down and took hold of the hopper by the wings. He turned him up, all his legs walking in the air, and looked at his jointed belly. Yes, it was black too, iridescent where the back and head were dusty.

"Go on, hopper," Nick said, speaking out loud for the first time. "Fly away somewhere."

He tossed the grasshopper up into the air and watched him sail away to a charcoal stump across the road.

Nick stood up. He leaned his back against the weight of his pack where it rested upright on the stump and got his arms through the shoulder straps. He stood with the pack on his back on the brow of the hill looking out across the country, toward the distant river and then struck down the hillside away from the road. Underfoot the ground was good walking. Two hundred yards down the hillside the fire line stopped. Then it was sweet fern, growing ankle high, to walk through, and clumps of jack pines; a long undulating country with frequent rises and descents, sandy underfoot and the country alive again.

Nick kept his direction by the sun. He knew where he wanted to strike the river and he kept on through the pine plain, mounting small rises to see other rises ahead of him and sometimes from the top of a rise a great solid island of pines off to his right or his left. He broke off some sprigs of the heathery sweet fern, and put them under his pack straps. The chafing crushed it and he smelled it as he walked.

He was tired and very hot, walking across the uneven, shadeless pine plain. At any time he knew he could strike the river by turning off to his left. It could not be more than a mile away. But he kept on toward the north to hit the river as far upstream as he could go in one day's walking.

For some time as he walked Nick had been in sight of one of the big islands of pine standing out above the rolling high ground he was crossing. He dipped down and then as he came slowly up to the crest of the bridge he turned and made toward the pine trees.

There was no underbrush in the island of pine trees. The trunks of the trees went straight up or slanted toward each other. The trunks were straight and brown without branches. The branches were high above. Some interlocked to make a solid shadow on the brown forest floor. Around the grove of trees was a bare space. It was brown and soft underfoot as Nick walked on it. This was the over-lapping of the pine needle floor, extending out beyond the width of the high branches. The trees had grown tall and the branches moved high, leaving in the sun this bare space they had once covered with shadow. Sharp at the edge of this extension of the forest floor commenced the sweet fern.

Nick slipped off his pack and lay down in the shade. He lay on his back and looked up into the pine trees. His neck and back and the small of his back rested as he stretched. The earth felt good against his back. He looked up at the sky, through the branches, and then shut his eyes. He opened them and looked up again. There was a wind high up in the branches. He shut his eyes again and went to sleep.

Nick woke stiff and cramped. The sun was nearly down. His pack was heavy and the straps painful as he lifted it on. He leaned over with the pack on and picked up the leather rod-case and started out from the pine trees across the sweet fern swale, toward the river. He knew it could not be more than a mile.

He came down a hillside covered with stumps into a meadow. At the edge of the meadow flowed the river. Nick was glad to get to the river. He walked upstream through the meadow. His trousers were soaked with the dew as he walked. After the hot day, the dew had come quickly and heavily. The river made no sound. It was too fast and smooth. At the edge of the meadow, before he mounted to a piece of high ground to make camp, Nick looked down the river at the trout rising. They were rising to insects come from the swamp on the other side of the stream when the sun went down. The trout jumped out of water to take them. While Nick walked through the little stretch of meadow alongside the stream, trout had jumped high out of water. Now as he looked down the river, the insects must be settling on the surface, for the trout were feeding steadily all down the stream. As far down the long stretch as he could see, the trout were rising, making circles all down the surface of the water, as though it were starting to rain.

The ground rose, wooded and sandy, to overlook the meadow, the stretch of river and the swamp. Nick dropped his pack and rod-case and looked for a level piece of ground. He was very hungry and he wanted to make his camp before he cooked. Between two jack pines, the ground was quite level. He took the ax out of the pack and chopped out two projecting roots. That leveled a piece of ground large enough to sleep on. He smoothed out the sandy soil with his hand and pulled all the sweet fern bushes by their roots. His hands smelled good from the sweet fern. He smoothed the uprooted earth. He did not want anything making lumps under the blankets. When he had the ground smooth, he spread his three blankets. One he folded double, next to the ground. The other two he spread on top.

With the ax he slit off a bright slab of pine from one of the stumps and split it into pegs for the tent. He wanted them long and solid to hold in the ground.

With the tent unpacked and spread on the ground, the pack, leaning against a jackpine, looked much smaller. Nick tied the rope that served the tent for a ridge-pole to the trunk of one of the pine trees and pulled the tent up off the ground with the other end of the rope and tied it to the other pine. The tent hung on the rope like a canvas blanket on a clothesline. Nick poked a pole he had cut up under the back peak of the canvas and then made it a tent by pegging out the sides. He pegged the sides out taut and drove the pegs deep, hitting them down into the ground with the flat of the ax until the rope loops were buried and the canvas was drum tight.

Across the open mouth of the tent Nick fixed cheesecloth to keep out mosquitoes. He crawled inside under the mosquito bar with various things from the pack to put at the head of the bed under the slant of the canvas. Inside the tent the light came through the brown canvas. It smelled pleasantly of canvas. Already there was something mysterious and homelike. Nick was happy as he crawled inside the tent. He had not been unhappy all day. This was different though. Now things were done. There had been this to do. Now it was done. It had been a hard trip. He was very tired. That was done. He had made his camp. He was settled. Nothing could touch him. It was a good place to camp. He was there, in the good place. He was in his home where he had made it. Now he was hungry.

He came out, crawling under the cheesecloth. It was quite dark outside. It was lighter in the tent.

Nick went over to the pack and found, with his fingers, a long nail in the paper sack of nails, in the bottom of the pack. He drove it into the pine tree, holding it close and hitting it gently with the flat of the ax. He hung the pack up on the nail. All his supplies were in the pack. They were off the ground and sheltered now.

Nick was hungry. He did not believe he had ever been hungrier. He opened and emptied a can of pork and beans and a can of spaghetti into the frying pan.

"I've got a right to eat this kind of stuff, if I'm willing to carry it," Nick said. His voice sounded strange in the darkening woods. He did not speak again.

He started a fire with some chunks of pine he got with the ax from a stump. Over the fire he stuck a wire grill, pushing the four legs down into the ground with his boot. Nick put the frying pan on the grill over the flames. He was hungrier. The beans and spaghetti warmed. Nick stirred them and mixed them together. They began to bubble, making little bubbles that rose with difficulty to the surface. There was a good smell. Nick got out a bottle of tomato catchup and cut four slices of bread. The little bubbles were coming faster now. Nick sat down beside the fire and lifted the frying pan off. He poured about half the contents out into the tin plate. It spread slowly on the plate. Nick knew it was too hot. He poured on some tomato catchup. He knew the beans and spaghetti were still too hot. He looked at the fire, then at the tent, he was not going to spoil it all by burning his tongue. For years he had never enjoyed fried bananas because he had never been able to wait for them to cool. His tongue was very sensitive. He was very hungry. Across the river in the swamp, in the almost dark, he saw a mist rising. He looked at the tent once more. All right. He took a full spoonful from the plate.

"Chrise," Nick said, "Geezus Chrise," he said happily.

He ate the whole plateful before he remembered the bread. Nick finished the second plateful with the bread, mopping the plate shiny. He had not eaten since a cup of coffee and a ham sandwich in the station restaurant at St. Ignace. It had been a very fine experience. He had been that hungry before, but had not been able to satisfy it. He could have made camp hours before if he had wanted to. There were plenty of good places to camp on the river. But this was good.

Nick tucked two big chips of pine under the grill. The fire flared up. He had forgotten to get water for the coffee. Out of the pack he got a folding canvas bucket and walked down the hill, across the edge of the meadow, to the stream. The other bank was in the white mist. The grass was wet and cold as he knelt on the bank and dipped the canvas bucket into the stream. It bellied and pulled hard in the current. The water was ice cold. Nick rinsed the bucket and carried it full up to the camp. Up away from the stream it was not so cold.

Nick drove another big nail and hung up the bucket full of water. He dipped the coffee pot half full, put some more chips under the grill onto the fire and put the pot on. He could not remember which way he made coffee. He could remember an argument about it with Hopkins, but not which side he had taken. He decided to bring it to a boil. He remembered now that was Hopkins's way. He had once argued about everything with Hopkins. While he waited for the coffee to boil, he opened a small can of apricots. He liked to open cans. He emptied the can of apricots out into a tin cup. While he watched the coffee on the fire, he drank the juice syrup of the apricots, carefully at first to keep from spilling, then meditatively, sucking the apricots down. They were better than fresh apricots.

The coffee boiled as he watched. The lid came up

and coffee and grounds ran down the side of the pot. Nick took it off the grill. It was a triumph for Hopkins. He put sugar in the empty apricot cup and poured some of the coffee out to cool. It was too hot to pour and he used his hat to hold the handle of the coffee pot. He would not let it steep in the pot at all. Not the first cup. It should be straight Hopkins all the way. Hop deserved that. He was a very serious coffee drinker. He was the most serious man Nick had ever known. Not heavy, serious. That was a long time ago. Hopkins spoke without moving his lips. He had played polo. He made millions of dollars in Texas. He had borrowed carfare to go to Chicago, when the wire came that his first big well had come in. He could have wired for money. That would have been too slow. They called Hop's girl the Blonde Venus. Hop did not mind because she was not his real girl. Hopkins said very confidently that none of them would make fun of his real girl. He was right. Hopkins went away when the telegram came. That was on the Black River. It took eight days for the telegram to reach him. Hopkins gave away his .22 caliber Colt automatic pistol to Nick. He gave his camera to Bill. It was to remember him always by. They were all going fishing again next summer. The Hop Head was rich. He would get a yacht and they would all cruise along the north shore of Lake Superior. He was excited but serious. They said goodbye and all felt bad. It broke up the trip. They never saw Hopkins again. That was a long time ago on the Black River.

Nick drank the coffee, the coffee according to Hopkins. The coffee was bitter. Nick laughed. It made a good ending to the story. His mind was starting to work. He knew he could choke it because he was tired enough. He spilled the coffee out of the pot and shook the grounds loose into the fire. He lit a cigarette and went inside the tent. He took off his shoes and trousers, sitting on the blankets, rolled the shoes up inside the trousers for a pillow and got in between the blankets.

Out through the front of the tent he watched the glow of the fire, when the night wind blew on it. It was a quiet night. The swamp was perfectly quiet. Nick stretched under the blanket comfortably. A mosquito hummed close to his ear. Nick sat up and lit a match. The mosquito was on the canvas, over his head. Nick moved the match quickly up to it. The mosquito made a satisfactory hiss in the flame. The match went out. Nick lay down again under the blanket. He turned on his side and shut his eyes. He was sleepy. He felt sleep coming. He curled up under the blanket and went to sleep.

PART II

In the morning the sun was up and the tent was starting to get hot. Nick crawled out under the mosquito netting stretched across the mouth of the tent, to look at the morning. The grass was wet on his hands as he came out. The sun was just up over the hill. There was the meadow, the river and the swamp. There were birch trees in the green of the swamp on the other side of the river.

The river was clear and smoothly fast in the early morning. Down about two hundred yards were three logs all the way across the stream. They made the water smooth and deep above them. As Nick watched, a mink crossed the river on the logs and went into the swamp. Nick was excited. He was excited by the early morning and the river. He was really too hurried to eat breakfast, but he knew he must. He built a little fire and put on the coffee pot.

While the water was heating in the pot he took an empty bottle and went down over the edge of the high ground to the meadow. The meadow was wet with dew and Nick wanted to catch grasshoppers for bait before the sun dried the grass. He found plenty of good grasshoppers. They were at the base of the grass stems. Sometimes they clung to a grass stem. They were cold and wet with the dew, and could not jump until the sun warmed them. Nick picked them up, taking only the medium-sized brown ones, and put them into the bottle. He turned over a log and just under the shelter of the edge were several hundred hoppers. It was a grasshopper lodging house. Nick put about fifty of the medium browns into the bottle. While he was picking up the hoppers the others warmed in the sun and commenced to hop away. They flew when they hopped. At first they made one flight and stayed stiff when they landed, as though they were dead.

Nick knew that by the time he was through with breakfast they would be as lively as ever. Without dew in the grass it would take him all day to catch a bottle full of good grasshoppers and he would have to crush many of them, slamming at them with his hat. He washed his hands at the stream. He was excited to be near it. Then he walked up to the tent. The hoppers were already jumping stiffly in the grass. In the bottle, warmed by the sun, they were jumping in a mass. Nick put in a pine stick as a cork. It plugged the mouth of the bottle enough, so the hoppers could not get out and left plenty of air passage.

He had rolled the log back and knew he could get grasshoppers there every morning.

Nick laid the bottle full of jumping grasshoppers

against a pine trunk. Rapidly he mixed some buckwheat flour with water and stirred it smooth, one cup of flour, one cup of water. He put a handful of coffee in the pot and dipped a lump of grease out of a can and slid it sputtering across the hot skillet. On the smoking skillet he poured smoothly the buckwheat batter. It spread like lava, the grease spitting sharply. Around the edges the buckwheat cake began to firm, then brown, then crisp. The surface was bubbling slowly to porousness. Nick pushed under the browned under surface with a fresh pine chip. He shook the skillet sideways and the cake was loose on the surface. I won't try and flop it, he thought. He slid the chip of clean wood all the way under the cake, and flopped it over onto its face. It sputtered in the pan.

When it was cooked Nick regreased the skillet. He used all the batter. It made another big flapjack and one smaller one.

Nick ate a big flapjack and a smaller one, covered with apple butter. He put apple butter on the third cake, folded it over twice, wrapped it in oiled paper and put it in his shirt pocket. He put the apple butter jar back in the pack and cut bread for two sandwiches.

In the pack he found a big onion. He sliced it in two and peeled the silky outer skin. Then he cut one half into slices and made onion sandwiches. He wrapped them in oiled paper and buttoned them in the other pocket of his khaki shirt. He turned the skillet upside down on the grill, drank the coffee, sweetened and yellow brown with the condensed milk in it, and tidied up the camp. It was a good camp.

Nick took his fly rod out of the leather rod-case, jointed it, and shoved the rod-case back into the tent. He put on the reel and threaded the line through the guides. He had to hold it from hand to hand, as he threaded it, or it would slip back through its own weight. It was a heavy, double tapered fly line. Nick had paid eight dollars for it a long time ago. It was made heavy to lift back in the air and come forward flat and heavy and straight to make it possible to cast a fly which has no weight. Nick opened the aluminum leader box. The leaders were coiled between the damp flannel pads. Nick had wet the pads at the water cooler on the train up to St. Ignace. In the damp pads the gut leaders had softened and Nick unrolled one and tied it by a loop at the end to the heavy fly line. He fastened a hook on the end of the leader. It was a small hook; very thin and springy.

Nick took it from his hook book, sitting with the rod across his lap. He tested the knot and the spring of the rod by pulling the line taut. It was a good feeling. He was careful not to let the hook bite into his finger.

He started down to the stream, holding his rod, the bottle of grasshoppers hung from his neck by a thong tied in half hitches around the neck of the bottle. His landing net hung by a hook from his belt. Over his shoulder was a long flour sack tied at each corner into an ear. The cord went over his shoulder. The sack flapped against his legs.

Nick felt awkward and professionally happy with all his equipment hanging from him. The grasshopper bottle swung against his chest. In his shirt the breast pockets bulged against him with the lunch and his fly book.

He stepped into the stream. It was a shock. His trousers clung tight to his legs. His shoes felt the gravel. The water was a rising cold shock.

Rushing, the current sucked against his legs. Where he stepped in, the water was over his knees. He waded with the current. The gravel slid under his shoes. He looked down at the swirl of water below each leg and tipped up the bottle to get a grasshopper.

The first grasshopper gave a jump in the neck of the bottle and went out into the water. He was sucked under in the whirl by Nick's right leg and came to the surface a little way down stream. He floated rapidly, kicking. In a quick circle, breaking the smooth surface of the water, he disappeared. A trout had taken him.

Another hopper poked his face out of the bottle. His antennæ wavered. He was getting his front legs out of the bottle to jump. Nick took him by the head and held him while he threaded the slim hook under his chin, down through his thorax and into the last segments of his abdomen. The grasshopper took hold of the hook with his front feet, spitting tobacco juice on it. Nick dropped him into the water.

Holding the rod in his right hand he let out line against the pull of the grasshopper in the current. He stripped off line from the reel with his left hand and let it run free. He could see the hopper in the little waves of the current. It went out of sight.

There was a tug on the line. Nick pulled against the taut line. It was his first strike. Holding the now living rod across the current, he brought in the line with his left hand. The rod bent in jerks, the trout pumping against the current. Nick knew it was a small one. He lifted the rod straight up in the air. It bowed with the pull.

He saw the trout in the water jerking with his head and body against the shifting tangent of the line in the stream.

Nick took the line in his left hand and pulled the trout, thumping tiredly against the current, to the surface. His back was mottled the clear, water-over-gravel color, his side flashing in the sun. The rod under his right arm, Nick stopped, dipping his right hand into the current. He held the trout, never still, with his moist right hand, while he unhooked the barb from his mouth, then dropped him back into the stream.

He hung unsteadily in the current, then settled to the bottom beside a stone. Nick reached down his hand to touch him, his arm to the elbow under water. The trout was steady in the moving stream, resting on the gravel, beside a stone. As Nick's fingers touched him, touched his smooth, cool, underwater feeling he was gone, gone in a shadow across the bottom of the stream.

He's all right, Nick thought. He was only tired.

He had wet his hand before he touched the trout, so he would not disturb the delicate mucus that covered him. If a trout was touched with a dry hand, a white fungus attacked the unprotected spot. Years before when he had fished crowded streams, with fly fishermen ahead of him and behind him, Nick had again and again come on dead trout, furry with white fungus, drifted against a rock, or floating belly up in some pool. Nick did not like to fish with other men on the river. Unless they were of your party, they spoiled it.

He wallowed down the stream, above his knees in the current, through the fifty yards of shallow water above the pile of logs that crossed the stream. He did not rebait his hook and held it in his hand as he waded. He was certain he could catch small trout in the shallows, but he did not want them. There would be no big trout in the shallows this time of day.

Now the water deepened up his thighs sharply and coldly. Ahead was the smooth dammed-back flood of water above the logs. The water was smooth and dark; on the left, the lower edge of the meadow; on the right the swamp.

Nick leaned back against the current and took a hopper from the bottle. He threaded the hopper on the hook and spat on him for good luck. Then he pulled several yards of line from the reel and tossed the hopper out ahead onto the fast, dark water. It floated down towards the logs, then the weight of the line pulled the bait under the surface. Nick held the rod in his right hand, letting the line run out through his fingers.

There was a long tug. Nick struck and the rod came alive and dangerous, bent double, the line tightening, coming out of water, tightening, all in a heavy, dangerous, steady pull. Nick felt the moment when the leader would break if the strain increased and let the line go.

The reel ratcheted into a mechanical shriek as the line went out in a rush. Too fast. Nick could not check it, the line rushing out, the reel note rising as the line ran out.

With the core of the reel showing, his heart feeling stopped with the excitement, leaning back against the current that mounted icily his thighs, Nick thumbed the reel hard with his left hand. It was awkward getting his thumb inside the fly reel frame.

As he put on pressure the line tightened into sudden hardness and beyond the logs a huge trout went high out of water. As he jumped, Nick lowered the tip of the rod. But he felt, as he dropped the tip to ease the strain, the moment when the strain was too great; the hardness too tight. Of course, the leader had broken. There was no mistaking the feeling when all spring left the line and it became dry and hard. Then it went slack.

His mouth dry, his heart down, Nick reeled in. He had never seen so big a trout. There was a heaviness, a power not to be held, and then the bulk of him, as he jumped. He looked as broad as a salmon.

Nick's hand was shaky. He reeled in slowly. The thrill had been too much. He felt, vaguely, a little sick, as though it would be better to sit down.

The leader had broken where the hook was tied to it. Nick took it in his hand. He thought of the trout somewhere on the bottom, holding himself steady over the gravel, far down below the light, under the logs, with the hook in his jaw. Nick knew the trout's teeth would cut through the snell of the hook. The hook would imbed itself in his jaw. He'd bet the trout was angry. Anything that size would be angry. That was a trout. He had been solidly hooked. Solid as a rock. He felt like a rock, too, before he started off. By God, he was a big one. By God, he was the biggest one I ever heard of.

Nick climbed out onto the meadow and stood, water running down his trousers and out of his shoes, his shoes squlchy. He went over and sat on the logs. He did not want to rush his sensations any.

He wriggled his toes in the water, in his shoes, and got out a cigarette from his breast pocket. He lit it and tossed the match into the fast water below the logs. A tiny trout rose at the match, as it swung around in the fast current. Nick laughed. He would finish the cigarette.

He sat on the logs, smoking, drying in the sun, the sun warm on his back, the river shallow ahead entering the woods, curving into the woods, shallows, light glittering, bit water-smooth rocks, cedars along the bank and white birches, the logs warm in the sun, smooth to sit on, without bark, gray to the touch; slowly the feeling of disappointment left him. It went away slowly, the feeling of disappointment that came sharply after the thrill that made his shoulders ache. It was all right now. His rod lying out on the logs, Nick tied a new hook on the leader, pulling the gut tight until it grimped into itself in a hard knot.

He baited up, then picked up the rod and walked to the far end of the logs to get into the water, where it was not too deep. Under and beyond the logs was a deep pool. Nick walked around the shallow shelf near the swamp shore until he came out on the shallow bed of the stream.

On the left, where the meadow ended and the woods began, a great elm tree was uprooted. Gone over in a storm, it lay back into the woods, its roots clotted with dirt, grass growing in them, rising a solid bank beside the stream. The river cut to the edge of the uprooted tree. From where Nick stood he could see deep channels, like ruts, cut in the shallow bed of the stream by the flow of the current. Pebbly where he stood and pebbly and full of boulders beyond; where it curved near the tree roots, the bed of the stream was marly and between the ruts of deep water green weed fronds swung in the current.

Nick swung the rod back over his shoulder and forward, and the line, curving forward, laid the grasshopper down on one of the deep channels in the weeds. A trout struck and Nick hooked him.

Holding the rod far out toward the uprooted tree and sloshing backward in the current, Nick worked the trout, plunging, the rod bending alive, out of the danger of the weeds into the open river. Holding the rod, pumping alive against the current, Nick brought the trout in. He rushed, but always came, the spring of the rod yielding to the rushes, sometimes jerking under water, but always bringing him in. Nick eased downstream with the rushes. The rod above his head he led the trout over the net, then lifted.

The trout hung heavy in the net, mottled trout back and silver sides in the meshes. Nick unhooked him; heavy sides, good to hold, big undershot jaw, and slipped him, heaving and big sliding, into the long sack that hung from his shoulders in the water.

Nick spread the mouth of the sack against the current and it filled, heavy with water. He held it up, the bottom in the stream, and the water poured out through the sides. Inside at the bottom was the big trout, alive in the water.

Nick moved downstream. The sack out ahead of him sunk heavy in the water, pulling from his shoulders.

It was getting hot, the sun hot on the back of his neck.

Nick had one good trout. He did not care about getting many trout. Now the stream was shallow and wide. There were trees along both banks. The trees of the left bank made short shadows on the current in the forenoon sun. Nick knew there were trout in each shadow. In the afternoon, after the sun had crossed toward the hills, the trout would be in the cool shadows on the other side of the stream.

The very biggest ones would lie up close to the bank. You could always pick them up there on the Black. When the sun was down they all moved out into the current. Just when the sun made the water blinding in the glare before it went down, you were liable to strike a big trout anywhere in the current. It was almost impossible to fish then, the surface of the water was blinding as a mirror in the sun. Of course, you could fish upstream, but in a stream like the Black, or this, you had to wallow against the current and in a deep place, the water piled up on you. It was no fun to fish upstream with this much current.

Nick moved along through the shallow stretch watching the banks for deep holes. A beech tree grew close beside the river, so that the branches hung down into the water. The stream went back in under the leaves. There were always trout in a place like that.

Nick did not care about fishing that hole. He was sure he would get hooked in the branches.

It looked deep though. He dropped the grasshopper so the current took it under water, back in under the overhanging branch. The line pulled hard and Nick struck. The trout threshed heavily, half out of water in the leaves and branches. The line was caught. Nick pulled hard and the trout was off. He reeled in and holding the hook in his hand, walked down the stream.

Ahead, close to the left bank, was a big log. Nick saw it was hollow; pointing up river the current entered it smoothly, only a little ripple spread each side of the log. The water was deepening. The top of the hollow log was gray and dry. It was partly in the shadow.

Nick took the cork out of the grasshopper bottle and a hopper clung to it. He picked him off, hooked him and tossed him out. He held the rod far out so that the hopper on the water moved into the current flowing into the hollow log. Nick lowered the rod and the hopper floated in. There was a heavy strike. Nick swung the rod against the pull. It felt as though he were hooked into the log itself, except for the live feeling.

He tried to force the fish out into the current. It came, heavily.

The line went slack and Nick thought the trout was gone. Then he saw him, very near, in the current, shaking his head, trying to get the hook out. His mouth was clamped shut. He was fighting the hook in the clear flowing current.

Looping in the line with his left hand, Nick swung the rod to make the line taut and tried to lead the trout toward the net, but he was gone, out of sight, the line pumping. Nick fought him against the current, letting him thump in the water against the spring of the rod. He shifted the rod to his left hand, worked the trout upstream, holding his weight, fighting on the rod, and then let him down into the net. He lifted him clear of the water, a heavy half circle in the net, the net dripping, unhooked him and slid him into the sack.

He spread the mouth of the sack and looked down in at the two big trout alive in the water.

Through the deepening water, Nick waded over to the hollow log. He took the sack off, over his head, the trout flopping as it came out of water, and hung it so the trout were deep in the water. Then he pulled himself up on the log and sat, the water from his trouser and boots running down into the stream. He laid his rod down, moved along to the shady end of the log and took the sandwiches out of his pocket. He dipped the sandwiches in the cold water. The current carried away the crumbs. He ate the sandwiches and dipped his hat full of water to drink, the water running out through his hat just ahead of his drinking.

It was cool in the shade, sitting on the log. He took a cigarette out and struck a match to light it. The match sunk into the gray wood, making a tiny furrow. Nick leaned over the side of the log, found a hard place and lit the match. He sat smoking and watching the river.

Ahead the river narrowed and went into a swamp. The river became smooth and deep and the swamp looked solid with cedar trees, their trunks close together, their branches solid. It would not be possible to walk through a swamp like that. The branches grew so low. You would have to keep almost level with the ground to move at all. You could not crash through the branches. That must be why the animals that lived in swamps were built the way they were, Nick thought.

He wished he had brought something to read. He felt like reading. He did not feel like going on into the swamp. He looked down the river. A big cedar slanted all the way across the stream. Beyond that the river went into the swamp.

Nick did not want to go in there now. He felt a reaction against deep wading with the water deepening up under his armpits, to hook big trout in places impossible to land them. In the swamp the banks were bare, the big cedars came together overhead, the sun did not come through, except in patches; in the fast deep water, in the half light, the fishing would be tragic. In the swamp fishing was a tragic adventure. Nick did not want it. He did not want to go down the stream any further today.

He took out his knife, opened it and stuck it in the log. Then he pulled up the sack, reached into it and brought out one of the trout. Holding him near the tail, hard to hold, alive, in his hand, he whacked him against the log. The trout quivered, rigid. Nick laid him on the log in the shade and broke the neck of the other fish the same way. He laid them side by side on the log. They were fine trout.

Nick cleaned them, slitting them from the vent to the tip of the jaw. All the insides and the gills and tongue came out in one piece. They were both males; long gray-white strips of milt, smooth and clean. All the insides clean and compact, coming out all together. Nick tossed the offal ashore for the minks to find.

He washed the trout in the stream. When he held them back up in the water they looked like live fish. Their color was not gone yet. He washed his hands and dried them on the log. Then he laid the trout on the sack spread out on the log, rolled them up in it, tied the bundle and put it in the landing net. His knife was still standing, blade stuck in the log. He cleaned it on the wood and put it in his pocket.

Nick stood up on the log, holding his rod, the landing net hanging heavy, then stepped into the water and splashed ashore. He climbed the bank and cut up into the woods, toward the high ground. He was going back to camp. He looked back. The river just showed through the trees. There were plenty of days coming when he could fish the swamp.

Babylon Revisited

F. Scott Fitzgerald (1896–1940)

Francis Scott Key Fitzgerald was born in St. Paul, Minnesota, and received his education in private schools. He entered Princeton in 1913, where he became a friend of Edmund Wilson and John Peale Bishop, but left before graduation to join the army. While stationed near Montgomery, Alabama, he met the beautiful and vivacious Zelda Sayre; they were married in 1920, after Fitzgerald had finished his first novel, *This Side of Paradise* (1920), a largely autobiographical account of the manners and morals of the new postwar generation. Its success and that of his early stories made Fitzgerald instantly famous as the spokesman for the "Jazz Age." The best of these stories are collected in *Flappers and Philosophers* (1921), *Tales of the Jazz Age* (1922), and *All the Sad Young Men* (1926). In 1924 the Fitzgeralds left New York for the Riviera and Paris, where they joined the expatriate world described in *Tender Is the Night. The Great Gatsby* (1925) was the culmination of the first half of Fitzgerald's career: in it the tragic limitations of the "American Dream" are movingly dramatized.

As the 1920s came to a frenzied close, Fitzgerald succumbed to personal and financial pressures, finding it more and more difficult to write. This sense of collapse is embodied in his last finished novel, *Tender Is the Night* (1934), and in stories such as "Babylon Revisited" (1931). During the early 1930s Zelda Fitzgerald suffered a mental breakdown and spent the rest of her life in a sanatorium. Fitzgerald moved to Hollywood, where he worked on films and began a novel, *The Last Tycoon,* based on his Hollywood experiences. It was unfinished at the time of his death in 1940. His last years were marked by a steady physical and psychological decline that Fitzgerald often handled with tragic dignity.

I

"And where's Mr. Campbell?" Charlie asked.

"Gone to Switzerland. Mr. Campbell's a pretty sick man, Mr. Wales."

"I'm sorry to hear that. And George Hardt?" Charlie inquired.

"Back in America, gone to work."

"And where is the Snow Bird?"

"He was in here last week. Anyway, his friend, Mr. Schaeffer, is in Paris."

Two familiar names from the long list of a year and a half ago. Charlie scribbled an address in his notebook and tore out the page.

"If you see Mr. Schaeffer, give him this," he said. "It's my brother-in-law's address. I haven't settled on a hotel yet."

He was not really disappointed to find Paris was so empty. But the stillness in the Ritz bar was strange and portentous. It was not an American bar any more—he felt polite in it, and not as if he owned it. It had gone back into France. He felt the stillness from the moment he got out of the taxi and saw the doorman, usually in a frenzy of activity at this hour, gossiping with a *chasseur* by the servants' entrance.

Passing through the corridor, he heard only a single, bored voice in the once-clamorous women's room. When he turned into the bar he travelled the twenty feet of green carpet with his eyes fixed straight ahead by old habit; and then, with his foot firmly on the rail, he turned and surveyed the room, encountering only a single pair of eyes that fluttered up from a newspaper in the corner. Charlie asked for the head barman, Paul, who in the latter days of the bull market had come to work in his own custom-built car—disembarking, however, with due nicety at the nearest corner. But Paul was at his country house today and Alix giving him information.

"No, no more," Charlie said, "I'm going slow these days."

Alix congratulated him: "You were going pretty strong a couple of years ago."

"I'll stick to it all right," Charlie assured him. "I've stuck to it for over a year and a half now."

"How do you find conditions in America?"

"I haven't been to America for months. I'm in business in Prague, representing a couple of concerns there. They don't know about me down there."

Alix smiled.

"Remember the night of George Hardt's bachelor dinner here?" said Charlie. "By the way, what's become of Claude Fessenden?"

Alix lowered his voice confidentially: "He's in Paris, but he doesn't come here any more. Paul doesn't allow it. He ran up a bill of thirty thousand francs, charging all his drinks and his lunches, and usually his dinner, for more than a year. And when Paul finally told him he had to pay, he gave him a bad check."

Alix shook his head sadly.

"I don't understand it, such a dandy fellow. Now he's all bloated up—" He made a plump apple of his hands.

Charlie watched a group of strident queens installing themselves in a corner.

"Nothing affects them," he thought. "Stocks rise and fall, people loaf or work, but they go on forever." The place oppressed him. He called for the dice and shook with Alix for the drink.

"Here for long, Mr. Wales?"

"I'm here for four or five days to see my little girl."

"Oh-h! You have a little girl?"

Outside, the fire-red, gas-blue, ghost-green signs shone smokily through the tranquil rain. It was late afternoon and the streets were in movement; the *bistros* gleamed. At the corner of the Boulevard des Capucines he took a taxi. The Place de la Concorde moved by in pink majesty; they crossed the logical Seine, and Charlie felt the sudden provincial quality of the left bank.

Charlie directed his taxi to the Avenue de l'Opera, which was out of his way. But he wanted to see the blue hour spread over the magnificent facade, and imagine that the cab horns, playing endlessly the first few bars of *Le Plus que Lent,* were the trumpets of the Second Empire. They were closing the iron grill in front of Brentano's Book-store, and people were already at dinner behind the trim little bourgeois hedge of Duvan's. He had never eaten at a really cheap restaurant in Paris. Five-course dinner, four francs fifty, eighteen cents, wine included. For some odd reason he wished that he had.

As they rolled on to the Left Bank and he felt its sudden provincialism, he thought, "I spoiled this city for myself. I didn't realize it, but the days came along one after another, and then two years were gone, and everything was gone, and I was gone."

He was thirty-five, and good to look at. The Irish mobility of his face was sobered by a deep wrinkle between his eyes. As he rang his brother-in-law's bell in the Rue Palatine, the wrinkle deepened till it pulled down his brows; he felt a cramping sensation in his belly. From behind the maid who opened the door darted a lovely little girl of nine who shrieked "Daddy!" and flew up, struggling like a fish, into his arms. She pulled his head around by one ear and set her cheek against his.

"My old pie," he said.

"Oh, daddy, daddy, daddy, daddy, dads, dads, dads!"

She drew him into the salon, where the family waited, a boy and girl his daughter's age, his sister-in-law and her husband. He greeted Marion with his voice pitched carefully to avoid either feigned enthusiasm or dislike, but her response was more frankly tepid, though she minimized her expression of unalterable distrust by directing her regard toward his child. The two men clasped hands in a friendly way and Lincoln Peters rested his for a moment on Charlie's shoulder. The room was warm and comfortably American. The three children moved intimately about, playing through the yellow oblongs that led to other rooms; the cheer of six o'clock spoke in the eager smacks of the fire and the sounds of French activity in the kitchen. But Charlie did not relax; his heart sat up rigidly in his body and he drew confidence from his daughter, who from time to time came close to him, holding in her arms the doll he had brought.

"Really extremely well," he declared in the answer to Lincoln's question. "There's a lot of business there that isn't moving at all, but we're doing even better than ever. In fact, damn well. I'm bringing my sister over from America next month to keep house for me. My income last year was bigger than it was when I had money. You see, the Czechs—"

His boasting was for a specific purpose; but after a moment, seeing a faint restiveness in Lincoln's eye, he changed the subject:

"Those are fine children of yours, well brought up, good manners."

"We think Honoria's a great little girl too."

Marion Peters came back from the kitchen. She was a tall woman with worried eyes, who had once possessed a fresh American loveliness. Charlie had never been sensitive to it and was always surprised when people spoke of how pretty she had been. From the first there had been an instinctive antipathy between them.

"Well, how do you find Honoria?" she asked.

"Wonderful. I was astonished how much she's grown in ten months. All the children are looking well."

"We haven't had a doctor for a year. How do you like being back in Paris?"

"It seems very funny to see so few Americans around."

"I'm delighted," Marion said vehemently. "Now at least you can go into a store without their assuming you're a millionaire. We've suffered like everybody, but on the whole it's a good deal pleasanter."

"But it was nice while it lasted," Charlie said. "We were sort of royalty, almost infallible, with a sort of magic around us. In the bar this afternoon"—he stumbled, seeing his mistake—"there wasn't a man I knew."

She looked at him keenly. "I should think you'd have had enough of bars."

"I only stayed a minute. I take one drink every afternoon, and no more."

"Don't you want a cocktail before dinner?" Lincoln asked.

"I take only one drink every afternoon, and I've had that."

"I hope you keep to it," said Marion.

Her dislike was evident in the coldness with which she spoke, but Charlie only smiled; he had larger plans. Her very aggressiveness gave him an advantage, and he knew enough to wait. He wanted them to initiate the discussion of what they knew had brought him to Paris.

At dinner he couldn't decide whether Honoria was most like him or her mother. Fortunate if she didn't combine the traits of both that had brought them to disaster. A great wave of protectiveness went over him. He thought he knew what to do for her. He believed in character; he wanted to jump back a whole generation and trust in character again as the eternally valuable element. Everything wore out.

He left soon after dinner, but not to go home. He was curious to see Paris by night with clearer and more judicious eyes than those of other days. He bought a *strapontin* for the Casino and watched Josephine Baker go through her chocolate arabesques.

After an hour he left and strolled toward Montmartre, up the Rue Pigalle into the Place Blanche. The rain had stopped and there were a few people in evening clothes disembarking from taxis in front of cabarets, and *cocottes* prowling singly or in pairs, and many Negroes. He passed a lighted door from which issued music, and stopped with a sense of familiarity; it was Bricktop's, where he had parted with so many hours and so much money. A few doors farther on he found another ancient rendezvous and incautiously put his head inside. Immediately an eager orchestra burst into sound, a pair of professional dancers leaped to their feet and a maître d'hôtel swooped toward him, crying, "Crowd just arriving, sir!" But he withdrew quickly.

"You have to be damn drunk," he thought.

Zelli's was closed, the bleak and sinister cheap hotels surrounding it were dark; up in the Rue Blanche there was more light and a local, colloquial French crowd. The Poet's Cave had disappeared, but the two great mouths of the Café of Heaven and Café of Hell still yawned—even devoured, as he watched, the meagre contents of a tourist bus—a German, a Japanese, and an American couple who glanced at him with frightened eyes.

So much for the effort and ingenuity of Montmartre. All the catering to vice and waste was on an utterly childish scale, and he suddenly realized the meaning of the word "dissipate"—to dissipate into thin air; to make nothing out of something. In the little hours of the night every move from place to place was an enormous human jump, an increase of paying for the privilege of slower and slower motion.

He remembered thousand-franc notes given to an orchestra for playing a single number, hundred-franc notes tossed to a doorman for calling a cab.

But it hadn't been given for nothing.

It had been given, even the most wildly squandered sum, as an offering to destiny that he might not remember the things most worth remembering, the things that now he would always remember—his child taken from his control, his wife escaped to a grave in Vermont.

In the glare of a *brasserie* a woman spoke to him. He bought her some eggs and coffee, and then, eluding her encouraging stare, gave her a twenty-franc note and took a taxi to his hotel.

II

He woke upon a fine fall day—football weather. The depression of yesterday was gone and he liked the people on the streets. At noon he sat opposite Honoria at Le Grand Vatel, the only restaurant he could think of not reminiscent of champagne dinners and long luncheons that began at two and ended in a blurred and vague twilight.

"Now, how about vegetables? Oughtn't you to have some vegetables?"

"Well, yes."

"Here's *épinards* and *chou-fleur* and carrots and *haricots.*"

"I'd like *chou-fleur.*"

"Wouldn't you like to have two vegetables?"

"I usually only have one at lunch."

The waiter was pretending to be inordinately fond of children. *"Qu'elle est mignonne la petite! Elle parle exactement comme une française."*

"How about dessert? Shall we wait and see?"

The waiter disappeared. Honoria looked at her father expectantly.

"What are we going to do?"

"First, we're going to that toy store in the Rue Saint-Honoré and buy you anything you like. And then we're going to the vaudeville at the Empire."

She hesitated. "I like it about the vaudeville, but not the toy store."

"Why not?"

"Well, you brought me this doll." She had it with her. "And I've got lots of things. And we're not rich any more, are we?"

"We never were. But today you are to have anything you want."

"All right," she agreed resignedly.

When there had been her mother and a French nurse he had been inclined to be strict; now he extended himself, reached out for a new tolerance; he must be both parents to her and not shut any of her out of communication.

"I want to get to know you," he said gravely. "First let me introduce myself. My name is Charles J. Wales, of Prague."

"Oh, daddy!" her voice cracked with laughter.

"And who are you, please?" he persisted, and she accepted a rôle immediately: "Honoria Wales, Rue Palatine, Paris."

"Married or single?"

"No, not married. Single."

He indicated the doll. "But I see you have a child, madame."

Unwilling to disinherit it, she took it to her heart and thought quickly: "Yes, I've been married, but I'm not married now. My husband is dead."

He went on quickly, "And the child's name?"

"Simone. That's after my best friend at school."

"I'm very pleased that you're doing so well at school."

"I'm third this month," she boasted. "Elsie"—that was her cousin—"is only about eighteenth, and Richard is about at the bottom."

"You like Richard and Elsie, don't you?"

"Oh, yes. I like Richard quite well and I like her all right."

Cautiously and casually he asked: "And Aunt Marion and Uncle Lincoln—which do you like best?"

"Oh, Uncle Lincoln, I guess."

He was increasingly aware of her presence. As they came in, a murmur of ". . . adorable" followed them, and now the people at the next table bent all their silences upon her, staring as if she were something no more conscious than a flower.

"Why don't I live with you?" she asked suddenly. "Because mama's dead?"

"You must stay here and learn more French. It would have been hard for daddy to take care of you so well."

"I don't really need much taking care of any more. I do everything for myself."

Going out of the restaurant, a man and a woman unexpectedly hailed him!

"Well, the old Wales!"

"Hello there, Lorraine. . . . Dunc."

Sudden ghosts out of the past: Duncan Schaeffer, a friend from college. Lorraine Quarrles, a lovely, pale blonde of thirty; one of a crowd who had helped them make months into days in the lavish times of three years ago.

"My husband couldn't come this year," she said, in answer to his question. "We're poor as hell. So he gave me two hundred a month and told me I could do my worst on that. . . . This your little girl?"

"What about coming back and sitting down?" Duncan asked.

"Can't do it." He was glad for an excuse. As always, he felt Lorraine's passionate, provocative attraction, but his own rhythm was different now.

"Well, how about dinner?" she asked.

"I'm not free. Give me your address and let me call you."

"Charlie, I believe you're sober," she said judicially. "I honestly believe he's sober, Dunc. Pinch him and see if he's sober."

Charlie indicated Honoria with his head. They both laughed.

"What's your address?" said Duncan sceptically.

He hesitated, unwilling to give the name of his hotel.

"I'm not settled yet. I'd better call you. We're going to see the vaudeville at the Empire."

"There! That's what I want to do," Lorraine said. "I want to see some clowns and acrobats and jugglers. That's just what we'll do, Dunc."

"We've got to do an errand first," said Charlie. "Perhaps we'll see you there."

"All right, you snob. . . . Good-by, beautiful little girl."

"Good-by."

Honoria bobbed politely.

Somehow, an unwelcome encounter. They liked him because he was functioning, because he was serious; they wanted to see him, because he was stronger than they were now, because they wanted to draw a certain sustenance from his strength.

At the Empire, Honoria proudly refused to sit upon her father's folded coat. She was already an individual with a code of her own, and Charlie was more and more absorbed by the desire of putting a little of himself into her before she crystallized utterly. It was hopeless to try to know her in so short a time.

Between the acts they came upon Duncan and Lorraine in the lobby where the band was playing.

"Have a drink?"

"All right, but not up at the bar. We'll take a table."

"The perfect father."

Listening abstractedly to Lorraine, Charlie watched Honoria's eyes leave their table, and he followed them wistfully about the room, wondering what they saw. He met her glance and she smiled.

"I like that lemonade," she said.

What had she said? What had he expected? Going home in a taxi afterward, he pulled her over until her head rested against his chest.

"Darling, do you ever think about your mother?"

"Yes, sometimes," she answered vaguely.

"I don't want you to forget her. Have you got a picture of her?"

"Yes, I think so. Anyhow, Aunt Marion has. Why don't you want me to forget her?"

"She loved you very much."

"I loved her too."

They were silent for a moment.

"Daddy, I want to come and live with you," she said suddenly.

His heart leaped; he had wanted it to come like this.

"Aren't you perfectly happy?"

"Yes, but I love you better than anybody. And you love me better than anybody, don't you, now that mummy's dead?"

"Of course I do. But you won't always like me best, honey. You'll grow up and meet somebody your own age and go marry him and forget you ever had a daddy."

"Yes, that's true," she agreed tranquilly.

He didn't go in. He was coming back at nine o'clock and he wanted to keep himself fresh and new for the thing he must say then.

"When you're safe inside, just show yourself in that window."

"All right. Good-by, dads, dads, dads, dads."

He waited in the dark street until she appeared, all warm and glowing, in the window above and kissed her fingers out into the night.

III

They were waiting. Marion sat behind the coffee service in a dignified black dinner dress that just faintly suggested mourning. Lincoln was walking up and down with the animation of one who had already been talking. They were as anxious as he was to get into the question. He opened it almost immediately:

"I suppose you know what I want to see you about—why I really came to Paris."

Marion played with the black stars on her necklace and frowned.

"I'm awfully anxious to have a home," he continued. "And I'm awfully anxious to have Honoria in it. I appreciate your taking in Honoria for her mother's sake, but things have changed now"—he hesitated and then continued more forcibly—"changed radically with me, and I want to ask you to reconsider the matter. It would be silly for me to deny that about three years ago I was acting badly—"

Marion looked up at him with hard eyes.

"—but all that's over. As I told you, I haven't had more than a drink a day for over a year, and I take that drink deliberately, so that the idea of alcohol won't get too big in my imagination. You see the idea?"

"No," said Marion succinctly.

"It's a sort of stunt I set myself. It keeps the matter in proportion."

"I get you," said Lincoln. "You don't want to admit it's got any attraction for you."

"Something like that. Sometimes I forget and don't take it. But I try to take it. Anyhow, I couldn't afford to drink in my position. The people I represent are more than satisfied with what I've done, and I'm bringing my sister over from Burlington to keep house for me, and I want awfully to have Honoria too. You know that even when her mother and I weren't getting along well we never let anything that happened touch Honoria. I know she's fond of me and I know I'm able to take care of her and—well, there you are. How do you feel about it?"

He knew that now he would have to take a beating. It would last an hour or two hours, and it would be difficult, but if he modulated his inevitable resentment to the chastened attitude of the reformed sinner, he might win his point in the end.

Keep your temper, he told himself. You don't want to be justified. You want Honoria.

Lincoln spoke first: "We've been talking it over ever since we got your letter last month. We're happy to have Honoria here. She's a dear little thing, and we're glad to be able to help her, but of course that isn't the question—"

Marion interrupted suddenly. "How long are you going to stay sober, Charlie?" she asked.

"Permanently, I hope."

"How can anybody count on that?"

"You know I never did drink heavily until I gave up business and came over here with nothing to do. Then Helen and I began to run around with—"

"Please leave Helen out of it. I can't bear to hear you talk about her like that."

He stared at her grimly; he had never been certain how fond of each other the sisters were in life.

"My drinking only lasted about a year and a half—from the time we came over until I—collapsed."

"It was time enough."

"It was time enough," he agreed.

"My duty is entirely to Helen," she said. "I try to think what she would have wanted me to do. Frankly, from the night you did that terrible thing you haven't really existed for me. I can't help that. She was my sister."

"Yes."

"When she was dying she asked me to look out for Honoria. If you hadn't been in a sanitarium then, it might have helped matters."

He had no answer.

"I'll never in my life be able to forget the morning when Helen knocked at my door, soaked to the skin and shivering, and said you'd locked her out."

Charlie gripped the sides of the chair. This was more difficult than he expected; he wanted to launch out into a long expostulation and explanation, but he only said: "The night I locked her out—" and she interrupted, "I don't feel up to going over that again."

After a moment's silence Lincoln said: "We're getting off the subject. You want Marion to set aside her legal guardianship and give you Honoria. I think the main point for her is whether she has confidence in you or not."

"I don't blame Marion," Charlie said slowly, "but I think she can have entire confidence in me. I had a good record up to three years ago. Of course, it's within human possibilities I might go wrong any time. But if we wait much longer I'll lose Honoria's childhood and my chance for a home." He shook his head, "I'll simply lose her, don't you see?"

"Yes, I see," said Lincoln.

"Why didn't you think of all this before?" Marion asked.

"I suppose I did, from time to time, but Helen and I were getting along badly. When I consented to the guardianship, I was flat on my back in a sanitarium and the market had cleaned me out. I knew I'd acted badly, and I thought if it would bring any peace to Helen, I'd agree to anything. But now it's different, I'm functioning, I'm behaving damn well, so far as—"

"Please don't swear at me," Marion said.

He looked at her, startled. With each remark the force of her dislike became more and more apparent. She had built up all her fear of life into one wall and faced it toward him. This trivial reproof was possibly the result of some trouble with the cook several hours before. Charlie became increasingly alarmed at leaving Honoria in this atmosphere of hostility against himself; sooner or later it would come out, in a word here, a shake of the head there, and some of that distrust would be irrevocably implanted in Honoria. But he pulled his temper down out of his face and shut it up inside him; he had won a point, for Lincoln realized the absurdity of Marion's remark and asked her lightly since when she had objected to the word "damn."

"Another thing," Charlie said: "I'm able to give her certain advantages now. I'm going to take a French governess to Prague with me. I've got a lease on a new apartment—"

He stopped, realizing that he was blundering. They couldn't be expected to accept with equanimity the fact that his income was again twice as large as their own.

"I suppose you can give her more luxuries than we can," said Marion. "When you were throwing away money we were living along watching every ten francs. . . . I suppose you'll start doing it again."

"Oh, no," he said. "I've learned. I worked hard for ten years, you know—until I got lucky in the market, like so many people. Terribly lucky. It didn't seem any use working any more, so I quit. It won't happen again."

There was a long silence. All of them felt their nerves straining, and for the first time in a year Charlie wanted a drink. He was sure now that Lincoln Peters wanted him to have his child.

Marion shuddered suddenly; part of her saw that Charlie's feet were planted on the earth now, and her own maternal feeling recognized the naturalness of his desire; but she had lived for a long time with a prejudice—a prejudice founded on a curious disbelief in her sister's happiness, and which, in the shock of one terrible night, had turned to hatred for him. It had all happened at a point in her life where the discouragement of ill health and adverse circumstances made it necessary for her to believe in tangible villainy and a tangible villain.

"I can't help what I think!" she cried out suddenly. "How much you were responsible for Helen's death, I don't know. It's something you'll have to square with your own conscience."

An electric current of agony surged through him; for a moment he was almost on his feet, an unuttered sound echoing in his throat. He hung on to himself for a moment, another moment.

"Hold on there," said Lincoln uncomfortably. "I never thought you were responsible for that."

"Helen died of heart trouble," Charlie said dully.

"Yes, heart trouble." Marion spoke as if the phrase had another meaning for her.

Then, in the flatness that followed her outburst, she saw him plainly and she knew he had somehow arrived at control over the situation. Glancing at her husband, she found no help from him, and as abruptly as if it were a matter of no importance, she threw up the sponge.

"Do what you like!" she cried, springing up from her chair. "She's your child. I'm not the person to stand in your way. I think if it were my child I'd rather see her—" She managed to check herself. "You two decide it. I can't stand this. I'm sick. I'm going to bed."

She hurried from the room; after a moment Lincoln said:

"This has been a hard day for her. You know how strongly she feels—" His voice was almost apologetic: "When a woman gets an idea in her head."

"Of course."

"It's going to be all right. I think she sees now that you—can provide for the child, and so we can't very well stand in your way or Honoria's way."

"Thank you, Lincoln."

"I'd better go along and see how she is."

"I'm going."

He was still trembling when he reached the street, but a walk down the Rue Bonaparte to the quais set him up, and as he crossed the Seine, fresh and new by the quai lamps, he felt exultant. But back in his room he couldn't sleep. The image of Helen haunted him. Helen whom he had loved so until they had senselessly begun to abuse each other's love, tear it into shreds. On that terrible February night that Marion remembered so vividly, a slow quarrel had gone on for hours. There was a scene at the Florida, and then he attempted to take her home, and then she kissed young Webb at a table; after that there was what she had hysterically said. When he arrived home alone he turned the key in the lock in wild anger. How could he know she would arrive an hour later alone, that there would be a snowstorm in which she wandered about in slippers, too confused to find a taxi? Then the aftermath, her escaping pneumonia by a miracle, and all the attendant horror. They were "reconciled," but that was the beginning of the end, and Marion, who had seen with her own eyes and who imagined it to be one of many scenes from her sister's martyrdom, never forgot.

Going over it again brought Helen nearer, and in the white, soft light that steals upon half sleep near morning he found himself talking to her again. She said that he was perfectly right about Honoria and she wanted Honoria to be with him. She said she was glad he was being good and doing better. She said a lot of other things—very friendly things—but she was in a swing in a white dress, and swinging faster and faster all the time, so that at the end he could not hear clearly all that she said.

IV

He woke up feeling happy. The door of the world was open again. He made plans, vistas, futures for Honoria and himself, but suddenly he grew sad, remembering all the plans he and Helen had made. She had not planned to die. The present was the thing—work to do and someone to love. But not to love too much, for he knew the injury that a father can do to a daughter or a mother to a son by attaching them too closely; afterward, out in the world, the child would seek in the marriage partner the same blind tenderness and, failing probably to find it, turn against love and life.

It was another bright, crisp day. He called Lincoln Peters at the bank where he worked and asked if he could count on taking Honoria when he left for Prague. Lincoln agreed that there was no reason for delay. One thing—the legal guardianship. Marion wanted to retain that a while longer. She was upset by the whole matter, and it would oil things if she felt that the situation was still in her control for another year.

Charlie agreed, wanted only the tangible, visible child.

Then the question of a governess. Charlie sat in a gloomy agency and talked to a cross Bernaise and to a buxom Breton peasant, neither of whom he could have endured. There were others whom he would see tomorrow.

He lunched with Lincoln Peters at Griffons, trying to keep down his exultation.

"There's nothing quite like your own child," Lincoln said. "But you understand how Marion feels too."

"She's forgotten how hard I worked for seven years there," Charlie said. "She just remembers one night."

"There's another thing." Lincoln hesitated. "While you and Helen were tearing around Europe throwing money away, we were just getting along. I didn't touch any of the prosperity because I never got ahead enough to carry anything but my insurance. I think Marion felt there was some kind of injustice in it—you not even working toward the end, and getting richer and richer."

"It went just as quick as it came," said Charlie.

"Yes, a lot of it stayed in the hands of *chasseurs* and saxophone players and maîtres d'hôtel—well, the big party's over now. I just said that to explain Marion's feeling about those crazy years. If you drop in about six o'clock tonight before Marion's too tired, we'll settle the details on the spot."

Back at his hotel, Charlie found a *pneumatique* that had been redirected from the Ritz bar where Charlie had left his address for the purpose of finding a certain man.

DEAR CHARLIE: You were so strange when we saw you the other day that I wondered if I did something to offend you. If so, I'm not conscious of it. In fact, I have thought about you too much for the last year, and it's always been in the back of my mind that I might see you if I came over here. We *did* have such good times that crazy spring, like the night you and I stole the butcher's tricycle, and the time we tried to call on the president and you had the old derby rim and the wire cane. Everybody seems so old lately, but I don't feel old a bit. Couldn't we get together some time today for old time's sake? I've got a vile hang-over for the moment, but will be feeling better this afternoon and will look for you about five in the sweat-shop at the Ritz.

Always devotedly,
LORRAINE.

His first feeling was one of awe that he had actually, in his mature years, stolen a tricycle and pedalled Lorraine all over the Étoile between the small hours and dawn. In retrospect it was a nightmare, Locking out Helen didn't fit in with any other act of his life, but the tricycle incident did—it was one of many. How many weeks or months of dissipation to arrive at that condition of utter irresponsibility?

He tried to picture how Lorraine had appeared to him then—very attractive; Helen was unhappy about it, though she said nothing. Yesterday, in the restaurant, Lorraine had seemed trite, blurred, worn away. He emphatically did not want to see her, and he was glad Alix had not given away his hotel address. It was a relief to think, instead, of Honoria, to think of Sundays spent with her and of saying good morning to her and of knowing she was there in his house at night, drawing her breath in the darkness.

At five he took a taxi and bought presents for all the Peters—a piquant cloth doll, a box of Roman soldiers, flowers for Marion, big linen hankerchiefs for Lincoln.

He saw, when he arrived in the apartment, that Marion had accepted the inevitable. She greeted him now as though he were a recalcitrant member of the family, rather than a menacing outsider. Honoria had been told she was going; Charlie was glad to see that her tact made her conceal her excessive happiness. Only on his lap did she whisper her delight and the question "When?" before she slipped away with the other children.

He and Marion were alone for a minute in the room, and on an impulse he spoke out boldly:

"Family quarrels are bitter things. They don't go according to any rules. They're not like aches or wounds; they're more like splits in the skin that won't heal because there's not enough material. I wish you and I could be on better terms."

"Some things are hard to forget," she answered. "It's a question of confidence." There was no answer to this and presently she asked, "When do you propose to take her?

"As soon as I can get a governess. I hoped the day after tomorrow."

"That's impossible. I've got to get her things in shape. Not before Saturday."

He yielded. Coming back into the room, Lincoln offered him a drink.

"I'll take my daily whisky," he said.

It was warm here, it was a home, people together by a fire. The children felt very safe and important; the mother and father were serious, watchful. They had things to do for the children more important than his visit here. A spoonful of medicine was, after all, more important than the strained relations between Marion and himself. They were not dull people, but they were very much in the grip of life and circumstances. He wondered if he couldn't do something to get Lincoln out of his rut at the bank.

A long peal at the door-bell; the *bonne à toute faire* passed through and went down the corridor. The door opened upon another long ring, and then voices, and the three in the salon looked up expectantly; Richard moved to bring the corridor within his range of vision, and Marion rose. Then the maid came back along the corridor, closely followed by the voices, which developed under the light into Duncan Schaeffer and Lorraine Quarrles.

They were gay, they were hilarious, they were roaring with laughter. For a moment Charlie was astounded; unable to understand how they ferreted out the Peters' address.

"Ah-h-h!" Duncan wagged his finger roguishly at Charlie. "Ah-h-h!"

They both slid down another cascade of laughter. Anxious and at a loss, Charlie shook hands with them quickly and presented them to Lincoln and Marion. Marion nodded, scarcely speaking. She had drawn back a step toward the fire; her little girl stood beside her, and Marion put an arm about her shoulder.

With growing annoyance at the intrusion, Charlie waited for them to explain themselves. After some concentration Duncan said: "We came to invite you out to dinner. Lorraine and I insist that all this shishi, cagy business 'bout your address got to stop."

Charlie came closer to them, as if to force them backward down the corridor.

"Sorry, but I can't. Tell me where you'll be and I'll phone you in half an hour.

This made no impression. Lorraine sat down suddenly on the side of a chair, and focusing her eyes on Richard, cried, "Oh, what a nice little boy! Come here, little boy." Richard glanced at his mother, but did not move. With a perceptible shrug of her shoulders, Lorraine turned back to Charlie:

"Come and dine. Sure your cousins won' mine. See you so sel'om. Or solemn."

"I can't," said Charlie sharply. "You two have dinner and I'll phone you."

Her voice became suddenly unpleasant. "All right, we'll go. But I remember once when you hammered on my door at four A.M. I was enough of a good sport to give you a drink. Come on, Dunc."

Still in slow motion, with blurred, angry faces, with uncertain feet, they retired along the corridor.

"Good night," Charlie said.

"Good night!" responded Lorraine emphatically.

When he went back into the salon Marion had not moved, only now her son was standing in the circle of her other arm. Lincoln was still swinging Honoria back and forth like a pendulum from side to side.

"What an outrage!" Charlie broke out. "What an absolute outrage!"

Neither of them answered. Charlie dropped into an armchair, picked up his drink, set it down again and said:

"People I haven't seen for two years having the colossal nerve—"

He broke off. Marion had made the sound "Oh!" in one swift, furious breath, turned her body from him with a jerk and left the room.

Lincoln set down Honoria carefully.

"You children go in and start your soup," he said, and when they obeyed, he said to Charlie:

"Marion's not well and she can't stand shocks. That kind of people make her really physically sick."

"I didn't tell them to come here. They wormed your name out of somebody. They deliberately—"

"Well, it's too bad. It doesn't help matters. Excuse me a minute."

Left alone, Charlie sat tense in his chair. In the next room he could hear the children eating, talking in monosyllables, already oblivious to the scene between their elders. He heard a murmur of conversation from a farther room and then the ticking bell of a telephone receiver picked up, and in a panic he moved to the other side of the room and out of earshot.

In a minute Lincoln came back. "Look here, Charlie. I think we'd better call off dinner for tonight. Marion's in bad shape."

"Is she angry with me?"

"Sort of," he said, almost roughly. "She's not strong and—"

"You mean she's changed her mind about Honoria?"

"She's pretty bitter right now. I don't know. You phone me at the bank tomorrow."

"I wish you'd explain to her I never dreamed these people would come here. I'm just as sore as you are."

"I couldn't explain anything to her now."

Charlie got up. He took his coat and hat and started down the corridor. Then he opened the door of the dining room and said in a strange voice, "Good night, children."

Honoria rose and ran around the table to hug him.

"Good night, sweetheart," he said vaguely, and then trying to make his voice more tender, trying to conciliate something, "Good night, dear children."

V

Charlie went directly to the Ritz bar with the furious idea of finding Lorraine and Duncan, but they were not there, and he realized that in any case there was nothing he could do. He had not touched his drink at the Peters', and now he ordered a whisky-and-soda. Paul came over to say hello.

"It's a great change," he said sadly. "We do about half the business we did. So many fellows I hear about back in the States lost everything, maybe not in the first crash, but then in the second. Your friend George Hardt lost every cent, I hear. Are you back in the States?"

"No, I'm in business in Prague."

"I heard that you lost a lot in the crash."

"I did," and he added grimly, "but I lost everything I wanted in the boom."

"Selling short."

"Something like that."

Again the memory of those days swept over him like a nightmare—the people they had met travelling; the people who couldn't add a row of figures or speak a coherent sentence. The little man Helen had consented to dance with at the ship's party, who had insulted her ten feet from the table; the women and girls carried screaming with drink or drugs out of public places—

—The men who locked their wives out in the snow, because the snow of twenty-nine wasn't real snow. If you didn't want it to be snow, you just paid some money.

He went to the phone and called the Peters' apartment; Lincoln answered.

"I called up because this thing is on my mind. Has Marion said anything definite?"

"Marion's sick," Lincoln answered shortly. "I know this thing isn't altogether your fault, but I can't have her go to pieces about it. I'm afraid we'll have to let it slide for six months; I can't take the chance of working her up to this state again."

"I see."

"I'm sorry, Charlie."

He went back to his table. His whisky glass was empty, but he shook his head when Alix looked at it questionably. There wasn't much he could do now except send Honoria some things; he would send her a lot of things tomorrow. He thought rather angrily that this was just money—he had given so many people money. . . .

"No, no more," he said to another waiter. "What do I owe you?"

He would come back some day; they couldn't make him pay forever. But he wanted his child, and nothing was much good now, beside that fact. He wasn't young any more, with a lot of nice thoughts and dreams to have by himself. He was absolutely sure Helen wouldn't have wanted him to be so alone.

Dry September

William Faulkner (1897–1962)

William Faulkner was born in New Albany, Mississippi, but his family soon moved to nearby Oxford (the "Jefferson" of his stories and novels). Faulkner's ancestors had been active in Mississippi life for three generations, and his great-grandfather had written a romantic novel. Faulkner left high school before graduation and enlisted in the Royal Canadian Flying Corps, but the war ended before he could see active service. After the war he entered the University of Mississippi for a time, worked as postmaster in Oxford, and then moved to New Orleans, where he came to know Sherwood Anderson. After a trip to Europe he settled in Oxford, which remained his home for the greater part of his career.

The early novels, *Soldier's Pay* (1926) and *Mosquitoes* (1927), reveal the influence of Hemingway and Fitzgerald; but in *Sartoris* (1929) and *The Sound and the Fury* (1929) Faulkner began to flesh out his mythical world, Yoknapatawpha County, "William Faulkner, sole owner & proprietor." Stories of this world dominate his first two collections, *These 13*

(1931, which contains "Dry September") and *Doctor Martino and Other Stories* (1934). Between 1929 and 1942, when the *Go Down, Moses* story cycle was published, Faulkner explored his legendary county in eight novels and four collections of stories. Among his greatest works are *The Sound and the Fury, As I Lay Dying* (1930), *Light in August* (1932), and *Absalom, Absalom!* (1936). His works published after 1942, such as *Intruder in the Dust* (1948), *A Fable* (1954), and the last two Snopes novels, *The Town* (1957) and *The Mansion* (1959), often lack the intensity of vision found in his greatest fiction. He was awarded the Nobel Prize for Literature in 1950.

1

Through the bloody September twilight, aftermath of sixty-two rainless days, it had gone like a fire in dry grass—the rumor, the story, whatever it was. Something about Miss Minnie Cooper and a Negro. Attacked, insulted, frightened: none of them, gathered in the barber shop on that Saturday evening where the ceiling fan stirred, without freshening it, the vitiated air, sending back upon them, in recurrent surges of stale pomade and lotion, their own stale breath and odors, knew exactly what had happened.

"Except it wasn't Will Mayes," a barber said. He was a man of middle age; a thin, sand-colored man with a mild face, who was shaving a client. "I know Will Mayes. He's a good nigger. And I know Miss Minnie Cooper, too."

"What do you know about her?" a second barber said.

"Who is she?" the client said. "A young girl?"

"No," the barber said. "She's about forty, I reckon. She aint married. That's why I dont believe—"

"Believe, hell!" a hulking youth in a sweat-stained silk shirt said. "Wont you take a white woman's word before a nigger's?"

"I dont believe Will Mayes did it," the barber said. "I know Will Mayes."

"Maybe you know who did it, then. Maybe you already got him out of town, you damn niggerlover."

"I dont believe anybody did anything. I dont believe anything happened. I leave it to you fellows if them ladies that get old without getting married dont have notions that a man cant—"

"Then you are a hell of a white man," the client said. He moved under the cloth. The youth had sprung to his feet.

"You dont?" he said. "Do you accuse a white woman of lying?"

The barber held the razor poised above the half-risen client. He did not look around.

"It's this durn weather," another said. "It's enough to make a man do anything. Even to her."

Nobody laughed. The barber said in his mild, stubborn tone: "I aint accusing nobody of nothing. I just know and you fellows know how a woman that never—"

"You damn niggerlover!" the youth said.

"Shut up, Butch," another said. "We'll get the facts in plenty of time to act."

"Who is? Who's getting them?" the youth said. "Facts, hell! I—"

"You're a fine white man," the client said. "Aint you?" In his frothy beard he looked like a desert rat in the moving pictures. "You tell them, Jack," he said to the youth. "If there aint any white men in this town, you can count on me, even if I aint only a drummer and a stranger."

"That's right, boys," the barber said. "Find out the truth first. I know Will Mayes."

"Well, by God!" the youth shouted. "To think that a white man in this town—"

"Shut up, Butch," the second speaker said. "We got plenty of time."

The client sat up. He looked at the speaker. "Do you claim that anything excuses a nigger attacking a white woman? Do you mean to tell me you are a white man and you'll stand for it? You better go back North where you came from. The South dont want your kind here."

"North what?" the second said. "I was born and raised in this town."

"Well, by God!" the youth said. He looked about with a strained, baffled gaze, as if he was trying to remember what it was he wanted to say or to do. He drew his sleeve across his sweating face. "Damn if I'm going to let a white woman—"

"You tell them, Jack," the drummer said. "By God, if they—"

The screen door crashed open. A man stood in the floor, his feet apart and his heavy-set body poised easily. His white shirt was open at the throat; he wore a felt hat. His hot, bold glance swept the group. His name was McLendon. He had commanded troops at the front in France and had been decorated for valor.

"Well," he said, "are you going to sit there and let a black son rape a white woman on the streets of Jefferson?"

Butch sprang up again. The silk of his shirt clung flat to his heavy shoulders. At each armpit was a dark halfmoon. "That's what I been telling them! That's what I—"

"Did it really happen?" a third said. "This aint the first man scare she ever had, like Hawkshaw says. Wasn't there something about a man on the kitchen roof, watching her undress, about a year ago?"

"What?" the client said. "What's that?" The barber had been slowly forcing him back into the chair; he arrested himself reclining, his head lifted, the barber still pressing him down.

McLendon whirled on the third speaker. "Happen? What the hell difference does it make? Are you going to let the black sons get away with it until one really does it?"

"That's what I'm telling them!" Butch shouted. He cursed, long and steady, pointless.

"Here, here," a fourth said. "Not so loud. Dont talk so loud."

"Sure," McLendon said; "no talking necessary at all. I've done my talking. Who's with me?" He poised on the balls of his feet, roving his gaze.

The barber held the drummer's face down, the razor poised. "Find out the facts first, boys. I know Willy Mayes. It wasn't him. Let's get the sheriff and do this thing right."

McLendon whirled upon him his furious, rigid face. The barber did not look away. They looked like men of different races. The other barbers had ceased also above their prone clients. "You mean to tell me," McLendon said, "that you'd take a nigger's word before a white woman's? Why, you damn nigger-loving—"

The third speaker rose and grasped McLendon's arm; he too had been a soldier. "Now, now. Let's figure this thing out. Who knows anything about what really happened?"

"Figure out hell!" McLendon jerked his arm free. "All that're with me get up from there. The ones that aint—" He roved his gaze, dragging his sleeve across his face.

Three men rose. The drummer in the chair sat up. "Here," he said, jerking at the cloth about his neck; "get this rag off me. I'm with him. I dont live here, but by God, if our mothers and wives and sisters—" He smeared the cloth over his face and flung it to the floor. McLendon stood in the floor and cursed the others. Another rose and moved toward him. The remainder sat uncomfortable, not looking at one another, then one by one they rose and joined him.

The barber picked the cloth from the floor. He began to fold it neatly. "Boys, dont do that. Will Mayes never done it. I know."

"Come on," McLendon said. He whirled. From his hip pocket protruded the butt of a heavy automatic pistol. They went out. The screen door crashed behind them reverberant in the dead air.

The barber wiped the razor carefully and swiftly, and put it away, and ran to the rear, and took his hat from the wall. "I'll be back as soon as I can," he said to the other barbers. "I cant let—" He went out, running. The two other barbers followed him to the door and caught it on the rebound, leaning out and looking up the street after him. The air was flat and dead. It had a metallic taste at the base of the tongue.

"What can he do?" the first said. The second one was saying "Jees Christ, Jees Christ" under his breath. "I'd just as lief be Will Mayes as Hawk, if he gets McLendon riled."

"Jees Christ, Jees Christ," the second whispered.

"You reckon he really done it to her?" the first said.

2

She was thirty-eight or thirty-nine. She lived in a small frame house with her invalid mother and a thin, sallow, unflagging aunt, where each morning between ten and eleven she would appear on the porch in a lace-trimmed boudoir cap, to sit swinging in the porch swing until noon. After dinner she lay down for a while, until the afternoon began to cool. Then, in one of the three or four new voile dresses which she had each summer, she would go downtown to spend the afternoon in the stores with the other ladies, where they would handle the goods and haggle over the prices in cold, immediate voices, without any intention of buying.

She was of comfortable people—not the best in Jefferson, but good people enough—and she was still on the slender side of ordinary looking, with a bright, faintly haggard manner and dress. When she was young she had had a slender, nervous body and a sort of hard vivacity which had enabled her for a time to ride upon the crest of the town's social life as exemplified by the high school party and church social period of her contemporaries while still children enough to be unclassconscious.

She was the last to realize that she was losing ground; that those among whom she had been a little brighter and louder flame than any other were beginning to learn the pleasure of snobbery—male—and retaliation—female. That was when her face began to wear that bright, haggard look. She still carried it to parties on shadowy porticoes and summer lawns, like a mask or a flag, with that bafflement of furious repudiation of truth in her eyes. One evening at a party she heard a boy and two girls, all schoolmates, talking. She never accepted another invitation.

She watched the girls with whom she had grown up as they married and got homes and children, but no man ever called on her steadily until the children of the other girls had been calling her "aunty" for several years, the while their mothers told them in bright voices about how popular Aunt Minnie had been as a girl. Then the town began to see her driving on Sunday afternoons with the cashier in the bank. He was a widower of about forty—a high-colored man, smelling always faintly of the barber shop or of whisky. He owned the first automobile in town, a red runabout; Minnie had the first motoring bonnet and veil the town ever saw. Then the town began to say: "Poor Minnie." "But she is old enough to take care of herself," others said. That was when she began to ask her old schoolmates that their children call her "cousin" instead of "aunty."

It was twelve years now since she had been relegated into adultery by public opinion, and eight years since the cashier had gone to a Memphis bank, returning for one day each Christmas, which he spent at an annual bachelors' party at a hunting club on the river. From behind their curtains the neighbors would see the party pass, and during the over-the-way Christmas day visiting they would tell her about him, about how well he looked, and how they heard that he was prospering in the city, watching with bright, secret eyes her haggard, bright face. Usually by that hour there would be the scent of whisky on her breath. It was supplied her by a youth, a clerk at the soda fountain: "Sure; I buy it for the old gal. I reckon she's entitled to a little fun."

Her mother kept to her room altogether now; the gaunt aunt ran the house. Against that background Minnie's bright dresses, her idle and empty days, had a quality of furious unreality. She went out in the evenings only with women now, neighbors, to the moving pictures. Each afternoon she dressed in one of the new dresses and went downtown alone, where her young "cousins" were already strolling in the late afternoons with their delicate, silken heads and thin, awkward arms and conscious hips, clinging to one another or shrieking and giggling with paired boys in the soda fountain when she passed and went on along the serried store fronts, in the doors of which the sitting and lounging men did not even follow her with their eyes any more.

3

The barber went swiftly up the street where the sparse lights, insect-swirled, glared in rigid and violent suspension in the lifeless air. The day had died in a pall of dust; above the darkened square, shrouded by the spent dust, the sky was as clear as the inside of a brass bell. Below the east was a rumor of the twice-waxed moon.

When he overtook them McLendon and three others were getting into a car parked in an alley. McLendon stooped his thick head, peering out beneath the top. "Changed your mind, did you?" he said. "Damn good thing; by God, tomorrow when this town hears about how you talked tonight—"

"Now, now," the other ex-soldier said. "Hawkshaw's all right. Come on, Hawk; jump in."

"Will Mayes never done it, boys," the barber said. "If anybody done it. Why, you all know well as I do there aint any town where they got better niggers than us. And you know how a lady will kind of think things about men when there aint any reason to, and Miss Minnie anyway—"

"Sure, sure," the soldier said. "We're just going to talk to him a little; that's all."

"Talk hell!" Butch said. "When we're through with the—"

"Shut up, for God's sake!" the soldier said. "Do you want everybody in town—"

"Tell them, by God!" McLendon said. "Tell every one of the sons that'll let a white woman—"

"Let's go; let's go: here's the other car." The second car slid squealing out of a cloud of dust at the alley mouth. McLendon started his car and took the lead. Dust lay like fog in the street. The street lights hung nimbused as in water. They drove on out of town.

A rutted lane turned at right angles. Dust hung above it too, and above all the land. The dark bulk of the ice plant, where the Negro Mayes was night watchman, rose against the sky. "Better stop here, hadn't we?" the soldier said. McLendon did not reply. He hurled the car up and slammed to a stop, the headlights glaring on the blank wall.

"Listen here, boys," the barber said; "if he's here, dont that prove he never done it? Dont it? If it was him, he would run. Dont you see he would?" The second car came up and stopped. McLendon got down; Butch sprang down beside him. "Listen, boys," the barber said.

"Cut the lights off!" McLendon said. The breathless dark rushed down. There was no sound in it save their lungs as they sought air in the parched dust in which for two months they had lived; then the diminishing crunch of McLendon's and Butch's feet, and a moment later McLendon's voice:

"Will! . . . Will!"

Below the east the wan hemorrhage of the moon increased. It heaved above the ridge, silvering the air, the dust, so that they seemed to breathe, live, in a bowl of molten lead. There was no sound of nightbird nor insect, no sound save their breathing and a faint ticking of contracting metal about the cars. Where their bodies touched one another they seemed to sweat dryly, for no moisture came. "Christ!" a voice said; "let's get out of here."

But they didn't move until vague noises began to grow out of the darkness ahead; then they got out and waited tensely in the breathless dark. There was another sound: a blow, a hissing expulsion of breath and McLendon cursing in undertone. They stood a moment longer, then they ran forward. They ran in a stumbling clump, as though they were fleeing something. "Kill him, kill the son," a voice whispered. McLendon flung them back.

"Not here," he said. "Get him into the car." "Kill him, kill the black son!" the voice murmured. They dragged the Negro to the car. The barber had waited beside the car. He could feel himself sweating and he knew he was going to be sick at the stomach.

"What is it, captains?" the Negro said. "I aint done nothing. 'Fore God, Mr John." Someone produced handcuffs. They worked busily about the Negro as though he were a post, quiet, intent, getting in one another's way. He submitted to the handcuffs, looking swiftly and constantly from dim face to dim face. "Who's here, captains?" he said, leaning to peer into the faces until they could feel his breath and smell his sweaty reek. He spoke a name or two. "What you all say I done, Mr John?"

McLendon jerked the car door open. "Get in!" he said.

The Negro did not move. "What you all going to do with me, Mr John? I aint done nothing. White folks, captains, I aint done nothing: I swear 'fore God." He called another name.

"Get in!" McLendon said. He struck the Negro. The others expelled their breath in a dry hissing and struck him with random blows and he whirled and cursed them, and swept his manacled hands across their faces and slashed the barber upon the mouth, and the barber struck him also. "Get him in there," McLendon said. They pushed at him. He ceased struggling and got in and sat quietly as the others took their places. He sat between the barber and the soldier, drawing his limbs in so as not to touch them, his eyes going swiftly and constantly from face to face. Butch clung to the running board. The car moved on. The barber nursed his mouth with his handkerchief.

"What's the matter, Hawk?" the soldier said.

"Nothing," the barber said. They regained the highroad and turned away from town. The second car dropped back out of the dust. They went on, gaining speed; the final fringe of houses dropped behind.

"Goddamn, he stinks!" the soldier said.

"We'll fix that," the drummer in front beside McLendon said. On the running board Butch cursed into the hot rush of air. The barber leaned suddenly forward and touched McLendon's arm.

"Let me out, John," he said.

"Jump out, niggerlover," McLendon said without turning his head. He drove swiftly. Behind them the sourceless lights of the second car glared in the dust. Presently McLendon turned into a narrow road. It was rutted with disuse. It led back to an abandoned brick kiln—a series of reddish mounds and weed- and vine-choked vats without bottom. It had been used for pasture once, until one day the owner missed one of his mules. Although he prodded carefully in the vats with a long pole, he could not even find the bottom of them.

"John," the barber said.

"Jump out, then," McLendon said, hurling the car along the ruts. Beside the barber the Negro spoke:

"Mr Henry."

The barber sat forward. The narrow tunnel of the road rushed up and past. Their motion was like an extinct furnace blast: cooler, but utterly dead. The car bounded from rut to rut.

"Mr Henry," the Negro said.

The barber began to tug furiously at the door. "Look out, there!" the soldier said, but the barber had already kicked the door open and swung onto the running board. The soldier leaned across the Negro and grasped at him, but he had already jumped. The car went on without checking speed.

The impetus hurled him crashing through dust-sheathed weeds, into the ditch. Dust puffed about him, and in a thin, vicious crackling of sapless stems he lay choking and retching until the second car passed and died away. Then he rose and limped on until he reached the highroad and turned toward town, brushing at his clothes with his hands. The moon was higher, riding high and clear of the dust at last, and after a while the town began to glare beneath the dust. He went on, limping. Presently he heard cars and the glow of them grew in the dust behind him and he left the road and crouched again in the weeds until they passed. McLendon's car came last now. There were four people in it and Butch was not on the running board.

They went on; the dust swallowed them; the glare and the sound died away. The dust of them hung for a while, but soon the eternal dust absorbed it again. The barber climbed back onto the road and limped on toward town.

4

As she dressed for supper on that Saturday evening, her own flesh felt like fever. Her hands trembled among the hooks and eyes, and her eyes had a feverish look, and her hair swirled crisp and crackling under the comb. While she was still dressing the friends called for her and sat while she donned her sheerest underthings and stockings and a new voile dress. "Do you feel strong enough to go out?" they said, their eyes bright too, with a dark glitter. "When you have had time to get over the shock, you must tell us what happened. What he said and did; everything."

In the leafed darkness, as they walked toward the square, she began to breathe deeply, something like a swimmer preparing to dive, until she ceased trembling, the four of them walking slowly because of the terrible heat and out of solicitude for her. But as they neared the square she began to tremble again, walking with her head up, her hands clenched at her sides, their voices about her murmurous, also with that feverish, glittering quality of their eyes.

They entered the square, she in the center of the group, fragile in her fresh dress. She was trembling worse. She walked slower and slower, as children eat ice cream, her head up and her eyes bright in the haggard banner of her face, passing the hotel and the coatless drummers in chairs along the curb looking around at her: "That's the one: see? The one in pink in the middle." "Is that her? What did they do with the nigger? Did they—?" "Sure. He's all right." "All right, is he?" "Sure. He went on a little trip." Then the drug store, where even the young men lounging in the doorway tipped their hats and followed with their eyes the motion of her hips and legs when she passed.

They went on, passing the lifted hats of the gentlemen, the suddenly ceased voices, deferent, protective. "Do you see?" the friends said. Their voices sounded like long, hovering sighs of hissing exultation. "There's not a Negro on the square. Not one."

They reached the picture show. It was like a miniature fairyland with its lighted lobby and colored lithographs of life caught in its terrible and beautiful mutations. Her lips began to tingle. In the dark, when the picture began, it would be all right; she could hold back the laughing so it would not waste away so fast and so soon. So she hurried on before the turning faces, the undertones of low astonishment, and they took their accustomed places where she could see the aisle against the silver glare and the young men and girls coming in two and two against it.

The lights flicked away; the screen glowed silver, and soon life began to unfold, beautiful and passionate and sad, while still the young men and girls entered, scented and sibilant in the half dark, their paired backs in silhouette delicate and sleek, their slim, quick bodies awkward, divinely young, while beyond them the silver dream accumulated, inevitably on and on. She began to laugh. In trying to suppress it, it made more noise than ever; heads began to turn. Still laughing, her friends raised her and led her out, and she stood at the curb, laughing on a high, sustained note, until the taxi came up and they helped her in.

They removed the pink voile and the sheer underthings and the stockings, and put her to bed, and cracked ice for her temples, and sent for the doctor. He was hard to locate, so they ministered to her with hushed ejaculations, renewing the ice and fanning her. While the ice was fresh and cold she stopped laughing and lay still for a time, moaning only a little. But soon the laughing welled again and her voice rose screaming.

"Shhhhhhhhhhh! Shhhhhhhhhhhhhh!" they said, freshening the icepack, smoothing her hair, examining it for gray; "poor girl!" Then to one another: "Do you suppose anything really happened?" their eyes darkly aglitter, secret and passionate. "Shhhhhhhhhh! Poor girl! Poor Minnie!"

5

It was midnight when McLendon drove up to his neat new house. It was trim and fresh as a birdcage and almost as small, with its clean, green-and-white paint. He locked the car and mounted the porch and entered. His wife rose from a chair beside the reading lamp. McLendon stopped in the floor and stared at her until she looked down.

"Look at that clock," he said, lifting his arm, pointing. She stood before him, her face lowered, a magazine in her hands. Her face was pale, strained, and weary-looking. "Haven't I told you about sitting up like this, waiting to see when I come in?"

"John," she said. She laid the magazine down. Poised on the balls of his feet, he glared at her with his hot eyes, his sweating face.

"Didn't I tell you?" He went toward her. She looked up then. He caught her shoulder. She stood passive, looking at him.

"Don't, John. I couldn't sleep . . . The heat; something. Please, John. You're hurting me."

"Didn't I tell you?" He released her and half struck, half flung her across the chair, and she lay there and watched him quietly as he left the room.

He went on through the house, ripping off his shirt, and on the dark, screened porch at the rear he stood and mopped his head and shoulders with the shirt and flung it away. He took the pistol from his hip and laid it on the table beside the bed, and sat on the bed and removed his shoes, and rose and slipped his trousers off. He was sweating again already, and he stooped and hunted furiously for the shirt. At last he found it and wiped his body again, and, with his body pressed against the dusty screen, he stood panting. There was no movement, no sound, not even an insect. The dark world seemed to lie stricken beneath the cold moon and the lidless stars.

Flowering Judas

Katherine Anne Porter (1890–)

Born in Indian Creek, Texas, Katherine Anne Porter was educated in a convent and at Southern girls' schools. She worked on a newspaper in Chicago and later played bit parts in movies. In 1921 she travelled to Mexico to study Aztec and Mayan art, and Mexico became the setting for several of her tales. Her first published story, "Maria Conception," appeared when she was thirty. Always a fastidious artist, Katherine Anne Porter did not rush into print, and her first collection of stories, *Flowering Judas* (1930), marked the appearance of a mature writer. It was followed by *Pale Horse, Pale Rider* (1939) and *The Leaning Tower* (1944). Her only novel, *Ship of Fools,* was published in 1962, although it had been conceived as early as 1931. During most of her career Katherine Anne Porter has worked as a university lecturer and free-lance essayist. Her *Collected Short Stories* (1965) won the National Book Award and the Pulitzer Prize for fiction.

Braggioni sits heaped upon the edge of a straight-backed chair much too small for him, and sings to Laura in a furry, mournful voice. Laura has begun to find reasons for avoiding her own house until the latest possible moment, for Braggioni is there almost every night. No matter how late she is, he will be sitting there with a surly, waiting expression, pulling at his kinky yellow hair, thumbing the strings of his guitar, snarling a tune under his breath. Lupe the Indian maid meets Laura at the door, and says with a flicker of a glance towards the upper room, "He waits."

Laura wishes to lie down, she is tired of her hairpins and the feel of her long tight sleeves, but she says to him, "Have you a new song for me this evening?" If he says yes, she asks him to sing it. If he says no, she remembers his favorite one, and asks him to sing it again. Lupe brings her a cup of chocolate and a plate of rice, and Laura eats at the small table under the lamp, first inviting Braggioni, whose answer is always the same: "I have eaten, and besides, chocolate thickens the voice."

Laura says, "Sing, then," and Braggioni heaves himself into song. He scratches the guitar familiarly as though it were a pet animal, and sings passionately off key, taking the high notes in a prolonged painful squeal. Laura, who haunts the markets listening to the ballad singers, and stops every day to hear the blind boy playing his reed-flute in Sixteenth of September Street, listens to Braggioni with pitiless courtesy, because she dares not smile at his miserable performance. Nobody dares to smile at him. Braggioni is cruel to everyone, with a kind of specialized insolence, but he is so vain of his talents, and so sensitive to slights, it would require a cruelty and vanity greater than his own to lay a finger on the vast cureless wound of his self-esteem. It would require courage, too, for it is dangerous to offend him, and nobody has this courage.

Braggioni loves himself with such tenderness and amplitude and eternal charity that his followers—for he is a leader of men, a skilled revolutionist, and his skin has been punctured in honorable warfare—warm themselves in the reflected glow, and say to each other: "He has a real nobility, a love of humanity raised above mere personal affections." The excess of this self-love has flowed out, inconveniently for her, over Laura, who, with so many others, owes her comfortable situation and her salary to him. When he is in a very good humor, he tells her, "I am tempted to forgive you for being a *gringa. Gringita!*" and Laura, burning, imagines herself leaning forward suddenly, and with a sound back-handed slap wiping the suety smile from his face. If he notices her eyes at these moments he gives no sign.

She knows what Braggioni would offer her, and she must resist tenaciously without appearing to resist, and if she could avoid it she would not admit even to herself the slow drift of his intention. During these long evenings which have spoiled a long month for her, she sits in her deep chair with an open book on her knees, resting her eyes on the consoling rigidity of the printed page when the sight and sound of Braggioni singing threaten to identify themselves with all her remembered afflictions and to add their weight to her uneasy premonitions of the future. The gluttonous bulk of Braggioni has become a symbol of her many disillusions, for a revolutionist should be lean, animated by heroic faith, a vessel of abstract virtues. This is nonsense, she knows it now and is ashamed of it. Revolution must have leaders, and leadership is a career for energetic men. She is, her comrades tell her, full of romantic error, for what she defines as cynicism in them is merely "a developed sense of reality." She is almost too willing to say, "I am wrong, I suppose I don't really understand the principles," and afterward she makes a secret truce with herself, determined not to surrender her will to such expedient logic. But she cannot help feeling that she has been betrayed irreparably by the disunion between her way of living and her feeling of what life should be, and at times she is almost contented to rest in this sense of grievance as a private store of consolation. Sometimes she wishes to run away, but she stays. Now she longs to fly out of this room, down the narrow stairs, and into the street where the houses lean together like conspirators under a single mottled lamp, and leave Braggioni singing to himself.

Instead she looks at Braggioni, frankly and clearly, like a good child who understands the rules of behavior. Her knees cling together under sound blue serge, and her round white collar is not purposely nun-like. She wears the uniform of an idea, and has renounced vanities. She was born Roman Catholic, and in spite of her fear of being seen by someone who might make a scandal of it, she slips now and again into some crumbling little church, kneels on the chilly stone, and says a Hail Mary on the gold rosary she bought in Tehuantepec. It is no good and she ends by examining the altar with its tinsel flowers and ragged brocades, and feels tender about the battered doll-shape of some male saint whose white, lace-trimmed drawers hang limply around his ankles below the hieratic dignity of his velvet robe. She has encased herself in a set of principles derived from her early training, leaving no detail of gesture or of personal taste untouched, and for this reason she will not wear lace made on machines. This is her private heresy, for in her special group the machine is sacred, and will be the salvation of the workers. She loves fine lace, and there is a tiny edge of fluted cobweb on this collar, which is one of twenty precisely alike, folded in blue tissue paper in the upper drawer of her clothes chest.

Braggioni catches her glance solidly as if he had been waiting for it, leans forward, balancing his paunch between his spread knees, and sings with tremendous emphasis, weighing his words. He has, the song relates, no father and no mother, nor even a friend to console him; lonely as a wave of the sea he comes and goes, lonely as a wave. His mouth opens round and yearns sideways, his balloon cheeks grow oily with the labor of song. He bulges marvelously in his expensive garments. Over his lavender collar, crushed upon a purple necktie, held by a diamond hoop: over his ammunition belt of tooled leather worked in silver, buckled cruelly around his gasping middle: over the tops of his glossy yellow shoes Braggioni swells with ominous ripeness, his mauve silk hose stretched taut, his ankles bound with the stout leather thongs of his shoes.

When he stretches his eyelids at Laura she notes

again that his eyes are the true tawny yellow cat's eyes. He is rich, not in money, he tells her, but in power, and this power brings with it the blameless ownership of things, and the right to indulge his love of small luxuries. "I have a taste for the elegant refinements," he said once, flourishing a yellow silk handkerchief before her nose. "Smell that? It is Jockey Club, imported from New York." Nonetheless he is wounded by life. He will say so presently. "It is true everything turns to dust in the hand, to gall on the tongue." He sighs and his leather belt creaks like a saddle girth. "I am disappointed in everything as it comes. Everything." He shakes his head. "You, poor thing, you will be disappointed too. You are born for it. We are more alike than you realize in some things. Wait and see. Some day you will remember what I have told you, you will know that Braggioni was your friend."

Laura feels a slow chill, a purely physical sense of danger, a warning in her blood that violence, mutilation, a shocking death, wait for her with lessening patience. She has translated this fear into something homely, immediate, and sometimes hesitates before crossing the street. "My personal fate is nothing, except as the testimony of a mental attitude," she reminds herself, quoting from some forgotten philosophic primer, and is sensible enough to add, "Anyhow, I shall not be killed by an automobile if I can help it."

"It may be true I am as corrupt, in another way, as Braggioni," she thinks in spite of herself, "as callous, as incomplete," and if this is so, any kind of death seems preferable. Still she sits quietly, she does not run. Where could she go? Uninvited she has promised herself to this place; she can no longer imagine herself as living in another country, and there is no pleasure in remembering her life before she came here.

Precisely what is the nature of this devotion, its true motives, and what are its obligations? Laura cannot say. She spends part of her days in Xochimilco, near by, teaching Indian children to say in English, "The cat is on the mat." When she appears in the classroom they crowd about her with smiles on their wise, innocent, clay-colored faces, crying, "Good morning, my titcher!" in immaculate voices, and they make of her desk a fresh garden of flowers every day.

During her leisure she goes to union meetings and listens to busy important voices quarreling over tactics, methods, internal politics. She visits the prisoners of her own political faith in their cells, where they entertain themselves with counting cockroaches, repenting of their indiscretions, composing their memoirs, writing out manifestoes and plans for their comrades who are still walking about free, hands in pockets, sniffing fresh air. Laura brings them food and cigarettes and a little money, and she brings messages disguised in equivocal phrases from the men outside who dare not set foot in the prison for fear of disappearing into the cells kept empty for them. If the prisoners confuse night and day, and complain, "Dear little Laura, time doesn't pass in this infernal hole, and I won't know when it is time to sleep unless I have a reminder," she brings them their favorite narcotics, and says in a tone that does not wound them with pity, "Tonight will really be night for you," and though her Spanish amuses them, they find her comforting, useful. If they lose patience and all faith, and curse the slowness of their friends in coming to their rescue with money and influence, they trust her not to repeat everything, and if she inquires, "Where do you think we can find money, or influence?" they are certain to answer, "Well, there is Braggioni, why doesn't he do something?"

She smuggles letters from headquarters to men hiding from firing squads in back streets in mildewed houses, where they sit in tumbled beds and talk bitterly as if all Mexico were at their heels, when Laura knows positively they might appear at the band concert in the Alameda on Sunday morning, and no one would notice them. But Braggioni says, "Let them sweat a little. The next time they may be careful. It is very restful to have them out of the way for a while." She is not afraid to knock on any door in any street after midnight, and enter in the darkness, and say to one of these men who is really in danger: "They will be looking for you—seriously—tomorrow morning after six. Here is some money from Vicente. Go to Vera Cruz and wait."

She borrows money from the Roumanian agitator to give to his bitter enemy the Polish agitator. The favor of Braggioni is their disputed territory, and Braggioni holds the balance nicely, for he can use them both. The Polish agitator talks love to her over café tables, hoping to exploit what he believes is her secret sentimental preference for him, and he gives her misinformation which he begs her to repeat as the solemn truth to certain persons. The Roumanian is more adroit. He is generous with his money in all good causes, and lies to her with an air of ingenuous candor, as if he were her good friend and confidant. She never repeats anything they may say. Braggioni never asks questions. He has other ways to discover all that he wishes to know about them.

Nobody touches her, but all praise her gray eyes, and the soft, round under lip which promises gayety, yet is always grave, nearly always firmly closed: and they cannot understand why she is in Mexico. She walks back and forth on her errands, with puzzled eyebrows, carrying her little folder of drawings and music and school papers. No dancer dances more beautifully than Laura walks, and she inspires some amusing, unexpected ardors, which cause little gossip, because nothing comes of them. A young captain who had been a soldier in Zapata's army attempted, during a horseback ride near Cuernavaca, to express his desire for her with the noble simplicity befitting a rude folk-hero: but gently, because he was gentle. This gentleness was his defeat, for when he alighted, and removed her foot from the stirrup, and essayed to draw her down into his arms, her horse, ordinarily a tame one, shied fiercely, reared and plunged away. The young hero's horse careered blindly after his stablemate, and the hero did not return to the hotel until rather late that evening. At breakfast he came to her table in full charro dress, gray buckskin jacket and trousers with strings of silver buttons down the leg, and he was in a humorous, careless mood. "May I sit with you?" and "You are a wonderful rider. I was terrified that you might be thrown and dragged. I should never have forgiven myself. But I cannot admire you enough for your riding!"

"I learned to ride in Arizona," said Laura.

"If you will ride with me again this morning, I promise you a horse that will not shy with you," he said. But Laura remembered that she must return to Mexico City at noon.

Next morning the children made a celebration and spent their playtime writing on the blackboard, "We lov ar ticher," and with tinted chalks they drew wreaths of flowers around the words. The young hero wrote her a letter: "I am a very foolish, wasteful, impulsive man. I should have first said I love you, and then you would not have run away. But you shall see me again." Laura thought, "I must send him a box of colored crayons," but she was trying to forgive herself for having spurred her horse at the wrong moment.

A brown, shock-haired youth came and stood in her patio one night and sang like a lost soul for two hours, but Laura could think of nothing to do about it. The moonlight spread a wash of gauzy silver over the clear spaces of the garden, and the shadows were cobalt blue. The scarlet blossoms of the Judas tree were dull purple, and the names of the colors repeated themselves automatically in her mind, while she watched not the boy, but his shadow, fallen like a dark garment across the fountain rim, trailing in the water. Lupe came silently and whispered expert counsel in her ear: "If you will throw him one little flower, he will sing another song or two and go away." Laura threw the flower, and he sang a last song and went away with the flower tucked in the band of his hat. Lupe said, "He is one of the organizers of the Typographers Union, and before that he sold corridos in the Merced market, and before that, he came from Guanajuato, where I was born. I would not trust any man, but I trust least those from Guanajuato."

She did not tell Laura that he would be back again the next night, and the next, nor that he would follow her at a certain fixed distance around the Merced market, through the Zócolo, up Francisco I. Madero Avenue, and so along the Paseo de la Reforma to Chapultepec Park, and into the Philosopher's Footpath, still with that flower withering in his hat, and an indivisible attention in his eyes.

Now Laura is accustomed to him, it means nothing except that he is nineteen years old and is observing a convention with all propriety, as though it were founded on a law of nature, which in the end it might well prove to be. He is beginning to write poems which he prints on a wooden press, and he leaves them stuck like handbills in her door. She is pleasantly disturbed by the abstract, unhurried watchfulness of his black eyes which will in time turn easily towards another object. She tells herself that throwing the flower was a mistake, for she is twenty-two years old and knows better; but she refuses to regret it, and persuades herself that her negation of all external events as they occur is a sign that she is gradually perfecting herself in the stoicism she strives to cultivate against that disaster she fears, though she cannot name it.

She is not at home in the world. Every day she teaches children who remain strangers to her, though she loves their tender round hands and their charming opportunist savagery. She knocks at unfamiliar doors not knowing whether a friend or a stranger shall answer, and even if a known face emerges from the sour gloom of that unknown interior, still it is the face of a stranger. No matter what this stranger says to her, nor what her message to him, the very cells of her flesh reject knowledge and kinship in one monotonous word. No. No. No. She draws her strength from this one holy talismanic word which does not suffer her to be led into evil. Denying everything, she may walk anywhere in safety, she looks at everything without amazement.

No, repeats this firm unchanging voice of her blood; and she looks at Braggioni without amazement. He is a great man, he wishes to impress this simple girl who covers her great round breasts with thick dark cloth, and who hides long, invaluably beautiful legs under a heavy skirt. She is almost thin except for the incomprehensible fullness of her breasts, like a nursing mother's, and Braggioni, who considers himself a judge of women, speculates again on the puzzle of her notorious virginity, and takes the liberty of speech which she permits without a sign of modesty, indeed, without any sort of sign, which is disconcerting.

"You think you are so cold, *gringita!* Wait and see. You will surprise yourself some day! May I be there to advise you!" He stretches his eyelids at her, and his ill-humored cat's eyes waver in a separate glance for the two points of light marking the opposite ends of a smoothly drawn path between the swollen curve of her breasts. He is not put off by that blue serge, nor by her resolutely fixed gaze. There is all the time in the world. His cheeks are bellying with the wind of song. "O girl with the dark eyes," he sings, and reconsiders. "But yours are not dark. I can change all that. O girl with the green eyes, you have stolen my heart away!" then his mind wanders to the song, and Laura feels the weight of his attention being shifted elsewhere. Singing thus, he seems harmless, he is quite harmless, there is nothing to do but sit patiently and say "No," when the moment comes. She draws a full breath, and her mind wanders also, but not far. She dares not wander too far.

Not for nothing has Braggioni taken pains to be a good revolutionist and a professional lover of humanity. He will never die of it. He has the malice, the cleverness, the wickedness, the sharpness of wit, the hardness of heart, stipulated for loving the world profitably. *He will never die of it.* He will live to see himself kicked out from his feeding trough by other hungry world-saviors. Traditionally he must sing in spite of his life which drives him to bloodshed, he tells Laura, for his father was a Tuscany peasant who drifted to Yucatan and married a Maya woman: a woman of race, an aristocrat. They gave him the love and knowledge of music, thus: and under the rip of his thumbnail, the strings of the instrument complain like exposed nerves.

Once he was called Delgadito by all the girls and married women who ran after him; he was so scrawny all his bones showed under his thin cotton clothing, and he could squeeze his emptiness to the very backbone with his two hands. He was a poet and the revolution was only a dream then; too many women loved him and sapped away his youth, and he could never find enough to eat anywhere, anywhere! Now he is a leader of men, crafty men who whisper in his ear, hungry men who wait for hours outside his office for a word with him, emaciated men with wild faces who waylay him at the street gate with a timid, "Comrade, let me tell you . . ." and they blow the foul breath from their empty stomachs in his face.

He is always sympathetic. He gives them handfuls of small coins from his own pocket, he promises them work, there will be demonstrations, they must join the unions and attend the meetings, above all they must be on the watch for spies. They are closer to him than his own brothers, without them he can do nothing—until tomorrow, comrade!

Until tomorrow. "They are stupid, they are lazy, they are treacherous, they would cut my throat for nothing," he says to Laura. He has good food and abundant drink, he hires an automobile and drives in the Paseo on Sunday morning, and enjoys plenty of sleep in a soft bed beside a wife who dares not disturb him; and he sits pampering his bones in easy billows of fat, singing to Laura, who knows and thinks these things about him. When he was fifteen, he tried to drown himself because he loved a girl, his first love, and she laughed at him. "A thousand women have paid for that," and his tight little mouth turns down at the corners. Now he perfumes his hair with Jockey Club, and confides to Laura: "One woman is really as good as another for me, in the dark. I prefer them all."

His wife organizes unions among the girls in the cigarette factories, and walks in picket lines, and even speaks at meetings in the evening. But she cannot be brought to acknowledge the benefits of true liberty. "I tell her I must have my freedom, net. She does not understand my point of view." Laura has heard this many times. Braggioni scratches the guitar and meditates. "She is an instinctively virtuous woman, pure gold, no doubt of that. If she were not, I should lock her up, and she knows it."

His wife, who works so hard for the good of the factory girls, employs part of her leisure lying on the floor weeping because there are so many women in the world, and only one husband for her, and she never knows where nor when to look for him. He told her: "Unless you can learn to cry when I am not here, I must go away for good." That day he went away and took a room at the Hotel Madrid.

It is this month of separation for the sake of higher principles that has been spoiled not only for Mrs. Braggioni, whose sense of reality is beyond criticism, but for Laura, who feels herself bogged in a nightmare. Tonight Laura envies Mrs. Braggioni, who is alone, and free to weep as much as she pleases about a concrete wrong. Laura has just come from a visit to the prison, and she is waiting for tomorrow with a bitter anxiety as if tomorrow may not come, but time may be caught immovably in this hour, with herself transfixed, Braggioni singing on forever, and Eugenio's body not yet discovered by the guard.

Braggioni says: "Are you going to sleep?" Almost before she can shake her head, he begins telling her about the May-day disturbances coming on in Morelia, for the Catholics hold a festival in honor of the Blessed Virgin, and the Socialists celebrate their martyrs on that day. "There will be two independent processions, starting from either end of town, and they will march until they meet, and the rest depends . . ." He asks her to oil and load his pistols. Standing up, he unbuckles his ammunition belt, and spreads it laden across her knees. Laura sits with the shells slipping through the cleaning cloth dipped in oil, and he says again he cannot understand why she works so hard for the revolutionary idea unless she loves some man who is in it. "Are you not in love with someone?" "No," says Laura. "And no one is in love with you?" "No." "Then it is your own fault. No woman need go begging. Why, what is the matter with you? The legless beggar woman in the Alameda has a perfectly faithful lover. Did you know that?"

Laura peers down the pistol barrel and says nothing, but a long, slow faintness rises and subsides in her; Braggioni curves his swollen fingers around the throat of the guitar and softly smothers the music out of it, and when she hears him again he seems to have forgotten her, and is speaking in the hypnotic voice he uses when talking in small rooms to a listening, close-gathered crowd. Some day this world, now seemingly so composed and eternal, to the edges of every sea shall be merely a tangle of gaping trenches, of crashing walls and broken bodies. Everything must be torn from its accustomed place where it has rotted for centuries, hurled skyward and distributed, cast down again clean as rain, without separate identity. Nothing shall survive that the stiffened hands of poverty have created for the rich and no one shall be left alive except the elect spirits destined to procreate a new world cleansed of cruelty and injustice, ruled by benevolent anarchy: "Pistols are good, I love them, cannon are even better, but in the end I pin my faith to good dynamite," he concludes, and strokes the pistol lying in her hands. "Once I dreamed of destroying this city, in case it offered resistance to General Ortíz, but it fell into his hands like an overripe pear."

He is made restless by his own words, rises and stands waiting. Laura holds up the belt to him: "Put that on, and go kill somebody in Morelia, and you will be happier," she says softly. The presence of death in the room makes her bold. "Today, I found Eugenio going into a stupor. He refused to allow me to call the prison doctor. He had taken all the tablets I brought him yesterday. He said he took them because he was bored."

"He is a fool, and his death is his own business," says Braggioni, fastening his belt carefully.

"I told him if he had waited only a little while longer, you would have got him set free," says Laura. "He said he did not want to wait."

"He is a fool and we are well rid of him," says Braggioni, reaching for his hat.

He goes away. Laura knows his mood has changed, she will not see him any more for a while. He will send word when he needs her to go on errands into strange streets, to speak to the strange faces that will appear, like clay masks with the power of human speech, to mutter their thanks to Braggioni for his help. Now she is free, and she thinks, I must run while there is time. But she does not go.

Braggioni enters his own house where for a month his wife has spent many hours every night weeping and tangling her hair upon her pillow. She is weeping now, and she weeps more at the sight of him, the cause of all her sorrows. He looks about the room. Nothing is changed, the smells are good and familiar, he is well acquainted with the woman who comes toward him with no reproach except grief on her face. He says to her tenderly: "You are so good, please don't cry any more, you dear good creature." She says, "Are you tired, my angel? Sit here and I will wash your feet." She brings a bowl of water, and kneeling, unlaces his shoes, and when from her knees she raises her sad eyes under her blackened lids, he is sorry for everything, and bursts into tears. "Ah, yes, I am hungry, I am tired, let us eat something together," he says, between sobs. His wife leans her head on his arm and says, "Forgive me!" and this time he is refreshed by the solemn, endless rain of her tears.

Laura takes off her serge dress and puts on a white linen nightgown and goes to bed. She turns her head a little to one side, and lying still, reminds herself that it is time to sleep. Numbers tick in her brain like little clocks, soundless doors close of themselves around her. If you would sleep, you must not remember anything, the children will say tomorrow, good morning, my teacher, the poor prisoners who come every day bringing flowers to their jailor. 1-2-3-4-5—it is monstrous to confuse love with revolution, night with day, life with death—ah, Eugenio!

The tolling of the midnight bell is a signal, but what does it mean? Get up, Laura, and follow me: come out of your sleep, out of your bed, out of this strange house. What are you doing in this house? Without a word, without fear she rose and reached for Eugenio's hand, but he eluded her with a sharp, sly smile and drifted away. This is not all, you shall see—Murderer, he said, follow me, I will show you a new country, but it is far away and we must hurry. No, said Laura, not unless you take my hand, no; and she clung first to the stair rail, and then to the topmost branch of the Judas tree that bent down slowly and set her upon the earth, and then to the rocky ledge of a cliff, and then to the jagged wave of a sea that was not water but a desert of crumbling stone. Where are you taking me, she asked in wonder but without fear. To death, and it is a long way off, and we must hurry, said Eugenio. No, said Laura, not unless you take my hand. Then eat these flowers, poor prisoner, said Eugenio in a voice of pity, take and eat: and from the Judas tree he stripped the warm bleeding flowers, and held them to her lips. She saw that his hand was fleshless, a cluster of small white petrified branches, and his eye sockets were without light, but she ate the flowers greedily for they satisfied both hunger and thirst. Murderer! said Eugenio, and Cannibal! This is my body and my blood. Laura cried No! and at the sound of her own voice, she awoke trembling, and was afraid to sleep again.

Why I Live at the P.O.

Eudora Welty (1909–)

Except for the years she spent as a student at the University of Wisconsin and Columbia University (1927–31), Eudora Welty has lived most of her life in Mississippi, drawing upon the history and manners of her native Jackson as William Faulkner drew upon his native Oxford. She has published five novels, including *Delta Wedding* (1946), a tale of contemporary Southern life; *The Ponder Heart* (1954), which became a play; and the more recent *Losing Battles* (1970) and *The Optimist's Daughter* (1972), which won a Pulitzer Prize. Her great achievement, however, has been in the writing of short stories. *A Curtain of Green* (1941), which contains "Why I Live at the P.O.," was followed by *The Wide Net* (1943), *The Golden Apples* (1949), and *The Bride of Innisfallen* (1955).

I was getting along fine with Mama, Papa-Daddy and Uncle Rondo until my sister Stella-Rondo just separated from her husband and came back home again. Mr Whitaker! Of course I went with Mr Whitaker first, when he first appeared here in China Grove, taking "Pose Yourself" photos, and Stella-Rondo broke us up. Told him I was one sided. Bigger on one side than the other, which is a deliberate, calculated falsehood: I'm the same. Stella-Rondo is exactly twelve months to the day younger than I am and for that reason she's spoiled.

She's always had anything in the world she wanted and then she'd throw it away. Papa-Daddy gave her this gorgeous Add-a-Pearl necklace when she was eight years old and she threw it away playing baseball when she was nine, with only two pearls.

So as soon as she got married and moved away from home the first thing she did was separate! From Mr Whitaker! This photographer with the popeyes she said she trusted. Came home from one of those towns up in Illinois and to our complete surprise brought this child of two.

Mama said she like to made her drop dead for a second. "Here you had this marvelous blonde child and never so much as wrote your mother a word about it," says Mama. "I'm thoroughly ashamed of you." But of course she wasn't.

Stella-Rondo just calmly takes off this *hat,* I wish you could see it. She says, "Why, Mama, Shirley-T.'s adopted, I can prove it."

"How?" says Mama, but all I says was, "H'm!" There I was over the hot stove, trying to stretch two chickens over five people and a completely unexpected child into the bargain, without one moment's notice.

"What do you mean—'H'm!'?" says Stella-Rondo, and Mama says, "I heard that, Sister."

I said that oh, I didn't mean a thing, only that whoever Shirley-T. was, she was the spit-image of Papa-Daddy if he'd cut off his beard, which of course he'd never do in the world. Papa-Daddy's Mama's papa and sulks.

Stella-Rondo got furious! She said, "Sister, I don't need to tell you you got a lot of nerve and always did have and I'll thank you to make no future reference to my adopted child whatsoever."

"Very well," I said. "Very well, very well. Of course I noticed at once she looks like Mr Whitaker's side too. That frown. She looks like a cross between Mr Whitaker and Papa-Daddy."

"Well, all I can say is she isn't."

"She looks exactly like Shirley Temple to me," says Mama, but Shirley-T. just ran away from her.

So the first thing Stella-Rondo did at the table was turn Papa-Daddy against me.

"Papa-Daddy," she says. He was trying to cut up his meat. "Papa-Daddy!" I was taken completely by surprise. Papa-Daddy is about a million years old and's got this long-long beard. "Papa-Daddy, Sister says she fails to understand why you don't cut off your beard."

So Papa-Daddy l-a-y-s down his knife and fork! He's real rich. Mama says he is, he says he isn't. So he says, "Have I heard correctly? You don't understand why I don't cut off my beard?"

"Why," I says, "Papa-Daddy, of course I understand, I did not say any such of a thing, the idea!"

He says, "Hussy!"

I says, "Papa-Daddy, you know I wouldn't any more want you to cut off your beard than the man in the moon. It was the farthest thing from my mind! Stella-Rondo sat there and made that up while she was eating breast of chicken."

But he says, "So the postmistress fails to understand why I don't cut off my beard. Which job I got you through my influence with the government. 'Bird's nest'—is that what you call it?"

Not that it isn't the next to smallest P.O. in the entire state of Mississippi.

I says, "Oh, Papa-Daddy," I says, "I didn't say any such of a thing, I never dreamed it was a bird's nest, I have always been grateful though this is the next to smallest P.O. in the state of Mississippi, and I do not enjoy being referred to as a hussy by my own grandfather."

But Stella-Rondo says, "Yes, you did say it too. Anybody in the world could of heard you, that had ears."

"Stop right there," says Mama, looking at *me*.

So I pulled my napkin straight back through the napkin ring and left the table.

As soon as I was out of the room Mama says, "Call her back, or she'll starve to death," but Papa-Daddy says, "This is the beard I started growing on the Coast when I was fifteen years old." He would of gone on till nightfall if Shirley-T. hadn't lost the Milky Way she ate in Cairo.

So Papa-Daddy says, "I am going out and lie in the hammock, and you can all sit here and remember my words: I'll never cut off my beard as long as I live, even one inch, and I don't appreciate it in you at all." Passed right by me in the hall and went straight out and got in the hammock.

It would be a holiday. It wasn't five minutes before Uncle Rondo suddenly appeared in the hall in one of Stella-Rondo's flesh-colored kimonos, all cut on the bias, like something Mr Whitaker probably thought was gorgeous.

"Uncle Rondo!" I says. "I didn't know who that was! Where are you going?"

"Sister," he says, "get out of my way, I'm poisoned."

"If you're poisoned stay away from Papa-Daddy," I says. "Keep out of the hammock. Papa-Daddy will certainly beat you on the head if you come within forty miles of him. He thinks I deliberately said he ought to cut off his beard after he got me the P.O., and I've told him and told him and told him, and he acts like he just don't hear me. Papa-Daddy must of gone stone deaf."

"He picked a fine day to do it then," says Uncle Rondo, and before you could say "Jack Robinson" flew out in the yard.

What he'd really done, he'd drunk another bottle of that prescription. He does it every single Fourth of July as sure as shooting, and it's horribly expensive. Then he falls over in the hammock and snores. So he insisted on zigzagging right on out to the hammock, looking like a half-wit.

Papa-Daddy woke up with this horrible yell and right there without moving an inch he tried to turn Uncle Rondo against me. I heard every word he said. Oh, he told Uncle Rondo I didn't learn to read till I was eight years old and he didn't see how in the world I ever got the mail put up at the P.O., much less read it all, and he said if Uncle Rondo could only fathom the lengths he had gone to to get me that job! And he said on the other hand he thought Stella-Rondo had a brilliant mind and deserved credit for getting out of town. All the time he was just lying there swinging as pretty as you please and looping out his beard, and poor Uncle Rondo was *pleading* with him to slow down the hammock, it was making him as dizzy as a witch to watch it. But that's what Papa-Daddy likes about a hammock. So Uncle Rondo was too dizzy to get turned against me for the time being. He's Mama's only brother and is a good case of a one-track mind. Ask anybody. A certified pharmacist.

Just then I heard Stella-Rondo raising the upstairs window. While she was married she got this peculiar idea that it's cooler with the windows shut and locked. So she has to raise the window before she can make a soul hear her outdoors.

So she raises the window and says, *"Oh!"* You would have thought she was mortally wounded.

Uncle Rondo and Papa-Daddy didn't even look up, but kept right on with what they were doing. I had to laugh.

I flew up the stairs and threw the door open! I says, "What in the wide world's the matter, Stella-Rondo? You mortally wounded?"

"No," she says, "I am not mortally wounded but I wish you would do me the favor of looking out that window there and telling me what you see."

So I shade my eyes and look out the window.

"I see the front yard," I says.

"Don't you see any human beings?" she says.

"I see Uncle Rondo trying to run Papa-Daddy out of the hammock," I says. "Nothing more. Naturally, it's so suffocating-hot in the house, with all the windows shut and locked, everybody who cares to stay in their right mind will have to go out and get in the hammock before the Fourth of July is over."

"Don't you notice anything different about Uncle Rondo?" asks Stella-Rondo.

"Why, no, except he's got on some terrible-looking flesh-colored contraption I wouldn't be found dead in, is all I can see," I says.

"Never mind, you won't be found dead in it, because it happens to be part of my trousseau, and Mr Whitaker took several dozen photographs of me in it," says Stella-Rondo. "What on earth could Uncle Rondo *mean* by wearing part of my trousseau out in the broad open daylight without saying so much as 'Kiss my foot,' *knowing* I only got home this morning after my separation and hung my negligee up on the bathroom door, just as nervous as I could be?"

"I'm sure I don't know, and what do you expect me to do about it?" I says. "Jump out the window?"

"No, I expect nothing of the kind. I simply declare that Uncle Rondo looks like a fool in it, that's all," she says. "It makes me sick to my stomach."

"Well, he looks as good as he can," I says. "As good as anybody in reason could." I stood up for Uncle Rondo, please remember. And I said to Stella-Rondo, "I think I would do well not to criticize so freely if I were you and came home with a two-year-old child I had never said a word about, and no explanation whatever about my separation."

"I asked you the instant I entered this house not to refer one more time to my adopted child, and you gave me your word of honor you would not," was all Stella-Rondo would say, and started pulling out every one of her eyebrows with some cheap Kress tweezers.

So I merely slammed the door behind me and went down and made some green-tomato pickle. Somebody had to do it. Of course Mama had turned both the niggers loose; she always said no earthly power could hold one anyway on the Fourth of July, so she wouldn't even try. It turned out that Jaypan fell in the lake and came within a very narrow limit of drowning.

So Mama trots in. Lifts up the lid and says, "H'm! Not very good for your Uncle Rondo in his precarious condition, I must say. Or poor little adopted Shirley-T. Shame on you!"

That made me tired. I says, "Well, Stella-Rondo had better thank her lucky stars it was her instead of me came trotting in with that very peculiar-looking child. Now if it had been me that trotted in from Illinois and brought a peculiar-looking child of two, I shudder to think of the reception I'd of got, much less controlled the diet of an entire family."

"But you must remember, Sister, that you were never married to Mr Whitaker in the first place and didn't go up to Illinois to live," says Mama, shaking a spoon in my face. "If you had I would of been just as overjoyed to see you and your little adopted girl as I was to see Stella-Rondo, when you wound up with your separation and came on back home."

"You would not," I says.

"Don't contradict me, I would," says Mama.

But I said she couldn't convince me though she talked till she was blue in the face. Then I said, "Besides, you know as well as I do that that child is not adopted."

"She most certainly is adopted," says Mama, stiff as a poker.

I says, "Why, Mama, Stella-Rondo had her just as sure as anything in this world, and just too stuck up to admit it."

"Why, Sister," said Mama. "Here I thought we were going to have a pleasant Fourth of July, and you start right out not believing a word your own baby sister tells you!"

"Just like Cousin Annie Flo. Went to her grave denying the facts of life," I remind Mama.

"I told you if you ever mentioned Annie Flo's name I'd slap your face," says Mama, and slaps my face.

"All right, you wait and see," I says.

"I," says Mama, *"I* prefer to take my children's word for anything when it's humanly possible." You ought to see Mama, she weighs two hundred pounds and has real tiny feet.

Just then something perfectly horrible occurred to me.

"Mama," I says, "can that child talk?" I simply had to whisper! "Mama, I wonder if that child can be—you know—in any way? Do you realize," I says, "that she hasn't spoken one single, solitary word to a human being up to this minute? This is the way she looks," I says, and I looked like this.

Well, Mama and I just stood there and stared at each other. It was horrible!

"I remember well that Joe Whitaker frequently drank like a fish," says Mama. "I believed to my soul he drank *chemicals."* And without another word she marches to the foot of the stairs and calls Stella-Rondo.

"Stella-Rondo? O-o-o-o-o! Stella-Rondo!"

"What?" says Stella-Rondo from upstairs. Not even the grace to get up off the bed.

"Can that child of yours talk?" asks Mama.

Stella-Rondo says, "Can she what?"

"Talk! Talk!" says Mama. "Burdyburdyburdyburdy!"

So Stella-Rondo yells back, "Who says she can't talk?"

"Sister says so," says Mama.

"You didn't have to tell me, I know whose word of honor don't mean a thing in this house," says Stella-Rondo.

And in a minute the loudest Yankee voice I ever heard in my life yells out, "OE'm Pop-OE the Sailor-r-r-r Ma-a-an!" and then somebody jumps up and down in the upstairs hall. In another second the house would of fallen down.

"Not only talks, she can tap-dance!" calls Stella-Rondo. "Which is more than some people I won't name can do."

"Why, the little precious darling thing!" Mama says, so surprised. "Just as smart as she can be!" Starts talking baby talk right there. Then she turns on me. "Sister, you ought to be thoroughly ashamed! Run upstairs this instant and apologize to Stella-Rondo and Shirley-T."

"Apologize for what?" I says. "I merely wondered if the child was normal, that's all. Now that she's proved she is, why, I have nothing further to say."

But Mama just turned on her heel and flew out, furious. She ran right upstairs and hugged the baby. She believed it was adopted. Stella-Rondo hadn't done a thing but turn her against me from upstairs while I stood there helpless over the hot stove. So that made Mama, Papa-Daddy and the baby all on Stella-Rondo's side.

Next, Uncle Rondo.

I must say that Uncle Rondo has been marvelous to me at various times in the past and I was completely unprepared to be made to jump out of my skin, the way it turned out. Once Stella-Rondo did something perfectly horrible to him—broke a chain letter from Flanders Field—and he took the radio back he had given her and gave it to me. Stella-Rondo was furious! For six months we all had to call her Stella instead of Stella-Rondo, or she wouldn't answer. I always thought Uncle Rondo had all the brains of the entire family. Another time he sent me to Mammoth Cave, with all expenses paid.

But this would be the day he was drinking that prescription, the Fourth of July.

So at supper Stella-Rondo speaks up and says she thinks Uncle Rondo ought to try to eat a little something. So finally Uncle Rondo said he would try a little cold bisquits and ketchup, but that was all. So *she* brought it to him.

"Do you think it wise to disport with ketchup in Stella-Rondo's flesh-colored kimono?" I says. Trying to be considerate! If Stella-Rondo couldn't watch out for her trousseau, somebody had to.

"Any objections?" asks Uncle Rondo, just about to pour out all the ketchup.

"Don't mind what she says, Uncle Rondo," says Stella-Rondo. "Sister has been devoting this solid afternoon to sneering out my bedroom window at the way you look."

"What's that?" says Uncle Rondo. Uncle Rondo has got the most terrible temper in the world. Anything is liable to make him tear the house down if it comes at the wrong time.

So Stella-Rondo says, "Sister says, 'Uncle Rondo certainly does look like a fool in that pink kimono!' "

Do you remember who it was really said that?

Uncle Rondo spills out all the ketchup and jumps out of his chair and tears off the Kimono and throws it down on the dirty floor and puts his foot on it. It had to be sent all the way to Jackson to the cleaners and re-pleated.

"So that's your opinion of your Uncle Rondo, is it?" he says. "I look like a fool, do I? Well, that's the last straw. A whole day in this house with nothing to do, and then to hear you come out with a remark like that behind my back!"

"I didn't say any such of a thing, Uncle Rondo," I says, "and I'm not saying who did, either. Why, I think you look all right. Just try to take care of yourself and not talk and eat at the same time," I says. "I think you better go lie down."

"Lie down my foot," says Uncle Rondo. I ought to of known by that he was fixing to do something perfectly horrible.

So he didn't do anything that night in the precarious state he was in—just played Casino with Mama and Stella-Rondo and Shirley-T. and gave Shirley-T. a nickel with a head on both sides. It tickled her nearly to death, and she called him "Papa." But at 6:30 A.M. the next morning, he threw a whole five-cent package of some unsold one-inch firecrackers from the store as hard as he could into my bedroom and they every one went off. Not one bad one in the string. Anybody else, there 'd be one that wouldn't go off.

Well, I'm just terribly susceptible to noise of any kind, the doctor has always told me I was the most sensitive person he had ever seen in his whole life, and I was simply prostrated. I couldn't eat! People tell me they heard it as far as the cemetery, and old Aunt Jep Patterson, that had been holding her own so good, thought it was Judgment Day and she was going to meet her whole family. It's usually so quiet here.

And I'll tell you it didn't take me any longer than a minute to make up my mind what to do. There I was with the whole entire house on Stella-Rondo's side and turned against me. If I have anything at all I have pride.

So I just decided I'd go straight down to the P.O. There's plenty of room there in the back, I says to myself.

Well! I made no bones about letting the family catch on to what I was up to. I didn't try to conceal it.

The first thing they knew, I marched in where they were all playing Old Maid and pulled the electric oscillating fan out by the plug, and everything got real hot. Next I snatched the pillow I'd done the needlepoint on right off the davenport from behind Papa-Daddy. He went "Ugh!" I beat Stella-Rondo up the stairs and finally found my charm bracelet in her bureau drawer under a picture of Nelson Eddy.

"So that's the way the land lies," says Uncle Rondo. There he was, piecing on the ham. "Well, Sister, I'll be glad to donate my army cot if you got any place to set it up, providing you'll leave right this minute and let me get some peace." Uncle Rondo was in France.

"Thank you kindly for the cot and 'peace' is hardly the word I would select if I had to resort to firecrackers at 6:30 A.M. in a young girl's bedroom," I says back to him. "And as to where I intend to go, you seem to forget my position as postmistress of China Grove, Mississippi," I says. "I've always got the P.O."

Well, that made them all sit up and take notice.

I went out front and started digging up some four-o'clocks to plant around the P.O.

"Ah-ah-ah!" says Mama, raising the window. "Those happen to be my four-o'clocks. Everything planted in that star is mine. I've never known you to make anything grow in your life."

"Very well," I says. "But I take the fern. Even you, Mama, can't stand there and deny that I'm the one watered that fern. And I happen to know where I can send in a box top and get a packet of one thousand mixed seeds, no two the same kind, free."

"Oh, where?" Mama wants to know.

But I says, "Too late. You 'tend to your house, and I'll 'tend to mine. You hear things like that all the time if you know how to listen to the radio. Perfectly marvelous offers. Get anything you want free."

So I hope to tell you I marched in and got that radio, and they could of all bit a nail in two, especially Stella-Rondo, that it used to belong to, and she well knew she couldn't get back, I'd sue for it like a shot. And I very politely took the sewing-machine motor I helped pay the most on to give Mama for Christmas back in 1929, and a good big calendar, with the first-aid remedies on it. The thermometer and the Hawaiian ukelele certainly were rightfully mine, and I stood on the step-ladder and got all my watermelon-rind preserves and every fruit and vegetable I'd put up, every jar. Then I began to pull the tacks out of the bluebird wall vases on the archway to the dining room.

"Who told you you could have those, Miss Priss?" says Mama, fanning as hard as she could.

"I bought 'em and I'll keep track of 'em," I says. "I'll tack 'em up one on each side the post-office window, and you can see 'em when you come to ask me for your mail, if you're so dead to see 'em."

"Not I! I'll never darken the door to that post office again if I live to be a hundred," Mama says. "Ungrateful child! After all the money we spent on you at the Normal."

"Me either," says Stella-Rondo. "You can just let my mail lie there and *rot,* for all I care. I'll never come and relieve you of a single, solitary piece."

"I should worry," I says. "And who you think's going to sit down and write you all those big fat letters and postcards, by the way? Mr Whitaker? Just because he was the only man ever dropped down in China Grove and you got him—unfairly—is he going to sit down and write you a lengthy correspondence after you come home giving no rhyme nor reason whatsoever for your separation and no explanation for the presence of that child? I may not have your brilliant mind, but I fail to see it."

So Mama says, "Sister, I've told you a thousand

times that Stella-Rondo simply got homesick, and this child is far too big to be hers," and she says, "Now, why don't you all just sit down and play Casino?"

Then Shirley-T. sticks out her tongue at me in this perfectly horrible way. She has no more manners than the man in the moon. I told her she was going to cross her eyes like that some day and they'd stick.

"It's too late to stop me now," I says. "You should have tried that yesterday. I'm going to the P.O. and the only way you can possibly see me is to visit me there."

So Papa-Daddy says, "You'll never catch me setting foot in that post office, even if I should take a notion into my head to write a letter some place." He says, "I won't have you reachin' out of that little old window with a pair of shears and cuttin' off any beard of mine. I'm too smart for you!"

"We all are," says Stella-Rondo.

But I said, "If you're so smart, where's Mr Whitaker?"

So then Uncle Rondo says, "I'll thank you from now on to stop reading all the orders I get on postcards and telling everybody in China Grove what you think is the matter with them," but I says, "I draw my own conclusions and will continue in the future to draw them." I says, "If people want to write their inmost secrets on penny postcards, there's nothing in the wide world you can do about it, Uncle Rondo."

"And if you think we'll ever *write* another postcard you're sadly mistaken," says Mama.

"Cutting off your nose to spite your face then," I says. "But if you're all determined to have no more to do with the U.S. mail, think of this: What will Stella-Rondo do now, if she wants to tell Mr Whitaker to come after her?"

"Wah!" says Stella-Rondo. I knew she'd cry. She had a conniption fit right there in the kitchen.

"It will be interesting to see how long she holds out," I says. "And now—I am leaving."

"Good-by," says Uncle Rondo.

"Oh, I declare," says Mama, "to think that a family of mine should quarrel on the Fourth of July, or the day after, over Stella-Rondo leaving old Mr Whitaker and having the sweetest little adopted child! It looks like we'd all be glad!"

"Wah!" says Stella-Rondo, and has a fresh conniption fit.

"*He* left *her*—you mark my words," I says. "That's Mr Whitaker. I know Mr Whitaker. After all, I knew him first. I said from the beginning he'd up and leave her. I foretold every single thing that's happened."

"Where did he go?" asks Mama.

"Probably to the North Pole, if he knows what's good for him," I says.

But Stella-Rondo just bawled and wouldn't say another word. She flew to her room and slammed the door.

"Now look what you've gone and done, Sister," says Mama. "You go apologize."

"I haven't got time, I'm leaving," I says.

"Well, what are you waiting around for?" asks Uncle Rondo.

So I just picked up the kitchen clock and marched off, without saying "Kiss my foot" or anything, and never did tell Stella-Rondo good-by.

There was a nigger girl going along on a little wagon right in front.

"Nigger girl," I says, "come help me haul these things down the hill, I'm going to live in the post office."

Took her nine trips in her express wagon. Uncle Rondo came out on the porch and threw her a nickel.

And that's the last I've laid eyes on any of my family or my family laid eyes on me for five solid days and nights. Stella-Rondo may be telling the most horrible tales in the world about Mr Whitaker, but I haven't heard them. As I tell everybody, I draw my own conclusions.

But oh, I like it here. It's ideal, as I've been saying. You see, I've got everything cater-cornered, the way I like it. Hear the radio? All the war news. Radio, sewing machine, book ends, ironing board and that great big piano lamp—peace, that's what I like. Butter-bean vines planted all along the front where the strings are.

Of course, there's not much mail. My family are naturally the main people in China Grove, and if they prefer to vanish from the face of the earth, for all the mail they get or the mail they write, why, I'm not going to open my mouth. Some of the folks here in town are taking up for me and some turned against me. I know which is which. There are always people who will quit buying stamps just to get on the right side of Papa-Daddy.

But here I am, and here I'll stay. I want the world to know I'm happy.

And if Stella-Rondo should come to me this minute, on bended knees, and *attempt* to explain the incidents of her life with Mr Whitaker, I'd simply put my fingers in both my ears and refuse to listen.

The Basement Room

Graham Greene (1904–   )

Born in Berkhamsted, Hertfordshire (his father was headmaster of the Berkhamsted School), Greene was educated at Oxford, where he wrote a volume of poetry, *Babbling April* (1925). During the next four years he worked as a reporter in Nottingham and London; it was at this time that he converted from the Anglo-Catholic church to Roman Catholicism. Beginning in 1929, Greene wrote a number of "thrillers," among them *Orient Express* (1932), *This Gun for Hire* (1936), *The Ministry of Fear* (1943), *The Third Man* (1949), and a take-off on the genre, *Our Man in Havana* (1958). Most of these "thrillers" were turned into films, a sign that Greene, perhaps more than any other modern novelist, learned many of his narrative techniques from the cinema. Combining these cinematic effects with the conventions of the detective story and spy tale, Greene developed a powerful form that was able to express the political and social anxieties of his time. His so-called "thrillers" have depth and shade, and his more ambitious works on Catholic themes, such as *Brighton Rock* (1938), *The Power and the Glory* (1940), *The Heart of the Matter* (1948), and *The End of the Affair* (1951), owe much to the popular forms. Greene has also been a prolific writer of plays and short stories. "The Basement Room" (1936) appeared in *Twenty-One Stories* (1947, 1954). His *Collected Stories* were published in 1973.

I

When the front door had shut the two of them out and the butler Baines had turned back into the dark and heavy hall, Philip began to live. He stood in front of the nursery door, listening until he heard the engine of the taxi die out along the street. His parents were safely gone for a fortnight's holiday; he was 'between nurses', one dismissed and the other not arrived; he was alone in the great Belgravia house with Baines and Mrs Baines.

He could go anywhere, even through the green baize door to the pantry or down the stairs to the basement living-room. He felt a happy stranger in his home because he could go into any room and all the rooms were empty.

You could only guess who had once occupied them: the rack of pipes in the smoking-room beside the elephant tusks, the carved wood tobacco jar; in the bedroom the pink hangings and the pale perfumes and three-quarter finished jars of cream which Mrs Baines had not yet cleared away for her own use; the high glaze on the never-opened piano in the drawing-room, the china clock, the silly little tables and the silver. But here Mrs Baines was already busy, pulling down the curtains, covering the chairs in dust-sheets.

'Be off out of here, Master Philip,' and she looked at him with her peevish eyes, while she moved round, getting everything in order, meticulous and loveless and doing her duty.

Philip Lane went downstairs and pushed at the baize door; he looked into the pantry, but Baines was not there, then he set foot for the first time on the stairs to the basement. Again he had the sense: this is life. All his seven nursery years vibrated with the strange, the new experience. His crowded brain was like a city which feels the earth tremble at a distant earthquake shock. He was apprehensive, but he was happier than he had ever been. Everything was more important than before.

Baines was reading a newspaper in his shirt-sleeves. He said, 'Come in, Phil, and make yourself at home. Wait a moment and I'll do the honours,' and going to a white cleaned cupboard he brought out a bottle of ginger-beer and half a Dundee cake. 'Half past eleven in the morning,' Baines said. 'It's opening time, my boy,' and he cut the cake and poured out the ginger-beer. He was more genial than Philip had ever known him, more at his ease, a man in his own home.

'Shall I call Mrs Baines?' Philip asked, and he was glad when Baines said no. She was busy. She liked to be busy, so why interfere with her pleasure?

'A spot of drink at half-past eleven,' Baines said, pouring himself out a glass of ginger-beer, 'gives an appetite for chop and does no man any harm.'

'A chop?' Philip asked.

'Old Coasters,' Baines said, 'they call all food chop.'

'But it's not a chop?'

'Well, it might be, you know, if cooked with palm oil. And then some paw-paw to follow.'

Philip looked out of the basement window at the dry stone yard, the ash-can and the legs going up and down beyond the railings.

'Was it hot there?'

'Ah, you never felt such heat. Not a nice heat, mind, like you get in the park on a day like this. Wet,' Baines said, 'corruption.' He cut himself a slice of cake. 'Smelling of rot,' Baines said, rolling his eyes round the small basement room, from clean cupboard to clean cupboard, the sense of bareness, of nowhere to hide a man's secrets. With an air of regret for something lost he took a long draught of ginger-beer.

'Why did father live out there?'

'It was his job,' Baines said, 'same as this is mine now. And it was mine then too. It was a man's job. You wouldn't believe it now, but I've had forty niggers under me, doing what I told them to.'

'Why did you leave?'

'I married Mrs Baines.'

Philip took the slice of Dundee cake in his hand and munched it round the room. He felt very old, independent and judicial; he was aware that Baines was talking to him as man to man. He never called him Master Philip as Mrs Baines did, who was servile when she was not authoritative.

Baines had seen the world; he had seen beyond the railings. He sat there over his ginger pop with the resigned dignity of an exile; Baines didn't complain; he had chosen his fate, and if his fate was Mrs Baines he had only himself to blame.

But today—the house was almost empty and Mrs Baines was upstairs and there was nothing to do—he allowed himself a little acidity.

'I'd go back tomorrow if I had the chance.'

'Did you ever shoot a nigger?'

'I never had any call to shoot,' Baines said. 'Of course I carried a gun. But you didn't need to treat them bad. That just made them stupid. Why,' Baines said, bowing his thin grey hair with embarrassment over the ginger pop, 'I loved some of those damned niggers. I couldn't help loving them. There they'd be laughing, holding hands; they liked to touch each other; it made them feel fine to know the other fellow was around. It didn't mean anything we could understand; two of them would go about all day without loosing hold, grown men; but it wasn't love; it didn't mean anything we could understand.'

'Eating between meals,' Mrs Baines said. 'What would your mother say, Master Philip?'

She came down the steep stairs to the basement, her hands full of pots of cream and salve, tubes of grease and paste. 'You oughtn't to encourage him, Baines,' she said, sitting down in a wicker armchair and screwing up her small ill-humoured eyes at the Coty lipstick, Pond's cream, the Leichner rouge and Cyclax powder and Elizabeth Arden astringent.

She threw them one by one into the wastepaper basket. She saved only the cold cream. 'Telling the boy stories,' she said. 'Go along to the nursery, Master Philip, while I get lunch.'

Philip climbed the stairs to the baize door. He heard Mrs Baines's voice like the voice in a nightmare when the small Price light has guttered in the saucer and the curtains move; it was sharp and shrill and full of malice, louder than people ought to speak, exposed.

'Sick to death of your ways, Baines, spoiling the boy. Time you did some work about the house,' but he couldn't hear what Baines said in reply. He pushed open the baize door, came up like a small earth animal in his grey flannel shorts into a wash of sunlight on a parquet floor, the gleam of mirrors dusted and polished and beautified by Mrs Baines.

Something broke downstairs, and Philip sadly mounted the stairs to the nursery. He pitied Baines; it occurred to him how happily they could live together in the empty house if Mrs Baines were called away. He didn't want to play with his Meccano sets; he wouldn't take out his train or his soldiers; he sat at the table with his chin on his hands: this is life; and suddenly he felt responsible for Baines, as if he were the master of the house and Baines an ageing servant who deserved to be cared for. There was not much one could do; he decided at least to be good.

He was not surprised when Mrs Baines was agreeable at lunch; he was used to her changes. Now it was 'another helping of meat, Master Philip', or 'Master Philip, a little more of this nice pudding'. It was a pudding he liked, Queen's pudding with a perfect meringue, but he wouldn't eat a second helping lest she might count that a victory. She was the kind of woman who thought that any injustice could be counterbalanced by something good to eat.

She was sour, but she liked making sweet things; one never had to complain of a lack of jam or plums; she ate well herself and added soft sugar to the meringue and the strawberry jam. The half-light through the basement window set the motes moving above her pale hair like dust as she sifted the sugar, and Baines crouched over his plate saying nothing.

Again Philip felt responsibility. Baines had looked forward to this, and Baines was disappointed: everything was being spoilt. The sensation of disappointment was one which Philip could share; he could understand better than anyone this grief, something hoped for not happening, something promised not fulfilled, something exciting which turned dull. 'Baines,' he said, 'will you take me for a walk this afternoon?'

'No,' Mrs Baines said, 'no. That he won't. Not with all the silver to clean.'

'There's a fortnight to do it in,' Baines said.

'Work first, pleasure afterwards.'

Mrs Baines helped herself to some more meringue.

Baines put down his spoon and fork and pushed his plate away. 'Blast,' he said.

'Temper,' Mrs Baines said, 'temper. Don't you go breaking any more things, Baines, and I won't have you swearing in front of the boy. Master Philip, if you've finished you can get down.'

She skinned the rest of the meringue off the pudding.

'I want to go for a walk,' Philip said.

'You'll go and have a rest.'

'I want to go for a walk.'

'Master Philip,' Mrs Baines said. She got up from the table, leaving her meringue unfinished, and came towards him, thin, menacing, dusty in the basement room. 'Master Philip, you just do as you're told.' She took him by the arm and squeezed it; she watched him with a joyless passionate glitter and above her head the feet of typists trudged back to the Victoria offices after the lunch interval.

'Why shouldn't I go for a walk?'

But he weakened; he was scared and ashamed of being scared. This was life; a strange passion he couldn't understand moving in the basement room. He saw a small pile of broken glass swept into a corner by the wastepaper basket. He looked at Baines for help and only intercepted hate; the sad hopeless hate of something behind bars.

'Why shouldn't I?' he repeated.

'Master Philip,' Mrs Baines said, 'you've got to do as you're told. You mustn't think just because your father's away there's nobody here to—'

'You wouldn't dare,' Philip cried, and was startled by Baines's low interjection:

'There's nothing she wouldn't dare.'

'I hate you,' Philip said to Mrs Baines. He pulled away from her and ran to the door, but she was there before him; she was old, but she was quick.

'Master Philip,' she said, 'you'll say you're sorry.' She stood in front of the door quivering with excitement. 'What would your father do if he heard you say that?'

She put a hand out to seize him, dry and white with constant soda, the nails cut to the quick, but he backed away and put the table between them, and suddenly to his surprise she smiled; she became again as servile as she had been arrogant. 'Get along with you, Master Philip,' she said with glee, 'I see I'm going to have my hands full till your father and mother come back.'

She left the door unguarded and when he passed her she slapped him playfully. 'I've got too much to do today to trouble about you. I haven't covered half the chairs,' and suddenly even the upper part of the house became unbearable to him as he thought of Mrs Baines moving around shrouding the sofas, laying out the dust-sheets.

So he wouldn't go upstairs to get his cap but walked straight out across the shining hall into the street, and again, as he looked this way and looked that way, it was life he was in the middle of.

2

The pink sugar cakes in the window on a paper doily, the ham, the slab of mauve sausage, the wasps driving like small torpedoes across the pane caught Philip's attention. His feet were tired by pavements; he had been afraid to cross the road, had simply walked first in one direction, then in the other. He was nearly home now; the square was at the end of the street; this was a shabby outpost of Pimlico, and he smudged the pane with his nose looking for sweets, and saw between the cakes and ham a different Baines. He hardly recognized the bulbous eyes, the bald forehead. This was a happy, bold and buccaneering Baines, even though it was, when you looked closer, a desperate Baines.

Philip had never seen the girl, but he remembered

Baines had a niece. She was thin and drawn, and she wore a white mackintosh; she meant nothing to Philip; she belonged to a world about which he knew nothing at all. He couldn't make up stories about her, as he could make them up about withered Sir Hubert Reed, the Permanent Secretary, about Mrs Wince-Dudley who came up once a year from Penstanley in Suffolk with a green umbrella and an enormous black handbag, as he could make them up about the upper servants in all the houses where he went to tea and games. She just didn't belong. He thought of mermaids and Undine, but she didn't belong there either, nor to the adventures of Emil, nor to the Bastables. She sat there looking at an iced pink cake in the detachment and mystery of the completely disinherited, looking at the half-used pots of powder which Baines had set out on the marble-topped table between them.

Baines was urging, hoping, entreating, commanding, and the girl looked at the tea and the china pots and cried. Baines passed his handkerchief across the table, but she wouldn't wipe her eyes; she screwed it in her palm and let the tears run down, wouldn't do anything, wouldn't speak, would only put up a silent resistance to what she dreaded and wanted and refused to listen to at any price. The two brains battled over the tea-cups loving each other, and there came to Philip outside, beyond the ham and wasps and dusty Pimlico pane, a confused indication of the struggle.

He was inquisitive and he didn't understand and he wanted to know. He went and stood in the doorway to see better, he was less sheltered than he had ever been; other people's lives for the first time touched and pressed and moulded. He would never escape that scene. In a week he had forgotten it, but it conditioned his career, the long austerity of his life; when he was dying, rich and alone, it was said that he asked: 'Who is she?'

Baines had won; he was cocky and the girl was happy. She wiped her face, she opened a pot of powder, and their fingers touched across the table. It occurred to Philip that it might be amusing to imitate Mrs Baines's voice and to call 'Baines' to him from the door.

His voice shrivelled them; you couldn't describe it in any other way, it made them smaller, they weren't together any more. Baines was the first to recover and trace the voice, but that didn't make things as they were. The sawdust was spilled out of the afternoon; nothing you did could mend it, and Philip was scared. 'I didn't mean . . .' He wanted to say that he loved Baines, that he had only wanted to laugh at Mrs Baines. But he had discovered you couldn't laugh at Mrs Baines. She wasn't Sir Hubert Reed, who used steel nibs and carried a pen-wiper in his pocket; she wasn't Mrs Wince-Dudley; she was darkness when the night-light went out in a draught; she was the frozen blocks of earth he had seen one winter in a graveyard when someone said, 'They need an electric drill'; she was the flowers gone bad and smelling in the little closet room at Penstanley. There was nothing to laugh about. You had to endure her when she was there and forget about her quickly when she was away, suppress the thought of her, ram it down deep.

Baines said, 'It's only Phil,' beckoned him in and gave him the pink iced cake the girl hadn't eaten, but the afternoon was broken, the cake was like dry bread in the throat. The girl left them at once: she even forgot to take the powder. Like a blunt icicle in her white mackintosh she stood in the doorway with her back to them, then melted into the afternoon.

'Who is she?' Philip asked. 'Is she your niece?'

'Oh, yes,' Baines said, 'that's who she is; she's my niece,' and poured the last drops of water on to the coarse black leaves in the teapot.

'May as well have another cup,' Baines said.

'The cup that cheers,' he said hopelessly, watching the bitter black fluid drain out of the spout.

'Have a glass of ginger pop, Phil?'

'I'm sorry. I'm sorry, Baines.'

'It's not your fault, Phil. Why, I could really believe it wasn't you at all, but her. She creeps in everywhere.' He fished two leaves out of his cup and laid them on the back of his hand, a thin soft flake and a hard stalk. He beat them with his hand: 'Today,' and the stalk detached itself, 'tomorrow, Wednesday, Thursday, Friday, Saturday, Sunday,' but the flake wouldn't come, stayed where it was, drying under his blows, with a resistance you wouldn't believe it to possess. 'The tough one wins,' Baines said.

He got up and paid the bill and out they went into the street. Baines said, 'I don't ask you to say what isn't true. But you needn't actually *tell* Mrs Baines you met us here.'

'Of course not,' Philip said, and catching something of Sir Hubert Reed's manner, 'I understand, Baines.' But he didn't understand a thing; he was caught up in other people's darkness.

'It was stupid,' Baines said. 'So near home, but I hadn't time to think, you see. I'd got to see her.'

'Of course, Baines.'

'I haven't time to spare,' Baines said. 'I'm not young. I've got to see that she's all right.'

'Of course you have, Baines.'

'Mrs Baines will get it out of you if she can.'

'You can trust me, Baines,' Philip said in a dry important Reed voice; and then, 'Look out. She's at the window watching.' And there indeed she was, looking up at them, between the lace curtains, from the basement room, speculating. 'Need we go in, Baines?' Philip asked, cold lying heavy on his stomach like too much pudding; he clutched Baines's arm.

'Careful,' Baines said softly, 'careful.'

'But need we go in, Baines? It's early. Take me for a walk in the park.'

'Better not.'

'But I'm frightened, Baines.'

'You haven't any cause,' Baines said. 'Nothing's going to hurt you. You just run along upstairs to the nursery. I'll go down by the area and talk to Mrs Baines.' But he stood hesitating at the top of the stone steps pretending not to see her, where she watched between the curtains. 'In at the front door, Phil, and up the stairs.'

Philip didn't linger in the hall; he ran, slithering on the parquet Mrs Baines had polished, to the stairs. Through the drawing-room doorway on the first floor he saw the draped chairs; even the china clock on the mantel was covered like a canary's cage. As he passed, it chimed the hour, muffled and secret under the duster. On the nursery table he found his supper laid out: a glass of milk and a piece of bread and butter, a sweet biscuit, and a little cold Queen's pudding without the meringue. He had no appetite; he strained his ears for Mrs Baines's coming, for the sound of voices, but the basement held its secrets; the green baize door shut off that world. He drank the milk and ate the biscuit, but he didn't touch the rest, and presently he could hear the soft precise footfalls of Mrs Baines on the stairs: she was a good servant, she walked softly; she was a determined woman, she walked precisely.

But she wasn't angry when she came in; she was ingratiating as she opened the night nursery door—'Did you have a good walk, Master Philip?'—pulled down the blinds, laid out his pyjamas, came back to clear his supper. 'I'm glad Baines found you. Your mother wouldn't have liked your being out alone.' She examined the tray. 'Not much appetite, have you, Master Philip? Why don't you try a little of this nice pudding? I'll bring you up some more jam for it.'

'No, no, thank you, Mrs Baines,' Philip said.

'You ought to eat more,' Mrs Baines said. She sniffed round the room like a dog. 'You didn't take any pots out of the wastepaper basket in the kitchen, did you, Master Philip?'

'No,' Philip said.

'Of course you wouldn't. I just wanted to make sure.' She patted his shoulder and her fingers flashed to his lapel; she picked off a tiny crumb of pink sugar. 'Oh, Master Philip,' she said, 'that's why you haven't any appetite. You've been buying sweet cakes. That's not what your pocket money's for.'

'But I didn't,' Philip said, 'I didn't.'

She tasted the sugar with the tip of her tongue.

'Don't tell lies to me, Master Philip. I won't stand for it any more than your father would.'

'I didn't, I didn't,' Philip said. 'They gave it me. I mean Baines,' but she had pounced on the word 'they'. She had got what she wanted; there was no doubt about that, even when you didn't know what it was she wanted. Philip was angry and miserable and disappointed because he hadn't kept Baines's secret. Baines oughtn't to have trusted him; grown-up people should keep their own secrets, and yet here was Mrs Baines immediately entrusting him with another.

'Let me tickle your palm and see if you can keep a secret.' But he put his hand behind him; he wouldn't be touched. 'It's a secret between us, Master Philip, that I know all about them. I suppose she was having tea with him,' she speculated.

'Why shouldn't she?' he asked, the responsibility for Baines weighing on his spirit, the idea that he had got to keep her secret when he hadn't kept Baines's making him miserable with the unfairness of life. 'She was nice.'

'She was nice, was she?' Mrs Baines said in a bitter voice he wasn't used to.

'And she's his niece.'

'So that's what he said,' Mrs Baines struck softly back at him like the clock under the duster. She tried to be jocular. 'The old scoundrel. Don't you tell him I know, Master Philip.' She stood very still between the table and the door, thinking very hard, planning something. 'Promise you won't tell. I'll give you that Meccano set, Master Philip . . .'

He turned his back on her; he wouldn't promise, but he wouldn't tell. He would have nothing to do with their secrets, the responsibilities they were determined to lay on him. He was only anxious to forget. He had received already a larger dose of life than he had bargained for, and he was scared. 'A 2A Meccano set, Master Philip.' He never opened his Meccano set again, never built anything, never created anything, died the old dilettante, sixty years later with nothing to show rather than preserve the memory of Mrs Baines's malicious voice saying good night, her soft determined footfalls on the stairs to the basement, going down, going down.

3

The sun poured in between the curtains and Baines was beating a tattoo on the water-can. 'Glory, glory,' Baines said. He sat down on the end of the bed and said, 'I beg to announce that Mrs Baines has been called away. Her mother's dying. She won't be back till tomorrow.'

'Why did you wake me up so early?' Philip complained. He watched Baines with uneasiness; he wasn't going to be drawn in; he'd learnt his lesson. It wasn't right for a man of Baines's age to be so merry. It made a grown person human in the same way that you were human. For if a grown-up could behave so childishly, you were liable to find yourself in their world. It was enough that it came at you in dreams: the witch at the corner, the man with a knife. So 'It's very early,' he whined, even though he loved Baines, even though he couldn't help being glad that Baines was happy. He was divided by the fear and the attraction of life.

'I want to make this a long day,' Baines said. 'This is the best time.' He pulled the curtains back. 'It's a bit misty. The cat's been out all night. There she is, sniffing round the area. They haven't taken in any milk at 59. Emma's shaking out the mats at 63.' He said, 'This was what I used to think about on the Coast: somebody shaking mats and the cat coming home. I can see it today,' Baines said, 'just as if I was still in Africa. Most days you don't notice what you've got. It's a good life if you don't weaken.' He put a penny on the washstand. 'When you've dressed, Phil, run and get a *Mail* from the barrow at the corner. I'll be cooking the sausages.'

'Sausages?'

'Sausages,' Baines said. 'We're going to celebrate today.' He celebrated at breakfast, restless, cracking jokes, unaccountably merry and nervous. It was going to be a long, long day, he kept on coming back to that: for years he had waited for a long day, he had sweated in the damp Coast heat, changed shirts, gone down with fever, lain between the blankets and sweated, all in the hope of this long day, that cat sniffing round the area, a bit of mist, the mats beaten at 63. He propped the *Mail* in front of the coffee-pot and read pieces aloud. He said, 'Cora Down's been married for the fourth time.' He was amused, but it wasn't his idea of a long day. His long day was the Park, watching the riders in the Row, seeing Sir Arthur Stillwater pass beyond the rails ('He dined with us once in Bo; up from Freetown; he was governor there'), lunch at the Corner House for Philip's sake (he'd have preferred himself a glass of stout and some oysters at the York bar), the Zoo, the long bus ride home in the last summer light: the leaves in the Green Park were beginning to turn and the motors nuzzled out of Berkeley Street with the low sun gently glowing on their wind-screens. Baines envied no one, not Cora Down, or Sir Arthur Stillwater, or Lord Sandale, who came out on to the steps of the Army and Navy and then went back again—he hadn't anything to do and might as well look at another paper. 'I said don't let me see you touch that black again.' Baines had led a man's life; everyone on top of the bus pricked his ears when he told Philip all about it.

'Would you have shot him?' Philip asked, and Baines put his head back and tilted his dark respectable man-servant's hat to a better angle as the bus swerved round the Artillery Memorial.

'I wouldn't have thought twice about it. I'd have shot to kill,' he boasted, and the bowed figure went by, the steel helmet, the heavy cloak, the down-turned rifle and the folded hands.

'Have you got the revolver?'

'Of course I've got it,' Baines said. 'Don't I need it with all the burglaries there've been?' This was the Baines whom Philip loved: not Baines singing and carefree, but Baines responsible, Baines behind barriers, living his man's life.

All the buses streamed out from Victoria like a convoy of aeroplanes to bring Baines home with honour. 'Forty blacks under me,' and there waiting near the area steps was the proper reward, love at lighting-up time.

'It's your niece,' Philip said, recognizing the white mackintosh, but not the happy sleepy face. She frightened him like an unlucky number; he nearly told Baines what Mrs Baines had said; but he didn't want to bother, he wanted to leave things alone.

'Why, so it is,' Baines said. 'I shouldn't wonder if she was going to have a bit of supper with us.' But, he said, they'd play a game, pretend they didn't know her, slip down the area steps, 'and here,' Baines said, 'we are,' lay the table, put out the cold sausages, a bottle of beer, a bottle of ginger pop, a flagon of harvest burgundy. 'Everyone his own drink,' Baines said. 'Run upstairs, Phil, and see if there's been a post.'

Phillip didn't like the empty house at dusk before the lights went on. He hurried. He wanted to be back with Baines. The hall lay there in quiet and shadow prepared to show him something he didn't want to see. Some letters rustled down and someone knocked. 'Open in the name of the Republic.' The tumbrils rolled, the head bobbed in the bloody basket. Knock, knock, and the postman's footsteps going away. Philip gathered the letters. The slit in the door was like the grating in a jeweller's window. He remembered the policeman he had seen peer through. He had said to his nurse, 'What's he doing?' and when she said, 'He's seeing if everything's all right,' his brain immediately filled with images of all that might be wrong. He ran to the baize door and the stairs. The girl was already there and Baines was kissing her. She leant breathless against the dresser.

'Here's Emmy, Phil.'

'There's a letter for you, Baines.'

'Emmy,' Baines said, 'it's from her.' But he wouldn't open it. 'You bet she's coming back.'

'We'll have supper, anyway,' Emmy said. 'She can't harm that.'

'You don't know her,' Baines said. 'Nothing's safe. Damn it,' he said, 'I was a man once,' and he opened the letter.

'Can I start?' Philip asked, but Baines didn't hear; he presented in his stillness an example of the importance grown-up people attached to the written word: you had to write your thanks, not wait and speak them, as if letters couldn't lie. But Philip knew better than that, sprawling his thanks across a page to Aunt Alice who had given him a teddy bear he was too old for. Letters could lie all right, but they made the lie permanent. They lay as evidence against you: they made you meaner than the spoken word.

'She's not coming back till tomorrow night,' Baines said. He opened the bottles, he pulled up the chairs, he kissed Emmy again against the dresser.

'You oughtn't to,' Emmy said, 'with the boy here.'

'He's got to learn,' Baines said, 'like the rest of us,' and he helped Philip to three sausages. He only took one himself; he said he wasn't hungry, but when Emmy said she wasn't hungry either he stood over her and made her eat. He was timid and rough with her and made her drink the harvest burgundy because he said she needed building up; he wouldn't take no for an answer, but when he touched her his hands were light and clumsy too, as if he was afraid to damage something delicate and didn't know how to handle anything so light.

'This is better than milk and biscuits, eh?'

'Yes,' Philip said, but he was scared, scared for Baines as much as for himself. He couldn't help wondering at every bite, at every draught of the ginger pop, what Mrs Baines would say if she ever learnt of this meal; he couldn't imagine it, there was a depth of bitterness and rage in Mrs Baines you couldn't sound. He said, 'She won't be coming back tonight?' but you could tell by the way they immediately understood him that she wasn't really away at all; she was there in the basement with them, driving them to longer drinks and louder talk, biding her time for the right cutting word. Baines wasn't really happy; he was only watching happiness from close to instead of from far away.

'No,' he said, 'she'll not be back till late tomorrow.' He couldn't keep his eyes off happiness. He'd played around as much as other men; he kept on reverting to the Coast as if to excuse himself for his innocence. He wouldn't have been so innocent if he'd lived his life in London, so innocent when it came to tenderness. 'If it was you, Emmy,' he said, looking at the white dresser, the scrubbed chairs, 'this'd be like a home.' Already the room was not quite so harsh; there was a little dust in corners, the silver needed a final polish, the morning's paper lay untidily on a chair. 'You'd better go to bed, Phil; it's been a long day.'

They didn't leave him to find his own way up through the dark shrouded house; they went with him, turning on lights, touching each other's fingers on the switches. Floor after floor they drove the night back. They spoke softly among the covered chairs. They watched him undress, they didn't make him wash or clean his teeth, they saw him into bed and lit his night-light and left his door ajar. He could hear their voices on the stairs, friendly like the guests he heard at dinner-parties when they moved down the hall, saying good night. They belonged; wherever they were they made a home. He heard a door open and a clock strike, he heard their voices for a long while, so that he felt they were not far away and he was safe. The voices didn't dwindle, they simply went out, and he could be sure that they were still somewhere not far from him, silent together in one of the many empty rooms, growing sleepy together as he grew sleepy after the long day.

He just had time to sigh faintly with satisfaction, because this too perhaps had been life, before he slept and the inevitable terrors of sleep came round him: a man with a tricolour hat beat at the door on His Majesty's service, a bleeding head lay on the kitchen table in a basket, and the Siberian wolves crept closer. He was bound hand and foot and couldn't move; they leapt round him breathing heavily; he opened his eyes and Mrs Baines was there, her grey untidy hair in threads over his face, her black hat askew. A loose hairpin fell on the pillow and one musty thread brushed his mouth. 'Where are they?' she whispered. 'Where are they?'

4

Philip watched her in terror. Mrs Baines was out of breath as if she had been searching all the empty rooms, looking under loose covers.

With her untidy grey hair and her black dress buttoned to her throat, her gloves of black cotton, she was so like the witches of his dreams that he didn't dare to speak. There was a stale smell in her breath.

'She's here,' Mrs Baines said, 'you can't deny she's

here.' Her face was simultaneously marked with cruelty and misery; she wanted to 'do things' to people, but she suffered all the time. It would have done her good to scream, but she daren't do that: it would warn them. She came ingratiatingly back to the bed where Philip lay rigid on his back and whispered, 'I haven't forgotten the Meccano set. You shall have it tomorrow, Master Philip. We've got secrets together, haven't we? Just tell me where they are.'

He couldn't speak. Fear held him as firmly as any nightmare. She said, 'Tell Mrs Baines, Master Philip. You love your Mrs Baines, don't you?' That was too much; he couldn't speak, but he could move his mouth in terrified denial, wince away from her dusty image.

She whispered, coming closer to him, 'Such deceit. I'll tell your father. I'll settle with you myself when I've found them. You'll smart; I'll see you smart.' Then immediately she was still, listening. A board had creaked on the floor below, and a moment later, while she stooped listening above his bed, there came the whispers of two people who were happy and sleepy together after a long day. The night-light stood beside the mirror and Mrs Baines could see there her own reflection, misery and cruelty wavering in the glass, age and dust and nothing to hope for. She sobbed without tears, a dry, breathless sound, but her cruelty was a kind of pride which kept her going; it was her best quality, she would have been merely pitiable without it. She went out of the door on tiptoe, feeling her way across the landing, going so softly down the stairs that no one behind a shut door could hear her. Then there was complete silence again; Philip could move; he raised his knees; he sat up in bed; he wanted to die. It wasn't fair, the walls were down again between his world and theirs, but this time it was something worse than merriment that the grown people made him share; a passion moved in the house he recognized but could not understand.

It wasn't fair, but he owed Baines everything: the Zoo, the ginger pop, the bus ride home. Even the supper called to his loyalty. But he was frightened; he was touching something he touched in dreams; the bleeding head, the wolves, the knock, knock, knock. Life fell on him with savagery, and you couldn't blame him if he never faced it again in sixty years. He got out of bed. Carefully from habit he put on his bedroom slippers and tiptoed to the door: it wasn't quite dark on the landing below because the curtains had been taken down for the cleaners and the light from the street washed in through the tall windows. Mrs Baines had her hand on the glass door-knob; she was very carefully turning it; he screamed: 'Baines, Baines.'

Mrs Baines turned and saw him cowering in his pyjamas by the banisters; he was helpless, more helpless even than Baines, and cruelty grew at the sight of him and drove her up the stairs. The nightmare was on him again and he couldn't move; he hadn't any more courage left, he couldn't even scream.

But the first cry brought Baines out of the best spare bedroom and he moved quicker than Mrs Baines. She hadn't reached the top of the stairs before he'd caught her round the waist. She drove her black cotton gloves at his face and he bit her hand. He hadn't time to think, he fought her like a stranger, but she fought back with knowledgeable hate. She was going to teach them all and it didn't really matter whom she began with; they had all deceived her; but the old image in the glass was by her side, telling her she must be dignified, she wasn't young enough to yield her dignity; she could beat his face, but she mustn't bite; she could push, but she mustn't kick.

Age and dust and nothing to hope for were her handicaps. She went over the banisters in a flurry of black clothes and fell into the hall; she lay before the front door like a sack of coals which should have gone down the area into the basement. Philip saw; Emmy saw; she sat down suddenly in the doorway of the best spare bedroom with her eyes open as if she were too tired to stand any longer. Baines went slowly down into the hall.

It wasn't hard for Philip to escape; they'd forgotten him completely. He went down the back, the servants' stairs, because Mrs Baines was in the hall. He didn't understand what she was doing lying there; like the pictures in a book no one had read to him, the things he didn't understand terrified him. The whole house had been turned over to the grown-up world; he wasn't safe in the night nursery; their passions had flooded in. The only thing he could do was to get away, by the back stairs, and up through the area, and never come back. He didn't think of the cold, of the need for food and sleep; for an hour it would seem quite possible to escape from people for ever.

He was wearing pyjamas and bedroom slippers when he came up into the square, but there was no one to see him. It was that hour of the evening in a residential district when everyone is at the theatre or at home. He climbed over the iron railings into the little garden: the plane-trees spread their large pale palms between him and the sky. It might have been an illimitable forest into which he had escaped. He crouched behind a trunk and the wolves retreated; it seemed to him between the little iron seat and the tree-trunk that no one would ever find him again. A kind of embittered happiness and self-pity made him cry; he was lost; there wouldn't be any more secrets to keep; he surrendered responsibility once and for all. Let grown-up people keep to their world and he would keep to his, safe in the small garden between the plane-trees.

Presently the door of 48 opened and Baines looked this way and that; then he signalled with his hand and Emmy came; it was as if they were only just in time for a train, they hadn't a chance of saying good-bye. She went quickly by like a face at a window swept past the platform, pale and unhappy and not wanting to go. Baines went in again and shut the door; the light was lit in the basement, and a policeman walked round the square, looking into the areas. You could tell how many families were at home by the lights behind the first-floor curtains.

Philip explored the garden: it didn't take long: a twenty-yard square of bushes and plane-trees, two iron seats and a gravel path, a padlocked gate at either end, a scuffle of old leaves. But he couldn't say: something stirred in the bushes and two illuminated eyes peered out at him like a Serbian wolf, and he though how terrible it would be if Mrs Baines found him there. He'd have no time to climb the railings; she'd seize him from behind.

He left the square at the unfashionable end and was immediately among the fish-and-chip shops, the little stationers selling *Bagatelle,* among the accommodation addresses and the dingy hotels with open doors. There were few people about because the pubs were open, but a blowsy woman carrying a parcel called out to him across the street and the commissionaire outside a cinema would have stopped him if he hadn't crossed the road. He went deeper: you could go farther and lose yourself more completely here than among the plane-trees. On the fringe of the square he was in danger of being stopped and taken back: it was obvious where he belonged; but as he went deeper he lost the marks of his origin. It was a warm night: any child in those free-living parts might be expected to play truant from bed. He found a kind of camaraderie even among grown-up people; he might have been a neighbour's child as he went quickly by, but they weren't going to tell on him, they'd been young once themselves. He picked up a protective coating of dust from the pavements, of smuts from the trains which passed along the backs in a spray of fire. Once he was caught in a knot of children running away from something or somebody, laughing as they ran; he was whirled with them round a turning and abandoned, with a sticky fruit-drop in his hand.

He couldn't have been more lost, but he hadn't the stamina to keep on. At first he feared that someone would stop him; after an hour he hoped that someone would. He couldn't find his way back, and in any case he was afraid of arriving home alone; he was afraid of Mrs Baines, more afraid than he had ever been. Baines was his friend, but something had happened which gave Mrs Baines all the power. He began to loiter on purpose to be noticed, but no one noticed him. Families were having a last breather on the doorsteps, the refuse bins had been put out and bits of cabbage stalks soiled his slippers. The air was full of voices, but he was cut off; these people were strangers and would always now be strangers; they were marked by Mrs Baines and he shied away from them into a deep class-consciousness. He had been afriad of policemen, but now he wanted one to take him home; even Mrs Baines could do nothing against a policeman. He sidled past a constable who was directing traffic, but he was too busy to pay him any attention. Philip sat down against a wall and cried.

It hadn't occurred to him that that was the easiest way, that all you had to do was to surrender, to show you were beaten and accept kindness. . . . It was lavished on him at once by two women and a pawnbroker. Another policeman appeared, a young man with a sharp incredulous face. He looked as if he noted everything he saw in pocket-books and drew conclusions. A woman offered to see Philip home, but he didn't trust her: she wasn't a match for Mrs Baines immobile in the hall. He wouldn't give his address; he said he was afraid to go home. He had his way; he got his protection. 'I'll take him to the station,' the policeman said, and holding him awkwardly by the hand (he wasn't married; he had his career to make) he led him round the corner, up the stone stairs into the little bare over-heated room where Justice lived.

5

Justice waited behind a wooden counter on a high stool; it wore a heavy moustache; it was kindly and had six children ('three of them nippers like yourself'); it wasn't really interested in Philip, but it pretended to be, it wrote the address down and sent a constable to fetch a glass of milk. But the young constable was interested; he had a nose for things.

'Your home's on the telephone, I suppose,' Justice said. 'We'll ring them up and say you are safe. They'll fetch you very soon. What's your name, sonny?'

'Philip.'

'Your other name?'

'I haven't got another name.' He didn't want to be fetched; he wanted to be taken home by someone who would impress even Mrs Baines. The constable watched him, watched the way he drank the milk, watched him when he winced away from questions.

'What made you run away? Playing truant, eh?'

'I don't know.'

'You oughtn't to do it, young fellow. Think how anxious your father and mother will be.'

'They are away.'

'Well, your nurse.'

'I haven't got one.'

'Who looks after you, then?' The question went home. Philip saw Mrs Baines coming up the stairs at him, the heap of black cotton in the hall. He began to cry.

'Now, now, now,' the sergeant said. He didn't know what to do; he wished his wife were with him; even a policewoman might have been useful.

'Don't you think it's funny,' the constable said, 'that there hasn't been an inquiry?'

'They think he's tucked up in bed.'

'You are scared, aren't you?' the constable said. 'What scared you?'

'I don't know.'

'Somebody hurt you?'

'No.'

'He's had bad dreams,' the sergeant said. 'Thought the house was on fire, I expect. I've brought up six of them. Rose is due back. She'll take him home.'

'I want to go home with you,' Philip said; he tried to smile at the constable, but the deceit was immature and unsuccessful.

'I'd better go,' the constable said. 'There may be something wrong.'

'Nonsense,' the sergeant said. 'It's a woman's job. Tact is what you need. Here's Rose. Pull up your stockings, Rose. You're a disgrace to the Force. I've got a job of work for you.' Rose shambled in: black cotton stockings drooping over her boots, a gawky Girl Guide manner, a hoarse hostile voice. 'More tarts, I suppose.'

'No, you've got to see this young man home.' She looked at him owlishly.

'I won't go with her,' Philip said. He began to cry again. 'I don't like her.'

'More of that womanly charm, Rose,' the sergeant said. The telephone rang on his desk. He lifted the receiver. 'What? What's that?' he said. 'Number 48? You've got a doctor?' He put his hand over the telephone mouth. 'No wonder this nipper wasn't reported,' he said. 'They've been too busy. An accident. Woman slipped on the stairs.'

'Serious?' the constable asked. The sergeant mouthed at him; you didn't mention the word death before a child (didn't he know? he had six of them), you made noises in the throat, you grimaced, a complicated shorthand for a word of only five letters anyway.

'You'd better go, after all,' he said, 'and make a report. The doctor's there.'

Rose shambled from the stove; pink apply-dapply cheeks, loose stockings. She stuck her hands behind her. Her large morgue-like mouth was full of blackened teeth. 'You told me to take him and now just because something interesting . . . I don't expect justice from a man . . .'

'Who's at the house?' the constable asked.

'The butler.'

'You don't think,' the constable said, 'he saw . . .'

'Trust me,' the sergeant said. 'I've brought up six. I know 'em through and through. You can't teach me anything about children.'

'He seemed scared about something.'

'Dreams,' the sergeant said.

'What name?'

'Baines.'

'This Mr Baines,' the constable said to Philip, 'you like him, eh? He's good to you?' They were trying to get something out of him; he was suspicious of the whole roomful of them; he said 'yes' without conviction because he was afraid at any moment of more responsibilities, more secrets.

'And Mrs Baines?'

'Yes.'

They consulted together by the desk. Rose was hoarsely aggrieved; she was like a female impersonator, she bore her womanhood with an unnatural emphasis even while she scorned it in her creased stockings and her weather-exposed face. The charcoal shifted in the stove; the room was over-heated in the mild late summer evening. A notice on the wall described a body found in the Thames, or rather the body's clothes: wool vest, wool pants, wool shirt with blue stripes, size ten boots, blue serge suit worn at the elbows, fifteen and a half celluloid collar. They couldn't find anything to say about the body, except its measurements, it was just an ordinary body.

'Come along,' the constable said. He was interested, he was glad to be going, but he couldn't help being embarrassed by his company, a small boy in pyjamas. His nose smelt something, he didn't know what, but he smarted at the sight of the amusement they caused: the pubs had closed and the streets were full again of men making as long a day of it as they could. He hurried through the less frequented streets, chose the darker pavements, wouldn't loiter, and Philip wanted more and more to loiter, pulling at his hand, dragging with his feet. He dreaded the sight of Mrs Baines waiting in the hall: he knew now that she was dead. The sergeant's mouthing had conveyed that; but she wasn't buried, she wasn't out of sight; he was going to see a dead person in the hall when the door opened.

The light was on in the basement, and to his relief the constable made for the area steps. Perhaps he wouldn't have to see Mrs Baines at all. The constable knocked on the door because it was too dark to see the bell, and Baines answered. He stood there in the doorway of the neat bright basement room and you could see the sad complacent plausible sentence he had prepared wither at the sight of Philip; he hadn't expected Philip to return like that in the policeman's company. He had to begin thinking all over again; he wasn't a deceptive man. If it hadn't been for Emmy he would have been quite ready to let the truth lead him where it would.

'Mr Baines?' the constable asked.

He nodded; he hadn't found the right words; he was daunted by the shrewd knowing face, the sudden appearance of Philip there.

'This little boy from here?'

'Yes,' Baines said. Philip could tell that there was a message he was trying to convey, but he shut his mind to it. He loved Baines, but Baines had involved him in secrets, in fears he didn't understand. That was what happened when you loved—you got involved; and Philip extricated himself from life, from love, from Baines.

'The doctor's here,' Baines said. He nodded at the door, moistened his mouth, kept his eyes on Philip, begging for something like a dog you can't understand, 'There's nothing to be done. She slipped on these stone basement stairs. I was in here. I heard her fall.' He wouldn't look at the notebook, at the constable's spidery writing which got a terrible lot on one page.

'Did the boy see anything?'

'He can't have done. I thought he was in bed. Hadn't he better go up? It's a shocking thing. O,' Baines said, losing control, 'it's a shocking thing for a child.'

'She's through there?' the constable asked.

'I haven't moved her an inch,' Baines said.

'He'd better then—'

'Go up the area and through the hall,' Baines said, and again he begged dumbly like a dog: one more secret, keep this secret, do this for old Baines, he won't ask another.

'Come along,' the constable said. 'I'll see you up to bed. You're a gentleman. You must come in the proper way through the front door like the master should. Or will you go along with him, Mr Baines, while I see the doctor?'

'Yes,' Baines said, 'I'll go.' He came across the room to Philip, begging, begging, all the way with his old soft stupid expression: this is Baines, the old Coaster; what about a palm-oil chop, eh?; a man's life; forty niggers; never used a gun; I tell you I couldn't help loving them; it wasn't what we call love, nothing we could understand. The messages flickered out from the last posts at the border, imploring, beseeching, reminding: this is your old friend Baines; what about an elevenses; a glass of ginger pop won't do you any harm; sausages; a long day. But the wires were out, the messages just faded out into the vacancy of the scrubbed room in which there had never been a place where a man could hide his secrets.

'Come along, Phil, it's bedtime. We'll just go up the steps . . .' Tap, tap, tap, at the telegraph; you may get through, you can't tell, somebody may mend the right wire. 'And in at the front door.'

'No,' Philip said, 'no. I won't go. You can't make me go. I'll fight. I won't see her.'

The constable turned on them quickly. 'What's that? Why won't you go?'

'She's in the hall,' Philip said. 'I know she's in the hall. And she's dead. I won't see her.'

'You moved her then?' the constable said to Baines. 'All the way down here? You've been lying, eh? That means you had to tidy up. . . . Were you alone?'

'Emmy,' Philip said, 'Emmy.' He wasn't going to keep any more secrets: he was going to finish once and for all with everything, with Baines and Mrs Baines and the grown-up life beyond him. 'It was all Emmy's fault,' he protested with a quaver which reminded Baines that after all he was only a child; it had been hopeless to expect help there; he was a child; he didn't understand what it all meant; he couldn't read this shorthand of terror; he'd had a long day and he was tired out. You could see him dropping asleep where he stood against the dresser, dropping back into the comfortable nursery peace. You couldn't blame him. When he woke in the morning, he'd hardly remember a thing.

'Out with it,' the constable said, addressing Baines with professional ferocity, 'who is she?' just as the old man sixty years later startled his secretary, his only watcher, asking, 'Who is she? Who is she?' dropping lower and lower into death, passing on the way perhaps the image of Baines: Baines hopeless, Baines letting his head drop, Baines 'coming clean'.

Looking for Mr. Green

Saul Bellow (1915–   )

The son of Russian parents, Saul Bellow was brought up in Montreal and Chicago and educated at the University of Chicago and Northwestern University. In the 1930s he worked for a time on the WPA Writers Project. After World War II he taught at a number of universities including Princeton, Minnesota, and New York University. Since 1962 he has been a teaching member of the Committee on Social Thought at the University of Chicago. Primarily a novelist who has taken the American Jewish experience for his central theme, Bellow has published *Dangling Man* (1944), *The Victim* (1947), *The Adventures of Augie March* (1953), *Henderson the Rain King* (1959), *Herzog* (1964), *Mr. Sammler's Planet* (1969), and *Humboldt's Gift* (1975). His collections of short fiction are *Seize the Day* (1956) and *Mosby's Memoirs* (1968) which includes "Looking for Mr. Green," first published in 1951. In 1976 Bellow received the Nobel Prize for Literature.

Whatsoever thy hand findeth to do, do it with thy might. . . .

Hard work? No, it wasn't really so hard. He wasn't used to walking and stair-climbing, but the physical difficulty of his new job was not what George Grebe felt most. He was delivering relief checks in the Negro district, and although he was a native Chicagoan this was not a part of the city he knew much about—it needed a depression to introduce him to it. No, it wasn't literally hard work, not as reckoned in foot-pounds, but yet he was beginning to feel the strain of it, to grow aware of its peculiar difficulty. He could find the streets and numbers, but the clients were not where they were supposed to be, and he felt like a hunter inexperienced in the camouflage of his game. It was an unfavorable day, too—fall, and cold, dark weather, windy. But, anyway, instead of shells in his deep trenchcoat pocket he had the cardboard of checks, punctured for the spindles of the file, the holes reminding him of the holes in player-piano paper. And he didn't look much like a hunter, either; his was a city figure entirely, belted up in this Irish conspirator's coat. He was slender without being tall, stiff in the back, his legs looking shabby in a pair of old tweed pants gone through and fringy at the cuffs. With this stiffness, he kept his head forward, so that his face was red from the sharpness of the weather; and it was an indoors sort of face with gray eyes that persisted in some kind of thought and yet seemed to avoid definiteness of conclusion. He wore sideburns that surprised you somewhat by the tough curl of the blond hair and the effect of assertion in their length. He was not so mild as he looked, nor so youthful; and nevertheless there was no effort on his part to seem what he was not. He was an educated man; he was a bachelor; he was in some ways simple; without lushing, he liked a drink; his luck had not been good. Nothing was deliberately hidden.

He felt that his luck was better than usual today. When he had reported for work that morning he had expected to be shut up in the relief office at a clerk's job, for he had been hired downtown as a clerk, and he was glad to have, instead, the freedom of the streets and welcomed, at least at first, the vigor of the cold and even the blowing of the hard wind. But on the other hand he was not getting on with the distribution of the checks. It was true that it was a city job; nobody expected you to push too hard at a city job. His supervisor, that young Mr. Raynor, had practically told him that. Still, he wanted to do well at it. For one thing, when he knew how quickly he could deliver a batch of checks, he would know also how much time he could expect to clip for himself. And then, too, the clients would be waiting for their money. That was not the most important consideration, though it certainly mattered to him. No, but he wanted to do well, simply for doing-well's sake, to acquit himself decently of a job because he so rarely had a job to do that required just this sort of energy. Of this peculiar energy he now had a superabundance; once it had started to flow, it flowed all too heavily. And, for the time being anyway, he was balked. He could not find Mr. Green.

So he stood in his big-skirted trenchcoat with a large envelope in his hand and papers showing from his pocket, wondering why people should be so hard to locate who were too feeble or sick to come to the station to collect their own checks. But Raynor had told him that tracking them down was not easy at first and had offered him some advice on how to proceed. "If you can see the postman, he's your first man to ask, and your best bet. If you can't connect with him, try the stores and tradespeople around. Then the janitor and the neighbors. But you'll find the closer you come to your man the less people will tell you. They don't want to tell you anything."

"Because I'm a stranger."

"Because you're white. We ought to have a Negro doing this, but we don't at the moment, and of course you've got to eat, too, and this is public employment. Jobs have to be made. Oh, that holds for me too. Mind you, I'm not letting myself out. I've got three years of seniority on you, that's all. And a law degree. Otherwise, you might be back of the desk and I might be going out into the field this cold day. The same dough pays us both and for the same, exact, identical reason. What's my law degree got to do with it? But you have to pass out these checks, Mr. Grebe, and it'll help if you're stubborn, so I hope you are."

"Yes, I'm fairly stubborn."

Raynor sketched hard with an eraser in the old dirt of his desk, left-handed, and said, "Sure, what else can you answer to such a question. Anyhow, the trouble you're going to have is that they don't like to give information about anybody. They think you're a plainclothes dick or an installment collector, or summons-server or something like that. Till you've been seen around the neighborhood for a few months and people know you're only from the relief."

It was dark, ground-freezing, pre-Thanksgiving weather; the wind played hob with the smoke, rushing it down, and Grebe missed his gloves, which he had left in Raynor's office. And no one would admit knowing Green. It was past three o'clock and the postman had made his last delivery. The nearest grocer, himself a Negro, had never heard the name Tulliver Green, or said he hadn't. Grebe was inclined to think that it was true, that he had in the end convinced the man that he wanted only to deliver a check. But he wasn't sure. He needed experience in interpreting looks and signs and, even more, the will not to be put off or denied and even the force to bully if need be. If the grocer did know, he had got rid of him easily. But since most of his trade was with reliefers, why should he prevent the delivery of a check? Maybe Green, or Mrs. Green, if there was a Mrs. Green, patronized another grocer. And was there a Mrs. Green? It was one of Grebe's great handicaps that he hadn't looked at any of the case records. Raynor should have let him read files for a few hours. But he apparently saw no need for that, probably considering the job unimportant. Why prepare systematically to deliver a few checks?

But now it was time to look for the janitor. Grebe took in the building in the wind and gloom of the late November day—trampled, frost-hardened lots on one side; on the other, an automobile junk yard and then the infinite work of Elevated frames, weak-looking, gaping with rubbish fires; two sets of leaning brick porches three stories high and a flight of cement stairs to the cellar. Descending, he entered the underground passage, where he tried the doors until one opened and he found himself in the furnace room. There someone rose toward him and approached, scraping on the coal grit and bending under the canvas-jacketed pipes.

"Are you the janitor?"

"What do you want?"

"I'm looking for a man who's supposed to be living here. Green."

"What Green?"

"Oh, you maybe have more than one Green?" said Grebe with new, pleasant hope. "This is Tulliver Green."

"I don't think I c'n help you, mister. I don't know any."

"A crippled man."

The janitor stood bent before him. Could it be that he was crippled? Oh, God! what if he was. Grebe's gray eyes sought with excited difficulty to see. But no, he was only very short and stooped. A head awakened from meditation, a strong-haired beard, low, wide shoulders. A staleness of sweat and coal rose from his black shirt and the burlap sack he wore as an apron.

"Crippled how?"

Grebe thought and then answered with the light voice of unmixed candor, "I don't know. I've never seen him." This was damaging, but his only other choice was to make a lying guess, and he was not up to it. "I'm delivering checks for the relief to shut-in cases. If he weren't crippled he'd come to collect himself. That's why I said crippled. Bedridden, chair-ridden—is there anybody like that?"

This sort of frankness was one of Grebe's oldest talents, going back to childhood. But it gained him nothing here.

"No suh. I've got four buildin's same as this that I take care of. I don' know all the tenants, leave alone the tenants' tenants. The rooms turn over so fast, people movin' in and out every day. I can't tell you."

The janitor opened his grimy lips but Grebe did not hear him in the piping of the valves and the consuming pull of air to flame in the body of the furnace. He knew, however, what he had said.

"Well, all the same, thanks. Sorry I bothered you. I'll prowl around upstairs again and see if I can turn up someone who knows him."

Once more in the cold air and early darkness he made the short circle from the cellarway to the entrance crowded between the brickwork pillars and began to climb to the third floor. Pieces of plaster ground under his feet; strips of brass tape from which the carpeting had been torn away marked old boundaries at the sides. In the passage, the cold reached him worse than in the street; it touched him to the bone. The hall toilets ran like springs. He thought grimly as he heard the wind burning around the building with a sound like that of the furnace, that this was a great piece of constructed shelter. Then he struck a match in the gloom and searched for names and numbers among the writings and scribbles on the walls. He saw WHOODY-DOODY GO TO JESUS, and zigzags, caricatures, sexual scrawls, and curses. So the sealed rooms of pyramids were also decorated, and the caves of human dawn.

The information on his card was, TULLIVER GREEN—APT 3D. There were no names, however, and no numbers. His shoulders drawn up, tears of cold in his eyes, breathing vapor, he went the length of the corridor and told himself that if he had been lucky enough to have the temperament for it he would bang on one of the doors and bawl out "Tulliver Green!" until he got results. But it wasn't in him to make an uproar and he continued to burn matches, passing the light over the walls. At the rear, in a corner off the hall, he discovered a door he had not seen before and he thought it best to investigate. It sounded empty when he knocked, but a young Negress answered, hardly more than a girl. She opened only a bit, to guard the warmth of the room.

"Yes suh?"

"I'm from the district relief station on Prairie Avenue. I'm looking for a man named Tulliver Green to give him his check. Do you know him?"

No, she didn't; but he thought she had not understood anything of what he had said. She had a dream-bound, dream-blind face, very soft and black, shut off. She wore a man's jacket and pulled the ends together at her throat. Her hair was parted in three directions, at the sides and transversely, standing up at the front in a dull puff.

"Is there somebody around here who might know?"

"I jus' taken this room las' week."

He observed that she shivered, but even her shiver was somnambulistic and there was no sharp consciousness of cold in the big smooth eyes of her handsome face.

"All right, miss, thank you. Thanks," he said, and went to try another place.

Here he was admitted. He was grateful, for the room was warm. It was full of people, and they were silent as he entered—ten people, or a dozen, perhaps more, sitting on benches like a parliament. There was no light, properly speaking, but a tempered darkness that the window gave, and everyone seemed to him enormous, the men padded out in heavy work clothes and winter coats, and the women huge, too, in their sweaters, hats, and old furs. And, besides, bed and bedding, a black cooking range, a piano piled towering to the ceiling with papers, a dining-room table of the old style of prosperous Chicago. Among these people Grebe, with his cold-heightened fresh color and his smaller stature, entered like a schoolboy. Even though he was met with smiles and good will, he knew, before a single word was spoken, that all the currents ran against him and that he would make no headway. Nevertheless he began. "Does anybody here know how I can deliver a check to Mr. Tulliver Green?"

"Green?" It was the man that had let him in who answered. He was in short sleeves, in a checkered shirt, and had a queer, high head, profusely overgrown and long as a shako; the veins entered it strongly from his forehead. "I never heard mention of him. Is this where he live?"

"This is the address they gave me at the station. He's a sick man, and he'll need his check. Can't anybody tell me where to find him?"

He stood his ground and waited for a reply, his crimson wool scarf wound about his neck and drooping outside his trenchcoat, pockets weighted with the block of checks and official forms. They must have realized that he was not a college boy employed afternoons by a bill collector, trying foxily to pass for a relief clerk, recognized that he was an older man who knew himself what need was, who had had more than an average seasoning in hardship. It was evident enough if you looked at the marks under his eyes and at the sides of his mouth.

"Anybody know this sick man?"

"No suh." On all sides he saw heads shaken and smiles of denial. No one knew. And maybe it was true, he considered, standing silent in the earthen, musky human gloom of the place as the rumble continued. But he could never really be sure.

"What's the matter with this man?" said shako-head.

"I've never seen him. All I can tell you is that he can't come in person for his money. It's my first day in this district."

"Maybe they given you the wrong number?"

"I don't believe so. But where else can I ask about him?" He felt that this persistence amused them deeply, and in a way he shared their amusement that he should stand up so tenaciously to them. Though smaller, though slight, he was his own man, he retracted nothing about himself and he looked back at them, gray-eyed, with amusement and also with a sort of courage. On the bench some man spoke in his throat, the words impossible to catch, and a woman answered with a wild, shrieking laugh, which was quickly cut off.

"Well, so nobody will tell me?"

"Ain't nobody who knows."

"At least, if he lives here, he pays rent to someone. Who manages the building?"

"Greatham Company. That's on Thirty-ninth Street."

Grebe wrote it in his pad. But, in the street again, a sheet of wind-driven paper clinging to his leg while he deliberated what direction to take next, it seemed a feeble lead to follow. Probably this Green didn't rent a flat, but a room. Sometimes there were as many as twenty people in an apartment; the real-estate agent would know only the lessee. And not even the agent could tell you who the renters were. In some places the beds were even used in shifts, watchmen or jitney drivers or short-order cooks in night joints turning out after a day's sleep and surrendering their beds to a sister, a nephew, or perhaps a stranger, just off the bus. There were large numbers of newcomers in this terrific, blight-bitten portion of the city between Cottage Grove and Ashland, wandering from house to house and room to room. When you saw them, how could you know them? They didn't carry bundles on their backs or look picturesque. You only saw a man, a Negro, walking in the street or riding in the car, like everyone else, with his thumb closed on a transfer. And therefore how were you supposed to tell? Grebe thought the Greatham agent would only laugh at his question.

But how much it would have simplifed the job to be able to say that Green was old, or blind, or comsumptive. An hour in the files, taking a few notes, and he needn't have been at such a disadvantage. When Raynor gave him the block of checks he asked, "How much should I know about these people?" Then Raynor had looked as though he were preparing to accuse him of trying to make the job more important than it was. He smiled, because by then they were on fine terms, but nevertheless he had been getting ready to say something like that when the confusion began in the station over Staika and her children.

Grebe had waited a long time for this job. It came to him through the pull of an old schoolmate in the Corporation Counsel's office, never a close friend, but suddenly sympathetic and interested—pleased to show, moreover, how well he had done, how strongly he was coming on even in these miserable times. Well, he was coming through strongly, along with the Democratic administration itself. Grebe had gone to see him in City Hall, and they had had a counter lunch or beers at least once a month for a year; and finally it had been possible to swing the job. He didn't mind being assigned the lowest clerical grade, nor even being a messenger, though Raynor thought he did.

This Raynor was an original sort of guy and Grebe had taken to him immediately. As was proper on the first day, Grebe had come early, but he waited long, for Raynor was late. At last he darted into his cubicle of an office as though he had just jumped from one of those hurtling huge red Indiana Avenue cars. His thin, rough face was wind-stung and he was grinning and saying something breathlessly to himself. In his hat, a small fedora, and his coat, the velvet collar a neat fit about his neck, and his silk muffler that set off the nervous twist of his chin, he swayed and turned himself in his swivel chair, feet leaving the ground; so that he pranced a little as he sat. Meanwhile he took Grebe's measure out of his eyes, eyes of an unusual vertical length and slightly sardonic. So the two men sat for a while, saying nothing, while the supervisor raised his hat from his miscombed hair and put it in his lap. His cold-darkened hands were not clean. A steel beam passed through the little makeshift room, from which machine belts once had hung. The building was an old factory.

"I'm younger than you; I hope you won't find it

hard taking orders from me," said Raynor. "But I don't make them up, either. You're how old, about?"

"Thirty-five."

"And you thought you'd be inside doing paper work. But it so happens I have to send you out."

"I don't mind."

"And it's mostly a Negro load we have in this district."

"So I thought it would be."

"Fine. You'll get along. *C'est un bon boulot.* Do you know French?"

"Some."

"I thought you'd be a university man."

"Have you been in France?" said Grebe.

"No, that's the French of the Berlitz School. I've been at it for more than a year, just as I'm sure people have been, all over the world, office boys in China and braves in Tanganyika. In fact, I damn well know it. Such is the attractive power of civilization. It's overrated, but what do you want? *Que voulez-vous?* I get *Le Rire* and all the spicy papers, just like in Tanganyika. It must be mystifying, out there. But my reason is that I'm aiming at the diplomatic service. I have a cousin who's a courier, and the way he describes it is awfully attractive. He rides in the *wagon-lits* and reads books. While we—What did you do before?"

"I sold."

"Where?"

"Canned meat at Stop and Shop. In the basement."

"And before that?"

"Window shades, at Goldblatt's."

"Steady work?"

"No, Thursdays and Saturdays. I also sold shoes."

"You've been a shoe-dog too. Well. And prior to that? Here it is in your folder." He opened the record. "Saint Olaf's College, instructor in classical languages. Fellow, University of Chicago, 1926–27. I've had Latin, too. Let's trade quotations—*'Dum spiro spero.'* "

" *'Da dextram misero.'* "

" *'Alea jacta est.'* "

" *'Excelsior.'* "

Raynor shouted with laughter, and other workers came to look at him over the partition. Grebe also laughed, feeling pleased and easy. The luxury of fun on a nervous morning.

When they were done and no one was watching or listening, Raynor said rather seriously, "What made you study Latin in the first place? Was it for the priesthood?"

"No."

"Just for the hell of it? For the culture? Oh, the things people think they can pull!" He made his cry hilarious and tragic. "I ran my pants off so I could study for the bar, and I've passed the bar, so I get twelve dollars a week more than you as a bonus for having seen life straight and whole. I'll tell you, as a man of culture, that even though nothing looks to be real, and everything stands for something else, and that thing for another thing, and that thing for a still further one—there ain't any comparison between twenty-five and thirty-seven dollars a week, regardless of the last reality. Don't you think that was clear to your Greeks? They were a thoughtful people, but they didn't part with their slaves."

This was a great deal more than Grebe had looked for in his first interview with his supervisor. He was too shy to show all the astonishment he felt. He laughed a little, aroused, and brushed at the sunbeam that covered his head with its dust. "Do you think my mistake was so terrible?"

"Damn right it was terrible, and you know it now that you've had the whip of hard times laid on your back. You should have been preparing yourself for trouble. Your people must have been well off to send you to the university. Stop me, if I'm stepping on your toes. Did your mother pamper you? Did your father give in to you? Were you brought up tenderly, with permission to go and find out what were the last things that everything else stands for while everybody else labored in the fallen world of appearances?"

"Well, no, it wasn't exactly like that." Grebe smiled. *The fallen world of appearances!* no less. But now it was his turn to deliver a surprise. "We weren't rich. My father was the last genuine English butler in Chicago—"

"Are you kidding?"

"Why should I be?"

"In a livery?"

"In livery. Up on the Gold Coast."

"And he wanted you to be educated like a gentleman?"

"He did not. He sent me to the Armour Institute to study chemical engineering. But when he died I changed schools."

He stopped himself, and considered how quickly Raynor had reached him. In no time he had your valise on the table and all your stuff unpacked. And afterward, in the streets, he was still reviewing how far he might have gone, and how much he might have been led to tell if they had not been interrupted by Mrs. Staika's great noise.

But just then a young woman, one of Raynor's workers, ran into the cubicle exclaiming, "Haven't you heard all the fuss?"

"We haven't heard anything."

"It's Staika, giving out with all her might. The reporters are coming. She said she phoned the papers, and you know she did."

"But what is she up to?" said Raynor.

"She brought her wash and she's ironing it here, with our current, because the relief won't pay her electric bill. She has her ironing board set up by the admitting desk, and her kids are with her, all six. They never are in school more than once a week. She's always dragging them around with her because of her reputation."

"I don't want to miss any of this," said Raynor, jumping up. Grebe, as he followed with the secretary, said, "Who is this Staika?"

"They call her the 'Blood Mother of Federal Street.' She's a professional donor at the hospitals. I think they pay ten dollars a pint. Of course it's no joke, but she makes a very big thing out of it and she and the kids are in the papers all the time."

A small crowd, staff and clients divided by a plywood barrier, stood in the narrow space of the entrance, and Staika was shouting in a gruff, mannish voice, plunging the iron on the board and slamming it on the metal rest.

"My father and mother came in a steerage, and I was born in our house, Robey by Huron. I'm no dirty immigrant. I'm a U.S. citizen. My husband is a gassed veteran from France with lungs weaker'n paper, that hardly can he go to the toilet by himself. These six children of mine, I have to buy the shoes for their feet with my own blood. Even a lousy little white Communion necktie, that's a couple of drops of blood; a little piece of mosquito veil for my Vadja so she won't be ashamed in church for the other girls, they take my blood for it by Goldblatt. That's how I keep goin'. A fine thing if I had to depend on the relief. And there's plenty of people on the rolls—fakes! There's nothin' *they* can't get, that can go and wrap bacon at Swift and Armour any time. They're lookin' for them by the Yards. They never have to be out of work. Only they rather lay in their lousy beds and eat the public's money." She was not afraid, in a predominantly Negro station, to shout this way about Negroes.

Grebe and Raynor worked themselves forward to get a closer view of the woman. She was flaming with anger and with pleasure at herself, broad and huge, a golden-headed woman who wore a cotton cap laced with pink ribbon. She was barelegged and had on black gym shoes, her Hoover apron was open and her great breasts, not much restrained by a man's undershirt, hampered her arms as she worked at the kid's dress on the ironing board. And the children, silent and white, with a kind of locked obstinacy, in sheepskins and lumberjackets, stood behind her. She had captured the station, and the pleasure this gave her was enormous. Yet her grievances were true grievances. She was telling the truth. But she behaved like a liar. The look of her small eyes was hidden, and while she raged she also seemed to be spinning and planning.

"They send me out college case workers in silk pants to talk me out of what I got comin'. Are they better'n me? Who told them? Fire them. Let 'em go and get married, and then you won't have to cut electric from people's budget."

The chief supervisor, Mr. Ewing, couldn't silence her and he stood with folded arms at the head of his staff, bald, bald-headed, saying to his subordinates like the ex-school principal he was, "Pretty soon she'll be tired and go."

"No she won't," said Raynor to Grebe. "She'll get what she wants. She knows more about the relief even then Ewing. She's been on the rolls for years, and she always gets what she wants because she puts on a noisy show. Ewing knows it. He'll give in soon. He's only saving face. If he gets bad publicity, the Commissioner'll have him on the carpet, downtown. She's got him submerged; she'll submerge everybody in time, and that includes nations and governments."

Grebe replied with his characteristic smile, disagreeing completely. Who would take Staika's orders, and what changes could her yelling ever bring about?

No, what Grebe saw in her, the power that made people listen, was that her cry expressed the war of flesh and blood, perhaps turned a little crazy and certainly ugly, on this place and this condition. And at first, when he went out, the spirit of Staika somehow presided over the whole district for him, and it took color from her; he saw her color, in the spotty curb fires, and the fires under the El, the straight alley of flamy gloom. Later, too, when he went into a tavern for a shot of rye, the sweat of beer, association with West Side Polish streets, made him think of her again.

He wiped the corners of his mouth with his muffler, his handkerchief being inconvenient to reach for, and went out again to get on with the delivery of his checks. The air bit cold and hard and a few flakes of snow formed near him. A train struck by and left a quiver in the frames and a bristling icy hiss over the rails.

Crossing the street, he descended a flight of board steps into a basement grocery, setting off a little bell. It was a dark, long store and it caught you with its stinks of smoked meat, soap, dried peaches, and fish. There was a fire wrinkling and flapping in the little stove, and the proprietor was waiting, an Italian with a long, hollow face and stubborn bristles. He kept his hands warm under his apron.

No, he didn't know Green. You knew people but not names. The same man might not have the same name twice. The police didn't know, either, and mostly didn't care. When somebody was shot or knifed they took the body away and didn't look for the murderer. In the first place, nobody would tell them anything. So they made up a name for the coroner and called it quits. And in the second place, they didn't give a goddamn anyhow. But they couldn't get to the bottom of a thing even if they wanted to. Nobody would get to know even a tenth of what went on among these people. They stabbed and stole, they did every crime and abomination you ever heard of, men and men, women and women, parents and children, worse than the animals. They carried on their own way, and the horrors passed off like a smoke. There was never anything like it in the history of the whole world.

It was a long speech, deepening with every word in its fantasy and passion and becoming increasingly senseless and terrible: a swarm amassed by suggestion and invention, a huge, hugging, despairing knot, a human wheel of heads, legs, bellies, arms, rolling through his shop.

Grebe felt that he must interrupt him. He said sharply, "What are you talking about! All I asked was whether you knew this man."

"That isn't even the half of it. I been here six years. You probably don't want to believe this. But suppose it's true?"

"All the same," said Grebe, "there must be a way to find a person."

The Italian's close-spaced eyes had been queerly concentrated, as were his muscles, while he leaned across the counter trying to convince Grebe. Now he gave up the effort and sat down on his stool. "Oh—I suppose. Once in a while. But I been telling you, even the cops don't get anywhere."

"They're always after somebody. It's not the same thing."

"Well, keep trying if you want. I can't help you."

But he didn't keep trying. He had no more time to spend on Green. He slipped Green's check to the back of the block. The next name on the list was FIELD, WINSTON.

He found the back-yard bungalow without the least trouble; it shared a lot with another house, a few feet of yard between. Grebe knew these two-shack arrangements. They had been built in vast numbers in the days before the swamps were filled and the streets raised, and they were all the same—a boardwalk along the fence, well under street level, three or four ball-headed posts for clotheslines, greening wood, dead shingles, and a long, long flight of stairs to the rear door.

A twelve-year-old boy let him into the kitchen, and there the old man was, sitting by the table in a wheel chair.

"Oh, it's d' Government man," he said to the boy when Grebe drew out his checks. "Go bring me my box of papers." He cleared a space on the table.

"Oh, you don't have to go to all that trouble," said Grebe. But Field laid out his papers: Social Security card, relief certification, letters from the state hospital in Manteno, and a naval discharge dated San Diego, 1920.

"That's plenty," Grebe said. "Just sign."

"You got to know who I am," the old man said. "You're from the Government. It's not your check, it's a Government check and you got no business to hand it over till everything is proved."

He loved the ceremony of it, and Grebe made no more objections. Field emptied his box and finished out the circle of cards and letters.

"There's everything I done and been Just the death certificate and they can close book on me." He said this with a certain happy pride and magnificence. Still he did not sign; he merely held the little pen upright on the golden-green corduroy of his thigh. Grebe did not hurry him. He felt the old man's hunger for conversation.

"I got to get better coal," he said. "I send my little gran'son to the yard with my order and they fill his wagon with screening. The stove ain't made for it. It fall through the grate. The order says Franklin County egg-size coal."

"I'll report it and see what can be done."

"Nothing can be done, I expect. You know and I know. There ain't no little ways to make things better, and the only thing big is money. That's the only sunbeams, money. Nothing is black where it shines, and the only place you see black is where it ain't shining. What we colored have to have is our own rich. There ain't no other way."

Grebe sat, his reddened forehead bridged levelly by his close-cut hair and his cheeks lowered in the wings of his collar—the caked fire shone hard within the isinglass-and-iron frames but the room was not comfortable—sat and listened while the old man unfolded his scheme. This was to create one Negro millionaire a month by subscription. One clever, good-hearted young fellow elected every month would sign a contract to use the money to start a business employing Negroes. This would be advertised by chain letters and word of mouth, and every Negro wage earner would contribute a dollar a month. Within five years there would be sixty millionaires.

"That'll fetch respect," he said with a throat-stopped sound that came out like a foreign syllable. "You got to take and organize all the money that gets thrown away on the policy wheel and horse race. As long as they can take it away from you, they got no respect for you. Money, that's d' sun of human kind!" Field was a Negro of mixed blood, perhaps Cherokee, or Natchez; his skin was reddish. And he sounded, speaking about a golden sun in this dark room, and looked, shaggy and slab-headed, with the mingled blood of his face and broad lips, the little pen still upright in his hand, like one of the underground kings of mythology, old judge Minos himself.

And now he accepted the check and signed. Not to soil the slip, he held it down with his knuckles. The table budged and creaked, the center of the gloomy, heathen midden of the kitchen covered with bread, meat, and cans, and the scramble of papers.

"Don't you think my scheme'd work?"

"It's worth thinking about. Something ought to be done, I agree."

"It'll work if people will do it. That's all. That's the only thing, any time. When they understand it in the same way, all of them."

"That's true," said Grebe, rising. His glance met the old man's.

"I know you got to go," he said. "Well, God bless you, boy, you ain't been sly with me. I can tell it in a minute."

He went back through the buried yard. Someone nursed a candle in a shed, where a man unloaded kindling wood from a sprawl-wheeled baby buggy and two voices carried on a high conversation. As he came up the sheltered passage he heard the hard boost of the wind in the branches and against the house fronts, and then, reaching the sidewalk, he saw the needle-eye red of cable towers in the open icy height hundreds of feet above the river and the factories—those keen points. From here, his view was obstructed all the way to the South Branch and its timber banks, and the cranes beside the water. Rebuilt after the Great Fire, this part of the city was, not fifty years later, in ruins again, factories boarded up, buildings deserted or fallen, gaps of prairie between. But it wasn't desolation that this made you feel, but rather a faltering of organization that set free a huge energy, an escaped, unattached, unregulated power from the giant raw place. Not only must people feel it but, it seemed to Grebe, they were compelled to match it. In their very bodies. He no less than others, he realized. Say that his parents had been servants in their time, whereas he was not supposed to be one. He thought that they had never done any service like this, which no one visible asked for, and probably flesh and blood could not even perform. Nor could anyone show why it should be performed; or see where the performance would lead. That did not mean that he wanted to be released from it, he realized with a grimly pensive face. On the contrary. He had something to do. To be compelled to feel this energy and yet have no task to do—that was horrible; that was suffering; he knew what that was. It was now quitting time. Six o'clock. He could go home if he liked, to his room, that is, to wash in hot water, to pour a drink, lie down on his quilt, read the paper, eat some liver paste on crackers before going out to dinner. But to think of this actually made him feel a little sick, as though he had swallowed hard air. He had six checks left, and he was determined to deliver at least one of these: Mr. Green's check.

So he started again. He had four or five dark blocks to go, past open lots, condemned houses, old foundations, closed schools, black churches, mounds, and he reflected that there must be many people alive who had once seen the neighborhood rebuilt and new. Now there was a second layer of ruins; centuries of history accomplished through human massing. Numbers had given the place forced growth; enormous numbers had also broken it down. Objects once so new, so concrete that it could have occurred to anyone they stood for other things, had crumbled. Therefore, reflected Grebe, the secret of them was out. It was that they stood for themselves by agreement, and were natural and not unnatural by agreement, and when the things themselves collapsed the agreement became visible. What was it, otherwise, that kept cities from looking peculiar? Rome, that was almost permanent, did not give rise to thoughts like these. And was it abidingly real? But in Chicago, where the cycles were so fast and the familiar died out, and again rose changed, and died again in thirty years, you saw the common agreement or covenant, and you were forced to think about appearances and realities. (He remembered Raynor and he smiled. Raynor was a clever boy.) Once you had grasped this, a great many things became intelligible. For instance, why Mr. Field should conceive such a scheme. Of course, if people were to agree to create a millionaire, a real millionaire would come into existence. And if you wanted to know how Mr. Field was inspired to think of this, why, he had within sight of his kitchen window the chart, the very bones of a successful scheme—the El with its blue and green confetti of signals. People consented to pay dimes and ride the crash-box cars, and so it was a success. Yet how absurd it looked; how little reality there was to start with. And yet Yerkes, the great financier who built it, had known that he could get people to agree to do it. Viewed as itself, what a scheme of a scheme it seemed, how close to an appearance. Then why wonder at Mr. Field's idea? He had grasped a principle. And then Grebe remembered, too, that Mr. Yerkes had established the Yerkes Observatory and endowed it with millions. Now how did the notion come to him in his New York museum of a palace or his Aegean-bound yacht to give money to astronomers? Was he awed by the success of his bizarre enterprise and therefore ready to spend money to find out where in the universe being and seeming were identical? Yes, he wanted to know what abides; and whether flesh is Bible grass; and he offered money to be burned in the fire of suns. Okay, then, Grebe thought further, these things exist because people consent to exist with them—we have got so far—and also there is a reality which doesn't depend on consent but within which consent is a game. But what about need, the need that keeps so many vast thousands in position? You tell me that, you *private* little gentleman and decent soul—he used these words against himself scornfully. Why is the consent given to misery? And why so painfully ugly? Because there is *something* that is dismal and permanently ugly? Here he sighed and gave it up, and thought it was enough for the present moment that he had a real check in his pocket for a Mr. Green who must be real beyond question. If only his neighbors didn't think they had to conceal him.

This time he stopped at the second floor. He struck a match and found a door. Presently a man answered his knock and Grebe had the check ready and showed it even before he began. "Does Tulliver Green live here? I'm from the relief."

The man narrowed the opening and spoke to someone at his back.

"Does he live here?"

"Uh-uh. No."

"Or anywhere in this building? He's a sick man and he can't come for his dough." He exhibited the check in the light, which was smoky—the air smelled of charred lard—and the man held off the brim of his cap to study it.

"Uh-uh. Never seen the name."

"There's nobody around here that uses crutches?"

He seemed to think, but it was Grebe's impression that he was simply waiting for a decent interval to pass.

"No, suh. Nobody I ever see."

"I've been looking for this man all afternoon"—Grebe spoke out with sudden force—"and I'm going to have to carry this check back to the station. It seems strange not to be able to find a person to *give* him something when you're looking for him for a good reason. I suppose if I had bad news for him I'd find him quick enough."

There was a responsive motion in the other man's face. "That's right, I reckon."

"It almost doesn't do any good to have a name if you can't be found by it. It doesn't stand for anything. He might as well not have any," he went on, smiling. It was as much of a concession as he could make to his desire to laugh.

"Well, now, there's a little old knot-back man I see once in a while. He might be the one you lookin' for. Downstairs."

"Where? Right side or left? Which door?"

"I don't know which. Thin-face little knot-back with a stick."

But no one answered at any of the doors on the first floor. He went to the end of the corridor, searching by matchlight, and found only a stairless exit to the yard, a drop of about six feet. But there was a bungalow near the alley, an old house like Mr. Field's. To jump was unsafe. He ran from the front door, through the underground passage and into the yard. The place was occupied. There was a light through the curtains, upstairs. The name on the ticket under the broken, scoop-shaped mailbox was Green! He exultantly rang the bell and pressed against the locked door. Then the lock clicked faintly and a long staircase opened before him. Someone was slowly coming down—a woman. He had the impression in the weak light that she was shaping her hair as she came, making herself presentable, for he saw her arms raised. But it was for support that they were raised; she was feeling her way downward, down the wall, stumbling. Next he wondered about the pressure of her feet on the treads; she did not seem to be wearing shoes. And it was a freezing stairway. His ring had got her out of bed, perhaps, and she had forgotten to put them on. And then he saw that she was not only shoeless but naked; she was entirely naked, climbing down while she talked to herself, a heavy woman, naked and drunk. She blundered into him. The contact of her breasts, though they touched only his coat, made him go back against the door with a blind shock. See what he had tracked down, in his hunting game!

The woman was saying to herself, furious with insult, "So I cain't ——k, huh? I'll show that son-of-a-bitch kin I, cain't I."

What should he do now? Grebe asked himself. Why, he should go. He should turn away and go. He couldn't talk to this woman. He couldn't keep her standing naked in the cold. But when he tried he found himself unable to turn away.

He said, "Is this where Mr. Green lives?"

But she was still talking to herself and did not hear him.

"Is this Mr. Green's house?"

At last she turned her furious drunken glance on him. "What do you want?"

Again her eyes wandered from him; there was a dot of blood in their enraged brilliance. He wondered why she didn't feel the cold.

"I'm from the relief."

"Awright, what?"

"I've got a check for Tulliver Green."

This time she heard him and put out her hand.

"No, no, for *Mr.* Green. He's got to sign," he said. How was he going to get Green's signature tonight!

"I'll take it. He cain't."

He desperately shook his head, thinking of Mr. Field's precautions about identification. "I can't let you have it. It's for him. Are you Mrs. Green?"

"Maybe I is, and maybe I ain't. Who want to know?"

"Is he upstairs?"

"Awright. Take it up yourself, you goddamn fool."

Sure, he was a goddamn fool. Of course he could not go up because Green would probably be drunk and naked, too. And perhaps he would appear on the landing soon. He looked eagerly upward. Under the light was a high narrow brown wall. Empty! It remained empty!

"Hell with you, then!" he heard her cry. To deliver a check for coal and clothes, he was keeping her in the cold. She did not feel it, but his face was burning with frost and self-ridicule. He backed away from her.

"I'll come tomorrow, tell him."

"Ah, hell with you. Don' never come. What you doin' here in the nighttime? Don' come back." She yelled so that he saw the breadth of her tongue. She stood astride in the long cold box of the hall and held on to the banister and the wall. The bungalow itself was shaped something like a box, a clumsy, high box pointing into the freezing air with its sharp, wintry lights.

"If you are Mrs. Green, I'll give you the check," he said, changing his mind.

"Give here, then." She took it, took the pen offered with it in her left hand, and tried to sign the receipt on the wall. He looked around, almost as though to see whether his madness was being observed, and came near believing that someone was standing on a mountain of used tires in the auto-junking shop next door.

"But are you Mrs. Green?" he now thought to ask. But she was already climbing the stairs with the check, and it was too late, if he had made an error, if he was now in trouble, to undo the thing. But he wasn't going to worry about it. Though she might not be Mrs. Green, he was convinced that Mr. Green was upstairs. Whoever she was, the woman stood for Green, whom he was not to see this time. Well, you silly bastard, he said to himself, so you think you found him. So what? Maybe you really did find him—what of it? But it was important that there was a real Mr. Green whom they could not keep him from reaching because he seemed to come as an emissary from hostile appearances. And though the self-ridicule was slow to diminish, and his face still blazed with it, he had, nevertheless, a feeling of elation, too. "For after all," he said, "he *could* be found!"

Revelation

Flannery O'Connor (1925–1964)

Mary Flannery O'Connor was brought up in a Roman Catholic household in Savannah, Georgia. She received her education at parochial schools and at the Women's College of Georgia. By the early 1950s it was clear that she had inherited the same incurable disease that killed her father, and during the last ten years of her life she was a semi-invalid. In her stories the violence and eccentricity of Southern life are examined from a Catholic viewpoint that never interferes with her delicate sense of individual character. *A Good Man Is Hard To Find* (1955) was the only volume of stories published during her lifetime. A posthumous collection, *Everything That Rises Must Converge* (which includes "Revelation") was published in 1965, and was followed by *The Complete Stories* (1971), which contains twelve stories previously uncollected.

The doctor's waiting room, which was very small, was almost full when the Turpins entered and Mrs. Turpin, who was very large, made it look even smaller by her presence. She stood looming at the head of the magazine table set in the center of it, a living demonstration that the room was inadequate and ridiculous. Her little bright black eyes took in all the patients as she sized up the seating situation. There was one vacant chair and a place on the sofa occupied by a blond child in a dirty blue romper who should have been told to move over and make room for the lady. He was five or six, but Mrs. Turpin saw at once that no one was going to tell him to move over. He was slumped down in the seat, his arms idle at his sides and his eyes idle in his head; his nose ran unchecked.

Mrs. Turpin put a firm hand on Claud's shoulder and said in a voice that included anyone who wanted to listen, "Claud, you sit in that chair there," and gave him a push down into the vacant one. Claud was florid and bald and sturdy, somewhat shorter than Mrs. Turpin, but he sat down as if he were accustomed to doing what she told him to.

Mrs. Turpin remained standing. The only man in the room besides Claud was a lean stringy old fellow with a rusty hand spread out on each knee, whose eyes were closed as if he were asleep or dead or pretending to be so as not to get up and offer her his seat. Her gaze settled agreeably on a well-dressed grey-haired lady whose eyes met hers and whose expression said: if that child belonged to me, he would have some manners and move over—there's plenty of room there for you and him too.

Claud looked up with a sigh and made as if to rise.

"Sit down," Mrs. Turpin said. "You know you're not supposed to stand on that leg. He has an ulcer on his leg," she explained.

Claud lifted his foot onto the magazine table and rolled his trouser leg up to reveal a purple swelling on a plump marble-white calf.

"My!" the pleasant lady said. "How did you do that?"

"A cow kicked him," Mrs. Turpin said.

"Goodness!" said the lady.

Claud rolled his trouser leg down.

"Maybe the little boy would move over," the lady suggested, but the child did not stir.

"Somebody will be leaving in a minute," Mrs. Turpin said. She could not understand why a doctor—with as much money as they made charging five dollars a day to just stick their head in the hospital door and look at you—couldn't afford a decent-sized waiting room. This one was hardly bigger than a garage. The table was cluttered with limp-looking magazines and at one end of it there was a big green glass ash tray full of cigaret butts and cotton wads with little blood spots on them. If she had had anything to do with the running of the place, that would have been emptied every so often. There were no chairs against the wall at the head of the room. It had a rectangular-shaped panel in it that permitted a view of the office where the nurse came and went and the secretary listened to the radio. A plastic fern in a gold pot sat in the opening and trailed its fronds down almost to the floor. The radio was softly playing gospel music.

Just then the inner door opened and a nurse with the highest stack of yellow hair Mrs. Turpin had ever seen put her face in the crack and called for the next patient. The woman sitting beside Claud grasped the two arms of her chair and hoisted herself up; she pulled her dress free from her legs and lumbered through the door where the nurse had disappeared.

Mrs. Turpin eased into the vacant chair, which held her tight as a corset. "I wish I could reduce," she said, and rolled her eyes and gave a comic sigh.

"Oh, *you* aren't fat," the stylish lady said.

"Ooooo I am too," Mrs. Turpin said. "Claud he eats all he wants to and never weighs over one hundred and seventy-five pounds, but me I just look at something good to eat and I gain some weight," and her stomach and shoulders shook with laughter. "You can eat all you want to, can't you, Claud?" she asked, turning to him.

Claud only grinned.

"Well, as long as you have such a good disposition," the stylish lady said, "I don't think it makes a bit of difference what size you are. You just can't beat a good disposition."

Next to her was a fat girl of eighteen or nineteen, scowling into a thick blue book which Mrs. Turpin saw was entitled *Human Development*. The girl raised her head and directed her scowl at Mrs. Turpin as if she did not like her looks. She appeared annoyed that anyone should speak while she tried to read. The poor girl's face was blue with acne and Mrs. Turpin thought how pitiful it was to have a face like that at that age. She gave the girl a friendly smile but the girl only scowled the harder. Mrs. Turpin herself was fat but she had always had good skin, and, though she was forty-seven years old, there was not a wrinkle in her face except around her eyes from laughing too much.

Next to the ugly girl was the child, still in exactly the same position, and next to him was a thin leathery old woman in a cotton print dress. She and Claud had three sacks of chicken feed in their pump house that was in the same print. She had seen from the first that the child belonged with the old woman. She could tell by the way they sat—kind of vacant and white-trashy, as if they would sit there until Doomsday if nobody called and told them to get up. And at right angles but next to the well-dressed pleasant lady was a lank-faced woman who was certainly the child's mother. She had on a yellow sweat shirt and wine-colored slacks, both gritty-looking, and the rims of her lips were stained with snuff. Her dirty yellow hair was tied behind with a little piece of red paper ribbon. Worse than niggers any day, Mrs. Turpin thought.

The gospel hymn playing was, "When I looked up and He looked down," and Mrs. Turpin, who knew it, supplied the last line mentally, "And wona these days I know I'll we-eara crown."

Without appearing to, Mrs. Turpin always noticed people's feet. The well-dressed lady had on red and grey suede shoes to match her dress. Mrs. Turpin had on her good black patent leather pumps. The ugly girl had on Girl Scout shoes and heavy socks. The old woman had on tennis shoes and the white-trashy mother had on what appeared to be bedroom slippers, black straw with gold braid threaded through them—exactly what you would have expected her to have on.

Sometimes at night when she couldn't go to sleep, Mrs. Turpin would occupy herself with the question of who she would have chosen to be if she couldn't have been herself. If Jesus had said to her before he made her, "There's only two places available for you. You can either be a nigger or white-trash," what would she have said? "Please, Jesus, please," she would have said, "just let me wait until there's another place available," and he would have said, "No, you have to go right now and I have only those two places so make up your mind." She would have wiggled and squirmed and begged and pleaded but it would have been no use and finally she would have said, "All right, make me a nigger then—but that don't mean a trashy one." And he would have made her a neat clean respectable Negro-woman, herself but black.

Next to the child's mother was a red-headed youngish woman, reading one of the magazines and working a piece of chewing gum, hell for leather, as Claud would say. Mrs. Turpin could not see the woman's feet. She was not white-trash, just common. Sometimes Mrs. Turpin occupied herself at night naming the classes of people. On the bottom of the heap were most colored people, not the kind she would have been if she had been one, but most of them; then next to them—not above, just away from—were the white-trash; then above them were the home-owners, and above them the home-and-land owners, to which she and Claud belonged. Above she and Claud were people with a lot of money and much bigger houses and much more land. But here the complexity of it would begin to bear in on her, for some of the people with a lot of money were common and ought to be below she and Claud and some of the people who had good blood had lost their money and had to rent and then there were colored people who owned their homes and land as well. There was a colored dentist in town who had two red Lincolns and a swimming pool and a farm with registered white-face cattle on it. Usually by the time she had fallen asleep all the classes of people were moiling and roiling around in her head, and she would dream they were all crammed in together in a box car, being ridden off to be put in a gas oven.

"That's a beautiful clock," she said and nodded to her right. It was a big wall clock, the face encased in a brass sunburst.

"Yes, it's very pretty," the stylish lady said agreeably. "And right on the dot too," she added, glancing at her watch.

The ugly girl beside her cast an eye upward at the clock, smirked, then looked directly at Mrs. Turpin and smirked again. Then she returned her eyes to her book. She was obviously the lady's daughter because, although they didn't look anything alike as to disposition, they both had the same shape of face and the same blue eyes. On the lady they sparkled pleasantly but in the girl's seared face they appeared alternately to smolder and to blaze.

What if Jesus had said, "All right, you can be white-trash or a nigger or ugly"!

Mrs. Turpin felt an awful pity for the girl, though she thought it was one thing to be ugly and another to act ugly.

The woman with the snuff-stained lips turned around in her chair and looked up at the clock. Then she turned back and appeared to look a little to the side of Mrs. Turpin. There was a cast in one of her eyes. "You want to know wher you can get you one of themther clocks?" she asked in a loud voice.

"No, I already have a nice clock," Mrs. Turpin said.

Once somebody like her got a leg in the conversation, she would be all over it.

"You can get you one with green stamps," the woman said. "That's most likely wher he got hisn. Save you up enough, you can get you most anythang. I got me some joo'ry."

Ought to have got you a wash rag and some soap, Mrs. Turpin thought.

"I get contour sheets with mine," the pleasant lady said.

The daughter slammed her book shut. She looked straight in front of her, directly through Mrs. Turpin and on through the yellow curtain and the plate glass window which made the wall behind her. The girl's eyes seemed lit all of a sudden with a peculiar light, an unnatural light like night road signs give. Mrs. Turpin turned her head to see if there was anything going on outside that she should see, but she could not see anything. Figures passing cast only a pale shadow through the curtain. There was no reason the girl should single her out for her ugly looks.

"Miss Finley," the nurse said, cracking the door. The gum-chewing woman got up and passed in front of her and Claud and went into the office. She had on red high-heeled shoes.

Directly across the table, the ugly girl's eyes were fixed on Mrs. Turpin as if she had some very special reason for disliking her.

"This is wonderful weather, isn't it?" the girl's mother said.

"It's good weather for cotton if you can get the niggers to pick it," Mrs. Turpin said, "but niggers don't want to pick cotton any more. You can't get the white folks to pick it and now you can't get the niggers—because they got to be right up there with the white folks."

"They gonna *try* anyways," the white-trash woman said, leaning forward.

"Do you have one of those cotton-picking machines?" the pleasant lady asked.

"No," Mrs. Turpin said, "they leave half the cotton in the field. We don't have much cotton anyway. If you want to make it farming now, you have to have a little of everything. We got a couple of acres of cotton and a few hogs and chickens and just enough whiteface that Claud can look after them himself."

"One thang I don't want," the white-trash woman said, wiping her mouth with the back of her hands. "Hogs. Nasty stinking things, a-gruntin and a-rootin all over the place."

Mrs. Turpin gave her the merest edge of her attention. "Our hogs are not dirty and they don't stink," she said. "They're cleaner than some children I've seen. Their feet never touch the ground. We have a pig-parlor—that's where you raise them on concrete," she explained to the pleasant lady, "and Claud scoots them down with the hose every afternoon and washes off the floor." Cleaner by far than that child right there, she thought. Poor nasty little thing. He had not moved except to put the thumb of his dirty hand into his mouth.

The woman turned her face away from Mrs. Turpin. "I know I wouldn't scoot down no hog with no hose," she said to the wall.

You wouldn't have no hog to scoot down, Mrs. Turpin said to herself.

"A-gruntin and a-rootin and a-groanin," the woman muttered.

"We got a little of everything," Mrs. Turpin said to the pleasant lady. "It's no use in having more than you can handle yourself with help like it is. We found enough niggers to pick our cotton this year but Claud he has to go after them and take them home again in the evening. They can't walk that half a mile. No they can't. I tell you," she said and laughed merrily, "I sure am tired of buttering up niggers, but you got to love em if you want em to work for you. When they come in the morning, I run out and I say, 'Hi yawl this morning?' and when Claud drives them off to the field I just wave to beat the band and they just wave back." And she waved her hand rapidly to illustrate.

"Like you read out of the same book," the lady said, showing she understood perfectly.

"Child, yes," Mrs. Turpin said. "And when they come in from the field, I run out with a bucket of icewater. That's the way it's going to be from now on," she said. "You may as well face it."

"One thang I know," the white-trash woman said. "Two thangs I ain't going to do: love no niggers or scoot down no hog with no hose." And she let out a bark of contempt.

The look that Mrs. Turpin and the pleasant lady exchanged indicated they both understood that you had to *have* certain things before you could *know* certain things. But every time Mrs. Turpin exchanged a look with the lady, she was aware that the ugly girl's peculiar eyes were still on her, and she had trouble bringing her attention back to the conversation.

"When you got something," she said, "you got to look after it." And when you ain't got a thing but breath and britches, she added to herself, you can afford to come to town every morning and just sit on the Court House coping and spit.

A grotesque revolving shadow passed across the curtain behind her and was thrown palely on the opposite wall. Then a bicycle clattered down against the outside of the building. The door opened and a colored boy glided in with a tray from the drug store. It had two large red and white paper cups on it with tops on them. He was a tall, very black boy in discolored white pants and a green nylon shirt. He was chewing gum slowly, as if to music. He set the tray down in the office opening next to the fern and stuck his head through to look for the secretary. She was not in there. He rested his arms on the ledge and waited, his narrow bottom stuck out, swaying slowly to the left and right. He raised a hand over his head and scratched the base of his skull.

"You see that button there, boy?" Mrs. Turpin said. "You can punch that and she'll come. She's probably in the back somewhere."

"Is thas right?" the boy said agreeably, as if he had never seen the button before. He leaned to the right and put his finger on it. "She sometime out," he said and twisted around to face his audience, his elbows behind him on the counter. The nurse appeared and he twisted back again. She handed him a dollar and he rooted in his pocket and made the change and counted it out to her. She gave him fifteen cents for a tip and he went out with the empty tray. The heavy door swung to slowly and closed at length with the sound of suction. For a moment no one spoke.

"They ought to send all them niggers back to Africa," the white-trash woman said. "That's wher they come from in the first place."

"Oh, I couldn't do without my good colored friends," the pleasant lady said.

"There's a heap of things worse than a nigger," Mrs. Turpin agreed. "It's all kinds of them just like it's all kinds of us."

"Yes; and it takes all kinds to make the world go round," the lady said in her musical voice.

As she said it, the raw-complexioned girl snapped her teeth together. Her lower lip turned downwards and inside out, revealing the pale pink inside of her mouth. After a second it rolled back up. It was the ugliest face Mrs. Turpin had ever seen anyone make and for a moment she was certain that the girl had made it at her. She was looking at her as if she had known and disliked her all her life—all of Mrs. Turpin's life, it seemed too, not just all the girl's life. Why, girl, I don't even know you, Mrs. Turpin said silently.

She forced her attention back to the discussion. "It wouldn't be practical to send them back to Africa," she said. "They wouldn't want to go. They got it too good here."

"Wouldn't be what they wanted—if I had anythang to do with it," the woman said.

"It wouldn't be a way in the world you could get all the niggers back over there," Mrs. Turpin said. "They'd be hiding out and lying down and turning sick on you and wailing and hollering and raring and pitching. It wouldn't be a way in the world to get them over there."

"They got over here," the trashy woman said. "Get back like they got over."

"It wasn't so many of them then," Mrs. Turpin explained.

The woman looked at Mrs. Turpin as if here was an idiot indeed but Mrs. Turpin was not bothered by the look, considering where it came from.

"Nooo," she said, "they're going to stay here where they can go to New York and marry white folks and improve their color. That's what they all want to do, every one of them, improve their color."

"You know what comes of that, don't you?" Claud asked.

"No, Claud, what?" Mrs. Turpin said.

Claud's eyes twinkled. "White-faced niggers," he said with never a smile.

Everybody in the office laughed except the white-trash and the ugly girl. The girl gripped the book in her lap with white fingers. The trashy woman looked around her from face to face as if she thought they were all idiots. The old woman in the feed sack dress continued to gaze expressionless across the floor at the high-top shoes of the man opposite her, the one who had been pretending to be asleep when the Turpins came in. He was laughing heartily, his hands still spread out on his knees. The child had fallen to the side and was lying now almost face down in the old woman's lap.

When they recovered from their laughter, the nasal chorus on the radio kept the room from silence.

"You go to blank blank
And I'll go to mine
But we'll all blank along
To-geth-ther,
And all along the blank
We'll hep each other out
Smile-ling in any kind of
Weath-ther!"

Mrs. Turpin didn't catch every word but she caught enough to agree with the spirit of the song and it turned her thoughts sober. To help anybody out that needed it was her philosophy of life. She never spared herself when she found somebody in need, whether they were white or black, trash or decent. And of all she had to be thankful for, she was most thankful that this was so. If Jesus had said, "You can be high society and have all the money you want and be thin and svelte-like, but you can't be a good woman with it," she would have had to say, "Well don't make me that then. Make me a good woman and it don't matter what else, how fat or how ugly or how poor!" Her heart rose. He had not made her a nigger or white-trash or ugly! He had made her herself and given her a little of everything. Jesus, thank you! she said. Thank you thank you thank you! Whenever she counted her blessings she felt as buoyant as if she weighed one hundred and twenty-five pounds instead of one hundred and eighty.

"What's wrong with your little boy?" the pleasant lady asked the white-trashy woman.

"He has a ulcer," the woman said proudly. "He ain't give me a minute's peace since he was born. Him and her are just alike," she said, nodding at the old woman, who was running her leathery fingers through the child's pale hair. "Look like I can't get nothing down them two but Co' Cola and candy."

That's all you try to get down em, Mrs. Turpin said to herself. Too lazy to light the fire. There was nothing you could tell her about people like them that she didn't know already. And it was not just that they didn't have anything. Because if you gave them everything, in two weeks it would all be broken or filthy or they would have chopped it up for lightwood. She knew all this from her own experience. Help them you must, but help them you couldn't.

All at once the ugly girl turned her lips inside out again. Her eyes were fixed like two drills on Mrs. Turpin. This time there was no mistaking that there was something urgent behind them.

Girl, Mrs. Turpin exclaimed silently, I haven't done a thing to you! The girl might be confusing her with somebody else. There was no need to sit by and let herself be intimidated. "You must be in college," she said boldly, looking directly at the girl. "I see you reading a book there."

The girl continued to stare and pointedly did not answer.

Her mother blushed at this rudeness. "The lady asked you a question, Mary Grace," she said under her breath.

"I have ears," Mary Grace said.

The poor mother blushed again. "Mary Grace goes to Wellesley College," she explained. She twisted one of the buttons on her dress. "In Massachusetts," she added with a grimace. "And in the summer she just keeps right on studying. Just reads all the time, a real book worm. She's done real well at Wellesley; she's taking English and Math and History and Psychology and Social Studies," she rattled on, "and I think it's too much. I think she ought to get out and have fun."

The girl looked as if she would like to hurl them all through the plate glass window.

"Way up north," Mrs. Turpin murmured and thought, well, it hasn't done much for her manners.

"I'd almost rather to have him sick," the white-trash woman said, wrenching the attention back to herself. "He's so mean when he ain't. Look like some children just take natural to meanness. It's some gets bad when they get sick but he was the opposite. Took sick and turned good. He don't give me no trouble now. It's me waitin to see the doctor," she said.

If I was going to send anybody back to Africa, Mrs. Turpin thought, it would be your kind, woman. "Yes, indeed," she said aloud, but looking up at the ceiling, "it's a heap of things worse than a nigger." And dirtier than a hog, she added to herself.

"I think people with bad dispositions are more to be pitied than anyone on earth," the pleasant lady said in a voice that was decidedly thin.

"I thank the Lord he has blessed me with a good one," Mrs. Turpin said. "The day has never dawned that I couldn't find something to laugh at."

"Not since she married me anyways," Claud said with a comical straight face.

Everybody laughed except the girl and the white-trash.

Mrs. Turpin's stomach shook. "He's such a caution," she said, "that I can't help but laugh at him."

The girl made a loud ugly noise through her teeth.

Her mother's mouth grew thin and tight. "I think the worst thing in the world," she said, "is an ungrateful person. To have everything and not appreciate it. I know a girl," she said, "who has parents who would give her anything, a little brother who loves her dearly, who is getting a good education, who wears the best clothes, but who can never say a kind word to anyone, who never smiles, who just criticizes and complains all day long."

"Is she too old to paddle?" Claud asked.

The girl's face was almost purple.

"Yes," the lady said, "I'm afraid there's nothing to do but leave her to her folly. Some day she'll wake up and it'll be too late."

"It never hurt anyone to smile," Mrs. Turpin said. "It just makes you feel better all over."

"Of course," the lady said sadly, "but there are just some people you can't tell anything to. They can't take criticism."

"If it's one thing I am," Mrs. Turpin said with feeling, "it's grateful. When I think who all I could have been besides myself and what all I got, a little of everything, and a good disposition besides, I just feel like shouting, 'Thank you, Jesus, for making everything the way it is!' It could have been different!" For one thing, somebody else could have got Claud. At the thought of this, she was flooded with gratitude and a terrible pang of joy ran through her. "Oh thank you, Jesus, Jesus, thank you!" she cried aloud.

The book struck her directly over her left eye. It struck almost at the same instant that she realized the girl was about to hurl it. Before she could utter a sound, the raw face came crashing across the table toward her, howling. The girl's fingers sank like clamps into the soft flesh of her neck. She heard the mother cry out and Claud shout, "Whoa!" There was an instant when she was certain that she was about to be in an earthquake.

All at once her vision narrowed and she saw everything as if it were happening in a small room far away, or as if she were looking at it through the wrong end of a telescope. Claud's face crumpled and fell out of sight. The nurse ran in, then out, then in again. Then the gangling figure of the doctor rushed out of the inner door. Magazines flew this way and that as the table turned over. The girl fell with a thud and Mrs. Turpin's vision suddenly reversed itself and she saw everything large instead of small. The eyes of the white-trashy woman were staring hugely at the floor. There the girl, held down on one side by the nurse and on the other by her mother, was wrenching and turning in their grasp. The doctor was kneeling astride her, trying to hold her arm down. He managed after a second to sink a long needle into it.

Mrs. Turpin felt entirely hollow except for her heart which swung from side to side as if it were agitated in a great empty drum of flesh.

"Somebody that's not busy call for the ambulance," the doctor said in the off-hand voice young doctors adopt for terrible occasions.

Mrs. Turpin could not have moved a finger. The old man who had been sitting next to her skipped nimbly into the office and made the call, for the secretary still seemed to be gone.

"Claud!" Mrs. Turpin called.

He was not in his chair. She knew she must jump up and find him but she felt like some one trying to catch a train in a dream, when everything moves in slow motion and the faster you try to run the slower you go.

"Here I am," a suffocated voice, very unlike Claud's, said.

He was doubled up in the corner on the floor, pale as paper, holding his leg. She wanted to get up and go to him but she could not move. Instead, her gaze was drawn slowly downward to the churning face on the floor, which she could see over the doctor's shoulder.

The girl's eyes stopped rolling and focused on her. They seemed a much lighter blue than before, as if a door that had been tightly closed behind them was now open to admit light and air.

Mrs. Turpin's head cleared and her power of motion returned. She leaned forward until she was looking directly into the fierce brilliant eyes. There was no doubt in her mind that the girl did know her, knew her in some intense and personal way, beyond time and place and condition. "What you got to say to me?" she asked hoarsely and held her breath, waiting, as for a revelation.

The girl raised her head. Her gaze locked with Mrs. Turpin's. "Go back to hell where you came from, you old wart hog," she whispered. Her voice was low but clear. Her eyes burned for a moment as if she saw with pleasure that her message had struck its target.

Mrs. Turpin sank back in her chair.

After a moment the girl's eyes closed and she turned her head wearily to the side.

The doctor rose and handed the nurse the empty syringe. He leaned over and put both hands for a moment on the mother's shoulders, which were shaking. She was sitting on the floor, her lips pressed together, holding Mary Grace's hand in her lap. The girl's fingers were gripped like a baby's around her thumb. "Go on to the hospital," he said. "I'll call and make the arrangements."

"Now let's see that neck," he said in a jovial voice to Mrs. Turpin. He began to inspect her neck with his first two fingers. Two little moon-shaped lines like pink fish bones were indented over her windpipe. There was the beginning of an angry red swelling above her eye. His fingers passed over this also.

"Lea' me be," she said thickly and shook him off. "See about Claud. She kicked him."

"I'll see about him in a minute," he said and felt her pulse. He was a thin grey-haired man, given to pleasantries. "Go home and have yourself a vacation the rest of the day," he said and patted her on the shoulder.

Quit your pattin me, Mrs. Turpin growled to herself.

"And put an ice pack over that eye," he said. Then he went and squatted down beside Claud and looked at his leg. After a moment he pulled him up and Claud limped after him into the office.

Until the ambulance came, the only sounds in the room were the tremulous moans of the girl's mother, who continued to sit on the floor. The white-trash woman did not take her eyes off the girl. Mrs. Turpin looked straight ahead at nothing. Presently the ambulance drew up, a long dark shadow, behind the curtain. The attendants came in and set the stretcher down beside the girl and lifted her expertly onto it and carried her out. The nurse helped the mother gather up her things. The shadow of the ambulance moved silently away and the nurse came back in the office.

"That ther girl is going to be a lunatic, ain't she?" the white-trash woman asked the nurse, but the nurse kept on to the back and never answered her.

"Yes, she's going to be a lunatic," the white-trash woman said to the rest of them.

"Po' critter," the old woman murmured. The child's face was still in her lap. His eyes looked idly out over her knees. He had not moved during the disturbance except to draw one leg up under him.

"I thank Gawd," the white-trash woman said fervently, "I ain't a lunatic."

Claud came limping out and the Turpins went home.

As their pick-up truck turned into their own dirt road and made the crest of the hill, Mrs. Turpin gripped the window ledge and looked out suspiciously. The land sloped gracefully down through a field dotted with lavender weeds and at the start of the rise their small yellow frame house, with its little flower beds spread out around it like a fancy apron, sat primly in its accustomed place between two giant hickory trees. She would not have been startled to see a burnt wound between two blackened chimneys.

Neither of them felt like eating so they put on their house clothes and lowered the shade in the bedroom and lay down, Claud with his leg on a pillow and herself with a damp washcloth over her eye. The instant she was flat on her back, the image of a razor-backed hog with warts on its face and horns coming out behind its ears snorted into her head. She moaned, a low quiet moan.

"I am not," she said tearfully, "a wart hog. From hell." But the denial had no force. The girl's eyes and her words, even the tone of her voice, low but clear, directed only to her, brooked no repudiation. She had been singled out for the message, though there was trash in the room to whom it might justly have been applied. The full force of this fact struck her only now. There was a woman there who was neglecting her own child but she had been overlooked. The message had been given to Ruby Turpin, a respectable, hardworking, church-going woman. The tears dried. Her eyes began to burn instead with wrath.

She rose on her elbow and the washcloth fell into her hand. Claud was lying on his back, snoring. She wanted to tell him what the girl had said. At the same time, she did not wish to put the image of herself as a wart hog from hell into his mind.

"Hey, Claud," she muttered and pushed his shoulder.

Claud opened one pale baby blue eye.

She looked into it warily. He did not think about anything. He just went his way.

"Wha, whasit?" he said and closed the eye again.

"Nothing," she said. "Does your leg pain you?"

"Hurts like hell," Claud said.

"It'll quit terreckly," she said and lay back down. In a moment Claud was snoring again. For the rest of the afternoon they lay there. Claud slept. She scowled at the ceiling. Occasionally she raised her fist and made a small stabbing motion over her chest as if she was defending her innocence to invisible guests who were like the comforters of Job, reasonable-seeming but wrong.

About five-thirty Claud stirred. "Got to go after those niggers," he sighed, not moving.

She was looking straight up as if there were unintelligible handwriting on the ceiling. The protuberance over the eye had turned a greenish-blue. "Listen here," she said.

"What?"

"Kiss me."

Claud leaned over and kissed her loudly on the mouth. He pinched her side and their hands interlocked. Her expression of ferocious concentration did not change. Claud got up, groaning and growling, and limped off. She continued to study the ceiling.

She did not get up until she heard the pick-up truck coming back with the Negroes. Then she rose and thrust her feet in her brown oxfords, which she did not bother to lace, and stumped out onto the back porch and got her red plastic bucket. She emptied a tray of ice cubes into it and filled it half full of water and went out into the back yard. Every afternoon after Claud brought the hands in, one of the boys helped him put out hay and the rest waited in the back of the truck until he was ready to take them home. The truck was parked in the shade under one of the hickory trees.

"Hi yawl this evening?" Mrs. Turpin asked grimly, appearing with the bucket and the dipper. There were three women and a boy in the truck.

"Us doin nicely," the oldest woman said. "Hi you doin?" and her gaze stuck immediately on the dark lump on Mrs. Turpin's forehead. "You done fell down, ain't you?" she asked in a solicitous voice. The old woman was dark and almost toothless. She had on an old felt hat of Claud's set back on her head. The other two women were younger and lighter and they both had new bright green sun hats. One of them had hers on her head; the other had taken hers off and the boy was grinning beneath it.

Mrs. Turpin set the bucket down on the floor of the truck. "Yawl hep yourselves," she said. She looked around to make sure Claud had gone. "No. I didn't fall down," she said, folding her arms. "It was something worse than that."

"Ain't nothing bad happen to you!" the old woman

said. She said it as if they all knew that Mrs. Turpin was protected in some special way by Divine Providence. "You just had you a little fall."

"We were in town at the doctor's office for where the cow kicked Mr. Turpin," Mrs. Turpin said in a flat tone that indicated they could leave off their foolishness. "And there was this girl there. A big fat girl with her face all broke out. I could look at that girl and tell she was peculiar but I couldn't tell how. And me and her mama were just talking and going along and all of a sudden WHAM! She throws this big book she was reading at me and . . ."

"Naw!" the old woman cried out.

"And then she jumps over the table and commences to choke me."

"Naw!" they all exclaimed, "naw!"

"Hi come she do that?" the old woman asked. "What ail her?"

Mrs. Turpin only glared in front of her.

"Somethin ail her," the old woman said.

"They carried her off in an ambulance," Mrs. Turpin continued, "but before she went she was rolling on the floor and they were trying to hold her down to give her a shot and she said something to me." She paused. "You know what she said to me?"

"What she say?" they asked.

"She said," Mrs. Turpin began, and stopped, her face very dark and heavy. The sun was getting whiter and whiter, blanching the sky overhead so that the leaves of the hickory tree were black in the face of it. She could not bring forth the words. "Something real ugly," she muttered.

"She sho shouldn't said nothin ugly to you," the old woman said. "You so sweet. You the sweetest lady I know."

"She pretty too," the one with the hat on said.

"And stout," the other one said. "I never knowed no sweeter white lady."

"That's the truth befo' Jesus," the old woman said. "Amen! You des as sweet and pretty as you can be."

Mrs. Turpin knew just exactly how much Negro flattery was worth and it added to her rage. "She said," she began again and finished this time with a fierce rush of breath, "that I was an old wart hog from hell."

There was an astounded silence.

"Where she at?" the youngest woman cried in a piercing voice.

"Lemme see her. I'll kill her!"

"I'll kill her with you!" the other one cried.

"She b'long in the sylum," the old woman said emphatically. "You the sweetest white lady I know."

"She pretty too," the other two said. "Stout as she can be and sweet. Jesus satisfied with her!"

"Deed he is," the old woman declared.

Idiots! Mrs Turpin growled to herself. You could never say anything intelligent to a nigger. You could talk at them but not with them. "Yawl ain't drunk your water," she said shortly. "Leave the bucket in the truck when you're finished with it. I got more to do than just stand around and pass the time of day," and she moved off and into the house.

She stood for a moment in the middle of the kitchen. The dark protuberance over her eye looked like a miniature tornado cloud which might any moment sweep across the horizon of her brow. Her lower lip protruded dangerously. She squared her massive shoulders. Then she marched into the front of the house and out the side door and started down the road to the pig parlor. She had the look of a woman going single-handed, weaponless, into battle.

The sun was a deep yellow now like a harvest moon and was riding westward very fast over the far tree line as if it meant to reach the hogs before she did. The road was rutted and she kicked several good-sized stones out of her path as she strode along. The pig parlor was on a little knoll at the end of a lane that ran off from the side of the barn. It was a square of concrete as large as a small room, with a board fence about four feet high around it. The concrete floor sloped slightly so that the hog wash could drain off into a trench where it was carried to the field for fertilizer. Claud was standing on the outside, on the edge of the concrete, hanging onto the top board, hosing down the floor inside. The hose was connected to the faucet of a water trough nearby.

Mrs. Turpin climbed up beside him and glowered down at the hogs inside. There were seven long-snouted bristly shoats in it—tan with liver-colored spots—and an old sow a few weeks off from farrowing. She was lying on her side grunting. The shoats were running about shaking themselves like idiot children, their little slit pig eyes searching the floor for anything left. She had read that pigs were the most intelligent animal. She doubted it. They were supposed to be smarter than dogs. There had even been a pig astronaut. He had performed his assignment perfectly but died of a heart attack afterwards because they left him in his electric suit, sitting upright throughout his examination when naturally a hog should be on all fours.

A-gruntin and a-rootin and a-groanin.

"Gimme that hose," she said, yanking it away from Claud. "Go on and carry them niggers home and then get off that leg."

"You look like you might have swallowed a mad dog," Claud observed, but he got down and limped off. He paid no attention to her humors.

Until he was out of earshot, Mrs. Turpin stood on the side of the pen, holding the hose and pointing the stream of water at the hind quarters of any shoat that looked as if it might try to lie down. When he had had time to get over the hill, she turned her head slightly and her wrathful eyes scanned the path. He was nowhere in sight. She turned back again and seemed to gather herself up. Her shoulders rose and she drew in her breath.

"What do you send me a message like that for?" she said in a low fierce voice, barely above a whisper but with the force of a shout in its concentrated fury. "How am I a hog and me both? How am I saved and from hell too?" Her free fist was knotted and with the other she gripped the hose, blindly pointing the stream of water in and out of the eye of the old sow whose outraged squeal she did not hear.

The pig parlor commanded a view of the back pasture where their twenty beef cows were gathered around the hay-bales Claud and the boy had put out. The freshly cut pasture sloped down to the highway. Across it was their cotton field and beyond that a dark green dusty wood which they owned as well. The sun was behind the wood, very red, looking over the paling of trees like a farmer inspecting his own hogs.

"Why me?" she rumbled. "It's no trash around here, black or white, that I haven't given to. And break my back to the bone every day working. And do for the church."

She appeared to be the right size woman to command the arena before her. "How am I a hog?" she demanded. "Exactly how am I like them?" and she jabbed the stream of water at the shoats. "There was plenty of trash there. It didn't have to be me.

"If you like trash better, go get yourself some trash then," she railed. "You could have made me trash. Or a nigger. If trash is what you wanted why didn't you make me trash?" She shook her fist with the hose in it and a watery snake appeared momentarily in the air. "I could quit working and take it easy and be filthy," she growled. "Lounge about the sidewalks all day drinking root beer. Dip snuff and spit in every puddle and have it all over my face. I could be nasty.

"Or you could have made me a nigger. It's too late for me to be a nigger," she said with deep sarcasm, "but I could act like one. Lay down in the middle of the road and stop traffic. Roll on the ground."

In the deepening light everything was taking on a mysterious hue. The pasture was growing a peculiar glassy green and the streak of highway had turned lavender. She braced herself for a final assault and this time her voice rolled out over the pasture. "Go on," she yelled, "call me a hog! Call me a hog again. From hell. Call me a wart hog from hell. Put that bottom rail on top. There'll still be a top and bottom!"

A garbled echo returned to her.

A final surge of fury shook her and she roared, "Who do you think you are?"

The color of everything, field and crimson sky, burned for a moment with a transparent intensity. The question carried over the pasture and across the highway and the cotton field and returned to her clearly like an answer from beyond the wood.

She opened her mouth but no sound came out of it.

A tiny truck, Claud's, appeared on the highway, heading rapidly out of sight. Its gears scraped thinly. It looked like a child's toy. At any moment a bigger truck might smash into it and scatter Claud's and the niggers' brains all over the road.

Mrs. Turpin stood there, her gaze fixed on the highway, all her muscles rigid, until in five or six minutes the truck reappeared, returning. She waited until it had had time to turn into their own road. Then like a monumental statue coming to life, she bent her head slowly and gazed, as if through the very heart of mystery, down into the pig parlor at the hogs. They had settled all in one corner around the old sow who was grunting softly. A red glow suffused them. They appeared to pant with a secret life.

Until the sun slipped finally behind the tree line, Mrs. Turpin remained there with her gaze bent to them as if she were absorbing some abysmal life-giving knowledge. At last she lifted her head. There was only a purple streak in the sky, cutting through a field of crimson and leading, like an extension of the highway, into the descending dusk. She raised her hands from the side of the pen in a gesture hieratic and profound. A visionary light settled in her eyes. She saw the streak as a vast swinging bridge extending upward from the earth through a field of living fire. Upon it a vast horde of souls were rumbling toward heaven. There were whole companies of white-trash, clean for the first time in their lives, and bands of black niggers in white robes, and battalions of freaks and lunatics shouting and clapping and leaping like frogs. And bringing up the end of the procession was a tribe of people whom she recognized at once as those who, like herself and Claud, had always had a little of everything and the God-given wit to use it right. She leaned forward to observe them closer. They were marching behind the others with great dignity, accountable as they had always been for good order and common sense and respectable behavior. They alone were on key. Yet she could see by their shocked and altered faces that even their virtues were being burned away. She lowered her hands and gripped the rail of the hog pen, her eyes small but fixed unblinkingly on what lay ahead. In a moment the vision faded but she remained where she was, immobile.

At length she got down and turned off the faucet and made her slow way on the darkening path to the house. In the woods around her the invisible cricket choruses had struck up, but what she heard were the voices of the souls climbing upward into the starry field and shouting hallelujah.

Sonny's Blues

James Baldwin (1924–)

The eldest of nine children, James Arthur Baldwin was reared in poverty in the Harlem ghetto of New York. After graduation from high school he supported himself with odd jobs while learning to write fiction. In 1948 he moved to Paris where he remained for nine years. *Go Tell It On The Mountain* (1953), his semi-autobiographical first novel based on his experience as a revivalist preacher, had a considerable success; it was followed in 1956 by *Giovanni's Room,* a novel set in Paris. After Baldwin returned to the United States in 1957 he committed himself to the civil rights movement, which became the subject of many essays and his 1962 novel, *Another Country.* In 1962 Baldwin wrote a long magazine essay on the Black Muslims and the civil rights struggle which was published in book form as *The Fire Next Time* (1963). *Going to Meet the Man,* a collection of short stories including "Sonny's Blues," appeared in 1965. Baldwin's most recent publications are *Tell Me How Long the Train's Been Gone* (a novel, 1968); *If Beale Street Could Talk* (1974); and *The Devil Finds Work: An Essay* (1976).

I read about it in the paper, in the subway, on my way to work. I read it, and I couldn't believe it, and I read it again. Then perhaps I just stared at it, at the newsprint spelling out his name, spelling out the story. I stared at it in the swinging lights of the subway car, and in the faces and bodies of the people, and in my own face, trapped in the darkness which roared outside.

It was not to be believed and I kept telling myself that, as I walked from the subway station to the high school. And at the same time I couldn't doubt it. I was scared, scared for Sonny. He became real to me again. A great block of ice got settled in my belly and kept melting there slowly all day long, while I taught my classes algebra. It was a special kind of ice. It kept melting, sending trickles of ice water all up and down my veins, but it never got less. Sometimes it hardened and seemed to expand until I felt my guts were going to come spilling out or that I was going to choke or scream. This would always be at a moment when I was remembering some specific thing Sonny had once said or done.

When he was about as old as the boys in my classes his face had been bright and open, there was a lot of copper in it; and he'd had wonderfully direct brown eyes, and great gentleness and privacy. I wondered what he looked like now. He had been picked up, the evening before, in a raid on an apartment downtown, for peddling and using heroin.

I couldn't believe it: but what I mean by that is that I couldn't find any room for it anywhere inside me. I had kept it outside me for a long time. I hadn't wanted to know. I had had suspicions, but I didn't name them, I kept putting them away. I told myself that Sonny was wild, but he wasn't crazy. And he'd always been a good boy, he hadn't ever turned hard or evil or disrespectful, the way kids can, so quick, so quick, especially in Harlem. I didn't want to believe that I'd ever see my brother going down, coming to nothing, all that light in his face gone out, in the condition I'd already seen so many others. Yet it had happened and here I was, talking about algebra to a lot of boys who might, every one of them for all I knew, be popping off needles every time they went to the head. Maybe it did more for them than algebra could.

I was sure that the first time Sonny had ever had horse, he couldn't have been much older than these boys were now. These boys, now, were living as we'd been living then, they were growing up with a rush and their heads bumped abruptly against the low ceiling of their actual possibilities. They were filled with rage. All they really knew were two darknesses, the darkness of their lives, which was now closing in on them, and the darkness of the movies, which had blinded them to that other darkness, and in which they now, vindictively, dreamed, at once more together than they were at any other time, and more alone.

When the last bell rang, the last class ended, I let out my breath. It seemed I'd been holding it for all that time. My clothes were wet—I may have looked as though I'd been sitting in a steam bath, all dressed up, all afternoon. I sat alone in the classroom a long time. I listened to the boys outside, downstairs, shouting and cursing and laughing. Their laughter struck me for perhaps the first time. It was not the joyous laughter which—God knows why—one associates with children. It was mocking and insular, its intent was to denigrate. It was disenchanted, and in this, also, lay the authority of their curses. Perhaps I was listening to them because I was thinking about my brother and in them I heard my brother. And myself.

One boy was whistling a tune, at once very complicated and very simple, it seemed to be pouring out of him as though he were a bird, and it sounded very cool and moving through all that harsh, bright air, only just holding its own through all those other sounds.

I stood up and walked over to the window and looked down into the courtyard. It was the beginning of the spring and the sap was rising in the boys. A teacher passed through them every now and again, quickly, as though he or she couldn't wait to get out of that courtyard, to get those boys out of their sight and off their minds. I started collecting my stuff. I thought I'd better get home and talk to Isabel.

The courtyard was almost deserted by the time I got downstairs. I saw this boy standing in the shadow of a doorway, looking just like Sonny. I almost called his name. Then I saw that it wasn't Sonny, but somebody we used to know, a boy from around our block. He'd been Sonny's friend. He'd never been mine, having been too young for me, and, anyway, I'd never liked him. And now, even though he was a grown-up man, he still hung around that block, still spent hours on the street corners, was always high and raggy. I used to run into him from time to time and he'd often work around to asking me for a quarter or fifty cents. He always had some real good excuse, too, and I always gave it to him, I don't know why.

But now, abruptly, I hated him. I couldn't stand the way he looked at me, partly like a dog, partly like a cunning child. I wanted to ask him what the hell he was doing in the school courtyard.

He sort of shuffled over to me, and he said, "I see you got the papers. So you already know about it."

"You mean about Sonny? Yes, I already know about it. How come they didn't get you?"

He grinned. It made him repulsive and it also brought to mind what he'd looked like as a kid. "I wasn't there. I stay away from them people."

"Good for you." I offered him a cigarette and I watched him through the smoke. "You come all the way down here just to tell me about Sonny?"

"That's right." He was sort of shaking his head and his eyes looked strange, as though they were about to cross. The bright sun deadened his damp dark brown skin and it made his eyes look yellow and showed up the dirt in his kinked hair. He smelled funky. I moved a little away from him and I said, "Well, thanks. But I already know about it and I got to get home."

"I'll walk you a little ways," he said. We started walking. There were a couple of kids still loitering in the courtyard and one of them said goodnight to me and looked strangely at the boy beside me.

"What're you going to do?" he asked me. "I mean, about Sonny?"

"Look. I haven't seen Sonny for over a year, I'm not sure I'm going to do anything. Anyway, what the hell *can* I do?"

"That's right," he said quickly, "ain't nothing you can do. Can't much help old Sonny no more, I guess."

It was what I was thinking and so it seemed to me he had no right to say it.

"I'm surprised at Sonny, though," he went on—he had a funny way of talking, he looked straight ahead as though he were talking to himself—"I thought Sonny was a smart boy, I thought he was too smart to get hung."

"I guess he thought so too," I said sharply, "and that's how he got hung. And now about you? You're pretty goddamn smart, I bet."

Then he looked directly at me, just for a minute. "I ain't smart," he said. "If I was smart, I'd have reached for a pistol a long time ago."

"Look. Don't tell *me* your sad story, if it was up to

me, I'd give you one." Then I felt guilty—guilty, probably, for never having supposed that the poor bastard *had* a story of his own, much less a sad one, and I asked, quickly, "What's going to happen to him now?"

He didn't answer this. He was off by himself some place. "Funny thing," he said, and from his tone we might have been discussing the quickest way to get to Brooklyn, "when I saw the papers this morning, the first thing I asked myself was if I had anything to do with it. I felt sort of responsible."

I began to listen more carefully. The subway station was on the corner, just before us, and I stopped. He stopped, too. We were in front of a bar and he ducked slightly, peering in, but whoever he was looking for didn't seem to be there. The juke box was blasting away with something black and bouncy and I half watched the barmaid as she danced her way from the juke box to her place behind the bar. And I watched her face as she laughingly responded to something someone said to her, still keeping time to the music. When she smiled one saw the little girl, one sensed the doomed, still-struggling woman beneath the battered face of the semi-whore.

"I never *give* Sonny nothing," the boy said finally, "but a long time ago I come to school high and Sonny asked me how it felt." He paused, I couldn't bear to watch him, I watched the barmaid, and I listened to the music which seemed to be causing the pavement to shake. "I told him it felt great." The music stopped, the barmaid paused and watched the juke box until the music began again. "It did."

All this was carrying me some place I didn't want to go. I certainly didn't want to know how it felt. It filled everything, the people, the houses, the music, the dark, quicksilver barmaid, with menace; and this menace was their reality.

"What's going to happen to him now?" I asked again.

"They'll send him away some place and they'll try to cure him." He shook his head. "Maybe he'll even think he's kicked the habit. Then they'll let him loose"—he gestured, throwing his cigarette into the gutter. "That's all."

"What do you mean, that's *all?*"

But I knew what he meant.

"I *mean,* that's *all.*" He turned his head and looked at me, pulling down the corners of his mouth. "Don't you know what I mean?" he asked, softly.

"How the hell *would* I know what you mean?" I almost whispered it, I don't know why.

"That's right," he said to the air, "how would *he* know what I mean?" He turned toward me again, patient and calm, and yet I somehow felt him shaking, shaking as though he were going to fall apart. I felt that ice in my guts again, the dread I'd felt all afternoon; and again I watched the barmaid, moving about the bar, washing glasses, and singing. "Listen. They'll let him out and then it'll just start all over again. That's what I mean."

"You mean—they'll let him out. And then he'll just start working his way back in again. You mean he'll never kick the habit. Is that what you mean?"

"That's right," he said, cheerfully. "*You* see what I mean."

"Tell me," I said at last, "why does he want to die? He must want to die, he's killing himself, why does he want to die?"

He looked at me in surprise. He licked his lips. "He don't want to die. He wants to live. Don't nobody want to die, ever."

Then I wanted to ask him—too many things. He could not have answered, or if he had, I could not have borne the answers. I started walking. "Well, I guess it's none of my business."

"It's going to be rough on old Sonny," he said. We reached the subway station. "This is your station?" he asked. I nodded. I took one step down. "Damn!" he said, suddenly. I looked up at him. He grinned again. "Damn it if I didn't leave all my money home. You ain't got a dollar on you, have you? Just for a couple of days, is all."

All at once something inside gave and threatened to come pouring out of me. I didn't hate him any more. I felt that in another moment I'd start crying like a child.

"Sure," I said. "Don't sweat." I looked in my wallet and didn't have a dollar, I only had a five. "Here," I said. "That hold you?"

He didn't look at it—he didn't want to look at it. A terrible, closed look came over his face, as though he were keeping the number on the bill a secret from him and me. "Thanks," he said, and now he was dying to see me go. "Don't worry about Sonny. Maybe I'll write him or something."

"Sure," I said. "You do that. So long."

"Be seeing you," he said. I went on down the steps.

And I didn't write Sonny or send him anything for a long time. When I finally did, it was just after my little girl died, he wrote me back a letter which made me feel like a bastard.

Here's what he said:

> Dear brother,
>
> You don't know how much I needed to hear from you. I wanted to write you many a time but I dug how much I must have hurt you and so I didn't write. But now I feel like a man who's been trying to

climb up out of some deep, real deep and funky hole and just saw the sun up there, outside. I got to get outside.

I can't tell you much about how I got here. I mean I don't know how to tell you. I guess I was afraid of something or I was trying to escape from something and you know I have never been very strong in the head (smile). I'm glad Mama and Daddy are dead and can't see what's happened to their son and I swear if I'd known what I was doing I would never have hurt you so, you and a lot of other fine people who were nice to me and who believed in me.

I don't want you to think it had anything to do with me being a musician. It's more than that. Or maybe less than that. I can't get anything straight in my head down here and I try not to think about what's going to happen to me when I get outside again. Sometime I think I'm going to flip and *never* get outside and sometime I think I'll come straight back. I tell you one thing, though, I'd rather blow my brains out than go through this again. But that's what they all say, so they tell me. If I tell you when I'm coming to New York and if you could meet me, I sure would appreciate it. Give my love to Isabel and the kids and I was sure sorry to hear about little Gracie. I wish I could be like Mama and say the Lord's will be done, but I don't know it seems to me that trouble is the one thing that never does get stopped and I don't know what good it does to blame it on the Lord. But maybe it does some good if you believe it.

Your brother,
Sonny

Then I kept in constant touch with him and I sent him whatever I could and I went to meet him when he came back to New York. When I saw him many things I thought I had forgotten came flooding back to me. This was because I had begun, finally, to wonder about Sonny, about the life that Sonny lived inside. This life, whatever it was, had made him older and thinner and it had deepened the distant stillness in which he had always moved. He looked very unlike my baby brother. Yet, when he smiled, when we shook hands, the baby brother I'd never known looked out from the depths of his private life, like an animal waiting to be coaxed into the light.

"How you been keeping?" he asked me.

"All right. And you?"

"Just fine." He was smiling all over his face. "It's good to see you again."

"It's good to see you."

The seven years' difference in our ages lay between us like a chasm: I wondered if these years would ever operate between us as a bridge. I was remembering, and it made it hard to catch my breath, that I had been there when he was born; and I had heard the first words he had ever spoken. When he started to walk, he walked from our mother straight to me. I caught him just before he fell when he took the first steps he ever took in this world.

"How's Isabel?"

"Just fine. She's dying to see you."

"And the boys?"

"They're fine, too. They're anxious to see their uncle."

"Oh, come on. You know they don't remember me."

"Are you kidding? Of course they remember you."

He grinned again. We got into a taxi. We had a lot to say to each other, far too much to know how to begin.

As the taxi began to move, I asked, "You still want to go to India?"

He laughed. "You still remember that. Hell, no. This place is Indian enough for me."

"It used to belong to them," I said.

And he laughed again. "They damn sure knew what they were doing when they got rid of it."

Years ago, when he was around fourteen, he'd been all hipped on the idea of going to India. He read books about people sitting on rocks, naked, in all kinds of weather, but mostly bad, naturally, and walking barefoot through hot coals and arriving at wisdom. I used to say that it sounded to me as though they were getting away from wisdom as fast as they could. I think he sort of looked down on me for that.

"Do you mind," he asked, "if we have the driver drive alongside the park? On the west side—I haven't seen the city in so long."

"Of course not," I said. I was afraid that I might sound as though I were humoring him, but I hoped he wouldn't take it that way.

So we drove along, between the green of the park and the stony, lifeless elegance of hotels and apartment buildings, toward the vivid, killing streets of our childhood. These streets hadn't changed, though housing projects jutted up out of them now like rocks in the middle of a boiling sea. Most of the houses in which we had grown up had vanished, as had the stores from which we had stolen, the basements in which we had first tried sex, the rooftops from which we had hurled tin cans and bricks. But houses exactly like the houses of our past yet dominated the landscape, boys exactly like the boys we once had been found themselves smothering in these houses, came down into the streets for light and air and found themselves encircled by disaster. Some escaped the trap, most didn't. Those who got out always left something of themselves behind, as some animals amputate a leg and leave it in the trap. It might be said, perhaps, that I had escaped, after all, I was a school teacher; or that Sonny had, he hadn't lived in Harlem for years. Yet, as the cab moved uptown through streets which seemed, with a rush, to darken with dark people, and as I covertly studied Sonny's face, it came to me that what we both were seeking through our separate cab windows was that part of ourselves which had been left behind. It's always at the hour of trouble and confrontation that the missing member aches.

We hit 110th Street and started rolling up Lenox Avenue. And I'd known this avenue all my life, but it seemed to me again, as it had seemed on the day I'd first heard about Sonny's trouble, filled with a hidden menace which was its very breath of life.

"We almost there," said Sonny.

"Almost." We were both too nervous to say anything more.

We live in a housing project. It hasn't been up long. A few days after it was up it seemed uninhabitably new, now, of course, it's already rundown. It looks like a parody of the good, clean, faceless life—God knows the people who live in it do their best to make it a parody. The beat-looking grass lying around isn't enough to make their lives green, the hedges will never hold out the streets, and they know it. The big windows fool no one, they aren't big enough to make space out of no space. They don't bother with the windows, they watch the TV screen instead. The playground is most popular with the children who don't play at jacks, or skip rope, or roller skate, or swing, and they can be found in it after dark. We moved in partly because it's not too far from where I teach, and partly for the kids; but it's really just like the houses in which Sonny and I grew up. The same things happen, they'll have the same things to remember. The moment Sonny and I started into the house I had the feeling that I was simply bringing him back into the danger he had almost died trying to escape.

Sonny has never been talkative. So I don't know why I was sure he'd be dying to talk to me when supper was over the first night. Everything went fine, the oldest boy remembered him, and the youngest boy liked him, and Sonny had remembered to bring something for each of them; and Isabel, who is really much nicer than I am, more open and giving, had gone to a lot of trouble about dinner and was genuinely glad to see him. And she's always been able to tease Sonny in a way that I haven't. It was nice to see her face so vivid again and to hear her laugh and watch her make Sonny laugh. She wasn't, or, anyway, she didn't seem to be, at all uneasy or embarrassed. She chatted as though there were no subject which had to be avoided and she got Sonny past his first, faint stiffness. And thank God she was there, for I was filled with that icy dread again. Everything I did seemed awkward to me, and everything I said sounded freighted with hidden meaning. I was trying to remember everything I'd heard about dope addiction and I couldn't help watching Sonny for signs. I wasn't doing it out of malice. I was trying to find out something about my brother. I was dying to hear him tell me he was safe.

"Safe!" my father grunted, whenever Mama suggested trying to move to a neighborhood which might be safer for children. "Safe, hell! Ain't no place safe for kids, nor nobody."

He always went on like this; but he wasn't, ever, really as bad as he sounded, not even on weekends, when he got drunk. As a matter of fact, he was always on the lookout for "something a little better," but he died before he found it. He died suddenly, during a drunken weekend in the middle of the war, when Sonny was fifteen. He and Sonny hadn't ever got on too well. And this was partly because Sonny was the apple of his father's eye. It was because he loved Sonny so much and was frightened for him, that he was always fighting with him. It doesn't do any good to fight with Sonny. Sonny just moves back, inside himself, where he can't be reached. But the principal reason that they never hit it off is that they were so much alike. Daddy was big and rough and loud-talking, just the opposite of Sonny, but they both had—that same privacy.

Mama tried to tell me something about this, just after Daddy died. I was home on leave from the army.

This was the last time I ever saw my mother alive. Just the same this picture gets all mixed up in my mind with pictures I had of her when she was younger. The way I always see her is the way she used to be on a Sunday afternoon, say, when the old folks were talking after the big Sunday dinner. I always see her wearing pale blue. She'd be sitting on the sofa. And my father would be sitting in the easy chair, not far from her. And the living room would be full of church folks and relatives. There they sit, in chairs all around the living room, and the night is creeping up outside, but nobody knows it yet. You can see the darkness growing against the windowpanes and you hear the street noises every now and again, or maybe the jangling beat of a tambourine from one of the churches close by, but it's real quiet in the room. For a moment nobody's talking, but every face looks darkening, like the sky outside. And my mother rocks a little from the waist, and my father's eyes are closed. Everyone is looking at something a child can't see. For a minute they've forgotten the children. Maybe a kid is lying on the rug, half asleep. Maybe somebody's got a kid in his lap and is absent-mindedly stroking the kid's head. Maybe there's a kid, quiet and big-eyed, curled up in a big chair in the corner. The silence, the darkness coming, and the darkness in the faces frightens the child obscurely. He hopes that the hand which strokes his forehead will never stop—will never die. He hopes that there will never come a time when the old folks won't be sitting around the living room, talking about where they've come from, and what they've seen, and what's happened to them and their kinfolk.

But something deep and watchful in the child knows that this is bound to end, is already ending. In a moment someone will get up and turn on the light. Then the old folks will remember the children and they won't talk any more that day. And when light fills the room, the child is filled with darkness. He knows that every time this happens he's moved just a little closer to that darkness outside. The darkness outside is what the old folks have been talking about. It's what they've come from. It's what they endure. The child knows that they won't talk any more because if he knows too much about what's happened to *them,* he'll know too much too soon, about what's going to happen to *him.*

The last time I talked to my mother, I remember I was restless. I wanted to get out and see Isabel. We weren't married then and we had a lot to straighten out between us.

There Mama sat, in black, by the window. She was humming an old church song, *Lord, you brought me from a long ways off.* Sonny was out somewhere. Mama kept watching the streets.

"I don't know," she said, "if I'll ever see you again, after you go off from here. But I hope you'll remember the things I tried to teach you."

"Don't talk like that," I said, and smiled. "You'll be here a long time yet."

She smiled, too, but she said nothing. She was quiet for a long time. And I said, "Mama, don't you worry about nothing. I'll be writing all the time, and you be getting the checks. . . ."

"I want to talk to you about your brother," she said, suddenly. "If anything happens to me he ain't going to have nobody to look out for him."

"Mama," I said, "ain't nothing going to happen to you *or* Sonny. Sonny's all right. He's a good boy and he's got good sense."

"It ain't a question of his being a good boy," Mama said, "nor of his having good sense. It ain't only the bad ones, nor yet the dumb ones that gets sucked under." She stopped, looking at me. "Your Daddy once had a brother," she said, and she smiled in a way that made me feel she was in pain. "You didn't never know that, did you?"

"No," I said, "I never knew that," and I watched her face.

"Oh, yes," she said, "your Daddy had a brother." She looked out of the window again. "I know you never saw your Daddy cry. But *I* did—many a time, through all these years."

I asked her, "What happened to his brother? How come nobody's ever talked about him?"

This was the first time I ever saw my mother look old.

"His brother got killed," she said, "when he was just a little younger than you are now. I knew him. He was a fine boy. He was maybe a little full of the devil, but he didn't mean nobody no harm."

Then she stopped and the room was silent, exactly as it had sometimes been on those Sunday afternoons. Mama kept looking out into the streets.

"He used to have a job in the mill," she said, "and, like all young folks, he just liked to perform on Saturday nights. Saturday nights, him and your father would drift around to different places, go to dances and things like that, or just sit around with people they knew, and your father's brother would sing, he had a fine voice, and play along with himself on his guitar. Well, this particular Saturday night, him and your father was coming home from some place, and they were both a little drunk and there was a moon that night, it was bright like day. Your father's brother was feeling kind of good, and he was whistling to himself, and he had his guitar slung over his shoulder. They was coming down a hill and beneath them was a road that turned off from the highway. Well, your father's brother, being always kind of frisky, decided to run down this hill, and he did, with that guitar banging and clanging behind him, and he ran across the road, and he was making water behind a tree. And your father was sort of amused at him and he was still coming down the hill, kind of slow. Then he heard a car motor and that same minute his brother stepped from behind the tree, into the road, in the moonlight. And he started to cross the road. And your father started to run down the hill, he says he don't know why. This car was full of white men. They was all drunk, and when they seen your father's brother they let out a great whoop and holler and they aimed the car straight at him. They was having fun, they just wanted to scare him, the way they do sometimes, you know. But they was drunk. And I guess the boy, being drunk, too, and scared, kind of lost his head. By the time he jumped it was too late. Your father says he heard his brother scream when the car rolled over him, and he heard the wood of that guitar when it give, and he heard them strings go flying, and he heard them white men shouting, and the car kept on a-going and it ain't stopped till this day. And, time your father got down the hill, his brother weren't nothing but blood and pulp."

Tears were gleaming on my mother's face. There wasn't anything I could say.

"He never mentioned it," she said, "because I never let him mention it before you children. Your Daddy was like a crazy man that night and for many a night thereafter. He says he never in his life seen anything as dark as that road after the lights of that car had gone away. Weren't nothing, weren't nobody on that road, just your Daddy and his brother and that busted guitar. Oh, yes. Your Daddy never did really get right again. Till the day he died he weren't sure but that every white man he saw was the man that killed his brother."

She stopped and took out her handkerchief and dried her eyes and looked at me.

"I ain't telling you all this," she said, "to make you scared or bitter or to make you hate nobody. I'm telling you this because you got a brother. And the world ain't changed."

I guess I didn't want to believe this. I guess she saw this in my face. She turned away from me, toward the window again, searching those streets.

"But I praise my Redeemer," she said at last, "that He called your Daddy home before me. I ain't saying it to throw no flowers at myself, but, I declare, it keeps me from feeling too cast down to know I helped your father get safely through this world. Your father always acted like he was the roughest, strongest man on earth. And everybody took him to be like that. But if he hadn't had *me* there—to see his tears!"

She was crying again. Still, I couldn't move. I said, "Lord, Lord, Mama, I didn't know it was like that."

"Oh, honey," she said, "there's a lot that you don't know. But you are going to find it out." She stood up from the window and came over to me. "You got to hold on to your brother," she said, "and don't let him fall, no matter what it looks like is happening to him and no matter how evil you gets with him. You going to be evil with him many a time. But don't you forget what I told you, you hear?"

"I won't forget," I said. "Don't you worry, I won't forget. I won't let nothing happen to Sonny."

My mother smiled as though she were amused at something she saw in my face. Then, "You may not be able to stop nothing from happening. But you got to let him know you's *there.*"

Two days later I was married, and then I was gone. And I had a lot of things on my mind and I pretty well forgot my promise to Mama until I got shipped home on a special furlough for her funeral.

And, after the funeral, with just Sonny and me alone in the empty kitchen, I tried to find out something about him.

"What do you want to do?" I asked him.

"I'm going to be a musician," he said.

For he had graduated, in the time I had been away, from dancing to the juke box to finding out who was playing what, and what they were doing with it, and he had bought himself a set of drums.

"You mean, you want to be a drummer?" I somehow had the feeling that being a drummer might be all right for other people but not for my brother Sonny.

"I don't think," he said, looking at me very gravely, "that I'll ever be a good drummer. But I think I can play a piano."

I frowned. I'd never played the role of the older brother quite so seriously before, had scarcely ever, in fact, *asked* Sonny a damn thing. I sensed myself in the presence of something I didn't really know how to handle, didn't understand. So I made my frown a little deeper as I asked: "What kind of musician do you want to be?"

He grinned. "How many kinds do you think there are?"

"Be *serious,*" I said.

He laughed, throwing his head back, and then looked at me. "I *am* serious."

"Well, then, for Christ's sake, stop kidding around and answer a serious question. I mean, do you want to be a concert pianist, you want to play classical music and all that, or—or what?" Long before I finished he was laughing again. "For Christ's *sake,* Sonny!"

He sobered, but with difficulty. "I'm sorry, but you sound so—*scared!*" and he was off again.

"Well, you may think it's funny now, baby, but it's not going to be so funny when you have to make your living at it, let me tell you *that.*" I was furious because I knew he was laughing at me and I didn't know why.

"No," he said, very sober now, and afraid, perhaps, that he'd hurt me, "I don't want to be a classical pianist. That isn't what interests me. I mean"—he paused, looking hard at me, as though his eyes would help me to understand, and then gestured helplessly, as though perhaps his hand would help—"I mean, I'll have a lot of studying to do, and I'll have to study *everything,* but, I mean, I want to play *with*—jazz musicians." He stopped. "I want to play jazz," he said.

Well, the word had never before sounded as heavy, as real, as it sounded that afternoon in Sonny's mouth. I just looked at him and I was probably frowning a real frown by this time. I simply couldn't see why on earth he'd want to spend his time hanging around nightclubs, clowning around on bandstands, while people pushed each other around a dance floor. It seemed—beneath him, somehow. I had never thought about it before, had never been forced to, but I suppose I had always put jazz musicians in a class with what Daddy called "good-time people."

"Are you *serious?"*

"Hell, *yes,* I'm serious."

He looked more helpless than ever, and annoyed, and deeply hurt.

I suggested, helpfully: "You mean—like Louis Armstrong?"

His face closed as though I'd struck him. "No. I'm not talking about none of that old-time, down home crap."

"Well, look, Sonny, I'm sorry, don't get mad. I just don't altogether get it, that's all. Name somebody—you know, a jazz musician you admire."

"Bird."

"Who?"

"Bird! Charlie Parker! Don't they teach you nothing in the goddamn army?"

I lit a cigarette. I was surprised and then a little amused to discover that I was trembling. "I've been out of touch," I said. "You'll have to be patient with me. Now. Who's this Parker character?"

"He's just one of the greatest jazz musicians alive," said Sonny, sullenly, his hands in his pockets, his back to me. "Maybe *the* greatest," he added, bitterly, "that's probably why *you* never heard of him."

"All right," I said, "I'm ignorant. I'm sorry. I'll go out and buy all the cat's records right away, all right?"

"It don't," said Sonny, with dignity, "make any difference to me. I don't care what you listen to. Don't do me no favors."

I was beginning to realize that I'd never seen him so upset before. With anotther part of my mind I was thinking that this would probably turn out to be one of those things kids go through and that I shouldn't make it seem important by pushing it too hard. Still, I didn't think it would do any harm to ask: "Doesn't all this take a lot of time? Can you make a living at it?"

He turned back to me and half leaned, half sat, on the kitchen table. "Everything takes time," he said, "and—well, yes, sure, I can make a living at it. But what I don't seem to be able to make you understand is that it's the only thing I want to do."

"Well, Sonny," I said, gently, "you know people can't always do exactly what they *want* to do—"

"*No,* I don't know that," said Sonny, surprising me. "I think people *ought* to do what they want to do, what else are they alive for?"

"You getting to be a big boy," I said desperately, "it's time you started thinking about your future."

"I'm thinking about my future," said Sonny, grimly. "I think about it all the time."

I gave up. I decided, if he didn't change his mind, that we could always talk about it later. "In the meantime," I said, "you got to finish school." We had already decided that he'd have to move in with Isabel and her folks. I knew this wasn't the ideal arrangement because Isabel's folks are inclined to be dicty and they hadn't especially wanted Isabel to marry me. But I didn't know what else to do. "And we have to get you fixed up at Isabel's."

There was a long silence. He moved from the kitchen table to the window. "That's a terrible idea. You know it yourself."

"Do you have a *better* idea?"

He just walked up and down the kitchen for a minute. He was as tall as I was. He had started to shave. I suddenly had the feeling that I didn't know him at all.

He stopped at the kitchen table and picked up my cigarettes. Looking at me with a kind of mocking, amused defiance, he put one between his lips. "You mind?"

"You smoking already?"

He lit the cigarette and nodded, watching me through the smoke. "I just wanted to see if I'd have the courage to smoke in front of you." He grinned and blew a great cloud of smoke to the ceiling. "It was easy." He looked at my face. "Come on, now. I bet you was smoking at my age, tell the truth."

I didn't say anything but the truth was on my face, and he laughed. But now there was something very strained in his laugh. "Sure. And I bet that ain't all you was doing."

He was frightening me a little. "Cut the crap," I said. "We already decided that you was going to go and live at Isabel's. Now what's got into you all of a sudden?"

"*You* decided it," he pointed out. "*I* didn't decide nothing." He stopped in front of me, leaning against the stove, arms loosely folded. "Look, brother. I don't want to stay in Harlem no more, I really don't." He was very earnest. He looked at me, then over toward the kitchen window. There was something in his eyes I'd never seen before, some thoughtfulness, some worry all his own. He rubbed the muscle of one arm. "It's time I was getting out of here."

"Where do you want to *go,* Sonny?"

"I want to join the army. Or the navy, I don't care. If I say I'm old enough, they'll believe me."

Then I got mad. It was because I was so scared. "You must be crazy. You goddamn fool, what the hell do you want to go and join the *army* for?"

"I just told you. To get out of Harlem."

"Sonny, you haven't even finshed *school.* And if you really want to be a musician, how do you expect to study if you're in the *army?"*

He looked at me, trapped, and in anguish. "There's ways. I might be able to work out some kind of deal. Anyway, I'll have the G.I. Bill when I come out."

"If you come out." We stared at each other. "Sonny, please. Be reasonable. I know the setup is far from perfect. But we got to do the best we can."

"I ain't learning nothing in school," he said. "Even when I go." He turned away from me and opened the window and threw his cigarette out into the narrow alley. I watched his back. "At least, I ain't learning nothing you'd want me to learn." He slammed the window so hard I thought the glass would fly out, and turned back to me. "And I'm sick of the stink of these garbage cans!"

"Sonny," I said, "I know how you feel. But if you don't finish school now, you're going to be sorry later that you didn't." I grabbed him by the shoulders. "And you only got another year. It ain't so bad. And I'll come back and I swear I'll help you do *whatever* you want to do. Just try to put up with it till I come back. Will you please do that? For me? "

He didn't answer and he wouldn't look at me.

"Sonny. You hear me?"

He pulled away. "I hear you. But you never hear anything *I* say."

I didn't know what to say to that. He looked out of the window and then back at me. "OK," he said, and sighed. "I'll try."

Then I said, trying to cheer him up a little, "They got a piano at Isabel's. You can practice on it."

And as a matter of fact, it did cheer him up for a minute. "That's right," he said to himself. "I forgot that." His face relaxed a little. But the worry, the thoughtfulness, played on it still, the way shadows play on a face which is staring into the fire.

But I thought I'd never hear the end of that piano. At first, Isabel would write me, saying how nice it was that Sonny was so serious about his music and how, as soon as he came in from school, or wherever he had been when he was supposed to be at school, he went straight to that piano and stayed there until suppertime. And, after supper, he went back to that piano and stayed there until everybody went to bed. He was at the piano all day Saturday and all day Sunday. Then he bought a record player and started playing records. He'd play one record over and over again, all day long sometimes, and he'd improvise along with it on the piano. Or he'd play one section of the record, one chord, one change, one progression, then he'd do it on the piano. Then back to the record. Then back to the piano.

Well, I really don't know how they stood it. Isabel finally confessed that it wasn't like living with a person at all, it was like living with sound. And the sound didn't make any sense to her, didn't make any sense to any of them—naturally. They began, in a way, to be afflicted by this presence that was living in their home. It was as though Sonny were some sort of god, or monster. He moved in an atmosphere which wasn't like theirs at all. They fed him and he ate, he washed himself, he walked in and out of their door; he certainly wasn't nasty or unpleasant or rude, Sonny isn't any of those things; but it was as though he were all wrapped up in some cloud, some fire, some vision all his own; and there wasn't any way to reach him.

At the same time, he wasn't really a man yet, he was still a child, and they had to watch out for him in all kinds of ways. They certainly couldn't throw him out. Neither did they dare to make a great scene about that piano because even they dimly sensed, as I sensed, from so many thousands of miles away, that Sonny was at that piano playing for his life.

But he hadn't been going to school. One day a letter came from the school board and Isabel's mother got it—there had, apparently, been other letters but Sonny had torn them up. This day, when Sonny came in, Isabel's mother showed him the letter and asked where he'd been spending his time. And she finally got it out of him that he'd been down in Greenwich Village, with musicians and other characters, in a white girl's apartment. And this scared her and she started to scream at him and what came up, once she began—though she denies it to this day—was what sacrifices they were making to give Sonny a decent home and how little he appreciated it.

Sonny didn't play the piano that day. By evening, Isabel's mother had calmed down but then there was the old man to deal with, and Isabel herself. Isabel says she did her best to be calm but she broke down and started crying. She says she just watched Sonny's face. She could tell, by watching him, what was happening with him. And what was happening was that they penetrated his cloud, they had reached him. Even if their fingers had been a thousand times more gentle than human fingers ever are, he could hardly help feeling that they had stripped him naked and were spitting on that nakedness. For he also had to see that his presence, that music, which was life or death to him, had been torture for them and that they had endured it, not at all for his sake, but only for mine. And Sonny couldn't take that. He can take it a little better today than he could then but he's still not very good at it and, frankly, I don't know anybody who is.

The silence of the next few days must have been louder than the sound of all the music ever played since time began. One morning, before she went to work, Isabel was in his room for something and she suddenly realized that all of his records were gone. And she knew for certain that he was gone. And he was. He went as far as the navy would carry him. He finally sent me a postcard from some place in Greece and that was the first I knew that Sonny was still alive. I didn't see him any more until we were both back in New York and the war had long been over.

He was a man by then, of course, but I wasn't willing to see it. He came by the house from time to time, but we fought almost every time we met. I didn't like the way he carried himself, loose and dreamlike all the time, and I didn't like his friends, and his music seemed to be merely an excuse for the life he led. It sounded just that weird and disordered.

Then we had a fight, a pretty awful fight, and I didn't see him for months. By and by I looked him up, where he was living, in a furnished room in the Village, and I tried to make it up. But there were lots of other people in the room and Sonny just lay on his bed, and he wouldn't come downstairs with me, and he treated these other people as though they were his family and I weren't. So I got mad and then he got mad, and then I told him that he might just as well be dead as live the way he was living. Then he stood up and told me not to worry about him any more in life, that he *was* dead as far as I was concerned. Then he pushed me to the door and the other people looked on as though nothing were happening, and he slammed the door behind me. I stood in the hallway, staring at the door. I heard somebody laugh in the room and then the tears came to my eyes. I started down the steps, whistling to keep from crying, I kept whistling to myself, *You going to need me, baby, one of these cold, rainy days.*

I read about Sonny's trouble in the spring. Little Grace died in the fall. She was a beautiful little girl. But she only lived a little over two years. She died of polio and she suffered. She had a slight fever for a couple of days, but it didn't seem like anything and we just kept her in bed. And we would certainly have called the doctor, but the fever dropped, she seemed to be all right. So we thought it had just been a cold. Then, one day, she was up, playing, Isabel was in the kitchen fixing lunch for the two boys when they'd come in from school, and she heard Grace fall down in the living room. When you have a lot of children you don't always start running when one of them falls, unless they start screaming or something. And, this time, Grace was quiet. Yet, Isabel says that when she heard that *thump* and then that silence, something happened in her to make her afraid. And she ran to the living room and there was little Grace on the floor, all twisted up, and the reason she hadn't screamed was that she couldn't get her breath. And when she did scream, it was the worst sound, Isabel says, that she'd ever heard in all her life, and she still hears it sometimes in her dreams. Isabel will sometimes wake me up with a low, moaning, strangled sound and I have to be quick to awaken her and hold her to me and where Isabel is weeping against me seems a mortal wound.

I think I may have written Sonny the very day that little Grace was buried. I was sitting in the living room in the dark, by myself, and I suddenly thought of Sonny. My trouble made his real.

One Saturday afternoon, when Sonny had been living with us, or, anyway, been in our house, for nearly two weeks, I found myself wandering aimlessly about the living room, drinking from a can of beer, and trying to work up the courage to search Sonny's room. He was out, he was usually out whenever I was home, and Isabel had taken the children to see their grandparents. Suddenly I was standing still in front of the living room window, watching Seventh Avenue. The idea of searching Sonny's room made me still. I scarcely dared to admit to myself what I'd be searching for. I didn't know what I'd do if I found it. Or if I didn't.

On the sidewalk across from me, near the entrance to a barbecue joint, some people were holding an old-fashioned revival meeting. The barbecue cook, wearing a dirty white apron, his conked hair reddish and metallic in the pale sun, and a cigarette between his lips, stood in the doorway, watching them. Kids and older people paused in their errands and stood there, along with some older men and a couple of very tough-looking women who watched everything that happened on the avenue, as though they owned it, or were maybe owned by it. Well, they were watching this, too. The revival was being carried on by three sisters in black, and a brother. All they had were their voices and their Bibles and a tambourine. The brother was testifying and while he testified two of the sisters stood together, seeming to say, amen, and the third sister walked around with the tambourine outstretched and a couple of people dropped coins into it. Then the brother's testimony ended and the sister who had been taking up the collection dumped the coins into her palm and transferred them to the pocket of her long black robe. Then she raised both hands, striking the tambourine against the air, and then against one hand, and she started to sing. And the two other sisters and the brother joined in.

It was strange, suddenly, to watch, though I had been seeing these street meetings all my life. So, of course, had everybody else down there. Yet, they paused and watched and listened and I stood still at the window. *"Tis the old ship of Zion,"* they sang, and the sister with the tambourine kept a steady, jangling beat, *"it has rescued many a thousand!"* Not a soul under the sound of their voices was hearing this song for the first time, not one of them had been rescued. Nor had they seen much in the way of rescue work being done around them. Neither did they especially believe in the holiness of the three sisters and the brother, they knew too much about them, knew where they lived, and how. The woman with the tambourine, whose voice dominated the air, whose face was bright with joy, was divided by very little from the woman who stood watching her, a cigarette between her heavy, chapped lips, her hair a cuckoo's nest, her face scarred and swollen from many beatings, and her black eyes glittering like coal. Perhaps they both knew this, which was why, when, as rarely, they addressed each other, they addressed each other as Sister. As the singing filled the air the watching, listening faces underwent a change, the eyes focusing on something within; the music seemed to soothe a poison out of them; and time seemed, nearly, to fall away from the sullen, belligerent, battered faces, as though they were fleeing back to their first condition, while dreaming of their last. The barbecue cook half shook his head and smiled, and dropped his cigarette and disappeared into his joint. A man fumbled in his pockets for change and stood holding it in his hand impatiently, as though he had just remembered a pressing appointment further up the avenue. He looked furious. Then I saw Sonny, standing on the edge of the crowd. He was carrying a wide, flat notebook with a green cover, and it made him look, from where I was standing, almost like a schoolboy. The coppery sun brought out the copper in his skin, he was very faintly smiling, standing very still. Then the singing stopped, the tambourine turned into a collection plate again. The furious man dropped in his coins and vanished, so did a couple of the women, and Sonny dropped some change in the plate, looking directly at the woman with a little smile. He started across the avenue, toward the house. He has a slow, loping walk, something like the way Harlem hipsters walk, only he's imposed on this his own half-beat. I had never really noticed it before.

I stayed at the window, both relieved and apprehensive. As Sonny disappeared from my sight, they began singing again. And they were still singing when his key turned in the lock.

"Hey," he said.

"Hey, yourself. You want some beer?"

"No. Well, maybe." But he came up to the window and stood beside me, looking out. "What a warm voice," he said.

They were singing *If I could only hear my mother pray again!*

"Yes," I said, "and she can sure beat that tambourine."

"But what a terrible song," he said, and laughed. He dropped his notebook on the sofa and disappeared into the kitchen. "Where's Isabel and the kids?"

"I think they went to see their grandparents. You hungry?"

"No." He came back into the living room with his can of beer. "You want to come some place with me tonight?"

I sensed, I don't know how, that I couldn't possibly say no. "Sure. Where?"

He sat down on the sofa and picked up his notebook and started leafing through it. "I'm going to sit in with some fellows in a joint in the Village."

"You mean, you're going to play, tonight?"

"That's right." He took a swallow of his beer and moved back to the window. He gave me a sidelong look. "If you can stand it."

"I'll try," I said.

He smiled to himself and we both watched as the meeting across the way broke up. The three sisters and the brother, heads bowed, were singing *God be with you till we meet again.* The faces around them were very quiet. Then the song ended. The small crowd dispersed. We watched the three women and the lone man walk slowly up the avenue.

"When she was singing before," said Sonny, abruptly, "her voice reminded me for a minute of what heroin feels like sometimes—when it's in your veins. It makes you feel sort of warm and cool at the same time. And distant. And—and sure." He sipped his beer, very deliberately not looking at me. I watched his face. "It makes you feel—in control. Sometimes you've got to have that feeling."

"Do you?" I sat down slowly in the easy chair.

"Sometimes." He went to the sofa and picked up his notebook again. "Some people do."

"In order," I asked, "to play?" And my voice was very ugly, full of contempt and anger.

"Well"—he looked at me with great, troubled eyes, as though, in fact, he hoped his eyes would tell me things he could never otherwise say—"they *think* so. And *if* they think so—!"

"And what do *you* think?" I asked.

He sat on the sofa and put his can of beer on the floor. "I don't know," he said, and I couldn't be sure if he were answering my question or pursuing his thoughts. His face didn't tell me. "It's not so much to *play*. It's to *stand* it, to be able to make it at all. On any level." He frowned and smiled: "In order to keep from shaking to pieces."

"But these friends of yours," I said, "they seem to shake themselves to pieces pretty goddamn fast."

"Maybe." He played with the notebook. And something told me that I should curb my tongue, that Sonny was doing his best to talk, that I should listen. "But of course you only know the ones that've gone to pieces. Some don't—or at least they haven't *yet* and that's just about all *any* of us can say." He paused. "And then there are some who just live, really, in hell, and they know it and they see what's happening and they go right on. I don't know." He sighed, dropped the notebook, folded his arms. "Some guys, you can tell from the way they play, they on something *all* the time. And you can see that, well, it makes something real for them. But of course," he picked up his beer from the floor and sipped it and put the can down again, "they *want* to, too, you've got to see that. Even some of them that say they don't—*some,* not all."

"And what about you?" I asked—I couldn't help it. "What about you? Do *you* want to?"

He stood up and walked to the window and remained silent for a long time. Then he sighed. "Me," he said. Then: "While I was downstairs before, on my way here, listening to that woman sing, it struck me all of a sudden how much suffering she must have had to go through—to sing like that. It's *repulsive* to think you have to suffer that much."

I said: "But there's no way not to suffer—is there, Sonny?"

"I believe not," he said and smiled, "but that's never stopped anyone from trying." He looked at me. "Has it?" I realized, with this mocking look, that there stood between us, forever, beyond the power of time or forgiveness, the fact that I had held silence—so long!—when he had needed human speech to help him. He turned back to the window. "No, there's no way not to suffer. But you try all kinds of ways to keep from drowning in it, to keep on top of it, and to make it seem—well, like *you*. Like you did something, all right, and now you're suffering for it. You know?" I said nothing. "Well you know," he said, impatiently, "why *do* people suffer? Maybe it's better to do something to give it a reason, *any* reason."

"But we just agreed," I said, "that there's no way not to suffer. Isn't it better, then, just to—take it?"

"But nobody just takes it," Sonny cried, "that's what I'm telling you! *Everybody* tries not to. You're just hung up on the *way* some people try—it's not *your* way!"

The hair on my face began to itch, my face felt wet. "That's not true," I said, "that's not true. I don't give a damn what other people do, I don't even care how they suffer. I just care how *you* suffer." And he looked at me. "Please believe me," I said, "I don't want to see you—die—trying not to suffer."

"I won't," he said, flatly, "die trying not to suffer. At least, not any faster than anybody else."

"But there's no need," I said, trying to laugh, "is there? in killing yourself."

I wanted to say more, but I couldn't. I wanted to talk about will power and how life could be—well, beautiful. I wanted to say that it was all within; but was it? or, rather, wasn't that exactly the trouble? And I wanted to promise that I would never fail him again. But it would all have sounded—empty words and lies.

So I made the promise to myself and prayed that I would keep it.

"It's terrible sometimes, inside," he said, "that's what's the trouble. You walk these streets, black and funky and cold, and there's not really a living ass to talk to, and there's nothing shaking, and there's no way of getting it out—that storm inside. You can't talk it and you can't make love with it, and when you finally try to get with it and play it, you realize *nobody's* listening. So *you've* got to listen. You got to find a way to listen."

And then he walked away from the window and sat on the sofa again, as though all the wind had suddenly been knocked out of him. "Sometimes you'll do *anything* to play, even cut your mother's throat." He laughed and looked at me. "Or your brother's." Then he sobered. "Or your own." Then: "Don't worry. I'm all right now and I think I'll *be* all right. But I can't forget—where I've been. I don't mean just the physical place I've been, I mean where I've *been*. And *what* I've been."

"What have you been, Sonny?" I asked.

He smiled—but sat sideways on the sofa, his elbow resting on the back, his fingers playing with his mouth and chin, not looking at me. "I've been something I didn't recognize, didn't know I could be. Didn't know anybody could be." He stopped, looking inward, looking helplessly young, looking old. "I'm not talking about it now because I feel *guilty* or anything like that—maybe it would be better if I did, I don't know. Anyway, I can't really talk about it. Not to you, not to anybody," and now he turned and faced me. "Sometimes, you know, and it was actually when I was most *out* of the world, I felt that I was in it, that I was *with* it, really, and I could play or I didn't really have to *play,* it just came out of me, it was there. And I don't know how I played, thinking about it now, but I know I did awful things, those times, sometimes, to people. Or it wasn't that I *did* anything to them—it was that they weren't real." He picked up the beer can; it was empty; he rolled it between his palms: "And other times—well, I needed a fix, I needed to find a place to lean, I needed to clear a space to *listen*—and I couldn't find it, and I—went crazy, I did terrible things to *me,* I was terrible *for* me." He began pressing the beer can between his hands, I watched the metal begin to give. It glittered, as he played with it, like a knife, and I was afraid he would cut himself, but I said nothing. "Oh well. I can never tell you. I was all by myself at the bottom of something, stinking and sweating and crying and shaking, and I smelled it, you know? *my* stink, and I thought I'd die if I couldn't get away from it and yet, all the same, I knew that everything I was doing was just locking me in with it. And I didn't know," he paused, still flattening the beer can, "I didn't know, I still *don't* know, something kept telling me that maybe it was good to smell your own stink, but I didn't think that *that* was what I'd been trying to do—and—who can stand it?" and he abruptly dropped the ruined beer can, looking at me with a small, still smile, and then rose, walking to the window as though it were the lodestone rock. I watched his face, he watched the avenue. "I couldn't tell you when Mama died—but the reason I wanted to leave Harlem so bad was to get away from drugs. And then, when I ran away, that's what I was running from—really. When I came back, nothing had changed, *I* hadn't changed, I was just—older." And he stopped, drumming with his fingers on the windowpane. The sun had vanished, soon darkness would fall. I watched his face. "It can come again," he said, almost as though speaking to himself. Then he turned to me. "It can come again," he repeated. "I just want you to know that."

"All right," I said, at last. "So it can come again. All right."

He smiled, but the smile was sorrowful. "I had to try to tell you," he said.

"Yes," I said. "I understand that."

"You're my brother," he said, looking straight at me, and not smiling at all.

"Yes," I repeated, "yes. I understand that."

He turned back to the window, looking out. "All that hatred down there," he said, "all that hatred and misery and love. It's a wonder it doesn't blow the avenue apart."

We went to the only nightclub on a short, dark street, downtown. We squeezed through the narrow, chattering, jam-packed bar to the entrance of the big room, where the bandstand was. And we stood there for a moment, for the lights were very dim in this room and we couldn't see. Then, "Hello, boy," said a voice and an enormous black man, much older than Sonny or myself, erupted out of all that atmospheric lighting and put an arm around Sonny's shoulder. "I been sitting right here," he said, "waiting for you."

He had a big voice, too, and heads in the darkness turned toward us.

Sonny grinned and pulled a little away, and said, "Creole, this is my brother. I told you about him."

Creole shook my hand. "I'm glad to meet you, son," he said, and it was clear that he was glad to meet me *there,* for Sonny's sake. And he smiled, "You got a real musician in *your* family," and he took his arm from Sonny's shoulder and slapped him, lightly, affectionately, with the back of his hand.

"Well. Now I've heard it all," said a voice behind us. This was another musician, and a friend of Sonny's, a coal-black, cheerful-looking man, built close to the ground. He immediately began confiding to me, at the top of his lungs, the most terrible things about Sonny, his teeth gleaming like a lighthouse and his laugh coming up out of him like the beginning of an earthquake. And it turned out that everyone at the bar knew Sonny, or almost everyone; some were musicians, working there, or nearby, or not working, some were simply hangers-on, and some were there to hear Sonny play. I was introduced to all of them and they were all very polite to me. Yet, it was clear that, for them, I was only Sonny's brother. Here, I was in Sonny's world. Or, rather: his kingdom. Here, it was not even a question that his veins bore royal blood.

They were going to play soon and Creole installed me, by myself, at a table in a dark corner. Then I watched them, Creole, and the little black man, and Sonny, and the others, while they horsed around, standing just below the bandstand. The light from the bandstand spilled just a little short of them and, watching them laughing and gesturing and moving about, I had the feeling that they, nevertheless, were being most careful not to step into that circle of light too suddenly: that if they moved into the light too suddenly, without thinking, they would perish in flame. Then, while I watched, one of them, the small, black man, moved into the light and crossed the bandstand and started fooling around with his drums. Then—being funny and being, also, extremely ceremonious—Creole took Sonny by the arm and led him to the piano. A woman's voice called Sonny's name and a few hands started clapping. And Sonny, also being funny and being ceremonious, and so touched, I think, that he could have cried, but neither hiding it nor showing it, riding it like a man, grinned, and put both hands to his heart and bowed from the waist.

Creole then went to the bass fiddle and a lean, very bright-skinned brown man jumped up on the bandstand and picked up his horn. So there they were, and the atmosphere on the bandstand and in the room began to change and tighten. Someone stepped up to the microphone and announced them. Then there were all kinds of murmurs. Some people at the bar shushed others. The waitress ran around, frantically getting in the last orders, guys and chicks got closer to each other, and the lights on the bandstand, on the quartet, turned to a kind of indigo. Then they all looked different there. Creole looked about him for the last time, as though he were making certain that all his chickens were in the coop, and then he—jumped and struck the fiddle. And there they were.

All I know about music is that not many people ever really hear it. And even then, on the rare occasions when something opens within, and the music enters, what we mainly hear, or hear corroborated, are personal, private, vanishing evocations. But the man who creates the music is hearing something else, is dealing with the roar rising from the void and imposing order on it as it hits the air. What is evoked in him, then, is of another order, more terrible because it has no words, and triumphant, too, for that same reason. And his triumph, when he triumphs, is ours. I just watched Sonny's face. His face was troubled, he was working hard, but he wasn't with it. And I had the feeling that, in a way, everyone on the bandstand was waiting for him, both waiting for him and pushing him along. But as I began to watch Creole, I realized that it was Creole who held them all back. He had them on a short rein. Up there, keeping the beat with his whole body, wailing on the fiddle, with his eyes half closed, he was listening to everything, but he was listening to Sonny. He was having a dialogue with Sonny. He wanted Sonny to leave the shoreline and strike out for the deep water. He was Sonny's witness that deep water and drowning were not the same thing—he had been there, and he knew. And he wanted Sonny to know. He was waiting for Sonny to do the things on the keys which would let Creole know that Sonny was in the water.

And, while Creole listened, Sonny moved, deep within, exactly like someone in torment. I had never before thought of how awful the relationship must be between the musician and his instrument. He has to fill it, this instrument, with the breath of life, his own. He has to make it do what he wants it to do. And a piano is just a piano. It's made out of so much wood and wires and little hammers and big ones, and ivory. While there's only so much you can do with it, the only way to find this out is to try; to try and make it do everything.

And Sonny hadn't been near a piano for over a year. And he wasn't on much better terms with his life, not the life that stretched before him now. He and the piano stammered, started one way, got scared, stopped; started another way, panicked, marked time, started again; then seemed to have found a direction, panicked again, got stuck. And the face I saw on Sonny I'd never seen before. Everything had been burned out of it, and, at the same time, things usually hidden were being burned in, by the fire and fury of the battle which was occurring in him up there.

Yet, watching Creole's face as they neared the end of the first set, I had the feeling that something had happened, something I hadn't heard. Then they finished, there was scattered applause, and then, without an instant's warning, Creole started into something else, it was almost sardonic, it was *Am I Blue*. And, as though he commanded, Sonny began to play. Something began to happen. And Creole let out the reins. The dry, low, black man said something awful on the drums, Creole answered, and the drums talked back. Then the horn insisted, sweet and high, slightly detached perhaps, and Creole listened, commenting now and then, dry, and driving, beautiful and calm and old. Then they all came together again, and Sonny was part of the family again. I could tell this from his face. He seemed to have found, right there beneath his fingers, a damn brand-new piano. It seemed that he couldn't get over it. Then, for awhile, just being happy with Sonny, they seemed to be agreeing with him that brand-new pianos certainly were a gas.

Then Creole stepped forward to remind them that what they were playing was the blues. He hit something in all of them, he hit something in me, myself, and the music tightened and deepened, apprehension began to beat the air. Creole began to tell us what the blues were all about. They were not about anything very new. He and his boys up there were keeping it new, at the risk of ruin, destruction, madness, and death, in order to find new ways to make us listen. For, while the tale of how we suffer, and how we are delighted, and how we may triumph is never new, it always must be heard. There isn't any other tale to tell, it's the only light we've got in all this darkness.

And this tale, according to that face, that body, those strong hands on those strings, has another aspect in every country, and a new depth in every generation. Listen, Creole seemed to be saying, listen. Now these are Sonny's blues. He made the little black man on the drums know it, and the bright, brown man on the horn. Creole wasn't trying any longer to get Sonny in the water. He was wishing him Godspeed. Then he stepped back, very slowly, filling the air with the immense suggestion that Sonny speak for himself.

Then they all gathered around Sonny and Sonny played. Every now and again one of them seemed to say, amen. Sonny's fingers filled the air with life, his life. But that life contained so many others. And Sonny went all the way back, he really began with the spare, flat statement of the opening phrase of the song. Then he began to make it his. It was very beautiful because it wasn't hurried and it was no longer a lament. I seemed to hear with what burning he had made it his, with what burning we had yet to make it ours, how we could cease lamenting. Freedom lurked around us and I understood, at last, that he could help us to be free if we would listen, that he would never be free until we did. Yet, there was no battle in his face now. I heard what he had gone through, and would continue to go through until he came to rest in earth. He had made it his: that long line, of which we knew only Mama and Daddy. And he was giving it back, as everything must be given back, so that, passing through death, it can live forever. I saw my mother's face again, and felt, for the first time, how the stones of the road she had walked on must have bruised her feet. I saw the moonlit road where my father's brother died. And it brought something else back to me, and carried me past it, I saw my little girl again and felt Isabel's tears again, and I felt my own tears begin to rise. And I was yet aware that this was only a moment, that the world waited outside, as hungry as a tiger, and that trouble stretched above us, longer than the sky.

Then it was over. Creole and Sonny let out their breath, both soaking wet, and grinning. There was a lot of applause and some of it was real. In the dark, the girl came by and I asked her to take drinks to the bandstand. There was a long pause, while they talked up there in the indigo light and after awhile I saw the girl put a Scotch and milk on top of the piano for Sonny. He didn't seem to notice it, but just before they started playing again, he sipped from it and looked toward me, and nodded. Then he put it back on top of the piano. For me, then, as they began to play again, it glowed and shook above my brother's head like the very cup of trembling.

Snow

Ted Hughes (1930–)

Born in the West Riding part of Yorkshire, England, Ted Hughes studied folklore and anthropology at Cambridge University, laying a foundation for the uses of myth and ritual in his later poetry. In 1956 he married Sylvia Plath, the young American poet who committed suicide in 1963. His first volume of poems, *The Hawk in the Rain* (1957), announced a sharp departure from the English "Movement" poets of the 1950s who had emphasized plain language and understated emotion: like his American contemporaries, Hughes did not avoid violence and personal confession. His second volume of verse, *Lupercal* (1960), was followed by *Wodwo* (1967), a collection of poetry and prose which contains the story "Snow." In the "Crow" poems of the late 1960s and early 1970s, published in several small volumes, Hughes has created a personal mythology of darkness and deprivation based on traditional materials. His *Selected Poems, 1957–67* appeared in 1972.

And let me repeat this over and over again: beneath my feet is the earth, some part of the surface of the earth. Beneath the snow, beneath my feet, that is. What else could it be? It is firm, I presume, and level. If it is not actually soil and rock, it must be ice. It is very probably ice. Whichever it may be, it is proof—the most substantial proof possible—that I am somewhere on the earth, the known earth. It would be absurd to dig down through the snow, just to determine exactly what is underneath, earth or ice. This bedded snow may well be dozens of feet deep. Besides, the snow filling all the air and rivering along the ground would pour into the hole as fast as I could dig, and cover me too—very quickly.

This could be no other planet: the air is perfectly natural, perfectly good.

Our aircraft was forced down by this unusual storm. The pilot tried to make a landing, but misjudged the extraordinary power of the wind and the whereabouts of the ground. The crash was violent. The fuselage buckled and gaped, and I was flung clear. Unconscious of everything save the need to get away from the disaster, I walked farther off into the blizzard and collapsed, which explains why when I came to full consciousness and stood up out of the snow that was burying me I could see nothing of either the aircraft or my fellow passengers. All around me was what I have been looking at every since. The bottomless dense motion of snow. I started to walk.

Of course, everything previous to that first waking may have been entirely different since I don't remember a thing about it. Whatever chance dropped me here in the snow evidently destroyed my memory. That's one thing of which there is no doubt whatsoever. It is, so to speak, one of my facts. The aircraft crash is a working hypothesis, that merely.

There's no reason why I should not last quite a long time yet. I seem to have an uncommon reserve of energy. To keep my mind firm, that is the essential thing, to fix it firmly in my reasonable hopes, and lull it there, encourage it. Mesmerize it slightly with a sort of continuous prayer. Because when my mind is firm, my energy is firm. And that's the main thing here—energy. No matter how circumspect I may be, or how lucid, without energy I am lost on the spot. Useless to think about it. Where my energy ends I end, and all circumspection and all lucidity end with me. As long as I have energy I can correct my mistakes, outlast them, outwalk them—for instance the unimaginable error that as far as I know I am making at this very moment. This step, this, the next five hundred, or five thousand—all mistaken, all absolute waste, back to where I was ten hours ago. But we recognize that thought. My mind is not my friend. My support, my defence, but my enemy too—not perfectly intent on getting me out of this. If I were mindless perhaps there would be no difficulty whatsoever. I would simply go on aware of nothing but my step by step success in getting over the ground. The thing to do is to keep alert, keep my mind fixed in alertness, recognize these treacherous paralysing, yes, lethal thoughts the second they enter, catch them before they can make that burrowing plunge down the spinal cord.

Then gently and without any other acknowledgment push them back—out into the snow where they belong. And that *is* where they belong. They are infiltrations of the snow, encroachments of this immensity of lifelessness. But they enter so slyly! We are true, they say, or at least very probably true, and on that account you must entertain us and even give us the run of your life, since above all things you are dedicated to the truth. That is the air they have, that's how they come in. What do I know about the truth? As if simpleminded dedication to truth were the final law of existence! I only know more and more clearly what is good for me. It's my mind that has this contemptible awe for the probably true, and my mind, I know, I prove it every minute, is not me and is by no means sworn to help me. Am I to lie? I must survive—that's a truth sacred as any, and as the hungry truths devour the sleepy truths I shall digest every other possible truth to the substance and health and energy of my own, and the ones I can't digest I shall spit out, since in this situation my intention to survive is the one mouth, the one digestive tract, so to speak, by which I live. But those others! I relax for a moment, I leave my mind to itself for a moment—and they are in complete possession. They plunge into me, exultantly, mercilessly. There is no question of their intention or their power. Five seconds of carelessness, and they have struck. The strength melts from me, my bowels turn to water, my consciousness darkens and shrinks, I have to stop.

What are my facts? I do have some definite facts.

Taking six steps every five seconds, I calculate—allowing for my brief regular sleeps—that I have been walking through this blizzard for five months and during that time have covered something equal to the breadth of the Atlantic between Southampton and New York. Two facts. And a third: throughout those five months this twilight of snow has not grown either darker or brighter.

So.

There seems no reason to doubt that I am somewhere within either the Arctic or the Antarctic Circle. That's a comfort, it means my chances of survival are not uniquely bad. Men have walked the length of Asia simply to amuse themselves.

Obviously I am not travelling in a straight line. But that needn't give me any anxiety. Perhaps I made a mistake when I first started walking, setting my face against the wind instead of downwind. Coming against the wind I waste precious energy and there is always this wearisome snow blocking my eyes and mouth. But I had to trust the wind. This resignation to the wind's guidance is the very foundation of my firmness of mind. The wind is not simply my compass. In fact, I must not think of it as a compass at all. The wind is my law. As a compass nothing could be more useless. No need to dwell on that. It's extremely probable indeed and something I need not hide from myself that this wind is leading me to and fro in quite a tight little maze—always shifting too stealthily for me to notice the change. Or, if the sun is circling the horizon, it seems likely that the wind is swinging with it through the three hundred and sixty degrees once in every twenty-four hours, turning me as I keep my face against it in a perfect circle not more than seven miles across. This would explain the otherwise strange fact that in spite of the vast distance I have covered the terrain is still dead level, exactly as when I started. A frozen lake, no doubt. This is a strong possibility and I must get used to it without letting it overwhelm me, and without losing sight of its real advantages.

The temptation to trust to luck and instinct and cut out across wind is to be restricted. The effect on my system of confidence would be disastrous. My own judgment would naturally lead me in a circle. I would have to make deliberate changes of direction to break out of that circle—only to go in a larger circle in the opposite direction. So more changes. Wilder and more sudden changes, changes of my changes—all to evade an enemy that showed so little sign of itself it might as well not have existed. It's clear where all that would end. Shouting and running and so on. Staggering round like a man beset by a mob. Falling, grovelling. So on. The snow.

No. All I have to do is endure: that is, keep my face to the wind. My face to the wind, a firm grip on my mind, and everything else follows naturally. There is not the slightest need to be anxious. Any time now the Polar night will arrive, bringing a drastic change of climate—inevitable. Clearing the sky and revealing the faultless compass of the stars.

The facts are overwhelmingly on my side. I could almost believe in Providence. After all, if one single circumstance were slightly—only slightly—other than it is! If, for instance, instead of waking in a blizzard on a firm level place I had come to consciousness falling endlessly through snow-cloud. Then I might have wondered very seriously whether I were in the gulf or not. Or if the atmosphere happened to consist of, say, ammonia. I could not have existed. And in the moment before death by asphyxiation I would certainly have been convinced I was out on some lifeless planet. Or if I had no body but simply arms and legs growing out of a head, my whole system of confidence would have been disoriented from the start. My dreams, for instance, would have been meaningless to me, or rather an argument of my own meaninglessness. I would have died almost immediately, out of sheer bewilderment. It wouldn't need nearly such extreme differences either. If I had been without those excellent pigskin boots, trousers, jacket, gloves and hood, the cold would have extinguished me at once.

And even if I had double the clothing that I have, where would I be without my chair? My chair is quite as important as one of my lungs. As both my lungs, indeed, for without it I should be dead. Where would I have slept? Lying in the snow. But lying flat, as I have discovered, I am buried by the snow in just under a minute, and cold begins to take over my hands and my feet and my face. Sleep would be impossible. In other words, I would very soon collapse of exhaustion and be buried. As it is, I unsnap my chair harness, plant the chair in the snow, sit on it, set my feet on the rung between the front legs, my arms folded over my knees and my head resting on my arms, and am able in this way to take a sleep of fully ten minutes before the snow piles over me.

The chain of providential coincidences is endless. Or rather, like a chain mail, it is complete without one missing link to betray and annul the rest. Even my dreams are part of it. They are as tough and essential a link as any, since there can no longer be any doubt that they are an accurate reproduction of my whole previous life, of the world as it is and as I knew it—all without one contradictory detail. Yet if my amnesia had been only a little bit stronger!—it needed only that. Because without this evidence of the world and my identity I could have known no purpose in continuing the ordeal. I could only have looked, breathed and died, like a nestling fallen from the nest.

Everything fits together. And the result—my survival, and my determination to survive. I should rejoice.

The chair is of conventional type: nothing in the least mystifying about it. A farmhouse sort of chair: perfectly of a piece with my dreams, as indeed are my clothes, my body and all the inclinations of my mind. It is of wood, painted black, though in places showing a coat of brown beneath the black. One of the nine struts in the back is missing and some child—I suppose it was a child—has stuck a dab of chewing-gum into the empty socket. Obviously the chair has been well used, and not too carefully. The right foreleg has been badly chewed, evidently by a puppy, and on the seat both black and brown paints are wearing through showing the dark grain of the pale wood. If all this is not final evidence of a reality beyond my own, of the reality of the world it comes from, the world I re-dream in my sleeps—I might as well lie down in the snow and be done with.

The curious harness needn't worry me. The world, so far as I've dreamed it at this point, contains no such harness, true. But since I've not yet dreamed anything from after my twenty-sixth birthday, the harness might well have been invented between that time and the time of my disaster. Probably it's now in general use. Or it may be the paraphernalia of some fashionable game that came in during my twenty-seventh or later year, and to which I got addicted. Sitting on snow peaks in nineteenth-century chairs. Or perhaps I developed a passion for painting polar scenery and along with that a passion for this particular chair as my painting seat, and had the harness designed specially. A lucky eccentricity! It is perfectly adapted to my present need. But all that's in the dark still. There's a lot I haven't dreamed yet. From my twenty-third and twenty-fourth years I have almost nothing—a few insignificant episodes. Nothing at all after my twenty-sixth birthday. The rest, though, is about complete, which suggests that any time now I ought to be getting my twenty-third and twenty-fourth years in full and, more important, my twenty-seventh year, or as much of it as there is, along with the accurate account of my disaster and the origin of my chair.

There seems little doubt of my age. Had I been dreaming my life chronologically there would have been real cause for worry. I could have had no idea how much was still to come. Of course, if I were suddenly to dream something from the middle of my sixtieth year I would have to reorganize all my ideas. What really convinces me of my youth is my energy. The appearance of my body tells me nothing. Indeed, from my hands and feet—which are all I have dared to uncover—one could believe I was several hundred years old, or even dead, they are so black and shrunken on the bone. But the emaciation is understandable, considering that for five months I have been living exclusively on will-power, without the slightest desire for food.

I have my job to get back to, and my mother and father will be in despair. And God knows what will have happened to Helen. Did I marry her? I have no wedding ring. But we were engaged. And it is another confirmation of my youth that my feelings for her are as they were then—stronger, in fact, yes a good deal stronger, though speaking impartially these feelings that seem to be for her might easily be nothing but my desperate longing to get back to the world in general—a longing that is using my one-time affection for Helen as a sort of form or model. It's possible, very possible, that I have in reality forgotten her, even that I am sixty years old, that she has been dead for thirty-four years. Certain things may be very different from what I imagine. If I were to take this drift of thoughts to the logical extreme there is no absolute proof that my job, my parents, Helen and the whole world are not simply my own invention, fantasies my imagination has improvised on the simple themes of my own form, my clothes, my chair, and the properties of my present environment. I am in no position to be sure about anything.

But there is more to existence, fortunately, than consideration of possibilities. There is conviction, faith. If there were not, where would I be? The moment I allow one of these 'possibilities' the slightest intimacy—a huge futility grips me, as it were physically, by the heart, as if the organ itself were despairing of this life and ready to give up.

Courageous and calm. That should be my prayer. I should repeat that, repeat it like the Buddhists with their 'O jewel of the lotus'. Repeat it till it repeats itself in my very heart, till every heartbeat drives it through my whole body. Courageous and calm. This is the world, think no more about it.

My chair will keep me sane. My chair, my chair, my chair—I might almost repeat that. I know every mark on it, every grain. So near and true! It alone predicates a Universe, the entire Universe, with its tough carpentering, its sprightly, shapely design—so delicate, so strong. And while I have the game I need be afraid of nothing. Though it is dangerous. Tempting, dangerous, but—it is enough to know that the joy is mine. I set the chair down in the snow, letting myself think I am going to sleep, but instead of sitting I step back a few paces into the snow. How did I think of that? The first time, I did not dare look away from it. I had never before let it out of my hand, never let it go for a fraction between unbuckling it and sitting down on it. But then I let it go and stepped back into the snow. I had never heard my voice before. I was astonished at the sound that struggled up out of me. Well, I need the compensations. And this game does rouse my energies, so it is, in a sense, quite practical. After the game, I could run. That's the moment of danger, though, the moment of overpowering impatience when I could easily lose control and break out, follow my instinct, throw myself on luck, run out across the wind.

But there is a worse danger. If I ran out across the wind I would pretty soon come to my senses, turn my face back into the wind. It is the game itself, the stage of development it has reached, that is dangerous now, I no longer simply step back. I set the chair down, turn my face away and walk off into the blizzard, counting my steps carefully. At fourteen paces I stop. Fifteen is the limit of vision in this dense flow of snow, so at fourteen I stop, and turn. Let those be the rules. Let me fix the game at that. Because at first I see nothing. That should be enough for me. Everywhere, pouring silent grey, a silence like a pressure, like the slow coming to bear of some incalculable pressure, too gradual to detect. If I were simply to stand there my mind would crack in a few moments. But I concentrate, I withdraw my awe from the emptiness and look pointedly into it. At first, everything is as usual—as I have seen it for five months. Then my heart begins to thump unnaturally, because I seem to make out a dimness, a shadow that wavers deep in the grey turmoil, vanishes and darkens, rises and falls. I step one pace forward and using all my will-power stop again. The shadow is as it was. Another step. The shadow seems to be a little darker. Then it vanishes and I lunge two steps forward but immediately stop because there it is, quite definite, no longer moving. Slowly I walk towards it. The rules are that I keep myself under control, that I restrain all sobs or shouts though of course it is impossible to keep the breathing regular—at this stage at least, and right up to the point where the shadow resolves into a chair. In that vast grey dissolution—my chair! The snowflakes are drifting against the legs and gliding between the struts, bumping against them, clinging and crawling over the seat. To control myself then is not within human power. Indeed I seem to more or less lose consciousness at that point. I'm certainly not responsible for the weeping, shouting thing that falls on my chair, embracing it, kissing it, bruising his cheeks against it. As the snowflakes tap and run over my gloves and over the chair I begin to call them names. I peer into each one as if it were a living face, full of speechless recognition, and I call to them—Willy, Joanna, Peter, Jesus, Ferdinand, anything that comes into my head, and shout to them and nod and laugh. Well, it's a harmless enough madness.

The temptation to go beyond the fourteen paces is now becoming painful. To go deep into the blizzard. Forty paces. Then come back, peering. Fifteen paces, twenty paces. Stop. A shadow.

That would not be harmless madness. If I were to leave my chair like that the chances are I would never find it again. My footprints do not exist in this undertow of snow. Weeks later, I would still be searching, casting in great circles, straining at every moment to pry a shadow out of the grey sameness. My chair meanwhile a hundred miles away in the blizzard, motionless—neat legs and elegant back, sometimes buried, sometimes uncovering again. And for centuries, long after I'm finished, still sitting there, intact with its toothmarks and missing strut, waiting for a darkening shape to come up out of the nothingness and shout to it and fall on it and possess it.

But my chair is here, on my back, here. There's no danger of my ever losing it. Never so long as I keep control, keep my mind firm. All the facts are on my side. I have nothing to do but endure.

See the Moon?

Donald Barthelme (1933–   )

Born in Philadelphia and brought up in Texas, Donald Barthelme has been a reporter, a museum director, and editor of a journal of art and literature, *Location.* He has written a novel, *Snow White* (1967), and has published five collections of stories, parodies, and fables: *Come Back, Dr. Caligari* (1964); *Unspeakable Practices, Unnatural Acts* (1968, containing "See the Moon?"); *City Life* (1970); *Sadness* (1972); and *Guilty Pleasures* (1974). His most recent publication is *Amateurs* (1976).

I know you think I'm wasting my time. You've made that perfectly clear. But I'm conducting these very important lunar hostility studies. And it's not you who'll have to leave the warm safe capsule. And dip a toe into the threatening lunar surround.

I am still wearing my yellow flower which has lasted wonderfully.

My methods may seem a touch irregular. Have to do chiefly with folded paper airplanes at present. But the paper must be folded *in the right way.* Lots of calculations and worrying about edges.

Show me a man who worries about edges and I'll show you a natural-born winner. Cardinal Y agrees. Columbus himself worried, the Admiral of the Ocean Sea. But he kept it quiet.

The sun so warm on this screened porch, it reminds me of my grandmother's place in Tampa. The same rusty creaky green glider and the same faded colored canvas cushions. And at night the moon graphed by the screen wire, if you squint. The Sea of Tranquillity occupying squares 47 through 108.

See the moon? It hates us.

My methods are homely but remember Newton and the apple. And when Rutherford started out he didn't even have a decently heated laboratory. And then there's the matter of my security check—I'm waiting for the government. Somebody told it I'm insecure. *That's true.*

I suffer from a frightful illness of the mind, light-mindedness. It's not catching. You needn't shrink.

You've noticed the wall? I pin things on it, souvenirs. There is the red hat, there the book of instructions for the Ant Farm. And this is a traffic ticket written on a saint's day (which saint? I don't remember) in 1954 just outside a fat little town (which town? I don't remember) in Ohio by a cop who asked me what I did. I said I wrote poppycock for the president of a university, true then.

You can see how far I've come. Lunar hostility studies aren't for everyone.

It's my hope that these . . . souvenirs . . . will someday merge, blur—cohere is the word, maybe—into something meaningful. A grand word, meaningful. What do I look for? A work of art, I'll not accept anything less. Yes I know it's shatteringly ingenuous but I wanted to be a painter. They get away with murder in my view; Mr. X. on the *Times* agrees with me. You don't know how I envy them. They can pick up a Baby Ruth wrapper on the street, glue it to the canvas (in the *right place,* of course, there's that), and lo! people crowd about and cry, "A real Baby Ruth wrapper, by God, what could be realer than that!" Fantastic metaphysical advantage. You hate them, if you're ambitious.

The Ant Farm instructions are a souvenir of Sylvia. The red hat came from Cardinal Y. We're friends, in a way.

I wanted to be one, when I was young, a painter. But I couldn't stand stretching the canvas. Does things to the fingernails. And that's the first place people look.

Fragments are the only forms I trust.

Light-minded or no, I'm . . . riotous with mental health. I measure myself against the Russians, that's fair. I have here a clipping datelined Moscow, four young people apprehended strangling a swan. *That's* boredom. The swan's name, Borka. The sentences as follows: Tsarev, metalworker, served time previously for stealing public property, four years in a labor camp, strict regime. Roslavtsev, electrician, jailed previously for taking a car on a joyride, three years and four months in a labor camp, semi-strict regime. Tatyana Voblikova (only nineteen and a Komsomol member too), technician, one and a half years in a labor camp, degree of strictness unspecified. Anna G. Kirushina, technical worker, fine of twenty per cent of salary for one year. Anna objected to the strangulation, but softly: she helped stuff the carcass in a bag.

The clipping is tacked up on my wall. I inspect it from time to time, drawing the moral. Strangling swans is wrong.

My brother who is a very distinguished pianist . . . has no fingernails at all. Don't look it's horrible. He plays under another name. And tunes his piano peculiarly, some call it sour. And renders *ragas* he wrote himself. A night *raga* played at noon can cause darkness, did you know that? It's extraordinary.

He wanted to be an Untouchable, Paul did. That was his idea of a contemporary career. But then a girl walked up and touched him (slapped him, actually; it's a complicated story). And he joined us, here in the imbroglio.

My father on the other hand is perfectly comfortable, and that's not a criticism. He makes flags, banners, bunting (sometimes runs me up a shirt). There was never any question of letting my father drink from the public well. He was on the Well Committee, he decided who dipped and who didn't. That's not a criticism. Exercises his creativity, nowadays, courtesy the emerging nations. Green for the veldt that nourishes the gracile Grant's gazelle, white for the purity of our revolutionary aspirations. The red for blood is understood. That's not a criticism. It's what they all ask for.

A call tonight from Gregory, my son by my first wife. Seventeen and at M.I.T. already. Recently he's been asking questions. Suddenly he's conscious of himself as a being with a history.

The telephone rings. Then, without a greeting: *Why did I have to take those little pills?* What little pills? *Little white pills with a "W" on them.* Oh. Oh yes. You had some kind of a nervous disorder, for a while. *How old was I?* Eight. Eight or nine. *What was it? Was it epilepsy?* Good God no, nothing so fancy. We never found out what it was. It went away. *What did I do? Did I fall down?* No no. Your mouth trembled, that was all. You couldn't control it. *Oh, O.K. See you.*

The receiver clicks.

Or: *What did my great-grandfather do? For a living I mean?* He was a ballplayer, semi-pro ballplayer, for a while. Then went into the building business. *Who'd he play for?* A team called the St. Augustine Rowdies, I think it was. *Never heard of them.* Well . . . *Did he make any money? In the building business?* Quite a bit. *Did your father inherit it?* No, it was tied up in a lawsuit. When the suit was over there wasn't anything left. *Oh. What was the lawsuit?* Great-grandfather diddled a man in a land deal. So the story goes. *Oh. When did he die?* Let's see, 1938 I think. *What of?* Heart attack. *Oh. O.K. See you.*

End of conversation.

Gregory, you didn't listen to my advice. I said try the Vernacular Isles. Where fish are two for a penny and women two for a fish. But you wanted M.I.T. and electron-spin-resonance spectroscopy. You didn't even crack a smile in your six-ply heather hopsacking.

Gregory you're going to have a half brother now. You'll like that, won't you? Will you half like it?

We talked about the size of the baby, Ann and I. What could be deduced from the outside.

I said it doesn't look very big to me. She said it's big enough for *us.* I said we don't need such a great roaring big one after all. She said they cost the earth, those extra-large sizes. Our holdings in Johnson's Baby Powder to be considered too. We'd need acres and acres. I said we'll put it in a Skinner box maybe. She said no child of hers. Displayed under glass like a rump roast. I said you haven't wept lately. She said I keep getting bigger whether I laugh or cry.

Dear Ann. I don't think you've quite . . .

What you don't understand is, it's like somebody walks up to you and says, I have a battleship I can't use, would you like to have a battleship. And you say, yes yes, I've never had a battleship, I've always wanted one. And he says, it has four sixteen-inch guns forward, and a catapult for launching scout planes. And you say, I've always wanted to launch scout planes. And he says, *it's yours,* and then you have this battleship. And then you have to paint it, because it's rusting, and clean it, because it's dirty, and anchor it somewhere, because the Police Department wants you to get it off the streets. And the crew is crying, and there are silverfish in the chartroom and a funny knocking noise in Fire Control, water rising in the No. 2 hold, and the chaplain can't find the Palestrina tapes for the Sunday service. And you can't get anybody to sit with it. And finally you discover that what you have here is this great, big, pink-and-blue rockabye *battleship.*

Ann. I'm going to keep her ghostly. Just the odd bit of dialogue:

"What is little Gog doing."

"Kicking."

I don't want her bursting in on us with the freshness and originality of her observations. What we need here is *perspective.* She's good with Gregory though. I think he half likes her.

Don't go. The greased-pig chase and balloon launchings come next.

I was promising once. After the Elgar, a *summa cum laude.* The university was proud of me. It was a bright shy white new university on the Gulf Coast. Gulls and oleanders and quick howling hurricanes. The teachers brown burly men with power boats and beer cans. The president a retired admiral who'd done beautiful things in the Coral Sea.

"You will be a credit to us, George," the admiral said. That's not my name. I'm protecting my identity, what there is of it.

Applause from the stands filled with mothers and brothers. Then following the mace in a long line back to the field house to ungown. Ready to take my place at the top.

But a pause at Pusan, and the toy train to the Chorwon Valley. Walking down a road wearing green clothes. Korea green and black and silent. The truce had been signed. I had a carbine to carry. My buddy Bo Tagliabue the bonus baby, for whom the Yanks had paid thirty thousand. We whitewashed rocks to enhance our area. Colonels came crowding to feel Bo's hurling arm. Mine the whitest rocks.

I lunched with Thais from Thailand, hot curry from great galvanized washtubs. Engineers banging down the road in six-by-sixes raising red dust. My friend Gib Mandell calling Elko, Nevada on his canvas-covered field telephone. "Operator I crave Elko, Nevada."

Then I was a sergeant with stripes, getting the troops out of the sun. Tagliabue a sergeant too. *Triste* in the Tennessee Tea Room in Tokyo, yakking it up in Yokohama. Then back to our little tent town on the side of a hill, boosting fifty-gallon drums of heating oil tentward in the snow.

Ozzie the jeep driver waking me in the middle of the night. "They got Julian in the Tango Tank." And up and alert as they taught us in Leadership School, over the hills to Tango, seventy miles away. Whizzing through Teapot, Tempest, Toreador, with the jeep's canvas top flapping. Pfc. Julian drunk and disorderly and beaten up. The M.P. sergeant held out a receipt book. I signed for the bawdy remains.

Back over the pearly Pacific in a great vessel decorated with oranges. A trail of orange peel on the plangent surface. Sitting in the bow fifty miles out of San Francisco, listening to the Stateside disc jockeys chattering cha cha cha. Ready to grab my spot at the top.

My clothes looked old and wrong. The city looked new with tall buildings raised while my back was turned. I rushed here and there visiting friends. They were burning beef in their back yards, brown burly men with beer cans. The beef black on the outside, red on the inside. My friend Horace had fidelity. "Listen to that bass. That's sixty watts worth of bass, boy."

I spoke to my father. "How is business?" "If Alaska makes it," he said, "I can buy a Hasselblad. And we're keeping an eye on Hawaii." Then he photographed my veteran face, f.6 at 300. My father once a cheerleader at a great Eastern school. Jumping in the air and making fierce angry down-the-field gestures at the top of his leap.

That's not a criticism. We have to have cheerleaders.

I presented myself at the Placement Office. I was on file. My percentile was the percentile of choice.

"How come you were headman of only one student organization, George?" the Placement Officer asked. Many hats for top folk was the fashion then.

I said I was wounded, and showed him my slash. From the Fencing Club.

"But you served your country in an overseas post."

"And regard my career plan on neatly typed pages with wide margins."

"Exemplary," the Placement Officer said. "You seem married, mature, malleable, how would you like to affiliate yourself with us here at the old school? We have a spot for a poppycock man, to write the admiral's speeches. Have you ever done poppycock?"

I said no but maybe I could fake it.

"Excellent, excellent," the Placement Officer said. "I see you have grasp. And you can sup at the Faculty Club. And there is a ten-per-cent discount on tickets for all home games."

The admiral shook my hand. "You will be a credit to us, George," he said. I wrote poppycock, sometimes cockypap. At four o'clock the faculty hoisted the cocktail flag. We drank Daiquiris on each other's sterns. I had equipped myself—a fibre-glass runabout, someplace to think. In the stadia of friendly shy new universities we went down the field on Gulf Coast afternoons with gulls, or exciting nights under the tall toothpick lights. The crowd roared. Sylvia roared. Gregory grew.

There was no particular point at which I stopped being promising.

Moonstruck I was, after a fashion. Sitting on a bench by the practice field, where the jocks chanted secret signals in their underwear behind tall canvas blinds.

Lay-about babies loafing on blankets, some staked out on twelve-foot dog chains. Brown mothers squatting knee to knee in shifts of scarlet and green. I stared at the moon's pale daytime presence. It seemed . . . inimical.

Moonstruck.

We're playing Flinch. You flinched.

The simplest things are the most difficult to explain, all authorities agree. Say I was tired of p***yc**k, if that pleases you. It's true enough.

Sylvia went up in a puff of smoke. She didn't like unsalaried life. And couldn't bear a male acquaintance moon-staring in the light of day. Decent people look at night.

We had trouble with Gregory: who would get which part. She settled for three-fifths, and got I think the worst of it, the dreaming raffish Romany part that thinks science will save us. I get matter-of-fact midnight telephone calls: *My E.E. instructor shot me down.* What happened? *I don't know, he's an ass anyhow.* Well that may be but still—*When's the baby due?* January, I told you. *Yeah, can I go to Mexico City for the holidays?* Ask your mother, you know she—*There's this guy, his old man has a villa. . . .* Well, we can talk about it. *Yea, was grandmother a Communist?* Nothing so distinguished, she—*You said she was kicked out of Germany.* Her family was anti-Nazi. *Adler means eagle in German.* That's true. There was something called the Weimar Republic, her father—*I read about it.*

We had trouble with Gregory, we wanted to be scientific. Toys from Procreative Playthings of Princeton. O Gregory, that Princeton crowd got you coming and going. Procreative Playthings at one end and the Educational Testing Service at the other. And that serious-minded co-op nursery, that was a mistake. "A growing understanding between parent and child through shared group experience." I still remember poor Henry Harding III. Under "Sibs" on the membership roll they listed his, by age:

26
25
23
20
19
15
10
9
8
6

O Mrs. Harding, haven't you heard? They have these little Christmas-tree ornaments for the womb now, they work wonders.

Did we do "badly" by Gregory? Will we do "better" with Gog? Such questions curl the hair. It's wiser not to ask.

I mentioned Cardinal Y (the red hat). He's a friend, in a way. Or rather, the subject of one of my little projects.

I set out to study cardinals, about whom science knows nothing. It seemed to me that cardinals could be known in the same way we know fishes or roses, by classification and enumeration. A perverse project, perhaps, but who else has embraced this point of view? Difficult nowadays to find a point of view kinky enough to call one's own, with Sade himself being carried through the streets on the shoulders of sociologists, cheers and shouting, ticker tape unwinding from high windows . . .

The why of Cardinal Y. You're entitled to an explanation.

The Cardinal rushed from the Residence waving in the air his hands, gloved in yellow pigskin it appeared, I grasped a hand, "Yes, yellow pigskin!" the Cardinal cried. I wrote in my book, *yellow pigskin.*

Significant detail. The pectoral cross contains nine diamonds, the scarlet soutane is laundered right on the premises.

I asked the Cardinal questions, we had a conversation.

"I am thinking of a happy island more beautiful than can be imagined," I said.

"I am thinking of a golden mountain which does not exist," he said.

"Upon what does the world rest?" I asked.

"Upon an elephant," he said.

"Upon what does the elephant rest?"

"Upon a tortoise."

"Upon what does the tortoise rest?"

"Upon a red lawnmower."

I wrote in my book, *playful.*

"Is there any value that has value?" I asked.

"If there is any value that has value, then it must lie outside the whole sphere of what happens and is the case, for all that happens and is the case is accidental," he said. He was not serious. I wrote in my book, *knows the drill.*

(Oh I had heard reports, how he slunk about in the snow telling children he was Santa Claus, how he disbursed funds in unauthorized disbursements to unshaven men who came to the kitchen door, how his housekeeper pointedly rolled his red socks together and black socks together hinting red with red and black with black, the Cardinal patiently unrolling a red ball to get a red sock and a black ball to get a black sock, which he then wore together. . . .)

Cardinal Y. He's sly.

I was thorough. I popped the Cardinal on the patella with a little hammer, and looked into his eyes with a little light. I tested the Cardinal's stomach acidity using Universal Indicator Paper, a scale of one to ten, a spectrum of red to blue. The pH value was 1 indicating high acidity. I measured the Cardinal's ego strength using the Minnesota Multiphastic Muzzle Map, he had an M.M.M.M. of four over three. I sang to the Cardinal, the song was "Stella by Starlight," he did not react in any way. I calculated the number of gallons needed to fill the Cardinal's bath to a depth of ten inches (beyond which depth, the Cardinal said, he never ventured). I took the Cardinal to the ballet, the ballet was "The Conservatory." The Cardinal applauded at fifty-seven points. Afterward, backstage, the Cardinal danced with Plenosova, holding her at arm's length with a good will and an ill grace. The skirts of the scarlet soutane stood out to reveal high-button shoes, and the stagehands clapped.

I asked the Cardinal his views on the moon, he said they were the conventional ones, and that is how I know all I know about cardinals. Not enough perhaps to rear a science of cardinalogy upon, but enough perhaps to form a basis for the investigations of other investigators. My report is over there, in the blue binding, next to my copy of *La Géomancie et la Néomancie des Anciens* by the Seigneur of Salerno.

Cardinal Y. One can measure and measure and miss the most essential thing. I liked him. I still get the odd blessing in the mail now and then.

Too, maybe I was trying on the role. Not for myself. When a child is born, the locus of one's hopes . . . shifts, slightly. Not altogether, not all at once. But you feel it, this displacement. You speak up, strike attitudes, like the mother of a tiny Lollobrigida. Drunk with possibility once more.

I am still wearing my yellow flower which has lasted wonderfully.

"What is Gog doing."

"Sleeping."

You see, Gog of mine, Gog o' my heart, I'm just trying to give you a little briefing here. I don't want you unpleasantly surprised. I can't stand a startled look. Regard me as a sort of Distant Early Warning System. Here is the world and here are the knowledgeable knowers knowing. What can I tell you? What has been pieced together from the reports of travellers.

Fragments are the only forms I trust.

Look at my wall, it's all there. That's a leaf, Gog, stuck up with Scotch Tape. No no, the Scotch Tape is the shiny transparent stuff, the leaf the veined irregularly shaped . . .

There are several sides to this axe, Gog, consider the photostat, "Mr. W. B. Yeats Presenting Mr. George Moore to the Queen of the Fairies." That's a civilized gesture. I mean Beerbohm's. And when the sculptor Aristide Maillol went into the print business he made the paper by *chewing the fibers himself.* That's dedication. And here is a Polaroid photo, shows your Aunt Sylvia and me putting an Ant Farm together. That's how close we were in those days. Just an Ant Farm apart.

See the moon? It hates us.

And now comes J. J. Sullivan's orange-and-blue Gulf Oil truck to throw kerosene into the space heater. Driver in green siren suit, red face, blond shaved head. The following rich verbal transaction:

"Beautiful day."

"Certainly is."

And now settling back in this green glider with a copy of *Man.* Dear Ann when I look at *Man* I don't want you. Unfolded Ursala Thigpen seems eversomuchmore desirable. A clean girl too and with interests, cooking, botany, pornographic novels. Someone new to show my slash to.

In another month Gog leaps fully armed from the womb. What can I do for him? I can get him into A.A., I have influence. And make sure no harsh moonlight falls on his new soft head.

Hello there Gog. We hope you'll be very happy here.

THE NOVEL

Novelists have always been uneasy about their reputation as the makers of "fictions." There is a real sense in which the novel can claim a completeness and self-sufficiency impossible in history or biography or the autobiographical memoir. The novelist lays down the rules of the game; he is the god of his creation, and what he chooses to leave out simply does not exist in his fictional world. At the same time, novelists have always tried to give their narratives the authority of common experience, to attach their works to something beyond themselves. Hence the popularity of first-person narrative, where the freedom of omniscient narration is deliberately sacrificed in order to attain the illusion of authenticity ("I was there. I saw it"); or the frequent attempts to disguise the novel as history; or the familiar strategy of crowding a fiction with journalistic details and "hard facts." This inevitable tension between the novel as a "model" of reality, with its own shape and laws of behavior, and the novel as an imperfect reflection of the disorderly world in which we all live, has made it an ideal form for dramatizing the disparities between illusion and fact, or between heroic aspiration and inevitable defeat. In the act of writing fiction the novelist, like so many of his characters, often creates an illusion which he must then destroy. From Cervantes onward, the problem of distinguishing appearance from reality (or the difficulty of identifying what is illusory and what is real) has been one of the novelist's major themes, and therefore a crucial factor in his choice of a narrative method.

The narrative structure of Conrad's *Heart of Darkness,* which might seem at first to "distance" the violent African experience from our ordinary lives, serves ultimately to implicate all of us in Kurtz's disintegration and Marlow's dark quest. In one sense Marlow is the detached observer, bringing us a strange tale from another world where the primitive landscape images the primitive forces civilization has managed to keep at bay. But on a deeper level *Heart of Darkness* tells of a voyage of self-exploration, Marlow discovering the darkness within himself as he penetrates the physical "heart of darkness," and the way in which the story is told involves us with this inner voyage. "And this also has been one of the dark places on the earth," says Marlow at the beginning of his tale, ostensibly referring to the countryside around the Pool of London as it looked in the "old days" of the Roman invasion, before the building of a recognizable city. By the end of the story we understand that the darkness of the Congo can also be found in the "monstrous town," that it is one of the constants of the human psyche.

Conrad's own journey to the Congo in 1890 left him with both physical and psychological wounds; the latter are exorcized in *Heart of Darkness.* We soon realize that Kurtz is Marlow's "other self," a dark double who uncomfortably reveals the destructive impulses within us all. The setting of *Heart of Darkness* is Africa at the height of European colonization and imperialism, and Conrad manages to expose the hypocrisy which masked economic expansion as moral improvement. The eloquent and altruistic report Kurtz has prepared for the International Society for the Suppression of Savage Customs, with a hasty afterthought scrawled on the last page ("Exterminate all the brutes!"), makes the point almost too plain. But Conrad is more interested in men than in a social system, and the man he is most concerned with is Marlow, who as trusted narrator becomes the surrogate for both Conrad and the reader. At first we feel that we have exhausted the story when we see the African experience as an emblem for the darkness within, those impulses toward violence and primitive behavior which, according to Freud, the civilized mind must constantly seek to restrain. Our cities are collective attempts to hold back the darkness. There is, however, a deeper reach to *Heart of Darkness,* where Conrad's concern is not so much the revelation of the primitive beneath the fragile surface of civilization as it is the exposure of "hollowness" and spiritual blankness. Apathy and indifference may be, on Conrad's scale of values, worse than an active commitment to evil. T. S. Eliot once thought of opening *The Waste Land,* his great poem of spiritual desolation, with a quotation from *Heart of Darkness:* Kurtz's final cry, "The horror! The horror!" It is easy to understand the connections Eliot saw between Conrad's novella, told in the harbor of the City of London, and his own tortured vision of the Unreal City. But in the end Eliot chose to use another line from *Heart of Darkness,* "Mistah Kurtz—he dead," as an epigraph for "The Hollow Men," a poem which goes beyond *The Waste Land* in its portrayal of spiritual "nothingness." In doing this he may have uncovered one of Conrad's most profound themes. *Heart of Darkness* speaks not only of civilization as a mere appearance, but of the possibility that modern man has lost even the ability to feel terror and despair.

Before starting work on *The Great Gatsby,* Fitzgerald re-read the preface to Conrad's *The Nigger of the 'Narcissus,'* where Conrad speaks of the necessary separation between "the man who suffers" and "the mind which creates," and calls for a work of art which can justify its existence in every line and every phrase. It is easy to trace the influence of Conrad in Fitzgerald's writing. Like Conrad, Fitzgerald divided himself in *The Great Gatsby* between his narrator and his hero: Nick Carraway, the aloof and somewhat skeptical observer, the type of the artist, and Jay Gatsby, who in his attempts to remake himself according to his "Platonic conception of himself" embodies the tragic innocence of the American character in its most idealized form. Fitzgerald himself had been a poor outsider from the Midwest, dazzled and disturbed by the world of the rich. He once told a friend that "the whole idea of Gatsby is the unfairness of a poor young man not being able to marry a girl with money. This theme comes up again and again because I lived it." More than any other American writer of his time,

Fitzgerald knew how money and social position can influence the way we think and behave, even the way we talk (there is the sound of money in Daisy's voice). But the magic of *The Great Gatsby* has to do with more than Fitzgerald's masterly description of a social world, although—as his editor, Maxwell Perkins, once said—the famous catalogue of those who came to Gatsby's house in the summer is the stuff of which greatness is made. Social observations and personal frustrations may have formed the "idea" of *Gatsby,* but beyond that lay Fitzgerald's ambition to write "something extraordinary and beautiful and simple and intricately patterned," a novel whose delicate form would mirror the impossible ideal sought by its hero. Fitzgerald told a friend, in the dark days of the 1930s, that he had never kept his artistic conscience so pure as during the writing of *The Great Gatsby,* and purity is the novel's deepest theme. Its "whole burden," Fitzgerald declared while writing it, is "the loss of those illusions that give such color to the world so that you don't care whether things are true or false as long as they partake of the magical glory." At the novel's elegiac close, when Nick Carraway broods upon the lost freshness of the New World and connects the aspirations of its first settlers with Gatsby's thwarted dreams, we feel that the failure of the American Dream—so darkly and violently acted out in the novel—is partly redeemed by a "magical glory" which lies beyond truth or falsehood. In holding this attitude Fitzgerald revealed himself as a true inheritor of the Romantic tradition and the most sympathetic witness to the America of the 1920s. We should not be surprised that he once thought of calling his novel *Under the Red White and Blue.*

In the first version of Hemingway's "The Snows of Kilimanjaro" the dying writer, all too obviously modeled after Ernest Hemingway, remembers with condescending pity "poor Scott Fitzgerald" and his "romantic awe" of the rich. Fitzgerald was indeed interested in the impact of money and social status upon behavior, but this was not a weakness, as Hemingway implies: it was the source of Fitzgerald's strength as a novelist of manners, absorbed in the codes that govern our social lives. Hemingway himself was obsessed with defining a code for living, but like a poet rather than a novelist he found this code best revealed in the interactions between man and nature. The solitary man and his vocations—hunting, fishing, war, the bullfight—provided Hemingway with his fictional laboratory, and since his heroes are less civilized and less articulate than most, the burden of narration must fall on the author. The young boy Manolo in *The Old Man and the Sea* is really a reincarnation of the young Santiago, at the exact age when he first sailed to Africa and saw the lions on the beach that now solace his dreams. So *The Old Man and the Sea* is really about one man alone, and Hemingway—not Santiago—must tell the story of this archetypal hero and his struggle with nature, which is really a struggle with himself.

In its style and form, *The Old Man and the Sea* stands at some distance from such early stories as "Big Two-Hearted River." In the early stories, which have become classic examples of the artistic power that can be released by a simplification of vocabulary and syntax, Hemingway confines himself to a description of the "sequence of motion and fact," allowing the reader to infer the emotions that result from this sequence. Value-words are kept to a minimum, so that when the literary phrase "tragic adventure" springs from the page near the end of "Big Two-Hearted River" we are brought up short by the deliberate change of style. The heroes of the early stories remain spiritually undefeated in the midst of their physical defeat because they carry themselves with the same restraint and simplicity found in Hemingway's language.

By the time Hemingway began to write *The Old Man and the Sea* in 1951, he had adopted a much more ornate style in which the "sequence of motion and fact" is combined with descriptions of feeling and emotion that are almost Biblical, and overt symbolism replaces the natural symbols of the early stories (such as the trout holding themselves against the current in "Big Two-Hearted River"). Hemingway had sighted the plot of *The Old Man and the Sea* as early as 1936, and he outlined its subject in a magazine article on the Gulf Stream:

> An old man fishing alone in a skiff out of Cabanas hooked a great marlin that, on the heavy sashcord handline, pulled the skiff far out to sea. Two days later the old man was picked up by fishermen 60 miles to the eastward, the head and the forward part of the marlin lashed alongside. What was left of the fish, less than half, weighed 800 pounds. The old man had stayed with him a day, a night, a day and another night while the fish swam deep and pulled the boat. When he had come up the old man had pulled the boat up on him and harpooned him. Lashed alongside the sharks had hit him and the old man had fought them out alone in the Gulf Stream in a skiff, clubbing them, stabbing at them, lunging at them with an oar until he was exhausted and the sharks had eaten all they could hold. He was crying in the boat when the fishermen picked him up, half crazy from his loss, and the sharks were still circling the boat.

This anecdote is told in the spare style of the early stories, and one can imagine it expanded into an austere tale like "The Undefeated" or "Big Two-Hearted River." Fifteen years later, however, Hemingway made the heroism implicit in the anecdote explicit through the use of Christian symbolism. Like the suffering of Christ, the battle with the great fish goes through three stages and three days. Santiago is named for St. James, who abandoned his vocation as fisherman to join Christ, and like Christ or St. James he has a last supper before his ordeal. As the story unfolds the pattern of suffering and personal atonement becomes even more obvious. When Santiago sees the sharks which foreshadow his tragic defeat he utters the sound *Ay*. "There is no translation for this word," says Hemingway, who then immediately translates it through a religious metaphor: "perhaps it is just a noise such as a man might make, involuntarily, feeling the nail go through his hands and into the wood." At the end of his martyrdom, Santiago unsteps the mast, furls the sail, and climbs the hill with the mast on his shoulder, acting out the ascent of Calvary which has been the hidden meaning of his ordeal. Hemingway was not a Christian writer, but in *The Old Man and the Sea* he used the language and symbols of Christianity to express his theme. In effect, he retold the story of the Crucifixion as a primitive, human tragedy. Many readers may feel that in doing this Hemingway went against the grain of his talent, which worked best through suggestion and understatement. But given its artistic premises *The Old Man and the Sea* must be viewed as a powerful fable of old age and victory-in-defeat.

Heart of Darkness

Joseph Conrad (1857–1924)

Józef Teodor Konrad Korzeniowski was born in Russian Poland, now the Soviet Ukraine. After the death of his mother in 1865 and his father in 1869, Conrad was reared by a maternal uncle. Bored with his studies, Conrad left Poland for Marseilles in 1874 and for four years served as a seaman in the French Merchant Navy. In 1878 he signed on a British ship and served sixteen years in the British merchant fleet, rising to first mate and eventually to captain. In 1893 illness and his literary ambitions (he had begun to write his first novel in 1889) caused Conrad to abandon life at sea and settle in England.

The many adventures of Conrad's sea life were to provide the substance for much of his later fiction. In 1890, for example, Conrad satisfied his lifelong interest in Africa by signing on a Congo River steamer. What he saw and felt in Africa—his experience of the physical and spiritual "heart of darkness"—was later transformed into his most famous short novel.

Conrad's first novel, *Almayer's Folly,* was published in 1895. In spite of the difficulty he found in thinking and writing in English, Conrad soon became one of the masters of English fiction. In the Preface to *The Nigger of the 'Narcissus'* (1897) he declares that the aim of his art is "by the power of the written word to make you hear, to make you feel—it is, before all, to make you *see.*" This aim was magnificently achieved in *Lord Jim* (1900), *Youth* (1902, including "Heart of Darkness"), *Nostromo* (1904), and *The Secret Agent* (1907), a novel of political intrigue. The decade 1897–1907 was Conrad's most productive period, but such later works as *Under Western Eyes* (1911) and *Victory* (1915) can stand with his best. Conrad was devoted to England, his adopted country, but he remained something of a cosmopolitan figure, just as his novels and stories belong both to the English tradition and to the wider currents of European literature.

I

The *Nellie,* a cruising yawl, swung to her anchor without a flutter of the sails, and was at rest. The flood had made, the wind was nearly calm, and being bound down the river, the only thing for it was to come to and wait for the turn of the tide.

The sea-reach of the Thames stretched before us like the beginning of an interminable waterway. In the offing the sea and the sky were welded together without a joint, and in the luminous space the tanned sails of the barges drifting up with the tide seemed to stand still in red clusters of canvas sharply peaked, with gleams of varnished sprits. A haze rested on the low shores that ran out to sea in vanishing flatness. The air was dark above Gravesend, and farther back still seemed condensed into a mournful gloom, brooding motionless over the biggest, and the greatest, town on earth.

The Director of Companies was our captain and our host. We four affectionately watched his back as he stood in the bows looking to seaward. On the whole river there was nothing that looked half so nautical. He resembled a pilot, which to a seaman is trustworthiness personified. It was difficult to realise his work was not out there in the luminous estuary, but behind him, within the brooding gloom.

Between us there was, as I have already said somewhere, the bond of the sea. Besides holding our hearts together through long periods of separation, it had the effect of making us tolerant of each other's yarns—and even convictions. The Lawyer—the best of old fellows—had, because of his many years and many virtues, the only cushion on deck, and was lying on the only rug. The Accountant had brought out already a box of dominoes, and was toying architecturally with the bones. Marlow sat cross-legged right aft, leaning against the mizzen-mast. He had sunken cheeks, a yellow complexion, a straight back, an ascetic aspect, and, with his arms dropped, the palms of hands outwards, resembled an idol. The Director, satisfied the anchor had good hold, made his way aft and sat down amongst us. We exchanged a few words lazily. Afterwards there was silence on board the yacht. For some reason or other we did not begin that game of dominoes. We felt meditative, and fit for nothing but placid staring. The day was ending in a serenity of still and exquisite brilliance. The water shone pacifically; the sky, without a speck, was a benign immensity of unstained light; the very mist on the Essex marshes was like a gauzy and radiant fabric, hung from the wooded rises inland, and draping the low shores in diaphanous folds. Only the gloom to the west, brooding over the upper reaches, became more sombre every minute, as if angered by the approach of the sun.

And at last, in its curved and imperceptible fall, the sun sank low, and from glowing white changed to a dull red without rays and without heat, as if about to go out suddenly, stricken to death by the touch of that gloom brooding over a crowd of men.

Forthwith a change came over the waters, and the serenity became less brilliant but more profound. The old river in its broad reach rested unruffled at the decline of day, after ages of good service done to the race that peopled its banks, spread out in the tranquil dignity of a waterway leading to the uttermost ends of the earth. We looked at the venerable stream not in the vivid flush of a short day that comes and departs for ever, but in the august light of abiding memories. And indeed nothing is easier for a man who has, as the phrase goes, "followed the sea" with reverence and affection, than to evoke the great spirit of the past upon the lower reaches of the Thames. The tidal current runs to and fro in its unceasing service, crowded with memories of men and ships it has borne to the rest of home or to the battles of the sea. It had known and served all the men of whom the nation is proud, from Sir Francis Drake to Sir John Franklin, knights all, titled and untitled—the great knights-errant of the sea. It had borne all the ships whose names are like jewels flashing in the night of time, from the *Golden Hind* returning with her round flanks full of treasure, to be visited by the Queen's Highness and thus pass out of the gigantic tale, to the *Erebus* and *Terror,* bound on other conquests—and that never returned. It had known the ships and the men. They had sailed from Deptford, from Greenwich, from Erith—the adventurers and the settlers; kings' ships and the ships of men on 'Change; captains, admirals, the dark "interlopers" of the Eastern trade, and the commissioned "generals" of East India fleets. Hunters for gold or pursuers of fame, they all had gone out on that stream, bearing the sword, and often the torch, messengers of the might within the land, bearers of a spark from the sacred fire. What greatness had not floated on the ebb of that river into the mystery of an unknown earth! . . . The dreams of men, the seed of commonwealths, the germs of empires.

The sun set; the dusk fell on the stream, and lights began to appear along the shore. The Chapman lighthouse, a three-legged thing erect on a mud-flat, shone strongly. Lights of ships moved in the fairway—a great stir of lights going up and going down. And farther west on the upper reaches the place of the monstrous town was still marked ominously on the sky, a brooding gloom in sunshine, a lurid glare under the stars.

"And this also," said Marlow suddenly, "has been one of the dark places of the earth."

He was the only man of us who still "followed the sea." The worst that could be said of him was that he did not represent his class. He was a seaman, but he was a wanderer too, while most seamen lead, if one may so express it, a sedentary life. Their minds are of the stay-at-home order, and their home is always with them—the ship; and so is their country—the sea. One ship is very much like another, and the sea is always the same. In the immutability of their surroundings the foreign shores, the foreign faces, the changing immensity of life, glide past, veiled not by a sense of mystery but by a slightly disdainful ignorance; for there is nothing mysterious to a seaman unless it be the sea itself, which is the mistress of his existence and as inscrutable as Destiny. For the rest, after his hours of work, a casual stroll or a casual spree on shore suffices to unfold for him the secret of a whole continent, and generally he finds the secret not worth knowing. The yarns of seamen have a direct simplicity, the whole meaning of which lies within the shell of a cracked nut. But Marlow was not typical (if his propensity to spin yarns be excepted), and to him the meaning of an episode was not inside like a kernel but outside, enveloping the tale which brought it out only as a glow brings out a haze, in the likeness of one of these misty halos that sometimes are made visible by the spectral illumination of moonshine.

His remark did not seem at all surprising. It was just like Marlow. It was accepted in silence. No one took the trouble to grunt even; and presently he said, very slow:

"I was thinking of very old times, when the Romans first came here, nineteen hundred years ago—the other day. . . . Light came out of this river since—you say Knights? Yes; but it is like a running blaze on a plain, like a flash of lightning in the clouds. We live in the flicker—may it last as long as the old earth keeps rolling! But darkness was here yesterday. Imagine the feelings of a commander of a fine—what d'ye call 'em?—trireme in the Mediterranean, ordered suddenly to the north; run overland across the Gauls in a hurry; put in charge of one of these craft the legionaries—a wonderful lot of handy men they must have been too—used to build, apparently by the hundred, in a month or two, if we may believe what we read. Imagine him here—the very end of the world, a sea the colour of lead, a sky the colour of smoke, a kind of ship about as rigid as a concertina—and going up this river with stores, or orders, or what you like. Sandbanks, marshes, forests, savages—precious little to eat fit for a civilised man, nothing but Thames water to drink. No Falernian wine here, no going ashore. Here and there a military camp lost in a wilderness, like a needle in a bundle of hay—cold, fog, tempests, disease, exile, and death—death skulking in the air, in the water, in the bush. They must have been dying like flies here. Oh yes—he did it. Did it very well, too, no doubt, and without thinking much about it either, except afterwards to brag of what he had gone through in his time, perhaps. They were men enough to face the darkness. And perhaps he was cheered by keeping his eye on a chance of promotion to the fleet at Ravenna by and by, if he had good friends in Rome and survived the awful climate. Or think of a decent young citizen in a toga—perhaps too much dice, you know—coming out here in the train of some prefect, or tax-gatherer, or trader, even, to mend his fortunes. Land in a swamp, march through the woods, and in some inland post feel the savagery, the utter savagery, had closed round him—all that mysterious life of the wilderness that stirs in the forest, in the jungles, in the hearts of wild men. There's no initiation either into such mysteries. He has to live in the midst of the incomprehensible, which is also detestable. And it has a fascination, too, that goes to work upon him. The fascination of the abomination—you know. Imagine the growing regrets, the longing to escape, the powerless disgust, the surrender, the hate."

He paused.

"Mind," he began again, lifting one arm from the elbow, the palm of the hand outwards, so that, with his legs folded before him, he had the pose of a Buddha preaching in European clothes and without a lotus-flower—"Mind, none of us would feel exactly like this. What saves us is efficiency—the devotion to efficiency. But these chaps were not much account, really. They were no colonists; their administration was merely a squeeze, and nothing more, I suspect. They were conquerors, and for that you want only brute force—nothing to boast of, when you have it, since your strength is just an accident arising from the weakness of others. They grabbed what they could get for the sake of what was to be got. It was just robbery with violence, aggravated murder on a great scale, and men going at it blind—as is very proper for those who tackle a darkness. The conquest of the earth, which mostly means the taking it away from those who have a different complexion or slightly flatter noses than ourselves, is not a pretty thing when you look into it too much. What redeems it is the idea only. An idea at the back of it; not a sentimental pretence but an idea; and an unselfish belief in the idea—something you can set up, and bow down before, and offer a sacrifice to. . . ."

He broke off. Flames glided in the river, small green flames, red flames, white flames, pursuing, overtaking, joining, crossing each other—then separating slowly or hastily. The traffic of the great city went on in the deepening night upon the sleepless river. We looked on, waiting patiently—there was nothing else to do till the end of the flood; but it was only after a long silence, when he said, in a hesitating voice, "I suppose you fellows remember I did once turn fresh-water sailor for a bit," that we knew we were fated, before the ebb began to run, to hear about one of Marlow's inconclusive experiences.

"I don't want to bother you much with what happened to me personally," he began, showing in this remark the weakness of many tellers of tales who seem so often unaware of what their audience would best like to hear; "yet to understand the effect of it on me you ought to know how I got out there, what I saw, how I went up that river to the place where I first met the poor chap. It was the farthest point of navigation and the culminating point of my experience. It seemed somehow to throw a kind of light on everything about me—and into my thoughts. It was sombre enough too—and pitiful—not extraordinary in any way—not very clear either. No, not very clear. And yet it seemed to throw a kind of light.

"I had then, as you remember, just returned to London after a lot of Indian Ocean, Pacific, China Seas—a regular dose of the East—six years or so, and I was loafing about, hindering you fellows in your work and invading your homes, just as though I had got a heavenly mission to civilise you. It was very fine for a time, but after a bit I did get tired of resting. Then I began to look for a ship—I should think the hardest work on earth. But the ships wouldn't even look at me. And I got tired of that game too.

"Now when I was a little chap I had a passion for maps. I would look for hours at South America, or Africa, or Australia, and lose myself in all the glories of exploration. At that time there were many blank spaces on the earth, and when I saw one that looked particularly inviting on a map (but they all look that) I would put my finger on it and say, When I grow up I will go there. The North Pole was one of these places, I remember. Well, I haven't been there yet, and shall not try now.The glamour's off. Other places were scattered about the Equator, and in every sort of latitude all over the two hemispheres. I have been in some of them, and . . . well, we won't talk about that. But there was one yet—the biggest, the most blank, so to speak—that I had a hankering after.

"True, by this time it was not a blank space any more. It had got filled since my boyhood with rivers and lakes and names. It had ceased to be a blank space of delightful mystery—a white patch for a boy to dream gloriously over. It had become a place of darkness. But there was in it one river especially, a mighty big river, that you could see on the map, resembling an immense snake uncoiled, with its head in the sea, its body at rest curving afar over a vast country, and its tail lost in the depths of the land. And as I looked at the map of it in a shop-window, it fascinated me as a snake would a bird—a silly little bird. Then I remembered there was a big concern, a Company for trade on that river. Dash it all! I thought to myself, they can't trade without using some kind of craft on that lot of fresh water—steamboats! Why shouldn't I try to get charge of one? I went on along Fleet Street, but could not shake off the idea. The snake had charmed me.

"You understand it was a Continental concern, that Trading Society; but I have a lot of relations living on the Continent, because it's cheap and not so nasty as it looks, they say.

"I am sorry to own I began to worry them. This was already a fresh departure for me. I was not used to get things that way, you know. I always went my own road and on my own legs where I had a mind to go. I wouldn't have believed it of myself; but, then—you see—I felt somehow I must get there by hook or by crook. So I worried them. The men said, 'My dear fellow,' and did nothing. Then—would you believe it?—I tried the women. I, Charlie Marlow, set the women to work—to get a job. Heavens! Well, you see, the notion drove me. I had an aunt, a dear enthusiastic soul. She wrote: 'It will be delightful. I am ready to do anything, anything for you. It is a glorious idea. I know the wife of a very high personage in the Administration, and also a man who has lots of influence with,' etc. etc. She was determined to make no end of fuss to get me appointed skipper of a river steamboat, if such was my fancy.

"I got my appointment—of course; and I got it very quick. It appears the Company had received news that one of their captains had been killed in a scuffle with the natives. This was my chance, and it made me the more anxious to go. It was only months and months afterwards, when I made the attempt to recover what was left of the body, that I heard the original quarrel arose from a misunderstanding about some hens. Yes, two black hens. Fresleven—that was the fellow's name, a Dane—thought himself wronged somehow in the bargain, so he went ashore and started to hammer the chief of the village with a stick. Oh, it didn't surprise me in the least to hear this, and at the same time to be told that Fresleven was the gentlest, quietest creature that ever walked on two legs. No doubt he was; but he had been a couple of years already out there engaged in the noble cause, you know, and he probably felt the need at last of asserting his self-respect in some way. Therefore he whacked the old nigger mercilessly, while a big crowd of his people watched him, thunderstruck, till some man—I was told the chief's son—in desperation at hearing the old chap yell, made a tentative jab with a spear at the white man—and of course it went quite easy between the shoulder-blades. Then the whole population cleared into the forest, expecting all kinds of calamities to happen, while, on the other hand, the steamer Fresleven commanded left also in a bad panic, in charge of the engineer, I believe. Afterwards nobody seemed to trouble much about Fresleven's remains, till I got out and stepped into his shoes. I couldn't let it rest, though; but when an opportunity offered at last to meet my predecessor, the grass growing through his ribs was tall enough to hide his bones. They were all there. The supernatural being had not been touched after he fell. And the village was deserted, the huts gaped black, rotting, all askew within the fallen enclosures. A calamity had come to it, sure enough. The people had vanished. Mad terror had scattered them, men, women, and children, through the bush, and they had never returned. What became of the hens I don't know either. I should think the cause of progress got them, anyhow. However, through this glorious affair I got my appointment, before I had fairly begun to hope for it.

"I flew around like mad to get ready, and before forty-eight hours I was crossing the Channel to show myself to my employers, and sign the contract. In a very few hours I arrived in a city that always makes me think of a whited sepulchre. Prejudice no doubt. I had no difficulty in finding the Company's offices. It was the biggest thing in the town, and everybody I met was full of it. They were going to run an oversea empire, and make no end of coin by trade.

"A narrow and deserted street in deep shadow, high houses, innumerable windows with venetian blinds, a dead silence, grass sprouting between the stones, imposing carriage archways right and left, immense double doors standing ponderously ajar. I slipped through one of these cracks, went up a swept and ungarnished staircase, as arid as a desert, and opened the first door I came to. Two women, one fat and the other slim, sat on straw-bottomed chairs, knitting black wool. The slim one got up and walked straight at me—still knitting with downcast eyes—and only just as I began to think of getting out of her way, as you would for a somnambulist, stood still, and looked up. Her dress was as plain as an umbrella-cover, and she turned round without a word and preceded me into a waiting-room. I gave my name, and looked about. Deal table in the middle, plain chairs all round the walls, on one end a large shining map, marked with all the colours of a rainbow. There was a vast amount of red—good to see at any time, because one knows that some real work is done in there, a deuce of a lot of blue, a little green, smears of orange, and, on the East Coast, a purple patch, to show where the jolly pioneers of progress drink the jolly lager-beer. However, I wasn't going into any of these. I was going into the yellow. Dead in the centre. And the river was there—fascinating—deadly—like a snake. Ough! A door opened, a white-haired secretarial head, but wearing a compassionate expression, appeared, and a skinny forefinger beckoned me into the sanctuary. Its light was dim, and a heavy writing-desk squatted in the middle. From behind that structure came out an impression of pale plumpness in a frock-coat. The great man himself. He was five feet six, I should judge, and had his grip on the handle-end of ever so many millions. He shook hands, I fancy, murmured vaguely, was satisfied with my French. *Bon voyage.*

"In about forty-five seconds I found myself again in the waiting-room with the compassionate secretary, who, full of desolation and sympathy, made me sign some document. I believe I undertook amongst other things not to disclose any trade secrets. Well, I am not going to.

"I began to feel slightly uneasy. You know I am not used to such ceremonies, and there was something ominous in the atmosphere. It was just as though I had been let into some conspiracy—I don't know—something not quite right; and I was glad to get out. In the outer room the two women knitted black wool feverishly. People were arriving, and the younger one was walking back and forth introducing them. The old one sat on her chair. Her flat cloth slippers were propped up on a foot-warmer, and a cat reposed on her lap. She wore a starched white affair on her head, had a wart on one cheek, and silver-rimmed spectacles hung on the tip of her nose. She glanced at me above the glasses. The swift and indifferent placidity of that look troubled me. Two youths with foolish cheery countenances were being piloted over, and she threw at them the same quick glance of unconcerned wisdom. She seemed to know all about them and about me too. An eerie feeling came over me. She seemed uncanny and fateful. Often far away there I thought of these two, guarding the door of Darkness, knitting black wool as for a warm pall, one introducing, introducing continuously to the unknown, the other scrutinising the cheery and foolish faces with unconcerned old eyes. *Ave!* Old knitter of black wool. *Morituri te salutant.* Not many of those she looked at ever saw her again—not half, by a long way.

"There was yet a visit to the doctor. 'A simple formality,' assured me the secretary, with an air of taking an immense part in all my sorrows. Accordingly a young chap wearing his hat over the left eyebrow, some clerk I suppose—there must have been clerks in the business, though the house was as still as a house in a city of the dead—came from somewhere upstairs, and led me forth. He was shabby and careless, with ink-stains on the sleeves of his jacket, and his cravat was large and billowy, under a chin shaped like the toe of an old boot. It was a little too early for the doctor, so I proposed a drink, and thereupon he developed a vein of joviality. As we sat over our vermouths he glorified the Company's business, and by and by I expressed casually my surprise at him not going out there. He became very cool and collected all at once. 'I am not such a fool as I look, quoth Plato to his disciples,' he said sententiously, emptied his glass with great resolution, and we rose.

"The old doctor felt my pulse, evidently thinking of something else the while. 'Good, good for there,' he mumbled, and then with a certain eagerness asked me whether I would let him measure my head. Rather surprised, I said Yes, when he produced a thing like callipers and got the dimensions back and front and every way, taking notes carefully. He was an unshaven little man in a thread-bare coat like a gaberdine, with his feet in slippers, and I thought him a harmless fool. 'I always ask leave, in the interests of science, to measure the crania of those going out there,' he said. 'And when they come back too?' I asked. 'Oh, I never see them,' he remarked; 'and, moreover, the changes take place inside, you know.' He smiled, as if at some quiet joke. 'So you are going out there. Famous. Interesting too.' He gave me a searching glance, and made another note. 'Ever any madness in your family?' he asked, in a matter-of-fact tone. I felt very annoyed. 'Is that question in the interests of science too?' 'It would be,' he said, without taking notice of my irritation, 'interesting for science to watch the mental changes of individuals, on the spot, but . . .' 'Are you an alienist?' I interrupted. 'Every doctor should be—a little,' answered that original imperturbably. 'I have a little theory which you Messieurs who go out there must help me to prove. This is my share in the advantages my country shall reap from the possession of such a magnificent dependency. The mere wealth I leave to others. Pardon my questions, but you are the first Englishman coming under my observation . . .' I hastened to assure him I was not in the least typical. 'If I were,' said I, 'I wouldn't be talking like this with you.' 'What you say is rather profound, and probably erroneous,' he said, with a laugh. 'Avoid irritation more than exposure to the sun. Adieu. How do you English say, eh? Good-bye. Ah! Good-bye. Adieu. In the tropics one must before everything keep calm.' . . . He lifted a warning forefinger. . . . *'Du calme, du calme. Adieu.'*

"One thing more remained to do—say good-bye to my excellent aunt. I found her triumphant. I had a cup of tea—the last decent cup of tea for many days—and in a room that most soothingly looked just as you would expect a lady's drawing-room to look, we had a long quiet chat by the fireside. In the course of these confidences it became quite plain to me I had been represented to the wife of the high dignitary, and goodness knows to how many more people besides, as an exceptional and gifted creature—a piece of good fortune for the Company—a man you don't get hold of every day. Good Heavens! and I was going to take charge of a two-penny-half-penny river-steamboat with a penny whistle attached! It appeared, however, I was also one of the Workers, with a capital—you know. Something like an emissary of light, something like a lower sort of apostle. There had been a lot of such rot let loose in print and talk just about that time, and the excellent woman, living right in the rush of all that humbug, got carried off her feet. She talked about 'weaning those ignorant millions from their horrid ways,' till, upon my word, she made me quite uncomfortable. I ventured to hint that the Company was run for profit.

" 'You forget, dear Charlie, that the labourer is worthy of his hire,' she said brightly. It's queer how out of touch with truth women are. They live in a world of their own, and there had never been anything like it, and never can be. It is too beautiful altogether, and if they were to set it up it would go to pieces before the first sunset. Some confounded fact we men have been living contentedly with ever since the day of creation would start up and knock the whole thing over.

"After this I got embraced, told to wear flannel, be sure to write often, and so on—and I left. In the street—I don't know why—a queer feeling came to me that I was an impostor. Odd thing that I, who used to clear out for any part of the world at twenty-four hours' notice, with less thought than most men give to the crossing of a street, had a moment—I won't say of hesitation, but of startled pause, before this commonplace affair. The best way I can explain it to you is by saying that, for a second or two, I felt as though, instead of going to the centre of a continent, I were about to set off for the centre of the earth.

"I left in a French steamer, and she called in every blamed port they have out there, for, as far as I could see, the sole purpose of landing soldiers and custom-house officers. I watched the coast. Watching a coast as it slips by the ship is like thinking about an enigma. There it is before you—smiling, frowning, inviting, grand, mean, insipid, or savage, and always mute with an air of whispering. Come and find out. This one was almost featureless, as if still in the making, with an aspect of monotonous grimness. The edge of a colossal jungle, so dark green as to be almost black, fringed with white surf, ran straight, like a ruled line, far, far away along a blue sea whose glitter was blurred by a creeping mist. The sun was fierce, the land seemed to glisten and drip with steam. Here and there greyish-whitish specks showed up clustered inside the white surf, with a flag flying above them perhaps—settlements some centuries old, and still no bigger than pin-heads on the untouched expanse of their background. We pounded along, stopped, landed soldiers; went on, landed custom-house clerks to levy toll in what looked like a God-forsaken wilderness, with a tin shed and a flag-pole lost in it; landed more soldiers—to take care of the custom-house clerks presumably.

Some, I heard, got drowned in the surf; but whether they did or not, nobody seemed particularly to care. They were just flung out there, and on we went. Every day the coast looked the same, as though we had not moved; but we passed various places—trading places—with names like Gran' Bassam, Little Popo; names that seemed to belong to some sordid farce acted in front of a sinister back-cloth. The idleness of a passenger, my isolation amongst all these men with whom I had no point of contact, the oily and languid sea, the uniform sombreness of the coast, seemed to keep me away from the truth of things, within the toil of a mournful and senseless delusion. The voice of the surf heard now and then was a positive pleasure, like the speech of a brother. It was something natural, that had its reason, that had a meaning. Now and then a boat from the shore gave one a monetary contact with reality. It was paddled by black fellows. You could see from afar the white of their eyeballs glistening. They shouted, sang; their bodies streamed with perspiration; they had faces like grotesque masks—these chaps; but they had bone, muscle, a wild vitality, an intense energy of movement, that was as natural and true as the surf along their coast. They wanted no excuse for being there. They were a great comfort to look at. For a time I would feel I belonged still to a world of straight-forward facts; but the feeling would not last long. Something would turn up to scare it away. Once, I remember, we came upon a man-of-war anchored off the coast. There wasn't even a shed there, and she was shelling the bush. It appears the French had one of their wars going on thereabouts. Her ensign dropped limp like a rag; the muzzles of the long six-inch guns stuck out all over the low hull; the greasy, slimy swell swung her up lazily and let her down, swaying her thin masts. In the empty immensity of earth, sky, and water, there she was, incomprehensible, firing into a continent. Pop, would go one of the six-inch guns; a small flame would dart and vanish, a little white smoke would disappear, a tiny projectile would give a feeble screech—and nothing happened. Nothing could happen. There was a touch of insanity in the proceeding, a sense of lugubrious drollery in the sight; and it was not dissipated by somebody on board assuring me earnestly there was a camp of natives—he called them enemies!—hidden out of sight somewhere.

"We gave her letters (I heard the men in that lonely ship were dying of fever at the rate of three a day) and went on. We called at some more places with farcical names, where the merry dance of death and trade goes on in a still and earthy atmosphere as of an overheated catacomb; all along the formless coast bordered by dangerous surf, as if Nature herself had tried to ward off intruders; in and out of rivers, streams of death in life, whose banks were rotting into mud, whose waters, thickened into slime, invaded the contorted mangroves, that seemed to writhe at us in the extremity of an impotent despair. Nowhere did we stop long enough to get a particularised impression, but the general sense of vague and oppressive wonder grew upon me. It was like a weary pilgrimage amongst hints for nightmares.

"It was upward of thirty days before I saw the mouth of the big river. We anchored off the seat of the government. But my work would not begin till some two hundred miles farther on. So as soon as I could I made a start for a place thirty miles higher up.

"I had my passage on a little sea-going steamer. Her captain was a Swede, and knowing me for a seaman, invited me on the bridge. He was a young man, lean, fair, and morose, with lanky hair and a shuffling gait. As we left the miserable little wharf, he tossed his head contemptuously at the shore. 'Been living there?' he asked. I said, 'Yes.' 'Fine lot these government chaps—are they not?' he went on, speaking English with great precision and considerable bitterness. 'It is funny what some people will do for a few francs a month. I wonder what becomes of that kind when it goes up country?' I said to him I expected to see that soon. 'So-o-o!' he exclaimed. He shuffled athwart, keeping one eye ahead vigilantly. 'Don't be too sure,' he continued. 'The other day I took up a man who hanged himself on the road. He was a Swede, too.' 'Hanged himself! Why, in God's name?' I cried. He kept on looking out watchfully. 'Who knows? The sun too much for him, or the country perhaps.'

"At last we opened a reach. A rocky cliff appeared, mounds of turned-up earth by the shore, houses on a hill, others with iron roofs, amongst a waste of excavations, or hanging to the declivity. A continuous noise of the rapids above hovered over this scene of inhabited devastation. A lot of people, mostly black and naked, moved about like ants. A jetty projected into the river. A blinding sunlight drowned all this at times in a sudden recrudescence of glare. 'There's your Company's station,' said the Swede, pointing to three wooden barrack-like structures on the rocky slope. 'I will send your things up. Four boxes did you say? So. Farewell.'

"I came upon a boiler wallowing in the grass, then found a path leading up the hill. It turned aside for the boulders, and also for an undersized railway truck lying there on its back with its wheels in the air. One was off. The thing looked as dead as the carcass of some animal. I came upon more pieces of decaying machinery, a stack of rusty rails. To the left a clump of trees made a shady spot, where dark things seemed to stir feebly. I blinked, the path was steep. A horn tooted to the right, and I saw the black people run. A heavy and dull detonation shook the ground, a puff of smoke came out of the cliff, and that was all. No change appeared on the face of the rock. They were building a railway. The cliff was not in the way or anything; but this objectless blasting was all the work going on.

"A slight clinking behind me made me turn my head. Six black men advanced in a file, toiling up the path. They walked erect and slow, balancing small baskets full of earth on their heads, and the clink kept time with their footsteps. Black rags were wound round their loins, and the short ends behind waggled to and fro like tails. I could see every rib, the joints of their limbs were like knots in a rope; each had an iron collar on his neck, and all were connected together with a chain whose bights swung between them, rhythmically clinking. Another report from the cliff made me think suddenly of that ship of war I had seen firing into a continent. It was the same kind of ominous voice; but these men could by no stretch of imagination be called enemies. They were called criminals, and the outraged law, like the bursting shells, had come to them, an insoluble mystery from the sea. All their meagre breasts panted together, the violently dilated nostrils quivered, the eyes stared stonily uphill. They passed me within six inches, without a glance, with that complete, deathlike indifference of unhappy savages. Behind this raw matter one of the reclaimed, the product of the new forces at work, strolled despondently, carrying a rifle by its middle. He had a uniform jacket with one button off, and seeing a white man on the path, hoisted his weapon to his shoulder with alacrity. This was simple prudence, white men being so much alike at a distance that he could not tell who I might be. He was speedily reassured, and with a large, white, rascally grin, and a glance at his charge, seemed to take me into partnership in his exalted trust. After all, I also was a part of the great cause of these high and just proceedings.

"Instead of going up, I turned and descended to the left. My idea was to let that chain-gang get out of sight before I climbed the hill. You know I am not particularly tender; I've had to strike and to fend off. I've had to resist and to attack sometimes—that's only one way of resisting—without counting the exact cost, according to the demands of such sort of life as I had blundered into. I've seen the devil of violence, and the devil of greed, and the devil of hot desire; but, by all the stars! these were strong, lusty, red-eyed devils, that swayed and drove men—men, I tell you. But as I stood on this hillside, I foresaw that in the blinding sunshine of that land I would become acquainted with a flabby, pretending, weak-eyed devil of a rapacious and pitiless folly. How insidious he could be, too, I was only to find out several months later and a thousand miles farther. For a moment I stood appalled, as though by a warning. Finally I decended the hill, obliquely, towards the trees I had seen.

"I avoided a vast artificial hole somebody had been digging on the slope, the purpose of which I found it impossible to divine. It wasn't a quarry or a sandpit, anyhow. It was just a hole. It might have been connected with the philanthropic desire of giving the criminals something to do. I don't know. Then I nearly fell into a very narrow ravine, almost no more than a scar in the hillside. I discovered that a lot of imported drainage-pipes for the settlement had been tumbled in there. There wasn't one that was not broken. It was a wanton smash-up. At last I got under the trees. My purpose was to stroll into the shade for a moment; but no sooner within than it seemed to me I had stepped into the gloomy circle of some Inferno. The rapids were near, and an uninterrupted, uniform, headlong, rushing noise filled the mournful stillness of the grove, where not a breath stirred, not a leaf moved, with a mysterious sound—as though the tearing pace of the launched earth had suddenly become audible.

"Black shapes crouched, lay, sat between the trees, leaning against the trunks, clinging to the earth, half coming out, half effaced within the dim light, in all the attitudes of pain, abandonment, and despair. Another mine on the cliff went off, followed by a slight shudder of the soil under my feet. The work was going on. The work! And this was the place where some of the helpers had withdrawn to die.

"They were dying slowly—it was very clear. They were not enemies, they were not criminals, they were nothing earthly now—nothing but black shadows of disease and starvation, lying confusedly in the greenish gloom. Brought from all the recesses of the coast in all the legality of time contracts, lost in uncongenial surroundings, fed on unfamiliar food, they sickened, became inefficient, and were then allowed to crawl away and rest. These moribund shapes were free as air—and nearly as thin. I began to distinguish the gleam of the eyes under the trees. Then, glancing down, I saw a face near my hand. The black bones reclined at full length with one shoulder against the tree, and slowly the eyelids rose and the sunken eyes looked up at me, enormous and vacant, a kind of blind, white flicker in the depths of the orbs, which died out slowly. The man seemed young—almost a boy—but you know with them it's hard to tell. I found nothing else to do but to offer him one of my good Swede's ship's biscuits I had in my pocket. The fingers closed slowly on it and held—there was no other movement and no other glance. He had tied a bit of white worsted round his neck—Why? Where did he get it? Was it a badge—an ornament—a charm—a propitiatory act? Was there any idea at all connected with it? It looked startling round his black neck, this bit of white thread from beyond the seas.

"Near the same tree two more bundles of acute angles sat with their legs drawn up. One, with his chin propped on his knees, stared at nothing, in an intolerable and appalling manner: his brother phantom rested its forehead, as if overcome with a great weariness; and all about others were scattered in every pose of contorted collapse, as in some picture of a massacre or a pestilence. While I stood horror-struck, one of these creatures rose to his hands and knees, and went off on all-fours towards the river to drink. He lapped out of his hand, then sat up in the sunlight, crossing his shins in front of him, and after a time let his woolly head fall on his breastbone.

"I didn't want any more loitering in the shade, and I made haste towards the station. When near the buildings I met a white man, in such an unexpected elegance of get-up that in the first moment I took him for a sort of vision. I saw a high starched collar, white cuffs, a light alpaca jacket, snowy trousers, a clean necktie, and varnished boots. No hat. Hair parted, brushed, oiled, under a green-lined parasol held in a big white hand. He was amazing, and had a penholder behind his ear.

"I shook hands with this miracle, and I learned he was the Company's chief accountant, and that all the book-keeping was done at this station. He had come out for a moment, he said, 'to get a breath of fresh air.' The expression sounded wonderfully odd, with its suggestion of sedentary desk-life. I wouldn't have mentioned the fellow to you at all, only it was from his lips that I first heard the name of the man who is so indissolubly connected with the memories of that time. Moreover, I respected the fellow. Yes; I respected his collars, his vast cuffs, his brushed hair. His appearance was certainly that of a hairdresser's dummy; but in the great demoralisation of the land he kept up his appearance. That's backbone. His starched collars and got-up shirt-fronts were achievements of character. He had been out nearly three years; and, later, I could not help asking him how he managed to sport such linen. He had just the faintest blush, and said modestly, 'I've been teaching one of the native women about the station. It was difficult. She had a distaste for the work.' Thus this man had verily accomplished something. And he was devoted to his books, which were in apple-pie order.

"Everything else in the station was in a muddle,—heads, things, buildings. Strings of dusty niggers with splay feet arrived and departed; a stream of manufactured goods, rubbishy cottons, beads, and brass-wire sent into the depths of darkness, and in return came a precious trickle of ivory.

"I had to wait in the station for ten days—an eternity. I lived in a hut in the yard, but to be out of the chaos I would sometimes get into the accountant's office. It was built of horizontal planks, and so badly put together that, as he bent over his high desk, he was barred from neck to heels with narrow strips of sunlight. There was no need to open the big shutter to see. It was hot there too; big flies buzzed fiendishly, and did not sting, but stabbed. I sat generally on the floor, while, of faultless appearance (and even slightly scented), perching on a high stool, he wrote, he wrote. Sometimes he stood up for exercise. When a truckle-bed with a sick man (some invalided agent from up-country) was put in there, he exhibited a gentle annoyance. 'The groans of this sick person,' he said, 'distract my attention. And without that it is extremely difficult to guard against clerical errors in this climate.'

"One day he remarked, without lifting his head, 'In the interior you will no doubt meet Mr. Kurtz.' On my asking who Mr. Kurtz was, he said he was a first-class agent; and seeing my disappointment at this information, he added slowly, laying down his pen, 'He is a very remarkable person.' Further questions elicited from him that Mr. Kurtz was at present in charge of a trading-post, a very important one, in the true ivory-country, at 'the very bottom of there. Sends in as much ivory as all the others put together . . .' He began to write again. The sick man was too ill to groan. The flies buzzed in a great peace.

"Suddenly there was a growing murmur of voices and a great tramping of feet. A caravan had come in. A violent babble of uncouth sounds burst out on the other side of the planks. All the carriers were speaking together, and in the midst of the uproar the lamentable voice of the chief agent was heard 'giving it up' tearfully for the twentieth time that day. . . . He rose slowly. 'What a frightful row,' he said. He crossed the room gently to look at the sick man, and returning, said to me, 'He does not hear.' 'What! Dead?' I asked, startled. 'No, not yet,' he answered, with great composure. Then, alluding with a toss of the head to the tumult in the station-yard, 'When one has got to make correct entries, one comes to hate those savages—hate them to the death.' He remained thoughtful for a moment. 'When you see Mr. Kurtz,' he went on, 'tell him from me that everything here'—he glanced at the desk—'is very satisfactory. I don't like to write to him—with those messengers of ours you never know who may get hold of your letter—at that Central Station.' He stared at me for a moment with his mild, bulging eyes. 'Oh, he will go far, very far,' he began again. 'He will be a somebody in the Administration before long. They, above—the Council in Europe, you know—mean him to be.'

"He turned to his work. The noise outside had ceased, and presently in going out I stopped at the door. In the steady buzz of flies the homeward-bound agent was lying flushed and insensible; the other, bent over his books, was making correct entries of perfectly correct transactions; and fifty feet below the doorstep I could see the still tree-tops of the grove of death.

"Next day I left that station at last, with a caravan of sixty men, for a two-hundred-mile tramp.

"No use telling you much about that. Paths, paths, everywhere; a stamped-in network of paths spreading over the empty land, through long grass, through burnt grass, through thickets, down and up chilly ravines, up and down stony hills ablaze with heat; and a solitude, a solitude, nobody, not a hut. The population had cleared out a long time ago. Well, if a lot of mysterious niggers armed with all kinds of fearful weapons suddenly took to travelling on the road between Deal and Gravesend, catching the yokels right and left to carry heavy loads for them, I fancy every farm and cottage thereabouts would get empty very soon. Only here the dwellings were gone too. Still, I passed through several abandoned villages. There's something pathetically childish in the ruins of grass walls. Day after day, with the stamp and shuffle of sixty pair of bare feet behind me, each pair under a 60-lb. load. Camp, cook, sleep; strike camp, march. Now and then a carrier dead in harness, at rest in the long grass near the path, with an empty water-gourd and his long staff lying by his side. A great silence around and above. Perhaps on some quiet night the tremor of far-off drums, sinking, swelling, a tremor vast, faint; a sound weird, appealing, suggestive, and wild—and perhaps with as profound a meaning as the sound of bells in a Christian country. Once a white man in an unbuttoned uniform, camping on the path with an armed escort of lank Zanzibaris, very hospitable and festive—not to say drunk. Was looking after the upkeep of the road, he declared. Can't say I saw any road or any upkeep, unless the body of a middle-aged negro, with a bullet-hole in the forehead, upon which I absolutely stumbled three miles farther on, may be considered as a permanent improvement. I had a white companion too, not a bad chap, but rather too fleshy and with the exasperating habit of fainting on the hot hillsides, miles away from the least bit of shade and water. Annoying, you know, to hold your own coat like a parasol over a man's head while he is coming to. I couldn't help asking him once what he meant by coming there at all. 'To make money, of course. What do you think?' he said scornfully. Then he got fever, and had to be carried in a hammock slung under a pole. As he weighed sixteen stone I had no end of rows with the carriers. They jibbed, ran away, sneaked off with their loads in the night—quite a mutiny. So, one evening, I made a speech in English with gestures, not one of which was lost to the sixty pairs of eyes before me, and the next morning I started the hammock off in front all right. An hour afterwards I came upon the whole concern wrecked in a bush—man, hammock, groans, blankets, horrors. The heavy pole had skinned his poor nose. He was very anxious for me to kill somebody, but there wasn't the shadow of a carrier near. I remembered the old doctor—'It would be interesting for science to watch the mental changes of individuals, on the spot.' I felt I was becoming scientifically interesting. However, all that is to no purpose. On the fifteenth day I came in sight of the big river again, and hobbled into the Central Station. It was on a back water surrounded by scrub and forest, with a pretty border of smelly mud on one side, and on the three others enclosed by a crazy fence of rushes. A neglected gap was all the gate it had, and the first glance at the place was enough to let you see the flabby devil was running that show. White men with long staves in their hands appeared languidly from amongst the buildings, strolling up to take a look at me, and then retired out of sight somewhere. One of them, a stout, excitable chap with black moustaches, informed me with great volubility and many digressions, as soon as I told him who I was, that my steamer was at the bottom of the river. I was thunderstruck. What, how, why? Oh, it was 'all right.' The 'manager himself' was there. All quite correct. 'Everybody had behaved splendidly! splendidly!'—'You must,' he said in agitation, 'go and see the general manager at once. He is waiting.'

"I did not see the real significance of that wreck at once. I fancy I see it now, but I am not sure—not at all. Certainly the affair was too stupid—when I think of it—to be altogether natural. Still . . . But at the moment it presented itself simply as a confounded nuisance. The steamer was sunk. They had started two days before in a sudden hurry up the river with the manager on board, in charge of some volunteer skipper, and before they had been out three hours they tore the bottom out of her on stones, and she sank near the south bank. I asked myself what I was to do there, now my boat was lost. As a matter of fact, I had plenty to do in fishing my command out of the river. I had to set about it the very next day. That, and the repairs when I brought the pieces to the station, took some months.

"My first interview with the manager was curious. He did not ask me to sit down after my twenty-mile walk that morning. He was commonplace in complexion, in feature, in manners, and in voice. He was of middle size and of ordinary build. His eyes, of the usual blue, were perhaps remarkably cold, and he certainly could make his glance fall on one as trenchant and heavy as an axe. But even at these times the rest of his person seemed to disclaim the intention. Otherwise there was only an indefinable, faint expression of his lips, something stealthy—a smile—not a smile—I remember it, but I can't explain. It was unconscious, this smile was, though just after he had said something it got intensified for an instant. It came at the end of his speeches like a seal applied on the words to make the meaning of the commonest phrase appear absolutely inscrutable. He was a common trader, from his youth up employed in these parts—nothing more. He was obeyed, yet he inspired neither love nor fear, nor even respect. He inspired uneasiness. That was it! Uneasiness. Not a definite mistrust—just uneasiness—nothing more. You have no idea how effective such a . . . a . . . faculty can be. He had no genius for organising, for initiative, or for order even. That was evident in such things as the deplorable state of the station. He had no learning, and no intelligence. His position had come to him—why? Perhaps because he was never ill . . . He had served three terms of three years out there . . . Because triumphant health in the general rout of constitutions is a kind of power in itself. When he went home on leave he rioted on a large scale—pompously. Jack ashore—with a difference—in externals only. This one could gather from his casual talk. He originated nothing, he could keep the routine going—that's all. But he was great. He was great by this little thing that it was impossible to tell what could control such a man. He never gave that secret away. Perhaps there was nothing within him. Such a suspicion made one pause—for out there there were no external checks. Once when various tropical diseases had laid low almost every 'agent' in the station, he was heard to say, 'Men who come out here should have no entrails.' He sealed the utterance with that smile of his, as though it had been a door opening into a darkness he had in his keeping. You fancied you had seen things—but the seal was on. When annoyed at meal-times by the constant quarrels of the white men about precedence, he ordered an immense round table to be made, for which a special house had to be built. This was the station's mess-room. Where he sat was the first place—the rest were nowhere. One felt this to be his unalterable conviction. He was neither civil or uncivil. He was quiet. He allowed his 'boy'—an overfed young negro from the coast—to treat the white men, under his very eyes, with provoking insolence.

"He began to speak as soon as he saw me. I had been very long on the road. He could not wait. Had to start without me. The up-river stations had to be relieved. There had been so many delays already that he did not know who was dead and who was alive, and how they got on—and so on, and so on. He paid no attention to my explanations, and, playing with a stick of sealing-wax, repeated several times that the situation was 'very grave, very grave.' There were rumours that a very important station was in jeopardy, and its chief, Mr. Kurtz, was ill. Hoped it was not true. Mr. Kurtz was . . . I felt weary and irritable. Hang Kurtz, I thought. I interrupted him by saying I had heard of Mr. Kurtz on the coast. 'Ah! So they talk of him down there,' he murmured to himself. Then he began again, assuring me Mr. Kurtz was the best agent he had, an exceptional man, of the greatest importance to the Company; therefore I could understand his anxiety. He was, he said, 'very, very uneasy.' Certainly he fidgeted on his chair a good deal, exclaimed, 'Ah, Mr. Kurtz!' broke the stick of sealing-wax and seemed dumbfounded by the accident. Next thing he wanted to know 'how long it would take to' . . . I interrupted him again. Being hungry, you know, and kept on my feet too, I was getting savage. 'How can I tell?' I said. 'I haven't even seen the wreck yet—some months, no doubt.' All this talk seemed to me so futile. 'Some months,' he said. 'Well, let us say three months before we can make a start. Yes. That ought to do the affair.' I flung out of his hut (he lived all alone in a clay hut with a sort of verandah) muttering to myself my opinion of him. He was a chattering idiot. Afterwards I took it back when it was borne in upon me startlingly with what extreme nicety he had estimated the time requisite for the 'affair.'

"I went to work the next day, turning, so to speak, my back on that station. In that way only it seemed to me I could keep my hold on the redeeming facts of life. Still, one must look about sometimes; and then I saw this station, these men strolling aimlessly about in the sunshine of the yard. I asked myself sometimes what it all meant. They wandered here and there with their absurd long staves in their hands, like a lot of faithless pilgrims bewitched inside a rotten face. The word 'ivory' rang in the air, was whispered, was sighed. You would think they were praying to it. A taint of imbecile rapacity blew through it all, like a whiff from some corpse. By Jove! I've never seen anything so unreal in my life. And outside, the silent wilderness surrounding this cleared speck on the earth struck me as something great and invincible, like evil or truth, waiting patiently for the passing away of this fantastic invasion.

"Oh, those months! Well, never mind. Various things happened. One evening a grass shed full of calico, cotton prints, beads, and I don't know what else, burst into a blaze so suddenly that you would have thought the earth had opened to let an avenging fire consume all that trash. I was smoking my pipe quietly by my dismantled steamer, and saw them all cutting capers in the light, with their arms lifted high, when the stout man with moustaches came tearing down to the river, a tin pail in his hand, assured me that everybody was 'behaving splendidly, splendidly,' dipped about a quart of water and tore back again. I noticed there was a hole in the bottom of his pail.

"I strolled up. There was no hurry. You see the thing had gone off like a box of matches. It had been hopeless from the very first. The flame had leaped high, driven everybody back, lighted up everything—and collapsed. The shed was already a heap of embers glowing fiercely. A nigger was being beaten near by. They said he had caused the fire in some way; be that as it may, he was screeching most horribly. I saw him, later, for several days, sitting in a bit of shade looking very sick and trying to recover himself: afterwards he arose and went out—and the wilderness without a sound took him into its bosom again. As I approached the glow from the dark I found myself at the back of two men, talking. I heard the name of Kurtz pronounced, then the words, 'take advantage of this unfortunate accident.' One of the men was the manager. I wished him a good evening. 'Did you ever see anything like it—eh? it is incredible,' he said, and walked off. The other man remained. He was a first-class agent, young, gentlemanly, a bit reserved, with a forked little beard and a hooked nose. He was stand-offish with the other agents, and they on their side said he was the manager's spy upon them. As to me, I had hardly ever spoken to him before. We got into talk, and by and by we strolled away from the hissing ruins. Then he asked me to his room, which was in the main building of the station. He struck a match, and I perceived that this young aristocrat had not only a silver-mounted dressing-case but also a whole candle all to himself. Just at that time the manager was the only man supposed to have any right to candles. Native mats covered the clay walls; a collection of spears, assegais, shields, knives, was hung up in trophies. The business entrusted to this fellow was the making of bricks—so I had been informed; but there wasn't a fragment of a brick anywhere in the station, and he had been there more than a year—waiting. It seems he could not make bricks without something, I don't know what—straw maybe. Anyway, it could not be found there, and as it was not likely to be sent from Europe, it did not appear clear to me what he was waiting for. An act of special creation perhaps. However, they were all waiting—all the sixteen or twenty pilgrims of them—for something; and upon my word it did not seem an uncongenial occupation, from the way they took it, though the only thing that ever came to them was disease—as far as I could see. They beguiled the time by backbiting and intriguing against each other in a foolish kind of way. There was an air of plotting about that station, but nothing came of it, of course. It was as unreal as everything else—as the philanthropic pretense of the whole concern, as their talk, as their government, as their show of work. The only real feeling was a desire to get appointed to a trading-post where ivory was to be had, so that they could earn percentages. They intrigued and slandered and hated each other only on that account—but as to effectually lifting a little finger—oh no. By Heavens! there is something after all in the world allowing one man to steal a horse while another must not look at a halter. Steal a horse straight out. Very well. He has done it. Perhaps he can ride. But there is a way of looking at a halter that would provoke the most charitable of saints into a kick.

"I had no idea why he wanted to be sociable, but as we chatted in there it suddenly occurred to me the fellow was trying to get at something—in fact, pumping me. He alluded constantly to Europe, to the people I was supposed to know there—putting leading questions as to my acquaintances in the sepulchral city, and so on. His little eyes glittered like mica discs—with curiosity—though he tried to keep up a bit of superciliousness. At first I was astonished, but very soon I became awfully curious to see what he would find out from me. I couldn't possibly imagine what I had in me to make it worth his while. It was very pretty to see how he baffled himself, for in truth my body was full only of chills, and my head had nothing in it but that wretched steamboat business. It was evident he took me for a perfectly shameless prevaricator. At last he got angry, and, to conceal a movement of furious annoyance, he yawned. I rose. Then I noticed a small sketch in oils, on a panel, representing a woman, draped and blindfolded, carrying a lighted torch. The background was sombre—almost black. The movement of the woman was stately, and the effect of the torchlight on the face was sinister.

"It arrested me, and he stood by civilly, holding an

empty half-pint champagne bottle (medical comforts) with the candle stuck in it. To my question he said Mr. Kurtz had painted this—in this very station more than a year ago—while waiting for means to go to his trading-post. 'Tell me, pray,' said I, 'who is this Mr. Kurtz?'

" 'The chief of the Inner Station,' he answered in a short tone, looking away. 'Much obliged,' I said, laughing. 'And you are the brickmaker of the Central Station. Every one knows that.' He was silent for a while. 'He is a prodigy,' he said at last. 'He is an emissary of pity, and science, and progress, and devil knows what else. We want,' he began to declaim suddenly, 'for the guidance of the cause entrusted to us by Europe, so to speak, higher intelligence, wide sympathies, a singleness of purpose.' 'Who says that?' I asked. 'Lots of them,' he replied. 'Some even write that; and so *he* comes here, a special being, as you ought to know.' 'Why ought I to know?' I interrupted, really surprised. He paid no attention. 'Yes. To-day he is chief of the best station, next year he will be assistant-manager, two years more and . . . but I daresay you know what he will be in two years' time. You are of the new gang—the gang of virtue. The same people who sent him specially also recommended you. Oh, don't say no. I've my own eyes to trust.' Light dawned upon me. My dear aunt's influential acquaintances were producing an unexpected effect upon that young man. I nearly burst into a laugh. 'Do you read the Company's confidential correspondence?' I asked. He hadn't a word to say. It was great fun. 'When Mr. Kurtz,' I continued severely, 'is General Manager, you won't have the opportunity.'

"He blew the candle out suddenly, and we went outside. The moon had risen. Black figures strolled about listlessly, pouring water on the glow, whence proceeded a sound of hissing; steam ascended in the moonlight; the beaten nigger groaned somewhere. 'What a row the brute makes!' said the indefatigable man with the moustaches, appearing near us. 'Serve him right. Transgression—punishment—bang! Pitiless, pitiless. That's the only way. This will prevent all conflagrations for the future. I was just telling the manager . . .' He noticed my companion, and became crestfallen all at once. 'Not in bed yet,' he said, with a kind of servile heartiness; 'it's so natural. Ha! Danger—agitation.' He vanished. I went on to the river-side, and the other followed me. I heard a scathing murmur at my ear, 'Heaps of muffs—go to.' The pilgrims could be seen in knots gesticulating, discussing. Several had still their staves in their hands. I verily believe they took these sticks to bed with them. Beyond the fence the forest stood up spectrally in the moonlight, and through the dim stir, through the faint sounds of that lamentable courtyard, the silence of the land went home to one's very heart—its mystery, its greatness, the amazing reality of its concealed life. The hurt nigger moaned feebly somewhere near by, and then fetched a deep sigh that made me mend my pace away from there. I felt a hand introducing itself under my arm. 'My dear sir,' said the fellow, 'I don't want to be misunderstood, and especially by you, who will see Mr. Kurtz long before I can have that pleasure. I wouldn't like him to get a false idea of my disposition. . . .'

"I let him run on, this papier-mâché Mephistopheles, and it seemed to me that if I tried I could poke my forefinger through him, and would find nothing inside but a little loose dirt, maybe. He, don't you see, had been planning to be assistant-manager by and by under the present man, and I could see that the coming of that Kurtz had upset them both not a little. He talked precipitately, and I did not try to stop him. I had my shoulders against the wreck of my steamer, hauled up on the slope like a carcass of some big river animal. The smell of mud, of primeval mud, by Jove! was in my nostrils, the high stillness of primeval forest was before my eyes; there were shiny patches on the black creek. The moon had spread over everything a thin layer of silver—over the rank grass, over the mud, upon the wall of matted vegetation standing higher than the wall of a temple, over the great river I could see through a sombre gap glittering, glittering, as it flowed broadly by without a murmur. All this was great, expectant, mute, while the man jabbered about himself. I wondered whether the stillness on the face of the immensity looking at us two were meant as an appeal or as a menace. What were we who had strayed in here? Could we handle that dumb thing, or would it handle us? I felt how big, how confoundedly big, was that thing that couldn't talk and perhaps was deaf as well. What was in there? I could see a little ivory coming out from there, and I had heard Mr. Kurtz was in there. I had heard enough about it too—God knows! Yet somehow it didn't bring any image with it—no more than if I had been told an angel or a fiend was in there. I believed it in the same way one of you might believe there are inhabitants in the planet Mars. I knew once a Scotch sailmaker who was certain, dead sure, there were people in Mars. If you asked him for some idea how they looked and behaved, he would get shy and mutter something about 'walking on all-fours.' If you as much as smiled, he would—though a man of sixty—offer to fight you. I would not have gone so far as to fight for Kurtz, but I went for him near enough to lie. You know I hate, detest, and can't bear a lie, not because I am straighter than the rest of us, but simply because it appals me. There is a taint of death, a flavour of mortality in lies—which is exactly what I hate and detest in the world—what I want to forget. It makes me miserable and sick, like biting something rotten would do. Temperament, I suppose. Well, I went near enough to it by letting the young fool there believe anything he liked to imagine as to my influence in Europe. I became in an instant as much of a pretence as the rest of the bewitched pilgrims. This simply because I had a notion it somehow would be of help to that Kurtz whom at the time I did not see—you understand. He was just a word for me. I did not see the man in the name any more than you do. Do you see him? Do you see the story? Do you see anything? It seems to me I am trying to tell you a dream—making a vain attempt, because no relation of a dream can convey the dream-sensation, that commingling of absurdity, surprise, and bewilderment in a tremor of struggling revolt, that notion of being captured by the incredible which is of the very essence of dreams. . . ."

He was silent for a while.

". . . No, it is impossible; it is impossible to convey the life-sensation of any given epoch of one's existence—that which makes its truth, its meaning—its subtle and penetrating essence. It is impossible. We live, as we dream—alone. . . ."

He paused again as if reflecting, then added:

"Of course in this you fellows see more than I could then. You see me, whom you know. . . ."

It had become so pitch dark that we listeners could hardly see one another. For a long time already he, sitting apart, had been no more to us than a voice. There was not a word from anybody. The others might have been asleep, but I was awake. I listened, I listened on the watch for the sentence, for the word, that would give me the clue to the faint uneasiness inspired by this narrative that seemed to shape itself without human lips in the heavy night-air of the river.

". . . Yes—I let him run on," Marlow began again, "and think what he pleased about the powers that were behind me. I did! And there was nothing behind me! There was nothing but that wretched, old, mangled steamboat I was leaning against, while he talked fluently about 'the necessity for every man to get on.' 'And when one comes out here, you conceive, it is not to gaze at the moon.' Mr. Kurtz was a 'universal genius,' but even a genius would find it easier to work with 'adequate tools—intelligent men.' He did not make bricks—why, there was a physical impossibility in the way—as I was well aware; and if he did secretarial work for the manager, it was because 'no sensible man rejects wantonly the confidence of his superiors.' Did I see it? I saw it. What more did I want? What I really wanted was rivets, by Heaven! Rivets. To get on with the work—to stop the hole. Rivets I wanted. There were cases of them down at the coast—cases—piled up—burst—split! You kicked a loose rivet at every second step in that station yard on the hillside. Rivets had rolled into the grove of death. You could fill your pockets with rivets for the trouble of stooping down—and there wasn't one rivet to be found where it was wanted. We had plates that would do, but nothing to fasten them with. And every week the messenger, a lone negro, letter-bag on shoulder and staff in hand, left our station for the coast. And several times a week a coast caravan came in with trade goods—ghastly glazed calico that made you shudder only to look at it, glass beads value about a penny a quart, confounded spotted cotton handkerchiefs. And no rivets. Three carriers could have brought all that was wanted to set that steamboat afloat.

"He was becoming confidential now, but I fancy my unresponsive attitude must have exasperated him at last, for he judged it necessary to inform me he feared neither God nor devil, let alone any mere man. I said I could see that very well, but what I wanted was a certain quality of rivets—the rivets were what really Mr. Kurtz wanted, if he had only known it. Now letters went to the coast every week. . . . 'My dear sir,' he cried, 'I write from dictation.' I demanded rivets. There was a way—for an intelligent man. He changed his manner; became very cold, and suddenly began to talk about a hippopotamus; wondered whether sleeping on board the steamer (I stuck to my salvage night and day) I wasn't disturbed. There was an old hippo that had the bad habit of getting out on the bank and roaming at night over the station grounds. The pilgrims used to turn out in body and empty every rifle they could lay hands on at him. Some even had sat up o' nights for him. All this energy was wasted, though. 'That animal has a charmed life,' he said; 'but you can say this only of brutes in this country. No man—you apprehend me?—no man here bears a charmed life.' He stood there for a moment in the moonlight with his delicate hooked nose set a little askew, and his mica eyes glittering without a wink, then, with a curt Good-night, he strode off. I could see he was disturbed and considerably puzzled, which made me feel more hopeful than I had been for days. It was a great comfort to turn from that chap to my influential friend, the battered, twisted, ruined, tin-pot steamboat. I clambered on board. She rang under my feet like an empty Huntley & Palmer biscuit-tin kicked along a gutter; she was nothing so solid in make, and rather less pretty in shape, but I had expended enough hard work on her to make me love her. No influential friend would have served me better. She had given me a chance to come out a bit—to find out what I could do. No, I don't like work. I had rather laze about and think of all the fine things that can be done. I don't like work—no man does—but I like what is in the work—the chance to find yourself. Your own reality—for yourself, not for others—what no other man can ever know. They can only see the mere show, and never can tell what it really means.

"I was not surprised to see somebody sitting aft, on the deck, with his legs dangling over the mud. You see I rather chummed with the few mechanics there were in that station, whom the other pilgrims naturally despised—on account of their imperfect manners, I suppose. This was the foreman—a boiler-maker by trade—a good worker. He was a lank, bony, yellow-faced man, with big intense eyes. His aspect was worried, and his head was as bald as the palm of my hand; but his hair in falling seemed to have stuck to his chin, and had prospered in the new locality, for his beard hung down to his waist. He was a widower with six young children (he had left them in charge of a sister of his to come out there), and the passion of his life was pigeon-flying. He was an enthusiast and a connoisseur. He would rave about pigeons. After work hours he used sometimes to come over from his hut for a talk about his children and his pigeons; at work, when he had to crawl in the mud under the bottom of the steamboat, he would tie up that beard of his in a kind of white serviette he brought for the purpose. It had loops to go over his ears. In the evening he could be seen squatted on the bank rinsing that wrapper in the creek with great care, then spreading it solemnly on a bush to dry.

"I slapped him on the back and shouted 'We shall have rivets!' He scrambled to his feet exclaiming 'No! Rivets!' as though he couldn't believe his ears. Then in a low voice, 'You . . . eh?' I don't know why we behaved like lunatics. I put my finger to the side of my nose and nodded mysteriously. 'Good for you!' he cried, snapped his fingers above his head, lifting one foot. I tried a jig. We capered on the iron deck. A frightful clatter came out of that hulk, and the virgin forest on the other bank of the creek sent it back in a thundering roll upon the sleeping station. It must have made some of the pilgrims sit up in their hovels. A dark figure obscured the lighted doorway of the manager's hut, vanished, then, a second or so after, the doorway itself vanished too. We stopped, and the silence driven away by the stamping of our feet flowed back again from the recesses of the land. The great wall of vegetation, an exuberant and entangled mass of trunks, branches, leaves, boughs, festoons, motionless in the moonlight, was like a rioting invasion of soundless life, a rolling wave of plants, piled up, crested, ready to topple over the creek, to sweep every little man of us out of his little existence. And it moved not. A deadened burst of mighty splashes and snorts reached us from afar, as though an ichthyosaurus had been taking a bath of glitter in the great river. 'After all,' said the boiler-maker in a reasonable tone, 'why shouldn't we get the rivets?' Why not, indeed! I did not know of any reason why we shouldn't. 'They'll come in three weeks,' I said confidently.

"But they didn't. Instead of rivets there came an invasion, an infliction, a visitation. It came in sections during the next three weeks, each section headed by a donkey carrying a white man in new clothes and tan shoes, bowing from that elevation right and left to the impressed pilgrims. A quarrelsome band of footsore sulky niggers trod on the heels of the donkey; a lot of tents, camp-stools, tin boxes, white cases, brown bales would be shot down in the courtyard, and the air of mystery would deepen a little over the muddle of the station. Five such instalments came, with their absurd air of disorderly flight with the loot of innumerable outfit shops and provision stores, that, one would think, they were lugging, after a raid, into the wilderness for equitable division. It was an inextricable mess of things decent in themselves but that human folly made look like the spoils of thieving.

"This devoted band called itself the Eldorado Exploring Expedition, and I believe they were sworn to secrecy. Their talk, however, was the talk of sordid buccaneers: it was reckless without hardihood, greedy without audacity, and cruel without courage; there was not an atom of foresight or of serious intention in the whole batch of them, and they did not seem aware these things are wanted for the work of the world. To tear treasure out of the bowels of the land was their desire, with no more moral purpose at the back of it than there is in burglars breaking into a safe. Who paid the expenses of the noble enterprise I don't know; but the uncle of our manager was leader of that lot.

"In exterior he resembled a butcher in a poor neighbourhood, and his eyes had a look of sleepy cunning. He carried his fat paunch with ostentation on his short legs, and during the time his gang infested the station spoke to no one but his nephew. You could see these two roaming about all day long with their heads close together in an everlasting confab.

"I had given up worrying myself about the rivets. One's capacity for that kind of folly is more limited than you would suppose. I said Hang!—and let things slide. I had plenty of time for meditation, and now and then I would give some thought to Kurtz. I wasn't very interested in him. No. Still, I was curious to see whether this man, who had come out equipped with moral ideas of some sort, would climb to the top after all, and how he would set about his work when there."

II

"One evening as I was lying flat on the deck of my steamboat, I heard voices approaching—and there were the nephew and the uncle strolling along the bank. I laid my head on my arm again, and had nearly lost myself in a doze, when somebody said in my ear, as it were: 'I am as harmless as a little child, but I don't like to be dictated to. Am I the manager—or am I not? I was ordered to send him there. It's incredible.' . . . I became aware that the two were standing on the shore alongside the forepart of the steamboat, just below my head. I did not move; it did not occur to me to move: I was sleepy. 'It *is* unpleasant,' grunted the uncle. 'He had asked the Administration to be sent there,' said the other, 'with the idea of showing what he could do; and I was instructed accordingly. Look at the influence that man must have. Is it not frightful?' They both agreed it was frightful, then made several bizarre remarks: 'Make rain and fine weather—one man—the Council—by the nose'—bits of absurd sentences that got the better of my drowsiness, so that I had pretty near the whole of my wits about me when the uncle said, 'The climate may do away with this difficulty for you. Is he alone there?' 'Yes,' answered the manager; 'he sent his assistant down the river with a note to me in these terms: "Clear this poor devil out of the country, and don't bother sending more of that sort. I had rather be alone than have the kind of men you can dispose of with me." It was more than a year ago. Can you imagine such impudence?' 'Anything since then?' asked the other hoarsely. 'Ivory,' jerked the nephew; 'lots of it—prime sort—lots—most annoying, from him.' 'And with that?' questioned the heavy rumble. 'Invoice,' was the reply fired out, so to speak. Then silence. They had been talking about Kurtz.

"I was broad awake by this time, but, lying perfectly at ease, remained still, having no inducement to change my position. 'How did that ivory come all this way?' growled the elder man, who seemed very vexed. The other explained that it had come with a fleet of canoes in charge of an English half-caste clerk Kurtz had with him; that Kurtz had apparently intended to return himself, the station being by that time bare of goods and stores, but after coming three hundred miles, had suddenly decided to go back, which he started to do alone in a small dugout with four paddlers, leaving the half-caste to continue down the river with the ivory. The two fellows there seemed astounded at anybody attempting such a thing. They were at a loss for an adequate motive. As for me, I seemed to see Kurtz for the first time. It was a distinct glimpse: the dugout, four paddling savages, and the lone white man turning his back suddenly on the headquarters, on relief, on thoughts of home—perhaps; setting his face towards the depths of the wilderness, towards his empty and desolate station. I did not know the motive. Perhaps he was just simply a fine fellow who stuck to his work for its own sake. His name, you understand, had not been pronounced once. He was 'that man.' The half-caste, who, as far as I could see, had conducted a difficult trip with great prudence and pluck, was invariably alluded to as 'that scoundrel.' The 'scoundrel' had reported that the 'man' had been very ill—had recovered imperfectly. . . . The two below me moved away then a few paces, and strolled back and forth at some little distance. I heard: 'Military post—doctor—two hundred miles—quite alone now—unavoidable delays—nine months—no news—strange rumours.' They approached again, just as the manager was saying, 'No one, as far as I know, unless a species of wandering trader—a pestilential fellow, snapping ivory from the natives.' Who was it they were talking about now? I gathered in snatches that this was some man supposed to be in Kurtz's district, and of whom the manager did not approve. 'We will not be free from unfair competition till one of these fellows is hanged for an example,' he said. 'Certainly,' grunted the other; 'get him hanged! Why not? Anything—anything can be done in this country. That's what I say; nobody here, you understand, *here,* can endanger your position. And why? You stand the climate—you outlast them all. The danger is in Europe; but there before I left I took care to——' They moved off and whispered, then their voices rose again. 'The extraordinary series of delays is not my fault. I did my possible.' The fat man sighed, 'Very sad.' 'And the pestiferous absurdity of his talk,' continued the other; 'he bothered me enough when he was here. "Each station should be like a beacon on the road towards better things, a centre for trade of course, but also for humanising, improving, instructing." Conceive you—that ass! And he wants to be manager! No, it's——' Here he got choked by excessive indignation, and I lifted my head the least bit. I was surprised to see how near they were—right under me. I could have spat upon their hats. They were looking on the ground, absorbed in thought. The manager was switching his leg with a slender twig: his sagacious relative lifted his head. 'You have been well since you came out this time?' he asked. The other gave a start. 'Who? I? Oh! Like a charm—like a charm. But the rest—oh, my goodness! All sick. They die so quick, too, that I haven't the time to send them out of the country—it's incredible!' 'H'm. Just so,' grunted the uncle. 'Ah! my boy, trust to this—I say, trust to this.' I saw him extend his short flipper of an arm for a gesture that took in the forest, the creek, the mud, the river—seemed to beckon with a dishonouring flourish before the sunlit face of the land a treacherous appeal to the lurking death, to the hidden evil, to the profound darkness of its heart. It was so startling that I leaped to my feet and looked back at the edge of the forest, as though I had expected an answer of some sort to that black display of confidence. You know the foolish notions that come to one sometimes. The high stillness confronted these two figures with its ominous patience, waiting for the passing away of a fantastic invasion.

"They swore aloud together—out of sheer fright, I believe—then, pretending not to know anything of my existence, turned back to the station. The sun was low; and leaning forward side by side, they seemed to be tugging painfully uphill their two ridiculous shadows of unequal length, that trailed behind them slowly over the tall grass without bending a single blade.

"In a few days the Eldorado Expedition went into the patient wilderness, that closed upon it as the sea closes over a diver. Long afterwards the news came that all the donkeys were dead. I know nothing as to the fate of the less valuable animals. They, no doubt, like the rest of us, found what they deserved. I did not inquire. I was then rather excited at the prospect of meeting Kurtz very soon. When I say very soon I mean it comparatively. It was just two months from the day we left the creek when we came to the bank below Kurtz's station.

"Going up that river was like travelling back to the earliest beginnings of the world, when vegetation rioted on the earth and the big trees were kings. An empty stream, a great silence, an impenetrable forest. The air was warm, thick, heavy, sluggish. There was no joy in the brilliance of sunshine. The long stretches of the waterway ran on, deserted, into the gloom of overshadowed distances. On silvery sandbanks hippos and alligators sunned themselves side by side. The broadening waters flowed through a mob of wooded islands; you lost your way on that river as you would in a desert, and butted all day long against shoals, trying to find the channel, till you thought yourself bewitched and cut off for ever from everything you had known once—somewhere—far away—in another existence perhaps. There were moments when one's past came back to one, as it will sometimes when you have not a moment to spare to yourself; but it came in the shape of an unrestful and noisy dream, remembered with wonder amongst the overwhelming realities of this strange world of plants, and water, and silence. And this stillness of life did not in the least resemble a peace. It was the stillness of an implacable force brooding over an inscrutable intention. It looked at you with a vengeful aspect. I got used to it afterwards; I did not see it any more; I had no time. I had to keep guessing at the channel; I had to discern, mostly by inspiration, the signs of hidden banks; I watched for sunken stones; I was learning to clap my teeth smartly before my heart flew out, when I shaved by a fluke some infernal sly old snag that would have ripped the life out of the tin-pot steamboat and drowned all the pilgrims; I had to keep a look-out for the signs of dead wood we could cut up in the night for next day's steaming. When you have to attend to things of that sort, to the mere incidents of the surface, the reality—the reality, I tell you—fades. The inner truth is hidden—luckily, luckily. But I felt it all the same; I felt often its mysterious stillness watching me at my monkey tricks, just as it watches you fellows performing on your respective tight-ropes for—what is it? half a crown a tumble——"

"Try to be civil, Marlow," growled a voice, and I knew there was at least one listener awake besides myself.

"I beg your pardon. I forgot the heartache which makes up the rest of the price. And indeed what does the price matter, if the trick be well done? You do your tricks very well. And I didn't do badly either, since I managed not to sink that steamboat on my first trip. It's a wonder to me yet. Imagine a blindfolded man set to drive a van over a bad road. I sweated and shivered over that business considerably, I can tell you. After all, for a seaman, to scrape the bottom of the thing that's supposed to float all the time under his care is the unpardonable sin. No one may know of it, but you never forget the thump—eh? A blow on the very heart. You remember it, you dream of it, you wake up at night and think of it—years after—and go hot and cold all over. I don't pretend to say that steamboat floated all the time. More than once she had to wade for a bit, with twenty cannibals splashing around and pushing. We had enlisted some of these chaps on the way for a crew. Fine fellows—cannibals—in their place. They were men one could work with, and I am grateful to them. And, after all, they did not eat each other before my face: they had brought along a provision of hippo-meat which went rotten, and made the mystery of the wilderness stink in my nostrils. Phoo! I can sniff it now. I had the manager on board and three or four pilgrims with their staves—all complete. Sometimes we came upon a station close by the bank, clinging to the skirts of the unknown, and the white men rushing out of a tumble-down hovel, with great gestures of joy and surprise and welcome, seemed very strange—had the appearance of being held there captive by a spell. The word 'ivory' would ring in the air for a while—and on we went again into the silence, along empty reaches, round the still bends, between the high walls of our winding way, reverberating in hollow claps the ponderous beat of the stern-wheel. Trees, trees, millions of trees, massive, immense, running up high; and at their foot, hugging the bank against the stream, crept the little begrimed steamboat, like a sluggish beetle crawling on the floor of a lofty portico. It made you feel very small, very lost, and yet it was not altogether depressing, that feeling. After all, if you were small, the grimy beetle crawled on—which was just what you wanted it to do. Where the pilgrims imagined it crawled to I don't know. To some place where they expected to get something, I bet! For me it crawled towards Kurtz—exclusively; but when the steam-pipes started leaking we crawled very slow. The reaches opened before us and closed behind, as if the forest had stepped leisurely across the water to bar the way for our return. We penetrated deeper and deeper into the heart of darkness. It was very quiet there. At night sometimes the roll of drums behind the curtain of trees would run up the river and remain sustained faintly, as if hovering in the air high over our heads, till the first break of day. Whether it meant war, peace, or prayer we could not tell. The dawns were heralded by the descent of a chill stillness; the woodcutters slept, their fires burned low; the snapping of a twig would make you start. We were wanderers on a prehistoric earth, on an earth that wore the aspect of an unknown planet. We could have fancied ourselves the first of men taking possession of an accursed inheritance, to be subdued at the cost of profound anguish and of excessive toil. But suddenly, as we struggled round a bend, there would be a glimpse of rush walls, of peaked grass-roofs, a burst of yells, a whirl of black limbs, a mass of hands clapping, of feet stamping, of bodies swaying, of eyes rolling, under the droop of heavy and motionless foliage. The steamer toiled along slowly on the edge of a black and incomprehensible frenzy. The prehistoric man was cursing us, praying to us, welcoming us—who could tell? We were cut off from the comprehension of our surroundings; we glided past like phantoms, wondering and secretly appalled, as sane men would be before an enthusiastic outbreak in a madhouse. We could not understand because we were too far and could not remember, because we were travelling in the night of first ages, of those ages that are gone, leaving hardly a sign—and no memories.

"The earth seemed unearthly. We are accustomed to look upon the shackled form of a conquered monster, but there—there you could look at a thing monstrous and free. It was unearthly, and the men were—— No, they were not inhuman. Well, you know, that was the worst of it—this suspicion of their not being inhuman. It would come slowly to one. They howled and leaped, and spun, and made horrid faces; but what thrilled you was just the thought of their humanity—like yours—the thought of your remote kinship with this wild and passionate uproar. Ugly. Yes, it was ugly enough; but if you were man enough you would admit to yourself that there was in you just the faintest trace of a response to the terrible frankness of that noise, a dim suspicion of there being a meaning in it which you—you so remote from the night of first ages—could comprehend. And why not? The mind of man is capable of anything—because everything is in it, all the past as well as all the future. What was there after all? Joy, fear, sorrow, devotion, valour, rage—who can tell?—but truth—truth stripped of its cloak of time. Let the fool gape and shudder—the man knows, and can look on without a wink. But he must at least be as much of a man as these on the shore. He must meet that truth with his own true stuff—with his own inborn strength. Principles? Principles won't do. Acquisitions, clothes, pretty rags—rags that would fly off at the first good shake. No; you want a deliberate belief. An appeal to me in this fiendish row—is there? Very well; I hear; I admit, but I have a voice too, and for good or evil mine is the speech that cannot be silenced. Of course, a fool, what with sheer fright and fine sentiments, is always safe. Who's that grunting? You wonder I didn't go ashore for a howl and a dance? Well, no—I didn't. Fine sentiments, you say? Fine sentiments be hanged! I had no time. I had to mess about with white-lead and strips of woollen blanket helping to put bandages on those leaky steam-pipes—I tell you. I had to watch the steering, and circumvent those snags, and get the tin-pot along by hook or by crook. There was surface-truth enough in these things to save a wiser man. And between whiles I had to look after the savage who was fireman. He was an improved specimen; he could fire up a vertical boiler. He was there below me, and, upon my word, to look at him was as edifying as seeing a dog in a parody of breeches and a feather hat, walking on his hind legs. A few months of training had done for that really fine chap. He squinted at the steam-gauge and at the water-gauge with an evident effort of intrepidity—and he had filed teeth too, the poor devil, and the wool of his pate shaved into queer patterns, and three ornamental scars on each of his cheeks. He ought to have been clapping his hands and stamping his feet on the bank, instead of which he was hard at work, a thrall to strange witchcraft, full of improving knowledge. He was useful because he had been instructed; and what he knew was this—that should the water in that transparent thing disappear, the evil spirit inside the boiler would get angry through the greatness of his thirst, and take a terrible vengeance. So he sweated and fired up and watched the glass fearfully (with an impromptu charm, made of rags, tied to his arm, and a piece of polished bone, as big as a watch, stuck flatways through his lower lip), while the wooded banks slipped past us slowly, the short noise was left behind, the interminable miles of silence—and we crept on, towards Kurtz. But the snags were thick, the water was treacherous and shallow, the boiler seemed indeed to have a sulky devil in it, and thus neither that fireman nor I had any time to peer into our creepy thoughts.

"Some fifty miles below the Inner Station we came upon a hut of reeds, an inclined and melancholy pole, with the unrecognisable tatters of what had been a flag of some sort flying from it, and a neatly stacked woodpile. This was unexpected. We came to the bank, and on the stack of firewood found a flat piece of board with some faded pencil-writing on it. When deciphered it said: 'Wood for you. Hurry up. Approach cautiously.' There was a signature, but it was illegible—not Kurtz—a much longer word. 'Hurry up.' Where? Up the river? 'Approach cautiously.' We had not done so. But the warning could not have been meant for the place where it could be only found after approach. Something was wrong above. But what—and how much? That was the question. We commented adversely upon the imbecility of that telegraphic style. The bush around said nothing, and would not let us look very far, either. A torn curtain of red twill hung in the doorway of the hut, and flapped sadly in our faces. The dwelling was dismantled; but we could see a white man had lived there not very long ago. There remained a rude table—a plank on two posts; a heap of rubbish reposed in a dark corner, and by the door I picked up a book. It had lost its covers, and the pages had been thumbed into a state of extremely dirty softness; but the back had been lovingly stitched afresh with white cotton thread, which looked clean yet. It was an extraordinary find. Its title was, *An Inquiry into some Points of Seamanship,* by a man Towser, Towson—some such name—Master in His Majesty's Navy. The matter looked dreary reading enough, with illustrative diagrams and repulsive tables of figures, and the copy was sixty years old. I handled this amazing antiquity with the greatest possible tenderness, lest it should dissolve in my hands. Within, Towson or Towser was inquiring earnestly into the breaking strain of ships' chains and tackle, and other such matters. Not a very enthralling book; but at the first glance you could see there a singleness of intention, an honest concern for the right way of going to work, which made these humble pages, thought out so many years ago, luminous with another than a professional light. The simple old sailor, with his talk of chains and purchases, made me forget the jungle and the pilgrims in a delicious sensation of having come upon something unmistakably real. Such a book being there was wonderful enough; but still more astounding were the notes pencilled in the margin, and plainly referring to the text. I couldn't believe my eyes! They were in cipher! Yes, it looked like cipher. Fancy a man lugging with him a book of that description into this nowhere and studying it—and making notes—in cipher at that! It was an extravagant mystery.

"I had been dimly aware for some time of a worrying noise, and when I lifted my eyes I saw the woodpile was gone, and the manager, aided by all the pilgrims, was shouting at me from the river-side. I slipped the book into my pocket. I assure you to leave off reading was like tearing myself away from the shelter of an old and solid friendship.

"I started the lame engine ahead. 'It must be this miserable trader—this intruder,' exclaimed the manager, looking back malevolently at the place we had left. 'He must be English,' I said. 'It will not save him from getting into trouble if he is not careful,' muttered the manager darkly. I observed with assumed innocence that no man was safe from trouble in this world.

"The current was more rapid now, the steamer seemed at her last gasp, the stern-wheel flopped languidly, and I caught myself listening on tiptoe for the next beat of the float, for in sober truth I expected the wretched thing to give up every moment. It was like watching the last flickers of a life. But still we crawled. Sometimes I would pick out a tree a little way ahead to measure our progress towards Kurtz by, but I lost it invariably before we got abreast. To keep the eyes so long on one thing was too much for human patience. The manager displayed a beautiful resignation. I fretted and fumed and took to arguing with myself whether or no I would talk openly with Kurtz; but before I could come to any conclusion it occurred to me that my speech or my silence, indeed any action of mine, would be a mere futility. What did it matter what any one knew or ignored? What did it matter who was manager? One gets sometimes such a flash of insight. The essentials of this affair lay deep under the surface, beyond my reach, and beyond my power of meddling.

"Towards the evening of the second day we judged ourselves about eight miles from Kurtz's station. I wanted to push on; but the manager looked grave, and told me the navigation up there was so dangerous that it would be advisable, the sun being very low already, to wait where we were till next morning. Moreover, he pointed out that if the warning to approach cautiously were to be followed, we must approach in daylight—not at dusk, or in the dark. This was sensible enough. Eight miles meant nearly three hours' steaming for us, and I could also see suspicious ripples at the upper end of the reach. Nevertheless, I was annoyed beyond expression at the delay, and most unreasonably too, since one night more could not matter much after so many months. As we had plenty of wood, and caution was the word, I brought up in the middle of the stream. The reach was narrow, straight, with high sides like a railway cutting. The dusk came gliding into it long before the sun had set. The current ran smooth and swift, but a dumb immobility sat on the banks. The living trees, lashed together by the creepers and every living bush of the undergrowth, might have been changed into stone, even to the slenderest twig, to the lightest leaf. It was not sleep—it seemed unnatural, like a state of trance. Not the faintest sound of any kind could be heard. You looked on amazed, and began to suspect yourself of being deaf—then the night came suddenly, and struck you blind as well. About three in the morning some large fish leaped, and the loud splash made me jump as though a gun had been fired. When the sun rose there was a white fog, very warm and clammy, and more blinding than the night. It did not shift or drive; it was just there, standing all round you like something solid. At eight or nine, perhaps, it lifted as a shutter lifts. We had a glimpse of the towering multitude of trees, of the immense matted jungle, with the blazing little ball of the sun hanging over it—all perfectly still—and then the white shutter came down again, smoothly, as if sliding in greased grooves. I ordered the chain, which we had begun to heave in, to be paid out again. Before it stopped running with a muffled rattle, a cry, a very loud cry, as of infinite desolation, soared slowly in the opaque air. It ceased. A complaining clamour, modulated in savage discords, filled our ears. The sheer unexpectedness of it made my hair stir under my cap. I don't know how it struck the others: to me it seemed as though the mist itself had screamed, so suddenly, and apparently from all sides at once, did this tumultuous and mournful uproar arise. It culminated in a hurried outbreak of almost intolerably excessive shrieking, which stopped short, leaving us stiffened in a variety of silly attitudes, and obstinately listening to the nearly as appalling and excessive silence. 'Good God! What is the meaning——?' stammered at my elbow one of the pilgrims—a little fat man, with sandy hair and red whiskers, who wore side-spring boots, and pink pyjamas tucked into his socks. Two others remained open-mouthed a whole minute, then dashed into the little cabin, to rush out incontinently and stand darting scared glances, with Winchesters at 'ready' in their hands. What we could see was just the steamer we were on, her outlines blurred as though she had been on the point of dissolving, and a misty strip of water, perhaps two feet broad, around her—and that was all. The rest of the world was nowhere, as far as our eyes and ears were concerned. Just nowhere. Gone, disappeared; swept off without leaving a whisper or a shadow behind.

"I went forward, and ordered the chain to be hauled in short, so as to be ready to trip the anchor and move the steamboat at once if necessary. 'Will they attack?' whispered an awed voice. 'We will all be butchered in this fog,' murmured another. The faces twitched with the strain, the hands trembled slightly, the eyes forgot to wink. It was very curious to see the contrast of expressions of the white men and of the black fellows of our crew, who were as much strangers to that part of the river as we, though their homes were only eight hundred miles away. The whites, of course greatly discomposed, had besides a curious look of being painfully shocked by such an outrageous row. The others had an alert, naturally interested expression; but their faces were essentially quiet, even those of the one or two who grinned as they hauled at the chain. Several exchanged short, grunting phrases, which seemed to settle the matter to their satisfaction. Their head-man, a young, broad-chested black, severely draped in dark-blue fringed cloths, with fierce nostrils and his hair all done up artfully in oily ringlets, stood near me. 'Aha!' I said, just for good fellowship's sake. 'Catch 'im,' he snapped, with a bloodshot widening of his eyes and a flash of sharp teeth—'catch 'im. Give 'im to us.' 'To you, eh?' I asked; 'what would you do with them?' 'Eat 'im!' he said curtly, and, leaning his elbow on the rail, looked out into the fog in a dignified and profoundly pensive attitude. I would no doubt have been properly horrified, had it not occurred to me that he and his chaps must be very hungry: that they must have been growing increasingly hungry for at least this month past. They had been engaged for six months (I don't think a single one of them had any clear idea of time, as we at the end of countless ages have. They still belonged to the beginnings of time—had no inherited experience to teach them, as it were), and of course, as long as there was a piece of paper written over in accordance with some farcical law or other made down the river, it didn't enter anybody's head to trouble how they would live. Certainly they had brought with them some rotten hippo-meat, which couldn't have lasted very long, anyway, even if the pilgrims hadn't, in the midst of a shocking hullabaloo, thrown a considerable quantity of it overboard. It looked like a high-handed proceeding; but it was really a case of legitimate self-defence. You can't breathe dead hippo waking, sleeping, and eating, and at the same time keep your precarious grip on existence. Besides that, they had given them every week three pieces of brass wire, each about nine inches long; and the theory was they were to buy their provisions with that currency in river-side villages. You can see how *that* worked. There were either no villages, or the people were hostile, or the director, who like the rest of us fed out of tins, with an occasional old he-goat thrown in, didn't want to stop the steamer for some more or less recondite reason. So, unless they swallowed the wire itself, or made loops of it to snare the fishes with, I don't see what good their extravagant salary could be to them. I must say it was paid with a regularity worthy of a large and honourable trading company. For the rest, the only thing to eat—though it didn't look eatable in the least—I saw in their possession was a few lumps of some stuff like half-cooked dough, of a dirty lavender colour, they kept wrapped in leaves, and now and then swallowed a piece of, but so small that it seemed done more for the look of the thing than for any serious purpose of sustenance. Why in the name of all the gnawing devils of hunger they didn't go for us—they were thirty to five—and have a good tuck-in for once, amazes me now when I think of it. They were big powerful men, with not much capacity to weigh the consequences, with courage, with strength, even yet, though their skins were no longer glossy and their muscles no longer hard. And I saw that something restraining, one of those human secrets that baffle probability, had come into play there. I looked at them with a swift quickening of interest—not because it occurred to me I might be eaten by them before very long, though I own to you that just then I perceived—in a new light, as it were—how unwholesome the pilgrims looked, and I hoped, yes, I positively hoped, that my aspect was not so—what shall I say?—so—unappetising: a touch of fantastic vanity which fitted well with the dream-sensation that pervaded all my days at that time. Perhaps I had a little fever too. One can't live with one's finger everlastingly on one's pulse. I had often 'a little fever,' or a little touch of other things—the playful paw-strokes of the wilderness, the preliminary trifling before the more serious onslaught which came in due course. Yes; I looked at them as you would on any human being, with a curiosity of their impulses, motives, capacities, weaknesses, when brought to the test of an inexorable physical necessity. Restraint! What possible restraint? Was it superstition, disgust, patience, fear—or some kind of primitive honour? No fear can stand up to hunger, no patience can wear it out, disgust simply does not exist where hunger is; and as to superstition, beliefs, and what you may call principles, they are less than chaff in a breeze. Don't you know the devilry of lingering starvation, its exasperating torment, its black thoughts, its sombre and brooding ferocity? Well, I do. It takes a man all his inborn strength to fight hunger properly. It's really easier to face bereavement, dishonour, and the perdition of one's soul—than this kind of prolonged hunger. Sad, but true. And these chaps too had no earthly reason for any kind of scruple. Restraint! I would just as soon have expected restraint from a hyena prowling amongst the corpses of a battlefield. But there was the fact facing me—the fact dazzling, to be seen, like the foam on the depths of the sea, like a ripple on an unfathomable enigma, a mystery greater—when I thought of it—than the curious, inexplicable note of desperate grief in this savage clamour that had swept by us on the river-bank, behind the blind whiteness of the fog.

"Two pilgrims were quarreling in hurried whispers as to which bank. 'Left.' 'No, no; how can you? Right, right, of course.' 'It is very serious,' said the manager's voice behind me; 'I would be desolated if anything should happen to Mr. Kurtz before we came up.' I looked at him, and had not the slightest doubt he was sincere. He was just the kind of man who would wish to preserve appearances. That was his restraint. But when he muttered something about going on at once, I did not even take the trouble to answer him. I knew, and he knew, that it was impossible. Were we to let go our hold of the bottom, we would be absolutely in the air—in space. We wouldn't be able to tell where we were going to—whether up or down stream, or across—till we fetched against one bank or the other—and then we wouldn't know at first which it was. Of course I made no move. I had no mind for a smash-up. You couldn't imagine a more deadly place for a shipwreck. Whether drowned at once or not, we were sure to perish speedily in one way or another. 'I authorise you to take all the risks,' he said, after a short silence. 'I refuse to take any,' I said shortly; which was just the answer he expected, though its tone might have surprised him. 'Well, I must defer to your judgment. You are captain,' he said, with marked civility. I turned my shoulder to him in sign of my appreciation, and looked into the fog. How long would it last? It was the most hopeless look-out. The approach to this Kurtz grubbing for ivory in the wretched bush was beset by as many dangers as though he had been an enchanted princess sleeping in a fabulous castle. 'Will they attack, do you think?' asked the manager, in a confidential tone.

"I did not think they would attack, for several obvious reasons. The thick fog was one. If they left the bank in their canoes they would get lost in it, as we would be if we attempted to move. Still, I had also judged the jungle of both banks quite impenetrable—and yet eyes were in it, eyes that had seen us. The river-side bushes were certainly very thick; but the undergrowth behind was evidently penetrable. However, during the short lift I had seen no canoes anywhere in the reach—certainly not abreast of the steamer. But what made the idea of attack inconceivable to me was the nature of the noise—of the cries we had heard. They had not the fierce character boding of immediate hostile intention. Unexpected, wild, and violent as they had been, they had given me an irresistible impression of sorrow. The glimpse of the steamboat had for some reason filled those savages with unrestrained grief. The danger, if any, I expounded, was from our proximity to a great human passion let loose. Even extreme grief may ultimately vent itself in violence—but more generally takes the form of apathy. . . .

"You should have seen the pilgrims stare! They had no heart to grin, or even to revile me; but I believe they thought me gone mad—with fright, maybe. I delivered a regular lecture. My dear boys, it was no good bothering. Keep a look-out? Well, you may guess I watched the fog for the signs of lifting as a cat watches a mouse; but for anything else our eyes were of no more use to us than if we had been buried miles deep in a heap of cotton-wool. It felt like it too—choking, warm, stifling. Besides, all I said, though it sounded extravagant, was absolutely true to fact. What we afterwards alluded to as an attack was really an attempt at repulse. The action was very far from being aggressive—it was not even defensive, in the usual sense: it was undertaken under the stress of desperation, and in its essence was purely protective.

"It developed itself, I should say, two hours after the fog lifted, and its commencement was at a spot, roughly speaking, about a mile and a half below Kurtz's station. We had just floundered and flopped round a bend, when I saw an islet, a mere grassy hummock of bright green, in the middle of the stream. It was the only thing of the kind; but as we opened the reach more, I perceived it was the head of a long sandbank, or rather of a chain of shallow patches stretching down the middle of the river. They were discoloured, just awash, and the whole lot was seen just under the water, exactly as a man's backbone is seen running down the middle of his back under the skin. Now, as far as I did see, I could go to the right or to the left of this. I didn't know either channel, of course. The banks looked pretty well alike, the depth appeared the same; but as I had been informed the station was on the west side, I naturally headed for the western passage.

"No sooner had we fairly entered it than I became aware it was much narrower than I had supposed. To the left of us there was the long uninterrupted shoal, and to the right a high steep bank heavily overgrown with bushes. Above the bush the trees stood in serried ranks. The twigs overhung the current thickly, and from distance to distance a large limb of some tree projected rigidly over the stream. It was then well on in the afternoon, the face of the forest was gloomy, and a broad strip of shadow had already fallen on the water. In this shadow we steamed up—very slowly, as you may imagine. I sheered her well inshore—the water being deepest near the bank, as the sounding-pole informed me.

"One of my hungry and forbearing friends was sounding in the bows just below us. This steamboat was exactly like a decked scow. On the deck there were two little teak-wood houses, with doors and windows. The boiler was in the fore-end, and the machinery right astern. Over the whole there was a light roof, supported on stanchions. The funnel projected through that roof, and in front of the funnel a small cabin built of light planks served for a pilot-house. It contained a couch, two camp-stools, a loaded Martini-Henry leaning in one corner, a tiny table, and the steering-wheel. It had a wide door in front and a broad shutter at each side. All these were always thrown open, of course. I spent my days perched up there on the extreme fore-end of that roof, before the door. At night I slept, or tried to, on the couch. An athletic black belonging to some coast tribe, and educated by my poor predecessor, was the helmsman. He sported a pair of brass earrings, wore a blue cloth wrapper from the waist to the ankles, and thought all the world of himself. He was the most unstable kind of fool I had ever seen. He steered with no end of a swagger while you were by; but if he lost sight of you, he became instantly the prey of an abject funk, and would let that cripple of a steamboat get the upper hand of him in a minute.

"I was looking down at the sounding-pole, and feeling much annoyed to see at each try a little more of it stick out of that river, when I saw my poleman give up the business suddenly, and stretch himself flat on the deck, without even taking the trouble to haul his pole in. He kept hold on it though, and it trailed in the water. At the same time the fireman, whom I could also see below me, sat down abruptly before his furnace and ducked his head. I was amazed. Then I had to look at the river mighty quick, because there was a snag in the fairway. Sticks, little sticks, were flying about—thick: they were whizzing before my nose, dropping below me, striking behind me against my pilot-house. All this time the river, the shore, the woods, were very quiet—perfectly quiet. I could only hear the heavy splashing thump of the stern-wheel and the patter of these things. We cleared the snag clumsily. Arrows, by Jove! We were being shot at! I stepped in quickly to close the shutter on the land-side. That fool-helmsman, his hands on the spokes, was lifting his knees high, stamping his feet, champing his mouth, like a reined-in horse. Confound him! And we were staggering within ten feet of the bank. I had to lean right out to swing the heavy shutter, and I saw a face amongst the leaves on the level with my own, looking at me very fierce and steady; and then suddenly, as though a veil had been removed from my eyes, I made out, deep in the tangled gloom, naked breasts, legs, glaring eyes—the bush was swarming with human limbs in movement, glistening, of bronze colour. The twigs shook, swayed, and rustled, the arrows flew out of them, and then the shutter came to. 'Steer her straight,' I said to the helmsman. He held his head rigid, face forward; but his eyes rolled, he kept on lifting and setting down his feet gently, his mouth foamed a little. 'Keep quiet!' I said in a fury. I might just as well have ordered a tree not to sway in the wind. I darted out. Below me there was a great scuffle of feet on the iron deck; confused exclamations; a voice screamed, 'Can you turn back?' I caught sight of a V-shaped ripple on the water ahead. What? Another snag! A fusillade burst out under my feet. The pilgrims had opened with their Winchesters, and were simply squirting lead into that bush. A deuce of a lot of smoke came up and drove slowly forward. I swore at it. Now I couldn't see the ripple or the snag either. I stood in the doorway, peering, and the arrows came in swarms. They might have been poisoned, but they looked as though they wouldn't kill a cat. The bush began to howl. Our wood-cutters raised a war-like whoop; the report of a rifle just at my back deafened me. I glanced over my shoulder, and the pilot-house was yet full of noise and smoke when I made a dash at the wheel. The fool-nigger had dropped everything, to throw the shutter open and let off that Martini-Henry. He stood before the wide opening, glaring, and I yelled at him to come back, while I straightened the sudden twist out of that steamboat. There was no room to turn even if I had wanted to, the snag was somewhere very near ahead in that confounded smoke, there was no time to lose, so I just crowded her into the bank—right into the bank, where I knew the water was deep.

"We tore slowly along the overhanging bushes in a whirl of broken twigs and flying leaves. The fusillade below stopped short, as I had foreseen it would when the squirts got empty. I threw my head back to avoid a glinting whiz that traversed the pilot-house, in at one shutter-hole and out at the other. Looking past that mad helmsman, who was shaking the empty rifle and yelling at the shore, I saw vague forms of men running bent double, leaping, gliding, distinct, incomplete, evanescent. Something big appeared in the air before the shutter, the rifle went overboard, and the man stepped back swiftly, looked at me over his shoulder in an extraordinary, profound, familiar manner, and fell upon my feet. The side of his head hit the wheel twice, and the end of what appeared a long cane clattered round and knocked over a little camp-stool. It looked as though after wrenching that thing from somebody ashore he had lost his balance in the effort. The thin smoke had blown away, we were clear of the snag, and looking ahead I could see that in another hundred yards or so I would be free to sheer off, away from the bank; but my feet felt so very warm and wet that I had to look down. The man had rolled on his back and stared straight up at me; both his hands clutched that cane. It was the shaft of a spear that, either thrown or lunged through the opening, had caught him in the side just below the ribs; the blade had gone in out of sight, after making a frightful gash; my shoes were full; a pool of blood lay very still, gleaming dark-red under the wheel; his eyes shone with an amazing lustre. The fusillade burst out again. He looked at me anxiously, gripping the spear like something precious, with an air of being afraid I would try to take it away from him. I had to make an effort to free my eyes from his gaze and attend to the steering. With one hand I felt above my head for the line of the steam whistle, and jerked out screech after screech hurriedly. The tumult of angry and warlike yells was checked instantly, and then from the depths of the woods went out such a tremulous and prolonged wail of mournful fear and utter despair as may be imagined to follow the flight of the last hope from the earth. There was a great commotion in the bush; the shower of arrows stopped, a few dropping shots rang out sharply—then silence, in which the languid beat of the stern-wheel came plainly to my ears. I put the helm hard a-starboard at the moment when the pilgrim in pink pyjamas, very hot and agitated, appeared in the doorway. 'The manager sends me——' he began in an official tone, and stopped short. 'Good God!' he said, glaring at the wounded man.

"We two whites stood over him, and his lustrous and inquiring glance enveloped us both. I declare it looked as though he would presently put to us some question in an understandable language; but he died without uttering a sound, without moving a limb, without twitching a muscle. Only in the very last moment, as though in response to some sign we could not see, to some whisper we could not hear, he frowned heavily, and that frown gave to his black death-mask an inconceivably sombre, brooding, and menacing expression. The lustre of inquiring glance faded swiftly into vacant glassiness. 'Can you steer?' I asked the agent eagerly. He looked very dubious; but I made a grab at his arm, and he understood at once I meant him to steer whether or no. To tell you the truth, I was morbidly anxious to change my shoes and socks. 'He is dead,' murmured the fellow, immensely impressed. 'No doubt about it,' said I, tugging like mad at the shoe-laces. 'And by the way, I suppose Mr. Kurtz is dead as well by this time.'

"For the moment that was the dominant thought. There was a sense of extreme disappointment, as though I had found out I had been striving after something altogether without a substance. I couldn't have been more disgusted if I had travelled all this way for the sole purpose of talking with Mr. Kurtz. Talking with . . . I flung one shoe overboard, and became aware that that was exactly what I had been looking forward to—a talk with Kurtz. I made the strange discovery that I had never imagined him as doing, you know, but as discoursing. I didn't say to myself, 'Now I will never see him,' or 'Now I will never shake him by the hand,' but, 'Now I will never hear him.' The man presented himself as a voice. Not of course that I did not connect him with some sort of action. Hadn't I been told in all the tones of jealousy and admiration that he had collected, bartered, swindled, or stolen more ivory than all the other agents together? That was not the point. The point was in his being a gifted creature, and that of all his gifts the one that stood out pre-eminently, that carried with it a sense of real presence, was his ability to talk, his words—the gift of expression, the bewildering, the illuminating, the most exalted and the most contemptible, the pulsating stream of light, or the deceitful flow from the heart of an impenetrable darkness.

"The other shoe went flying unto the devil-god of that river. I thought, By Jove! it's all over. We are too late; he has vanished—the gift has vanished, by means of some spear, arrow, or club. I will never hear that chap speak after all—and my sorrow had a startling extravagance of emotion, even such as I had noticed in the howling sorrow of these savages in the bush. I couldn't have felt more of lonely desolation somehow, had I been robbed of a belief or had missed my destiny in life. . . . Why do you sigh in this beastly way, somebody? Absurd? Well, absurd. Good Lord! mustn't a man ever—— Here, give me some tobacco." . . .

There was a pause of profound stillness, then a match flared, and Marlow's lean face appeared, worn, hollow, with downward folds and dropped eyelids, with an aspect of concentrated attention; and as he took vigorous draws at his pipe, it seemed to retreat and advance out of the night in the regular flicker of the tiny flame. The match went out.

"Absurd!" he cried. "This is the worst of trying to tell . . . Here you all are, each moored with two good addresses, like a hulk with two anchors, a butcher round one corner, a policeman round another, excellent appetities, and temperature normal—you hear—normal from year's end to year's end. And you say, Absurd! Absurd be—exploded! Absurd! My dear boys, what can you expect from a man who out of sheer nervousness had just flung overboard a pair of new shoes? Now I think of it, it is amazing I did not shed tears. I am, upon the whole, proud of my fortitude. I was cut to the quick at the idea of having lost the inestimable privilege of listening to the gifted Kurtz. Of course I was wrong. The privilege was waiting for me. Oh yes, I heard more than enough. And I was right, too. A voice. He was very little more than a voice. And I heard—him—it—this voice—other voices—all of them were so little more than voices—and the memory of that time itself lingers around me, impalpable, like a dying vibration of one immense jabber, silly, atrocious, sordid, savage, or simply mean, without any kind of sense. Voices, voices—even the girl herself—now—"

He was silent for a long time.

"I laid the ghost of his gifts at last with a lie," he began suddenly. "Girl! What? Did I mention a girl? Oh, she is out of it—completely. They—the women I mean—are out of it—should be out of it. We must help them to stay in that beautiful world of their own, lest ours gets worse. Oh, she had to be out of it. You should have heard the disinterred body of Mr. Kurtz saying, 'My Intended.' You would have perceived directly then how completely she was out of it. And the lofty frontal bone of Mr. Kurtz! They say the hair goes on growing sometimes, but this—ah—specimen was impressively bald. The wilderness had patted him on the head, and, behold, it was like a ball—an ivory ball; it had caressed him, and—lo!—he had withered; it had taken him, loved him, embraced him, got into his veins, consumed his flesh, and sealed his soul to its own by the inconceivable ceremonies of some devilish initiation. He was its spoiled and pampered favourite. Ivory? I should think so. Heaps of it, stacks of it. The old mud shanty was bursting with it. You would think there was not a single tusk left either above or below the ground in the whole country. 'Mostly fossil,' the manager had remarked disparagingly. It was no more fossil than I am; but they call it fossil when it is dug up. It appears these niggers do bury the tusks sometimes—but evidently they couldn't bury this parcel deep enough to save the gifted Mr. Kurtz from his fate. We filled the steamboat with it, and had to pile a lot on the deck. Thus he could see and enjoy as long as he could see, because the appreciation of this favour had remained with him to the last. You should have heard him say, 'My ivory.' Oh yes, I heard him. 'My Intended, my ivory, my station, my river, my——' everything belonged to him. It made me hold my breath in expectation of hearing the wilderness burst into a prodigious peal of laughter that would shake the fixed stars in their places. Everything belonged to him—but that was a trifle. The thing was to know what he belonged to, how many powers of darkness claimed him for their own. That was the reflection that made you creepy all over. It was impossible—it was not good for one either—trying to imagine. He had taken a high seat amongst the devils of the land—I mean literally. You can't understand. How could you?—with solid pavement under your feet, surrounded by kind neighbours ready to cheer you or to fall on you, stepping delicately between the butcher and the policeman, in the holy terror of scandal and gallows and lunatic asylums—how can you imagine what particular region of the first ages a man's untrammelled feet may take him into by the way of solitude—utter solitude without a policeman—by the way of silence—utter silence, where no warning voice of a kind neighbour can be heard whispering of public opinion? These little things make all the great difference. When they are gone you must fall back upon your own innate strength, upon your own capacity for faithfulness. Of course you may be too much of a fool to go wrong—too dull even to know you are being assaulted by the powers of darkness. I take it, no fool ever made a bargain for his soul with the devil: the fool is too much of a fool, or the devil too much of a devil—I don't know which. Or you may be such a thunderingly exalted creature as to be altogether deaf and blind to anything but heavenly sights and sounds. Then the earth for you is only a standing place—and whether to be like this is your loss or your gain I won't pretend to say. But most of us are neither one nor the other. The earth for us is a place to live in, where we must put up with sights, with sounds, with smells, too, by Jove!—breathe dead hippo, so to speak, and not be contaminated. And there, don't you see? your strength comes in, the faith in your ability for the digging of unostentatious holes to bury the stuff in—your power of devotion, not to yourself, but to an obscure, back-breaking business. And that's difficult enough. Mind, I am not trying to excuse or even explain—I am trying to account to myself for—for—Mr. Kurtz—for the shade of Mr. Kurtz. This initiated wraith from the back of Nowhere honoured me with its amazing confidence before it vanished altogether. This was because it could speak English to me. The original Kurtz had been educated partly in England, and—as he was good enough to say himself—his sympathies were in the right place. His mother was half-English, his father was half-French. All Europe contributed to the making of Kurtz; and by and by I learned that, most appropriately, the International Society for the Suppression of Savage Customs had entrusted him with the making of a report, for its future guidance. And he had written it too. I've seen it. I've read it. It was eloquent, vibrating with eloquence, but too high-strung, I think. Seventeen pages of close writing he had found time for! But this must have been before his—let us say—nerves went wrong, and caused him to preside at certain midnight dances ending with unspeakable rites, which—as far as I reluctantly gathered from what I heard at various times—were offered up to him—do you understand?—to Mr. Kurtz himself. But it was a beautiful piece of writing. The opening paragraph, however, in the light of later information, strikes me now as ominous. He began with the argument that we whites, from the point of development we had arrived at, 'must necessarily appear to them [savages] in the nature of supernatural beings—we approach them with the might as of a deity,' and so on, and so on. 'By the simple exercise of our will we can exert a power for good practically unbounded,' etc. etc. From that point he soared and took me with him. The peroration was magnificent, though difficult to remember, you know. It gave me the notion of an exotic Immensity ruled by an august Benevolence. It made me tingle with enthusiasm. This was the unbounded power of eloquence—of words—of burning noble words. There were no practical hints to interrupt the magic current of phrases, unless a kind of note at the foot of the last page, scrawled evidently much later, in an unsteady hand, may be regarded as the exposition of a method. It was very simple, and at the end of that moving appeal to every altruistic sentiment it blazed at you, luminous and terrifying, like a flash of lightning in a serene sky: 'Exterminate all the brutes!' The curious part was that he had apparently forgotten all about that valuable postscriptum, because, later on, when he in a sense came to himself, he repeatedly entreated me to take good care of 'my pamphlet' (he called it), as it was sure to have in the future a good influence upon his career. I had full information about all these things, and, besides, as it turned out, I was to have the care of his memory. I've done enough for it to give me the indisputable right to lay it, if I choose, for an everlasting rest in the dust-bin of progress, amongst all the sweepings and, figuratively speaking, all the dead cats of civilisation. But then, you see, I can't choose. He won't be forgotten. Whatever he was, he was not common. He had the power to charm or frighten rudimentary souls into an aggravated witch-dance in his honour; he could also fill the small souls of the pilgrims with bitter misgivings: he had one devoted friend at least, and he had conquered one soul in the world that was neither rudimentary nor tainted with self-seeking. No; I can't forget him, though I am not prepared to affirm the fellow was exactly worth the life we lost in getting to him. I missed my late helmsman awfully—I missed him even while his body was still lying in the pilot-house. Perhaps you will think it passing strange this regret for a savage who was no more account than a grain of sand in a black Sahara. Well, don't you see, he had done something, he had steered; for months I had him at my back—a help—an instrument. It was a kind of partnership. He steered for me—I had to look after him, I worried about his deficiencies, and thus a subtle bond had been created, of which I only became aware when it was suddenly broken. And the intimate profundity of that look he gave me when he received his hurt remains to this day in my memory—like a claim of distant kinship affirmed in a supreme moment.

"Poor fool! If he had only left that shutter alone. He had no restraint, no restraint—just like Kurtz—a tree swayed by the wind. As soon as I had put on a dry pair of slippers, I dragged him out, after first jerking the spear out of his side, which operation I confess I performed with my eyes shut tight. His heels leaped together over the little door-step; his shoulders were pressed to my breast; I hugged him from behind desperately. Oh! he was heavy, heavy; heavier than any man on earth, I should imagine. Then without more ado I tipped him overboard. The current snatched him as though he had been a wisp of grass, and I saw the body roll over twice before I lost sight of it for ever. All the pilgrims and the manager were then congregated on the awning-deck about the pilot-house, chattering at each other like a flock of excited magpies, and there was a scandalised murmur at my heartless promptitude. What they wanted to keep that body hanging about for I can't guess. Embalm it, maybe. But I had also heard another, and a very ominous, murmur on the deck below. My friends the wood-cutters were likewise scandalised, and with a better show of reason—though I admit that the reason itself was quite inadmissible. Oh, quite! I had made up my mind that if my late helmsman was to be eaten, the fishes alone should have him. He had been a very second-rate helmsman while alive, but now he was dead he might have become a first-class temptation, and possibly cause some startling trouble. Besides, I was anxious to take the wheel, the man in pink pyjamas showing himself a hopeless duffer at the business.

"This I did directly the simple funeral was over. We were going half-speed, keeping right in the middle of the stream, and I listened to the talk about me. They had given up Kurtz, they had given up the station; Kurtz was dead, and the station had been burnt—and so on, and so on. The red-haired pilgrim was beside himself with the thought that at least this poor Kurtz had been properly revenged. 'Say! We must have made a glorious slaughter of them in the bush. Eh? What do you think? Say?' He positively danced, the bloodthirsty little gingery beggar. And he had nearly fainted when he saw the wounded man! I could not help saying, 'You made a glorious lot of smoke, anyhow.' I had seen, from the way the tops of the bushes rustled and flew, that almost all the shots had gone too high. You can't hit anything unless you take aim and fire from the shoulder; but these chaps fired from the hip with their eyes shut. The retreat, I maintained—and I was right—was caused by the screeching of the steam-whistle. Upon this they forgot Kurtz, and began to howl at me with indignant protests.

"The manager stood by the wheel murmuring confidentially about the necessity of getting well away down the river before dark at all events, when I saw in the distance a clearing on the river-side and the outlines of some sort of building. 'What's this?' I asked. He clapped his hands in wonder. 'The station!' he cried. I edged in at once, still going half-speed.

"Through my glasses I saw the slope of a hill interspersed with rare trees and perfectly free from undergrowth. A long decaying building on the summit was half buried in the high grass; the large holes in the peaked roof gaped black from afar; the jungle and the woods made a background. There was no enclosure or fence of any kind; but there had been one apparently, for near the house half a dozen slim posts remained in a row, roughly trimmed, and with their upper ends ornamented with round carved balls. The rails, or whatever there had been between, had disappeared. Of course the forest surrounded all that. The river-bank was clear, and on the water side I saw a white man under a hat like a cart-wheel beckoning persistently with his whole arm. Examining the edge of the forest above and below, I was almost certain I could see movements—human forms gliding here and there, I steamed past prudently, then stopped the engines and let her drift down. The man on the shore began to shout, urging us to land. 'We have been attacked,' screamed the manager. 'I know—I know. It's all right,' yelled back the other, as cheerful as you please. 'Come along. It's all right. I am glad.'

"His aspect reminded me of something I had seen—something funny I had seen somewhere. As I manœuvred to get alongside, I was asking myself, 'What does this fellow look like?' Suddenly I got it. He looked like a harlequin. His clothes had been made of some stuff that was brown holland probably, but it was covered with patches all over, with bright patches, blue, red, and yellow—patches on the back, patches on the front, patches on elbows, on knees; coloured binding round his jacket, scarlet edging at the bottom of his trousers; and the sunshine made him look extremely gay and wonderfully neat withal, because you could see how beautifully all this patching had been done. A beardless, boyish face, very fair, no features to speak of, nose peeling, little blue eyes, smiles and frowns chasing each other over that open countenance like sunshine and shadow on a wind-swept plain. 'Look out, captain!' he cried; 'there's a snag lodged in here last night.' What! Another snag? I confess I swore shamefully. I had nearly holed my cripple, to finish off that charming trip. The harlequin on the bank turned his little pug-nose up to me. 'You English?' he asked, all smiles. 'Are you?' I shouted from the wheel. The smiles vanished, and he shook his head as if sorry for my disappointment. Then he brightened up. 'Never mind!' he cried encouragingly. 'Are we in time?' I asked. 'He is up there,' he replied, with a toss of the head up the hill, and becoming gloomy all of a sudden. His face was like the autumn sky, overcast one moment and bright the next.

"When the manager, escorted by the pilgrims, all of them armed to the teeth, had gone to the house, this chap came on board. 'I say, I don't like this. These natives are in the bush,' I said. He assured me earnestly it was all right. 'They are simple people,' he added; 'well, I am glad you came. It took me all my time to keep them off.' 'But you said it was all right,' I cried. 'Oh, they meant no harm,' he said; and as I stared he corrected himself, 'Not exactly.' Then vivaciously, 'My faith, your pilot-house wants a clean-up!' In the next breath he advised me to keep enough steam on the boiler to blow the whistle in case of any trouble. 'One good screech will do more for you than all your rifles. They are simple people,' he repeated. He rattled away at such a rate he quite overwhelmed me. He seemed to be trying to make up for lots of silence, and actually hinted, laughing, that such was the case. 'Don't you talk with Mr. Kurtz?' I said. 'You don't talk with that man—you listen to him,' he exclaimed with severe exaltation. 'But now——' He waved his arm, and in the twinkling of an eye was in the uttermost depths of despondency. In a moment he came up again with a jump, possessed himself of both my hands, shook them continuously, while he gabbled: 'Brother sailor . . . honour . . . pleasure . . . delight . . . introduce myself . . . Russian . . . son of an arch-priest . . . Government of Tambov . . . What? Tobacco! English tobacco; the excellent English tobacco! Now, that's brotherly. Smoke? Where's a sailor that does not smoke?'

"The pipe soothed him, and gradually I made out he had run away from school, had gone to sea in a Russian ship; ran away again; served some time in English ships; was now reconciled with the arch-priest. He made a point of that. 'But when one is young one must see things, gather experience, ideas; enlarge the mind.' 'Here!' I interrupted. 'You can never tell! Here I met Mr. Kurtz,' he said, youthfully solemn and reproachful. I held my tongue after that. It appears he had persuaded a Dutch trading-house on the coast to fit him out with stores and goods, and had started for the interior with a light heart, and no more idea of what would happen to him than a baby. He had been wandering about that river for nearly two years alone, cut off from everybody and everything. 'I am not so young as I look. I am twenty-five,' he said. 'At first old Van Shuyten would tell me to go to the devil,' he narrated with keen enjoyment; 'but I stuck to him, and talked and talked, till at last he got afraid I would talk the hind-leg off his favourite dog, so he gave me some cheap things and a few guns, and told me he hoped he would never see my face again. Good old Dutchman, Van Shuyten. I sent him one small lot of ivory a year ago, so that he can't call me a little thief when I get back. I hope he got it. And for the rest, I don't care. I had some wood stacked for you. That was my old house. Did you see?'

"I gave him Towson's book. He made as though he

would kiss me, but restrained himself. 'The only book I had left, and I thought I had lost it,' he said, looking at it ecstatically. 'So many accidents happen to a man going about alone, you know. Canoes get upset sometimes—and sometimes you've got to clear out so quick when the people get angry.' He thumbed the pages. 'You made notes in cipher,' I said. He laughed, then became serious. 'I had lots of trouble to keep these people off,' he said. 'Did they want to kill you?' I asked. 'Oh no!' he cried, and checked himself. 'Why did they attack us?' I pursued. He hesitated, then said shamefacedly, 'They don't want him to go.' 'Don't they?' I said curiously. He nodded a nod full of mystery and wisdom. 'I tell you,' he cried, 'this man has enlarged my mind.' He opened his arms wide, staring at me with his little blue eyes that were perfectly round."

III

"I looked at him, lost in astonishment. There he was before me, in motley, as though he had absconded from a troupe of mimes, enthusiastic, fabulous. His very existence was improbable, inexplicable, and altogether bewildering. He was an insoluble problem. It was inconceivable how he had existed, how he had succeeded in getting so far, how he had managed to remain—why he did not instantly disappear. 'I went a little farther,' he said, 'then still a little farther—till I had gone so far that I don't know how I'll ever get back. Never mind. Plenty time. I can manage. You take Kurtz away quick—quick—I tell you.' The glamour of youth enveloped his parti-coloured rags, his destitution, his loneliness, the essential desolation of his futile wanderings. For months—for years—his life hadn't been worth a day's purchase; and there he was gallantly, thoughtlessly alive, to all appearance indestructible solely by the virtue of his few years and of his unreflecting audacity. I was seduced into something like admiration—like envy. Glamour urged him on, glamour kept him unscathed. He surely wanted nothing from the wilderness but space to breathe in and to push on through. His need was to exist, and to move onwards at the greatest possible risk, and with a maximum of privation. If the absolutely pure, uncalculating, unpractical spirit of adventure had ever ruled a human being, it ruled this be-patched youth. I almost envied him the possession of this modest and clear flame. It seemed to have consumed all thought of self so completely, that, even while he was talking to you, you forgot that it was he—the man before your eyes—who had gone through these things. I did not envy him his devotion to Kurtz, though. He had not meditated over it. It came to him, and he accepted it with a sort of eager fatalism. I must say that to me it appeared about the most dangerous thing in every way he had come upon so far.

"They had come together unavoidably, like two ships becalmed near each other, and lay rubbing sides at last. I suppose Kurtz wanted an audience, because on a certain occasion, when encamped in the forest, they had talked all night, or more probably Kurtz had talked. 'We talked of everything,' he said, quite transported at the recollection. 'I forgot there was such a thing as sleep. The night did not seem to last an hour. Everything! Everything! . . . Of love too.' 'Ah, he talked to you of love!' I said, much amused. 'It isn't what you think,' he cried, almost passionately. 'It was in general. He made me see things—things.'

"He threw his arms up. We were on deck at the time, and the head-man of my wood-cutters, lounging near by, turned upon him his heavy and glittering eyes. I looked around, and I don't know why, but I assure you that never, never before, did this land, this river, this jungle, the very arch of this blazing sky, appear to me so hopeless and so dark, so impenetrable to human thought, so pitiless to human weakness. 'And, ever since, you have been with him, of course?' I said.

"On the contrary. It appears their intercourse had been very much broken by various causes. He had, as he informed me proudly, managed to nurse Kurtz through two illnesses (he alluded to it as you would to some risky feat), but as a rule Kurtz wandered alone, far in the depths of the forest. 'Very often coming to this station, I had to wait days and days before he would turn up,' he said. 'Ah, it was worth waiting for!—sometimes.' 'What was he doing? exploring or what?' I asked. 'Oh yes, of course'; he had discovered lots of villages, a lake too—he did not know exactly in what direction; it was dangerous to inquire too much—but mostly his expeditions had been for ivory. 'But he had no goods to trade with by that time,' I objected. 'There's a good lot of cartridges left even yet,' he answered, looking away. 'To speak plainly, he raided the country,' I said. He nodded. 'Not alone, surely!' He muttered something about the villages round that lake. 'Kurtz got the tribe to follow him, did he?' I suggested. He fidgeted a little. 'They adored him,' he said. The tone of these words was so extraordinary that I looked at him searchingly. It was curious to see his mingled eagerness and reluctance to speak of Kurtz. The man filled his life, occupied his thoughts, swayed his emotions. 'What can you expect?' he burst out; 'he came to them with thunder and lightning, you know—and they had never seen anything like it—and very terrible. He could be very terrible. You can't judge Mr. Kurtz as you would an ordinary man. No, no, no! Now—just to give you an idea—I don't mind telling you, he wanted to shoot me too one day—but I don't judge him.' 'Shoot you!' I cried. 'What for?' 'Well, I had a small lot of ivory the chief of that village near my house gave me. You see I used to shoot game for them. Well, he wanted it, and wouldn't hear reason. He declared he would shoot me unless I gave him the ivory and then cleared out of the country, because he could do so, and had a fancy for it, and there was nothing on earth to prevent him killing whom he jolly well pleased. And it was true too. I gave him the ivory. What did I care! But I didn't clear out. No, no. I couldn't leave him. I had to be careful, of course, till we got friendly again for a time. He had his second illness then. Afterwards I had to keep out of the way; but I didn't mind. He was living for the most part in those villages on the lake. When he came down to the river, sometimes he would take to me and sometimes it was better for me to be careful. This man suffered too much. He hated all this, and somehow he couldn't get away. When I had a chance I begged him to try and leave while there was time; I offered to go back with him. And he would say yes, and then he would remain; go off on another ivory hunt; disappear for weeks; forget himself amongst these people—forget himself—you know.' 'Why! he's mad,' I said. He protested indignantly. Mr. Kurtz couldn't be mad. If I had heard him talk, only two days ago, I wouldn't dare hint at such a thing. . . . I had taken up my binoculars while we talked, and was looking at the shore, sweeping the limit of the forest at each side and at the back of the house. The consciousness of there being people in that bush, so silent, so quiet—as silent and quiet as the ruined house on the hill—made me uneasy. There was no sign on the face of nature of this amazing tale that was not so much told as suggested to me in desolate exclamations, completed by shrugs, in interrupted phrases, in hints ending in deep sighs. The woods were unmoved, like a mask—heavy, like the closed door of a prison—they looked with their air of hidden knowledge, of patient expectation, of unapproachable silence. The Russian was explaining to me that it was only lately that Mr. Kurtz had come down to the river, bringing along with him all the fighting men of that lake tribe. He had been absent for several months—getting himself adored, I suppose—and had come down unexpectedly, with the intention to all appearance of making a raid either across the river or down stream. Evidently the appetite for more ivory had got the better of the—what shall I say?—less material aspirations. However, he had got much worse suddenly. 'I heard he was lying helpless, and so I came up—took my chance,' said the Russian. 'Oh, he is bad, very bad.' I directed my glass to the house. There were no signs of life, but there were the ruined roof, the long mud wall peeping above the grass, with three little square window-holes, no two of the same size; all this brought within reach of my hand, as it were. And then I made a brusque movement, and one of the remaining posts of that vanished fence leaped up in the field of my glass. You remember I told you I had been struck at the distance by certain attempts at ornamentation, rather remarkable in the ruinous aspect of the place. Now I had suddenly a nearer view, and its first result was to make me throw my head back as if before a blow. Then I went carefully from post to post with my glass, and I saw my mistake. These round knobs were not ornamental but symbolic; they were expressive and puzzling, striking and disturbing—food for thought and also for vultures if there had been any looking down from the sky; but at all events for such ants as were industrious enough to ascend the pole. They would have been even more impressive, those heads on the stakes, if their faces had not been turned to the house. Only one, the first I had made out, was facing my way. I was not so shocked as you may think. The start back I had given was really nothing but a movement of surprise. I had expected to see a knob of wood there, you know. I returned deliberately to the first I had seen—and there it was, black, dried, sunken, with closed eyelids—a head that seemed to sleep at the top of that pole, and, with the shrunken dry lips showing a narrow white line of the teeth, was smiling too, smiling continuously at some endless and jocose dream of that eternal slumber.

"I am not disclosing any trade secrets. In fact the manager said afterwards that Mr. Kurtz's methods had ruined the district. I have no opinion on that point, but I want you clearly to understand that there was nothing exactly profitable in these heads being there. They only showed that Mr. Kurtz lacked restraint in the gratification of his various lusts, that there was something wanting in him—some small matter which, when the pressing need arose, could not be found under his magnificent eloquence. Whether he knew of this deficiency himself I can't say. I think the knowledge came to him at last—only at the very last. But the wilderness had found him out early, and had taken on him a terrible vengeance for the fantastic invasion. I think it had whispered to him things about himself which he did not know, things of which he had no conception till he took counsel with this great solitude—and the whisper had proved irresistibly fascinating. It echoed loudly within him because he was hollow at the core. . . . I put down the glass, and the head that had appeared near enough to be spoken to seemed at once to have leaped away from me into inaccessible distance.

"The admirer of Mr. Kurtz was a bit crestfallen. In a hurried, indistinct voice he began to assure me he had not dared to take these—say, symbols—down. He was not afraid of the natives; they would not stir till Mr. Kurtz gave the word. His ascendancy was extraordinary. The camps of these people surrounded the place, and the chiefs came every day to see him. They would crawl . . . 'I don't want to know anything of the ceremonies used when approaching Mr. Kurtz,' I shouted. Curious, this feeling that came over me that such details would be more intolerable than those heads drying on the stakes under Mr. Kurtz's windows. After all, that was only a savage sight, while I seemed at one bound to have been transported into some lightless region of subtle horrors, where pure, uncomplicated savagery was a positive relief, being something that had a right to exist—obviously—in the sunshine. The young man looked at me with surprise. I suppose it did not occur to him that Mr. Kurtz was no idol of mine. He forgot I hadn't heard any of these splendid monologues on, what was it? on love, justice, conduct of life—or what not. If it had come to crawling before Mr. Kurtz, he crawled as much as the veriest savage of them all. I had no idea of the conditions, he said: these heads were the heads of rebels. I shocked him excessively by laughing. Rebels! What would be the next definition I was to hear? There had been enemies, criminals, workers—and these were rebels. Those rebellious heads looked very subdued to me on their sticks. 'You don't know how such a life tries a man like Kurtz,' cried Kurtz's last disciple. 'Well, and you?' I said. "I! I! I am a simple man. I have no great thoughts. I want nothing from anybody. How can you compare me to . . .?' His feelings were too much for speech, and suddenly he broke down. 'I don't understand,' he groaned. 'I've been doing my best to keep him alive, and that's enough. I had no hand in all this. I have no abilities. There hasn't been a drop of medicine or a mouthful of invalid food for months here. He was shamefully abandoned. A man like this, with such ideas. Shamefully! Shamefully! I—I—haven't slept for the last ten nights. . . .'

"His voice lost itself in the calm of the evening. The long shadows of the forest had slipped downhill while we talked, had gone far beyond the ruined hovel, beyond the symbolic row of stakes. All this was in the gloom, while we down there were yet in the sunshine, and the stretch of the river abreast of the clearing glittered in a still and dazzling splendour, with a murky and overshadowed bend above and below. Not a living soul was seen on the shore. The bushes did not rustle.

"Suddenly round the corner of the house a group of men appeared, as though they had come up from the ground. They waded waist-deep in the grass, in a compact body, bearing an improvised stretcher in their midst. Instantly, in the emptiness of the landscape, a cry arose whose shrillness pierced the still air like a sharp arrow flying straight to the very heart of the land; and, as if by enchantment, streams of human beings—of naked human beings—with spears in their hands, with bows, with shields, with wild glances and savage movements, were poured into the clearing by the dark-faced and pensive forest. The bushes shook, the grass swayed for a time, and then everything stood still in attentive immobility.

" 'Now, if he does not say the right thing to them we are all done for,' said the Russian at my elbow. The knot of men with the stretcher had stopped too, halfway to the steamer, as if petrified. I saw the man on the stretcher sit up, lank and with an uplifted arm, above the shoulders of the bearers. 'Let us hope that the man who can talk so well of love in general will find some particular reason to spare us this time,' I said. I resented bitterly the absurd danger of our situation, as if to be at the mercy of that atrocious phantom had been a dishonouring necessity. I could not hear a sound, but through my glasses I saw the thin arm extended commandingly, the lower jaw moving, the eyes of that apparition shining darkly far in its bony head that nodded with grotesque jerks. Kurtz—Kurtz—that means 'short' in German—don't it? Well, the name was as true as everything else in his life—and death. He looked at least seven feet long. His covering had fallen off, and his body emerged from it pitiful and appalling as from a winding-sheet. I could see the cage of his ribs all astir, the bones of his arm waving. It was as though an animated image of death carved out of old ivory had been shaking its hand with menaces at a motionless crowd of men made of dark and glittering bronze. I saw him open his mouth wide—it gave him a weirdly voracious aspect, as though he had wanted to swallow all the air, all the earth, all the men before him. A deep voice reached me faintly. He must have been shouting. He fell back suddenly. The stretcher shook as the bearers staggered forward again, and almost at the same time I noticed that the crowd of savages was vanishing without any perceptible movement of retreat, as if the forest that had ejected these beings so suddenly had drawn them in again as the breath is drawn in a long aspiration.

"Some of the pilgrims behind the stretcher carried his arms—two shot-guns, a heavy rifle, and a light revolver-carbine—the thunderbolts of that pitiful Jupiter. The manager bent over him murmuring as he walked beside his head. They laid him down in one of the little cabins—just a room for a bed-place and a camp-stool or two, you know. We had brought his belated correspondence, and a lot of torn envelopes and open letters littered his bed. His hand roamed feebly amongst these papers. I was struck by the fire of his eyes and the composed languor of his expression. It was not so much the exhaustion of disease. He did not seem in pain. This shadow looked satiated and calm, as though for the moment it had had its fill of all the emotions.

"He rustled one of the letters, and looking straight in my face said, 'I am glad.' Somebody had been writing to him about me. These special recommendations were turning up again. The volume of tone he emitted without effort, almost without the trouble of moving his lips, amazed me. A voice! a voice! It was grave, profound, vibrating, while the man did not seem capable of a whisper. However, he had enough strength in him—factitious no doubt—to very nearly make an end of us, as you shall hear directly.

"The manager appeared silently in the doorway; I stepped out at once and he drew the curtain after me. The Russian, eyed curiously by the pilgrims, was staring at the shore. I followed the direction of his glance.

"Dark human shapes could be made out in the distance, flitting indistinctly against the gloomy border of the forest, and near the river two bronze figures, leaning on tall spears, stood in the sunlight under fantastic head-dresses of spotted skins, warlike and still in statuesque repose. And from right to left along the lighted shore moved a wild and gorgeous apparition of a woman.

"She walked with measured steps, draped in striped and fringed cloths, treading the earth proudly, with a slight jingle and flash of barbarous ornaments. She carried her head high; her hair was done in the shape of a helmet; she had brass leggings to the knees, brass wire gauntlets to the elbow, a crimson spot on her tawny cheek, innumerable necklaces of glass beads on her neck; bizarre things, charms, gifts of witch-men, that hung about her, glittered and trembled at every step. She must have had the value of several elephant tusks upon her. She was savage and superb, wild-eyed and magnificent; there was something ominous and stately in her deliberate progress. And in the hush that had fallen suddenly upon the whole sorrowful land, the immense wilderness, the colossal body of the fecund and mysterious life seemed to look at her, pensive, as though it had been looking at the image of its own tenebrous and passionate soul.

"She came abreast of the steamer, stood still, and faced us. Her long shadow fell to the water's edge. Her face had a tragic and fierce aspect of wild sorrow and of dumb pain mingled with the fear of some struggling, half-shaped resolve. She stood looking at us without a stir, and like the wilderness itself, with an air of brooding over an inscrutable purpose. A whole minute passed, and then she made a step forward. There was a low jingle, a glint of yellow metal, a way of fringed draperies, and she stopped as if her heart had failed her. The young fellow by my side growled. The pilgrims murmured at my back. She looked at us all as if her life had depended upon the unswerving steadiness of her glance. Suddenly she opened her bared arms and threw them up rigid above her head, as though in an uncontrollable desire to touch the sky, and at the same time the swift shadows darted out on the earth, swept around on the river, gathering the steamer in a shadowy embrace. A formidable silence hung over the scene.

"She turned away slowly, walked on, following the bank, and passed into the bushes to the left. Once only her eyes gleamed back at us in the dusk of the thickets before she disappeared.

" 'If she had offered to come aboard I really think I would have tried to shoot her,' said the man of patches nervously. 'I had been risking my life every day for the last fortnight to keep her out of the house. She got in one day and kicked up a row about those miserable rags I picked up in the storeroom to mend my clothes with. I wasn't decent. At least it must have been that, for she talked like a fury to Kurtz for an hour, pointing at me now and then. I don't understand the dialect of this tribe. Luckily for me, I fancy Kurtz felt too ill that day to care, or there would have been mischief. I don't understand. . . . No—it's too much for me. Ah, well, it's all over now.'

"At this moment I heard Kurtz's deep voice behind the curtain: 'Save me!—save the ivory, you mean. Don't tell me. Save *me!* Why, I've had to save you. You are interrupting my plans now. Sick! Sick! Not so sick as you would like to believe. Never mind. I'll carry my ideas out yet—I will return. I'll show you what can be done. You with your little peddling notions—you are interfering with me. I will return. I . . .'

"The manager came out. He did me the honour to take me under the arm and lead me aside. 'He is very low, very low,' he said. He considered it necessary to sigh, but neglected to be consistently sorrowful. 'We have done all we could for him—haven't we? But there is no disguising the fact, Mr. Kurtz has done more harm than good to the Company. He did not see the time was not ripe for vigorous action. Cautiously, cautiously—that's my principle. We must be cautious yet. The district is closed to us for a time. Deplorable! Upon the whole, the trade will suffer. I don't deny there is a remarkable quantity of ivory—mostly fossil. We must save it, at all events—but look how precarious the position is—and why? Because the method is unsound.' 'Do you,' said I, looking at the shore, 'call it "unsound method"?' 'Without doubt,' he exclaimed hotly. 'Don't you?' . . . 'No method at all,' I murmured after a while. 'Exactly,' he exulted. 'I anticipated this. Shows a complete want of judgment. It is my duty to point it out in the proper quarter.' 'Oh,' said I, 'that fellow—what's his name?—the brickmaker, will make a readable report for you.' He appeared confounded for a moment. It seemed to me I had never breathed an atmosphere so vile, and I turned mentally to Kurtz for relief—positively for relief. 'Nevertheless, I think Mr. Kurtz is a remarkable man,' I said with emphasis. He started, dropped on me a cold heavy glance, said very quietly, 'He *was,*' and turned his back on me. My hour of favour was over; I found myself lumped along with Kurtz as a partisan of methods for which the time was not ripe: I was unsound! Ah! but it was something to have at least a choice of nightmares.

"I had turned to the wilderness really, not to Mr. Kurtz, who, I was ready to admit, was as good as buried. And for a moment it seemed to me as if I also were buried in a vast grave full of unspeakable secrets. I felt an intolerable weight oppressing my breast, the smell of the damp earth, the unseen presence of victorious corruption, the darkness of an impenetrable night. . . . The Russian tapped me on the shoulder. I heard him mumbling and stammering something about 'brother seaman—couldn't conceal—knowledge of matters that would affect Mr. Kurtz's reputation.' I waited. For him evidently Mr. Kurtz was not in his grave; I suspect that for him Mr. Kurtz was one of the immortals. 'Well!' said I at last, 'speak out. As it happens, I am Mr. Kurtz's friend—in a way.'

"He stated with a good deal of formality that had we not been 'of the same profession,' he would have kept the matter to himself without regard to consequences. He suspected 'there was an active ill-will towards him on the part of these white men that——' 'You are right,' I said, remembering a certain conversation I had overheard. 'The manager thinks you ought to be hanged.' He showed a concern at this intelligence which amused me at first. 'I had better get out of the way quietly,' he said earnestly. 'I can do no more for Kurtz now, and they would soon find some excuse. What's to stop them? There's a military post three hundred miles from here.' 'Well, upon my word,' said I, 'perhaps you had better go if you have any friends amongst the savages near by.' 'Plenty,' he said. 'They are simple people—and I want nothing, you know.' He stood biting his lip, then: 'I don't want any harm to happen to these whites here, but of course I was thinking of Mr. Kurtz's reputation—but you are a brother seaman and——' 'All right,' said I, after a time. 'Mr. Kurtz's reputation is safe with me.' I did not know how truly I spoke.

"He informed me, lowering his voice, that it was Kurtz who had ordered the attack to be made on the steamer. 'He hated sometimes the idea of being taken away—and then again . . . But I don't understand these matters. I am a simple man. He thought it would scare you away—that you would give it up, thinking him dead. I could not stop him. Oh, I had an awful time of it this last month.' 'Very well,' I said. 'He is all right now.' 'Ye-e-es,' he muttered, not very convinced apparently. 'Thanks,' said I; 'I shall keep my eyes open.' 'But quiet—eh?' he urged anxiously. 'It would be awful for his reputation if anybody here——' I promised a complete discretion with great gravity. 'I have a canoe and three black fellows waiting not very far. I am off. Could you give me a few Martini-Henry cartridges?' I could, and did, with proper secrecy. He helped himself, with a wink at me, to a handful of my tobacco. 'Between sailors—you know—good English tobacco.' At the door of the pilot-house he turned round—'I say, haven't you a pair of shoes you could spare?' He raised one leg. 'Look.' The soles were tied with knotted strings sandal-wise under his bare feet. I rooted out an old pair, at which he looked with admiration before tucking it under his left arm. One of his pockets (bright red) was bulging with cartridges, from the other (dark blue) peeped 'Towson's Inquiry,' etc. etc. He seemed to think himself excellently well equipped for a renewed encounter with the wilderness. 'Ah! I'll never, never meet such a man again. You ought to have heard him recite poetry—his own too it was, he told me. Poetry!' He rolled his eyes at the recollection of these delights. 'Oh, he enlarged my mind!' 'Good-bye,' said I. He shook hands and vanished in the night. Sometimes I ask myself whether I had ever really seen him—whether it was possible to meet such a phenomenon! . . .

"When I woke up shortly after midnight his warning came to my mind with its hint of danger that seemed, in the starred darkness, real enough to make me get up for the purpose of having a look round. On the hill a big fire burned, illuminating fitfully a crooked corner of the station-house. One of the agents with a picket of a few of our blacks, armed for the purpose, was keeping guard over the ivory; but deep within the forest, red gleams that wavered, that seemed to sink and rise from the ground amongst confused columnar shapes of intense blackness, showed the exact position of the camp where Mr. Kurtz's adorers were keeping their uneasy vigil. The monotonous beating of a big drum filled the air with muffled shocks and a lingering vibration. A steady droning sound of many men chanting each to himself some weird incantation came out from the black, flat wall of the woods as the humming of bees comes out of a hive, and had a strange narcotic effect upon my half-awake senses. I believe I dozed off leaning over the rail, till an abrupt burst of yells, an overwhelming outbreak of a pent-up and mysterious frenzy, woke me up in a bewildered wonder. It was cut short all at once, and the low droning went on with an effect of audible and soothing silence. I glanced casually into the little cabin. A light was burning within, but Mr. Kurtz was not there.

"I think I would have raised an outcry if I had believed my eyes. But I didn't believe them at first—the thing seemed so impossible. The fact is, I was completely unnerved by a sheer blank fright, pure abstract terror, unconnected with any distinct shape of physical danger. What made this emotion so overpowering was—how shall I define it?—the moral shock I received, as if something altogether monstrous, intolerable to thought and odious to the soul, had been thrust upon me unexpectedly. This lasted of course the merest fraction of a second, and then the usual sense of commonplace, deadly danger, the possibility of a sudden onslaught and massacre, or something of the kind, which I saw impending, was positively welcome and composing. It pacified me, in fact, so much, that I did not raise an alarm.

"There was an agent buttoned up inside an ulster and sleeping on a chair on deck within three feet of me. The yells had not awakened him; he snored very slightly; I left him to his slumbers and leaped ashore. I did not betray Mr. Kurtz—it was ordered I should never betray him—it was written I should be loyal to the nightmare of my choice. I was anxious to deal with this shadow by myself alone—and to this day I don't know why I was so jealous of sharing with any one the peculiar blackness of that experience.

"As soon as I got on the bank I saw a trail—a broad trail through the grass. I remember the exultation with which I said to myself, 'He can't walk—he is crawling on all-fours—I've got him.' The grass was wet with dew. I strode rapidly with clenched fists. I fancy I had some vague notion of falling upon him and giving him a drubbing. I don't know. I had some imbecile thoughts. The knitting old woman with the cat obtruded herself upon my memory as a most improper person to be sitting at the other end of such an affair. I saw a row of pilgrims squirting lead in the air out of Winchesters held to the hip. I thought I would never get back to the steamer, and imagined myself living alone and unarmed in the woods to an advanced age. Such silly things—you know. And I remember I confounded the beat of the drum with the beating of my heart, and was pleased at its calm regularity.

"I kept to the track though—then stopped to listen. The night was very clear; a dark blue space, sparkling with dew and starlight, in which black things stood very still. I thought I could see a kind of motion ahead of me. I was strangely cocksure of everything that night. I actually left the track and ran in a wide semicircle (I verily believe chuckling to myself) so as to get in front of that stir, of that motion I had seen—if indeed I had seen anything. I was circumventing Kurtz as though it had been a boyish game.

"I came upon him, and, if he had not heard me coming, I would have fallen over him too, but he got up in time. He rose, unsteady, long, pale, indistinct, like a vapour exhaled by the earth, and swayed slightly, misty and silent before me; while at my back the fires loomed between the trees, and the murmur of many voices issued from the forest. I had cut him off cleverly; but when actually confronting him I seemed to come to my senses, I saw the danger in its right proportion. It was by no means over yet. Suppose he began to shout? Though he could hardly stand, there was still plenty of vigour in his voice. 'Go away—hide yourself,' he said, in that profound tone. It was very awful. I glanced back. We were within thirty yards from the nearest fire. A black figure stood up, strode on long black legs, waving long black arms, across the glow. It had horns—antelope horns, I think—on its head. Some sorcerer, some witch-man, no doubt: it looked fiend-like enough. 'Do you know what you are doing?' I whispered. 'Perfectly,' he answered, raising his voice for that single word: it sounded to me far off and yet loud, like a hail through a speaking-trumpet. If he makes a row we are lost, I thought to myself. This clearly was not a case for fisticuffs, even apart from the very natural aversion I had to beat that Shadow—this wandering and tormented thing. 'You will be lost,' I said—'utterly lost.' One gets sometimes such a flash of inspiration, you know. I did say the right thing, though indeed he could not have been more irretrievably lost than he was at this very moment, when the foundations of our intimacy were being laid—to endure—to endure—even to the end—even beyond.

" 'I had immense plans,' he muttered irresolutely. 'Yes,' said I; 'but if you try to shout I'll smash your head with——' There was not a stick or a stone near. 'I will throttle you for good,' I corrected myself. 'I was on the threshold of great things,' he pleaded, in a voice of longing, with a wistfulness of tone that made my blood run cold. 'And now for this stupid scoundrel——' 'Your success in Europe is assured in any case,' I affirmed steadily. I did not want to have the throttling of him, you understand—and indeed it would have been very little use for any practical purpose. I tried to break the spell—the heavy, mute spell of the wilderness—that seemed to draw him to its pitiless breast by the awakening of forgotten and brutal instincts, by the memory of gratified and monstrous passions. This alone, I was convinced, had driven him out to the edge of the forest, to the bush, towards the gleam of fires, the throb of drums, the drone of weird incantations; this alone had beguiled his unlawful soul beyond the bounds of permitted aspirations. And, don't you see, the terror of the position was not in being knocked on the head—though I had a very lively sense of that danger too—but in this, that I had to deal with a being to whom I could not appeal in the name of anything high or low. I had, even like the niggers, to invoke him—himself—his own exalted and incredible degradation. There was nothing either above or below him, and I knew it. He had kicked himself loose of the earth. Confound the man! he had kicked the very earth to pieces. He was alone, and I before him did not know whether I stood on the ground or floated in the air. I've been telling you what we said—repeating the phrases we pronounced—but what's the good? They were common everyday words—the familiar, vague sounds exchanged on every waking day of life. But what of that? They had behind them, to my mind, the terrific suggestiveness of words heard in dreams, of phrases spoken in nightmares. Soul! If anybody had ever struggled with a soul, I am the man. And I wasn't arguing with a lunatic either. Believe me or not, his intelligence was perfectly clear—concentrated, it is true, upon himself with horrible intensity, yet clear; and therein was my only chance—barring, of course, the killing him there and then, which wasn't so good, on account of unavoidable noise. But his soul was mad. Being alone in the wilderness, it had looked within itself, and, by Heavens! I tell you, it had gone mad. I had—for my sins, I suppose, to go through the ordeal of looking into it myself. No eloquence could have been so withering to one's belief in mankind as his final burst of sincerity. He struggled with himself too. I saw it—I heard it. I saw the inconceivable mystery of a soul that knew no restraint, no faith, and no fear, yet struggling blindly with itself. I kept my head pretty well; but when I had him at last stretched on the couch, I wiped my forehead, while my legs shook under me as though I had carried half a ton on my back down that hill. And yet I had only supported him, his bony arm clasped round my neck—and he was not much heavier than a child.

"When next day we left at noon, the crowd, of whose presence behind the curtain of trees I had been acutely conscious all the time, flowed out of the woods again, filled the clearing, covered the slope with a mass of naked, breathing, quivering, bronze bodies. I steamed up a bit, then swung down-stream, and two thousand eyes followed the evolutions of the splashing, thumping, fierce river-demon beating the water with its terrible tail and breathing black smoke into the air. In front of the first rank, along the river, three men, plastered with bright red earth from head to foot, strutted to and fro restlessly. When we came abreast again, they faced the river, stamped their feet, nodded their horned heads, swayed their scarlet bodies; they shook towards the fierce river-demon a bunch of black feathers, a mangy skin with a pendent tail—something that looked like a dried gourd; they shouted periodically together strings of amazing words that resembled no sounds of human language; and the deep murmurs of the crowd, interrupted suddenly, were like the responses of some satanic litany.

"We had carried Kurtz into the pilot-house; there was more air there. Lying on the couch, he stared through the open shutter. There was an eddy in the mass of human bodies, and the woman with helmeted head and tawny cheeks rushed out to the very brink of the stream. She put out her hands, shouted something, and all that wild mob took up the shout in a roaring chorus of articulated, rapid, breathless utterance.

" 'Do you understand this?' I asked.

"He kept on looking out past me with fiery, longing eyes, with a mingled expression of wistfulness and hate. He made no answer, but I saw a smile, a smile of indefinable meaning, appear on his colourless lips that a moment after twitched convulsively. 'Do I not?' he said slowly, gasping, as if the words had been torn out of him by a supernatural power.

"I pulled the string of the whistle, and I did this because I saw the pilgrims on deck getting out their rifles with an air of anticipating a jolly lark. At the sudden screech there was a movement of abject terror through that wedged mass of bodies. 'Don't! don't you frighten them away,' cried some one on deck disconsolately. I pulled the string time after time. They broke and ran, they leaped, they crouched, they swerved, they dodged the flying terror of the sound. The three red chaps had fallen flat, face down on the shore, as though they had been shot dead. Only the barbarous and superb woman did not so much as flinch, and stretched tragically her bare arms after us over the sombre and glittering river.

"And then that imbecile crowd down on the deck started their little fun, and I could see nothing more for smoke.

"The brown current ran swiftly out of the heart of darkness, bearing us down towards the sea with twice the speed of our upward progress; and Kurtz's life was running swiftly too, ebbing, ebbing out of his heart into the sea of inexorable time. The manager was very placid, he had no vital anxieties now, he took us both in with a comprehensive and satisfied glance: the 'affair' had come off as well as could be wished. I saw the time approaching when I would be left alone of the party of 'unsound method.' The pilgrims looked upon me with disfavour. I was, so to speak, numbered with the dead. It is strange how I accepted this unforeseen partnership, this choice of nightmares forced upon me in the tenebrous land invaded by these mean and greedy phantoms.

"Kurtz discoursed. A voice! a voice! It rang deep to the very last. It survived his strength to hide in the magnificent folds of eloquence the barren darkness of his heart. Oh, he struggled! he struggled! The wastes of his weary brain were haunted by shadowy images now—images of wealth and fame revolving obsequiously round his unextinguishable gift of noble and lofty expression. My Intended, my station, my career, my ideas—these were the subjects for the occasional utterances of elevated sentiments. The shade of the original Kurtz frequented the bedside of the hollow sham, whose fate it was to be buried presently in the mould of primeval earth. But both the diabolic love and the unearthly hate of the mysteries it had penetrated fought for the possession of that soul satiated with primitive emotions, avid of lying fame, of sham distinction, of all the appearances of success and power.

"Sometimes he was contemptibly childish. He desired to have kings meet him at railway stations on his return from some ghastly Nowhere, where he intended to accomplish great things. 'You show them you have in you something that is really profitable, and then there will be no limits to the recognition of your ability,' he would say. 'Of course you must take care of the motives—right motives—always.' The long reaches that were like one and the same reach, monotonous bends that were exactly alike, slipped past the steamer with their multitude of secular trees looking patiently after this grimy fragment of another world, the forerunner of change, of conquest, of trade, of massacres, of blessings. I looked ahead—piloting. 'Close the shutter,' said Kurtz suddenly one day; 'I can't bear to look at this.' I did so. There was a silence. 'Oh, but I will wring your heart yet!'' he cried at the invisible wilderness.

"We broke down—as I had expected—and had to lie up for repairs at the head of an island. This delay was the first thing that shook Kurtz's confidence. One morning he gave me a packet of papers and a photograph—the lot tied together with a shoe-string. 'Keep this for me,' he said. 'This noxious fool' (meaning the manager) 'is capable of prying into my boxes when I am not looking.' In the afternoon I saw him. He was lying on his back with closed eyes, and I withdrew quietly, but I heard him mutter, 'Live rightly, die, die . . .' I listened. There was nothing more. Was he rehearsing some speech in his sleep, or was it a fragment of a phrase from some newspaper article? He had been writing for the papers and meant to do so again, 'for the furthering of my ideas. It's a duty.'

"His was an impenetrable darkness. I looked at him as you peer down at a man who is lying at the bottom of a precipice where the sun never shines. But I had not much time to give him, because I was helping the engine-driver to take to pieces the leaky cylinders, to straighten a bent connecting-rod, and in other such matters. I lived in an infernal mess of rust, filings, nuts, bolts, spanners, hammers, ratchet-drills—things I abominate, because I don't get on with them. I tended the little forge we fortunately had aboard; I toiled wearily in a wretched scrap-heap—unless I had the shakes too bad to stand.

"One evening coming in with a candle I was startled to hear him say a little tremulously, 'I am lying here in the dark waiting for death.' The light was within a foot of his eyes. I forced myself to murmur, 'Oh, nonsense!' and stood over him as if transfixed.

"Anything approaching the change that came over his features I have never seen before, and hope never to see again. Oh, I wasn't touched. I was fascinated. It was as though a veil had been rent. I saw on that ivory face the expression of sombre pride, of ruthless power, of craven terror—of an intense and hopeless despair. Did he live his life again in every detail of desire, temptation, and surrender during that supreme moment of complete knowledge? He cried in a whisper at some image, at some vision—he cried out twice, a cry that was no more than a breath:

" 'The horror! The horror!'

"I blew the candle out and left the cabin. The pilgrims were dining in the mess-room, and I took my place opposite the manager, who lifted his eyes to give me a questioning glance, which I successfully ignored. He leaned back, serene, with that peculiar smile of his sealing the unexpressed depths of his meanness. A continuous shower of small flies streamed upon the lamp, upon the cloth, upon our hands and faces. Suddenly the manager's boy put his insolent black head in the doorway, and said in a tone of scathing contempt:

" 'Mistah Kurtz—he dead.'

"All the pilgrims rushed out to see. I remained, and went on with my dinner. I believe I was considered brutally callous. However, I did not eat much. There was a lamp in there—light, don't you know—and outside it was so beastly, beastly dark. I went no more near the remarkable man who had pronounced a judgment upon the adventures of his soul on this earth. The voice was gone. What else had been there? But I am of course aware that next day the pilgrims buried something in a muddy hole.

"And then they very nearly buried me.

"However, as you see, I did not go to join Kurtz there and then. I did not. I remained to dream the nightmare out to the end, and to show my loyalty to Kurtz once more. Destiny. My destiny! Droll thing life is—that mysterious arrangement of merciless logic for a futile purpose. The most you can hope from it is some knowledge of yourself—that comes too late—a crop of unextinguishable regrets. I have wrestled with death. It is the most unexciting contest you can imagine. It takes place in an impalpable greyness, with nothing underfoot, with nothing around, without spectators, without clamour, without glory, without the great desire of victory, without the great fear of defeat, in a sickly atmosphere of tepid scepticism, without much belief in your own right, and still less in that of your adversary. If such is the form of ultimate wisdom, then life is a greater riddle than some of us think it to be. I was within a hair's-breadth of the last opportunity for pronouncement, and I found with humiliation that probably I would have nothing to say. This is the reason why I affirm that Kurtz was a remarkable man. He had something to say. He said it. Since I had peeped over the edge myself, I understand better the meaning of his stare, that could not see the flame of the candle, but was wide enough to embrace the whole universe, piercing enough to penetrate all the hearts that beat in the darkness. He had summed up—he had judged. 'The horror!' He was a remarkable man. After all, this was the expression of some sort of belief; it had candour, it had conviction, it had a vibrating note of revolt in its whisper, it had the appalling face of a glimpsed truth—the strange commingling of desire and hate. And it is not my own extremity I remember best—a vision of greyness without form filled with physical pain, and a careless contempt for the evanescence of all things—even of this pain itself. No! It is his extremity that I seem to have lived through. True, he had made that last stride, he had stepped over the edge, while I had been permitted to draw back my hesitating foot. And perhaps in this is the whole difference; perhaps all the wisdom, and all truth, and all sincerity, are just compressed into that inappreciable moment of time in which we step over the threshold of the invisible. Perhaps! I like to think my summing-up would not have been a word of careless contempt. Better his cry—much better. It was an affirmation, a moral victory paid for by innumerable defeats by abominable terrors, by abominable satisfactions. But it was a victory! That is why I have remained loyal to Kurtz to the last, and even beyond, when a long time after I heard once more, not his own voice, but the echo of his magnificent eloquence thrown to me from a soul as translucently pure as a cliff of crystal.

"No, they did not bury me, though there is a period of time which I remember mistily, with a shuddering wonder, like a passage through some inconceivable world that had no hope in it and no desire. I found myself back in the sepulchral city resenting the sight of people hurrying through the streets to filch a little money from each other, to devour their infamous cookery, to gulp their unwholesome beer, to dream their insignificant and silly dreams. They trespassed upon my thoughts. They were intruders whose knowledge of life was to me an irritating pretence, because I felt so sure they could not possibly know the things I knew. Their bearing, which was simply the bearing of commonplace individuals going about their business in the assurance of perfect safety, was offensive to me like the outrageous flauntings of folly in the face of a danger it is unable to comprehend. I had no particular desire to enlighten them, but I had some difficulty in restraining myself from laughing in their faces, so full of stupid importance. I daresay I was not very well at that time. I tottered about the streets—there were various affairs to settle—grinning bitterly at perfectly respectable persons. I admit my behaviour was inexcusable, but then my temperature was seldom normal in these days. My dear aunt's endeavours to 'nurse up my strength' seemed altogether beside the mark. It was not my strength that wanted nursing, it was my imagination that wanted soothing. I kept the bundle of papers given me by Kurtz, not knowing exactly what to do with it. His mother had died lately, watched over, as I was told, by his Intended. A clean-shaved man, with an official manner and wearing gold-rimmed spectacles, called on me one day and made inquiries, at first circuitous, afterwards suavely pressing, about what he was pleased to denominate certain 'documents.' I was not surprised, because I had had two rows with the manager on the subject out there. I had refused to give up the smallest scrap out of that package, and I took the same attitude with the spectacled man. He became darkly menacing at last, and with much heat argued that the Company had the right to every bit of information about its 'territories.' And, said he, 'Mr. Kurtz's knowledge of unexplored regions must have been necessarily extensive and peculiar—owing to his great abilities and to the deplorable circumstances in which he had been placed: therefore——' I assured him Mr. Kurtz's knowledge, however extensive, did not bear upon the problems of commerce or administration. He invoked then the name of science. 'It would be an incalculable loss if,' etc. etc. I offered him the report on the 'Suppression of Savage Customs,' with the postscriptum torn off. He took it up eagerly, but ended by sniffing at it with an air of contempt. 'This is not what we had a right to expect,' he remarked. 'Expect nothing else,' I said. 'There are only private letters.' He withdrew upon some threat of legal proceedings, and I saw him no more; but another fellow, calling himself Kurtz's cousin, appeared two days later, and was anxious to hear all the details about his dear relative's last moments. Incidentally he gave me to understand that Kurtz had been essentially a great musician. 'There was the making of an immense success,' said the man, who was an organist, I believe, with lank grey hair flowing over a greasy coat-collar. I had no reason to doubt his statement; and to this day I am unable to say what was Kurtz's profession, whether he ever had any—which was the greatest of his talents. I had taken him for a painter who wrote for the papers, or else for a journalist who could paint—but even the cousin (who took snuff during the interview) could not tell me what he had been—exactly. He was a universal genius—on that point I agreed with the old chap, who thereupon blew his nose noisily into a large cotton handkerchief and withdrew in senile agitation, bearing off some family letters and memoranda without importance. Ultimately a journalist anxious to know something of the fate of his 'dear colleague' turned up. This visitor informed me Kurtz's proper sphere ought to have been politics 'on the popular side.' He had furry straight eyebrows, bristly hair cropped short, an eyeglass on a broad ribbon, and, becoming expansive, confessed his opinion that Kurtz really couldn't write a bit—'but Heavens! how that man could talk! He electrified large meetings. He had faith—don't you see?—he had the faith. He could get himself to believe anything—anything. He would have been a splendid leader of an extreme party.' 'What party?' I asked. 'Any party,' answered the other. 'He was an—an—extremist.' Did I not think so? I assented. Did I know, he asked, with a sudden flash of curiosity, 'what it was that had induced him to go out there?' 'Yes,' said I, and forthwith handed him the famous Report for publication, if he thought fit. He glanced through it hurriedly, mumbling all the time, judged 'it would do,' and took himself off with this plunder.

"Thus I was left at last with a slim packet of letters and the girl's portrait. She struck me as beautiful—I mean she had a beautiful expression. I know that the sunlight can be made to lie too, yet one felt that no manipulation of light and pose could have conveyed the delicate shade of truthfulness upon those features. She seemed ready to listen without mental reservation, without suspicion, without a thought for herself. I concluded I would go and give her back her portrait and those letters myself. Curiosity? Yes; and also some other feeling perhaps. All that had been Kurtz's had passed out of my hands: his soul, his body, his station, his plans, his ivory, his career. There remained only his memory and his Intended—and I wanted to give that up too to the past, in a way—to surrender personally all that remained of him with me to that oblivion which is the last word of our common fate. I don't defend myself. I had no clear perception of what it was I really wanted. Perhaps it was an impulse of unconscious loyalty, or the fulfilment of one of those ironic necessities that lurk in the fact of human existence. I don't know. I can't tell. But I went.

"I thought his memory was like the other memories of the dead that accumulate in every man's life—a vague impress on the brain of shadows that had fallen on it in their swift and final passage; but before the high and ponderous door, between the tall houses of a street as still and decorous as a well-kept alley in a cemetery, I had a vision of him on the stretcher, opening his mouth voraciously, as if to devour all the earth with all its mankind. He lived then before me; he lived as much as he had ever lived—a shadow insatiable of splendid appearances, of frightful realities; a shadow darker than the shadow of the night, and draped nobly in the folds of a gorgeous eloquence. The vision seemed to enter the house with me—the stretcher, the phantom-bearers, the wild crowd of obedient worshippers, the gloom of the forests, the glitter of the reach between the murky bends, the beat of the drum, regular and muffled like the beating of a heart—the heart of a conquering darkness. It was a moment of triumph for the wilderness, an invading and vengeful rush which, it seemed to me, I would have to keep back alone for the salvation of another soul. And the memory of what I had heard him say afar there, with the horned shapes stirring at my back, in the glow of fires, within the patient woods, those broken phrases came back to me, were heard again in their ominous and terrifying simplicity. I remembered his abject pleading, his abject threats, the colossal scale of his vile desires, the meanness, the torment, the tempestuous anguish of his soul. And later on I seemed to see his collected languid manner, when he said one day, 'This lot of ivory now is really mine. The Company did not pay for it. I collected it myself at a very great personal risk. I am afraid they will try to claim it as theirs though. H'm. It is a difficult case. What do you think I ought to do—resist? Eh? I want no more than justice.' . . . He wanted no more than justice—no more than justice. I rang the bell before a mahogany door on the first floor, and while I waited he seemed to stare at me out of the glassy panel—stare with that wide and immense stare embracing, condemning, loathing all the universe. I seemed to hear the whispered cry, 'The horror! The horror!'

"The dusk was falling. I had to wait in a lofty drawing-room with three long windows from floor to ceiling that were like three luminous and bedraped columns. The bent gilt legs and backs of the furniture shone in indistinct curves. The tall marble fireplace had a cold and monumental whiteness. A grand piano stood massively in a corner; with dark gleams on the flat surfaces like a sombre and polished sarcophagus. A high door opened—closed. I rose.

"She came forward, all in black, with a pale head, floating towards me in the dusk. She was in mourning. It was more than a year since his death, more than a year since the news came; she seemed as though she would remember and mourn for ever. She took both my hands in hers and murmured, 'I had heard you were coming.' I noticed she was not very young—I mean not girlish. She had a mature capacity for fidelity, for belief, for suffering. The room seemed to have grown darker, as if all the sad light of the cloudy evening had taken refuge on her forehead. This fair hair, this pale visage, this pure brow, seemed surrounded by an ashy halo from which the dark eyes looked out at me. Their glance was guileless, profound, confident, and trustful. She carried her sorrowful head as though she were proud of that sorrow, as though she would say, I—I alone know how to mourn for him as he deserves. But while we were still shaking hands, such a look of awful desolation came upon her face that I perceived she was one of those creatures that are not the playthings of Time. For her he had died only yesterday. And, by Jove! the impression was so powerful that for me too he seemed to have died only yesterday—nay, this very minute. I saw her and him in the same instant of time—his death and her sorrow—I saw her sorrow in the very moment of his death. Do you understand? I saw them together—I heard them together. She had said, with a deep catch of the breath, 'I have survived'; while my strained ears seemed to hear distinctly, mingled with her tone of despairing regret, the summing-up whisper of his eternal condemnation. I asked myself what I was doing there, with a sensation of panic in my heart as though I had blundered into a place of cruel and absurd mysteries not fit for a human being to behold. She motioned me to a chair. We sat down. I laid the packet gently on the little table, and she put her hand over it. . . . 'You knew him well,' she murmured, after a moment of mourning silence.

" 'Intimacy grows quickly out there,' I said. 'I knew him as well as it is possible for one man to know another.'

" 'And you admired him,' she said. 'It was impossible to know him and not to admire him. Was it?'

" 'He was a remarkable man,' I said unsteadily. Then before the appealing fixity of her gaze, that seemed to watch for more words on my lips, I went on, 'It was impossible not to——'

" 'Love him,' she finished eagerly, silencing me into an appalled dumbness. 'How true! how true! But when you think that no one knew him so well as I! I had all his noble confidence. I knew him best.'

" 'You knew him best,' I repeated. And perhaps she did. But with every word spoken the room was growing darker, and only her forehead, smooth and white, remained illumined by the unextinguishable light of belief and love.

" 'You were his friend,' she went on. 'His friend,' she repeated, a little louder. 'You must have been, if he had given you this, and sent you to me. I feel I can speak to you—and oh! I must speak. I want you—you who have heard his last words—to know I have been worthy of him. . . . It is not pride. . . . Yes! I am proud to know I understood him better than any one on earth—he told me so himself. And since his mother died I have had no one—no one—to—to——'

"I listened. The darkness deepened. I was not even sure whether he had given me the right bundle. I rather suspect he wanted me to take care of another batch of his papers which, after his death, I saw the manager examining under the lamp. And the girl talked, easing her pain in the certitude of my sympathy; she talked as thirsty men drink. I had heard that her engagement with Kurtz had been disapproved by her people. He wasn't rich enough or something. And indeed I don't know whether he had not been a pauper all his life. He had given me some reason to infer that it was his impatience of comparative poverty that drove him out there.

" '. . . Who was not his friend who had heard him speak once?' she was saying. 'He drew men towards him by what was best in them.' She looked at me with intensity. 'It is the gift of the great,' she went on, and the sound of her low voice seemed to have the accompaniment of all the other sounds, full of mystery, desolation, and sorrow, I had ever heard—the ripple of the river, the soughing of the trees swayed by the wind, the murmurs of the crowds, the faint ring of incomprehensible words cried from afar, the whisper of a voice speaking from beyond the threshold of an eternal darkness. 'But you have heard him! You know!' she cried.

" 'Yes, I know,' I said with something like despair in my heart, but bowing my head before the faith that was in her, before that great and saving illusion that shone with an unearthly glow in the darkness, in the triumphant darkness from which I could not have defended her—from which I could not even defend myself.

" 'What a loss to me—to us!'—she corrected herself with beautiful generosity; then added in a murmur, 'To the world.' By the last gleams of twilight I could see the glitter of her eyes, full of tears—of tears that would not fall.

" 'I have been very happy—very fortunate—very proud,' she went on. 'Too fortunate. Too happy for a little while. And now I am unhappy for—for life.'

"She stood up; her fair hair seemed to catch all the remaining light in a glimmer of gold. I rose too.

" 'And of all this,' she went on mournfully, 'of all his promise, and of all his greatness, of his generous mind, of his noble heart, nothing remains—nothing but a memory. You and I——'

" 'We shall always remember him,' I said hastily.

" 'No!' she cried. 'It is impossible that all this should be lost—that such a life should be sacrificed to leave nothing—but sorrow. You know what vast plans he had. I knew of them too—I could not perhaps understand—but others knew of them. Something must remain. His words, at least, have not died.'

" 'His words will remain,' I said.

" 'And his example,' she whispered to herself. 'Men looked up to him—his goodness shone in every act. His example——'

" 'True,' I said; 'his example too. Yes, his example. I forgot that.'

" 'But I do not. I cannot—I cannot believe—not yet. I cannot believe that I shall never see him again, that nobody will see him again, never, never, never.'

"She put out her arms as if after a retreating figure, stretching them back and with clasped pale hands across the fading and narrow sheen of the window. Never see him! I saw him clearly enough then. I shall see this eloquent phantom as long as I live, and I shall see her too, a tragic and familiar Shade, resembling in this gesture another one, tragic also, and bedecked with powerless charms, stretching bare brown arms over the glitter of the infernal stream, the stream of darkness. She said suddenly very low, 'He died as he lived.'

" 'His end,' said I, with dull anger stirring in me, 'was in every way worthy of his life.'

" 'And I was not with him,' she murmured. My anger subsided before a feeling of infinite pity.

" 'Everything that could be done——' I mumbled.

" 'Ah, but I believed in him more than any one on earth—more than his own mother, more than—himself. He needed me! Me! I would have treasured every sigh, every word, every sign, every glance.'

"I felt like a chill grip on my chest. 'Don't,' I said, in a muffled voice.

" 'Forgive me. I—I—have mourned so long in silence—in silence. . . . You were with him—to the last? I think of his loneliness. Nobody near to understand him as I would have understood. Perhaps no one to hear . . .'

" 'To the very end,' I said shakily. 'I heard his very last words. . . .' I stopped in a fright.

" 'Repeat them,' she murmured in a heart-broken tone. 'I want—I want—something—something—to—to live with.'

"I was on the point of crying at her, 'Don't you hear them?' The dusk was repeating them in a persistent whisper all around us, in a whisper that seemed to swell menacingly like the first whisper of a rising wind. 'The horror! The horror!'

" 'His last word—to live with,' she insisted. 'Don't you understand I loved him—I loved him—I loved him!'

"I pulled myself together and spoke slowly.

" 'The last word he pronounced was—your name.'

"I heard a light sigh and then my heart stood still, stopped dead short by an exulting and terrible cry, by the cry of inconceivable triumph and of unspeakable pain. 'I knew it—I was sure!' . . . she knew. She was sure. I heard her weeping; she had hidden her face in her hands. It seemed to me that the house would collapse before I could escape, that the heavens would fall upon my head. But nothing happened. The heavens do not fall for such a trifle. Would they have fallen, I wonder, if I had rendered Kurtz that justice which was his due? Hadn't he said he wanted only justice? But I couldn't. I could not tell her. It would have been too dark—too dark altogether. . . ."

Marlow ceased, and sat apart, indistinct and silent, in the pose of a meditating Buddha. Nobody moved for a time. "We have lost the first of the ebb," said the Director suddenly. I raised my head. The offing was barred by a black bank of clouds, and the tranquil waterway leading to the uttermost ends of the earth flowed sombre under an overcast sky—seemed to lead into the heart of an immense darkness.

The Great Gatsby

F. Scott Fitzgerald (1896–1940)

Francis Scott Key Fitzgerald was born in St. Paul, Minnesota, and received his education in private schools. He entered Princeton in 1913, where he became a friend of Edmund Wilson and John Peale Bishop, but left before graduation to join the army. While stationed near Montgomery, Alabama, he met the beautiful and vivacious Zelda Sayre; they were married in 1920, after Fitzgerald had finished his first novel, *This Side of Paradise* (1920), a largely autobiographical account of the manners and morals of the new postwar generation. Its success and that of his early stories made Fitzgerald instantly famous as the spokesman for the "Jazz Age." The best of these stories are collected in *Flappers and Philosophers* (1921), *Tales of the Jazz Age* (1922), and *All the Sad Young Men* (1926). In 1924 the Fitzgeralds left New York for the Riviera and Paris, where they joined the expatriate world described in *Tender Is the Night*. *The Great Gatsby* (1925) was the culmination of the first half of Fitzgerald's career: in it the tragic limitations of the "American Dream" are movingly dramatized.

As the 1920s came to a frenzied close, Fitzgerald succumbed to personal and financial pressures, finding it more and more difficult to write. This sense of collapse is embodied in his last finished novel, *Tender Is the Night* (1934), and in stories such as "Babylon Revisited" (1931). During the early 1930s Zelda Fitzgerald suffered a mental breakdown and spent the rest of her life in a sanatorium. Fitzgerald moved to Hollywood, where he worked on films and began a novel, *The Last Tycoon*, based on his Hollywood experiences. It was unfinished at the time of his death in 1940. His last years were marked by a steady physical and psychological decline that Fitzgerald often handled with tragic dignity.

CHAPTER I

In my younger and more vulnerable years my father gave me some advice that I've been turning over in my mind ever since.

"Whenever you feel like criticizing anyone," he told me, "just remember that all the people in this world haven't had the advantages that you've had."

He didn't say any more, but we've always been unusually communicative in a reserved way, and I understood that he meant a great deal more than that. In consequence, I'm inclined to reserve all judgments, a habit that has opened up many curious natures to me and also made me the victim of not a few veteran bores. The abnormal mind is quick to detect and attach itself to this quality when it appears in a normal person, and so it came about that in college I was unjustly accused of being a politician, because I was privy to the secret griefs of wild, unknown men. Most of the confidences were unsought—frequently I have feigned sleep, preoccupation, or a hostile levity when I realized by some unmistakable sign that an intimate revelation was quivering on the horizon; for the intimate revelations of young men, or at least the terms in which they express them, are usually plagiaristic and marred by obvious suppressions. Reserving judgments is a matter of infinite hope. I am still a little afraid of missing something if I forget that, as my father snobbishly suggested, and I snobbishly repeat, a sense of the fundamental decencies is parceled out unequally at birth.

And, after boasting this way of my tolerance, I come to the admission that it has a limit. Conduct may be founded on the hard rock or the wet marshes, but after a certain point I don't care what it's founded on. When I came back from the East last autumn I felt that I wanted the world to be in uniform and at a sort of moral attention forever; I wanted no more riotous excursions with privileged glimpses into the human heart. Only Gatsby, the man who gives his name to this book, was exempt from my reaction—Gatsby, who represented everything for which I have an unaffected scorn. If personality is an unbroken series of successful gestures, then there was something gorgeous about him, some heightened sensitivity to the promises of life, as if he were related to one of those intricate machines that register earthquakes ten thousand miles away. This responsiveness had nothing to do with that flabby impressionability which is dignified under the name of the "creative temperament"—it was an extraordinary gift for hope, a romantic readiness such as I have never found in any other person and which it is not likely I shall ever find again. No—Gatsby turned out all right at the end; it is what preyed on Gatsby, what foul dust floated in the wake of his dreams that temporarily closed out my interest in the abortive sorrows and short-winded elations of men.

My family have been prominent, well-to-do people in this Middle Western city for three generations. The Carraways are something of a clan, and we have a tradition that we're descended from the Dukes of Buccleuch, but the actual founder of my line was my grandfather's brother, who came here in fifty-one, sent a substitute to the Civil War, and started the wholesale hardware business that my father carries on today.

I never saw this great-uncle, but I'm supposed to look like him—with special reference to the rather hard-boiled painting that hangs in father's office. I graduated from New Haven in 1915, just a quarter of a century after my father, and a little later I participated in that delayed Teutonic migration known as the Great War. I enjoyed the counterraid so thoroughly that I came back restless. Instead of being the warm center of the world, the Middle West now seemed like the ragged edge of the universe—so I decided to go East and learn the bond business. Everybody I knew was in the bond business, so I supposed it could support one more single man. All my aunts and uncles talked it over as if they were choosing a prep school for me, and finally said, "Why—ye-es," with very grave, hesitant faces. Father agreed to finance me for a year, and after various delays I came East, permanently, I thought, in the spring of twenty-two.

The practical thing was to find rooms in the city, but it was a warm season, and I had just left a country of wide lawns and friendly trees, so when a young man at the office suggested that we take a house together in a commuting town, it sounded like a great idea. He found the house, a weatherbeaten cardboard bungalow at eighty a month, but at the last minute the firm ordered him to Washington, and I went out to the country alone. I had a dog—at least I had him for a few days until he ran away—and an old Dodge and a Finnish woman, who made my bed and cooked breakfast and muttered Finnish wisdom to herself over the electric stove.

It was lonely for a day or so until one morning some man, more recently arrived than I, stopped me on the road.

"How do you get to West Egg Village?" he asked helplessly.

I told him. And as I walked on I was lonely no longer. I was a guide, a pathfinder, an original settler. He had casually conferred on me the freedom of the neighborhood.

And so with the sunshine and the great bursts of leaves growing on the trees, just as things grow in fast movies, I had that familiar conviction that life was beginning over again with the summer.

There was so much to read, for one thing, and so much fine health to be pulled down out of the young breath-giving air. I bought a dozen volumes on banking and credit and investment securities, and they stood on my shelf in red and gold like new money from the mint, promising to unfold the shining secrets that only Midas and Morgan and Maecenas knew. And I had the high intention of reading many other books besides. I was rather literary in college—one year I wrote a series of very solemn and obvious editorials for the *Yale News*—and now I was going to bring back all such things into my life and become again that most limited of all specialists, the "well-rounded man." This isn't just an epigram—life is much more successfully looked at from a single window, after all.

It was a matter of chance that I should have rented a house in one of the strangest communities in North America. It was on that slender riotous island which extends itself due east of New York—and where there are, among other natural curiosities, two unusual formations of land. Twenty miles from the city a pair of enormous eggs, identical in contour and separated only by a courtesy bay, jut out into the most domesticated body of salt water in the Western Hemisphere, the great wet barnyard of Long Island Sound. They are not perfect ovals—like the egg in the Columbus story, they are both crushed flat at the contact end—but their physical resemblance must be a source of perpetual confusion to the gulls that fly overhead. To the wingless a more arresting phenomenon is their dissimilarity in every particular except shape and size.

I lived at West Egg, the—well, the less fashionable of the two, though this is a most superficial tag to express the bizarre and not a little sinister contrast between them. My house was at the very tip of the egg, only fifty yards from the Sound, and squeezed between two huge places that rented for twelve or fifteen thousand a season. The one on my right was a colossal affair by any standard—it was a factual imitation of some *hôtel de ville* in Normandy, with a tower on one side, spanking new under a thin beard of raw ivy, and a marble swimming pool, and more than forty acres of lawn and garden. It was Gatsby's mansion. Or, rather, as I didn't know Mr. Gatsby, it was a mansion, inhabited by a gentleman of that name. My own house was an eyesore, but it was a small eyesore, and it had been overlooked, so I had a view of the water, a partial view of my neighbor's lawn, and the consoling proximity of millionaires—all for eighty dollars a month.

Across the courtesy bay the white palaces of fashionable East Egg glittered along the water, and the history of the summer really begins on the evening I drove over there to have dinner with the Tom Buchanans. Daisy was my second cousin once removed, and I'd known Tom in college. And just after the war I spent two days with them in Chicago.

Her husband, among various physical accomplishments, had been one of the most powerful ends that ever played football at New Haven—a national figure in a way, one of those men who reach such an acute limited excellence at twenty-one that everything afterward savors of anticlimax. His family were enormously wealthy—even in college his freedom with money was a matter for reproach—but now he'd left Chicago and come East in a fashion that rather took your breath away; for instance, he'd brought down a string of polo ponies from Lake Forest. It was hard to realize that a man in my own generation was wealthy enough to do that.

Why they came East I don't know. They had spent a year in France for no particular reason, and then drifted here and there unrestfully wherever people played polo and were rich together. This was a permanent move, said Daisy over the telephone, but I didn't believe it—I had no sight into Daisy's heart, but I felt that Tom would drift on forever seeking, a little wistfully, for the dramatic turbulence of some irrecoverable football game.

And so it happened that on a warm windy evening I drove over to East Egg to see two old friends whom I scarcely knew at all. Their house was even more elaborate than I expected, a cheerful red-and-white Georgian Colonial mansion, overlooking the bay. The lawn started at the beach and ran toward the front door for a quarter of a mile, jumping over sundials and brick walls and burning gardens—finally when it reached the house drifting up the side in bright vines as though from the momentum of its run. The front was broken by a line of French windows, glowing now with reflected gold and wide open to the warm windy afternoon, and Tom Buchanan in riding clothes was standing with his legs apart on the front porch.

He had changed since his New Haven years. Now he was a sturdy straw-haired man of thirty with a rather hard mouth and a supercilious manner. Two shining arrogant eyes had established dominance over his face and gave him the appearance of always leaning aggressively forward. Not even the effeminate swank of his riding clothes could hide the enormous power of that body—he seemed to fill those glistening boots until he strained the top lacing, and you could see a great pack of muscle shifting when his shoulder moved under his thin coat. It was a body capable of enormous leverage—a cruel body.

His speaking voice, a gruff husky tenor, added to the impression of fractiousness he conveyed. There was a touch of paternal contempt in it, even toward people he liked—and there were men at New Haven who had hated his guts.

"Now, don't think my opinion on these matters is final," he seemed to say, "just because I'm stronger and more of a man than you are." We were in the same senior society, and while we were never intimate I always had the impression that he approved of me and wanted me to like him with some harsh, defiant wistfulness of his own.

We talked for a few minutes on the sunny porch.

"I've got a nice place here," he said, his eyes flashing about restlessly.

Turning me around by one arm, he moved a broad flat hand along the front vista, including in its sweep a sunken Italian garden, a half acre of deep, pungent roses, and a snub-nosed motorboat that bumped the tide offshore.

"It belonged to Demaine, the oil man." He turned me around again, politely and abruptly. "We'll go inside."

We walked through a high hallway into a bright rosy-colored space, fragilely bound into the house by French windows at either end. The windows were ajar and gleaming white against the fresh grass outside that seemed to grow a little way into the house. A breeze blew through the room, blew curtains in at one end and out the other like pale flags, twisting them up toward the frosted wedding cake of the ceiling, and then rippled over the wine-colored rug, making a shadow on it as wind does on the sea.

The only completely stationary object in the room was an enormous couch on which two young women were buoyed up as though upon an anchored balloon. They were both in white, and their dresses were rippling and fluttering as if they had just been blown back in after a short flight around the house. I must have stood for a few moments listening to the whip and snap of the curtains and the groan of a picture on the wall. Then there was a boom as Tom Buchanan shut the rear windows and the caught wind died out about the room, and the curtains and the rugs and the two young women ballooned slowly to the floor.

The younger of the two was a stranger to me. She was extended full length at her end of the divan, completely motionless, and with her chin raised a little, as if she were balancing something on it which was quite likely to fall. If she saw me out of the corner of her eyes she gave no hint of it—indeed, I was almost surprised into murmuring an apology for having disturbed her by coming in.

The other girl, Daisy, made an attempt to rise—she leaned slightly forward with a conscientious expression—then she laughed, an absurd, charming little laugh, and I laughed too and came forward into the room.

"I'm p-paralyzed with happiness."

She laughed again, as if she said something very witty, and held my hand for a moment, looking up into my face, promising that there was no one in the world she so much wanted to see. That was a way she had. She hinted in a murmur that the surname of the balancing girl was Baker. (I've heard it said that Daisy's murmur was only to make people lean toward her; an irrelevant criticism that made it no less charming.)

At any rate, Miss Baker's lips fluttered, she nodded at me almost imperceptibly, and then quickly tipped her head back again—the object she was balancing had obviously tottered a little and given her something of a fright. Again a sort of apology arose to my lips. Almost any exhibition of complete self-sufficiency draws a stunned tribute from me.

I looked back at my cousin, who began to ask me questions in her low, thrilling voice. It was the kind of voice that the ear follows up and down, as if each speech is an arrangement of notes that will never be played again. Her face was sad and lovely with bright things in it, bright eyes and a bright passionate mouth, but there was an excitement in her voice that men who had cared for her found difficult to forget: a singing compulsion, a whispered "Listen," a promise that she had done gay, exciting things just a while since and that there were gay, exciting things hovering in the next hour.

I told her how I had stopped off in Chicago for a day on my way East, and how a dozen people had sent their love through me.

"Do they miss me?" she cried ecstatically.

"The whole town is desolate. All the cars have the left rear wheel painted black as a mourning wreath, and there's a persistent wail all night along the North Shore."

"How gorgeous! Let's go back, Tom. Tomorrow!" Then she added irrelevantly: "You ought to see the baby."

"I'd like to."

"She's asleep. She's three years old. Haven't you ever seen her?"

"Never."

"Well, you ought to see her. She's——"

Tom Buchanan, who had been hovering restlessly about the room, stopped and rested his hand on my shoulder.

"What you doing, Nick?"

"I'm a bond man."

"Who with?"

I told him.

"Never heard of them," he remarked decisively.

This annoyed me.

"You will," I answered shortly. "You will if you stay in the East."

"Oh, I'll stay in the East, don't you worry," he said, glancing at Daisy and then back at me, as if he were alert for something more. "I'd be a God-damned fool to live anywhere else."

At this point Miss Baker said: "Absolutely!" with such suddenness that I started—it was the first word she had uttered since I came into the room. Evidently it surprised her as much as it did me, for she yawned and with a series of rapid, deft movements stood up into the room.

"I'm stiff," she complained, "I've been lying on that sofa for as long as I can remember."

"Don't look at me," Daisy retorted, "I've been trying to get you to New York all afternoon."

"No, thanks," said Miss Baker to the four cocktails just in from the pantry, "I'm absolutely in training."

Her host looked at her incredulously.

"You are!" He took down his drink as if it were a drop in the bottom of a glass. "How you ever get anything done is beyond me."

I looked at Miss Baker, wondering what it was she "got done." I enjoyed looking at her. She was a slender, small-breasted girl, with an erect carriage, which she accentuated by throwing her body backward at the shoulders like a young cadet. Her gray sun-strained eyes looked back at me with polite reciprocal curiosity out of a wan, charming, discontented face. It occurred to me now that I had seen her, or a picture of her, somewhere before.

"You live in West Egg," she remarked contemptuously. "I know somebody there."

"I don't know a single——"

"You must know Gatsby."

"Gatsby?" demanded Daisy. "What Gatsby?"

Before I could reply that he was my neighbor, dinner was announced; wedging his tense arm imperatively under mine, Tom Buchanan compelled me from the room as though he were moving a checker to another square.

Slenderly, languidly, their hands set lightly on their hips, the two young women preceded us out onto a rosy-colored porch, open toward the sunset, where four candles flickered on the table in the diminished wind.

"Why *candles?"* objected Daisy, frowning. She snapped them out with her fingers. "In two weeks it'll be the longest day in the year." She looked at us all radiantly. "Do you always watch for the longest day of the year and then miss it? I always watch for the longest day in the year and then miss it."

"We ought to plan something," yawned Miss Baker, sitting down at the table as if she were getting into bed.

"All right," said Daisy. "What'll we plan?" She turned to me helplessly: "What do people plan?"

Before I could answer her eyes fastened with an awed expression on her little finger.

"Look!" she complained; "I hurt it."

We all looked—the knuckle was black and blue.

"You did it, Tom," she said accusingly. "I know you didn't meant to, but you *did* do it. That's what I get for marrying a brute of a man, a great, big, hulking physical specimen of a——"

"I hate that word hulking," objected Tom crossly, "even in kidding."

"Hulking," insisted Daisy.

Sometimes she and Miss Baker talked at once, unobtrusively and with a bantering inconsequence that was never quite chatter, that was as cool as their white dresses and their impersonal eyes in the absence of all desire. They were here, and they accepted Tom and me, making only a polite pleasant effort to entertain or to be entertained. They knew that presently dinner would be over and a little later the evening, too, would be over and casually put away. It was sharply different from the West, where an evening was hurried from phase to phase toward its close, in a continually disappointed anticipation or else in sheer nervous dread of the moment itself.

"You make me feel uncivilized, Daisy," I confessed on my second glass of corky but rather impressive claret. "Can't you talk about crops or something?"

I meant nothing in particular by this remark, but it was taken up in an unexpected way.

"Civilization's going to pieces," broke out Tom violently. "I've gotten to be a terrible pessimist about things. Have you read *The Rise of the Colored Empires* by this man Goddard?"

"Why, no," I answered, rather surprised by his tone.

"Well, it's a fine book, and everybody ought to read it. The idea is if we don't look out the white race will be—will be utterly submerged. It's all scientific stuff; it's been proved."

"Tom's getting very profound," said Daisy, with an expression of unthoughtful sadness. "He reads deep books with long words in them. What was that word we——"

"Well, these books are all scientific," insisted Tom, glancing at her impatiently. "This fellow has worked out the whole thing. It's up to us, who are the dominant race, to watch out or these other races will have control of things."

"We've got to beat them down," whispered Daisy, winking ferociously toward the fervent sun.

"You ought to live in California—" began Miss Baker, but Tom interrupted her by shifting heavily in his chair.

"This idea is that we're Nordics. I am, and you are, and you are, and—" After an infinitesimal hesitation he included Daisy with a slight nod, and she winked at me again. "—And we've produced all the things that go to make civilization—oh, science and art, and all that. Do you see?"

There was something pathetic in his concentration, as if his complacency, more acute than of old, was not enough to him any more. When, almost immediately, the telephone rang inside and the butler left the porch Daisy seized upon the momentary interruption and leaned toward me.

"I'll tell you a family secret," she whispered enthusiastically. "It's about the butler's nose. Do you want to hear about the butler's nose?"

"That's why I came over tonight."

"Well, he wasn't always a butler; he used to be the silver polisher for some people in New York that had a silver service for two hundred people. He had to polish it from morning till night, until finally it began to affect his nose——"

"Things went from bad to worse," suggested Miss Baker.

"Yes. Things went from bad to worse, until finally he had to give up his position."

For a moment the last sunshine fell with romantic affection upon her glowing face; her voice compelled me forward breathlessly as I listened—then the glow faded, each light deserting her with lingering regret, like children leaving a pleasant street at dusk.

The butler came back and murmured something close to Tom's ear, whereupon Tom frowned, pushed back his chair, and without a word went inside. As if his absence quickened something within her, Daisy leaned forward again, her voice glowing and singing.

"I love to see you at my table, Nick. You remind me of a—of a rose, an absolute rose. Doesn't he?" She turned to Miss Baker for confirmation: "An absolute rose?"

This was untrue. I am not even faintly like a rose. She was only extemporizing, but a stirring warmth flowed from her, as if her heart was trying to come out to you concealed in one of those breathless, thrilling words. Then suddenly she threw her napkin on the table and excused herself and went into the house.

Miss Baker and I exchanged a short glance consciously devoid of meaning. I was about to speak when she sat up alertly and said "Sh!" in a warning voice. A subdued impassioned murmur was audible in the room beyond, and Miss Baker leaned forward unashamed, trying to hear. The murmur trembled on the verge of coherence, sank down, mounted excitedly, and then ceased altogether.

"This Mr. Gatsby you spoke of is my neighbor——" I began.

"Don't talk. I want to hear what happens."

"Is something happening?" I inquired innocently.

"You mean to say you don't know?" said Miss Baker, honestly surprised. "I thought everybody knew."

"I don't."

"Why—" she said hesitantly, "Tom's got some woman in New York."

"Got some woman?" I repeated blankly.

Miss Baker nodded.

"She might have the decency not to telephone him at dinnertime. Don't you think?"

Almost before I had grasped her meaning there was the flutter of a dress and the crunch of leather boots, and Tom and Daisy were back at the table.

"It couldn't be helped!" cried Daisy with tense gaiety.

She sat down, glanced searchingly at Miss Baker and then at me, and continued: "I looked outdoors for a minute, and it's very romantic outdoors. There's a bird on the lawn that I think must be a nightingale come over on the Cunard or White Star Line. He's singing away—" Her voice sang: "It's romantic, isn't it, Tom?"

"Very romantic," he said, and then miserably to me: "If it's light enough after dinner, I want to take you down to the stables."

The telephone rang inside, startlingly, and as Daisy shook her head decisively at Tom the subject of the stables, in fact all subjects, vanished into air. Among the broken fragments of the last five minutes at table I remember the candles being lit again, pointlessly, and I was conscious of wanting to look squarely at everyone, and yet to avoid all eyes. I couldn't guess what Daisy and Tom were thinking, but I doubt if even Miss Baker, who seemed to have mastered a certain hardy skepticism, was able utterly to put this fifth guest's shrill metallic urgency out of mind. To a certain temperament the situation might have seemed intriguing—my own instinct was to telephone immediately for the police.

The horses, needless to say, were not mentioned again. Tom and Miss Baker, with several feet of twilight between them, strolled back into the library, as if to a vigil beside a perfectly tangible body, while, trying to look pleasantly interested and a little deaf, I followed Daisy around a chain of connecting verandas to the porch in front. In its deep gloom we sat down side by side on a wicker settee.

Daisy took her face in her hands as if feeling its lovely shape, and her eyes moved gradually out into the velvet dusk. I saw that turbulent emotions possessed her, so I asked what I thought would be some sedative questions about her little girl.

"We don't know each other very well, Nick," she said suddenly. "Even if we are cousins. You didn't come to my wedding."

"I wasn't back from the war."

"That's true." She hesitated. "Well, I've had a very bad time, Nick, and I'm pretty cynical about everything."

Evidently she had reason to be. I waited but she didn't say any more, and after a moment I returned rather feebly to the subject of her daughter.

"I suppose she talks, and—eats, and everything."

"Oh, yes." She looked at me absently. "Listen, Nick; let me tell you what I said when she was born. Would you like to hear?"

"Very much."

"It'll show you how I've gotten to feel about—

things. Well, she was less than an hour old and Tom was God knows where. I woke up out of the ether with an utterly abandoned feeling, and asked the nurse right away if it was a boy or a girl. She told me it was a girl, and so I turned my head away and wept. 'All right,' I said, 'I'm glad it's a girl. And I hope she'll be a fool—that's the best thing a girl can be in this world, a beautiful little fool.'

"You see I think everything's terrible anyhow," she went on in a convinced way. "Everybody thinks so—the most advanced people. And I *know*. I've been everywhere and seen everything and done everything." Her eyes flashed around her in a defiant way, rather like Tom's, and she laughed with thrilling scorn. "Sophisticated—God, I'm sophisticated!"

The instant her voice broke off, ceasing to compel my attention, my belief, I felt the basic insincerity of what she had said. It made me uneasy, as though the whole evening had been a trick of some sort to exact a contributary emotion from me. I waited, and sure enough, in a moment she looked at me with an absolute smirk on her lovely face, as if she had asserted her membership in a rather distinguished secret society to which she and Tom belonged.

Inside, the crimson room bloomed with light. Tom and Miss Baker sat at either end of the long couch and she read aloud to him from the *Saturday Evening Post*—the words, murmurous and uninflected, running together in a soothing tune. The lamplight, bright on his boots and dull on the autumn-leaf yellow of her hair, glinted along the paper as she turned a page with a flutter of slender muscles in her arms.

When we came in she held us silent for a moment with a lifted hand.

"To be continued," she said, tossing the magazine on the table, "in our very next issue."

Her body asserted itself with a restless movement of her knee, and she stood up.

"Ten o'clock," she remarked, apparently finding the time on the ceiling. "Time for this good girl to go to bed."

"Jordan's going to play in the tournament tomorrow," explained Daisy, "over at Westchester."

"Oh—you're *Jor*dan Baker."

I knew now why her face was familiar—its pleasing contemptuous expression had looked out at me from many rotogravure pictures of the sporting life at Asheville and Hot Springs and Palm Beach. I had heard some story of her too, a critical, unpleasant story, but what it was I had forgotten long ago.

"Good night," she said softly. "Wake me at eight, won't you?"

"If you'll get up."

"I will. Good night, Mr. Carraway. See you anon."

"Of course you will," confirmed Daisy. "In fact, I think I'll arrange a marriage. Come over often, Nick, and I'll sort of—oh—fling you together. You know—lock you up accidentally in linen closets and push you out to sea in a boat, and all that sort of thing——"

"Good night," called Miss Baker from the stairs. "I haven't heard a word."

"She's a nice girl," said Tom after a moment. "They oughtn't to let her run around the country this way."

"Who oughtn't to?" inquired Daisy coldly.

"Her family."

"Her family is one aunt about a thousand years old. Besides, Nick's going to look after her, aren't you, Nick? She's going to spend lots of week ends out here this summer. I think the home influence will be very good for her."

Daisy and Tom looked at each other for a moment in silence.

"Is she from New York?" I asked quickly.

"From Louisville. Our white girlhood was passed together there. Our beautiful white——"

"Did you give Nick a little heart-to-heart talk on the veranda?" demanded Tom suddenly.

"Did I?" She looked at me. "I can't seem to remember, but I think we talked about the Nordic race. Yes, I'm sure we did. It sort of crept up on us and first thing you know——"

"Don't believe everything you hear, Nick," he advised me.

I said lightly that I had heard nothing at all, and a few minutes later I got up to go home. They came to the door with me and stood side by side in a cheerful square of light. As I started my motor Daisy peremptorily called: "Wait!

"I forgot to ask you something, and it's important. We heard you were engaged to a girl out West."

"That's right," corroborated Tom kindly. "We heard that you were engaged."

"It's a libel. I'm too poor."

"But we heard it," insisted Daisy, surprising me by opening up again in a flowerlike way. "We heard it from three people, so it must be true."

Of course I knew what they were referring to, but I wasn't even vaguely engaged. The fact that gossip had published the banns was one of the reasons I had come East. You can't stop going with an old friend on account of rumors, and on the other hand I had no intention of being rumored into marriage.

Their interest rather touched me and made them less remotely rich—nevertheless, I was confused and a little disgusted as I drove away. It seemed to me that the thing for Daisy to do was to rush out of the house, child in arms—but apparently there were no such intentions in her head. As for Tom, the fact that he "had some woman in New York" was really less surprising than that he had been depressed by a book. Something was making him nibble at the edge of stale ideas as if his sturdy physical egotism no longer nourished his peremptory heart.

Already it was deep summer on roadhouse roofs and in front of wayside garages, where new red gas pumps sat out in pools of light, and when I reached my estate at West Egg I ran the car under its shed and sat for a while on an abandoned grass roller in the yard. The wind had blown off, leaving a loud, bright night, with wings beating in the trees and a persistent organ sound as the full bellows of the earth blew the frogs full of life. The silhouette of a moving cat wavered across the moonlight, and turning my head to watch it, I saw that I was not alone—fifty feet away a figure had emerged from the shadow of my neighbor's mansion and was standing with his hands in his pockets regarding the silver pepper of the stars. Something in his leisurely movements and the secure position of his feet upon the lawn suggested that it was Mr. Gatsby himself, come out to determine what share was his of our local heavens.

I decided to call to him. Miss Baker had mentioned him at dinner, and that would do for an introduction. But I didn't call to him, for he gave a sudden intimation that he was content to be alone—he stretched out his arms toward the dark water in a curious way, and, far as I was from him, I could have sworn he was trembling. Involuntarily I glanced seaward—and distinguished nothing except a single green light, minute and far away, that might have been the end of a dock. When I looked once more for Gatsby he had vanished, and I was alone again in the unquiet darkness.

CHAPTER II

About half way between West Egg and New York the motor road hastily joins the railroad and runs beside it for a quarter of a mile, so as to shrink away from a certain desolate area of land. This is a valley of ashes—a fantastic farm where ashes grow like wheat into ridges and hills and grotesque gardens; where ashes take the forms of houses and chimneys and rising smoke and, finally, with a transcendent effort, of men who move dimly and already crumbling through the powdery air. Occasionally a line of gray cars crawls along an invisible track, gives out a ghastly creak, and comes to rest, and immediately the ash-gray men swarm up with leaden spades and stir up an impenetrable cloud, which screens their obscure operations from your sight.

But above the gray land and the spasms of bleak dust which drift endlessly over it, you perceive, after a moment, the eyes of Doctor T. J. Eckleburg. The eyes of Doctor T. J. Eckleburg are blue and gigantic—their retinas are one yard high. They look out of no face, but, instead, from a pair of enormous yellow spectacles which pass over a nonexistent nose. Evidently some wild wag of an oculist set them there to fatten his practice in the borough of Queens, and then sank down himself into eternal blindness, or forgot them and moved away. But his eyes, dimmed a little by many paintless days under sun and rain, brood on over the solemn dumping ground.

The valley of ashes is bounded on one side by a small foul river, and, when the drawbridge is up to let barges through, the passengers on waiting trains can stare at the dismal scene for as long as half an hour. There is always a halt there of at least a minute, and it was because of this that I first met Tom Buchanan's mistress.

The fact that he had one was insisted upon wherever he was known. His acquaintances resented the fact that he turned up in popular cafés with her and, leaving her at a table, sauntered about, chatting with whomsoever he knew. Though I was curious to see her, I had no desire to meet her—but I did. I went up to New York with Tom on the train one afternoon and when we stopped by the ashheaps he jumped to his feet and, taking hold of my elbow, literally forced me from the car.

"We're getting off," he insisted. "I want you to meet my girl."

I think he'd tanked up a good deal at luncheon, and his determination to have my company bordered on violence. The supercilious assumption was that on Sunday afternoon I had nothing better to do.

I followed him over a low whitewashed railroad fence, and we walked back a hundred yards along the road under Doctor Eckleburg's persistent stare. The only building in sight was a small block of yellow brick sitting on the edge of the wasteland, a sort of compact Main Street ministering to it, and contiguous to absolutely nothing. One of the three shops it contained was for rent and another was an all-night restaurant, approached by a trail of ashes; the third was a garage—*Repairs.* GEORGE B. WILSON. *Cars bought and sold.*—and I followed Tom inside.

The interior was unprosperous and bare; the only car visible was the dust-covered wreck of a Ford which crouched in a dim corner. It had occurred to me that this shadow of a garage must be a blind, and that sumptuous and romantic apartments were concealed overhead, when the proprietor himself appeared in the door of an office, wiping his hands on a piece of waste. He was a blond, spiritless man, anemic, and faintly handsome. When he saw us a damp gleam of hope sprang into his light blue eyes.

"Hello, Wilson, old man," said Tom, slapping him jovially on the shoulder. "How's business?"

"I can't complain," answered Wilson unconvincingly. "When are you going to sell me that car?"

"Next week; I've got my man working on it now."

"Works pretty slow, don't he?"

"No, he doesn't," said Tom coldly. "And if you feel that way about it, maybe I'd better sell it somewhere else after all."

"I don't mean that," explained Wilson quickly. "I just meant——"

His voice faded off and Tom glanced impatiently around the garage. Then I heard footsteps on a stairs, and in a moment the thickish figure of a woman blocked out the light from the office door. She was in the middle thirties, and faintly stout, but she carried her surplus flesh sensuously as some women can. Her face, above a spotted dress of dark blue crepe de Chine, contained no facet or gleam of beauty, but there was an immediately perceptible vitality about her as if the nerves of her body were continually smoldering. She smiled slowly and, walking through her husband as if he were a ghost, shook hands with Tom, looking him flush in the eye. Then she wet her lips, and without turning around spoke to her husband in a soft, coarse voice:

"Get some chairs, why don't you, so somebody can sit down."

"Oh, sure," agreed Wilson hurriedly, and went toward the little office, mingling immediately with the cement color of the walls. A white ashen dust veiled his dark suit and his pale hair as it veiled everything in the vicinity—except his wife, who moved close to Tom.

"I want to see you," said Tom intently. "Get on the next train."

"All right."

"I'll meet you by the newsstand on the lower level."

She nodded and moved away from him just as George Wilson emerged with two chairs from his office door.

We waited for her down the road and out of sight. It was a few days before the Fourth of July, and a gray, scrawny Italian child was setting torpedoes in a row along the railroad track.

"Terrible place, isn't it," said Tom, exchanging a frown with Doctor Eckleburg.

"Awful."

"It does her good to get away."

"Doesn't her husband object?"

"Wilson? He thinks she goes to see her sister in New York. He's so dumb he doesn't know he's alive."

So Tom Buchanan and his girl and I went up together to New York—or not quite together, for Mrs. Wilson sat discreetly in another car. Tom deferred that much to the sensibilities of those East Eggers who might be on the train.

She had changed her dress to a brown figured muslin, which stretched tight over her rather wide hips as Tom helped her to the platform in New York. At the newsstand she bought a copy of *Town Tattle* and a moving-picture magazine, and in the station drugstore some cold cream and a small flask of perfume. Upstairs, in the solemn echoing drive she let four taxicabs drive away before she selected a new one, lavender-colored with gray upholstery, and in this we slid out from the mass of the station into the glowing sunshine. But immediately she turned sharply from the window and, leaning forward, tapped on the front glass.

"I want to get one of those dogs," she said earnestly. "I want to get one for the apartment. They're nice to have—a dog."

We backed up to a gray old man who bore an absurd resemblance to John D. Rockefeller. In a basket swung from his neck cowered a dozen very recent puppies of an indeterminate breed.

"What kind are they?" asked Mrs. Wilson eagerly, as he came to the taxi window.

"All kinds. What kind do you want, lady?"

"I'd like to get one of those police dogs; I don't suppose you got that kind?"

The man peered doubtfully into the basket, plunged in his hand and drew one up, wriggling, by the back of the neck.

"That's no police dog," said Tom.

"No, it's not exactly a *police* dog," said the man with disappointment in his voice. "It's more of an Airedale." He passed his hand over the brown washrag of a back. "Look at that coat. Some coat. That's a dog that'll never bother you with catching cold."

"I think it's cute," said Mrs. Wilson enthusiastically. "How much is it?"

"That dog?" He looked at it admiringly. "That dog will cost you ten dollars."

The Airedale—undoubtedly there was an Airedale concerned in it somewhere, though its feet were startlingly white—changed hands and settled down into Mrs. Wilson's lap, where she fondled the weatherproof coat with rapture.

"Is it a boy or a girl?" she asked delicately.

"That dog? That dog's a boy."

"It's a bitch," said Tom decisively. "Here's your money. Go and buy ten more dogs with it."

We drove over to Fifth Avenue, so warm and soft, almost pastoral, on the summer Sunday afternoon that I wouldn't have been surprised to see a great flock of white sheep turn the corner.

"Hold on," I said, "I have to leave you here."

"No, you don't," interposed Tom quickly. "Myrtle'll be hurt if you don't come up to the apartment. Won't you, Myrtle?"

"Come on," she urged. "I'll telephone my sister Catherine. She's said to be very beautiful by people who ought to know."

"Well, I'd like to, but——"

We went on, cutting back again over the Park toward the West Hundreds. At 158th Street the cab stopped at one slice in a long white cake of apartment houses. Throwing a regal home-coming glance around the neighborhood, Mrs. Wilson gathered up her dog and her other purchases, and went haughtily in.

"I'm going to have the McKees come up," she announced as we rose in the elevator. "And, of course, I got to call up my sister, too."

The apartment was on the top floor—a small living room, a small dining room, a small bedroom, and a bath. The living room was crowded to the doors with a set of tapestried furniture entirely too large for it, so that to move about was to stumble continually over scenes of ladies swinging in the gardens of Versailles. The only picture was an overenlarged photograph, apparently a hen sitting on a blurred rock. Looked at from a distance, however, the hen resolved itself into a bonnet, and the countenance of a stout old lady beamed down into the room. Several old copies of *Town Tattle* lay on the table together with a copy of *Simon Called Peter,* and some of the small scandal magazines of Broadway. Mrs. Wilson was first concerned with the dog. A reluctant elevator boy went for a box full of straw and some milk, to which he added on his own initiative a tin of large, hard dog biscuits—one of which decomposed apathetically in the saucer of milk all afternoon. Meanwhile Tom brought out a bottle of whiskey from a locked bureau door.

I have been drunk just twice in my life, and the second time was that afternoon; so everything that happened has a dim, hazy cast over it, although until after eight o'clock the apartment was full of cheerful sun. Sitting on Tom's lap Mrs. Wilson called up several people on the telephone; then there were no cigarettes, and I went out to buy some at the drugstore on the corner. When I came back they had disappeared, so I sat down discreetly in the living room and read a chapter of *Simon Called Peter*—either it was terrible stuff or the whiskey distorted things, because it didn't make any sense to me.

Just as Tom and Myrtle (after the first drink Mrs. Wilson and I called each other by our first names) reappeared, company commenced to arrive at the apartment door.

The sister, Catherine, was a slender, worldly girl of about thirty, with a solid, sticky bob of red hair, and a complexion powdered milky white. Her eyebrows had been plucked and then drawn on again at a more rakish angle but the efforts of nature toward the restoration of the old alignment gave a blurred air to her face. When she moved about there was an incessant clicking as innumerable pottery bracelets jingled up and down upon her arms. She came in with such a proprietary haste, and looked around so possessively at the furniture that I wondered if she lived here. But when I asked her she laughed immoderately, repeated my question aloud, and told me she lived with a girl friend at a hotel.

Mr. McKee was a pale, feminine man from the flat below. He had just shaved, for there was a white spot of lather on his cheekbone, and he was most respectful in his greeting to everyone in the room. He informed me that he was in the "artistic game," and I gathered later that he was a photographer and had made the dim enlargement of Mrs. Wilson's mother which hovered like an ectoplasm on the wall. His wife was shrill, languid, handsome, and horrible. She told me with pride that her husband had photographed her a hundred and twenty-seven times since they had been married.

Mrs. Wilson had changed her costume some time before, and was now attired in an elaborate afternoon dress of cream-colored chiffon, which gave out a continual rustle as she swept about the room. With the influence of the dress her personality had also undergone a change. The intense vitality that had been so remarkable in the garage was converted into impressive hauteur. Her laughter, her gestures, her assertions became more violently affected moment by moment, and as she expanded the room grew smaller around her, until she seemed to be revolving on a noisy, creaking pivot through the smoky air.

"My dear," she told her sister in a high, mincing shout, "most of these fellas will cheat you every time. All they think of is money. I had a woman up here last week to look at my feet, and when she gave me the bill you'd of thought she had my appendicitis out."

"What was the name of the woman?" asked Mrs. McKee.

"Mrs. Eberhardt. She goes around looking at people's feet in their own homes."

"I like your dress," remarked Mrs. McKee, "I think it's adorable."

Mrs. Wilson rejected the compliment by raising her eyebrow in disdain.

"It's just a crazy old thing," she said. "I just slip it on sometimes when I don't care what I look like."

"But it looks wonderful on you, if you know what I mean," pursued Mrs. McKee. "If Chester could only get you in that pose I think he could make something of it."

We all looked in silence at Mrs. Wilson, who removed a strand of hair from over her eyes and looked back at us with a brilliant smile. Mr. McKee regarded her intently with his head on one side, and then moved his hand back and forth slowly in front of his face.

"I should change the light," he said after a moment. "I'd like to bring out the modeling of the features. And I'd try to get hold of all the back hair."

"I wouldn't think of changing the light," cried Mrs. McKee. "I think it's——"

Her husband said *"Sh!"* and we all looked at the subject again, whereupon Tom Buchanan yawned audibly and got to his feet.

"You McKees have something to drink," he said. "Get some more ice and mineral water, Myrtle, before everybody goes to sleep."

"I told that boy about the ice." Myrtle raised her eyebrows in despair at the shiftlessness of the lower orders. "These people! You have to keep after them all the time."

She looked at me and laughed pointlessly. Then she flounced over to the dog, kissed it with ecstasy, and swept into the kitchen, implying that a dozen chefs awaited her orders there.

"I've done some nice things out on Long Island," asserted Mr. McKee.

Tom looked at him blankly.

"Two of them we have framed downstairs."

"Two what?" demanded Tom.

"Two studies. One of them I call 'Montauk Point—The Gulls,' and the other I call 'Montauk Point—The Sea.' "

The sister Catherine sat down beside me on the couch.

"Do you live down on Long Island, too?" she inquired.

"I live at West Egg."

"Really? I was down there at a party about a month ago. At a man named Gatsby's. Do you know him?"

"I live next door to him."

"Well, they say he's a nephew or a cousin of Kaiser Wilhelm's. That's where all his money comes from."

"Really?"

She nodded.

"I'm scared of him. I'd hate to have him get anything on me."

This absorbing information about my neighbor was interrupted by Mrs. McKee's pointing suddenly at Catherine:

"Chester, I think you could do something with *her,"* she broke out, but Mr. McKee only nodded in a bored way, and turned his attention to Tom.

"I'd like to do more work on Long Island, if I could get the entry. All I ask is that they should give me a start."

"Ask Myrtle," said Tom, breaking into a short shout of laughter as Mrs. Wilson entered with a tray. "She'll give you a letter of introduction, won't you, Myrtle?"

"Do what?" she asked, startled.

"You'll give McKee a letter of introduction to your husband, so he can do some studies of him." His lips moved silently for a moment as he invented. " 'George B. Wilson at the Gasoline Pump,' or something like that."

Catherine leaned close to me and whispered in my ear:

"Neither of them can stand the person they're married to."

"Can't they?"

"Can't *stand* them." She looked at Myrtle and then at Tom. "What I say is, why go on living with them if they can't stand them? If I was them I'd get a divorce and get married to each other right away."

"Doesn't she like Wilson either?"

The answer to this was unexpected. It came from Myrtle, who had overheard the question, and it was violent and obscene.

"You see," cried Catherine triumphantly. She lowered her voice again. "It's really his wife that's keeping them apart. She's a Catholic, and they don't believe in divorce."

Daisy was not a Catholic, and I was a little shocked at the elaborateness of the lie.

"When they do get married," continued Catherine, "they're going West to live for a while until it blows over."

"It'd be more discreet to go to Europe."

"Oh, do you like Europe?" she exclaimed surprisingly. "I just got back from Monte Carlo."

"Really."

"Just last year. I went over there with another girl."

"Stay long?"

"No, we just went to Monte Carlo and back. We went by way of Marseilles. We had over twelve hundred dollars when we started, but we got gypped out of it all in two days in the private rooms. We had an awful time getting back, I can tell you. God, how I hated that town!"

The late afternoon sky bloomed in the window for a moment like the blue honey of the Mediterranean—then the shrill voice of Mrs. McKee called me back into the room.

"I almost made a mistake, too," she declared vigorously. "I almost married a little kike who'd been after me for years. I knew he was below me. Everybody kept saying to me: 'Lucille, that man's 'way below you!' But if I hadn't met Chester, he'd of got me sure."

"Yes, but listen," said Myrtle Wilson, nodding her head up and down, "at least you didn't marry him."

"I know I didn't."

"Well, I married him," said Myrtle, ambiguously. "And that's the difference between your case and mine."

"Why did you, Myrtle?" demanded Catherine. "Nobody forced you to."

Myrtle considered.

"I married him because I thought he was a gentleman," she said finally. "I thought he knew something about breeding, but he wasn't fit to lick my shoe."

"You were crazy about him for a while," said Catherine.

"Crazy about him!" cried Myrtle incredulously. "Who said I was crazy about him? I never was any more crazy about him than I was about that man there."

She pointed suddenly at me, and everyone looked at me accusingly. I tried to show by my expression that I had played no part in her past.

"The only *crazy* I was was when I married him. I knew right away I made a mistake. He borrowed somebody's best suit to get married in, and never even told me about it, and the man came after it one day when he was out." She looked around to see who was listening. " 'Oh, is that your suit?' I said. 'This is the first I ever heard about it.' But I gave it to him and then I lay down and cried to beat the band all afternoon."

"She really ought to get away from him," resumed Catherine to me. "They've been living over that garage for eleven years. And Tom's the first sweetie she ever had."

The bottle of whiskey—a second one—was now in constant demand by all present, excepting Catherine, who "felt just as good on nothing at all." Tom rang for the janitor and sent him for some celebrated sandwiches, which were a complete supper in themselves. I wanted to get out and walk eastward toward the Park through the soft twilight, but each time I tried to go I became entangled in some wild, strident argument which pulled me back, as if with ropes, into my chair. Yet high over the city our line of yellow windows must have contributed their share of human secrecy to the casual watcher in the darkening streets, and I saw him too, looking up and wondering. I was within and without, simultaneously enchanted and repelled by the inexhaustible variety of life.

Myrtle pulled her chair close to mine, and suddenly her warm breath poured over me the story of her first meeting with Tom.

"It was on the two little seats facing each other that are always the last ones left on the train. I was going up to New York to see my sister and spend the night. He had on a dress suit and patent leather shoes, and I couldn't keep my eyes off him, but every time he looked at me I had to pretend to be looking at the advertisement over his head. When we came into the station he was next to me, and his white shirt front pressed against my arm, and so I told him I'd have to call a policeman, but he knew I lied. I was so excited that when I got into a taxi with him I didn't hardly know I wasn't getting into a subway train. All I kept thinking about, over and over, was 'You can't live forever; you can't live forever.' "

She turned to Mrs. McKee and the room rang full of her artificial laughter.

"My dear," she cried, "I'm going to give you this dress as soon as I'm through with it. I've got to get another one tomorrow. I'm going to make a list of all the things I've got to get. A massage and a wave, and a collar for the dog, and one of those cute little ash trays where you touch a spring, and a wreath with a black silk bow for mother's grave that'll last all summer. I got to write down a list so I won't forget all the things I got to do."

It was nine o'clock—almost immediately afterward I looked at my watch and found it was ten. Mr. McKee was asleep on a chair with his fists clenched in his lap, like a photograph of a man of action. Taking out my handkerchief I wiped from his cheek the remains of the spot of dried lather that had worried me all the afternoon.

The little dog was sitting on the table looking with blind eyes through the smoke, and from time to time groaning faintly. People disappeared, reappeared, made plans to go somewhere, and then lost each other, searched for each other, found each other a few feet away. Sometime toward midnight Tom Buchanan and Mrs. Wilson stood face to face, discussing in impassioned voices whether Mrs. Wilson had any right to mention Daisy's name.

"Daisy! Daisy! Daisy!" shouted Mrs. Wilson. "I'll say it whenever I want to! Daisy! Dai——"

Making a short deft movement, Tom Buchanan broke her nose with his open hand.

Then there were bloody towels upon the bathroom floor, and women's voices scolding, and high over the confusion a long broken wail of pain. Mr. McKee awoke from his doze and started in a daze toward the door. When he had gone halfway he turned around and stared at the scene—his wife and Catherine scolding and consoling as they stumbled here and there among the crowded furniture with articles of aid, and the despairing figure on the couch, bleeding fluently, and trying to spread a copy of *Town Tattle* over the tapestry scenes of Versailles. Then Mr. McKee turned and continued on out the door. Taking my hat from the chandelier, I followed.

"Come to lunch some day," he suggested, as we groaned down in the elevator.

"Where?"

"Anywhere."

"Keep your hands off the lever," snapped the elevator boy.

"I beg your pardon," said Mr. McKee with dignity, "I didn't know I was touching it."

"All right," I agreed, "I'll be glad to."

. . . I was standing beside his bed and he was sitting up between the sheets, clad in his underwear, with a great portfolio in his hands.

"Beauty and the Beast . . . Loneliness . . . Old Grocery Horse . . . Brook'n Bridge. . . ."

Then I was lying half asleep in the cold lower level of the Pennsylvania Station, staring at the morning *Tribune,* and waiting for the four o'clock train.

CHAPTER III

There was music from my neighbor's house through the summer nights. In his blue gardens men and girls came and went like moths among the whisperings and the champagne and the stars. At high tide in the afternoon I watched his guests diving from the tower of his raft, or taking the sun on the hot sand of his beach while his two motorboats slit the waters of the Sound, drawing aquaplanes over cataracts of foam. On week ends his Rolls-Royce became an omnibus, bearing parties to and from the city between nine in the morning and long past midnight, while his station wagon scampered like a brisk yellow bug to meet all trains. And on Mondays eight servants, including an extra gardener, toiled all day with mops and scrubbing brushes and hammers and garden shears, repairing the ravages of the night before.

Every Friday five crates of oranges and lemons arrived from a fruiterer in New York—every Monday these same oranges and lemons left his back door in a pyramid of pulpless halves. There was a machine in the kitchen which could extract the juice of two hundred oranges in half an hour if a little button was pressed two hundred times by a butler's thumb.

At least once a fortnight a corps of caterers came down with several hundred feet of canvas and enough colored lights to make a Christmas tree of Gatsby's enormous garden. On buffet tables, garnished with glistening hors d'oeuvres, spiced baked hams crowded against salads of harlequin designs and pastry pigs and turkeys bewitched to a dark gold. In the main hall a bar with a real brass rail was set up, and stocked with gins and liquors and with cordials so long forgotten that most of his female guests were too young to know one from another.

By seven o'clock the orchestra has arrived, no thin five-piece affair, but a whole pitful of oboes and trombones and saxophones and viols and cornets and piccolos, and low and high drums. The last swimmers have come in from the beach now and are dressing upstairs; the cars from New York are parked five deep in the drive, and already the halls and salons and verandas are gaudy with primary colors, and hair bobbed in strange new ways, and shawls beyond the dreams of Castile. The bar is in full swing, and floating rounds of cocktails permeate the garden outside, until the air is alive with chatter and laughter, and casual innuendo and introductions forgotten on the spot, and enthusiastic meetings between women who never knew each other's names.

The lights grow brighter as the earth lurches away from the sun, and now the orchestra is playing yellow cocktail music, and the opera of voices pitches a key higher. Laughter is easier minute by minute, spilled with prodigality, tipped out at a cheerful word. The groups change more swiftly, swell with new arrivals, dissolve and form in the same breath; already there are wanderers, confident girls who weave here and there among the stouter and more stable, become for a sharp, joyous moment the center of a group, and then, excited with triumph, glide on through the sea change of faces and voices and color under the constantly changing light.

Suddenly one of these gypsies, in trembling opal, seizes a cocktail out of the air, dumps it down for courage and, moving her hands like Frisco, dances out alone on the canvas platform. A momentary hush; the orchestra leader varies his rhythm obligingly for her, and there is a burst of chatter as the erroneous news goes around that she is Gilda Gray's understudy from the Follies. The party has begun.

I believe that on the first night I went to Gastby's house I was one of the few guests who had actually been invited. People were not invited—they went there. They got into automobiles which bore them out to Long Island, and somehow they ended up at Gatsby's door. Once there they were introduced by somebody who knew Gatsby, and after that they conducted themselves according to the rules of behavior associated with an amusement park. Sometimes they came and went without having met Gatsby at all, came for the party with a simplicity of heart that was its own ticket of admission.

I had been actually invited. A chauffeur in a uniform of robin's-egg blue crossed my lawn early that Saturday morning with a surprisingly formal note from his employer: the honor would be entirely Gatsby's, it said, if I would attend his "little party" that night. He had seen me several times, and had intended to call on me long before, but a peculiar combination of circumstances had prevented it—signed Jay Gatsby, in a majestic hand.

Dressed up in white flannels I went over to his lawn a little after seven, and wandered around rather ill at ease among swirls and eddies of people I didn't know—though here and there was a face I had noticed on the commuting train. I was immediately struck by the number of young Englishmen dotted about; all well dressed, all looking a little hungry, and all talking in low, earnest voices to solid and prosperous Americans. I was sure that they were selling something: bonds or insurance or automobiles. They were at least agonizingly aware of the easy money in the vicinity and convinced that it was theirs for a few words in the right key.

As soon as I arrived I made an attempt to find my host, but the two or three people of whom I asked his whereabouts stared at me in such an amazed way, and denied so vehemently any knowledge of his movements, that I slunk off in the direction of the cocktail table—the only place in the garden where a single man could linger without looking purposeless and alone.

I was on my way to get roaring drunk from sheer embarrassment when Jordan Baker came out of the house and stood at the head of the marble steps, leaning a little backward and looking with contemptuous interest down into the garden.

Welcome or not, I found it necessary to attach myself to someone before I should begin to address cordial remarks to the passers-by.

"Hello!" I roared, advancing toward her. My voice seemed unnaturally loud across the garden.

"I thought you might be here," she responded absently as I came up. "I remembered you lived next door to——"

She held my hand impersonally, as a promise that she'd take care of me in a minute, and gave ear to two girls in twin yellow dresses, who stopped at the foot of the steps.

"Hello!" they cried together. "Sorry you didn't win."

That was for the golf tournament. She had lost in the finals the week before.

"You don't know who we are," said one of the girls in yellow, "but we met you here about a month ago."

"You've dyed your hair since then," remarked Jordan, and I started, but the girls had moved casually on and her remark was addressed to the premature moon, produced like the supper, no doubt, out of a caterer's basket. With Jordan's slender golden arm resting in mine, we descended the steps and sauntered about the garden. A tray of cocktails floated at us through the twilight, and we sat down at a table with the two girls in yellow and three men, each one introduced to us as Mr. Mumble.

"Do you come to these parties often?" inquired Jordan of the girl beside her.

"The last one was the one I met you at," answered the girl, in an alert confident voice. She turned to her companion: "Wasn't it for you, Lucille?"

It was for Lucille, too.

"I like to come," Lucille said. "I never care what I do, so I always have a good time. When I was here last I tore my gown on a chair, and he asked me my name and address—inside of a week I got a package from Croirier's with a new evening gown in it."

"Did you keep it?" asked Jordan.

"Sure I did. I was going to wear it tonight, but it was too big in the bust and had to be altered. It was gas blue with lavender beads. Two hundred and sixty-five dollars."

"There's something funny about a fellow that'll do a thing like that," said the other girl eagerly. "He doesn't want any trouble with *any*body."

"Who doesn't?" I inquired.

"Gatsby. Somebody told me——"

The two girls and Jordan leaned together confidentially.

"Somebody told me they thought he killed a man once."

A thrill passed over all of us. The three Mr. Mumbles bent forward and listened eagerly.

"I don't think it's so much *that,*" argued Lucille

skeptically; "it's more that he was a German spy during the war."

One of the men nodded in confirmation.

"I heard that from a man who knew all about him, grew up with him in Germany," he assured us positively.

"Oh, no," said the first girl, "it couldn't be that, because he was in the American army during the war." As our credulity switched back to her she leaned forward with enthusiasm. "You look at him sometimes when he thinks nobody's looking at him. I'll bet he killed a man."

She narrowed her eyes and shivered. Lucille shivered. We all turned and looked around for Gatsby. It was testimony to the romantic speculation he inspired that there were whispers about him from those who had found little that it was necessary to whisper about in this world.

The first supper—there would be another one after midnight—was now being served, and Jordan invited me to join her own party, who were spread around a table on the other side of the garden. There were three married couples and Jordan's escort, a persistent undergraduate given to violent innuendo, and obviously under the impression that sooner or later Jordan was going to yield him up her person to a greater or lesser degree. Instead of rambling, this party had preserved a dignified homogeneity, and assumed to itself the function of representing the staid nobility of the countryside—East Egg condescending to West Egg, and carefully on guard against its spectroscopic gaiety.

"Let's get out," whispered Jordan, after a somehow wasteful and inappropriate half-hour; "this is much too polite for me."

We got up, and she explained that we were going to find the host: I had never met him, she said, and it was making me uneasy. The undergraduate nodded in a cynical, melancholy way.

The bar, where we glanced first, was crowded, but Gatsby was not there. She couldn't find him from the top of the steps, and he wasn't on the veranda. On a chance we tried an important-looking door, and walked into a high Gothic library, paneled with carved English oak, and probably transported complete from some ruin overseas.

A stout, middle-aged man, with enormous owl-eyed spectacles, was sitting somewhat drunk on the edge of a great table, staring with unsteady concentration at the shelves of books. As we entered he wheeled excitedly around and examined Jordan from head to foot.

"What do you think?" he demanded impetuously.

"About what?"

He waved his hand toward the bookshelves.

"About that. As a matter of fact you needn't bother to ascertain. I ascertained. They're real."

"The books?"

He nodded.

"Absolutely real—have pages and everything. I thought they'd be a nice durable cardboard. Matter of fact, they're absolutely real. Pages and—Here! Lemme show you."

Taking our skepticism for granted, he rushed to the bookcases and returned with Volume One of the *Stoddard Lectures.*

"See!" he cried triumphantly. "It's a bona fide piece of printed matter. It fooled me. This fella's a regular Belasco. It's a triumph. What thoroughness! What realism! Knew when to stop, too—didn't cut the pages. But what do you want? What do you expect?"

He snatched the book from me and replaced it hastily on its shelf, muttering that if one brick was removed the whole library was liable to collapse.

"Who brought you?" he demanded. "Or did you just come? I was brought. Most people were brought."

Jordan looked at him alertly, cheerfully, without answering.

"I was brought by a woman named Roosevelt," he continued. "Mrs. Claude Roosevelt. Do you know her? I met her somewhere last night. I've been drunk for about a week now, and I thought it might sober me up to sit in a library."

"Has it?"

"A little bit, I think. I can't tell yet. I've only been here an hour. Did I tell you about the books? They're real. They're——"

"You told us."

We shook hands with him gravely and went back outdoors.

There was dancing now on the canvas in the garden; old men pushing young girls backward in eternal graceless circles, superior couples holding each other tortuously, fashionably, and keeping in the corners—and a great number of single girls dancing individualistically or relieving the orchestra for a moment of the burden of the banjo or the traps. By midnight the hilarity had increased. A celebrated tenor had sung in Italian, and a notorious contralto had sung in jazz, and between the numbers people were doing "stunts" all over the garden, while happy, vacuous bursts of laughter rose toward the summer sky. A pair of stage twins, who turned out to be the girls in yellow, did a baby act in costume, and champagne was served in glasses bigger than finger bowls. The moon had risen higher, and floating in the Sound was a triangle of silver scales, trembling a little to the stiff, tinny drip of the banjos on the lawn.

I was still with Jordan Baker. We were sitting at a table with a man of about my age and a rowdy little girl, who gave way upon the slightest provocation to uncontrollable laughter. I was enjoying myself now. I had taken two finger bowls of champagne, and the scene had changed before my eyes into something significant, elemental, and profound.

At a lull in the entertainment the man looked at me and smiled.

"Your face is familiar," he said, politely. "Weren't you in the Third Division during the war?"

"Why, yes. I was in the Ninth Machine-Gun Battalion."

"I was in the Seventh Infantry until June nineteen-eighteen. I knew I'd seen you somewhere before."

We talked for a moment about some wet, gray little villages in France. Evidently he lived in this vicinity, for he told me that he had just bought a hydroplane, and was going to try it out in the morning.

"Want to go with me, old sport? Just near the shore along the Sound."

"What time?"

"Any time that suits you best."

It was on the tip of my tongue to ask his name when Jordan looked around and smiled.

"Having a gay time now?" she inquired.

"Much better." I turned again to my new acquaintance. "This is an unusual party for me. I haven't even seen the host. I live over there—" I waved my hand at the invisible hedge in the distance, "and this man Gatsby sent over his chauffeur with an invitation."

For a moment he looked at me as if he failed to understand.

"I'm Gatsby," he said suddenly.

"What!" I exclaimed. "Oh, I beg your pardon."

"I thought you knew, old sport. I'm afraid I'm not a very good host."

He smiled understandingly—much more than understandingly. It was one of those rare smiles with a quality of eternal reassurance in it, that you may come across four or five times in life. It faced—or seemed to face—the whole external world for an instant, and then concentrated on *you* with an irresistible prejudice in your favor. It understood you just as far as you wanted to be understood, believed in you as you would like to believe in yourself, and assured you that it had precisely the impression of you that, at your best, you hoped to convey. Precisely at that point it vanished—and I was looking at an elegant young roughneck, a year or two over thirty, whose elaborate formality of speech just missed being absurd. Sometime before he introduced himself I'd got a strong impression that he was picking his words with care.

Almost at the moment when Mr. Gatsby identified himself, a butler hurried toward him with the information that Chicago was calling him on the wire. He excused himself with a small bow that included each of us in turn.

"If you want anything just ask for it, old sport," he urged me. "Excuse me. I will rejoin you later."

When he was gone I turned immediately to Jordan—constrained to assure her of my surprise. I had expected that Mr. Gatsby would be a florid and corpulent person in his middle years.

"Who is he?" I demanded. "Do you know?"

"He's just a man named Gatsby."

"Where is he from, I mean? And what does he do?"

"Now *you're* started on the subject," she answered with a wan smile. "Well, he told me once he was an Oxford man."

A dim background started to take shape behind him, but at her next remark it faded away.

"However, I don't believe it."

"Why not?"

"I don't know," she insisted, "I just don't think he went there."

Something in her tone reminded me of the other girl's "I think he killed a man," and had the effect of stimulating my curiosity. I would have accepted without question the information that Gatsby sprang from the swamps of Louisiana or from the Lower East Side of New York. That was comprehensible. But young men didn't—at least in my provincial inexperience I believed they didn't—drift coolly out of nowhere and buy a palace on Long Island Sound.

"Anyhow, he gives large parties," said Jordan, changing the subject with an urban distaste for the concrete. "And I like large parties. They're so intimate. At small parties there isn't any privacy."

There was the boom of a bass drum, and the voice of the orchestra leader rang out suddenly above the echolalia of the garden.

"Ladies and gentlemen," he cried. "At the request of Mr. Gatsby we are going to play for you Mr. Vladimir Tostoff's latest work, which attracted so much attention at Carnegie Hall last May. If you read the papers, you know there was a big sensation." He smiled with jovial condescension, and added: "Some sensation!" Whereupon everybody laughed.

"The piece is known," he concluded lustily, "as Vladimir Tostoff's 'Jazz History of the World.' "

The nature of Mr. Tostoff's composition eluded me, because just as it began my eyes fell on Gatsby, standing alone on the marble steps and looking from one group to another with approving eyes. His tanned skin was drawn attractively tight on his face and his short hair looked as though it were trimmed every day. I could see nothing sinister about him. I wondered if the fact that he was not drinking helped to set him off from his guests, for it seemed to me that he grew more correct as the fraternal hilarity increased. When the "Jazz History of the World" was over, girls were putting their heads on men's shoulders in a puppyish, convivial way, girls were swooning backward playfully into men's arms, even into groups, knowing that someone would arrest their falls—but no one swooned backward on Gatsby, and no French bob touched Gatsby's shoulder, and no singing quartets were formed with Gatsby's head for one link.

"I beg your pardon."

Gatsby's butler was suddenly standing beside us.

"Miss Baker?" he inquired. "I beg your pardon, but Mr. Gatsby would like to speak to you alone."

"With me?" she exclaimed in surprise.

"Yes, madame."

She got up slowly, raising her eyebrows at me in astonishment, and followed the butler toward the house. I noticed that she wore her evening dress, all her dresses, like sports clothes—there was a jauntiness about her movements as if she had first learned to walk upon golf courses on clean, crisp mornings.

I was alone and it was almost two. For some time confused and intriguing sounds had issued from a long, many-windowed room which overhung the terrace. Eluding Jordan's undergraduate, who was now engaged in an obstetrical conversation with two chorus girls, and who implored me to join him, I went inside.

The large room was full of people. One of the girls in yellow was playing the piano, and beside her stood a tall, red-haired young lady from a famous chorus, engaged in song. She had drunk a quantity of champagne, and during the course of her song she had decided, ineptly, that everything was very, very sad—she was not only singing, she was weeping too. Whenever there was a pause in the song she filled it with gasping, broken sobs, and then took up the lyric in a quavering soprano. The tears coursed down her cheeks—not freely, however, for when they came into contact with her heavily beaded eyelashes they assumed an inky color, and pursued the rest of their way in slow black rivulets. A humorous suggestion was made that she sing the notes on her face, whereupon she threw up her hands, sank into a chair, and went off into a deep vinous sleep.

"She had a fight with a man who says he's her husband," explained a girl at my elbow.

I looked around. Most of the remaining women were now having fights with men said to be their husbands. Even Jordan's party, the quartet from East Egg, were rent asunder by dissension. One of the men was talking with curious intensity to a young actress, and his wife after attempting to laugh at the situation in a dignified and indifferent way, broke down entirely and resorted to flank attacks—at intervals she appeared suddenly at his side like an angry diamond, and hissed: "You promised!" into his ear.

The reluctance to go home was not confined to wayward men. The hall was at present occupied by two deplorably sober men and their highly indignant wives. The wives were sympathizing with each other in slightly raised voices.

"Whenever he sees I'm having a good time he wants to go home."

"Never heard anything so selfish in my life."

"We're always the first ones to leave."

"So are we."

"Well, we're almost the last tonight," said one of the men sheepishly. "The orchestra left half an hour ago."

In spite of the wives' agreement that such malevolence was beyond credibility, the dispute ended in a short struggle, and both wives were lifted, kicking, into the night.

As I waited for my hat in the hall the door of the library opened and Jordan Baker and Gatsby came out together. He was saying some last word to her, but the eagerness in his manner tightened abruptly into formality as several people approached him to say good-by.

Jordan's party were calling impatiently to her from the porch, but she lingered for a moment to shake hands.

"I've just heard the most amazing thing," she whispered. "How long were we in there?"

"Why, about an hour."

"It was . . . simply amazing," she repeated abstractedly. "But I swore I wouldn't tell it and here I am tantalizing you." She yawned gracefully in my face. "Please come and see me. . . . Phone book. . . . Under the name of Mrs. Sigourney Howard. . . . My aunt. . . ." She was hurrying off as she talked—her brown hand waved a jaunty salute as she melted into her party at the door.

Rather ashamed that on my first appearance I had stayed so late, I joined the last of Gatsby's guests, who were clustered around him. I wanted to explain that I'd hunted for him early in the evening and to apologize for not having known him in the garden.

"Don't mention it," he enjoined me eagerly. "Don't give it another thought, old sport." The familiar expression held no more familiarity than the hand which reassuringly brushed my shoulder. "And don't forget we're going up in the hydroplane tomorrow morning, at nine o'clock."

Then the butler, behind his shoulder:

"Philadelphia wants you on the phone, sir."

"All right, in a minute. Tell them I'll be right there. . . . Good night."

"Good night."

"Good night." He smiled—and suddenly there seemed to be a pleasant significance in having been among the last to go, as if he had desired it all the time. "Good night, old sport. . . . Good night."

But as I walked down the steps I saw that the evening was not quite over. Fifty feet from the door a dozen headlights illuminated a bizarre and tumultuous scene. In the ditch beside the road, right side up, but violently shorn on one wheel, rested a new coupé which had left Gatsby's drive not two minutes before. The sharp jut of a wall accounted for the detachment of the wheel, which was now getting considerable attention from half a dozen curious chauffeurs. However, as they had left their cars blocking the road, a harsh, discordant din from those in the rear had been audible for some time, and added to the already violent confusion of the scene.

A man in a long duster had dismounted from the wreck and now stood in the middle of the road, looking from the car to the tire and from the tire to the observers in a pleasant, puzzled way.

"See!" he explained. "It went in the ditch."

The fact was infinitely astonishing to him, and I recognized first the unusual quality of wonder, and then the man—it was the late patron of Gatsby's library.

"How'd it happen?"

He shrugged his shoulders.

"I know nothing whatever about mechanics," he said decisively.

"But how did it happen? Did you run into the wall?"

"Don't ask me," said Owl Eyes, washing his hands of the whole matter. "I know very little about driving—next to nothing. It happened, and that's all I know."

"Well, if you're a poor driver you oughtn't to try driving at night."

"But I wasn't even trying," he explained indignantly, "I wasn't even trying."

An awed hush fell upon the bystanders.

"Do you want to commit suicide?"

"You're lucky it was just a wheel! A bad driver and not even *trying*!"

"You don't understand," explained the criminal. "I wasn't driving. There's another man in the car."

The shock that followed this declaration found voice in a sustained "Ah-h-h!" as the door of the coupé swung slowly open. The crowd—it was now a crowd—stepped back involuntarily, and when the door had opened wide there was a ghostly pause. Then, very gradually, part by part, a pale, dangling individual stepped out of the wreck, pawing tentatively at the ground with a large uncertain dancing shoe.

Blinded by the glare of the headlights and confused by the incessant groaning of the horns, the apparition stood swaying for a moment before he perceived the man in the duster.

"Wha's matter?" he inquired calmly. "Did we run outa gas?"

"Look!"

Half a dozen fingers pointed at the amputated wheel—he stared at it for a moment, and then looked upward as though he suspected that it had dropped from the sky.

"It came off," someone explained.

He nodded.

"At first I din' notice we'd stopped."

A pause. Then, taking a long breath and straightening his shoulders, he remarked in a determined voice:

"Wonder'ff tell me where there's a gas'line station?"

At least a dozen men, some of them little better off than he was, explained to him that wheel and car were no longer joined by any physical bond.

"Back out," he suggested after a moment. "Put her in reverse."

"But the *wheel's* off!"

He hesitated.

"No harm in trying," he said.

The caterwauling horns had reached a crescendo and I turned away and cut across the lawn toward home. I glanced back once. A wafer of a moon was shining over Gatsby's house, making the night fine as before, and surviving the laughter and the sound of his still glowing garden. A sudden emptiness seemed to flow now from the windows and the great doors, endowing with complete isolation the figure of the host, who stood on the porch, his hand up in a formal gesture of farewell.

Reading over what I have written so far, I see I have given the impression that the events of three nights several weeks apart were all that absorbed me. On the contrary, they were merely casual events in a crowded summer, and, until much later, they absorbed me infinitely less than my personal affairs.

Most of the time I worked. In the early morning the sun threw my shadow westward as I hurried down the white chasms of lower New York to the Probity Trust. I knew the other clerks and young bond salesmen, by their first names, and lunched with them in dark, crowded restaurants on little pig sausages and mashed potatoes and coffee. I even had a short affair with a girl who lived in Jersey City and worked in the accounting department, but her brother began throwing mean looks in my direction, so when she went on her vacation in July I let it blow quietly away.

I took dinner usually at the Yale Club—for some reason it was the gloomiest event of my day—and then I went upstairs to the library and studied investments and securities for a conscientious hour. There were generally a few rioters around, but they never came into the library, so it was a good place to work. After that, if the night was mellow, I strolled down Madison Avenue past the old Murray Hill Hotel, and over Thirty-third Street to the Pennsylvania Station.

I began to like New York, the racy, adventurous feel of it at night, and the satisfaction that the constant flicker of men and women and machines gives to the restless eye. I liked to walk up Fifth Avenue and pick out romantic women from the crowd and imagine that in a few minutes I was going to enter into their lives, and no one would ever know or disapprove. Sometimes, in my mind, I followed them to their apartments on the corners of hidden streets, and they turned and smiled back at me before they faded through a door into warm darkness. At the enchanted metropolitan twilight I felt a haunting loneliness sometimes, and felt it in others—poor young clerks who loitered in front of windows waiting until it was time for a solitary restaurant dinner—young clerks in the dusk, wasting the most poignant moments of night and life.

Again at eight o'clock, when the dark lanes of the Forties were five deep with throbbing taxicabs, bound for the theater district, I felt a sinking in my heart. Forms leaned together in the taxis as they waited, and voices sang, and there was laughter from unheard jokes, and lighted cigarettes outlined unintelligible gestures inside. Imagining that I, too, was hurrying toward gaiety and sharing their intimate excitement, I wished them well.

For a while I lost sight of Jordan Baker, and then in midsummer I found her again. At first I was flattered to go places with her, because she was a golf champion, and everyone knew her name. Then it was something more. I wasn't actually in love, but I felt a sort of tender curiosity. The bored haughty face that she turned to the world concealed something—most affectations conceal something eventually, even though they don't in the beginning—and one day I found what it was. When we were on a house party together up in Warwick, she left a borrowed car out in the rain with the top down, and then lied about it—and suddenly I remembered the story about her that had eluded me that night at Daisy's. At her first big golf tournament there was a row that nearly reached the newspapers—a suggestion that she had moved her ball from a bad lie in the semifinal round. The thing approached the proportions of a scandal—then died away. A caddy retracted his statement, and the only other witness admitted that he might have been mistaken. The incident and the name had remained together in my mind.

Jordan Baker instinctively avoided clever, shrewd men, and now I saw that this was because she felt safer on a plane where any divergence from a code would be thought impossible. She was incurably dishonest. She wasn't able to endure being at a disadvantage and, given this unwillingness, I suppose she had begun dealing in subterfuges when she was very young in order to keep that cool, insolent smile turned to the world and yet satisfy the demands of her hard, jaunty body.

It made no difference to me. Dishonesty in a woman is a thing you never blame deeply—I was casually sorry, and then I forgot. It was on that same house party that we had a curious conversation about driving a car. It started because she passed so close to some workmen that our fender flicked a button on one man's coat.

"You're a rotten driver," I protested. "Either you ought to be more careful, or you oughtn't to drive at all."

"I am careful."

"No, you're not."

"Well, other people are," she said lightly.

"What's that got to do with it?"

"They'll keep out of my way," she insisted. "It takes two to make an accident."

"Suppose you met somebody just as careless as yourself."

"I hope I never will," she answered. "I hate careless people. That's why I like you."

Her gray, sun-strained eyes stared straight ahead, but she had deliberately shifted our relations, and for a moment I thought I loved her. But I am slow-thinking and full of interior rules that act as brakes on my desires, and I knew that first I had to get myself definitely out of that tangle back home. I'd been writing letters once a week and signing them: "Love, Nick," and all I could think of was how, when that certain girl played tennis, a faint mustache of perspiration appeared on her upper lip. Nevertheless there was a vague understanding that had to be tactfully broken off before I was free.

Everyone suspects himself of at least one of the cardinal virtues, and this is mine: I am one of the few honest people that I have ever known.

CHAPTER IV

On Sunday morning while church bells rang in the villages alongshore, the world and its mistress returned to Gatsby's house and twinkled hilariously on his lawn.

"He's a bootlegger," said the young ladies, moving somewhere between his cocktails and his flowers. "One time he killed a man who had found out that he was nephew to Von Hindenburg and second cousin to the devil. Reach me a rose, honey, and pour me a last drop into that there crystal glass."

Once I wrote down on the empty spaces of a timetable the names of those who came to Gatsby's house that summer. It is an old timetable now, disintegrating at its folds, and headed "This schedule in effect July 5th, 1922." But I can still read the gray names, and they will give you a better impression than my generalities of those who accepted Gatsby's hospitality and paid him the subtle tribute of knowing nothing whatever about him.

From East Egg, then, came the Chester Beckers and the Leeches, and a man named Bunsen, whom I knew at Yale, and Doctor Webster Civet, who was drowned last summer up in Maine. And the Hornbeams and the Willie Voltaires, and a whole clan named Blackbuck, who always gathered in a corner and flipped up their noses like goats at whosoever came near. And the Ismays and the Chrysties (or rather Hubert Auerbach and Mr. Chrystie's wife), and Edgar Beaver, whose hair, they say, turned cotton-white one winter afternoon for no good reason at all.

Clarence Endive was from East Egg, as I remember. He came only once, in white knickerbockers, and had a fight with a bum named Etty in the garden. From farther out on the Island came the Cheadles and the O. R. P. Schraeders, and the Stonewall Jackson Abrams of Georgia, and the Fishguards and the Ripley Snells. Snell was there three days before he went to the penitentiary, so drunk out on the gravel drive that Mrs. Ulysses Swett's automobile ran over his right hand. The Dancies came, too, and S. B. Whitebait, who was well over sixty, and Maurice A. Flink, and the Hammerheads, and Beluga the tobacco importer, and Beluga's girls.

From West Egg came the Poles and the Mulreadys and Cecil Roebuck and Cecil Schoen and Gulick the state senator and Newton Orchid, who controlled Films Par Excellence, and Eckhaust and Clyde Cohen and Don S. Schwartze (the son) and Arthur McCarty, all connected with the movies in one way or another. And the Catlips and the Bembergs and G. Earl Muldoon, brother to that Muldoon who afterward strangled his wife. Da Fontano the promoter came there, and Ed Legros and James B. ("Rot-Gut") Ferret and the De Jongs and Ernest Lilly—they came to gamble, and when Ferret wandered into the garden it meant he was cleaned out and Associated Traction would have to fluctuate profitably next day.

A man named Klipspringer was there so often and so long that he became known as "the boarder"—I doubt if he had any other home. Of theatrical people there were Gus Waize and Horace O'Donavan and Lester Myer and George Duckweed and Francis Bull. Also from New York were the Chromes and the Backhyssons and the Dennickers and Russel Betty and the Corrigans and the Kellehers and the Dewars and the Scullys and S. W. Belcher and the Smirkes and the young Quinns, divorced now, and Henry L. Palmetto, who killed himself by jumping in front of a subway train in Times Square.

Benny McClenahan arrived always with four girls. They were never quite the same ones in physical person, but they were so identical one with another that it inevitably seemed they had been there before. I have forgotten their names—Jaqueline, I think, or else Consuela, or Gloria or Judy or June, and their last names were either the melodious names of flowers and months or the sterner ones of the great American capitalists whose cousins, if pressed, they would confess themselves to be.

In addition to all these I can remember that Faustina O'Brien came there at least once and the Baedeker girls and young Brewer, who had his nose shot off in the war, and Mr. Albrucksburger and Miss Haag, his financée, and Ardita Fitz-Peters and Mr. P. Jewett, once head of the American Legion, and Miss Claudia Hip, with a man reputed to be her chauffeur, and a prince of something, whom we called Duke, and whose name, if I ever knew it, I have forgotten.

All these people came to Gatsby's house in the summer.

At nine o'clock, one morning late in July, Gatsby's gorgeous car lurched up the rocky drive to my door and gave out a burst of melody from its three-noted horn. It was the first time he had called on me, though I had gone to two of his parties, mounted in his hydroplane, and, at his urgent invitation, made frequent use of his beach.

"Good morning, old sport. You're having lunch with me today and I thought we'd ride up together."

He was balancing himself on the dashboard of his car with that resourcefulness of movement that is so peculiarly American—that comes, I suppose, with the absence of lifting work or rigid sitting in youth and, even more, with the formless grace of our nervous, sporadic games. This quality was continually breaking through his punctilious manner in the shape of restlessness. He was never quite still; there was always a tapping foot somewhere or the impatient opening and closing of a hand.

He saw me looking with admiration at his car.

"It's pretty, isn't it, old sport!" He jumped off to give me a better view. "Haven't you ever seen it before?"

I'd seen it. Everybody had seen it. It was a rich cream color, bright with nickel, swollen here and there in its monstrous length with triumphant hatboxes and supper boxes and toolboxes, and terraced with a labyrinth of windshields that mirrored a dozen suns. Sitting down behind many layers of glass in a sort of green leather conservatory, we started to town.

I had talked with him perhaps six times in the past month and found, to my disappointment, that he had little to say. So my first impression, that he was a person of some undefined consequence, had gradually faded and he had become simply the proprietor of an elaborate roadhouse next door.

And then came that disconcerting ride. We hadn't reached West Egg Village before Gatsby began leaving his elegant sentences unfinished and slapping himself indecisively on the knee of his caramel-colored suit.

"Look here, old sport," he broke out surprisingly, "what's your opinion of me, anyhow?"

A little overwhelmed, I began the generalized evasions which that question deserves.

"Well, I'm going to tell you something about my life," he interrupted. "I don't want you to get a wrong idea of me from all these stories you hear."

So he was aware of the bizarre accusations that flavored conversation in his halls.

"I'll tell you God's truth." His right hand suddenly ordered divine retribution to stand by. "I am the son of some wealthy people in the Middle West—all dead now. I was brought up in America but educated at Oxford, because all my ancestors have been educated there for many years. It is a family tradition."

He looked at me sideways—and I knew why Jordan Baker had believed he was lying. He hurried the phrase "educated at Oxford," or swallowed it, or choked on it, as though it had bothered him before. And with this doubt, his whole statement fell to pieces, and I wondered if there wasn't something a little sinster about him after all.

"What part of the Middle West?" I inquired casually.

"San Francisco."

"I see."

"My family all died and I came into a good deal of money."

His voice was solemn, as if the memory of that sudden extinction of a clan still haunted him. For a moment I suspected that he was pulling my leg, but a glance at him convinced me otherwise.

"After that I lived like a young rajah in all the capitals of Europe—Paris, Venice, Rome—collecting jewels, chiefly rubies, hunting big game, painting a little, things for myself only, and trying to forget something very sad that had happened to me long ago."

With an effort I managed to restrain my incredulous laughter. The very phrases were worn so threadbare that they evoked no image except that of a turbaned "character" leaking sawdust at every pore as he pursued a tiger through the Bois de Boulogne.

"Then came the war, old sport. It was a great relief, and I tried very hard to die, but I seemed to bear an enchanted life. I accepted a commission as first lieutenant when it began. In the Argonne Forest I took two machine-gun detachments so far forward that there was a half mile gap on either side of us where the infantry couldn't advance. We stayed there two days and two nights, a hundred and thirty men with sixteen Lewis guns, and when the infantry came up at last they found the insignia of three German divisions among the piles of dead. I was promoted to be a major, and every Allied government gave me a decoration—even Montenegro, little Montenegro down on the Adriatic Sea!"

Little Montenegro! He lifted up the words and nodded at them—with his smile. The smile comprehended Montenegro's troubled history and sympathized with the brave struggles of the Montenegrin people. It appreciated fully the chain of national circumstances which had elicited this tribute from Montenegro's warm little heart. My incredulity was submerged in fascination now; it was like skimming hastily through a dozen magazines.

He reached in his pocket, and a piece of metal, slung on a ribbon, fell into my palm.

"That's the one from Montenegro."

To my astonishment, the thing had an authentic look. "Orderi de Danilo," ran the circular legend, "Montenegro, Nicolas Rex."

"Turn it."

"Major Jay Gatsby," I read, "For Valour Extraordinary."

"Here's another thing I always carry. A souvenir of Oxford days. It was taken in Trinity Quad—the man on my left is now the Earl of Doncaster."

It was a photograph of half a dozen young men in blazers loafing in an archway through which were visible a host of spires. There was Gatsby, looking a little, not much, younger—with a cricket bat in his hand.

Then it was all true. I saw the skins of tigers flaming in his palace on the Grand Canal; I saw him opening a chest of rubies to ease, with their crimson-lighted depths, the gnawings of his broken heart.

"I'm going to make a big request of you today," he said, pocketing his souvenirs with satisfaction, "so I thought you ought to know something about me. I didn't want you to think I was just some nobody. You see, I usually find myself among strangers because I drift here and there trying to foget the sad thing that happened to me." He hesitated. "You'll hear about it this afternoon."

"At lunch?"

"No, this afternoon. I happened to find out that you're taking Miss Baker to tea."

"Do you mean you're in love with Miss Baker?"

"No, old sport, I'm not. But Miss Baker has kindly consented to speak to you about this matter."

I hadn't the faintest idea what "this matter" was, but I was more annoyed than interested. I hadn't asked Jordan to tea in order to discuss Mr. Jay Gatsby. I was sure the request would be something utterly fantastic, and for a moment I was sorry I'd ever set foot upon his overpopulated lawn.

He wouldn't say another word. His correctness grew on him as we neared the city. We passed Port Roosevelt, where there was a glimpse of red-belted ocean-going ships, and sped along a cobbled slum lined with the dark, undeserted saloons of the faded-gilt nineteen-hundreds. Then the valley of ashes opened out on both sides of us, and I had a glimpse of Mrs. Wilson straining at the garage pump with panting vitality as we went by.

With fenders spread like wings we scattered light through half Astoria—only half, for as we twisted among the pillars of the elevated I heard the familiar "jug-jug-*spat!*" of a motorcycle, and a frantic policeman rode alongside.

"All right, old sport," called Gatsby. We slowed down. Taking a white card from his wallet, he waved it before the man's eyes.

"Right you are," agreed the policeman, tipping his cap. "Know you next time, Mr. Gatsby. Excuse *me!*"

"What was that?" I inquired. "The picture of Oxford?"

"I was able to do the commissioner a favor once, and he sends me a Christmas card every year."

Over the great bridge, with the sunlight through the girders making a constant flicker upon the moving cars, with the city rising up across the river in white heaps and sugar lumps all built with a wish out of nonolfactory money. The city seen from the Queensboro Bridge is always the city seen for the first time, in its first wild promise of all the mystery and the beauty in the world.

A dead man passed us in a hearse heaped with blooms, followed by two carriages with drawn blinds, and by more cheerful carriages for friends. The friends looked out at us with the tragic eyes and short upper lips of southeastern Europe, and I was glad that the sight of Gatsby's splendid car was included in their somber holiday. As we crossed Blackwell's Island a limousine passed us, driven by a white chauffeur, in which sat three modish Negroes, two bucks and a girl. I laughed aloud as the yolks of their eyeballs rolled toward us in haughty rivalry.

"Anything can happen now that we've slid over this bridge," I thought; "anything at all. . . ."

Even Gatsby could happen, without any particular wonder.

Roaring noon. In a well-fanned Forty-second Street cellar I met Gatsby for lunch. Blinking away the brightness of the street outside, my eyes picked him out obscurely in the anteroom, talking to another man.

"Mr. Carraway, this is my friend Mr. Wolfsheim."

A small, flat-nosed Jew raised his large head and regarded me with two fine growths of hair which luxuriated in either nostril. After a moment I discovered his tiny eyes in the half-darkness.

"—So I took one look at him," said Mr. Wolfsheim, shaking my hand earnestly, "and what do you think I did?"

"What?" I inquired politely.

But evidently he was not addressing me, for he dropped my hand and covered Gatsby with his expressive nose.

"I handed the money to Katspaugh and I said: 'All right, Katspaugh, don't pay him a penny till he shuts his mouth.' He shut it then and there."

Gatsby took an arm of each of us and moved forward into the restaurant, whereupon Mr. Wolfsheim swallowed a new sentence he was starting and lapsed into a somnambulatory abstraction.

"Highballs?" asked the head waiter.

"This is a nice restaurant here," said Mr. Wolfsheim, looking at the Presbyterian nymphs on the ceiling. "But I like across the street better!"

"Yes, highballs," agreed Gatsby, and then to Mr. Wolfsheim: "It's too hot over there."

"Hot and small—yes," said Mr. Wolfsheim, "but full of memories."

"What place is that?" I asked.

"The old Metropole.

"The old Metropole," brooded Mr. Wolfsheim gloomily. "Filled with faces dead and gone. Filled with friends gone now forever. I can't forget so long as I live the night they shot Rosy Rosenthal there. It was six of us at the table, and Rosy had eat and drunk a lot all evening. When it was almost morning the waiter came up to him with a funny look and says somebody wants to speak to him outside. 'All right,' says Rosy, and begins to get up, and I pulled him down in his chair.

" 'Let the bastards come in here if they want you, Rosy, but don't you, so help me, move outside this room.'

"It was four o'clock in the morning then, and if we'd of raised the blinds we'd of seen daylight."

"Did he go?" I asked innocently.

"Sure he went." Mr. Wolfsheim's nose flashed at me indignantly. "He turned around in the door and says: "Don't let that waiter take away my coffee!" Then he went out on the sidewalk, and they shot him three times in his full belly and drove away."

"Four of them were electrocuted," I said, remembering.

"Five, with Becker." His nostrils turned to me in an interested way. "I understand you're looking for a business gonnegtion."

The juxtaposition of these two remarks was startling. Gatsby answered for me:

"Oh, no," he exclaimed, "this isn't the man."

"No?" Mr. Wolfsheim seemed disappointed.

"This is just a friend. I told you we'd talk about that some other time."

"I beg your pardon," said Mr. Wolfsheim, "I had a wrong man."

A succulent hash arrived, and Mr. Wolfsheim, forgetting the more sentimental atmosphere of the old Metropole, began to eat with ferocious delicacy. His eyes, meanwhile, roved very slowly all around the room—he completed the arc by turning to inspect the people directly behind. I think that, except for my presence, he would have taken one short glance beneath our own table.

"Look here, old sport," said Gatsby, leaning toward me, "I'm afraid I made you a little angry this morning in the car."

There was the smile again, but this time I held out against it.

"I don't like mysteries," I answered, "and I don't understand why you won't come out frankly and tell me what you want. Why has it all got to come through Miss Baker?"

"Oh, it's nothing underhand," he assured me. "Miss Baker's a great sportswoman, you know, and she'd never do anything that wasn't all right."

Suddenly he looked at his watch, jumped up, and hurried from the room, leaving me with Mr. Wolfsheim at the table.

"He has to telphone," said Mr. Wolfsheim following him with his eyes. "Fine fellow, isn't he? Handsome to look at and a perfect gentleman."

"Yes."

"He's an Oggsford man."

"Oh!"

"He went to Oggsford College in England. You know Oggsford College?"

"I've heard of it."

"It's one of the most famous colleges in the world."

"Have you known Gatsby for a long time?" I inquired.

"Several years," he answered in a gratified way. "I made the pleasure of his acquaintance just after the war. But I knew I had discovered a man of fine breeding after I talked with him an hour. I said to myself: 'There's the kind of man you'd like to take home and introduce to your mother and sister.' " He paused. "I see you're looking at my cuff buttons."

I hadn't been looking at them, but I did now. They were composed of oddly familiar pieces of ivory.

"Finest specimens of human molars," he informed me.

"Well!" I inspected them. "That's a very interesting idea."

"Yeah." He flipped his sleeves up under his coat. "Yeah, Gatsby's very careful about women. He would never so much as look at a friend's wife."

When the subject of this instinctive trust returned to the table and sat down Mr. Wolfsheim drank his coffee with a jerk and got to his feet.

"I have enjoyed my lunch," he said, "and I'm going to run off from you two young men before I outstay my welcome."

"Don't hurry, Meyer," said Gatsby, without enthusiasm. Mr. Wolfsheim raised his hand in a sort of benediction.

"You're very polite, but I belong to another generation," he announced solemnly. "You sit here and discuss your sports and your young ladies and your——" He supplied an imaginary noun with another wave of his hand. "As for me, I am fifty years old, and I won't impose myself on you any longer."

As he shook hands and turned away his tragic nose was trembling. I wondered if I had said anything to offend him.

"He becomes very sentimental sometimes," explained Gatsby. "This is one of his sentimental days. He's quite a character around New York—a denizen of Broadway."

"Who is he, anyhow, an actor?"

"No."

"A dentist?"

"Meyer Wolfsheim? No, he's a gambler." Gatsby

hesitated, then added coolly: "He's the man who fixed the world's series back in 1919."

"Fixed the world's series?" I repeated.

The idea staggered me. I remembered, of course, that the world's series had been fixed in 1919, but if I had thought of it at all I would have thought of it as a thing that merely *happened,* the end of some inevitable chain. It never occurred to me that one man could play with the faith of fifty million people—with the single-mindedness of a burglar blowing a safe.

"How did he happen to do that?" I asked after a minute.

"He just saw the opportunity."

"Why isn't he in jail?"

"They can't get him, old sport. He's a smart man."

I insisted on paying the check. As the waiter brought my change I caught sight of Tom Buchanan across the crowded room.

"Come along with me for a minute," I said: "I've got to say hello to someone."

When he saw us Tom jumped up and took half a dozen steps in our direction.

"Where've you been?" he demanded eagerly. "Daisy's furious because you haven't called up."

"This is Mr. Gatsby, Mr. Buchanan."

They shook hands briefly, and a strained, unfamiliar look of embarrassment came over Gatsby's face.

"How've you been, anyhow?" demanded Tom of me. "How'd you happen to come up this far to eat?"

"I've been having lunch with Mr. Gatsby."

I turned toward Mr. Gatsby, but he was no longer there.

One October day in nineteen-seventeen——

(said Jordan Baker that afternoon, sitting up very straight on a straight chair in the teagarden at the Plaza Hotel)

—I was walking along from one place to another, half on the sidewalks and half on the lawns. I was happier on the lawns because I had on shoes from England with rubber nobs on the soles that bit into the soft ground. I had on a new plaid skirt also that blew a little in the wind, and whenever this happened the red, white, and blue banners in front of all the houses stretched out stiff and said *tut-tut-tut-tut,* in a disapproving way.

The largest of the banners and the largest of the lawns belonged to Daisy Fay's house. She was just eighteen, two years older than me, and by far the most popular of all the young girls in Louisville. She dressed in white, and had a little white roadster, and all day long the telephone rang in her house and excited young officers from Camp Taylor demanded the privilege of monopolizing her that night. "Anyways, for an hour!"

When I came opposite her house that morning her white roadster was beside the curb, and she was sitting in it with a lieutenant I had never seen before. They were so engrossed in each other that she didn't see me until I was five feet away.

"Hello, Jordan," she called unexpectedly. "Please come here."

I was flattered that she wanted to speak to me, because of all the older girls I admired her most. She asked me if I was going to the Red Cross and make bandages. I was. Well, then, would I tell them that she couldn't come that day? The officer looked at Daisy while she was speaking, in a way that every young girl wants to be looked at sometime, and because it seemed romantic to me I have remembered the incident ever since. His name was Jay Gatsby, and I didn't lay eyes on him again for over four years—even after I'd met him on Long Island I didn't realize it was the same man.

That was nineteen-seventeen. By the next year I had a few beaux myself, and I began to play in tournaments, so I didn't see Daisy very often. She went with a slightly older crowd—when she went with anyone at all. Wild rumors were circulating about her—how her mother had found her packing her bag one winter night to go to New York and say good-by to a soldier who was going overseas. She was effectually prevented, but she wasn't on speaking terms with her family for several weeks. After that she didn't play around with the soldiers any more, but only with a few flat-footed short-sighted young men in town, who couldn't get into the army at all.

By the next autumn she was gay again, gay as ever. She had a debut after the Armistice, and in February she was presumably engaged to a man from New Orleans. In June she married Tom Buchahan of Chicago, with more pomp and circumstance than Louisville ever knew before. He came down with a hundred people in four private cars, and hired a whole floor of the Seelbach Hotel, and the day before the wedding he gave her a string of pearls valued at three hundred and fifty thousand dollars.

I was a bridesmaid. I came into her room half an hour before the bridal dinner, and found her lying on her bed as lovely as the June night in her flowered dress—and as drunk as a monkey. She had a bottle of Sauterne in one hand and a letter in the other.

"'Gratulate me," she muttered. "Never had a drink before, but oh how I do enjoy it."

"What's the matter, Daisy?"

I was scared, I can tell you; I'd never seen a girl like that before.

"Here, deares'." She groped around in a wastebasket she had with her on the bed and pulled out the string of pearls. "Take 'em downstairs and give 'em back to whoever they belong to. Tell 'em all Daisy's change' her mine. Say: 'Daisy's change' her mine!' "

She began to cry—she cried and cried. I rushed out and found her mother's maid, and we locked the door and got her into a cold bath. She wouldn't let go of the letter. She took it into the tub with her and squeezed it up into a wet ball, and only let me leave it in the soap dish when she saw that it was coming to pieces like snow.

But she didn't say another word. We gave her spirits of ammonia and put ice on her forehead and hooked her back into her dress, and half an hour later, when we walked out of the room, the pearls were around her neck and the incident was over. Next day at five o'clock she married Tom Buchanan without so much as a shiver, and started off on a three months' trip to the South Seas.

I saw them in Santa Barbara when they came back, and I thought I'd never seen a girl so mad about her husband. If he left the room for a minute she'd look around uneasily, and say: "Where's Tom gone?" and wear the most abstracted expression until she saw him coming in the door. She used to sit on the sand with his head in her lap by the hour, rubbing her fingers over his eyes and looking at him with unfathomable delight. It was touching to see them together—it made you laugh in a hushed, fascinated way. That was in August. A week after I left Santa Barbara Tom ran into a wagon on the Ventura road one night, and ripped a front wheel off his car. The girl who was with him got into the papers, too, because her arm was broken—she was one of the chambermaids in the Santa Barbara Hotel.

The next April Daisy had her little girl, and they went to France for a year. I saw them one spring in Cannes, and later in Deauville, and then they came back to Chicago to settle down. Daisy was popular in Chicago, as you know. They moved with a fast crowd, all of them young and rich and wild, but she came out with an absolutely perfect reputation. Perhaps because she doesn't drink. It's a great advantage not to drink among hard-drinking people. You can hold your tongue, and, moreover, you can time any little irregularity of your own so that everybody else is so blind that they don't see or care. Perhaps Daisy never went in for amour at all—and yet there's something in that voice of hers. . . .

Well, about six weeks ago, she heard the name Gatsby for the first time in years. It was when I asked you—do you remember?—if you knew Gatsby in West Egg. After you had gone home she came into my room and woke me up, and said: "What Gatsby?" and when I described him—I was half asleep—she said in the strangest voice that it must be the man she used to know. It wasn't until then that I connected this Gatsby with the officer in her white car.

When Jordan Baker had finished telling all this we had left the Plaza for half an hour and were driving in a victoria through Central Park. The sun had gone down behind the tall apartments of the movie stars in the West Fifties, and the clear voices of little girls already gathered like crickets on the grass, rose through the hot twilight:

"I'm the Sheik of Araby.
Your love belongs to me.
At night when you're asleep
Into your tent I'll creep——"

"It was a strange coincidence," I said.

"But it wasn't a coincidence at all."

"Why not?"

"Gatsby bought that house so that Daisy would be just across the bay."

Then it had not been merely the stars to which he had aspired on that June night. He came alive to me, delivered suddenly from the womb of his purposeless splendor.

"He wants to know," continued Jordan, "if you'll invite Daisy to your house some afternoon and then let him come over."

The modesty of the demand shook me. He had waited five years and bought a mansion where he dispensed starlight to casual moths—so that he could "come over" some afternoon to a stranger's garden.

"Did I have to know all this before he could ask such a little thing?"

"He's afraid, he's waited so long. He thought you might be offended. You see, he's a regular tough underneath it all."

Something worried me.

"Why didn't he ask you to arrange a meeting?"

"He wants her to see his house," she explained. "And your house is right next door."

"Oh!"

"I think he half expected her to wander into one of his parties, some night," went on Jordan, "but she never did. Then he began asking people casually if they knew her, and I was the first one he found. It was that night he sent for me at his dance, and you should have heard the elaborate way he worked up to it. Of course, I immediately suggested a luncheon in New York—and I thought he'd go mad:

" 'I don't want to do anything out of the way!' he kept saying. 'I want to see her right next door.'

"When I said you were a particular friend of Tom's, he started to abandon the whole idea. He doesn't know very much about Tom, though he says he's read a Chicago paper for years just on the chance of catching a glimpse of Daisy's name."

It was dark now, and as we dipped under a little bridge I put my arm around Jordan's golden shoulder and drew her toward me and asked her to dinner. Suddenly I wasn't thinking of Daisy and Gatsby any more, but of this clean, hard, limited person, who dealt in universal skepticism, and who leaned back jauntily just within the circle of my arm. A phrase began to beat in my ears with a sort of heady excitement: "There are only the pursued, the pursuing, the busy, and the tired."

"And Daisy ought to have something in her life," murmured Jordan to me.

"Does she want to see Gatsby?"

"She's not to know about it. Gatsby doesn't want her to know. You're just supposed to invite her to tea."

We passed a barrier of dark trees, and then the façade of Fifty-ninth Street, a block of delicate pale light, beamed down into the Park. Unlike Gatsby and Tom Buchanan, I had no girl whose disembodied face floated along the dark cornices and blinding signs, and so I drew up the girl beside me, tightening my arms. Her wan, scornful mouth smiled, and so I drew her up again closer, this time to my face.

CHAPTER V

When I came home to West Egg that night I was afraid for a moment that my house was on fire. Two o'clock and the whole corner of the peninsula was blazing with light, which fell unreal on the shrubbery and made thin elongating glints upon the roadside wires. Turning a corner, I saw that it was Gatsby's house, lit from tower to cellar.

At first I thought it was another party, a wild rout that had resolved itself into "hide-and-go-seek" or "sardines-in-the-box" with all the house thrown open to the game. But there wasn't a sound. Only wind in the trees, which blew the wires and made the lights go off and on again as if the house had winked into the darkness. As my taxi groaned away I saw Gatsby walking toward me across his lawn.

"Your place looks like the World's Fair," I said.

"Does it?" He turned his eyes toward it absently. "I have been glancing into some of the rooms. Let's go to Coney Island, old sport. In my car."

"It's too late."

"Well, suppose we take a plunge in the swimming pool? I haven't made use of it all summer."

"I've got to go to bed."

"All right."

He waited, looking at me with suppressed eagerness.

"I talked with Miss Baker," I said after a moment. "I'm going to call up Daisy tomorrow and invite her over here to tea."

"Oh, that's all right," he said carelessly. "I don't want to put you to any trouble."

"What day would suit you?"

"What day would suit *you?*" he corrected me quickly. "I don't want to put you to any trouble, you see."

"How about the day after tomorrow?"

He considered for a moment. Then, with reluctance:

"I want to get the grass cut," he said.

We both looked at the grass—there was a sharp line where my ragged lawn ended and the darker, well-kept expanse of his began. I suspected that he meant my grass.

"There's another little thing," he said uncertainly, and hesitated.

"Would you rather put it off for a few days?" I asked.

"Oh, it isn't about that. At least—" He fumbled with a series of beginnings. "Why, I thought—why, look here, old sport, you don't make much money, do you?"

"Not very much."

This seemed to reassure him and he continued more confidently.

"I thought you didn't, if you'll pardon my—you see, I carry on a little business on the side, a sort of side line, you understand. And I thought that if you don't make very much—You're selling bonds, aren't you, old sport?"

"Trying to."

"Well, this would interest you. It wouldn't take up much of your time and you might pick up a nice bit of money. It happens to be a rather confidential sort of thing."

I realize now that under different circumstances that conversation might have been one of the crises of my life. But, because the offer was obviously and tactlessly for a service to be rendered, I had no choice except to cut him off there.

"I've got my hands full," I said. "I'm much obliged but I couldn't take on any more work."

"You wouldn't have to do any business with Wolfsheim." Evidently he thought that I was shying away from the "gonnegtion" mentioned at lunch, but I assured him he was wrong. He waited a moment longer, hoping I'd begin a conversation, but I was too absorbed to be responsive, so he went unwillingly home.

The evening had made me light-headed and happy; I think I walked into a deep sleep as I entered my front door. So I don't know whether or not Gatsby went to Coney Island, or for how many hours he "glanced into rooms" while his house blazed gaudily on. I called up Daisy from the office next morning, and invited her to come to tea.

"Don't bring Tom," I warned her.

"What?"

"Don't bring Tom."

"Who is 'Tom'?" she asked innocently.

The day agreed upon was pouring rain. At eleven o'clock a man in a raincoat, dragging a lawnmower, tapped at my front door and said that Mr. Gatsby had sent him over to cut my grass. This reminded me that I had forgotten to tell my Finn to come back, so I drove into West Egg Village to search for her among soggy whitewashed alleys and to buy some cups and lemons and flowers.

The flowers were unnecessary, for at two o'clock a greenhouse arrived from Gatsby's, with innumerable receptacles to contain it. An hour later the front door opened nervously, and Gatsby, in a white flannel suit, silver shirt, and gold-colored tie, hurried in. He was pale, and there were dark signs of sleeplessness beneath his eyes.

"Is everything all right?" he asked immediately.

"The grass looks fine, if that's what you mean."

"What grass?" he inquired blankly. "Oh, the grass in the yard." He looked out the window at it, but, judging from his expression, I don't believe he saw a thing.

"Looks very good," he remarked vaguely. "One of the papers said they thought the rain would stop about four. I think it was *The Journal.* Have you got everything you need in the shape of—of tea?"

I took him into the pantry, where he looked a little reproachfully at the Finn. Together we scrutinized the twelve lemon cakes from the delicatessen shop.

"Will they do?" I asked.

"Of course, of course! They're fine!" and he added hollowly, ". . . old sport."

The rain cooled about half past three to a damp mist, through which occasional thin drops swam like dew. Gatsby looked with vacant eyes through a copy of Clay's *Economics,* starting at the Finnish tread that shook the kitchen floor, and peering toward the bleared windows from time to time as if a series of invisible but alarming happenings were taking place outside. Finally he got up and informed me, in an uncertain voice, that he was going home.

"Why's that?"

"Nobody's coming to tea. It's too late!" He looked at his watch as if there was some pressing demand on his time elsewhere. "I can't wait all day."

"Don't be silly; it's just two minutes to four."

He sat down miserably, as if I had pushed him, and simultaneously there was the sound of a motor turning into my lane. We both jumped up, and, a little harrowed myself, I went out into the yard.

Under the dripping bare lilac trees a large open car was coming up the drive. It stopped. Daisy's face, tipped sideways beneath a three-cornered lavender hat, looked out at me with a bright ecstatic smile.

"Is this absolutely where you live, my dearest one?"

The exhilarating ripple of her voice was a wild tonic in the rain. I had to follow the sound of it for a moment, up and down, with my ear alone, before any words came through. A damp streak of hair lay like a dash of blue paint across her cheek, and her hand was wet with glistening drops as I took it to help her from the car.

"Are you in love with me," she said low in my ear, "or why did I have to come alone?"

"That's the secret of Castle Rackrent. Tell your chauffeur to go far away and spend an hour."

"Come back in an hour, Ferdie." Then in a grave murmur: "His name is Ferdie."

"Does the gasoline affect his nose?"

"I don't think so," she said innocently. "Why?"

We went in. To my overwhelming surprise the living room was deserted.

"Well, that's funny," I exclaimed.

"What's funny?"

She turned her head as there was a light dignified knocking at the front door. I went out and opened it. Gatsby, pale as death, with his hands plunged like weights in his coat pockets, was standing in a puddle of water glaring tragically into my eyes.

With his hands still in his coat pockets he stalked by me into the hall, turned sharply as if he were on a wire, and disappeared into the living room. It wasn't a bit funny. Aware of the loud beating of my own heart I pulled the door to against the increasing rain.

For half a minute there wasn't a sound. Then from the living room I heard a sort of choking murmur and part of a laugh, followed by Daisy's voice on a clear artificial note:

"I certainly am awfully glad to see you again."

A pause; it endured horribly. I had nothing to do in the hall, so I went into the room.

Gatsby, his hands still in his pockets, was reclining

against the mantlepiece in a strained counterfeit of perfect ease, even of boredom. His head leaned back so far that it rested against the face of a defunct mantelpiece clock, and from this position his distraught eyes stared down at Daisy, who was sitting, frightened but graceful, on the edge of a stiff chair.

"We've met before," muttered Gatsby. His eyes glanced momentarily at me, and his lips parted with an abortive attempt at a laugh. Luckily the clock took this moment to tilt dangerously at the pressure of his head, whereupon he turned and caught it with trembling fingers and set it back in place. Then he sat down, rigidly, his elbow on the arm of the sofa and his chin in his hand.

"I'm sorry about the clock," he said.

My own face had now assumed a deep tropical burn. I couldn't muster up a single commonplace out of the thousand in my head.

"It's an old clock," I told them idiotically.

I think we all believed for a moment that it had smashed in pieces on the floor.

"We haven't met for many years," said Daisy, her voice as matter-of-fact as it could ever be.

"Five years next November."

The automatic quality of Gatsby's answer set us all back at least another minute. I had them both on their feet with the desperate suggestion that they help me make tea in the kitchen when the demoniac Finn brought it in on a tray.

Amid the welcome confusion of cups and cakes a certain physical decency established itself. Gatsby got himself into a shadow and, while Daisy and I talked, looked conscientiously from one to the other of us with tense, unhappy eyes. However, as calmness wasn't an end in itself, I made an excuse at the first possible moment, and got to my feet.

"Where are you going?" demanded Gatsby in immediate alarm.

"I'll be back."

"I've got to speak to you about something before you go."

He followed me wildly into the kitchen, closed the door, and whispered: "Oh, God!" in a miserable way.

"What's the matter?"

"This is a terrible mistake," he said, shaking his head from side to side, "a terrible, terrible mistake."

"You're just embarrassed, that's all," and luckily I added: "Daisy's embarrassed too."

"She's embarrassed?" he repeated incredulously.

"Just as much as you are."

"Don't talk so loud."

"You're acting like a little boy," I broke out impatiently. "Not only that, but you're rude. Daisy's sitting in there all alone."

He raised his hand to stop my words, looked at me with unforgettable reproach, and, opening the door cautiously, went back into the other room.

I walked out the back way—just as Gatsby had when he had made his nervous circuit of the house half an hour before—and ran for a huge black knotted tree, whose massed leaves made a fabric against the rain. Once more it was pouring, and my irregular lawn, well-shaved by Gatsby's gardener, abounded in small muddy swamps and prehistoric marshes. There was nothing to look at from under the tree except Gatsby's enormous house, so I stared at it, like Kant at his church steeple, for half an hour. A brewer had built it early in the "period" craze, a decade before, and there was a story that he'd agreed to pay five years' taxes on all the neighboring cottages if the owners would have their roofs thatched with straw. Perhaps their refusal took the heart out of his plan to Found a Family—he went into an immediate decline. His children sold his house with the black wreath still on the door. Americans, while occasionally willing to be serfs, have always been obstinate about being peasantry.

After half an hour, the sun shone again, and the grocer's automobile rounded Gatsby's drive with the raw material for his servants' dinner—I felt sure he wouldn't eat a spoonful. A maid began opening the upper windows of his house, appeared momentarily in each, and, leaning from a large central bay, spat meditatively into the garden. It was time I went back. While the rain continued it had seemed like the murmur of their voices, rising and swelling a little now and then with gusts of emotion. But in the new silence I felt that silence had fallen within the house too.

I went in—after making every possible noise in the kitchen, short of pushing over the stove—but I don't believe they heard a sound. They were sitting at either end of the couch, looking at each other as if some question had been asked, or was in the air, and every vestige of embarrassment was gone. Daisy's face was smeared with tears, and when I came in she jumped up and began wiping at it with her handkerchief before a mirror. But there was a change in Gatsby that was simply confounding. He literally glowed; without a word or a gesture of exultation a new well-being radiated from him and filled the little room.

"Oh, hello, old sport," he said, as if he hadn't seen me for years. I thought for a moment he was going to shake hands.

"It's stopped raining."

"Has it?" When he realized what I was talking about, that there were twinkle-bells of sunshine in the room, he smiled like a weatherman, like an ecstatic patron of recurrent light, and repeated the news to Daisy. "What do you think of that? It's stopped raining."

"I'm glad, Jay." Her throat, full of aching, grieving beauty, told only of her unexpected joy.

"I want you and Daisy to come over to my house," he said, "I'd like to show her around."

"You're sure you want me to come?"

"Absolutely, old sport."

Daisy went upstairs to wash her face—too late I thought with humiliation of my towels—while Gatsby and I waited on the lawn.

"My house looks well, doesn't it?" he demanded. "See how the whole front of it catches the light."

I agreed that it was splendid.

"Yes." His eyes went over it, every arched door and square tower. "It took me just three years to earn the money that bought it."

"I thought you inherited your money."

"I did, old sport," he said automatically, "but I lost most of it in the big panic—the panic of the war."

I think he hardly knew what he was saying, for when I asked him what business he was in he answered: "That's my affair," before he realized that it wasn't an appropriate reply.

"Oh, I've been in several things," he corrected himself. "I was in the drug business and then I was in the oil business. But I'm not in either one now." He looked at me with more attention. "Do you mean you've been thinking over what I proposed the other night?"

Before I could answer, Daisy came out of the house and two rows of brass buttons on her dress gleamed in the sunlight.

"That huge place *there?*" she cried pointing.

"Do you like it?"

"I love it, but I don't see how you live there all alone."

"I keep it always full of interesting people, night and day. People who do interesting things. Celebrated people."

Instead of taking the short cut along the Sound we went down to the road and entered by the big postern. With enchanting murmurs Daisy admired this aspect or that of the feudal silhouette against the sky, admired the gardens, the sparkling odor of jonquils and the frothy odor of hawthorn and plum blossoms and the pale gold odor of kiss-me-at-the-gate. It was strange to reach the marble steps and find no stir of bright dresses in and out of the door, and hear no sound but bird voices in the trees.

And inside, as we wandered through Marie Antionette music rooms and Restoration salons, I felt that there were guests concealed behind every couch and table, under orders to be breathlessly silent until we had passed through. As Gatsby closed the door of "the Merton College Library" I could have sworn I heard the owl-eyed man break into ghostly laughter.

We went upstairs, through period bedrooms swathed in rose and lavender silk and vivid with new flowers, through dressing rooms and poolrooms, and bathrooms, with sunken baths—intruding into one chamber where a disheveled man in pajamas was doing liver exercises on the floor. It was Mr. Klipspringer, the "boarder." I had seen him wandering hungrily about the beach that morning. Finally we came to Gatsby's own apartment, a bedroom and a bath, and an Adam study, where we sat down and drank a glass of some chartreuse he took from a cupboard in the wall.

He hadn't once ceased looking at Daisy, and I think he revalued everything in his house according to the measure of response it drew from her well-loved eyes. Sometimes, too, he stared around at his possessions in a dazed way, as though in her actual and astounding presence none of it was any longer real. Once he nearly toppled down a flight of stairs.

His bedroom was the simplest room of all—except where the dresser was garnished with a toilet set of pure dull gold. Daisy took the brush with delight, and smoothed her hair, whereupon Gatsby sat down and shaded his eyes and began to laugh.

"It's the funniest thing, old sport," he said hilariously. "I can't—when I try to——"

He had passed visibly through two states and was entering upon a third. After his embarrassment and his unreasoning joy he was consumed with wonder at her presence. He had been full of the idea so long, dreamed it right through to the end, waited with his teeth set, so to speak, at an inconceivable pitch of intensity. Now, in the reaction, he was running down like an overwound clock.

Recovering himself in a minute he opened for us two hulking patent cabinets which held his massed suits and dressing gowns and ties, and his shirts, piled like bricks in stacks a dozen high.

"I've got a man in England who buys me clothes. He sends over a selection of things at the beginning of each season, spring and fall."

He took out a pile of shirts and began throwing them, one by one, before us, shirts of sheer linen and thick silk and fine flannel, which lost their folds as they fell and covered the table in many-colored disarray. While we admired he brought more and the soft rich heap mounted higher—shirts with stripes and scrolls and plaids in coral and apple-green and lavender and faint orange, with monograms of Indian blue. Suddenly, with a strained sound, Daisy bent her head into the shirts and began to cry stormily.

"They're such beautiful shirts," she sobbed, her voice muffled in the thick folds. "It makes me sad because I've never seen such—such beautiful shirts before."

After the house, we were to see the grounds and the swimming pool, and the hydroplane and the midsummer flowers—but outside Gatsby's window it began to rain again, so we stood in a row looking at the corrugated surface of the Sound.

"If it wasn't for the mist we could see your home across the bay," said Gatsby. "You always have a green light that burns all night at the end of your dock."

Daisy put her arm through his abruptly, but he seemed absorbed in what he had just said. Possibly it had occurred to him that the colossal significance of that light had now vanished forever. Compared to the great distance that had separated him from Daisy it had seemed very near to her, almost touching her. It had seemed as close as a star to the moon. Now it was again a green light on a dock. His count of enchanted objects had diminished by one.

I began to walk about the room, examining various indefinite objects in the half darkness. A large photograph of an elderly man in yachting costume attracted me, hung on the wall over his desk.

"Who's this?"

"That? That's Mr. Dan Cody, old sport."

The name sounded faintly familiar.

"He's dead now. He used to be my best friend years ago."

There was a small picture of Gatsby, also in yachting costume, on the bureau—Gatsby with his head thrown back defiantly—taken apparently when he was about eighteen.

"I adore it," exclaimed Daisy. "The pompadour! You never told me you had a pompadour—or a yacht."

"Look at this," said Gatsby quickly. "Here's a lot of clippings—about you."

They stood side by side examining it. I was going to ask to see the rubies when the phone rang, and Gatsby took up the receiver.

"Yes. . . . Well, I can't talk now. . . . I can't talk now, old sport. . . . I said a *small* town. . . . He must know what a small town is. . . . Well, he's no use to us if Detroit is his idea of a small town. . . ."

He rang off.

"Come here *quick!*" cried Daisy at the window.

The rain was still falling, but the darkness had parted in the west, and there was a pink and golden billow of foamy clouds above the sea.

"Look at that," she whispered, and then after a moment: "I'd like to just get one of those pink clouds and put you in it and push you around."

I tried to go then, but they wouldn't hear of it; perhaps my presence made them feel more satisfactorily alone.

"I know what we'll do," said Gatsby, "we'll have Klipspringer play the piano."

He went out of the room calling "Ewing!" and returned in a few minutes accompanied by an embarrassed, slightly worn young man, with shell-rimmed glasses and scanty blond hair. He was now decently clothed in a sport shirt, open at the neck, sneakers, and duck trousers of a nebulous hue.

"Did we interrupt your exercises?" inquired Daisy politely.

"I was asleep," cried Mr. Klipspringer, in a spasm of embarrassment. "That is, I'd *been* asleep. Then I got up. . . ."

"Klipspringer plays the piano," said Gatsby, cutting him off. "Don't you, Ewing, old sport?"

"I don't play well. I don't—I hardly play at all. I'm all out of prac——"

"We'll go downstairs," interrupted Gatsby. He flipped a switch. The gray windows disappeared as the house glowed full of light.

In the music room Gatsby turned on a solitary lamp beside the piano. He lit Daisy's cigarette from a trembling match, and sat down with her on a couch far across the room, where there was no light save what the gleaming floor bounced in from the hall.

When Klipspringer had played "The Love Nest" he turned around on the bench and searched unhappily for Gatsby in the gloom.

"I'm all out of practice, you see. I told you I couldn't play. I'm all out of prac——"

"Don't talk so much, old sport," commanded Gatsby. "Play!"

"In the morning,
 In the evening,
  Ain't we got fun——"

Outside the wind was loud and there was a faint flow of thunder along the Sound. All the lights were going on in West Egg now; the electric trains, men-carrying, were plunging home through the rain from New York. It was the hour of a profound human change, and excitement was generating on the air.

"One thing's sure and nothing's surer
 The rich get richer and the poor get—children.
  In the meantime,
  In between time——"

As I went over to say good-by I saw that the expression of bewilderment had come back into Gatsby's face, as though a faint doubt had occurred to him as to the quality of his present happiness. Almost five years! There must have been moments even that afternoon when Daisy tumbled short of his dreams—not through her own fault, but because of the colossal vitality of his illusion. It had gone beyond her, beyond everything. He had thrown himself into it with a creative passion, adding to it all the time, decking it out with every bright feather that drifted his way. No amount of fire or freshness can challenge what a man will store up in his ghostly heart.

As I watched him he adjusted himself a little, visibly. His hand took hold of hers, and as she said something low in his ear he turned toward her with a rush of emotion. I think that voice held him most, with its fluctuating, feverish warmth, because it couldn't be overdreamed—that voice was a deathless song.

They had forgotten me, but Daisy glanced up and held out her hand; Gatsby didn't know me now at all. I looked once more at them and they looked back at me, remotely, possessed by intense life. Then I went out of the room and down the marble steps into the rain, leaving them there together.

CHAPTER VI

About this time an ambitious young reporter from New York arrived one morning at Gatsby's door and asked him if he had anything to say.

"Anything to say about what?" inquired Gatsby politely.

"Why—any statement to give out."

It transpired after a confused five minutes that the man had heard Gatsby's name around his office in a connection which he either wouldn't reveal or didn't fully understand. This was his day off and with laudable initiative he had hurried out "to see."

It was a random shot, and yet the reporter's instinct was right. Gatsby's notoriety, spread about by the hundreds who had accepted his hospitality and so become authorities upon his past, had increased all summer until he fell just short of being news. Contemporary legends such as the "underground pipeline to Canada" attached themselves to him, and there was one persistent story that he didn't live in a house at all, but in a boat that looked like a house and was moved secretly up and down the Long Island shore. Just why these inventions were a source of satisfaction to James Gatz of North Dakota isn't easy to say.

James Gatz—that was really, or at least legally, his name. He had changed it at the age of seventeen and at the specific moment that witnessed the beginning of his career—when he saw Dan Cody's yacht drop anchor over the most insidious flat on Lake Superior. It was James Gatz who had been loafing along the beach that afternoon in a torn green jersey and a pair of canvas pants, but it was already Jay Gatsby who borrowed a rowboat, pulled out to the *Tuolumee,* and informed Cody that a wind might catch him and break him up in half an hour.

I suppose he'd had the name ready for a long time, even then. His parents were shiftless and unsuccessful farm people—his imagination had never really accepted them as his parents at all. The truth was that Jay Gatsby of West Egg, Long Island, sprang from his Platonic conception of himself. He was a son of God—a phrase which, if it means anything, means just that—and he must be about His Father's business, the service of a vast, vulgar, and meretricious beauty. So he invented just the sort of Jay Gatsby that a seventeen-year-old boy would be likely to invent, and to this conception he was faithful to the end.

For over a year he had been beating his way along the south shore of Lake Superior as a clam digger and a salmon fisher or in any other capacity that brought him food and bed. His brown, hardening body lived naturally through the half-fierce, half-lazy work of the bracing days. He knew women early, and since they spoiled him he became contemptuous of them, of young virgins because they were ignorant, of the others because they were hysterical about things which in his overwhelming self-absorption he took for granted.

But his heart was in a constant, turbulent riot. The most grotesque and fantastic conceits haunted him in his bed at night. A universe of ineffable gaudiness spun itself out in his brain while the clock ticked on the washstand and the moon soaked with wet light his tangled clothes upon the floor. Each night he added to the pattern of his fancies until drowsiness closed down upon some vivid scene with an oblivious embrace. For a while these reveries provided an outlet for his imagination; they were a satisfactory hint of the unreality of reality, a promise that the rock of the world was founded securely on a fairy's wing.

An instinct toward his future glory had led him, some months before, to the small Lutheran college of St. Olaf's in southern Minnesota. He stayed there two weeks, dismayed at its ferocious indifference to the drums of his destiny, to destiny itself, and despising the janitor's work with which he was to pay his way through. Then he drifted back to Lake Superior, and he was still searching for something to do on the day that Dan Cody's yacht dropped anchor in the shallows alongshore.

Cody was fifty years old then, a product of the Nevada silver fields, of the Yukon, of every rush for metal since seventy-five. The transactions in Montana copper that made him many times a millionaire found him physically robust but on the verge of soft-mindedness, and, suspecting this, an infinite number of women tried to separate him from his money. The none too savory ramifications by which Ella Kaye, the newspaperwoman, played Madame de Maintenon to his weakness and sent him to sea in a yacht were common property of the turgid journalism of 1902. He had been coasting along all too hospitable shores for five years when he turned up as James Gatz's destiny in Little Girl Bay.

To young Gatz, resting on his oars and looking up at the railed deck, that yacht represented all the beauty and glamour in the world. I suppose he smiled at Cody—he had probably discovered that people liked him when he smiled. At any rate Cody asked him a few questions (one of them elicited the brand-new name) and found that he was quick and extravagantly ambitious. A few days later he took him to Duluth and bought him a blue coat, six pairs of white duck trousers, and a yachting cap. And when the *Tuolomee* left for the West Indies and the Barbary Coast Gatsby left too.

He was employed in a vague personal capacity—while he remained with Cody he was in turn steward, mate, skipper, secretary, and even jailer, for Dan Cody sober knew what lavish doings Dan Cody drunk might soon be about, and he provided for such contingencies by reposing more and more trust in Gatsby. The arrangement lasted five years, during which the boat went three times around the Continent. It might have have lasted indefinitely except for the fact that Ella Kaye came on board one night in Boston and a week later Dan Cody inhospitably died.

I remember the portrait of him up in Gatsby's bedroom, a gray, florid man with a hard, empty face—the pioneer debauchee, who during one phase of American life brought back to the Eastern seaboard the savage violence of the frontier brothel and saloon. It was indirectly due to Cody that Gatsby drank so little. Sometimes in the course of gay parties women used to rub champagne into his hair; for himself he formed the habit of letting liquor alone.

And it was from Cody that he inherited money—a legacy of twenty-five thousand dollars. He didn't get it. He never understood the legal device that was used against him, but what remained of the millions went intact to Ella Kaye. He was left with his singularly appropriate education; the vague contour of Jay Gatsby had filled out to the substantiality of a man.

He told me all this very much later, but I've put it down here with the idea of exploding those first wild rumors about his antecedents, which weren't even faintly true. Moreover he told it to me at a time of confusion, when I had reached the point of believing everything and nothing about him. So I take advantage of this short halt, while Gatsby, so to speak, caught his breath, to clear this set of misconceptions away.

It was a halt, too, in my association with his affairs. For several weeks I didn't see him or hear his voice on the phone—mostly I was in New York, trotting around with Jordan and trying to ingratiate myself with her senile aunt—but finally I went over to his house one Sunday afternoon. I hadn't been there two minutes when somebody brought Tom Buchanan in for a drink. I was startled, naturally, but the really surprising thing was that it hadn't happened before.

They were a party of three on horseback—Tom and a man named Sloane and a pretty woman in a brown riding habit, who had been there previously.

"I'm delighted to see you," said Gatsby, standing on his porch. "I'm delighted that you dropped in."

As though they cared!

"Sit right down. Have a cigarette or a cigar." He walked around the room quickly, ringing bells. "I'll have something to drink for you in just a minute."

He was profoundly affected by the fact that Tom was there. But he would be uneasy anyhow until he had given them something, realizing in a vague way that that was all they came for. Mr. Sloane wanted nothing. A lemonade? No, thanks. A little champagne? Nothing at all, thanks. . . . I'm sorry——

"Did you have a nice ride?"

"Very good roads around here."

"I suppose the automobiles——"

"Yeah."

Moved by an irresistible impulse, Gatsby turned to Tom, who had accepted the introduction as a stranger.

"I believe we've met somewhere before, Mr. Buchanan."

"Oh, yes," said Tom, gruffly polite, but obviously not remembering. "So we did. I remember very well."

"About two weeks ago."

"That's right. You were with Nick here."

"I know your wife," continued Gatsby, almost aggressively.

"That so?"

Tom turned to me.

"You live near here, Nick?"

"Next door."

"That so?"

Mr. Sloane didn't enter into the conversation, but lounged back haughtily in his chair; the woman said nothing either—until unexpectedly, after two highballs, she became cordial.

"We'll all come over to your next party, Mr. Gatsby," she suggested. "What do you say?"

"Certainly; I'd be delighted to have you."

"Be ver' nice," said Mr. Sloane, without gratitude. "Well—think ought to be starting home."

"Please don't hurry," Gatsby urged them. He had control of himself now, and he wanted to see more of Tom. "Why don't you—why don't you stay for supper? I wouldn't be surprised if some other people dropped in from New York."

"You come to supper with *me,*" said the lady enthusiastically. "Both of you."

This included me. Mr. Sloane got to his feet.

"Come along," he said—but to her only.

"I mean it," she insisted. "I'd love to have you. Lots of room."

Gatsby looked at me questioningly. He wanted to go, and he didn't see that Mr. Sloane had determined he shouldn't.

"I'm afraid I won't be able to," I said.

"Well, you come," she urged, concentrating on Gatsby.

Mr. Sloane murmured something close to her ear.

"We won't be late if we start now," she insisted aloud.

"I haven't got a horse," said Gatsby. "I used to ride in the army, but I've never bought a horse. I'll have to follow you in my car. Excuse me for just a minute."

The rest of us walked out on the porch, where Sloane and the lady began an impassioned conversation aside.

"My, God, I believe the man's coming," said Tom. "Doesn't he know she doesn't want him?"

"She says she does want him."

"She has a big dinner party and he won't know a soul there." He frowned. "I wonder where in the devil he met Daisy. By God, I may be old-fashioned in my ideas, but women run around too much these days to suit me. They meet all kinds of crazy fish."

Suddenly Mr. Sloane and the lady walked down the steps and mounted their horses.

"Come on," said Mr. Sloane to Tom, "we're late. We've got to go." And then to me: "Tell him we couldn't wait, will you?"

Tom and I shook hands, the rest of us exchanged a cool nod, and they trotted quickly down the drive, disappearing under the August foliage just as Gatsby, with hat and light overcoat in hand, came out the front door.

Tom was evidently perturbed at Daisy's running around alone, for on the following Saturday night he came with her to Gatsby's party. Perhaps his presence gave the evening its peculiar quality of oppressiveness—it stands out in my memory from Gatsby's other parties that summer. There were the same people, or at least the same sort of people, the same profusion of champagne, the same many-colored, many-keyed commotion, but I felt an unpleasantness in the air, a pervading harshness that hadn't been there before. Or perhaps I had merely grown used to it, grown to accept West Egg as a world complete in itself, with its own standards and its own great figures, second to nothing because it had no consciousness of being so, and now I was looking at it again, through Daisy's eyes. It is invariably saddening to look through new eyes at things upon which you have expended your own powers of adjustment.

They arrived at twilight, and, as we strolled out among the sparkling hundreds, Daisy's voice was playing murmurous tricks in her throat.

"These things excite me *so,*" she whispered. "If you want to kiss me any time during the evening, Nick, just let me know and I'll be glad to arrange it for you. Just mention my name. Or present a green card. I'm giving out green——"

"Look around," suggested Gatsby.

"I'm looking around. I'm having a marvelous——"

"You must see the faces of many people you've heard about."

Tom's arrogant eyes roamed the crowd.

"We don't go around very much," he said; "in fact, I was just thinking I don't know a soul here."

"Perhaps you know that lady," Gatsby indicated a gorgeous, scarcely human orchid of a woman who sat in state under a white-plum tree. Tom and Daisy stared, with that particularly unreal feeling that accompanies the recognition of a hitherto ghostly celebrity of the movies.

"She's lovely," said Daisy.

"The man bending over her is her director."

He took them ceremoniously from group to group:

"Mrs. Buchanan . . . and Mr. Buchanan—" After an instant's hesitation he added: "the polo player."

"Oh, no," objected Tom quickly, "not me."

But evidently the sound of it pleased Gatsby, for Tom remained "the polo player" for the rest of the evening.

"I've never met so many celebrities," Daisy exclaimed. "I liked that man—what was his name?—with the sort of blue nose."

Gatsby identified him, adding that he was a small producer.

"Well, I liked him anyhow."

"I'd a little rather not be the polo player," said Tom pleasantly, "I'd rather look at all these famous people in—in oblivion."

Daisy and Gatsby danced. I remembered being surprised by his graceful, conservative fox trot—I had never seen him dance before. Then they sauntered over to my house and sat on the steps for half an hour, while at her request I remained watchfully in the garden. "In case there's a fire or a flood," she explained, "or any act of God."

Tom appeared from his oblivion as we were sitting down to supper together. "Do you mind if I eat with some people over here?" he said. "A fellow's getting off some funny stuff."

"Go ahead," answered Daisy genially, "and if you want to take down any addresses here's my little gold pencil." . . . She looked around after a moment and told me the girl was "common but pretty," and I knew that except for the half-hour she'd been alone with Gatsby she wasn't having a good time.

We were at a particularly tipsy table. That was my fault—Gatsby had been called to the phone, and I'd enjoyed these same people only two weeks before. But what had amused me then turned septic on the air now.

"How do you feel, Miss Baedeker?"

The girl addressed was trying, unsuccessfully, to slump against my shoulder. At this inquiry she sat up and opened her eyes.

"Wha'?"

A massive and lethargic woman, who had been urging Daisy to play golf with her at the local club tomorrow, spoke in Miss Baedeker's defense:

"Oh, she's all right now. When she's had five or six cocktails she always starts screaming like that. I tell her she ought to leave it alone."

"I do leave it alone," affirmed the accused hollowly.

"We heard you yelling, so I said to Doc Civet here: 'There's somebody that needs your help, Doc.' "

"She's much obliged, I'm sure," said another friend, without gratitude, "but you got her dress all wet when you stuck her head in the pool."

"Anything I hate is to get my head stuck in a pool," mumbled Miss Baedeker. "They almost drowned me once over in New Jersey."

"Then you ought to leave it alone," countered Doctor Civet.

"Speak for yourself!" cried Miss Baedeker violently. "Your hand shakes. I wouldn't let you operate on me!"

It was like that. Almost the last thing I remember was standing with Daisy and watching the moving-picture director and his Star. They were still under the white-plum tree and their faces were touching except for a pale, thin ray of moonlight between. It occurred to me that he had been very slowly bending toward her all evening to attain this proximity, and even while I watched I saw him stoop one ultimate degree and kiss at her cheek.

"I like her," said Daisy, "I think she's lovely."

But the rest offended her—and inarguably, because it wasn't a gesture but an emotion. She was appalled by West Egg, this unprecedented "place" that Broadway had begotten upon a Long Island fishing village—appalled by its raw vigor that chafed under the old euphemisms and by the too obtrusive fate that herded its inhabitants along a short cut from nothing to nothing. She saw something awful in the very simplicity she failed to understand.

I sat on the front steps with them while they waited for their car. It was dark here in front; only the bright door sent ten square feet of light volleying out into the soft black morning. Sometimes a shadow moved against a dressing-room blind above, gave way to another shadow, an indefinite procession of shadows, that rouged and powdered in an invisible glass.

"Who is this Gatsby anyhow?" he demanded suddenly. "Some big bootlegger?"

"Where'd you hear that?" I inquired.

"I didn't hear it. I imagined it. A lot of these newly rich people are just big bootleggers, you know."

"Not Gatsby," I said shortly.

He was silent for a moment. The pebbles of the drive crunched under his feet.

"Well, he certainly must have strained himself to get this menagerie together."

A breeze stirred the gray haze of Daisy's fur collar.

"At least they're more interesting than the people we know," she said with an effort.

"You didn't look so interested."

"Well, I was."

Tom laughed and turned to me.

"Did you notice Daisy's face when that girl asked her to put her under a cold shower?"

Daisy began to sing with the music in a husky, rhythmic whisper, bringing out a meaning in each word that it had never had before and would never have again. When the melody rose, her voice broke up sweetly, following it, in a way contralto voices have, and each change tipped out a little of her warm human magic upon the air.

"Lots of people come who haven't been invited," she said suddenly. "That girl hadn't been invited. They simply force their way in and he's too polite to object."

"I'd like to know who he is and what he does," insisted Tom. "And I think I'll make a point of finding out."

"I can tell you right now," she answered. "He

owned some drugstores, a lot of drugstores. He built them up himself."

The dilatory limousine came rolling up the drive.

"Good night, Nick," said Daisy.

Her glance left me and sought the lighted top of the steps, where "Three O'Clock in the Morning," a neat, sad little waltz of that year, was drifting out the open door. After all, in the very casualness of Gatsby's party there were romantic possibilities totally absent from her world. What was it up there in the song that seemed to be calling her back inside? What would happen now in the dim incalculable hours? Perhaps some unbelievable guest would arrive, a person infinitely rare and to be marveled at, some authentically radiant young girl who with one fresh glance at Gatsby, one moment of magical encounter, would blot out those five years of unwavering devotion.

I stayed late that night, Gatsby asked me to wait until he was free, and I lingered in the garden until the inevitable swimming party had run up, chilled and exalted, from the black beach, until the lights were extinguished in the guest rooms overhead. When he came down the steps at last the tanned skin was drawn unusually tight on his face, and his eyes were bright and tired.

"She didn't like it," he said immediately.

"Of course she did."

"She didn't like it," he insisted. "She didn't have a good time."

He was silent, and I guessed at his unutterable depression.

"I feel far away from her," he said. "It's hard to make her understand."

"You mean about the dance?"

"The dance?" He dismissed all the dances he had given with a snap of his fingers. "Old sport, the dance is unimportant."

He wanted nothing less of Daisy than that she should go to Tom and say: "I never loved you." After she had obliterated four years with that sentence they could decide upon the more practical measures to be taken. One of them was that, after she was free, they were to go back to Louisville and be married from her house—just as if it were five years ago.

"And she doesn't understand," he said. "She used to be able to understand. We'd sit for hours——"

He broke off and began to walk up and down a desolate path of fruit rinds and discarded favors and crushed flowers.

"I wouldn't ask too much of her," I ventured. "You can't repeat the past."

"Can't repeat the past?" he cried incredulously. "Why of course you can!"

He looked around him wildly, as if the past were lurking here in the shadow of his house, just out of reach of his hand.

"I'm going to fix everything just the way it was before," he said, nodding determinedly. "She'll see."

He talked a lot about the past, and I gathered that he wanted to recover something, some idea of himself perhaps, that had gone into loving Daisy. His life had been confused and disordered since then, but if he could once return to a certain starting place and go over it all slowly, he could find out what that thing was. . . .

. . . One autumn night, five years before, they had been walking down the street when the leaves were falling, and they came to a place where there were no trees and the sidewalk was white with moonlight. They stopped here and turned toward each other. Now it was a cool night with that mysterious excitement in it which comes at the two changes of the year. The quiet lights in the houses were humming out into the darkness and there was a stir and bustle among the stars. Out of the corner of his eye Gatsby saw that the blocks of the sidewalks really formed a ladder and mounted to a secret place above the trees—he could climb to it, if he climbed alone, and once there he could suck on the pap of life, gulp down the incomparable milk of wonder.

His heart beat faster and faster as Daisy's white face came up to his own. He knew that when he kissed this girl, and forever wed his unutterable visions to her perishable breath, his mind would never romp again like the mind of God. So he waited, listening for a moment longer to the tuning-fork that had been struck upon a star. Then he kissed her. At his lips' touch she blossomed for him like a flower and the incarnation was complete.

Through all he said, even through his appalling sentimentality, I was reminded of something—an elusive rhythm, a fragment of lost words, that I had heard somewhere a long time ago. For a moment a phrase tried to take shape in my mouth and my lips parted like a dumb man's, as though there was more struggling upon them than a wisp of startled air. But they made no sound, and what I had almost remembered was uncommunicable forever.

CHAPTER VII

It was when curiosity about Gatsby was at its highest that the lights in his house failed to go on one Saturday night—and, as obscurely as it had begun, his career as Trimalchio was over. Only gradually did I become aware that the automobiles which turned expectantly into his drive stayed for just a minute and then drove sulkily away. Wondering if he were sick I went over to find out—an unfamiliar butler with a villainous face squinted at me suspiciously from the door.

"Is Mr. Gatsby sick?"

"Nope." After a pause he added "sir" in a dilatory, grudging way.

"I hadn't seen him around, and I was rather worried. Tell him Mr. Carraway came over."

"Who?" he demanded rudely.

"Carraway."

"Carraway. All right, I'll tell him."

Abruptly he slammed the door.

My Finn informed me that Gatsby had dismissed every servant in his house a week ago and replaced them with half a dozen others, who never went into West Egg Village to be bribed by the tradesmen, but ordered moderate supplies over the telephone. The grocery boy reported that the kitchen looked like a pigsty, and the general opinion in the village was that the new people weren't servants at all.

Next day Gatsby called me on the phone.

"Going away?" I inquired.

"No, old sport."

"I hear you fired all your servants."

"I wanted somebody who wouldn't gossip. Daisy comes over quite often—in the afternoons."

So the whole caravansary had fallen in like a card house at the disapproval in her eyes.

"They're some people Wolfsheim wanted to do something for. They're all brothers and sisters. They used to run a small hotel."

"I see."

He was calling up at Daisy's request—would I come to lunch at her house tomorrow? Miss Baker would be there. Half an hour later Daisy herself telephoned and seemed relieved to find that I was coming. Something was up. And yet I couldn't believe that they would choose this occasion for a scene—especially for the rather harrowing scene that Gatsby had outlined in the garden.

The next day was broiling, almost the last, certainly the warmest, of the summer. As my train emerged from the tunnel into sunlight, only the hot whistles of the National Biscuit Company broke the simmering hush at noon. The straw seats of the car hovered on the edge of combustion; the woman next to me perspired delicately for a while into her white shirtwaist, and then, as her newspaper dampened under her fingers, lapsed despairingly into deep heat with a desolate cry. Her pocketbook slapped to the floor.

"Oh, my!" she gasped.

I picked it up with a weary bend and handed it back to her, holding it at arm's length and by the extreme tip of the corners to indicate that I had no designs upon it—but everyone nearby, including the woman, suspected me just the same.

"Hot!" said the conductor to familiar faces. "Some weather! . . . Hot! . . . Hot! . . . Hot! . . . Is it hot enough for you? Is it hot? Is it . . . ?"

My commutation ticket came back to me with a dark stain from his hand. That anyone should care in this heat whose flushed lips he kissed, whose head made damp the pajama pocket over his heart!

. . . Through the hall of the Buchanans' house blew a faint wind, carrying the sound of the telephone bell out to Gatsby and me as we waited at the door.

"The master's body!" roared the butler into the mouthpiece. "I'm sorry madame, but we can't furnish it—it's far too hot to touch this noon!"

What he really said was: "Yes . . . Yes . . . I'll see."

He set down the receiver and came toward us, glistening slightly, to take our stiff straw hats.

"Madame expects you in the salon!" he cried, needlessly indicating the direction. In this heat every extra gesture was an affront to the common store of life.

The room, shadowed well with awnings, was dark and cool. Daisy and Jordan lay upon an enormous couch, like silver idols weighing down their own white dresses against the singing breeze of the fans.

"We can't move," they said together.

Jordan's fingers, powdered white over their tan, rested for a moment in mine.

"And Mr. Thomas Buchanan, the athlete?" I inquired.

Simultaneously I heard his voice, gruff, muffled, husky, at the hall telephone.

Gatsby stood in the center of the crimson carpet and gazed around with fascinated eyes. Daisy watched him and laughed, her sweet, exciting laugh; a tiny gust of powder rose from her bosom into the air.

"The rumor is," whispered Jordan, "that that's Tom's girl on the telephone."

We were silent. The voice in the hall rose high with annoyance: "Very well, then, I won't sell you the car at all. . . . I'm under no obligations to you at all . . . and as for your bothering me about it at lunchtime, I won't stand that at all!"

"Holding down the receiver," said Daisy cynically.

"No, he's not," I assured her. "It's a bona fide deal. I happen to know about it."

Tom flung open the door, blocked out its space for a moment with his thick body, and hurried into the room.

"Mr. Gatsby!" He put out his broad, flat hand with well-concealed dislike. "I'm glad to see you, sir. . . . Nick. . . ."

"Make us a cold drink," cried Daisy.

As he left the room again she got up and went over to Gatsby and pulled his face down, kissing him on the mouth.

"You know I love you," she murmured.

"You forget there's a lady present," said Jordan.

Daisy looked around doubtfully.

"You kiss Nick too."

"What a low, vulgar girl!"

"I don't care!" cried Daisy, and began to clog on the brick fireplace. Then she remembered the heat and sat down guiltily on the couch just as a freshly laundered nurse leading a little girl came into the room.

"Bles-sed pre-cious," she crooned, holding out her arms. "Come to your own mother that loves you."

The child, relinquished by the nurse, rushed across the room and rooted shyly into her mother's dress.

"The bles-sed pre-cious! Did Mother get powder on your old yellowy hair! Stand up now, and say—How-de-do."

Gatsby and I in turn leaned down and took the small reluctant hand. Afterward he kept looking at the child with surprise. I don't think he had ever really believed in its existence before.

"I got dressed before luncheon," said the child, turning eagerly to Daisy.

"That's because your mother wanted to show you off." Her face bent into the single wrinkle of the small white neck. "You dream, you. You absolute little dream."

"Yes," admitted the child calmly. "Aunt Jordan's got on a white dress too."

"How do you like Mother's friends?" Daisy turned her around so that she faced Gatsby. "Do you think they're pretty?"

"Where's Daddy?"

"She doesn't look like her father," explained Daisy. "She looks like me. She's got my hair and shape of the face."

Daisy sat back upon the couch. The nurse took a step forward and held out her hand.

"Come, Pammy."

"Good-by, sweetheart!"

With a reluctant backward glance the well-disciplined child held to her nurse's hand and was pulled out the door, just as Tom came back, preceding four gin rickeys that clicked full of ice.

Gatsby took up his drink.

"They certainly look cool," he said, with visible tension.

We drank in long, greedy swallows.

"I read somewhere that the sun's getting hotter every year," said Tom genially. "It seems that pretty soon the earth's going to fall into the sun—or wait a minute—it's just the opposite—the sun's getting colder every year."

"Come outside," he suggested to Gatsby, "I'd like you to have a look at the place."

I went with them out to the veranda. On the green Sound, stagnant in the heat, one small sail crawled slowly toward the fresher sea. Gatsby's eyes followed it momentarily; he raised his hand and pointed across the bay.

"I'm right across from you."

"So you are."

Our eyes lifted over the rose beds and the hot lawn and the weedy refuse of the dog days along-shore. Slowly the white wings of the boat moved against the blue cool limit of the sky. Ahead lay the scalloped ocean and the abounding blessed isles.

"There's sport for you," said Tom, nodding. "I'd like to be out there with him for about an hour."

We had luncheon in the dining room, darkened too against the heat, and drank down nervous gaiety with the cold ale.

"What'll we do with ourselves this afternoon?" cried Daisy, "and the day after that, and the next thirty years?"

"Don't be morbid," Jordan said. "Life starts all over again when it gets crisp in the fall."

"But it's so hot," insisted Daisy, on the verge of tears, "and everything's so confused. Let's all go to town!"

Her voice struggled on through the heat, beating against it, molding its senselessness into forms.

"I've heard of making a garage out of a stable," Tom was saying to Gatsby, "but I'm the first man who ever made a stable out of a garage."

"Who wants to go to town?" demanded Daisy insistently. Gatsby's eyes floated toward her. "Ah," she cried, "you look so cool."

Their eyes met, and they stared together at each other, alone in space. With an effort she glanced down at the table.

"You always look so cool," she repeated.

She had told him that she loved him, and Tom Buchanan saw. He was astounded. His mouth opened a little, and he looked at Gatsby, and then back at Daisy as if he had just recognized her as someone he knew a long time ago.

"You resemble the advertisement of the man," she went on innocently. "You know the advertisement of the man——"

"All right," broke in Tom quickly, "I'm perfectly willing to go to town. Come on—we're all going to town."

He got up, his eyes still flashing between Gatsby and his wife. No one moved.

"Come on!" His temper cracked a little. "What's the matter, anyhow? If we're going to town, let's start."

His hand, trembling with his effort at self-control, bore to his lips the last glass of ale. Daisy's voice got us to our feet and out on to the blazing gravel drive.

"Are we just going to go?" she objected. "Like this? Aren't we going to let anyone smoke a cigarette first?"

"Everybody smoked all through lunch."

"Oh, let's have fun," she begged him. "It's too hot to fuss."

He didn't answer.

"Have it your own way," she said. "Come on, Jordan."

They went upstairs to get ready while we three men stood there shuffling the hot pebbles with our feet. A silver curve of the moon hovered already in the western sky. Gatsby started to speak, changed his mind, but not before Tom wheeled and faced him expectantly.

"Have you got your stables here?" asked Gatsby with an effort.

"About a quarter of a mile down the road."

"Oh."

A pause.

"I don't see the idea of going to town," broke out Tom savagely. "Women get these notions in their heads——"

"Shall we take anything to drink?" called Daisy from an upper window.

"I'll get some whiskey," answered Tom. He went inside.

Gatsby turned to me rigidly:

"I can't say anything in his house, old sport."

"She's got an indiscreet voice," I remarked. "It's full of—" I hesitated.

"Her voice is full of money," he said suddenly.

That was it. I'd never understood before. It was full of money—that was the inexhaustible charm that rose and fell in it, the jingle of it, the cymbals' song of it. . . . High in a white palace the king's daughter, the golden girl. . . .

Tom came out of the house wrapping a quart bottle in a towel, followed by Daisy and Jordan wearing small tight hats of metallic cloth and carrying light capes over their arms.

"Shall we all go in my car?" suggested Gatsby. He felt the hot, green leather of the seat. "I ought to have left it in the shade."

"Is it standard shift?" demanded Tom.

"Yes."

"Well, you take my coupé and let me drive your car to town."

The suggestion was distasteful to Gatsby.

"I don't think there's much gas," he objected.

"Plenty of gas," said Tom boisterously. He looked at the gauge. "And if it runs out I can stop at a drugstore. You can buy anything at a drugstore nowadays."

A pause followed this apparently pointless remark. Daisy looked at Tom frowning, and an indefinable expression, at once definitely unfamiliar and vaguely recognizable, as if I had only heard it described in words, passed over Gatsby's face.

"Come on, Daisy," said Tom, pressing her with his hand toward Gatsby's car. "I'll take you in this circus wagon."

He opened the door, but she moved out from the circle of his arm.

"You take Nick and Jordan. We'll follow you in the coupé."

She walked close to Gatsby, touching his coat with her hand. Jordan and Tom and I got into the front seat of Gatsby's car, Tom pushed the unfamiliar gears tentatively, and we shot off into the oppressive heat, leaving them out of sight behind.

"Did you see that?" demanded Tom.

"See what?"

He looked at me keenly, realizing that Jordan and I must have known all along.

"You think I'm pretty dumb, don't you?" he suggested. "Perhaps I am, but I have a—almost a second sight, sometimes, that tells me what to do. Maybe you don't believe that, but science——"

He paused. The immediate contingency overtook him, pulled him back from the edge of the theoretical abyss.

"I've made a small investigation of this fellow," he continued. "I could have gone deeper if I'd known——"

"Do you mean you've been to a medium?" inquired Jordan humorously.

"What?" Confused, he stared at us as we laughed. "A medium?"

"About Gatsby."

"About Gatsby! No, I haven't. I said I'd been making a small investigation of his past."

"And you found he was an Oxford man," said Jordan helpfully.

"An Oxford man!" He was incredulous. "Like hell he is! He wears a pink suit."

"Nevertheless he's an Oxford man."

"Oxford, New Mexico," snorted Tom contemptuously, "or something like that."

"Listen, Tom. If you're such a snob, why did you invite him to lunch?" demanded Jordan crossly.

"Daisy invited him; she knew him before we were married—God knows where!"

We were all irritable now with the fading ale, and aware of it we drove for a while in silence. Then as Doctor T. J. Eckleburg's faded eyes came into sight down the road, I remembered Gatsby's caution about gasoline.

"We've got enough to get us to town," said Tom.

"But there's a garage right here," objected Jordan. "I don't want to get stalled in this baking heat."

Tom threw on both brakes impatiently, and we slid to an abrupt dusty stop under Wilson's sign. After a moment the proprietor emerged from the interior of his establishment and gazed hollow-eyed at the car.

"Let's have some gas!" cried Tom roughly. "What do you think we stopped for—to admire the view?"

"I'm sick," said Wilson without moving. "Been sick all day."

"What's the matter?"

"I'm all run down."

"Well, shall I help myself?" Tom demanded. "You sounded well enough on the phone."

With an effort Wilson left the shade and support of the doorway and, breathing hard, unscrewed the cap of the tank. In the sunlight his face was green.

"I didn't mean to interrupt your lunch," he said. "But I need money pretty bad, and I was wondering what you were going to do with your old car."

"How do you like this one?" inquired Tom. "I bought it last week."

"It's a nice yellow one," said Wilson, as he strained at the handle.

"Like to buy it?"

"Big chance," Wilson smiled faintly. "No, but I could make some money on the other."

"What do you want money for, all of a sudden?"

"I've been here too long. I want to get away. My wife and I want to go West."

"Your wife does," exclaimed Tom, startled.

"She's been talking about it for ten years." He rested for a moment against the pump, shading his eyes. "And now she's going whether she wants to or not. I'm going to get her away."

The coupé flashed by us with a flurry of dust and the flash of a waving hand.

"What do I owe you?" demanded Tom harshly.

"I just got wised up to something funny the last two days," remarked Wilson. "That's why I want to get away. That's why I been bothering you about the car."

"What do I owe you?"

"Dollar twenty."

The relentless beating heat was beginning to confuse me and I had a bad moment there before I realized that so far his suspicions hadn't alighted on Tom. He had discovered that Myrtle had some sort of life apart from him in another world, and the shock had made him physically sick. I stared at him and then at Tom, who had made a parallel discovery less than an hour before—and it occurred to me that there was no difference between men, in intelligence or race, so profound as the difference between the sick and the well. Wilson was so sick that he looked guilty, unforgivably guilty—as if he had just got some poor girl with child.

"I'll let you have that car," said Tom. "I'll send it over tomorrow afternoon."

That locality was always vaguely disquieting, even in the broad glare of afternoon, and now I turned my head as though I had been warned of something behind. Over the ashheaps the giant eyes of Doctor T. J. Eckleburg kept their vigil, but I perceived, after a moment, that other eyes were regarding us less than twenty feet away.

In one of the windows over the garage the curtains had been moved aside a little, and Myrtle Wilson was peering down at the car. So engrossed was she that she had no consciousness of being observed, and one emotion after another crept into her face like objects into a slowly developing picture. Her expression was curiously familiar—it was an expression I had often seen on women's faces, but on Myrtle Wilson's face it seemed purposeless and inexplicable until I realized that her eyes, wide with jealous terror, were fixed not on Tom, but on Jordan Baker, whom she took to be his wife.

There is no confusion like the confusion of a simple mind, and as we drove away Tom was feeling the hot whips of panic. His wife and his mistress, until an hour ago secure and inviolate, were slipping precipitately from his control. Instinct made him step on the accelerator with the double purpose of overtaking Daisy and leaving Wilson behind, and we sped along toward Astoria at fifty miles an hour, until, among the spidery girders of the elevated, we came in sight of the easygoing blue coupé.

"Those big movies around Fiftieth Street are cool," suggested Jordan. "I love New York on summer afternoons when everyone's away. There's something very sensuous about it—overripe, as if all sorts of funny fruits were going to fall into your hands."

The word "sensuous" had the effect of further disquieting Tom, but before he could invent a protest the coupé came to a stop, and Daisy signaled us to draw up alongside.

"Where are we going?" she cried.

"How about the movies?"

"It's so hot," she complained. "You go. We'll ride around and meet you after." With an effort her wit rose faintly, "We'll meet you on some corner. I'll be the man smoking two cigarettes."

"We can't argue about it here," Tom said impatiently, as a truck gave out a cursing whistle behind us. "You follow me to the south side of Central Park, in front of the Plaza."

Several times he turned his head and looked back for their car, and if the traffic delayed them he slowed up until they came into sight. I think he was afraid they would dart down a side street and out of his life forever.

But they didn't. And we all took the less explicable step of engaging the parlor of a suite in the Plaza Hotel.

The prolonged and tumultuous argument that ended by herding us into that room eludes me, though I have a sharp physical memory that, in the course of it, my underwear kept climbing like a damp snake around my legs and intermittent beads of sweat raced cool across my back. The notion originated with Daisy's suggestion that we hire five bathrooms and take cold baths, and then assumed more tangible form as "a place to have a mint julep." Each of us said over and over that it was a "crazy idea"—we all talked at once to a baffled clerk and thought, or pretended to think, that we were being very funny . . .

The room was large and stifling, and, though it was already four o'clock, opening the windows admitted only a gust of hot shrubbery from the Park. Daisy went to the mirror and stood with her back to us, fixing her hair.

"It's a swell suite," whispered Jordan respectfully, and everyone laughed.

"Open another window," commanded Daisy, without turning around.

"There aren't any more."

"Well, we'd better telephone for an ax——"

"The thing to do is to forget about the heat," said Tom impatiently. "You make it ten times worse by crabbing about it."

He unrolled the bottle of whiskey from the towel and put it on the table.

"Why not let her alone, old sport?" remarked Gatsby. "You're the one that wanted to come to town."

There was a moment of silence. The telephone book slipped from its nail and splashed to the floor, whereupon Jordan whispered, "Excuse me"—but this time no one laughed.

"I'll pick it up," I offered.

"I've got it." Gatsby examined the parted string, muttered "Hum!" in an interested way, and tossed the book on a chair.

"That's a great expression of yours, isn't it?" said Tom sharply.

"What is?"

"All this 'old sport' business. Where'd you pick that up?"

"Now see here, Tom," said Daisy, turning around from the mirror, "if you're going to make personal remarks I won't stay here a minute. Call up and order some ice for the mint julep."

As Tom took up the receiver the compressed heat exploded into sound and we were listening to the portentous chords of Mendelssohn's Wedding March from the ballroom below.

"Imagine marrying anybody in this heat!" cried Jordan dismally.

"Still—I was married in the middle of June," Daisy remembered, "Louisville in June! Somebody fainted. Who was it fainted, Tom?"

"Biloxi," he answered shortly.

"A man named Biloxi. 'Blocks' Biloxi, and he made boxes—that's a fact—and he was from Biloxi, Mississippi."

"They carried him into my house," appended Jordan, "because we lived just two doors from the church. And he stayed three weeks, until Daddy told him he had to get out. The day after he left Daddy died." After a moment she added as if she might have sounded irreverent, "There wasn't any connection."

"I used to know a Bill Biloxi from Memphis," I remarked.

"That was his cousin. I knew his whole family history before he left. He gave me an aluminum putter that I use today."

The music had died down as the ceremony began and now a long cheer floated in at the window, followed by intermittent cries of "Yea—ea—ea!" and finally by a burst of jazz as the dancing began.

"We're getting old," said Daisy. "If we were young we'd rise and dance."

"Remember Biloxi," Jordan warned her. "Where'd you know him, Tom?"

"Biloxi?" He concentrated with an effort. "I didn't know him. He was a friend of Daisy's."

"He was not," she denied. "I'd never seen him before. He came down in the private car."

"Well, he said he knew you. He said he was raised

in Louisville. Asa Bird brought him around at the last minute and asked if we had room for him."

Jordan smiled. "He was probably bumming his way home. He told me he was president of your class at Yale."

Tom and I looked at each other blankly.

"Biloxi?"

"First place, we didn't have any president——"

Gatsby's foot beat a short, restless tattoo and Tom eyed him suddenly.

"By the way, Mr. Gatsby, I understand you're an Oxford man."

"Not exactly."

"Oh, yes, I understand you went to Oxford."

"Yes—I went there."

A pause. Then Tom's voice incredulous and insulting:

"You must have gone there about the time Biloxi went to New Haven."

Another pause. A waiter knocked and came in with crushed mint and ice, but the silence was unbroken by his "thank you" and the soft closing of the door. This tremendous detail was to be cleared up at last.

"I told you I went there," said Gatsby.

"I heard you, but I'd like to know when."

"It was in nineteen-nineteen. I only stayed five months. That's why I can't really call myself an Oxford man."

Tom glanced around to see if we mirrored his unbelief. But we were all looking at Gatsby.

"It was an opportunity they gave to some of the officers after the Armstice," he continued. "We could go to any of the universities in England or France."

I wanted to get up and slap him on the back. I had one of those renewals of complete faith in him that I'd experienced before.

Daisy rose, smiling faintly, and went to the table.

"Open the whiskey, Tom," she ordered, "and I'll make you a mint julep. Then you won't seem so stupid to yourself. . . . Look at the mint!"

"Wait a minute," snapped Tom, "I want to ask Mr. Gatsby one more question."

"Go on," Gatsby said politely.

"What kind of a row are you trying to cause in my house anyhow?"

They were out in the open at last and Gatsby was content.

"He isn't causing a row," Daisy looked desperately from one to the other. "You're causing a row. Please have a little self-control."

"Self-control!" repeated Tom incredulously. "I suppose the latest thing is to sit back and let Mr. Nobody from Nowhere make love to your wife. Well, if that's the idea you can count me out. . . . Nowadays people begin by sneering at family life and family institutions, and next they'll throw everything overboard and have intermarriage between black and white."

Flushed with his impassioned gibberish, he saw himself standing alone on the last barrier of civilization.

"We're all white here," murmured Jordan.

"I know I'm not very popular. I don't give big parties. I suppose you've got to make your house into a pigsty in order to have any friends—in the modern world."

Angry as I was, as we all were, I was tempted to laugh whenever he opened his mouth. The transition from libertine to prig was so complete.

"I've got something to tell *you,* old sport—" began Gatsby. But Daisy guessed at his intention.

"Please don't!" she interrupted helplessly. "Please let's all go home. Why don't we all go home?"

"That's a good idea." I got up. "Come on, Tom. Nobody wants a drink."

"I want to know what Mr. Gatsby has to tell me."

"Your wife doesn't love you," said Gatsby. "She never loved you. She loves me."

"You must be crazy!" exclaimed Tom automatically.

Gatsby sprang to his feet, vivid with excitement.

"She never loved you, do you hear?" he cried. "She only married you because I was poor and she was tired of waiting for me. It was a terrible mistake, but in her heart she never loved anyone except me!"

At this point Jordan and I tried to go, but Tom and Gatsby insisted with competitive firmness that we remain—as though neither of them had anything to conceal and it would be a privilege to partake vicariously of their emotions.

"Sit down, Daisy," Tom's voice groped unsuccessfully for the paternal note. "What's been going on? I want to hear all about it."

"I told you what's been going on," said Gatsby. "Going on for five years—and you didn't know."

Tom turned to Daisy sharply.

"You've been seeing this fellow for five years?"

"Not seeing," said Gatsby. "No, we couldn't meet. But both of us loved each other all that time, old sport, and you didn't know. I used to laugh sometimes"—but there was no laughter in his eyes—"to think that you didn't know."

"Oh—that's all." Tom tapped his thick fingers together like a clergyman and leaned back in his chair.

"You're crazy!" he exploded. "I can't speak about what happened five years ago, because I didn't know Daisy then—and I'll be damned if I see how you got within a mile of her unless you brought the groceries to the back door. But all the rest of that's a God-damned lie. Daisy loved me when she married me and she loves me now."

"No," said Gatsby, shaking his head.

"She does, though. The trouble is that sometimes she gets foolish ideas in her head and doesn't know what she's doing." He nodded sagely. "And what's more, I love Daisy too. Once in a while I go off on a spree and make a fool of myself, but I always come back, and in my heart I love her all the time."

"You're revolting," said Daisy. She turned to me, and her voice, dropping an octave lower, filled the room with thrilling scorn: "Do you know why we left Chicago? I'm surprised that they didn't treat you to the story of that little spree."

Gatsby walked over and stood beside her.

"Daisy, that's all over now," he said earnestly. "It doesn't matter any more. Just tell him the truth—that you never loved him—and it's all wiped out forever."

She looked at him blindly. "Why—how could I love him—possibly?"

"You never loved him."

She hesitated. Her eyes fell on Jordan and me with a sort of appeal, as though she realized at last what she was doing—and as though she had never, all along, intended doing anything at all. But it was done now. It was too late.

"I never loved him," she said, with perceptible reluctance.

"Not at Kapiolani?" demanded Tom suddenly.

"No."

From the ballroom beneath, muffled and suffocating chords were drifting up on hot waves of air.

"Not that day I carried you down from the Punch Bowl to keep your shoes dry?" There was a husky tenderness in his tone. . . . "Daisy?"

"Please don't." Her voice was cold, but the rancor was gone from it. She looked at Gatsby. "There, Jay," she said—but her hand as she tried to light a cigarette was trembling. Suddenly she threw the cigarette and the burning match on the carpet.

"Oh, you want too much!" she cried to Gatsby. "I love you now—isn't that enough? I can't help what's past." She began to sob helplessly. "I did love him once—but I love you too."

Gatsby's eyes opened and closed.

"You loved me *too?*" he repeated.

"Even that's a lie," said Tom savagely. "She didn't know you were alive. Why—there're things between Daisy and me that you'll never know, things that neither of us can ever forget."

The words seemed to bite physically into Gatsby.

"I want to speak to Daisy alone," he insisted. "She's all excited now——"

"Even alone I can't say I never loved Tom,"she admitted in a pitiful voice. "It wouldn't be true."

"Of course it wouldn't," agreed Tom.

She turned to her husband.

"As if it mattered to you," she said.

"Of course it matters. I'm going to take better care of you from now on."

"You don't understand," said Gatsby, with a touch of panic. "You're not going to take care of her any more."

"I'm not?" Tom opened his eyes wide and laughed. He could afford to control himself now. "Why's that?"

"Daisy's leaving you."

"Nonsense."

"I am, though," she said with a visible effort.

"She's not leaving me!" Tom's words suddenly leaned down over Gatsby. "Certainly not for a common swindler who'd have to steal the ring he put on her finger."

"I won't stand this!" cried Daisy. "Oh, please let's get out."

"Who are you, anyhow?" broke out Tom. "You're one of that bunch that hangs around with Meyer Wolfsheim—that much I happen to know. I've made a little investigation into your affairs—and I'll carry it further tomorrow."

"You can suit yourself about that, old sport," said Gatsby steadily.

"I found out what your 'drugstores' were." He turned to us and spoke rapidly. "He and this Wolfsheim bought up a lot of side-street drugstores here and in Chicago and sold grain alcohol over the counter. That's one of his little stunts. I picked him for a bootlegger the first time I saw him, and I wasn't far wrong."

"What about it?" said Gatsby politely. "I guess your friend Walter Chase wasn't too proud to come in on it."

"And you left him in the lurch, didn't you? You let him go to jail for a month over in New Jersey. God! You ought to hear Walter on the subject of *you.*"

"He came to us dead broke. He was very glad to pick up some money, old sport."

"Don't you call me 'old sport'!" cried Tom. Gatsby said nothing. "Walter could have you up on the betting laws too, but Wolfsheim scared him into shutting his mouth."

That unfamiliar yet recognizable look was back again in Gatsby's face.

"That drugstore business was just small change," continued Tom slowly, "but you've got something on now that Walter's afraid to tell me about."

I glanced at Daisy, who was staring terrified between

Gatsby and her husband, and at Jordan, who had begun to balance an invisible but absorbing object on the tip of her chin. Then I turned back to Gatsby—and was startled at his expression. He looked—and this is said in all contempt for the babbled slander of his garden—as if he had "killed a man." For a moment the set of his face could be described in just that fantastic way.

It passed, and he began to talk excitedly to Daisy, denying everything, defending his name against accuations that had not been made. But with every word she was drawing further and further into herself, so he gave that up, and only the dead dream fought on as the afternoon slipped away, trying to touch what was no longer tangible, struggling unhappily, undespairingly, toward that lost voice across the room.

The voice begged again to go.

"Please, Tom! I can't stand this any more."

Her frightened eyes told that whatever intentions, whatever courage she had had, were definitely gone.

"You two start on home, Daisy," said Tom. "In Mr. Gatsby's car."

She looked at Tom, alarmed now, but he insisted with magnanimous scorn.

"Go on. He won't annoy you. I think he realizes that his presumptuous little flirtation is over."

They were gone, without a word, snapped out, made accidental, isolated, like ghosts, even from our pity.

After a moment Tom got up and began wrapping the unopened bottle of whiskey in the towel.

"Want any of this stuff? Jordan? . . . Nick?"

I didn't answer.

"Nick?" He asked again.

"What?"

"Want any?"

"No . . . I just remembered that today's my birthday."

I was thirty. Before me stretched the portentous, menacing road of a new decade.

It was seven o'clock when we got into the coupé with him and started for Long Island. Tom talked incessantly, exulting and laughing, but his voice was as remote from Jordan and me as the foreign clamor on the sidewalk or the tumult of the elevated overhead. Human sympathy has its limits, and we were content to let all their tragic arguments fade with the city lights behind. Thirty—the promise of a decade of loneliness, a thinning list of single men to know, a thinning briefcase of enthusiasm, thinning hair. But there was Jordan beside me, who, unlike Daisy, was too wise ever to carry well-forgotten dreams from age to age. As we passed over the dark bridge her wan face fell lazily against my coat's shoulder and the formidable stroke of thirty died away with the reassuring pressure of her hand.

So we drove on toward death through the cooling twilight.

The young Greek, Michaelis, who ran the coffee joint beside the ashheaps was the principal witness at the inquest. He had slept through the heat until after five, when he strolled over to the garage, and found George Wilson sick in his office—really sick, pale as his own pale hair and shaking all over. Michaelis advised him to go to bed, but Wilson refused, saying that he'd miss a lot of business if he did. While his neighbor was trying to persuade him a violent racket broke out overhead.

"I've got my wife locked in up there," explained Wilson calmly. "She's going to stay there till the day after tomorrow, and then we're going to move away."

Michaelis was astonished; they had been neighbors for four years, and Wilson had never seemed faintly capable of such a statement. Generally he was one of these worn-out men: when he wasn't working, he sat on a chair in the doorway and stared at the people and the cars that passed along the road. When anyone spoke to him he invariably laughed in an agreeable, colorless way. He was his wife's man and not his own.

So naturally Michaelis tried to find out what had happened, but Wilson wouldn't say a word—instead he began to throw curious, suspicious glances at his visitor and ask him what he'd been doing at certain times on certain days. Just as the latter was getting uneasy, some workmen came past the door bound for his restaurant, and Michaelis took the opportunity to get away, intending to come back later. But he didn't. He supposed he forgot to, that's all. When he came outside again, a little after seven, he was reminded of the conversation because he heard Mrs. Wilson's voice, loud and scolding, downstairs in the garage.

"Beat me!" he heard her cry. "Throw me down and beat me, you dirty little coward!"

A moment later she rushed out into the dusk, waving her hands and shouting—before he could move from his door the business was over.

The "death car" as the newspapers called it, didn't stop; it came out of the gathering darkness, wavered tragically for a moment, and then disappeared around the next bend. Michaelis wasn't even sure of its color—he told the first policeman that it was light green. The other car, the one going toward New York, came to rest a hundred yards beyond, and its driver hurried back to where Myrtle Wilson, her life violently extinguished, knelt in the road and mingled her thick dark blood with the dust.

Michaelis and this man reached her first, but when

they had torn open her shirtwaist, still damp with perspiration, they saw that her left breast was swinging loose like a flap, and there was no need to listen for the heart beneath. The mouth was wide open and ripped at the corners, as though she had choked a little in giving up the tremendous vitality she had stored so long.

We saw the three or four automobiles and the crowd when we were still some distance away.

"Wreck!" said Tom. "That's good. Wilson'll have a little business at last."

He slowed down, but still without any intention of stopping, until, as we came nearer, the hushed, intent faces of the people at the garage door made him automatically put on the brakes.

"We'll take a look," he said doubtfully, "just a look."

I became aware now of a hollow, wailing sound which issued incessantly from the garage, a sound which as we got out of the coupé and walked toward the door resolved itself into the words "Oh, my God!" uttered over and over in a gasping moan.

"There's some bad trouble here," said Tom excitedly.

He reached up on tiptoes and peered over a circle of heads into the garage, which was lit only by a yellow light in a swinging wire basket overhead. Then he made a harsh sound in his throat, and with a violent thrusting movement of his powerful arms pushed his way through.

The circle closed up again with a running murmur of expostulation; it was a minute before I could see anything at all. Then new arrivals deranged the line, and Jordan and I were pushed suddenly inside.

Myrtle Wilson's body, wrapped in a blanket, and then in another blanket, as though she suffered from a chill in the hot night, lay on a worktable by the wall, and Tom, with his back to us, was bending over it, motionless. Next to him stood a motorcycle policeman taking down names with much sweat and correction in a little book. At first I couldn't find the source of the high, groaning words that echoed clamorously through the bare garage—then I saw Wilson standing on the raised threshold of his office, swaying back and forth and holding to the doorposts with both hands. Some man was talking to him in a low voice and attempting, from time to time, to lay a hand on his shoulder, but Wilson neither heard nor saw. His eyes would drop slowly from the swinging light to the laden table by the wall, and then jerk back to the light again, and he gave out incessantly his high, horrible call:

"Oh, my Ga-od! Oh, my Ga-od! Oh, Ga-od! Oh, my Ga-od!"

Presently Tom lifted his head with a jerk and, after staring around the garage with glazed eyes, addressed a mumbled incoherent remark to the policeman.

"M-a-v—" the policeman was saying, "—o——"

"No, r—" corrected the man, "M-a-v-r-o——"

"Listen to me!" muttered Tom fiercely.

"r" said the policeman, "o——"

"g——"

"g—" He looked up as Tom's broad hand fell sharply on his shoulder. "What you want, fella?"

"What happened?—that's what I want to know."

"Auto hit her. Ins'antly killed."

"Instantly killed," repeated Tom, staring.

"She ran out ina road. Son-of-a-bitch didn't even stopus car."

"There was two cars," said Michaelis, "one comin', one goin', see?"

"Going where?" asked the policeman keenly.

"One goin' each way. Well, she"—his hand rose toward the blankets but stopped halfway and fell to his side—"she ran out there an' the one comin' from N'York knock right into her, goin' thirty or forty miles an hour."

"What's the name of this place here?" demanded the officer.

"Hasn't got any name."

A pale well-dressed Negro stepped near.

"It was a yellow car," he said, "big yellow car. New."

"See the accident?" asked the policeman.

"No, but the car passed me down the road, going faster'n forty. Going fifty, sixty."

"Come here and let's have your name. Look out now. I want to get his name."

Some words of this conversation must have reached Wilson, swaying in the office door, for suddenly a new theme found voice among his gasping cries:

"You don't have to tell me what kind of car it was! I know what kind of car it was!"

Watching Tom, I saw the wad of muscle back of his shoulder tighten under his coat. He walked quickly over to Wilson and, standing in front of him, seized him firmly by the upper arms.

"You've got to pull yourself together," he said with soothing gruffness.

Wilson's eyes fell upon Tom; he started up on his tiptoes and then would have collapsed to his knees had not Tom held him upright.

"Listen," said Tom, shaking him a little. "I just got here a minute ago, from New York. I was bringing you that coupé we've been talking about. That yellow car I was driving this afternoon wasn't mine—do you hear? I haven't seen it all afternoon."

Only the Negro and I were near enough to hear

what he said, but the policeman caught something in the tone and looked over with truculent eyes.

"What's all that?" he demanded.

"I'm a friend of his." Tom turned his head but kept his hands firm on Wilson's body. "He says he knows the car that did it. . . . It was a yellow car."

Some dim impulse moved the policeman to look suspiciously at Tom.

"And what color's your car?"

"It's a blue car, a coupé."

"We've come straight from New York," I said.

Someone who had been driving a little behind us confirmed this, and the policeman turned away.

"Now, if you'll let me have that name again correct——"

Picking up Wilson like a doll, Tom carried him into the office, set him down in a chair, and came back.

"If somebody'll come here and sit with him," he snapped authoritatively. He watched while the two men standing closest glanced at each other and went unwillingly into the room. Then Tom shut the door on them and came down the single step, his eyes avoiding the table. As he passed close to me he whispered: "Let's get out."

Self-consciously, with his authoritative arms breaking the way, we pushed through the still-gathering crowd, passing a hurried doctor, case in hand, who had been sent for in wild hope half an hour ago.

Tom drove slowly until we were beyond the bend—then his foot came down hard, and the coupé raced along through the night. In a little while I heard a low husky sob, and saw that the tears were overflowing down his face.

"The God-damned coward!" he whimpered. "He didn't even stop his car."

The Buchanans' house floated suddenly toward us through the dark rustling trees. Tom stopped beside the porch and looked up at the second floor, where two windows bloomed with light among the vines.

"Daisy's home," he said. As we got out of the car he glanced at me and frowned slightly.

"I ought to have dropped you in West Egg, Nick. There's nothing we can do tonight."

A change had come over him, and he spoke gravely, and with decision. As we walked across the moonlight gravel to the porch he disposed of the situation in a few brisk phrases.

"I'll telephone for a taxi to take you home, and while you're waiting you and Jordan better go in the kitchen and have them get you some supper—if you want any." He opened the door. "Come in."

"No, thanks. But I'd be glad if you'd order me the taxi. I'll wait outside."

Jordan put her hand on my arm.

"Won't you come in, Nick?"

"No, thanks."

I was feeling a little sick and I wanted to be alone. But Jordan lingered for a moment more.

"It's only half past nine," she said.

I'd be damned if I'd go in; I'd had enough of all of them for one day, and suddenly that included Jordan too. She must have seen something of this in my expression, for she turned abruptly away and ran up the porch steps into the house. I sat down for a few minutes with my head in my hands, until I heard the phone taken up inside and the butler's voice calling a taxi. Then I walked slowly down the drive away from the house, intending to wait by the gate.

I hadn't gone twenty yards when I heard my name and Gatsby stepped from between two bushes into the path. I must have felt pretty weird by that time, because I could think of nothing except the luminosity of his pink suit under the moon.

"What are you doing?" I inquired.

"Just standing here, old sport."

Somehow, that seemed a despicable occupation. For all I knew he was going to rob the house in a moment; I wouldn't have been surprised to see sinister faces, the faces of "Wolfsheim's people," behind him in the dark shrubbery.

"Did you see any trouble on the road?" he asked after a minute.

"Yes."

He hesitated.

"Was she killed?"

"Yes."

"I thought so: I told Daisy I thought so. It's better that the shock should all come at once. She stood it pretty well."

He spoke as if Daisy's reaction was the only thing that mattered.

"I got to West Egg by a side road," he went on, "and left the car in my garage. I don't think anybody saw us, but of course I can't be sure."

I disliked him so much by this time that I didn't find it necessary to tell him he was wrong.

"Who was the woman?" he inquired.

"Her name was Wilson. Her husband owns the garage. How the devil did it happen?"

"Well, I tried to swing the wheel—" He broke off, and suddenly I guessed at the truth.

"Was Daisy driving?"

"Yes," he said after a moment, "but of course I'll say I was. You see, when we left New York she was very nervous and she thought it would steady her to drive—and this woman rushed out at us just as we were passing a car coming the other way. It all happened in a minute, but it seemed to me that she wanted to speak to us, thought we were somebody she knew. Well, first Daisy turned away from the woman toward the other car, and then she lost her nerve and turned back. The second my hand reached the wheel I felt the shock—it must have killed her instantly."

"It ripped her open——"

"Don't tell me, old sport." He winced. "Anyhow—Daisy stepped on it. I tried to make her stop, but she couldn't, so I pulled on the emergency brake. Then she fell over into my lap and I drove on.

"She'll be all right tomorrow," he said presently. "I'm just going to wait here and see if he tries to bother her about that unpleasantness this afternoon. She's locked herself into her room, and if he tries any brutality she's going to turn the light out and on again."

"He won't touch her," I said. "He's not thinking about her."

"I don't trust him, old sport."

"How long are you going to wait?"

"All night, if necessary. Anyhow, till they all go to bed."

A new point of view occurred to me. Suppose Tom found out that Daisy had been driving. He might think he saw a connection in it—he might think anything. I looked at the house; there were two or three bright windows downstairs and the pink glow from Daisy's room on the second floor.

"You wait here," I said. "I'll see if there's any sign of a commotion."

I walked back along the border of the lawn, traversed the gravel softly, and tiptoed up the veranda steps. The drawing-room curtains were open, and I saw that the room was empty. Crossing the porch where we had dined that June night three months before, I came to a small rectangle of light which I guessed was the pantry window. The blind was drawn, but I found a rift at the sill.

Daisy and Tom were sitting opposite each other at the kitchen table, with a plate of cold fried chicken between them, and two bottles of ale. He was talking intently across the table at her, and in his earnestness his hand had fallen upon and covered her own. Once in a while she looked up at him and nodded in agreement.

They weren't happy, and neither of them had touched the chicken or the ale—and yet they weren't unhappy either. There was an unmistakable air of natural intimacy about the picture, and anybody would have said that they were conspiring together.

As I tiptoed from the porch I heard my taxi feeling its way along the dark road toward the house. Gatsby was waiting where I had left him in the drive.

"Is it all quiet up there?" he asked anxiously.

"Yes, it's all quiet." I hesitated. "You'd better come home and get some sleep."

He shook his head.

"I want to wait here till Daisy goes to bed. Good night, old sport."

He put his hands in his coat pockets and turned back eagerly to his scrutiny of the house, as though my presence marred the sacredness of the vigil. So I walked away and left him standing there in the moonlight—watching over nothing.

CHAPTER VIII

I couldn't sleep all night; a foghorn was groaning incessantly on the Sound, and I tossed half sick between grotesque reality and savage, frightening dreams. Toward dawn I heard a taxi go up Gatsby's drive, and immediately I jumped out of bed and began to dress—I felt that I had something to tell him, something to warn him about, and morning would be too late.

Crossing his lawn, I saw that his front door was still open and he was leaning against a table in the hall, heavy with dejection or sleep.

"Nothing happened," he said wanly. "I waited, and about four o'clock she came to the window and stood there for a minute and then turned out the light."

His house had never seemed so enormous to me as it did that night when we hunted through the great rooms for cigarettes. We pushed aside curtains that were like pavilions, and felt over innumerable feet of dark wall for electric light switches—once I tumbled with a sort of splash upon the keys of a ghostly piano. There was an inexplicable amount of dust everywhere, and the rooms were musty, as though they hadn't been aired for many days. I found the humidor on an unfamiliar table, with two stale, dry cigarettes inside. Throwing open the French windows of the drawing room, we sat smoking out into the darkness.

"You ought to go away," I said. "It's pretty certain they'll trace your car."

"Go away *now,* old sport?"

"Go to Atlantic City for a week, or up to Montreal."

He wouldn't consider it. He couldn't possibly leave Daisy until he knew what she was going to do. He was clutching at some last hope and I couldn't bear to shake him free.

It was this night that he told me the strange story of his youth with Dan Cody—told it to me because "Jay Gatsby" had broken up like glass against Tom's hard malice, and the long secret extravaganza was played out. I think that he would have acknowledged anything now, without reserve, but he wanted to talk about Daisy.

She was the first "nice" girl he had ever known. In various unrevealed capacities he had come in contact with such people, but always with indiscernible barbed wire between. He found her excitingly desirable. He went to her house, at first with other officers from Camp Taylor, then alone. It amazed him—he had never been in such a beautiful house before. But what gave it an air of breathless intensity was that Daisy lived there—it was as casual a thing to her as his tent out at camp was to him. There was a ripe mystery about it, a hint of bedrooms upstairs more beautiful and cool than other bedrooms, of gay and radiant activities taking place through its corridors, and of romances that were not musty and laid away already in lavender, but fresh and breathing and redolent of this year's shining motorcars and of dances whose flowers were scarcely withered. It excited him, too, that many men had already loved Daisy—it increased her value in his eyes. He felt their presence all about the house, pervading the air with the shades and echoes of still vibrant emotions.

But he knew that he was in Daisy's house by a colossal accident. However glorious might be his future as Jay Gatsby, he was at present a penniless young man without a past, and at any moment the invisible cloak of his uniform might slip from his shoulders. So he made the most of his time. He took what he could get, ravenously and unscrupulously—eventually he took Daisy one still October night, took her because he had no real right to touch her hand.

He might have despised himself, for he had certainly taken her under false pretenses. I don't mean that he had traded on his phantom millions, but he had deliberately given Daisy a sense of security; he let her believe that he was a person from much the same stratum as herself—that he was fully able to take care of her. As a matter of fact, he had no such facilities—he had no comfortable family standing behind him, and he was liable at the whim of an impersonal government to be blown anywhere about the world.

But he didn't despise himself and didn't turn out as he had imagined. He had intended, probably, to take what he could and go—but now he found that he had committed himself to the following of a grail. He knew that Daisy was extraordinary, but he didn't realize just how extraordinary a "nice" girl could be. She vanished into her rich house, into her rich, full life, leaving Gatsby—nothing. He felt married to her, that was all.

When they met again, two days later, it was Gatsby who was breathless, who was, somehow, betrayed. Her porch was bright with the bought luxury of starshine; the wicker of the settee squeaked fashionably as she turned toward him and he kissed her curious and lovely mouth. She had caught a cold, and it made her voice huskier and more charming than ever, and Gatsby was overwhelmingly aware of the youth and mystery that wealth imprisons and preserves, of the freshness of many clothes, and of Daisy, gleaming like silver, safe and proud above the hot struggles of the poor.

"I can't describe to you how surprised I was to find out I loved her, old sport. I even hoped for a while that she'd throw me over, but she didn't, because she was in love with me too. She thought I knew a lot because I knew different things from her . . . Well, there I was, 'way off my ambitions, getting deeper in love every minute, and all of a sudden I didn't care. What was the use of doing great things if I could have a better time telling her what I was going to do?"

On the last afternoon before he went abroad, he sat with Daisy in his arms for a long, silent time. It was a cold fall day, with fire in the room and her cheeks flushed. Now and then she moved and he changed his arm a little, and once he kissed her dark shining hair. The afternoon had made them tranquil for a while, as if to give them a deep memory for the long parting the next day promised. They had never been closer in their month of love, nor communicated more profoundly one with another, than when she brushed silent lips against his coat's shoulder or when he touched the end of her fingers, gently, as though she were asleep.

He did extraordinarily well in the war. He was a captain before he went to the front, and following the Argonne battles he got his majority and the command of the divisional machine guns. After the Armistice he tried frantically to get home, but some complication or misunderstanding sent him to Oxford instead. He was worried now—there was a quality of nervous despair in Daisy's letters. She didn't see why he couldn't come. She was feeling the pressure of the world outside, and she wanted to see him and feel his presence beside her and be reassured that she was doing the right thing after all.

For Daisy was young and her artificial world was redolent of orchids and pleasant, cheerful snobbery and orchestras which set the rhythm of the year, summing up the sadness and suggestiveness of life in new tunes. All night the saxophones wailed the hopeless comment of the "Beale Street Blues" while a hundred pairs of golden and silver slippers shuffled the shining dust. At the gray tea hour there were always rooms that throbbed incessantly with this low, sweet fever, while fresh faces drifted here and there like rose petals blown by the sad horns around the floor.

Through this twilight universe Daisy began to move again with the season; suddenly she was again keeping half a dozen dates a day with half a dozen men, and drowsing asleep at dawn with the beads and chiffon of an evening dress tangled among dying orchids on the floor beside her bed. And all the time something within her was crying for a decision. She wanted her life shaped now, immediately—and the decision must be made by some force—of love, of money, of unquestionable practicality—that was close at hand.

That force took shape in the middle of spring with the arrival of Tom Buchanan. There was a wholesome bulkiness about his person and his position, and Daisy was flattered. Doubtless there was a certain struggle and a certain relief. The letter reached Gatsby while he was still at Oxford.

It was dawn now on Long Island and we went about opening the rest of the windows downstairs, filling the house with gray-turning, gold-turning light. The shadow of a tree fell abruptly across the dew and ghostly birds began to sing among the blue leaves. There was a slow, pleasant movement in the air, scarcely a wind, promising a cool, lovely day.

"I don't think she ever loved him," Gatsby turned around from a window and looked at me challengingly. "You must remember, old sport, she was very excited this afternoon. He told her those things in a way that frightened her—that made it look as if I was some kind of cheap sharper. And the result was she hardly knew what she was saying."

He sat down gloomily.

"Of course she might have loved him just for a minute, when they were first married—and loved me more even then, do you see?"

Suddenly he came out with a curious remark.

"In any case," he said, "it was just personal."

What could you make of that, except to suspect some intensity in his conception of the affair that couldn't be measured?

He came back from France when Tom and Daisy were still on their wedding trip, and made a miserable but irresistible journey to Louisville on the last of his army pay. He stayed there a week, walking the streets where their footsteps had clicked together through the November night and revisiting the out-of-the-way places to which they had driven in her white car. Just as Daisy's house had always seemed to him more mysterious and gay than other houses, so his idea of the city itself, even though she was gone from it, was pervaded with a melancholy beauty.

He left, feeling that if he had searched harder, he might have found her—that he was leaving her behind. The day coach—he was penniless now—was hot. He went out to the open vestibule and sat down on a folding chair, and the station slid away and the backs of unfamiliar buildings moved by. Then out into the spring fields, where a yellow trolley raced them for a minute with the people in it who might once have seen the pale magic of her face along the casual street.

The track curved and now it was going away from the sun, which, as it sank lower, seemed to spread itself in benediction over the vanishing city where she had drawn her breath. He stretched out his hand desperately as if to snatch only a wisp of air, to save a fragment of the spot that she had made lovely for him. But it was all going by too fast now for his blurred eyes and he knew that he had lost that part of it, the freshest and the best, forever.

It was nine o'clock when we finished breakfast and went out on the porch. The night had made a sharp difference in the weather and there was an autumn flavor in the air. The gardener, the last one of Gatsby's former servants, came to the foot of the steps.

"I'm going to drain the pool today, Mr. Gatsby. Leaves'll start falling pretty soon, and then there's always trouble with the pipes."

"Don't do it today," Gatsby answered. He turned to me apologetically. "You know, old sport, I've never used that pool all summer?"

I looked at my watch and stood up.

"Twelve minutes to my train."

I didn't want to go to the city. I wasn't worth a decent stroke of work, but it was more than that—I didn't want to leave Gatsby. I missed that train, and then another, before I could get myself away.

"I'll call you up," I said finally.

"Do, old sport."

"I'll call you about noon."

We walked slowly down the steps.

"I suppose Daisy'll call too." He looked at me anxiously, as if he hoped I'd corroborate this.

"I suppose so."

"Well, good-by."

We shook hands and I started away. Just before I reached the hedge I remembered something and turned around.

"They're a rotten crowd," I shouted across the lawn. "You're worth the whole damn bunch put together."

I've always been glad I said that. It was the only

compliment I ever gave him, because I disapproved of him from beginning to end. First he nodded politely, and then his face broke into that radiant and understanding smile, as if we'd been in ecstatic cahoots on that fact all the time. His gorgeous pink rag of a suit made a bright spot of color against the white steps, and I thought of the night when I first came to his ancestral home, three months before. The lawn and drive had been crowded with the faces of those who guessed at his corruption—and he had stood on those steps, concealing his incorruptible dream, as he waved them good-by.

I thanked him for his hospitality. We were always thanking him for that—I and the others.

"Good-by," I called. "I enjoyed breakfast, Gatsby."

Up in the city, I tried for a while to list the quotations on an interminable amount of stock, then I fell asleep in my swivel chair. Just before noon the phone woke me, and I started up with sweat breaking out on my forehead. It was Jordan Baker; she often called me up at this hour because the uncertainty of her own movements between hotels and clubs and private houses made her hard to find in any other way. Usually her voice came over the wire as something fresh and cool, as if a divot from a green golf links had come sailing in at the office window, but this morning it seemed harsh and dry.

"I've left Daisy's house," she said. "I'm at Hempstead, and I'm going down to Southampton this afternoon."

Probably it had been tactful to leave Daisy's house, but the act annoyed me, and her next remark made me rigid.

"You weren't so nice to me last night."

"How could it have mattered then?"

Silence for a moment. Then:

"However—I want to see you."

"I want to see you, too."

"Suppose I don't go to Southampton, and come into town this afternoon?"

"No—I don't think this afternoon."

"Very well."

"It's impossible this afternoon. Various——"

We talked like that for a while, and then abruptly we weren't talking any longer. I don't know which of us hung up with a sharp click, but I know I didn't care. I couldn't have talked to her across a tea table that day if I never talked to her again in this world.

I called Gatsby's house a few minutes later, but the line was busy. I tried four times; finally an exasperated central told me the wire was being kept open for long-distance from Detroit. Taking out my timetable, I drew a small circle around the three-fifty train. Then I leaned back in my chair and tried to think. It was just noon.

When I passed the ashheaps on the train that morning I had crossed deliberately to the other side of the car. I supposed there'd be a curious crowd around there all day with little boys searching for dark spots in the dust, and some garrulous man telling over and over what had happened, until it became less and less real even to him and he could tell it no longer, and Myrtle Wilson's tragic achievement was forgotten. Now I want to go back a little and tell what happened at the garage after we left there the night before.

They had difficulty in locating the sister, Catherine. She must have broken her rule against drinking that night, for when she arrived she was stupid with liquor and unable to understand that the ambulance had already gone to Flushing. When they convinced her of this, she immediately fainted, as if that was the intolerable part of the affair. Someone, kind or curious, took her in his car and drove her in the wake of her sister's body.

Until long after midnight a changing crowd lapped up against the front of the garage, while George Wilson rocked himself back and forth on the couch inside. For a while the door of the office was open, and everyone who came into the garage glanced irresistibly through it. Finally someone said it was a shame, and closed the door. Michaelis and several other men were with him; first, four or five men, later two or three men. Still later Michaelis had to ask the last stranger to wait there fifteen minutes longer, while he went back to his own place and made a pot of coffee. After that, he stayed there alone with Wilson until dawn.

About three o'clock the quality of Wilson's incoherent muttering changed—he grew quieter and began to talk about the yellow car. He announced that he had a way of finding out whom the yellow car belonged to, and then he blurted out that a couple of months ago his wife had come from the city with her face bruised and her nose swollen.

But when he heard himself say this, he flinched and began to cry "Oh, my God!" again in his groaning voice. Michaelis made a clumsy attempt to distract him.

"How long have you been married, George? Come on there, try and sit still a minute and answer my question. How long have you been married?"

"Twelve years."

"Ever had any children? Come on, George, sit still—I asked you a question. Did you ever have any children?"

The hard brown beetles kept thudding against the

dull light, and whenever Michaelis heard a car go tearing along the road outside it sounded to him like the car that hadn't stopped a few hours before. He didn't like to go into the garage, because the workbench was stained where the body had been lying, so he moved uncomfortably around the office—he knew every object in it before morning—and from time to time sat down beside Wilson trying to keep him more quiet.

"Have you got a church you go to sometimes, George? Maybe even if you haven't been there for a long time? Maybe I could call up the church and get a priest to come over and he could talk to you, see?"

"Don't belong to any."

"You ought to have a church, George, for times like this. You must have gone to church once. Didn't you get married in a church? Listen, George, listen to me. Didn't you get married in a church?"

"That was a long time ago."

The effort of answering broke the rhythm of his rocking—for a moment he was silent. Then the same half-knowing, half-bewildered look came back into his faded eyes.

"Look in the drawer there," he said, pointing at the desk.

"Which drawer?"

"That drawer—that one."

Michaelis opened the drawer nearest his hand. There was nothing in it but a small, expensive dog leash, made of leather and braided silver. It was apparently new.

"This?" he inquired, holding it up.

Wilson stared and nodded.

"I found it yesterday afternoon. She tried to tell me about it, but I knew it was something funny."

"You mean your wife bought it?"

"She had it wrapped in tissue paper on her bureau."

Michaelis didn't see anything odd in that, and he gave Wilson a dozen reasons why his wife might have bought the dog leash. But conceivably Wilson had heard some of these same explanations before, from Myrtle, because he began saying "Oh my God!" again in a whisper—his comforter left several explanations in the air.

"Then he killed her," said Wilson. His mouth dropped open suddenly.

"Who did?"

"I have a way of finding out."

"You're morbid, George," said his friend. "This has been a strain to you and you don't know what you're saying. You'd better try and sit quiet till morning."

"He murdered her."

"It was an accident, George."

Wilson shook his head. His eyes narrowed and his mouth widened slightly with the ghost of a superior "Hm!"

"I know," he said definitely, "I'm one of these trusting fellas and I don't think any harm to *no*body, but when I get to know a thing I know it. It was the man in that car. She ran out to speak to him and he wouldn't stop."

Michaelis had seen this too, but it hadn't occurred to him that there was any special significance in it. He believed that Mrs. Wilson had been running away from her husband, rather than trying to stop any particular car.

"How could she of been like that?"

"She's a deep one," said Wilson, as if that answered the question. "Ah-h-h——"

He began to rock again, and Michaelis stood twisting the leash in his hand.

"Maybe you got some friend that I could telephone for, George?"

This was a forlorn hope—he was almost sure that Wilson had no friend: there was not enough of him for his wife. He was glad a little later when he noticed a change in the room, a blue quickening by the window, and realized that dawn wasn't far off. About five o'clock it was blue enough outside to snap off the light.

Wilson's glazed eyes turned out to the ashheaps, where small gray clouds took on fantastic shapes and scurried here and there in the faint dawn wind.

"I spoke to her," he muttered, after a long silence. "I told her she might fool me but she couldn't fool God. I took her to the window"—with an effort he got up and walked to the rear window and leaned with his face pressed against it—"and I said 'God knows what you've been doing, everything you've been doing. You may fool me, but you can't fool God!' "

Standing behind him, Michaelis saw with a shock that he was looking at the eyes of Doctor T. J. Eckleburg, which had just emerged, pale and enormous, from the dissolving night.

"God sees everything," repeated Wilson.

"That's an advertisement," Michaelis assured him. Something made him turn away from the window and look back into the room. But Wilson stood there a long time, his face close to the windowpane, nodding into the twilight.

By six o'clock Michaelis was worn out, and grateful for the sound of a car stopping outside. It was one of the watchers of the night before who had promised to come back, so he cooked breakfast for three, which he and the other man ate together. Wilson was quieter now, and Michaelis went home to sleep; when he awoke four hours later and hurried back to the garage, Wilson was gone.

His movements—he was on foot all the time—were afterward traced to Port Roosevelt and then to Gad's Hill, where he bought a sandwich that he didn't eat, and a cup of coffee. He must have been tired and walking slowly, for he didn't reach Gad's Hill until noon. Thus far there was no difficulty in accounting for his time—there were boys who had seen a man "acting sort of crazy," and motorists at whom he stared oddly from the side of the road. Then for three hours he disappeared from view. The police, on the strength of what he said to Michaelis, that he "had a way of finding out," supposed that he spent that time going from garage to garage thereabout, inquiring for a yellow car. On the other hand, no garage man who had seen him ever came forward, and perhaps he had an easier, surer way of finding out what he wanted to know. By half past two he was in West Egg, where he asked someone the way to Gatsby's house. So by that time he knew Gatsby's name.

At two o'clock Gatsby put on his bathing suit and left word with the butler that if anyone phoned word was to be brought to him at the pool. He stopped at the garage for a pneumatic mattress that had amused his guests during the summer, and the chauffeur helped him pump it up. Then he gave instructions that the open car wasn't to be taken out under any circumstances—and this was strange, because the front right fender needed repair.

Gatsby shouldered the mattress and started for the pool. Once he stopped and shifted it a little, and the chauffeur asked him if he needed help, but he shook his head and in a moment disappeared among the yellowing trees.

No telephone message arrived, but the butler went without his sleep and waited for it until four o'clock—until long after there was anyone to give it to if it came. I have an idea that Gatsby himself didn't believe it would come, and perhaps he no longer cared. If that was true he must have felt that he had lost the old warm world, paid a high price for living too long with a single dream. He must have looked up at an unfamiliar sky through frightening leaves and shivered as he found what a grotesque thing a rose is and how raw the sunlight was upon the scarcely created grass. A new world, material without being real, where poor ghosts, breathing dreams like air, drifted fortuitously about . . . like that ashen, fantastic figure gliding toward him through the amorphous trees.

The chauffeur—he was one of Wolfsheim's protégés—heard the shots—afterward he could only say that he hadn't thought anything much about them. I drove from the station directly to Gatsby's house and my rushing anxiously up the front steps was the first thing that alarmed anyone. But they knew then, I firmly believe. With scarcely a word said, four of us, the chauffeur, butler, gardener, and I, hurried down to the pool.

There was a faint, barely perceptible movement of the water as the fresh flow from one end urged its way toward the drain at the other. With little ripples that were hardly the shadows of waves, the laden mattress moved irregularly down the pool. A small gust of wind that scarcely corrugated the surface was enough to disturb its accidental course with its accidental burden. The touch of a cluster of leaves revolved it slowly, tracing, like the leg of transit, a thin red circle in the water.

It was after we started with Gatsby toward the house that the gardener saw Wilson's body a little way off in the grass, and the holocaust was complete.

CHAPTER IX

After two years I remember the rest of that day, and that night and the next day, only as an endless drill of police and photographers and newspapermen in and out of Gatsby's front door. A rope stretched across the main gate and a policeman by it kept out the curious, but little boys soon discovered that they could enter through my yard, and there were always a few of them clustered open-mouthed about the pool. Someone with a positive manner, perhaps a detective, used the expression "madman" as he bent over Wilson's body that afternoon, and the adventitious authority of his voice set the key for the newspaper reports next morning.

Most of those reports were a nightmare—grotesque, circumstantial, eager, and untrue. When Michaelis' testimony at the inquest brought to light Wilson's suspicions of his wife I thought the whole tale would shortly be served up in racy pasquinade—but Catherine, who might have said anything, didn't say a word. She showed a surprising amount of character about it too—looked at the coroner with determined eyes under that corrected brow of hers, and swore that her sister had never seen Gatsby, that her sister was completely happy with her husband, that her sister had been into no mischief whatever. She convinced herself of it, and cried into her handkerchief, as if the very suggestion was more than she could endure. So Wilson was reduced to a man "deranged by grief" in order that the case might remain in its simplest form. And it rested there.

But all this part of it seemed remote and unessential. I found myself on Gatsby's side, and alone. From the moment I telephoned news of the catastrophe to West Egg Village, every surmise about him, and every practical question, was referred to me. At first I was surprised and confused; then, as he lay in his house and didn't move or breathe or speak, hour upon hour, it grew upon me that I was responsible, because no one else was interested—interested, I mean, with that intense personal interest to which everyone has some vague right at the end.

I called up Daisy half an hour after we found him, called her instinctively and without hesitation. But she and Tom had gone away early that afternoon, and taken baggage with them.

"Left no address?"

"No."

"Say when they'd be back?"

"No."

"Any idea where they are? How I could reach them?"

"I don't know. Can't say."

I wanted to get somebody for him. I wanted to go into the room where he lay and reassure him: "I'll get somebody for you, Gatsby. Don't worry. Just trust me and I'll get somebody for you——"

Meyer Wolfsheim's name wasn't in the phone book. The butler gave me his office address on Broadway, and I called Information, but by the time I had the number it was long after five, and no one answered the phone.

"Will you ring again?"

"I've rung them three times."

"It's very important."

"Sorry. I'm afraid no one's there."

I went back to the drawing room and thought for an instant that they were chance visitors, all these official people who suddenly filled it. But, as they drew back the sheet and looked at Gatsby with unmoved eyes, his protest continued in my brain:

"Look here, old sport, you've got to get somebody for me. You've got to try hard. I can't go through this alone."

Someone started to ask me questions, but I broke away and going upstairs looked hastily through the unlocked parts of his desk—he'd never told me definitely that his parents were dead. But there was nothing—only the picture of Dan Cody, a token of forgotten violence, staring down from the wall.

Next morning I sent the butler to New York with a letter to Wolfsheim, which asked for information and urged him to come out on the next train. That request seemed superfluous when I wrote it. I was sure he'd start when he saw the newspapers, just as I was sure there'd be a wire from Daisy before noon—but neither a wire nor Mr. Wolfsheim arrived; no one arrived except more police and photographers and newspapermen. When the butler brought back Wolfsheim's answer I began to have a feeling of defiance, of scornful solidarity between Gatsby and me against them all.

> Dear Mr. Carraway. This has been one of the most terrible shocks of my life to me I hardly can believe it that it is true at all. Such a mad act as that man did should make us all think. I cannot come down now as I am tied up in some very important business and cannot get mixed up in this thing now. If there is anything I can do a little later let me know in a letter by Edgar. I hardly know where I am when I hear about a thing like this and am completely knocked down and out.
>
> Yours truly
> MEYER WOLFSHEIM

and then hasty addenda beneath:

> Let me know about the funeral etc do not know his family at all.

When the phone rang that afternoon and long-distance said Chicago was calling I thought this would be Daisy at last. But the connection came through as a man's voice, very thin and far away.

"This is Slagle speaking . . ."

"Yes?" The name was unfamiliar.

"Hell of a note, isn't it? Get my wire?"

"There haven't been any wires."

"Young Parke's in trouble," he said rapidly. "They picked him up when he handed the bonds over the counter. They got a circular from New York giving 'em the numbers just five minutes before. What d'you know about that, hey? You never can tell in these hick towns—"

"Hello!" I interrupted breathlessly. "Look here—this isn't Mr. Gatsby. Mr. Gatsby's dead."

There was a long silence on the other end of the wire, followed by an exclamation . . . then a quick squawk as the connection was broken.

I think it was on the third day that a telegram signed Henry C. Gatz arrived from a town in Minnesota. It said only that the sender was leaving immediately and to postpone the funeral until he came.

It was Gatsby's father, a solemn old man, very helpless and dismayed, bundled up in a long cheap ulster against the warm September day. His eyes leaked continuously with excitement, and when I took the bag and umbrella from his hands he began to pull so incessantly at his sparse gray beard that I had difficulty in getting off his coat. He was on the point of collapse, so I took him into the music room and made him sit down while I sent for something to eat. But he wouldn't eat, and the glass of milk spilled from his trembling hand.

"I saw it in the Chicago newspaper," he said. "It was all in the Chicago newspaper. I started right away."

"I didn't know how to reach you."

His eyes, seeing nothing, moved ceaselessly about the room.

"It was a madman," he said. "He must have been mad."

"Would you like some coffee?" I urged him.

"I don't want anything. I'm all right now, Mr.——"

"Carraway."

"Well, I'm all right now. Where have they got Jimmy?"

I took him into the drawing room, where his son lay, and left him there. Some little boys had come up on the steps and were looking into the hall; when I told them who had arrived, they went reluctantly away.

After a little while Mr. Gatz opened the door and came out, his mouth ajar, his face flushed slightly, his eyes leaking isolated and unpunctual tears. He had reached an age where death no longer has the quality of ghastly surprise, and when he looked around him now for the first time and saw the height and splendor of the hall and the great rooms opening out from it into other rooms, his grief began to be mixed with an awed pride. I helped him to a bedroom upstairs; while he took off his coat and vest I told him that all arrangements had been deferred until he came.

"I didn't know what you'd want, Mr. Gatsby——"

"Gatz is my name."

"—Mr. Gatz. I thought you might want to take the body West."

He shook his head.

"Jimmy always liked it better down East. He rose up to his position in the East. Were you a friend of my boy's, Mr.——?"

"We were close friends."

"He had a big future before him, you know. He was only a young man, but he had a lot of brain power here."

He touched his head impressively, and I nodded.

"If he'd of lived, he'd of been a great man. A man like James J. Hill. He'd of helped build up the country."

"That's true," I said, uncomfortably.

He fumbled at the embroidered coverlet, trying to take it from the bed, and lay down stiffly—was instantly asleep.

That night an obviously frightened person called up, and demanded to know who I was before he would give his name.

"This is Mr. Carraway," I said.

"Oh!" He sounded relieved. "This is Klipspringer."

I was relieved too, for that seemed to promise another friend at Gatsby's grave. I didn't want it to be in the papers and draw a sight-seeing crowd, so I'd been calling up a few people myself. They were hard to find.

"The funeral's tomorrow," I said. "Three o'clock, here at the house. I wish you'd tell anybody who'd be interested."

"Oh, I will," he broke out hastily. "Of course I'm not likely to see anybody, but if I do."

His tone made me suspicious.

"Of course you'll be there yourself."

"Well, I'll certainly try. What I called up about is——"

"Wait a minute," I interrupted. "How about saying you'll come?"

"Well, the fact is—the truth of the matter is that I'm staying with some people up here in Greenwich, and they rather expect me to be with them tomorrow. In fact, there's a sort of picnic or something. Of course I'll do my very best to get away."

I ejaculated an unrestrained "Huh!" and he must have heard me, for he went on nervously:

"What I called up about was a pair of shoes I left there. I wonder if it'd be too much trouble to have the butler send them on. You see, they're tennis shoes, and I'm sort of helpless without them. My address is care of B. F.——"

I didn't hear the rest of the name, because I hung up the receiver.

After that I felt a certain shame for Gatsby—one gentleman to whom I telephoned implied that he had got what he deserved. However, that was my fault, for he was one of those who used to sneer most bitterly at Gatsby on the courage of Gatsby's liquor, and I should have known better than to call him.

The morning of the funeral I went up to New York to see Meyer Wolfsheim; I couldn't seem to reach him any other way. The door that I pushed open, on the advice of an elevator boy, was marked "The Swastika Holding Company," and at first there didn't seem to be anyone inside. But when I'd shouted "hello" several times in vain, an argument broke out behind a partition, and presently a lovely Jewess appeared at an interior door and scrutinized me with black hostile eyes.

"Nobody's in," she said. "Mr. Wolfsheim's gone to Chicago."

The first part of this was obviously untrue, for someone had begun to whistle "The Rosary," tunelessly, inside.

"Please say that Mr. Carraway wants to see him."

"I can't get him back from Chicago, can I?"

At this moment a voice, unmistakably Wolfsheim's, called "Stella!" from the other side of the door.

"Leave your name on the desk," she said quickly. "I'll give it to him when he gets back."

"But I know he's there."

She took a step toward me and began to slide her hands indignantly up and down her hips.

"You young men think you can force your way in here any time," she scolded. "We're getting sickantired of it. When I say he's in Chicago, he's in Chicago."

I mentioned Gatsby.

"Oh-h!" She looked at me over again. "Will you just—What was your name?"

She vanished. In a moment Meyer Wolfsheim stood solemnly in the doorway, holding out both hands. He drew me into his office, remarking in a reverent voice that it was a sad time for all of us, and offered me a cigar.

"My memory goes back to when first I met him," he said. "A young major just out of the army and covered over with medals he got in the war. He was so hard up he had to keep on wearing his uniform because he couldn't buy some regular clothes. First time I saw him was when he come into Winebrenner's poolroom, at Forty-third Street and asked for a job. He hadn't eat anything for a couple of days. 'Come on have some lunch with me,' I said. He ate more than four dollars' worth of food in half an hour."

"Did you start him in business?" I inquired.

"Start him! I made him."

"Oh."

"I raised him up out of nothing, right out of the gutter. I saw right away he was a fine-appearing, gentlemanly young man, and when he told me he was an Oggsford I knew I could use him good. I got him to join up in the American Legion and he used to stand high there. Right off he did some work for a client of mine up to Albany. We were so thick like that in everything"—he held up two bulbous fingers—"always together."

I wondered if this partnership had included the world's series transaction in 1919.

"Now he's dead," I said after a moment. "You were his closest friend, so I know you'll want to come to his funeral this afternoon."

"I'd like to come."

"Well, come then."

The hair in his nostrils quivered slightly, and as he shook his head his eyes filled with tears.

"I can't do it—I can't get mixed up in it," he said.

"There's nothing to get mixed up in. It's all over now."

"When a man gets killed I never like to get mixed up in it in any way. I keep out. When I was a young man it was different—if a friend of mine died, no matter how, I stuck with them to the end. You may think that's sentimental, but I mean it—to the bitter end."

I saw that for some reason of his own he was determined not to come, so I stood up.

"Are you a college man?" he inquired suddenly.

For a moment I thought he was going to suggest a "gonnegtion," but he only nodded and shook my hand.

"Let us learn to show our friendship for a man when he is alive and not after he is dead," he suggested. "After that, my own rule is to let everything alone."

When I left his office the sky had turned dark and I got back to West Egg in a drizzle. After changing my clothes I went next door and found Mr. Gatz walking up and down excitedly in the hall. His pride in his son and in his son's possessions was continually increasing and now he had something to show me.

"Jimmy sent me this picture." He took out his wallet with trembling fingers. "Look there."

It was a photograph of the house, cracked in the corners and dirty with many hands. He pointed out every detail to me eagerly. "Look there!" and then sought admiration from my eyes. He had shown it so often that I think it was more real to him now than the house itself.

"Jimmy sent it to me. I think it's a very pretty picture. It shows up well."

"Very well. Had you seen him lately?"

"He come out to see me two years ago and bought me the house I live in now. Of course we was broke up when he run off from home, but I see now there was a reason for it. He knew he had a big future in front of him. And ever since he made a success he was very generous with me."

He seemed reluctant to put away the picture, held it for another minute, lingeringly, before my eyes. Then he returned the wallet and pulled from his pocket a ragged old copy of a book called *Hopalong Cassidy*. "Look here, this is a book he had when he was a boy. It just shows you."

He opened it at the back cover and turned it around for me to see. On the last flyleaf was printed the word SCHEDULE, and the date September 12, 1906. And underneath:

Rise from bed	6.00	A.M.
Dumbbell exercise and wall-scaling	6.15–6.30	"

Study electricity, etc.	7.15–8.15	"
Work	8.30–4.30	P.M.
Baseball and sports	4.30–5.00	"
Practice elocution, poise and how to attain it	5.00–6.00	"
Study needed inventions	7.00–9.00	"

GENERAL RESOLVES

No wasting time at Shafters or [a name, indecipherable]
No more smokeing or chewing.
Bath every other day
Read one improving book or magazine per week
Save $5.00 [crossed out] $3.00 per week
Be better to parents

"I come across this book by accident," said the old man. "It just shows you, don't it?

"Jimmy was bound to get ahead. He always had some resolves like this or something. Do you notice what he's got about improving his mind? He was always great for that. He told me I et like a hog once, and I beat him for it."

He was reluctant to close the book, reading each item aloud and then looking eagerly at me. I think he rather expected me to copy down the list for my own use.

A little before three the Lutheran minister arrived from Flushing, and I began to look involuntarily out the windows for other cars. So did Gatsby's father. And as the time passed and the servants came in and stood waiting in the hall, his eyes began to blink anxiously, and he spoke of the rain in a worried, uncertain way. The minister glanced several times at his watch, so I took him aside and asked him to wait for half an hour. But it wasn't any use. Nobody came.

About five o'clock our procession of three cars reached the cemetery and stopped in a thick drizzle beside the gate—first a motor hearse, horribly black and wet, then Mr. Gatz and the minister and I in the limousine, and a little later four or five servants and the postman from West Egg, in Gatsby's station wagon, all wet to the skin. As we started through the gate into the cemetery I heard a car stop and then the sound of someone splashing after us over the soggy ground. I looked around. It was the man with owl-eyed glasses whom I had found marveling over Gatsby's books in the library one night three months before.

I'd never seen him since then. I don't know how he knew about the funeral, or even his name. The rain poured down his thick glasses, and he took them off and wiped them to see the protecting canvas unrolled from Gatsby's grave.

I tried to think about Gatsby then for a moment, but he was already too far away, and I could only remember, without resentment, that Daisy hadn't sent a message or a flower. Dimly I heard someone murmur "Blessed are the dead that the rain falls on," and then the owl-eyed man said "Amen to that," in a brave voice.

We straggled down quickly through the rain to the cars. Owl Eyes spoke to me by the gate.

"I couldn't get to the house," he remarked.

"Neither could anybody else."

"Go on!" He started. "Why, my God! they used to go there by the hundreds."

He took off his glasses and wiped them again, outside and in.

"The poor son-of-a-bitch," he said.

One of my most vivid memories is of coming back West from prep school and later from college at Christmas time. Those who went farther than Chicago would gather in the old dim Union Station at six o'clock of a December evening, with a few Chicago friends, already caught up into their own holiday gaieties, to bid them a hasty good-by. I remember the fur coats of the girls returning from Miss This-or-That's and the chatter of frozen breath and the hands waving overhead as we caught sight of old acquaintances, and the matchings of invitations: "Are you going to the Ordways'? the Herseys'? the Schultzes'?" and the long green tickets clasped tight in our gloved hands. And last the murky yellow cars of the Chicago, Milwaukee & St. Paul Railroad looking cheerful as Christmas itself on the tracks beside the gate.

When we pulled out into the winter night and the real snow, our snow, began to stretch out beside us and twinkle against the windows, and the dim lights of small Wisconsin stations moved by, a sharp wild brace came suddenly into the air. We drew in deep breaths of it as we walked back from dinner through the cold vestibules, unutterably aware of our identity with this country for one strange hour, before we melted indistinguishably into it again.

That's my Middle West—not the wheat or the prairies or the lost Swede towns, but the thrilling returning trains of my youth, and the street lamps and sleigh bells in the frosty dark and the shadows of holly wreaths thrown by lighted windows on the snow. I am part of that, a little solemn with the feel of those long winters, a little complacent from growing up in the Carraway house in a city where dwellings are still called through decades by a family's name. I see now that this has been a story of the West, after all—Tom and Gatsby, Daisy and Jordan and I, were all Westerners, and perhaps we possessed some deficiency in common which made us subtly unadaptable to Eastern life.

Even when the East excited me most, even when I was most keenly aware of its superiority to the bored, sprawling, swollen towns beyond the Ohio, with their interminable inquisitions which spared only the children and the very old—even then it had always for me a quality of distortion. West Egg, especially, still figures in my more fantastic dreams. I see it as a night scene by El Greco: a hundred houses, at once conventional and grotesque, crouching under a sullen, overhanging sky and a lusterless moon. In the foreground four solemn men in dress suits are walking along the sidewalk with a stretcher on which lies a drunken woman in a white evening dress. Her hand, which dangles over the side, sparkles cold with jewels. Gravely the men turn in at a house—the wrong house. But no one knows the woman's name, and no one cares.

After Gatsby's death the East was haunted for me like that, distorted beyond my eyes' power of correction. So when the blue smoke of brittle leaves was in the air and the wind blew the wet laundry stiff on the line I decided to come back home.

There was one thing to be done before I left, an awkward, unpleasant thing that perhaps had better have been let alone. But I wanted to leave things in order and not just trust that obliging and indifferent sea to sweep my refuse away. I saw Jordan Baker and talked over and around what had happened to us together, and what had happened afterward to me, and she lay perfectly still, listening, in a big chair.

She was dressed to play golf, and I remember thinking she looked like a good illustration, her chin raised a little jauntily, her hair the color of an autumn leaf, her face the same brown tint as the fingerless glove on her knee. When I had finished she told me without comment that she was engaged to another man. I doubted that, though there were several she could have married at a nod of her head, but I pretended to be surprised. For just a minute I wondered if I wasn't making a mistake, then I thought it all over again quickly and got up to say good-by.

"Nevertheless you did throw me over," said Jordan suddenly. "You threw me over on the telephone. I don't give a damn about you now, but it was a new experience for me, and I felt a little dizzy for a while."

We shook hands.

"Oh, and do you remember"—she added—"a conversation we had once about driving a car?"

"Why—not exactly."

"You said a bad driver was only safe until she met another bad driver? Well, I met another bad driver, didn't I? I mean it was careless of me to make such a wrong guess. I thought you were rather an honest, straightforward person. I thought it was your secret pride."

"I'm thirty," I said. "I'm five years too old to lie to myself and call it honor."

She didn't answer. Angry, and half in love with her, and tremendously sorry, I turned away.

One afternoon late in October I saw Tom Buchanan. He was walking ahead of me along Fifth Avenue in his alert, aggressive way, his hands out a little from his body as if to fight off interference, his head moving sharply here and there, adapting itself to his restless eyes. Just as I slowed up to avoid overtaking him he stopped and began frowning into the windows of a jewelry store. Suddenly he saw me and walked back, holding out his hand.

"What's the matter, Nick? Do you object to shaking hands with me?"

"Yes. You know what I think of you."

"You're crazy, Nick," he said quickly. "Crazy as hell. I don't know what's the matter with you."

"Tom," I inquired, "what did you say to Wilson that afternoon?"

He stared at me without a word, and I knew I had guessed right about those missing hours. I started to turn away, but he took a step after me and grabbed my arm.

"I told him the truth," he said. "He came to the door while we were getting ready to leave, and when I sent down word that we weren't in he tried to force his way upstairs. He was crazy enough to kill me if I hadn't told him who owned the car. His hand was on a revolver in his pocket every minute he was in the house—" He broke off defiantly. "What if I did tell him? That fellow had it coming to him. He threw dust into your eyes just like he did in Daisy's, but he was a tough one. He ran over Myrtle like you'd run over a dog and never even stopped his car."

There was nothing I could say except the one unutterable fact that it wasn't true.

"And if you think I didn't have my share of suffering—look here, when I went to give up that flat and saw that damn box of dog biscuits sitting there on the sideboard, I sat down and cried like a baby. By God it was awful——"

I couldn't forgive him or like him, but I saw that what he had done was, to him, entirely justified. It was all very careless and confused. They were careless people, Tom and Daisy—they smashed up things and creatures and then retreated back into their money or their vast carelessness, or whatever it was that kept them together, and let other people clean up the mess they had made. . . .

I shook hands with him; it seemed silly not to, for I

felt suddenly as though I were talking to a child. Then he went into the jewelry store to buy a pearl necklace—or perhaps only a pair of cuff buttons—rid of my provincial squeamishness forever.

Gatsby's house was still empty when I left—the grass on his lawn had grown as long as mine. One of the taxi drivers in the village never took a fare past the entrance gate without stopping for a minute and pointing inside; perhaps it was he who drove Daisy and Gatsby over to East Egg the night of the accident, and perhaps he had made a story about it all his own. I didn't want to hear it and I avoided him when I got off the train.

I spent my Saturday nights in New York, because those gleaming, dazzling parties of his were with me so vividly that I could still hear the music and the laughter, faint and incessant, from his garden, and the cars going up and down his drive. One night I did hear a material car there, and saw its lights stop at his front steps. But I didn't investigate. Probably it was some final guest who had been away at the ends of the earth and didn't know that the party was over.

On the last night, with my trunk packed and my car sold to the grocer, I went over and looked at that huge incoherent failure of a house once more. On the white steps an obscene word, scrawled by some boy with a piece of brick, stood out clearly in the moonlight, and I erased it, drawing my shoe raspingly along the stone. Then I wandered down to the beach and sprawled out on the sand.

Most of the big shore places were closed now and there were hardly any lights except the shadowy, moving glow of a ferryboat across the Sound. And as the moon rose higher the inessential houses began to melt away until gradually I became aware of the old island here that flowered once for Dutch sailors' eyes—a fresh, green breast of the new world. Its vanished trees, the trees that had made way for Gatsby's house, had once pandered in whispers to the last and greatest of all human dreams; for a transitory enchanted moment man must have held his breath in the presence of this continent, compelled into an aesthetic contemplation he neither understood nor desired, face to face for the last time in history with something commensurate to his capacity for wonder.

And as I sat there brooding on the old, unknown world, I thought of Gatsby's wonder when he first picked out the green light at the end of Daisy's dock. He had come a long way to this blue lawn, and his dream must have seemed so close that he could hardly fail to grasp it. He did not know that it was already behind him, somewhere back in that vast obscurity beyond the city, where the dark fields of the republic rolled on under the night.

Gatsby believed in the green light, the orgiastic future that year by year recedes before us. It eluded us then, but that's no matter—tomorrow we will run faster, stretch out our arms farther. . . . And one fine morning——

So we beat on, boats against the current, borne back ceaselessly into the past.

The Old Man and the Sea

Ernest Hemingway (1899–1961)

Born and reared in Oak Park, Illinois, a suburb of Chicago, Hemingway graduated from high school in 1917 and worked for a brief period as a reporter for the Kansas City *Star*. When the United States entered World War I he volunteered for the ambulance service and was severely wounded at the Italian front. After the armistice he became a foreign correspondent for the Toronto *Star* and soon settled into the life of an expatriate writer in Paris. His first important volume of short stories, *In Our Time* (1925), is characterized by the austerity and precision found in "Big Two-Hearted River." Hemingway's first novel, *The Sun Also Rises* (1926), based on his experiences in Paris and Spain, was followed in 1929 by his great novel of the first World War, *A Farewell to Arms.* Between 1923 and 1933 Heminway wrote most of his important short stories. *The Fifth Column and the First Forty-nine Stories* (1938) collects the stories of *In Our Time, Men Without Women* (1927), and *Winner Take Nothing* (1933), along with a few later stories and a play about the Spanish Civil War.

The 1930s was a difficult decade for Hemingway: essentially an aloof stylist, he did not adjust easily to the climate of political activism and social commitment. However, his experience as a reporter and partisan in the Spanish Civil War did produce a highly successful novel, *For Whom the Bell Tolls* (1940). During the later days of World War II Hemingway was a reporter and participant on the Western front, but the novel based partly on this experience, *Across the River and Into the Trees* (1950), lacks the clean objectivity of *A Farewell to Arms* and the healthy romanticism of *For Whom the Bell Tolls.* In *The Old Man and the Sea* (1952), however, Hemingway produced a fable which combines his famous gift for realistic description with a new-found interest in overt symbolism. He was awarded the Nobel Prize for Literature in 1954, but the success of *The Old Man and the Sea* was not repeated. His last years were marked by a steady physical and mental disintegration, and he committed suicide in 1961.

He was an old man who fished alone in a skiff in the Gulf Stream and he had gone eighty-four days now without taking a fish. In the first forty days a boy had been with him. But after forty days without a fish the boy's parents had told him that the old man was now definitely and finally *salao,* which is the worst form of unlucky, and the boy had gone at their orders in another boat which caught three good fish the first week. It made the boy sad to see the old man come in each day with his skiff empty and he always went down to help him carry either the coiled lines or the gaff and harpoon and the sail that was furled around the mast. The sail was patched with flour sacks and, furled, it looked like the flag of permanent defeat.

The old man was thin and gaunt with deep wrinkles in the back of his neck. The brown blotches of the benevolent skin cancer the sun brings from its reflection on the tropic sea were on his cheeks. The blotches ran well down the sides of his face and his hands had the deep-creased scars from handling heavy fish on the cords. But none of these scars were fresh. They were as old as erosions in a fishless desert.

Everything about him was old except his eyes and they were the same color as the sea and were cheerful and undefeated.

"Santiago," the boy said to him as they climbed the bank from where the skiff was hauled up. "I could go with you again. We've made some money."

The old man had taught the boy to fish and the boy loved him.

"No," the old man said. "You're with a lucky boat. Stay with them."

"But remember how you went eighty-seven days without fish and then we caught big ones every day for three weeks."

"I remember," the old man said. "I know you did not leave me because you doubted."

"It was papa made me leave. I am a boy and I must obey him."

"I know," the old man said. "It is quite normal."

"He hasn't much faith."

"No," the old man said. "But we have. Haven't we?"

"Yes," the boy said. "Can I offer you a beer on the Terrace and then we'll take the stuff home."

"Why not?" the old man said. "Between fishermen."

They sat on the Terrace and many of the fishermen made fun of the old man and he was not angry. Others, of the older fishermen, looked at him and were sad. But they did not show it and they spoke politely about the current and the depths they had drifted their lines at and the steady good weather and of what they had seen. The successful fishermen of that day were already in and had butchered their marlin out and carried them laid full length across two planks, with two men staggering at the end of each plank, to the fish house where they waited for the ice truck to carry them to the market in Havana. Those who had caught sharks had taken them to the shark factory on the other side of the cove where they were hoisted on a block and tackle, their livers removed, their fins cut off and their hides skinned out and their flesh cut into strips for salting.

When the wind was in the east a smell came across the harbour from the shark factory; but today there was only the faint edge of the odour because the wind had backed into the north and then dropped off and it was pleasant and sunny on the Terrace.

"Santiago," the boy said.

"Yes," the old man said. He was holding his glass and thinking of many years ago.

"Can I go out to get sardines for you for tomorrow?"

"No. Go and play baseball. I can still row and Rogelio will throw the net."

"I would like to go. If I cannot fish with you, I would like to serve in some way."

"You bought me a beer," the old man said. "You are already a man."

"How old was I when you first took me in a boat?"

"Five and you nearly were killed when I brought the fish in too green and he nearly tore the boat to pieces. Can you remember?"

"I can remember the tail slapping and banging and the thwart breaking and the noise of the clubbing. I can remember you throwing me into the bow where the wet coiled lines were and feeling the whole boat shiver and the noise of you clubbing him like chopping a tree down and the sweet blood smell all over me."

"Can you really remember that or did I just tell it to you?"

"I remember everything from when we first went together."

The old man looked at him with his sun-burned, confident loving eyes.

"If you were my boy I'd take you out and gamble," he said. "But you are your father's and your mother's and you are in a lucky boat."

"May I get the sardines? I know where I can get four baits too."

"I have mine left from today. I put them in salt in the box."

"Let me get four fresh ones."

"One," the old man said. His hope and his confidence had never gone. But now they were freshening as when the breeze rises.

"Two," the boy said.

"Two," the old man agreed. "You didn't steal them?"

"I would," the boy said. "But I bought these."

"Thank you," the old man said. He was too simple to wonder when he had attained humility. But he knew he had attained it and he knew it was not disgraceful and it carried no loss of true pride.

"Tomorrow is going to be a good day with this current," he said.

"Where are you going?" the boy asked.

"Far out to come in when the wind shifts. I want to be out before it is light."

"I'll try to get him to work far out," the boy said. "Then if you hook something truly big we can come to your aid."

"He does not like to work too far out."

"No," the boy said. "But I will see something that he cannot see such as a bird working and get him to come out after dolphin."

"Are his eyes that bad?"

"He is almost blind."

"It is strange," the old man said. "He never went turtle-ing. That is what kills the eyes."

"But you went turtle-ing for years off the Mosquito Coast and your eyes are good."

"I am a strange old man."

"But are you strong enough now for a truly big fish?"

"I think so. And there are many tricks."

"Let us take the stuff home," the boy said. "So I can get the cast net and go after the sardines."

They picked up the gear from the boat. The old man carried the mast on his shoulder and the boy carried the wooden box with the coiled, hard-braided brown lines, the gaff and the harpoon with its shaft. The box with the baits was under the stern of the skiff along with the club that was used to subdue the big fish when they were brought alongside. No one would steal from the old man but it was better to take the sail and the heavy lines home as the dew was bad for them and, though he was quite sure no local people would steal from him, the old man thought that a gaff and a harpoon were needless temptations to leave in a boat.

They walked up the road together to the old man's shack and went in through its open door. The old man leaned the mast with its wrapped sail against the wall and the boy put the box and the other gear beside it. The mast was nearly as long as the one room of the shack. The shack was made of the tough budshields of the royal palm which are called *guano* and in it there was a bed, a table, one chair, and a place on the dirt floor to cook with charcoal. On the brown walls of the flattened, overlapping leaves of the sturdy fibered *guano* there was a picture in color of the Sacred Heart of Jesus and another of the Virgin of Cobre. These were relics of his wife. Once there had been a tinted photograph of his wife on the wall but he had taken it down because it made him too lonely to see it and it was on the shelf in the corner under his clean shirt.

"What do you have to eat?" the boy asked.

"A pot of yellow rice with fish. Do you want some?"

"No. I will eat at home. Do you want me to make the fire?"

"No. I will make it later on. Or I may eat the rice cold."

"May I take the cast net?"

"Of course."

There was no cast net and the boy remembered when they had sold it. But they went through this fiction every day. There was no pot of yellow rice and fish and the boy knew this too.

"Eighty-five is a lucky number," the old man said. "How would you like to see me bring one in that dressed out over a thousand pounds?"

"I'll get the cast net and go for sardines. Will you sit in the sun in the doorway?"

"Yes. I have yesterday's paper and I will read the baseball."

The boy did not know whether yesterday's paper was a fiction too. But the old man brought it out from under the bed.

"Perico gave it to me at the *bodega,*" he explained.

"I'll be back when I have the sardines. I'll keep yours and mine together on ice and we can share them in the morning. When I come back you can tell me about the baseball."

"The Yankees cannot lose."

"But I fear the Indians of Cleveland."

"Have faith in the Yankees my son. Think of the great DiMaggio."

"I fear both the Tigers of Detroit and the Indians of Cleveland."

"Be careful or you will fear even the Reds of Cincinnati and the White Sox of Chicago."

"You study it and tell me when I come back."

"Do you think we should buy a terminal of the lottery with an eight-five? Tomorrow is the eighty-fifth day."

"We can do that," the boy said. "But what about the eighty-seven of your great record?"

"It could not happen twice. Do you think you can find an eighty-five?"

"I can order one."

"One sheet. That's two dollars and a half. Who can we borrow that from?"

"That's easy. I can always borrow two dollars and a half."

"I think perhaps I can too. But I try not to borrow. First you borrow. Then you beg."

"Keep warm old man," the boy said. "Remember we are in September."

"The month when the great fish come," the old man said. "Anyone can be a fisherman in May."

"I go now for the sardines," the boy said.

When the boy came back the old man was asleep in the chair and the sun was down. The boy took the old army blanket off the bed and spread it over the back of the chair and over the old man's shoulders. They were strange shoulders, still powerful although very old, and the neck was still strong too and the creases did not show so much when the old man was asleep and his head fallen forward. His shirt had been patched so many times that it was like the sail and the patches were faded to many different shades by the sun. The old man's head was very old though and with his eyes closed there was no life in his face. The newspaper lay across his knees and the weight of his arm held it there in the evening breeze. He was barefooted.

The boy left him there and when he came back the old man was still asleep.

"Wake up old man," the boy said and put his hand on one of the old man's knees.

The old man opened his eyes and for a moment he was coming back from a long way away. Then he smiled.

"What have you got?" he asked.

"Supper," said the boy. "We're going to have supper."

"I'm not very hungry."

"Come on and eat. You can't fish and not eat."

"I have," the old man said getting up and taking the newspaper and folding it. Then he started to fold the blanket.

"Keep the blanket around you," the boy said. "You'll not fish without eating while I'm alive."

"Then live a long time and take care of yourself," the old man said. "What are we eating?"

"Black beans and rice, fried bananas, and some stew."

The boy had brought them in a two-decker metal container from the Terrace. The two sets of knives and forks and spoons were in his pocket with a paper napkin wrapped around each set.

"Who gave this to you?"

"Martin. The owner."

"I must thank him."

"I thanked him already," the boy said. "You don't need to thank him."

"I'll give him the belly meat of a big fish," the old man said. "Has he done this for us more than once?"

"I think so."

"I must give him something more than the belly meat then. He is very thoughtful for us."

"He sent two beers."

"I like the beer in cans best."

"I know. But this is in bottles, Hatuey beer, and I take back the bottles."

"That's very kind of you," the old man said. "Should we eat?"

"I've been asking you to," the boy told him gently. "I have not wished to open the container until you were ready."

"I'm ready now," the old man said. "I only needed time to wash."

Where did you wash? the boy thought. The village water supply was two streets down the road. I must have water here for him, the boy thought, and soap and a good towel. Why am I so thoughtless? I must get him another shirt and a jacket for the winter and some sort of shoes and another blanket.

"Your stew is excellent," the old man said.

"Tell me about the baseball," the boy asked him.

"In the American League it is the Yankees as I said," the old man said happily.

"They lost today," the boy told him.

"That means nothing. The great DiMaggio is himself again."

"They have other men on the team."

"Naturally. But he makes the difference. In the other league, between Brooklyn and Philadelphia I must take Brooklyn. But then I think of Dick Sisler and those great drives in the old park."

"There was nothing ever like them. He hits the longest ball I have ever seen."

"Do you remember when he used to come to the Terrace? I wanted to take him fishing but I was too timid to ask him. Then I asked you to ask him and you were too timid."

"I know. It was a great mistake. He might have gone with us. Then we would have that for all of our lives."

"I would like to take the great DiMaggio fishing," the old man said. "They say his father was a fisherman. Maybe he was as poor as we are and would understand."

"The great Sisler's father was never poor and he, the father, was playing in the Big Leagues when he was my age."

"When I was your age I was before the mast on a square rigged ship that ran to Africa and I have seen lions on the beaches in the evening."

"I know. You told me."

"Should we talk about Africa or about baseball?"

"Baseball I think," the boy said. "Tell me about the great John J. McGraw." He said *Jota* for J.

"He used to come to the Terrace sometimes too in the older days. But he was rough and harsh-spoken and difficult when he was drinking. His mind was on horses as well as baseball. At least he carried lists of horses at all times in his pocket and frequently spoke the names of horses on the telephone."

"He was a great manager," the boy said. "My father thinks he was the greatest."

"Because he came here the most times," the old man said. "If Durocher had continued to come here each year your father would think him the greatest manager."

"Who is the greatest manager, really, Luque or Mike Gonzalez?"

"I think they are equal."

"And the best fisherman is you."

"No. I know others better."

"Qué va," the boy said. "There are many good fishermen and some great ones. But there is only you."

"Thank you. You make me happy. I hope no fish will come along so great that he will prove us wrong."

"There is no such fish if you are still strong as you say."

"I may not be as strong as I think," the old man said. "But I know many tricks and I have resolution."

"You ought to go to bed now so that you will be fresh in the morning. I will take the things back to the Terrace."

"Good night then. I will wake you in the morning."

"You're my alarm clock," the boy said.

"Age is my alarm clock," the old man said. "Why do old men wake so early? Is it to have one longer day?"

"I don't know," the boy said. "All I know is that young boys sleep late and hard."

"I can remember it," the old man said. "I'll waken you in time."

"I do not like for him to waken me. It is as though I were inferior."

"I know."

"Sleep well old man."

The boy went out. They had eaten with no light on the table and the old man took off his trousers and went to bed in the dark. He rolled his trousers up to make a pillow, putting the newspaper inside them. He rolled himself in the blanket and slept on the other old newspaper that covered the springs of the bed.

He was asleep in a short time and he dreamed of Africa when he was a boy and the long golden beaches and the white beaches, so white they hurt your eyes, and the high capes and the great brown mountains. He lived along that coast now every night and in his dreams he heard the surf roar and saw the native boats come riding through it. He smelled the tar and oakum of the deck as he slept and he smelled the smell of Africa that the land breeze brought at morning.

Usually when he smelled the land breeze he woke up and dressed to go and wake the boy. But tonight the smell of the land breeze came very early and he knew it was too early in his dream and went on dreaming to see the white peaks of the Islands rising from the sea and then he dreamed of the different harbours and roadsteads of the Canary Islands.

He no longer dreamed of storms, nor of women, nor of great occurrences, nor of great fish, nor fights, nor contests of strength, nor of his wife. He only dreamed of places now and of the lions on the beach. They played like young cats in the dusk and he loved them as he loved the boy. He never dreamed about the boy. He simply woke, looked out the open door at the moon and unrolled his trousers and put them on. He urinated outside the shack and then went up the road to wake the boy. He was shivering with the morning cold. But he knew he would shiver himself warm and that soon he would be rowing.

The door of the house where the boy lived was unlocked and he opened it and walked in quietly with his bare feet. The boy was asleep on a cot in the first room and the old man could see him clearly with the light that came in from the dying moon. He took hold of one foot gently and held it until the boy woke and turned and looked at him. The old man nodded and the boy took his trousers from the chair by the bed and, sitting on the bed, pulled them on.

The old man went out the door and the boy came after him. He was sleepy and the old man put his arm across his shoulders and said, "I am sorry."

"Qué va," the boy said. "It is what a man must do."

They walked down the road to the old man's shack and all along the road, in the dark, barefoot men were moving, carrying the masts of their boats.

When they reached the old man's shack the boy took the rolls of line in the basket and the harpoon and gaff and the old man carried the mast with the furled sail on his shoulder.

"Do you want coffee?" the boy asked.

"We'll put the gear in the boat and then get some."

They had coffee from condensed milk cans at an early morning place that served fishermen.

"How did you sleep old man?" the boy asked. He was waking up now although it was still hard for him to leave his sleep.

"Very well, Manolin," the old man said. "I feel confident today."

"So do I," the boy said. "Now I must get your sardines and mine and your fresh baits. He brings our gear himself. He never wants anyone to carry anything."

"We're different," the old man said. "I let you carry things when you were five years old."

"I know it," the boy said. "I'll be right back. Have another coffee. We have credit here."

He walked off, bare-footed on the coral rocks, to the ice house where the baits were stored.

The old man drank his coffee slowly. It was all he would have all day and he knew that he should take it. For a long time now eating had bored him and he never carried a lunch. He had a bottle of water in the bow of the skiff and that was all he needed for the day.

The boy was back now with the sardines and the two baits wrapped in a newspaper and they went down the trail to the skiff, feeling the pebbled sand under their feet, and lifted the skiff and slid her into the water.

"Good luck old man."

"Good luck," the old man said. He fitted the rope

lashings of the oars onto the thole pins and, leaning forward against the thrust of the blades in the water, he began to row out of the harbour in the dark. There were other boats from the other beaches going out to sea and the old man heard the dip and push of their oars even though he could not see them now the moon was below the hills.

Sometimes someone would speak in a boat. But most of the boats were silent except for the dip of the oars. They spread apart after they were out of the mouth of the harbour and each one headed for the part of the ocean where he hoped to find fish. The old man knew he was going far out and he left the smell of the land behind and rowed out into the clean early morning smell of the ocean. He saw the phosphorescence of the Gulf weed in the water as he rowed over the part of the ocean that the fishermen called the great well because there was a sudden deep of seven hundred fathoms where all sorts of fish congregated because of the swirl the current made against the steep walls of the floor of the ocean. Here there were concentrations of shrimp and bait fish and sometimes schools of squid in the deepest holes and these rose close to the surface at night where all the wandering fish fed on them.

In the dark the old man could feel the morning coming and as he rowed he heard the trembling sound as flying fish left the water and the hissing that their stiff set wings made as they soared away in the darkness. He was very fond of flying fish as they were his principal friends on the ocean. He was sorry for the birds, especially the small delicate dark terns that were always flying and looking and almost never finding, and he thought, the birds have a harder life than we do except for the robber birds and the heavy strong ones. Why did they make birds so delicate and fine as those sea swallows when the ocean can be so cruel? She is kind and very beautiful. But she can be so cruel and it comes so suddenly and such birds that fly, dipping and hunting, with their small sad voices are made too delicately for the sea.

He always thought of the sea as *la mar* which is what people call her in Spanish when they love her. Sometimes those who love her say bad things of her but they are always said as though she were a woman. Some of the younger fishermen, those who used buoys as floats for their lines and had motorboats, bought when the shark livers had brought much money, spoke of her as *el mar* which is masculine. They spoke of her as a contestant or a place or even an enemy. But the old man always thought of her as feminine and as something that gave or withheld great favours, and if she did wild or wicked things it was because she could not help them. The moon affects her as it does a woman, he thought.

He was rowing steadily and it was no effort for him since he kept well within his speed and the surface of the ocean was flat except for the occasional swirls of the current. He was letting the current do a third of the work and as it started to be light he saw he was already further out than he had hoped to be at this hour.

I worked the deep wells for a week and did nothing, he thought. Today I'll work out where the schools of bonito and albacore are and maybe there will be a big one with them.

Before it was really light he had his baits out and was drifting with the current. One bait was down forty fathoms. The second was at seventy-five and the third and fourth were down in the blue water at one hundred and one hundred and twenty-five fathoms. Each bait hung head down with the shank of the hook inside the bait fish, tied and sewed solid and all the projecting part of the hook, the curve and the point, was covered with fresh sardines. Each sardine was hooked through both eyes so that they made a half-garland on the projecting steel. There was no part of the hook that a great fish could feel which was not sweet smelling and good tasting.

The boy had given him two fresh small tunas, or albacores, which hung on the two deepest lines like plummets and, on the others, he had a big blue runner and a yellow jack that had been used before; but they were in good condition still and had the excellent sardines to give them scent and attractiveness. Each line, as thick around as a big pencil, was looped onto a green-sapped stick so that any pull or touch on the bait would make the stick dip and each line had two forty-fathom coils which could be made fast to the other spare coils so that, if it were necessary, a fish could take out over three hundred fathoms of line.

Now the man watched the dip of the three sticks over the side of the skiff and rowed gently to keep the lines straight up and down and at their proper depths. It was quite light and any moment now the sun would rise.

The sun rose thinly from the sea and the old man could see the other boats, low on the water and well in toward the shore, spread out across the current. Then the sun was brighter and the glare came on the water and then, as it rose clear, the flat sea sent it back at his eyes so that it hurt sharply and he rowed without looking into it. He looked down into the water and watched the lines that went straight down into the dark of the water. He kept them straighter than anyone did, so that at each level in the darkness of the stream there would be a bait waiting exactly where he wished it to be for any fish that swam there. Others let them drift with the current and sometimes they were at sixty fathoms when the fishermen thought they were at a hundred.

But, he thought, I keep them with precision. Only I have no luck any more. But who knows? Maybe today. Every day is a new day. It is better to be lucky. But I would rather be exact. Then when luck comes you are ready.

The sun was two hours higher now and it did not hurt his eyes so much to look into the east. There were only three boats in sight now and they showed very low and far inshore.

All my life the early sun has hurt my eyes, he thought. Yet they are still good. In the evening I can look straight into it without getting the blackness. It has more force in the evening too. But in the morning it is painful.

Just then he saw a man-of-war bird with his long black wings circling in the sky ahead of him. He made a quick drop, slanting down on his back-swept wings, and then circled again.

"He's got something," the old man said aloud. "He's not just looking."

He rowed slowly and steadily toward where the bird was circling. He did not hurry and he kept his lines straight up and down. But he crowded the current a little so that he was still fishing correctly though faster than he would have fished if he was not trying to use the bird.

The bird went higher in the air and circled again, his wings motionless. Then he dove suddenly and the old man saw flying fish spurt out of the water and sail desperately over the surface.

"Dolphin," the old man said aloud. "Big dolphin."

He shipped his oars and brought a small line from under the bow. It had a wire leader and a medium-sized hook and he baited it with one of the sardines. He let it go over the side and then made it fast to a ring bolt in the stern. Then he baited another line and left it coiled in the shade of the bow. He went back to rowing and to watching the long-winged black bird who was working, now, low over the water.

As he watched the bird dipped again slanting his wings for the dive and then swinging them wildly and ineffectually as he followed the flying fish. The old man could see the slight bulge in the water that the big dolphin raised as they followed the escaping fish. The dolphin were cutting through the water below the flight of the fish and would be in the water, driving at speed, when the fish dropped. It is a big school of dolphin, he thought. They are widespread and the flying fish have little chance. The bird has no chance. The flying fish are too big for him and they go too fast.

He watched the flying fish burst out again and again and the ineffectual movements of the bird. That school has gotten away from me, he thought. They are moving out too fast and too far. But perhaps I will pick up a stray and perhaps my big fish is around them. My big fish must be somewhere.

The clouds over the land now rose like mountains and the coast was only a long green line with the gray blue hills behind it. The water was a dark blue now, so dark that it was almost purple. As he looked down into it he saw the red sifting of the plankton in the dark water and the strange light the sun made now. He watched his lines to see them go straight down out of sight into the water and he was happy to see so much plankton because it meant fish. The strange light the sun made in the water, now that the sun was higher, meant good weather and so did the shape of the clouds over the land. But the bird was almost out of sight now and nothing showed on the surfce of the water but some patches of yellow, sun-bleached Sargasso weed and the purple, formalized, iridescent, gelatinous bladder of a Portuguese man-of-war floating close beside the boat. It turned on its side and then righted itself. It floated cheerfully as a bubble with its long deadly purple filaments trailing a yard behind it in the water.

"Agua mala," the man said. "You whore."

From where he swung lightly against his oars he looked down into the water and saw the tiny fish that were coloured like the trailing filaments and swam between them and under the small shade the bubble made as it drifted. They were immune to its poison. But men were not and when some of the filaments would catch on a line and rest there slimy and purple while the old man was working a fish, he would have welts and sores on his arms and hands of the sort that poison oak can give. But these poisonings from the *agua mala* came quickly and struck like a whiplash.

The iridescent bubbles were beautiful. But they were the falsest thing in the sea and the old man loved to see the big sea turtles eating them. The turtles saw them, approached them from the front, then shut their eyes so they were completely carapaced and ate them filaments and all. The old man loved to see the turtles eat them and he loved to walk on them on the beach after a storm and hear them pop when he stepped on them with the horny soles of his feet.

He loved green turtles and hawk-bills with their elegance and speed and their great value and he had a friendly contempt for the huge, stupid loggerheads, yellow in their armour-plating, strange in their love-making, and happily eating the Portuguese men-of-war with their eyes shut.

He had no mysticism about turtles although he had gone in turtle boats for many years. He was sorry for them all, even the great trunk backs that were as long as the skiff and weighed a ton. Most people are heartless about turtles because a turtle's heart will beat for hours after he has been cut up and butchered. But the old man thought, I have such a heart too and my feet and hands are like theirs. He ate the white eggs to give himself strength. He ate them all through May to be strong in September and October for the truly big fish.

He also drank a cup of shark liver oil each day from the big drum in the shack where many of the fishermen kept their gear. It was there for all fishermen who wanted it. Most fishermen hated the taste. But it was no worse than getting up at the hours that they rose and it was very good against all colds and grippes and it was good for the eyes.

Now the old man looked up and saw that the bird was circling again.

"He's found fish," he said aloud. No flying fish broke the surface and there was no scattering of bait fish. But as the old man watched, a small tuna rose in the air, turned and dropped head first into the water. The tuna shone silver in the sun and after he had dropped back into the water another and another rose and they were jumping in all directions, churning the water and leaping in long jumps after the bait. They were circling it and driving it.

If they don't travel too fast I will get into them, the old man thought, and he watched the school working the water white and the bird now dropping and dipping into the bait fish that were forced to the surface in their panic.

"The bird is a great help," the old man said. Just then the stern line came taut under his foot, where he had kept a loop of the line, and he dropped his oars and felt the weight of the small tuna's shivering pull as he held the line firm and commenced to haul it in. The shivering increased as he pulled in and he could see the blue back of the fish in the water and the gold of his sides before he swung him over the side and into the boat. He lay in the stern in the sun, compact and bullet shaped, his big, unintelligent eyes staring as he thumped his life out against the planking of the boat with the quick shivering strokes of his neat, fast-moving tail. The old man hit him on the head for kindness and kicked him, his body still shuddering, under the shade of the stern.

"Albacore," he said aloud. "He'll make a beautiful bait. He'll weigh ten pounds."

He did not remember when he had first started to talk aloud when he was by himself. He had sung when he was by himself in the old days and he had sung at night sometimes when he was alone steering on his watch in the smacks or in the turtle boats. He had probably started to talk aloud, when alone, when the boy had left. But he did not remember. When he and the boy fished together they usually spoke only when it was necessary. They talked at night or when they were storm-bound by bad weather. It was considered a virtue not to talk unnecessarily at sea and the old man had always considered it so and respected it. But now he said his thoughts aloud many times since there was no one that they could annoy.

"If the others heard me talking out loud they would think that I am crazy," he said aloud. "But since I am not crazy, I do not care. And the rich have radios to talk to them in their boats and to bring them the baseball."

Now is no time to think of baseball, he thought. Now is the time to think of only one thing. That which I was born for. There might be a big one around that school, he thought. I picked up only a straggler from the albacore that were feeding. But they are working far out and fast. Everything that shows on the surface today travels very fast and to the north-east. Can that be the time of day? Or is it some sign of weather that I do not know?

He could not see the green of the shore now but only the tops of the blue hills that showed white as though they were snow-capped and the clouds that looked like high snow mountains above them. The sea was very dark and the light made prisms in the water. The myriad flecks of the plankton were annulled now by the high sun and it was only the great deep prisms in the blue water that the old man saw now with his lines going straight down into the water that was a mile deep.

The tuna, the fishermen called all the fish of that species tuna and only distinguished among them by their proper names when they came to sell them or to trade them for baits, were down again. The sun was hot now and the old man felt it on the back of his neck and felt the sweat trickle down his back as he rowed.

I could just drift, he thought, and sleep and put a bight of line around my toe to wake me. But today is eighty-five days and I should fish the day well.

Just then, watching his lines, he saw one of the projecting green sticks dip sharply.

"Yes," he said. "Yes," and shipped his oars without bumping the boat. He reached out for the line and held it softly between the thumb and forefinger of his right hand. He felt no strain nor weight and he held the line lightly. Then it came again. This time it was a tentative pull, not solid nor heavy, and he knew exactly what it was. One hundred fathoms down a marlin was eating the sardines that covered the point and the shank of the hook where the hand-forged hook projected from the head of the small tuna.

The old man held the line delicately, and softly, with his left hand, unleashed it from the stick. Now he could let it run through his fingers without the fish feeling any tension.

This far out, he must be huge in this month, he thought. Eat them, fish. Eat them. Please eat them. How fresh they are and you down there six hundred feet in that cold water in the dark. Make another turn in the dark and come back and eat them.

He felt the light delicate pulling and then a harder pull when a sardine's head must have been more difficult to break from the hook. Then there was nothing.

"Come on," the old man said aloud. "Make another turn. Just smell them. Aren't they lovely? Eat them good now and then there is the tuna. Hard and cold and lovely. Don't be shy, fish. Eat them."

He waited with the line between his thumb and his finger, watching it and the other lines at the same time for the fish might have swum up or down. Then came the same delicate pulling touch again.

"He'll take it," the old man said aloud. "God help him to take it."

He did not take it though. He was gone and the old man felt nothing.

"He can't have gone," he said. "Christ knows he can't have gone. He's making a turn. Maybe he has been hooked before and he remembers something of it."

Then he felt the gentle touch on the line and he was happy.

"It was only his turn," he said. "He'll take it."

He was happy feeling the gentle pulling and then he felt something hard and unbelievably heavy. It was the weight of the fish and he let the line slip down, down, down, unrolling off the first of the two reserve coils. As it went down, slipping lightly through the old man's fingers, he still could feel the great weight, though the pressure of his thumb and finger were almost imperceptible.

"What a fish," he said. "He has it sideways in his mouth now and he is moving off with it."

Then he will turn and swallow it, he thought. He did not say that because he knew that if you said a good thing it might not happen. He knew what a huge fish this was and he thought of him moving away in the darkness with the tuna held crosswise in his mouth. At that moment he felt him stop moving but the weight was still there. Then the weight increased and he gave more line. He tightened the pressure of his thumb and finger for a moment and the weight increased and was going straight down.

"He's taken it," he said. "Now I'll let him eat it well."

He let the line slip through his fingers while he reached down with his left hand and made fast the free end of the two reserve coils to the loop of the two reserve coils of the next line. Now he was ready. He had three forty-fathom coils of line in reserve now, as well as the coil he was using.

"Eat it a little more," he said. "Eat it well."

Eat it so that the point of the hook goes into your heart and kills you, he thought. Come up easy and let me put the harpoon into you. All right. Are you ready? Have you been long enough at table?

"Now!" he said aloud and struck hard with both hands, gained a yard of line and then struck again and again, swinging with each arm alternately on the cord with all the strength of his arms and the pivoted weight of his body.

Nothing happened. The fish just moved away slowly and the old man could not raise him an inch. His line was strong and made for heavy fish and he held it against his back until it was so taut that beads of water were jumping from it. Then it began to make a slow hissing sound in the water and he still held it, bracing himself against the thwart and leaning back against the pull. The boat began to move slowly off toward the north-west.

The fish moved steadily and they travelled slowly on the calm water. The other baits were still in the water but there was nothing to be done.

"I wish I had the boy," the old man said aloud. "I'm being towed by a fish and I'm the towing bitt. I could make the line fast. But then he could break it. I must hold him all I can and give him line when he must have it. Thank God he is travelling and not going down."

What I will do if he decides to go down, I don't know. What I'll do if he sounds and dies I don't know. But I'll do something. There are plenty of things I can do.

He held the line against his back and watched its slant in the water and the skiff moving steadily to the north-west.

This will kill him, the old man thought. He can't do this forever. But four hours later the fish was still swimming steadily out to sea, towing the skiff, and the old man was still braced solidly with the line across his back.

"It was noon when I hooked him," he said. "And I have never seen him."

He had pushed his straw hat hard down on his head before he hooked the fish and it was cutting his forehead. He was thirsty too and he got down on his knees and, being careful not to jerk on the line, moved as far into the bow as he could get and reached the water bottle with one hand. He opened it and drank a little. Then he rested against the bow. He rested sitting on the un-stepped mast and sail and tried not to think but only to endure.

Then he looked behind him and saw that no land was visible. That makes no difference, he thought. I can always come in on the glow from Havana. There are two more hours before the sun sets and maybe he will come up before that. If he doesn't maybe he will come up with the moon. If he does not do that maybe he will come up with the sunrise. I have no cramps and I feel strong. It is he that has the hook in his mouth. But what a fish to pull like that. He must have his mouth shut tight on the wire. I wish I could see him. I wish I could see him only once to know what I have against me.

The fish never changed his course nor his direction all that night as far as the man could tell from watching the stars. It was cold after the sun went down and the old man's sweat dried cold on his back and his arms and his old legs. During the day he had taken the sack that covered the bait box and spread it in the sun to dry. After the sun went down he tied it around his neck so that it hung down over his back and he cautiously worked it down under the line that was across his shoulders now. The sack cushioned the line and he had found a way of leaning forward against the bow so that he was almost comfortable. The position actually was only somewhat less intolerable; but he thought of it as almost comfortable.

I can do nothing with him and he can do nothing with me, he thought. Not as long as he keeps this up.

Once he stood up and urinated over the side of the skiff and looked at the stars and checked his course. The line showed like a phosphorescent streak in the water straight out from his shoulders. They were moving more slowly now and the glow of Havana was not so strong, so that he knew the current must be carrying them to the eastward. If I lose the glare of Havana we must be going more to the eastward, he thought. For if the fish's course held true I must see it for many more hours. I wonder how the baseball came out in the grand leagues today, he thought. It would be wonderful to do this with a radio. Then he thought, think of it always. Think of what you are doing. You must do nothing stupid.

Then he said aloud, "I wish I had the boy. To help me and to see this."

No one should be alone in their old age, he thought. But it is unavoidable. I must remember to eat the tuna before he spoils in order to keep strong. Remember, no matter how little you want to, that you must eat him in the morning. Remember, he said to himself.

During the night two porpoises came around the boat and he could hear them rolling and blowing. He could tell the difference between the blowing noise the male made and the sighing blow of the female.

"They are good," he said. "They play and make jokes and love one another. They are our brothers like the flying fish."

Then he began to pity the great fish that he had hooked. He is wonderful and strange and who knows how old he is, he thought. Never have I had such a strong fish nor one who acted so strangely. Perhaps he is too wise to jump. He could ruin me by jumping or by a wild rush. But perhaps he has been hooked many times before and he knows that this is how he should make his fight. He cannot know that it is only one man against him, nor that it is an old man. But what a great fish he is and what will he bring in the market if the flesh is good. He took the bait like a male and he pulls like a male and his fight has no panic in it. I wonder if he has any plans or if he is just as desperate as I am?

He remembered the time he had hooked one of a pair of marlin. The male fish always let the female fish feed first and the hooked fish, the female, made a wild, panic-stricken, despairing fight that soon exhausted her, and all the time the male had stayed with her, crossing the line and circling with her on the surface. He had stayed so close that the old man was afraid he would cut the line with his tail which was sharp as a scythe and almost of that size and shape. When the old man had gaffed her and clubbed her, holding the rapier bill with its sandpaper edge and clubbing her across the top of her head until her colour turned to a colour almost like the backing of mirrors, and then, with the boy's aid, hoisted her aboard, the male fish had stayed by the side of the boat. Then, while the old man was clearing the lines and preparing the harpoon, the male fish jumped high into the air beside the boat to see where the female was and then went down deep, his lavender wings, that were his pectoral fins, spread wide and all his wide lavender stripes showing. He was beautiful, the old man remembered, and he had stayed.

That was the saddest thing I ever saw with them, the old man thought. The boy was sad too and we begged her pardon and butchered her promptly.

"I wish the boy was here," he said aloud and settled himself against the rounded planks of the bow and felt the strength of the great fish through the line he held across his shoulders moving steadily toward whatever he had chosen.

When once, through my treachery, it had been necessary to him to make a choice, the old man thought.

His choice had been to stay in the deep dark water far out beyond all snares and traps and treacheries. My choice was to go there to find him beyond all people. Beyond all people in the world. Now we are joined together and have been since noon. And no one to help either one of us.

Perhaps I should not have been a fisherman, he thought. But that was the thing that I was born for. I must surely remember to eat the tuna after it gets light.

Some time before daylight something took one of the baits that were behind him. He heard the stick break and the line begin to rush out over the gunwale of the skiff. In the darkness he loosened his sheath knife and taking all the strain of the fish on his left shoulder he leaned back and cut the line against the wood of the gunwale. Then he cut the other line closest to him and in the dark made the loose ends of the reserve coils fast. He worked skillfully with the one hand and put his foot on the coils to hold them as he drew his knots tight. Now he had six reserve coils of line. There were two from each bait he had severed and the two from the bait the fish had taken and they were all connected.

After it is light, he thought, I will work back to the forty-fathom bait and cut it away too and link up the reserve coils. I will have lost two hundred fathoms of good Catalan *cardel* and the hooks and leaders. That can be replaced. But who replaces this fish if I hook some fish and it cuts him off? I don't know what that fish was that took the bait just now. It could have been a marlin or a broadbill or a shark. I never felt him. I had to get rid of him too fast.

Aloud he said, "I wish I had the boy."

But you haven't got the boy, he thought. You have only yourself and you had better work back to the last line now, in the dark or not in the dark, and cut it away and hook up the two reserve coils.

So he did it. It was difficult in the dark and once the fish made a surge that pulled him down on his face and made a cut below his eye. The blood ran down his cheek a little way. But it coagulated and dried before it reached his chin and he worked his way back to the bow and rested against the wood. He adjusted the sack and carefully worked the line so that it came across a new part of his shoulders and, holding it anchored with his shoulders, he carefully felt the pull of the fish and then felt with his hand the progress of the skiff through the water.

I wonder what he made that lurch for, he thought. The wire must have slipped on the great hill of his back. Certainly his back cannot feel as badly as mine does. But he cannot pull this skiff forever, no matter how great he is. Now everything is cleared away that might make trouble and I have a big reserve of line; all that a man can ask.

"Fish," he said softly, aloud, "I'll stay with you until I am dead."

He'll stay with me too, I suppose, the old man thought and he waited for it to be light. It was cold now in the time before daylight and he pushed against the wood to be warm. I can do it as long as he can, he thought. And in the first light the line extended out and down into the water. The boat moved steadily and when the first edge of the sun rose it was on the old man's right shoulder.

"He's headed north," the old man said. The current will have set us far to the eastward, he thought. I wish he would turn with the current. That would show that he was tiring.

When the sun had risen further the old man realized that the fish was not tiring. There was only one favorable sign. The slant of the line showed he was swimming at a lesser depth. That did not necessarily mean that he would jump. But he might.

"God let him jump," the old man said. "I have enough line to handle him."

Maybe if I can increase the tension just a little it will hurt him and he will jump, he thought. Now that it is daylight let him jump so that he'll fill the sacks along his backbone with air and then he cannot go deep to die.

He tried to increase the tension, but the line had been taut up to the very edge of the breaking point since he had hooked the fish and he felt the harshness as he leaned back to pull and knew he could put no more strain on it. I must not jerk it ever, he thought. Each jerk widens the cut the hook makes and then when he does jump he might throw it. Anyway I feel better with the sun and for once I do not have to look into it.

There was yellow weed on the line but the old man knew that only made an added drag and he was pleased. It was the yellow Gulf weed that had made so much phosphorescence in the night.

"Fish," he said, "I love you and respect you very much. But I will kill you dead before this day ends."

Let us hope so, he thought.

A small bird came toward the skiff from the north. He was a warbler and flying very low over the water. The old man could see that he was very tired.

The bird made the stern of the boat and rested there. Then he flew around the old man's head and rested on the line where he was more comfortable.

"How old are you?" the old man asked the bird. "Is this your first trip?"

The bird looked at him when he spoke. He was too tired even to examine the line and he teetered on it as his delicate feet gripped it fast.

"It's steady," the old man told him. "It's too steady. You shouldn't be that tired after a windless night. What are birds coming to?"

The hawks, he thought, that come out to sea to meet them. But he said nothing of this to the bird who could not understand him anyway and who would learn about the hawks soon enough.

"Take a good rest, small bird," he said. "Then go in and take your chance like any man or bird or fish."

It encouraged him to talk because his back had stiffened in the night and it hurt truly now.

"Stay at my house if you like, bird," he said. "I am sorry I cannot hoist the sail and take you in with the small breeze that is rising. But I am with a friend."

Just then the fish gave a sudden lurch that pulled the old man down onto the bow and would have pulled him overboard if he had not braced himself and given some line.

The bird had flown up when the line jerked and the old man had not even seen him go. He felt the line carefully with his right hand and noticed his hand was bleeding.

"Something hurt him then," he said aloud and pulled back on the line to see if he could turn the fish. But when he was touching the breaking point he held steady and settled back against the strain of the line.

"You're feeling it now, fish," he said. "And so, God knows, am I."

He looked around for the bird now because he would have liked him for company. The bird was gone.

You did not stay long, the man thought. But it is rougher where you are going until you make the shore. How did I let the fish cut me with that one quick pull he made? I must be getting very stupid. Or perhaps I was looking at the small bird and thinking of him. Now I will pay attention to my work and then I must eat the tuna so that I will not have a failure of strength.

"I wish the boy were here and that I had some salt," he said aloud.

Shifting the weight of the line to his left shoulder and kneeling carefully he washed his hand in the ocean and held it there, submerged, for more than a minute watching the blood trail away and the steady movement of the water against his hand as the boat moved.

"He has slowed much," he said.

The old man would have liked to keep his hand in the salt water longer but he was afraid of another sudden lurch by the fish and he stood up and braced himself and held his hand up against the sun. It was only a line burn that had cut his flesh. But it was in the working part of his hand. He knew he would need his hands before this was over and he did not like to be cut before it started.

"Now," he said, when his hand had dried, "I must eat the small tuna. I can reach him with the gaff and eat him here in comfort."

He knelt down and found the tuna under the stern with the gaff and drew it toward him keeping it clear of the coiled lines. Holding the line with his left shoulder again, and bracing on his left hand and arm, he took the tuna off the gaff hook and put the gaff back in place. He put one knee on the fish and cut strips of dark red meat longitudinally from the back of the head to the tail. They were wedge-shaped strips and he cut them from next to the back bone down to the edge of the belly. When he had cut six strips he spread them out on the wood of the bow, wiped his knife on his trousers, and lifted the carcass of the bonito by the tail and dropped it overboard.

"I don't think I can eat an entire one," he said and drew his knife across one of the strips. He could feel the steady hard pull of the line and his left hand was cramped. It drew up tight on the heavy cord and he looked at it in disgust.

"What kind of a hand is that," he said. "Cramp then if you want. Make yourself into a claw. It will do you no good."

Come on, he thought and looked down into the dark water at the slant of the line. Eat it now and it will strengthen the hand. It is not the hand's fault and you have been many hours with the fish. But you can stay with him forever. Eat the bonito now.

He picked up a piece and put it in his mouth and chewed it slowly. It was not unpleasant.

Chew it well, he thought, and get all the juices. It would not be bad to eat with a little lime or with lemon or with salt.

"How do you feel, hand?" he asked the cramped hand that was almost as stiff as rigor mortis. "I'll eat some more for you."

He ate the other part of the piece that he had cut in two. He chewed it carefully and then spat out the skin.

"How does it go, hand? Or is it too early to know?"

He took another full piece and chewed it.

"It is a strong full-blooded fish," he thought. "I was lucky to get him instead of dolphin. Dolphin is too sweet. This is hardly sweet at all and all the strength is still in it."

There is no sense in being anything but practical though, he thought. I wish I had some salt. And I do not know whether the sun will rot or dry what is left, so I had better eat it all although I am not hungry. The fish is calm and steady. I will eat it all and then I will be ready.

"Be patient, hand," he said. "I do this for you."

I wish I could feed the fish, he thought. He is my brother. But I must kill him and keep strong to do it. Slowly and conscientiously he ate all of the wedge-shaped strips of fish.

He straightened up, wiping his hand on his trousers.

"Now," he said. "You can let the cord go, hand, and I will handle him with the right arm alone until you stop that nonsense." He put his left foot on the heavy line that the left hand had held and lay back against the pull against his back.

"God help me to have the cramp go," he said. "Because I do not know what the fish is going to do."

But he seems calm, he thought, and following his plan. But what is his plan, he thought. And what is mine? Mine I must improvise to his because of his great size. If he will jump I can kill him. But he stays down forever. Then I will stay down with him forever.

He rubbed the cramped hand against his trousers and tried to gentle the fingers. But it would not open. Maybe it will open with the sun, he thought. Maybe it will open when the strong raw tuna is digested. If I have to have it, I will open it, cost whatever it costs. But I do not want to open it now by force. Let it open by itself and come back of its own accord. After all I abused it much in the night when it was necessary to free and untie the various lines.

He looked across the sea and knew how alone he was now. But he could see the prisms in the deep dark water and the line stretching ahead and the strange undulation of the calm. The clouds were building up now for the trade wind and he looked ahead and saw a flight of wild ducks etching themselves against the sky over the water, then blurring, then etching again and he knew no man was ever alone on the sea.

He thought of how some men feared being out of sight of land in a small boat and knew they were right in the months of sudden bad weather. But now they were in hurricane months and, when there are no hurricanes, the weather of hurricane months is the best of all the year.

If there is a hurricane you always see the signs of it in the sky for days ahead, if you are at sea. They do not see it ashore because they do not know what to look for, he thought. The land must make a difference too, in the shape of the clouds. But we have no hurricane coming now.

He looked at the sky and saw the white cumulus built like friendly piles of ice cream and high above were the thin feathers of the cirrus against the high September sky.

"Light *brisa,*" he said. "Better weather for me than for you, fish."

His left hand was still cramped, but he was unknotting it slowly.

I hate a cramp, he thought. It is a treachery of one's own body. It is humiliating before others to have a diarrhoea from ptomaine poisoning or to vomit from it. But a cramp, he thought of it as a *calambre,* humiliates oneself especially when one is alone.

If the boy were here he could rub it for me and loosen it down from the forearm, he thought. But it will loosen up.

Then, with his right hand he felt the difference in the pull of the line before he saw the slant change in the water. Then, as he leaned against the line and slapped his left hand hard and fast against his thigh he saw the line slanting slowly upward.

"He's coming up," he said. "Come on hand. Please come on."

The line rose slowly and steadily and then the surface of the ocean bulged ahead of the boat and the fish came out. He came out unendingly and water poured from his sides. He was bright in the sun and his head and back were dark purple and in the sun the stripes on his sides showed wide and a light lavender. His sword was as long as a baseball bat and tapered like a rapier and he rose his full length from the water and then re-entered it, smoothly, like a diver and the old man saw the great scythe-blade of his tail go under and the line commenced to race out.

"He is two feet longer than the skiff," the old man said. The line was going out fast but steadily and the fish was not panicked. The old man was trying with both hands to keep the line just inside of breaking strength. He knew that if he could not slow the fish with a steady pressure the fish could take out all the line and break it.

He is a great fish and I must convince him, he thought. I must never let him learn his strength nor what he could do if he made his run. If I were him I would put in everything now and go until something broke. But, thank God, they are not as intelligent as we who kill them; although they are more noble and more able.

The old man had seen many great fish. He had seen many that weighed more than a thousand pounds and he had caught two of that size in his life, but never alone. Now alone, and out of sight of land, he was fast to the biggest fish that he had ever seen and bigger than he had ever heard of, and his left hand was still as tight as the gripped claws of an eagle.

It will uncramp though, he thought. Surely it will uncramp to help my right hand. There are three things that are brothers: the fish and my two hands. It must uncramp. It is unworthy of it to be cramped. The fish had slowed again and was going at his usual pace.

I wonder why he jumped, the old man thought. He jumped almost as though to show me how big he was. I know now, anyway, he thought. I wish I could show him what sort of man I am. But then he would see the cramped hand. Let him think I am more man than I am and I will be so. I wish I was the fish, he thought, with everything he has against only my will and my intelligence.

He settled comfortably against the wood and took his suffering as it came and the fish swam steadily and the boat moved slowly through the dark water. There was a small sea rising with the wind coming up from the east and at noon the old man's left hand was uncramped.

"Bad news for you, fish," he said and shifted the line over the sacks that covered his shoulders.

He was comfortable but suffering, although he did not admit the suffering at all.

"I am not religious," he said. "But I will say ten Our Fathers and ten Hail Marys that I should catch this fish, and I promise to make a pilgrimage to the Virgin of Cobre if I catch him. That is a promise."

He commenced to say his prayers mechanically. Sometimes he would be so tired that he could not remember the prayer and then he would say them fast so that they would come automatically. Hail Marys are easier to say than Our Fathers, he thought.

"Hail Mary full of Grace the Lord is with thee. Blessed art thou among women and blessed is the fruit of thy womb, Jesus. Holy Mary, Mother of God, pray for us sinners now and at the hour of our death. Amen." Then he added, "Blessed Virgin, pray for the death of this fish. Wonderful though he is."

With his prayers said, and feeling much better, but suffering exactly as much, and perhaps a little more, he leaned against the wood of the bow and began, mechanically, to work the fingers of his left hand.

The sun was hot now although the breeze was rising gently.

"I had better re-bait that little line out over the stern," he said. "If the fish decides to stay another night I will need to eat again and the water is low in the bottle. I don't think I can get anything but a dolphin here. But if I eat him fresh enough he won't be bad. I wish a flying fish would come on board tonight. But I have no light to attract them. A flying fish is excellent to eat raw and I would not have to cut him up. I must save all my strength now. Christ, I did not know he was so big."

"I'll kill him though," he said. "In all his greatness and his glory."

Although it is unjust, he thought. But I will show him what a man can do and what a man endures.

"I told the boy I was a strange old man," he said. "Now is when I must prove it."

The thousand times that he had proved it meant nothing. Now he was proving it again. Each time was a new time and he never thought about the past when he was doing it.

I wish he'd sleep and I could sleep and dream about the lions, he thought. Why are the lions the main thing that is left? Don't think, old man, he said to himself. Rest gently now against the wood and think of nothing. He is working. Work as little as you can.

It was getting into the afternoon and the boat still moved slowly and steadily. But there was an added drag now from the easterly breeze and the old man rode gently with the small sea and the hurt of the cord across his back came to him easily and smoothly.

Once in the afternoon the line started to rise again. But the fish only continued to swim at a slightly higher level. The sun was on the old man's left arm and shoulder and on his back. So he knew the fish had turned east of north.

Now that he had seen him once, he could picture the fish swimming in the water with his purple pectoral fins set wide as wings and the great erect tail slicing through the dark. I wonder how much he sees at that depth, the old man thought. His eye is huge and a horse, with much less eye, can see in the dark. Once I could see quite well in the dark. Not in the absolute dark. But almost as a cat sees.

The sun and his steady movement of his fingers had uncramped his left hand now completely and he began to shift more of the strain to it and he shrugged the muscles of his back to shift the hurt of the cord a little.

"If you're not tired, fish," he said aloud, "you must be very strange."

He felt very tired now and he knew the night would come soon and he tried to think of other things. He thought of the Big Leagues, to him they were the *Gran Ligas,* and he knew that the Yankees of New York were playing the *Tigres* of Detroit.

This is the second day now that I do not know the result of the *juegos,* he thought. But I must have confidence and I must be worthy of the great DiMaggio who does all things perfectly even with the pain of the bone spur in his heel. What is a bone spur? he asked himself. *Un espuela de hueso.* We do not have them. Can it be as painful as the spur of a fighting cock in one's heel? I do not think I could endure that or the loss of the eye and of both eyes and continue to fight as the fighting cocks do. Man is not much beside the great birds and beasts. Still I would rather be that beast down there in the darkness of the sea.

"Unless sharks come," he said aloud. "If sharks come, God pity him and me."

Do you believe the great DiMaggio would stay with a fish as long as I will stay with this one? he thought. I am sure he would and more since he is young and strong. Also his father was a fisherman. But would the bone spur hurt him too much?

"I do not know," he said aloud. "I never had a bone spur."

As the sun set he remembered, to give himself more confidence, the time in the tavern at Casablanca when he had played the hand game with the great negro from Cienfuegos who was the strongest man on the docks. They had gone one day and one night with their elbows on a chalk line on the table and their forearms straight up and their hands gripped tight. Each one was trying to force the other's hand down onto the table. There was much betting and people went in and out of the room under the kerosene lights and he had looked at the arm and hand of the negro and at the negro's face. They changed the referees every four hours after the first eight so that the referees could sleep. Blood came out from under the fingernails of both his and the negro's hands and they looked each other in the eye and at their hands and forearms and the bettors went in and out of the room and sat on high chairs against the wall and watched. The walls were painted bright blue and were of wood and the lamps threw their shadows against them. The negro's shadow was huge and it moved on the wall as the breeze moved the lamps.

The odds would change back and forth all night and they fed the negro rum and lighted cigarettes for him. Then the negro, after the rum, would try for a tremendous effort and once he had the old man, who was not an old man then but was Santiago *El Campeón,* nearly three inches off balance. But the old man had raised his hand up to dead even again. He was sure then that he had the negro, who was a fine man and a great athlete, beaten. And at daylight when the bettors were asking that it be called a draw and the referee was shaking his head, he had unleashed his effort and forced the hand of the negro down and down until it rested on the wood. The match had started on a Sunday morning and ended on a Monday morning. Many of the bettors had asked for a draw because they had to go to work on the docks loading sacks of sugar or at the Havana Coal Company. Otherwise everyone would have wanted it to go to a finish. But he had finished it anyway and before anyone had to go to work.

For a long time after that everyone had called him The Champion and there had been a return match in the spring. But not much money was bet and he had won it quite easily since he had broken the confidence of the negro from Cienfuegos in the first match. After that he had a few matches and then no more. He decided that he could beat anyone if he wanted to badly enough and he decided that it was bad for his right hand for fishing. He had tried a few practice matches with his left hand. But his left hand had always been a traitor and would not do what he called on it to do and he did not trust it.

The sun will bake it out well now, he thought. It should not cramp on me again unless it gets too cold in the night. I wonder what this night will bring.

An airplane passed overhead on its course to Miami and he watched its shadow scaring up the schools of flying fish.

"With so much flying fish there should be dolphin," he said, and leaned back on the line to see if it was possible to gain any on his fish. But he could not and it stayed at the hardness and water-drop shivering that preceded breaking. The boat moved ahead slowly and he watched the airplane until he could no longer see it.

It must be very strange in an airplane, he thought. I wonder what the sea looks like from that height? They should be able to see the fish well if they do not fly too high. I would like to fly very slowly at two hundred fathoms high and see the fish from above. In the turtle boats I was in the cross-trees of the mast-head and even at that height I saw much. The dolphin look greener from there and you can see their stripes and their purple spots and you can see all of the school as they swim. Why is it that all the fast-moving fish of the dark current have purple backs and usually purple stripes or spots? The dolphin looks green of course because he is really golden. But when he comes to feed, truly hungry, purple stripes show on his sides as on a marlin. Can it be anger, or the greater speed he makes that brings them out?

Just before it was dark, as they passed a great island of Sargasso weed that heaved and swung in the light sea as though the ocean were making love with something under a yellow blanket, his small line was taken by a dolphin. He saw it first when it jumped in the air, true gold in the last of the sun and bending and flapping wildly in the air. It jumped again and again in the acrobatics of its fear and he worked his way back to the stern and crouching and holding the big line with his right hand and arm, he pulled the dolphin in with his left hand, stepping on the gained line each time with his bare left foot. When the fish was at the stern, plunging and cutting from side to side in desperation, the old man leaned over the stern and lifted the burnished gold fish with its purple spots over the stern. Its jaws were working convulsively in quick bites against the hook and it pounded the bottom of the skiff with its long flat body, its tail and its head until he clubbed it across the shining golden head until it shivered and was still.

The old man unhooked the fish, rebaited the line with another sardine and tossed it over. Then he worked his way slowly back to the bow. He washed his left hand and wiped it on his trousers. Then he shifted the heavy line from his right hand to his left and washed his right hand in the sea while he watched the sun go into the ocean and the slant of the big cord.

"He hasn't changed at all," he said. But watching the movement of the water against his hand he noted that it was perceptibly slower.

"I'll lash the two oars together across the stern and that will slow him in the night," he said. "He's good for the night and so am I."

It would be better to gut the dolphin a little later to save the blood in the meat, he thought. I can do that a little later and lash the oars to make a drag at the same time. I had better keep the fish quiet now and not disturb him too much at sunset. The setting of the sun is a difficult time for all fish.

He let his hand dry in the air then grasped the line with it and eased himself as much as he could and allowed himself to be pulled forward against the wood so that the boat took the strain as much, or more, than he did.

I'm learning how to do it, he thought. This part of it anyway. Then too, remember he hasn't eaten since he took the bait and he is huge and needs much food. I have eaten the whole bonito. Tomorrow I will eat the dolphin. He called it *dorado*. Perhaps I should eat some of it when I clean it. It will be harder to eat than the bonito. But, then, nothing is easy.

"How do you feel, fish?" he asked aloud. "I feel good and my left hand is better and I have food for a night and a day. Pull the boat, fish."

He did not truly feel good because the pain from the cord across his back had almost passed pain and gone into a dullness that he mistrusted. But I have had worse things than that, he thought. My hand is only cut a little and the cramp is gone from the other. My legs are all right. Also now I have gained on him in the question of sustenance.

It was dark now as it becomes dark quickly after the sun sets in September. He lay against the worn wood of the bow and rested all that he could. The first stars were out. He did not know the name of Rigel but he saw it and knew soon they would all be out and he would have all his distant friends.

"The fish is my friend too," he said aloud. "I have never seen or heard of such a fish. But I must kill him. I am glad we do not have to try to kill the stars."

Imagine if each day a man must try to kill the moon, he thought. The moon runs away. But imagine if a man each day should have to try to kill the sun? We were born lucky, he thought. Then he was sorry for the great fish that had nothing to eat and his determination to kill him never relaxed in his sorrow for him. How many people will he feed, he thought. But are they worthy to eat him? No, of course not. There is no one worthy of eating him from the manner of his behaviour and his great dignity.

I do not understand these things, he thought. But it is good that we do not have to try to kill the sun or the moon or the stars. It is enough to live on the sea and kill our true brothers.

Now, he thought, I must think about the drag. It has its perils and its merits. I may lose so much line that I will lose him, if he makes his effort and the drag made by the oars is in place and the boat loses all her lightness. Her lightness prolongs both our suffering but it is my safety since he has great speed that he has never yet employed. No matter what passes I must gut the dolphin so he does not spoil and eat some of him to be strong.

Now I will rest an hour more and feel that he is solid and steady before I move back to the stern to do the work and make the decision. In the meantime I can see how he acts and if he shows any changes. The oars are a good trick; but it has reached the time to play for safety. He is much fish still and I saw that the hook was in the corner of his mouth and he has kept his mouth tight shut. The punishment of the hook is nothing. The punishment of hunger, and that he is against something that he does not comprehend, is everything. Rest now, old man, and let him work until your next duty comes.

He rested for what he believed to be two hours. The moon did not rise now until late and he had no way of judging the time. Nor was he really resting except comparatively. He was still bearing the pull of the fish across his shoulders but he placed his left hand on the gunwhale of the bow and confided more and more of the resistance to the fish to the skiff itself.

How simple it would be if I could make the line fast, he thought. But with one small lurch he could break it. I must cushion the pull of the line with my body and at all times be ready to give line with both hands.

"But you have not slept yet, old man," he said

aloud. "It is half a day and a night and now another day and you have not slept. You must devise a way so that you sleep a little if he is quiet and steady. If you do not sleep you might become unclear in the head."

I'm clear enough in the head, he thought. Too clear. I am as clear as the stars that are my brothers. Still I must sleep. They sleep and the moon and the sun sleep and even the ocean sleeps sometimes on certain days when there is no current and a flat calm.

But remember to sleep, he thought. Make yourself do it and devise some simple and sure way about the lines. Now go back and prepare the dolphin. It is too dangerous to rig the oars as a drag if you must sleep.

I could go without sleeping, he told himself. But it would be too dangerous.

He started to work his way back to the stern on his hands and knees, being careful not to jerk against the fish. He may be half asleep himself, he thought. But I do not want him to rest. He must pull until he dies.

Back in the stern he turned so that his left hand held the strain of the line across his shoulders and drew his knife from its sheath with his right hand. The stars were bright now and he saw the dolphin clearly and he pushed the blade of his knife into his head and drew him out from under the stern. He put one of his feet on the fish and slit him quickly from the vent up to the tip of his lower jaw. Then he put his knife down and gutted him with his right hand, scooping him clean and pulling the gills clear. He felt the maw heavy and slippery in his hands and he slit it open. There were two flying fish inside. They were fresh and hard and he laid them side by side and dropped the guts and the gills over the stern. They sank leaving a trail of phosphorescence in the water. The dolphin was cold and a leprous gray-white now in the starlight and the old man skinned one side of him while he held his right foot on the fish's head. Then he turned him over and skinned the other side and cut each side off from the head down to the tail.

He slid the carcass overboard and looked to see if there was any swirl in the water. But there was only the light of its slow descent. He turned then and placed the two flying fish inside the two fillets of fish and putting his knife back in its sheath, he worked his way slowly back to the bow. His back was bent with the weight of the line across it and he carried the fish in his right hand.

Back in the bow he laid the two fillets of fish out on the wood with the flying fish beside them. After that he settled the line across his shoulders in a new place and held it again with his left hand resting on the gunwale. Then he leaned over the side and washed the flying fish in the water, noting the speed of the water against his hand. His hand was phosphorescent from skinning the fish and he watched the flow of the water against it. The flow was less strong and as he rubbed the side of his hand against the planking of the skiff, particles of phosphorus floated off and drifted slowly astern.

"He is tiring or he is resting," the old man said. "Now let me get through the eating of this dolphin and get some rest and a little sleep."

Under the stars and with the night colder all the time he ate half of one of the dolphin fillets and one of the flying fish, gutted and with its head cut off.

"What an excellent fish dolphin is to eat cooked," he said. "And what a miserable fish raw. I will never go in a boat again without salt or limes."

If I had brains I would have splashed water on the bow all day and drying, it would have made salt, he thought. But then I did not hook the dolphin until almost sunset. Still it was a lack of preparation. But I have chewed it all well and I am not nauseated.

The sky was clouding over to the east and one after another the stars he knew were gone. It looked now as though he were moving into a great canyon of clouds and the wind had dropped.

"There will be bad weather in three or four days," he said. "But not tonight and not tomorrow. Rig now to get some sleep, old man, while the fish is calm and steady."

He held the line tight in his right hand and then pushed his thigh against his right hand as he leaned all his weight against the wood of the bow. Then he passed the line a little lower on his shoulders and braced his left hand on it.

My right hand can hold it as long as it is braced, he thought. If it relaxes in sleep my left hand will wake me as the line goes out. It is hard on the right hand. But he is used to punishment. Even if I sleep twenty minutes or a half an hour it is good. He lay forward cramping himself against the line with all of his body, putting all his weight onto his right hand, and he was asleep.

He did not dream of the lions but instead of a vast school of porpoises that stretched for eight or ten miles and it was in the time of their mating and they would leap high into the air and return into the same hole they had made in the water when they leaped.

Then he dreamed that he was in the village on his bed and there was a norther and he was very cold and his right arm was asleep because his head had rested on it instead of a pillow.

After that he began to dream of the long yellow beach and he saw the first of the lions come down onto it in the early dark and then the other lions came and he rested his chin on the wood of the bows where the ship lay anchored with the evening off-shore breeze and he waited to see if there would be more lions and he was happy.

The moon had been up for a long time but he slept on and the fish pulled on steadily and the boat moved into the tunnel of clouds.

He woke with the jerk of his right fist coming up against his face and the line burning out through his right hand. He had no feeling of his left hand but he braked all he could with his right and the line rushed out. Finally his left hand found the line and he leaned back against the line and now it burned his back and his left hand, and his left hand was taking all the strain and cutting badly. He looked back at the coils of line and they were feeding smoothly. Just then the fish jumped making a great bursting of the ocean and then a heavy fall. Then he jumped again and again and the boat was going fast although line was still racing out and the old man was raising the strain to breaking point and raising it to breaking point again and again. He had been pulled down tight onto the bow and his face was in the cut slice of dolphin and he could not move.

This is what we waited for, he thought. So now let us take it.

Make him pay for the line, he thought. Make him pay for it.

He could not see the fish's jumps but only heard the breaking of the ocean and the heavy splash as he fell. The speed of the line was cutting his hands badly but he had always known this would happen and he tried to keep the cutting across the calloused parts and not let the line slip into the palm nor cut the fingers.

If the boy was here he would wet the coils of line, he thought. Yes. If the boy were here. If the boy were here.

The line went out and out and out but it was slowing now and he was making the fish earn each inch of it. Now he got his head up from the wood and out of the slice of fish that his cheek had crushed. Then he was on his knees and then he rose slowly to his feet. He was ceding line but more slowly all the time. He worked back to where he could feel with his foot the coils of line that he could not see. There was plenty of line still and now the fish had to pull the friction of all that new line through the water.

Yes, he thought. And now he has jumped more than a dozen times and filled the sacks along his back with air and he cannot go down deep to die where I cannot bring him up. He will start circling soon and then I must work on him. I wonder what started him so suddenly? Could it have been hunger that made him desperate, or was he frightened by something in the night? Maybe he suddenly felt fear. But he was such a calm, strong fish and he seemed so fearless and so confident. It is strange.

"You better be fearless and confident yourself, old man," he said. "You're holding him again but you cannot get line. But soon he has to circle."

The old man held him with his left hand and his shoulders now and stooped down and scooped up water in his right hand to get the crushed dolphin flesh off of his face. He was afraid that it might nauseate him and he would vomit and lose his strength. When his face was cleaned he washed his right hand in the water over the side and then let it stay in the salt water while he watched the first light come before the sunrise. He's headed almost east, he thought. That means he is tired and going with the current. Soon he will have to circle. Then our true work begins.

After he judged that his right hand had been in the water long enough he took it out and looked at it.

"It is not bad," he said. "And pain does not matter to a man."

He took hold of the line carefully so that it did not fit into any of the fresh line cuts and shifted his weight so that he could put his left hand into the sea on the other side of the skiff.

"You did not do so badly for something worthless," he said to his left hand. "But there was a moment when I could not find you."

Why was I not born with two good hands? he thought. Perhaps it was my fault in not training that one properly. But God knows he has had enough chances to learn. He did not do so badly in the night, though, and he has only cramped once. If he cramps again let the line cut him off.

When he thought that he knew that he was not being clear-headed and he thought he should chew some more of the dolphin. But I can't, he told himself. It is better to be light-headed than to lose your strength from nausea. And I know I cannot keep it if I eat it since my face was in it. I will keep it for an emergency until it goes bad. But it is too late to try for strength now through nourishment. You're stupid, he told himself. Eat the other flying fish.

It was there, cleaned and ready, and he picked it up with his left hand and ate it chewing the bones carefully and eating all of it down to the tail.

It has more nourishment than almost any fish, he thought. At least the kind of strength that I need. Now I have done what I can, he thought. Let him begin to circle and let the fight come.

The sun was rising for the third time since he had put to sea when the fish started to circle.

He could not see by the slant of the line that the fish was circling. It was too early for that. He just felt a faint slackening of the pressure of the line and he commenced to pull on it gently with his right hand. It tightened, as always, but just when he reached the point where it would break, line began to come in. He slipped his shoulders and head from under the line and began to pull in line steadily and gently. He used both of his hands in a swinging motion and tried to do the pulling as much as he could with his body and his legs. His old legs and shoulders pivoted with the swinging of the pulling.

"It is a very big circle," he said. "But he is circling."

Then the line would not come in any more and he held it until he saw the drops jumping from it in the sun. Then it started out and the old man knelt down and let it go grudgingly back into the dark water.

"He is making the far part of his circle now," he said. I must hold all I can, he thought. The strain will shorten his circle each time. Perhaps in an hour I will see him. Now I must convince him and then I must kill him.

But the fish kept on circling slowly and the old man was wet with sweat and tired deep into his bones two hours later. But the circles were much shorter now and from the way the line slanted he could tell the fish had risen steadily while he swam.

For an hour the old man had been seeing black spots before his eyes and the sweat salted his eyes and salted the cut over his eye and on his forehead. He was not afraid of the black spots. They were normal as the tension that he was pulling on the line. Twice, though, he had felt faint and dizzy and that had worried him.

"I could not fail myself and die on a fish like this," he said. "Now that I have him coming so beautifully, God help me endure. I'll say a hundred Our Fathers and a hundred Hail Marys. But I cannot say them now."

Consider them said, he thought. I'll say them later.

Just then he felt a sudden banging and jerking on the line he held with his two hands. It was sharp and hard-feeling and heavy.

He is hitting the wire leader with his spear, he thought. That was bound to come. He had to do that. It may make him jump though and I would rather he stayed circling now. The jumps were necessary for him to take air. But after that each one can widen the opening of the hook wound and he can throw the hook.

"Don't jump, fish," he said. "Don't jump."

The fish hit the wire several times more and each time he shook his head the old man gave up a little line.

I must hold his pain where it is, he thought. Mine does not matter. I can control mine. But his pain could drive him mad.

After a while the fish stopped beating at the wire and started circling slowly again. The old man was gaining line steadily now. But he felt faint again. He lifted some sea water with his left hand and put it on his head. Then he put more on and rubbed the back of his neck.

"I have no cramps," he said. "He'll be up soon and I can last. You have to last. Don't even speak of it."

He kneeled against the bow and, for a moment, slipped the line over his back again. I'll rest now while he goes out on the circle and then stand up and work on him when he comes in, he decided.

It was a great temptation to rest in the bow and let the fish make one circle by himself without recovering any line. But when the strain showed the fish had turned to come toward the boat, the old man rose to his feet and started the pivoting and the weaving pulling that brought in all the line he gained.

I'm tireder than I have ever been, he thought, and now the trade wind is rising. But that will be good to take him in with. I need that badly.

"I'll rest on the next turn as he goes out," he said. "I feel much better. Then in two or three turns more I will have him."

His straw hat was far on the back of his head and he sank down into the bow with the pull of the line as he felt the fish turn.

The sea had risen considerably. But it was a fair-weather breeze and he had to have it to get home.

"I'll just steer south and west," he said. "A man is never lost at sea and it is a long island."

It was on the third turn that he saw the fish first.

He saw him first as a dark shadow that took so long to pass under the boat that he could not believe its length.

"No," he said. "He can't be that big."

But he was that big and at the end of this circle he came to the surface only thirty yards away and the man saw his tail out of water. It was higher than a big scythe blade and a very pale lavender above the dark blue water. It raked back and as the fish swam just below the surface the old man could see his huge bulk and the purple stripes that banded him. His dorsal fin was down and his huge pectorals were spread wide.

On this circle the old man could see the fish's eye and the two gray sucking fish that swam around him. Sometimes they attached themselves to him. Sometimes they darted off. Sometimes they would swim easily in his shadow. They were each over three feet long and when they swam fast they lashed their whole bodies like eels.

The old man was sweating now but from something else besides the sun. On each calm placid turn the fish made he was gaining line and he was sure that in two turns more he would have a chance to get the harpoon in.

But I must get him close, close, close, he thought. I mustn't try for the head. I must get the heart.

"Be calm and strong, old man," he said.

On the next circle the fish's back was out but he was a little too far from the boat. On the next circle he was still too far away but he was higher out of water and the old man was sure that by gaining some more line he could have him alongside.

He had rigged his harpoon long before and its coil of light rope was in a round basket and the end was made fast to the bitt in the bow.

The fish was coming in on his circle now calm and beautiful looking and only his great tail moving. The old man pulled on him all that he could to bring him closer. For just a moment the fish turned a little on his side. Then he straightened himself and began another circle.

"I moved him," the old man said. "I moved him then."

He felt faint again now but he held on the great fish all the strain that he could. I moved him, he thought. Maybe this time I can get him over. Pull, hands, he thought. Hold up, legs. Last for me, head. Last for me. You never went. This time I'll pull him over.

But when he put all of his effort on, starting it well out before the fish came alongside and pulling with all his strength, the fish pulled part way over and then righted himself and swam away.

"Fish," the old man said. "Fish, you are going to have to die anyway. Do you have to kill me too?"

That way nothing is accomplished, he thought. His mouth was too dry to speak but he could not reach for the water now. I must get him alongside this time, he thought. I am not good for many more turns. Yes you are, he told himself. You're good for ever.

On the next turn, he nearly had him. But again the fish righted himself and swam slowly away.

You are killing me, fish, the old man thought. But you have a right to. Never have I seen a greater, or more beautiful, or a calmer or more noble thing than you, brother. Come on and kill me. I do not care who kills who.

Now you are getting confused in the head, he thought. You must keep your head clear. Keep your head clear and know how to suffer like a man. Or a fish, he thought.

"Clear up, head," he said in a voice he could hardly hear. "Clear up."

Twice more it was the same on the turns.

I do not know, the old man thought. He had been on the point of feeling himself go each time. I do not know. But I will try it once more.

He tried it once more and he felt himself going when he turned the fish. The fish righted himself and swam off again slowly with the great tail weaving in the air.

I'll try it again, the old man promised, although his hands were mushy now and he could only see well in flashes.

He tried it again and it was the same. So he thought, and he felt himself going before he started; I will try it once again.

He took all his pain and what was left of his strength and his long gone pride and he put it against the fish's agony and the fish came over onto his side and swam gently on his side, his bill almost touching the planking of the skiff and started to pass the boat, long, deep, wide, silver and barred with purple and interminable in the water.

The old man dropped the line and put his foot on it and lifted the harpoon as high as he could and drove it down with all his strength, and more strength he had just summoned, into the fish's side just behind the great chest fin that rose high in the air to the altitude of the man's chest. He felt the iron go in and he leaned on it and drove it further and then pushed all his weight after it.

Then the fish came alive, with his death in him, and rose high out of the water showing all his great length and width and all his power and his beauty. He seemed to hang in the air above the old man in the skiff. Then he fell into the water with a crash that sent spray over the old man and over all of the skiff.

The old man felt faint and sick and he could not see well. But he cleared the harpoon line and let it run slowly through his raw hands and, when he could see, he saw the fish was on his back with his silver belly up. The shaft of the harpoon was projecting at an angle from the fish's shoulder and the sea was discolouring with the red of the blood from his heart. First it was dark as a shoal in the blue water that was more than a mile deep. Then it spread like a cloud. The fish was silvery and still and floated with the waves.

The old man looked carefully in the glimpse of vision that he had. Then he took two turns of the harpoon line around the bitt in the bow and laid his head on his hands.

"Keep my head clear," he said against the wood of the bow. "I am a tired old man. But I have killed this fish which is my brother and now I must do the slave work."

Now I must prepare the nooses and the rope to lash

him alongside, he thought. Even if we were two and swamped her to load him and bailed her out, this skiff would never hold him. I must prepare everything, then bring him in and lash him well and step the mast and set sail for home.

He started to pull the fish in to have him alongside so that he could pass a line through his gills and out his mouth and make his head fast alongside the bow. I want to see him, he thought, and to touch and to feel him. He is my fortune, he thought. But that is not why I wish to feel him. I think I felt his heart, he thought. When I pushed on the harpoon shaft the second time. Bring him in now and make him fast and get the noose around his tail and another around his middle to bind him to the skiff.

"Get to work, old man," he said. He took a very small drink of the water. "There is very much slave work to be done now that the fight is over."

He looked up at the sky and then out to his fish. He looked at the sun carefully. It is not much more than noon, he thought. And the trade wind is rising. The lines all mean nothing now. The boy and I will splice them when we are home.

"Come on, fish," he said. But the fish did not come. Instead he lay there wallowing now in the seas and the old man pulled the skiff up onto him.

When he was even with him and had the fish's head against the bow he could not believe his size. But he untied the harpoon rope from the bitt, passed it through the fish's gills and out his jaws, made a turn around his sword then passed the rope through the other gill, made another turn around the bill and knotted the double rope and made it fast to the bitt in the bow. He cut the rope then and went astern to noose the tail. The fish had turned silver from his original purple and silver, and the stripes showed the same pale violet colour as his tail. They were wider than a man's hand with his fingers spread and the fish's eye looked as detached as the mirrors in a periscope or as a saint in a procession.

"It was the only way to kill him," the old man said. He was feeling better since the water and he knew he would not go away and his head was clear. He's over fifteen hundred pounds the way he is, he thought. Maybe much more. If he dresses out two-thirds of that at thirty cents a pound?

"I need a pencil for that," he said. "My head is not that clear. But I think the great DiMaggio would be proud of me today. I had no bone spurs. But the hands and the back hurt truly." I wonder what a bone spur is, he thought. Maybe we have them without knowing of it.

He made the fish fast to bow and stern and to the middle thwart. He was so big it was like lashing a much bigger skiff alongside. He cut a piece of line and tied the fish's lower jaw against his bill so his mouth would not open and they would sail as cleanly as possible. Then he stepped the mast and, with the stick that was his gaff and with his boom rigged, the patched sail drew, the boat began to move, and half lying in the stern he sailed south-west.

He did not need a compass to tell him where south-west was. He only needed the feel of the trade wind and the drawing of the sail. I better put a small line out with a spoon on it and try and get something to eat and drink for the moisture. But he could not find a spoon and his sardines were rotten. So he hooked a patch of yellow Gulf weed with the gaff as they passed and shook it so that the small shrimps that were in it fell onto the planking of the skiff. There were more than a dozen of them and they jumped and kicked like sand fleas. The old man pinched their heads off with his thumb and forefinger and ate them chewing up the shells and the tails. They were very tiny but he knew they were nourishing and they tasted good.

The old man still had two drinks of water in the bottle and he used half of one after he had eaten the shrimps. The skiff was sailing well considering the handicaps and he steered with the tiller under his arm. He could see the fish and he had only to look at his hands and feel his back against the stern to know that this had truly happened and was not a dream. At one time when he was feeling so badly toward the end, he had thought perhaps it was a dream. Then when he had seen the fish come out of the water and hang motionless in the sky before he fell, he was sure there was some great strangeness and he could not believe it. Then he could not see well, although now he saw as well as ever.

Now he knew there was the fish and his hands and back were no dream. The hands cure quickly, he thought. I bled them clean and the salt water will heal them. The dark water of the true gulf is the greatest healer that there is. All I must do is keep the head clear. The hands have done their work and we sail well. With his mouth shut and his tail straight up and down we sail like brothers. Then his head started to become a little unclear and he thought, is he bringing me in or am I bringing him in? If I were towing him behind there would be no question. Nor if the fish were in the skiff, with all dignity gone, there would be no question either. But they were sailing together lashed side by side and the old man thought, let him bring me in if it pleases him. I am only better than him through trickery and he meant me no harm.

They sailed well and the old man soaked his hands

in the salt water and tried to keep his head clear. There were high cumulus clouds and enough cirrus above them so that the old man knew the breeze would last all night. The old man looked at the fish constantly to make sure it was true. It was an hour before the first shark hit him.

The shark was not an accident. He had come up from deep down in the water as the dark cloud of blood had settled and dispersed in the mile deep sea. He had come up so fast and absolutely without caution that he broke the surface of the blue water and was in the sun. Then he fell back into the sea and picked up the scent and started swimming on the course the skiff and fish had taken.

Sometimes he lost the scent. But he would pick it up again, or have just a trace of it, and he swam fast and hard on the course. He was a very big Mako shark built to swim as fast as the fastest fish in the sea and everything about him was beautiful except his jaws. His back was as blue as a sword fish's and his belly was silver and his hide was smooth and handsome. He was built as a sword fish except for his huge jaws which were tight shut now as he swam fast, just under the surface with his high dorsal fin knifing through the water without wavering. Inside the closed double lip of his jaws all of his eight rows of teeth were slanted inwards. They were not the ordinary pyramid-shaped teeth of most sharks. They were shaped like a man's fingers when they are crisped like claws. They were nearly as long as the fingers of the old man and they had razor-sharp cutting edges on both sides. This was a fish built to feed on all the fishes in the sea, that were so fast and strong and well armed that they had no other enemy. Now he speeded up as he smelled the fresher scent and his blue dorsal fin cut the water.

When the old man saw him coming he knew that this was a shark that had no fear at all and would do exactly what he wished. He prepared the harpoon and made the rope fast while he watched the shark come on. The rope was short as it lacked what he had cut away to lash the fish.

The old man's head was clear and good now and he was full of resolution but he had little hope. It was too good to last, he thought. He took one look at the great fish as he watched the shark close in. It might as well have been a dream, he thought. I cannot keep him from hitting me but maybe I can get him. *Dentuso,* he thought. Bad luck to your mother.

The shark closed fast astern and when he hit the fish the old man saw his mouth open and his strange eyes and the clicking chop of the teeth as he drove forward in the meat just above the tail. The shark's head was out of the water and his back was coming out and the old man could hear the noise of skin and flesh ripping on the big fish when he rammed the harpoon down onto the shark's head at a spot where the line between his eyes intersected with the line that ran straight back from his nose. There were no such lines. There was only the heavy sharp blue head and the big eyes and the clicking, thrusting all-swallowing jaws. But that was the location of the brain and the old man hit it. He hit it with his blood mushed hands driving a good harpoon with all his strength. He hit it without hope but with resolution and complete malignancy.

The shark swung over and the old man saw his eye was not alive and then he swung over once again, wrapping himself in two loops of the rope. The old man knew that he was dead but the shark would not accept it. Then, on his back, with his tail lashing and his jaws clicking, the shark plowed over the water as a speed-boat does. The water was white where his tail beat it and three-quarters of his body was clear above the water when the rope came taut, shivered, and then snapped. The shark lay quietly for a little while on the surface and the old man watched him. Then he went down very slowly.

"He took about forty pounds," the old man said aloud. He took my harpoon too and all the rope, he thought, and now my fish bleeds again and there will be others.

He did not like to look at the fish anymore since he had been mutilated. When the fish had been hit it was as though he himself were hit.

But I killed the shark that hit my fish, he thought. And he was the biggest *dentuso* that I have ever seen. And God knows that I have seen big ones.

It was too good to last, he thought. I wish it had been a dream now and that I had never hooked the fish and was alone in bed on the newspapers.

"But man is not made for defeat," he said. "A man can be destroyed but not defeated." I am sorry that I killed the fish though, he thought. Now the bad time is coming and I do not even have the harpoon. The *dentuso* is cruel and able and strong and intelligent. But I was more intelligent than he was. Perhaps not, he thought. Perhaps I was only better armed.

"Don't think, old man," he said aloud. "Sail on this course and take it when it comes."

But I must think, he thought. Because it is all I have left. That and baseball. I wonder how the great DiMaggio would have liked the way I hit him in the brain? It was no great thing, he thought. Any man could do it. But do you think my hands were as great a handicap as the bone spurs? I cannot know. I never had anything wrong with my heel except the time the sting ray stung it when I stepped on him when swimming and paralyzed the lower leg and made the unbearable pain.

"Think about something cheerful, old man," he said. "Every minute now you are closer to home. You sail lighter for the loss of forty pounds."

He knew quite well the pattern of what could happen when he reached the inner part of the current. But there was nothing to be done now.

"Yes there is," he said aloud. "I can lash my knife to the butt of one of the oars."

So he did that with the tiller under his arm and the sheet of the sail under his foot.

"Now," he said. "I am still an old man. But I am not unarmed."

The breeze was fresh now and he sailed on well. He watched only the forward part of the fish and some of his hope returned.

It is silly not to hope, he thought. Besides I believe it is a sin. Do not think about sin, he thought. There are enough problems now without sin. Also I have no understanding of it.

I have no understanding of it and I am not sure that I believe in it. Perhaps it was a sin to kill the fish. I suppose it was even though I did it to keep me alive and feed many people. But then everything is a sin. Do not think about sin. It is much too late for that and there are people who are paid to do it. Let them think about it. You were born to be a fisherman as the fish was born to be a fish. San Pedro was a fisherman as was the father of the great DiMaggio.

But he liked to think about all things that he was involved in and since there was nothing to read and he did not have a radio, he thought much and he kept on thinking about sin. You did not kill the fish only to keep alive and to sell for food, he thought. You killed him for pride and because you are a fisherman. You loved him when he was alive and you loved him after. If you love him, it is not a sin to kill him. Or is it more?

"You think too much, old man," he said aloud.

But you enjoyed killing the *dentuso,* he thought. He lives on the live fish as you do. He is not a scavenger nor just a moving appetite as some sharks are. He is beautiful and noble and knows no fear of anything.

"I killed him in self-defense," the old man said aloud. "And I killed him well."

Besides, he thought, everything kills everything else in some way. Fishing kills me exactly as it keeps me alive. The boy keeps me alive, he thought. I must not deceive myself too much.

He leaned over the side and pulled loose a piece of the meat of the fish where the shark had cut him. He chewed it and noted its quality and its good taste. It was firm and juicy, like meat, but it was not red. There was no stringiness in it and he knew that it would bring the highest price in the market. But there was no way to keep its scent out of the water and the old man knew that a very bad time was coming.

The breeze was steady. It had backed a little further into the north-east and he knew that meant that it would not fall off. The old man looked ahead of him but he could see no sails nor could he see the hull nor the smoke of any ship. There were only the flying fish that went up from his bow sailing away to either side and the yellow patches of Gulf weed. He could not even see a bird.

He had sailed for two hours, resting in the stern and sometimes chewing a bit of the meat from the marlin, trying to rest and to be strong, when he saw the first of the two sharks.

"Ay," he said aloud. There is no translation for this word and perhaps it is just a noise such as a man might make, involuntarily, feeling the nail go through his hands and into the wood.

"Galanos," he said aloud. He had seen the second fin now coming up behind the first and had identified them as shovel-nosed sharks by the brown, triangular fin and the sweeping movements of the tail. They had the scent and were excited and in the stupidity of their great hunger they were losing and finding the scent in their excitement. But they were closing all the time.

The old man made the sheet fast and jammed the tiller. Then he took up the oar with the knife lashed to it. He lifted it as lightly as he could because his hands rebelled at the pain. Then he opened and closed them on it lightly to loosen them. He closed them firmly so they would take the pain now and would not flinch and watched the sharks come. He could see their wide, flattened, shovel-pointed heads now and their white-tipped wide pectoral fins. They were hateful sharks, bad smelling, scavengers as well as killers, and when they were hungry they would bite at an oar or the rudder of a boat. It was these sharks that would cut the turtles' legs and flippers off when the turtles were asleep on the surface, and they would hit a man in the water, if they were hungry, even if the man had no smell of fish blood nor of fish slime on him.

"Ay," the old man said. *"Galanos.* Come on *galanos."*

They came. But they did not come as the Mako had come. One turned and went out of sight under the skiff and the old man could feel the skiff shake as he jerked and pulled on the fish. The other watched the old man with his slitted yellow eyes and then came in fast with his half circle of jaws wide to hit the fish where he had already been bitten. The line showed clearly on the top of his brown head and back where the brain joined the spinal cord and the old man drove the knife on the oar into the juncture, withdrew it, and drove it in again into the shark's yellow cat-like eyes. The shark let go of the fish and slid down, swallowing what he had taken as he died.

The skiff was still shaking with the destruction the other shark was doing to the fish and the old man let go the sheet so that the skiff would swing broadside and bring the shark out from under. When he saw the shark he leaned over the side and punched at him. He hit only meat and the hide was set hard and he barely got the knife in. The blow hurt not only his hands but his shoulder too. But the shark came up fast with his head out and the old man hit him squarely in the center of his flat-topped head as his nose came out of water and lay against the fish. The old man withdrew the blade and punched the shark exactly in the same spot again. He still hung to the fish with his jaws hooked and the old man stabbed him in his left eye. The shark still hung there.

"No?" the old man said and he drove the blade between the vertebrae and the brain. It was an easy shot now and he felt the cartilage sever. The old man reversed the oar and put the blade between the shark's jaws to open them. He twisted the blade and as the shark slid loose he said, "Go on, *galano*. Slide down a mile deep. Go see your friend, or maybe it's your mother."

The old man wiped the blade of his knife and laid down the oar. Then he found the sheet and the sail filled and he brought the skiff onto her course.

"They must have taken a quarter of him and of the best meat," he said aloud. "I wish it were a dream and that I had never hooked him. I'm sorry about it, fish. It makes everything wrong." He stopped and he did not want to look at the fish now. Drained of blood and awash he looked the colour of the silver backing of a mirror and his stripes still showed.

"I shouldn't have gone out so far, fish," he said. "Neither for you nor for me. I'm sorry, fish."

Now, he said to himself. Look to the lashing on the knife and see if it has been cut. Then get your hand in order because there still is more to come.

"I wish I had a stone for the knife," the old man said after he had checked the lashing on the oar butt. "I should have brought a stone." You should have brought many things, he thought. But you did not bring them, old man. Now is no time to think of what you do not have. Think of what you can do with what there is.

"You give me much good counsel," he said aloud. "I'm tired of it."

He held the tiller under his arm and soaked both his hands in the water as the skiff drove forward.

"God knows how much that last one took," he said. "But she's much lighter now." He did not want to think of the mutilated under-side of the fish. He knew that each of the jerking bumps of the shark had been meat torn away and that the fish now made a trail for all sharks as wide as a highway through the sea.

He was a fish to keep a man all winter, he thought. Don't think of that. Just rest and try to get your hands in shape to defend what is left of him. The blood smell from my hands means nothing now with all that scent in the water. Besides they do not bleed much. There is nothing cut that means anything. The bleeding may keep the left from cramping.

What can I think of now? he thought. Nothing. I must think of nothing and wait for the next ones. I wish it had really been a dream, he thought. But who knows? It might have turned out well.

The next shark that came was a single shovelnose. He came like a pig to the trough if a pig had a mouth so wide that you could put your head in it. The old man let him hit the fish and then drove the knife on the oar down into his brain. But the shark jerked backwards as he rolled and the knife blade snapped.

The old man settled himself to steer. He did not even watch the big shark sinking slowly in the water, showing first life-size, then small, then tiny. That always fascinated the old man. But he did not even watch it now.

"I have the gaff now," he said. "But it will do no good. I have the two oars and the tiller and the short club."

Now they have beaten me, he thought. I am too old to club sharks to death. But I will try it as long as I have the oars and the short club and the tiller.

He put his hands in the water again to soak them. It was getting late in the afternoon and he saw nothing but the sea and the sky. There was more wind in the sky than there had been, and soon he hoped that he would see land.

"You're tired, old man," he said. "You're tired inside."

The sharks did not hit him again until just before sunset.

The old man saw the brown fins coming along the wide trail the fish must make in the water. They were not even quartering on the scent. They were headed straight for the skiff swimming side by side.

He jammed the tiller, made the sheet fast and reached under the stern for the club. It was an oar handle from a broken oar sawed off to about two and a half feet in length. He could only use it effectively with one hand because of the grip of the handle and he took good hold of it with his right hand, flexing his hand on it, as he watched the sharks come. They were both *galanos.*

I must let the first one get a good hold and hit him on the point of the nose or straight across the top of the head, he thought.

The two sharks closed together and as he saw the one nearest him open his jaws and sink them into the silver side of the fish, he raised the club high and brought it down heavy and slamming onto the top of the shark's broad head. He felt the rubbery solidity as the club came down. But he felt the rigidity of bone too and he struck the shark once more hard across the point of the nose as he slid down from the fish.

The other shark had been in and out and now came in again with his jaws wide. The old man could see pieces of the meat of the fish spilling white from the corner of his jaws as he bumped the fish and closed his jaws. He swung at him and hit only the head and the shark looked at him and wrenched the meat loose. The old man swung the club down on him again as he slipped away to swallow and hit only the heavy solid rubberiness.

"Come on, *galano,*" the old man said. "Come in again."

The shark came in a rush and the old man hit him as he shut his jaws. He hit him solidly and from as high up as he could raise the club. This time he felt the bone at the base of the brain and he hit him again in the same place while the shark tore the meat loose sluggishly and slid down from the fish.

The old man watched for him to come again but neither shark showed. Then he saw one on the surface swimming in circles. He did not see the fin of the other.

I could not expect to kill them, he thought. I could have in my time. But I have hurt them both badly and neither one can feel very good. If I could have used a bat with two hands I could have killed the first one surely. Even now, he thought.

He did not want to look at the fish. He knew that half of him had been destroyed. The sun had gone down while he had been in the fight with the sharks.

"It will be dark soon," he said. "Then I should see the glow of Havana. If I am too far to the eastward I will see the lights of one of the new beaches."

I cannot be too far out now, he thought. I hope no one has been too worried. There is only the boy to worry, of course. But I am sure he would have confidence. Many of the older fishermen will worry. Many others too, he thought. I live in a good town.

He could not talk to the fish anymore because the fish had been ruined too badly. Then something came into his head.

"Half-fish," he said. "Fish that you were. I am sorry that I went too far out. I ruined us both. But we have killed many sharks, you and I, and ruined many others. How many did you ever kill, old fish? You do not have that spear on your head for nothing."

He liked to think of the fish and what he could do to a shark if he were swimming free. I should have chopped the bill off to fight them with, he thought. But there was no hatchet and then there was no knife.

But if I had, and could have lashed it to an oar butt, what a weapon. Then we might have fought them together. What will you do now if they come in the night? What can you do?

"Fight them," he said. "I'll fight them until I die."

But in the dark now and no glow showing and no lights and only the wind and the steady pull of the sail he felt that perhaps he was already dead. He put his two hands together and felt the palms. They were not dead and he could bring the pain of life by simply opening and closing them. He leaned his back against the stern and knew he was not dead. His shoulders told him.

I have all those prayers I promised if I caught the fish, he thought. But I am too tired to say them now. I better get the sack and put it over my shoulders.

He lay in the stern and steered and watched for the glow to come in the sky. I have half of him, he thought. Maybe I'll have the luck to bring the forward half in. I should have some luck. No, he said. You violated your luck when you went too far outside.

"Don't be silly," he said aloud. "And keep awake and steer. You may have much luck yet.

"I'd like to buy some if there's any place they sell it," he said.

What could I buy it with? he asked himself. Could I buy it with a lost harpoon and a broken knife and two bad hands?

"You might," he said. "You tried to buy it with eighty-four days at sea. They nearly sold it to you too."

I must not think nonsense, he thought. Luck is a thing that comes in many forms and who can recognize her? I would take some though in any form and pay what they asked. I wish I could see the glow from the lights, he thought. I wish too many things. But that is the thing I wish for now. He tried to settle more comfortably to steer and from his pain he knew he was not dead.

He saw the reflected glare of the lights of the city at what must have been around ten o'clock at night. They were only perceptible at first as the light is in the sky before the moon rises. Then they were steady to see across the ocean which was rough now with the increasing breeze. He steered inside of the glow and he thought that now, soon, he must hit the edge of the stream.

Now it is over, he thought. They will probably hit me again. But what can a man do against them in the dark without a weapon?

He was stiff and sore now and his wounds and all of the strained parts of his body hurt with the cold of the night. I hope I do not have to fight again, he thought. I hope so much I do not have to fight again.

But by midnight he fought and this time he knew the fight was useless. They came in a pack and he could only see the lines in the water that their fins made and their phosphorescence as they threw themselves on the fish. He clubbed at heads and heard the jaws chop and the shaking of the skiff as they took hold below. He clubbed desperately at what he could only feel and hear and he felt something seize the club and it was gone.

He jerked the tiller free from the rudder and beat and chopped with it, holding it in both hands and driving it down again and again. But they were up to the bow now and driving in one after the other and together, tearing off the pieces of meat that showed glowing below the sea as they turned to come once more.

One came, finally, against the head itself and he knew that it was over. He swung the tiller across the shark's head where the jaws were caught in the heaviness of the fish's head which would not tear. He swung it once and twice and again. He heard the tiller break and he lunged at the shark with the splintered butt. He felt it go in and knowing it was sharp he drove it in again. The shark let go and rolled away. That was the last shark of the pack that came. There was nothing more for them to eat.

The old man could hardly breathe now and he felt a strange taste in his mouth. It was coppery and sweet and he was afraid of it for a moment. But there was not much of it.

He spat into the ocean and said, "Eat that, *galanos.* And make a dream you've killed a man."

He knew he was beaten now finally and without remedy and he went back to the stern and found the jagged end of the tiller would fit in the slot of the rudder well enough for him to steer. He settled the sack around his shoulders and put the skiff on her course. He sailed lightly now and he had no thoughts nor any feelings of any kind. He was past everything now and he sailed the skiff to make his home port as well and as intelligently as he could. In the night sharks hit the carcass as someone might pick up crumbs from the table. The old man paid no attention to them and did not pay any attention to anything except steering. He only noticed how lightly and how well the skiff sailed now there was no great weight beside her.

She's good, he thought. She is sound and not harmed in any way except for the tiller. That is easily replaced.

He could feel he was inside the current now and he could see the lights of the beach colonies along the shore. He knew where he was now and it was nothing to get home.

The wind is our friend, anyway, he thought. Then he added, sometimes. And the great sea with our friends and our enemies. And bed, he thought. Bed is my friend. Just bed, he thought. Bed will be a great thing. It is easy when you are beaten, he thought. I never knew how easy it was. And what beat you, he thought.

"Nothing," he said aloud. "I went out too far."

When he sailed into the little harbour the lights of the Terrace were out and he knew everyone was in bed. The breeze had risen steadily and was blowing strongly now. It was quiet in the harbour though and he sailed up onto the little patch of shingle below the rocks. There was no one to help him so he pulled the boat up as far as he could. Then he stepped out and made her fast to a rock.

He unstepped the mast and furled the sail and tied it. Then he shouldered the mast and started to climb. It was then he knew the depth of his tiredness. He stopped for a moment and looked back and saw in the reflection from the street light the great tail of the fish standing up well behind the skiff's stern. He saw the white naked line of his backbone and the dark mass of the head with the projecting bill and all the nakedness between.

He started to climb again and at the top he fell and lay for some time with the mast across his shoulder. He tried to get up. But it was too difficult and he sat there with the mast on his shoulder and looked at the road. A cat passed on the far side going about its business and the old man watched it. Then he just watched the road.

Finally he put the mast down and stood up. He picked the mast up and put it on his shoulder and started up the road. He had to sit down five times before he reached his shack.

Inside the shack he leaned the mast against the wall. In the dark he found a water bottle and took a drink. Then he lay down on the bed. He pulled the blanket over his shoulders and then over his back and legs and he slept face down on the newspapers with his arms out straight and the palms of his hands up.

He was asleep when the boy looked in the door in

the morning. It was blowing so hard that the drifting-boats would not be going out and the boy had slept late and then come to the old man's shack as he had come each morning. The boy saw that the old man was breathing and then he saw the old man's hands and he started to cry. He went out very quietly to go to bring some coffee and all the way down the road he was crying.

Many fishermen were around the skiff looking at what was lashed beside it and one was in the water, his trousers rolled up, measuring the skeleton with a length of line.

The boy did not go down. He had been there before and one of the fishermen was looking after the skiff for him.

"How is he?" one of the fishermen shouted.

"Sleeping," the boy called. He did not care that they saw him crying. "Let no one disturb him."

"He was eighteen feet from nose to tail," the fisherman who was measuring him called.

"I believe it," the boy said.

He went into the Terrace and asked for a can of coffee.

"Hot and with plenty of milk and sugar in it."

"Anything more?"

"No. Afterwards I will see what he can eat."

"What a fish it was," the proprietor said. "There has never been such a fish. Those were two fine fish you took yesterday too."

"Damn my fish," the boy said and he started to cry again.

"Do you want a drink of any kind?" the proprietor asked.

"No," the boy said. "Tell them not to bother Santiago. I'll be back."

"Tell him how sorry I am."

"Thanks," the boy said.

The boy carried the hot can of coffee up to the old man's shack and sat by him until he woke. Once it looked as though he were waking. But he had gone back into heavy sleep and the boy had gone across the road to borrow some wood to heat the coffee.

Finally the old man woke.

"Don't sit up," the boy said. "Drink this." He poured some of the coffee in a glass.

The old man took it and drank it.

"They beat me, Manolin," he said. "They truly beat me."

"*He* didn't beat you. Not the fish."

"No. Truly. It was afterwards."

"Pedrico is looking after the skiff and the gear. What do you want done with the head?"

"Let Pedrico chop it up to use in fish traps."

"And the spear?"

"You keep it if you want it."

"I want it," the boy said. "Now we must make our plans about the other things."

"Did they search for me?"

"Of course. With coast guard and with planes."

"The ocean is very big and a skiff is small and hard to see," the old man said. He noticed how pleasant it was to have someone to talk to instead of speaking only to himself and to the sea. "I missed you," he said. "What did you catch?"

"One the first day. One the second and two the third."

"Very good."

"Now we fish together again."

"No. I am not lucky. I am not lucky anymore."

"The hell with luck," the boy said. "I'll bring the luck with me."

"What will your family say?"

"I do not care. I caught two yesterday. But we will fish together now for I still have much to learn."

"We must get a good killing lance and always have it on board. You can make the blade from a spring leaf from an old Ford. We can grind it in Guanabacoa. It should be sharp and not tempered so it will break. My knife broke."

"I'll get another knife and have the spring ground. How many days of heavy *brisa* have we?"

"Maybe three. Maybe more."

"I will have everything in order," the boy said. "You get your hands well old man."

"I know how to care for them. In the night I spat something strange and felt something in my chest was broken."

"Get that well too," the boy said. "Lie down, old man, and I will bring you your clean shirt. And something to eat."

"Bring any of the papers of the time that I was gone," the old man said.

"You must get well fast for there is much that I can learn and you can teach me everything. How much did you suffer?"

"Plenty," the old man said.

"I'll bring the food and the papers," the boy said. "Rest well, old man. I will bring stuff from the drugstore for your hands."

"Don't forget to tell Pedrico the head is his."

"No. I will remember."

As the boy went out the door and down the worn coral rock road he was crying again.

That afternoon there was a party of tourists at the Terrace and looking down in the water among the empty beer cans and dead barracudas a woman saw a great long white spine with a huge tail at the end that lifted and swung with the tide while the east wind blew a heavy steady sea outside the entrance to the harbour.

"What's that?" she asked a waiter and pointed to the long backbone of the great fish that was now just garbage waiting to go out with the tide.

"Tiburon," the waiter said. "Eshark." He was meaning to explain what had happened.

"I didn't know sharks had such handsome, beautifully formed tails."

"I didn't either," her male companion said.

Up the road, in his shack, the old man was sleeping again. He was still sleeping on his face and the boy was sitting by him watching him. The old man was dreaming about the lions.

THE DRAMA

Drama is the most social of the arts, since its creation involves a group enterprise—director and actors interpreting the author's text—while its success depends on a sympathetic interaction between actors and audience. Thus drama is a highly protean form, a mixture of the text we read, the productions we may see, and the ideal performance we imagine. Faced with this fluidity in the drama, scholars and critics have developed a passion for classification and definition. In their anxiety to bring order out of such a rambunctious art, and to make sense out of its history, they speak confidently of trends and movements: Realism, Naturalism, Expressionism, Symbolism, Surrealism, Poetic Theater, The Theater of Cruelty, The Theater of the Absurd, and many more. When handled in a tactful way such classifications are extremely useful (see the articles by Kernan and Albee reprinted in the Essay section), but individual plays have a stubborn tendency to resist labels, and although we must never forget the climate of social and artistic ideas within which a dramatist works, we must also learn to take each play on its own terms. This point seems worth making as a prelude to any general statements about the development of modern drama in England and America.

We can locate the beginnings of modern drama in the last half of the nineteenth century, when an exhausted romanticism and a mechanical notion of the "well-made play" (which tended to give an idealized view of life) gave way to more realistic forms that sought to achieve on the stage the same effects found in realistic fiction. Whether this realism took the form of unsentimental social commentary, as in the plays of Ibsen's middle period, or whether it shaded into a more doctrinaire naturalism that aimed at a "scientific" analysis of the cultural and psychological causes for human behavior, it represented a new dramatic ideal which is still powerful a hundred years later. No matter how diverse and subjective the works of our playwrights may be, we still measure their achievements by reference to the norm of realistic drama.

Pure realism, with its tedious stage directions, its illusion of the four-sided stage, and its assumption that the language of the actors must be the language of the audience, had a limited appeal and was, in fact, rarely achieved on the stage. As Tennessee Williams once remarked, a form which must use "a genuine frigidaire and authentic ice-cubes" puts the playwright in an artistic straitjacket. No sooner had the philosophy of realism been asserted than playwrights began to resist it, whether through a return to symbolism and poetic language, as in William Butler Yeats and the playwrights of the Irish Renaissance, or through the expressionistic style which emerged at the turn of the century. In a deliberate rejection of external realism, the expressionists (such as Strindberg) set out to dramatize the inner lives of their characters, acting out dreams or fantasies on the stage and employing all the resources of dramatic illusion to break down our realistic sense of space and time. Expressionism and its later, more radical, mutations—such as Dadaism and Surrealism—spurned objective action and sought to dramatize the irrational forms of the unconscious mind. This reaction to realism was, paradoxically, encouraged by the rise of the cinema, with its sophisticated technology for manipulating time and space. Yet throughout all these changes, modern drama has never lost sight of the realistic norm: like the basic rhythm of a freely constructed poem, it is the point of departure for even the most subjective plays, always present as the "other" way of presenting life. Which may be simply to say that the theater always asserts its double status as an actual place—a physical setting—and a place of illusions.

Shaw's *Pygmalion* brilliantly explores this basic theme of reality and illusion. As a satire on contemporary manners, it exposes the perversions of "correct" English in Edwardian life: the "language of Shakespeare" has become a means of maintaining class distinctions, which is another way of saying that class distinctions have lost their natural authority. If a flower girl can be transformed into a duchess through a change in diction, then class has become a sham. Yet Shaw is more than a didactic social critic, he is an activist: language can be a way of changing society, and in *Pygmalion* "proper English" is also a symbol of that ideal world where we will all behave "as if there are no third-class carriages, and one soul is as good as another." In its emphasis on the scientific nature of phonetics, *Pygmalion* reflects Shaw's persistent desire to improve society through art.

But a deeper and darker theme runs counter to this emphasis on improvement. Pygmalion was a mythical sculptor who created his ideal woman in ivory and then fell in love with her; the statue became human. Henry Higgins takes a real woman and tries to turn her into an ideal, with mixed results. Shaw will not allow the romantic ending that we all sentimentally desire (and that the film and musical versions so neatly provide). As the epilogue tells us, Eliza will marry Freddy and become mistress of a fashionable flower shop. One may argue that the epilogue is not part of the play, but that is to deny the nature of Shavian drama. In writing about his hero, Henrik Ibsen, Shaw always emphasized Ibsen's realism (or naturalism) and his introduction of discussion into drama. Both elements are essential to *Pygmalion*. The play is subtitled "A Romance in Five Acts," but Shaw's real purpose is to subvert the romantic conventions through a realistic account of human behavior. This involves the presentation of complex characters and the avoidance of neat solutions. Just as (according to Shaw) Ibsen had replaced the conventional denouement of the well-made play with "discussion," so *Pygmalion* avoids the conventional comic ending and trails off into a nondramatic discussion of the realistic alternatives. Part of the play's enduring appeal lies in the fact that Shaw both admires and criticizes his self-sufficient hero, his scientific "superman," and has created superb comedy without yielding to the basic convention of a happy ending.

Eugene O'Neill's *Desire Under the Elms* is both a starkly realistic account of New England farm life and a poetic exploration of the tragic rhythms that underlie everyday existence. It was the climax of O'Neill's early attempts to render a naturalistic action, where the psychological and economic determinants of human behavior would be exposed in almost elemental form. The characters are powerfully developed as believable individuals, but they are also translated into types or symbols through O'Neill's sense of tragedy. It is this sense of tragedy which counterbalances the hopelessness that would appear to result from the realistic situation. Joy-out-of-despair has always been the theme of writers on tragedy, from Aristotle to Yeats, and O'Neill gave his own version of the theme in a public statement made in 1922, two years before he began *Desire Under the Elms.* Responding to the popular complaint that he did not write about "happiness," O'Neill defined the deeper joy of tragic art.

> Sure I'll write about happiness if I can happen to meet up with that luxury, and find it sufficiently dramatic and in harmony with any deep rhythm in life. But happiness is a word. What does it mean? Exaltation; an intensified feeling of the significant worth of man's being and becoming? Well, if it means that—and not a mere smirking contentment with one's lot—I know there is more of it in one real tragedy than in all the happy-ending plays ever written. It's mere present-day judgment to think of tragedy as unhappy! The Greeks and the Elizabethans knew better. They felt the tremendous lift to it. It roused them spiritually to a deeper understanding of life. Through it they found release from the petty consideration of everyday existence. They saw their lives ennobled by it. A work of art is always happy; all else is unhappy. . . . I don't love life because it's pretty. Prettiness is only clothes-deep. I am a truer lover than that. I love it naked. There is a beauty to me even in its ugliness.

In this passage O'Neill places himself squarely in the tradition of the great tragic realists. Tennessee Williams, by contrast, is a master of poetic realism, whose works veer toward pathos and sentiment but are usually rescued by the playwright's fine sense of the limits of illusion. The delicate pathos of *The Glass Menagerie* is the result of its narrative frame: the drama is a reminiscence by the poetic son, who is Williams' other self in the play (the entire story is deeply autobiographical). As Tom says, "memory always seems to move to music," and the music of *The Glass Menagerie* is the music of nostalgic reverie. Although it remains in touch with the social realities of American life through the tough-minded Amanda, the play reserves its most moving moments for the dreamlike fantasies of the crippled Laura. We oscillate between the realities of a disintegrating American family trapped by the Great Depression and the fantasy world of the "glass menagerie," and the emotional balance is clearly on the side of these shining symbols. The opening stage direction emphasizes that although the setting of the play is a tawdry urban apartment, the fire escape upon which Tom appears is "a structure whose name is a touch of accidental poetic truth." In *The Glass Menagerie* the "fourth wall" of realistic drama has become a "transparent fourth wall," and the moments of personal transfiguration within the play have the transparency of poetic truth.

The Gentleman Caller of *The Glass Menagerie,* with his pathetic faith in success through popularity, embodies the American Dream in its classic form. By the time of *The Zoo Story* (1958), the American Dream had dwindled to the few symbols of domestic security that solace Peter's life. If life is like a zoo, "everyone separated by bars from everyone else," then Jerry's frantic attempts at communication may seem more admirable than Peter's defensive isolation. Very little "happens" in *The Zoo Story* until we reach the shocking violence of its conclusion, but through a subtle interweaving of sharp symbolism and apparently aimless dialogue Albee has established Jerry and Peter as dependent yet incomplete figures, two halves of the divided modern mind. "THE STORY OF JERRY AND THE DOG," which so disturbs Peter, is a parable of sexual and spiritual frustration, portraying a world in which even cruelty or violence can be a needed means of communication. The self-willed death of Jerry may seem pointless and absurd, but there are strong overtones of a sacrificial death ("So be it!"). In Albee's world the ennobling tragic vision of O'Neill has been greatly diminished, but it has not been extinguished.

The label "Theater of the Absurd" has been given to those modern dramas which provide a tragi-comic view of man's existence in an irrational universe. The term "absurd" has metaphysical connotations, as in Albert Camus' definition of the word in "The Myth of Sisyphus," where it is defined as a divorce between modern man and his traditional role in the world. This divorce is finely imaged in plays where actors are sundered from their traditional rôles, and both Albee and Pinter may be said to employ techniques from the Theater of the Absurd; but there is nothing nihilistic about their plays. The repetitiveness of the dialogue and the apparent randomness of the action reflect a moral viewpoint and suggest our tragic distance from a world (and a theater) which were not absurd. In *A Slight Ache* the maddening repetition of the opening dialogue gives us a sense of personal and social sterility: words have lost their root meanings and become part of a ritual without substance. The matchseller, like Jerry in *The Zoo Story,* represents the intrusion of a disturbing sexual and metaphysical energy, a menacing irrationality. Edward's sterile rationality (he is writing on space and time) has cut him off from the natural beauty of midsummer, giving him the "slight ache" behind the eyes that develops through the play. By means of poetic suggestion and intricate symbolism, Pinter establishes an atmosphere of generalized but acute anxiety, in which his characters seem less and less able to make contact with the solid world of the senses. But that solid world is there, built into the descriptive language and the very nature of the physical stage. We feel the great power of *A Slight Ache* only because we see in its violent deformations of the dramatic tradition an image of man's separation from a more orderly and purposeful world.

Pygmalion

A Romance in Five Acts

Bernard Shaw (1856–1950)

George Bernard Shaw was born in Dublin, the son of Protestant parents. He read widely as a child and was intensely interested in music, but resisted all formal education. In 1876 he joined his mother in London (she had separated from her husband some time before) and spent a decade in genteel poverty, writing five novels that were rejected by the publishers. He became involved in the Socialist movement and in 1884 was one of the founders of the Fabian Society. In the 1880s and 1890s Shaw was unusually active in politics, making speeches and writing pamphlets on the subject of Socialism, but after the turn of the century his political ideas became more complex and idiosyncratic. Beginning in 1885 Shaw worked industriously for some years as a music and drama critic, championing the plays of the Norwegian dramatist Ibsen, and through this he gradually became interested in writing plays. *Widowers' House* (1892) reflected his earlier interest in Socialism, but in succeeding works the "thesis" (often summarized in a didactic preface) became more personal and complicated. Between 1893 and 1930 Shaw wrote over twenty major plays, most on social themes, including *Mrs. Warren's Profession, Arms and the Man, The Devil's Disciple, Caesar and Cleopatra, Man and Superman, Major Barbara, The Doctor's Dilemma, Androcles and the Lion, Heartbreak House, St. Joan,* and *The Apple Cart.* He won the Nobel Prize for Literature in 1925, and during the remaining twenty-five years of his life continued to produce political essays and minor dramas.

Pygmalion (1913), Shaw's comic study of language and class, was the first of the plays he allowed to be filmed (1938). It was later turned into the popular musical comedy *My Fair Lady* (1956).

Preface to Pygmalion

A PROFESSOR OF PHONETICS

As will be seen later on, Pygmalion needs, not a preface, but a sequel, which I have supplied in its due place.

The English have no respect for their language, and will not teach their children to speak it. They cannot spell it because they have nothing to spell it with but an old foreign alphabet of which only the consonants—and not all of them—have any agreed speech value. Consequently no man can teach himself what it should sound like from reading it; and it is impossible for an Englishman to open his mouth without making some other Englishman despise him. Most European languages are now accessible in black and white to foreigners: English and French are not thus accessible even to Englishmen and Frenchmen. The reformer we need most today is an energetic enthusiast: that is why I have made such a one the hero of a popular play.

There have been heroes of that kind crying in the wilderness for many years past. When I became interested in the subject towards the end of the eighteen-seventies, the illustrious Alexander Melville Bell, the inventor of Visible Speech, had emigrated to Canada, where his son invented the telephone; but Alexander J. Ellis was still a London Patriarch, with an impressive head always covered by a velvet skull cap, for which he would apologize to public meetings in a very courtly manner. He and Tito Pagliardini, another phonetic veteran, were men whom it was impossible to dislike. Henry Sweet, then a young man, lacked their sweetness of character: he was about as conciliatory to conventional mortals as Ibsen or Samuel Butler. His great ability as a phonetician (he was, I think, the best of them all at his job) would have entitled him to high official recognition, and perhaps enabled him to popularize his subject, but for his Satanic contempt for all academic dignitaries and persons in general who thought more of Greek than of phoentics. Once, in the days when the Imperial Institute rose in South Kensington, and Joseph Chamberlain was booming the Empire, I induced the editor of a leading monthly review to commission an article from Sweet on the imperial importance of his subject. When it arrived, it contained nothing but a savagely derisive attack on a professor of language and literature whose chair Sweet regarded as proper to a phonetic expert only. The article, being libellous, had to be returned as impossible; and I had to renounce my dream of dragging its author into the limelight. When I met him afterwards, for the first time for many years, I found to my astonishment that he, who had been a quite tolerably presentable young man, had actually managed by sheer scorn to alter his personal appearance until he had become a sort of walking repudiation of Oxford and all its traditions. It must have been largely in his own despite that he was squeezed into something called a Readership of phonetics there. The future of phonetics rests probably with his pupils, who all swore by him; but nothing could bring the man himself into any sort of compliance with the university to which he nevertheless clung by divine right in an intensely Oxonian way. I daresay his papers, if he has left any, include some satires that may be published without too destructive results fifty years hence. He was, I believe, not in the least an ill-natured man: very much the opposite, I should say; but he would not suffer fools gladly; and to him all scholars who were not rabid phoneticians were fools.

Those who knew him will recognize in my third act the allusion to the Current Shorthand in which he used to write postcards. It may be acquired from a four and sixpenny manual published by the Clarendon Press. The postcards which Mrs. Higgins describes are such as I have received from Sweet. I would decipher a sound which a cockney would represent by *zerr,* and a Frenchman by *seu,* and then write demanding with some heat what on earth it meant. Sweet, with boundless contempt for my stupidity, would reply that it not only meant but obviously was the word Result, as no other word containing that sound, and capable of making sense with the context, existed in any language spoken on earth. That less expert mortals should require fuller indications was beyond Sweet's patience. Therefore, though the whole point of his Current Shorthand is that it can express every sound in the language perfectly, vowels as well as consonants, and that your hand has to make no stroke except the easy and current ones with which you write m, n, and u, l, p, and q, scribbling them at whatever angle comes easiest to you, his unfortunate determination to make this remarkable and quite legible script serve also as a shorthand reduced it in his own practice to the most inscrutable of cryptograms. His true objective was the provision of a full, accurate, legible script for our language; but he was led past that by his contempt for the popular Pitman system of shorthand, which he called the Pitfall system. The triumph of Pitman was a triumph of business organization: there was a weekly paper to persuade you to learn Pitman: there were cheap textbooks and exercise books and transcripts of speeches for you to copy, and schools where experienced teachers coached you up to the necessary proficiency. Sweet could not organize his market in that fashion. He might as well have been the Sybil who tore up the leaves of prophecy that nobody would attend to. The four and sixpenny manual, mostly in his lithographed handwriting, that was never vulgarly advertized, may perhaps some day be taken up by a syndicate and pushed upon the public as The Times pushed the Encyclopædia Britannica; but until then it will certainly not prevail against Pitman. I have bought three copies of it during my lifteime; and I am informed by the publishers that its cloistered existence is still a steady and healthy one. I actually learned the system two several times; and yet the shorthand in which I am writing these lines is Pitman's. And the reason is that my secretary cannot transcribe Sweet, having been perforce taught in the schools of Pitman. In America I could use the commercially organized Gregg shorthand, which has taken a hint from Sweet by making its letters writable (current, Sweet would have called them) instead of having to be geometrically drawn like Pitman's; but all these systems, including Sweet's, are spoilt by making them available for verbatim reporting, in which complete and exact spelling and word division are impossible. A complete and exact phonetic script is neither practicable nor necessary for ordinary use; but if we enlarge our alphabet to the Russian size, and make our spelling as phonetic as Spanish, the advance will be prodigious.

Pygmalion Higgins is not a portrait of Sweet, to whom the adventure of Eliza Doolittle would have been impossible; still, as will be seen, there are touches of Sweet in the play. With Higgins's physique and temperament Sweet might have set the Thames on fire. As it was, he impressed himself professionally on Europe to an extent that made his comparative personal obscurity, and the failure of Oxford to do justice to his eminence, a puzzle to foreign specialists in his subject. I do not blame Oxford, because I think Oxford is quite right in demanding a certain social amenity from its nurslings (heaven knows it is not exorbitant in its requirement!); for although I well know how hard it is for a man of genius with a seriously underrated subject to maintain serene and kindly relations with the men who underrate it, and who keep all the best places for less important subjects which they profess without originality and sometimes without much capacity for them, still, if he overwhelms them with wrath and disdain, he cannot expect them to heap honors on him.

Of the later generations of phoneticians I know little. Among them towered Robert Bridges, to whom perhaps Higgins may owe his Miltonic sympathies, though here again I must disclaim all portraiture. But if the play makes the public aware that there are such people as phoneticians, and that they are among the most important people in England at present, it will serve its turn.

I wish to boast that Pygmalion has been an extremely successful play, both on stage and screen, all over Europe and North America as well as at home. It is so intensely and deliberately didactic, and its subject is esteemed so dry, that I delight in throwing it at the heads of the wiseacres who repeat the parrot cry that art should never be didactic. It goes to prove my contention that great art can never be anything else.

Finally, and for the encouragement of people troubled with accents that cut them off from all high employment, I may add that the change wrought by Professor Higgins in the flower-girl is neither impossible nor uncommon. The modern concierge's daughter who fulfills her ambition by playing the Queen of Spain in Ruy Blas at the Théâtre Français is only one of many thousands of men and women who have sloughed off their native dialects and acquired a new tongue. Our West End shop assistants and domestic servants are bilingual. But the thing has to be done scientifically, or the last state of the aspirant may be worse than the first. An honest slum dialect is more tolerable than the attempts of phonetically untaught persons to imitate the plutocracy. Ambitious flower-girls who read this play must not imagine that they can pass themselves off as fine ladies by untutored imitation. They must learn their alphabet over again, and differently, from a phonetic expert. Imitation will only make them ridiculous.

Note for technicians. A complete representation of the play as printed in this edition is technically possible only on the cinema screen or on stages furnished with exceptionally elaborate machinery. For ordinary theatrical use the scenes separated by rows of asterisks are to be omitted. In the dialogue an e upside down indicates the indefinite vowel, sometimes called obscure or neutral, for which, though it is one of the commonest sounds in English speech, our wretched alphabet has no letter.

ACT I

London at 11.15 p.m. Torrents of heavy summer rain. Cab whistles blowing frantically in all directions. Pedestrians running for shelter into the portico of St. Paul's church (not Wren's cathedral but Inigo Jones's church in Covent Garden vegetable market), among them a lady and her daughter in evening dress. All are peering out gloomily at the rain, except one man with his back turned to the rest, wholly preoccupied with a notebook in which he is writing.

The church clock strikes the first quarter.

THE DAUGHTER [*in the space between the central pillars, close to the one on her left*]: I'm getting chilled to the bone. What can Freddy be doing all this time? He's been gone twenty minutes.

THE MOTHER [*on her daughter's right*]: Not so long. But he ought to have got us a cab by this.

A BYSTANDER [*on the lady's right*]: He wont get no cab not until half-past eleven, missus, when they come back after dropping their theatre fares.

THE MOTHER: But we must have a cab. We cant stand here until half-past eleven. It's too bad.

THE BYSTANDER: Well, it ain't my fault, missus.

THE DAUGHTER: If Freddy had a bit of gumption, he would have got one at the theatre door.

THE MOTHER: What could he have done, poor boy?

THE DAUGHTER: Other people got cabs. Why couldnt he?

[FREDDY *rushes in out of the rain from the Southampton Street side, and comes between them closing a dripping umbrella. He is a young man of twenty, in evening dress, very wet round the ankles.*]

THE DAUGHTER: Well, havnt you got a cab?

FREDDY: Theres not one to be had for love or money.

THE MOTHER: Oh, Freddy, there must be one. You cant have tried.

THE DAUGHTER: It's too tiresome. Do you expect us to go and get one ourselves?

FREDDY: I tell you theyre all engaged. The rain was so sudden: nobody was prepared; and everybody had to take a cab. Ive been to Charing Cross one way and nearly to Ludgate Circus the other; and they were all engaged.

THE MOTHER: Did you try Trafalgar Square?

FREDDY: There wasn't one at Trafalgar Square.

THE DAUGHTER: Did you try?

FREDDY: I tried as far as Charing Cross Station. Did you expect me to walk to Hammersmith?

THE DAUGHTER: You havnt tried at all.

THE MOTHER: You really are very helpless, Freddy. Go again; and dont come back until you have found a cab.

FREDDY: I shall simply get soaked for nothing.

THE DAUGHTER: And what about us? Are we to stay here all night in this draught, with next to nothing on? You selfish pig—

FREDDY: Oh, very well: I'll go, I'll go. [*He opens his umbrella and dashes off Strandwards, but comes into collision with a flower girl who is hurrying in for shelter, knocking her basket out of her hands. A blinding flash of lightning, followed instantly by a rattling peal of thunder, orchestrates the incident*].

THE FLOWER GIRL: Nah then, Freddy: look wh'y' gowin, deah.

FREDDY: Sorry [*he rushes off*].

THE FLOWER GIRL [*picking up her scattered flowers and replacing them in the basket*]: Theres menners f' yer! Tə-oo banches o voylets trod into the mad. [*She sits down on the plinth of the column, sorting her flowers, on the lady's right. She is not at all a romantic figure. She is perhaps eighteen, perhaps twenty, hardly older. She wears a little sailor hat of black straw that has long been exposed to the dust and soot of London and has seldom if ever been brushed. Her hair needs washing rather badly: its mousy color can hardly be natural. She wears a shoddy black coat that reaches nearly to her knees and is shaped to her waist. She has a brown skirt with a coarse apron. Her boots are much the worse for wear. She is no doubt as clean as she can afford to be; but compared to the ladies she is very dirty. Her features are no worse than theirs; but their condition leaves something to be desired; and she needs the services of a dentist*].

THE MOTHER: How do you know that my son's name is Freddy, pray?

THE FLOWER GIRL: Ow, eez yə-ooa san, is e? Wal, fewd dan y' də-ooty bawmz a mather should, eed now bettern to spawl a pore gel's flahrzn than ran awy athaht pyin. Will ye-oo py me f'them? [*Here, with apologies, this desperate attempt to represent her dialect without a phonetic alphabet must be abandoned as unintelligible outside London*].

THE DAUGHTER: Do nothing of the sort, mother. The idea!

THE MOTHER: Please allow me, Clara. Have you any pennies?

THE DAUGHTER: No. Ive nothing smaller than sixpence.

THE FLOWER GIRL [*hopefully*]: I can give you change for a tanner, kind lady.

THE MOTHER [*to* CLARA]: Give it to me. [CLARA *parts reluctantly.*] Now [*to the girl*] This is for your flowers.

THE FLOWER GIRL: Thank you kindly, lady.

THE DAUGHTER: Make her give you the change. These things are only a penny a bunch.

THE MOTHER: Do hold your tongue, Clara. [*To the girl*] You can keep the change.

THE FLOWER GIRL: Oh, thank you, lady.

THE MOTHER: Now tell me how you know that young gentleman's name.

THE FLOWER GIRL: I didnt.

THE MOTHER: I heard you call him by it. Dont try to deceive me.

THE FLOWER GIRL [*protesting*]: Who's trying to deceive you? I called him Freddy or Charlie same as you might yourself if you was talking to a stranger and wished to be pleasant.

THE DAUGHTER: Sixpence thrown away! Really, mamma, you might have spared Freddy that. [*She retreats in disgust behind the pillar*].

[*An elderly gentleman of the amiable military type rushes into the shelter, and closes a dripping umbrella. He is in the same plight as* FREDDY, *very wet about the ankles. He is in evening dress, with a light overcoat. He takes the place left vacant by the daughter.*]

THE GENTLEMAN: Phew!

THE MOTHER [*to the gentleman*]: Oh, sir, is there any sign of its stopping?

THE GENTLEMAN: I'm afraid not. It started worse than ever about two minutes ago [*he goes to the plinth beside the flower girl: puts up his foot on it; and stoops to turn down his trouser ends*].

THE MOTHER: Oh dear! [*She retires sadly and joins her daughter*].

THE FLOWER GIRL [*taking advantage of the military gentleman's proximity to establish friendly relations with him*]: If it's worse, it's a sign it's nearly over. So cheer up, Captain; and buy a flower off a poor girl.

THE GENTLEMAN: I'm sorry. I havent any change.

THE FLOWER GIRL: I can give you change, Captain.

THE GENTLEMAN: For a sovereign? Ive nothing less.

THE FLOWER GIRL: Garn! Oh do buy a flower off me, Captain. I can change half-a-crown. Take this for tuppence.

THE GENTLEMAN: Now dont be troublesome: theres a good girl. [*Trying his pockets*] I really havnt any change—Stop: heres three hapence, if thats any use to you [*he retreats to the other pillar*].

THE FLOWER GIRL [*disappointed, but thinking three half-pence better than nothing*]: Thank you, sir.

THE BYSTANDER [*to the girl*]: You be careful: give him a flower for it. Theres a bloke here behind taking down every blessed word youre saying. [*All turn to the man who is taking notes*].

THE FLOWER GIRL [*springing up terrified*]: I aint done nothing wrong by speaking to the gentleman. Ive a right to sell flowers if I keep off the kerb. [*Hysterically*] I'm a respectable girl: so help me, I never spoke to him except to ask him to buy a flower off me.

General hubbub, mostly sympathetic to the flower girl, but deprecating her excessive sensibility. Cries of Dont start hollerin. Who's hurting you? Nobody's going to touch you. Whats the good of fussing? Steady on. Easy easy, etc., *come from the elderly staid spectators, who pat her comfortingly. Less patient ones bid her shut her head, or ask her roughly what is wrong with her. A remoter group, not knowing what the matter is, crowd in and increase the noise with questions and answer:* Whats the row? What-she do? Where is he? A tec taking her down. What! him? Yes: him over there: Took money off the gentleman, etc.

THE FLOWER GIRL [*breaking through them to the gentleman, crying wildly*]: Oh, sir, dont let him charge me. You dunno what it means to me. Theyll take away my character and drive me on the streets for speaking to gentlemen. They—

THE NOTE TAKER [*coming forward on her right, the rest crowding after him*]: There! there! there! there! who's hurting you, you silly girl? What do you take me for?

THE BYSTANDER: It's aw rawt: e's a genleman: look at his bə-oots. [*Explaining to the note taker*] She thought you was a copper's nark, sir.

THE NOTE TAKER [*with quick interest*]: Whats a copper's nark?

THE BYSTANDER [*inapt at definition*]: It's a—well, it's a copper's nark, as you might say. What else would you call it? A sort of informer.

THE FLOWER GIRL [*still hysterical*]: I take my Bible oath I never said a word—

THE NOTE TAKER [*overbearing but good-humored*]: Oh, shut up, shut up. Do I look like a policeman?

THE FLOWER GIRL [*far from reassured*]: Then what did you take down my words for? How do I know whether you took me down right? You just shew me what youve wrote about me. [*The note taker opens his book and holds it steadily under her nose, though the pressure of the mob trying to read it over his shoulders would upset a weaker man*]. What's that? That aint proper writing. I cant read that.

THE NOTE TAKER: I can. [*Reads, reproducing her pronunciation exactly*] "Cheer ap, Keptin; n'baw ya flahr orf a pore gel."

THE FLOWER GIRL [*much distressed*]: It's because I called him Captain. I meant no harm. [*To the gentleman*] Oh, sir, dont let him lay a charge agen me for a word like that. You—

THE GENTLEMAN: Charge! I make no charge. [*To the note taker*] Really, sir, if you are a detective, you need not begin protecting me against molestation by young women until I ask you. Anybody could see that the girl meant no harm.

THE BYSTANDERS GENERALLY [*demonstrating against police espionage*]: Course they could. What business is it of yours? You mind your own affairs. He wants promotion, he does. Taking down people's words! Girl never said a word to him. What harm if she did? Nice thing a girl cant shelter from the rain without being insulted, etc. etc., etc. [*She is conducted by the more sympathetic demonstrators back to her plinth, where she resumes her seat and struggles with her emotion*].

THE BYSTANDER: He aint a tec. He's a bloming busybody: thats what he is. I tell you, look at his bə-oots.

THE NOTE TAKER [*turning on him genially*]: And how are all your people down at Selsey?

THE BYSTANDER [*suspiciously*]: Who told you my people come from Selsey?

THE NOTE TAKER: Never you mind. They did. [*To the girl*] How do you come to be up so far east? You were born in Lisson Grove.

THE FLOWER GIRL [*appalled*]: Oh, what harm is there in my leaving Lisson Grove? It wasnt fit for a pig to live in; and I had to pay four-and-six a week. [*In tears*] Oh, boo—hoo—oo—

THE NOTE TAKER: Live where you like; but stop that noise.

THE GENTLEMAN [*to the girl*]: Come, come! he cant touch you: you have a right to live where you please.

A SARCASTIC BYSTANDER [*thrusting himself between the note taker and the gentleman*]: Park Lane, for instance. I'd like to go into the Housing Question with you, I would.

THE FLOWER GIRL [*subsiding into a brooding melancholy over her basket, and talking very low-spiritedly to herself*]: I'm a good girl, I am.

THE SARCASTIC BYSTANDER [*not attending to her*]: Do you know where *I* come from?

THE NOTE TAKER [*promptly*]: Hoxton.

[*Titterings. Popular interest in the note taker's performance increases*].

THE SARCASTIC ONE [*amazed*]: Well, who said I didnt? Bly me! you know everything, you do.

THE FLOWER GIRL [*still nursing her sense of injury*]: Aint no call to meddle with me, he aint.

THE BYSTANDER [*to her*]: Of course he aint. Dont you stand it from him. [*To the note taker*] See here: what call have you to know about people what never offered to meddle with you?

THE FLOWER GIRL: Let him say what he likes. I don't want to have no truck with him.

THE BYSTANDER: You take us for dirt under your feet, don't you? Catch you taking liberties with a gentleman!

THE SARCASTIC BYSTANDER: Yes: tell him where he come from if you want to go fortune-telling.

THE NOTE TAKER: Cheltenham, Harrow, Cambridge, and India.

THE GENTLEMAN: Quite right.

[*Great laughter. Reaction in the note taker's favor. Exclamations of* He knows all about it. Told him proper. Hear him tell the toff where he come from? etc.].

THE GENTLEMAN: May I ask, sir, do you do this for your living at a music hall?

THE NOTE TAKER: I've thought of that. Perhaps I shall some day.

[*The rain has stopped; and the persons on the outside of the crowd begin to drop off*].

THE FLOWER GIRL [*resenting the reaction*]: He's no gentleman, he aint, to interfere with a poor girl.

THE DAUGHTER [*out of patience, pushing her way rudely to the front and displacing the gentleman who politely retires to the other side of the pillar*]: What on earth is Freddy doing? I shall get pneumownia if I stay in this draught any longer.

THE NOTE TAKER [*to himself, hastily making a note of her pronunciation of "monia"*]: Earlscourt.

THE DAUGHTER [*violently*]: Will you please keep your impertinent remarks to yourself.

THE NOTE TAKER: Did I say that out loud? I didnt mean to. I beg your pardon. Your mother's Epsom, unmistakeably.

THE MOTHER [*advancing between the daughter and the note taker*]: How very curious! I was brought up in Largelady Park, near Epsom.

THE NOTE TAKER [*uproariously amused*]: Ha! ha! What a devil of a name! Excuse me. [*To the daughter*] You want a cab, do you?

THE DAUGHTER: Dont dare speak to me.

THE MOTHER: Oh please, please, Clara. [*Her daughter repudiates her with an angry shrug and retires haughtily*] We should be so grateful to you, sir, if you found us a cab. [*The note taker produces a whistle*] Oh, thank you. [*She joins her daughter*].

[*The note taker blows a piercing blast*].

THE SARCASTIC BYSTANDER: There! I knowed he was a plainclothes copper.

THE BYSTANDER: That aint a police whistle: thats a sporting whistle.

THE FLOWER GIRL [*still preoccupied with her wounded feelings*]: He's no right to take away my character. My character is the same to me as any lady's.

THE NOTE TAKER: I dont know whether youve noticed it; but the rain stopped about two minutes ago.

THE BYSTANDER: So it has. Why didn't you say so before? and us losing our time listening to your silliness! [*He walks off towards the Strand*].

THE SARCASTIC BYSTANDER: I can tell where you come from. You come from Anwell. Go back there.

THE NOTE TAKER [*helpfully*]: *H*anwell.

THE SARCASTIC BYSTANDER [*affecting great distinction of speech*]: Thenk you, teacher. Haw haw! So long [*he touches his hat with mock respect and strolls off*].

THE FLOWER GIRL: Frightening people like that! How would he like it himself?

THE MOTHER: It's quite fine now, Clara. We can walk to a motor bus. Come. [*She gathers her skirts above her ankles and hurries off towards the Strand*].

THE DAUGHTER: But the cab—[*her mother is out of hearing*]. Oh, how tiresome! [*She follows angrily*].

[*All the rest have gone except the note taker, the gentleman, and the flower girl, who sits arranging her basket, and still pitying herself in murmurs*].

THE FLOWER GIRL: Poor girl! Hard enough for her to live without being worrited and chivied.

THE GENTLEMAN [*returning to his former place on the note taker's left*]: How do you do it, if I may ask?

THE NOTE TAKER: Simply phonetics. The science of

speech. Thats my profession: also my hobby. Happy is the man who can make a living by his hobby! You can spot an Irishman or a Yorkshireman by his brogue. *I* can place any man within six miles. I can place him within two miles in London. Sometimes within two streets.

THE FLOWER GIRL: Ought to be ashamed of himself, unmanly coward!

THE GENTLEMAN: But is there a living in that?

THE NOTE TAKER: Oh yes. Quite a fat one. This is an age of upstarts. Men begin in Kentish Town with £80 a year, and end in Park Lane with a hundred thousand. They want to drop Kentish Town; but they give themselves away every time they open their mouths. Now I can teach them—

THE FLOWER GIRL: Let him mind his own business and leave a poor girl—

THE NOTE TAKER [*explosively*]: Woman: cease this detestable boohooing instantly; or else seek the shelter of some other place of worship.

THE FLOWER GIRL [*with feeble defiance*]: Ive a right to be here if I like, same as you.

THE NOTE TAKER: A woman who utters such depressing and disgusting sounds has no right to be anywhere—no right to live. Remember that you are a human being with a soul and the divine gift of articulate speech: that your native language is the language of Shakespear and Milton and The Bible; and dont sit there crooning like a bilious pigeon.

THE FLOWER GIRL [*quite overwhelmed, looking up at him in mingled wonder and deprecation without daring to raise her head*]: Ah-ah-ah-ow-ow-ow-oo!

THE NOTE TAKER [*whipping out his book*]: Heavens! what a sound! [*He writes; then holds out the book and reads, reproducing her vowels exactly*] Ah-ah-ah-ow-ow-ow-oo!

THE FLOWER GIRL [*tickled by the performance, and laughing in spite of herself*]: Garn!

THE NOTE TAKER: You see this creature with her kerbstone English: the English that will keep her in the gutter to the end of her days. Well, sir, in three months I could pass that girl off as a duchess at an ambassador's garden party. I could even get her a place as lady's maid or shop assistant, which requires better English.

THE FLOWER GIRL: What's that you say?

THE NOTE TAKER: Yes, you squashed cabbage leaf, you disgrace to the noble architecture of these columns, you incarnate insult to the English language: I could pass you off as the Queen of Sheba. [*To the Gentleman*] Can you believe that?

THE GENTLEMAN: Of course I can. I am myself a student of Indian dialects; and—

THE NOTE TAKER [*eagerly*]: Are you? Do you know Colonel Pickering, the author of Spoken Sanscrit?

THE GENTLEMAN: I am Colonel Pickering. Who are you?

THE NOTE TAKER: Henry Higgins, author of Higgins's Universal Alphabet.

PICKERING [*with enthusiasm*]: I came from India to meet you.

HIGGINS: I was going to India to meet you.

PICKERING: Where do you live?

HIGGINS: 27A Wimpole Street. Come and see me tomorrow.

PICKERING: I'm at the Carlton. Come with me now and lets have a jaw over some supper.

HIGGINS: Right you are.

THE FLOWER GIRL [*to* PICKERING, *as he passes her*]: Buy a flower, kind gentleman. I'm short for my lodging.

PICKERING: I really havnt any change. I'm sorry [*he goes away*].

HIGGINS [*shocked at the girl's mendacity*]: Liar. You said you could change half-a-crown.

THE FLOWER GIRL [*rising in desperation*]: You ought to be stuffed with nails, you ought. [*Flinging the basket at his feet*] Take the whole blooming basket for sixpence.

[*The church clock strikes the second quarter*].

HIGGINS [*hearing in it the voice of God, rebuking him for his Pharisaic want of charity to the poor girl*]: A reminder. [*He raises his hat solemnly; then throws a handful of money into the basket and follows* PICKERING].

THE FLOWER GIRL [*picking up a half-crown*]: Ah-ow-ooh! [*Picking up a couple of florins*] Aaah-ow-ooh! [*Picking up several coins*] Aaaaah-ow-ooh! [*Picking up a half-sovereign*] Aaaaaaaaaaaah-ow-ooh!!!

FREDDY [*springing out of a taxicab*]: Got one at last. Hallo! [*To the girl*] Where are the two ladies that were here?

THE FLOWER GIRL: They walked to the bus when the rain stopped.

FREDDY: And left me with a cab on my hands! Damnation!

THE FLOWER GIRL [*with grandeur*]: Never mind, young man. *I'm* going home in a taxi. [*She sails off to the cab. The driver puts his hand behind him and holds the door firmly shut against her. Quite understanding his mistrust, she shews him her handful of money.*] A taxi fare aint no object to me, Charlie. [*He grins and opens the door*]. Here. What about the basket?

THE TAXIMAN: Give it here. Tuppence extra.

LIZA: No: I dont want nobody to see it. [*She

crushes it into the cab and gets in, continuing the conversation through the window] Goodbye, Freddy.

FREDDY [*dazedly raising his hat*]: Goodbye.

TAXIMAN: Where to?

LIZA: Bucknam Pellis [Buckingham Palace].

TAXIMAN: What d'ye mean—Bucknam Pellis?

LIZA: Dont you know where it is? In the Green Park, where the King lives. Goodbye, Freddy. Dont let me keep you standing there. Goodbye.

FREDDY: Goodbye. [*He goes*].

TAXIMAN: Here? Whats this about Bucknam Pellis? What business have you at Bucknam Pellis?

LIZA: Of course I havnt none. But I wasn't going to let him know that. You drive me home.

TAXIMAN: And wheres home?

LIZA: Angel Court, Drury Lane, next Meiklejohn's oil shop.

TAXIMAN: That sounds more like it, Judy. [*He drives off*].

* * * * *

Let us follow the taxi to the entrance to Angel Court, a narrow little archway between two shops, one of them Meiklejohn's oil shop. When it stops there, Eliza gets out, dragging her basket with her.

LIZA: How much?

TAXIMAN [*indicating the taximeter*]: Cant you read? A shilling.

LIZA: A shilling for two minutes!!

TAXIMAN: Two minutes or ten: it's all the same.

LIZA: Well, I dont call it right.

TAXIMAN: Ever been in a taxi before?

LIZA [*with dignity*]: Hundreds and thousands of times, young man.

TAXIMAN [*laughing at her*]: Good for you, Judy. Keep the shilling, darling, with best love from all at home. Good luck! [*He drives off*].

LIZA [*humiliated*]: Impidence!

[*She picks up the basket and trudges up the alley with it to her lodging: a small room with very old wall paper hanging loose in the damp places. A broken pane in the window is mended with paper. A portrait of a popular actor and a fashion plate of ladies' dresses, all wildly beyond poor* ELIZA'S *means, both torn from newspapers, are pinned up on the wall. A birdcage hangs in the window; but its tenant died long ago: it remains as a memorial only*].

[*These are the only visible luxuries: the rest is the irreducible minimum of poverty's needs: a wretched bed heaped with all sorts of coverings that have any warmth in them, a draped packing case with a basin and jug on it and a little looking glass over it, a chair and table, the refuse of some suburban kitchen, and an American alarum clock on the shelf above the unused fireplace: the whole lighted with a gas lamp with a penny in the slot meter. Rent: four shillings a week*].

Here Eliza, chronically weary, but too excited to go to bed, sits, counting her new riches and dreaming and planning what to do with them, until the gas goes out, when she enjoys for the first time the sensation of being able to put in another penny without grudging it. This prodigal mood does not extinguish her gnawing sense of the need for economy sufficiently to prevent her from calculating that she can dream and plan in bed more cheaply and warmly than sitting up without a fire. So she takes off her shawl and skirt and adds them to the miscellaneous bedclothes. Then she kicks off her shoes and gets into bed without any further change.

ACT II

Next day at 11 a.m. HIGGINS'S *laboratory in Wimpole Street. It is a room on the first floor, looking on the street, and was meant for the drawing room. The double doors are in the middle of the back wall; and persons entering find in the corner to their right two tall file cabinets at right angles to one another against the walls. In this corner stands a flat writing-table, on which are a phonograph, a laryngoscope, a row of tiny organ pipes with a bellows, a set of lamp chimneys for singing flames with burners attached to a gas plug in the wall by an indiarubber tube, several tuning-forks of different sizes, a life-size image of half a human head, shewing in section the vocal organs, and a box containing a supply of wax cylinders for the phonograph.*

Further down the room, on the same side, is a fireplace, with a comfortable leather-covered easy-chair at the side of the hearth nearest the door, and a coal-scuttle. There is a clock on the mantelpiece. Between the fireplace and the phonograph table is a stand for newspapers.

On the other side of the central door, to the left of the visitor, is a cabinet of shallow drawers. On it is a telephone and the telephone directory. The corner beyond, and most of the side wall, is occupied by a grand piano, with the keyboard at the end furthest from the door, and a bench for the players extending the full length of the keyboard. On the piano is a dessert dish heaped with fruit and sweets, mostly chocolates.

The middle of the room is clear. Besides the easy-chair, the piano bench, and two chairs at the phonograph table, there is one stray chair. It stands near the fireplace. On the walls, engravings: mostly Piranesis and mezzotint portraits. No paintings.

PICKERING *is seated at the table, putting down some cards and a tuning-fork which he has been using.* HIGGINS *is standing up near him, closing two or three file drawers which are hanging out. He appears in the morning light as a robust, vital, appetizing sort of man of forty or thereabouts, dressed in a professional-looking black frock-coat with a white linen collar and black silk tie. He is of energetic, scientific type, heartily, even violently interested in everything that can be studied as a scientific subject, and careless about himself and other people, including their feelings. He is, in fact, but for his years and size, rather like a very impetuous baby "taking notice" eagerly and loudly, and requiring almost as much watching to keep him out of unintended mischief. His manner varies from genial bullying when he is in a good humor to stormy petulance when anything goes wrong; but he is so entirely frank and void of malice that he remains likeable even in his least reasonable moments.*

HIGGINS [*as he shuts the last drawer*]: Well, I think thats the whole show.

PICKERING: It's really amazing. I havnt taken half of it in, you know.

HIGGINS: Would you like to go over any of it again?

PICKERING [*rising and coming to the fireplace, where he plants himself with his back to the fire*]: No, thank you: not now. I'm quite done up for this morning.

HIGGINS [*following him, and standing beside him on his left*]: Tired of listening to sounds?

PICKERING: Yes. It's a fearful strain. I rather fancied myself because I can pronounce twenty-four distinct vowel sounds; but your hundred and thirty beat me. I cant hear a bit of difference between most of them.

HIGGINS [*chuckling, and going over to the piano to eat sweets*]: Oh, that comes with practice. You hear no difference at first; but you keep on listening, and presently you find theyre all as different as A from B. [MRS. PEARCE *looks in: she is* HIGGINS'S *housekeeper*]. Whats the matter?

MRS. PEARCE [*hesitating, evidently perplexed*]: A young woman asks to see you, sir.

HIGGINS: A young woman! What does she want?

MRS. PEARCE: Well, sir, she says youll be glad to see her when you know what she's come about. She's quite a common girl, sir. Very common indeed. I should have sent her away, only I thought perhaps you wanted her to talk into your machines. I hope Ive not done wrong; but really you see such queer people sometimes—youll excuse me, I'm sure, sir—

HIGGINS: Oh, thats all right, Mrs. Pearce. Has she an interesting accent?

MRS. PEARCE: Oh, something dreadful, sir, really. I dont know how you can take an interest in it.

HIGGINS [*to* PICKERING]: Lets have her up. Shew her up, Mrs. Pearce [*he rushes across to his working table and picks out a cylinder to use on the phonograph*].

MRS. PEARCE [*only half resigned to it*]: Very well, sir. It's for you to say. [*She goes downstairs*].

HIGGINS: This is rather a bit of luck. I'll shew you how I make records. We'll set her talking; and I'll take it down first in Bell's Visible Speech; then in broad Romic; and then we'll get her on the phonograph so that you can turn her on as often as you like with the written transcript before you.

MRS. PEARCE [*returning*]: This is the young woman, sir.

[*The flower girl enters in state. She has a hat with three ostrich feathers, orange, sky-blue, and red. She has a nearly clean apron, and the shoddy coat has been tidied a little. The pathos of this deplorable figure, with its innocent vanity and consequential air, touches* PICKERING, *who has already straightened himself in the presence of* MRS. PEARCE. *But as to* HIGGINS, *the only distinction he makes between men and women is that when he is neither bullying nor exclaiming to the heavens against some feather-weight cross, he coaxes women as a child coaxes its nurse when it wants to get anything out of her*].

HIGGINS [*brusquely, recognizing her with unconcealed disappointment, and at once, babylike, making an intolerable grievance of it*]: Why, this is the girl I jotted down last night. She's no use: I've got all the records I want of the Lisson Grove lingo; and I'm not going to waste another cylinder on it. [*To the girl*] Be off with you: I dont want you.

THE FLOWER GIRL: Dont you be so saucy. You aint

heard what I come for yet. [*To* MRS. PEARCE, *who is waiting at the door for further instructions*] Did you tell him I come in a taxi?

MRS. PEARCE: Nonsense, girl! what do you think a gentleman like Mr. Higgins cares what you came in?

THE FLOWER GIRL: Oh, we are proud! He aint above giving lessons, not him: I heard him say so. Well, I aint come here to ask for any compliment; and if my money's not good enough I can go elsewhere.

HIGGINS: Good enough for what?

THE FLOWER GIRL: Good enough for yə-oo. Now you know, dont you? I've come to have lessons, I am. And to pay for em tə-oo: make no mistake.

HIGGINS [*stupent*]: Well!!! [*Recovering his breath with a gasp*] What do you expect me to say to you?

THE FLOWER GIRL: Well, if you was a gentleman, you might ask me to sit down, I think. Dont I tell you I'm bringing you business?

HIGGINS: Pickering: shall we ask this baggage to sit down, or shall we throw her out of the window?

THE FLOWER GIRL [*running away in terror to the piano, where she turns at bay*]: Ah-ah-oh-ow-ow-ow-oo! [*Wounded and whimpering*] I wont be called a baggage when Ive offered to pay like any lady.

[*Motionless, the two men stare at her from the other side of the room, amazed*].

PICKERING [*gently*]: But what is it you want?

THE FLOWER GIRL: I want to be a lady in a flower shop stead of sellin at the corner of Tottenham Court Road. But they wont take me unless I can talk more genteel. He said he could teach me. Well, here I am ready to pay him—not asking any favor—and he treats me zif I was dirt.

MRS. PEARCE: How can you be such a foolish ignorant girl as to think you could afford to pay Mr. Higgins?

THE FLOWER GIRL: Why shouldnt I? I know what lessons cost as well as you do; and I'm ready to pay.

HIGGINS: How much?

THE FLOWER GIRL [*coming back to him, triumphant*]: Now youre talking! I thought youd come off it when you saw a chance of getting back a bit of what you chucked at me last night. [*Confidentially*] Youd had a drop in, hadnt you?

HIGGINS [*peremptorily*]: Sit down.

THE FLOWER GIRL: Oh, if youre going to make a compliment of it—

HIGGINS [*thundering at her*]: Sit down.

MRS. PEARCE [*severely*]: Sit down, girl. Do as youre told.

THE FLOWER GIRL: Ah-ah-ah-ow-ow-oo! [*She stands, half rebellious, half bewildered*].

PICKERING [*very courteous*]: Wont you sit down? [*He places the stray chair near the hearthrug between himself and* HIGGINS.]

LIZA [*coyly*]: Dont mind if I do. [*She sits down.* PICKERING *returns to the hearthrug*].

HIGGINS: Whats your name?

THE FLOWER GIRL: Liza Doolittle.

HIGGINS [*declaiming gravely*]:

Eliza, Elizabeth, Betsy and Bess,
They went to the woods to get a bird's nes':

PICKERING: They found a nest with four eggs in it:

HIGGINS: They took one apiece, and left three in it.

[*They laugh heartily at their own fun*].

LIZA: Oh, dont be silly.

MRS. PEARCE [*placing herself behind* ELIZA'S *chair*]: You mustnt speak to the gentleman like that.

LIZA: Well, why wont he speak sensible to me?

HIGGINS: Come back to business. How much do you propose to pay me for the lessons?

LIZA: Oh, I know whats right. A lady friend of mine gets French lessons for eighteenpence an hour from a real French gentleman. Well, you wouldnt have the face to ask me the same for teaching me my own language as you would for French; so I wont give more than a shilling. Take it or leave it.

HIGGINS [*walking up and down the room, rattling his keys and his cash in his pockets*]: You know, Pickering, if you consider a shilling, not as a simple shilling, but as a percentage of this girl's income, it works out as fully equivalent to sixty or seventy guineas from a millionaire.

PICKERING: How so?

HIGGINS: Figure it out. A millionaire has about £150 a day. She earns about half-a-crown.

LIZA [*haughtily*]: Who told you I only—

HIGGINS [*continuing*]: She offers me two-fifths of her day's income for a lesson. Two-fifths of a millionaire's income for a day would be somewhere about £60. It's handsome. By George, it's enormous! it's the biggest offer I ever had.

LIZA [*rising, terrified*]: Sixty pounds! What are you talking about? I never offered you sixty pounds. Where would I get—

HIGGINS. Hold your tongue.

LIZA [*weeping*]: But I aint got sixty pounds. Oh—

MRS. PEARCE. Dont cry, you silly girl. Sit down. Nobody is going to touch your money.

HIGGINS: Somebody is going to touch you, with a broomstick, if you dont stop snivelling. Sit down.

LIZA [*obeying slowly*]: Ah-ah-ah-ow-oo-o! One would think you was my father.

HIGGINS: If I decide to teach you, I'll be worse than two fathers to you. Here [*he offers her his silk handkerchief*]!

LIZA: Whats this for?

HIGGINS: To wipe your eyes. To wipe any part of your face that feels moist. Remember: thats your handkerchief; and thats your sleeve. Dont mistake the one for the other if you wish to become a lady in a shop.

[LIZA, *utterly bewildered, stares helplessly at him*].

MRS. PEARCE: It's no use talking to her like that, Mr. Higgins: she doesnt understand you. Besides, youre quite wrong: she doesnt do it that way at all [*she takes the handkerchief*].

LIZA [*snatching it*]: Here! You give me that handkerchief. He gev it to me, not to you.

PICKERING [*laughing*]: He did. I think it must be regarded as her property, Mrs. Pearce.

MRS. PEARCE [*resigning herself*]: Serve you right, Mr. Higgins.

PICKERING: Higgins: I'm interested. What about the ambassador's garden party? I'll say youre the greatest teacher alive if you make that good. I'll bet you all the expenses of the experiment you cant do it. And I'll pay for the lessons.

LIZA: Oh, you are real good. Thank you, Captain.

HIGGINS [*tempted, looking at her*]: It's almost irresistible. She's so deliciously low—so horribly dirty—

LIZA [*protesting extremely*]: Ah-ah-ah-ah-ow-ow-oo-oo!!! I aint dirty: I washed my face and hands afore I come, I did.

PICKERING: Youre certainly not going to turn her head with flattery, Higgins.

MRS. PEARCE [*uneasy*]: Oh, dont say that, sir: theres more ways than one of turning a girl's head; and nobody can do it better than Mr. Higgins, though he may not always mean it. I do hope, sir, you wont encourage him to do anything foolish.

HIGGINS [*becoming excited as the idea grows on him*]: What is life but a series of inspired follies? The difficulty is to find them to do. Never lose a chance: it doesnt come every day. I shall make a duchess of this draggletailed guttersnipe.

LIZA [*strongly deprecating this view of her*]: Ah-ah-ah-ow-ow-oo!

HIGGINS [*carried away*]: Yes: in six months—in three if she has a good ear and a quick tongue—I'll take her anywhere and pass her off as anything. We'll start today: now! this moment! Take her away and clean her, Mrs. Pearce. Monkey Brand, if it wont come off any other way. Is there a good fire in the kitchen?

MRS. PEARCE [*protesting*]: Yes; but—

HIGGINS [*storming on*]: Take all her clothes off and burn them. Ring up Whitely or somebody for new ones. Wrap her up in brown paper til they come.

LIZA: Youre no gentleman, youre not, to talk of such things. I'm a good girl, I am; and I know what the like of you are, I do.

HIGGINS: We want none of your Lisson Grove prudery here, young woman. Youve got to learn to behave like a duchess. Take her away, Mrs. Pearce. If she gives you any trouble, wallop her.

LIZA [*springing up and running between* PICKERING *and* MRS. PEARCE *for protection*]: No! I'll call the police, I will.

MRS. PEARCE: But Ive no place to put her.

HIGGINS: Put her in the dustbin.

LIZA: Ah-ah-ah-ow-ow-oo!

PICKERING: Oh come, Higgins! be reasonable.

MRS. PEARCE [*resolutely*]: You must be reasonable, Mr. Higgins: really you must. You cant walk over everybody like this.

[HIGGINS, *thus scolded, subsides. The hurricane is succeeded by a zephyr of amiable surprise*].

HIGGINS [*with professional exquisiteness of modulation*]: *I* walk over everybody! My dear Mrs. Pearce, my dear Pickering, I never had the slightest intention of walking over anyone. All I propose is that we should be kind to this poor girl. We must help her to prepare and fit herself for her new station in life. If I did not express myself clearly it was because I did not wish to hurt her delicacy, or yours.

[LIZA, *reassured, steals back to her chair*].

MRS. PEARCE [*to* PICKERING]: Well, did you ever hear anything like that, sir?

PICKERING [*laughing heartily*]: Never, Mrs. Pearce: never.

HIGGINS [*patiently*]: Whats the matter?

MRS. PEARCE: Well, the matter is, sir, that you cant take a girl up like that as if you were picking up a pebble on the beach.

HIGGINS: Why not?

MRS. PEARCE: Why not! But you dont know anything about her. What about her parents? She may be married.

LIZA: Garn!

HIGGING: There! As the girl very properly says, Garn! Married indeed! Dont you know that a woman of that class looks a worn out drudge of fifty a year after she's married?

LIZA: Whood marry me?

HIGGINS [*suddenly resorting to the most thrilling beautiful low tones in his best elocutionary style*]: By George, Eliza, the streets will be strewn with the bodies of men shooting themselves for your sake before Ive done with you.

MRS. PEARCE: Nonsense, sir. You mustnt talk like that to her.

LIZA [*rising and squaring herself determinedly*]: I'm

going away. He's off his chump, he is. I dont want no balmies teaching me.

HIGGINS [*wounded in his tenderest point by her insensibility to his elocution*]: Oh, indeed! I'm mad, am I? Very well, Mrs. Pearce: you neednt order the new clothes for her. Throw her out.

LIZA [*whimpering*]: Nah-ow. You got no right to touch me.

MRS. PEARCE: You see now what comes of being saucy. [*Indicating the door*] This way, please.

LIZA [*almost in tears*]: I didnt want no clothes. I wouldnt have taken them [*she throws away the handkerchief*]. I can buy my own clothes.

HIGGINS [*deftly retrieving the handkerchief and intercepting her on her reluctant way to the door*]: Youre an ungrateful wicked girl. This is my return for offering to take you out of the gutter and dress you beautifully and make a lady of you.

MRS. PEARCE: Stop, Mr. Higgins. I wont allow it. It's you that are wicked. Go home to your parents, girl; and tell them to take better care of you.

LIZA: I aint got no parents. They told me I was big enough to earn my own living and turned me out.

MRS. PEARCE: Wheres your mother?

LIZA: I aint got no mother. Her that turned me out was my sixth stepmother. But I done without them. And I'm a good girl, I am.

HIGGINS: Very well, then, what on earth is all this fuss about? The girl doesnt belong to anybody—is no use to anybody but me. [*He goes to* MRS. PEARCE *and begins coaxing*]. You can adopt her, Mrs. Pearce: I'm sure a daughter would be a great amusement to you. Now dont make any more fuss. Take her downstairs; and—

MRS. PEARCE: But whats to become of her? Is she to be paid anything? Do be sensible, sir.

HIGGINS: Oh, pay her whatever is necessary: put it down in the housekeeping book. [*Impatiently*] What on earth will she want with money? She'll have her food and her clothes. She'll only drink if you give her money.

LIZA [*turning on him*]: Oh you are a brute. It's a lie: nobody ever saw the sign of liquor on me. [*To* PICKERING] Oh, sir: youre a gentleman: dont let him speak to me like that.

PICKERING [*in good-humored remonstrance*]: Does it occur to you, Higgins, that the girl has some feelings?

HIGGINS [*looking critically at her*]: Oh no, I dont think so. Not any feelings that we need bother about. [*Cheerily*] Have you, Eliza?

LIZA: I got my feelings same as anyone else.

HIGGINS [*to* PICKERING, *reflectively*]: You see the difficulty?

PICKERING: Eh? What difficulty?

HIGGINS: To get her to talk grammar. The mere pronunciation is easy enough.

LIZA: I don't want to talk grammar. I want to talk like a lady in a flower-shop.

MRS. PEARCE: Will you please keep to the point, Mr. Higgins. I want to know on what terms the girl is to be here. Is she to have any wages? And what is to become of her when youve finished your teaching? You must look ahead a little.

HIGGINS [*impatiently*]: Whats to become of her if I leave her in the gutter? Tell me that, Mrs. Pearce.

MRS. PEARCE: Thats her own business, not yours, Mr. Higgins.

HIGGINS: Well, when Ive done with her, we can throw her back into the gutter; and then it will be her own business again; so thats all right.

LIZA: Oh, youve no feeling heart in you: you dont care for nothing but yourself. [*She rises and takes the floor resolutely*]. Here! Ive had enough of this. I'm going [*making for the door*]. You ought to be ashamed of yourself, you ought.

HIGGINS [*snatching a chocolate cream from the piano, his eyes suddenly beginning to twinkle with mischief*]: Have some chocolates, Eliza.

LIZA [*halting, tempted*]: How do I know what might be in them? Ive heard of girls being drugged by the like of you.

[HIGGINS *whips out his penknife; cuts a chocolate in two; puts one half into his mouth and bolts it; and offers her the other half.*]

HIGGINS: Pledge of good faith, Eliza. I eat one half: you eat the other. [LIZA *opens her mouth to retort: he pops the half chocolate into it*]. You shall have boxes of them, barrels of them, every day. You shall live on them. Eh?

LIZA [*who has disposed of the chocolate after being nearly choked by it*]: I wouldnt have ate it, only I'm too ladylike to take it out of my mouth.

HIGGINS: Listen, Eliza. I think you said you came in a taxi.

LIZA: Well, what if I did? Ive as good a right to take a taxi as anyone else.

HIGGINS: You have, Eliza; and in future you shall have as many taxis as you want. You shall go up and down and round the town in a taxi every day. Think of that, Eliza.

MRS. PEARCE: Mr. Higgins: youre tempting the girl. It's not right. She should think of the future.

HIGGINS: At her age! Nonsense! Time enough to think of the future when you havnt any future to think of. No, Eliza: do as this lady does: think of other people's futures; but never think of your own. Think of chocolates, and taxis, and gold, and diamonds.

LIZA: No: I dont want no gold and no diamonds. I'm

a good girl, I am. [*She sits down again, with an attempt at dignity*].

HIGGINS: You shall remain so, Eliza, under the care of Mrs. Pearce. And you shall marry an officer in the Guards, with a beautiful moustache: the son of a marquis, who will disinherit him for marrying you, but will relent when he sees your beauty and goodness—

PICKERING: Excuse me, Higgins; but I really must interfere. Mrs. Pearce is quite right. If this girl is to put herself in your hands for six months for an experiment in teaching, she must understand thoroughly what she's doing.

HIGGINS: How can she? She's incapable of understanding anything. Besides, do any of us understand what we are doing? If we did, would we ever do it?

PICKERING: Very clever, Higgins; but not to the present point. [*To* ELIZA] Miss Doolittle—

LIZA [*overwhelmed*]: Ah-ah-ow-oo!

HIGGINS: There! Thats all youll get out of Eliza. Ah-ah-ow-oo! No use explaining. As a military man you ought to know that. Give her her orders: thats enough for her. Eliza: you are to live here for the next six months, learning how to speak beautifully, like a lady in a florist's shop. If youre good and do whatever youre told, you shall sleep in a proper bedroom, and have lots to eat, and money to buy chocolates and take rides in taxis. If youre naughty and idle you will sleep in the back kitchen among the black beetles, and be walloped by Mrs. Pearce with a broomstick. At the end of six months you shall go to Buckingham Palace in a carriage, beautifully dressed. If the King finds out youre not a lady, you will be taken by the police to the Tower of London, where your head will be cut off as a warning to other presumptuous flower girls. If you are not found out, you shall have a present of seven-and-sixpence to start life with as a lady in a shop. If you refuse this offer you will be a most ungrateful wicked girl; and the angels will weep for you. [*To* PICKERING]. Now are you satisfied, Pickering? [*To* MRS. PEARCE] Can I put it more plainly and fairly, Mrs. Pearce?

MRS. PEARCE [*patiently*]: I think youd better let me speak to the girl properly in private. I dont know that I can take charge of her or consent to the arrangement at all. Of course I know you dont mean her any harm; but when you get what you call interested in people's accents, you never think or care what may happen to them or you. Come with me, Eliza.

HIGGINS: Thats all right. Thank you, Mrs. Pearce. Bundle her off to the bath-room.

LIZA [*rising reluctantly and suspiciously*]: Youre a great bully, you are. I wont stay here if I dont like. I wont let nobody wallop me. I never asked to go to Bucknam Palace, I didnt. I was never in trouble with the police, not me. I'm a good girl—

MRS. PEARCE: Dont answer back, girl. You dont understand the gentleman. Come with me. [*She leads the way to the door, and holds it open for* ELIZA].

LIZA [*as she goes out*]: Well, what I say is right. I wont go near the King, not if I'm going to have my head cut off. If I'd known what I was letting myself in for, I wouldnt have come here. I always been a good girl; and I never offered to say a word to him; and I dont owe him nothing; and I dont care; and I wont be put upon; and I have my feelings the same as anyone else—

[MRS. PEARCE *shuts the door; and* LIZA'S *plaints are no longer audible*].

* * * * *

Eliza is taken upstairs to the third floor greatly to her surprise; for she expected to be taken down to the scullery. There Mrs. Pearce opens a door and takes her into a spare bedroom.

MRS. PEARCE: I will have to put you here. This will be your bedroom.

LIZA: O-h, I couldnt sleep here, missus. It's too good for the likes of me. I should be afraid to touch anything. I aint a duchess yet, you know.

MRS. PEARCE: You have got to make yourself as clean as the room: then you wont be afraid of it. And you must call me Mrs. Pearce, not missus. [*She throws open the door of the dressingroom, now modernized as a bathroom*].

LIZA: Gawd! whats this? Is this where you wash clothes? Funny sort of copper I call it.

MRS. PEARCE: It is not a copper. This is where we wash ourselves, Eliza, and where I am going to wash you.

LIZA: You expect me to get into that and wet myself all over! Not me. I should catch my death. I knew a woman did it every Saturday night; and she died of it.

MRS. PEARCE: Mr. Higgins has the gentlemen's bathroom downstairs; and he has a bath every morning, in cold water.

LIZA: Ugh! He's made of iron, that man.

MRS. PEARCE: If you are to sit with him and the Colonel and be taught you will have to do the same. They wont like the smell of you if you dont. But you can have the water as hot as you like. There are two taps: hot and cold.

LIZA [*weeping*]: I couldnt. I dursnt. Its not natural: it would kill me. Ive never had a bath in my life: not what youd call a proper one.

MRS. PEARCE: Well, dont you want to be clean and sweet and decent, like a lady? You know you cant be a nice girl inside if youre a dirty slut outside.

LIZA: Boohoo!!!!

MRS. PEARCE: Now stop crying and go back into your room and take off all your clothes. Then wrap yourself in this [*Taking down a gown from its peg and handing it to her*] and come back to me. I will get the bath ready.

LIZA [*all tears*]: I cant. I wont. I'm not used to it. Ive never took off all my clothes before. It's not right: it's not decent.

MRS. PEARCE: Nonsense, child. Dont you take off all your clothes every night when you go to bed?

LIZA [*amazed*]: No. Why should I? I should catch my death. Of course I take off my skirt.

MRS. PEARCE: Do you mean that you sleep in the underclothes you wear in the daytime?

LIZA: What else have I to sleep in?

MRS. PEARCE: You will never do that again so long as you live here. I will get you a proper nightdress.

LIZA: Do you mean change into cold things and lie awake shivering half the night? You want to kill me, you do.

MRS. PEARCE: I want to change you from a frowzy slut to a clean respectable girl fit to sit with the gentlemen in the study. Are you going to trust me and do what I tell you or be thrown out and sent back to your flower basket?

LIZA: But you dont know what the cold is to me. You dont know how I dread it.

MRS. PEARCE: Your bed won't be cold here: I will put a hot water bottle in it. [*Pushing her into the bedroom*] Off with you and undress.

LIZA: Oh, if only I'd known what a dreadful thing it is to be clean I'd never have come. I didnt know when I was well off. I—[MRS. PEARCE *pushes her through the door, but leaves it partly open lest her prisoner should take to flight*].

[MRS. PEARCE *puts on a pair of white rubber sleeves, and fills the bath, mixing hot and cold, and testing the result with the bath thermometer. She perfumes it with a handful of bath salts and adds a palmful of mustard. She then takes a formidable looking long handled scrubbing brush and soaps it profusely with a ball of scented soap*]. [ELIZA *comes back with nothing on but the bath gown huddled tightly round her, a piteous spectacle of abject terror*].

MRS. PEARCE: Now come along. Take that thing off.

LIZA: Oh I couldnt, Mrs. Pearce: I reely couldnt. I never done such a thing.

MRS. PEARCE: Nonsense. Here: step in and tell me whether its hot enough for you.

LIZA: Ah-oo! Ah-oo! It's too hot.

MRS. PEARCE [*deftly snatching the gown away and throwing* ELIZA *down on her back*]: It wont hurt you. [*She sets to work with the scrubbing brush*].

[ELIZA'S *screams are heartrending*].

* * * * *

Meanwhile the Colonel has been having it out with Higgins about Eliza. Pickering has come from the hearth to the chair and seated himself astride of it with his arms on the back to cross-examine him.

PICKERING: Excuse the straight question, Higgins. Are you a man of good character where women are concerned?

HIGGINS [*moodily*]: Have you ever met a man of good character where women are concerned?

PICKERING: Yes: very frequently.

HIGGINS [*dogmatically, lifting himself on his hands to the level of the piano, and sitting on it with a bounce*]: Well, I havnt. I find that the moment I let a woman make friends with me, she becomes jealous, exacting, suspicious, and a damned nuisance. I find that the moment I let myself make friends with a woman, I become selfish and tyrannical. Women upset everything. When you let them into your life, you find that the woman is driving at one thing and youre driving at another.

PICKERING: At what, for example?

HIGGINS [*coming off the piano restlessly*]: Oh, Lord knows! I suppose the woman wants to live her own life; and the man wants to live his; and each tries to drag the other on to the wrong track. One wants to go north and the other south; and the result is that both have to go east, though they both hate the east wind. [*He sits down on the bench at the keyboard*]. So here I am, a confirmed old bachelor, and likely to remain so.

PICKERING [*rising and standing over him gravely*]: Come, Higgins! You know what I mean. If I'm to be in this business I shall feel responsible for that girl. I hope it's understood that no advantage is to be taken of her position.

HIGGINS: What! That thing! Sacred, I assure you. [*Rising to explain*] You see, she'll be a pupil; and teaching would be impossible unless pupils were sacred. Ive taught scores of American millionairesses how to speak English: the best looking women in the world. I'm seasoned. They might as well be blocks of wood. *I* might as well be a block of wood. It's—

[MRS. PEARCE *opens the door. She has* ELIZA'S *hat in her hand.* PICKERING *retires to the easy-chair at the hearth and sits down*].

HIGGINS [*eagerly*]: Well, Mrs. Pearce: is it all right?

MRS. PEARCE [*at the door*]: I just wish to trouble you with a word, if I may, Mr. Higgins.

HIGGINS: Yes, certainly. Come in. [*She comes forward*]. Dont burn that, Mrs. Pearce. I'll keep it as a curiosity. [*He takes the hat*].

MRS. PEARCE: Handle it carefully, sir, please. I had to promise her not to burn it; but I had better put it in the oven for a while.

HIGGINS [*putting it down hastily on the piano*]: Oh! thank you. Well, what have you to say to me?

PICKERING: Am I in the way?

MRS. PEARCE: Not in the least, sir. Mr. Higgins: will you please be very particular what you say before the girl?

HIGGINS [*sternly*]: Of course, I'm always particular about what I say. Why do you say this to me?

MRS. PEARCE [*unmoved*]: No, sir: youre not at all particular when youve mislaid anything or when you get a little impatient. Now it doesnt matter before me: I'm used to it. But you really must not swear before the girl.

HIGGINS [*indignantly*]: *I* swear! [*Most emphatically*] I never swear. I detest the habit. What the devil do you mean?

MRS. PEARCE [*stolidly*]: Thats what I mean, sir. You swear a great deal too much. I dont mind your damning and blasting, and what the devil and where the devil and who the devil—

HIGGINS: Mrs. Pearce: this language from your lips! Really!

MRS. PEARCE [*not to be put off*]:—but there is a certain word I must ask you not to use. The girl used it herself when she began to enjoy the bath. It begins with the same letter as bath. She knows no better: she learnt it at her mother's knee. But she must not hear it from your lips.

HIGGINS [*loftily*]: I cannot charge myself with having ever uttered it, Mrs. Pearce. [*She looks at him steadfastly. He adds, hiding an uneasy conscience with a judicial air*] Except perhaps in a moment of extreme and justifiable excitement.

MRS. PEARCE: Only this morning sir, you applied it to your boots, to the butter, and to the brown bread.

HIGGINS: Oh, that! Mere alliteration, Mrs. Pearce, natural to a poet.

MRS. PEARCE: Well, sir, whatever you choose to call it, I beg you not to let the girl hear you repeat it.

HIGGINS: Oh, very well, very well. Is that all?

MRS. PEARCE: No, sir. We shall have to be very particular with this girl as to personal cleanliness.

HIGGINS: Certainly. Quite right. Most important.

MRS. PEARCE: I mean not to be slovenly about her dress or untidy in leaving things about.

HIGGINS [*going to her solemnly*]: Just so. I intended to call your attention to that. [*He passes on to* PICKERING, *who is enjoying the conversation immensely*]. It is these little things that matter, Pickering. Take care of the pence and the pounds will take care of themselves is as true of personal habits as of money. [*He comes to anchor on the hearthrug, with the air of a man in an unassailable position*].

MRS. PEARCE: Yes, sir. Then might I ask you not to come down to breakfast in your dressing-gown, or at any rate not to use it as a napkin to the extent you do, sir. And if you would be so good as not to eat everything off the same plate, and remember not to put the porridge saucepan out of your hand on the clean tablecloth, it would be a better example to the girl. You know you nearly choked yourself with a fishbone in a jam only last week.

HIGGINS [*routed from the hearthrug and drifting back to the piano*]: I may do these things sometimes in absence of mind; but surely I dont do them habitually. [*Angrily*] By the way: my dressing-gown smells most damnably of benzine.

MRS. PEARCE: No doubt it does, Mr. Higgins. But if you will wipe your fingers—

HIGGINS [*yelling*]: Oh very well, very well: I'll wipe them in my hair in future.

MRS. PEARCE: I hope youre not offended, Mr. Higgins.

HIGGINS [*shocked at finding himself thought capable of an unamiable sentiment*]: Not at all, not at all. Youre quite right, Mrs. Pearce: I shall be particularly careful before the girl. Is that all?

MRS. PEARCE: No, sir. Might she use some of those Japanese dresses you brought from abroad? I really cant put her back into her old things.

HIGGINS: Certainly. Anything you like. Is that all?

MRS. PEARCE: Thank you, sir. Thats all. [*She goes out*].

HIGGINS: You know, Pickering, that woman has the most extraordinary ideas about me. Here I am, a shy, diffident sort of man. Ive never been able to feel really grown-up and tremendous, like other chaps. And yet she's firmly persuaded that I'm an arbitrary overbearing bossing kind of person. I cant account for it.

[MRS. PEARCE *returns*].

MRS. PEARCE: If you please, sir, the trouble's beginning already. Theres a dustman downstairs, Alfred Doolittle, wants to see you. He says you have his daughter here.

PICKERING [*rising*]: Phew! I say!

HIGGINS [*promptly*]: Send the blackguard up.

MRS. PEARCE: Oh, very well, sir. [*She goes out*].

PICKERING: He may not be a blackguard, Higgins.

HIGGINS: Nonsense. Of course he's a blackguard.

PICKERING: Whether he is or not, I'm afraid we shall have some trouble with him.

HIGGINS [*confidently*]: Oh no: I think not. If theres any trouble he shall have it with me, not I with him. And we are sure to get something interesting out of him.

PICKERING: About the girl?

HIGGINS: No. I mean his dialect.

PICKERING: Oh!

MRS. PEARCE [*at the door*]: Doolittle, sir. [*She admits* DOOLITTLE *and retires*].

[ALFRED *is an elderly but vigorous dustman, clad in the costume of his profession, including a hat with a back brim covering his neck and shoulders. He has well marked and rather interesting features, and seems equally free from fear and conscience. He has a remarkably expressive voice, the result of a habit of giving vent to his feelings without reserve. His present pose is that of wounded honor and stern resolution*].

DOOLITTLE [*at the door, uncertain which of the two gentlemen is his man*]: Professor Iggins?

HIGGINS: Here. Good morning. Sit down.

DOOLITTLE: Morning, Governor. [*He sits down magisterially*] I come about a very serious matter, Governor.

HIGGINS [*to* PICKERING]: Brought up in Hounslow. Mother Welsh, I should think. [DOOLITTLE *opens his mouth, amazed.* HIGGINS *continues*] What do you want, Doolittle?

DOOLITTLE [*menacingly*]: I want my daughter: thats what I want. See?

HIGGINS: Of course you do. Youre her father, arnt you? You dont suppose anyone else wants her, do you? I'm glad to see you have some spark of family feeling left. She's upstairs. Take her away at once.

DOOLITTLE [*rising, fearfully taken aback*]: What!

HIGGINS: Take her away. Do you suppose I'm going to keep your daughter for you?

DOOLITTLE [*remonstrating*]: Now, now, look here, Governor. Is this reasonable? Is it fairity to take advantage of a man like this? The girl belongs to me. You got her. Where do I come in? [*He sits down again*].

HIGGINS: Your daughter had the audacity to come to my house and ask me to teach her how to speak properly so that she could get a place in a flowershop. This gentleman and my housekeeper have been here all the time. [*Bullying him*] How dare you come here and attempt to blackmail me? You sent her here on purpose.

DOOLITTLE [*protesting*]: No, Governor.

HIGGINS: You must have. How else could you possibly know that she is here?

DOOLITTLE: Don't take a man up like that, Governor.

HIGGINS: The police shall take you up. This is a plant—a plot to extort money by threats. I shall telephone for the police [*he goes resolutely to the telephone and opens the directory*].

DOOLITTLE: Have I asked you for a brass farthing? I leave it to the gentleman here: have I said a word about money?

HIGGINS [*throwing the book aside and marching down on* DOOLITTLE *with a poser*]: What else did you come for?

DOOLITTLE [*sweetly*]: Well, what would a man come for? Be human, Governor.

HIGGINS [*disarmed*]: Alfred: did you put her up to it?

DOOLITTLE: So help me, Governor, I never did. I take my Bible oath I aint seen the girl these two months past.

HIGGINS: Then how did you know she was here?

DOOLITTLE [*"most musical, most melancholy"*]: I'll tell you, Governor, if youll only let me get a word in. I'm willing to tell you. I'm wanting to tell you. I'm waiting to tell you.

HIGGINS: Pickering: this chap has a certain natural gift of rhetoric. Observe the rhythm of his native woodnotes wild. "I'm willing to tell you: I'm wanting to tell you: I'm waiting to tell you." Sentimental rhetoric! thats the Welsh strain in him. It also accounts for his mendacity and dishonesty.

PICKERING: Oh, please, Higgins: I'm west country myself. [*To* DOOLITTLE] How did you know the girl was here if you didnt send her?

DOOLITTLE: It was like this, Governor. The girl took a boy in the taxi to give him a jaunt. Son of her landlady, he is. He hung about on the chance of her giving him another ride home. Well, she sent him back for her luggage when she heard you was willing for her to stop here. I met the boy at the corner of Long Acre and Endell Street.

HIGGINS: Public house. Yes?

DOOLITTLE: The poor man's club, Governor: why shouldnt I?

PICKERING: Do let him tell his story, Higgins.

DOOLITTLE: He told me what was up. And I ask you, what was my feelings and my duty as a father? I says to the boy, "You bring me the luggage," I says—

PICKERING: Why didnt you go for it yourself?

DOOLITTLE: Landlady wouldnt have trusted me with it, Governor. She's that kind of woman: you know. I had to give the boy a penny afore he trusted me with it, the little swine. I brought it to her just to oblige you like, and make myself agreeable. Thats all.

HIGGINS: How much luggage?

DOOLITTLE: Musical instrument, Governor. A few pictures, a trifle of jewelry, and a bird-cage. She said she didnt want no clothes. What was I to think from that, Governor? I ask you as a parent what was I to think?

HIGGINS: So you came to rescue her from worse than death, eh?

DOOLITTLE [*appreciatively: relieved at being so well understood*]: Just so, Governor. Thats right.

PICKERING: But why did you bring her luggage if you intended to take her away?

DOOLITTLE: Have I said a word about taking her away? Have I now?

HIGGINS [*determinedly*]: Youre going to take her away, double quick. [*He crosses to the hearth and rings the bell*].

DOOLITTLE [*rising*]: No, Governor. Dont say that. I'm not the man to stand in my girl's light. Heres a career opening for her, as you might say; and—

[MRS. PEARCE *opens the door and awaits orders*].

HIGGINS: Mrs. Pearce: this is Eliza's father. He has come to take her away. Give her to him. [*He goes back to the piano, with an air of washing his hands of the whole affair*].

DOOLITTLE: No. This is a misunderstanding. Listen here—

MRS. PEARCE: He cant take her away, Mr. Higgins: how can he? You told me to burn her clothes.

DOOLITTLE: Thats right. I cant carry the girl through the streets like a blooming monkey, can I? I put it to you.

HIGGINS: You have put it to me that you want your daughter. Take your daughter. If she has no clothes go out and buy her some.

DOOLITTLE [*desperate*]: Wheres the clothes she come in? Did I burn them or did your missus here?

MRS. PEARCE: I am the housekeeper, if you please. I have sent for some clothes for your girl. When they come you can take her away. You can wait in the kitchen. This way, please.

[DOOLITTLE, *much troubled, accompanies her to the door; then hesitates; finally turns confidentially to* HIGGINS].

DOOLITTLE: Listen here, Governor. You and me is men of the world, aint we?

HIGGINS: Oh! Men of the world, are we? Youd better go, Mrs. Pearce.

MRS. PEARCE: I think so, indeed, sir. [*She goes, with dignity*].

PICKERING: The floor is yours, Mr. Doolittle.

DOOLITTLE [*to* PICKERING]: I thank you, Governor. [*To* HIGGINS, *who takes refuge on the piano bench, a little overwhelmed by the proximity of his visitor; for* DOOLITTLE *has a professional flavour of dust about him*]. Well, the truth is, I've taken a sort of fancy to you, Governor; and if you want the girl, I'm not so set on having her back home again but what I might be open to an arrangement. Regarded in the light of a young woman, she's a fine handsome girl. As a daughter she's not worth her keep; and so I tell you straight. All I ask is my rights as a father; and youre the last man alive to expect me to let her go for nothing; for I can see youre one of the straight sort, Governor. Well, whats a five-pound note to you? and whats Eliza to me? [*He turns to his chair and sits down judicially*].

PICKERING: I think you ought to know, Doolittle, that Mr. Higgins's intentions are entirely honorable.

DOOLITTLE: Course they are, Governor. If I thought they wasn't, I'd ask fifty.

HIGGINS [*revolted*]: Do you mean to say that you would sell your daughter for £50?

DOOLITTLE: Not in a general way I would; but to oblige a gentleman like you I'd do a good deal, I do assure you.

PICKERING: Have you no morals, man?

DOOLITTLE [*unabashed*]: Cant afford them, Governor. Neither could you if you was as poor as me. Not that I mean any harm, you know. But if Liza is going to have a bit out of this, why not me too?

HIGGINS [*troubled*]: I dont know what to do, Pickering. There can be no question that as a matter of morals it's a positive crime to give this chap a farthing. And yet I feel a sort of rough justice in his claim.

DOOLITTLE: Thats it, Governor. Thats all I say. A father's heart, as it were.

PICKERING: Well, I know the feeling; but really it seems hardly right—

DOOLITTLE: Dont say that, Governor. Dont look at it that way. What am I, Governors both? I ask you, what am I? I'm one of the undeserving poor: thats what I am. Think of what that means to a man. It means that he's up agen middle class morality all the time. If theres anything going, and I put in for a bit of it, it's always the same story: "Youre undeserving; so you cant have it." But my needs is as great as the most deserving widow's that ever got money out of six different charities in one week for the death of the same husband. I dont need less than a deserving man: I need more. I dont eat less hearty than him; and I drink a lot more. I want a bit of amusement, cause I'm a thinking man. I want cheerfulness and a song and a band when I feel low. Well, they charge me just the same for everything as they charge the deserving. What is middle class morality? Just an excuse for never giving me anything. Therefore, I ask you, as two gentlemen, not to play that game on me. I'm playing straight with you. I aint pretending to be deserving. I'm undeserving; and I mean to go on being undeserving. I like it; and thats the truth. Will you take advantage of a man's nature to do him out of the price of his own daughter what he's brought up and fed and clothed by the sweat of his brow until she's growed big enough to be interesting to you two gentlemen? Is five pounds unreasonable? I put it to you; and I leave it to you.

HIGGINS [*rising, and going over to* PICKERING]:

Pickering: if we were to take this man in hand for three months, he could choose between a seat in the Cabinet and a popular pulpit in Wales.

PICKERING: What do you say to that, Doolittle?

DOOLITTLE: Not me, Governor, thank you kindly. Ive heard all the preachers and all the prime ministers—for I'm a thinking man and game for politics or religion or social reform same as all the other amusements—and I tell you it's a dog's life any way you look at it. Undeserving poverty is my line. Taking one station in society with another, it's—it's—well, it's the only one that has any ginger in it, to my taste.

HIGGINS: I suppose we must give him a fiver.

PICKERING: He'll make a bad use of it, I'm afraid.

DOOLITTLE: Not me, Governor, so help me I wont. Dont you be afraid that I'll save it and spare it and live idle on it. There wont be a penny of it left by Monday: I'll have to go to work same as if I'd never had it. It wont pauperize me, you bet. Just one good spree for myself and the missus, giving pleasure to ourselves and employment to others, and satisfaction to you to think it's not been throwed away. You couldnt spend it better.

HIGGINS [*taking out his pocket book and coming between* DOOLITTLE *and the piano*]: This is irresistible. Lets give him ten. [*He offers two notes to the dustman*].

DOOLITTLE: No, Governor. She wouldnt have the heart to spend ten; and perhaps I shouldnt neither. Ten pounds is a lot of money: it makes a man feel prudent like; and then goodbye to happiness. You give me what I ask you, Governor: not a penny more, and not a penny less.

PICKERING: Why dont you marry that missus of yours? I rather draw the line at encouraging that sort of immorality.

DOOLITTLE: Tell her so, Governor: tell her so. *I*'m willing. It's me that suffers by it. Ive no hold on her. I got to be agreeable to her. I got to give her presents. I got to buy her clothes something sinful. I'm a slave to that woman, Governor, just because I'm not her lawful husband. And she knows it too. Catch her marrying me! Take my advice, Governor: marry Eliza while she's young and dont know no better. If you dont you'll be sorry for it after. If you do, she'll be sorry for it after; but better her than you, because youre a man, and she's only a woman and dont know how to be happy anyhow.

HIGGINS: Pickering: if we listen to this man another minute, we shall have no convictions left. [*To* DOOLITTLE] Five pounds I think you said.

DOOLITTLE: Thank you kindly, Governor.

HIGGINS: Youre sure you wont take ten?

DOOLITTLE: Not now. Another time, Governor.

HIGGINS [*handing him a five-pound note*]: Here you are.

DOOLITTLE: Thank you, Governor. Good morning. [*He hurries to the door, anxious to get away with his booty. When he opens it he is confronted with a dainty and exquisitely clean young Japanese lady in a simple blue cotton kimono printed cunningly with small white jasmine blossoms.* MRS. PEARCE *is with her. He gets out of her way deferentially and apologizes*]. Beg pardon, miss.

THE JAPANESE LADY: Garn! Dont you know your own daughter?

DOOLITTLE	*exclaiming*	Bly me! it's Eliza!
HIGGINS	*simul-*	Whats that? This!
PICKERING	*taneously*	By Jove!

LIZA: Dont I look silly?

HIGGINS: Silly?

MRS. PEARCE [*at the door*]: Now, Mr. Higgins, please dont say anything to make the girl conceited about herself.

HIGGINS [*conscientiously*]: Oh! Quite right, Mrs. Pearce. [*To* ELIZA] Yes: damned silly.

MRS. PEARCE: Please, sir.

HIGGINS [*correcting himself*]: I mean extremely silly.

LIZA: I should look all right with my hat on. [*She takes up her hat; puts it on; and walks across the room to the fireplace with a fashionable air*].

HIGGINS: A new fashion, by George! And it ought to look horrible!

DOOLITTLE [*with fatherly pride*]: Well, I never thought she'd clean up as good looking as that, Governor. She's a credit to me, aint she?

LIZA: I tell you, it's easy to clean up here. Hot and cold water on tap, just as much as you like, there is. Woolly towels, there is; and a towel horse so hot, it burns your fingers. Soft brushes to scrub yourself, and a wooden bowl of soap smelling like primroses. Now I know why ladies is so clean. Washing's a treat for them. Wish they could see what it is for the like of me!

HIGGINS: I'm glad the bathroom met with your approval.

LIZA: It didnt: not all of it; and I dont care who hears me say it. Mrs. Pearce knows.

HIGGINS: What was wrong, Mrs. Pearce?

MRS. PEARCE [*blandly*]: Oh, nothing, sir. It doesnt matter.

LIZA: I had a good mind to break it. I didnt know which way to look. But I hung a towel over it, I did.

HIGGINS: Over what?

MRS. PEARCE: Over the looking-glass, sir.

HIGGINS: Doolittle: you have brought your daughter up too strictly.

DOOLITTLE: Me! I never brought her up at all, except to give her a lick of a strap now and again. Dont put it on me, Governor. She aint accustomed to it, you see: thats all. But she'll soon pick up your free-and-easy ways.

LIZA: I'm a good girl, I am; and I wont pick up no free-and-easy ways.

HIGGINS: Eliza: if you say again that youre a good girl, your father shall take you home.

LIZA: Not him. You dont know my father. All he come here for was to touch you for some money to get drunk on.

DOOLITTLE: Well, what else would I want money for? To put into the plate in church, I suppose. [*She puts out her tongue at him. He is so incensed by this that* PICKERING *presently finds it necessary to step between them*]. Dont you give me none of your lip; and dont let me hear you giving this gentleman any of it neither, or youll hear from me about it. See?

HIGGINS: Have you any further advice to give her before you go, Doolittle? Your blessing, for instance.

DOOLITTLE: No, Governor: I aint such a mug as to put up my children to all I know myself. Hard enough to hold them in without that. If you want Eliza's mind improved, Governor, you do it yourself with a strap. So long, gentlemen. [*He turns to go*].

HIGGINS [*impressively*]: Stop. Youll come regularly to see your daughter. It's your duty, you know. My brother is a clergyman; and he could help you in your talks with her.

DOOLITTLE [*evasively*]: Certainly, I'll come, Governor. Not just this week, because I have a job at a distance. But later on you may depend on me. Afternoon, gentlemen. Afternoon, maam. [*He touches his hat to* MRS. PEARCE, *who disdains the salutation and goes out. He winks at* HIGGINS, *thinking him probably a fellow-sufferer from* MRS. PEARCE'S *difficult disposition, and follows her*].

LIZA: Dont you believe the old liar. He'd as soon you set a bulldog on him as a clergyman. You wont see him again in a hurry.

HIGGINS: I dont want to, Eliza. Do you?

LIZA: Not me. I don't want never to see him again, I dont. He's a disgrace to me, he is, collecting dust, instead of working at his trade.

PICKERING: What is his trade, Eliza?

LIZA: Talking money out of other people's pockets into his own. His proper trade's a navvy; and he works at it sometimes too—for exercise—and earns good money at it. Aint you going to call me Miss Doolittle any more?

PICKERING: I beg your pardon, Miss Doolittle. It was a slip of the tongue.

LIZA: Oh, I dont mind; only it sounded so genteel. I should just like to take a taxi to the corner of Tottenham Court Road and get out there and tell it to wait for me, just to put the girls in their place a bit. I wouldnt speak to them, you know.

PICKERING: Better wait til we get you something really fashionable.

HIGGINS: Besides, you shouldnt cut your old friends now that you have risen in the world. Thats what we call snobbery.

LIZA: You dont call the like of them my friends now, I should hope. Theyve took it out of me often enough with their ridicule when they had the chance; and now I mean to get a bit of my own back. But if I'm to have fashionable clothes, I'll wait. I should like to have some. Mrs. Pearce says youre going to give me something to wear in bed at night different to what I wear in the daytime; but it do seem a waste of money when you could get something to shew. Besides, I never could fancy changing into cold things on a winter night.

MRS. PEARCE [*coming back*]: Now, Eliza. The new things have come for you to try on.

LIZA: Ah-ow-oo-ooh! [*She rushes out*].

MRS. PEARCE [*following her*]: Oh, dont rush about like that, girl. [*She shuts the door behind her*].

HIGGINS: Pickering: we have taken on a stiff job.

PICKERING [*with conviction*]: Higgins: we have.

* * * * *

There seems to be some curiosity as to what Higgins's lessons to Eliza were like. Well, here is a sample: the first one.

Picture Eliza, in her new clothes, and feeling her inside put out of step by a lunch, dinner, and breakfast of a kind to which it is unaccustomed, seated with Higgins and the Colonel in the study, feeling like a hospital out-patient at a first encounter with the doctors.

Higgins, constitutionally unable to sit still, discomposes her still more by striding restlessly about. But for the reassuring presence and quietude of her friend the Colonel she would run for her life, even back to Drury Lane.

HIGGINS: Say your alphabet.

LIZA: I know my alphabet. Do you think I know nothing? I dont need to be taught like a child.

HIGGINS [*thundering*]: Say your alphabet.

PICKERING: Say it, Miss Doolittle. You will understand presently. Do what he tells you; and let him teach you in his own way.

LIZA: Oh well if you put it like that—Ahyee, bəyee, cəyee, dəyee—

HIGGINS [*with the roar of a wounded lion*]: Stop.

Listen to this, Pickering. This is what we pay for as elementary education. This unfortunate animal has been locked up for nine years in school at our expense to teach her to speak and read the language of Shakespear and Milton. And the result is Ahyee, Bə-yee, Cə-yee, Dəyee. [*To* ELIZA] Say, A, B, C, D.

LIZA [*almost in tears*]: But I'm sayin it. Ahyee, Bəyee, Cəyee—

HIGGINS: Stop. Say a cup of tea.

LIZA: A cappətə-ee.

HIGGINS: Put your tongue forward until it squeezes against the top of your lower teeth. Now say cup.

LIZA: C-c-c—I cant. C-Cup.

PICKERING: Good. Splendid, Miss Doolittle.

HIGGINS: By Jupiter, she's done it the first shot. Pickering: We shall make a duchess of her. [*To* ELIZA] Now do you think you could possibly say tea? Not tə-yee, mind: if you ever say bə-yee cə-yee dəyee again you shall be dragged round the room three times by the hair of your head. [*Fortissimo*] T, T, T, T.

LIZA [*weeping*]: I cant hear no difference cep that it sounds more genteel-like when you say it.

HIGGINS: Well, if you can hear that difference, what the devil are you crying for? Pickering: give her a chocolate.

PICKERING: No, no. Never mind crying a little, Miss Doolittle: you are doing very well; and the lessons wont hurt. I promise you I wont let him drag you round the room by your hair.

HIGGINS: Be off with you to Mrs. Pearce and tell her about it. Think about it. Try to do it by yourself: and keep your tongue well forward in your mouth instead of trying to roll it up and swallow it. Another lesson at half-past four this afternoon. Away with you.

[ELIZA, *still sobbing, rushes from the room*].

And that is the sort of ordeal poor Eliza has to go through for months before we meet her again on her first appearance in London society of the professional class.

ACT III

It is MRS. HIGGINS'S *at-home day. Nobody has yet arrived. Her drawing room, in a flat on Chelsea Embankment, has three windows looking on the river; and the ceiling is not so lofty as it would be in an older house of the same pretension. The windows are open, giving access to a balcony with flowers in pots. If you stand with your face to the windows, you have the fireplace on your left and the door in the right-hand wall close to the corner near the windows.*

MRS. HIGGINS *was brought up on Morris and Burne Jones; and her room, which is very unlike her son's room in Wimpole Street, is not crowded with furniture and little tables and nicknacks. In the middle of the room there is a big ottoman; and this, with the carpet, the Morris wall-papers, and the Morris chintz window curtains and brocade covers of the ottoman and its cushions, supply all the ornament, and are much too handsome to be hidden by odds and ends of useless things. A few good oil-paintings from the exhibitions in the Grosvenor Gallery thirty years ago (the Burne Jones, not the Whistler side of them) are on the walls. The only landscape is a Cecil Lawson on the scale of a Rubens. There is a portrait of* MRS. HIGGINS *as she was when she defied the fashion in her youth in one of the beautiful Rossettian costumes which, when caricatured by people who did not understand, led to the absurdities of popular estheticism in the eighteen-seventies.*

In the corner diagonally opposite the door MRS. HIGGINS, *now over sixty and long past taking the trouble to dress out of the fashion, sits writing at an elegantly simple writing-table with a bell button within reach of her hand. There is a Chippendale chair further back in the room between her and the window nearest her side. At the other side of the room, further forward, is an Elizabethan chair roughly carved in the taste of Inigo Jones. On the same side a piano in a decorated case. The corner between the fireplace and the window is occupied by a divan cushioned in Morris chintz.*

It is between four and five in the afternoon.

The door is opened violently; and HIGGINS *enters with his hat on.*

MRS. HIGGINS [*dismayed*]: Henry! [*Scolding him*] What are you doing here today? It is my at-home day: you promised not to come. [*As he bends to kiss her, she takes his hat off, and presents it to him*].

HIGGINS: Oh bother! [*He throws the hat down on the table*].

MRS. HIGGINS: Go home at once.

HIGGINS [*kissing her*]: I know, mother. I came on purpose.

MRS. HIGGINS: But you mustnt. I'm serious, Henry. You offend all my friends: they stop coming whenever they meet you.

HIGGINS: Nonsense! I know I have no small talk; but people dont mind. [*He sits on the settee*].

MRS. HIGGINS: Oh! dont they? Small talk indeed! What about your large talk? Really, dear, you mustnt stay.

HIGGINS: I must. Ive a job for you. A phonetic job.

MRS. HIGGINS: No use, dear. I'm sorry: but I cant get round your vowels; and though I like to get pretty postcards in your patent shorthand, I always have to read the copies in ordinary writing you so thoughtfully send me.

HIGGINS: Well, this isnt a phonetic job.

MRS. HIGGINS: You said it was.

HIGGINS: Not your part of it. Ive picked up a girl.

MRS. HIGGINS: Does that mean that some girl has picked you up?

HIGGINS: Not at all. I dont mean a love affair.

MRS. HIGGINS: What a pity!

HIGGINS: Why?

MRS. HIGGINS: Well, you never fall in love with anyone under forty-five. When will you discover that there are some rather nice-looking young women about?

HIGGINS: Oh, I cant be bothered with young women. My idea of a lovable woman is somebody as like you as possible. I shall never get into the way of seriously liking young women: some habits lie too deep to be changed. [*Rising abruptly and walking about, jingling his money and his keys in his trouser pockets*] Besides, theyre all idiots.

MRS. HIGGINS: Do you know what you would do if you really loved me, Henry?

HIGGINS: Oh bother! What? Marry, I suppose.

MRS. HIGGINS: No. Stop fidgeting and take your hands out of your pockets. [*With a gesture of despair, he obeys and sits down again*]. Thats a good boy. Now tell me about the girl.

HIGGINS: She's coming to see you.

MRS. HIGGINS: I dont remember asking her.

HIGGINS: You didnt. *I* asked her. If youd known her you wouldnt have asked her.

MRS. HIGGINS: Indeed! Why?

HIGGINS: Well, it's like this. She's a common flower girl. I picked her off the kerbstone.

MRS. HIGGINS: And invited her to my at-home!

HIGGINS [*rising and coming to her to coax her*]: Oh, thatll be all right. Ive taught her to speak properly; and she has strict orders as to her behavior. She's to keep to two subjects: the weather and everybody's health—Fine day and How do you do, you know—and not to let herself go on things in general. That will be safe.

MRS. HIGGINS: Safe! To talk about our health! about our insides! perhaps about our outsides! How could you be so silly, Henry?

HIGGINS [*impatiently*]: Well, she must talk about something. [*He controls himself and sits down again*]. Oh, she'll be all right: dont you fuss. Pickering is in it with me. Ive a sort of bet on that I'll pass her off as a duchess in six months. I started on her some months ago; and she's getting on like a house on fire. I shall win my bet. She has a quick ear; and she's easier to teach than my middle-class pupils because she's had to learn a complete new language. She talks English almost as you talk French.

MRS. HIGGINS: Thats satisfactory, at all events.

HIGGINS: Well, it is and it isnt.

MRS. HIGGINS: What does that mean?

HIGGINS: You see, Ive got her pronunciation all right; but you have to consider not only how a girl pronounces, but what she pronounces; and that's where—

[*They are interrupted by the parlor-maid, announcing guests*].

THE PARLOR-MAID: Mrs. and Miss Eynsford Hill. [*She withdraws*].

HIGGINS: Oh Lord! [*He rises; snatches his hat from the table; and makes for the door; but before he reaches it his mother introduces him*].

[MRS. *and* MISS EYNSFORD HILL *are the mother and daughter who sheltered from the rain in Covent Garden. The mother is well bred, quiet, and has the habitual anxiety of straitened means. The daughter has acquired a gay air of being very much at home in society: the bravado of genteel poverty*].

MRS. EYNSFORD HILL [*to* MRS. HIGGINS]: How do you do? [*They shake hands*].

MISS EYNSFORD HILL: How d'you do? [*She shakes*].

MRS. HIGGINS [*introducing*]: My son Henry.

MRS. EYNSFORD HILL: Your celebrated son! I have so longed to meet you, Professor Higgins.

HIGGINS [*glumly, making no movement in her direction*]: Delighted. [*He backs against the piano and bows brusquely*].

MISS EYNSFORD HILL [*going to him with confident familiarity*]: How do you do?

HIGGINS [*staring at her*]: Ive seen you before somewhere. I havnt the ghost of a notion where; but Ive heard your voice. [*Drearily*] It doesn't matter. Youd better sit down.

MRS. HIGGINS: I'm sorry to say that my celebrated son has no manners. You mustnt mind him.

MISS EYNSFORD HILL [*gaily*]: I don't. [*She sits in the Elizabethan chair*].

MRS. EYNSFORD HILL [*a little bewildered*]: Not at all. [*She sits on the ottoman between her daughter and* MRS. HIGGINS, *who has turned her chair away from the writing-table*].

HIGGINS: Oh, have I been rude? I didnt mean to be.

[*He goes to the central window, through which, with his back to the company, he contemplates the river and the flowers in Battersea Park on the opposite bank as if they were a frozen desert*].

[*The parlor-maid returns, ushering in* PICKERING].

THE PARLOR-MAID: Colonel Pickering. [*She withdraws*].

PICKERING: How do you do, Mrs. Higgins?

MRS. HIGGINS: So glad youve come. Do you know Mrs. Eynsford Hill—Miss Eynsford Hill? [*Exchange of bows. The Colonel brings the Chippendale chair a little forward between* MRS. HILL *and* MRS. HIGGINS, *and sits down*].

PICKERING: Has Henry told you what weve come for?

HIGGINS [*over his shoulder*]: We were interrupted: damn it!

MRS. HIGGINS: Oh Henry, Henry, really!

MRS. EYNSFORD HILL [*half rising*]: Are we in the way?

MRS. HIGGINS [*Rising and making her sit down again*]: No, no. You couldnt have come more fortunately: we want you to meet a friend of ours.

HIGGINS [*turning hopefully*]: Yes, by George! We want two or three people. You'll do as well as anybody else.

[*The parlor-maid returns, ushering* FREDDY].

THE PARLOR-MAID: Mr. Eynsford Hill.

HIGGINS [*almost audibly, past endurance*]: God of Heaven! another of them.

FREDDY [*shaking hands with* MRS. HIGGINS]: Ahdedo?

MRS. HIGGINS: Very good of you to come. [*Introducing*] Colonel Pickering.

FREDDY [*bowing*]: Ahdedo?

MRS. HIGGINS: I dont think you know my son, Professor Higgins.

FREDDY [*going to* HIGGINS]: Ahdedo?

HIGGINS [*looking at him much as if he were a pickpocket*]: I'll take my oath Ive met you before somewhere. Where was it?

FREDDY: I dont think so.

HIGGINS [*resignedly*]: It dont matter, anyhow. Sit down.

[*He shakes* FREDDY'S *hand, and almost slings him on to the ottoman with his face to the window; then comes around to the other side of it*].

HIGGINS: Well, here we are, anyhow! [*He sits down on the ottoman next* MRS. EYNSFORD HILL, *on her left*] And now, what the devil are we going to talk about until Eliza comes?

MRS. HIGGINS: Henry: you are the life and soul of the Royal Society's soirées; but really youre rather trying on more commonplace occasions.

HIGGINS: Am I? Very sorry. [*Beaming suddenly*] I suppose I am, you know. [*Uproariously*] Ha, ha!

MISS EYNSFORD HILL [*who considers* HIGGINS *quite eligible matrimonially*]: I sympathize. *I* havnt any small talk. If people would only be frank and say what they really think!

HIGGINS [*relapsing into gloom*]: Lord forbid!

MRS. EYNSFORD HILL [*taking up her daughter's cue*]: But why?

HIGGINS: What they think they ought to think is bad enough, Lord knows; but what they really think would break up the whole show. Do you suppose it would be really agreeable if I were to come out now with what *I* really think?

MISS EYNSFORD HILL [*gaily*]: Is it so very cynical?

HIGGINS: Cynical! Who the dickens said it was cynical? I mean it wouldnt be decent.

MRS. EYNSFORD HILL [*seriously*]: Oh! I'm sure you dont mean that, Mr. Higgins.

HIGGINS: You see, we're all savages, more or less. We're supposed to be civilized and cultured—to know all about poetry and philosophy and art and science, and so on; but how many of us know even the meanings of these names? [*To* MISS HILL] What do you know of poetry? [*To* MRS. HILL] What do you know of science? [*Indicating* FREDDY] What does he know of art or science or anything else? What the devil do you imagine I know of philosophy?

MRS. HIGGINS [*warningly*]: Or of manners, Henry?

THE PARLOR-MAID [*opening the door*]: Miss Doolittle. [*She withdraws*].

HIGGINS [*rising hastily and running to* MRS. HIGGINS]: Here she is, mother. [*He stands on tiptoe and makes signs over his mother's head to* ELIZA *to indicate to her which lady is her hostess*].

[ELIZA, *who is exquisitely dressed, produces an impression of such remarkable distinction and beauty as she enters that they all rise, quite fluttered. Guided by* HIGGINS'S *signals, she comes to* MRS. HIGGINS *with studied grace*].

LIZA [*speaking with pedantic correctness of pronunciation and great beauty of tone*]: How do you do, Mrs. Higgins? [*She gasps slightly in making sure of the H in* HIGGINS, *but is quite successful*]. Mr. Higgins told me I might come.

MRS. HIGGINS [*cordially*]: Quite right: I'm very glad indeed to see you.

PICKERING: How do you do, Miss Doolittle?

LIZA [*shaking hands with him*]: Colonel Pickering, is it not?

MRS. EYNSFORD HILL: I feel sure we have met before, Miss Doolittle. I remember your eyes.

LIZA: How do you do? [*She sits down on the ottoman gracefully in the place just left vacant by* HIGGINS].

MRS. EYNSFORD HILL [*introducing*]: My daughter Clara.

LIZA: How do you do?

CLARA [*impulsively*]: How do you do? [*She sits down on the ottoman beside* ELIZA, *devouring her with her eyes*].

FREDDY [*coming to their side of the ottoman*]: Ive certainly had the pleasure.

MRS. EYNSFORD HILL [*introducing*]: My son Freddy.

LIZA: How do you do?

[FREDDY *bows and sits down in the Elizabethan chair, infatuated*].

HIGGINS [*suddenly*]: By George, yes: it all comes back to me! [*They stare at him*]. Covent Garden! [*Lamentably*] What a damned thing!

MRS. HIGGINS: Henry, please! [*He is about to sit on the edge of the table*] Dont sit on my writing-table: youll break it.

HIGGINS [*sulkily*]: Sorry.

[*He goes to the divan, stumbling into the fender and over the fire-irons on his way; extricating himself with muttered imprecations; and finishing his disastrous journey by throwing himself so impatiently on the divan that he almost breaks it.* MRS. HIGGINS *looks at him, but controls herself and says nothing*].

[*A long and painful pause ensues*].

MRS. HIGGINS [*at last, conversationally*]: Will it rain, do you think?

LIZA: The shallow depression in the west of these islands is likely to move slowly in an easterly direction. There are no indications of any great change in the barometrical situation.

FREDDY: Ha! ha! how awfully funny!

LIZA: What is wrong with that, young man? I bet I got it right.

FREDDY: Killing!

MRS. EYNSFORD HILL: I'm sure I hope it wont turn cold. Theres so much influenza about. It runs right through our whole family regularly every spring.

LIZA [*darkly*]: My aunt died of influenza: so they said.

MRS. EYNSFORD HILL [*clicks her tongue sympathetically*]: !!!

LIZA [*in the same tragic tone*]: But it's my belief they done the old woman in.

MRS. HIGGINS [*puzzled*]: Done her in?

LIZA: Y-e-e-e-es, Lord love you! Why should she die of influenza? She come through diphtheria right enough the year before. I saw her with my own eyes. Fairly blue with it, she was. They all thought she was dead; but my father he kept ladling gin down her throat til she came to so sudden that she bit the bowl off the spoon.

MRS. EYNSFORD HILL [*startled*]: Dear me!

LIZA [*piling up the indictment*]: What call would a woman with that strength in her have to die of influenza? What become of her new straw hat that should have come to me? Somebody pinched it; and what I say is, them as pinched it done her in.

MRS. EYNSFORD HILL: What does doing her in mean?

HIGGINS [*hastily*]: Oh, thats the new small talk. To do a person in means to kill them.

MRS. EYNSFORD HILL [*to* ELIZA, *horrified*]: You surely dont believe that your aunt was killed?

LIZA: Do I not! Them she lived with would have killed her for a hat-pin, let alone a hat.

MRS. EYNSFORD HILL: But it cant have been right for your father to pour spirits down her throat like that. It might have killed her.

LIZA: Not her. Gin was mother's milk to her. Besides, he'd poured so much down his own throat that he knew the good of it.

MRS. EYNSFORD HILL: Do you mean that he drank?

LIZA: Drank! My word! Something chronic.

MRS. EYNSFORD HILL: How dreadful for you!

LIZA: Not a bit. It never did him no harm what I could see. But then he did not keep it up regular. [*Cheerfully*] On the burst, as you might say, from time to time. And always more agreeable when he had a drop in. When he was out of work, my mother used to give him fourpence and tell him to go out and not come back until he'd drunk himself cheerful and loving-like. Theres lots of women has to make their husbands drunk to make them fit to live with. [*Now quite at her ease*] You see it's like this. If a man has a bit of conscience, it always takes him when he's sober; and then it makes him low-spirited. A drop of booze just takes that off and makes him happy. [*To* FREDDY, *who is in convulsions of suppressed laughter*] Here! What are you sniggering at?

FREDDY: The new small talk. You do it so awfully well.

LIZA: If I was doing it proper, what was you laughing at? [*To* HIGGINS] Have I said anything I oughtnt?

MRS. HIGGINS [*interposing*]: Not at all, Miss Doolittle.

LIZA: Well, thats a mercy, anyhow. [*Expansively*] What I always say is—

HIGGINS [*rising and looking at his watch*]: Ahem!

LIZA [*looking round at him; taking the hint; and ris-*

ing]: Well: I must go. [*They all rise.* FREDDY *goes to the door*]. So pleased to have met you. Goodbye. [*She shakes hands with* MRS. HIGGINS].

MRS. HIGGINS: Goodbye.

LIZA: Goodbye, Colonel Pickering.

PICKERING: Goodbye, Miss Doolittle. [*They shake hands*].

LIZA [*nodding to the others*]: Goodbye, all.

FREDDY [*opening the door for her*]: Are you walking across the Park, Miss Doolittle? If so—

LIZA [*with perfectly elegant diction*]: Walk! Not bloody likely. [*Sensation*]. I am going in a taxi. [*She goes out*].

[PICKERING *gasps and sits down.* FREDDY *goes out on the balcony to catch another glimpse of* ELIZA].

MRS. EYNSFORD HILL [*suffering from shock*]: Well, I really cant get used to the new ways.

CLARA [*throwing herself discontentedly into the Elizabethan chair*]: Oh, it's all right, mamma, quite right. People will think we never go anywhere or see anybody if you are so old-fashioned.

MRS. EYNSFORD HILL: I daresay I am very old-fashioned; but I do hope you wont begin using that expression, Clara. I have got accustomed to hear you talking about men as rotters, and calling everything filthy and beastly; though I do think it horrible and unladylike. But this last is really too much. Dont you think so, Colonel Pickering?

PICKERING: Dont ask me. Ive been away in India for several years; and manners have changed so much that I sometimes dont know whether I'm at a respectable dinnertable or in a ship's forecastle.

CLARA: It's all a matter of habit. Theres no right or wrong in it. Nobody means anything by it. And it's so quaint, and gives such a smart emphasis to things that are not in themselves very witty. I find the new small talk delightful and quite innocent.

MRS. EYNSFORD HILL [*rising*]: Well, after that, I think it's time for us to go.

[PICKERING *and* HIGGINS *rise*].

CLARA [*rising*]: Oh yes: we have three at-homes to go to still. Goodbye, Mrs. Higgins. Goodbye, Colonel Pickering. Goodbye, Professor Higgins.

HIGGINS [*coming grimly at her from the divan, and accompanying her to the door*]: Goodbye. Be sure you try on that small talk at the three at-homes. Dont be nervous about it. Pitch it in strong.

CLARA [*all smiles*]: I will. Goodbye. Such nonsense, all this early Victorian prudery!

HIGGINS [*tempting her*]: Such damned nonsense!

CLARA: Such bloody nonsense!

MRS. EYNSFORD HILL [*convulsively*]: Clara!

CLARA: Ha! ha! [*She goes out radiant, conscious of being thoroughly up to date, and is heard descending the stairs in a stream of silvery laughter*].

FREDDY [*to the heavens at large*]: Well, I ask you— [*He gives it up, and comes to* MRS. HIGGINS]. Goodbye.

MRS. HIGGINS [*shaking hands*]: Goodbye. Would you like to meet Miss Doolittle again?

FREDDY [*eagerly*]: Yes, I should, most awfully.

MRS. HIGGINS: Well, you know my days.

FREDDY: Yes, Thanks awfully. Goodbye. [*He goes out*].

MRS. EYNSFORD HILL: Goodbye, Mr. Higgins.

HIGGINS: Goodbye. Goodbye.

MRS. EYNSFORD HILL [*to* PICKERING]: It's no use. I shall never be able to bring myself to use that word.

PICKERING: Dont. It's not compulsory, you know. Youll get on quite well without it.

MRS. EYNSFORD HILL: Only, Clara is so down on me if I am not positively reeking with the latest slang. Goodbye.

PICKERING: Goodbye [*They shake hands*].

MRS. EYNSFORD HILL [*to* MRS. HIGGINS]: You mustnt mind Clara. [PICKERING, *catching from her lowered tone that this is not meant for him to hear, discreetly joins* HIGGINS *at the window*]. We're so poor! and she gets so few parties, poor child! She doesnt quite know. [MRS. HIGGINS, *seeing that her eyes are moist, takes her hand sympathetically and goes with her to the door*]. But the boy is nice. Dont you think so?

MRS. HIGGINS: Oh, quite nice. I shall always be delighted to see him.

MRS. EYNSFORD HILL: Thank you, dear. Goodbye. [*She goes out*].

HIGGINS [*eagerly*]: Well? Is Eliza presentable [*he swoops on his mother and drags her to the ottoman, where she sits down in* ELIZA'S *place with her son on her left*]?

[PICKERING *returns to his chair on her right*].

MRS. HIGGINS: You silly boy, of course she's not presentable. She's a triumph of your art and of her dressmaker's; but if you suppose for a moment that she doesn't give herself away in every sentence she utters, you must be perfectly cracked about her.

PICKERING: But dont you think something might be done? I mean something to eliminate the sanguinary element from her conversation.

MRS. HIGGINS: Not as long as she is in Henry's hands.

HIGGINS [*aggrieved*]: Do you mean that my language is improper?

MRS. HIGGINS: No, dearest: it would be quite proper—say on a canal barge; but it would not be proper for her at a garden party.

HIGGINS [*deeply injured*]: Well I must say—

PICKERING [*interrupting him*]: Come, Higgins: you must learn to know yourself. I havent heard such language as yours since we used to review the volunteers in Hyde Park twenty years ago.

HIGGINS [*sulkily*]: Oh, well, if you say so, I suppose I dont always talk like a bishop.

MRS. HIGGINS [*quieting* HENRY *with a touch*]: Colonel Pickering: will you tell me what is the exact state of things in Wimpole Street?

PICKERING [*cheerfully: as if this completely changed the subject*]: Well, I have come to live there with Henry. We work together at my Indian Dialects; and we think it more convenient—

MRS. HIGGINS: Quite so. I know all about that: it's an excellent arrangement. But where does this girl live?

HIGGINS: With us, of course. Where should she live?

MRS. HIGGINS: But on what terms? Is she a servant? If not, what is she?

PICKERING [*slowly*]: I think I know what you mean, Mrs. Higgins.

HIGGINS: Well, dash me if *I* do! Ive had to work at the girl every day for months to get her to her present pitch. Besides, she's useful. She knows where my things are, and remembers my appointments and so forth.

MRS. HIGGINS: How does your housekeeper get on with her?

HIGGINS: Mrs. Pearce? Oh, she's jolly glad to get so much taken off her hands; for before Eliza came, she used to have to find things and remind me of my appointments. But she's got some silly bee in her bonnet about Eliza. She keeps saying "You dont think, sir": doesnt she, Pick?

PICKERING: Yes: thats the formula. "You dont think, sir." Thats the end of every conversation about Eliza.

HIGGINS: As if I ever stop thinking about the girl and her confounded vowels and consonants. I'm worn out, thinking about her, and watching her lips and her teeth and her tongue, not to mention her soul, which is the quaintest of the lot.

MRS. HIGGINS: You certainly are a pretty pair of babies, playing with your live doll.

HIGGINS: Playing! The hardest job I ever tackled: make no mistake about that, mother. But you have no idea how frightfully interesting it is to take a human being and change her into a quite different human being by creating a new speech for her. It's filling up the deepest gulf that separates class from class and soul from soul.

PICKERING [*drawing his chair closer to* MRS. HIGGINS *and bending over to her eagerly*]: Yes: it's enormously interesting. I assure you, Mrs. Higgins, we take Eliza very seriously. Every week—every day almost—there is some new change. [*Closer again*] We keep records of every stage—dozens of gramophone disks and photographs—

HIGGINS [*assailing her at the other ear*]: Yes, by George: it's the most absorbing experiment I ever tackled. She regularly fills our lives up: doesnt she, Pick?

PICKERING: We're always talking Eliza.

HIGGINS: Teaching Eliza.

PICKERING: Dressing Eliza.

MRS. HIGGINS: What!

HIGGINS: Inventing new Elizas.

HIGGINS:	[*speaking together*]	You know, she has the most extraordinary quickness of ear:
PICKERING:		I assure you, my dear Mrs. Higgins, that girl
HIGGINS:		just like a parrot. Ive tried her with every
PICKERING:		is a genius. She can play the piano quite beautifully.
HIGGINS:		possible sort of sound that a human being can make—
PICKERING:		We have taken her to classical concerts and to music
HIGGINS:		Continental dialects, African dialects, Hottentot
PICKERING:		halls; and it's all the same to her: she plays everything
HIGGINS:		clicks, things it took me years to get hold of; and
PICKERING:		she hears right off when she comes home, whether it's
HIGGINS:		she picks them up like a shot, right away, as if she had
PICKERING:		Beethoven and Brahms or Lehar and Lionel Monckton;
HIGGINS:		been at it all her life.
PICKERING:		though six months ago, she'd never as much as touched a piano—

MRS. HIGGINS [*putting her fingers in her ears, as they are by this time shouting one another down with an intolerable noise*]: Sh-sh-sh—sh! [*They stop*].

PICKERING: I beg your pardon. [*He draws his chair back apologetically*].

HIGGINS: Sorry. When Pickering starts shouting nobody can get a word in edgeways.

MRS. HIGGINS: Be quiet, Henry. Colonel Pickering: dont you realize that when Eliza walked in Wimpole Street, something walked in with her?

PICKERING: Her father did. But Henry soon got rid of him.

MRS. HIGGINS: It would have been more to the point if her mother had. But as her mother didn't something else did.

PICKERING: But what?

MRS. HIGGINS [*unconsciously dating herself by the word*]: A problem.

PICKERING: Oh, I see. The problem of how to pass her off as a lady.

HIGGINS: I'll solve that problem. Ive half solved it already.

MRS. HIGGINS: No, you two infinitely stupid male creatures: the problem of what is to be done with her afterwards.

HIGGINS: I dont see anything in that. She can go her own way, with all the advantages I have given her.

MRS. HIGGINS: The advantages of that poor woman who was here just now! The manners and habits that disqualify a fine lady from earning her own living without giving her a fine lady's income! Is that what you mean?

PICKERING [*indulgently, being rather bored*]: Oh, that will be all right, Mrs. Higgins. [*He rises to go*].

HIGGINS [*rising also*]: We'll find her some light employment.

PICKERING: She's happy enough. Dont you worry about her. Goodbye. [*He shakes hands as if he were consoling a frightened child, and makes for the door*].

HIGGINS: Anyhow, theres no good bothering now. The thing's done. Goodbye, mother. [*He kisses her, and follows* PICKERING].

PICKERING [*turning for a final consolation*]: There are plenty of openings. We'll do whats right. Goodbye.

HIGGINS [*to* PICKERING *as they go out together*]: Lets take her to the Shakespear exhibition at Earls Court.

PICKERING: Yes: lets. Her remarks will be delicious.

HIGGINS: She'll mimic all the people for us when we get home.

PICKERING: Ripping. [*Both are heard laughing as they go downstairs*].

MRS. HIGGINS [*rises with an impatient bounce, and returns to her work at the writing-table. She sweeps a litter of disarranged papers out of the way; snatches a sheet of paper from her stationery case; and tries resolutely to write. At the third time she gives it up; flings down her pen; grips the table angrily and exclaims*]: Oh, men! men!! men!!!

* * * * *

Clearly Eliza will not pass as a duchess yet; and Higgins's bet remains unwon. But the six months are not yet exhausted; and just in time Eliza does actually pass as a princess. For a glimpse of how she did it imagine an Embassy in London one summer evening after dark. The hall door has an awning and a carpet across the sidewalk to the kerb, because a grand reception is in progress. A small crowd is lined up to see the guests arrive.

A Rolls-Royce car drives up. Pickering in evening dress, with medals and orders, alights, and hands out Eliza, in opera cloak, evening dress, diamonds, fan, flowers and all accessories. Higgins follows. The car drives off; and the three go up the steps and into the house, the door opening for them as they approach.

Inside the house they find themselves in a spacious hall from which the grand staircase rises. On the left are the arrangements for the gentlemen's cloaks. The male guests are depositing their hats and wraps there.

On the right is a door leading to the ladies' cloakroom. Ladies are going in cloaked and coming out in splendor. Pickering whispers to Eliza and points out the ladies' room. She goes into it. Higgins and Pickering take off their overcoats and take tickets for them from the attendant.

One of the guests, occupied in the same way, has his back turned. Having taken his ticket, he turns round and reveals himself as an important looking young man with an astonishingly hairy face. He has an enormous moustache, flowing out into luxuriant whiskers. Waves of hair cluster on his brow. His hair is cropped closely at the back, and glows with oil. Otherwise he is very smart. He wears several worthless orders. He is evidently a foreigner, guessable as a whiskered Pandour from Hungary; but in spite of the ferocity of his moustache he is amiable and genially voluble.

Recognizing Higgins, he flings his arms wide apart and approaches him enthusiastically.

WHISKERS: Maestro, maestro [*he embraces* HIGGINS *and kisses him on both cheeks*]. You remember me?

HIGGINS: No I dont. Who the devil are you?

WHISKERS: I am your pupil: your first pupil, your best and greatest pupil. I am little Nepommuck, the marvellous boy. I have made your name famous throughout Europe. You teach me phonetic. You cannot forget ME.

HIGGINS: Why dont you shave?

NEPOMMUCK: I have not your imposing appearance, your chin, your brow. Nobody notice me when I shave. Now I am famous: they call me Hairy Faced Dick.

HIGGINS: And what are you doing here among all these swells?

NEPOMMUCK: I am interpreter. I speak 32 languages. I am indispensable at these international parties. You are great cockney specialist: you place a man anywhere in London the moment he open his mouth. I place any man in Europe.

[*A footman hurries down the grand staircase and comes to* NEPOMMUCK].

FOOTMAN: You are wanted upstairs. Her Excellency cannot understand the Greek gentleman.

NEPOMMUCK: Thank you, yes, immediately.

[*The footman goes and is lost in the crowd*].

NEPOMMUCK [*to* HIGGINS]: This Greek diplomatist pretends he cannot speak nor understand English. He cannot deceive me. He is the son of a Clerkenwell watchmaker. He speaks English so villainously that he dare not utter a word of it without betraying his origin. I help him to pretend; but I make him pay through the nose. I make them all pay. Ha ha! [*He hurries upstairs*].

PICKERING: Is this fellow really an expert? Can he find out Eliza and blackmail her?

HIGGINS: We shall see. If he finds her out I lost my bet.

[ELIZA *comes from the cloakroom and joins them*].

PICKERING: Well, Eliza, now for it. Are you ready?

LIZA: Are you nervous, Colonel?

PICKERING: Frightfully. I feel exactly as I felt before my first battle. It's the first time that frightens.

LIZA: It is not the first time for me, Colonel. I have done this fifty times—hundreds of times—in my little piggery in Angel Court in my day-dreams. I am in a dream now. Promise me not to let Professor Higgins wake me; for if he does I shall forget everything and talk as I used to in Drury Lane.

PICKERING: Not a word, Higgins. [*To* ELIZA] Now, ready?

LIZA: Ready.

PICKERING: Go.

[*They mount the stairs,* HIGGINS *last.* PICKERING *whispers to the footman on the first landing*].

FIRST LANDING FOOTMAN: Miss Doolittle, Colonel Pickering, Professor Higgins.

SECOND LANDING FOOTMAN: Miss Doolittle, Colonel Pickering, Professor Higgins.

[*At the top of the staircase the Ambassador and his wife, with* NEPOMMUCK *at her elbow, are receiving*].

HOSTESS [*taking* ELIZA'S *hand*]: How d'ye do?

HOST [*same play*]: How d'ye do? How d'ye do, Pickering?

LIZA [*with a beautiful gravity that awes her hostess*]: How do you do? [*She passes on to the drawingroom*].

HOSTESS: Is that your adopted daughter, Colonel Pickering? She will make a sensation.

PICKERING: Most kind of you to invite her for me. [*He passes on*].

HOSTESS [*to* NAPOMMUCK]: Find out all about her.

NEPOMMUCK [*bowing*]: Excellency—[*he goes into the crowd*].

HOST: How d'ye do, Higgins? You have a rival here tonight. He introduced himself as your pupil. Is he any good?

HIGGINS: He can learn a language in a fortnight—knows dozens of them. A sure mark of a fool. As a phonetician, no good whatever.

HOSTESS: How d'ye do, Professor?

HIGGINS: How do you do? Fearful bore for you this sort of thing. Forgive my part in it. [*He passes on*].

In the drawingroom and its suite of salons the reception is in full swing. Eliza passes through. She is so intent on her ordeal that she walks like a somnambulist in a desert instead of a débutante in a fashionable crowd. They stop talking to look at her, admiring her dress, her jewels, and her strangely attractive self. Some of the younger ones at the back stand on their chairs to see.

The Host and Hostess come in from the staircase and mingle with their guests. Higgins, gloomy and contemptuous of the whole business, comes into the group where they are chatting.

HOSTESS: Ah, here is Professor Higgins: he will tell us. Tell us all about the wonderful young lady, Professor.

HIGGINS [*almost morosely*]: What wonderful young lady?

HOSTESS: You know very well. They tell me there has been nothing like her in London since people stood on their chairs to look at Mrs. Langtry.

[NEPOMMUCK *joins the group, full of news*].

HOSTESS: Ah, here you are at last, Nepommuck. Have you found out all about the Doolittle lady?

NEPOMMUCK: I have found out all about her. She is a fraud.

HOSTESS: A fraud! Oh no.

NEPOMMUCK: YES, yes. She cannot deceive me. Her name cannot be Doolittle.

HIGGINS: Why?

NEPOMMUCK: Because Doolittle is an English name. And she is not English.

HOSTESS: Oh, nonsense! She speaks English perfectly.

NEPOMMUCK: Too perfectly. Can you shew me any English woman who speaks English as it should be spoken? Only foreigners who have been taught to speak it speak it well.

HOSTESS: Certainly she terrified me by the way she said How d'ye do. I had a schoolmistress who talked like that; and I was mortally afraid of her. But if she is not English what is she?

NEPOMMUCK: Hungarian.

ALL THE REST: Hungarian!

NEPOMMUCK: Hungarian. And of royal blood. I am Hungarian. My blood is royal.

HIGGINS: Did you speak to her in Hungarian?

NEPOMMUCK: I did. She was very clever. She said "Please speak to me in English: I do not understand French." French! She pretend not to know the difference between Hungarian and French. Impossible: she knows both.

HIGGINS: And the blood royal? How did you find that out?

NEPOMMUCK: Instinct, maestro, instinct. Only the Magyar races can produce that air of the divine right, those resolute eyes. She is a princess.

HOST: What do you say, Professor?

HIGGINS: I say an ordinary London girl out of the gutter and taught to speak by an expert. I place her in Drury Lane.

NEPOMMUCK: Ha ha ha! Oh, maestro, maestro, you are mad on the subject of cockney dialects. The London gutter is the whole world for you.

HIGGINS [*to the Hostess*]: What does your Excellency say?

HOSTESS: Oh, of course I agree with Nepommuck. She must be a princess at least.

HOST: Not necessarily legitimate, of course. Morganatic perhaps. But that is undoubtedly her class.

HIGGINS: I stick to my opinion.

HOSTESS: Oh, you are incorrigible.

[*The group breaks up, leaving* HIGGINS *isolated.* PICKERING *joins him*].

PICKERING: Where is Eliza? We must keep an eye on her.

[ELIZA *joins them*].

LIZA: I dont think I can bear much more. The people all stare so at me. An old lady has just told me that I speak exactly like Queen Victoria. I am sorry if I have lost your bet. I have done my best; but nothing can make me the same as these people.

PICKERING: You have not lost it, my dear. You have won it ten times over.

HIGGINS: Let us get out of this. I have had enough of chattering to these fools.

PICKERING: Eliza is tired; and I am hungry. Let us clear out and have supper somewhere.

ACT IV

The Wimpole Street laboratory. Midnight. Nobody in the room. The clock on the mantelpiece strikes twelve. The fire is not alight: it is a summer night. Presently HIGGINS *and* PICKERING *are heard on the stairs.*

HIGGINS [*calling down to* PICKERING]: I say, Pick: lock up, will you? I shant be going out again.

PICKERING: Right. Can Mrs. Pearce go to bed? We dont want anything more, do we?

HIGGINS: Lord, no!

[ELIZA *opens the door and is seen on the lighted landing in all the finery in which she has just won* HIGGINS'S *bet for him. She comes to the hearth, and switches on the electric lights there. She is tired: her pallor contrasts strongly with her dark eyes and hair; and her expression is almost tragic. She takes off her cloak; puts her fan and gloves on the piano; and sits down on the bench, brooding and silent.* HIGGINS, *in evening dress, with overcoat and hat, comes in, carrying a smoking jacket which he has picked up downstairs. He takes off the hat and overcoat; throws them carelessly on the newspaper stand; disposes of his coat in the same way; puts on the smoking jacket; and throws himself wearily into the easy-chair at the hearth.* PICKERING, *similarly attired, comes in. He also takes off his hat and overcoat, and is about to throw them on* HIGGINS'S *when he hesitates*].

PICKERING: I say: Mrs. Pearce will row if we leave these things lying about in the drawing room.

HIGGINS: Oh, chuck them over the bannisters into the hall. She'll find them there in the morning and put them away all right. She'll think we were drunk.

PICKERING: We are, slightly. Are there any letters?

HIGGINS: I didnt look. [PICKERING *takes the overcoats and hats and goes downstairs.* HIGGINS *begins half singing half yawning an air from La Fanciulla del Golden West. Suddenly he stops and exclaims*] I wonder where the devil my slippers are!

[ELIZA *looks at him darkly; then rises suddenly and leaves the room.*

HIGGINS *yawns again, and resumes his song.*

PICKERING *returns, with the contents of the letter-box in his hand*].

PICKERING: Only circulars, and this coroneted billet-doux for you. [*He throws the circulars into the fender, and posts himself on the hearth-rug, with his back to the grate*].

HIGGINS [*glancing at the billet-doux*]: Money-lender. [*He throws the letter after the circulars*].

[ELIZA *returns with a pair of large down-at-heel slippers. She places them on the carpet before* HIGGINS, *and sits as before without a word*].

HIGGINS [*yawning again*]: Oh Lord! What an evening! What a crew! What a silly tomfoolery! [*He raises his shoe to unlace it, and catches sight of the slippers. He stops unlacing and looks at them as if they had appeared there of their own accord*]. Oh! they're there, are they?

PICKERING [*stretching himself*]: Well, I feel a bit tired. It's been a long day. The garden party, a dinner party, and the reception! Rather too much of a good thing. But youve won your bet, Higgins. Eliza did the trick, and something to spare, eh?

HIGGINS [*fervently*]: Thank God it's over!

[ELIZA *flinches violently; but they take no notice of her; and she recovers herself and sits stonily as before*].

PICKERING: Were you nervous at the garden party? *I* was. Eliza didnt seem a bit nervous.

HIGGINS: Oh, she wasnt nervous. I knew she'd be all right. No: it's the strain of putting the job through all these months that has told on me. It was interesting enough at first, while we were at the phonetics; but after that I got deadly sick of it. If I hadnt backed myself to do it I should have chucked the whole thing up two months ago. It was a silly notion: the whole thing has been a bore.

PICKERING: Oh come! the garden party was frightfully exciting. My heart began beating like anything.

HIGGINS: Yes, for the first three minutes. But when I saw we were going to win hands down, I felt like a bear in a cage, hanging about doing nothing. The dinner was worse: sitting gorging there for over an hour, with nobody but a damned fool of a fashionable woman to talk to! I tell you, Pickering, never again for me. No more artificial duchesses. The whole thing has been simple purgatory.

PICKERING: Youve never been broken in properly to the social routine. [*Strolling over to the piano*] I rather enjoy dipping into it occasionally myself: it makes me feel young again. Anyhow, it was a great success: an immense success. I was quite frightened once or twice because Eliza was doing it so well. You see, lots of the real people cant do it at all: theyre such fools that they think style comes by nature to people in their position; and so they never learn. Theres always something professional about doing a thing superlatively well.

HIGGINS: Yes: thats what drives me mad: the silly people dont know their own silly business. [*Rising*] However, it's over and done with; and now I can go to bed at last without dreading tomorrow.

[ELIZA'S *beauty becomes murderous*].

PICKERING: I think I shall turn in too. Still, it's been a great occasion: a triumph for you. Goodnight. [*He goes*].

HIGGINS [*following him*]: Goodnight. [*Over his shoulder, at the door*] Put out the lights, Eliza; and tell Mrs. Pearce not to make coffee for me in the morning: I'll take tea. [*He goes out*].

[ELIZA *tries to control herself and feel indifferent as she rises and walks across to the hearth to switch off the lights. By the time she gets there she is on the point of screaming. She sits down in* HIGGINS'S *chair and holds on hard to the arms. Finally she gives away and flings herself furiously on the floor, raging*].

HIGGINS [*in despairing wrath outside*]: What the devil have I done with my slippers? [*He appears at the door*].

LIZA [*snatching up the slippers, and hurling them at him one after the other with all her force*]: There are your slippers. And there. Take your slippers; and may you never have a day's luck with them!

HIGGINS [*astounded*]: What on earth—! [*He comes to her*]. Whats the matter? Get up. [*He pulls her up*]. Anything wrong?

LIZA [*breathless*]: Nothing wrong—with you. Ive won your bet for you, havnt I? Thats enough for you. *I* dont matter, I suppose.

HIGGINS: You won my bet! You! Presumptuous insect! *I* won it. What did you throw those slippers at me for?

LIZA: Because I wanted to smash your face. I'd like to kill you, you selfish brute. Why didnt you leave me where you picked me out of—in the gutter? You thank

God it's all over, and that now you can throw me back again there, do you? [*She crisps her fingers frantically*].

HIGGINS [*looking at her in cool wonder*]: The creature is nervous, after all.

LIZA [*gives a suffocated scream of fury, and instinctively darts her nails at his face*]:!!

HIGGINS [*catching her wrists*]: Ah! would you? Claws in, you cat. How dare you shew your temper to me? Sit down and be quiet. [*He throws her roughly into the easy-chair*].

LIZA [*crushed by superior strength and weight*]: Whats to become of me? Whats to become of me?

HIGGINS: How the devil do I know whats to become of you? What does it matter what becomes of you?

LIZA: You dont care. I know you dont care. You wouldnt care if I was dead. I'm nothing to you—not so much as them slippers.

HIGGINS [*thundering*]: Those slippers.

LIZA [*with better submission*]: Those slippers. I didnt think it made any difference now.

[*A pause.* ELIZA *hopeless and crushed.* HIGGINS *a little uneasy.*]

HIGGINS [*in his loftiest manner*]: Why have you begun going on like this? May I ask whether you complain of your treatment here?

LIZA: No.

HIGGINS: Has anybody behaved badly to you? Colonel Pickering? Mrs. Pearce? Any of the servants?

LISA: No.

HIGGINS I presume you dont pretend that *I* have treated you badly?

LISA: No.

HIGGINS: I am glad to hear it. [*He moderates his tone*]. Perhaps youre tired after the strain of the day. Will you have a glass of champagne? [*He moves towards the door*].

LIZA: No. [*Recollecting her manners*] Thank you.

HIGGINS [*good-humored again*]: This has been coming on you for some days. I suppose it was natural for you to be anxious about the garden party. But thats all over now. [*He pats her kindly on the shoulder. She writhes*]. Theres nothing more to worry about.

LIZA: No. Nothing more for you to worry about. [*She suddenly rises and gets away from him by going to the piano bench, where she sits and hides her face.*] Oh God! I wish I was dead.

HIGGINS [*staring after her in sincere surprise*]: Why? In heaven's name, why? [*Reasonably, going to her*] Listen to me, Eliza. All this irritation is purely subjective.

LIZA: I dont understand. I'm too ignorant.

HIGGINS: It's only imagination. Low spirits and nothing else. Nobody's hurting you. Nothing's wrong. You go to bed like a good girl and sleep it off. Have a little cry and say your prayers: that will make you comfortable.

LIZA: I heard your prayers. "Thank God it's all over!"

HIGGINS [*impatiently*]: Well, dont you thank God it's all over? Now you are free and can do what you like.

LIZA [*pulling herself together in desperation*]: What am I fit for? What have you left me fit for? Where am I to go? What am I to do? Whats to become of me?

HIGGINS [*enlightened, but not at all impressed*]: Oh, thats whats worrying you, is it? [*He thrusts his hands into his pockets, and walks about in his usual manner, rattling the contents of his pockets, as if condescending to a trivial subject out of pure kindness*]. I shouldnt bother about it if I were you. I should imagine you wont have much difficulty in settling yourself somewhere or other, though I hadnt quite realized that you were going away. [*She looks quickly at him: he does not look at her, but examines the dessert stand on the piano and decides that he will eat an apple*]. You might marry, you know. [*He bites a large piece out of the apple and munches it noisily*]. You see, Eliza, all men are not confirmed old bachelors like me and the Colonel. Most men are the marrying sort (poor devils!); and youre not bad-looking: it's quite a pleasure to look at you sometimes—not now, of course, because youre crying and looking as ugly as the very devil; but when youre all right and quite yourself, youre what I should call attractive. That is, to the people in the marrying line, you understand. You go to bed and have a good nice rest; and then get up and look at yourself in the glass; and you wont feel so cheap.

[ELIZA *again looks at him, speechless, and does not stir.*

The look is quite lost on him: He eats his apple with a dreamy expression of happiness, as it is quite a good one].

HIGGINS [*a genial afterthought occurring to him*]: I daresay my mother could find some chap or other who would do very well.

LIZA: We were above that at the corner of Tottenham Court Road.

HIGGINS [*waking up*]: What do you mean?

LIZA: I sold flowers. I didnt sell myself. Now youve made a lady of me I'm not fit to sell anything else. I wish youd left me where you found me.

HIGGINS [*slinging the core of the apple decisively into the grate*]: Tosh, Eliza. Dont you insult human relations by dragging all this cant about buying and selling into it. You neednt marry the fellow if you dont like him.

LIZA: What else am I to do?

HIGGINS: Oh, lots of thing. What about your old idea of a florist's shop? Pickering could set you up in one: he has lots of money. [*Chuckling*] He'll have to pay for all those togs you have been wearing today; and that, with the hire of the jewellery, will make a big hole in two hundred pounds. Why, six months ago you would have thought it the millennium to have a flower shop of your own. Come! youll be all right. I must clear off to bed: I'm devilish sleepy. By the way, I came down for something: I forget what it was.

LIZA: Your slippers.

HIGGINS: Oh yes, of course. You shied them at me. [*He picks them up, and is going out when she rises and speaks to him*].

LIZA: Before you go, sir—

HIGGINS [*dropping the slippers in his surprise at her calling him Sir*]: Eh?

LIZA: Do my clothes belong to me or to Colonel Pickering?

HIGGINS [*coming back into the room as if her question were the very climax of unreason*]: What the devil use would they be to Pickering?

LIZA: He might want them for the next girl you pick up to experiment on.

HIGGINS [*shocked and hurt*]: Is that the way you feel towards us?

LIZA: I dont want to hear anything more about that. All I want to know is whether anything belongs to me. My own clothes were burnt.

HIGGINS: But what does it matter? Why need you start bothering about that in the middle of the night?

LIZA: I want to know what I may take away with me. I dont want to be accused of stealing.

HIGGINS [*now deeply wounded*]: Stealing! You shouldnt have said that, Eliza. That shews a want of feeling.

LIZA: I'm sorry. I'm only a common ignorant girl; and in my station I have to be careful. There cant be any feelings between the like of you and the like of me. Please will you tell me what belongs to me and what doesnt?

HIGGINS [*very sulky*]: You may take the whole damned houseful if you like. Except the jewels. Theyre hired. Will that satisfy you? [*He turns on his heel and is about to go in extreme dudgeon*].

LIZA [*drinking in his emotion like nectar, and nagging him to provoke a further supply*]: Stop, please. [*She takes off her jewels*]. Will you take these to your room and keep them safe? I dont want to run the risk of their being missing.

HIGGINS [*furious*]: Hand them over. [*She puts them into his hands*]. If these belonged to me instead of to the jeweller, I'd ram them down your ungrateful throat. [*He perfunctorily thrusts them into his pockets, unconsciously decorating himself with the protruding ends of the chains*].

LIZA [*taking a ring off*]: This ring isnt the jeweller's: it's the one you bought me in Brighton. I dont want it now. [HIGGINS *dashes the ring violently into the fireplace, and turns on her so threateningly that she crouches over the piano with her hands over her face, and exclaims*] Dont you hit me.

HIGGINS: Hit you! You infamous creature, how dare you accuse me of such a thing? It is you who have hit me. You have wounded me to the heart.

LIZA [*thrilling with hidden joy*]: I'm glad. Ive got a little of my own back, anyhow.

HIGGINS [*with dignity, in his finest professional style*]: You have caused me to lose my temper: a thing that has hardly ever happened to me before. I prefer to say nothing more tonight. I am going to bed.

LIZA [*pertly*]: Youd better leave a note for Mrs. Pearce about the coffee; for she wont be told by me.

HIGGINS [*formally*]: Damn Mrs. Pearce; and damn the coffee; and damn you; and [*wildly*] damn my own folly in having lavished my hard-earned knowledge and the treasure of my regard and intimacy on a heartless guttersnipe. [*He goes out with impressive decorum, and spoils it by slamming the door savagely*].

[ELIZA *goes down on her knees on the hearthrug to look for the ring. When she finds it she considers for a moment what to do with it. Finally she flings it down on the dessert stand and goes upstairs in a tearing rage*].

* * * * *

The furniture of Eliza's room has been increased by a big wardrobe and a sumptuous dressing-table. She comes in and switches on the electric light. She goes to the wardrobe; opens it; and pulls out a walking dress, a hat, and a pair of shoes, which she throws on the bed. She takes off her evening dress and shoes; then takes a padded hanger from the wardrobe; adjusts it carefully in the evening dress; and hangs it in the wardrobe, which she shuts with a slam. She puts on her walking shoes, her walking dress, and hat. She takes her wrist watch from the dressing-table and fastens it on. She pulls on her gloves; takes her vanity bag; and looks into it to see that her purse is there before hanging it on her wrist. She makes for the door. Every movement expresses her furious resolution.

She takes a last look at herself in the glass.

She suddenly puts out her tongue at herself; then leaves the room, switching off the electric light at the door.

Meanwhile, in the street outside, Freddy Eynsford

Hill, lovelorn, is gazing up at the second floor, in which one of the windows is still lighted.

FREDDY: Goodnight, darling, darling, darling.

[ELIZA *comes out, giving the door a considerable bang behind her.*]

LIZA: Whatever are you doing here?

FREDDY: Nothing. I spend most of my nights here. It's the only place where I'm happy. Dont laugh at me, Miss Doolittle.

LIZA: Dont you call me Miss Doolittle, do you hear? Liza's good enough for me. [*She breaks down and grabs him by the shoulders*] Freddy: you dont think I'm a heartless guttersnipe, do you?

FREDDY: Oh no, no, darling: how can you imagine such a thing? You are the loveliest, dearest—

[*He loses all self-control and smothers her with kisses. She, hungry for comfort, responds. They stand there in one another's arms*].

[*An elderly police constable arrives*].

CONSTABLE [*scandalized*]: Now then! Now then!! Now then!!!

[*They release one another hastily*].

FREDDY: Sorry, constable. Weve only just become engaged.

[*They run away*].

The constable shakes his head, reflecting on his own courtship and on the vanity of human hopes. He moves off in the opposite direction with slow professional steps.

The flight of the lovers takes them to Cavendish Square. There they halt to consider their next move.

LIZA [*out of breath*]: He didnt half give me a fright, that copper. But you answered him proper.

FREDDY: I hope I havent taken you out of your way. Where were you going?

LIZA: To the river.

FREDDY: What for?

LIZA: To make a hole in it.

FREDDY [*horrified*]: Eliza, darling. What do you mean? What's the matter?

LIZA: Never mind. It doesnt matter now. There's nobody in the world now but you and me, is there?

FREDDY: Not a soul.

[*They indulge in another embrace, and are again surprised by a much younger constable*].

SECOND CONSTABLE: Now then, you two! What's this? Where do you think you are? Move along here, double quick.

FREDDY: As you say, sir, double quick.

They run away again, and are in Hanover Square before they stop for another conference.

FREDDY: I had no idea the police were so devilishly prudish.

LIZA: It's their business to hunt girls off the streets.

FREDDY: We must go somewhere. We cant wander about the streets all night.

LIZA: Cant we? I think it'd be lovely to wander about for ever.

FREDDY: Oh, darling.

[*They embrace again, oblivious of the arrival of a crawling taxi. It stops*].

TAXIMAN: Can I drive you and the lady anywhere, sir?

[*They start asunder*].

LIZA: Oh, Freddy, a taxi. The very thing.

FREDDY: But, damn it, I've no money.

LIZA: I have plenty. The Colonel thinks you should never go out without ten pounds in your pocket. Listen. We'll drive about all night; and in the morning I'll call on old Mrs. Higgins and ask her what I ought to do. I'll tell you all about it in the cab. And the police wont touch us there.

FREDDY: Righto! Ripping. [*To the Taximan*] Wimbledon Common. [*They drive off*].

ACT V

MRS. HIGGINS'S *drawing room. She is at her writing-table. As before. The parlormaid comes in.*

THE PARLORMAID [*at the door*]: Mr. Henry, maam, is downstairs with Colonel Pickering.

MRS. HIGGINS: Well, shew them up.

THE PARLORMAID: Theyre using the telephone, maam. Telephoning to the police, I think.

MRS. HIGGINS: What!

THE PARLORMAID [*coming further in and lowering her voice*]: Mr. Henry is in a state, maam. I thought I'd better tell you.

MRS. HIGGINS: If you had told me that Mr. Henry was not in a state it would have been more surprising. Tell them to come up when theyve finished with the police. I suppose he's lost something.

THE PARLORMAID: Yes, maam [*going*].

MRS. HIGGINS: Go upstairs and tell Miss Doolittle that Mr. Henry and the Colonel are here. Ask her not to come down til I send for her.

THE PARLORMAID: Yes, maam.

[HIGGINS *bursts in. He is, as the parlormaid has said, in a state*].

HIGGINS: Look here, mother: heres a confounded thing!

MRS. HIGGINS: Yes, dear. Good morning. [*He checks his impatience and kisses her, whilst the parlormaid goes out*]. What is it?

HIGGINS: Eliza's bolted.

MRS. HIGGINS [*calmly continuing her writing*]: You must have frightened her.

HIGGINS: Frightened her! nonsense! She was left last night, as usual, to turn out the lights and all that; and instead of going to bed she changed her clothes and went right off: her bed wasnt slept in. She came in a cab for her things before seven this morning; and that fool Mrs. Pearce let her have them without telling me a word about it. What am I to do?

MRS. HIGGINS: Do without, I'm afraid, Henry. The girl has a perfect right to leave if she chooses.

HIGGINS [*wandering distractedly across the room*]: But I cant find anything. I dont know what appointments Ive got. I'm—[PICKERING *comes in.* MRS. HIGGINS *puts down her pen and turns away from the writing-table*].

PICKERING [*shaking hands*]: Good morning, Mrs. Higgins. Has Henry told you? [*He sits down on the ottoman*].

HIGGINS: What does that ass of an inspector say? Have you offered a reward?

MRS. HIGGINS [*rising in indignant amazement*]: You dont mean to say you have set the police after Eliza.

HIGGINS: Of course. What are the police for? What else could we do? [*He sits in the Elizabethan chair*].

PICKERING: The inspector made a lot of difficulties. I really think he suspected us of some improper purpose.

MRS. HIGGINS: Well, of course he did. What right have you to go to the police and give the girl's name as if she were a thief, or a lost umbrella, or something? Really! [*She sits down again, deeply vexed*].

HIGGINS: But we want to find her.

PICKERING: We cant let her go like this, you know, Mrs. Higgins. What were we to do?

MRS. HIGGINS: You have no more sense, either of you, than two children. Why—

[*The parlormaid comes in and breaks off the conversation*].

THE PARLORMAID: Mr. Henry: a gentleman wants to see you very particular. He's been sent on from Wimpole Street.

HIGGINS: Oh, bother! I cant see anyone now. Who is it?

THE PARLORMAID: A Mr. Doolittle, sir.

PICKERING: Doolittle! Do you mean the dustman?

THE PARLORMAID: Dustman! Oh, no, sir: a gentleman.

HIGGINS [*springing up excitedly*]: By George, Pick, it's some relative of hers that she's gone to. Somebody we know nothing about. [*To the parlormaid*] Send him up, quick.

THE PARLORMAID: Yes, sir. [*She goes*].

HIGGINS [*eagerly, going to his mother*]: Genteel relatives! now we shall hear something. [*He sits down in the Chippendale chair*].

MRS. HIGGINS: Do you know any of her people?

PICKERING: Only her father: the fellow we told you about.

THE PARLORMAID [*announcing*]: Mr. Doolittle. [*She withdraws*].

[DOOLITTLE *enters. He is resplendently dressed as for a fashionable wedding, and might, in fact, be the bridegroom. A flower in his buttonhole, a dazzling silk hat, and patent leather shoes complete the effect. He is too concerned with the business he has come on to notice* MRS. HIGGINS. *He walks straight to* HIGGINS, *and accosts him with vehement reproach*].

DOOLITTLE [*indicating his own person*] See here! Do you see this? You done this.

HIGGINS: Done what, man?

DOOLITTLE: This, I tell you. Look at it. Look at this hat. Look at this coat.

PICKERING: Has Eliza been buying you clothes?

DOOLITTLE: Eliza! not she. Why would she buy me clothes?

MRS. HIGGINS: Good morning, Mr. Doolittle. Wont you sit down?

DOOLITTLE [*taken aback as he becomes conscious that he has forgotten his hostess*]: Asking your pardon, maam. [*He approaches her and shakes her proffered hand*]. Thank you [*He sits down on the ottoman, on* PICKERING'S *right*]. I am that full of what has happened to me that I cant think of anything else.

HIGGINS: What the dickens has happened to you?

DOOLITTLE: I shouldnt mind if it had only happened to me: anything might happen to anybody and nobody to blame but Providence, as you might say. But this is something that you done to me: yes, you, Enry Iggins.

HIGGINS: Have you found Eliza?

DOOLITTLE: Have you lost her?

HIGGINS: Yes.

DOOLITTLE: You have all the luck, you have. I aint found her; but she'll find me quick enough now after what you done to me.

MRS. HIGGINS: But what has my son done to you, Mr. Doolittle?

DOOLITTLE: Done to me! Ruined me. Destroyed my happiness. Tied me up and delivered me into the hands of middle class morality.

HIGGINS [*rising intolerantly and standing over* DOO-

LITTLE]: Youre raving. Youre drunk. Youre mad. I gave you five pounds. After that I had two conversations with you, at half-a-crown an hour. Ive never seen you since.

DOOLITTLE: Oh! Drunk am I? Mad am I? Tell me this. Did you or did you not write a letter to an old blighter in America that was giving five millions to found Moral Reform Societies all over the world, and that wanted you to invent a universal language for him?

HIGGINS: What! Ezra D. Wannafeller! He's dead. [*He sits down again carelessly*].

DOOLITTLE: Yes: he's dead; and I'm done for. Now did you or did you not write a letter to him to say that the most original moralist at present in England, to the best of your knowledge, was Alfred Doolittle, a common dustman?

HIGGINS: Oh, after your first visit I remember making some silly joke of the kind.

DOOLITTLE: Ah! you may well call it a silly joke. It put the lid on me right enough. Just give him the chance he wanted to shew that Americans is not like us: that they reckonize and respect merit in every class of life, however humble. Them words is in his blooming will, in which, Henry Higgins, thanks to your silly joking, he leaves me a share in his Pre-digested Cheese Trust worth four thousand a year on condition that I lecture for his Wannafeller Moral Reform World League as often as they ask me up to six times a year.

HIGGINS: The devil he does! Whew! [*Brightening suddenly*] What a lark!

PICKERING: A safe thing for you, Doolittle. They wont ask you twice.

DOOLITTLE: It aint the lecturing I mind. I'll lecture them blue in the face, I will, and not turn a hair. It's making a gentleman of me that I object to. Who asked him to make a gentleman of me? I was happy. I was free. I touched pretty nigh everybody for money when I wanted it, same as I touched you, Enry Iggins. Now I am worrited; tied neck and heels; and everybody touches me for money. It's a fine thing for you, says my solicitor. Is it? says I. You mean it's a good thing for you, I says. When I was a poor man and had a solicitor once when they found a pram in the dust cart, he got me off, and got shut of me and got me shut of him as quick as he could. Same with the doctors: used to shove me out of the hospital before I could hardly stand on my legs, and nothing to pay. Now they finds out that I'm not a healthy man and cant live unless they looks after me twice a day. In the house I'm not let do a hand's turn for myself: somebody else must do it and touch me for it. A year ago I hadnt a relative in the world except two or three that wouldnt speak to me. Now Ive fifty, and not a decent week's wages among the lot of them. I have to live for others and not for myself: that middle class morality. You talk of losing Eliza. Dont you be anxious: I bet she's on my doorstep by this: she that could support herself easy by selling flowers if I wasnt respectable. And the next one to touch me will be you, Enry Iggins. I'll have to learn to speak middle class languge from you, instead of speaking proper English. Thats where youll come in; and I daresay thats what you done it for.

MRS. HIGGINS: But, my dear Mr. Doolittle, you need not suffer all this if you are really in earnest. Nobody can force you to accept this bequest. You can repudiate it. Isnt that so, Colonel Pickering?

PICKERING: I believe so.

DOOLITTLE [*softening his manner in deference to her sex*]: Thats the tragedy of it, maam. It's easy to say chuck it; but I havnt the nerve. Which of us has? We're all intimidated. Intimidated, maam: thats what we are. What is there for me if I chuck it but the workhouse in my old age? I have to dye my hair already to keep my job as a dustman. If I was one of the deserving poor, and had put by a bit, I could chuck it; but then why should I, acause the deserving poor might as well be millionaires for all the happiness they ever has. They dont know what happiness is. But I, as one of the undeserving poor, have nothing between me and the pauper's uniform but this here blasted four thousand a year that shoves me into the middle class. (Excuse the expression, maam; youd use it yourself if you had my provocation.) Theyve got you every way you turn: it's a choice between the Skilly of the workhouse and the Char Bydis of the middle class; and I havnt the nerve for the workhouse. Intimidated: thats what I am. Broke. Bought up. Happier men than me will call for my dust, and touch me for their tip; and I'll look on helpless, and envy them. And thats what your son has brought me to. [*He is overcome by emotion*].

MRS. HIGGINS: Well, I'm very glad youre not going to do anything foolish, Mr. Doolittle. For this solves the problem of Eliza's future. You can provide for her now.

DOOLITTLE [*with melancholy resignation*]: Yes, maam: I'm expected to provide for everyone now, out of four thousand a year.

HIGGINS [*jumping up*]: Nonsense! he cant provide for her. He shant provide for her. She doesnt belong to him. I paid him five pounds for her. Doolittle: either youre an honest man or a rogue.

DOOLITTLE [*tolerantly*]: A little of both, Henry, like the rest of us: a little of both.

HIGGINS: Well, you took that money for the girl; and you have no right to take her as well.

MRS. HIGGINS: Henry: dont be absurd. If you want to know where Eliza is, she is upstairs.

HIGGINS [*amazed*]: Upstairs!!! Then I shall jolly soon fetch her downstairs. [*He makes resolutely for the door*].

MRS. HIGGINS [*rising and following him*]: Be quiet, Henry. Sit down.

HIGGINS: I—

MRS. HIGGINS: Sit down, dear; and listen to me.

HIGGINS: Oh very well, very well, very well. [*He throws himself ungraciously on the ottoman, with his face towards the windows*]. But I think you might have told us this half an hour ago.

MRS. HIGGINS: Eliza came to me this morning. She told me of the brutal way you two treated her.

HIGGINS [*bounding up again*]: What!

PICKERING [*rising also*]: My dear Mrs. Higgins, she's been telling you stories. We didnt treat her brutally. We hardly said a word to her; and we parted on particularly good terms. [*Turning on* HIGGINS] Higgins: did you bully her after I went to bed?

HIGGINS: Just the other way about. She threw my slippers in my face. She behaved in the most outrageous way. I never gave her the slightest provocation. The slippers came bang into my face the moment I entered the room—before I had uttered a word. And used perfectly awful language.

PICKERING [*astonished*]: But why? What did we do to her?

MRS. HIGGINS: I think I know pretty well what you did. The girl is naturally rather affectionate, I think. Isnt she, Mr. Doolittle?

DOOLITTLE: Very tender-hearted, maam. Takes after me.

MRS. HIGGINS: Just so. She had become attached to you both. She worked very hard for you, Henry. I dont think you quite realize what anything in the nature of brain work means to a girl of her class. Well, it seems that when the great day of trial came, and she did this wonderful thing for you without making a single mistake, you two sat there and never said a word to her, but talked together of how glad you were that it was all over and how you had been bored with the whole thing. And then you were surprised because she threw your slippers at you! I should have thrown the fire-irons at you.

HIGGINS: We said nothing except that we were tired and wanted to go to bed. Did we, Pick?

PICKERING [*shrugging his shoulders*]: That was all.

MRS. HIGGINS [*ironically*]: Quite sure?

PICKERING: Absolutely. Really, that was all.

MRS. HIGGINS: You didnt thank her, or pet her, or admire her, or tell her how splendid she'd been.

HIGGINS [*impatiently*]: But she knew all about that. We didnt make speeches to her, if thats what you mean.

PICKERING [*conscience stricken*]: Perhaps we were a little inconsiderate. Is she very angry?

MRS. HIGGINS [*returning to her place at the writing-table*]: Well, I'm afraid she wont go back to Wimpole Street, especially now that Mr. Doolittle is able to keep up the position you have thrust on her; but she says she is quite willing to meet you on friendly terms and to let bygones be bygones.

HIGGINS [*furious*]: Is she, by George? Ho!

MRS. HIGGINS: If you promise to behave yourself, Henry, I'll ask her to come down. If not, go home; for you have taken up quite enough of my time.

HIGGINS: Oh, all right. Very well. Pick: you behave yourself. Let us put on our best Sunday manners for this creature that we picked out of the mud. [*He flings himself sulkily into the Elizabethan chair*].

DOOLITTLE [*remonstrating*]: Now, now, Enry Iggins! Have some consideration for my feelings as a middle class man.

MRS. HIGGINS: Remember your promise, Henry. [*She presses the bell-button on the writing-table*]. Mr. Doolittle: will you be so good as to step out on the balcony for a moment. I dont want Eliza to have the shock of your news until she has made it up with these two gentelmen. Would you mind?

DOOLITTLE: As you wish, lady. Anything to help Henry to keep her off my hands. [*He disappears through the window*].

[*The parlormaid answers the bell.* PICKERING *sits down in* DOOLITTLE'S *place*].

MRS. HIGGINS: Ask Miss Doolittle to come down, please.

THE PARLORMAID: Yes, maam. [*She goes out*].

MRS. HIGGINS: Now, Henry: be good.

HIGGINS: I am behaving myself perfectly.

PICKERING: He is doing his best, Mrs. Higgins.

[*A pause.* HIGGINS *throws back his head; stretches out his legs; and begins to whistle*].

MRS. HIGGINS: Henry, dearest, you dont look at all nice in that attitude.

HIGGINS [*pulling himself together*]: I was not trying to look nice, mother.

MRS. HIGGINS: It doesnt matter, dear. I only wanted to make you speak.

HIGGINS: Why?

MRS. HIGGINS: Because you cant speak and whistle at the same time.

[HIGGINS *groans. Another very trying pause*].

HIGGINS [*springing up, out of patience*]: Where the devil is that girl? Are we to wait here all day?

[ELIZA *enters, sunny, self-possessed, and giving a staggeringly convincing exhibition of ease of manner. She carries a little workbasket, and is very much at home.* PICKERING *is too much taken aback to rise*].

LIZA: How do you do, Professor Higgins? Are you quite well?

HIGGINS [*choking*]: Am I—[*He can say no more*].

LIZA: But of course you are: you are never ill. So glad to see you again, Colonel Pickering. [*He rises hastily; and they shake hands*]. Quite chilly this morning, isnt it? [*She sits down on his left. He sits beside her*].

HIGGINS: Dont you dare try this game on me. I taught it to you; and it doesnt take me in. Get up and come home; and dont be a fool.

[ELIZA *takes a piece of needlework from her basket, and begins to stitch at it, without taking the least notice of this outburst*].

MRS. HIGGINS: Very nicely put, indeed, Henry. No woman could resist such an invitation.

HIGGINS: You let her alone, mother. Let her speak for herself. You will jolly soon see whether she has an idea that I havnt put into her head or a word that I havnt put into her mouth. I tell you I have created this thing out of the squashed cabbage leaves of Covent Garden; and now she pretends to play the fine lady with me.

MRS. HIGGINS [*placidly*]: Yes, dear; but youll sit down, wont you?

[HIGGINS *sits down again, savagely*].

LIZA [*to* PICKERING, *taking no apparent notice of* HIGGINS, *and working away deftly*]: Will you drop me altogether now that the experiment is over, Colonel Pickering?

PICKERING: Oh dont. You mustnt think of it as an experiment. It shocks me, somehow.

LIZA: Oh, I'm only a squashed cabbage leaf—

PICKERING [*impulsively*]: No.

LIZA [*continuing quietly*]: —but I owe so much to you that I should be very unhappy if your forgot me.

PICKERING: It's very kind of you to say so, Miss Doolittle.

LIZA: It's not because you paid for my dresses. I know you are generous to everybody with money. But it was from you that I learnt really nice manners; and that is what makes one a lady, isnt it? You see it was so very difficult for me with the example of Professor Higgins always before me. I was brought up to be just like him, unable to control myself, and using bad language on the slightest provocation. And I should never have known that ladies and gentlemen didnt behave like that if you hadnt been there.

HIGGINS: Well!!

PICKERING: Oh, thats only his way, you know. He doesnt mean it.

LIZA: Oh, *I* didnt mean it either, when I was a flower girl. It was only my way. But you see I did it; and thats what makes the difference after all.

PICKERING: No doubt. Still, he taught you to speak; and I couldnt have done that, you know.

LIZA [*trivially*]: Of course: that is his profession.

HIGGINS: Damnation!

LIZA [*continuing*]: It was just like learning to dance in the fashionable way: there was nothing more than that in it. But do you know what began my real education?

PICKERING: What?

LIZA [*stopping her work for a moment*]: Your calling me Miss Doolittle that day when I first came to Wimpole Street. That was the beginning of self-respect for me. [*She resumes her stitching*] And there were a hundred little things you never noticed, because they came naturally to you. Things about standing up and taking off your hat and opening doors—

PICKERING: Oh, that was nothing.

LIZA: Yes: things that shewed you thought and felt about me as if I were something better than a scullery-maid; though of course I know you would have been just the same to a scullery-maid if she had been let into the drawing room. You never took off your boots in the dining room when I was there.

PICKERING: You mustnt mind that. Higgins takes off his boots all over the place.

LIZA: I know. I am not blaming him. It is his way, isnt it? But it made such a difference to me that you didnt do it. You see, really and truly, apart from the things anyone can pick up (the dressing and the proper way of speaking, and so on), the difference between a lady and a flower girl is not how she behaves, but how she's treated. I shall always be a flower girl to Professor Higgins, because he always treats me as a flower girl, and always will; but I know I can be a lady to you, because you always treat me as a lady, and always will.

MRS. HIGGINS: Please dont grind your teeth, Henry.

PICKERING: Well, this is really very nice of you, Miss Doolittle.

LIZA: I should like you to call me Eliza, now, if you would.

PICKERING: Thank you. Eliza, of course.

LIZA: And I should like Professor Higgins to call me Miss Doolittle.

HIGGINS: I'll see you damned first.

MRS. HIGGINS: Henry! Henry!

PICKERING [*laughing*]: Why dont you slang back at him? Dont stand it. It would do him a lot of good.

LIZA: I cant. I could have done it once; but now I

cant go back to it. You told me, you know, that when a child is brought to a foreign country, it picks up the language in a few weeks, and forgets its own. Well, I am a child in your country. I have forgotten my own language, and can speak nothing but yours. Thats the real break-off with the corner of Tottenham Court Road. Leaving Wimpole Street finishes it.

PICKERING [*much alarmed*]: Oh! but youre coming back to Wimpole Street, arnt you? Youll forgive Higgins?

HIGGINS [*rising*]: Forgive! Will she, by George! Let her go. Let her find out how she can get on without us. She will relapse into the gutter in three weeks without me at her elbow.

[DOOLITTLE *appears at the centre window. With a look of dignified reproach at* HIGGINS, *he comes slowly and silently to his daughter, who, with her back to the window, is unconscious of his approach*].

PICKERING: He's incorrigible, Eliza. You wont relapse, will you?

LIZA: No: not now. Never again. I have learnt my lesson. I dont believe I could utter one of the old sounds if I tried. [DOOLITTLE *touches her on the left shoulder. She drops her work, losing her self-possession utterly at the spectacle of her father's splendor*] A-a-a-a-ah-ow-ooh!

HIGGINS [*with a crow of triumph*]: Aha! Just so. A-a-a-a-ahowooh! A-a-a-a-ahowooh! A-a-a-a-ahowooh! Victory! Victory! [*He throws himself on the divan, folding his arms, and spraddling arrogantly*].

DOOLITTLE: Can you blame the girl? Dont look at me like that, Eliza. It aint my fault. Ive come into some money.

LIZA: You must have touched a millionaire this time, dad.

DOOLITTLE: I have. But I'm dressed something special today. I'm going to St. George's, Hanover Square. Your stepmother is going to marry me.

LIZA [*angrily*]: Youre going to let yourself down to marry that low common woman!

PICKERING [*quietly*]: He ought to, Eliza. [*To* DOOLITTLE] Why has she changed her mind?

DOOLITTLE [*sadly*]: Intimidated, Governor. Intimidated. Middle class morality claims its victim. Wont you put on your hat, Liza, and come and see me turned off?

LIZA: If the Colonel says I must, I—I'll [*almost sobbing*] I'll demean myself. And get insulted for my pains, like enough.

DOOLITTLE: Dont be afraid: she never comes to words with anyone now, poor woman! respectability has broke all the spirit out of her.

PICKERING [*squeezing* ELIZA'S *elbow gently*]: Be kind to them, Eliza. Make the best of it.

LIZA [*forcing a little smile for him through her vexation*]: Oh well, just to shew theres no ill feeling. I'll be back in a moment. [*She goes out*].

DOOLITTLE [*sitting down beside* PICKERING]: I feel uncommon nervous about the ceremony, Colonel. I wish youd come and see me through it.

PICKERING: But youve been through it before, man. You were married to Eliza's mother.

DOOLITTLE: Who told you that, Colonel?

PICKERING: Well, nobody told me. But I concluded—naturally—

DOOLITTLE: No: that aint the natural way, Colonel: it's only the middle class way. My way was always the undeserving way. But dont say nothing to Eliza. She dont know: I always had a delicacy about telling her.

PICKERING: Quite right. We'll leave it so, if you dont mind.

DOOLITTLE: And youll come to the church, Colonel, and put me through straight?

PICKERING: With pleasure. As far as a bachelor can.

MRS. HIGGINS: May I come, Mr. Doolittle? I should be very sorry to miss your wedding.

DOOLITTLE: I should indeed be honored by your condescension, maam; and my poor old woman would take it as a tremenjous compliment. She's been very low, thinking of the happy days that are no more.

MRS. HIGGINS [*rising*]: I'll order the carriage and get ready. [*The men rise, except* HIGGINS]. I shant be more than fifteen minutes. [*As she goes to the door* ELIZA *comes in, hatted and buttoning her gloves*]. I'm going to the church to see your father married, Eliza. You had better come in the brougham with me. Colonel Pickering can go on with the bridegroom.

[MRS. HIGGINS *goes out.* ELIZA *comes to the middle of the room between the centre window and the ottoman.* PICKERING *joins her*].

DOOLITTLE: Bridegroom. What a word! It makes a man realize his position, somehow. [*He takes up his hat and goes towards the door*].

PICKERING: Before I go, Eliza, do forgive Higgins and come back to us.

LIZA: I dont think dad would allow me. Would you, dad?

DOOTLITTLE [*sad but magnanimous*]: They played you off very cunning, Eliza, them two sportsmen. If it had been only one of them, you could have nailed him. But you see, there was two; and one of them chaperoned the other, as you might say. [*To* PICKERING] It was artful of you, Colonel; but I bear no malice: I should have done the same myself. I been the victim of one woman after another all my life, and I dont grudge you two getting the better of Liza. I shant interfere. It's time for us to go, Colonel. So long, Henry. See you in St. George's, Eliza. [*He goes out*].

PICKERING [*coaxing*]: Do stay with us, Eliza. [*He follows* DOOLITTLE].

[ELIZA *goes out on the balcony to avoid being alone with* HIGGINS. *He rises and joins her there. She immediately comes back into the room and makes for the door; but he goes along the balcony and gets his back to the door before she reaches it*].

HIGGINS: Well, Eliza, youve had a bit of your own back, as you call it. Have you had enough? and are you going to be reasonable? Or do you want any more?

LIZA: You want me back only to pick up your slippers and put up with your tempers and fetch and carry for you.

HIGGINS: I havnt said I wanted you back at all.

LIZA: Oh, indeed. Then what are we talking about?

HIGGINS: About you, not about me. If you come back I shall treat you just as I have always treated you. I cant change my nature; and I dont intend to change my manners. My manners are exactly the same as Colonel Pickering's.

LIZA: Thats not true. He treats a flower girl as if she was a duchess.

HIGGINS: And I treat a duchess as if she was a flower girl.

LIZA: I see [*She turns away composedly, and sits on the ottoman, facing the window*]. The same to everybody.

HIGGINS: Just so.

LIZA: Like father.

HIGGINS [*grinning, a little taken down*]: Without accepting the comparison at all points, Eliza, it's quite true that your father is not a snob, and that he will be quite at home in any station of life to which his eccentric destiny may call him. [*Seriously*] The great secret, Eliza, is not having bad manners or good manner or any other particular sort of manners, but having the same manner for all human souls: in short, behaving as if you were in Heaven, where there are no third-class carriages, and one soul is as good as another.

LIZA: Amen. You are a born preacher.

HIGGINS [*irritated*]: The question is not whether I treat you rudely, but whether you ever heard me treat anyone else better.

LIZA [*with sudden sincerity*]: I dont care how you treat me. I dont mind your swearing at me. I shouldnt mind a black eye: Ive had one before this. But [*standing up and facing him*] I wont be passed over.

HIGGINS: Then get out of my way; for I wont stop for you. You talk about me as if I were a motor bus.

LIZA: So you are a motor bus: all bounce and go, and no consideration for anyone. But I can do without you: dont think I cant.

HIGGINS: I know you can. I told you you could.

LIZA [*wounded, getting away from him to the other side of the ottoman with her face to the hearth*]: I know you did, you brute. You wanted to get rid of me.

HIGGINS: Liar.

LIZA: Thank you. [*She sits down with dignity*].

HIGGINS: You never asked yourself, I suppose, whether *I* could do without you.

LIZA [*earnestly*]: Dont you try to get round me. Youll have to do without me.

HIGGINS [*arrogant*]: I can do without anybody. I have my own soul: my own spark of divine fire. But [*with sudden humility*] I shall miss you, Eliza. [*He sits down near her on the ottoman*] I have learnt something from your idiotic notions: I confess that humbly and gratefully. And I have grown accustomed to your voice and appearance. I like them, rather.

LIZA: Well, you have both of them on your gramophone and in your book of photographs. When you feel lonely without me, you can turn the machine on. It's got no feelings to hurt.

HIGGINS: I cant turn your soul on. Leave me those feelings; and you can take away the voice and the face. They are not you.

LIZA: Oh, you are a devil. You can twist the heart in a girl as easy as some could twist her arms to hurt her. Mrs. Pearce warned me. Time and again she has wanted to leave you; and you always got round her at the last minute. And you dont care a bit for her. And you dont care a bit for me.

HIGGINS: I care for life, for humanity; and you are a part of it that has come my way and been built into my house. What more can you or anyone ask?

LIZA: I wont care for anybody that doesnt care for me.

HIGGINS: Commercial principles, Eliza. Like [*reproducing her Covent Garden pronunciation with professional exactness*] s'yollin voylets [selling violets], isnt it?

LIZA: Dont sneer at me. It's mean to sneer at me.

HIGGINS: I have never sneered in my life. Sneering doesnt become either the human face or the human soul. I am expressing my righteous contempt for Commercialism. I dont and wont trade in affection. You call me a brute because you couldnt buy a claim on me by fetching my slippers and finding my spectacles. You were a fool: I think a woman fetching a man's slippers is a disgusting sight: did I ever fetch your slippers? I think a good deal more of you for throwing them in my face. No use slaving for me and then saying you want to be cared for: who cares for a slave? If you come back, come back for the sake of good fellowship;

for youll get nothing else. Youve had a thousand times as much out of me as I have out of you; and if you dare to set up your little dog's tricks of fetching and carrying slippers against my creation of a Duchess Eliza, I'll slam the door in your silly face.

LIZA: What did you do it for if you didnt care for me?

HIGGINS [*heartily*]: Why, because it was my job.

LIZA: You never thought of the trouble it would make for me.

HIGGINS: Would the world ever have been made if its maker had been afraid of making trouble? Making life means making trouble. Theres only one way of escaping trouble; and thats killing things. Cowards, you notice, are always shrieking to have troublesome people killed.

LIZA: I'm no preacher: I dont notice things like that. I notice that you dont notice me.

HIGGINS [*jumping up and walking about intolerantly*]: Eliza: youre an idot. I waste the treasures of my Miltonic mind by spreading them before you. Once for all, understand that I go my way and do my work without caring twopence what happens to either of us. I am not intimidated, like your father and your stepmother. So you can come back or go to the devil: which you please.

LIZA: What am I to come back for?

HIGGINS [*bouncing up on his knees on the ottoman and leaning over it to her*]: For the fun of it. Thats why I took you on.

LIZA [*with averted face*]: And you may throw me out tomorrow if I dont do everything you want me to?

HIGGINS: Yes; and you may walk out tomorrow if I dont do everything you want me to.

LIZA: And live with my stepmother?

HIGGINS: Yes, or sell flowers.

LIZA: Oh! if I only could go back to my flower basket! I should be independent of both you and father and all the world! Why did you take my independence from me? Why did I give it up? I'm a slave now, for all my fine clothes.

HIGGINS: Not a bit. I'll adopt you as my daughter and settle money on you if you like. Or would you rather marry Pickering?

LIZA [*looking fiercely round at him*]: I wouldnt marry you if you asked me; and youre nearer my age than what he is.

HIGGINS [*gently*]: Than he is: not "than what he is."

LIZA [*losing her temper and rising*]: I'll talk as I like. Youre not my teacher now.

HIGGINS [*reflectively*]: I dont suppose Pickering would, though. He's as confirmed an old bachelor as I am.

LIZA: Thats not what I want; and dont you think it. I've always had chaps enough wanting me that way. Freddy Hill writes to me twice and three times a day, sheets and sheets.

HIGGINS [*disagreeably surprised*]: Damn his impudence! [*He recoils and finds himself sitting on his heels.*]

LIZA: He has a right to if he likes, poor lad. And he does love me.

HIGGINS [*getting off the ottoman*]: You have no right to encourage him.

LIZA: Every girl has a right to be loved.

HIGGINS: What! By fools like that?

LIZA: Freddy's not a fool. And if he's weak and poor and wants me, may be he'd make me happier than my betters that bully me and dont want me.

HIGGINS: Can he make anything of you? Thats the point.

LIZA: Perhaps I could make something of him. But I never thought of us making anything of one another; and you never think of anything else. I only want to be natural.

HIGGINS: In short, you want me to be as infatuated about you as Freddy? Is that it?

LIZA: No I dont. Thats not the sort of feeling I want from you. And dont you be too sure of yourself or of me. I could have been a bad girl if I'd liked. Ive seen more of some things than you, for all your learning. Girls like me can drag gentlemen down to make love to them easy enough. And they wish each other dead the next minute.

HIGGINS: Of course they do. Then what in thunder are we quarrelling about?

LIZA [*much troubled*]: I want a little kindness. I know I'm a common ignorant girl, and you a book-learned gentleman; but I'm not dirt under your feet. What I done [*correcting herself*] what I did was not for the dresses and the taxis: I did it because we were pleasant together and I come—came—to care for you; not to want you to make love to me, and not forgetting the difference between us, but more friendly like.

HIGGINS: Well, of course. Thats just how I feel. And how Pickering feels. Eliza: youre a fool.

LIZA: Thats not a proper answer to give me [*she sinks on the chair at the writing-table in tears*].

HIGGINS: It's all youll get until you stop being a common idiot. If youre going to be a lady, youll have to give up feeling neglected if the men you know dont spend half their time snivelling over you and the other half giving you black eyes. If you cant stand the coldness of my sort of life, and the strain of it, go back to the gutter. Work til youre more a brute than a human being; and then cuddle and squabble and drink til you fall asleep. Oh, it's a fine life, the life of the gutter. It's real: it's warm: it's violent: you can feel it through the thickest skin: you can taste it and smell it without any training or any work. Not like Science and Literature and Classical Music and Philosophy and Art. You find me cold, unfeeling, selfish, dont you? Very well: be off with you to the sort of people you like. Marry some sentimental hog or other with lots of money, and a thick pair of lips to kiss you with and a thick pair of boots to kick you with. If you cant appreciate what youve got, youd better get what you can appreciate.

LIZA [*desperate*]: Oh, you are a cruel tyrant. I cant talk to you: you turn everything against me: I'm always in the wrong. But you know very well all the time that youre nothing but a bully. You know I cant go back to the gutter, as you call it, and that I have no real friends in the world but you and the Colonel. You know well I couldnt bear to live with a low common man after you two; and it's wicked and cruel of you to insult me by pretending I could. You think I must go back to Wimpole Street because I have nowhere else to go but father's. But dont you be too sure that you have me under your feet to be trampled on and talked down. I'll marry Freddy, I will, as soon as I'm able to support him.

HIGGINS [*thunderstuck*]: Freddy!!! that young fool! That poor devil who couldnt get a job as an errand boy even if he had the guts to try for it! Woman: do you not understand that I have made you a consort for a king?

LIZA: Freddy loves me: that makes him king enough for me. I dont want him to work: he wasnt brought up to it as I was. I'll go and be a teacher.

HIGGINS: Whatll you teach, in heaven's name?

LIZA: What you taught me. I'll teach phonetics.

HIGGINS: Ha! ha! ha!

LIZA: I'll offer myself as an assistant to that hairy-faced Hungarian.

HIGGINS [*rising in a fury*]: What! That imposter! that humbug! that toadying ignoramus! Teach him my methods! my discoveries! You take one step in his direction and I'll wring your neck. [*He lays hands on her*]. Do you hear?

LIZA [*defiantly non-resistant*]: Wring away. What do I care? I knew youd strike me some day. [*He lets her go, stamping with rage at having forgotten himself, and recoils so hastily that he stumbles back into his seat on the ottoman*]. Aha! Now I know how to deal with you. What a fool I was not to think of it before! You cant take away the knowledge you gave me. You said I had a finer ear than you. And I can be civil and kind to people, which is more than you can. Aha! [*purposely dropping her aitches to annoy him*] Thats done you, Enry Iggins, it az. Now I dont care that [*snapping her fingers*] for your bullying and your big talk. I'll advertize it in the papers that your duchess is only a flower girl that you taught, and that she'll teach anybody to be a duchess just the same in six months for a thousand guineas. Oh, when I think of myself crawling under your feet and being trampled on and called names, when all the time I had only to lift up my finger to be as good as you, I could just kick myself.

HIGGINS [*wondering at her*]: You damned impudent slut, you! But it's better than snivelling; better than fetching slippers and finding spectacles, isnt it? [*Rising*] By George, Eliza, I said I'd make a woman of you; and I have. I like you like this.

LIZA: Yes: you turn round and make up to me now that I'm not afraid of you, and can do without you.

HIGGINS: Of course I do, you little fool. Five minutes ago you were like a millstone round my neck. Now youre a tower of strength: a consort battleship. You and I and Pickering will be three old bachelors instead of only two men and a silly girl.

[MRS. HIGGINS *returns, dressed for the wedding.* ELIZA *instantly becomes cool and elegant*].

MRS. HIGGINS: The carriage is waiting, Eliza. Are you ready?

LIZA: Quite. Is the Professor coming?

MRS. HIGGINS: Certainly not. He cant behave himself in church. He makes remarks out loud all the time on the clergyman's pronunciation.

LIZA: Then I shall not see you again, Professor. Goodbye. [*She goes to the door*].

MRS. HIGGINS [*coming to* HIGGINS]: Goodbye, dear.

HIGGINS: Goodbye, mother. [*He is about to kiss her, when he recollects something*]. Oh, by the way, Eliza, order a ham and a Stilton cheese, will you? And buy me a pair of reindeer gloves, number eights, and a tie to match that new suit of mine. You can choose the color. [*His cheerful, careless, vigorous voice shews that he is incorrigible*].

LIZA [*disdainfully*]: Number eights are too small for you if you want them lined with lamb's wool. You have three new ties that you have forgotten in the drawer of your washstand. Colonel Pickering prefers double Gloucester to Stilton; and you dont notice the difference. I telephoned Mrs. Pearce this morning not to forget the ham. What you are to do without me I cannot imagine. [*She sweeps out*].

MRS. HIGGINS: I'm afraid youve spoilt that girl, Henry. I should be uneasy about you and her if she were less fond of Colonel Pickering.

HIGGINS: Pickering! Nonsense: she's going to marry Freddy. Ha ha! Freddy! Freddy!! Ha ha ha ha ha!!!! [*He roars with laughter as the play ends*].

The rest of the story need not be shewn in action, and indeed, would hardly need telling if your imaginations were not so enfeebled by their lazy dependence on the ready-mades and reach-me-downs of the ragshop in which Romance keeps its stock of "happy endings" to misfit all stories. Now, the history of Eliza Doolittle, though called a romance because the transfiguration it records seems exceedingly improbable, is common enough. Such transfigurations have been achieved by hundreds of resolutely ambitious young women since Nell Gwynne set them the example by playing queens and fascinating kings in the theatre in which she began by selling oranges. Nevertheless, people in all directions have assumed, for no other reason than that she became the heroine of a romance, that she must have married the hero of it. This is unbearable, not only because her little drama, if acted on such a thoughtless assumption, must be spoiled, but because the true sequel is patent to anyone with a sense of human nature in general, and of feminine instinct in particular.

Eliza, in telling Higgins she would not marry him if he asked her, was not coquetting: she was announcing a well-considered decision. When a bachelor interests, and dominates, and teaches, and becomes important to a spinster, as Higgins with Eliza, she always, if she has character enough to be capable of it, considers very seriously indeed whether she will play for becoming that bachelor's wife, especially if he is so little interested in marriage that a determined and devoted woman might capture him if she set herself resolutely to do it. Her decision will depend a good deal on whether she is really free to choose; and that, again, will depend on her age and income. If she is at the end of her youth, and has no security for her livelihood, she will marry him because she must marry anybody who will provide for her. But at Eliza's age a good-looking girl does not feel that pressure: she feels free to pick and choose. She is therefore guided by her instinct in the matter. Eliza's instinct tells her not to marry Higgins. It does not tell her to give him up. It is not in the slightest doubt as to his remaining one of the strongest personal interests in her life. It would be very sorely strained if there was another woman likely to supplant her with him. But as she feels sure of him on that last point, she has no doubt at all as to her course, and would not have any, even if the difference of twenty years in age, which seems so great to youth, did not exist between them.

As our own instincts are not appealed to by her conclusion, let us see whether we cannot discover some reason in it. When Higgins excused his indifference to young women on the ground that they had an irresistible rival in his mother, he gave the clue to his inveterate old-bachelordom. The case is uncommon only to the extent that remarkable mothers are uncommon. If an imaginative boy has a sufficiently rich mother who has intelligence, personal grace, dignity of character without harshness, and a cultivated sense of the best art of her time to enable her to make her house beautiful, she sets a standard for him against which very few women can struggle, besides effecting for him a disengagement of his affections, his sense of beauty, and his idealism from his specifically sexual impulses. This makes him a standing puzzle to the huge number of uncultivated people who have been brought up in tasteless homes by commonplace or disagreeable parents, and to whom, consequently, literature, painting, sculpture, music, and affectionate personal relations come as modes of sex if they come at all. The word passion means nothing else to them; and that Higgins could have a passion for phonetics and idealize his mother instead of Eliza, would seem to them absurd and unnatural. Nevertheless, when we look round and see that hardly anyone is too ugly or disagreeable to find a wife or a husband if he or she wants one, whilst many old maids and bachelors are above the average in quality and culture, we cannot help suspecting that the disentanglement of sex from the associations with which it is so commonly confused, a disentanglement which persons of genius achieve by sheer intellectual analysis, is sometimes produced or aided by parental fascination.

Now, though Eliza was incapable of thus explaining to herself Higgins's formidable powers of resistance to the charm that prostrated Freddy at the first glance, she was instinctively aware that she could never obtain a complete grip of him, or come between him and his mother (the first necessity of the married woman). To put it shortly, she knew that for some mysterious reason he had not the makings of a married man in him, according to her conception of a husband as one to whom she would be his nearest and fondest and warmest interest. Even had there been no mother-rival, she would still have refused to accept an interest in herself that was secondary to philosophic interests. Had Mrs. Higgins died, there would still have been Milton and the Universal Alphabet. Landor's remark that to those who have the greatest power of loving, love is a secondary affair, would not have recommended Landor to Eliza. Put that along with her resentment of Higgins's domineering superiority, and her mistrust of his coaxing cleverness in getting round her and evading her wrath when he had gone too far with his impetuous bullying, and you will see that Eliza's instinct had good grounds for warning her not to marry her Pygmalion.

And now, whom did Eliza marry? For if Higgins was a predestinate old bachelor, she was most certainly not a predestinate old maid. Well, that can be told very shortly to those who have not guessed it from the indications she has herself given them.

Almost immediately after Eliza is stung into proclaiming her considered determination not to marry Higgins, she mentions the fact that young Mr. Frederick Eynsford Hill is pouring out his love for her daily through the post. Now Freddy is young, practically twenty years younger than Higgins: he is a gentleman (or, as Eliza would qualify him, a toff), and speaks like one. He is nicely dressed, is treated by the Colonel as an equal, loves her unaffectedly, and is not her master, nor ever likely to dominate her in spite of his advantage of social standing. Eliza has no use for the foolish romantic tradition that all women love to be mastered, if not actually bullied and beaten. "When you go to women" says Nietzsche "take your whip with you." Sensible despots have never confined that precaution to women: they have taken their whips with them when they have dealt with men, and been slavishly idealized by the men over whom they have flourished the whip much more than by women. No doubt there are slavish women as well as slavish men; and women, like men, admire those that are stronger than themselves. But to admire a strong person and to live under that strong person's thumb are two different things. The weak may not be admired and hero-worshipped; but they are by no means disliked or shunned; and they never seem to have the least difficulty in marrying people who are too good for them. They may fail in emergencies; but life is not one long emergency: it is mostly a string of situations for which no exceptional strength is needed, and with which even rather weak people can cope if they have a stronger partner to help them out. Accordingly, it is a truth everywhere in evidence that strong people, masculine or feminine, not only do not marry stronger people, but do not shew any preference for them in selecting their friends. When a lion meets another with a louder roar "the first lion thinks the last a bore." The man or woman who feels strong enough for two, seeks for every other quality in a partner than strength.

The converse is also true. Weak people want to marry strong people who do not frighten them too much; and this often leads them to make the mistake we describe metaphorically as "biting off more than they can chew." They want too much for too little; and when the bargain is unreasonable beyond all bearing, the union becomes impossible: it ends in the weaker party being either discarded or borne as a cross, which is worse. People who are not only weak, but silly or obtuse as well, are often in these difficulties.

This being the state of human affairs, what is Eliza fairly sure to do when she is placed between Freddy and Higgins? Will she look forward to a lifetime of fetching Higgins's slippers or to a lifetime of Freddy fetching hers? There can be no doubt about the answer. Unless Freddy is biologically repulsive to her, and Higgins biologically attractive to a degree that overwhelms all her other instincts, she will, if she marries either of them, marry Freddy.

And that is just what Eliza did.

Complications ensued; but they were economic, not romantic. Freddy had no money and no occupation. His mother's jointure, a last relic of the opulence of Largelady Park, had enabled her to struggle along in Earlscourt with an air of gentility, but not to procure any serious secondary education for her children, much less give the boy a profession. A clerkship at thirty shillings a week was beneath Freddy's dignity, and extremely distasteful to him besides. His prospects consisted of a hope that if he kept up appearances somebody would do something for him. The something appeared vaguely to his imagination as a private secretaryship or a sinecure of some sort. To his mother it perhaps appeared as a marriage to some lady of means who could not resist her boy's niceness. Fancy her feelings when he married a flower girl who had become disclassed under extraordinary circumstances which were now notorious!

It is true that Eliza's situation did not seem wholly ineligible. Her father, though formerly a dustman, and now fantastically disclassed, had become extremely popular in the smartest society by a social talent which triumphed over every prejudice and every disadvantage. Rejected by the middle class, which he loathed, he had shot up at once into the highest circles by his wit, his dustmanship (which he carried like a banner), and his Nietzschean transcendence of good and evil. At intimate ducal dinners he sat on the right hand of the Duchess; and in country houses he smoked in the pantry and was made much of by the butler when he was not feeding in the dining room and being consulted by cabinet ministers. But he found it almost as hard to do all this on four thousand a year as Mrs. Eynsford Hill to live in Earlscourt on an income so pitiably smaller that I have not the heart to disclose its exact figure. He absolutely refused to add the last straw to his burden by contributing to Eliza's support.

Thus Freddy and Eliza, now Mr. and Mrs. Eynsford Hill, would have spent a penniless honeymoon but for a wedding present of £500 from the Colonel to Eliza. It lasted a long time because Freddy did not know how to spend money, never having had any to spend, and Eliza, socially trained by a pair of old bachelors, wore her clothes as long as they held together and looked pretty, without the least regard to their being many months out of fashion. Still, £500 will not last two young people for ever; and they both knew, and Eliza felt as well, that they must shift for themselves in the end. She could quarter herself on Wimpole Street because it had come to be her home; but she was quite aware that she ought not to quarter Freddy there, and that it would not be good for his character if she did.

Not that the Wimpole Street bachelors objected. When she consulted them, Higgins declined to be bothered about her housing problem when that solution was so simple. Eliza's desire to have Freddy in the house with her seemed of no more importance than if she had wanted an extra piece of bedroom furniture. Pleas as to Freddy's character, and the moral obligation on him to earn his own living, were lost on Higgins. He denied that Freddy had any character, and declared that if he tried to do any useful work some competent person would have the trouble of undoing it: a procedure involving a net loss to the community, and great unhappiness to Freddy himself, who was obviously intended by Nature for such light work as amusing Eliza, which, Higgins declared, was a much more useful and honorable occupation than working in the city. When Eliza referred again to her project of teaching phonetics, Higgins abated not a jot of his violent opposition to it. He said she was not within ten years of being qualified to meddle with his pet subject; and as it was evident that the Colonel agreed with him, she felt she could not go against them in this grave matter, and that she had no right, without Higgins's consent, to exploit the knowledge he had given her; for his knowledge seemed to her as much his private property as his watch: Eliza was no communist. Besides, she was superstitiously devoted to them both, more entirely and frankly after her marriage than before it.

It was the Colonel who finally solved the problem, which had cost him much perplexed cogitation. He one day asked Eliza, rather shyly, whether she had quite given up her notion of keeping a flower shop. She replied that she had thought of it, but had put it out of her head, because the Colonel had said, that day at Mrs. Higgins's, that it would never do. The Colonel confessed that when he said that, he had not quite recovered from the dazzling impression of the day before. They broke the matter to Higgins that evening. The sole comment vouchsafed by him very nearly led to a serious quarrel with Eliza. It was to the effect that she would have in Freddy an ideal errand boy.

Freddy himself was next sounded on the subject. He said he had been thinking of a shop himself; though it had presented itself to his pennilessness as a small place in which Eliza should sell tobacco at one counter whilst he sold newspapers at the opposite one. But he agreed that it would be extraordinarily jolly to go early every morning with Eliza to Covent Garden and buy flowers on the scene of their first meeting: a sentiment which earned him many kisses from his wife. He added that he had always been afraid to propose anything of the sort, because Clara would make an awful row about a step that must damage her matrimonial chances, and his mother could not be expected to like it after clinging for so many years to that step of the social ladder on which retail trade is impossible.

This difficulty was removed by an event highly unexpected by Freddy's mother. Clara, in the course of her incursions into those artistic circles which were the highest within her reach, discovered that her conversational qualifications were expected to include a grounding in the novels of Mr. H. G. Wells. She borrowed them in various directions so energetically that she swallowed them all within two months. The result was a conversion of a kind quite common today. A modern Acts of the Apostles would fill fifty whole Bibles if anyone were capable of writing it.

Poor Clara, who appeared to Higgins and his mother as a disagreeable and ridiculous person, and to her own mother as in some inexplicable way a social failure, had never seen herself in either light; for, though to some extent ridiculed and mimicked in West Kensington like everybody else there, she was accepted as a rational and normal—or shall we say inevitable?—sort of human being. At worst they called her The Pusher; but to them no more than to herself had it ever occurred that she was pushing the air, and pushing it in a wrong direction. Still, she was not happy. She was growing desperate. Her one asset, the fact that her mother was what the Epsom greengrocer called a carriage lady, had no exchange value, apparently. It had prevented her from getting educated because the only education she could have afforded was education with the Earlscourt greengrocer's daughter. It had led her to seek the society of her mother's class; and that class simply would not have her, because she was much poorer than the greengrocer, and, far from being able to afford a maid, could not afford even a housemaid, and had to scrape along at home with an illiberally treated general servant. Under such circumstances nothing could give her an air of being a genuine product of Largelady Park. And yet its tradition made her regard a marriage with anyone within her reach as an unbearable humiliation. Commercial people and professional people in a small way were odious to her. She ran after painters and novelists; but she did not charm them; and her bold attempts to pick up and practise artistic and literary talk irritated them. She was, in short, an utter failure, an ignorant, incompetent, pretentious, unwelcome, penniless, useless little snob; and though she did not admit these disqualifications (for nobody ever faces unpleasant truths of this kind until the possibility of a way out dawns on them) she felt their effects too keenly to be satisfied with her position.

Clara had a startling eyeopener when, on being suddenly wakened to enthusiasm by a girl of her own age who dazzled her and produced in her a gushing desire to take her for a model, and gain her friendship, she discovered that this exquisite apparition had graduated from the gutter in a few months time. It shook her so violently, that when Mr. H. G. Wells lifted her on the point of his puissant pen, and placed her at the angle of view from which the life she was leading and the society to which she clung appeared in its true relation to real human needs and worthy social structure, he effected a conversion and a conviction of sin comparable to the most sensational feats of General Booth or Gypsy Smith. Clara's snobbery went bang. Life suddenly began to move with her. Without knowing how or why, she began to make friends and enemies. Some of the acquaintances to whom she had been a tedious or indifferent or ridiculous affliction, dropped her: others became cordial. To her amazement she found that some "quite nice" people were saturated with Wells, and that this accessibility to ideas was the secret of their niceness. People she had thought deeply religious, and had tried to conciliate on that tack with disastrous results, suddenly took an interest in her, and revealed a hostility to conventional religion which she had never conceived possible except among the most desperate characters. They made her read Galsworthy; and Galsworthy exposed the vanity of Largelady Park and finished her. It exasperated her to think that the dungeon in which she had languished for so many unhappy years had been unlocked all the time, and that the impulses she had so carefully struggled with and stifled for the sake of keeping well with society, were precisely those by which alone she could have come into any sort of sincere human contact. In the radiance of these discoveries, and the tumult of their reaction, she made a fool of herself as freely and conspicuously as when she so rashly adopted Eliza's expletive in Mrs. Higgins's drawing room; for the newborn Wellsian had to find her bearings almost as ridiculously as a baby; but nobody hates a baby for its ineptitudes, or thinks the worse of it for trying to eat the matches; and Clara lost no friends by her follies. They laughed at her to her face this time; and she had to defend herself and fight it out as best she could.

When Freddy paid a visit to Earlscourt (which he never did when he could possibly help it) to make the desolating announcement that he and his Eliza were thinking of blackening the Largelady scutcheon by opening a shop, he found the little household already convulsed by a prior announcement from Clara that she also was going to work in an old furniture shop in Dover Street, which had been started by a fellow Wellsian. This appointment Clara owed, after all, to her old social accomplishment of Push. She had made up her mind that, cost what it might, she would see Mr. Wells in the flesh; and she had achieved her end at a garden party. She had better luck than so rash an enterprise deserved. Mr. Wells came up to her expectations. Age had not withered him, nor could custom stale his infinite variety in half an hour. His pleasant neatness and compactness, his small hands and feet, his teeming ready brain, his unaffected accessibility, and a certain fine apprehensiveness which stamped him as susceptible from his topmost hair to his tipmost toe, proved irresistible. Clara talked of nothing else for weeks and weeks afterwards. And as she happened to talk to the lady of the furniture shop, and that lady also desired above all things to know Mr. Wells and sell pretty things to him, she offered Clara a job on the chance of achieving that end through her.

And so it came about that Eliza's luck held, and the expected opposition to the flower shop melted away. The shop is in the arcade of a railway station not very far from the Victoria and Albert Museum; and if you live in that neighbourhood you may go there any day and buy a buttonhole from Eliza.

Now here is a last opportunity for romance. Would you not like to be assured that the shop was an immense success, thanks to Eliza's charms and her early business experience in Covent Garden? Alas! the truth is the truth: the shop did not pay for a long time, simply because Eliza and her Freddy did not know how to keep it. True, Eliza had not to begin at the very beginning: she knew the names and prices of the cheaper flowers; and her elation was unbounded when she found that Freddy, like all youths educated at cheap, pretentious, and thoroughly inefficient schools, knew a little Latin. It was very little, but enough to make him appear to her a Porson or Bentley, and to put him at his ease with botanical nomenclature. Unfortunately he knew nothing else; and Eliza, though she could count money up to eighteen shillings or so, and had acquired a certain familiarity with the language of Milton from her struggles to qualify herself for winning Higgins's bet, could not write out a bill without utterly disgracing the establishment. Freddy's power of stating in Latin that Balbus built a wall and that Gaul was divided into three parts did not carry with it the slightest knowledge of accounts or business: Colonel

Pickering had to explain to him what a cheque book and a bank account meant. And the pair were by no means easily teachable. Freddy backed up Eliza in her obstinate refusal to believe that they could save money by engaging a bookkeeper with some knowledge of the business. How, they argued, could you possibly save money by going to extra expense when you already could not make both ends meet? But the Colonel, after making the ends meet over and over again, at last gently insisted; and Eliza, humbled to the dust by having to beg from him so often, and stung by the uproarious derision of Higgins, to whom the notion of Freddy succeeding at anything was a joke that never palled, grasped the fact that business, like phonetics, has to be learned.

On the piteous spectacle of the pair spending their evenings in shorthand schools and polytechnic classes, learning bookkeeping and typewriting with incipient junior clerks, male and female, from the elementary schools, let me not dwell. There were even classes at the London School of Economics, and a humble personal appeal to the director of that institution to recommend a course bearing on the flower business. He, being a humorist, explained to them the method of the celebrated Dickensian essay on Chinese Metaphysics by the gentleman who read an article on China and an article on Metaphysics and combined the information. He suggested that they should combine the London School with Kew Gardens. Eliza, to whom the procedure of the Dickensian gentleman seemed perfectly correct (as in fact it was) and not in the least funny (which was only her ignorance), took the advice with entire gravity. But the effort that cost her the deepest humiliation was a request to Higgins, whose pet artistic fancy, next to Milton's verse, was caligraphy, and who himself wrote a most beautiful Italian hand, that he would teach her to write. He declared that she was congenitally incapable of forming a single letter worthy of the least of Milton's words; but she persisted; and again he suddenly threw himself into the task of teaching her with a combination of stormy intensity, concentrated patience, and occasional bursts of interesting disquisition on the beauty and nobility, the august mission and destiny, of human handwriting. Eliza ended by acquiring an extremely uncommercial script which was a positive extension of her personal beauty, and spending three times as much on stationery as anyone else because certain qualities and shapes on paper became indispensable to her. She could not even address an envelope in the usual way because it made the margins all wrong.

Their commercial schooldays were a period of disgrace and despair for the young couple. They seemed to be learning nothing about flower shops. At last they gave it up as hopeless, and shook the dust of the shorthand schools, and the polytechnics, and the London School of Economics from their feet for ever. Besides, the business was in some mysterious way beginning to take care of itself. They had somehow forgotten their objections to employing other people. They came to the conclusion that their own way was the best, and that they had really a remarkable talent for business. The Colonel, who had been compelled for some years to keep a sufficient sum on current account at his bankers to make up their deficits, found that the provision was unnecessary: the young people were prospering. It is true that there was not quite fair play between them and their competitors in trade. Their week-ends in the country cost them nothing, and saved them the price of their Sunday dinners; for the motor car was the Colonel's; and he and Higgins paid the hotel bills. Mr. F. Hill, florist and greengrocer (they soon discovered that there was money in asparagus; and asparagus led to other vegetables), had an air which stamped the business as classy; and in private life he was still Frederick Eynsford Hill, Esquire. Not that there was any swank about him: nobody but Eliza knew that he had been christened Frederick Challoner. Eliza herself swanked like anything.

That is all. That is how it has turned out. It is astonishing how much Eliza still manages to meddle in the housekeeping at Wimpole Street in spite of the shop and her own family. And it is notable that though she never nags her husband, and frankly loves the Colonel as if she were his favorite daughter, she has never got out of the habit of nagging Higgins that was established on the fatal night when she won his bet for him. She snaps his head off on the faintest provocation, or on none. He no longer dares to tease her by assuming an abysmal inferiority of Freddy's mind to his own. He storms and bullies and derides; but she stands up to him so ruthlessly that the Colonel has to ask her from time to time to be kinder to Higgins; and it is the only request of his that brings a mulish expression into her face. Nothing but some emergency or calamity great enough to break down all likes and dislikes, and throw them both back on their common humanity—and may they be spared any such trial!—will ever alter this. She knows that Higgins does not need her, just as her father did not need her. The very scrupulousness with which he told her that day that he had become used to having her there, and dependent on her for all sorts of little services, and that he should miss her if she went away (it would never have occurred to Freddy or the Colonel to say anything of the sort) deepens her inner certainty that she is "no more to him than them slippers"; yet she has a sense, too, that his indifference is deeper than the infatuation of commoner souls. She is immensely interested in him. She has even secret mischievous moments in which she wishes she could get him alone, on a desert island, away from all ties and with nobody else in the world to consider, and just drag him off his pedestal and see him making love like any common man. We all have private imaginations of that sort. But when it comes to business, to the life that she really leads as distinguished from the life of dreams and fancies, she likes Freddy and she likes the Colonel; and she does not like Higgins and Mr. Doolittle. Galatea never does quite like Pygmalion; his relation to her is too godlike to be altogether agreeable.

Desire Under the Elms

Eugene O'Neill (1888–1953)

The son of a well-known actor, James O'Neill, Eugene O'Neill entered Princeton University in 1906 but was forced to withdraw the following year. He travelled for the next few years, working for a time as a sailor and later as a reporter. He took a course in playwriting at Harvard (1914–15), and the next year joined the newly formed Provincetown Players, who performed his one-act play *Bound East for Cardiff. Beyond the Horizon* (1920) won a Pulitzer Prize, as did *Anna Christie* (1922) and *Strange Interlude* (1928). *Desire Under the Elms* appeared in 1924, at the height of O'Neill's interest in tragic realism. Between 1920 and the early 1940s O'Neill wrote some twenty long plays, among the best known being *Mourning Becomes Electra* (1931), a trilogy which counterpoints New England at the time of the American Civil War with the world of Aeschylus' *Oresteia.* From 1934 to 1946 O'Neill lived in California, writing plays but withholding them from performance. In 1936 he became the first American playwright to win a Nobel Prize. After his death in 1953 his great autobiographical play, *Long Day's Journey into Night,* was published and performed.

CHARACTERS

EPHRAIM CABOT
SIMEON, PETER, EBEN — *His sons*
ABBIE PUTNAM
Young Girl, Two Farmers, The Fiddler, A Sheriff, and other folk from the neighboring farms.

The action of the entire play takes place in, and immediately outside of, the Cabot farmhouse in New England, in the year 1850. The south end of the house faces front to a stone wall with a wooden gate at center opening on a country road. The house is in good condition but in need of paint. Its walls are sickly grayish, the green of the shutters faded. Two enormous elms are on each side of the house. They bend their trailing branches down over the roof. They appear to protect and at the same time subdue. There is a sinister maternity in their aspect, a crushing, jealous absorption. They have developed from their intimate contact with the life of man in the house an appalling humaneness. They brood oppressively over the house. They are like exhausted women resting their sagging breasts and hands and hair on its roof, and when it rains their tears trickle down monotonously and rot on the shingles.

There is a path running from the gate around the right corner of the house to the front door. A narrow porch is on this side. The end wall facing us has two windows in its upper story, two larger ones on the floor below. The two upper are those of the father's bedroom and that of the brothers. On the left, ground floor, is the kitchen—on the right, the parlor, the shades of which are always drawn down.

PART ONE

Scene One

Exterior of the Farmhouse. It is sunset of a day at the beginning of summer in the year 1850. There is no wind and everything is still. The sky above the roof is suffused with deep colors, the green of the elms glows, but the house is in a shadow, seeming pale and washed out by contrast.

A door opens and EBEN CABOT *comes to the end of the porch and stands looking down the road to the right. He has a large bell in his hand and this he swings mechanically, awakening a deafening clangor. Then he puts his hands on his hips and stares up at the sky. He sighs with a puzzled awe and blurts out with halting appreciation.*

EBEN: God! Purty! [*His eyes fall and he stares about him frowningly. He is twenty-five, tall and sinewy. His face is well-formed, good-looking, but its expression is resentful and defensive. His defiant, dark eyes remind one of a wild animal's in captivity. Each day is a cage in which he finds himself trapped but inwardly unsubdued. There is a fierce repressed vitality about him. He has black hair, mustache, a thin curly trace of beard. He is dressed in rough farm clothes.*

He spits on the ground with intense disgust, turns and goes back into the house.

SIMEON *and* PETER *come in from their work in the fields. They are tall men, much older than their half-brother* (SIMEON *is thirty-nine and* PETER *thirty-seven*), *built on a squarer, simpler model, fleshier in body, more bovine and homelier in face, shrewder and more practical. Their shoulders stoop a bit from years of farm work. They clump heavily along in their clumsy thick-soled boots caked with earth. Their clothes, their faces, hands, bare arms and throats are earth-stained. They smell of earth. They stand together for a moment in front of the house and, as if with the one impulse, stare dumbly up at the sky, leaning on their hoes. Their faces have a compressed, unresigned expression. As they look upward, this softens.*]

SIMEON [*grudgingly*]: Purty.

PETER: Ay-eh.

SIMEON [*suddenly*]: Eighteen year ago.

PETER: What?

SIMEON: Jenn. My woman. She died.

PETER: I'd fergot.

SIMEON: I rec'lect—now an' again. Makes it lonesome. She'd hair long's a hoss' tail—an' yaller like gold!

PETER: Waal—she's gone. [*This with indifferent finality—then after a pause*] They's gold in the West, Sim.

SIMEON [*still under the influence of sunset—vaguely*]: In the sky?

PETER: Waal—in a manner o' speakin'—thar's the promise. [*Growing excited*] Gold in the sky—in the West—Golden Gate—Californi-a!—Goldest West!—fields o' gold!

SIMEON [*excited in his turn*]: Fortunes layin' just atop o' the ground waitin' t' be picked! Solomon's mines, they says! [*For a moment they continue looking up at the sky—then their eyes drop.*]

PETER [*with sardonic bitterness*]: Here—it's stones atop o' the ground—stones atop o' stones—makin' stone walls—year atop o' year—him 'n' yew 'n' me 'n' then Eben—makin' stone walls fur him to fence us in!

SIMEON: We've wuked. Give our strength. Give our years. Plowed 'em under the ground,—[*he stamps rebelliously*]—rottin'—makin' soil for his crops! [*A pause*] Waal—the farm pays good for hereabouts.

PETER: If we plowed in Californi-a, they'd be lumps o' gold in the furrow!

SIMEON: Californi-a's t'other side o'earth, a'most. We got t' calc'late—

PETER [*after a pause*]: 'Twould be hard fur me, too, to give up what we've 'arned here by our sweat. [*A pause.* EBEN *sticks his head out of the dining-room window, listening.*]

SIMEON: Ay-eh. [*A pause*] Mebbe—he'll die soon.

PETER [*doubtfully*]: Mebbe.

SIMEON: Mebbe—fur all we knows—he's dead now.

PETER: Ye'd need proof.

SIMEON: He's been gone two months—with no word.

PETER: Left us in the fields an evenin' like this. Hitched up an' druv off into the West. That's plum onnateral. He hain't never been off this farm 'ceptin' t' the village in thirty year or more, not since he married Eben's maw. [*A pause. Shrewdly*] I calc'late we might git him declared crazy by the court.

SIMEON: He skinned 'em too slick. He got the best o' all on 'em. They'd never b'lieve him crazy. [*A pause*] We got t' wait—till he's under ground.

EBEN [*with a sardonic chuckle*]: Honor thy father! [*They turn, startled, and stare at him. He grins, then scowls*] I pray he's died. [*They stare at him. He continues matter-of-factly*] Supper's ready.

SIMEON *and* PETER [*together*]: Ay-eh.

EBEN [*gazing up at the sky*]: Sun's downin' purty.

SIMEON *and* PETER [*together*]: Ay-eh. They's gold in the West.

EBEN: Ay-eh. [*Pointing*] Yonder atop o' the hill pasture, ye mean?

SIMEON *and* PETER [*together*]: In Californi-a!

EBEN: Hunh? [*Stares at them indifferently for a second, then drawls*] Waal—supper's gitten' cold. [*He turns back into kitchen.*]

SIMEON [*startled—smacks his lips*]: I air hungry!

PETER [*sniffing*]: I smells bacon!

SIMEON [*with hungry appreciation*]: Bacon's good!

PETER [*in same tone*]: Bacon's bacon! [*They turn, shouldering each other, their bodies bumping and rubbing together as they hurry clumsily to their food, like two friendly oxen toward their evening meal. They disappear around the right corner of house and can be heard entering the door.*]

Curtain

Scene Two

The color fades from the sky. Twilight begins. The interior of the kitchen is now visible. A pine table is at center, a cookstove in the right rear corner, four rough wooden chairs, a tallow candle on the table. In the middle of the rear wall is fastened a big advertising poster with a ship in full sail and the word "California" in big letters. Kitchen utensils hang from nails. Everything is neat and in order but the atmosphere is of a men's camp kitchen rather than that of a home.

Places for three are laid. EBEN *takes boiled potatoes and bacon from the stove and puts them on the table, also a loaf of bread and a crock of water.* SIMEON *and* PETER *shoulder in, slump down in their chairs without a word.* EBEN *joins them. The three eat in silence for a moment, the two elder as naturally unrestrained as beasts of the field,* EBEN *picking at his food without appetite, glancing at them with a tolerant dislike.*

SIMEON [*suddenly turns to* EBEN]: Looky here! Ye'd oughtn't t' said that, Eben.

PETER: 'Twa'n't righteous.

EBEN: What?

SIMEON: Ye prayed he'd died.

EBEN: Waal—don't yew pray it? [*A pause.*]

PETER: He's our Paw.

EBEN [*violently*]: Not mine!

SIMEON [*dryly*]: Ye'd not let no one else say that about yer Maw! Ha! [*He gives one abrupt sardonic guffaw.* PETER *grins.*]

EBEN [*very pale*]: I meant—I hain't his'n— hain't like him—he hain't me!

PETER [*dryly*]: Wait till ye've growed his age!

EBEN [*intensely*]: I'm Maw—every drop o' blood! [*A pause. They stare at him with indifferent curiosity.*]

PETER [*reminiscently*]: She was good t' Sim 'n' me. A good Stepmaw's scurse.

SIMEON: She was good t' everyone.

EBEN: [*greatly moved, gets to his feet and makes an awkward bow to each of them—stammering*]: I be thankful t' ye. I'm her—her heir. [*He sits down in confusion.*]

PETER [*after a puse—judicially*]: She was good even t' him.

EBEN [*fiercely*]: An' fur thanks he killed her!

SIMEON [*after a pause*]: No one never kills nobody. It's allus somethin'. That's the murderer.

EBEN: Didn't he slave Maw t' death?

PETER: He's slaved himself t' death. He's slaved Sim 'n' me 'n' yew t' death—on'y none o' us hain't died—yit.

SIMEON: It's somethin'—drivin' him—t' drive us!

EBEN [*vengefully*]: Waal—I hold him t' jedgment! [*Then scornfully*] Somethin'! What's somethin'?

SIMEON: Dunno.

EBEN [*sardonically*]: What's drivin' yew to Californi-a, mebbee? [*They look at him in surprise*] Oh, I've heerd ye! [*Then, after a pause*] But ye'll never go t' the gold fields!

PETER [*assertively*]: Mebbee!

EBEN: Whar'll ye git the money?

PETER: We kin walk. It's an a'mighty ways—Californi-a—but if yew was t' put all the steps we've walked on this farm end t' end we'd be in the moon!

EBEN: The Injuns'll skulp ye on the plains.

SIMEON [*with grim humor*]: We'll mebbe make 'em pay a hair fur a hair!

EBEN [*decisively*]: But t'aint that. Ye won't never go because ye'll wait here fur yer share o' the farm, thinkin' allus he'll die soon.

SIMEON [*after a pause*]: We've a right.

PETER: Two-thirds belong t'us.

EBEN [*jumping to his feet*]: Ye've no right! She wa'n't yewr Maw! It was her farm! Didn't he steal it from her? She's dead. It's my farm.

SIMEON [*sardonically*]: Tell that t' Paw—when he comes! I'll bet ye a dollar he'll laugh—fur once in his life. Ha! [*He laughs himself in one single mirthless bark*].

PETER [*amused in turn, echoes his brother*]: Ha!

SIMEON [*after a pause*]: What've ye got held agin us, Eben? Year arter year it's skulked in yer eye—somethin'.

PETER: Ay-eh.

EBEN: Ay-eh. They's somethin'. [*Suddenly exploding*] Why didn't ye never stand between him 'n' Maw when he was slavin' her to her grave—t' pay her back fur the kindness she done t' yew? [*There is a long pause. They stare at him in surprise.*]

SIMEON: Waal—the stock'd got t' be watered.

PETER: 'R they was woodin' t' do.

SIMEON: 'R plowin'.

PETER: 'R hayin'.

SIMEON: 'R spreadin' manure.

PETER: 'R weedin'.

SIMEON: 'R prunin'.

PETER: 'R milkin'.

EBEN [*breaking in harshly*]: An' makin' walls—stone atop o' stone—makin' walls till yer heart's a stone ye heft up out o' the way o' growth onto a stone wall t' wall in yer heart!

SIMEON [*matter-of-factly*]: We never had no time t' meddle.

PETER [*to* EBEN]: Yew was fifteen afore yer Maw died—an' big fur yer age. Why didn't ye never do nothin'?

EBEN [*harshly*]: They was chores t' do, wa'n't they? [*A pause—then slowly*] It was on'y arter she died I come to think o' it. Me cookin'—doin' her work—that made me know her, suffer her sufferin'—she'd come back t' help—come back t' bile potatoes—come back t' fry bacon—come back t' bake biscuits—come back all cramped up t' shake the fire, an' carry ashes, her eyes weepin' an' bloody with smoke an' cinders same's they used t' be. She still comes back—stands by the stove thar in the evening'—she can't find it natural sleepin' an restin' in peace. She can't git used t' bein' free—even in her grave.

SIMEON: She never complained none.

EBEN: She'd got too tired. She'd got too used t' bein' too tired. That was what he done. [*With vengeful passion*] An' sooner'r later, I'll meddle. I'll say the thin's I didn't say then t' him! I'll yell 'em at the top o' my lungs. I'll see t' it my Maw gits some rest an' sleep in her grave! [*He sits down again, relapsing into a brooding silence. They look at him with a queer indifferent curiosity.*]

PETER [*after a pause*]: Whar in tarnation d'ye s'pose he went, Sim?

SIMEON: Dunno. He druv off in the buggy, all spick an' span, with the mare all breshed an' shiny, druv off clackin' his tongue an' wavin' his whip. I remember it right well. I was finishin' plowin', it was spring an' May an' sunset, an' gold in the West, an' he druv off into it. I yells "Whar ye goin,' Paw?" an' he hauls up by the stone wall a jiffy. His old snake's eyes was glitterin' in the sun like he'd been drinkin' a jugful an' he says with a mule's grin: "Don't ye run away till I come back!"

PETER: Wonder if he knowed we was wantin' fur Californi-a?

SIMEON: Mebbe. I didn't say nothin' and he says, lookin' kinder queer an' sick: "I been hearin' the hens cluckin' an' the roosters crowin' all the durn day. I been listenin' t' the cows lowin' an' everythin' else kickin' up till I can't stand it no more. It's spring an' I'm feelin' damned," he says. "Damned like an old bare hickory tree fit on'y fur burnin'," he says. An' then I calc'late I must've looked a mite hopeful, fur he adds real spry and vicious: "But don't git no fool idee I'm dead. I've sworn t' live a hundred an' I'll do it, if on'y t' spite yer sinful greed! An' now I'm ridin' out t' learn God's message t' me in the spring, like the prophets done. An' yew git back t' yer plowin'," he says. An' he druv off singin' a hymn. I thought he was drunk—'r I'd stopped him goin'.

EBEN [*scornfully*]: No, ye wouldn't! Ye're scared o' him. He's stronger—inside—than both o' ye put together!

PETER [*sardonically*]: An' yew—be yew Samson?

EBEN: I'm gittin' stronger. I kin feel it growin' in me—growin' an' growin'—till it'll bust out—! [*He gets up and puts on his coat and a hat. They watch him, gradually breaking into grins.* EBEN *avoids their eyes sheepishly*] I'm goin' out fur a spell—up the road.

PETER: T' the village?

SIMEON: T' see Minnie?

EBEN [*defiantly*]: Ay-eh!

PETER [*jeeringly*]: The Scarlet Woman!

SIMEON: Lust—that's what's growin' in ye!

EBEN: Waal—she's purty!

PETER: She's been purty fur twenty year!

SIMEON: A new coat o' paint'll make a heifer out of forty.

EBEN: She hain't forty!

PETER: If she hain't, she's teeterin' on the edge.

EBEN [*desperately*]: What d'yew know—

PETER: All they is . . . Sim knew her—an' then me arter—

SIMEON: An' Paw kin tell yew somethin' too! He was fust!

EBEN: D'ye mean t' say he . . . ?

SIMEON [*with a grin*]: Ay-eh! We air his heirs in everythin'!

EBEN [*intensely*]: That's more to it! That grows on it! It'll bust soon! [*Then violently*] I'll go smash my fist in her face! [*He pulls open the door in rear violently.*]

SIMEON [*with a wink at* PETER—*drawlingly*]: Mebbe—but the night's wa'm—purty—by the time ye git thar mebbe ye'll kiss her instead!

PETER: Sart'n he will! [*They both roar with coarse laughter.* EBEN *rushes out and slams the door—then the outside front door*—comes around the corner of *the house and stands still by the gate, staring up at the sky.*]

SIMEON [*looking after him*]: Like his Paw.

PETER: Dead spit an' image!

SIMEON: Dog'll eat dog!

PETER: Ay-eh. [*Pause. With yearning*] Mebbe a year from now we'll be in Californi-a.

SIMEON: Ay-eh. [*A pause. Both yawn*] Let's git t'bed. [*He blows out the candle. They go out door in rear.* EBEN *stretches his arms up to the sky—rebelliously.*]

EBEN: Waal—thar's a star, an' somewhar's they's him, an' here's me, an' thar's Min up the road—in the same night. What if I does kiss her? She's like t'night, she's soft 'n' wa'm, her eyes kin wink like a star, her mouth's wa'm, her arms're wa'm, she smells like a wa'm plowed field, she's purty . . . Ay-eh! By God A'mighty she's purty, an' I don't give a damn how many sins she's sinned afore mine or who she's sinned 'em with, my sin's as purty as any one on 'em! [*He strides off down the road to the left.*]

Scene Three

It is the pitch darkness just before dawn. EBEN *comes in from the left and goes around to the porch, feeling his way, chuckling bitterly and cursing half-aloud to himself.*

EBEN: The cussed old miser! [*He can be heard going in the front door. There is a pause as he goes upstairs, then a loud knock on the bedroom door of the brothers*] Wake up!

SIMEON [*startedly*]: Who's thar?

EBEN [*pushing open the door and coming in, a lighted candle in his hand. The bedroom of the brothers is revealed. Its ceiling is the sloping roof. They can stand upright only close to the center dividing wall of the upstairs.* SIMEON *and* PETER *are in a double bed, front.* EBEN'S *cot is to the rear.* EBEN *has a mixture of silly grin and vicious scowl on his face*]: I be!

PETER [*angrily*]: What in hell's-fire . . . ?

EBEN: I got news fur ye! Ha! [*He gives one abrupt sardonic guffaw.*]

SIMEON [*angrily*]: Couldn't ye hold it 'til we'd got our sleep?

EBEN: It's nigh sunup. [*Then explosively*] He's gone an' married agen!

SIMEON *and* PETER [*explosively*]: Paw?

EBEN: Got himself hitched to a female 'bout thirty-five—an' purty, they says . . .

SIMEON [*aghast*]: It's a durn lie!

PETER: Who says?

SIMEON: They been stringin' ye!

EBEN: Think I'm a dunce, do ye? The hull village says. The preacher from New Dover, he brung the news—told it t'our preacher—New Dover, that's whar the old loon got himself hitched—that's whar the woman lived—

PETER [*no longer doubting—stunned*]: Waal . . . !

SIMEON [*the same*]: Waal . . . !

EBEN [*sitting down on a bed—with vicious hatred*]: Ain't he a devil out o' hell? It's jest t' spite us—the damned old mule!

PETER [*after a pause*]: Everythin'll go t' her now.

SIMEON: Ay-eh. [*A pause—dully*] Waal—if it's done—

PETER: It's done us. [*Pause—then persuasively*] They's gold in the fields o' Californi-a, Sim. No good a-stayin' here now.

SIMEON: Jest what I was a-thinkin'. [*Then with decision*] S'well fust's last. Let's light out and git this mornin'.

PETER: Suits me.

EBEN: Ye must like walkin'.

SIMEON [*sardonically*]: If ye'd grow wings on us we'd fly thar!

EBEN: Ye'd like ridin' better—on a boat, wouldn't ye? [*Fumbles in his pocket and takes out a crumpled sheet of foolscap*] Waal, if ye sign this ye kin ride on a boat. I've had it writ out an' ready in case ye'd ever go. It says fur three hundred dollars t' each ye agree yewr shares o' the farm is sold t' me. [*They look suspiciously at the paper. A pause.*]

SIMEON [*wonderingly*]: But if he's hitched agen—

PETER: An' whar'd yew git that sum o' money, anyways?

EBEN [*cunningly*]: I know whar it's hid. I been waitin'—Maw told me. She knew whar it lay fur years, but she was waitin' . . . It's her'n—the money he hoarded from her farm an' hid from Maw. It's my money by rights now.

PETER: Whar's it hid?

EBEN [*cunningly*]: Whar yew won't never find it without me. Maw spied on him—'r she'd never knowed. [*A pause. They look at him suspiciously, and he at them*] Waal, is it fa'r trade?

SIMEON: Dunno.

PETER: Dunno.

SIMEON [*looking at window*]: Sky's grayin'.

PETER: Ye better start the fire, Eben.

SIMEON: An' fix some vittles.

EBEN: Ay-eh. [*Then with a forced jocular heartiness*] I'll git ye a good one. If ye're startin' t' hoof it t' Californi-a ye'll need somethin' that'll stick t' yer ribs. [*He turns to the door, adding meaningly*] But ye kin ride on a boat if ye'll swap. [*He stops at the door and pauses. They stare at him.*]

SIMEON [*suspiciously*]: Whar was ye all night?

EBEN [*defiantly*]: Up t' Min's. [*Then slowly*] Walkin' thar, fust I felt 's if I'd kiss her; then I got a-thinkin' o' what ye'd said o' him an' her an' I says, I'll bust her nose fur that! Then I got t' the village an' heerd the news an' I got madder'n hell an' run all the way t' Min's not knowin' what I'd do—[*He pauses—then sheepishly but more defiantly*] Waal—when I seen her, I didn't hit her—nor I didn't kiss her nuther—I begun t' beller like a calf an' cuss at the same time, I was so durn mad—an' she got scared—an' I jest grabbed holt an' tuk her! [*Proudly*] Yes, sirree! I tuk her. She may've been his'n—an' your'n, too—but she's mine now!

SIMEON [*dryly*]: In love, air yew?

EBEN [*with lofty scorn*]: Love! I don't take no stock in sech slop!

PETER [*winking at* SIMEON]: Mebbe Eben's aimin' t' marry, too.

SIMEON: Min'd make a true faithful he'pmeet! [*They snicker.*]

EBEN: What do I care fur her—'ceptin' she's round an' wa'm? The p'int is she was his'n—an' now she b'longs t' me! [*He goes to the door—then turns—rebelliously*] An' Min hain't sech a bad un. They's worse'n Min in the world, I'll bet ye! Wait'll we see this cow the Old Man's hitched t'! She'll beat Min, I got a notion! [*He starts to go out.*]

SIMEON [*suddenly*]: Mebbe ye'll try t' make her your'n, too?

PETER: Ha! [*He gives a sardonic laugh of relish at this idea.*]

EBEN [*spitting with disgust*]: Her—here—sleepin' with him—stealin' my Maw's farm! I'd as soon pet a skunk 'r kiss a snake! [*He goes out. The two stare after him suspiciously. A pause. They listen to his steps receding.*]

PETER: He's startin' the fire.

SIMEON: I'd like t' ride t' Californi-a—but—

PETER: Min might o' put some scheme in his head.

SIMEON: Mebbe it's all a lie 'bout Paw marryin'. We'd best wait an' see the bride.

PETER: An' don't sign nothin' till we does!

SIMEON: Nor till we've tested it's good money! [*Then with a grin*] But if Paw's hitched we'd be sellin' Eben somethin' we'd never git nohow!

PETER: We'll wait an' see. [*Then with sudden vindictive anger*] An' till he comes, let's yew 'n' me not wuk a lick, let Eben tend to thin's if he's a mind t', let's us jest sleep an' eat an' drink likker, an' let the hull damned farm go t' blazes!

SIMEON [*excitedly*]: By God, we've 'arned a rest! We'll play rich fur a change. I hain't a-goin to stir outa bed till breakfast's ready.

PETER: An' on the table!

SIMEON [*after a pause—thoughtfully*]: What d'ye calc'late she'll be like—our new Maw? Like Eben thinks?

PETER: More'n' likely.

SIMEON [*vindictively*]: Waal—I hope she's a shedevil that'll make him wish he was dead an' livin' in the pit o' hell fur comfort!

PETER [*fervently*]: Amen!

SIMEON [*imitating his father's voice*]: "I'm ridin' out t' learn God's message t' me in the spring like the prophets done," he says. I'll bet right then an' thar he knew plumb well he was goin' whorin', the stinkin' old hypocrite!

Scene Four

Same as Scene Two—shows the interior of the kitchen with a lighted candle on table. It is gray dawn outside. SIMEON *and* PETER *are just finishing their breakfast.* EBEN *sits before his plate of untouched food, brooding frowningly.*

PETER [*glancing at him rather irritably*]: Lookin' glum don't help none.

SIMEON [*sarcastically*]: Sorrowin' over his lust o' the flesh!

PETER [*with a grin*]: Was she yer fust?

EBEN [*angrily*]: None o' yer business. [*A pause*] I was thinkin' o' him. I got a notion he's gittin' near—I kin feel him comin' on like yew kin feel malaria chill afore it takes ye.

PETER: It's too early yet.

SIMEON: Dunno. He'd like t' catch us nappin'—jest t' have somethin' t' hoss us 'round over.

PETER [*mechanically gets to his feet.* SIMEON *does the same*]: Waal—let's git t' wuk. [*They both plod mechanically toward the door before they realize. Then they stop short.*]

SIMEON [*grinning*]: Ye're a cussed fool, Pete—and I be wuss! Let him see we hain't wukin'! We don't give a durn!

PETER [*as they go back to the table*]: Not a damned durn! It'll serve t' show him we're done with him. [*They sit down again.* EBEN *stares from one to the other with surprise.*]

SIMEON [*grins at him*]: We're aimin' t' start bein' lilies o' the field.

PETER: Nary a toil 'r spin 'r lick o' wuk do we put in!

SIMEON: Ye're sole owner—till he comes—that's what ye wanted. Waal, ye got t' be sole hand, too.

PETER: The cows air bellerin'. Ye better hustle at the milkin'.

EBEN [*with excited joy*]: Ye mean ye'll sign the paper?

SIMEON [*dryly*]: Mebbe.

PETER: Mebbe.

SIMEON: We're considerin'. [*Peremptorily*] Ye better git t' wuk.

EBEN [*with queer excitement*]: It's Maw's farm agen! It's my farm! Them's my cows! I'll milk my durn fingers off fur cows o' mine! [*He goes out door in rear, they stare after him indifferently.*]

SIMEON: Like his Paw.

PETER: Dead spit 'n' image!

SIMEON: Waal—let dog eat dog! [EBEN *comes out of front door and around the corner of the house. The sky is beginning to grow flushed with sunrise.* EBEN *stops by the gate and stares around him with glowing, possessive eyes. He takes in the whole farm with his embracing glance of desire.*]

EBEN: It's purty! It's damned purty! It's mine! [*He suddenly throws his head back boldly and glares with hard, defiant eyes at the sky*] Mine, d'ye hear? Mine! [*He turns and walks quickly off left, rear, toward the barn. The two brothers light their pipes.*]

SIMEON [*putting his muddy boots up on the table, tilting back his chair, and puffing defiantly*]: Waal—this air solid comfort—fur once.

PETER: Ay-eh. [*He follows suit. A pause. Unconsciously they both sigh.*]

SIMEON [*suddenly*]: He never was much o' a hand at milkin', Eben wa'n't.

PETER [*with a snort*]: His hands air like hoofs! [*A pause.*]

SIMEON: Reach down the jug thar! Let's take a swaller. I'm feelin' kind o' low.

PETER: Good idee! [*He does so—gets two glasses—they pour out drinks of whisky*] Here's t' the gold in Californi-a!

SIMEON: An' luck t' find it! [*They drink—puff resolutely—sigh—take their feet down from the table.*]

PETER: Likker don't pear t' sot right.

SIMEON: We hain't used t' it this early. [*A pause. They become very restless.*]

PETER: Gittin' close in this kitchen.

SIMEON [*with immense relief*] Let's git a breath o' air. [*They arise briskly and go out rear—appear around house and stop by the gate. They stare up at the sky with a numbed appreciation.*]

PETER: Purty!

SIMEON: Ay-eh. Gold's t' the East now.

PETER: Sun's startin' with us fur the Golden West.

SIMEON [*staring around the farm, his compressed face tightened, unable to conceal his emotion*]: Waal—it's our last mornin'—mebbe.

PETER [*the same*]: Ay-eh.

SIMEON [*stamps his foot on the earth and addresses it desperately*]: Waal—ye've thirty year o' me buried in ye—spread out over ye—blood an' bone an' sweat—rotted away—fertilizin' ye—richin' yer soul—prime manure, by God, that's what I been t' ye!

PETER: Ay-eh! An' me!

SIMEON: An' yew, Peter. [*He sighs—then spits*] Waal—no use'n cryin' over spilt milk.

PETER: They's gold in the West—an' freedom, mebbe. We been slaves t' stone walls here.

SIMEON [*defiantly*]: We hain't nobody's slaves from this out—nor no thin's slaves nuther. [*A pause—restlessly*] Speakin' o' milk, wonder how Eben's managin'?

PETER: I s'pose he's managin'.

SIMEON: Mebbe we'd ought t' help—this once.

PETER: Mebbe. The cows know us.

SIMEON: An' likes us. They don't know him much.

PETER: An' the hosses, an' pigs, an' chickens. They don't know him much.

SIMEON: They knows us like brothers—an' likes us! [*Proudly*] Hain't we raised 'em t' be fust-rate, number one prize stock?

PETER: We hain't—not no more.

SIMEON [*dully*]: I was fergittin'. [*Then resignedly*] Waal, let's go help Eben a spell an' git waked up.

PETER: Suits me. [*They are starting off down left, rear, for the barn when* EBEN *appears from there hurrying toward them, his face excited.*]

EBEN [*breathlessly*]: Waal—har they be! The old mule an' the bride! I seen 'em from the barn down below at the turnin'.

PETER: How could ye tell that far?

EBEN: Hain't I as far-sight as he's near-sight? Don't I know the mare 'n' buggy, an' two people settin' in it? Who else . . . ? An' I tell ye I kin feel 'em a-comin', too! [*He squirms as if he had the itch.*]

PETER [*beginning to be angry*]: Waal—let him do his own unhitchin'!

SIMEON [*angry in his turn*]: Let's hustle in an' git our bundles an' be a-goin' as he's a-comin'. I don't want never t' step inside the door agen arter he's back. [*They both start back around the corner of the house.* EBEN *follows them.*]

EBEN [*anxiously*]: Will ye sign it afore ye go?

PETER: Let's see the color o' the old skinflint's money an' we'll sign. [*They disappear left. The two brothers clump upstairs to get their bundles.* EBEN *appears in the kitchen, runs to window, peers out, comes back and pulls up a strip of flooring in under stove, takes out a canvas bag and puts it on table, then sets the floorboard back in place. The two brothers appear a moment after. They carry old carpet bags.*]

EBEN [*puts his hand on bag guardingly*]: Have ye signed?

SIMEON [*shows paper in his hand*]: Ay-eh. [*Greedily*] Be that the money?

EBEN [*opens bag and pours out pile of twenty-dollar gold pieces*]: Twenty-dollar pieces—thirty on 'em. Count 'em. [*Peter does so, arranging them in stacks of five, biting one or two to test them.*]

PETER: Six hundred [*He puts them in bag and puts it inside his shirt carefully.*]

SIMEON [*handing paper to* EBEN]: Har ye be.

EBEN [*after a glance, folds it carefully and hides it under his shirt—gratefully*]: Thank yew.

PETER: Thank yew fur the ride.

SIMEON: We'll send ye a lump o' gold fur Christmas. [*A pause.* EBEN *stares at them and they at him.*]

PETER [*awkardly*]: Waal—we're a-goin'.

SIMEON: Comin' out t' the yard?

EBEN: No. I'm waitin' in here a spell. [*Another silence. The brothers edge awkwardly to door in rear—then turn and stand.*]

SIMEON: Waal—good-by.

PETER: Good-by.

EBEN: Good-by. [*They go out. He sits down at the table, faces the stove and pulls out the paper. He looks from it to the stove. His face, lighted up by the shaft of sunlight from the window, has an expression of trance. His lips move. The two brothers come out to the gate.*]

PETER [*looking off toward barn*]: Thar he be—unhitchin'.

SIMEON [*with a chuckle*]: I'll bet ye he's riled!

PETER: An' thar she be.

SIMEON: Let's wait 'n' see what our new Maw looks like.

PETER [*with a grin*]: An' give him our partin' cuss!

SIMEON [*grinning*]: I feel like raisin' fun. I feel light in my head an' feet.

PETER: Me, too. I feel like laffin' till I'd split up the middle.

SIMEON: Reckon it's the likker?

PETER: No. My feet feel itchin' t' walk an' walk—an' jump high over thin's—an'. . . .

SIMEON: Dance? [*A pause.*]

PETER [*puzzled*]: It's plumb onnateral.

SIMEON [*a light coming over his face*]: I calc'late it's 'cause school's out. It's holiday. Fur once we're free!

PETER [*dazedly*]: Free?

SIMEON: The halter's broke—the harness is busted—the fence bars is down—the stone walls air crumblin' an' tumblin'! We'll be kickin' up an' tearin' away down the road!

PETER [*drawing a deep breath—oratorically*]: Anybody that wants this stinkin' old rock-pile of a farm kin hev it. T'ain't ou'n, no siree!

SIMEON [*takes the gate off its hinges and puts it under his arm*]: We harby 'bolishes shet gates, an' open gates, an' all gates, by thunder!

PETER: We'll take it with us fur luck an' let 'er sail free down some river.

SIMEON [*as a sound of voices comes from left, rear*]: Har they comes! [*The two brothers congeal into two stiff, grim-visaged statues.* EPHRAIM CABOT *and* ABBIE PUTNAM *come in.* CABOT *is seventy-five, tall and gaunt, with great, wiry, concentrated power, but stoop-shouldered from toil. His face is as hard as if it were hewn out of a boulder, yet there is a weakness in it, a petty pride in its own narrow strength. His eyes are small, close together, and extremely near-sighted, blinking continually in the effort to focus on objects, their stare having a straining, ingrowing quality. He is dressed in his dismal black Sunday suit.* ABBIE *is thirty-five, buxom, full of vitality. Her round face is pretty but marred by its rather gross sensuality. There is strength and obstinacy in her jaw, a hard determination in her eyes, and about her whole personality the same unsettled, untamed, desperate quality which is so apparent in* EBEN.]

CABOT [*as they enter—a queer strangled emotion in his dry cracking voice*]: Har we be t' hum, Abbie.

ABBIE [*with lust for the word*]: Hum! [*Her eyes gloating on the house without seeming to see the two stiff figures at the gate*] It's purty—purty! I can't b'lieve it's r'ally mine.

CABOT [*sharply*]: Yewr'n? Mine! [*He stares at her penetratingly. She stares back. He adds relentingly*] Our'n—mebbe! It was lonesome too long. I was growin' old in the spring. A hum's got t' hev a woman.

ABBIE [*her voice taking possession*]: A woman's got t' hev a hum!

CABOT [*nodding uncertainly*]: Ay-eh. [*Then irritably*] Whar be they? Ain't thar nobody about—'r wukin'—r' nothin'?

ABBIE [*sees the brothers. She returns their stare of cold appraising contempt with interest—slowly*]: Thar's two men loafin' at the gate an' starin' at me like a couple o' strayed hogs.

CABOT [*straining his eyes*]: I kin see 'em—but I can't make out. . . .

SIMEON: It's Simeon.

PETER: It's Peter.

CABOT [*exploding*]: Why hain't ye wukin'?

SIMEON [*dryly*]: We're waitin' t' welcome ye hum—yew an' the bride!

CABOT [*confusedly*]: Huh? Waal—this be yer new Maw, boys. [*She stares at them and they at her.*]

SIMEON [*turns away and spits contemptuously*]: I see her!

PETER [*spits also*]: An' I see her!

ABBIE [*with the conqueror's conscious superiority*]: I'll go in an' look at *my* house. [*She goes slowly around to porch.*]

SIMEON [*with a snort*]: *Her* house!

PETER [*calls after her*]: Ye'll find Eben inside. Ye better not tell him it's *yewr* house.

ABBIE [*mouthing the name*]: Eben. [*Then quietly*] I'll tell Eben.

CABOT [*with a contemptuous sneer*]: Ye needn't heed Eben. Eben's a dumb fool—like his Maw—soft an' simple!

SIMEON [*with his sardonic burst of laughter*]: Ha! Eben's a chip o' yew—spit 'n' image—hard 'n' bitter's a hickory tree! Dog'll eat dog. He'll eat ye yet, old man!

CABOT [*commandingly*]: Ye git t' wuk!

SIMEON [*as* ABBIE *disappears in house—winks at* PETER *and says tauntingly*]: So that thar's our new Maw, be it? Whar in hell did ye dig her up? [*He and* PETER *laugh.*]

PETER: Ha! Ye'd better turn her in the pen with the other sows. [*They laugh uproariously, slapping their thighs.*]

CABOT [*so amazed at their effrontery that he stutters in confusion*]: Simeon! Peter! What's come over ye? Air ye drunk?

SIMEON: We're free, old man—free o' yew an' the hull damned farm! [*They grow more and more hilarious and excited.*]

PETER: An' we're startin' out fur the gold fields o' Californi-a!

SIMEON: Ye kin take this place an' burn it!

PETER: An' bury it—fur all we cares!

SIMEON: We're free, old man! [*He cuts a caper.*]

PETER: Free! [*He gives a kick in the air.*]

SIMEON [*in a frenzy*]: Whoop!

PETER: Whoop! [*They do an absurd Indian war dance about the old man who is petrified between rage and the fear that they are insane.*]

SIMEON: We're free as Injuns! Lucky we don't skulp ye!

PETER: An' burn yer barn an' kill the stock!

SIMEON: An' rape yer new woman! Whoop! [*He and* PETER *stop their dance, holding their sides, rocking with wild laughter.*]

CABOT [*edging away*]: Lust fur gold—fur the sinful, easy gold o' Californi-a! It's made ye mad!

SIMEON [*tauntingly*]: Wouldn't ye like us to send ye back some sinful gold, ye old sinner?

PETER: They's gold besides what's in Californi-a! [*He retreats back beyond the vision of the old man and takes the bag of money and flaunts it in the air above his head, laughing.*]

SIMEON: And sinfuller, too!

PETER: We'll be voyagin' on the sea! Whoop! [*He leaps up and down.*]

SIMEON: Livin' free! Whoop! [*He leaps in turn.*]

CABOT [*suddenly roaring with rage*]: My cuss on ye!

SIMEON: Take our'n in trade fur it! Whoop!

CABOT: I'll hev ye both chained up in the asylum!

PETER: Ye old skinflint! Good-by!

SIMEON: Ye old blood sucker! Good-by!

CABOT: Go afore I . . . !

PETER: Whoop! [*He picks a stone from the road.* SIMEON *does the same.*]

SIMEON: Maw'll be in the parlor.

PETER: Ay-eh! One! Two!

CABOT [*frightened*]: What air ye . . . ?

PETER: Three! [*They both throw, the stones hitting the parlor window with a crash of glass, tearing the shade.*]

SIMEON: Whoop!

PETER: Whoop!

CABOT [*in a fury now, rushing toward them*]: If I kin lay hands on ye—I'll break yer bones fur ye! [*But they beat a capering retreat before him,* SIMEON *with the gate still under his arm.* CABOT *comes back, panting with impotent rage. Their voices as they go off take up the song of the gold-seekers to the old tune of "Oh, Susannah!"*]

"I jumped aboard the Liza ship,
And traveled on the sea,
And every time I thought of home
I wished it wasn't me!
Oh! Californi-a,
That's the land fur me!
I'm off to Californi-a!
With my wash bowl on me knee."

[*In the meantime, the window of the upper bedroom on right is raised and* ABBIE *sticks her head out. She looks down at* CABOT*—with a sigh of relief.*]

ABBIE: Waal—that's the last o' them two, hain't it? [*He doesn't answer. Then in possessive tones*] This here's a nice bedroom, Ephraim. It's a r'al nice bed. Is it my room, Ephraim?

CABOT [*grimly—without looking up*]: Our'n! [*She cannot control a grimace of aversion and pulls back her head slowly and shuts the window. A sudden horrible thought seems to enter* CABOT'S *head*] They been up to somethin'! Mebbe—mebbe they've pizened the stock—'r somethin'! [*He almost runs off down toward the barn. A moment later the kitchen door is slowly pushed open and* ABBIE *enters. For a moment she stands looking at* EBEN. *He does not notice her at first. Her eyes take him in penetratingly with a calculating appraisal of his strength as against hers. But under this her desire is dimly awakened by his youth and good looks. Suddenly he becomes conscious of her presence and looks up. Their eyes meet. He leaps to his feet, glowering at her speechlessly.*]

ABBIE [*in her most seductive tones which she uses all through this scene*]: Be you—Eben? I'm Abbie—[*She laughs*] I mean, I'm yer new Maw.

EBEN [*viciously*]: No, damn ye!

ABBIE [*as if she hadn't heard—with a queer smile*]: Yer Paw's spoke a lot o' yew. . . .

EBEN: Ha!

ABBIE: Ye mustn't mind him. He's an old man. [*A long pause. They stare at each other*] I don't want t' pretend playin' Maw t' ye, Eben. [*Admiringly*] Ye're too big an' too strong fur that. I want t' be frens with ye. Mebbe with me fur a fren ye'd find ye'd like livin' here better. I kin make it easy fur ye with him, mebbe. [*With a scornful sense of power*] I calc'late I kin git him t' do most anythin' fur me.

EBEN [*with bitter scorn*]: Ha! [*They stare again,* EBEN *obscurely moved, physically attracted to her—in forced stilted tones*] Yew kin go t' the devil!

ABBIE [*calmly*]: If cussin' me does ye good, cuss all ye've a mind t'. I'm all prepared t' have ye agin me—at fust. I don't blame ye nuther. I'd feel the same at any stranger comin' t' take my Maw's place. [*He shudders. She is watching him carefully*] Yew must've cared a lot fur yewr Maw, didn't ye? My Maw died afore I'd growed. I don't remember her none. [*A pause*] But yew won't hate me long, Eben. I'm not the wust in the world—an' yew an' me've got a lot in common. I kin tell that by lookin' at ye. Waal—I've had a hard life, too—oceans o' trouble an' nuthin' but wuk fur reward. I was a orphan early an' had t' wuk fur others in other folks' hums. Then I married an' he turned out a drunken spreer an' so he had to wuk fur others an' me too agen in other folks' hums, an' the baby died, an' my husband got sick an' died too, an' I was glad sayin' now I'm free fur once, on'y I diskivered right away all I was free fur was t' wuk agen in other folks' hums, doin' other folks' wuk till I'd most give up hope o' ever doin' my own wuk in my own hum, an' then your Paw come. . . . [CABOT *appears returning from the barn. He comes to the gate and looks down the road the brothers have gone. A faint strain of their retreating voices is heard: "Oh, Californi-a! That's the place for me." He stands glowering, his fist clenched, his face grim with rage.*]

EBEN [*fighting against his growing attraction and sympathy—harshly*]: An' bought yew—like a harlot! [*She is stung and flushes angrily. She has been sincerely moved by the recital of her troubles. He adds furiously*] An' the price he's payin' ye—this farm—was my Maw's, damn ye!—an' mine now!

ABBIE [*with a cool laugh of confidence*]: Yewr'n? We'll see 'bout that! [*Then strongly*] Waal—what if I did need a hum? What else'd I marry an old man like him fur?

EBEN [*maliciously*]: I'll tell him ye said that!

ABBIE [*smiling*]: I'll say ye're lyin' a-purpose—an' he'll drive ye off the place!

EBEN: Ye devil!

ABBIE [*defying him*]: This be my farm—this be my hum—this be my kitchen—!

EBEN [*furiously, as if he were going to attack her*]: Shut up, damn ye!

ABBIE [*walks up to him—a queer coarse expression of desire in her face and body—slowly*]: An' upstairs—that be my bedroom—an' my bed! [*He stares into her eyes, terribly confused and torn. She adds softly*] I hain't bad nor mean—'ceptin' fur an enemy—but I got t' fight fur what's due me out o' life, if I ever 'spect t' git it. [*Then putting her hand on his arm—seductively*] let's yew 'n' me be frens, Eben.

EBEN [*stupidly—as if hypnotized*]: Ay-eh. [*Then furiously flinging off her arm*] No, ye durned old witch! I hate ye! [*He rushes out the door.*]

ABBIE [*looks after him smiling satisfiedly—then half to herself, mouthing the word*]: Eben's nice. [*She looks at the table, proudly*] I'll wash up *my* dishes now. [EBEN *appears outside, slamming the door behind him. He comes around corner, stops on seeing his father, and stands staring at him with hate.*]

CABOT [*raising his arms to heaven in the fury he can no longer control*]: Lord God o' Hosts, smite the undutiful sons with Thy wust cuss!

EBEN [*breaking in violently*]: Yew 'n' yewr God! Allus cussin' folks—allus naggin' 'em!

CABOT [*oblivious to him—summoningly*]: God o' the old! God o' the lonesome!

EBEN [*mockingly*]: Naggin' His sheep t' sin! T' hell with yewr God! [CABOT *turns. He and* EBEN *glower at each other.*]

CABOT [*harshly*]: So it's yew. I might've knowed it. [*Shaking his finger threateningly at him*] Blasphemin' fool! [*Then quickly*] Why hain't ye t' wuk?

EBEN: Why hain't yew? They've went. I can't wuk it all alone.

CABOT [*contemptuously*]: Nor noways! I'm wuth ten o' ye yit, old's I be! Ye'll never be more'n half a man! [*Then, matter-of-factly*] Waal—let's git t' the barn. [*They go. A last faint note of the "Californi-a" song is heard from the distance.* ABBIE *is washing her dishes.*]

Curtain

PART TWO

Scene One

The exterior of the farmhouse, as in Part One—a hot Sunday afternoon two months later. ABBIE, *dressed in her best, is discovered sitting in a rocker at the end of the porch. She rocks listlessly, enervated by the heat, staring in front of her with bored, half-closed eyes.*

EBEN *sticks his head out of his bedroom window. He looks around furtively and tries to see—or hear—if anyone is on the porch, but although he has been careful to make no noise,* ABBIE *has sensed his movement. She stops rocking, her face grows animated and eager, she waits attentively.* EBEN *seems to feel her presence, he scowls back his thoughts of her and spits with exaggerated disdain—then withdraws back into the room.* ABBIE *waits, holding her breath as she listens with passionate eagerness for every sound within the house.*

EBEN *comes out. Their eyes meet. His falter, he is confused, he turns away and slams the door resentfully. At this gesture,* ABBIE *laughs tantalizingly, amused but at the same time piqued and irritated. He scowls, strides off the porch to the path and starts to walk past her to the road with a grand swagger of ignoring her existence. He is dressed in his store suit, spruced up, his face shines from soap and water.* ABBIE *leans forward on her chair, her eyes hard and angry now, and, as he passes her, gives a sneering, taunting chuckle.*

EBEN [*stung—turns on her furiously*]: What air yew cacklin' 'bout?

ABBIE [*triumphant*]: Yew!

EBEN: What about me?

ABBIE: Ye look all slicked up like a prize bull.

EBEN [*with a sneer*]: Waal—ye hain't so durned purty yerself, be ye? [*They stare into each other's eyes, his held by hers in spite of himself, hers glowingly possessive. Their physical attraction becomes a palpable force quivering in the hot air.*]

ABBIE [*softly*]: Ye don't mean that, Eben. Ye may think ye mean it, mebbe, but ye don't. Ye can't. It's agin nature, Eben. Ye been fightin' yer nature ever since the day I come—tryin' t' tell yerself I hain't purty t'ye. [*She laughs a low humid laugh without taking her eyes from his. A pause—her body squirms desirously—she murmurs languorously*] Hain't the sun strong an' hot? Ye kin feel it burnin' into the earth —Nature—makin' thin's grow—bigger 'n' bigger— burnin' inside ye—makin' ye want t' grow—into somethin' else—till ye're jined with it—an' it's your'n—but it owns ye, too—an' makes ye grow bigger—like a tree—like them elums— [*She laughs again softly, holding his eyes. He takes a step toward her, compelled against his will*] Nature'll beat ye, Eben. Ye might's well own up t' it fust 's last.

EBEN [*trying to break from her spell—confusedly*]: If Paw'd hear ye goin' on. . . . [*Resentfully*] But ye've made such a damned idjit out o' the old devil. . . ! [ABBIE *laughs.*]

ABBIE: Wall—hain't it easier fur yew with him changed softer?

EBEN [*defiantly*]: No. I'm fightin' him—fightin' yew— fightin' fur Maw's rights t' her hum! [*This breaks her spell for him. He glowers at her*] An' I'm onto ye. Ye hain't foolin' me a mite. Ye're aimin' t' swaller up everythin' an' make it your'n. Waal, you'll find I'm a heap sight bigger hunk nor yew kin chew! [*He turns from her with a sneer.*]

ABBIE [*trying to regain her ascendancy—seductively*]: Eben!

EBEN: Leave me be! [*He starts to walk away*].

ABBIE [*more commandingly*]: Eben!

EBEN [*stops—resentfully*]: What d'ye want?

ABBIE [*trying to conceal a growing excitement*]: Whar air ye goin'?

EBEN [*with malicious nonchalance*]: Oh—up the road a spell.

ABBIE: T' the village?

EBEN [*airily*]: Mebbe.

ABBIE [*excitedly*]: T' see that Min, I s'pose?

EBEN: Mebbe.

ABBIE [*weakly*]: What d'ye want t' waste time on her fur?

EBEN [*revenging himself now—grinning at her*]: Ye can't beat Nature, didn't ye say? [*He laughs and again starts to walk away.*]

ABBIE [*bursting out*]: An ugly old hake!

EBEN [*with a tantalizing sneer*]: She's purtier'n yew be!

ABBIE: That every wuthless drunk in the county has. . . .

EBEN [*tauntingly*]: Mebbe—but she's better'n yew. She owns up fa'r 'n' squar' t' her doin's.

ABBIE [*furiously*]: Don't ye dare compare. . . .

EBEN: She don't go sneakin' an' stealin'—what's mine.

ABBIE [*savagely seizing on his weak point*]: Your'n? yew mean—my farm?

EBEN: I mean the farm yew sold yerself fur like any other old whore—my farm!

ABBIE [*stung—fiercely*]: Ye'll never live t' see the day when even a stinkin' weed on it 'll belong t' ye! [*Then in a scream*] Git out o' my sight! Go on t' yer slut— disgracin' yer Paw 'n' me! I'll git yer Paw t' horsewhip ye off the place if I want t'! Ye're only livin' here 'cause I tolerate ye! Git along! I hate the sight o' ye! [*She stops, panting and glaring at him.*]

EBEN [*returning her glance in kind*]: An' I hate the sight o' yew!

[*He turns and strides off up the road. She follows his retreating figure with concentrated hate. Old* CABOT *appears coming up from the barn. The hard, grim expression of his face has changed. He seems in some queer way softened, mellowed. His eyes have taken on a strange, incongruous dreamy quality. Yet there is no hint of physical weakness about him—rather he looks more robust and younger.* ABBIE *sees him and turns away quickly with unconcealed aversion. He comes slowly up to her.*]

CABOT [*mildly*]: War yew an' Eben quarrelin' agen?

ABBIE [*shortly*]: No.

CABOT: Ye was talkin' a'mighty loud. [*He sits down on the edge of porch.*]

ABBIE [*snappishly*]: If ye heerd us they hain't no need askin' questions.

CABOT: I didn't hear what ye said.

ABBIE [*relieved*]: Waal—it wa'n't nothin' t' speak on.

CABOT [*after a pause*]: Eben's queer.

ABBIE [*bitterly*]: He's the dead spit 'n' image o' yew!

CABOT [*queerly interested*]: D'ye think so, Abbie? [*After a pause, ruminatingly*] Me 'n' Eben's allus fit 'n' fit. I never could b'ar him noways. He's so thunderin' soft—like his Maw.

ABBIE [*scornfully*]: Ay-eh! 'Bout as soft as yew be!

CABOT [*as if he hadn't heard*]: Mebbe I been too hard on him.

ABBIE [*jeeringly*]: Waal—ye're gittin' soft now—soft as slop! That's what Eben was sayin'.

CABOT [*his face instantly grim and ominous*]: Eben was sayin'? Waal, he'd best not do nothin' t' try me 'r he'll soon diskiver. . . . [*A pause. She keeps her face turned away. He gradually softens. He stares up at the sky*] Purty, hain't it?

ABBIE [*crossly*]: I don't see nothin' purty.

CABOT: The sky. Feels like a wa'm field up thar.

ABBIE [*sarcastically*]: Air yew aimin' t' buy up over the farm too? [*She snickers contemptuously.*]

CABOT [*strangely*]: I'd like t' own my place up thar. [*A pause*] I'm gittin' old, Abbie. I'm gittin' ripe on the bough. [*A pause. She stares at him mystified. He goes on*] It's allus lonesome cold in the house—even when it's bilin' hot outside. Hain't yew noticed?

ABBIE: No.

CABOT: It's wa'm down t' the barn—nice smellin' an' warm—with the cows. [*A pause*] Cows is queer.

ABBIE: Like yew?

CABOT: Like Eben. [*A pause*] I'm gittin' t' feel resigned t' Eben—jest as I got t' feel 'bout his Maw. I'm gittin' t' learn to b'ar his softness—jest like her'n. I calc'late I c'd a'most take t' him—if he wa'n't sech a dumb fool! [*A pause*] I s'pose it's old age a-creepin' in my bones.

ABBIE [*indifferently*]: Waal—ye hain't dead yet.

CABOT [*roused*]: No, I hain't, yew bet—not by a hell of a sight—I'm sound 'n' tough as hickory! [*Then moodily*] But arter three score and ten the Lord warns ye t' prepare. [*A pause*] That's why Eben's come in my head. Now that his cussed sinful brothers is gone their path t' hell, they's no one left but Eben.

ABBIE [*resentfully*]: They's me, hain't they? [*Agitatedly*] What's all this sudden likin' ye've tuk to Eben? Why don't ye say nothin' 'bout me? Hain't I yer lawful wife?

CABOT [*simply*]: Ay-eh. Ye be. [*A pause—he stares at her desirously—his eyes grow avid—then with a sudden movement he seizes her hands and squeezes them, declaiming in a queer camp meeting preacher's tempo*] Yew air my Rose o' Sharon! Behold, yew air fair; yer eyes air doves; yer lips air like scarlet; yer two breasts air like two fawns; yer navel be like a round goblet; yer belly be like a heap o' wheat. . . . [*He covers her hand with kisses. She does not seem to notice. She stares before her with hard angry eyes.*]

ABBIE [*jerking her hands away—harshly*]: So ye're plannin' t' leave the farm t' Eben, air ye?

CABOT [*dazedly*]: Leave. . . ? [*Then with resentful obstinacy*] I hain't a-givin' it t' no one!

ABBIE [*remorselessly*]: Ye can't take it with ye.

CABOT [*thinks a moment—then reluctantly*]: No, I calc'late not. [*After a pause—with a strange passion*] But if I could, I would, by the Etarnal! 'R if I could, in my dyin' hour, I'd set it afire an' watch it burn—this house an' every ear o' corn an' every tree down t' the last blade o' hay! I'd sit an' know it was all a-dying with me an' no one else'd ever own what was mine, what I'd made out o' nothin' with my own sweat 'n' blood! [*A pause—then he adds with a queer affection*] 'Ceptin' the cows. Them I'd turn free.

ABBIE [*harshly*]: An' me?

CABOT [*with a queer smile*]: Ye'd be turned free, too.

ABBIE [*furiously*]: So that's the thanks I git fur marryin' ye—t' have ye change kind to Eben who hates ye, an' talk o' turnin' me out in the road.

CABOT [*hastily*]: Abbie! Ye know I wa'n't. . . .

ABBIE [*vengefully*]: Just let me tell ye a thing or two 'bout Eben! Whar's he gone? T' see that harlot, Min! I tried fur t' stop him. Disgracin' yew an' me—on the Sabbath, too!

CABOT [*rather guiltily*]: He's a sinner—nateral-born. It's lust eatin' his heart.

ABBIE [*enraged beyond endurance—wildly vindictive*]: An' his lust fur me! Kin ye find excuses fur that?

CABOT [*stares at her—after a dead pause*]: Lust—fur yew?

ABBIE [*defiantly*]: He was tryin' t' make love t' me—when ye heerd us quarrelin'.

CABOT [*stares at her—then a terrible expression of rage comes over his face—he springs to his feet shaking all over*]: By the A'mighty God—I'll end him!

ABBIE [*frightened now for Eben*]: No! Don't ye!

CABOT [*violently*]: I'll git the shotgun an' blow his soft brains t' the top o' them elums!

ABBIE [*throwing her arms around him*]: No, Ephraim!

CABOT [*pushing her away violently*]: I will, by God!

ABBIE [*in a quieting tone*]: Listen, Ephraim. 'Twa'n't nothin' bad—on'y a boy's foolin'—'twa'n't meant serious—jest jokin' an' teasin'. . . .

CABOT: Then why did ye say—lust?

ABBIE: It must hev sounded wusser'n I meant. An' I was mad at thinkin'—ye'd leave him the farm.

CABOT [*quieter but still grim and cruel*]: Waal then, I'll horsewhip him off the place if that much'll content ye.

ABBIE [*reaching out and taking his hand*]: No. Don't think o' me! Ye mustn't drive him off. 'Tain't sensible. Who'll ye get to help ye on the farm? They's no one hereabouts.

CABOT [*considers this—then nodding his appreciation*]: Ye got a head on ye. [*Then irritably*] Waal, let him stay. [*He sits down on the edge of the porch. She sits beside him. He murmurs contemptuously*] I oughtn't t' git riled so—at that 'ere fool calf. [*A pause*] But har's the p'int. What son o' mine'll keep on here t' the farm—when the Lord does call me? Simeon an' Peter air gone t' hell—an' Eben's follerin' 'em.

ABBIE: They's me.

CABOT: Ye're on'y a woman.

ABBIE: I'm yewr wife.

CABOT: That hain't me. A son is me—my blood—mine. Mine ought t' git mine. An' then it's still mine—even though I be six foot under. D'ye see?

ABBIE [*giving him a look of hatred*]: Ay-eh. I see. [*She becomes very thoughtful, her face growing shrewd, her eyes studying* CABOT *craftily.*]

CABOT: I'm gittin' old—ripe on the bough. [*Then with a sudden forced reassurance*] Not but what I hain't a hard nut t' crack even yet—an' fur many a year t' come! By the Etarnal, I kin break most o' the young fellers' backs at any kind o' work any day o' the year!

ABBIE [*suddenly*]: Mebbe the Lord'll give us a son.

CABOT [*turns and stares at her eagerly*]: Ye mean—a son—t' me 'n' yew?

ABBIE [*with a cajoling smile*]: Ye're a strong man yet, hain't ye? 'Tain't noways impossible, be it? We know that. Why d'ye stare so? Hain't ye never thought o' that afore? I been thinkin' o' it all along. Ay-eh—an' I been prayin' it'd happen, too.

CABOT [*his face growing full of joyous pride and a sort of religious ecstasy*]: Ye been prayin', Abbie?—fur a son?—t' us?

ABBIE: Ay-eh. [*With a grim resolution*] I want a son now.

CABOT [*excitedly clutching both of her hands in his*]: It'd be the blessin' o' God, Abbie—the blessin' o' God A'mighty on me—in my old age—in my lonesomeness! They hain't nothin' I wouldn't do fur ye then, Abbie. Ye'd hev on'y t' ask it—anythin' ye'd a mind t'!

ABBIE [*interrupting*]: Would ye will the farm t' me then—t' me an' it. . . ?

CABOT [*vehemently*]: I'd do anythin' ye axed, I tell ye! I swar it! May I be everlastin' damned t' hell if I wouldn't! [*He sinks to his knees pulling her down with him. He trembles all over with the fervor of his hopes*] Pray t' the Lord agen, Abbie. It's the Sabbath! I'll jine ye! Two prayers air better nor one. "An' God hearkened unto Rachel"! An' God hearkened unto Abbie! Pray, Abbie! Pray fur him to hearken! [*He bows his head, mumbling. She pretends to do likewise but gives him a side glance of scorn and triumph.*]

Scene Two

About eight in the evening. The interior of the two bedrooms on the top floor is shown. EBEN *is sitting on the side of his bed in the room on the left. On account of the heat he has taken off everything but his undershirt and pants. His feet are bare. He faces front, brooding moodily, his chin propped on his hands, a desperate expression on his face.*

In the other room CABOT *and* ABBIE *are sitting side by side on the edge of their bed, an old four-poster with feather mattress. He is in his night shirt, she in her nightdress. He is still in the queer, excited mood into which the notion of a son has thrown him. Both rooms are lighted dimly and fickeringly by tallow candles.*

CABOT: The farm needs a son.

ABBIE: I need a son.

CABOT: Ay-eh. Sometimes ye air the farm an' sometimes the farm be yew. That's why I clove t' ye in my lonesomeness. [*A pause. He pounds his knee with his fist*] Me an' the farm has got t' beget a son!

ABBIE: Ye'd best go t' sleep. Ye're gittin' thin's all mixed.

CABOT [*with an impatient gesture*]: No, I haint. My mind's clear's a well. Ye don't know me, that's it. [*He stares hopelessly at the floor.*]

ABBIE [*indifferently*]: Mebbe. [*In the next room* EBEN *gets up and paces up and down distractedly.* ABBIE *hears him. Her eyes fasten on the intervening wall with concentrated attention.* EBEN *stops and stares. Their hot glances seem to meet through the wall. Unconsciously he stretches out his arms for her and she half rises. Then aware, he mutters a curse at himself and flings himself face downward on the bed, his clenched fists above his head, his face buried in the pillow.* ABBIE *relaxes with a faint sigh but her eyes remain fixed on the wall; she listens with all her attention for some movement from* EBEN.]

CABOT [*suddenly raises his head and looks at her—scornfully*]: Will ye ever know me—'r will any man 'r woman? [*Shaking his head*] No. I calc'late 't wa'n't t' be. [*He turns away.* ABBIE *looks at the wall. Then, evidently unable to keep silent about his thoughts, without looking at his wife, he puts out his hand and clutches her knee. She starts violently, looks at him, sees he is not watching her, concentrates again on the wall and pays no attention to what he says*] Listen, Abbie. When I come here fifty odd year ago—I was jest twenty an' the strongest an' hardest ye ever seen—ten times as strong an' fifty times as hard as Eben. Waal—this place was nothin' but fields o' stones. Folks laughed when I tuk it. They couldn't know what I knowed. When ye kin make corn sprout out o' stones, God's livin' in yew! They wa'n't strong enuf fur that! They reckoned God was easy. They laughed. They don't laugh no more. Some died hereabouts. Some went West an' died. They're all under ground—fur follerin' arter an easy God. God hain't easy. [*He shakes his head slowly*] An' I growed hard.

Folks kept allus sayin' he's a hard man like 'twas sinful t' be hard, so's at last I said back at 'em: Waal then, by thunder, ye'll git me hard an' see how ye like it! [*Then suddenly*] But I give in t' weakness once. 'Twas arter I'd been here two year. I got weak—despairful—they was so many stones. They was a party leavin', givin' up, goin' West. I jined 'em. We tracked on 'n' on. We come t' broad medders, plains, whar the soil was black an' rich as gold. Nary a stone. Easy. Ye'd on'y to plow an' sow an' then set an' smoke yer pipe an' watch thin's grow. I could o' been a rich man—but somethin' in me fit me an' fit me—the voice o' God sayin': "This hain't wuth nothin' t' Me. Git ye back t' hum!" I got afeerd o' that voice an' I lit out back t' hum here, leavin' my claim an' crops t' whoever'd a mind t' take 'em. Ay-eh. I actoolly give up what was rightful mine! God's hard, not easy! God's in the stones! Build my church on a rock—out o' stones an' I'll be in them! That's what He meant t' Peter! [*He sighs heavily—a pause*] Stones. I picked 'em up an' piled 'em into walls. Ye kin read the years o' my life in them walls, every day a hefted stone, climbin' over the hills up and down, fencin' in the fields that was mine, whar I'd made thin's grow out o' nothin'—like the will o' God, like the servant o' His hand. It wa'n't easy. It was hard an' He made me hard fur it. [*He pauses*] All the time I kept gittin' lonesomer. I tuk a wife. She bore Simeon an' Peter. She was a good woman. She wuked hard. We was married twenty year. She never knowed me. She helped but she never knowed what she was helpin'. I was allus lonesome. She died. After that it wa'n't so lonesome fur a spell. [*A pause*] I lost count o' the years. I had no time t' fool away countin' 'em. Sim an' Peter helped. The farm growed. It was all mine! When I thought o' that I didn't feel lonesome. [*A pause*] But ye can't hitch yer mind t' one thin' day an' night. I tuk another wife—Eben's Maw. Her folks was contestin' me at law over my deeds t' the farm—my farm! That's why Eben keeps a-talkin' his fool talk o' this bein' his Maw's farm. She bore Eben. She was purty—but soft. She tried t' be hard. She couldn't. She never knowed me nor nothin'. It was lonesomer 'n hell with her. After a matter o' sixteen odd years, she died. [*A pause*] I lived with the boys. They hated me 'cause I was hard. I hated them 'cause they was soft. They coveted the farm without knowin' what it meant. It made me bitter 'n wormwood. It aged me—them coveting what I'd made fur mine. Then this spring the call come—the voice o' God cryin' in my wilderness, in my lonesomeness—t' go out an' seek an' find! [*Turning to her with strange passion*] I sought ye an' I found ye! Yew air my Rose o' Sharon! Yer eyes air like. . . . [*She has turned a blank face, resentful eyes to his. He stares at her for a moment—then harshly*] Air ye any the wiser fur all I've told ye?

ABBIE [*confusedly*]: Mebbe.

CABOT [*pushing her away from him—angrily*]: Ye don't know nothing'—nor never will. If ye don't hev a son t' redeem ye. . . . [*This in a tone of cold threat.*]

ABBIE [*resentfully*]: I've prayed, hain't I?

CABOT [*bitterly*]: Pray agen—fur understandin'!

ABBIE [*a veiled threat in her tone*]: Ye'll have a son out o' me, I promise ye.

CABOT: How kin ye promise?

ABBIE: I got second-sight mebbe. I kin foretell. [*She gives a queer smile.*]

CABOT: I believe ye have. Ye give me the chills sometimes. [*He shivers*] It's cold in this house. It's oneasy. They's thin's pokin' about in the dark—in the corners. [*He pulls on his trousers, tucking in his night shirt, and pulls on his boots.*]

ABBIE [*surprised*]: Whar air ye goin'?

CABOT [*queerly*]: Down whar it's restful—whar it's warm—down t' the barn. [*Bitterly*] I kin talk t' the cows. They know. They know the farm an' me. They'll give me peace. [*He turns to go out the door.*]

ABBIE [*a bit frightenedly*]: Air ye ailin' tonight, Ephraim?

CABOT: Growin'. Growin' ripe on the bough. [*He turns and goes, his boots clumping down the stairs.* EBEN *sits up with a start, listening.* ABBIE *is conscious of his movement and stares at the wall.* CABOT *comes out of the house around the corner and stands by the gate, blinking at the sky. He stretches up his hands in a tortured gesture*] God A'mighty, call from the dark! [*He listens as if expecting an answer. Then his arms drop, he shakes his head and plods off toward the barn.* EBEN *and* ABBIE *stare at each other through the wall.* EBEN *sighs heavily and* ABBIE *echoes it. Both become terribly nervous, uneasy. Finally* ABBIE *gets up and listens, her ear to the wall. He acts as if he saw every move she was making, he becomes resolutely still. She seems driven into a decision—goes out the door in rear determinedly. His eyes follow her. Then as the door of his room is opened softly, he turns away, waits in an attitude of strained fixity.* ABBIE *stands for a second staring at him, her eyes burning with desire. Then with a little cry she runs over and throws her arms about his neck, she pulls his head back and covers his mouth with kisses. At first, he submits dumbly; then he puts his arms about her neck and returns her kisses, but finally, suddenly aware of his hatred, he hurls her away from him, springing to his feet. They stand speechless and breathless, panting like two animals.*]

ABBIE [*at last—painfully*]: Ye shouldn't, Eben—ye shouldn't—I'd make ye happy!

EBEN [*harshly*]: I don't want t' be happy—from yew!

ABBIE [*helplessly*]: Ye do, Eben! Ye do! Why d'ye lie?

EBEN [*viciously*]: I don't take t'ye, I tell ye! I hate the sight o' ye!

ABBIE [*with an uncertain troubled laugh*]: Waal, I kissed ye anyways—an' ye kissed back—yer lips was burnin'—ye can't lie 'bout that! [*Intensely*] If ye don't care, why did ye kiss me back—why was yer lips burnin'?

EBEN [*wiping his mouth*]: It was like pizen on 'em. [*Then tauntingly*] When I kissed ye back, mebbe I thought 'twas someone else.

ABBIE [*wildly*]: Min?

EBEN: Mebbe.

ABBIE [*torturedly*]: Did ye go t' see her? Did ye r'ally go? I thought ye mightn't. Is that why ye throwed me off jest now?

EBEN [*sneeringly*]: What if it be?

ABBIE [*raging*]: Than ye're a dog, Eben Cabot!

EBEN [*threateningly*]: Ye can't talk that way t' me!

ABBIE [*with a shrill laugh*]: Can't I? Did ye think I was in love with ye—a weak thin' like yew? Not much! I on'y wanted ye fur a purpose o' my own—an' I'll hev ye fur it yet 'cause I'm stronger'n yew be!

EBEN [*resentfully*]: I knowed well it was on'y part o' yer plan t' swaller everythin'!

ABBIE [*tauntingly*]: Mebbe!

EBEN [*furious*]: Git out o' my room!

ABBIE: This air my room an' ye're on'y hired help!

EBEN [*threateningly*]: Git out afore I murder ye!

ABBIE [*quite confident now*]: I hain't a mite afeerd. Ye want me, don't ye? Yes, ye do! An' yer Paw's son'll never kill what he wants! Look at yer eyes! They's lust fur me in 'em, burnin' 'em up! Look at yer lips now! They're tremblin' an' longin' t' kiss me, an' yer teeth t' bite! [*He is watching her now with a horrible fascination. She laughs a crazy triumphant laugh*] I'm a-goin' t' make all o' this hum my hum! They's one room hain't mine yet, but it's a-goin' t' be tonight. I'm a-goin' down now an' light up! [*She makes him a mocking bow*] Won't ye come courtin' me in the best parlor, Mister Cabot?

EBEN [*staring at her—horribly confused—dully*]: Don't ye dare! It hain't been opened since Maw died an' was laid out thar! Don't ye. . . ! [*But her eyes are fixed on his so burningly that his will seems to wither before hers. He stands swaying toward her helplessly.*]

ABBIE [*holding his eyes and putting all her will into her words as she backs out the door*]: I'll expect ye afore long, Eben.

EBEN [*stares after her for a while, walking toward the door. A light appears in the parlor window. He murmurs*]: In the parlor? [*This seems to arouse connotations for he comes back and puts on his white shirt, collar, half ties the tie mechanically, puts on coat, takes his hat, stands barefooted looking about him in bewilderment, mutters wonderingly*] Maw! Whar air yew? [*Then goes slowly toward the door in rear.*]

Scene Three

A few minutes later. The interior of the parlor is shown. A grim, repressed room like a tomb in which the family has been interred alive. ABBIE *sits on the edge of the horsehair sofa. She has lighted all the candles and the room is revealed in all its preserved ugliness. A change has come over the woman. She looks awed and frightened now, ready to run away.*

The door is opened and EBEN *appears. His face wears an expression of obsessed confusion. He stands staring at her, his arms hanging disjointedly from his shoulders, his feet bare, his hat in his hand.*

ABBIE [*after a pause—with a nervous, formal politeness*]: Won't ye set?

EBEN [*dully*]: Ay-eh. [*Mechanically he places his hat carefully on the floor near the door and sits stiffly beside her on the edge of the sofa. A pause. They both remain rigid, looking straight ahead with eyes full of fear.*]

ABBIE: When I fust come in—in the dark—they seemed somethin' here.

EBEN [*simply*]: Maw.

ABBIE: I kin still feel—somethin'. . . .

EBEN: It's Maw.

ABBIE: At fust I was feered o' it. I wanted t' yell an' run. Now—since yew come—seems like it's growin' soft an' kind t' me. [*Addressing the air—queerly*] Thank yew.

EBEN: Maw allus loved me.

ABBIE: Mebbe it knows I love yew, too. Mebbe that makes it kind t' me.

EBEN [*dully*]: I dunno. I should think she'd hate ye.

ABBIE [*with certainty*]: No. I kin feel it don't—not no more.

EBEN: Hate ye fur stealin' her place—here in her

hum—settin' in her parlor whar she was laid— [*He suddenly stops, staring stupidly before him.*]

ABBIE: What is it, Eben?

EBEN [*in a whisper*]: Seems like Maw didn't want me t' remind ye.

ABBIE [*excitedly*]: I knowed, Eben! It's kind t' me! It don't b'ar me no grudges fur what I never knowed an' couldn't help!

EBEN: Maw b'ars him a grudge.

ABBIE: Waal, so does all o' us.

EBEN: Ay-eh. [*With passion*] I does, by God!

ABBIE [*taking one of his hands in hers and patting it*]: Thar! Don't git riled thinkin' o' him. Think o' yer Maw who's kind t' us. Tell me about yer Maw, Eben.

EBEN: They hain't nothin' much. She was kind. She was good.

ABBIE [*putting one arm over his shoulder. He does not seem to notice—passionately*]: I'll be kind an' good t' ye!

EBEN: Sometimes she used t' sing fur me.

ABBIE: I'll sing fur ye!

EBEN: This was her hum. This was her farm.

ABBIE: This is my hum! This is my farm!

EBEN: He married her t' steal 'em. She was soft an' easy. He couldn't 'preciate her.

ABBIE: He can't 'preciate me!

EBEN: He murdered her with his hardness.

ABBIE: He's murderin' me!

EBEN: She died. [*A pause*] Sometimes she used to sing fur me. [*He bursts into a fit of sobbing.*]

ABBIE [*both her arms around him—with wild passion*]: I'll sing fur ye! I'll die fur ye! [*In spite of her overwhelming desire for him, there is a sincere maternal love in her manner and voice—a horribly frank mixture of lust and mother love*] Don't cry, Eben! I'll take yer Maw's place! I'll be everythin' she was t' ye! Let me kiss ye, Eben! [*She pulls his head around. He makes a bewildered pretense of resistance. She is tender*] Don't be afeered! I'll kiss ye pure, Eben—same 's if I was a Maw t' ye—an' ye kin kiss me back 's if yew was my son—my boy—sayin' good-night t' me! Kiss me, Eben. [*They kiss in restrained fashion. Then suddenly wild passion overcomes her. She kisses him lustfully again and again and he flings his arms about her and returns her kisses. Suddenly, as in the bedroom, he frees himself from her violently and springs to his feet. He is trembling all over, in a strange state of terror.* ABBIE *strains her arms toward him with fierce pleading*] Don't ye leave me, Eben! Can't ye see it hain't enuf—lovin' ye like a Maw—can't ye see it's got t' be that an' more—much more—a hundred times more—fur me t' be happy—fur yew t' be happy?

EBEN [*to the presence he feels in the room*]: Maw! Maw! What d'ye want? What air ye tellin' me?

ABBIE: She's tellin' ye t' love me. She knows I love ye an' I'll be good t' ye. Can't ye feel it? Don't ye know? She's tellin' ye t' love me, Eben!

EBEN: Ay-eh. I feel—mebbe she—but—I can't figger out—why—when ye've stole her place—here in her hum—in the parlor whar she was—

ABBIE [*fiercely*]: She knows I love ye!

EBEN [*his face suddenly lighting up with a fierce, triumphant grin*]: I see it! I sees why. It's her vengeance on him—so's she kin rest quiet in her grave!

ABBIE [*wildly*]: Vengeance o' God on the hull o' us! What d'we give a durn? I love ye, Eben! God knows I love ye! [*She stretches out her arms for him.*]

EBEN [*throws himself on his knees beside the sofa and grabs her in his arms—releasing all his pent-up passion*]: An' I love yew, Abbie!—now I kin say it! I been dyin' fur want o' ye—every hour since ye come! I love ye! [*Their lips meet in a fierce, bruising kiss.*]

Scene Four

Exterior of the farmhouse. It is just dawn. The front door at right is opened and EBEN *comes out and walks around to the gate. He is dressed in his working clothes. He seems changed. His face wears a bold and confident expression, he is grinning to himself with evident satisfaction. As he gets near the gate, the window of the parlor is heard opening and the shutters are flung back and* ABBIE *sticks her head out. Her hair tumbles over her shoulders in disarray, her face is flushed, she looks at* EBEN *with tender, languorous eyes and calls softly.*

ABBIE: Eben. [*As he turns—playfully*] Jest one more kiss afore ye go. I'm goin' to miss ye fearful all day.

EBEN: An' me yew, ye kin bet! [*He goes to her. They kiss several times. He draws away, laughingly*] Thar. That's enuf, hain't it? Ye won't hev none left fur next time.

ABBIE: I got a million o' 'em left fur yew! [*Then a bit anxiously*] D'ye r'ally love me, Eben?

EBEN [*emphatically*]: I like ye better'n any gal I ever knowed! That's gospel!

ABBIE: Likin' hain't lovin'.

EBEN: Waal then—I love ye. Now air yew satisfied?

ABBIE: Ay-eh, I be. [*She smiles at him adoringly.*]

EBEN: I better git t' the barn. The old critter's liable t' suspicion an' come sneakin' up.

ABBIE [*with a confident laugh*]: Let him! I kin allus pull the wool over his eyes. I'm goin' t' leave the shutters open and let in the sun 'n' air. This room's been dead long enuf. Now it's goin' t' be my room!

EBEN [*frowning*]: Ay-eh.

ABBIE [*hastily*]: I meant—our room.

EBEN: Ay-eh.

ABBIE: We made it our'n last night, didn't we? We give it life—our lovin' did. [*A pause.*]

EBEN [*with a strange look*]: Maw's gone back t' her grave. She kin sleep now.

ABBIE: May she rest in peace! [*Then tenderly rebuking*] Ye oughtn't t' talk o' sad thin's—this mornin'.

EBEN: It jest come up in my mind o' itself.

ABBIE: Don't let it. [*He doesn't answer. She yawns*] Waal, I'm a-goin' t' steal a wink o' sleep. I'll tell the Old Man I hain't feelin' pert. Let him git his own vittles.

EBEN: I see him comin' from the barn. Ye better look smart an' git upstairs.

ABBIE: Ay-eh. Good-by. Don't ferget me. [*She throws him a kiss. He grins—then squares his shoulders and awaits his father confidently.* CABOT *walks slowly up from the left, staring up at the sky with a vague face.*]

EBEN [*jovially*]: Mornin', Paw. Star-gazin' in daylight?

CABOT: Purty, hain't it?

EBEN [*looking around him possessively*]: It's a durned purty farm.

CABOT: I mean the sky.

EBEN [*grinning*]: How d'ye know? Them eyes o' your'n can't see that fur. [*This tickles his humor and he slaps his thigh and laughs*] Ho-ho! That's a good un!

CABOT [*grimly sarcastic*]: Ye're feelin' right chipper, hain't ye? Whar'd ye steal the likker?

EBEN [*good-naturedly*]: 'Tain't likker. Jest life. [*Suddenly holding out his hand—soberly*] Yew 'n' me is quits. Let's shake hands.

CABOT [*suspiciously*]: What's come over ye?

EBEN: Then don't. Mebbe it's jest as well. [*A moment's pause*] What's come over me? [*Queerly*] Didn't ye feel her passin'—goin' back t' her grave?

CABOT [*dully*]: Who?

EBEN: Maw. She kin rest now an' sleep content. She's quits with ye.

CABOT [*confusedly*]: I rested. I slept good—down with the cows. They know how t' sleep. They're teachin' me.

EBEN [*suddenly jovial again*]: Good fur the cows! Waal—ye better git t' work.

CABOT [*grimly amused*]: Air yew bossin' me, ye calf?

EBEN [*beginning to laugh*]: Ay-eh! I'm bossin' yew! Ha-ha-ha! See how ye like it! Ha-ha-ha! I'm the prize rooster o' this roost. Ha-ha-ha! [*He goes off toward the barn laughing.*]

CABOT [*looks after him with scornful pity*]: Softheaded. Like his Maw. Dead spit 'n' image. No hope in him! [*He spits with contemptuous disgust*] A born fool! [*Then matter-of-factly*] Waal—I'm gittin' peckish. [*He goes toward door.*]

Curtain

PART THREE

Scene One

A night in late spring the following year. The kitchen and the two bedrooms upstairs are shown. The two bedrooms are dimly lighted by a tallow candle in each. EBEN *is sitting on the side of the bed in his room, his chin propped on his fists, his face a study of the struggle he is making to understand his conflicting emotions. The noisy laughter and music from below where a kitchen dance is in progress annoy and distract him. He scowls at the floor.*

In the next room a cradle stands beside the double bed.

In the kitchen all is festivity. The stove has been taken down to give more room to the dancers. The chairs, with wooden benches added, have been pushed back against the walls. On these are seated, squeezed in tight against one another, farmers and their wives and their young folks of both sexes from the neighboring farms. They are all chattering and laughing loudly. They evidently have some secret joke in common. There is no end of winking, of nudging, of meaning nods of the head toward CABOT *who, in a state of extreme hilarious excitement increased by the amount he has drunk, is standing near the rear door where there is a small keg of whisky and serving drinks to all the men. In the left corner, front, dividing the attention with her husband,* ABBIE *is sitting in a rocking chair, a shawl wrapped about her shoulders. She is very pale, her face is thin and drawn, her eyes are fixed anxiously on the open door in rear as if waiting for someone.*

The musician is tuning up his fiddle, seated in the far right corner. He is a lanky young fellow with a long, weak face. His pale eyes blink incessantly and he grins about him slyly with a greedy malice.

ABBIE [*suddenly turning to a young girl on her right*]: What's Eben?

YOUNG GIRL [*eyeing her scornfully*]: I dunno, Mrs. Cabot. I hain't seen Eben in ages. [*Meaningly*] Seems like he's spent most o' his time t' hum since yew come.

ABBIE [*vaguely*]: I tuk his Maw's place.

YOUNG GIRL: Ay-eh. So I've heard. [*She turns away to retail his bit of gossip to her mother sitting next to her.* ABBIE *turns to her left to a big stoutish middle-aged man whose flushed face and starting eyes show the amount of "likker" he has consumed.*]

ABBIE: Ye hain't seen Eben, hev ye?

MAN: No, I hain't. [*Then he adds with a wink*] If yew hain't, who would?

ABBIE: He's the best dancer in the county. He'd ought t' come an' dance.

MAN [*with a wink*]: Mebbe he's doin' the dutiful an' walkin' the kid t' sleep. It's a boy, hain't it?

ABBIE [*nodding vaguely*]: Ay-eh—born two weeks back—purty's a picter.

MAN: They all is—t' their Maws. [*Then in a whisper, with a nudge and a leer*] Listen, Abbie—if ye ever git tired o' Eben, remember me! Don't fergit now! [*He looks at her uncomprehending face for a second—then grunts disgustedly*] Waal—guess I'll likker agin. [*He goes over and joins* CABOT *who is arguing noisily with an old farmer over cows. They all drink.*]

ABBIE [*this time appealing to nobody in particular*]: Wonder what Eben's a-doin'? [*Her remark is repeated down the line with many a guffaw and titter until it reaches the fiddler. He fastens his blinking eyes on* ABBIE.]

FIDDLER [*raising his voice*]: Bet I kin tell ye, Abbie, what Eben's doin'! He's down t' the church offerin' up prayers o' thanksgivin'. [*They all titter expectantly.*]

A MAN: What fur? [*Another titter.*]

FIDDLER: 'Cause unto him a—[*He hesitates just long enough*] brother is born! [*A roar of laughter. They all look from* ABBIE *to* CABOT. *She is oblivious, staring at the door.* CABOT, *although he hasn't heard the words, is irritated by the laughter and steps forward, glaring about him. There is an immediate silence.*]

CABOT: What're ye all bleatin' about— like a flock o' goats? Why don't ye dance, damn ye? I axed ye here t' dance—t' eat, drink an' be merry—an' thar ye set cacklin' like a lot o' wet hens with the pip! Ye've swilled my likker an' guzzled my vittles like hogs, hain't ye? Then dance fur me, can't ye? That's fa'r an' squar', hain't it? [*A grumble of resentment goes around but they are all evidently in too much awe of him to express it openly.*]

FIDDLER [*slyly*]: We're waitin' fur Eben. [*A suppressed laugh.*]

CABOT [*with a fierce exultation*]: T'hell with Eben! Eben's done fur now! I got a new son! [*His mood switching with drunken suddenness*] But ye needn't t' laugh at Eben, none o' ye! He's my blood, if he be a dumb fool. He's better nor any o' yew! He kin do a day's work a'most up t' what I kin—an' that'd put any o' yew pore critters t' shame!

FIDDLER: An' he kin do a good night's work, too! [*A roar of laughter.*]

CABOT: Laugh, ye damn fools! Ye're right jist the same, Fiddler. He kin work day an' night too, like I kin, if need be!

OLD FARMER [*from behind the keg where he is weaving drunkenly back and forth—with great simplicity*]: They hain't many t' touch ye, Ephraim—a son at seventy-six. That's a hard man fur ye! I be on'y sixty-eight an' I couldn't do it. [*A roar of laughter in which* CABOT *joins uproariously.*]

CABOT [*slapping him on the back*]: I'm sorry fur ye, Hi. I'd never suspicion sech weakness from a boy like yew!

OLD FARMER: An' I never reckoned yew had it in ye nuther, Ephraim. [*There is another laugh.*]

CABOT [*suddenly grim*]: I got a lot in me—a hell of a lot—folks don't know on. [*Turning to the fiddler*] Fiddle 'er up, durn ye! Give 'em somethin' t' dance t'! What air ye, an ornament? Hain't this a celebration? Then grease yer elbow an' go it!

FIDDLER [*seizes a drink which the* OLD FARMER *holds out to him and downs it*]: Here goes! [*He starts to fiddle "Lady of the Lake." Four young fellows and four girls form in two lines and dance a square dance. The* FIDDLER *shouts directions for the different movements, keeping his words in the rhythm of the music and interspersing them with jocular personal remarks to the dancers themselves. The people seated along the walls stamp their feet and clap their hands in unison.* CABOT *is especially active in this respect. Only* ABBIE *remains apathetic, staring at the door as if she were alone in a silent room.*]

FIDDLER: Swing your partner t' the right! That's it,

Jim! Give her a b'ar hug! Her Maw hain't lookin'. [*Laughter*] Change partners! That suits ye, don't it, Essie, now ye got Reub afore ye? Look at her redden up, will ye? Waal, life is short an' so's love, as the feller says. [*Laughter.*]

CABOT [*excitedly, stamping his foot*]: Go it, boys! Go it, gals!

FIDDLER [*with a wink at the others*]: Ye're the spryest seventy-six ever I sees, Ephraim! Now if ye'd on'y good eye-sight . . . ! [*Suppressed laughter. He gives* CABOT *no chance to retort but roars*] Promenade! Ye're walkin' like a bride down the aisle, Sarah! Waal, while they's life they's allus hope, I've heerd tell. Swing your partner to the left! Gosh A'mighty, look at Johnny Cook high-steppin'! They hain't goin' t'be much strength left fur howin' in the corn lot t'morrow. [*Laughter.*]

CABOT: Go it! Go it! [*Then suddenly, unable to restrain himself any longer, he prances into the midst of the dancers, scattering them, waving his arms about wildly*] Ye're all hoofs! Git out o' my road! Give me room! I'll show ye dancin'. Ye're all too soft! [*He pushes them roughly away. They crowd back toward the walls, muttering, looking at him resentfully.*]

FIDDLER [*jeeringly*]: Go it, Ephraim! Go it! [*He starts "Pop, Goes the Weasel," increasing the tempo with every verse until at the end he is fiddling crazily as fast as he can go.*]

CABOT [*starts to dance, which he does very well and with tremendous vigor. Then he begins to improvise, cuts incredibly grotesque capers, leaping up and cracking his heels together, prancing around in a circle with body bent in an Indian war dance, then suddenly straightening up and kicking as high as he can with both legs. He is like a monkey on a string. And all the while he intersperses his antics with shouts and derisive comments*]: Whoop! Here's dancin' fur ye! Whoop! See that! Seventy-six, if I'm a day! Hard as iron yet! Beatin' the young 'uns like I allus done! Look at me! I'd invite ye t' dance on my hundredth birthday on'y ye'll all be dead by then. Ye're a sickly generation! Yer hearts air pink, not red! Yer veins is full o' mud an' water! I be the on'y man in the county! Whoop! See that! I'm a Injun! I've killed Injuns in the West afore ye was born—an' skulped 'em too! They's a arrer wound on my backside I c'd show ye! The hull tribe chased me. I outrun 'em all—with the arrer stuck in me! An' I tuk vengeance on 'em. Ten eyes fur an eye, that was my motter! Whoop! Look at me! I kin kick the ceilin' off the room! Whoop!

FIDDLER [*stops playing—exhaustedly*]: God A'mighty, I got enuf. Ye got the devil's strength in ye.

CABOT [*delightedly*]: Did I beat yew, too? Wa'al, ye played smart. Hev a swig. [*He pours whisky for himself and* FIDDLER. *They drink. The others watch* CABOT *silently with cold, hostile eyes. There is a dead pause. The* FIDDLER *rests.* CABOT *leans against the keg, panting, glaring around him confusedly. In the room above,* EBEN *gets to his feet and tiptoes out the door in rear, appearing a moment later in the other bedroom. He moves silently, even frightenedly, toward the cradle and stands there looking down at the baby. His face is as vague as his reactions are confused, but there is a trace of tenderness, of interested discovery. At the same moment that he reaches the cradle,* ABBIE *seems to sense something. She gets up weakly and goes to* CABOT.]

ABBIE: I'm goin' up t' the baby.

CABOT [*with real solicitation*]: Air ye able fur the stairs? D'ye want me t' help ye, Abbie?

ABBIE: No. I'm able. I'll be down agen soon.

CABOT: Don't ye git wore out! He needs ye, remember—our son does! [*He grins affectionately, patting her on the back. She shrinks from his touch.*]

ABBIE [*dully*]: Don't—tech me. I'm goin'—up. [*She goes.* CABOT *looks after her. A whisper goes around the room.* CABOT *turns. It ceases. He wipes his forehead streaming with sweat. He is breathing pantingly.*]

CABOT: I'm a-goin' out t' git fresh air. I'm feelin' a mite dizzy. Fiddle up thar! Dance, all o' ye! Here's likker fur them as wants it. Enjoy yerselves. I'll be back. [*He goes, closing the door behing him.*]

FIDDLER [*sarcastically*]: Don't hurry none on our account! [*A suppressed laugh. He imitates* ABBIE] Whar's Eben? [*More laughter.*]

A WOMAN [*loudly*]: What's happened in this house is plain as the nose on yer face! [ABBIE *appears in the doorway upstairs and stands looking in surprise and adoration at* EBEN *who does not see her.*]

A MAN: Ssshh! He's li'ble t' be listenin' at the door. That'd be like him. [*Their voices die to an intensive whispering. Their faces are concentrated on this gossip. A noise as of dead leaves in the wind comes from the room.* CABOT *has come out from the porch and stands by the gate, leaning on it, staring at the sky blinkingly.* ABBIE *comes across the room silently.* EBEN *does not notice her until quite near.*]

EBEN [*starting*]: Abbie!

ABBIE: Ssshh! [*She throws her arms around him. They kiss—then bend over the cradle together*] Ain't he purty?—dead spit 'n' image o' yew!

EBEN [*pleased*]: Air he? I can't tell none.

ABBIE: E-zactly like!

EBEN [*frowningly*]: I don't like this. I don't like lettin' on what's mine's his'n. I been doin' that all my life. I'm gittin' t' the end o' b'arin' it!

ABBIE [*putting her finger on his lips*]: We're doin' the best we kin. We got t' wait. Somethin's bound t' happen. [*She puts her arms around him*] I got t' go back.

EBEN: I'm goin' out. I can't b'ar it with the fiddle playin' an' the laughin'.

ABBIE: Don't git feelin' low. I love ye, Eben. Kiss me. [*He kisses her. They remain in each other's arms.*]

CABOT [*at the gate, confusedly*]: Even the music can't drive it out—somethin'. Ye kin feel it droppin' off the elums, climbin' up the roof, sneakin' down the chimney, pokin' in the corners! They's no peace in houses, they's no rest livin' with folks. Somethin's always livin' with ye. [*With a deep sigh*] I'll go t' the barn an' rest a spell. [*He goes wearily toward the barn.*]

FIDDLER [*tuning up*]: Let's celebrate the old skunk gittin' fooled! We kin have some fun now he's went. [*He starts to fiddle "Turkey in the Straw." There is real merriment now. The young folks get up to dance*]

Scene Two

*A half hour later—Exterior—*EBEN *is standing by the gate looking up at the sky, an expression of dumb pain bewildered by itself on his face,* CABOT *appears, returning from the barn, walking wearily, his eyes on the ground. He sees* EBEN *and his whole mood immediately changes. He becomes excited, a cruel, triumphant grin comes to his lips, he strides up and slaps* EBEN *on the back. From within comes the whining of the fiddle and the noise of stamping feet and laughing voices.*

CABOT: So har ye be!

EBEN [*startled, stares at him with hatred for a moment—then dully*]: Ay-eh.

CABOT [*surveying him jeeringly*]: Why hain't ye been in t' dance? They was all axin' fur ye.

EBEN: Let 'em ax!

CABOT: They's a hull passel o' purty gals.

EBEN: T' hell with 'em!

CABOT: Ye'd ought t' be marryin' one o' 'em soon.

EBEN: I hain't marryin' no one.

CABOT: Ye might 'arn a share o' a farm that way.

EBEN [*with a sneer*]: Like yew did, ye mean? I hain't that kind.

CABOT [*stung*]: Ye lie! 'Twas yer Maw's folks aimed t' steal my farm from me.

EBEN: Other folks don't say so. [*After a pause—defiantly*] An' I got a farm, anyways!

CABOT [*derisively*]: Whar?

EBEN [*stamps a foot on the ground*]: Har!

CABOT [*throws his head back and laughs coarsely*]: Ho-ho! Ye hev, hev ye? Waal, that's a good un!

EBEN [*controlling himself—grimly*]: Ye'll see!

CABOT [*stares at him suspiciously, trying to make him out—a pause—then with scornful confidence*]: Ay-eh. I'll see. So'll ye. It's ye that's blind—blind as a mole underground. [EBEN *suddenly laughs one short sardonic bark: "Ha." A pause.* CABOT *peers at him with renewed suspicion*] Whar air ye hawin' 'bout? [EBEN *turns away without answering.* CABOT *grows angry*] God A'mighty, yew air a dumb dunce! They's nothin' in that thick skull o' your'n but noise—like a empty keg it be! [EBEN *doesn't seem to hear.* CABOT'S *rage grows*] Yewr farm! God A'mighty! If ye wa'n't a born donkey ye'd know ye'll never own stick nor stone on it, specially now arter him bein' born. It's his'n, I tell ye—his'n arter I die—but I'll live a hundred jest t' fool ye all—an' he'll be growed then—yewr age a'most! [EBEN *laughs again his sardonic "Ha." This drives* CABOT *into a fury*] Ha? Ye think ye kin git 'round that someways, do ye? Waal, it'll be her'n, too—Abbie's—ye won't git 'round her—she knows yer tricks—she'll be too much fur ye—she wants the farm her'n—she was afeerd o' ye—she told me ye was sneakin' 'round tryin' t' make love t' her t' git her on yer side . . . ye . . . ye mad fool, ye! [*He raises his clenched fists threateningly.*]

EBEN [*is confronting him, choking with rage*]: Ye lie, ye old skunk! Abbie never said no sech thing!

CABOT [*suddenly triumphant when he sees how shaken* EBEN *is*]: She did. An' I says, I'll blow his brains t' the top o' them elums—an' she says no, that hain't sense, who'll ye git t'help ye on the farm in his place—an' then she says yew'n me ought t' have a son—I know we kin, she says—an' I says, if we do, ye kin have anythin' I've got ye've a mind t'. An' she says, I wants Eben cut off so's this farm'll be mine when ye die! [*With terrible gloating*] An' that's what happened, hain't it? An' the farm's her'n! An' the dust o' the road—that's you'rn! Ha! Now who's hawin'?

EBEN [*has been listening, petrified with grief and rage—suddenly laughs wildly and brokenly*]: Ha-ha-ha! So that's her sneakin' game—all along!—like I suspicioned at fust—t' swaller it all—an' me, too . . . ! [*Madly*] I'll murder her! [*He springs toward the porch but* CABOT *is quicker and gets in between.*]

CABOT: No, ye don't!

EBEN: Git out o' my road! [*He tries to throw* CABOT *aside. They grapple in what becomes immediately a murderous struggle. The old man's concentrated strength is too much for* EBEN. CABOT *gets one hand on his throat and presses him back across the stone wall. At the same moment,* ABBIE *comes out on the porch. With a stifled cry she runs toward them.*]

ABBIE: Eben! Ephraim! [*She tugs at the hand on* EBEN'S *throat*] Let go, Ephraim! Ye're chokin' him!

CABOT [*removes his hand and flings* EBEN *sideways full length on the grass, gasping and choking. With a cry,* ABBIE *kneels beside him, trying to take his head on her lap, but he pushes her away.* CABOT *stands looking down with fierce triumph*]: Ye needn't t've fret, Abbie, I wa'n't aimin' t' kill him. He hain't wuth hangin' fur—not by a hell of a sight! [*More and more triumphantly*] Seventy-six an' him not thirty yit—an' look whar he be fur thinkin' his Paw was easy! No, by God, I hain't easy! An' him upstairs, I'll raise him t' be like me! [*He turns to leave them*] I'm goin' in an' dance!—sing an' celebrate! [*He walks to the porch—then turns with a great grin*] I don't calc'late it's left in him, but if he gits pesky, Abbie, ye jest sing out. I'll come a-runnin' an' by the Etarnal, I'll put him across my knee an' birch him! Ha-ha-ha! [*He goes into the house laughing. A moment later his loud "whoop" is heard.*]

ABBIE [*tenderly*]: Eben. Air ye hurt? [*She tries to kiss him but he pushes her violently away and struggles to a sitting position.*]

EBEN [*graspingly*]: T'hell—with ye!

ABBIE [*not believing her ears*]: It's me, Eben—Abbie—don't ye know me?

EBEN [*glowering at her with hatred*]: Ay-eh—I know ye—now! [*He suddenly breaks down, sobbing weakly.*]

ABBIE [*fearfully*]: Eben—what's happened t' ye—why did ye look at me 's if ye hated me?

EBEN [*violently, between sobs and gasps*]: I do hate ye! Ye're a whore—a damn trickin' whore!

ABBIE [*shrinking back horrified*]: Eben! Ye don't know what ye're sayin'!

EBEN [*scrambling to his feet and following her—accusingly*]: Ye're nothin' but a stinkin' passel o' lies! Ye've been lyin' t' me every word ye spoke, day an' night, since we fust—done it. Ye've kept sayin' ye loved me. . . .

ABBIE [*frantically*]: I do love ye! [*She takes his hand but he flings her away.*]

EBEN [*unheeding*]: Ye've made a fool o' me—a sick, dumb fool—a-purpose! Ye've been on'y playin' yer sneakin', stealin' game all along—gittin' me t'lie with ye, so's ye'd hev a son he'd think was his'n, an' makin' him promise he'd give ye the farm and let me eat dust, if ye git him a son! [*Staring at her with anguished, bewildered eyes*] They must be a devil livin' in ye! T'ain't human t' be as bad as that be!

ABBIE [*stunned—dully*]: He told yew . . . ?

EBEN: Hain't it true? It hain't no good in yew lyin'.

ABBIE [*pleadingly*]: Eben, listen—ye must listen—it was long ago—afore we done nothin'—yew was scornin' me—goin' t' see Min—when I was lovin' ye—an' I said it t' him t' git vengeance on ye!

EBEN [*unheedingly. With tortured passion*]: I wish ye was dead! I wish I was dead along with ye afore this come! [*Ragingly*] But I'll git my vengeance too! I'll pray Maw t' come back t' help me—t' put her cuss on yew an' him!

ABBIE [*brokenly*]: Don't ye, Eben! Don't ye! [*She throws herself on her knees before him, weeping*] I didn't mean t' do bad t'ye! Fergive me, won't ye?

EBEN [*not seeming to hear her—fiercely*]: I'll git squar' with the old skunk—an' yew! I'll tell him the truth 'bout the son he's so proud o'! Then I'll leave ye here t' pizen each other—with Maw comin' out o' her grave at nights—an' I'll go t' the gold fields o' Californi-a whar Sim an' Peter be!

ABBIE [*terrified*]: Ye won't—leave me? Ye can't!

EBEN [*with fierce determination*]: I'm a-goin', I tell ye! I'll git rich thar an' come back an' fight him fur the farm he stole—an' I'll kick ye both out in the road—t' beg an' sleep in the woods—an' yer son along with ye—t' starve an' die! [*He is hysterical at the end.*]

ABBIE [*with a shudder—humbly*]: He's yewr son, too, Eben.

EBEN [*torturedly*]: I wish he never was born! I wish he'd die this minit! I wish I'd never sot eyes on him! It's him—yew havin' him—a purpose t' steal—that's changed everythin'!

ABBIE [*gently*]: Did ye believe I loved ye—afore he come?

EBEN: Ay-eh—like a dumb ox!

ABBIE: An' ye don't believe no more?

EBEN: B'lieve a lyin' thief! Ha!

ABBIE [*shudders—then humbly*]: An' did ye r'ally love me afore?

EBEN [*brokenly*]: Ay-eh—an' ye was trickin' me!

ABBIE: An' ye don't love me now!

EBEN [*violently*]: I hate ye, I tell ye!

ABBIE: An' ye're truly goin' West—goin' t' leave me—all account o' him being born?

EBEN: I'm a-goin' in the mornin'—or may God strike me t' hell!

ABBIE [*after a pause—with a dreadful cold intensity—slowly*]: If that's what his comin's done t' me—killin' yewr love—takin' yew away—my on'y joy—the on'y joy I ever knowed—like heaven t' me—purtier'n heaven—then I hate him, too, even if I be his Maw!

EBEN [*bitterly*]: Lies! Ye love him! He'll steal the farm fur ye! [*Brokenly*] But t'ain't the farm so much—not no more—it's yew foolin' me—gittin' me t' love ye—lyin' yew loved me—jest t' git a son t'steal!

ABBIE [*distractedly*]: He won't steal! I'd kill him fust! I do love ye! I'll prove t' ye. . . !

EBEN [*harshly*]: T'ain't no use lyin' no more. I'm deaf t' ye! [*He turns away*] I hain't seein' ye agen. Good-by!

ABBIE [*pale with anguish*]: Hain't ye even goin' t' kiss me—not once—arter all we loved?

EBEN [*in a hard voice*]: I hain't wantin' t' kiss ye never agen! I'm wantin' t' forgit I ever sot eyes on ye!

ABBIE: Eben!—ye mustn't—wait a spell—I want t' tell ye. . . .

EBEN: I'm a-goin' in t' git drunk. I'm a-goin' t' dance.

ABBIE [*clinging to his arm—with passionate earnestness*]: If I could make it—'s if he'd never come up between us—if I could prove t' ye I wa'n't schemin' t' steal from ye—so's everythin' could be jest the same with us, lovin' each other jest the same, kissin' an' happy the same's we've been happy afore he come—if I could do it—ye'd love me agen, wouldn't ye? Ye'd kiss me agen? Ye wouldn't never leave me, would ye?

EBEN [*moved*]: I calc'late not. [*Then shaking her hand off his arm—with a bitter smile*] But ye hain't God, be ye?

ABBIE [*exultantly*]: Remember ye've promised! [*Then with strange intensity*] Mebbe I kin take back one thin' God does!

EBEN [*peering at her*]: Ye're gitten' cracked, hain't ye? [*Then going towards door*] I'm a-goin' t' dance.

ABBIE [*calls after him intensely*]: I'll prove t' ye! I'll prove I love ye better'n. . . . [*He goes in the door, not seeming to hear. She remains standing where she is, looking after him—then she finishes desperately*] Better'n everythin' else in the world!

Scene Three

Just before dawn in the morning—shows the kitchen and CABOT'S *bedroom. In the kitchen, by the light of a tallow candle on the table,* EBEN *is sitting, his chin propped on his hands, his drawn face blank and expressionless. His carpetbag is on the floor beside him. In the bedroom, dimly lighted by a small whale-oil lamp,* CABOT *lies asleep.* ABBIE *is bending over the cradle, listening, her face full of terror yet with an undercurrent of desperate triumph. Suddenly, she breaks down and sobs, appears about to throw herself on her knees beside the cradle; but the old man turns restlessly, groaning in his sleep and she controls herself, and shrinking away from the cradle with a gesture of horror, backs swiftly toward the door in rear and goes out. A moment later she comes into the kitchen and, running to* EBEN, *flings her arms about his neck and kisses him wildly. He hardens himself, he remains unmoved and cold, he keeps his eyes straight ahead.*

ABBIE [*hysterically*]: I done it, Eben! I told ye I'd do it! I've proved I love ye—better'n everythin'—so's ye can't never doubt me no more!

EBEN [*dully*]: Whatever ye done, it hain't no good now.

ABBIE [*wildly*]: Don't ye say that! Kiss me, Eben, won't ye? I need ye t' kiss me arter what I done! I need ye t' love me!

EBEN [*kisses her without emotion—dully*]: That's fur good-by. I'm a-goin' soon.

ABBIE: No! No! Ye won't go—not now!

EBEN [*going on with his own thoughts*]: I been a-thinkin'—an' I hain't goin' t' tell Paw nothin'. I'll leave Maw t' take vengeance on ye. If I told him, the old skunk'd jest be stinken' mean enuf to take it out on that baby. [*His voice showing emotion in spite of him*] An' I don't want nothin' bad t' happen t' him. He hain't t' blame fur yew. [*He adds with a certain queer pride*] An' he looks like me! An' by God, he's mine! An' some day I'll be a-comin' back an' . . . !

ABBIE [*too absorbed in her own thoughts to listen to him—pleadingly*]: They's no cause fur ye t' go now—they's no sense—it's all the same's it was—they's nothin' come b'tween us now—arter what I done!

EBEN [*something in her voice arouses him. He stares at her a bit frightenedly*]: Ye look mad, Abbie. What did ye do?

ABBIE: I—I killed him, Eben.

EBEN [*amazed*]: Ye killed him?

ABBIE [*dully*] Ay-eh.

EBEN [*recovering from his astonishment—savagely*]: An' serves him right! But we got t' do somethin' quick t' make it look s'if the old skunk'd killed himself when he was drunk. We kin prove by 'em all how drunk he got.

ABBIE [*wildly*]: No! No! Not him! [*Laughing distractedly*] But that's what I ought t' done, hain't it?

I oughter killed him instead! Why didn't ye tell me?

EBEN [*appalled*]: Instead? What d'ye mean?

ABBIE: Not him.

EBEN [*his face grown ghastly*]: Not—not that baby!

ABBIE [*dully*]: Ay-eh!

EBEN [*falls to his knees as if he'd been struck—his voice trembling with horror*]: Oh, God A'mighty! A'mighty God! Maw, whar was ye, why didn't ye stop her?

ABBIE [*simply*]: She went back t' her grave that night we fust done it, remember? I hain't felt her about since. [*A pause.* EBEN *hides his head in his hands, trembling all over as if he had the ague. She goes on dully*] I left the piller over his little face. Then he killed himself. He stopped breathin'. [*She begins to weep softly.*]

EBEN [*rage beginning to mingle with grief*]: He looked like me. He was mine, damn ye!

ABBIE [*slowly and brokenly*]: I didn't want t' do it. I hated myself fur doin' it. I loved him. He was so purty—dead spit 'n' image o' yew. But I loved yew more—an' yew was goin' away—far off whar I'd never see ye agen, never kiss ye, never feel ye pressed agin me agen—an' ye said ye hated me fur havin' him—ye said ye hated him an' wished he was dead—ye said if it hadn't been fur him comin' it'd be the same's afore between us.

EBEN [*unable to endure this, springs to his feet in a fury, threatening her, his twitching fingers seeming to reach out for her throat*]: Ye lie! I never said—I never dreamed ye'd—I'd cut off my head afore I'd hurt his finger!

ABBIE [*piteously, sinking on her knees*]: Eben, don't ye look at me like that—hatin' me—not after what I done fur ye—fur us—so's we could be happy agen—

EBEN [*furiously now*]: Shut up, or I'll kill ye! I see yer game now—the same old sneakin' trick—ye're aimin' t' blame me fur the murder ye done!

ABBIE [*moaning—putting her hands over her ears*]: Don't ye, Eben! Don't ye! [*She grasps his legs.*]

EBEN [*his mood suddenly changing to horror, shrinks away from her*]: Don't ye tech me! Ye're pizen! How could ye—t' murder a pore little critter—Ye must've swapped yer soul t' hell! [*Suddenly raging*] Ha! I kin see why ye done it! Not the lies ye jest told—but 'cause ye wanted t' steal agen—steal the last thin' ye'd left me—my part o' him—no, the hull o' him—ye saw he looked like me—ye knowed he was all mine—an' ye couldn't b'ar it—I know ye! Ye killed him fur bein' mine! [*All this has driven him almost insane. He makes a rush past her for the door—then turns—shaking both fists at her, violently*] But I'll take vengeance now! I'll git the Sheriff! I'll tell him everythin'! Then I'll sing "I'm off to Californi-a!" an' go—gold—Golden Gate—gold sun—fields o' gold in the West! [*This last he half shouts, half croons incoherently, suddenly breaking off passionately*] I'm a-goin' fur the Sheriff t' come an' git ye! I want ye tuk away, locked up from me! I can't stand t' luk at ye! Murderer an' thief 'r not, ye still tempt me! I'll give ye up t' the Sheriff! [*He turns and runs out, around the corner of house, panting and sobbing, and breaks into a swerving sprint down the road.*]

ABBIE [*struggling to her feet, runs to the door, calling after him*]: I love ye, Eben! I love ye! [*She stops at the door weakly, swaying, about to fall*] I don't care what ye do—if ye'll on'y love me agen— [*She falls limply to the floor in a faint.*]

Scene Four

About an hour later. Same as Scene Three. Shows the kitchen and CABOT'S *bedroom. It is after dawn. The sky is brilliant with the sunrise. In the kitchen,* ABBIE *sits at the table, her body limp and exhausted, her head bowed down over her arms, her face hidden. Upstairs,* CABOT *is still asleep but awakens with a start. He looks toward the window and gives a snort of surprise and irritation—throws back the covers and begins hurriedly pulling on his clothes. Without looking behind him, he begins talking to* ABBIE *whom he supposes beside him.*

CABOT: Thunder 'n' lightin', Abbie! I hain't slept this late in fifty year! Looks 's if the sun was full riz a'most. Must've been the dancin' and likker. Must be gitten' old. I hope Eben's t' wuk. Ye might've tuk the trouble t' rouse me, Abbie. [*He turns—sees no one there—surprised*] Waal—whar air she? Gittin' vittles, I calc'late. [*He tiptoes to the cradle and peers down—proudly*] Mornin', sonny. Purty's a picter! Sleepin' sound. He don't beller all night like most o' 'em. [*He goes quietly out the door in rear—a few moments later enters kitchen—sees* ABBIE*—with satisfaction*] So thar ye be. Ye got any vittles cooked?

ABBIE [*without moving*]: No.

CABOT [*coming to her, almost sympathetically*]: Ye feelin' sick?

ABBIE: No.

CABOT [*pats her on shoulder. She shudders*]: Ye'd

best lie down a spell. [*Half jocularly*] Yer son'll be needin' ye soon. He'd ought t' wake up with a gnashin' appetite, the sound way he's sleepin'.

ABBIE [*shudders—then in a dead voice*]: He hain't never goin' t' wake up.

CABOT [*jokingly*]: Takes after me this mornin'. I hain't slept so late in . . .

ABBIE: He's dead.

CABOT [*stares at her—bewilderedly*]: What. . . .

ABBIE: I killed him.

CABOT [*stepping back from her—aghast*]: Air ye drunk—'r crazy—'r . . . !

ABBIE [*suddenly lifts her head and turns on him—wildly*]: I killed him, I tell ye! I smothered him. Go up an' see if ye don't b'lieve me! [CABOT *stares at her a second, then bolts out the rear door, can be heard bounding up the stairs, and rushes into the bedroom and over to the cradle.* ABBIE *has sunk back lifelessly into her former position.* CABOT *puts his hand down on the body in the crib. An expression of fear and horror comes over his face.*]

CABOT [*shrinking away—trembling*]: God A'mighty! God A'mighty. [*He stumbles out the door—in a short while returns to the kitchen—comes to* ABBIE, *the stunned expression still on his face—hoarsely*] Why did ye do it? Why? [*As she doesn't answer, he grabs her violently by the shoulder and shakes her*] I ax ye why ye done it! Ye'd better tell me 'r . . . !

ABBIE [*gives him a furious push which sends him staggering back and springs to her feet—with wild rage and hatred*]: Don't ye dare tech me! What right hev ye t' question me 'bout him? He wa'n't yewr son! Think I'd have a son by yew? I'd die fust! I hate the sight o' ye an' allus did! It's yew I should've murdered, if I'd had good sense! I hate ye! I love Eben. I did from the fust. An' he was Eben's son—mine an' Eben's—not your'n!

CABOT [*stands looking at her dazedly—a pause—finding his words with an effort—dully*]: That was it—what I felt—pokin' round the corners—while ye lied—holdin' yerself from me—sayin' ye'd a'ready conceived— [*He lapses into crushed silence—then with a strange emotion*] He's dead, sart'n. I felt his heart. Pore little critter! [*He blinks back one tear, wiping his sleeve across his nose.*]

ABBIE [*hysterically*]: Don't ye! Don't ye! [*She sobs unrestrainedly.*]

CABOT [*with a concentrated effort that stiffens his body into a rigid line and hardens his face into a stony mask—through his teeth to himself*]: I got t' be—like a stone—a rock o' jedgment! [*A pause. He gets complete control over himself—harshly*] If he was Eben's, I be glad he air gone! An' mebbe I suspicioned it all along. I felt they was somethin' onnateral—somewhars—the house got so lonesome—an' cold—drivin' me down t' the barn—t' the beasts o' the field. . . . Ay-eh. I must've suspicioned—somethin'. Ye didn't fool me—not altogether, leastways—I'm too old a bird—growin' ripe on the bough. . . . [*He becomes aware he is wandering, straightens again, looks at* ABBIE *with a cruel grin*] So ye'd liked t' hev murdered me 'stead o' him, would ye? Waal, I'll live to a hundred! I'll live t' see ye hung! I'll deliver ye up t' the jedgment o' God an' the law! I'll git the Sheriff now. [*Starts for the door.*]

ABBIE [*dully*]: Ye needn't. Eben's gone fur him.

CABOT [*amazed*]: Eben—gone fur the Sheriff?

ABBIE: Ay-eh.

CABOT: T' inform agen ye?

ABBIE: Ay-eh.

CABOT [*considers this—a pause—then in a hard voice*]: Waal, I'm thankful fur him savin' me the trouble. I'll git t' wuk. [*He goes to the door—then turns—in a voice full of strange emotion*] He'd ought t' been my son, Abbie. Ye'd ought t' loved me. I'm a man. If ye'd loved me, I'd never told no Sheriff on ye no matter what ye did, if they was t' brile me alive!

ABBIE [*defensively*]: They's more to it nor yew know, makes him tell.

CABOT [*dryly*]: Fur yewr sake, I hope they be. [*He goes out—comes around to the gate—stares up at the sky. His control relaxes. For a moment he is old and weary. He murmurs despairingly*] God A'mighty, I be lonesomer'n ever! [*He hears running footsteps from the left, immediately is himself again.* EBEN *runs in, panting exhaustedly, wild-eyed and mad looking. He lurches through the gate.* CABOT *grabs him by the shoulder.* EBEN *stares at him dumbly*] Did ye tell the Sheriff?

EBEN [*nodding stupidly*]: Ay-eh.

CABOT [*gives him a push away that sends him sprawling—laughing with withering contempt*]: Good fur ye! A prime chip o' yer Maw ye be! [*He goes toward the barn, laughing harshly.* EBEN *scrambles to his feet. Suddenly* CABOT *turns—grimly threatening*] Git off this farm when the Sheriff takes her—or, by God, he'll have t' come back an' git me fur murder, too! [*He stalks off.* EBEN *does not appear to have heard him. He runs to the door and comes into the kitchen.* ABBIE *looks up with a cry of anguished joy.* EBEN *stumbles over and throws himself on his knees beside her—sobbing brokenly.*]

EBEN: Fergive me!

ABBIE [*happily*]: Eben! [*She kisses him and pulls his head over against her breast.*]

EBEN: I love ye! Fergive me!

ABBIE [*ecstatically*]: I'd fergive ye all the sins in hell fur sayin' that! [*She kisses his head, pressing it to her with a fierce passion of possession.*]

EBEN [*brokenly*]: But I told the Sheriff. He's comin' fur ye!

ABBIE: I kin b'ar what happens t' me—now!

EBEN: I woke him up. I told him. He says, wait 'til I git dressed. I was waiting. I got to thinkin' o' yew. I got to thinkin' how I'd loved ye. It hurt like somethin' was bustin' in my chest an' head. I got t' cryin'. I knowed sudden I loved ye yet, an' allus would love ye!

ABBIE [*caressing his hair—tenderly*]: My boy, hain't ye?

EBEN: I begun t' run back. I cut across the fields an' through the woods. I thought ye might have time t' run away—with me—an' . .

ABBIE [*shaking her head*]: I got t' take my punishment—t' pay fur my sin.

EBEN: Then I want t' share it with ye.

ABBIE: Ye didn't do nothin'.

EBEN: I put it in yer head. I wisht he was dead! I as much as urged ye t' do it!

ABBIE: No. It was me alone!

EBEN: I'm as guilty as yew be! He was the child o' our sin.

ABBIE [*lifting her head as if defying God*]: I don't repent that sin! I hain't askin' God t' fergive that!

EBEN: Nor me—but it led up t' the other—an' the murder ye did, ye did 'count o' me—an' it's my murder, too, I'll tell the Sheriff—an' if ye deny it, I'll say we planned it t'gether—an' they'll all b'lieve me, fur they suspicion everythin' we've done, an' it'll seem likely an' true to 'em. An' it is true—way down. I did help ye—somehow.

ABBIE [*laying her head on his—sobbing*]: No! I don't want yew t' suffer!

EBEN: I got t' pay fur my part o' the sin! An' I'd suffer wuss leavin' ye, goin' West, thinkin' o' ye day an' night, bein' out when yew was in— [*Lowering his voice*] 'r bein' alive when yew was dead. [*A pause*] I want t' share with ye, Abbie—prison 'r death 'r hell 'r anythin'! [*He looks into her eyes and forces a trembling smile*] If I'm sharin' with ye, I won't feel lonesome, leastways.

ABBIE [*weakly*]: Eben! I won't let ye! I can't let ye!

EBEN [*kissing her—tenderly*]: Ye can't he'p yerself. I got ye beat fur once!

ABBIE [*forcing a smile—adoringly*]: I hain't beat—s'long's I got ye!

EBEN [*hears the sound of feet outside*]: Ssshh! Listen! They've come t' take us!

ABBIE: No, it's him. Don't give him no chance to fight ye, Eben. Don't say nothin'—no matter what he says. An' I won't neither. [*It is* CABOT. *He comes up from the barn in a great state of excitement and strides into the house and then into the kitchen.* EBEN *is kneeling beside* ABBIE, *his arm around her, hers around him. They stare straight ahead.*]

CABOT [*stares at them, his face hard. A long pause—vindictively*]: Ye make a slick pair o' murderin' turtle doves! Ye'd ought t' be both hung on the same limb an' left thar t' swing in the breeze an' rot—a warnin' t' old fools like me t' b'ar their lonesomeness alone—an' fur young fools like ye t' hobble their lust. [*A pause. The excitement returns to his face, his eyes snap, he looks a bit crazy*] I couldn't work today. I couldn't take no interest. T' hell with the farm! I'm leavin' it! I've turned the cows an' other stock loose! I've druv 'em into the woods whar they kin be free! By freein' 'em, I'm freein' myself! I'm quittin' here today! I'll set fire t' house an' barn an' watch 'em burn, an' I'll leave yer Maw t' haunt the ashes, an' I'll will the fields back t' God, so that nothin' human kin never touch 'em! I'll be a-goin' to Californi-a—t' jine Simeon an' Peter—true sons o' mine if they be dumb fools—an' the Cabots'll find Solomon's Mines t'gether! [*He suddenly cuts a mad caper*] Whoop! What was the song they sung? "Oh, Californi-a! That's the land fur me." [*He sings this—then gets on his knees by the floorboard under which the money was hid*] An' I'll sail thar on one o' the finest clippers I kin find! I've got the money! Pity ye didn't know whar this was hidden so's ye could steal. . . . [*He has pulled up the board. He stares—feels—stares again. A pause of dead silence. He slowly turns, slumping into a sitting position on the floor, his eyes like those of a dead fish, his face the sickly green of an attack of nausea. He swallows painfully several times—forces a weak smile at last*] So—ye did steal it!

EBEN [*emotionlessly*]: I swapped it t' Sim an' Peter fur their share o' the farm—t' pay their passage t' Californi-a.

CABOT [*with one sardonic*]: Ha! [*He begins to recover. Gets slowly to his feet—strangely*] I calc'late God give it to 'em—not yew! God's hard, not easy! Mebbe they's easy gold in the West but it hain't God's gold. It hain't fur me. I kin hear His voice warnin' me agen t' be hard an' stay on my farm. I kin see his hand usin' Eben t' steal t' keep me from weakness. I kin feel I be in the palm o' His hand, His fingers guidin' me. [*A pause—then he mutters sadly*] It's a-goin' t' be lonesomer now than ever it war afore—an' I'm gittin' old, Lord—ripe on the bough. . . . [*Then stiffening*] Waal—what d'ye want? God's lonesome, hain't He? God's hard an' lonesome! [*A pause. The Sheriff with two men comes up the road from the left. They move cautiously to the door. The Sheriff knocks on it with the butt of his pistol.*]

SHERIFF: Open in the name o' the law! [*They start.*]

CABOT: They've come fur ye. [*He goes to the rear door*] Come in, Jim! [*The three men enter.* CABOT *meets them in doorway*] Jest a minit, Jim. I got 'em safe here. [*The Sheriff nods. He and his companions remain in the doorway.*]

EBEN [*suddenly calls*]: I lied this mornin', Jim. I helped her to do it. Ye kin take me, too.

ABBIE [*brokenly*]: No!

CABOT: Take 'em both. [*He comes forward—stares at* EBEN *with a trace of grudging admiration*] Purty good—fur yew! Waal, I got t' round up the stock. Good-by.

EBEN: Good-by.

ABBIE: Good-by. [*CABOT turns and strides past the men—comes out and around the corner of the house, his shoulders squared, his face stony, and stalks grimly toward the barn. In the meantime the Sheriff and men have come into the room.*]

SHERIFF [*embarrassedly*]: Waal—we'd best start.

ABBIE: Wait. [*Turns to* EBEN] I love ye, Eben.

EBEN: I love ye, Abbie. [*They kiss. The three men grin and shuffle embarrassedly.* EBEN *takes* ABBIE'S *hand. They go out the door in rear, the men following, and come from the house, walking hand in hand to the gate.* EBEN *stops there and points to the sunrise sky*] Sun's a-rizin'. Purty, hain't it?

ABBIE: Ay-eh. [*They both stand for a moment looking up raptly in attitudes strangely aloof and devout.*]

SHERIFF [*looking around at the farm enviously—to his companion*]: It's a jim-dandy farm, no denyin'. Wished I owned it!

Curtain

The Glass Menagerie

Tennessee Williams (1911–)

Born in Columbus, Mississippi, Thomas Lanier Williams (he adopted the penname "Tennessee Williams" in 1939) studied at the University of Missouri, Washington University (St. Louis), and the University of Iowa. The Depression interrupted his education at several points, and during the 1930s he worked as a manual laborer, clerk in a shoe factory, waiter, and elevator operator. He began to write in the late 1920s, and some of his plays were produced locally in the 1930s. His first important success came with the publication of *American Blues: Five Short Plays* in 1939, but *Battle of Angels,* a full-length play produced in 1940, had a short and disastrous run. The war years were difficult ones for Williams, and he worked at a variety of jobs until the spectacular success of *The Glass Menagerie* (1944), which ran on Broadway for over a year. It was followed by four plays—*A Streetcar Named Desire* (1947), *Camino Real* (1953), *Cat on a Hot Tin Roof* (1955), and *The Night of the Iguana* (1962)—that established Williams as a major American playwright. During the 1960s ill-health and a mental breakdown affected Williams' work, but in *Small Craft Warnings* (1972) he regained much of his old power to move an audience.

CHARACTERS

AMANDA WINGFIELD, *the mother.*

A little woman of great but confused vitality clinging frantically to another time and place. Her characterization must be carefully created, not copied from type. She is not paranoiac, but her life is paranoia. There is much to admire in AMANDA, *and as much to love and pity as there is to laugh at. Certainly she has endurance and a kind of heroism, and though her foolishness makes her unwittingly cruel at times, there is tenderness in her slight person.*

LAURA WINGFIELD, *her daughter.*

AMANDA, *having failed to establish contact with reality, continues to live vitally in her illusions, but* LAURA'S *situation is even graver. A childhood illness has left her crippled, one leg slightly shorter than the other, and held in a brace. This defect need not be more than suggested on the stage. Stemming from this,* LAURA'S *separation increases till she is like a piece of her own glass collection, too exquisitely fragile to move from the shelf.*

TOM WINGFIELD, *her son, and the narrator of the play.*

A poet with a job in a warehouse. His nature is not remorseless, but to escape from a trap he has to act without pity.

JIM O'CONNOR, *the gentleman caller.*

A nice, ordinary, young man.

SCENE

An Alley in St. Louis

PART I. Preparation for a Gentleman Caller.

PART II. The Gentleman calls.

Time: Now and the Past.

Production Notes

Being a "memory play," *The Glass Menagerie* can be presented with unusual freedom of convention. Because of its considerably delicate or tenuous material, atmospheric touches and subtleties of direction play a particularly important part. Expressionism and all other unconventional techniques in drama have only one valid aim, and that is a closer approach to truth. When a play employs unconventional techniques, it is not, or certainly shouldn't be, trying to escape its responsibility of dealing with reality, or interpreting experience, but is actually or should be attempting to find a closer approach, a more penetrating and vivid expression of things as they are. The straight realistic play with its genuine Frigidaire and authentic ice-cubes, its characters who speak exactly as its audience speaks, corresponds to the academic landscape and has the same virtue of a photographic likeness. Everyone should know nowadays the unimportance of the photographic in art: that truth, life, or reality is an organic thing which the poetic imagination can represent or suggest, in essence, only through transformation, through changing into other forms than those which were merely present in appearance.

These remarks are not meant as a preface only to this particular play. They have to do with a conception of a new, plastic theatre which must take the place of the exhausted theatre of realistic conventions if the theatre is to resume vitality as a part of our culture.

The Screen Device: There is *only one important difference between the original and the acting version of the play* and that is the *omission* in the latter of the device that I tentatively included in my *original* script. This device was the use of a screen on which were projected magic-lantern slides bearing images or titles. I do not regret the omission of this device from the original Broadway production. The extraordinary power of Miss Taylor's performance made it suitable to have the utmost simplicity in the physical production. But I think it may be interesting to some readers to see how this device was conceived. So I am putting it into the published manuscript. These images and legends, projected from behind, were cast on a section of wall between the front-room and dining-room areas, which should be indistinguishable from the rest when not in use.

The purpose of this will probably be apparent. It is to give accent to certain values in each scene. Each scene contains a particular point (or several) which is structurally the most important. In an episodic play, such as this, the basic structure or narrative line may be obscured from the audience; the effect may seem fragmentary rather than architectural. This may not be the fault of the play so much as a lack of attention in the audience. The legend or image upon the screen will strengthen the effect of what is merely allusion in the writing and allow the primary point to be made more simply and lightly than if the entire responsibility were on the spoken lines. Aside from this structural value, I think the screen will have a definite emotional appeal, less definable but just as important. An imaginative producer or director may invent many other uses for this device than those indicated in the present script. In fact the possibilities of the device seem much larger to me than the instance of this play can possibly utilize.

The Music: Another extra-literary accent in this play is provided by the use of music. A single recurring tune, "The Glass Menagerie," is used to give emotional emphasis to suitable passages. This tune is like circus music, not when you are on the grounds or in the immediate vicinity of the parade, but when you are at some distance and very likely thinking of something else. It seems under those circumstances to continue almost interminably and it weaves in and out of your preoccupied consciousness; then it is the lightest, most delicate music in the world and perhaps the saddest. It expresses the surface vivacity of life with the underlying strain of immutable and inexpressible sorrow. When you look at a piece of delicately spun glass you think of two things: how beautiful it is and how easily it can be broken. Both of those ideas should be woven into the recurring tune, which dips in and out of the play as if it were carried on a wind that changes. It serves as a thread of connection and allusion between the narrator with his separate point in time and space and the subject of his story. Between each episode it returns as reference to the emotion, nostalgia, which is the first condition of the play. It is primarily Laura's music and therefore comes out most clearly when the play focuses upon her and the lovely fragility of glass which is her image.

The Lighting: The lighting in the play is not realistic. In keeping with the atmosphere of memory, the stage is dim. Shafts of light are focused on selected areas or actors, sometimes in contradistinction to what is the apparent center. For instance, in the quarrel scene between Tom and Amanda, in which Laura has no active part, the clearest pool of light is on her figure. This is also true of the supper scene, when her silent figure on the sofa should remain the visual center. The light upon Laura should be distinct from the others, having a peculiar pristine clarity such as light used in early religious portraits of female saints or madonnas. A certain correspondence to light in religious paintings, such as El Greco's, where the figures are radiant in atmosphere that is relatively dusky, could be effectively used throughout the play. (It will also permit a more effective use of the screen.) A free, imaginative use of light can be of enormous value in giving a mobile, plastic quality to plays of a more or less static nature.

Tennessee Williams

Scene One

The Wingfield apartment is in the rear of the building, one of those vast hive-like conglomerations of cellular living-units that flower as warty growths in overcrowded urban centers of lower middle-class population and are symptomatic of the impulse of this largest and fundamentally enslaved section of American society to avoid fluidity and differentiation and to exist and function as one interfused mass of automatism.

The apartment faces an alley and is entered by a fire escape, a structure whose name is a touch of accidental poetic truth, for all of these huge buildings are always burning with the slow and implacable fires of human desperation. The fire escape is part of what we see—that is, the landing of it and steps descending from it.

The scene is memory and is therefore nonrealistic. Memory takes a lot of poetic license. It omits some details; others are exaggerated, according to the emotional value of the articles it touches, for memory is seated predominantly in the heart. The interior is therefore rather dim and poetic.

At the rise of the curtain, the audience is faced with the dark, grim rear wall of the Wingfield tenement. This building is flanked on both sides by dark, narrow alleys which run into murky canyons of tangled clotheslines, garbage cans, and the sinister latticework of neighboring fire escapes. It is up and down these side alleys that exterior entrances and exits are made during the play. At the end of TOM'S *opening commentary, the dark tenement wall slowly becomes transparent and reveals the interior of the ground-floor Wingfield apartment.*

Nearest the audience is the living room, which also serves as a sleeping room for LAURA, *the sofa unfolding to make her bed. Just beyond, separated from the living room by a wide arch or second proscenium with transparent faded portieres (or second curtain), is the dining room. In an old-fashioned whatnot in the living room are seen scores of transparent glass animals. A blown-up photograph of the father hangs on the wall of the living room, to the left of the archway. It is the face of a very handsome young man in a doughboy's First World War cap. He is gallantly smiling, ineluctably smiling, as if to say "I will be smiling forever."*

Also hanging on the wall, near the photograph, are a typewriter keyboard chart and a Gregg shorthand diagram. An upright typewriter on a small table stands beneath the charts.

The audience hears and sees the opening scene in the dining room through both the transparent fourth wall of the building and the transparent gauze portieres of the dining-room arch. It is during this revealing scene that the fourth wall slowly ascends, out of sight. This transparent exterior wall is not brought down again until the very end of the play, during TOM'S *final speech.*

The narrator is an undisguised convention of the play. He takes whatever license with dramatic convention is convenient to his purposes.

TOM *enters, dressed as a merchant sailor, and strolls across to the fire escape. There he stops and lights a cigarette. He addresses the audience.*

TOM: Yes, I have tricks in my pocket, I have things up my sleeve. But I am the opposite of a stage magician. He gives you illusion that has the appearance of truth. I give you truth in the pleasant disguise of illusion.

To begin with, I turn back time. I reverse it to that quaint period, the thirties, when the huge middle class of America was matriculating in a school for the blind. Their eyes had failed them, or they had failed their eyes, and so they were having their fingers pressed forcibly down on the fiery Braille alphabet of a dissolving economy.

In Spain there was revolution. Here there was only shouting and confusion. In Spain there was Guernica. Here there were disturbances of labor, sometimes pretty violent, in otherwise peaceful cities such as Chicago, Cleveland, Saint Louis . . .

This is the social background of the play.

[*Music begins to play.*]

The play is memory. Being a memory play, it is dimly lighted, it is sentimental, it is not realistic. In memory everything seems to happen to music. That explains the fiddle in the wings.

I am the narrator of the play, and also a character in it. The other characters are my mother, Amanda, my sister, Laura, and a gentleman caller who appears in the final scenes. He is the most realistic character in the play, being an emissary from a world of reality that we were somehow set apart from. But since I have a poet's weakness for symbols, I am using this character also as a symbol; he is the long-delayed but always expected something that we live for.

There is a fifth character in the play who doesn't appear except in this larger-than-life-size photograph over the mantel. This is our father who left us a long time ago. He was a telephone man who fell in love with long distances; he gave up his job with the telephone company and skipped the light fantastic out of town . . .

The last we heard of him was a picture postcard from Mazatlan, on the Pacific coast of Mexico, containing a message of two words: "Hello—Goodbye!" and no address.

I think the rest of the play will explain itself. . . .

[AMANDA'S *voice becomes audible through the portieres.*]

[*Legend on screen:* "Ou sont les neiges."]

[TOM *divides the portieres and enters the dining room.* AMANDA *and* LAURA *are seated at a drop-leaf table. Eating is indicated by gestures without food or utensils.* AMANDA *faces the audience.* TOM *and* LAURA *are seated in profile. The interior has lit up softly and through the scrim we see* AMANDA *and* LAURA *seated at the table.*]

AMANDA [*calling*]: Tom?

TOM: Yes, Mother.

AMANDA: We can't say grace until you come to the table!

TOM: Coming, Mother. [*He bows slightly and withdraws, reappearing a few moments later in his place at the table.*]

AMANDA [*to her son*]: Honey, don't *push* with your *fingers.* If you have to push with something, the thing to push with is a crust of bread. And chew—chew! Animals have secretions in their stomachs which enable them to digest food without mastication, but human beings are supposed to chew their food before they swallow it down. Eat food leisurely, son, and really enjoy it. A well-cooked meal has lots of delicate flavors that have to be held in the mouth for appreciation. So chew your food and give your salivary glands a chance to function!

[TOM *deliberately lays his imaginary fork down and pushes his chair back from the table.*]

TOM: I haven't enjoyed one bite of this dinner because of your constant directions on how to eat it. It's you that make me rush through meals with your hawk-like attention to every bite I take. Sickening—spoils my appetite—all this discussion of—animals' secretion—salivary glands—mastication!

AMANDA [*lightly*]: Temperament like a Metropolitan star!

[TOM *rises and walks toward the living room.*]

You're not excused from the table.

TOM: I'm getting a cigarette.

AMANDA: You smoke too much.

[LAURA *rises.*]

LAURA: I'll bring in the blanc mange.

[TOM *remains standing with his cigarette by the portieres.*]

AMANDA [*rising*]: No, sister, no, sister—you be the lady this time and I'll be the darky.

LAURA: I'm already up.

AMANDA: Resume your seat, little sister—I want you to stay fresh and pretty—for gentlemen callers!

LAURA [*sitting down*]: I'm not expecting any gentlemen callers.

AMANDA [*crossing out to the kitchenette, airily*]: Sometimes they come when they are least expected! Why, I remember one Sunday afternoon in Blue Mountain—

[*She enters the kitchenette.*]

TOM: I know what's coming!

LAURA: Yes. But let her tell it.

TOM: Again?

LAURA: She loves to tell it.

[AMANDA *returns with a bowl of dessert*].

AMANDA: One Sunday afternoon in Blue Mountain—your mother received—*seventeen!*—gentlemen callers! Why, sometimes there weren't chairs enough to accommodate them all. We had to send the nigger over to bring in folding chairs from the parish house.

TOM [*remaining at the portieres*]: How did you entertain those gentlemen callers?

AMANDA: I understood the art of conversation!

TOM: I bet you could talk.

AMANDA: Girls in those days *knew* how to talk, I can tell you.

TOM: Yes?

[*Image on screen:* Amanda as a girl on a porch, greeting callers.]

AMANDA: They knew how to entertain their gentlemen callers. It wasn't enough for a girl to be possessed of a pretty face and a graceful figure—although I wasn't slighted in either respect. She also needed to have a nimble wit and a tongue to meet all occasions.

TOM: What did you talk about?

AMANDA: Things of importance going on in the world! Never anything coarse or common or vulgar. [*She addresses* TOM *as though he were seated in the vacant chair at the table though he remains by the portieres. He plays this scene as though reading from a script.*] My callers were gentlemen—all! Among my callers were some of the most prominent young planters of the Mississippi Delta—planters and sons of planters!

[TOM *motions for music and a spot of light on* AMANDA. *Her eyes lift, her face glows, her voice becomes rich and elegiac.*]

[*Screen legend:* "Ou sont les neiges d'antan?"]

There was young Champ Laughlin who later became vice-president of the Delta Planters Bank. Hadley Stevenson who was drowned in Moon Lake and left his widow one hundred and fifty thousand in Government bonds. There were the Cutrere brothers, Wesley and Bates. Bates was one of my bright particular beaux! He got in a quarrel with that wild Wainwright boy. They shot it out on the floor of Moon Lake Casino. Bates was shot through the stomach. Died in the ambulance on his way to Memphis. His widow was also well provided-for, came into eight or ten thousand acres, that's all. She married him on the rebound—never loved her—carried my picture on him the night he died! And there was that boy that every girl in the Delta had set her cap for! That beautiful, brilliant young Fitzhugh boy from Greene County!

TOM: What did he leave his widow?

AMANDA: He never married! Gracious, you talk as though all of my old admirers had turned up their toes to the daisies!

TOM: Isn't this the first you've mentioned that still survives?

AMANDA: That Fitzhugh boy went North and made a fortune—came to be known as the Wolf of Wall Street! He had the Midas touch, whatever he touched turned to gold! And I could have been Mrs. Duncan J. Fitzhugh, mind you! But—I picked your *father!*

LAURA [*rising*]: Mother, let me clear the table.

AMANDA: No, dear, you go in front and study your typewriter chart. Or practice your shorthand a little. Stay fresh and pretty!—It's almost time for our gentlemen callers to start arriving. [*She flounces girlishly toward the kitchenette*] How many do you suppose we're going to entertain this afternoon?

[TOM *throws down the paper and jumps up with a groan.*]

LAURA [*alone in the dining room*]: I don't believe we're going to receive any, Mother.

AMANDA [*reappearing, airily*]: What? No one—not one? You must be joking!

[LAURA *nervously echoes her laugh. She slips in a fugitive manner through the half-open portieres and draws them gently behind her. A shaft of very clear light is thrown on her face against the faded tapestry of the curtains. Faintly the music of "The Glass Menagerie" is heard as she continues, lightly:*]

Not one gentleman caller? It can't be true! There must be a flood, there must have been a tornado!

LAURA: It isn't a flood, it's not a tornado, Mother. I'm just not popular like you were in Blue Mountain. . . .

[TOM *utters another groan.* LAURA *glances at him with a faint, apologetic smile. Her voice catches a little:*]

Mother's afraid I'm going to be an old maid.

[*The scene dims out with the "Glass Menagerie" music.*]

Scene Two

On the dark stage the screen is lighted with the image of blue roses. Gradually LAURA'S *figure becomes apparent and the screen goes out. The music subsides.*

LAURA *is seated in the delicate ivory chair at the small claw-foot table. She wears a dress of soft violet material for a kimono—her hair is tied back from her forehead with a ribbon. She is washing and polishing her collection of glass.* AMANDA *appears on the fire escape steps. At the sound of her ascent,* LAURA *catches her breath, thrusts the bowl of ornaments away, and seats herself stiffly before the diagram of the typewriter keyboard as though it held her spellbound. Something has happened to* AMANDA. *It is written in her face as she climbs to the landing: a look that is grim and hopeless and a little absurd. She has on one of those cheap or imitation velvety-looking cloth coats with imitation fur collar. Her hat is five or six years old, one of those dreadful cloche hats that were worn in the late Twenties, and she is clutching an enormous black patent-leather pocketbook with nickel clasps and initials. This is her full-dress outfit, the one she usually wears to the D.A.R. Before entering she looks through the door. She purses her lips, opens her eyes very wide, rolls them upward and shakes her head. Then she slowly lets herself in the door. Seeing her mother's expression* LAURA *touches her lips with a nervous gesture.*

LAURA: Hello, Mother, I was— [*She makes a nervous gesture toward the chart on the wall.* AMANDA *leans against the shut door and stares at* LAURA *with a martyred look.*]

AMANDA: Deception? Deception? [*She slowly removes her hat and gloves, continuing the sweet suffering stare. She lets the hat and gloves fall on the floor—a bit of acting.*]

LAURA [*shakily*]: How was the D.A.R. meeting?

[AMANDA *slowly opens her purse and removes a dainty white handkerchief which she shakes out delicately and delicately touches to her lips and nostrils.*]

Didn't you go to the D.A.R. meeting, Mother?

AMANDA [*faintly, almost inaudibly*]: —No.—No. [*then more forcibly:*] I did not have the strength—to go to the D.A.R. In fact, I did not have the courage! I wanted to find a hole in the ground and hide myself in it forever! [*She crosses slowly to the wall and removes the diagram of the typewriter keyboard. She holds it in front of her for a second, staring at it sweetly and sorrowfully—then bites her lips and tears it in two pieces.*]

LAURA [*faintly*]: Why did you do that, Mother?

[AMANDA *repeats the same procedure with the chart of the Gregg Alphabet.*]

Why are you—

AMANDA: Why? Why? How old are you, Laura?

LAURA: Mother, you know my age.

AMANDA: I thought that you were an adult; it seems that I was mistaken. [*She crosses slowly to the sofa and sinks down and stares at* LAURA.]

LAURA: Please don't stare at me, Mother.

[AMANDA *closes her eyes and lowers her head. There is a ten-second pause.*]

AMANDA: What are we going to do, what is going to become of us, what is the future?

[*There is another pause.*]

LAURA: Has something happened, Mother?

[AMANDA *draws a long breath, takes out the handkerchief again, goes though the dabbing process.*]

Mother, has—something happened?

AMANDA: I'll be all right in a minute, I'm just bewildered—[*She hesitates.*]—by life. . . .

LAURA: Mother, I wish that you would tell me what's happened!

AMANDA: As you know, I was supposed to be inducted into my office at the D.A.R. this afternoon.

[*Screen image:* A swarm of typewriters.]

But I stopped off at Rubicam's Business College to speak to your teachers about your having a cold and ask them what progress they thought you were making down there.

LAURA: Oh. . . .

AMANDA: I went to the typing instructor and introduced myself as your mother. She didn't know who you were. "Wingfield," she said, "We don't have any such student enrolled at the school!"

I assured her she did, that you had been going to classes since early in January.

"I wonder," she said, "If you could be talking about that terribly shy little girl who dropped out of school after only a few days' attendance?"

"No," I said, "Laura, my daughter, has been going to school every day for the past six weeks!"

"Excuse me," she said. She took the attendance book out and there was your name, unmistakably printed, and all the dates you were absent until they decided that you had dropped out of school.

I still said, "No, there must have been some mistake!

There must have been some mix-up in the records!"

And she said, "No—I remember her perfectly now. Her hands shook so that she couldn't hit the right keys! The first time we gave a speed test, she broke down completely—was sick at the stomach and almost had to be carried into the wash room! After that morning she never showed up any more. We phoned the house but never got any answer"—While I was working at Famous-Barr, I suppose, demonstrating those—

[*She indicates a brassiere with her hands.*]

Oh! I felt so weak I could barely keep on my feet! I had to sit down while they got me a glass of water! Fifty dollars' tuition, all of our plans—my hopes and ambitions for you—just gone up the spout, just gone up the spout like that.

[LAURA *draws a long breath and gets awkwardly to her feet. She crosses to the Victrola and winds it up.*]

What are you doing?

LAURA: Oh! [*She releases the handle and returns to her seat.*]

AMANDA: Laura, where have you been going when you've gone out pretending that you were going to business college?

LAURA: I've just been going out walking.

AMANDA: That's not true.

LAURA: It is. I just went walking.

AMANDA: Walking? Walking? In winter? Deliberately courting pneumonia in that light coat? Where did you walk to, Laura?

LAURA: All sorts of places—mostly in the park.

AMANDA: Even after you'd started catching that cold?

LAURA: It was the lesser of two evils, Mother.

[*Screen image:* Winter scene in a park.]

I couldn't go back there. I—threw up—on the floor!

AMANDA: From half past seven till after five every day you mean to tell me you walked around in the park, because you wanted to make me think that you were still going to Rubicam's Business College?

LAURA: It wasn't as bad as it sounds. I went inside places to get warmed up.

AMANDA: Inside where?

LAURA: I went in the art museum and the bird houses at the Zoo. I visited the penguins every day! Sometimes I did without lunch and went to the movies. Lately I've been spending most of my afternoons in the Jewel Box, that big glass house where they raise the tropical flowers.

AMANDA: You did all this to deceive me, just for deception? [LAURA *looks down.*] Why?

LAURA: Mother, when you're disappointed, you get that awful suffering look on your face, like the picture of Jesus' mother in the museum!

AMANDA: Hush!

LAURA: I couldn't face it.

[*There is a pause. A whisper of strings is heard. Legend on screen:* "The Crust of Humility."]

AMANDA [*hopelessly fingering the huge pocketbook*]: So what are we going to do the rest of our lives? Stay home and watch the parades go by? Amuse ourselves with the glass menagerie, darling? Eternally play those worn-out phonograph records your father left as a painful reminder of him? We won't have a business career—we've given that up because it gave us nervous indigestion! [*She laughs wearily.*] What is there left but dependency all our lives? I know so well what becomes of unmarried women who aren't prepared to occupy a position. I've seen such pitiful cases in the South—barely tolerated spinsters living upon the grudging patronage of sister's husband or brother's wife!—stuck away in some little mousetrap of a room—encouraged by one in-law to visit another—little birdlike women without any nest—eating the crust of humility all their life!

Is that the future that we've mapped out for ourselves? I swear it's the only alternative I can think of! [*She pauses.*] It isn't a very pleasant alternative, is it? [*She pauses again.*] Of course—some girls *do marry.*

[LAURA *twists her hands nervously.*]

Haven't you ever liked some boy?

LAURA: Yes. I liked one once. [*She rises.*] I came across his picture a while ago.

AMANDA [*with some interest*]: He gave you his picture?

LAURA: No, it's in the yearbook.

AMANDA [*disappointed*]: Oh—a high school boy.

[*Screen image:* Jim as the high school hero bearing a silver cup.]

LAURA: Yes. His name was Jim. [*She lifts the heavy annual from the claw-foot table.*] Here he is in *The Pirates of Penzance.*

AMANDA [*absently*]: The what?

LAURA: The operetta the senior class put on. He had a wonderful voice and we sat across the aisle from each other Mondays, Wednesdays and Fridays in the Aud. Here he is with the silver cup for debating! See his grin?

AMANDA [*absently*]: He must have had a jolly disposition.

LAURA: He used to call me—Blue Roses.

[*Screen image:* Blue roses.]

AMANDA: Why did he call you such a name as that?

LAURA: When I had that attack of pleurosis—he asked me what was the matter when I came back. I said pleurosis—he thought that I said Blue Roses! So that's what he always called me after that. Whenever he saw me, he'd holler, "Hello, Blue Roses!" I didn't care for the girl that he went out with. Emily Meisenbach. Emily was the best-dressed girl at Soldan. She never struck me, though, as being sincere . . . It says in the Personal Section—they're engaged. That's—six years ago! They must be married by now.

AMANDA: Girls that aren't cut out for business careers usually wind up married to some nice man. [*She gets up with a spark of revival.*] Sister, that's what you'll do!

[LAURA *utters a startled, doubtful laugh. She reaches quickly for a piece of glass.*]

LAURA: But, Mother—

AMANDA: Yes? [*She goes over to the photograph.*]

LAURA [*in a tone of frightened apology*]: I'm—crippled!

AMANDA: Nonsense! Laura, I've told you never, never to use that word. Why, you're not crippled, you just have a little defect—hardly noticeable, even! When people have some slight disadvantage like that, they cultivate other things to make up for it—develop charm—and vivacity—and—*charm!* That's all you have to do! [*She turns again to the photograph.*] One thing your father had *plenty of*—was *charm!*

[*The scene fades out with music.*]

Scene Three

Legend on screen: "After the fiasco—"
TOM *speaks from the fire escape landing.*

TOM: After the fiasco at Rubicam's Business College, the idea of getting a gentleman caller for Laura began to play a more and more important part in Mother's calculations. It became an obsession. Like some archetype of the universal unconscious, the image of the gentleman caller haunted our small apartment. . . .

[*Screen image:* A young man at the door of a house with flowers.]

An evening at home rarely passed without some allusion to this image, this specter, this hope. . . . Even when he wasn't mentioned, his presence hung in Mother's preoccupied look and in my sister's frightened, apologetic manner—hung like a sentence passed upon the Wingfields!

Mother was a woman of action as well as words. She began to take logical steps in the planned direction. Late that winter and in the early spring—realizing that extra money would be needed to properly feather the nest and plume the bird—she conducted a vigorous campaign on the telephone, roping in subscribers to one of those magazines for matrons called *The Homemaker's Companion,* the type of journal that features the serialized sublimations of ladies of letters who think in terms of delicate cuplike breasts, slim, tapering waists, rich, creamy thighs, eyes like wood smoke in autumn, fingers that soothe and caress like strains of music, bodies as powerful as Etruscan sculpture.

[*Screen image:* The cover of a glamor magazine.]

[AMANDA *enters with the telephone on a long extension cord. She is spotlighted in the dim stage.*]

AMANDA: Ida Scott? This is Amanda Wingfield! We *missed* you at the D.A.R. last Monday! I said to myself: She's probably suffering with that sinus condition! How is that sinus condition?

Horrors! Heaven have mercy!—You're a Christian martyr, yes, that's what your are, a Christian martyr!

Well, I just now happened to notice that your subscription to the *Companion*'s about to expire! Yes, it expires with the next issue, honey!—just when that wonderful new serial by Bessie Mae Hopper is getting off to such an exciting start. Oh, honey, it's something that you can't miss! You remember how *Gone with the Wind* took everybody by storm? You simply couldn't go out if you hadn't read it. All everybody *talked* was Scarlett O'Hara. Well, this is a book that critics already compare to *Gone with the Wind.* It's the *Gone with the Wind* of the post-World-War generation!—What?—Burning?—Oh, honey, don't let them burn, go take a look in the oven and I'll hold the wire! Heavens—I think she's hung up!

[*The scene dims out.*]

[*Legend on screen:* "You think I'm in love with Continental Shoemakers?"]

[*Before the lights come up again, the violent voices of* TOM *and* AMANDA *are heard. They are quarreling behind the portieres. In front of them stands* LAURA *with clenched hands and panicky expression. A clear pool of light is on her figure throughout this scene.*]

TOM: What in Christ's name am I—

AMANDA [*shrilly*]: Don't you use that—

TOM: —supposed to do!

AMANDA: —expression! Not in my—

TOM: Ohhh!

AMANDA: —presence! Have you gone out of your senses?

TOM: I have, that's true, *driven* out!

AMANDA: What is the matter with you, you—big—big—IDIOT!

TOM: Look!—I've got *no thing,* no single thing—

AMANDA: Lower your voice!

TOM: —in my life here that I can call my OWN! Everything is—

AMANDA: Stop that shouting!

TOM: Yesterday you confiscated my books! You had the nerve to—

AMANDA: I took that horrible novel back to the library—yes! That hideous book by that insane Mr. Lawrence.

[TOM *laughs wildly.*]

I cannot control the output of diseased minds or people who cater to them—

[TOM *laughs still more wildly.*]

BUT I WON'T ALLOW SUCH FILTH BROUGHT INTO MY HOUSE! No, no, no, no, no!

TOM: House, house! Who pays rent on it, who makes a slave of himself to—

AMANDA [*fairly screeching*]: Don't you DARE to—

TOM: No, no, *I* mustn't say things! *I've* got to just—

AMANDA: Let me tell you—

TOM: I don't want to hear any more!

[*He tears the portieres open. The dining-room area is lit with a turgid smoky red glow. Now we see* AMANDA; *her hair is in metal curlers and she is wearing a very old bathrobe, much too large for her slight figure, a relic of the faithless Mr. Wingfield. The upright typewriter now stands on the drop-leaf table, along with a wild disarray of manuscripts. The quarrel was probably precipitated by* AMANDA'S *interruption of* TOM'S *creative labor. A chair lies overthrown on the floor. Their gesticulating shadows are cast on the ceiling by the fiery glow.*]

AMANDA: You *will* hear more, you—

TOM: No, I won't hear more, I'm going out!

AMANDA: You come right back in—

TOM: Out, out, out! Because I'm—

AMANDA: Come back here, Tom Wingfield! I'm not through talking to you!

TOM: Oh, go—

LAURA [*desperately*]: —Tom!

AMANDA: You're going to listen, and no more insolence from you! I'm at the end of my patience!

[*He comes back toward her.*]

TOM: What do you think I'm at? Aren't I supposed to have any patience to reach the end of, Mother? I know, I know. It seems unimportant to you, what I'm *doing*—what I *want* to do—having a little *difference* between them! You don't think that—

AMANDA: I think you've been doing things that you're ashamed of. That's why you act like this. I don't believe that you go every night to the movies. Nobody goes to the movies night after night. Nobody in their right minds goes to the movies as often as you pretend to. People don't go to the movies at nearly midnight, and movies don't let out at two A.M. Come in stumbling. Muttering to yourself like a maniac! You get three hours' sleep and then go to work. Oh, I can picture the way you're doing down there. Moping, doping, because you're in no condition.

TOM [*wildly*]: No, I'm in no condition!

AMANDA: What right have you got to jeopardize your job? Jeopardize the security of us all? How do you think we'd manage if you were—

TOM: Listen! You think I'm crazy about the *warehouse?* [*He bends fiercely toward her slight figure.*] You think I'm in love with the Continental Shoemakers? You think I want to spend fifty-five *years* down there in that—*celotex interior!* with—*fluorescent—tubes!* Look! I'd rather somebody picked up a crowbar and battered out my brains—than go back mornings! I *go!* Every time you come in yelling that God-damn *"Rise and Shine!" "Rise and shine!"* I say to myself, "How *lucky dead* people are!" But I get up. I *go!* For sixty-five dollars a month I give up all that I dream of doing and being *ever!* And you say self—*self's* all I ever think of. Why, listen, if self is what I thought of, Mother, I'd be where he is—GONE! [*He points to his father's picture.*] As far as the system of transportation reaches! [*He starts past her. She grabs his arm.*] Don't grab at me, Mother!

AMANDA: Where are you going?

TOM: I'm going to the *movies!*

AMANDA: I don't believe that lie!

[*Tom crouches toward her, overtowering her tiny figure. She backs away, gasping.*]

TOM: I'm going to opium dens! Yes, opium dens, dens of vice and criminals' hangouts, Mother. I've joined the Hogan Gang, I'm a hired assassin, I carry a tommy gun in a violin case! I run a string of cat houses in the Valley! They call me Killer, Killer Wingfield, I'm leading a double-life, a simple, honest warehouse worker by day, by night a dynamic *czar* of the *underworld, Mother.* I go to gambling casinos, I spin away fortunes on the roulette table! I wear a patch over one eye and a false mustache, sometimes I put on green whiskers. On those occasions they call me—*El Diablo!* Oh, I could tell you many things to make you sleepless! My enemies plan to dynamite this place. They're going to blow us all sky-high some night! I'll be glad, very happy, and so will you! You'll go up, up on a broomstick, over Blue Mountain with seventeen gentlemen callers! You ugly—babbling old —*witch.* . . .

[He goes through a series of violent, clumsy movements, seizing his overcoat, lunging to the door, pulling it fiercely open. The women watch him, aghast. His arm catches in the sleeve of the coat as he struggles to pull it on. For a moment he is pinioned by the bulky garment. With an outraged groan he tears the coat off again, splitting the shoulder of it, and hurls it across the room. It strikes against the shelf of LAURA'S *glass collection, and there is a tinkle of shattering glass. Laura cries out as if wounded.]*

[Music.]

[Screen legend: "The Glass Menagerie."*]*

LAURA *[shrilly]*: *My glass!*—menagerie. . . . *[She covers her face and turns away.]*

[But AMANDA *is still stunned and stupefied by the "ugly witch" so that she barely notices this occurrence. Now she recovers her speech.]*

AMANDA *[in an awful voice]*: I won't speak to you—until you apologize!

[She crosses through the portieres and draws them together behind her. TOM *is left with* LAURA. LAURA *clings weakly to the mantel with her face averted.* TOM *stares at her stupidly for a moment. Then he crosses to the shelf. He drops awkwardly on his knees to collect the fallen glass, glancing at* LAURA *as if he would speak but couldn't.]*

["The Glass Menagerie" music steals in as the scene dims out.]

Scene Four

The interior of the apartment is dark. There is faint light in the alley. A deep-voiced bell in a church is tolling the hour of five.

TOM *appears at the top of the alley. After each solemn boom of the bell in the tower, he shakes a little noisemaker or rattle as if to express the tiny spasm of man in contrast to the sustained power and dignity of the Almighty. This and the unsteadiness of his advance make it evident that he has been drinking. As he climbs the few steps to the fire escape landing light steals up inside.* LAURA *appears in the front room in a nightdress. She notices that* TOM'S *bed is empty.* TOM *fishes in his pockets for his door key, removing a motley assortment of articles in the search, including a shower of movie ticket stubs and an empty bottle. At last he finds the key, but just as he is about to insert it, it slips from his fingers. He strikes a match and crouches below the door.*

TOM *[bitterly]*: One crack—and it falls through!

*[*LAURA *opens the door.]*

LAURA: Tom! Tom, what are you doing?

TOM: Looking for a door key.

LAURA: Where have you been all this time?

TOM: I have been to the movies.

LAURA: All this time at the movies?

TOM: There was a very long program. There was a Garbo picture and a Mickey Mouse and a travelogue and a newsreel and a preview of coming attractions. And there was an organ solo and a collection for the Milk Fund—simultaneously—which ended up in a terrible fight between a fat lady and an usher!

LAURA *[innocently]*: Did you have to stay through everything?

TOM: Of course! And, oh, I forgot! There was a big stage show! The headliner on this stage show was Malvolio the Magician. He performed wonderful tricks, many of them, such as pouring water back and forth between pitchers. First it turned to wine and then it turned to beer and then it turned to whisky. I know it was whisky it finally turned into because he needed somebody to come up out of the audience to help him, and I came up—both shows! It was Kentucky Straight Bourbon. A very generous fellow, he gave souvenirs. *[He pulls from his back pocket a shimmering rainbow-colored scarf.]* He gave me this. This is his magic scarf. You can have it, Laura. You wave it over a canary cage and you get a bowl of goldfish. You wave it over the goldfish bowl and they fly away canaries. . . . But the wonderfullest trick of all was the coffin trick. We nailed him into a coffin and he got out of the coffin without removing one nail. *[He has come inside.]* There is a trick that would come in handy for me—get me out of this two-by-four situation! *[He flops onto the bed and starts removing his shoes.]*

LAURA: Tom—shhh!

TOM: What're you shushing me for?

LAURA: You'll wake up Mother.

TOM: Goody, goody! Pay 'er back for all those "Rise an' Shines." *[He lies down, groaning.]* You know it don't take much intelligence to get yourself into a nailed-up coffin, Laura. But who in hell ever got himself out of one without removing one nail?

[As if in answer, the father's grinning photograph lights up. The scene dims out.]

[Immediately following, the church bell is heard striking six. At the sixth stroke the alarm clock goes off in AMANDA'S *room, and after a few moments we hear her calling: "Rise and Shine! Rise*

and Shine! Laura, go tell your brother to rise and shine!"]

TOM [*sitting up slowly*]: I'll rise—but I won't shine.

[*The light increases.*]

AMANDA: Laura, tell your brother his coffee is ready.

[LAURA *slips into the front room.*]

LAURA: Tom!—It's nearly seven. Don't make Mother nervous.

[*He stares at her stupidly.*]

[*beseechingly:*] Tom, speak to Mother this morning. Make up with her, apologize, speak to her!

TOM: She won't to me. It's her that started not speaking.

LAURA: If you just say you're sorry she'll start speaking.

TOM: Her not speaking—is that such a tragedy?

LAURA: Please—please!

AMANDA [*calling from the kitchenette*]: Laura, are you going to do what I asked you to do, or do I have to get dressed and go out myself?

LAURA: Going, going—soon as I get on my coat!

[*She pulls on a shapeless felt hat with a nervous, jerky movement, pleadingly glancing at* TOM. *She rushes awkwardly for her coat. The coat is one of* AMANDA'S, *inaccurately made-over, the sleeves too short for* LAURA.]

Butter and what else?

AMANDA [*entering from the kitchenette*]: Just butter. Tell them to charge it.

LAURA: Mother, they make such faces when I do that.

AMANDA: Sticks and stones can break our bones, but the expression on Mr. Garfinkel's face won't harm us! Tell your brother his coffee is getting cold.

LAURA [*at the door*]: Do what I asked you, will you, will you, Tom?

[*He looks sullenly away.*]

AMANDA: Laura, go now or just don't go at all!

LAURA [*rushing out*]: Going—going!

[*A second later she cries out.* TOM *springs up and crosses to the door.* TOM *opens the door.*]

TOM: Laura?

LAURA: I'm all right. I slipped, but I'm all right.

AMANDA [*peering anxiously after her*]: If anyone breaks a leg on those fire-escape steps, the landlord ought to be sued for every cent he possesses! [*She shuts the door. Now she remembers she isn't speaking to* TOM *and returns to the other room.*]

[*As* TOM *comes listlessly for his coffee, she turns her back to him and stands rigidly facing the window on the gloomy gray vault of the areaway. Its light on her face with its aged but childish features is cruelly sharp, satirical as a Daumier print.*]

[*The music of "Ave Maria," is heard softly.*]

[TOM *glances sheepishly but sullenly at her averted figure and slumps at the table. The coffee is scalding hot; he sips it and gasps and spits it back in the cup. At his gasp,* AMANDA *catches her breath and half turns. Then she catches herself and turns back to the window.* TOM *blows on his coffee, glancing sidewise at his mother. She clears her throat.* TOM *clears his. He starts to rise, sinks back down again, scratches his head, clears his throat again.* AMANDA *coughs.* TOM *raises his cup in both hands to blow on it, his eyes staring over the rim of it at his mother for several moments. Then he slowly sets the cup down and awkwardly and hesitantly rises from the chair.*]

TOM [*hoarsely*]: Mother. I—I apologize, Mother.

[AMANDA *draws a quick, shuddering breath. Her face works grotesquely. She breaks into childlike tears.*]

I'm sorry for what I said, for everything that I said, I didn't mean it.

AMANDA [*sobbingly*]: My devotion has made me a witch and so I make myself hateful to my children!

TOM: *No, you don't.*

AMANDA: I worry so much, don't sleep, it makes me nervous!

TOM [*gently*]: I understand that.

AMANDA: I've had to put up a solitary battle all these years. But you're my right-hand bower! Don't fall down, don't fail!

TOM [*gently*]: I try, Mother.

AMANDA [*with great enthusiasm*]: Try and you will *succeed!* [*The notion makes her breathless.*] Why, you—you're just *full* of natural endowments! Both of my children—they're *unusual* children! Don't you think I know it? I'm so—*proud!* Happy and—feel I've—so much to be thankful for but—promise me one thing, son!

TOM: What, Mother?

AMANDA: Promise, son, you'll—never be a drunkard!

TOM [*turns to her grinning*]: I will never be a drunkard, Mother.

AMANDA: That's what frightened me so, that you'd be drinking! Eat a bowl of Purina!

TOM: Just coffee, Mother.

AMANDA: Shredded wheat biscuit?

TOM: No. No, Mother, just coffee.

AMANDA: You can't put in a day's work on an empty stomach. You've got ten minutes—don't gulp! Drinking too-hot liquids makes cancer of the stomach. . . . Put cream in.

TOM: No, thank you.

AMANDA: To cool it.

TOM: No! No, thank you, I want it black.

AMANDA: I know, but it's not good for you. We have to do all that we can to build ourselves up. In these trying times we live in, all that we have to cling to is—each other. . . . That's why it's so important to—Tom, I—I sent out your sister so I could discuss something with you. If you hadn't spoken I would have spoken to you. [*She sits down.*]

TOM [*gently*]: What is it, Mother, that you want to discuss?

AMANDA: *Laura!*

[TOM *puts his cup down slowly.*]

[*Legend on screen:* "Laura." *Music: "The Glass Menagerie."*]

TOM: —Oh.—Laura . . .

AMANDA [*touching his sleeve*]: You know how Laura is. So quiet but—still water runs deep! She notices things and I think she—broods about them.

[TOM *looks up.*]

A few days ago I came in and she was crying.

TOM: What about?

AMANDA: You.

TOM: Me?

AMANDA: She has an idea that you're not happy here.

TOM: What gave her that idea?

AMANDA: What gives her any idea? However, you do act strangely. I—I'm not criticizing, understand *that!* I know your ambitions do not lie in the warehouse, that like everybody in the whole wide world—you've had to—make sacrifices, but—Tom—Tom life's not easy, it calls for—Spartan endurance! There's so many things in my heart that I cannot describe to you! I've never told you but I—*loved* your father. . . .

TOM [*gently*]: I know that, Mother.

AMANDA: And you—when I see you taking after his ways! Staying out late—and—well, you *had* been drinking the night you were in that—terrifying condition! Laura says that you hate the apartment and that you go out nights to get away from it! Is that true, Tom?

TOM: No. You say there's so much in your heart that you can't describe to me. That's true of me, too. There's so much in my heart that I can't describe to *you!* So let's respect each other's—

AMANDA: But, why—*why,* Tom—are you always so *restless?* Where do you go to, nights?

TOM: I—go to the movies.

AMANDA: Why do you go to the movies so much, Tom?

TOM: I go to the movies because—I like adventure. Adventure is something I don't have much of at work, so I go to the movies.

AMANDA: But, Tom, you go to the movies *entirely* too *much!*

TOM: I like a lot of adventure.

[AMANDA *looks baffled, then hurt. As the familiar inquisition resumes,* TOM *becomes hard and impatient again.* AMANDA *slips back into her querulous attitude toward him.*]

[*Image on screen:* A sailing vessel with Jolly Roger.]

AMANDA: Most young men find adventure in their careers.

TOM: Then most young men are not employed in a warehouse.

AMANDA: The world is full of young men employed in warehouses and offices and factories.

TOM: Do all of them find adventure in their careers?

AMANDA: They do or they do without it! Not everybody has a craze for adventure.

TOM: Man is by instinct a lover, a hunter, a fighter, and none of those instincts are given much play at the warehouse!

AMANDA: Man is by instinct! Don't quote instinct to me! Instinct is something that people have got away from! It belongs to animals! Christian adults don't want it!

TOM: What do Christian adults want, then, Mother?

AMANDA: Superior things! Things of the mind and the spirit! Only animals have to satisfy instincts! Surely your aims are somewhat higher than theirs! Than monkeys—pigs—

TOM: I reckon they're not.

AMANDA: You're joking. However, that isn't what I wanted to discuss.

TOM [*rising*]: I haven't much time.

AMANDA [*pushing his shoulders*]: Sit down.

TOM: You want me to punch in red at the warehouse, Mother?

AMANDA: You have five minutes. I want to talk about Laura.

[*Screen legend:* "Plans and Provisions."]

TOM: All right! What about Laura?

AMANDA: We have to be making some plans and provisions for her. She's older than you, two years, and nothing has happened. She just drifts along doing nothing. It frightens me terribly how she just drifts along.

TOM: I guess she's the type that people call home girls.

AMANDA: There's no such type, and if there is, it's a pity! That is unless the home is hers, with a husband!

TOM: What?

AMANDA: Oh, I can see the handwriting on the wall as plain as I see the nose in front of my face! It's terrifying! More and more you remind me of your father! He was out all hours without explanations!—Then *left! Goodbye!* And me with the bag to hold. I saw that letter you got from the Merchant Marine. I know what you're dreaming of. I'm not standing here blindfolded. [*She pauses.*] Very well, then. Then *do* it! But not till there's somebody to take your place.

TOM: What do you mean?

AMANDA: I mean that as soon as Laura has got somebody to take care of her, married, a home of her own, independent—why, then you'll be free to go wherever you please, on land, on sea, whichever way the wind blows you! But until that time you've got to look out for your sister. I don't say me because I'm old and don't matter! I say for your sister because she's young and dependent.

I put her in business college—a dismal failure! Frightened her so it made her sick at the stomach. I took her over to the Young People's League at the church. Another fiasco. She spoke to nobody, nobody spoke to her. Now all she does is fool with those pieces of glass and play those worn-out records. What kind of a life is that for a girl to lead?

TOM: What can I do about it?

AMANDA: Overcome selfishness! Self, self, self is all that you ever think of!

[TOM *springs up and crosses to get his coat. It is ugly and bulky. He pulls on a cap with earmuffs.*]

Where is your muffler? Put your wool muffler on!

[*He snatches it angrily from the closet, tosses it around his neck and pulls both ends tight.*]

Tom! I haven't said what I had in mind to ask you.

TOM: I'm too late to—

AMANDA [*catching his arm—very importunately; then shyly*]: Down at the warehouse, aren't there some—nice young men?

TOM: No!

AMANDA: There *must* be—*some* . . .

TOM: Mother— [*He gestures.*]

AMANDA: Find out one that's clean-living—doesn't drink and ask him out for sister!

TOM: What?

AMANDA: For *sister!* To *meet!* Get *acquainted!*

TOM [*stamping to the door*] Oh, my *go-osh!*

AMANDA: Will you?

[*He opens the door. She says, imploringly:*]

Will you?

[*He starts down the fire escape.*]

Will you? *Will* you, dear?

TOM [*calling back*]: *Yes!*

[AMANDA *closes the door hesitantly and with a troubled but faintly hopeful expression.*]

[*Screen image:* The cover of a glamor magazine.]

[*The spotlight picks up* AMANDA *at the phone.*]

AMANDA: Ella Cartwright? This is Amanda Wingfield!

How are you, honey?

How is that kidney condition?

[*There is a five-second pause.*]

Horrors!

[*There is another pause*]

You're a Christian martyr, yes, honey, that's what you are, a Christian martyr! Well, I just now happened to notice in my little red book that your subscription to the *Companion* has just run out! I knew that you wouldn't want to miss out on the wonderful serial starting in this new issue. It's by Bessie Mae Hopper, the first thing she's written since *Honeymoon for Three.* Wasn't that a strange and interesting story? Well, this one is even lovelier, I believe. It has a sophisticated, society background. It's all about the horsey set on Long Island!

[*The lights fades out.*]

Scene Five

Legend on the screen: "Annunciation."

Music is heard as the light slowly comes on.

It is early dusk of a spring evening. Supper has just been finished in the Wingfield apartment. AMANDA *and* LAURA, in light-colored dresses, are *removing dishes from the table in the dining room, which is shadowy, their movements formalized almost as a dance or ritual, their moving forms as pale and silent as moths.* TOM, *in white shirt and trousers, rises from the table and crosses toward the fire escape.*

AMANDA [*as he passes her*]: Son, will you do me a favor?

TOM: What?

AMANDA: Comb your hair! You look so pretty when your hair is combed!

[TOM *slouches on the sofa with the evening paper. Its enormous headline reads: "Franco Triumphs."*]

There is only one respect in which I would like you to emulate your father.

TOM: What respect is that?

AMANDA: The care he always took of his appearance. He never allowed himself to look untidy.

[*He throws down the paper and crosses to the fire escape.*]

Where are you going?

TOM: I'm going out to smoke.

AMANDA: You smoke too much. A pack a day at fifteen cents a pack. How much would that amount to in a month? Thirty times fifteen is how much, Tom? Figure it out and you will be astounded at what you could save. Enough to give you a night-school course in accounting at Washington U.! Just think what a wonderful thing that would be for you, son!

[TOM *is unmoved by the thought.*]

TOM: I'd rather smoke. [*He steps out on the landing, letting the screen door slam.*]

AMANDA [*sharply*]: I know! That's the tragedy of it. . . . [*Alone, she turns to look at her husband's picture.*]

[*Dance music: "The World Is Waiting for the Sunrise!"*]

TOM [*to the audience*]: Across the alley from us was the Paradise Dance Hall. On evenings in spring the windows and doors were open and the music came outdoors. Sometimes the lights were turned out except for a large glass sphere that hung from the ceiling. It would turn slowly about and filter the dusk with delicate rainbow colors. Then the orchestra played a waltz or a tango, something that had a slow and sensuous rhythm. Couples would come outside, to the relative privacy of the alley. You could see them kissing behind ash pits and telephone poles. This was the compensation for lives that passed like mine, without any change or adventure. Adventure and change were imminent in this year. They were waiting around the corner for all these kids. Suspended in the mist over Berchtesgaden, caught in the folds of Chamberlain's umbrella. In Spain there was Guernica! But here there was only hot swing music and liquor, dance halls, bars, and movies, and sex that hung in the gloom like a chandelier and flooded the world with brief, deceptive rainbows. . . . All the world was waiting for bombardments!

[AMANDA *turns from the picture and comes outside.*]

AMANDA [*sighing*]: A fire escape landing's a poor excuse for a porch. [*She spreads a newspaper on a step and sits down, gracefully and demurely as if she were settling into a swing on a Mississippi veranda.*] What are you looking at?

TOM: The moon.

AMANDA: Is there a moon this evening?

TOM: It's rising over Garfinkel's Delicatessen.

AMANDA: So it is! A little silver slipper of a moon. Have you made a wish on it yet?

TOM: Um-hum.

AMANDA: What did you wish for?

TOM: That's a secret.

AMANDA: A secret, huh? Well, I won't tell mine either. I will be just as mysterious as you.

TOM: I bet I can guess what yours is.

AMANDA: Is my head so transparent?

TOM: You're not a sphinx.

AMANDA: No, I don't have secrets. I'll tell you what I wished for on the moon. Success and happiness for my precious children! I wish for that whenever there's a moon, and when there isn't a moon, I wish for it, too.

TOM: I thought perhaps you wished for a gentleman caller.

AMANDA: Why do you say that?

TOM: Don't you remember asking me to fetch one?

AMANDA: I remember suggesting that it would be nice for your sister if you brought home some nice young man from the warehouse. I think that I've made that suggestion more than once.

TOM: Yes, you have made it repeatedly.

AMANDA: Well?

TOM: We are going to have one.

AMANDA: *What?*

TOM: A gentleman caller!

[*The annunciation is celebrated with music.*]

[AMANDA *rises*]

[*Image on screen:* A caller with a bouquet.]

AMANDA: You mean you have asked some nice young man to come over?

TOM: Yep. I've asked him to dinner.

AMANDA: You really did?

TOM: I did!

AMANDA: You did, and did he—*accept?*

TOM: He did!

AMANDA: Well, well—well, well! That's—lovely!

TOM: I thought that you would be pleased.

AMANDA: It's definite then?

TOM: Very definite.

AMANDA: Soon?

TOM: Very soon.

AMANDA: For heaven's sake, stop putting on and tell me some things, will you?

TOM: What things do you want me to tell you?

AMANDA: *Naturally* I would like to know when he's *coming!*

TOM: He's coming tomorrow.

AMANDA: *Tomorrow?*

TOM: Yep. Tomorrow.

AMANDA: But, Tom!

TOM: Yes, Mother?

AMANDA: Tomorrow gives me no time!

TOM: Time for what?

AMANDA: Preparations! Why didn't you phone me at once, as soon as you asked him, the minute that he accepted? Then, don't you see, I could have been getting ready!

TOM: You don't have to make any fuss.

AMANDA: Oh, Tom, Tom, Tom, of course I have to make a fuss! I want things nice, not sloppy! Not thrown together. I'll certainly have to do some fast thinking, won't I?

TOM: I don't see why you have to think at all.

AMANDA: You just don't know. We can't have a gentleman caller in a pigsty! All my wedding silver has to be polished, the monogrammed table linen ought to be laundered! The windows have to be washed and fresh curtains put up. And how about clothes? We have to *wear* something, don't we?

TOM: Mother, this boy is no one to make a fuss over!

AMANDA: Do you realize he's the first young man we've introduced to your sister? It's terrible, dreadful, disgraceful that poor little sister has never received a single gentleman caller! Tom, come inside! [*She opens the screen door.*]

TOM: What for?

AMANDA: I want to ask you some things.

TOM: If you're going to make such a fuss, I'll call it off, I'll tell him not to come!

AMANDA: You certainly won't do anything of the kind. Nothing offends people worse than broken engagements. It simply means I'll have to work like a Turk! We won't be brilliant, but we will pass inspection. Come on inside.

[TOM *follows her inside, groaning.*]

Sit down.

TOM: Any particular place you would like me to sit?

AMANDA: Thank heavens I've got that new sofa! I'm also making payments on a floor lamp I'll have sent out! And put the chintz covers on, they'll brighten things up! Of course I'd hoped to have these walls re-papered. . . . What is the young man's name?

TOM: His name is O'Connor.

AMANDA: That, of course, means fish—tomorrow is Friday! I'll have that salmon loaf—with Durkee's dressing! What does he do? He works at the warehouse?

TOM: Of course! How else would I—

AMANDA: Tom, he—doesn't drink?

TOM: Why do you ask me that?

AMANDA: Your father *did!*

TOM: Don't get started on that!

AMANDA: He *does* drink, then?

TOM: Not that I know of!

AMANDA: Make sure, be certain! The last thing I want for my daughter's a boy who drinks!

TOM: Aren't you being a little bit premature? Mr. O'Connor has not yet appeared on the scene!

AMANDA: But will tomorrow. To meet your sister, and what do I know about his character? Nothing! Old maids are better off than wives of drunkards!

TOM: Oh, my God!

AMANDA: Be still!

TOM [*leaning forward to whisper*]: Lots of fellows meet girls whom they don't marry!

AMANDA: Oh, talk sensibly, Tom—and don't be sarcastic! [*She has gotten a hairbrush.*]

TOM: What are you doing?

AMANDA: I'm brushing that cowlick down! [*She attacks his hair with the brush.*] What is this young man's position at the warehouse?

TOM [*submitting grimly to the brush and the interrogation*]: This young man's position is that of a shipping clerk, Mother.

AMANDA: Sounds to me like a fairly responsible job, the sort of a job *you* would be in if you just had more *get-up.* What is his salary? Have you any idea.

TOM: I would judge it to be approximately eighty-five dollars a month.

AMANDA: Well—not princely, but—

TOM: Twenty more than I make.

AMANDA: Yes, how well I know! But for a family man, eighty-five dollars a month is not much more than you can just get by on. . . .

TOM: Yes, but Mr. O'Connor is not a family man.

AMANDA: He might be, mightn't he? Some time in the future?

TOM: I see. Plans and provisions.

AMANDA: You are the only young man that I know of who ignores the fact that the future becomes the present, the present the past, and the past turns into everlasting regret if you don't plan for it!

TOM: I will think that over and see what I can make of it.

AMANDA: Don't be supercilious with your mother! Tell me some more about this—what do you call him?

TOM: James D. O'Connor. The D. is for Delaney.

AMANDA: Irish on *both* sides! *Gracious!* And doesn't drink?

TOM: Shall I call him up and ask him right this minute?

AMANDA: The only way to find out about those things is to make discreet inquiries at the proper moment. When I was a girl in Blue Mountain and it was suspected that a young man drank, the girl whose attentions he had been receiving, if any girl *was,* would sometimes speak to the minister of his church, or rather her father would if her father was living, and sort of feel him out on the young man's character. That is the way such things are discreetly handled to keep a young woman from making a tragic mistake!

TOM: Then how did you happen to make a tragic mistake?

AMANDA: That innocent look of your father's had everyone fooled! He *smiled*—the world was *enchanted!* No girl can do worse than put herself at the mercy of a handsome appearance! I hope that Mr. O'Connor is not too good-looking.

TOM: No, he's not too good-looking. He's covered with freckles and hasn't too much of a nose.

AMANDA: He's not right-down homely, though?

TOM: Not right-down homely. Just medium homely, I'd say.

AMANDA: Character's what to look for in a man.

TOM: That's what I've always said, Mother.

AMANDA: You've never said anything of the kind and I suspect you would never give it a thought.

TOM: Don't be so suspicious of me.

AMANDA: At least I hope he's the type that's up and coming.

TOM: I think he really goes in for self-improvement.

AMANDA: What reason have you to think so?

TOM: He goes to night school.

AMANDA [*beaming*]: Splendid! What does he do, I mean study?

TOM: Radio engineering and public speaking!

AMANDA: Then he has visions of being advanced in the world! Any young man who studies public speaking is aiming to have an executive job some day! And radio engineering? A thing for the future! Both of these facts are very illuminating. Those are the sort of things that a mother should know concerning any young man who comes to call on her daughter. Seriously or—not.

TOM: One little warning. He doesn't know about Laura. I didn't let on that we had dark ulterior motives. I just said, why don't you come and have dinner with us? He said okay and that was the whole conversation.

AMANDA: I bet it was! You're eloquent as an oyster. However, he'll know about Laura when he gets here. When he sees how lively and sweet and pretty she is, he'll thank his lucky stars he was asked to dinner.

TOM: Mother, you mustn't expect too much of Laura.

AMANDA: What do you mean?

TOM: Laura seems all those things to you and me because she's ours and we love her. We don't even notice she's crippled any more.

AMANDA: Don't say crippled! You know that I never allow that word to be used!

TOM: But face facts, Mother. She is and—that's not all—

AMANDA: What do you mean "not all"?

TOM: Laura is very different from other girls.

AMANDA: I think the difference is all to her advantage.

TOM: Not quite all—in the eyes of others—strangers—she's terribly shy and lives in a world of her own and those things make her seem a little peculiar to people outside the house.

AMANDA: Don't say peculiar.

TOM: Face the facts. She is.

[*The dance hall music changes to a tango that has a minor and somewhat onimous tone.*]

AMANDA: In what way is she peculiar—may I ask?

TOM [*gently*]: She lives in a world of her own—a world of little glass ornaments, Mother. . . .

[*He gets up.* AMANDA *remains holding the brush, looking at him, troubled.*]

She plays old phonograph records and—that's about all— [*He glances at himself in the mirror and crosses to the door.*]

AMANDA [*sharply*]: Where are you going?

TOM: I'm going to the movies. [*He goes out the screen door.*]

AMANDA: Not to the movies, every night to the movies! [*She follows quickly to the screen door.*] I don't believe you always go to the movies!

[*He is gone.* AMANDA *looks worriedly after him for a moment. Then vitality and optimism return and she turns from the door, crossing to the portieres.*]

Laura! Laura!

[LAURA *answers from the kitchenette.*]

LAURA: Yes, Mother.

AMANDA: Let those dishes go and come in front!

[LAURA *appears with a dish towel.* AMANDA *speaks to her gaily.*]

Laura, come here and make a wish on the moon!

[*Screen image:* The Moon.]

LAURA [*entering*]: Moon—moon?

AMANDA: A little silver slipper of a moon. Look over your left shoulder, Laura, and make a wish!

[LAURA *looks faintly puzzled as if called out of sleep.* AMANDA *seizes her shoulders and turns her at an angle by the door.*]

Now! Now, darling, *wish!*

LAURA: What shall I wish for, Mother?

AMANDA [*her voice trembling and her eyes suddenly filling with tears*]: Happiness! Good fortune!

[*The sound of the violin rises and the stage dims out.*]

Scene Six

The light comes up on the fire escape landing. TOM *is leaning against the grill, smoking.*

[*Screen image:* The high school hero.]

TOM: And so the following evening I brought Jim home to dinner. I had known Jim slightly in high school. In high school Jim was a hero. He had tremendous Irish good nature and vitality with the scrubbed and polished look of white chinaware. He seemed to move in a continual spotlight. He was a star in basketball, captain of the debating club, president of the senior class and the glee club and he sang the male lead in the annual light operas. He was always running or bounding, never just walking. He seemed always at the point of defeating the law of gravity. He was shooting with such velocity through his adolescence that you would logically expect him to arrive at nothing short of the White House by the time he was thirty. But Jim apparently ran into more interference after his graduation from Soldan. His speed had definitely slowed. Six years after he left high school he was holding a job that wasn't much better than mine.

[*Screen image:* The Clerk.]

He was the only one at the warehouse with whom I was on friendly terms. I was valuable to him as someone who could remember his former glory, who had seen him win basketball games and the silver cup in debating. He knew of my secret practice of retiring to a cabinet of the washroom to work on poems when business was slack in the warehouse. He called me Shakespeare. And while the other boys in the warehouse regarded me with suspicious hostility, Jim took a humorous attitude toward me. Gradually his attitude affected the others, their hostility wore off and they also began to smile at me as people smile at an oddly fashioned dog who trots across their path at some distance.

I knew that Jim and Laura had known each other at Soldan, and I had heard Laura speak admiringly of his voice. I didn't know if Jim remembered her or not. In high school Laura had been as unobtrusive as Jim had been astonishing. If he did remember Laura, it was not as my sister, for when I asked him to dinner, he grinned and said, "You know, Shakespeare, I never thought of you as having folks!"

He was about to discover that I did. . . .

[*Legend on screen:* "The accent of a coming foot."]

[*The light dims out on* TOM *and comes up in the Wingfield living room—a delicate lemony light. It is about five on a Friday evening of late spring which comes "scattering poems in the sky."*]

[AMANDA *has worked like a Turk in preparation for the gentleman caller. The results are astonishing. The new floor lamp with its rose silk shade is in place, a colored paper lantern conceals the broken light fixture in the ceiling, new billowing white curtains are at the windows, chintz covers are on the chairs and sofa, a pair of new sofa pillows make their initial appearance. Open boxes and tissue paper are scattered on the floor.*]

[LAURA *stands in the middle of the room with lifted arms while* AMANDA *crouches before her, adjusting the hem of a new dress, devout and ritualistic. The dress is colored and designed by memory. The arrangement of* LAURA'S *hair is changed; it is softer and more becoming. A fragile, unearthly prettiness has come out in* LAURA: *she is like a piece of translucent glass touched by light, given a momentary radiance, not actual, not lasting.*]

AMANDA [*impatiently*]: Why are you trembling?

LAURA: Mother, you've made me so nervous!

AMANDA: How have I made you nervous?

LAURA: By all this fuss! You make it seem so important!

AMANDA: I don't understand you, Laura. You couldn't be satisfied with just sitting home, and yet whenever I try to arrange something for you, you seem to resist it. [*She gets up.*] Now take a look at yourself. No, wait! Wait just a moment—I have an idea!

LAURA: What is it now?

[AMANDA *produces two powder puffs which she wraps in handkerchiefs and stuffs in* LAURA'S *bosom.*]

LAURA: Mother, what are you doing?

AMANDA: They call them "Gay Deceivers"!

LAURA: I won't wear them!

AMANDA: You will!

LAURA: Why should I?

AMANDA: Because, to be painfully honest, your chest is flat.

LAURA: You make it seem like we were setting a trap.

AMANDA: All pretty girls are a trap, a pretty trap, and men expect them to be.

[*Legend on screen:* "A pretty trap."]

Now look at yourself, young lady. This is the prettiest you will ever be! [*She stands back to admire* LAURA.]

I've got to fix myself now! You're going to be surprised by your mother's appearance!

[AMANDA *crosses through the portieres, humming gaily.* LAURA *moves slowly to the long mirror and stares solemnly at herself. A wind blows the white curtains inward in a slow, graceful motion and with a faint, sorrowful sighing.*]

AMANDA [*from somewhere behind the portieres*]: It isn't dark enough yet.

[LAURA *turns slowly before the mirror with a troubled look.*]

[*Legend on screen:* "This is my sister: Celebrate her with strings!" *Music plays.*]

AMANDA [*laughing, still not visible*]: I'm going to show you something. I'm going to make a spectacular appearance!

LAURA: What is it, Mother?

AMANDA: Possess your soul in patience—you will see! Something I've resurrected from that old trunk! Styles haven't changed so terribly much after all. . . . [*She parts the portieres.*] Now just look at your mother! [*She wears a girlish frock of yellowed voile with a blue silk sash. She carries a bunch of jonquils—the legend of her youth is nearly revived. Now she speaks feverishly:*] This is the dress in which I led the cotillion. Won the cakewalk twice at Sunset Hill, wore one Spring to the Governor's Ball in Jackson! See how I sashayed around the ballroom, Laura? [*She raises her skirt and does a mincing step around the room.*] I wore it on Sundays for my gentlemen callers! I had it on the day I met your father. . . . I had malaria fever all that Spring. The change of climate from East Tennessee to the Delta—weakened resistance. I had a little temperature all the time—not enough to be serious—just enough to make me restless and giddy! Invitations poured in—parties all over the Delta! "Stay in bed," said Mother, "you have a fever!"—but I just wouldn't. I took quinine but kept on going, going! Evenings, dances! Afternoons, long, long rides! Picnics—lovely! So lovely, that country in May—all lacy with dogwood, literally flooded with jonquils! That was the spring I had the craze for jonquils. Jonquils became an absolute obsession. Mother said, "Honey, there's no more room for jonquils." And still I kept on bringing in more jonquils. Whenever, wherever I saw them, I'd say, "Stop! Stop! I see jonquils!" I made the young men help me gather the jonquils! It was a joke, Amanda and her jonquils. Finally there were no more vases to hold them, every available space was filled with jonquils. No vases to hold them? All right, I'll hold them myself! And then I—[*She stops in front of the picture. Music plays.*] met your father! Malaria fever and jonquils and then—this—boy. . . . [*She switches on the rose-colored lamp.*] I hope they get here before it starts to rain. [*She crosses the room and places the jonquils in a bowl on the table.*] I gave your brother a little extra change so he and Mr. O'Connor could take the service car home.

LAURA [*with an altered look*]: What did you say his name was?

AMANDA: O'Connor.

LAURA: What is his first name?

AMANDA: I don't remember. Oh, yes, I do. It was—Jim!

[LAURA *sways slightly and catches hold of a chair.*]

[*Legend on screen:* "Not Jim!"]

LAURA [*faintly*]: Not—Jim!

AMANDA: Yes, that was it, it was Jim! I've never known a Jim that wasn't nice!

[*The music becomes ominous.*]

LAURA: Are you sure his name is Jim O'Connor?

AMANDA: Yes. Why?

LAURA: Is he the one that Tom used to know in high school?

AMANDA: He didn't say so. I think he just got to know him at the warehouse.

LAURA: There was a Jim O'Connor we both knew in high school—[*then, with effort*] If that is the one that Tom is bringing to dinner—you'll have to excuse me, I won't come to the table.

AMANDA: What sort of nonsense is this?

LAURA: You asked me once if I'd ever liked a boy. Don't you remember I showed you this boy's picture?

AMANDA: You mean the boy you showed me in the yearbook?

LAURA: Yes, that boy.

AMANDA: Laura, Laura, were you in love with that boy?

LAURA: I don't know, Mother. All I know is I couldn't sit at the table if it was him!

AMANDA: It won't be him! It isn't the least bit likely. But whether it is or not, you will come to the table. You will not be excused.

LAURA: I'll have to be, Mother.

AMANDA: I don't intend to humor your silliness, Laura. I've had too much from you and your brother, both! So just sit down and compose yourself till they come. Tom has forgotten his key so you'll have to let them in, when they arrive.

LAURA [*panicky*]: Oh, Mother—*you* answer the door!

AMANDA [*lightly*]: I'll be in the kitchen—busy!

LAURA: Oh, Mother, please answer the door, don't make me do it!

AMANDA [*crossing into the kitchenette*]: I've got to

fix the dressing for the salmon. Fuss, fuss—silliness!—over a gentleman caller!

[*The door swings shut.* LAURA *is left alone.*]

[*Legend on screen:* "Terror!"]

[*She utters a low moan and turns off the lamp—sits stiffly on the edge of the sofa, knotting her fingers together.*]

[*Legend on screen:* "The Opening of a Door!"]

[TOM and JIM *appear on the fire escape steps and climb to the landing. Hearing their approach,* LAURA *rises with a panicky gesture. She retreats to the portieres. The doorbell rings.* LAURA *catches her breath and touches her throat. Low drums sound.*]

AMANDA [*calling*]: Laura, sweetheart! The door!

[LAURA *stares at it without moving.*]

JIM: I think we just beat the rain.

TOM: Uh-huh. [*He rings again, nervously.* JIM *whistles and fishes for a cigarette.*]

AMANDA [*very, very gaily*]: Laura, that is your brother and Mr. O'Connor! Will you let them in, darling?

[LAURA *crosses toward the kitchenette door.*]

LAURA [*breathlessly*]: Mother—you go to the door!

[AMANDA *steps out of the kitchenette and stares furiously at* LAURA. *She points imperiously at the door.*]

LAURA: Please, please!

AMANDA [*in a fierce whisper*]: What is the matter with you, you silly thing?

LAURA [*desperately*]: Please, you answer it, *please!*

AMANDA: I told you I wasn't going to humor you, Laura. Why have you chosen this moment to lose your mind?

LAURA: Please, please, please, you go!

AMANDA: You'll have to go to the door because I can't!

LAURA [*despairingly*]: I can't either!

AMANDA: *Why?*

LAURA: I'm *sick!*

AMANDA: I'm sick, too—of your nonsense! Why can't you and your brother be normal people? Fantastic whims and behavior!

[TOM *gives a long ring.*]

Preposterous goings on! Can you give me one reason—[*She calls out lyrically.*] *Coming! Just one second!*—why you should be afraid to open a door? Now you answer it, Laura!

LAURA: Oh, oh, oh . . . [*She returns through the portieres, darts to the Victrola, winds it frantically and turns it on.*]

AMANDA: Laura Wingfield, you march right to that door!

LAURA: Yes—yes, Mother!

[*A faraway, scratchy rendition of "Dardanella" softens the air and gives her strength to move through it. She slips to the door and draws it cautiously open.* TOM *enters with the caller,* JIM O'CONNOR.]

TOM: Laura, this is Jim. Jim, this is my sister, Laura.

JIM [*stepping inside*]: I didn't know that Shakespeare had a sister!

LAURA [*retreating, stiff and trembling, from the door*]: How—how do you do?

JIM [*heartily, extending his hand*]: Okay!

[LAURA *touches it hesitantly with hers.*]

JIM: Your hand's *cold,* Laura!

LAURA: Yes, well—I've been playing the Victrola. . . .

JIM: Must have been playing classical music on it! You ought to play a little hot swing music to warm you up!

LAURA: Excuse me—I haven't finished playing the Victrola. . . . [*She turns awkwardly and hurries into the front room. She pauses a second by the Victrola. Then she catches her breath and darts through the portieres like a frightened deer.*]

JIM [*grinning*]: What was the matter?

TOM: Oh—with Laura? Laura is—terribly shy.

JIM: Shy, huh? It's unusual to meet a shy girl nowadays. I don't believe you ever mentioned you had a sister.

TOM: Well, now you know. I have one. Here is the *Post Dispatch.* You want a piece of it?

JIM: Uh-huh.

TOM: What piece? The comics?

JIM: Sports! [*He glances at it.*] Ole Dizzy Dean is on his bad behavior.

TOM [*uninterested*]: Yeah? [*He lights a cigarette and goes over to the fire-escape door.*]

JIM: Where are *you* going?

TOM: I'm going out on the terrace.

JIM [*going after him*]: You know, Shakespeare—I'm going to sell you a bill of goods!

TOM: What goods?

JIM: A course I'm taking.

TOM: Huh?

JIM: In public speaking! You and me, we're not the warehouse type.

TOM: Thanks—that's good news. But what has public speaking got to do with it?

JIM: It fits you for—executive positions!

TOM: Awww.

JIM: I tell you it's done a helluva lot for me.

[*Image on screen:* Executive at his desk.]

TOM: In what respect?

JIM: In every! Ask yourself what is the difference between you an' me and men in the office down front? Brains?—No!—Ability?—No! Then what? Just one little thing—

TOM: What is that one little thing?

JIM: Primarily it amounts to—social poise! Being able to square up to people and hold your own on any social level!

AMANDA [*from the kitchenette*]: Tom?

TOM: Yes, Mother?

AMANDA: Is that you and Mr. O'Connor?

TOM: Yes, Mother.

AMANDA: Well, you just make yourselves comfortable in there.

TOM: Yes, Mother.

AMANDA: Ask Mr. O'Connor if he would like to wash his hands.

JIM: Aw, no—no—thank you—I took care of that at the warehouse. Tom—

TOM: Yes?

JIM: Mr. Mendoza was speaking to me about you.

TOM: Favorably?

JIM: What do you think?

TOM: Well—

JIM: You're going to be out of a job if you don't wake up.

TOM: I am waking up—

JIM: You show no signs.

TOM: The signs are interior.

[*Image on screen:* The sailing vessel with the Jolly Roger again.]

TOM: I'm planning to change. [*He leans over the fire-escape rail, speaking with quiet exhilaration. The incandescent marquees and signs of the first-run movie houses light his face from across the alley. He looks like a voyager.*] I'm right at the point of committing myself to a future that doesn't include the warehouse and Mr. Mendoza or even a night-school course in public speaking.

JIM: What are you gassing about?

TOM: I'm tired of the movies.

JIM: Movies!

TOM: Yes, movies! Look at them—[*a wave toward the marvels of Grand Avenue*] All of those glamorous people—having adventures—hogging it all, gobbling the whole thing up! You know what happens? People go to the *movies* instead of *moving!* Hollywood characters are supposed to have all the adventures for everybody in America, while everybody in America sits in a dark room and watches them have them! Yes, until there's a war. That's when adventure becomes available to the masses! *Everyone's* dish, not only Gable's! Then the people in the dark room come out of the dark room to have some adventures themselves—goody, goody! It's our turn now, to go to the South Sea Island—to make a safari—to be exotic, far-off! But I'm not patient. I don't want to wait till then. I'm tired of the *movies* and I am *about* to *move!*

JIM [*incredulously*]: Move?

TOM: Yes.

JIM: When?

TOM: Soon!

JIM: Where? Where?

[*The music seems to answer the question, while* TOM *thinks it over. He searches in his pockets.*]

TOM: I'm starting to boil inside. I know I seem dreamy, but inside—well, I'm boiling! Whenever I pick up a shoe, I shudder a little thinking how short life is and what I am doing! Whatever that means, I know it doesn't mean shoes—except as something to wear on a traveler's feet! [*He finds what he has been searching for in his pockets and holds out a paper to* JIM.] Look—

JIM: What?

TOM: I'm a member.

JIM [*reading*]: The Union of Merchant Seamen.

TOM: I paid my dues this month, instead of the light bill.

JIM: You will regret it when they turn the lights off.

TOM: I won't be here.

JIM: How about your mother?

TOM: I'm like my father. The bastard son of a bastard! Did you notice how he's grinning in his picture in there? And he's been absent going on sixteen years!

JIM: You're just talking, you drip. How does your mother feel about it?

TOM: Shhh! Here comes Mother! Mother is not acquainted with my plans!

AMANDA [*coming through the portieres*]: Where are you all?

TOM: On the terrace, Mother.

[*They start inside. She advances to them.* TOM *is distinctly shocked at her appearance. Even* JIM *blinks a little. He is making his first contact with girlish Southern vivacity and in spite of the night-school course in public speaking is somewhat thrown off the beam by the unexpected outlay of social charm. Certain responses are attempted by* JIM *but are swept aside by* AMANDA'S *gay laughter and chatter.* TOM *is embarrassed but after the first shock* JIM *reacts very warmly. He grins and chuckles, is altogether won over.*]

[*Image on screen:* Amanda as a girl.]

AMANDA [*coyly smiling, shaking her girlish ringlets*]: Well, well, well, so this is Mr. O'Connor. Introductions entirely unnecessary. I've heard so much about you from my boy. I finally said to him, Tom—good gracious!—why don't you bring this paragon to supper? I'd like to meet this nice young man at the warehouse!—instead of just hearing him sing your praises so much! I don't know why my son is so stand-offish—that's not Southern behavior!

Let's sit down and—I think we could stand a little more air in here! Tom, leave the door open. I felt a nice fresh breeze a moment ago. Where has it gone to? Mmm, so warm already! And not quite summer, even. We're going to burn up when summer really gets started. However, we're having—we're having a very light supper. I think light things are better fo' this time of year. The same as light clothes are. Light clothes an' light food are what warm weather calls fo'. You know our blood gets so thick during th' winter—it takes a while fo' us to *adjust* ou'selves!—when the season changes . . . It's come so quick this year. I wasn't prepared. All of a sudden—heavens! Already summer! I ran to the trunk an' pulled out this light dress—terribly old! Historical almost! But feels so good—so good an' co-ol, y' know. . . .

TOM: Mother—

AMANDA: Yes, honey?

TOM: How about—supper?

AMANDA: Honey, you go ask Sister if supper is ready! You know that Sister is in full charge of supper! Tell her you hungry boys are waiting for it. [*to* JIM] Have you met Laura?

JIM: She—

AMANDA: Let you in? Oh, good, you've met already! It's rare for a girl as sweet an' pretty as Laura to be domestic! But Laura is, thank heavens, not only pretty but also very domestic. I'm not at all. I never was a bit. I never could make a thing but angel-food cake. Well, in the South we had so many servants. Gone, gone, gone. All vestige of gracious living! Gone completely! I wasn't prepared for what the future brought me. All of my gentlemen callers were sons of planters and so of course I assumed that I would be married to one and raise my family on a large piece of land with plenty of servants. But man proposes—and woman accepts the proposal! To vary that old, old saying a little bit—I married no planter! I married a man who worked for the telephone company! That gallantly smiling gentleman over there! [*She points to the picture.*] A telephone man who—fell in love with long-distance! Now he travels and I don't even know where! But what am I going on for about my—tribulations? Tell me yours—I hope you don't have any! Tom?

TOM [*returning*]: Yes, Mother?

AMANDA: Is supper nearly ready?

TOM: It looks to me like supper is on the table.

AMANDA: Let me look— [*She rises prettily and looks through the portieres.*] Oh, lovely! But where is Sister?

TOM: Laura is not feeling well and she says that she thinks she'd better not come to the table.

AMANDA: What? Nonsense! Laura? Oh, Laura!

LAURA [*from the kitchenette, faintly*]: Yes, Mother.

AMANDA: You really must come to the table. We won't be seated until you come to the table! Come in, Mr. O'Connor. You sit over there, and I'll. . . . Laura? Laura Wingfield! You're keeping us waiting, honey! We can't say grace until you come to the table!

[*The kitchenette door is pushed weakly open and* LAURA *comes in. She is obviously quite faint, her lips trembling, her eyes wide and staring. She moves unsteadily toward the table.*]

[*Screen legend:* "Terror!"]

[*Outside a summer storm is coming on abruptly. The white curtains billow inward at the windows and there is a sorrowful murmur from the deep blue dusk.*]

[LAURA *suddenly stumbles; she catches at a chair with a faint moan.*]

TOM: Laura!

AMANDA: Laura!

[*There is a clap of thunder.*]

[*Screen legend:* "Ah!"]

[*despairingly*] Why, Laura, you *are* ill, darling! Tom, help your sister into the living room, dear! Sit in the living room, Laura—rest on the sofa. Well! [*to* JIM *as* TOM *helps his sister to the sofa in the living room*] Standing over the hot stove made her ill! I told her that it was just too warm this evening, but—

[TOM *comes back to the table.*]

Is Laura all right now?

TOM: Yes.

AMANDA: What *is* that? Rain? A nice cool rain has come up [*She gives Jim a frightened look.*] I think we may—have grace—now . . .

[TOM *looks at her stupidly.*] Tom, honey—you say grace!

TOM: Oh . . . "For these and all thy mercies—"

[*They bow their heads,* AMANDA *stealing a nervous glance at* JIM. *In the living room* LAURA, *stretched on the sofa, clenches her hand to her lips, to hold back a shuddering sob.*]

God's Holy Name be praised—

[*The scene dims out.*]

Scene Seven

It is half an hour later. Dinner is just being finished in the dining room, LAURA *is still huddled upon the sofa, her feet drawn under her, her head resting on a pale blue pillow, her eyes wide and mysteriously watchful. The new floor lamp with its shade of rose-colored silk gives a soft, becoming light to her face, bringing out the fragile, unearthly prettiness which usually escapes attention. From outside there is a steady murmur of rain, but it is slackening and soon stops; the air outside becomes pale and luminous as the moon breaks through the clouds. A moment after the curtain rises, the lights in both rooms flicker and go out.*

JIM: Hey, there, Mr. Light Bulb!

[AMANDA *laughs nervously.*]

[*Legend on screen:* "Suspension of a public service."]

AMANDA: Where was Moses when the lights went out? Ha-ha. Do you know the answer to that one, Mr. O'Connor?

JIM: No, Ma'am, what's the answer?

AMANDA: In the dark!

[JIM *laughs appreciatively.*]

Everybody sit still. I'll light the candles. Isn't it lucky we have them on the table? Where's a match? Which of you gentlemen can provide a match?

JIM: Here.

AMANDA: Thank you, Sir.

JIM: Not at all, Ma'am!

AMANDA [*as she lights the candles*]: I guess the fuse has burnt out. Mr. O'Connor, can you tell a burnt-out fuse? I know I can't and Tom is a total loss when it comes to mechanics.

[*They rise from the table and go into the kitchenette, from where their voices are heard.*]

Oh, be careful you don't bump into something. We don't want our gentleman caller to break his neck. Now wouldn't that be a fine howdy-do?

JIM: Ha-ha! Where is the fuse-box?

AMANDA: Right here next to the stove. Can you see anything?

JIM: Just a minute.

AMANDA: Isn't electricity a mysterious thing? Wasn't it Benjamin Franklin who tied a key to a kite? We live in such a mysterious universe, don't we? Some people say that science clears up all the mysteries for us. In my opinion it only creates more! Have you found it yet?

JIM: No, Ma'am. All these fuses look okay to me.

AMANDA: Tom!

TOM: Yes, Mother?

AMANDA: That light bill I gave you several days ago. The one I told you we got the notices about?

[*Legend on screen:* "Ha!"]

TOM: Oh—yeah.

AMANDA: You didn't neglect to pay it by any chance?

TOM: Why, I—

AMANDA: Didn't! I might have known it!

JIM: Shakespeare probably wrote a poem on that light bill, Mrs. Wingfield.

AMANDA: I might have known better than to trust him with it! There's such a high price for negligence in this world!

JIM: Maybe the poem will win a ten-dollar prize.

AMANDA: We'll just have to spend the remainder of the evening in the nineteenth century, before Mr. Edison made the Mazda lamp!

JIM: Candlelight is my favorite kind of light.

AMANDA: That shows you're romantic! But that's no excuse for Tom. Well, we got through dinner. Very considerate of them to let us get through dinner before they plunged us into everlasting darkness, wasn't it, Mr. O'Connor?

JIM: Ha-ha!

AMANDA: Tom, as a penalty for your carelessness you can help me with the dishes.

JIM: Let me give you a hand.

AMANDA: Indeed you will not!

JIM: I ought to be good for something.

AMANDA: Good for something? [*Her tone is rhapsodic.*] *You?* Why, Mr. O'Connor, nobody, *nobody's* given me this much entertainment in years—as you have!

JIM: Aw, now, Mrs. Wingfield!

AMANDA: I'm not exaggerating, not one bit! But Sister is all by her lonesome. You go keep her company in the parlor! I'll give you this lovely old candelabrum that used to be on the altar at the Church of the Heavenly Rest. It was melted a little out of shape when the church burnt down. Lightning struck it one spring. Gypsy Jones was holding a revival at the time and he intimated that the church was destroyed because the Episcopalians gave card parties.

JIM: Ha-ha.

AMANDA: And how about you coaxing Sister to drink a little wine? I think it would be good for her! Can you carry both at once?

JIM: Sure. I'm Superman!

AMANDA: Now, Thomas, get into this apron!

[JIM *comes into the dining room, carrying the candelabrum, its candles lighted, in one hand and a glass of wine in the other. The door of the kitchenette swings closed on* AMANDA'S *gay laughter; the flickering light approaches the portieres.* LAURA *sits up nervously as* JIM *enters. She can hardly speak from the almost intolerable strain of being alone with a stranger.*]

[*Screen legend:* "I don't suppose you remember me at all!"]

[*At first, before* JIM'S *warmth overcomes her paralyzing shyness,* LAURA'S *voice is thin and breathless, as though she had just run up a steep flight of stairs.* JIM'S *attitude is gently humorous. While the incident is apparently unimportant, it is to* LAURA *the climax of her secret life.*]

JIM: Hello there, Laura.

LAURA [*faintly*]: Hello. [*She clears her throat.*]

JIM: How are you feeling now? Better?

LAURA: Yes. Yes, thank you.

JIM: This is for you. A little dandelion wine. [*He extends the glass toward her with extravagant gallantry.*].

LAURA: Thank you.

JIM: Drink it—but don't get drunk!

[*He laughs heartily.* LAURA *takes the glass uncertainly; she laughs shyly.*]

Where shall I set the candles?

LAURA: Oh—oh, anywhere . . .

JIM: How about here on the floor? Any objections?

LAURA: No.

JIM: I'll spread a newspaper under to catch the drippings. I like to sit on the floor. Mind if I do?

LAURA: Oh, no.

JIM: Give me a pillow?

LAURA: What?

JIM: A pillow!

LAURA: Oh . . . [*She hands him one quickly.*]

JIM: How about you? Don't you like to sit on the floor?

LAURA: Oh—yes.

JIM: Why don't you, then?

LAURA: I—will.

JIM: Take a pillow!

[LAURA *does. She sits on the floor on the other side of the candelabrum.* JIM *crosses his legs and smiles engagingly at her.*]

I can't hardly see you sitting way over there.

LAURA: I can—see you.

JIM: I know, but that's not fair, I'm in the limelight.

[LAURA *moves her pillow closer.*]

Good! Now I can see you! Comfortable?

LAURA: Yes.

JIM: So am I. Comfortable as a cow! Will you have some gum?

LAURA: No, thank you.

JIM: I think that I will indulge, with your permission. [*He musingly unwraps a stick of gum and holds it up.*] Think of the fortune made by the guy that invented the first piece of chewing gum. Amazing, huh? The Wrigley Building is one of the sights of Chicago—I saw it when I went up to the Century of Progress. Did you take in the Century of Progress?

LAURA: No, I didn't.

JIM: Well, it was quite a wonderful exposition. What impressed me most was the Hall of Science. Gives you an idea of what the future will be in America, even more wonderful than the present time is! [*There is a pause.* JIM *smiles at her.*] Your brother tells me you're shy. Is that right, Laura?

LAURA: I—don't know.

JIM: I judge you to be an old-fashioned type of girl. Well, I think that's a pretty good type to be. Hope you don't think I'm being too personal—do you?

LAURA [*hastily, out of embarrassment*]: I believe I *will* take a piece of gum, if you—don't mind. [*clearing her throat*] Mr. O'Connor, have you—kept up with your singing?

JIM: Singing? Me?

LAURA: Yes. I remember what a beautiful voice you had.

JIM: When did you hear me sing?

[LAURA *does not answer, and in the long pause which follows a man's voice is heard singing offstage.*]

Voice:

O blow, ye winds, heigh-ho,
A-roving I will go!
I'm off to my love
With a boxing glove—
Ten thousand miles away!

JIM: You say you've heard me sing?

LAURA: Oh, yes! Yes, very often . . . I—don't suppose—you remember me—at all?

JIM [*smiling doubtfully*]: You know I have an idea I've seen you before. I had that idea soon as you opened the door. It seemed almost like I was about to remember your name. But the name that I started to call you—wasn't a name! And so I stopped myself before I said it.

LAURA: Wasn't it—Blue Roses?

JIM [*springing up, grinning*]: Blue Roses! My gosh, yes—Blue Roses! That's what I had on my tongue when you opened the door! Isn't it funny what tricks your memory plays? I didn't connect you with high school somehow or other. But that's where it was; it was high school. I didn't even know you were Shakespeare's sister! Gosh, I'm sorry.

LAURA: I didn't expect you to. You—barely knew me!

JIM: But we did have a speaking acquaintance, huh?

LAURA: Yes, we—spoke to each other.

JIM: When did you recognize me?

LAURA: Oh, right away!

JIM: Soon as I came in the door?

LAURA: When I heard your name I thought it was probably you. I knew that Tom used to know you a little in high school. So when you came in the door—well, then I was—sure.

JIM: Why didn't you *say* something, then?

LAURA [*breathlessly*]: I didn't know what to say, I was—too surprised!

JIM: For goodness' sakes! You know, this sure is funny!

LAURA: Yes! Yes, isn't it, though . . .

JIM: Didn't we have a class in something together?

LAURA: Yes, we did.

JIM: What class was that?

LAURA: It was—singing—chorus!

JIM: Aw!

LAURA: I sat across the aisle from you in the Aud.

JIM: Aw.

LAURA: Mondays, Wednesdays, and Fridays.

JIM: Now I remember—you always came in late.

LAURA: Yes, it was so hard for me, getting upstairs. I had that brace on my leg—it clumped so loud!

JIM: I never heard any clumping.

LAURA [*wincing at the recollection*]: To me it sounded like—thunder!

JIM: Well, well, well, I never even noticed.

LAURA: And everybody was seated before I came in. I had to walk in front of all those people. My seat was in the back row. I had to go clumping all the way up the aisle with everyone watching!

JIM: You shouldn't have been self-conscious.

LAURA: I know, but I was. It was always such a relief when the singing started.

JIM: Aw, yes, I've placed you now! I used to call you Blue Roses. How was it that I got started calling you that?

LAURA: I was out of school a little while with pleurosis. When I came back you asked me what was the matter. I said I had pleurosis—you thought I said *Blue Roses.* That's what you always called me after that!

JIM: I hope you didn't mind.

LAURA: Oh, no—I liked it. You see, I wasn't acquainted with many people. . . .

JIM: As I remember you sort of stuck by yourself.

LAURA: I—I—never have had much luck at—making friends.

JIM: I don't see why you wouldn't.

LAURA: Well, I—started out badly.

JIM: You mean being—

LAURA: Yes, it sort of—stood between me—

JIM: You shouldn't have let it!

LAURA: I know, but it did, and—

JIM: You were shy with people!

LAURA: I tried not to be but never could—

JIM: Overcome it?

LAURA: No, I—I never could!

JIM: I guess being shy is something you have to work out of kind of gradually.

LAURA [*sorrowfully*]: Yes—I guess it—

JIM: Takes time!

LAURA: Yes—

JIM: People are not so dreadful when you know them. That's what you have to remember! And everybody has problems, not just you, but practically everybody has got some problems. You think of yourself as having the only problems, as being the only one who is disappointed. But just look around you and you will see lots of people as disappointed as you are. For instance, I hoped when I was going to high school that I would be further along at this time, six years later, than I am now. You remember that wonderful write-up I had in *The Torch?*

LAURA: Yes! [*She rises and crosses to the table.*]

JIM: It said I was bound to succeed in anything I went into!

[LAURA *returns with the high school yearbook.*]

Holy Jeez! *The Torch!*

[*He accepts it reverently. They smile across the book with mutual wonder.* LAURA *crouches beside him and they begin to turn the pages.* LAURA'S *shyness is dissolving in his warmth.*]

LAURA: Here you are in *The Pirates of Penzance!*

JIM [*wistfully*]: I sang the baritone lead in that operetta.

LAURA [*raptly*]: So—*beautifully!*

JIM [*protesting*]: Aw—

LAURA: Yes, yes—beatifully—beautifully!

JIM: You heard me?

LAURA: All three times!

JIM: No!

LAURA: Yes!

JIM: All three performances?

LAURA [*looking down*]: Yes.

JIM: Why?

LAURA: I—wanted to ask you to—autograph my program. [*She takes the program from the back of the yearbook and shows it to him.*]

JIM: Why didn't you ask me to?

LAURA: You were always surrounded by your own friends so much that I never had a chance to.

JIM: You should have just—

LAURA: Well, I—thought you might think I was—

JIM: Thought I might think you was—what?

LAURA: Oh—

JIM [*with reflective relish*]: I was beleaguered by females in those days.

LAURA: You were terribly popular!

JIM: Yeah—

LAURA: You had such a—friendly way—

JIM: I was spoiled in high school.

LAURA: Everybody—liked you!

JIM: Including you?

LAURA: I—yes, I—did, too— [*She gently closes the book in her lap.*]

JIM: Well, well, well! Give me that program, Laura.

[*She hands it to him. He signs it with a flourish.*]

There you are—better late than never!

LAURA: Oh, I—what a—surprise!

JIM: My signature isn't worth very much right now. But some day—maybe—it will increase in value! Being disappointed is one thing and being discouraged is something else. I am disappointed but I am not discouraged. I'm twenty-three years old. How old are you?

LAURA: I'll be twenty-four in June.

JIM: That's not old age!

LAURA: No, but—

JIM: You finished high school?

LAURA [*with difficulty*]: I didn't go back.

JIM: You mean you dropped out?

LAURA: I made bad grades in my final examinations. [*She rises and replaces the book and the program on the table. Her voice is strained.*] How is—Emily Meisenbach getting along?

JIM: Oh, that kraut-head!

LAURA: Why do you call her that?

JIM: That's what she was.

LAURA: You're not still—going with her?

JIM: I never see her.

LAURA: It said in the "Personal" section that you were—engaged!

JIM: I know, but I wasn't impressed by that—propaganda!

LAURA: It wasn't—the truth?

JIM: Only in Emily's optimistic opinion!

LAURA: Oh—

[*Legend:* "What have you done since high school?"]

[JIM *lights a cigarette and leans indolently back on his elbows smiling at* LAURA *with a warmth and charm which lights her inwardly with altar candles. She remains by the table, picks up a piece from the glass menagerie collection, and turns it in her hands to cover her tumult.*]

JIM [*after several reflective puffs on his cigarette*]: What have you done since high school?

[*She seems not to hear him.*]

Huh?

[LAURA *looks up.*]

I said what have you done since high school, Laura?

LAURA: Nothing much.

JIM: You must have been doing something these six long years.

LAURA: Yes.

JIM: Well, then, such as what?

LAURA: I took a business course at business college—

JIM: How did that work out?

LAURA: Well, not very—well—I had to drop out, it gave me—indigestion—

[JIM *laughs gently.*]

JIM: What are you doing now?

LAURA: I don't do anything—much. Oh, please don't think I sit around doing nothing! My glass collection takes up a good deal of time. Glass is something you have to take good care of.

JIM: What did you say—about glass?

LAURA: Collection I said—I have one— [*She clears her throat and turns away again, acutely shy.*]

JIM [*abruptly*]: You know what I judge to be the trouble with you? Inferiority complex! Know what that is? That's what they call it when someone low-rates himself! I understand it because I had it, too. Although my case was not so aggravated as yours seems to be. I had it until I took up public speaking, developed my voice, and learned that I had an aptitude for science. Before that time I never thought of myself as being outstanding in any way whatsoever! Now I've never made a regular study of it, but I have a friend who says I can analyze people better than doctors that make a profession of it. I don't claim that to be necessarily true, but I can sure guess a person's psychology, Laura! [*He takes out his gum.*] Excuse me, Laura. I always take it out when the flavor is gone. I'll use this scrap of paper to wrap it in. I know how it is to get it stuck on a shoe. [*He wraps the gum in paper and puts it in his pocket.*] Yep—that's what I judge to be your principal trouble. A lack of confidence in yourself as a person. You don't have the proper amount of faith in yourself. I'm basing that fact on a number of your remarks and also on certain observations I've made. For instance that clumping you thought was so awful in high school. You say that you even dreaded to walk into class. You see what you did? You dropped out of school, you gave up an education because of a clump, which as far as I know was practically non-existent! A little physical defect is what you have. Hardly noticeable even! Magnified thousands of times by imagination! You know what my strong advice to you is? Think of yourself as *superior* in some way!

LAURA: In what way would I think?

JIM: Why, man alive, Laura! Just look about you a little. What do you see? A world full of common people! All of 'em born and all of 'em going to die! Which of them has one-tenth of your good points! Or mine! Or anyone else's, as far as that goes—gosh! Everybody excels in some one thing. Some in many! [*He unconsciously glances at himself in the mirror.*] All you've got to do is discover in *what!* Take me, for instance. [*He adjusts his tie at the mirror.*] My interest happens to lie in electro-dynamics. I'm taking a course in radio engineering at night school, Laura, on top of a fairly responsible job at the warehouse. I'm taking that course and studying public speaking.

LAURA: Ohhhh.

JIM: Because I believe in the future of television! [*turning his back to her.*] I wish to be ready to go up right along with it. Therefore I'm planning to get in on the ground floor. In fact I've already made the right connections and all that remains is for the industry itself to get under way! Full steam—[*His eyes are starry.*] *Knowledge—Zzzzzp! Money—Zzzzzzp!—Power!* That's the cycle democracy is built on!

[*His attitude is convincingly dynamic.* LAURA *stares at him, even her shyness eclipsed in her absolute wonder. He suddenly grins.*]

I guess you think I think a lot of myself!

LAURA: No—o-o-o, I—

JIM: Now how about you? Isn't there something you take more interest in than anything else?

LAURA: Well, I do—as I said—have my—glass collection—

[*A peal of girlish laughter rings from the kitchenette.*]

JIM: I'm not right sure I know what you're talking about. What kind of glass is it?

LAURA: Little articles of it, they're ornaments mostly! Most of them are little animals made out of glass, the tiniest little animals in the world. Mother calls them a glass menagerie! Here's an example of one, if you'd like to see it! This one is one of the oldest. It's nearly thirteen.

[*Music:* "The Glass Menagerie."]

[*He stretches out his hand.*]

Oh, be careful—if you breathe, it breaks!

JIM: I'd better not take it. I'm pretty clumsy with things.

LAURA: Go on, I trust you with him! [*She places the piece in his palm.*] There now—you're holding him gently! Hold him over the light, he loves the light! You see how the light shines through him?

JIM: It sure does shine!

LAURA: I shouldn't be partial, but he is my favorite one.

JIM: What kind of a thing is this one supposed to be?

LAURA: Haven't you noticed the single horn on his forehead?

JIM: A unicorn, huh?

LAURA: Mmmm-hmmm!

JIM: Unicorns—aren't they extinct in the modern world?

LAURA: I know!

JIM: Poor little fellow, he must feel sort of lonesome.

LAURA [*smiling*]: Well, if he does, he doesn't complain about it. He stays on a shelf with some horses that don't have horns and all of them seem to get along nicely together.

JIM: How do you know?

LAURA [*lightly*]: I haven't heard any arguments among them!

JIM [*grinning*]: No arguments, huh? Well, that's a pretty good sign! Where shall I set him?

LAURA: Put him on the table. They all like a change of scenery once in a while!

JIM: Well, well, well, well—[*He places the glass piece on the table, then raises his arms and stretches.*] Look how big my shadow is when I stretch!

LAURA: Oh, oh, yes—it stretches across the ceiling!

JIM [*crossing to the door*]: I think it's stopped raining. [*He opens the fire-escape door and the background music changes to a dance tune.*] Where does the music come from?

LAURA: From the Paradise Dance Hall across the alley.

JIM: How about cutting the rug a little, Miss Wingfield?

LAURA: Oh, I—

JIM: Or is your program filled up? Let me have a look at it. [*He grasps an imaginary card.*] Why, every dance is taken! I'll just have to scratch some out.

[*Waltz music:* "La Golondrina."]

Ahhh, a waltz! [*He executes some sweeping turns by himself, then holds his arms toward* LAURA.]

LAURA [*breathlessly*]: I—can't dance!

JIM: There you go, that inferiority stuff!

LAURA: I've never danced in my life!

JIM: Come on, try!

LAURA: Oh, but I'd step on you!

JIM: I'm not made out of glass.

LAURA: How—how—how do we start?

JIM: Just leave it to me. You hold your arms out a little.

LAURA: Like this?

JIM [*taking her in his arms*]: A little bit higher. Right. Now don't tighten up, that's the main thing about it—relax.

LAURA [*laughing breathlessly*]: It's hard not to.

JIM: Okay.

LAURA: I'm afraid you can't budge me.

JIM: What do you bet I can't? [*He swings her into motion.*]

LAURA: Goodness, yes, you can!

JIM: Let yourself go, now, Laura, just let yourself go.

LAURA: I'm—

JIM: Come on!

LAURA: —trying!

JIM: Not so stiff—easy does it!

LAURA: I know but I'm—

JIM: Loosen th' backbone! There now, that's a lot better.

LAURA: Am I?

JIM: Lots, lots better! [*He moves her about the room in a clumsy waltz.*]

LAURA: Oh, my!

JIM: Ha-ha!

LAURA: Oh, my goodness!

JIM: Ha-ha-ha!

[*They suddenly bump into the table, and the glass piece on it falls to the floor.* JIM *stops the dance.*]

What did we hit on?

LAURA: Table.

JIM: Did something fall off it? I think—

LAURA: Yes.

JIM: I hope that it wasn't the little glass horse with the horn!

LAURA: Yes. [*She stoops to pick it up.*]

JIM: Aw, aw, aw. Is it broken?

LAURA: Now it is just like all the other horses.

JIM: It's lost its—

LAURA: Horn! It doesn't matter. Maybe it's a blessing in disguise.

JIM: You'll never forgive me. I bet that that was your favorite piece of glass.

LAURA: I don't have favorites much. It's no tragedy, Freckles. Glass breaks so easily. No matter how careful you are. The traffic jars the shelves and things fall off them.

JIM: Still I'm awfully sorry that I was the cause.

LAURA [*smiling*]: I'll just imagine he had an operation. The horn was removed to make him feel less—freakish!

[*They both laugh.*]

Now he will feel more at home with the other horses, the ones that don't have horns. . . .

JIM: Ha-ha, that's very funny! [*Suddenly he is serious.*] I'm glad to see that you have a sense of humor. You know—you're—well—very different! Surprisingly different from anyone else I know! [*His voice becomes soft and hesitant with a genuine feeling.*] Do you mind me telling you that?

[LAURA *is abashed beyond speech.*]

I mean it in a nice way—

[LAURA *nods shyly, looking away.*]

You make me feel sort of—I don't know how to put it! I'm usually pretty good at expressing things, but—this is something that I don't know how to say!

[LAURA *touches her throat and clears it—turns the broken unicorn in her hands. His voice becomes softer.*]

Has anyone ever told you that you were pretty?

[*There is a pause, and the music rises slightly.* LAURA *looks up slowly, with wonder, and shakes her head.*]

Well, you are! In a very different way from anyone else. And all the nicer because of the difference, too.

[*His voice becomes low and husky.* LAURA *turns away, nearly faint with the novelty of her emotions.*]

I wish that you were my sister. I'd teach you to have some confidence in yourself. The different people are not like other people, but being different is nothing to be ashamed of. Because other people are not such wonderful people. They're one hundred times one thousand. You're one times one! They walk all over the earth. You just stay here. They're common as—weeds, but—you—well, you're—*Blue Roses!*

[*Image on screen?* Blue Roses.]

[*The music changes.*]

LAURA: But blue is wrong for—roses. . . .

JIM: It's right for you! You're—pretty!

LAURA: In what respect am I pretty?

JIM: In all respects—believe me! Your eyes—your hair—are pretty! Your hands are pretty! [*He catches hold of her hand.*] You think I'm making this up because I'm invited to dinner and have to be nice. Oh, I could do that! I could put on an act for you, Laura, and say lots of things without being very sincere. But this time I am. I'm talking to you sincerely. I happened to notice you had this inferiority complex that keeps you from feeling comfortable with people. Somebody needs to build your confidence up and make you proud instead of shy and turning away and—blushing. Somebody—ought to—*kiss* you, Laura!

[*His hand slips slowly up her arm to her shoulder as the music swells tumultuously. He suddenly turns her about and kisses her on the lips. When he releases her,* LAURA *sinks on the sofa with a bright, dazed look.* JIM *backs away and fishes in his pocket for a cigarette.*]

[*Legend on screen:* "A souvenir."]

Stumblejohn!

[He lights the cigarette, avoiding her look. There is a peal of girlish laughter from AMANDA *in the kitchenette.* LAURA *slowly raises and opens her hand. It still contains the little broken glass animal. She looks at it with a tender, bewildered expression.]*

Stumblejohn! I shouldn't have done that—that was way off the beam. You don't smoke, do you?

[She looks up, smiling, not hearing the question. He sits beside her rather gingerly. She looks at him speechlessly—waiting. He coughs decorously and moves a little farther aside as he considers the situation and senses her feelings, dimly, with perturbation. He speaks gently.]

Would you—care for a—mint?

[She doesn't seem to hear him but her look grows brighter even.]

Peppermint? Life Saver? My pocket's a regular drugstore—wherever I go. . . . *[He pops a mint in his mouth. Then he gulps and decides to make a clean breast of it. He speaks slowly and gingerly.]* Laura, you know, if I had a sister like you, I'd do the same thing as Tom. I'd bring out fellows and—introduce her to them. The right type of boys—of a type to—appreciate her. Only—well—he made a mistake about me. Maybe I've got no call to be saying this. That may not have been the idea in having me over. But what if it was? There's nothing wrong about that. The only trouble is that in my case—I'm not in a situation to—do the right thing. I can't take down your number and say I'll phone. I can't call up next week and—ask for a date. I thought I had better explain the situation in case you—misunderstood it and—I hurt your feelings. . . .

[There is a pause. Slowly, very slowly, LAURA'S *look changes, her eyes returning slowly from his to the glass figure in her palm.* AMANDA *utters another gay laugh in the kitchenette.]*

LAURA *[faintly]*: You—won't—call again?

JIM: No, Laura, I can't. *[He rises from the sofa.]* As I was just explaining, I've—got strings on me. Laura, I've—been going steady! I go out all the time with a girl named Betty. She's a home-girl like you, and Catholic, and Irish, and in a great many ways we—get along fine. I met her last summer on a moonlight boat trip up the river to Alton, on the *Majestic.* Well—right away from the start it was—love!

[Legend: Love!]

*[*LAURA *sways slightly forward and grips the arm of the sofa. He fails to notice, now enrapt in his own comfortable being.]*

Being in love has made a new man of me!

[Leaning stiffly forward, clutching the arm of the sofa, LAURA *struggles visibly with her storm. But* JIM *is oblivious; she is a long way off.]*

The power of love is really pretty tremendous! Love is something that—changes the whole world, Laura!

[The storm abates a little and LAURA *leans back. He notices her again.]*

It happened that Betty's aunt took sick, she got a wire and had to go to Centralia. So Tom—when he asked me to dinner—I naturally just accepted the invitation, not knowing that you—that he—that I— *[He stops awkwardly.]* Huh—I'm a stumblejohn!

[He flops back on the sofa. The holy candles on the altar of LAURA'S *face have been snuffed out. There is a look of almost infinite desolation.* JIM *glances at her uneasily.]*

I wish that you would—say something.

[She bites her lip which was trembling and then bravely smiles. She opens her hand again on the broken glass figure. Then she gently takes his hand and raises it level with her own. She carefully places the unicorn in the palm of his hand, then pushes his fingers closed upon it.]

What are you—doing that for? You want me to have him? Laura?

[She nods.]

What for?

LAURA: A—souvenir. . . .

[She rises unsteadily and crouches beside the Victrola to wind it up.]

[Legend on screen: "Things have a way of turning out so badly!" *Or image:* "Gentleman caller waving goodbye—gaily."]

[At this moment AMANDA *rushes brightly back into the living room. She bears a pitcher of fruit punch in an old-fashioned cut-glass pitcher, and a plate of macaroons. The plate has a gold border and poppies painted on it.]*

AMANDA: Well, well, well! Isn't the air delightful after the shower? I've made you children a little liquid refreshment. *[She turns gaily to* JIM*]* Jim, do you know that song about lemonade?

"Lemonade, lemonade
Made in the shade and stirred with a spade—
Good enough for any old maid!"

JIM *[uneasily]*: Ha-ha! No—I never heard it.

AMANDA: Why, Laura! You look so serious!

JIM: We were having a serious conversation.

AMANDA: Good! Now you're better acquainted!

JIM *[uncertainly]*: Ha-ha! Yes.

AMANDA: You modern young people are much more serious-minded than my generation. I was so gay as a girl!

JIM: You haven't changed, Mrs. Wingfield.

AMANDA: Tonight I'm rejuvenated! The gaiety of the occasion, Mr. O'Connor! *[She tosses her head with a peal of laughter, spilling some lemonade.*] Oooo! I'm baptizing myself!

JIM: Here—let me—

AMANDA [*setting the pitcher down*]: There now. I discovered we had some maraschino cherries. I dumped them in, juice and all!

JIM: You shouldn't have gone to that trouble, Mrs. Wingfield.

AMANDA: Trouble, trouble? Why, it was loads of fun! Didn't you hear me cutting up in the kitchen? I bet your ears were burning! I told Tom how outdone with him I was for keeping you to himself so long a time! He should have brought you over much, much sooner! Well, now that you've found your way, I want you to be a very frequent caller! Not just occasional but all the time. Oh, we're going to have a lot of gay times together! I see them coming! Mmm, just breathe that air! So fresh, and the moon's so pretty! I'll skip back out—I know where my place is when young folks are having a—serious conversation!

JIM: Oh, don't go out, Mrs. Wingfield. The fact of the matter is I've got to be going.

AMANDA: Going, now? You're joking! Why, it's only the shank of the evening, Mr. O'Connor!

JIM: Well, you know how it is.

AMANDA: You mean you're a young workingman and have to keep workingmen's hours. We'll let you off early tonight. But only on the condition that next time you stay later. What's the best night for you? Isn't Saturday night the best night for you workingmen?

JIM: I have a couple of time-clocks to punch, Mrs. Wingfield. One at morning, another one at night!

AMANDA: My, but you *are* ambitious! You work at night, too?

JIM: No, Ma'am, not work but—Betty!

[*He crosses deliberately to pick up his hat. The band at the Paradise Dance Hall goes into a tender waltz.*]

AMANDA: Betty? Betty? Who's—Betty!

[*There is an ominous cracking sound in the sky.*]

JIM: Oh, just a girl. The girl I go steady with!

[*He smiles charmingly. The sky falls.*]

[*Legend:* "The Sky Falls."]

AMANDA [*a long-drawn exhalation*]: Ohhhh . . . Is it a serious romance, Mr. O'Connor?

JIM: We're going to be married the second Sunday in June.

AMANDA: Ohhhh—how nice! Tom didn't mention that you were engaged to be married.

JIM: The cat's not out of the bag at the warehouse yet. You know how they are. They call you Romeo and stuff like that. [*He stops at the oval mirror to put on his hat. He carefully shapes the brim and the crown to give a discreetly dashing effect.*] It's been a wonderful evening, Mrs. Wingfield. I guess this is what they mean by Southern hospitality.

AMANDA: It really wasn't anything at all.

JIM: I hope it don't seem like I'm rushing off. But I promised Betty I'd pick her up at the Wabash depot, an' by the time I get my jalopy down there her train'll be in. Some women are pretty upset if you keep 'em waiting.

AMANDA: Yes, I know—the tyranny of women! [*She extends her hand.*] Goodbye, Mr. O'Connor. I wish you luck—and happiness—and success! All three of them, and so does Laura! Don't you, Laura?

LAURA: Yes!

JIM [*taking* LAURA'S *hand*]: Goodbye, Laura. I'm certainly going to treasure that souvenir. And don't you forget the good advice I gave you. [*He raises his voice to a cheery shout.*] So long, Shakespeare! Thanks again, ladies. Good night!

[*He grins and ducks jauntily out. Still bravely grimacing,* AMANDA *closes the door on the gentleman caller. Then she turns back to the room with a puzzled expression. She and* LAURA *don't dare to face each other.* LAURA *crouches beside the Victrola to wind it.*]

AMANDA [*faintly*]: Things have a way of turning out so badly. I don't believe that I would play the Victrola. Well, well—well! Our gentleman caller was engaged to be married! [*She raises her voice.*] Tom!

TOM [*from the kitchenette*]: Yes, Mother?

AMANDA: Come in here a minute. I want to tell you something awfully funny.

TOM [*entering with a macaroon and a glass of the lemonade*]: Has the gentleman caller gotten away already?

AMANDA: The gentleman caller has made an early departure. What a wonderful joke you played on us!

TOM: How do you mean?

AMANDA: You didn't mention that he was engaged to be married.

TOM: Jim? Engaged?

AMANDA: That's what he just informed us.

TOM: I'll be jiggered! I didn't know about that.

AMANDA: That seems very peculiar.

TOM: What's peculiar about it?

AMANDA: Didn't you call him your best friend down at the warehouse?

TOM: He is, but how did I know?

AMANDA: It seems extremely peculiar that you wouldn't know your best friend was going to be married!

TOM: The warehouse is where I work, not where I know things about people!

AMANDA: You don't know things anywhere! You live in a dream; you manufacture illusions!

[He crosses to the door.]

Where are you going?

TOM: I'm going to the movies.

AMANDA: That's right, now that you've had us make such fools of ourselves. The effort, the preparations, all the expense! The new floor lamp, the rug, the clothes for Laura! All for what? To entertain some other girl's fiancé! Go to the movies, go! Don't think about us, a mother deserted, an unmarried sister who's crippled and has no job! Don't let anything interfere with your selfish pleasure! Just go, go, go—to the movies!

TOM: All right, I will! The more you shout about my selfishness to me the quicker I'll go, and I won't go to the movies!

AMANDA: Go, then! Go to the moon—you selfish dreamer!

[TOM *smashes his glass on the floor. He plunges out on the fire escape, slamming the door.* LAURA *screams in fright. The dance-hall music becomes louder.* TOM *stands on the fire escape, gripping the rail. The moon breaks through the storm clouds, illuminating his face.*]

[*Legend on screen:* "And so goodbye . . ."]

[TOM'S *closing speech is timed with what is happening inside the house. We see, as though through soundproof glass, that* AMANDA *appears to be making a comforting speech to* LAURA, *who is huddled upon the sofa. Now that we cannot hear the mother's speech, her silliness is gone and she has dignity and tragic beauty.* LAURA'S *hair hides her face until, at the end of the speech, she lifts her head to smile at her mother.* AMANDA'S *gestures are slow and graceful, almost dancelike, as she comforts her daughter. At the end of her speech she glances a moment at the father's picture—then withdraws through the portieres. At the close of* TOM'S *speech,* LAURA *blows out the candles, ending the play.*]

TOM: I didn't go to the moon, I went much further—for time is the longest distance between two places. Not long after that I was fired for writing a poem on the lid of a shoe-box. I left Saint Louis. I descended the steps of this fire escape for a last time and followed, from then on, in my father's footsteps, attempting to find in motion what was lost in space. I traveled around a great deal. The cities swept about me like dead leaves, leaves that were brightly colored but torn away from the branches. I would have stopped, but I was pursued by something. It always came upon me unawares, taking me altogether by surprise. Perhaps it was a familiar bit of music. Perhaps it was only a piece of transparent glass. Perhaps I am walking along a street at night, in some strange city, before I have found companions. I pass the lighted window of a shop where perfume is sold. The window is filled with pieces of colored glass, tiny transparent bottles in delicate colors, like bits of a shattered rainbow. Then all at once my sister touches my shoulder. I turn around and look into her eyes. Oh, Laura, Laura, I tried to leave you behind me, but I am more faithful than I intended to be! I reach for a cigarette, I cross the street. I run into the movies or a bar, I buy a drink, I speak to the nearest stranger—anything that can blow your candles out!

[LAURA *bends over the candles.*]

For nowadays the world is lit by lightning! Blow out your candles, Laura—and so goodbye. . . .

[*She blows the candles out.*]

The Zoo Story

A Play in One Scene

Edward Albee (1928–   )

Abandoned at an early age by his natural parents, Edward Albee was adopted by Reed A. Albee, the wealthy owner of the Keith-Albee chain of vaudeville theaters. He attended the Lawrenceville School, Valley Forge Military Academy, and the Choate School, graduating from the latter in 1946. He then attended Trinity College, Hartford, for two years. After leaving college he worked at a number of jobs for ten years, among them office boy for an advertising firm, record salesman at Bloomingdale's, counterman at a luncheonette, and Western Union messenger. He had begun to write fiction while at Choate, and in 1953 Thornton Wilder encouraged him to try his hand at drama. His first play, *The Zoo Story* (1959), was followed by among others *The Sandbox* (1959), *The American Dream* (1961), *Who's Afraid of Virginia Woolf?* (1961), *Tiny Alice* (1964), *A Delicate Balance* (1966), which won the Pulitzer Prize, *All Over* (1971), and *Seascape* (1975).

THE PLAYERS

PETER: *A man in his early forties, neither fat nor gaunt, neither handsome nor homely. He wears tweeds, smokes a pipe, carries horn-rimmed glasses. Although he is moving into middle age, his dress and his manner would suggest a man younger.*

JERRY: *A man in his late thirties, not poorly dressed, but carelessly. What was once a trim and lightly muscled body has begun to go to fat; and while he is no longer handsome, it is evident that he once was. His fall from physical grace should not suggest debauchery; he has, to come closest to it, a great weariness.*

THE SCENE

It is Central Park; a Sunday afternoon in summer; the present. There are two park benches, one toward either side of the stage; they both face the audience. Behind them: foliage, trees, sky. At the beginning, Peter is seated on one of the benches.

As the curtain rises, PETER *is seated on the bench stage-right. He is reading a book. He stops reading, cleans his glasses, goes back to reading.* JERRY *enters.*

JERRY: I've been to the zoo. [PETER *doesn't notice*] I said, I've been to the zoo. MISTER, I'VE BEEN TO THE ZOO!

PETER: Hm? . . . What? . . . I'm sorry, were you talking to me?

JERRY: I went to the zoo, and then I walked until I came here. Have I been walking north?

PETER [*puzzled*]: North? Why . . . I . . . I think so. Let me see.

JERRY: [*pointing past the audience*]: Is that Fifth Avenue?

PETER: Why yes; yes, it is.

JERRY: And what is that cross street there; that one, to the right?

PETER: That? Oh, that's Seventy-fourth Street.

JERRY: And the zoo is around Sixty-fifth Street; so, I've been walking north.

PETER [*anxious to get back to his reading*]: Yes; it would seem so.

JERRY: Good old north.

PETER [*lightly, by reflex*]: Ha, ha.

JERRY [*after a slight pause*]: But not due north.

PETER: I . . . well, no, not due north; but, we . . . call it north. It's northerly.

JERRY [*watches as* PETER, *anxious to dismiss him, prepares his pipe*]: Well, boy; *you're* not going to get lung cancer, are you?

PETER [*looks up, a little annoyed, then smiles*]: No, sir. Not from this.

JERRY: No, sir. What you'll probably get is cancer of the mouth, and then you'll have to wear one of those things Freud wore after they took one whole side of his jaw away. What do they call those things?

PETER [*uncomfortable*]: A prosthesis?

JERRY: The very thing! A prosthesis. You're an educated man, aren't you? Are you a doctor?

PETER: Oh, no; no. I read about it somewhere; *Time* magazine, I think. [*He turns to his book.*]

JERRY: Well, *Time* magazine isn't for blockheads.

PETER: No, I suppose not.

JERRY [*after a pause*]: Boy, I'm glad that's Fifth Avenue there.

PETER [*vaguely*]: Yes.

JERRY: I don't like the west side of the park much.

PETER: Oh? [*Then, slightly wary, but interested*] Why?

JERRY [*offhand*]: I don't know.

PETER: Oh. [*He returns to his book.*]

JERRY [*he stands for a few seconds, looking at* PETER, *who finally looks up again, puzzled*]: Do you mind if we talk?

PETER [*obviously minding*]: Why . . . no, no.

JERRY: Yes you do; you do.

PETER [*puts his book down, his pipe out and away, smiling*]: No, really; I don't mind.

JERRY: Yes you do.

PETER [*finally decided*]: No; I don't mind at all, really.

JERRY: It's . . . it's a nice day.

PETER [*stares unnecessarily at the sky*]: Yes. Yes, it is; lovely.

JERRY: I've been to the zoo.

PETER: Yes, I think you said so . . . didn't you?

JERRY: You'll read about it in the papers tomorrow, if you don't see it on your TV tonight. You have TV, haven't you?

PETER: Why yes, we have two; one for the children.

JERRY: You're married!

PETER [*with pleased emphasis*]: Why, certainly.

JERRY: It isn't a law, for God's sake.

PETER: No . . . no, of course not.

JERRY: And you have a wife.

PETER [*bewildered by the seeming lack of communication*]: Yes!

JERRY: And you have children.

PETER: Yes; two.

JERRY: Boys?

PETER: No, girls . . . both girls.

JERRY: But you wanted boys.

PETER: Well . . . naturally, every man wants a son, but . . .

JERRY [*lightly mocking*]: But that's the way the cookie crumbles?

PETER [*annoyed*]: I wasn't going to say that.

JERRY: And you're not going to have any more kids, are you?

PETER [*a bit distantly*]: No. No more. [*Then back, and irksome*] Why did you say that? How would you know about that?

JERRY: The way you cross your legs, perhaps; something in the voice. Or maybe I'm just guessing. Is it your wife?

PETER [*furious*]: That's none of your business! [*a silence*] Do you understand? [JERRY *nods.* PETER *is quiet now*] Well, you're right. We'll have no more children.

JERRY [*softly*]: That *is* the way the cookie crumbles.

PETER [*forgiving*]: Yes . . . I guess so.

JERRY: Well, now; what else?

PETER: What were you saying about the zoo . . . that I'd read about it, or see . . . ?

JERRY: I'll tell you about it, soon. Do you mind if I ask you questions?

PETER: Oh, not really.

JERRY: I'll tell you why I do it; I don't talk to many people—except to say like: give me a beer, or where's the john, or what time does the feature go on, or keep your hands to yourself, buddy. You know—things like that.

PETER: I must say I don't . . .

JERRY: But every once in a while I like to talk to

somebody, really *talk;* like to get to know somebody, know all about him.

PETER [*lightly laughing, still a little uncomfortable*]: And am I the guinea pig for today?

JERRY: On a sun-drenched Sunday afternoon like this? Who better than a nice married man with two daughters and . . . uh . . . a dog? [PETER *shakes his head*] No? Two dogs. [PETER *shakes his head again*] Hm. No dogs? [PETER *shakes his head, sadly*] Oh, that's a shame. But you look like an animal man. CATS? [PETER *nods his head, ruefully*] Cats! But, that can't be your idea. No, sir. Your wife and daughters? [PETER *nods his head*] Is there anything else I should know?

PETER [*he has to clear his throat*]: There are . . . there are two parakeets. One . . . uh . . . one for each of my daughters.

JERRY: Birds.

PETER: My daughters keep them in a cage in their bedroom.

JERRY: Do they carry disease? The birds.

PETER: I don't believe so.

JERRY: That's too bad. If they did you could set them loose in the house and the cats could eat them and die, maybe. [PETER *looks blank for a moment, then laughs*] And what else? What do you do to support your enormous household?

PETER: I . . . uh . . . I have an executive position with a . . . a small publishing house. We . . . uh . . . we publish textbooks.

JERRY: That sounds nice; very nice. What do you make?

PETER [*still cheerful*]: Now look here!

JERRY: Oh, come on.

PETER: Well, I make around eighteen thousand a year, but I don't carry more than forty dollars at any one time . . . in case you're a . . . a holdup man . . . ha, ha, ha.

JERRY [*ignoring the above*]: Where do you live? [PETER *is reluctant*] Oh, look; I'm not going to rob you, and I'm not going to kidnap your parakeets, your cats, or your daughters.

PETER [*too loud*]: I live between Lexington and Third Avenue, on Seventy-fourth Street.

JERRY: That wasn't so hard, was it?

PETER: I didn't mean to seem . . . ah . . . it's that you don't really carry on a conversation; you just ask questions. And I'm . . . I'm normally . . . uh . . . reticent. Why do you just stand there?

JERRY: I'll start walking around in a little while, and eventually I'll sit down. [*Recalling*] Wait until you see the expression on his face.

PETER: What? Whose face? Look here; is this something about the zoo?

JERRY [*distantly*]: The what?

PETER: The zoo; the zoo. Something about the zoo.

JERRY: The zoo?

PETER: You've mentioned it several times.

JERRY [*still distant, but returning abruptly*]: The zoo? Oh, yes; the zoo. I was there before I came here. I told you that. Say, what's the dividing line between upper-middle-middle-class and lower-upper-middle-class?

PETER: My dear fellow, I . . .

JERRY: Don't my dear fellow me.

PETER [*unhappily*]: Was I patronizing? I believe I was; I'm sorry. But, you see your question about the classes bewildered me.

JERRY: And when you're bewildered you become patronizing?

PETER: I . . . I don't express myself too well, sometimes. [*He attempts a joke on himself*] I'm in publishing, not writing.

JERRY [*amused, but not at the humor*]: So be it. The truth *is: I* was being patronizing.

PETER: Oh, now; you needn't say that.

[*It is at this point that* JERRY *may begin to move about the stage with slowly increasing determination and authority, but pacing himself, so that the long speech about the dog comes at the high point of the arc*]

JERRY: All right. Who are your favorite writers? Baudelaire and J. P. Marquand?

PETER [*wary*]: Well, I like a great many writers; I have a considerable . . . catholicity of taste, if I may say so. Those two men are fine, each in his way. [*warming up*] Baudelaire, of course . . . uh . . . is by far the finer of the two, but Marquand has a place . . . in our . . . uh . . . national . . .

JERRY: Skip it.

PETER: I . . . sorry.

JERRY: Do you know what I did before I went to the zoo today? I walked all the way up Fifth Avenue from Washington Square; all the way.

PETER: Oh; you live in the Village! [*This seems to enlighten* PETER]

JERRY: No, I don't. I took the subway down to the Village so I could walk all the way up Fifth Avenue to the zoo. It's one of those things a person has to do; sometimes a person has to go a very long distance out of his way to come back a short distance correctly.

PETER [*almost pouting*]: Oh, I thought you lived in the Village.

JERRY: What were you trying to do? Make sense out of things? Bring order? The old pigeonhole bit? Well, that's easy; I'll tell you. I live in a four-story brownstone roominghouse on the upper West Side between Columbus Avenue and Central Park West. I live on the top floor; rear; west. It's a laughably small room, and one of my walls is made of beaverboard; this beaverboard separates my room from another laughably small room, so I assume that the two rooms were once one room, a small room, but not necessarily laughable. The room beyond my beaverboard wall is occupied by a colored queen who always keeps his door open; well, not always but *always* when he's plucking his eyebrows, which he does with Buddhist concentration. This colored queen has rotten teeth, which is rare, and he has a Japanese kimono, which is also pretty rare; and he wears this kimono to and from the john in the hall, which is pretty frequent. I mean, he goes to the john a lot. He never bothers me, and he never brings anyone up to his room. All he does is pluck his eyebrows, wear his kimono and go to the john. Now, the two front rooms on my floor are a little larger, I guess; but they're pretty small, too. There's a Puerto Rican family in one of them, a husband, a wife, and some kids; I don't know how many. These people entertain a lot. And in the other front room, there's somebody living there, but I don't know who it is. I've never seen who it is. Never. Never ever.

PETER [*embarrassed*]: Why . . . why do you live there?

JERRY [*from a distance again*]: I don't know.

PETER: It doesn't sound like a very nice place . . . where you live.

JERRY: Well, no; it isn't an apartment in the East Seventies. But, then again, I don't have one wife, two daughters, two cats and two parakeets. What I do have, I have toilet articles, a few clothes, a hot plate that I'm not supposed to have, a can opener, one that works with a key, you know; a knife, two forks, and two spoons, one small, one large; three plates, a cup, a saucer, a drinking glass, two picture frames, both empty, eight or nine books, a pack of pornographic playing cards, regular deck, an old Western Union typewriter that prints nothing but capital letters, and a small strongbox without a lock which has in it . . . what? Rocks! Some rocks . . . sea-rounded rocks I picked up on the beach when I was a kid. Under which . . . weighed down . . . are some letters . . . please letters . . . please why don't you do this, and please when will you do that letters. And when letters, too. When will you write? When will you come? When? These letters are from more recent years.

PETER [*stares glumly at his shoes, then*]: About those two empty picture frames . . . ?

JERRY: I don't see why they need any explanation at all. Isn't it clear? I don't have pictures of anyone to put in them.

PETER: Your parents . . . perhaps . . . a girl friend . . .

JERRY: You're a very sweet man, and you're possessed of a truly enviable innocence. But good old Mom and good old Pop are dead . . . you know? . . . I'm broken up about it, too . . . I mean really. BUT. That particular vaudeville act is playing the cloud circuit now, so I don't see how I can look at them, all neat and framed. Besides, or, rather, to be pointed about it, good old Mom walked out on good old Pop when I was ten and a half years old; she embarked on an adulterous turn of our southern states . . . a journey of a year's duration . . . and her most constant companion . . . among others, among many others . . . was a Mr. Barleycorn. At least, that's what good old Pop told me after he went down . . . came back . . . brought her body north. We'd received the news between Christmas and New Year's, you see, that good old Mom had parted with the ghost in some dump in Alabama. And, without the ghost . . . she was less welcome. I mean, what was she? A stiff . . . a northern stiff. At any rate, good old Pop celebrated the New Year for an even two weeks and then slapped into the front of a somewhat moving city omnibus, which sort of cleaned things out family-wise. Well no; then there was Mom's sister, who was given neither to sin nor the consolations of the bottle. I moved in on her, and my memory of her is slight excepting I remember still that she did all things dourly: sleeping, eating, working, praying. She dropped dead on the stairs to her apartment, my apartment then, too, on the afternoon of my high school graduation. A terribly middle-European joke, if you ask me.

PETER: Oh, my; oh, my.

JERRY: Oh, your what? But that was a long time ago, and I have no feeling about any of it that I care to admit to myself. Perhaps you can see, though, why good old Mom and good old Pop are frameless. What's your name? Your first name?

PETER: I'm Peter.

JERRY: I'd forgotten to ask you. I'm Jerry.

PETER [*with a slight, nervous laugh*]: Hello, Jerry.

JERRY [*nods his hello*]: And let's see now; what's the point of having a girl's picture, especially in two frames? I have two picture frames, you remember. I never see the pretty little ladies more than once, and most of them wouldn't be caught in the same room with a camera. It's odd, and I wonder if it's sad.

PETER: The girls?

JERRY: No. I wonder if it's sad that I never see the little ladies more than once. I've never been able to have sex with, or, how is it put? . . . make love to anybody more than once. Once; that's it. . . . Oh, wait; for a week and a half, when I was fifteen . . . and I hang my head in shame that puberty was late . . . I was a h-o-m-o-s-e-x-u-a-l. I mean, I was queer . . . [*Very fast*] . . . queer, queer, queer . . . with bells ringing, banners snapping in the wind. And for those eleven days, I met at least twice a day with the park superintendent's son . . . a Greek boy, whose birthday was the same as mine, except he was a year older. I think I was very much in love . . . maybe just with sex. But that was the jazz of a very special hotel, wasn't it? And now; oh, do I love the little ladies; really, I love them. For about an hour.

PETER: Well, it seems perfectly simple to me. . . .

JERRY [*angry*]: Look! Are you going to tell me to get married and have parakeets?

PETER [*angry himself*]: Forget the parakeets! And stay single if you want to. It's no business of mine. I didn't start this conversation in the . . .

JERRY: All right, all right. I'm sorry. All right? You're not angry?

PETER [*laughing*]: No, I'm not angry.

JERRY [*relieved*]: Good. [*Now back to his previous tone*] Interesting that you asked me about the picture frames. I would have thought that you would have asked me about the pornographic playing cards.

PETER [*with a knowing smile*]: Oh, I've seen those cards.

JERRY: That's not the point. [*Laughs*] I suppose when you were a kid you and your pals passed them around, or you had a pack of your own.

PETER: Well, I guess a lot of us did.

JERRY: And you threw them away just before you got married.

PETER: Oh, now; look here. I didn't *need* anything like that when I got older.

JERRY: No?

PETER [*embarrassed*]: I'd rather not talk about these things.

JERRY: So? Don't. Besides, I wasn't trying to plumb your post-adolescent sexual life and hard times; what I wanted to get at is the value difference between pornographic playing cards when you're a kid, and pornographic playing cards when you're older. It's that when you're a kid you use the cards as a substitute for a real experience, and when you're older you use real experience as a substitute for the fantasy. But I imagine you'd rather hear about what happened at the zoo.

PETER [*enthusiastic*]: Oh, yes; the zoo. [*Then, awkward*] That is . . . if you. . . .

JERRY: Let me tell you about why I went . . . well, let me tell you some things. I've told you about the fourth floor of the roominghouse where I live. I think the rooms are better as you go down, floor by floor. I guess they are; I don't know. I don't know any of the people on the third and second floors. Oh, wait! I do know that there's a lady living on the third floor, in the front. I know because she cries all the time. Whenever I go out or come back in, whenever I pass her door, I always hear her crying, muffled, but . . . very determined. Very determined indeed. But the one I'm getting to, and all about the dog, is the landlady. I don't like to use words that are too harsh in describing people. I don't like to. But the landlady is a fat, ugly, mean, stupid, unwashed, misanthropic, cheap, drunken bag of garbage. And you may have noticed that I very seldom use profanity, so I can't describe her as well as I might.

PETER: You describe her . . . vividly.

JERRY: Well, thanks. Anyway, she has a dog, and I will tell you about the dog, and she and her dog are the gatekeepers of my dwelling. The woman is bad enough; she leans around in the entrance hall, spying to see that I don't bring in things or people, and when she's had her midafternoon pint of lemon-flavored gin she always stops me in the hall, and grabs ahold of my coat or my arm, and she presses her disgusting body up against me to keep me in a corner so she can talk to me. The smell of her body and her breath . . . you can't imagine it . . . and somewhere, somewhere in the back of that pea-sized brain of hers, an organ developed just enough to let her eat, drink, and emit, she has some foul parody of sexual desire. And I, Peter, I am the object of her sweaty lust.

PETER: That's disgusting. That's . . . horrible.

JERRY: But I have found a way to keep her off. When she talks to me, when she presses herself to my body and mumbles about her room and how I should come there, I merely say: but, Love; wasn't yesterday enough for you, and the day before? Then she puzzles, she makes slits of her tiny eyes, she sways a little, and then, Peter . . . and it is at this moment that I think I might be doing some good in that tormented house . . . a simple-minded smile begins to form on her unthinkable face, and she giggles and groans as she thinks about yesterday and the day before; as she believes and relives what never happened. Then, she motions to that black monster of a dog she has, and she goes back to her room. And I am safe until our next meeting.

PETER: It's so . . . unthinkable. I find it hard to believe that people such as that really *are*.

JERRY [*lightly mocking*]: It's for reading about, isn't it?

PETER [*seriously*]: Yes.

JERRY: And fact is better left to fiction. You're right, Peter. Well, what I have been meaning to tell you about is the dog; I shall, now.

PETER [*nervously*]: Oh, yes; the dog.

JERRY: Don't go. You're not thinking of going, are you?

PETER: Well . . . no, I don't think so.

JERRY [*as if to a child*]: Because after I tell you about the dog, do you know what then? Then . . . then I'll tell you about what happened at the zoo.

PETER [*laughing faintly*]: You're . . . you're full of stories, aren't you?

JERRY: You don't *have* to listen. Nobody is holding you here; remember that. Keep that in your mind.

PETER [*irritably*]: I know that.

JERRY: You do? Good.

[*The following long speech, it seems to me, should be done with a great deal of action, to achieve a hypnotic effect on* PETER, *and on the audience, too. Some specific actions have been suggested, but the director and the actor playing* JERRY *might best work it out for themselves*]

ALL RIGHT. [*As if reading from a huge billboard*] THE STORY OF JERRY AND THE DOG! [*Natural again*] What I am going to tell you has something to do with how sometimes it's necessary to go a long distance out of the way in order to come back a short distance correctly; or, maybe I only think that it has something to do with that. But, it's why I went to the zoo today, and why I walked north . . . northerly, rather . . . until I came here. All right. The dog, I think I told you, is a black monster of a beast: an oversized head, tiny, tiny ears, and eyes . . . bloodshot, infected, maybe; and a body you can see the ribs through the skin. The dog is black, all black; all black except for the bloodshot eyes, and . . . yes . . . and an open sore on its . . . *right* forepaw; that is red, too. And, oh yes; the poor monster, and I do believe it's an old dog . . . it's certainly a misused one . . . almost always has an erection . . . of sorts. That's red, too. And . . . what else? . . . oh, yes; there's a gray-yellow-white color, too, when he bares his fangs. Like this: Grrrrrr! Which is what he did when he saw me for the first time . . . the day I moved in. I worried about that animal the very first minute I met him. Now, animals don't take to me like Saint Francis had birds hanging off him all the time. What I mean is: animals are indifferent to me . . . like people [*He smiles slightly*] . . . most of the time. But this dog wasn't indifferent. From the very beginning he'd snarl and then go for me, to get one of my legs. Not like he was rabid, you know; he was sort of a stumbly dog, but he wasn't half-assed, either. It was a good, stumbly run; but I always got away. He got a piece of my trouser leg, look, you can see right here, where it's mended; he got that the second day I lived there; but, I kicked free and got upstairs fast, so that was that. [*Puzzles*] I still don't know to this day how the other roomers manage it, but you know what I *think:* I think it had to do only with me. Cozy. So. Anyway, this went on for over a week, whenever I came in; but never when I went out. That's funny. Or, it *was* funny. I could pack up and live in the street for all the dog cared. Well, I thought about it up in my room one day, one of the times after I'd bolted upstairs, and I made up my mind. I decided: First, I'll kill the dog with kindness, and if that doesn't work . . . I'll just kill him. [PETER *winces*] Don't react, Peter; just listen. So, the next day I went out and bought a bag of hamburgers, medium rare, no catsup, no onion; and on the way home I threw away all the rolls and kept just the meat.

[*Action for the following, perhaps*]

When I got back to the roominghouse the dog was waiting for me. I half opened the door that led into the entrance hall, and there he was; waiting for me. It figured. I went in, very cautiously, and I had the hamburgers, you remember; I opened the bag, and I set the meat down about twelve feet from where the dog was snarling at me. Like so! He snarled; stopped snarling; sniffed; moved slowly; then faster; then faster toward the meat. Well, when he got to it he stopped, and he looked at me. I smiled; but tentatively, you understand. He turned his face back to the hamburgers, smelled, sniffed some more, and then . . . RRRAAAAGGGGGHHHH, like that . . . he tore into them. It was as if he had never eaten anything in his life before, except like garbage. Which might very well have been the truth. I don't think the landlady ever eats anything but garbage. But. He ate all the hamburgers, almost all at once, making sounds in his throat like a woman. *Then,* when he'd finished the meat, the hamburger, and tried to eat the paper, too, he sat down and smiled. I think he smiled; I know cats do. It was a very gratifying few moments. Then, BAM, he snarled and made for me again. He didn't get me this time, either. So, I got upstairs, and I lay down on my bed and started to think about the dog again. To be truthful, I was offended, and I was damn mad, too. It was six perfectly good hamburgers with not enough pork in them to make it disgusting. I was offended. But, after a while, I decided to try it for a few more days. If you think about it, this dog had what amounted to an antipathy toward me; really. And, I wondered if I mightn't overcome this antipathy. So, I tried it for five more days, but it was always the same: snarl, sniff; move; faster; stare; gobble; RAAGGGHHH; smile; snarl; BAM. Well, now; by this time Columbus Avenue was strewn with hamburger rolls and I was less offended than disgusted. So, I decided to kill the dog.

[PETER *raises a hand in protest*]

Oh, don't be so alarmed, Peter; I didn't succeed. The

day I tried to kill the dog I bought only one hamburger and what I thought was a murderous portion of rat poison. When I bought the hamburger I asked the man not to bother with the roll, all I wanted was the meat. I expected some reaction from him, like: we don't sell no hamburgers without rolls; or, wha' d'ya wanna do, eat it out'a ya han's? But no; he smiled benignly, wrapped up the hamburger in waxed paper, and said: A bite for ya pussy-cat? I wanted to say: No, not really; it's part of a plan to poison a dog I know. But, you can't say "a dog I know" without sounding funny; so I said, a little too loud, I'm afraid, and too formally: YES, A BITE FOR MY PUSSY-CAT. People looked up. It always happens when I try to simplify things; people look up. But that's neither hither nor thither. So. On my way back to the roominghouse, I kneaded the hamburger and the rat poison together between my hands, at that point feeling as much sadness as disgust. I opened the door to the entrance hall, and there the monster was, waiting to take the offering and then jump me. Poor bastard; he never learned that the moment he took to smile before he went for me gave me time enough to get out of range. BUT, there he was; malevolence with an erection, waiting. I put the poison patty down, moved toward the stairs and watched. The poor animal gobbled the food down as usual, smiled, which made me almost sick, and then, BAM. But, I sprinted up the stairs, as usual, and the dog didn't get me, as usual. AND IT CAME TO PASS THAT THE BEAST WAS DEATHLY ILL. I knew this because he no longer attended me, and because the landlady sobered up. She stopped me in the hall the same evening of the attempted murder and confided the information that God had struck her puppy-dog a surely fatal blow. She had forgotten her bewildered lust, and her eyes were wide open for the first time. They looked like the dog's eyes. She sniveled and implored me to pray for the animal. I wanted to say to her: Madam, I have myself to pray for, the colored queen, the Puerto Rican family, the person in the front room whom I've never seen, the woman who cries deliberately behind her closed door, and the rest of the people in all roominghouses, everywhere; besides, Madam, I don't understand how to pray. But . . . to simplify things . . . I told her I would pray. She looked up. She said that I was a liar, and that I probably wanted the dog to die. I told her, and there was so much truth here, that I didn't want the dog to die. I didn't, and not just because I'd poisoned him. I'm afraid that I must tell you I wanted the dog to live so that I could see what our new relationship might come to.

[PETER *indicates his increasing displeasure and slowly growing antagonism*]

Please understand, Peter; that sort of thing is important. You must believe me; it *is* important. We have to know the effect of our actions. [*Another deep sigh*] Well, anyway; the dog recovered. I have no idea why, unless he was a descendant of the puppy that guarded the gates of hell or some such resort. I'm not up on my mythology. [*He pronounces the word myth-o-*logy] Are you?

[PETER *sets to thinking, but* JERRY *goes on*]

At any rate, and you've missed the eight-thousand-dollar question, Peter; at any rate, the dog recovered his health and the landlady recovered her thirst, in no way altered by the bow-wow's deliverance. When I came home from a movie that was playing on Forty-second Street, a movie I'd seen, or one that was very much like one or several I'd seen, after the landlady told me puppykins was better, I was so hoping for the dog to be waiting for me. I was . . . well, how would you put it . . . enticed? . . . fascinated? . . . no, I don't think so . . . heart-shatteringly anxious, that's it; I was heart-shatteringly anxious to confront my friend again.

[PETER *reacts scoffingly*]

Yes, Peter; friend. That's the only word for it. I was heart-shatteringly et cetera to confront my doggy friend again. I came in the door and advanced, unafraid, to the center of the entrance hall. The beast was there . . . looking at me. And, you know, he looked better for his scrape with the nevermind. I stopped; I looked at him; he looked at me. I think . . . I think we stayed a long time that way . . . still, stone-statue . . . just looking at one another. I looked more into his face than he looked into mine. I mean, I can concentrate longer at looking into a dog's face than a dog can concentrate at looking into mine, or into anybody else's face, for that matter. But during that twenty seconds or two hours that we looked into each other's face, we made contact. Now, here is what I had wanted to happen: I loved the dog now, and I wanted him to love me. I had tried to love, and I had tried to kill, and both had been unsuccessful by themselves. I hoped . . . and I don't really know why I expected the dog to understand anything, much less my motivations . . . I hoped that the dog would understand.

[PETER *seems to be hypnotized*]

It's just . . . it's just that . . . [JERRY *is abnormally tense, now*] . . . it's just that if you can't deal with people, you have to make a start somewhere. WITH ANIMALS! [*Much faster now, and like a conspirator*] Don't you see? A person has to have some way of dealing with SOMETHING. If not with people . . . if not with people . . . SOMETHING. With a bed, with a cockroach, with a mirror . . . no, that's too hard, that's one of the last steps. With a cockroach, with a

. . . with a . . . with a carpet, a roll of toilet paper . . . no, not that, either . . . that's a mirror, too; always check bleeding. You see how hard it is to find things? With a street corner, and too many lights, all colors reflecting on the oily-wet streets . . . with a wisp of smoke, a wisp . . . of smoke . . . with . . . with pornographic playing cards, with a strongbox . . . WITHOUT A LOCK . . . with love, with vomiting, with crying, with fury because the pretty little ladies aren't pretty little ladies, with making money with your body which is an act of love and I could prove it, with howling because you're alive; with God. How about that? WITH GOD WHO IS A COLORED QUEEN WHO WEARS A KIMONO AND PLUCKS HIS EYEBROWS, WHO IS A WOMAN WHO CRIES WITH DETERMINATION BEHIND HER CLOSED DOOR . . . with God who, I'm told, turned his back on the whole thing some time ago . . . with . . . some day, with people. [JERRY *sighs the next word heavily*] People. With an idea; a concept. And where better, where ever better in this humiliating excuse for a jail, where better to communicate one single, simple-minded idea than in an entrance hall? Where? It would be A START! Where better to make a beginning . . . to understand and just possibly be understood . . . a beginning of an understanding, than with . . .

[*Here* JERRY *seems to fall into almost grotesque fatigue*]

. . . than with A DOG. Just that; a dog.

[*Here there is a silence that might be prolonged for a moment or so; then* JERRY *wearily finishes his story*]

A dog. It seemed like a perfectly sensible idea. Man is a dog's best friend, remember. So: the dog and I looked at each other. I longer than the dog. And what I saw then has been the same ever since. Whenever the dog and I see each other we both stop where we are. We regard each other with a mixture of sadness and suspicion, and then we feign indifference. We walk past each other safely; we have an understanding. It's very sad, but you'll have to admit that it is an understanding. We had made many attempts at contact, and we had failed. The dog has returned to garbage, and I to solitary but free passage. I have not returned. I mean to say, I have *gained* solitary free passage, if that much further loss can be said to be gain. I have learned that neither kindness nor cruelty by themselves, independent of each other, creates any effect beyond themselves; and I have learned that the two combined, together, at the same time, are the teaching emotion. And what is gained is loss. And what has been the result: the dog and I have attained a compromise; more of a bargain, really. We neither love nor hurt because we do not try to reach each other. And, *was* trying to feed the dog an act of love? And, perhaps, was the dog's attempt to bite me *not* an act of love? If we can so misunderstand, well then, why have we invented the word love in the first place?

[*There is silence.* JERRY *moves to* PETER'S *bench and sits down beside him. This is the first time* JERRY *has sat down during the play*]

The Story of Jerry and the Dog: the end.

[PETER *is silent*]

Well, Peter? [JERRY *is suddenly cheerful*] Well, Peter? Do you think I could sell that story to the *Reader's Digest* and make a couple of hundred bucks for *The Most Unforgettable Character I've Ever Met?* Huh?

[JERRY *is animated, but* PETER *is disturbed*]

Oh, come on now, Peter; tell me what you think.

PETER [*numb*]: I . . . I don't understand what . . . I don't think I . . . [*Now, almost tearfully*] Why did you tell me all of this?

JERRY: Why not?

PETER: I DON'T UNDERSTAND!

JERRY [*furious, but whispering*]: That's a lie.

PETER: No. No, it's not.

JERRY [*quietly*]: I tried to explain it to you as I went along. I went slowly; it all has to do with . . .

PETER: I DON'T WANT TO HEAR ANY MORE. I don't understand you, or your landlady, or her dog. . . .

JERRY: *Her* dog! I thought it was my . . . No. No, you're right. It *is* her dog. [*Looks at* PETER *intently, shaking his head*] I don't know what I was thinking about; of course you don't understand. [*In a monotone, wearily*] I don't live in your block; I'm not married to two parakeets, or whatever your setup is. I am a *permanent transient,* and my home is the sickening roominghouses on the West Side of New York City, which is the greatest city in the world. Amen.

PETER: I'm . . . I'm sorry; I didn't mean to . . .

JERRY: Forget it. I suppose you don't quite know what to make of me, eh?

PETER [*a joke*]: We get all kinds in publishing. [*Chuckles*]

JERRY: You're a funny man. [*He forces a laugh*] You know that? You're a very . . . a richly comic person.

PETER [*modestly, but amused*]: Oh, now, not really. [*Still chuckling*]

JERRY: Peter, do I annoy you, or confuse you?

PETER [*lightly*]: Well, I must confess that this wasn't the kind of afternoon I'd anticipated.

JERRY: You mean, I'm not the gentleman you were expecting.

PETER: I wasn't expecting anybody.

JERRY: No, I don't imagine you were. But I'm here, and I'm not leaving.

PETER [*consulting his watch*]: Well, you may not be, but I must be getting home soon.

JERRY: Oh, come on; stay a while longer.

PETER: I really should get home; you see . . .

JERRY [*tickles* PETER'S *ribs with his fingers*]: Oh, come on.

PETTER [*he is very ticklish; as* JERRY *continues to tickle him his voice becomes falsetto*]: No, I . . . OHHHHH! Don't do that. Stop, Stop. Ohhh, no, no.

JERRY: Oh, come on.

PETER [*as* JERRY *tickles*]: Oh, hee, hee, hee. I must go. I . . . hee, hee, hee. After all, stop, stop, hee, hee, hee, after all, the parakeets will be getting dinner ready soon. Hee, hee. And the cats are setting the table. Stop, stop, and, and . . . [PETER *is beside himself now*] . . . and we're having . . . hee, hee . . . uh . . . ho, ho, ho.

[JERRY *stops tickling* PETER, *but the combination of the tickling and his own mad whimsy has* PETER *laughing almost hysterically. As his laughter continues, then subsides,* JERRY *watches him, with a curious fixed smile*]

JERRY: Peter?

PETER: Oh, ha, ha, ha, ha, ha. What? What?

JERRY: Listen, now.

PETER: Oh, ho, ho. What . . . what is it, Jerry? Oh, my.

JERRY [*mysteriously*]: Peter, do you want to know what happened at the zoo?

PETER: Ah, ha, ha. The what? Oh, yes; the zoo. Oh, ho, ho. Well, I had my own zoo there for a moment with . . . hee, hee, the parakeets getting dinner ready, and the . . . ha, ha, whatever it was, the . . .

JERRY [*calmly*]: Yes, that was very funny, Peter. I wouldn't have expected it. But do you want to hear about what happened at the zoo, or not?

PETER: Yes. Yes, by all means; tell me what happened at the zoo. Oh, my. I don't know what happened to me.

JERRY: Now I'll let you in on what happened at the zoo; but first, I should tell you why I went to the zoo. I went to the zoo to find out more about the way people exist with animals, and the way animals exist with each other, and with people too. It probably wasn't a fair test, what with everyone separated by bars from everyone else, the animals for the most part from each other, and always the people from the animals. But, if it's a zoo, that's the way it is. [*He pokes* PETER *on the arm*] Move over.

PETER [*friendly*]: I'm sorry, haven't you enough room? [*He shifts a little*]

JERRY [*smiling slightly*]: Well, all the animals are there, and all the people are there, and it's Sunday and all the children are there. [*He pokes* PETER *again*] Move over.

PETER [*patiently, still friendly*]: All right.

[*He moves some more, and* JERRY *has all the room he might need*]

JERRY: And it's a hot day, so all the stench is there, too, and all the balloon sellers, and all the ice cream sellers, and all the seals are barking, and all the birds are screaming. [*Pokes* PETER *harder*] Move over!

PETER [*beginning to be annoyed*]: Look here, you have more than enough room! [*But he moves more, and is now fairly cramped at one end of the bench.*]

JERRY: And I am there, and it's feeding time at the lions' house, and the lion keeper comes into the lion cage, one of the lion cages, to feed one of the lions. [*Punches* PETER *on the arm, hard*] MOVE OVER!

PETER [*very annoyed*]: I can't move over any more, and stop hitting me. What's the matter with you?

JERRY: Do you want to hear the story? [*Punches* PETER'S *arm again*]

PETER [*flabbergasted*]: I'm not so sure! I certainly don't want to be punched in the arm.

JERRY [*punches* PETER'S *arm again*]: Like that?

PETER: Stop it! What's the matter with you?

JERRY: I'm crazy, you bastard.

PETER: That isn't funny.

JERRY: Listen to me, Peter. I want this bench. You go sit on the bench over there, and if you're good I'll tell you the rest of the story.

PETER [*flustered*]: But . . . whatever for? What *is* the matter with you? Besides, I see no reason why I should give up this bench. I sit on this bench almost every Sunday afternoon, in good weather. It's secluded here; there's never anyone sitting here, so I have it all to myself.

JERRY [*softly*]: Get off this bench, Peter; I want it.

PETER [*almost whining*]: No.

JERRY: I said I want this bench, and I'm going to have it. Now get over there.

PETER: People can't have everything they want. You should know that; it's a rule; people can have some of the things they want, but they can't have everything.

JERRY [*laughs*]: Imbecile! You're slow-witted!

PETER: Stop that!

JERRY: You're a vegetable! Go lie down on the ground.

PETER [*intense*]: Now *you* listen to me. I've put up with you all afternoon.

JERRY: Not really.

PETER: LONG ENOUGH. I've put up with you long enough. I've listened to you because you seemed . . . well, because I thought you wanted to talk to somebody.

JERRY: You put things well; economically, and, yet . . . oh, what is the word I want to put justice to your . . . JESUS, you make me sick . . . get off here and give me my bench.

PETER: MY BENCH!

JERRY [*punches* PETER *almost, but not quite, off the bench*]: Get out of my sight.

PETER [*regaining his position*]: God da . . . mn you. That's enough! I've had enough of you. I will not give up this bench; you can't have it, and that's that. Now, go away.

[JERRY *snorts but he does not move*]

Go away, I said.

[JERRY *does not move*]

Get away from here. If you don't move on . . . you're a bum . . . that's what you are. . . . If you don't move on, I'll get a policeman here and make you go.

[JERRY *laughs, stays*]

I warn you, I'll call a policeman.

JERRY [*softly*]: You won't find a policeman around here; they're all over on the west side of the park chasing fairies down from trees or out of the bushes. That's all they do. That's their function. So scream your head off; it won't do you any good.

PETER: POLICE! I warn you, I'll have you arrested. POLICE! [*Pause*] I said POLICE! [*Pause*] I feel ridiculous.

JERRY: You look ridiculous: a grown man screaming for the police on a bright Sunday afternoon in the park with nobody harming you. If a policeman *did* fill his quota and come sludging over this way he'd probably take you in as a nut.

PETER [*with disgust and impotence*]: Great God, I just came here to read, and now you want me to give up the bench. You're mad.

JERRY: Hey, I got news for you, as they say. I'm on your precious bench, and you're never going to have it for yourself again.

PETER [*furious*]: Look, you; get off my bench. I don't care if it makes any sense or not. I want this bench to myself; I want you OFF IT!

JERRY [*mocking*]: Aw . . . look who's mad.

PETER: GET OUT!

JERRY: No.

PETER: I WARN YOU!

JERRY: Do you know how ridiculous you look *now?*

PETER [*his fury and self-consciousness have possessed him*]: It doesn't matter. [*He is almost crying*] GET AWAY FROM MY BENCH!

JERRY: Why? You have everything in the world you want; you've told me about your home, and your family, and *your own* little zoo. You have everything, and now you want this bench. Are these the things men fight for? Tell me, Peter, is this bench, this iron and this wood, is this your honor? Is this the thing in the world you'd fight for? Can you think of anything more absurd?

PETER: Absurd? Look, I'm not going to talk to you about honor, or even try to explain it to you. Besides, it isn't a question of honor; but even if it were, you wouldn't understand.

JERRY [*contemptuously*]: You don't even know what you're saying, do you? This is probably the first time in your life you've had anything more trying to face than changing your cats' toilet box. Stupid! Don't you have any idea, not even the slightest, what other people *need?*

PETER: Oh, boy, listen to you; well, you don't need this bench. That's for sure.

JERRY: Yes; yes, I do.

PETER [*quivering*]: I've come here for years; I have hours of great pleasure, great satisfaction, right here. And that's important to a man. I'm a responsible person, and I'm a GROWNUP. This is my bench, and you have no right to take it away from me.

JERRY: Fight for it, then. Defend yourself; defend your bench.

PETER: You've *pushed* me to it. Get up and fight.

JERRY: Like a man?

PETER [*still angry*]: Yes, like a man, if you insist on mocking me even further.

JERRY: I'll have to give you credit for one thing: you *are* a vegetable, and a slightly nearsighted one, I think . . .

PETER: THAT'S ENOUGH. . . .

JERRY: . . . but, you know, as they say on TV all the time—you know—and I mean this, Peter, you have a certain dignity; it surprises me. . . .

PETER: STOP!

JERRY [*rises lazily*]: Very well, Peter, we'll battle for the bench, but we're not evenly matched.

[*He takes out and clicks open an ugly-looking knife*]

PETER [*suddenly awakening to the reality of the situation*]: You *are* mad! You're stark raving mad! YOU'RE GOING TO KILL ME!

[*But before* PETER *has time to think what to do,* JERRY *tosses the knife at* PETER'S *feet*]

JERRY: There you go. Pick it up. You have the knife and we'll be more evenly matched.

PETER [*horrified*]: No!

JERRY [*rushes over to* PETER, *grabs him by the collar;* PETER *rises; their faces almost touch*]: Now you pick up that knife and you fight with me. You fight for your self-respect; you fight for that goddamned bench.

PETER [*struggling*]: No! Let . . . let go of me! He . . . Help!

JERRY [*slaps* PETER *on each "fight"*]: You fight, you miserable bastard; fight for that bench; fight for your parakeets; fight for your cats, fight for your two daughters; fight for your wife; fight for your manhood, you pathetic little vegetable. [*Spits in* PETER'S *face*] You couldn't even get your wife with a male child.

PETER [*breaks away, enraged*]: It's a matter of genetics, not manhood, you . . . you monster.

[*He darts down, picks up the knife and backs off a little; he is breathing heavily*]

I'll give you one last chance; get out of here and leave me alone!

[*He holds the knife with a firm arm, but far in front of him, not to attack, but to defend*]

JERRY [*sighs heavily*]: So be it!

[*With a rush he charges* PETER *and impales himself on the knife. Tableau: For just a moment, complete silence,* JERRY *impaled on the knife at the end of* PETER'S *still firm arm. Then* PETER *screams, pulls away, leaving the knife in* JERRY. JERRY *is motionless, on point. Then he, too, screams, and it must be the sound of an infuriated and fatally wounded animal. With the knife in him, he stumbles back to the bench that* PETER *had vacated. He crumbles there, sitting, facing* PETER, *his eyes wide in agony, his mouth open*]

PETER [*whispering*]: Oh my God, oh my God, oh my God. . . . [*He repeats these words many times, very rapidly*]

JERRY [JERRY *is dying; but now his expression seems to change. His features relax, and while his voice varies, sometimes wrenched with pain, for the most part he seems removed from his dying. He smiles*]: Thank you, Peter. I mean that, now; thank you very much.

[PETER'S *mouth drops open. He cannot move; he is transfixed*]

Oh, Peter, I was so afraid I'd drive you away. [*He laughs as best he can*] You don't know how afraid I was you'd go away and leave me. And now I'll tell you what happened at the zoo. I think . . . . I think this is what happened at the zoo . . . I think. I think that while I was at the zoo I decided that I would walk north . . . northerly, rather . . . until I found you . . . or somebody . . . and I decided that I would talk to you . . . I would tell you things . . . and things that I would tell you would . . . Well, here we are. You see? Here we *are*. But . . . I don't know . . . could I have planned all this? No . . . no, I couldn't have. But I think I did. And now I've told you what you wanted to know, haven't I? And now you know all about what happened at the zoo. And now you know what you'll see in your TV, and the face I told you about . . . you remember . . . the face I told you about . . . my face, the face you see right now. Peter . . . Peter? . . . Peter . . . thank you. I came unto you [*He laughs, so faintly*] and you have comforted me. Dear Peter.

PETER [*almost fainting*]: Oh my God!

JERRY: You'd better go now. Somebody might come by, and you don't want to be here when anyone comes.

PETER [*does not move, but begins to weep*]: Oh my God, oh my God.

JERRY [*most faintly, now; he is very near death*]: You won't be coming back here any more, Peter; you've been dispossessed. You've lost your bench, but you've defended your honor. And Peter, I'll tell you something now; you're not really a vegetable; it's all right, you're an animal. You're an animal, too. But you'd better hurry now, Peter. Hurry, you'd better go . . . see?

[JERRY *takes a handkerchief and with great effort and pain wipes the knife handle clean of fingerprints*]

Hurry away, Peter.

[PETER *begins to stagger away*]

Wait . . . wait, Peter. Take your book . . . book. Right here . . . beside me . . . on your bench . . . my bench, rather. Come . . . take your book.

[PETER *starts for the book, but retreats*]

Hurry . . . Peter.

[PETER *rushes to the bench, grabs the book, retreats*]

Very good, Peter . . . very good. Now . . . hurry away.

[PETER *hesitates for a moment, then flees, stage-left*]

Hurry away. . . . [*His eyes are closed now*] Hurry away, your parakeets are making the dinner . . . the cats . . . are setting the table . . .

PETER [*off stage; A pitiful howl*]: OH MY GOD!

JERRY [*his eyes still closed, he shakes his head and speaks; a combination of scornful mimicry and supplication*]: Oh . . . my . . . God.

[*He is dead*]

Curtain

A Slight Ache

Harold Pinter (1930–)

The son of a Jewish tailor, Harold Pinter grew up in a working-class district in the East End of London, where he witnessed some of the worst bombing of World War II. After leaving school Pinter studied acting at the Royal Academy of Dramatic Art, but left after a few months. When he was called up for military service he declared himself a conscientious objector, but not on the basis of religious belief; he was tried twice and eventually fined. From 1948 to 1958 Pinter worked at a number of odd jobs and continued his career as an actor. He began to publish poetry in 1950, and his first play, *The Room,* was produced in 1957. It and *The Birthday Party* (1958) were not initially successful, but *The Caretaker* (1960) made Pinter's reputation as the most difficult and exciting playwright to appear in England after World War II. *A Slight Ache,* originally a radio play, was produced in London in 1961 and published the same year. It was followed by *The Homecoming* (1965), *Old Times* (1971), and *No Man's Land* (1975). In addition to his major plays for the theater, Pinter has written for television and adapted his works and those of other writers for the cinema.

A country house, with two chairs and a table laid for breakfast at the centre of the stage. These will later be removed and the action will be focused on the scullery on the right and the study on the left, both indicated with a minimum of scenery and props. A large well kept garden is suggested at the back of the stage with flower beds, trimmed hedges, etc. The garden gate, which cannot be seen by the audience, is off right.

FLORA *and* EDWARD *are discovered sitting at the breakfast table.* EDWARD *is reading the paper.*

FLORA: Have you noticed the honeysuckle this morning?

EDWARD: The what?

FLORA: The honeysuckle.

EDWARD: Honeysuckle? Where?

FLORA: By the back gate, Edward.

EDWARD: Is that honeysuckle? I thought it was . . . convolvulus, or something.

FLORA: But you know it's honeysuckle.

EDWARD: I tell you I thought it was convolvulus.

[*Pause.*]

FLORA: It's in wonderful flower.

EDWARD: I must look.

FLORA: The whole garden's in flower this morning. The clematis. The convolvulus. Everything. I was out at seven. I stood by the pool.

EDWARD: Did you say—that the convolvulus was in flower?

FLORA: Yes.

EDWARD: But good God, you just denied there was any.

FLORA: I was talking about the honeysuckle.

EDWARD: About the what?

FLORA [*calmly*]: Edward—you know that shrub outside the toolshed . . .

EDWARD: Yes, yes.

FLORA: That's convolvulus.

EDWARD: That?

FLORA: Yes.

EDWARD: Oh.

[*Pause.*]

I thought it was japonica.

FLORA: Oh, good Lord no.

EDWARD: Pass the teapot, please.

[*Pause. She pours tea for him.*]

I don't see why I should be expected to distinguish between these plants. It's not my job.

FLORA: You know perfectly well what grows in your garden.

EDWARD: Quite the contrary. It is clear that I don't.

[*Pause.*]

FLORA [*rising*]: I was up at seven. I stood by the pool. The peace. And everything in flower. The sun was up. You should work in the garden this morning. We could put up the canopy.

EDWARD: The canopy? What for?

FLORA: To shade you from the sun.

EDWARD: Is there a breeze?

FLORA: A light one.

EDWARD: It's very treacherous weather, you know.

[*Pause.*]

FLORA: Do you know what today is?

EDWARD: Saturday.

FLORA: It's the longest day of the year.

EDWARD: Really?

FLORA: It's the height of summer today.

EDWARD: Cover the marmalade.

FLORA: What?

EDWARD: Cover the pot. There's a wasp. [*He puts the paper down on the table.*] Don't move. Keep still. What are you doing?

FLORA: Covering the pot.

EDWARD: Don't move. Leave it. Keep still.

[*Pause.*]

Give me the 'Telegraph'.

FLORA: Don't hit it. It'll bite.

EDWARD: Bite? What do you mean, bite? Keep still.

[*Pause.*]

It's landing.

FLORA: It's going in the pot.

EDWARD: Give me the lid.

FLORA: It's in.

EDWARD: Give me the lid.

FLORA: I'll do it.

EDWARD: Give it to me! Now . . . Slowly . . .

FLORA: What are you doing?

EDWARD: Be quiet. Slowly . . . carefully . . . on . . . the . . . pot! Ha-ha-ha. Very good.

[*He sits on a chair to the right of the table.*]

FLORA: Now he's in the marmalade.

EDWARD: Precisely.

[*Pause. She sits on a chair to the left of the table and reads the 'Telegraph'.*]

FLORA: Can you hear him?

EDWARD: Hear him?

FLORA: Buzzing.

EDWARD: Nonsense. How can you hear him? It's an earthenware lid.

FLORA: He's becoming frantic.

EDWARD: Rubbish. Take it away from the table.

FLORA: What shall I do with it?

EDWARD: Put it in the sink and drown it.

FLORA: It'll fly out and bite me.

EDWARD: It will not bite you! Wasps don't bite. Anyway, it won't fly out. It's stuck. It'll drown where it is, in the marmalade.

FLORA: What a horrible death.

EDWARD: On the contrary.

[*Pause.*]

FLORA: Have you got something in your eyes?

EDWARD: No. Why do you ask?

FLORA: You keep clenching them, blinking them.

EDWARD: I have a slight ache in them.

FLORA: Oh, dear.

EDWARD: Yes, a slight ache. As if I hadn't slept.

FLORA: Did you sleep, Edward?

EDWARD: Of course I slept. Uninterrupted. As always.

FLORA: And yet you feel tired.

EDWARD: I didn't say I felt tired. I merely said I had a slight ache in my eyes.

FLORA: Why is that, then?

EDWARD: I really don't know.

[*Pause.*]

FLORA: Oh goodness!

EDWARD: What is it?

FLORA: I can see it. It's trying to come out.

EDWARD: How can it?

FLORA: Through the hole. It's trying to crawl out, through the spoon-hole.

EDWARD: Mmmnn, yes. Can't do it, of course. [*Silent pause.*] Well, let's kill it, for goodness' sake.

FLORA: Yes, let's. But how?

EDWARD: Bring it out on the spoon and squash it on a plate.

FLORA: It'll fly away. It'll bite.

EDWARD: If you don't stop saying that word I shall leave this table.

FLORA: But wasps do bite.

EDWARD: They don't bite. They sting. It's snakes . . . that bite.

FLORA: What about horseflies?

[*Pause.*]

EDWARD [*to himself*]: Horseflies suck.

[*Pause.*]

FLORA: [*tentatively*]: If we . . . if we wait long

enough, I suppose it'll choke to death. It'll suffocate in the marmalade.

EDWARD [*briskly*]: You do know I've got work to do this morning, don't you? I can't spend the whole day worrying about a wasp.

FLORA: Well, kill it.

EDWARD: You want to kill it?

FLORA: Yes.

EDWARD: Very well. Pass me the hot water jug.

FLORA: What are you going to do?

EDWARD: Scald it. Give it to me.

[*She hands him the jug. Pause.*]

Now . . .

FLORA [*whispering*]: Do you want me to lift the lid?

EDWARD: No, no, no. I'll pour down the spoon hole. Right . . . down the spoon-hole.

FLORA: Listen!

EDWARD: What?

FLORA: It's buzzing.

EDWARD: Vicious creatures.

[*Pause.*]

Curious, but I don't remember seeing any wasps at all, all summer, until now. I'm sure I don't know why. I mean, there must have been wasps.

FLORA: Please.

EDWARD: This couldn't be the first wasp, could it?

FLORA: Please.

EDWARD: The first wasp of summer? No. It's not possible.

FLORA: Edward.

EDWARD: Mmmmnnn?

FLORA: Kill it.

EDWARD: Ah, yes. Tilt the pot. Tilt. Aah . . . down here . . . right down . . . blinding him . . . that's . . . it.

FLORA: Is it?

EDWARD: Lift the lid. All right, I will. There he is! Dead. What a monster. [*He squashes it on a plate.*]

FLORA: What an awful experience.

EDWARD: What a beautiful day it is. Beautiful. I think I shall work in the garden this morning. Where's that canopy?

FLORA: It's in the shed.

EDWARD: Yes, we must get it out. My goodness, just look at that sky. Not a cloud. Did you say it was the longest day of the year today?

FLORA: Yes.

EDWARD: Ah, it's a good day. I feel it in my bones. In my muscles. I think I'll stretch my legs in a minute. Down to the pool. My God, look at that flowering shrub over there. Clematis. What a wonderful . . . [*He stops suddenly.*]

FLORA: What?

[*Pause.*]

Edward, what is it?

[*Pause.*]

Edward . . .

EDWARD [*thickly*]: He's there.

FLORA: Who?

EDWARD [*low murmuring*]: Blast and damn it, he's there, he's there at the back gate.

FLORA: Let me see.

[*She moves over to him to look. Pause.*]

[*Lightly.*]. Oh, it's the matchseller.

EDWARD: He's back again.

FLORA: But he's always there.

EDWARD: Why? What is he doing there?

FLORA: But he's never disturbed you, has he? The man's been standing there for weeks. You've never mentioned it.

EDWARD: What is he doing there?

FLORA: He's selling matches, of course.

EDWARD: It's ridiculous. What's the time?

FLORA: Half past nine.

EDWARD: What in God's name is he doing with a tray full of matches at half past nine in the morning?

FLORA: He arrives at seven o'clock.

EDWARD: Seven o'clock?

FLORA: He's always there at seven.

EDWARD: Yes, but you've never . . . actually seen him arrive?

FLORA: No, I . . .

EDWARD: Well, how do you know he's . . . not been standing there all night?

[*Pause.*]

FLORA: Do you find him interesting, Edward?

EDWARD [*casually*]: Interesting? No. No, I . . . don't find him interesting.

FLORA: He's a very nice old man, really.

EDWARD: You've spoken to him?

FLORA: No. No, I haven't spoken to him. I've nodded.

EDWARD [*pacing up and down*]: For two months he's been standing on that spot, do you realize that? Two months. I haven't been able to step outside the back gate.

FLORA: Why on earth not?

EDWARD [*to himself*]: It used to give me great pleasure, such pleasure, to stroll along through the long grass, out through the back gate, pass into the lane. That pleasure is now denied me. It's my own house, isn't it? It's my own gate.

FLORA: I really can't understand this, Edward.

EDWARD: Damn. And do you know I've never seen him sell one box? Not a box. It's hardly surprising. He's on the wrong road. It's not a road at all. What is it?

It's a lane, leading to the monastery. Off everybody's route. Even the monks take a short cut to the village, when they want to go . . . to the village. No one goes up it. Why doesn't he stand on the main road if he wants to sell matches, by the *front* gate? The whole thing's preposterous.

FLORA [*going over to him*]: I don't know why you're getting so excited about it. He's a quiet, harmless old man, going about his business. He's quite harmless.

EDWARD: I didn't say he wasn't harmless. Of course he's harmless. How could he be other than harmless?

[*Fade out and silence.*]

[FLORA'S *voice, far in the house, drawing nearer.*]

FLORA [*Off*]: Edward, where are you? Edward? Where are you, Edward?

[*She appears.*]

Edward?

Edward, what are you doing in the scullery?

EDWARD [*looking through the scullery window*]: Doing?

FLORA: I've been looking everywhere for you. I put up the canopy ages ago. I came back and you were nowhere to be seen. Have you been out?

EDWARD: No.

FLORA: Where have you been?

EDWARD: Here.

FLORA: I looked in your study. I even went into the attic.

EDWARD [*tonelessly*]: What would I be doing in the attic?

FLORA: I couldn't imagine what had happened to you. Do you know it's twelve o'clock?

EDWARD: Is it?

FLORA: I even went to the bottom of the garden, to see if you were in the toolshed.

EDWARD [*tonelessly*]: What would I be doing in the toolshed?

FLORA: You must have seen me in the garden. You can see through this window.

EDWARD: Only part of the garden.

FLORA: Yes.

EDWARD: Only a corner of the garden. A very small corner.

FLORA: What are you doing in here?

EDWARD: Nothing. I was digging out some notes, that's all.

FLORA: Notes?

EDWARD: For my essay.

FLORA: Which essay?

EDWARD: My essay on space and time.

FLORA: But . . . I've never . . . I don't know that one.

EDWARD: You don't know it?

FLORA: I thought you were writing one about the Belgian Congo.

EDWARD: I've been engaged on the dimensionality and continuity of space . . . and time . . . for years.

FLORA: And the Belgian Congo?

EDWARD [*shortly*]: Never mind about the Belgian Congo.

[*Pause.*]

FLORA: But you don't keep notes in the scullery.

EDWARD: You'd be surprised. You'd be highly surprised.

FLORA: Good Lord, what's that? Is that a bullock let loose? No. It's the matchseller! My goodness, you can see him . . . through the hedge. He looks bigger. Have you been watching him? He looks . . . like a bullock.

[*Pause.*]

Edward?

[*Pause.*]

[*Moving over to him.*] Are you coming outside? I've put up the canopy. You'll miss the best of the day. You can have an hour before lunch.

EDWARD: I've no work to do this morning.

FLORA: What about your essay? You don't intend to stay in the scullery all day, do you?

EDWARD: Get out. Leave me alone.

[*A slight pause.*]

FLORA: Really Edward. You've never spoken to me like that in all your life.

EDWARD: Yes, I have.

FLORA: Oh, Weddie. Beddie-Weddie . . .

EDWARD: Do not call me that!

FLORA: Your eyes are bloodshot.

EDWARD: Damn it.

FLORA: It's too dark in here to peer . . .

EDWARD: Damn.

FLORA: It's so bright outside.

EDWARD: Damn.

FLORA: And it's dark in here.

[*Pause.*]

EDWARD: Christ blast it!

FLORA: You're frightened of him.

EDWARD: I'm not.

FLORA: You're frightened of a poor old man. Why?

EDWARD: I am not!

FLORA: He's a poor, harmless old man.

EDWARD: Aaah my eyes.

FLORA: Let me bathe them.

EDWARD: Keep away.

[*Pause.*]

[*Slowly.*] I want to speak to that man. I want to have a word with him.

[*Pause.*].

It's quite absurd, of course. I really can't tolerate something so . . . absurd, right on my doorstep. I shall not tolerate it. He's sold nothing all morning. No one passed. Yes. A monk passed. A non-smoker. In a loose garmet. It's quite obvious he was a non-smoker but still, the man made no effort. He made no effort to clinch a sale, to rid himself of one of his cursed boxes. His one chance, all morning, and he made no effort.

[*Pause.*]

I haven't wasted my time. I've hit, in fact, upon the truth. He's not a matchseller at all. The bastard isn't a matchseller at all. Curious I never realized that before. He's an impostor. I watched him very closely. He made no move towards the monk. As for the monk, the monk made no move towards him. The monk was moving along the lane. He didn't pause, or halt, or in any way alter his step. As for the matchseller—how ridiculous to go on calling him by that title. What a farce. No, there is something very false about that man. I intend to get to the bottom of it. I'll soon get rid of him. He can go and ply his trade somewhere else. Instead of standing like a bullock . . . a bullock, outside my back gate.

FLORA: But if he isn't a matchseller, what is his trade?

EDWARD: We'll soon find out.

FLORA: You're going out to speak to him?

EDWARD: Certainly not! Go out to *him?* Certainly . . . not. I'll invite him in here. Into my study. Then we'll . . . get to the bottom of it.

FLORA: Why don't you call the police and have him removed?

[*He laughs. Pause.*]

Why don't you call the police, Edward? You could say he was a public nuisance. Although I . . . I can't say I find him a nuisance.

EDWARD: Call him in.

FLORA: Me?

EDWARD: Go out and call him in.

FLORA: Are you serious?

[*Pause.*]

Edward, I could call the police. Or even the vicar.

EDWARD: Go and get him.

[*She goes out. Silence.*]

[EDWARD *waits.*]

FLORA [*in the garden*]: Good morning.

[*Pause.*]

We haven't met. I live in this house here. My husband and I.

[*Pause.*]

I wonder if you could . . . would you care for a cup of tea?

[*Pause.*]

Or a glass of lemon? It must be so dry, standing here.

[*Pause.*]

Would you like to come inside for a little while? It's much cooler. There's something we'd very much like to . . . tell you, that will benefit you. Could you spare a few moments? We won't keep you long.

[*Pause.*]

Might I buy your tray of matches, do you think? We've run out, completely, and we always keep a very large stock. It happens that way, doesn't it? Well, we can discuss it inside. Do come. This way. Ah now, do come. Our house is full of curios, you know. My husband's been rather a collector. We have goose for lunch. Do you care for goose?

[*She moves to the gate.*]

Come and have lunch with us. This way. That's . . . right. May I take your arm? There's a good deal of *nettle* inside the gate. [*The* MATCHSELLER *appears.*] Here. This way. Mind now. Isn't it beautiful weather? It's the longest day of the year today.

[*Pause.*]

That's honeysuckle. And that's convolvulus. There's clematis. And do you see that plant by the conservatory? That's japonica.

[*Silence. She enters the study.*]

FLORA: He's here.

EDWARD: I know.

FLORA: He's in the hall.

EDWARD: I know he's here. I can smell him.

FLORA: Smell him?

EDWARD: I smelt him when he came under my window. Can't you smell the house now?

FLORA: What are you going to do with him, Edward? You won't be rough with him in any way? He's very old. I'm not sure if he can hear, or even see. And he's wearing the oldest—

EDWARD: I don't want to know what he's wearing.

FLORA: But you'll see for yourself in a minute, if you speak to him.

EDWARD: I shall.

[*Slight pause.*]

FLORA: He's an old man. You won't . . . be rough with him?

EDWARD: If he's so old, why doesn't he seek shelter . . . from the storm?

FLORA: But there's no storm. It's summer, the longest day . . .

EDWARD: There was a storm, last week. A summer storm. He stood without moving, while it raged about him.

FLORA: When was this?

EDWARD: He remained quite still, while it thundered all about him.

[*Pause.*]

FLORA: Edward . . . are you sure it's wise to bother about all this?

EDWARD: Tell him to come in.

FLORA: I . . .

EDWARD: Now.

[*She goes and collects the* MATCHSELLER.]

FLORA: Hullo. Would you like to go in? I won't be long. Up these stairs here.

[*Pause.*]

You can have some sherry before lunch.

[*Pause.*]

Shall I take your tray? No. Very well, take it with you. Just . . . up those stairs. The door at the . . .

[*She watches him move.*]

the door . . .

[*Pause.*]

the door at the top. I'll join you . . . later. [*She goes out.*]

[*The* MATCHSELLER *stands on the threshold of the study.*]

EDWARD [*cheerfully*]: Here I am. Where are you?

[*Pause.*]

Don't stand out there, old chap. Come into my study.

[*He rises.*] Come in.

[*The* MATCHSELLER *enters.*]

That's right. Mind how you go. That's . . . it. Now. make yourself comfortable. Thought you might like some refreshment, on a day like this. Sit down, old man. What will you have? Sherry? Or what about a double scotch? Eh?

[*Pause.*]

I entertain the villagers annually, as a matter of fact. I'm not the squire, but they look upon me with some regard. Don't believe we've got a squire here any more, actually. Don't know what became of him. Nice old man he was. Great chess player, as I remember. Three daughters. The pride of the county. Flaming red hair. Alice was the eldest. Sit yourself down, old chap. Eunice I think was number two. The youngest one was the best of the bunch. Sally. No, no, wait a minute, no, it wasn't Sally, it was . . . Fanny. Fanny. A flower. You must be a stranger here. Unless you lived here once, went on a long voyage and have lately returned. Do you know the district?

[*Pause.*]

Now, now, you mustn't . . . stand about like that. Take a seat. Which one would you prefer? We have a great variety, as you see. Can't stand uniformity. Like different seats, different backs. Often when I'm working, you know, I draw up one chair, scribble a few lines, put it by, draw up another, sit back, ponder, put it by . . . [*absently*] . . . sit back . . . put it by . . .

[*Pause.*]

I write theological and philosophical essays . . .

[*Pause.*]

Now and again I jot down a few observations on certain tropical phenomena—not from the same standpoint, of course. [*Silent pause.*] Yes. Africa, now. Africa's always been my happy hunting ground. Fascinating country. Do you know it? I get the impression that you've . . . been around a bit. Do you by any chance know the Membunza Mountains? Great range south of Katambaloo. French Equatorial Africa, if my memory serves me right. Most extraordinary diversity of flora and fauna. Especially fauna. I understand in the Gobi Desert you can come across some very strange sights. Never been there myself. Studied the maps though. Fascinating things, maps.

[*Pause.*]

Do you live in the village? I don't often go down, of course. Or are you passing through? On your way to another part of the country? Well, I can tell you, in my opinion you won't find many prettier parts than here. We win the first prize regularly, you know, the best kept village in the area. Sit down.

[*Pause.*]

I say, can you hear me?

[*Pause.*]

I said, I say, can you hear me?

[*Pause.*]

You possess most extraordinary repose, for a man of your age, don't you? Well, perhaps that's not quite the right word . . . repose. Do you find it chilly in here? I'm sure it's chillier in here than out. I haven't been out yet, today, though I shall probably spend the whole afternoon working, in the garden, under my canopy, at my table, by the pool.

[*Pause.*]

Oh, I understand you met my *wife?* Charming woman, don't you think? Plenty of grit there, too. Stood by me through thick and thin, that woman. In season and out of season. Fine figure of a woman she was, too, in her youth. Wonderful carriage, flaming red hair. [*He stops abruptly.*]

[*Pause.*]

Yes, I . . . I was in much the same position myself then as you are now, you understand. Struggling to make my way in the world. I was in commerce too. [*With a chuckle.*] Oh, yes, I know what it's like—the weather, the rain, beaten from pillar to post, up hill and down dale . . . the rewards were few . . . winters in hovels . . . up till all hours working at your thesis . . . yes, I've done it all. Let me advise you. Get a good woman to stick by you. Never mind what the world says. Keep at it. Keep your shoulder to the wheel. It'll pay dividends.

[*Pause.*]

[*With a laugh.*] You must excuse my chatting away like this. We have few visitors this time of the year. All our friends summer abroad. I'm a home bird myself. Wouldn't mind taking a trip to Asia Minor, mind you, or to certain lower regions of the Congo, but Europe? Out of the question. Much too noisy. I'm sure you agree. Now look, what will you have to drink? A glass of ale? Curaçao Fockink Orange? Ginger beer? Tia Maria? A Wachenheimer Fuchsmantel Reisling Beeren Auslese? Gin and it? Chateauneuf-du-Pape? A little Asti Spumante? Or what do you say to a straightforward Piesporter Goldtropfschen Feine Auslese (Reichsgraf von Kesselstaff)? Any preference?

[*Pause.*]

You look a trifle warm. Why don't you take off your balaclava? I'd find that a little itchy myself. But then I've always been one for freedom of movement. Even in the depth of winter I wear next to nothing.

[*Pause.*]

I say, can I ask you a personal question? I don't want to seem inquisitive but aren't you rather on the wrong road for matchselling? Not terribly busy, is it? Of course you may not care for petrol fumes or the noise of traffic. I can quite understand that.

[*Pause.*]

Do forgive me peering but is that a glass eye you're wearing?

[*Pause.*]

Do take off your balaclava, there's a good chap, put your tray down and take your ease, as they say in this part of the world. [*He moves towards him.*] I must say you keep quite a good stock, don't you? Tell me, between ourselves, are those boxes full, or are there just a few half-empty ones among them? Oh yes, I used to be in commerce. Well now, before the good lady sounds the gong for petit déjeuner will you join me in an apéritif? I recommend a glass of cider. Now . . . just a minute . . . I know I've got some—Look out! Mind your tray!

[*The tray falls, and the matchboxes.*]

Good God, what . . .?

[*Pause.*]

You've dropped your tray.

[*Pause. He picks the matchboxes up.*]

[*Grunts.*] Eh, these boxes are all wet. You've no right to sell wet matches, you know. Uuuuugggh. This feels suspiciously like fungus. You won't get very far in this trade if you don't take care of your goods. [*Grunts, rising.*] Well, here you are.

[*Pause.*]

Here's your tray.

[*He puts the tray into the* MATCHSELLER'S *hands, and sits. Pause.*]

Now listen, let me be quite frank with you, shall I? I really cannot understand why you don't sit down. There are four chairs at your disposal. Not to mention the hassock. I can't possibly talk to you unless you're settled. Then and only then can I speak to you. Do you follow me? You're sweating. The sweat's pouring out of you. Take off that balaclava.

[*Pause.*]

Go into the corner then. Into the corner. Go on. Get into the shade of the corner. Back. Backward.

[*Pause.*]

Get back!

[*Pause.*]

Ah, you understand me. Forgive me for saying so, but I had decided that you had the comprehension of a bullock. I was mistaken. You understand me perfectly well. That's right. A little more. A little to the right. Aaah. Now you're there. In shade, in shadow. Good-o. Now I can get down to brass tacks. Can't I?

[*Pause.*]

No doubt you're wondering why I invited you into this house? You may think I was alarmed by the look of you. You would be quite mistaken. I was not alarmed by the look of you. I did not find you at all alarming. No, no. Nothing outside this room has ever alarmed me. You disgusted me, quite forcibly, if you want to know the truth.

[*Pause.*]

Why did you disgust me to that extent? That seems to be a pertinent question. You're no more disgusting than Fanny, the squire's daughter, after all. In appearance you differ but not in essence. There's the same . . .

[*Pause.*]

The same . . .

[*Pause.*]

[*In a low voice.*] I want to ask you a question. Why do you stand outside my back gate, from dawn till dusk, why do you pretend to sell matches, why . . .? What is it, damn you. You're shivering. You're sagging. Come here, come here . . . mind your tray! [EDWARD *rises and moves behind a chair*]. Come, quick quick. There. Sit here. Sit . . . sit in this.

[*The* MATCHSELLER *stumbles and sits. Pause.*]

Aaaah! You're sat. At last. What a relief. You must be tired. [*Slight pause.*] Chair comfortable? I bought it in a sale. I bought all the furniture in this house in a sale. The same sale. When I was a young man. You too, perhaps. You too, perhaps.

[*Pause.*]

At the same time, perhaps!

[*Pause.*]

[*Muttering.*] I must get some air. I must get a breath of air.

[*He goes to the door.*]

Flora!

FLORA: Yes?

EDWARD [*with great weariness*]: Take me into the garden.

[*Silence. They move from the study door to a chair under a canopy.*]

FLORA: Come under the canopy.

EDWARD: Ah. [*He sits.*]

[*Pause.*]

The peace. The peace out here.

FLORA: Look at our trees.

EDWARD: Yes.

FLORA: Our own trees. Can you hear the birds?

EDWARD: No, I can't hear them.

FLORA: But they're singing, high up, and flapping.

EDWARD: Good. Let them flap.

FLORA: Shall I bring your lunch out here? You can have it in peace, and a quiet drink, under your canopy.

[*Pause.*]

How are you getting on with your old man?

EDWARD: What do you mean?

FLORA: What's happening? How are you getting on with him?

EDWARD: Very well. We get on remarkably well. He's a little . . . reticent. Somewhat withdrawn. It's understandable. I should be the same, perhaps, in his place. Though, of course, I could not possibly find myself in his place.

FLORA: Have you found out anything about him?

EDWARD: A little. A little. He's had various trades, that's certain. His place of residence is unsure. He's . . . he's not a drinking man. As yet, I haven't discovered the reason for his arrival here. I shall in due course . . . by nightfall.

FLORA: Is it necessary?

EDWARD: Necessary?

FLORA [*quickly sitting on the right arm of the chair*]: I could show him out now, it wouldn't matter. You've seen him, he's harmless, unfortunate . . . old, that's all. Edward—listen—he's not here through any . . . design, or anything, I know it. I mean, he might just as well stand outside our back gate as anywhere else. He'll move on. I can . . . make him. I promise you. There's no point in upsetting yourself like this. He's an old man, weak in the head . . . that's all. [*Pause.*]

EDWARD: You're deluded.

FLORA: Edward—

EDWARD [*rising*]: You're deluded. And stop calling me Edward.

FLORA: You're not still frightened of him?

EDWARD: Frightened of him? Of *him?* Have you *seen* him?

[*Pause.*]

He's like jelly. A great bullockfat of jelly. He can't see straight. I think as a matter of fact he wears a glass eye. He's almost stone deaf . . . almost . . . not quite. He's very nearly dead on his feet. Why should he frighten me? No, you're a woman, you know nothing. [*Slight pause.*] But he possesses other faculties. Cunning. The man's an imposter and he knows I know it.

FLORA: I'll tell you what. Look. Let me speak to him. I'll speak to him.

EDWARD [*quietly*]: And I know he knows I know it.

FLORA: I'll find out all about him, Edward. I promise you I will.

EDWARD: And he knows I know.

FLORA: Edward! Listen to me! I can find out all about him, I promise you. I shall go and have a word with him now. I shall . . . get to the bottom of it.

EDWARD: You? It's laughable.

FLORA: You'll see—he won't bargain for me. I'll surprise him. He'll . . . he'll admit everything.

EDWARD [*softly*]: He'll admit everything, will he?

FLORA: You wait and see, you just—

EDWARD [*hissing*]: What are you plotting?

FLORA: I know exactly what I shall—

EDWARD: What are you plotting?

[*He seizes her arms.*]

FLORA: Edward, you're hurting me!

[*Pause.*]

[*With dignity.*] I shall wave from the window when I'm ready. Then you can come up. I shall get to the truth of it, I assure you. You're much too heavy-handed, in every way. You should trust your wife more, Edward. You should trust her judgment, and have a greater insight into her capabilities. A woman . . . a woman will often succeed, you know, where a man must invariably fail.

[*Silence. She goes into the study.*]

Do you mind if I come in?

[*The door closes.*]

Are you comfortable?

[*Pause.*]

Oh, the sun's shining directly on you. Wouldn't you rather sit in the shade?

[*She sits down.*]

It's the longest day of the year today, did you know that? Actually the year has flown. I can remember Christmas and that dreadful frost. And the floods! I hope you weren't here in the floods. We were out of danger up here, of course, but in the valleys whole families I remember drifted away on the current. The country was a lake. Everything stopped. We lived on our own preserves, drank elderberry wine, studied other cultures.

[*Pause.*]

Do you know, I've got a feeling I've seen you before, somewhere. Long before the flood. You were much younger. Yes, I'm really sure of it. Between ourselves, were you ever a poacher? I had an encounter with a poacher once. It was a ghastly rape, the brute. High up on a hillside cattle track. Early spring. I was out riding on my pony. And there on the verge a man lay—ostensibly injured, lying on his front, I remember, possibly the victim of a murderous assault, how was I to know? I dismounted, I went to him, he rose, I fell, my pony took off, down to the valley. I saw the sky through the trees, blue. Up to my ears in mud. It was a desperate battle.

[*Pause.*]

I lost.

[*Pause*]

Of course, life was perilous in those days. It was my first canter unchaperoned.

[*Pause.*]

Years later, when I was a Justice of the Peace for the county, I had him in front of the bench. He was there for poaching. That's how I know he was a poacher. The evidence though was sparse, inadmissible, I acquitted him, letting him off with a caution. He'd grown a red beard, I remember. Yes. A bit of a stinker.

[*Pause.*]

I say, you are perspiring, aren't you? Shall I mop your brow? With my chiffon? Is it the heat? Or the closeness? Or confined space? Or . . . ? [*She goes over to him.*] Actually, the day is cooling. It'll soon be dusk. Perhaps it is dusk. May I? You don't mind?

[*Pause. She mops his brow.*]

Ah, there, that's better. And your cheeks. It is a woman's job, isn't it? And I'm the only woman on hand. There.

[*Pause. She leans on the arm of chair.*]

[*Intimately.*] Tell me, have you a woman? Do you like women? Do you ever . . . think about women?

[*Pause.*]

Have you ever . . . stopped a woman?

[*Pause.*]

I'm sure you must have been quite attractive once. [*She sits.*] Not any more, of course. You've got a vile smell. Vile. Quite repellent, in fact.

[*Pause.*]

Sex, I suppose, means nothing to you. Does it ever occur to you that sex is a very vital experience for other people? Really, I think you'd amuse me if you weren't so hideous. You're probably quite amusing in your own way. [*Seductively.*] Tell me all about love. Speak to me of love.

[*Pause.*]

God knows what you're saying at this very moment. It's quite disgusting. Do you know when I was a girl I loved . . . I loved . . . I simply adored . . . what *have* you got on, for goodness sake? A jersey? It's clogged. Have you been rolling in mud? [*Slight pause.*] You haven't been rolling in mud, have you? [*She rises and goes over to him.*] And what have you got under your jersey? Let's see. [*Slight pause.*] I'm not tickling you, am I? No. Good . . . Lord, is this a vest? That's quite original. Quite original. [*She sits on the arm of his chair.*] Hmmnn, you're a solid old boy, I must say. Not at all like a jelly. All you need is a bath. A lovely lathery bath. And a good scrub. A lovely lathery scrub. [*Pause.*] Don't you? It will be a pleasure. [*She throws her arms round him.*] I'm going to keep you. I'm going to keep you, you dreadful chap, and call you Barnabas. Isn't it dark, Barnabas? Your eyes, your eyes, your great big eyes.

[*Pause.*]

My husband would never have guessed your name. Never. [*She kneels at his feet. Whispering.*] It's me you were waiting for, wasn't it? You've been standing waiting for me. You've seen me in the woods, picking daisies, in my apron, my pretty daisy apron, and you came and stood, poor creature, at my gate, till death us do part. Poor Barnabas. I'm going to put you to bed. I'm going to put you to bed and watch over you. But first you must have a good whacking great bath. And I'll buy you pretty little things that will suit you. And little toys to play with. On your deathbed. Why shouldn't you die happy?

[*A shout from the hall.*]

EDWARD: Well?

[*Footsteps upstage.*]

Well?

FLORA: Don't come in.

EDWARD: Well?

FLORA: He's dying.

EDWARD: Dying? He's not dying.

FLORA: I tell you, he's very ill.

EDWARD: He's not dying! Nowhere near. He'll see you cremated.

FLORA: The man is desperately ill!

EDWARD: Ill? You lying slut. Get back to your trough!

FLORA: Edward . . .

EDWARD [*violently*]: To your trough!

[*She goes out. Pause.*]

[*Coolly.*] Good evening to you. Why are you sitting in the gloom? Oh, you've begun to disrobe. Too warm? Let's open these windows, then, what?

[*He opens the windows.*]

Pull the blinds.

[*He pulls the blinds.*]

And close . . . the curtains . . . again.

[*He closes the curtains.*]

Ah. Air will enter through the side chinks. Of the blinds. And filter through the curtains. I hope. Don't want to suffocate, do we?

[*Pause.*]

More comfortable? Yes. You look different in darkness. Take off all your togs, if you like. Make yourself at home. Strip to your buff. Do as you would in your own house.

[*Pause.*]

Did you say something?

[*Pause.*]

Did you say something?

[*Pause.*]

Anything? Well then, tell me about your boyhood. Mmnn?

[*Pause.*]

What did you do with it? Run? Swim? Kick the ball? You kicked the ball? What position? Left back? Goalie? First reserve?

[*Pause.*]

I used to play myself. Country house matches, mostly. Kept wicket and batted number seven.

[*Pause.*]

Kept wicket and batted number seven. Man called—Cavendish, I think, had something of your style. Bowled left arm over the wicket, always kept his cap on, quite a dab hand at solo whist, preferred a good round of prop and cop to anything else.

[*Pause.*]

On wet days when the field was swamped.

[*Pause.*]

Perhaps you don't play cricket.

[*Pause.*]

Perhaps you never met Cavendish and never played cricket. You look less and less like a cricketer the more I see of you. Where did you live in those days? God damn it, I'm entitled to know something about you! You're in my blasted house, on my territory, drinking my wine, eating my duck! Now you've had your fill you sit like a hump, a mouldering heap. In my room. My den. I can rem . . . [*He stops abruptly.*]

[*Pause.*]

[*In disgust.*] Good Christ, is that a grin on your face? [*Further disgust.*] It's lopsided. It's all—done on one side. You're grinning. It amuses you, does it? When I tell you how well I remember this room, how well I remember this den. [*Muttering.*] Ha. Yesterday now, it was clear, clearly defined, so clearly.

[*Pause.*]

The garden, too, was sharp, lucid, in the rain, in the sun.

[*Pause.*]

My den, too, was sharp, arranged for my purpose . . . quite satisfactory.

[*Pause.*]

The house too, was polished, all the banisters were polished, and the stair rods, and the curtain rods.

[*Pause.*]

My desk was polished, and my cabinet.

[*Pause.*]

I was polished. [*Nostalgic.*] I could stand on the hill and look through my telescope at the sea. And follow the path of the three-masted schooner, feeling fit, well aware of my sinews, their suppleness, my arms lifted holding the telescope, steady, easily, no trembling, my aim was perfect, I could pour hot water down the spoon-hole, yes, easily, no difficulty, my grasp firm, my command established, my life was accounted for, I was ready for my excursions to the cliff, down the path to the back gate, through the long grass, no need to watch for the nettles, my progress was fluent, after my long struggling against all kinds of usurpers, disreputables, lists, literally lists of people anxious to do me down, and my reputation down, my command was established, all summer I would breakfast, survey my landscape, take my telescope, examine the overhanging of my hedges, pursue the narrow lane past the monastery, climb the hill, adjust the lens [*he mimes a telescope*], watch the progress of the three-masted schooner, my progress was as sure, as fluent . . .

[*Pause. He drops his arms.*]

Yes, yes, you're quite right, it is funny.

[*Pause.*]

Laugh your bloody head off! go on. Don't mind me. No need to be polite.

[*Pause.*]

That's right.

[*Pause.*]

You're quite right, it is funny. I'll laugh with you!

[*He laughs.*]

Ha-ha-ha! Yes! You're laughing with me, I'm laughing with you, we're laughing together!

[*He laughs and stops.*]

[*Brightly.*] Why did I invite you into this room? That's your next question, isn't it? Bound to be.

[*Pause.*]

Well, why not, you might say? My oldest acquaintance. My nearest and dearest. My kith and kin. But surely correspondence would have been as satisfactory . . . more satisfactory? We could have exchanged postcards, couldn't we? What? Views, couldn't we? Of sea and land, city and village, town and country, autumn and winter . . . clocktowers . . . museums . . . citadels . . . bridges . . . rivers . . .

[*Pause.*]

Seeing you stand, at the back gate, such close proximity, was not at all the same thing.

[*Pause.*]

What are you doing? You're taking off your balaclava . . . you've decided not to. No, very well then, all things considered, did I then invite you into this room with express intention of asking you to take off your balaclava, in order to determine your resemblance to—some other person? The answer is no, certainly not, I did not, for when I first saw you you wore no balaclava. No headcovering of any kind, in fact. You looked quite different without a head—I mean without a hat—I mean without a headcovering, of any kind. In fact every time I have seen you you have looked quite different to the time before.

[*Pause.*]

Even now you look different. Very different.

[*Pause.*]

Admitted that sometimes I viewed you through dark glasses, yes, and sometimes through light glasses, and on other occasions bare eyed, and on other occasions through the bars of the scullery window, or from the roof, the roof, yes in driving snow, or from the bottom of the drive in thick fog, or from the roof again in blinding sun, so blinding, so hot, that I had to skip and jump and bounce in order to remain in one place. Ah, that's good for a guffaw, is it? That's good for a belly laugh? Go on, then. Let it out. Let yourself go, for God's . . . [*He catches his breath.*] You're crying . . .

[*Pause.*]

[*Moved.*] You haven't been laughing. You're crying.

[*Pause.*]

You're weeping. You're shaking with grief. For me. I can't believe it. For my plight. I've been wrong.

[*Pause.*]

[*Briskly.*] Come, come, stop it. Be a man. Blow your nose for goodness sake. Pull yourself together.

[*He sneezes.*]

Ah.

[*He rises. Sneeze.*]

Ah. Fever. Excuse me.

[*He blows his nose.*]

I've caught a cold. A germ. In my eyes. It was this morning. In my eyes. My eyes.

[*Pause. He falls to the floor.*]

Not that I had any difficulty in seeing you, no, no, it was not so much my sight, my sight is excellent—in winter I run about with nothing on but a pair of polo shorts—no, it was not so much any deficiency in my sight as the airs between me and my object—don't weep—the change of air, the currents obtaining in the space between me and my object, the shades they make, the shapes they take, the quivering, the eternal quivering—please stop crying—nothing to do with heat-haze. Sometimes, of course, I would take shelter, shelter to compose myself. Yes, I would seek a tree, a cranny of bushes, erect my canopy and so make shelter. And rest. [*Low murmur.*] And then I no longer heard the wind or saw the sun. Nothing entered, nothing left my nook. I lay on my side in my polo shorts, my fingers lightly in contact with the blades of grass, the earthflowers, the petals of the earthflowers flaking, lying on my palm, the underside of all the great foliage dark, above me, but it is only afterwards I say the foliage was dark, the petals flaking, then I said nothing, I remarked nothing, things happened upon me, then in my times of shelter, the shades, the petals, carried themselves, carried their bodies upon me, and nothing entered my nook, nothing left it.

[*Pause.*]

But then, the time came. I saw the wind. I saw the wind, swirling, and the dust at my back gate, lifting, and the long grass, scything together . . . [*Slowly, in horror.*] You *are* laughing. You're laughing. Your face. Your body. [*Overwhelming nausea and horror.*] Rocking . . . gasping . . . rocking . . . shaking . . . rocking . . . heaving . . . rocking . . . You're laughing at me! Aaaaahhhh!

[*The* MATCHSELLER *rises. Silence.*]

You look younger. You look extraordinarily . . . youthful.

[*Pause.*]

You want to examine the garden? It must be very bright, in the moonlight. [*Becoming weaker.*] I would like to join you . . . explain . . . show you . . . the garden . . . explain . . . The plants . . . where I run . . . my track . . . in training . . . I was number one sprinter at Howells . . . when a stripling . . . no more than a stripling . . . licked . . . men twice my strength . . . when a stripling . . . like yourself.

[*Pause.*]

[*Flatly.*] The pool must be glistening. In the moonlight. And the lawn. I remember it well. The cliff. The sea. The three-masted schooner.

[*Pause.*]

[*With great, final effort—a whisper.*] Who are you?

FLORA [*off*]: Barnabas?

[*Pause.*]

[*She enters.*]

Ah, Barnabas. Everything is ready.

[*Pause.*]

I want to show you my garden, your garden. You must see my japonica, my convolvulus . . . my honeysuckle, my clematis.

[*Pause.*]

The summer is coming. I've put up your canopy for you. You can lunch in the garden, by the pool. I've polished the whole house for you.

[*Pause.*]

Take my hand.

[*Pause. The* MATCHSELLER *goes over to her.*]

Yes. Oh, wait a moment.

[*Pause.*]

Edward. Here is your tray.

She crosses to EDWARD *with the tray of matches, and puts it in his hands. Then she and the* MATCHSELLER *start to go out as the curtain falls slowly.*

POETRY

When William Butler Yeats began to compile *The Oxford Book of Modern Verse* (1936) he was faced with a difficult question. What poem should be the first in the anthology? Which selection would indicate most fully where, in his view, modern poetry really began? Finally Yeats settled upon the following:

> She is older than the rocks among which she sits;
> Like the Vampire,
> She has been dead many times,
> And learned the secrets of the grave;
> And has been a diver in deep seas,
> And keeps their fallen day about her;
> And trafficked for strange webs with Eastern merchants;
> And, as Leda,
> Was the mother of Helen of Troy,
> And, as Saint Anne,
> Was the mother of Mary;
> And all this has been to her but as the sound of lyres and flutes,
> And lives
> Only in the delicacy
> With which it has moulded the changing lineaments,
> And tinged the eyelids and the hands.

The passage is from Walter Pater's description of the Mona Lisa in *The Renaissance* (1873); but Yeats set up Pater's lyrical prose as if it were free verse in order to show "its revolutionary importance." With its mesmeric rhythms and symbolic suggestiveness, Pater's reverie over the

Mona Lisa (as recast by Yeats) reads much like one of Yeats's own mood poems of the 1890s. In his essay on Leonardo Da Vinci, Pater calls the Mona Lisa "the symbol of the modern idea," and for Yeats the "modern idea" was clearly international in scope. According to Yeats, modern poetry in English began when a native British aestheticism and an imported French symbolism were brought into alignment, and it was developed by poets from all the English-speaking countries, especially Ireland and the United States.

In contrast to Yeats's *Oxford Book of Modern Verse,* Philip Larkin's *Oxford Book of 20th Century English Verse* (1973) opens with a charming sonnet by the minor late-Victorian poet Wilfrid Scawen Blunt:

> I see you, Juliet, still, with your straw hat
> Loaded with vines, and with your dear pale face,
> On which those thirty years so lightly sat,
> And the white outline of your muslin dress.
> You wore a little *fichu* trimmed with lace
> And crossed in front, as was the fashion then,
> Bound at your waist with a broad band or sash,
> All white and fresh and virginally plain.
> There was a sound of shouting far away
> Down in the valley, as they called to us,
> And you, with hands clasped seeming still to pray
> Patience of fate, stood listening to me thus
> With heaving bosom. There a rose lay curled.
> It was the reddest rose in all the world.

To begin in this way is to emphasize the conventional and native strains in twentieth-century English poetry, its continuities with the past rather than its revolutionary nature. The word *modern,* with its suggestion of a European movement in all the arts, has even disappeared from the title, and Larkin cautiously defines his subject as "verse written in English by writers born in these islands (or resident here for an appreciable time) who were alive during the twentieth century and during it made or added to their reputations." These are minimal claims which contrast sharply with the grand sweep of Yeats's introduction to his anthology. This deliberate provinciality is, of course, partly a result of Larkin's own "little England" attitude, his conscious revolt against the large claims for poetry made by such "moderns" as Yeats and Ezra Pound. But it also reflects a real division between English and American poetry which developed in the generation that came after W. H. Auden. The coalition of English, American, and Irish writers we think of when we speak of "modern" poetry dominated the period between the two World Wars, but after World War II it gave way to more diverse and local concerns, so that we find it difficult to generalize about the recent history of either British or American poetry. Probably the dominant influence in recent American poetry has been the later work of William Carlos Williams, who in his early career was partially eclipsed by the more glamorous reputations of Pound and Eliot (see Williams' "Essay on *Leaves of Grass"* in the Essay section). Younger poets have looked to him rather than to the expatriate "moderns" for inspiration, admiring both his liberated verse-forms and his dedication to local experience. On the British side, many poets of Philip Larkin's generation turned to Thomas Hardy rather than Yeats or Pound or Eliot, admiring his emotional candor and finding in him a link with the great English poets of the eighteenth and nineteenth centuries who transformed local landscapes into structures of feeling. There are, of course, many exceptions to this simplified scheme. Ted Hughes and other younger British poets have gone to school to the American confessional poets of the 1950s and 1960s, while some younger American poets have emulated the understatement of Philip Larkin. In this scheme W. H. Auden, the British poet who became an American citizen, plays a fitting transitional role. Both Eliot and Hardy were his early masters, and his poetry combines the native British landscape tradition with the cosmopolitan allusiveness of the great "moderns."

An alternate model for the development of twentieth-century poetry in England and America would stress the perpetual struggle between a poetic which seeks to control emotion through formal restraints and a poetic which seeks to liberate emotion through looser and more expressive verse-forms. T. S. Eliot would be the type of the formal poet, D. H. Lawrence the type of the expressive, and the central critical texts would be Eliot's "Tradition and the Individual Talent" (1919; reprinted in the Essay section) and Lawrence's "Poetry of the Present" (1918; the introduction to the American edition of his *New Poems*). Eliot emphasizes the power of tradition and calls for a recognition of the continuities between past and present. Lawrence rejects the voices of both past and future, calling for a poetry of the present moment, the flux. In contrast to the poetry of the past, with its finality and symmetry, Lawrence believes "there is another kind of poetry: the poetry of that which is at hand: the immediate present."

> In the immediate present there is no perfection, no consummation, nothing finished. The strands are all flying, quivering, intermingling into the web, the waters are shaking the moon. There is no round, consummate moon on the face of running water, nor on the face of the unfinished tide. There are no gems of the living plasm. The living plasm vibrates unspeakably, it inhales the future, it exhales the past, it is the quick of both, and yet it is neither. There is no plasmic finality, nothing crystal, permanent. If we try to fix the living tissue, as the biologists fix it with formation, we have only a hardened bit of the past, the bygone life under our observation.

In Eliot's view, the traditional forms of poetry are means for changing private emotions into public feelings, the substance of art. For Lawrence, form must follow emotion and be shaped by its fluid nature. The differences between these two views are clearly exposed in the debate over "free verse." For Eliot and Pound, free verse (as in Eliot's "The Love Song of J. Alfred Prufrock" or Pound's "Portrait d'une Femme") always had an underlying traditional rhythm. It was a device they used to free themselves from the dead forms of late Victorian poetry, and when that liberation had been accomplished they returned to stricter patterns. Poems such as Eliot's "Sweeney Among the Nightingales" and Pound's "Medallion" were, in part, deliberate attempts to counteract the informality and loose technique of so much popular free verse. As Eliot said in 1917, there is obviously an escape from rhyme but "there is no escape from metre; there is only mastery."

For Lawrence, on the other hand, free verse was not a technical method but a way of life, almost a metaphysical idea. Traditional forms emphasize continuity with the past, while "in free verse we look for the insurgent naked throb of the instant moment. . . . free verse has its own *nature,* it is neither star nor pearl, but instantaneous like plasm."

> Much has been written about free verse. But all that can be said, first and last, is that free verse is, or should be, direct utterance from the instant, whole man. It is the soul and the mind and body surging at once, nothing left out. They speak all together.
>
> (From "Poetry of the Present")

So one way to view the history of poetry in this century is to see it as a long debate, sometimes with acrimonious exchanges, sometimes with accommodations, between two poetics that we might label "formalist" and "expressive."

These models for the development of twentieth-century poetry can be supported by the following selections, but so can many others. Within the space available we have tried to include poems which will illustrate different versions of the history of modern poetry and which are worthy in themselves of intensive study. The poets are, with two exceptions, presented in the order of their birth dates. The exceptions are Gerard Manley Hopkins and Emily Dickinson, since neither of them had a contemporary reputation: their poems are introduced at that point in literary history (c. 1918) when they became well known and exercised a decisive influence on other poets. An attempt has been made to represent the range in style and subject-matter of the major poets, but no effort has been made to preserve chronological balance within such brief selections. The policy throughout has been to reprint entire poems, rather than excerpts: thus there are no passages from *Four Quartets* or *Paterson* or Wallace Stevens' long poems. Wherever possible poems have been chosen that reinforce or comment upon other poems. Yeats's "Easter 1916" provides the essential background for Thomas Kinsella's "A Country Walk"; Auden's "Musée des Beaux Arts" and Williams' "Landscape with the Fall of Icarus" are two different treatments of the same Brueghel painting; Allen Tate's "Ode to the Confederate Dead" is counterpointed by Robert Lowell's "For the Union Dead"; Ted Hughes's "The Horses" may be interestingly contrasted with Philip Larkin's "At Grass" to show the differences between "expressive" and "formalist" poetry; and the "Portrait of a Lady" poems by Eliot, Pound, and Williams are included for comparison. These and many more interactions between poems should provide the basis for lively discussion.

The poems have been lightly annotated wherever they contain quotations or allusions which are not easily found in the standard reference works.

Thomas Hardy (1840–1928)

Thomas Hardy was born in Upper Bockhampton, Dorsetshire, the son of a builder and master mason. After leaving school he worked as an architect's apprentice for six years, then turned definitely to writing in the years after 1862. His most impressive early work was in poetry, but after 1870 he devoted twenty-five years of his life to the writing of fiction. Among his major novels are *The Return of the Native* (1878), *The Mayor of Casterbridge* (1886), *Tess of the D'Urbervilles* (1891), and *Jude the Obscure* (1895). In his fiction Hardy used the language and customs of his native southwest England, creating an imaginary "Wessex" which rivals in power and completeness William Faulkner's Yoknapatawpha County. In his best novels Hardy goes far beyond regionalism and manages to endow his local scenes with an almost mythological energy.

Hardy's pessimism and his honest attempts to portray sexual matters often offended the Victorian audience, and after the outraged reception of *Jude the Obscure* he returned to poetry. *Wessex Poems* was published in 1898, followed oy a series of volumes which culminated in *Winter Words in Various Moods and Metres* (1928). Hardy's finest achievements are his lyric poems, but between 1903 and 1908 he published *The Dynasts,* an epic dramatic poem about the Napoleonic Wars which displays many of his gifts as a novelist. Hardy's first wife, whom he met in 1870, died in 1912, and although Hardy had been estranged from her for many years her death was the occasion for his most moving sequence of poems, the elegies of 1912–13 which include "The Voice." In 1914 Hardy remarried, and his second wife—Florence Emily Hardy—completed the standard biography which Hardy had drafted during his last years. After his death on January 11, 1928, Hardy's ashes were placed in Westminster Abbey, but his heart was buried in the church at Stinsford, near his birthplace.

THE DARKLING THRUSH

I leant upon a coppice gate
    When Frost was spectre-gray,
And Winter's dregs made desolate
    The weakening eye of day.
The tangled bine-stems scored the sky
    Like strings of broken lyres,
And all mankind that haunted nigh
    Had sought their household fires.

The land's sharp features seemed to be
    The Century's corpse[1] outleant,
His crypt the cloudy canopy,
    The wind his death-lament.
The ancient pulse of germ and birth
    Was shrunken hard and dry,
And every spirit upon earth
    Seemed fervourless as I.

At once a voice arose among
    The bleak twigs overhead
In a full-hearted evensong
    Of joy illimited;
An aged thrush, frail, gaunt, and small,
    In blast-beruffled plume,
Had chosen thus to fling his soul
    Upon the growing gloom.

[1] The poem was written in the last days of the nineteenth century.

So little cause for carolings
Of such ecstatic sound
Was written on terrestrial things
Afar or nigh around,
That I could think there trembled through
His happy good-night air
Some blessed Hope, whereof he knew
And I was unaware.

CHANNEL FIRING[2]

That night your great guns, unawares,
Shook all our coffins as we lay,
And broke the chancel window-squares,
We thought it was the Judgment-day

And sat upright. While drearisome
Arose the howl of wakened hounds:
The mouse let fall the altar-crumb,
The worms drew back into the mounds,

The glebe cow drooled. Till God called, "No;
It's gunnery practice out at sea
Just as before you went below;
The world is as it used to be:

"All nations striving strong to make
Red war yet redder. Mad as hatters
They do no more for Christés sake
Than you who are helpless in such matters.

"That this is not the judgment-hour
For some of them's a blessed thing,
For if it were they'd have to scour
Hell's floor for so much threatening. . . .

"Ha, ha. It will be warmer when
I blow the trumpet (if indeed
I ever do; for you are men,
And rest eternal sorely need)."

So down we lay again. "I wonder,
Will the world ever saner be,"
Said one, "than when He sent us under
In our indifferent century!"

And many a skeleton shook his head.
"Instead of preaching forty year,"

[2] The setting for the poem is gunnery practice in the English Channel, just before the outbreak of World War I.

My neighbour Parson Thirdly said,
"I wish I had stuck to pipes and beer."

Again the guns disturbed the hour,
Roaring their readiness to avenge,
As far inland as Stourton Tower,
And Camelot, and starlit Stonehenge.[3]

THE VOICE

Woman much missed, how you call to me, call to me,
Saying that now you are not as you were
When you had changed from the one who was all to
me,
But as at first, when our day was fair.

Can it be you that I hear? Let me view you, then,
Standing as when I drew near to the town
Where you would wait for me: yes, as I knew you then,
Even to the original air-blue gown!

Or is it only the breeze, in its listlessness
Travelling across the wet mead to me here,
You being ever dissolved to wan wistlessness,
Heard no more again far or near?

Thus I; faltering forward,
Leaves around me falling,
Wind oozing thin through the thorn from norward,
And the woman calling.

IN TIME OF "THE BREAKING OF NATIONS"[4]

I

Only a man harrowing clods
In a slow silent walk
With an old horse that stumbles and nods
Half asleep as they stalk.

[3] Stourton Tower was built to commemorate King Alfred's victory over the Danes in the ninth century; Camelot was the legendary home of King Arthur; Stonehenge is the famous site of prehistoric megaliths. All are located in the south of England, and the movement of the gunfire through space is also a movement through time into the distant past.

[4] Jeremiah 51:20. "Thou art my battle axe and weapons of war: for with thee will I break in pieces the nations, and with thee will I destroy kingdoms." Written during the first World War, this poem incorporates an earlier experience that Hardy had during the Franco-Prussian War of 1870.

II

Only thin smoke without flame
  From the heaps of couch-grass;
Yet this will go onward the same
  Though Dynasties pass.

III

Yonder a maid and her wight
  Come whispering by:
War's annals will fade into night
  Ere their story die.

SNOW IN THE SUBURBS

Every branch big with it,
Bent every twig with it;
Every fork like a white web-foot;
Every street and pavement mute:
Some flakes have lost their way, and grope back
  upward, when
Meeting those meandering down they turn and
  descend again.
The palings are glued together like a wall,
And there is no waft of wind with the fleecy fall.

A sparrow enters the tree,
Whereon immediately
A snow-lump thrice his own slight size
Descends on him and showers his head and eyes,
And overturns him,
And near inurns him,
And lights on a nether twig, when its brush
Starts off a volley of other lodging lumps with a rush.

The steps are a blanched slope,
Up which, with feeble hope,
A black cat comes, wide-eyed and thin;
And we take him in.

A. E. Housman (1859–1936)

Born in Worcestershire, Alfred Edward Housman was educated at the local schools and at St. John's College, Oxford. At Oxford he failed to obtain an Honors degree, and this failure brought to the surface a melancholy strain which had previously been masked by his open and lively behavior. After leaving Oxford Housman worked in the Government Patent Office for ten years and then was appointed Professor of Latin at University College, London. In 1911 he became Professor of Latin at Trinity College, Cambridge, where he spent the rest of his life. Housman was one of the greatest classical scholars of his time, producing definitive work as an editor and textual critic. His first volume of poetry, *A Shropshire Lad,* was published in 1896. *Last Poems* (a title with characteristic irony) appeared in 1922, and the posthumous *More Poems* in 1936. His lectures on the art of poetry, *The Name and Nature of Poetry,* were published in 1933. Housman was a fastidious worker, and his poems combine the exactitude of a scholar with the intense feelings of a lyric poet. His range of tone and subject-matter was deliberately limited, but within that range Housman maintained total control, transmuting personal anxieties into impersonal and traditional forms.

LOVELIEST OF TREES

Loveliest of trees, the cherry now
Is hung with bloom along the bough,
And stands about the woodland ride
Wearing white for Eastertide.

Now, of my threescore years and ten,
Twenty will not come again,

And take from seventy springs a score,
It only leaves me fifty more.

And since to look at things in bloom
Fifty springs are little room,
About the woodlands I will go
To see the cherry hung with snow.

WHEN I WAS ONE-AND-TWENTY

When I was one-and-twenty
  I heard a wise man say,
'Give crowns and pounds and guineas
  But not your heart away;
Give pearls away and rubies
  But keep your fancy free.'
But I was one-and-twenty,
  No use to talk to me.

When I was one-and-twenty
  I heard him say again,
'The heart out of the bosom
  Was never given in vain;
'Tis paid with sighs a plenty
  And sold for endless rue.'
And I am two and-twenty,
  And oh, 'tis true, 'tis true.

TO AN ATHLETE DYING YOUNG

The time you won your town the race
We chaired you through the market-place;
Man and boy stood cheering by,
And home we brought you shoulder-high.

To-day, the road all runners come,
Shoulder-high we bring you home,
And set you at your threshold down,
Townsman of a stiller town.

Smart lad, to slip betimes away
From fields where glory does not stay
And early though the laurel grows
It withers quicker than the rose.

Eyes the shady night has shut
Cannot see the record cut,
And silence sounds no worse than cheers
After earth has stopped the ears:

Now you will not swell the rout
Of lads that wore their honours out,
Runners whom renown outran
And the name died before the man.

So set, before its echoes fade,
The fleet foot on the sill of shade,
And hold to the low lintel up
The still-defended challenge-cup.

And round that early-laurelled head
Will flock to gaze the strengthless dead
And find unwithered on its curls
The garland briefer than a girl's.

WITH RUE MY HEART IS LADEN

With rue my heart is laden
  For golden friends I had,
For many a rose-lipt maiden
  And many a lightfoot lad.

By brooks too broad for leaping
  The lightfoot boys are laid;
The rose-lipt girls are sleeping
  In fields where roses fade.

THE CHESTNUT CASTS HIS FLAMBEAUX

The chestnut casts his flambeaux, and the flowers
  Stream from the hawthorn on the wind away,
The doors clap to, the pane is blind with showers.
  Pass me the can, lad; there's an end of May.

There's one spoilt spring to scant our mortal lot,
  One season ruined of our little store.
May will be fine next year as like as not:
  Oh ay, but then we shall be twenty-four.

We for a certainty are not the first
  Have sat in taverns while the tempest hurled
Their hopeful plans to emptiness, and cursed
  Whatever brute and blackguard made the world.

It is in truth iniquity on high
  To cheat our sentenced souls of aught they crave,
And mar the merriment as you and I
  Fare on our long fool's-errand to the grave.

Iniquity it is; but pass the can.
  My lad, no pair of kings our mothers bore;
Our only portion is the estate of man:
  We want the moon, but we shall get no more.

If here to-day the cloud of thunder lours
  To-morrow it will hie on far behests;
The flesh will grieve on other bones than ours
  Soon, and the soul will mourn in other breasts.

The troubles of our proud and angry dust
  Are from eternity, and shall not fail.
Bear them we can, and if we can we must.
  Shoulder the sky, my lad, and drink your ale.

W. B. Yeats (1865–1939)

William Butler Yeats was born in Dublin, the son of a lawyer who eventually became a well-known painter. He was descended from a long line of Anglo-Irish Protestants, and in his later work he exalted this heritage, holding up the eighteenth-century Anglo-Irish world of Jonathan Swift, Edmund Burke, and Bishop Berkeley as a model for Ireland's future. Yeats spent much of his youth in London, but his summer holidays at Sligo, in the west of Ireland, had the most profound impact on his imagination (see "The Lake Isle of Innisfree"). When Yeats was fifteen the family returned to Dublin, where he entered art school and began to write lyric poetry. He early developed an interest in magic and the occult which was to become a lifelong obsession and a frequent support for his art.

Yeats's early works appeared in *The Wanderings of Oisin and Other Poems* (1889), a volume which shows his affinity with Pre-Raphaelite art. In the same year he met Maud Gonne, an Irish beauty devoted to the cause of Irish political freedom, and fell deeply in love with her. His passion for Maud Gonne dominated the next thirty years of his life, and many of his most moving poems, such as "No Second Troy," were written with her in mind. During the 1890s Yeats travelled between London and Dublin, his art vacillating between an interest in Irish legend and a fascination with the symbolic modes of the French and English "decadents." This phase of Yeats's poetic life culminated in *The Wind Among the Reeds* (1899), but even before the book appeared there was evidence of radical changes in Yeats's art. In 1897 he first visited Coole Park, the Galway home of the Irish writer and folklorist Lady Gregory (as he returned to Coole Park each summer it became an emblem of the grace and ceremony threatened by the modern world). Through Lady Gregory, Yeats became interested in popular drama and the founding of a National Theatre. As the new century opened he turned away from the *fin de siècle* mood of the 1890s and became a public figure, meanwhile seeking to infuse his art with new energy and precision. In the plays and poems of the years 1900–14 he tried to cast off the vague symbolism and langorous rhythms of his earlier work, enlarging the range of his poetry to include public affairs. The marriage of Maud Gonne to Major John MacBride in 1903 had increased his sense of personal isolation and frustration, and this was intensified by the many public controversies (such as that over John Millington Synge's *Playboy of the Western World*) which convinced Yeats that the Irish middle class could not be transfigured through national art, as he had once hoped. The poems of *Responsibilities* (1914) reflect this bitterness and discouragement, but in the years between 1914 and 1920 several events changed Yeats's life and art. The Easter Rebellion of 1916 and its tragic aftermath (see "Easter 1916") gave him a glimpse of heroic possibilities that he had thought lost to Ireland. At the same time, a revived interest in the occult led to his construction of that visionary system which gives strength and coherence to so many of the later poems, such as "Leda and the Swan" (in 1925 Yeats set forth his system for interpreting art and history in *A Vision*). Most important of all, his marriage in 1917 to George Hyde-Lees, and the birth of a daughter in 1919 and a son in 1921, gave Yeats new energy and purpose. His poetry stretching from *The Wild Swans at Coole* (1917) to *The Winding Stair* (1933) is among the greatest in the language, marked by dramatic intensity and a spectacular range of verse-forms. Perhaps the most important volume is *The Tower* (1928), named after the ruined Norman tower which Yeats had renovated and made his home. Its tone is set by the opening poem, "Sailing to Byzantium," and the entire volume balances the humiliations of old age against the glories of art and philosophy.

Yeats was desperately ill in the late 1920s, and when he recovered he remade his art once again, trying to attain in some of his last poems the simple, direct truth of the ballad or the nursery rhyme. In his last years he took an apocalyptic view of the social and political violence which surrounded him, but he never lost the gaiety and historical perspective that were part of his tragic vision and which are embodied in such poems as "Lapis Lazuli." The years since Yeats's death have confirmed the judgment made in 1940 by T. S. Eliot: "the greatest poet of our time—certainly the greatest in this language, and so far as I am able to judge, in any language."

THE LAKE ISLE OF INNISFREE[1]

I will arise and go now, and go to Innisfree,
And a small cabin build there, of clay and wattles made:
Nine bean-rows will I have there, a hive for the honey-bee,
And live alone in the bee-loud glade.

And I shall have some peace there, for peace comes dropping slow,
Dropping from the veils of the morning to where the cricket sings;
There midnight's all a glimmer, and noon a purple glow,
And evening full of the linnet's wings.

I will arise and go now, for always night and day
I hear lake water lapping with low sounds by the shore;
While I stand on the roadway, or on the pavements grey,
I hear it in the deep heart's core.

THE SORROW OF LOVE

The brawling of a sparrow in the eaves,
The brilliant moon and all the milky sky,
And all that famous harmony of leaves,
Had blotted out man's image and his cry.

A girl arose that had red mournful lips
And seemed the greatness of the world in tears,
Doomed like Odysseus and the labouring ships
And proud as Priam murdered with his peers;

Arose, and on the instant clamorous eaves,
A climbing moon upon an empty sky,
And all that lamentation of the leaves,
Could but compose man's image and his cry.

NO SECOND TROY

Why should I blame her that she filled my days
With misery, or that she would of late
Have taught to ignorant men most violent ways,
Or hurled the little streets upon the great,
Had they but courage equal to desire?
What could have made her peaceful with a mind
That nobleness made simple as a fire,
With beauty like a tightened bow, a kind
That is not natural in an age like this,
Being high and solitary and most stern?
Why, what could she have done, being what she is?
Was there another Troy for her to burn?

THE WILD SWANS AT COOLE[2]

The trees are in their autumn beauty,
The woodland paths are dry,

[1] Innisfree is an island near Sligo, in the west of Ireland, where Yeats spent some of the happiest times of his youth. The poem was written in London, and the first line echoes the parable of the prodigal son ("I will arise and go to my father . . .", Luke 15:18).

[2] Coole Park, the estate of Yeats's friend and patron Lady Gregory, became for him an emblem of ceremony and aristocratic support for the arts. Yeats first visited Coole in 1897, nineteen years before the poem was written.

Under the October twilight the water
Mirrors a still sky;
Upon the brimming water among the stones
Are nine-and-fifty swans.

The nineteenth autumn has come upon me
Since I first made my count;
I saw, before I had well finished,
All suddenly mount
And scatter wheeling in great broken rings
Upon their clamorous wings.

I have looked upon those brilliant creatures,
And now my heart is sore.
All's changed since I, hearing at twilight,
The first time on this shore,
The bell-beat of their wings above my head,
Trod with a lighter tread.

Unwearied still, lover by lover,
They paddle in the cold
Companionable streams or climb the air;
Their hearts have not grown old;
Passion or conquest, wander where they will,
Attend upon them still.

But now they drift on the still water,
Mysterious, beautiful;
Among what rushes will they build,
By what lake's edge or pool
Delight men's eyes when I awake some day
To find they have flown away?

EASTER 1916[3]

I have met them at close of day
Coming with vivid faces
From counter or desk among grey
Eighteenth-century houses.
I have passed with a nod of the head
Or polite meaningless words,
Or have lingered awhile and said
Polite meaningless words,
And thought before I had done
Of a mocking tale or a gibe
To please a companion
Around the fire at the club,
Being certain that they and I
But lived where motley is worn:
All changed, changed utterly:
A terrible beauty is born.

That woman's[4] days were spent
In ignorant good-will,
Her nights in argument
Until her voice grew shrill.
What voice more sweet than hers
When, young and beautiful,
She rode to harriers?
This man[5] had kept a school
And rode our wingèd horse;
This other[6] his helper and friend
Was coming into his force;
He might have won fame in the end,
So sensitive his nature seemed,
So daring and sweet his thought.
This other man[7] I had dreamed
A drunken, vainglorious lout.
He had done most bitter wrong
To some who are near my heart,
Yet I number him in the song;
He, too, has resigned his part
In the casual comedy;
He, too, has been changed in his turn,
Transformed utterly:
A terrible beauty is born.

Hearts with one purpose alone
Through summer and winter seem
Enchanted to a stone
To trouble the living stream.
The horse that comes from the road,
The rider, the birds that range
From cloud to tumbling cloud,
Minute by minute they change;
A shadow of cloud on the stream
Changes minute by minute;
A horse-hoof slides on the brim,

[3] The Easter Rebellion of 1916, when Irish republicans seized central Dublin and held it for several days against the English, was a "rebirth" which both fascinated and disturbed Yeats. It brought forth a "terrible beauty," both in the sense of a sublime heroism and a waste (perhaps futile) of promising lives. Some of the leaders of the rebellion were executed, and others imprisoned.

[4] Constance Gore-Booth (later Constance Markiewicz), one of the leaders of the rebellion, whose death sentence was later commuted. Yeats had first met her and her sister in 1894: "Two girls in silk kimonos, both / Beautiful, one a gazelle" (see Yeats's poem "In Memory of Eva Gore-Booth and Con Markiewicz").

[5] Patrick Pearse, schoolmaster and poet, one of the crucial figures in the Easter Rising.

[6] Thomas MacDonagh, poet and playwright.

[7] Major John MacBride, the husband of Maud Gonne. Yeats had loved Maud Gonne since his youth and idealized her in many of his poems. Married in 1903, Maud Gonne and Major MacBride later separated; Yeats felt that MacBride had misunderstood and mistreated her.

And a horse plashes within it;
The long-legged moor-hens dive,
And hens to moor-cocks call;
Minute by minute they live:
The stone's in the midst of all.

Too long a sacrifice
Can make a stone of the heart.
O when may it suffice?
That is Heaven's part, our part
To murmur name upon name,
As a mother names her child
When sleep at last has come
On limbs that had run wild.
What is it but nightfall?
No, no, not night but death;
Was it needless death after all?
For England may keep faith
For all that is done and said.
We know their dream; enough
To know they dreamed and are dead;
And what if excess of love
Bewildered them till they died?
I write it out in a verse—
MacDonagh and MacBride
And Connolly[8] and Pearse
Now and in time to be,
Wherever green is worn,
Are changed, changed utterly:
A terrible beauty is born.

LEDA AND THE SWAN[9]

A sudden blow: the great wings beating still
Above the staggering girl, her thighs caressed
By the dark webs, her nape caught in his bill,
He holds her helpless breast upon his breast.

How can those terrified vague fingers push
The feathered glory from her loosening thighs?
And how can body, laid in that white rush,
But feel the strange heart beating where it lies?

A shudder in the loins engenders there
The broken wall, the burning roof and tower
And Agamemnon dead.
Being so caught up,
So mastered by the brute blood of the air,
Did she put on his knowledge with his power
Before the indifferent beak could let her drop?

SAILING TO BYZANTIUM[10]

I

That is no country for old men. The young
In one another's arms, birds in the trees
—Those dying generations—at their song,
The salmon-falls, the mackerel-crowded seas,
Fish, flesh, or fowl, commend all summer long
Whatever is begotten, born, and dies.
Caught in that sensual music all neglect
Monuments of unaging intellect.

II

An aged man is but a paltry thing,
A tattered coat upon a stick, unless
Soul clap its hands and sing, and louder sing
For every tatter in its mortal dress,
Nor is there singing school but studying
Monuments of its own magnificence;
And therefore I have sailed the seas and come
To the holy city of Byzantium.

III

O sages standing in God's holy fire
As in the gold mosaic of a wall,
Come from the holy fire, perne in a gyre,
And be the singing-masters of my soul.
Consume my heart away; sick with desire
And fastened to a dying animal
It knows not what it is; and gather me
Into the artifice of eternity.

[8] James Connolly, union organizer and ardent republican, who organized the Citizen Army and commanded the captured Post Office during the Easter Rebellion.

[9] In his cyclic view of history, Yeats imagined the ancient world (a cycle of 2000 years) as having been initiated by the rape of Leda, when Zeus took the form of a swan. Out of this union came two eggs, one containing Castor and Pollux, the other Helen and Clytemnestra. Hence the Trojan War was conceived by Leda and Zeus, and Yeats is being mythologically accurate when he says: "A shudder in the loins engenders there / The broken wall, the burning roof and tower / And Agamemnon dead."

[10] Yeats imagined Byzantium (Constantinople) in its ancient glory as a place where spirit and matter were united, as in a perfect work of art, and where artisan, saint, and common man could work together to create a single image of perfection.

IV

Once out of nature I shall never take
My bodily form from any natural thing,
But such a form as Grecian goldsmiths make
Of hammered gold and gold enamelling
To keep a drowsy emperor awake;
Or set upon a golden bough to sing
To lords and ladies of Byzantium
Of what is past, or passing, or to come.

AMONG SCHOOL CHILDREN[11]

I

I walk through the long schoolroom questioning;
A kind old nun in a white hood replies;
The children learn to cipher and to sing,
To study reading-books and history,
To cut and sew, be neat in everything
In the best modern way—the children's eyes
In momentary wonder stare upon
A sixty-year-old smiling public man.

II

I dream of a Ledæan body, bent
Above a sinking fire, a tale that she
Told of a harsh reproof, or trivial event
That changed some childish day to tragedy—
Told, and it seemed that our two natures blent
Into a sphere from youthful sympathy,
Or else, to alter Plato's parable,
Into the yolk and white of the one shell.

III

And thinking of that fit of grief or rage
I look upon one child or t'other there
And wonder if she stood so at that age—
For even daughters of the swan can share
Something of every paddler's heritage—
And had that colour upon cheek or hair,
And thereupon my heart is driven wild:
She stands before me as a living child.

[11] While an Irish Senator in the 1920s Yeats occasionally visited schools and reported on their work.

IV

Her present image floats into the mind—
Did Quattrocento[12] finger fashion it
Hollow of cheek as though it drank the wind
And took a mess of shadows for its meat?
And I though never of Ledæan kind
Had pretty plumage once—enough of that,
Better to smile on all that smile, and show
There is a comfortable kind of old scarecrow.

V

What youthful mother, a shape upon her lap
Honey of generation had betrayed,
And that must sleep, shriek, struggle to escape
As recollection or the drug decide,
Would think her son, did she but see that shape
With sixty or more winters on its head,
A compensation for the pang of his birth,
Or the uncertainty of his setting forth?

VI

Plato thought nature but a spume that plays
Upon a ghostly paradigm of things;
Solider Aristotle played the taws
Upon the bottom of a king of kings;
World-famous golden-thighed Pythagoras[13]
Fingered upon a fiddle stick or strings
What a star sang and careless Muses heard:
Old clothes upon old sticks to scare a bird.

VII

Both nuns and mothers worship images,
But those the candles light are not as those
That animate a mother's reveries,
But keep a marble or a bronze repose.
And yet they too break hearts—O Presences
That passion, piety or affection knows,
And that all heavenly glory symbolise—
O self-born mockers of man's enterprise;

[12] The classic period of Italian painting, the fifteenth century.

[13] Plato's ideal forms, Aristotle's more practical theories of education (he was the tutor of Alexander the Great), and Pythagoras's mathematical theories of musical harmony, all are ideals compromised by the facts of mutability and old age.

VIII

Labour is blossoming or dancing where
The body is not bruised to pleasure soul,
Nor beauty born out of its own despair,
Nor blear-eyed wisdom out of midnight oil.
O chestnut-tree, great-rooted blossomer,
Are you the leaf, the blossom or the bole?
O body swayed to music, O brightening glance,
How can we know the dancer from the dance?

LAPIS LAZULI[14]

I have heard that hysterical women say
They are sick of the palette and fiddle-bow,
Of poets that are always gay,
For everybody knows or else should know
That if nothing drastic is done
Aeroplane and Zeppelin[15] will come out,
Pitch like King Billy[16] bomb-balls in
Until the town lie beaten flat.

All perform their tragic play,
There struts Hamlet, there is Lear,
That's Ophelia, that Cordelia;
Yet they, should the last scene be there,
The great stage curtain about to drop,
If worthy their prominent part in the play,
Do not break up their lines to weep.
They know that Hamlet and Lear are gay;
Gaiety transfiguring all that dread.
All men have aimed at, found and lost;
Black out; Heaven blazing into the head:
Tragedy wrought to its uttermost.
Though Hamlet rambles and Lear rages,
And all the drop-scenes drop at once
Upon a hundred thousand stages,
It cannot grow by an inch or an ounce.

On their own feet they came, or on shipboard,
Camel-back, horse-back, ass-back, mule-back,
Old civilisations put to the sword.
Then they and their wisdom went to rack:
No handiwork of Callimachus,[17]
Who handled marble as if it were bronze,
Made draperies that seemed to rise
When sea-wind swept the corner, stands;
His long lamp-chimney shaped like the stem
Of a slender palm, stood but a day;
All things fall and are built again,
And those that build them again are gay.

Two Chinamen, behind them a third,
Are carved in lapis lazuli,
Over them flies a long-legged bird,
A symbol of longevity;
The third, doubtless a serving-man,
Carries a musical instrument.

Every discoloration of the stone,
Every accidental crack or dent,
Seems a water-course or an avalanche,
Or lofty slope where it still snows
Though doubtless plum or cherry-branch
Sweetens the little half-way house
Those Chinamen climb towards, and I
Delight to imagine them seated there;
There, on the mountain and the sky,
On all the tragic scene they stare.
One asks for mournful melodies;
Accomplished fingers begin to play.
Their eyes mid many wrinkles, their eyes,
Their ancient, glittering eyes, are gay.

[14] The carving of lapis lazuli described at the end of the poem was given to Yeats in the 1930s. He said of it: "Ascetic, pupil, hard stone, eternal theme of the sensual east. The heroic cry in the midst of despair. But no, I am wrong, the east has its solutions always and therefore knows nothing of tragedy. It is we, not the east, that must raise the heroic cry."

[15] German dirigibles of the first World War.

[16] William III, who defeated James II at the Battle of the Boyne in 1690. Yeats is conflating the events of 1690 with those of 1914–18.

[17] Callimachus, Greek sculptor of the late fifth century B.C., reputed to be a master of elegance and elaboration. None of his works has survived.

Edwin Arlington Robinson (1869–1935)

Edwin Arlington Robinson was born in Maine and attended Harvard College, but financial difficulties forced him to leave after two years. He settled in New York where he suffered years of poverty and obscurity before his poetry became widely known. In 1905 President Theodore Roosevelt appointed him to a position in the Custom House which he held until 1910, when he was able to devote his full time to poetry. His early poems, found in the volumes from *The Children of the Night* (1897) to *The Man Against the Sky* (1916), are mainly dramatic lyrics in which traditional verse-forms are used to frame a realistic, contemporary diction. Many of these short dramatic poems characterize the inhabitants of an imaginary Maine village, Tilbury Town, which resembles Gardiner, Maine, where Robinson grew up. In the last years of his life Robinson turned to long blank-verse narratives on Arthurian subjects, although he continued to produce shorter works such as "Mr. Flood's Party." His *Collected Poems* (1921) was awarded a Pulitzer Prize, and he received two more Pulitzers in 1925 and 1928. His poetry had a deep impact on Robert Frost, who admired Robinson's mastery of "the old-fashioned way to be new."

MINIVER CHEEVY

Miniver Cheevy, child of scorn,
  Grew lean while he assailed the seasons;
He wept that he was ever born,
  And he had reasons.

Miniver loved the days of old
  When swords were bright and steeds were prancing;
The vision of a warrior bold
  Would set him dancing.

Miniver sighed for what was not,
  And dreamed, and rested from his labors;
He dreamed of Thebes and Camelot,
  And Priam's neighbors.[1]

Miniver mourned the ripe renown
  That made so many a name so fragrant;
He mourned Romance, now on the town,
  And Art, a vagrant.

[1] Reminders of Oedipus, King Arthur, and the fall of Troy.

Miniver loved the Medici,[2]
  Albeit he had never seen one;
He would have sinned incessantly
  Could he have been one.

Miniver cursed the commonplace
  And eyed a khaki suit with loathing;
He missed the mediæval grace
  Of iron clothing.

Miniver scorned the gold he sought,
  But sore annoyed was he without it;
Miniver thought, and thought, and thought,
  And thought about it.

Miniver Cheevy, born too late,
  Scratched his head and kept on thinking;
Miniver coughed, and called it fate,
  And kept on drinking.

[2] Italian bankers and statesmen of the Renaissance, patrons of the arts.

MR. FLOOD'S PARTY

Old Eben Flood, climbing alone one night
Over the hill between the town below
And the forsaken upland hermitage
That held as much as he should ever know
On earth again of home, paused warily.
The road was his with not a native near;
And Eben, having leisure, said aloud,
For no man else in Tilbury Town to hear:

"Well, Mr. Flood, we have the harvest moon
Again, and we may not have many more;
The bird is on the wing, the poet says,
And you and I have said it here before.
Drink to the bird." He raised up to the light
The jug that he had gone so far to fill,
And answered huskily: "Well, Mr. Flood,
Since you propose it, I believe I will."

Alone, as if enduring to the end
A valiant armor of scarred hopes outworn,
He stood there in the middle of the road
Like Roland's ghost winding a silent horn.[3]
Below him, in the town among the trees,
Where friends of other days had honored him,
A phantom salutation of the dead
Rang thinly till old Eben's eyes were dim.

Then, as a mother lays her sleeping child
Down tenderly, fearing it may awake,
He set the jug down slowly at his feet
With trembling care, knowing that most things break;
And only when assured that on firm earth
It stood, as the uncertain lives of men
Assuredly did not, he paced away,
And with his hand extended paused again:

"Well, Mr. Flood, we have not met like this
In a long time; and many a change has come
To both of us, I fear, since last it was
We had a drop together. Welcome home!"
Convivially returning with himself,
Again he raised the jug up to the light;
And with an acquiescent quaver said:
"Well, Mr. Flood, if you insist, I might.

"Only a very little, Mr. Flood—
For auld lang syne. No more, sir; that will do."
So, for the time, apparently it did,
And Eben evidently thought so too;
For soon amid the silver loneliness
Of night he lifted up his voice and sang,
Secure, with only two moons listening,
Until the whole harmonious landscape rang—

"For auld lang syne." The weary throat gave out,
The last word wavered, and the song was done.
He raised again the jug regretfully
And shook his head, and was again alone.
There was not much that was ahead of him,
And there was nothing in the town below—
Where strangers would have shut the many doors
That many friends had opened long ago.

[3] In the *Chanson de Roland,* a French medieval romance, Roland heroically refuses to blow his horn (a signal for help) until he is doomed to death.

Robert Frost (1874–1963)

Robert Lee Frost was born in San Francisco, California, on March 26, 1874. It seems only appropriate that this master of paradoxes who became the poet-laureate of rural New England should have been born in a city a continent away and named for a Confederate general. After the death of his father when Frost was eleven the family settled in New England, and he entered Dartmouth College in 1892 but stayed only a few months. For the next few years he taught school, tried his hand at farming, and wrote poetry on the side. Frost attended Harvard in 1897–99, but left without a degree and returned to farming and teaching. In 1912 he sold his farm at Derry, New Hampshire, and moved to England with his family. There he attracted the attention of other poets, notably Ezra Pound, and in 1913 his first collection of poetry, *A Boy's Will,* was published. It was followed in 1914 by *North of Boston,* and the two volumes secured Frost's reputation as a regional poet of universal appeal.

In 1915 Frost returned to the United States and became a farmer-poet, teaching frequently at Amherst, the University of Michigan, and the Bread Loaf School of English. Among his collections of poetry, *New Hampshire* (1923), *A Further Range* (1937), and *A Witness Tree* (1942) won Pulitzer Prizes. In his later years Frost became a national folk hero, creating a public image of serenity and canny wisdom which was often at variance with the darkness and isolation of his best poems. The climax to this phase of Frost's career came in 1961 when he was asked to read a poem at the inauguration of President John F. Kennedy.

AFTER APPLE-PICKING

My long two-pointed ladder's sticking through a tree
Toward heaven still,
And there's a barrel that I didn't fill
Beside it, and there may be two or three
Apples I didn't pick upon some bough.
But I am done with apple-picking now.
Essence of winter sleep is on the night,
The scent of apples: I am drowsing off.
I cannot rub the strangeness from my sight
I got from looking through a pane of glass
I skimmed this morning from the drinking trough
And held against the world of hoary grass.
It melted, and I let it fall and break.
But I was well
Upon my way to sleep before it fell,
And I could tell
What form my dreaming was about to take.
Magnified apples appear and disappear,
Stem end and blossom end,
And every fleck of russet showing clear.
My instep arch not only keeps the ache,
It keeps the pressure of a ladder-round.
I feel the ladder sway as the boughs bend.
And I keep hearing from the cellar bin
The rumbling sound
Of load on load of apples coming in.
For I have had too much
Of apple-picking: I am overtired
Of the great harvest I myself desired.
There were ten thousand thousand fruit to touch,
Cherish in hand, lift down, and not let fall.
For all
That struck the earth,
No matter if not bruised or spiked with stubble,
Went surely to the cider-apple heap
As of no worth.
One can see what will trouble
This sleep of mine, whatever sleep it is.
Were he not gone,
The woodchuck could say whether it's like his
Long sleep, as I describe its coming on,
Or just some human sleep.

MENDING WALL

Something there is that doesn't love a wall,
That sends the frozen-ground-swell under it
And spills the upper boulders in the sun,
And makes gaps even two can pass abreast.
The work of hunters is another thing:
I have come after them and made repair
Where they have left not one stone on a stone,
But they would have the rabbit out of hiding,
To please the yelping dogs. The gaps I mean,
No one has seen them made or heard them made,
But at spring mending-time we find them there.
I let my neighbor know beyond the hill;
And on a day we meet to walk the line
And set the wall between us once again.
We keep the wall between us as we go.
To each the boulders that have fallen to each.
And some are loaves and some so nearly balls
We have to use a spell to make them balance:
"Stay where you are until our backs are turned!"
We wear our fingers rough with handling them
Oh, just another kind of outdoor game,
One on a side. It comes to little more:
There where it is we do not need the wall:
He is all pine and I am apple orchard.
My apple trees will never get across
And eat the cones under his pines, I tell him.
He only says, "Good fences make good neighbors."
Spring is the mischief in me, and I wonder

If I could put a notion in his head:
"*Why* do they make good neighbors? Isn't it
Where there are cows? But here there are no cows.
Before I built a wall I'd ask to know
What I was walling in or walling out,
And to whom I was like to give offense.
Something there is that doesn't love a wall,
That wants it down." I could say "Elves" to him,
But it's not elves exactly, and I'd rather
He said it for himself. I see him there,
Bringing a stone grasped firmly by the top
In each hand, like an old-stone savage armed.
He moves in darkness as it seems to me,
Not of woods only and the shade of trees.
He will not go behind his father's saying,
And he likes having thought of it so well
He says again, "Good fences make good neighbors."

THE OVEN BIRD

There is a singer everyone has heard,
Loud, a mid-summer and a mid-wood bird,
Who makes the solid tree trunks sound again.
He says that leaves are old and that for flowers
Mid-summer is to spring as one to ten.
He says the early petal-fall is past,
When pear and cherry bloom went down in showers
On sunny days a moment overcast;
And comes that other fall we name the fall.
He says the highway dust is over all.
The bird would cease and be as other birds
But that he knows in singing not to sing.
The question that he frames in all but words
Is what to make of a diminished thing.

STOPPING BY WOODS ON A SNOWY EVENING

Whose woods these are I think I know.
His house is in the village, though;
He will not see me stopping here
To watch his woods fill up with snow.

My little horse must think it queer
To stop without a farmhouse near
Between the woods and frozen lake
The darkest evening of the year.

He gives his harness bells a shake
To ask if there is some mistake.
The only other sound's the sweep
Of easy wind and downy flake.

The woods are lovely, dark, and deep,
But I have promises to keep,
And miles to go before I sleep,
And miles to go before I sleep.

ACQUAINTED WITH THE NIGHT

I have been one acquainted with the night.
I have walked out in rain—and back in rain.
I have outwalked the furthest city light.

I have looked down the saddest city lane.
I have passed by the watchman on his beat
And dropped my eyes, unwilling to explain.

I have stood still and stopped the sound of feet
When far away an interrupted cry
Came over houses from another street,

But not to call me back or say good-bye;
And further still at an unearthly height,
One luminary clock against the sky

Proclaimed the time was neither wrong nor right.
I have been one acquainted with the night.

DESIGN

I found a dimpled spider, fat and white,
On a white heal-all,[1] holding up a moth
Like a white piece of rigid satin cloth—
Assorted characters of death and blight
Mixed ready to begin the morning right,
Like the ingredients of a witches' broth—
A snow-drop spider, a flower like a froth,
And dead wings carried like a paper kite.

What had that flower to do with being white,
The wayside blue and innocent heal-all?
What brought the kindred spider to that height,
Then steered the white moth thither in the night?
What but design of darkness to appall?—
If design govern in a thing so small.

[1] A plant believed to have healing properties, normally blue in color.

DIRECTIVE

Back out of all this now too much for us,
Back in a time made simple by the loss
Of detail, burned, dissolved, and broken off
Like graveyard marble sculpture in the weather,
There is a house that is no more a house
Upon a farm that is no more a farm
And in a town that is no more a town.
The road there, if you'll let a guide direct you
Who only has at heart your getting lost,
May seem as if it should have been a quarry—
Great monolithic knees the former town
Long since gave up pretense of keeping covered.
And there's a story in a book about it:
Besides the wear of iron wagon wheels
The ledges show lines ruled southeast-northwest,
The chisel work of an enormous Glacier
That braced his feet against the Arctic Pole.
You must not mind a certain coolness from him
Still said to haunt this side of Panther Mountain.
Nor need you mind the serial ordeal
Of being watched from forty cellar holes
As if by eye pairs out of forty firkins.
As for the woods' excitement over you
That sends light rustle rushes to their leaves,
Charge that to upstart inexperience.
Where were they all not twenty years ago?
They think too much of having shaded out
A few old pecker-fretted apple trees.
Make yourself up a cheering song of how
Someone's road home from work this once was,
Who may be just ahead of you on foot
Or creaking with a buggy load of grain.
The height of the adventure is the height
Of country where two village cultures faded
Into each other. Both of them are lost.
And if you're lost enough to find yourself
By now, pull in your ladder road behind you
And put a sign up CLOSED to all but me.
Then make yourself at home. The only field
Now left's no bigger than a harness gall.
First there's the children's house of make-believe,
Some shattered dishes underneath a pine,
The playthings in the playhouse of the children.
Weep for what little things could make them glad.
Then for the house that is no more a house,
But only a belilaced cellar hole,
Now slowly closing like a dent in dough.
This was no playhouse but a house in earnest.
Your destination and your destiny's
A brook that was the water of the house,
Cold as a spring as yet so near its source,
Too lofty and original to rage.
(We know the valley streams that when aroused
Will leave their tatters hung on barb and thorn.)
I have kept hidden in the instep arch
Of an old cedar at the waterside
A broken drinking goblet like the Grail
Under a spell so the wrong ones can't find it,
So can't get saved, as Saint Mark says they mustn't.[2]
(I stole the goblet from the children's playhouse.)
Here are your waters and your watering place.
Drink and be whole again beyond confusion.

[2] Mark 4:11—12. "And he [Jesus] said unto them, Unto you it is given to know the mystery of the kingdom of God: but unto them that are without, all these things are done in parables: That seeing they may see, and not perceive; and hearing they may hear, and not understand; lest at any time they should be converted, and their sins should be forgiven them."

Wallace Stevens (1879–1955)

Born in Reading, Pennsylvania, Wallace Stevens spent three years at Harvard and then, after a brief stint as a newspaper reporter in New York, took a law degree at the New York Law School. Stevens was a late-bloomer as a poet, and although he was intensely interested in the New York literary scene he always remained fastidiously aloof, pursuing his double career as public businessman and private poet. In 1916 he joined the legal staff of the Hartford

Accident and Indemnity Company and soon after moved to Hartford, Connecticut, where he remained until his death. His first major poems (including "Sunday Morning") were published in 1915, but it was not until 1923, when he was well over forty, that Stevens produced his first volume of poetry, *Harmonium.* After a silence of six years (1924–30), during which he consolidated his business career, Stevens returned to poetry and wrote the poems of *Ideas of Order* (1935) and *The Man with the Blue Guitar* (1937), where the gaudiness of many of the poems in *Harmonium* is replaced by a more sombre tone. During the 1930s Stevens sought to fashion a sustaining theory of poetry which found full expression in *Parts of a World* and *Notes toward a Supreme Fiction* (1942). In his last years he created a self-contained imaginative world in which the idea of poetry may take the place of religious belief (see "To an Old Philosopher in Rome"). *Transport to Summer* (1947) was followed by *The Auroras of Autumn* (1950) and *Collected Poems* (1954), which won the Pulitzer Prize. A collection of essays on the theory of poetry, *The Necessary Angel,* appeared in 1951, and after his death the uncollected poems and essays were published as *Opus Posthumous* (1957).

SUNDAY MORNING

I

Complacencies of the peignoir, and late
Coffee and oranges in a sunny chair,
And the green freedom of a cockatoo
Upon a rug mingle to dissipate
The holy hush of ancient sacrifice.
She dreams a little, and she feels the dark
Encroachment of that old catastrophe,
As a calm darkens among water-lights.
The pungent oranges and bright, green wings
Seem things in some procession of the dead,
Winding across wider water, without sound.
The day is like wide water, without sound,
Stilled for the passing of her dreaming feet
Over the seas, to silent Palestine,
Dominion of the blood and sepulchre.

II

Why should she give her bounty to the dead?
What is divinity if it can come
Only in silent shadows and in dreams?
Shall she not find in comforts of the sun,
In pungent fruit and bright, green wings, or else
In any balm or beauty of the earth,
Things to be cherished like the thought of heaven?
Divinity must live within herself:
Passions of rain, or moods in falling snow;
Grievings in loneliness, or unsubdued
Elations when the forest blooms; gusty
Emotions on wet roads on autumn nights;
All pleasures and all pains, remembering
The bough of summer and the winter branch.
These are the measures destined for her soul.

III

Jove in the clouds had his inhuman birth.
No mother suckled him, no sweet land gave
Large-mannered motions to his mythy mind
He moved among us, as a muttering king,
Magnificent, would move among his hinds,
Until our blood, commingling, virginal,
With heaven, brought such requital to desire
The very hinds discerned it, in a star.
Shall our blood fail? Or shall it come to be
The blood of paradise? And shall the earth
Seem all of paradise that we shall know?
The sky will be much friendlier then than now,
A part of labor and a part of pain,
And next in glory to enduring love,
Not this dividing and indifferent blue.

IV

She says, "I am content when wakened birds,
Before they fly, test the reality
Of misty fields, by their sweet questionings;
But when the birds are gone, and their warm fields
Return no more, where, then, is paradise?"
There is not any haunt of prophecy,
Nor any old chimera of the grave,
Neither the golden underground, nor isle
Melodious, where spirits gat them home,
Nor visionary south, nor cloudy palm
Remote on heaven's hill, that has endured

As April's green endures; or will endure
Like her remembrance of awakened birds,
Or her desire for June and evening, tipped
By the consummation of the swallow's wings.

V

She says, "But in contentment I still feel
The need of some imperishable bliss."
Death is the mother of beauty; hence from her,
Alone, shall come fulfilment to our dreams
And our desires. Although she strews the leaves
Of sure obliteration on our paths,
The path sick sorrow took, the many paths
Where triumph rang its brassy phrase, or love
Whispered a little out of tenderness,
She makes the willow shiver in the sun
For maidens who were wont to sit and gaze
Upon the grass, relinquished to their feet.
She causes boys to pile new plums and pears
On disregarded plate. The maidens taste
And stray impassioned in the littering leaves.

VI

Is there no change of death in paradise?
Does ripe fruit never fall? Or do the boughs
Hang always heavy in that perfect sky,
Unchanging, yet so like our perishing earth,
With rivers like our own that seek for seas
They never find, the same receding shores
That never touch with inarticulate pang?
Why set the pear upon those river-banks
Or spice the shores with odors of the plum?
Alas, that they should wear our colors there,
The silken weavings of our afternoons,
And pick the strings of our insipid lutes!
Death is the mother of beauty, mystical,
Within whose burning bosom we devise
Our earthly mothers waiting, sleeplessly.

VII

Supple and turbulent, a ring of men
Shall chant in orgy on a summer morn
Their boisterous devotion to the sun,
Not as a god, but as a god might be,
Naked among them, like a savage source.
Their chant shall be a chant of paradise,
Out of their blood, returning to the sky;
And in their chant shall enter, voice by voice,
The windy lake wherein their lord delights,
The trees, like serafin, and echoing hills,
That choir among themselves long afterward.
They shall know well the heavenly fellowship
Of men that perish and of summer morn.
And whence they came and whither they shall go
The dew upon their feet shall manifest.

VIII

She hears, upon that water without sound,
A voice that cries, "The tomb in Palestine
Is not the porch of spirits lingering.
It is the grave of Jesus, where he lay."
We live in an old chaos of the sun,
Or old dependency of day and night,
Or island solitude, unsponsored, free,
Of that wide water, inescapable.
Deer walk upon our mountains, and the quail
Whistle about us their spontaneous cries;
Sweet berries ripen in the wilderness;
And, in the isolation of the sky,
At evening, casual flocks of pigeons make
Ambiguous undulations as they sink,
Downward to darkness, on extended wings.

THIRTEEN WAYS OF LOOKING AT A BLACKBIRD

I

Among twenty snowy mountains,
The only moving thing
Was the eye of the blackbird.

II

I was of three minds,
Like a tree
In which there are three blackbirds.

III

The blackbird whirled in the autumn winds.
It was a small part of the pantomime.

IV

A man and a woman
Are one.
A man and a woman and a blackbird
Are one.

V

I do not know which to prefer,
The beauty of inflections
Or the beauty of innuendoes,
The blackbird whistling
Or just after.

VI

Icicles filled the long window
With barbaric glass.
The shadow of the blackbird
Crossed it, to and fro.
The mood
Traced in the shadow
An indecipherable cause.

VII

O thin men of Haddam,[1]
Why do you imagine golden birds?
Do you not see how the blackbird
Walks around the feet
Of the women about you?

VIII

I know noble accents
And lucid, inescapable rhythms;
But I know, too,
That the blackbird is involved
In what I know.

IX

When the blackbird flew out of sight,
It marked the edge
Of one of many circles.

[1] An actual town in Connecticut.

X

At the sight of blackbirds
Flying in a green light,
Even the bawds of euphony
Would cry out sharply.

XI

He rode over Connecticut
In a glass coach.
Once, a fear pierced him,
In that he mistook
The shadow of his equipage
For blackbirds.

XII

The river is moving.
The blackbird must be flying.

XIII

It was evening all afternoon.
It was snowing
And it was going to snow.
The blackbird sat
In the cedar-limbs.

THE EMPEROR OF ICE-CREAM

Call the roller of big cigars,
The muscular one, and bid him whip
In kitchen cups concupiscent curds.
Let the wenches dawdle in such dress
As they are used to wear, and let the boys
Bring flowers in last month's newspapers.
Let be be finale of seem.
The only emperor is the emperor of ice-cream.

Take from the dresser of deal
Lacking the three glass knobs, that sheet
On which she embroidered fantails once
And spread it so as to cover her face.
If her horny feet protrude, they come
To show how cold she is, and dumb.
Let the lamp affix its beam.
The only emperor is the emperor of ice-cream.

THE IDEA OF ORDER AT KEY WEST[2]

She sang beyond the genius of the sea.
The water never formed to mind or voice,
Like a body wholly body, fluttering
Its empty sleeves; and yet its mimic motion
Made constant cry, caused constantly a cry,
That was not ours although we understood,
Inhuman, of the veritable ocean.

The sea was not a mask. No more was she.
The song and water were not medleyed sound
Even if what she sang was what she heard,
Since what she sang was uttered word by word.
It may be that in all her phrases stirred
The grinding water and the gasping wind;
But it was she and not the sea we heard.

For she was the maker of the song she sang.
The ever-hooded, tragic-gestured sea
Was merely a place by which she walked to sing.
Whose spirit is this? we said, because we knew
It was the spirit that we sought and knew
That we should ask this often as she sang.

If it was only the dark voice of the sea
That rose, or even colored by many waves;
If it was only the outer voice of sky
And cloud, of the sunken coral water-walled,
However clear, it would have been deep air,
The heaving speech of air, a summer sound
Repeated in a summer without end
And sound alone. But it was more than that,
More even than her voice, and ours, among
The meaningless plungings of water and the wind,
Theatrical distances, bronze shadows heaped
On high horizons, mountainous atmospheres
Of sky and sea.
It was her voice that made
The sky acutest at its vanishing.
She measured to the hour its solitude.
She was the single artificer of the world
In which she sang. And when she sang, the sea,
Whatever self it had, became the self
That was her song, for she was the maker. Then we,
As we beheld her striding there alone,
Knew that there never was a world for her
Except the one she sang and, singing, made.

Ramon Fernandez,[3] tell me, if you know,
Why, when the singing ended and we turned
Toward the town, tell why the glassy lights,
The lights in the fishing boats at anchor there,
As the night descended, tilting in the air,
Mastered the night and portioned out the sea,
Fixing emblazoned zones and fiery poles,
Arranging, deepening, enchanting night.

Oh! Blessed rage for order, pale Ramon,
The maker's rage to order words of the sea,
Words of the fragrant portals, dimly-starred,
And of ourselves and of our origins,
In ghostlier demarcations, keener sounds.

[2]The title defines the limits of the poem: a generalized experience ("the idea of order") which can only occur at one time and place ("at Key West").

TO AN OLD PHILOSOPHER IN ROME[4]

On the threshold of heaven, the figures in the street
Become the figures of heaven, the majestic movement
Of men growing small in the distances of space,
Singing, with smaller and still smaller sound,
Unintelligible absolution and an end—

The threshold, Rome, and that more merciful Rome
Beyond, the two alike in the make of the mind.
It is as if in a human dignity
Two parallels become one, a perspective, of which
Men are part both in the inch and in the mile.

[3]Ramon Fernandez was a well-known French critic and aesthetician who came from the area between Spain and France. Stevens claimed that he chose the name at random.

[4]The philosopher of the title is George Santayana, the Spanish-born American philosopher who taught Stevens at Harvard and died in Rome, under the care of the Blue Nuns, in 1952. In his late essay "Imagination as Value" (1948) Stevens said: "There can be lives, nevertheless, which exist by the deliberate choice of those who live them. To use a single illustration: it may be assumed that the life of Professor Santayana is a life in which the function of the imagination has had a function similar to its function in any deliberate work of art or letters. We have only to think of this present phase of it, in which, in his old age, he dwells in the head of the world, in the company of devoted women, in their convent, and in the company of familiar saints, whose presence does so much to make any convent an appropriate refuge for a generous and human philosopher. To repeat, there can be lives in which the value of the imagination is the same as its value in arts and letters."

How easily the blown banners change to wings . . .
Things dark on the horizons of perception,
Become accompaniments of fortune, but
Of the fortune of the spirit, beyond the eye,
Not of its sphere, and yet not far beyond,

The human end in the spirit's greatest reach,
The extreme of the known in the presence of the
extreme
Of the unknown. The newsboys' muttering
Becomes another murmuring; the smell
Of medicine, a fragrantness not to be spoiled . . .

The bed, the books, the chair, the moving nuns,
The candle as it evades the sight, these are
The sources of happiness in the shape of Rome,
A shape within the ancient circles of shapes,
And these beneath the shadow of a shape

In a confusion on bed and books, a portent
On the chair, a moving transparence on the nuns,
A light on the candle tearing against the wick
To join a hovering excellence, to escape
From fire and be part only of that of which

Fire is the symbol: the celestial possible.
Speak to your pillow as if it was yourself.
Be orator but with an accurate tongue
And without eloquence, O, half-asleep,
Of the pity that is the memorial of this room,

So that we feel, in this illumined large,
The veritable small, so that each of us
Beholds himself in you, and hears his voice
In yours, master and commiserable man,
Intent on your particles of nether-do,

Your dozing in the depths of wakefulness,
In the warmth of your bed, at the edge of your chair,
alive
Yet living in two worlds, impenitent
As to one, and, as to one, most penitent,
Impatient for the grandeur that you need

In so much misery; and yet finding it
Only in misery, the afflatus of ruin,
Profound poetry of the poor and of the dead,
As in the last drop of the deepest blood,
As it falls from the heart and lies there to be seen,

Even as the blood of an empire, it might be,
For a citizen of heaven though still of Rome.
It is poverty's speech that seeks us out the most.
It is older than the oldest speech of Rome.
This is the tragic accent of the scene.

And you—it is you that speak it, without speech,
The loftiest syllables among loftiest things,
The one invulnerable man among
Crude captains, the naked majesty, if you like,
Of bird-nest arches and of rain-stained-vaults.

The sounds drift in. The buildings are remembered.
The life of the city never lets go, nor do you
Ever want it to. It is part of the life in your room.
Its domes are the architecture of your bed.
The bells keep on repeating solemn names

In choruses and choirs of choruses,
Unwilling that mercy should be a mystery
Of silence, that any solitude of sense
Should give you more than their peculiar chords
And reverberations clinging to whisper still.

It is a kind of total grandeur at the end,
With every visible thing enlarged and yet
No more than a bed, a chair and moving nuns,
The immensest theatre, the pillared porch,
The book and candle in your ambered room,

Total grandeur of a total edifice,
Chosen by an inquisitor of structures
For himself. He stops upon this threshold,
As if the design of all his words takes form
And frame from thinking and is realized.

THE COURSE OF A PARTICULAR

Today the leaves cry, hanging on branches swept by
wind,
Yet the nothingness of winter becomes a little less.
It is still full of icy shades and shapen snow.

The leaves cry . . . One holds off and merely hears
the cry.
It is a busy cry, concerning someone else.
And though one says that one is part of everything,

There is a conflict, there is a resistance involved;
And being part is an exertion that declines:
One feels the life of that which gives life as it is.

The leaves cry. It is not a cry of divine attention,
Nor the smoke-drift of puffed-out heroes, nor human
cry.
It is the cry of leaves that do not transcend themselves,
In the absence of fantasia, without meaning more
Than they are in the final finding of the ear, in the
thing
Itself, until, at last, the cry concerns no one at all.

William Carlos Williams (1883–1963)

Born in Rutherford, New Jersey, William Carlos Williams attended local schools until 1897 when his parents (who had emigrated from England and Puerto Rico) sent him to Geneva and Paris for two years of Lycée education. After returning to the United States he studied at Horace Mann High School in New York City and entered the University of Pennsylvania Medical School in 1902, where he later met Ezra Pound (then a graduate student in Romance languages). After obtaining his medical degree he was an intern in New York and spent a year in Leipzig, Germany, doing postgraduate work in pediatrics. He then returned to his native Rutherford where he pursued the double career of poet and physician for the rest of his life (except for a "sabbatical" year in Europe during the 1920s). Williams' early poems are weak and conventionally romantic, but beginning with *The Tempers* (1913) and *Al Que Quiere!* (1917) he entered the world of experimental modern poetry. Throughout his career Williams displayed an allegiance to both the European avant-garde and the native tradition in American poetry represented by Walt Whitman. Many of his poems, such as those of *Spring and All* (1923), reveal a strong cosmopolitan influence, yet Williams firmly rejected the international style and intellectual subject-matter of expatriate poets such as Pound and Eliot, seeking to ground his own art in the local landscape. *In the American Grain* (1925), a collection of essays on the American national character, was followed by poems which led ultimately to his five-volume epic of the Passaic valley, *Paterson* (1946–58), in which the industrial landscape of city and river becomes an archetype of modern man. In his last work on *Paterson* and in such late volumes as *The Desert Music* (1954) and *Pictures from Brueghel* (1962) Williams felt that he had discovered an expressive, musical form which could hold the natural rhythms of our speech. Throughout his life Williams was a prolific writer, stealing time from his work as a physician to produce poetry, plays, fiction, and autobiography. Just as he tried to domesticate a complex and cosmopolitan artistic vision, so he tried to make his language concrete ("No ideas but in things") while lifting concrete details to a level of general significance.

PORTRAIT OF A LADY[1]

Your thighs are appletrees
whose blossoms touch the sky.
Which sky? The sky
where Watteau hung a lady's
slipper.[2] Your knees
are a southern breeze—or

[1] Perhaps an allusion to Henry James's novel, *The Portrait of a Lady* (1881). See T. S. Eliot's "Portrait of a Lady" and Ezra Pound's "Portrait d'une Femme," both reprinted in this section.

[2] Williams has conflated the elegant paintings of Watteau (1684–1721) with "The Swing" by Fragonard (1723–1806). In Fragonard's painting a lady in a garden swing has kicked off her slipper, which hangs in mid-air.

a gust of snow. Agh! what
sort of man was Fragonard?
—as if that answered
anything. Ah, yes—below
the knees, since the tune
drops that way, it is
one of those white summer days,
the tall grass of your ankles
flickers upon the shore—
Which shore?—
the sand clings to my lips—
Which shore?
Agh, petals maybe. How
should I know?
Which shore? Which shore?
I said petals from an appletree.

QUEEN-ANN'S-LACE

Her body is not so white as
anemone petals nor so smooth—nor
so remote a thing. It is a field
of the wild carrot taking
the field by force; the grass
does not raise above it.
Here is no question of whiteness,
white as can be, with a purple mole
at the center of each flower.
Each flower is a hand's span
of her whiteness. Wherever
his hand has lain there is
a tiny purple blemish. Each part
is a blossom under his touch
to which the fibres of her being
stem one by one, each to its end,
until the whole field is a
white desire, empty, a single stem,
a cluster, flower by flower,
a pious wish to whiteness gone over—
or nothing.

THE RED WHEELBARROW

so much depends
upon

a red wheel
barrow

glazed with rain
water

beside the white
chickens.

THE YACHTS

contend in a sea which the land partly encloses
shielding them from the too-heavy blows
of an ungoverned ocean which when it chooses

tortures the biggest hulls, the best man knows
to pit against its beatings, and sinks them pitilessly.
Mothlike in mists, scintillant in the minute

brilliance of cloudless days, with broad bellying sails
they glide to the wind tossing green water
from their sharp prows while over them the crew
crawls

ant-like, solicitously grooming them, releasing,
making fast as they turn, lean far over and having
caught the wind again, side by side, head for the mark.

In a well guarded arena of open water surrounded by
lesser and greater craft which, sycophant, lumbering
and flittering follow them, they appear youthful, rare

as the light of a happy eye, live with the grace
of all that in the mind is fleckless, free and
naturally to be desired. Now the sea which holds them

is moody, lapping their glossy sides, as if feeling
for some slightest flaw but fails completely.
Today no race. Then the wind comes again. The
yachts

move, jockeying for a start, the signal is set and they
are off. Now the waves strike at them but they are too
well made, they slip through, though they take in
canvas.

Arms with hands grasping seek to clutch at the prows.
Bodies thrown recklessly in the way are cut aside.
It is a sea of faces about them in agony, in despair

until the horror of the race dawns staggering the mind,
the whole sea become an entanglement of watery
bodies
lost to the world bearing what they cannot hold.
Broken,

beaten, desolate, reaching from the dead to be taken
up
they cry out, failing, failing! their cries rising
in waves still as the skillful yachts pass over.

PROLETARIAN PORTRAIT

A big young bareheaded woman
in an apron

Her hair slicked back standing
on the street

One stockinged foot toeing
the sidewalk

Her shoe in her hand. Looking
intently into it

She pulls out the paper insole
to find the nail

That has been hurting her

LANDSCAPE WITH THE FALL OF ICARUS[3]

According to Brueghel
when Icarus fell
it was spring

a farmer was plowing
his field
the whole pageantry

of the year was
awake tingling
near

the edge of the sea
concerned
with itself

sweating in the sun
that melted
the wings' wax

unsignificantly
off the coast
there was

a splash quite unnoticed
this was
Icarus drowning

[3] In Greek mythology Icarus, the son of Daedalus, flew too near the sun after Daedalus had fashioned wings from feathers and wax in order to escape from their island prison. The wax melted and Icarus plunged into the sea, thus becoming the type of the "overreacher." In Pieter Brueghel's painting of the 16th century, the fall is presented as one small detail in a natural landscape. For another treatment of the same theme, see W. H. Auden's "Musée des Beaux Arts."

Ezra Pound (1885–1972)

Born in Hailey, Idaho, where his father was temporarily stationed as a Federal Land Office inspector, Ezra Loomis Pound was brought up in Philadelphia and educated at Hamilton College, New York, and the University of Pennsylvania. He did graduate work in Romance Languages and spent a disastrous few months as a teacher at Wabash College, Crawfordsville, Indiana. After dismissal from Wabash he left for Europe (which he had visited twice before) and published his first volume of poetry, *A Lume Spento* (1908), in Venice. He then settled in London, entering the literary world of William Butler Yeats, and with his second volume, *Personae* (1909), began to build a reputation as one of the leaders of the new movement in poetry. Between 1909 and 1920 Pound played a complicated role as innovative poet, revolutionary critic, and sponsor for some of the most important figures in modern literature. He was instrumental in organizing the "Imagist" movement which emphasized the precise visual image that could stand as a natural symbol without the support of conventional poetic diction (see "In a Station of the Metro"). He was an early admirer of Robert Frost and T. S. Eliot, and an indefatigable publicist for James Joyce. In his own criticism and poetry he stressed clarity and a sense of cosmopolitan values, often "translating" from Chinese, Greek, Latin, or the modern European languages in his search for a characteristic idiom. His semi-autobiographical suite of poems, *Hugh Selwyn Mauberley* (1920), is both a nostalgic farewell to the London literary world he had dominated for over a decade and a devastating critique of that world.

In 1920 Pound moved to Paris where he became a friend and supporter of Ernest Hemingway. In 1924 he settled in Rapallo, Italy, where he continued work on the *Cantos,* a long personal epic started ten years before in London. Pound became obsessed by the disastrous economic and artistic consequences of the first World War, and during the 1920s and 1930s he was increasingly caught up in right-wing politics. His literary criticism, which had once praised the detached perspective and the fastidious style, became more and more polemical. In the 1930s Pound was a defender of Mussolini, and during World War II he broadcast from Rome in support of the Fascist and Nazi regimes. In 1945 he was arrested by the advancing American army and imprisoned in a cage near Pisa; out of this harrowing time came his most moving late poems, the *Pisan Cantos* (1948). Pound was returned to the United States to face a charge of treason, but was declared "mentally unfit for trial" and sent to St. Elizabeth's Hospital for the criminally insane, where he remained—translating and writing the later *Cantos*—until 1958, when the charges against him were finally dropped. He then returned to Italy, living in Venice in virtual silence until his death.

PORTRAIT D'UNE FEMME[1]

Your mind and you are our Sargasso Sea,[2]
London has swept about you this score years
And bright ships left you this or that in fee:
Ideas, old gossip, oddments of all things,
Strange spars of knowledge and dimmed wares of
    price.
Great minds have sought you—lacking someone else.
You have been second always. Tragical?
No. You preferred it to the usual thing:
One dull man, dulling and uxorious,
One average mind—with one thought less, each year.
Oh, you are patient, I have seen you sit

[1] See T. S. Eliot's "Portrait of a Lady" and William Carlos Williams' "Portrait of a Lady."

[2] A still part of the north Atlantic where floating material tends to collect. It was, according to legend, the graveyard of many ships which became entangled in the dense seaweed.

Hours, where something might have floated up.
And now you pay one. Yes, you richly pay.
You are a person of some interest, one comes to you
And takes strange gain away:
Trophies fished up; some curious suggestion;
Fact that leads nowhere; and a tale or two,
Pregnant with mandrakes, or with something else
That might prove useful and yet never proves,
That never fits a corner or shows use,
Or finds its hour upon the loom of days:
The tarnished, gaudy, wonderful old work;
Idols and ambergris and rare inlays,
These are your riches, your great store; and yet
For all this sea-hoard of deciduous things,
Strange woods half sodden, and new brighter stuff:
In the slow float of differing light and deep,
No! there is nothing! In the whole and all,
Nothing that's quite your own.
Yet this is you.

IN A STATION OF THE METRO

The apparition of these faces in the crowd;
Petals on a wet, black bough.

THE RIVER-MERCHANT'S WIFE: A LETTER[3]

While my hair was still cut straight across my forehead
I played about the front gate, pulling flowers.
You came by on bamboo stilts, playing horse,
You walked about my seat, playing with blue plums.
And we went on living in the village of Chokan:
Two small people, without dislike or suspicion.

At fourteen I married My Lord you.
I never laughed, being bashful.
Lowering my head, I looked at the wall.
Called to, a thousand times, I never looked back.

At fifteen I stopped scowling,
I desired my dust to be mingled with yours
For ever and for ever and for ever.
Why should I climb the look out?

At sixteen you departed,
You went into far Ku-to-yen, by the river of swirling eddies,
And you have been gone five months.
The monkeys make sorrowful noise overhead.

You dragged your feet when you went out.
By the gate now, the moss is grown, the different mosses,
Too deep to clear them away!
The leaves fall early this autumn, in wind.
The paired butterflies are already yellow with August
Over the grass in the West garden;
They hurt me. I grow older.
If you are coming down through the narrows of the river Kiang,
Please let me know beforehand,
And I will come out to meet you
As far as Cho-fu-Sa.

By Rihaku

[3] This is one of Pound's early versions of a Chinese poem, made from the notes of the Orientalist Ernest Fenollosa. "Rihaku" is the Japanese for Li Po, a famous Chinese poet of the eighth century.

MEDALLION[4]

Luini[5] in porcelain!
The grand piano
Utters a profane
Protest with her clear soprano.

The sleek head emerges
From the gold-yellow frock
As Anadyomene in the opening
Pages of Reinach.[6]

Honey-red, closing the face-oval,
A basket-work of braids which seem as if they were
Spun in King Minos' hall[7]
From metal, or intractable amber;

The face-oval beneath the glaze,
Bright in its suave bounding-line, as,
Beneath half-watt rays,
The eyes turn topaz.

[4] This is the last poem of Part II of *Hugh Selwyn Mauberley*, Pound's long poem which describes and criticizes the London art world of 1918–20. It is a loving tribute to the mannered style which Pound felt he had to reject if he were to develop as an artist.
[5] Bernardino Luini (d. 1532), a Mannerist painter and follower of Leonardo da Vinci.
[6] Venus "Anadyomene" (born from the foam), an illustration in Salomon Reinach's work of art history, *Apollo* (1904). The magical Venus of Botticelli has been reduced to a plate in a textbook.
[7] The legendary king of Crete, associated with the richness of Minoan art.

D. H. Lawrence (1885–1930)

David Herbert Lawrence was born in a colliery village in Nottinghamshire, England, the son of a coal miner and a school teacher who, it was thought, had married "beneath her." After leaving Nottingham High School at the age of sixteen Lawrence held several jobs before entering University College, Nottingham, where he received a teaching certificate after two years. He took up a teaching position at Croyden, near London, and began to write verse and fiction. His first novel, *The White Peacock* (1911), was followed by his semi-autobiographical novel, *Sons and Lovers* (1913), and *The Prussian Officer and Other Stories* (1914). In April 1912 Lawrence met Frieda Weekley (born Frieda von Richthofen), the German wife of a university professor at Nottingham; they fell in love and soon left together for Germany, returning to England in 1913. Lawrence and Frieda were married in 1914 after she obtained a divorce. Their intense, nomadic relationship was to form one of the unifying designs in Lawrence's life and art.

The years of the first World War were difficult ones for Lawrence. He was looked upon with suspicion because of his German wife and bohemian ways, and he in turn felt a deep disgust for the war. It was, however, a period of great productivity. His first volume of verse, *Love Poems and Others* (1913), was followed by three more collections, *Amores* (1916), *Look! We Have Come Through* (1917), and *New Poems* (1918), while his major novels *The Rainbow* and *Women in Love* were completed in 1915–16 (published in 1916, 1920). After the war Lawrence's restless imagination led him to the Mediterranean countries, Ceylon, Australia, New Mexico, and Mexico, the settings for such works as *Kangaroo* (1923) and *The Plumed Serpent* (1926). Lawrence's production of poetry and fiction remained prodigious, but his health—always delicate—began to fail. After returning to Europe in 1925 he spent much of his time painting, studying Etruscan art, and writing and rewriting his last novel, *Lady Chatterley's Lover,* which was privately printed in Florence in 1928 and published in an expurgated edition in 1932 (the full text did not escape the English censor until 1960). In June 1928 Lawrence left Florence in failing health; he died in the south of France, of tuberculosis, on March 2, 1930.

During the period 1918–30 Lawrence published five volumes of verse, the most important being *Birds, Beasts and Flowers* (1923). His first *Collected Poems* appeared in 1928. The standard collection is *The Complete Poems of D. H. Lawrence,* edited by Vivian de Sola Pinto and Warren Roberts (1964).

LOVE ON THE FARM

What large, dark hands are those at the window
Grasping in the golden light
Which weaves its way through the evening wind
  At my heart's delight?

Ah, only the leaves! But in the west
I see a redness suddenly come
Into the evening's anxious breast—
  'Tis the wound of love goes home!

The woodbine creeps abroad
Calling low to her lover:

The sun-lit flirt who all the day
Has poised above her lips in play
And stolen kisses, shallow and gay
Of pollen, now has gone away—
She woos the moth with her sweet, low word;
And when above her his moth-wings hover
Then her bright breast she will uncover
And yield her honey-drop to her lover.

Into the yellow, evening glow
Saunters a man from the farm below;
Leans, and looks in at the low-built shed
Where the swallow has hung her marriage bed.
The bird lies warm against the wall.
She glances quick her startled eyes
Towards him, then she turns away
Her small head, making warm display
Of red upon the throat. Her terrors sway
Her out of the nest's warm, busy ball,
Whose plaintive cry is heard as she flies
In one blue swoop from out of the sties
Into the twilight's empty hall.

Oh, water-hen, beside the rushes
Hide your quaintly scarlet blushes,
Still your quick tail, lie still as dead,
Till the distance folds over his ominous tread!

The rabbit presses back her ears,
Turns back her liquid, anguished eyes
And crouches low; then with wild spring
Spurts from the terror of *his* oncoming;
To be choked back, the wire ring
Her frantic effort throttling:
Piteous brown ball of quivering fears!
Ah, soon in his large, hard hands she dies,
And swings all loose from the swing of his walk!
Yet calm and kindly are his eyes
And ready to open in brown surprise
Should I not answer to his talk
Or should he my tears surmise.

I hear his hand on the latch, and rise from my chair
Watching the door open; he flashes bare
His strong teeth in a smile, and flashes his eyes
In a smile like triumph upon me; then careless-wise
He flings the rabbit soft on the table board
And comes toward me: ah! the uplifted sword
Of his hand against my bosom! and oh, the broad
Blade of his glance that asks me to applaud
His coming! With his hand he turns my face to him
And caresses me with his fingers that still smell grim
Of rabbit's fur! God, I am caught in a snare!
I know not what fine wire is round my throat;
I only know I let him finger there
My pulse of life, and let him nose like a stoat
Who sniffs with joy before he drinks the blood.

And down his mouth comes to my mouth! and down
His bright dark eyes come over me, like a hood
Upon my mind! his lips meet mine, and a flood
Of sweet fire sweeps across me, so I drown
Against him, die, and find death good.

PIANO

Softly, in the dusk, a woman is singing to me;
Taking me back down the vista of years, till I see
A child sitting under the piano, in the boom of the
tingling strings
And pressing the small, poised feet of a mother who
smiles as she sings.

In spite of myself, the insidious mastery of song
Betrays me back, till the heart of me weeps to belong
To the old Sunday evenings at home, with winter
outside
And hymns in the cosy parlour, the tinkling piano our
guide.

So now it is vain for the singer to burst into clamour
With the great black piano appassionato. The glamour
Of childish days is upon me, my manhood is cast
Down in the flood of remembrance, I weep like a child
for the past.

SNAKE

A snake came to my water-trough
On a hot, hot day, and I in pyjamas for the heat,
To drink there.

In the deep, strange-scented shade of the great dark
carob-tree
I came down the steps with my pitcher
And must wait, must stand and wait, for there he was
at the trough before me.

He reached down from a fissure in the earth-wall in
the gloom
And trailed his yellow-brown slackness soft-bellied
down, over the edge of the stone trough
And rested his throat upon the stone bottom,

And where the water had dripped from the tap, in a small clearness,
He sipped with his straight mouth,
Softly drank through his straight gums, into his slack long body,
Silently.

Someone was before me at my water-trough,
And I, like a second comer, waiting.

He lifted his head from his drinking, as cattle do,
And looked at me vaguely, as drinking cattle do,
And flickered his two-forked tongue from his lips, and mused a moment,
And stooped and drank a little more,
Being earth-brown, earth-golden from the burning bowels of the earth
On the day of Sicilian July, with Etna smoking.

The voice of my education said to me
He must be killed,
For in Sicily the black black snakes are innocent, the gold are venomous.

And voices in me said, If you were a man
You would take a stick and break him now, and finish him off.

But must I confess how I liked him,
How glad I was he had come like a guest in quiet, to drink at my water-trough
And depart peaceful, pacified, and thankless,
Into the burning bowels of this earth?

Was it cowardice, that I dared not kill him?
Was it perversity, that I longed to talk to him?
Was it humility, to feel so honoured?
I felt so honoured.

And yet those voices:
If you were not afraid, you would kill him!

And truly I was afraid, I was most afraid,
But even so, honoured still more
That he should seek my hospitality
From out the dark door of the secret earth.

He drank enough
And lifted his head, dreamily, as one who has drunken,
And flickered his tongue like a forked night on the air, so black;
Seeming to lick his lips,
And looked around like a god, unseeing, into the air,
And slowly turned his head,
And slowly, very slowly, as if thrice adream,
Proceeded to draw his slow length curving round
And climb again the broken bank of my wall-face.

And as he put his head into that dreadful hole,
And as he slowly drew up, snake-easing his shoulders, and entered farther,
A sort of horror, a sort of protest against his withdrawing into that horrid black hole,
Deliberately going into the blackness, and slowly drawing himself after,
Overcame me now his back was turned.

I looked around, I put down my pitcher,
I picked up a clumsy log
And threw it at the water-trough with a clatter.

I think I did not hit him,
But suddenly that part of him that was left behind convulsed in undignified haste,
Writhed like lightning, and was gone
Into the black hole, the earth-lipped fissure in the wall-front,
At which, in the intense still noon, I stared with fascination.

And immediately I regretted it.
I thought how paltry, how vulgar, what a mean act!
I despised myself and the voices of my accursed human education.

And I thought of the albatross,[1]
And I wished he would come back, my snake.

For he seemed to me again like a king,
Like a king in exile, uncrowned in the underworld,
Now due to be crowned again.

And so, I missed my chance with one of the lords
Of life.
And I have something to expiate;
A pettiness.

BAVARIAN GENTIANS

Not every man has gentians in his house
In soft September, at slow, sad Michaelmas.[2]

[1] The bird of good omen that is killed by the Mariner in Coleridge's *Rime of the Ancient Mariner.* This sin against nature leads to his punishment and ultimate penance.

[2] Saint Michael's day, September 29.

Bavarian gentians, tall and dark, but dark
Darkening the day-time torch-like with the smoking
blueness of Pluto's gloom,[3]
Ribbed hellish flowers erect, with their blaze of
darkness spread blue,
Blown into points, by the heavy white draught of the
day.

Torch-flowers of the blue-smoking darkness, Pluto's
dark blue blaze
Black lamps from the halls of Dis, smoking dark blue
Giving off darkness, blue darkness, upon Demeter's
yellow-pale day
Whom have you come for, here in the white-cast day?

Reach me a gentian, give me a torch!
Let me guide myself with the blue, forked torch of a
flower
Down the darker and darker stairs, where blue is
darkened on blueness
Down the way Persephone goes, just now, in first-
frosted September.
To the sightless realm where darkness is married to
dark
And Persephone herself is but a voice, as a bride,
A gloom invisible enfolded in the deeper dark
Of the arms of Pluto as he ravishes her once again
And pierces her once more with his passion of the
utter dark.
Among the splendour of black-blue torches, shedding
fathomless darkness on the nuptials.

Give me a flower on a tall stem, and three dark flames,
For I will go to the wedding, and be wedding-guest
At the marriage of the living dark.

[3] Pluto (Hades), the god of the underworld, carried off Persephone, the daughter of Demeter, and made her his consort. She was allowed to return to the fertile world of her mother each spring, but had to re-enter the dark underworld in September. The myth is one variant of the archetypal story of the death and rebirth of the natural year.

T. S. Eliot (1888–1965)

Thomas Stearns Eliot was born in St. Louis, Missouri, where he spent the first seventeen years of his life. He came from an old New England family (his grandfather, a graduate of Harvard Divinity School, founded Washington University in St. Louis), and some of the happiest moments of Eliot's early life occurred during summer visits to the New England coast. In 1905 he was sent East to study at Milton Academy, and the following year he entered Harvard where he eventually did graduate work in philosophy and Oriental religions. As an undergraduate Eliot first wrote poetry heavily influenced by Tennyson and the late Victorian poets, but his encounter in 1909–10 with the new French poetry (especially that of Jules Laforgue) led to a more ironic and introspective style. In 1910–11 Eliot spent a year at the Sorbonne in Paris; in 1914 he was awarded a fellowship to a German university, but the outbreak of World War I caused a change of plans and he took up residence at Merton College, Oxford (1914–15). It was at this time that he met Ezra Pound, who was so impressed by "The Love Song of J. Alfred Prufrock" that he arranged for its publication. In 1915 Eliot moved to London, and for the next ten years produced a remarkable body of influential poetry and criticism, in spite of the difficulties surrounding his marriage (in 1915) to Vivien Haigh-Wood. A collection of poems, *Prufrock and Other Observations* (1917), was followed by *Poems* (1920), in which the looser and more personal form of the early verse was replaced by the strict quatrains of the Sweeney poems. In 1922 Eliot published his long poem *The Waste Land,* a personal testament to the spiritual dryness of the contemporary world which he put into final form with the help of Ezra Pound. In these same years Eliot was writing some of his most important literary criticism. *The Sacred Wood* (1920)—which contains his famous essay on the poet's role, "Tradition and the Individual Talent," first published a year earlier—was followed in 1924 by *Homage to John Dryden.* Between 1922 and 1939 Eliot edited *The Criterion,* probably the most influential literary journal of the time.

In 1928 Eliot announced that he was a classicist in literature, a Royalist in politics (he had become a British subject in 1927), and an Anglo-Catholic in religion, thus acknowledging changes which had been evident in his life and art for some time. In 1930 he published *Ash Wednesday,* a long poem on the theme of religious conversion. In 1932 Eliot returned to the United States for the first time in nearly twenty years to lecture at Harvard and the University of Virginia, and this renewal of early experience seems to have acted as a catalyst for his poetry. Between 1935 and 1941 he published *Four Quartets,* long meditative poems on British and American landscapes which are the glory of his later career. In the 1930s he also channeled his long-standing interest in drama into the writing of plays. *Murder in the Cathedral* (1935) was followed by *The Family Reunion* (1939) and a series of "comedies" on religious themes, *The Cocktail Party* (1950), *The Confidential Clerk* (1954), and *The Elder Statesman* (1959). Eliot continued to write literary criticism until his death, but his career as a poet was concluded with *Four Quartets.* In 1948 he received the Nobel Prize for literature.

THE LOVE SONG OF J. ALFRED PRUFROCK

S'io credesse che mia risposta fosse
A persona che mai tornasse al mondo,
Questa fiamma staria senza piu scosse.
Ma perciocche giammai di questo fondo
Non torno vivo alcun, s'i'odo il vero,
Senza tema d'infamia ti rispondo.[1]

Let us go then, you and I,
When the evening is spread out against the sky
Like a patient etherised upon a table;
Let us go, through certain half-deserted streets,
The muttering retreats
Of restless nights in one-night cheap hotels
And sawdust restaurants with oyster-shells:
Streets that follow like a tedious argument
Of insidious intent
To lead you to an overwhelming question . . .
Oh, do not ask, "What is it?"
Let us go and make our visit.

In the room the women come and go
Talking of Michelangelo.

The yellow fog that rubs its back upon the window-panes,
The yellow smoke that rubs its muzzle on the window-panes
Licked its tongue into the corners of the evening,
Lingered upon the pools that stand in drains,
Let fall upon its back the soot that falls from chimneys,
Slipped by the terrace, made a sudden leap,
And seeing that it was a soft October night,
Curled once about the house, and fell asleep.

And indeed there will be time
For the yellow smoke that slides along the street,
Rubbing its back upon the window-panes;
There will be time, there will be time
To prepare a face to meet the faces that you meet;
There will be time to murder and create,
And time for all the works and days of hands
That lift and drop a question on your plate;
Time for you and time for me,
And time yet for a hundred indecisions,
And for a hundred visions and revisions,
Before the taking of a toast and tea.

In the room the women come and go
Talking of Michelangelo.

And indeed there will be time
To wonder, "Do I dare?" and, "Do I dare?"
Time to turn back and descend the stair,
With a bald spot in the middle of my hair—
[They will say: "How his hair is growing thin!"]
My morning coat, my collar mounting firmly to the chin,

[1] Dante, *Inferno,* XXVII. Guido da Montefeltro, embodied in a flame like Ulysses and the other evil counsellors, speaks to Dante: "If I thought my answer were to one who ever could return to the world, this flame should shake no more; but since none ever did return alive from this depth, if what I hear is true, without fear of infamy I answer thee."

My necktie rich and modest, but asserted by a simple
pin—
[They will say: "But how his arms and legs are thin!"]
Do I dare
Disturb the universe?
In a minute there is time
For decisions and revisions which a minute will
reverse.

For I have known them all already, known them
all:—
Have known the evenings, mornings, afternoons,
I have measured out my life with coffee spoons;
I know the voices dying with a dying fall[2]
Beneath the music from a farther room.
So how should I presume?

And I have known the eyes already, known them
all—
The eyes that fix you in a formulated phrase,
And when I am formulated, sprawling on a pin,
When I am pinned and wriggling on the wall,
Then how should I begin
To spit out all the butt-ends of my days and ways?
And how should I presume?

And I have known the arms already, known them
all—
Arms that are braceleted and white and bare
[But in the lamplight, downed with light brown hair!]
Is it perfume from a dress
That makes me so digress?
Arms that lie along a table, or wrap about a shawl.
And should I then presume?
And how should I begin?

. . . . .

Shall I say, I have gone at dusk through narrow streets
And watched the smoke that rises from the pipes
Of lonely men in shirt-sleeves, leaning out of
windows? . . .

I should have been a pair of ragged claws
Scuttling across the floors of silent seas.

. . . . .

And the afternoon, the evening sleeps so peacefully!
Smoothed by long fingers,
Asleep . . . tired . . . or it malingers,
Stretched on the floor, here beside you and me.

[2] An allusion to Duke Orsino's lovesick speech at the opening of Shakespeare's *Twelfth Night,* which begins: "If music be the food of love, play on! / Give me excess of it, that, surfeiting, / The appetite may sicken, and so die. / That strain again! It had a dying fall."

Should I, after tea and cakes and ices,
Have the strength to force the moment to its crisis?
But though I have wept and fasted, wept and prayed,
Though I have seen my head [grown slightly bald]
brought in upon a platter,[3]
I am no prophet—and here's no great matter;
I have seen the moment of my greatness flicker,
And I have seen the eternal Footman hold my coat,
and snicker,
And in short, I was afraid.

And would it have been worth it, after all,
After the cups, the marmalade, the tea,
Among the porcelain, among some talk of you and
me,
Would it have been worth while,
To have bitten off the matter with a smile,
To have squeezed the universe into a ball[4]
To roll it toward some overwhelming question,
To say: "I am Lazarus,[5] come from the dead,
Come back to tell you all, I shall tell you all"—
If one, settling a pillow by her head,
Should say: "That is not what I meant at all.
That is not it, at all."

And would it have been worth it, after all,
Would it have been worth while,
After the sunsets and the dooryards and the sprinkled
streets,
After the novels, after the teacups, after the skirts that
trail along the floor—
And this, and so much more?—
It is impossible to say just what I mean!
But as if a magic lantern threw the nerves in patterns
on a screen:
Would it have been worth while
If one, settling a pillow or throwing off a shawl,
And turning toward the window, should say:
"That is not it at all,
That is not what I meant, at all."

. . . . .

No! I am not Prince Hamlet, nor was meant to be;
Am an attendant lord, one that will do
To swell a progress, start a scene or two,

[3] At the request of Herodias, King Herod had John the Baptist beheaded and his head brought in on a platter (Matthew 14: 1–12).

[4] Andrew Marvell (1621–78), "To His Coy Mistress": "Let us roll all our strength and all / Our sweetness up into one ball, / And tear our pleasures with rough strife / Through the iron gates of life: / Thus, though we cannot make our sun / Stand still, yet we will make him run."

[5] The man Christ raised from the dead (John 11:1–44).

Advise the prince; no doubt, an easy tool,
Deferential, glad to be of use,
Politic, cautious, and meticulous;
Full of high sentence, but a bit obtuse;
At times, indeed, almost ridiculous—
Almost, at times, the Fool.

I grow old . . . I grow old . . .
I shall wear the bottoms of my trousers rolled.

Shall I part my hair behind? Do I dare to eat a peach?
I shall wear white flannel trousers, and walk upon the beach.
I have heard the mermaids singing, each to each.

I do not think that they will sing to me.

I have seen them riding seaward on the waves
Combing the white hair of the waves blown back
When the wind blows the water white and black.

We have lingered in the chambers of the sea
By sea-girls wreathed with seaweed red and brown
Till human voices wake us, and we drown.

PORTRAIT OF A LADY[6]

Thou hast committed—
Fornication: but that was in another country,
And besides, the wench is dead.

The Jew of Malta.[7]

I

Among the smoke and fog of a December afternoon
You have the scene arrange itself—as it will seem to do—
With "I have saved this afternoon for you";
And four wax candles in the darkened room,
Four rings of light upon the ceiling overhead,
An atmosphere of Juliet's tomb
Prepared for all the things to be said, or left unsaid.

[6] The title recalls Henry James's novel *The Portrait of a Lady* (1881). See Ezra Pound's "Portrait d'une Femme" and William Carlos Williams' "Portrait of a Lady."

[7] From Christopher Marlowe's *The Jew of Malta,* Act IV, Scene 1. The first line is spoken by a Friar who is about to recount the sins of Barabas, the Jew of Malta; but Barabas interrupts with his own cynical confession. In fact, both the Friar and Barabas are engaged in an elaborate game of deceit.

We have been, let us say, to hear the latest Pole
Transmit the Preludes, through his hair and fingertips.
"So intimate, this Chopin, that I think his soul
Should be resurrected only among friends
Some two or three, who will not touch the bloom
That is rubbed and questioned in the concert room."
—And so the conversation slips
Among velleities and carefully caught regrets
Through attenuated tones of violins
Mingled with remote cornets
And begins.
"You do not know how much they mean to me, my friends,
And how, how rare and strange it is, to find
In a life composed so much, so much of odds and ends,
[For indeed I do not love it . . . you knew? you are not blind!
How keen you are!]
To find a friend who has these qualities,
Who has, and gives
Those qualities upon which friendship lives.
How much it means that I say this to you—
Without these friendships—life, what *cauchemar!*"[8]

Among the windings of the violins
And the ariettes
Of cracked cornets
Inside my brain a dull tom-tom begins
Absurdly hammering a prelude of its own,
Capricious monotone
That is at least one definite "false note."
—Let us take the air, in a tobacco trance,
Admire the monuments,
Discuss the late events,
Correct our watches by the public clocks.
Then sit for half an hour and drink our bocks.

II

Now that lilacs are in bloom
She has a bowl of lilacs in her room
And twists one in her fingers while she talks.
"Ah, my friend, you do not know, you do not know
What life is, you who hold it in your hands";
(Slowly twisting the lilac stalks)
"You let it flow from you, you let it flow,
And youth is cruel, and has no remorse
And smiles at situations which it cannot see."
I smile, of course,
And go on drinking tea.

[8] French for "nightmare."

"Yet with these April sunsets, that somehow recall
My buried life,[9] and Paris in the Spring,
I feel immeasurably at peace, and find the world
To be wonderful and youthful, after all."

The voice returns like the insistent out-of-tune
Of a broken violin on an August afternoon:
"I am always sure that you understand
My feelings, always sure that you feel,
Sure that across the gulf you reach your hand.

You are invulnerable, you have no Achilles' heel.
You will go on, and when you have prevailed
You can say: at this point many a one has failed.
But what have I, but what have I, my friend,
To give you, what can you receive from me?
Only the friendship and the sympathy
Of one about to reach her journey's end.

I shall sit here, serving tea to friends. . . ."

I take my hat: how can I make a cowardly amends
For what she has said to me?
You will see me any morning in the park
Reading the comics and the sporting page.
Particularly I remark
An English countess goes upon the stage.
A Greek was murdered at a Polish dance,
Another bank defaulter has confessed.
I keep my countenance,
I remain self-possessed
Except when a street piano, mechanical and tired
Reiterates some worn-out common song
With the smell of hyacinths across the garden
Recalling things that other people have desired.
Are these ideas right or wrong?

III

The October night comes down; returning as before
Except for a slight sensation of being ill at ease
I mount the stairs and turn the handle of the door
And feel as if I had mounted on my hands and knees.
"And so you are going abroad; and when do you
return?
But that's a useless question.
You hardly know when you are coming back,
You will find so much to learn."
My smile falls heavily among the bric-à-brac.

"Perhaps you can write to me."
My self-possession flares up for a second;
This is as I had reckoned.
"I have been wondering frequently of late
(But our beginnings never know our ends!)
Why we have not developed into friends."
I feel like one who smiles, and turning shall remark
Suddenly, his expression in a glass.
My self-possession gutters; we are really in the dark.

"For everybody said so, all our friends,
They all were sure our feelings would relate
So closely! I myself can hardly understand.
We must leave it now to fate.
You will write, at any rate.
Perhaps it is not too late.
I shall sit here, serving tea to friends."

And I must borrow every changing shape
To find expression . . . dance, dance
Like a dancing bear,
Cry like a parrot, chatter like an ape.
Let us take the air, in a tobacco trance—

Well! and what if she should die some afternoon,
Afternoon grey and smoky, evening yellow and rose;
Should die and leave me sitting pen in hand
With the smoke coming down above the housetops;
Doubtful, for a while
Not knowing what to feel or if I understand
Or whether wise or foolish, tardy or too soon . . .
Would she not have the advantage, after all?
This music is successful with a "dying fall"[10]
Now that we talk of dying—
And should I have the right to smile?

SWEENEY AMONG THE NIGHTINGALES

ωμοι, πέπληγμαι καιρίαν πληγὴν εσω.[11]

Apeneck Sweeney spreads his knees
Letting his arms hang down to laugh,
The zebra stripes along his jaw
Swelling to maculate[12] giraffe.

[9] Matthew Arnold's poem "The Buried Life" speaks of the "mystery of this heart which beats so wild, so deep in us"—the mystery of the buried emotions.

[10] See footnote 2.

[11] The words of Agamemnon as he is struck down by his wife Clytemnestra in Aeschylus' *Agamemnon:* "Alas, I am struck with a mortal blow."

[12] "Striped": the opposite of immaculate.

The circles of the stormy moon
Slide westward toward the River Plate,
Death and the Raven drift above
And Sweeney guards the hornèd gate.[13]

Gloomy Orion and the Dog[14]
Are veiled; and hushed the shrunken seas;
The person in the Spanish cape
Tries to sit on Sweeney's knees

Slips and pulls the table cloth
Overturns a coffee-cup,
Reorganized upon the floor
She yawns and draws a stocking up;

The silent man in mocha brown
Sprawls at the window-sill and gapes;
The waiter brings in oranges
Bananas figs and hothouse grapes;

The silent vertebrate in brown
Contracts and concentrates, withdraws;
Rachel *née* Rabinovitch
Tears at the grapes with murderous paws;

She and the lady in the cape
Are suspect, thought to be in league;
Therefore the man with heavy eyes
Declines the gambit, shows fatigue,

Leaves the room and reappears
Outside the window, leaning in,
Branches of wistaria
Circumscribe a golden grin;

The host with someone indistinct
Converses at the door apart,
The nightingales are singing near
The Convent of the Sacred Heart,

And sang within the bloody wood[15]
When Agamemnon cried aloud,
And let their liquid siftings fall
To stain the stiff dishonoured shroud.

[13] The River Plate is in South America, and the Raven (Corvus) is a southern constellation. In classical mythology, the gates of horn were the gates of Hades through which true dreams pass. In Eliot's early poetry, Sweeney is the type of instinctive, unthinking man.

[14] Orion, one of the brightest of the winter constellations, is a hunter who appears in the southern sky with his dog (marked by the dog star, Sirius).

[15] The sacred wood of primitive ritual in which the old king or priest is slain by his successor, who in turn is slain in the endless cycle of death and renewal.

THE HOLLOW MEN[16]

Mistah Kurtz—he dead.[17]

A penny for the Old Guy[18]

I

We are the hollow men
We are the stuffed men
Leaning together
Headpiece filled with straw. Alas!
Our dried voices, when
We whisper together
Are quiet and meaningless
As wind in dry grass
Or rats' feet over broken glass
In our dry cellar

Shape without form, shade without colour,
Paralysed force, gesture without motion;

Those who have crossed
With direct eyes, to death's other Kingdom[19]
Remember us—if at all—not as lost
Violent souls, but only
As the hollow men
The stuffed men.

II

Eyes I dare not meet in dreams
In death's dream kingdom
These do not appear:
There, the eyes are
Sunlight on a broken column
There, is a tree swinging
And voices are

[16] The title appears to come from *Julius Caesar* (IV, 2), where the phrase "hollow men" is used; but it also recalls the hollowness of Kurtz in Conrad's *Heart of Darkness.*

[17] The words of the black servant in *Heart of Darkness,* reporting the death of his master.

[18] On Guy Fawkes Day (November 5th) English children memorialize the defeat of the Gunpowder Plot against King James by preparing an effigy of the traitor, Guy Fawkes, and begging money for fireworks. The stuffed figure of "Old Guy" is still displayed on the streets of England on November 5th.

[19] Presumably the passage from Limbo, the world of those who were neither for or against God, the hollow men, to Hell or Purgatory. Dante's pilgrimage, as described in the *Divine Comedy,* is the essential background to the poem.

In the wind's singing
More distant and more solemn
Than a fading star.

Let me be no nearer
In death's dream kingdom
Let me also wear
Such deliberate disguises
Rat's coat, crowskin, crossed staves
In a field
Behaving as the wind behaves
No nearer—

Not that final meeting
In the twilight kingdom

III

This is the dead land
This is cactus land
Here the stone images
Are raised, here they receive
The supplication of a dead man's hand
Under the twinkle of a fading star.

Is it like this
In death's other kingdom
Waking alone
At the hour when we are
Trembling with tenderness
Lips that would kiss
Form prayers to broken stone.

IV

The eyes are not here
There are no eyes here
In this valley of dying stars
In this hollow valley
This broken jaw of our lost kingdoms

In this last of meeting places
We grope together
And avoid speech
Gathered on this beach of the tumid river[20]

Sightless, unless
The eyes reappear
As the perpetual star
Multifoliate rose[21]
Of death's twilight kingdom
The hope only
Of empty men.

V

Here we go round the prickly pear
Prickly pear prickly pear
Here we go round the prickly pear
At five o'clock in the morning.

Between the idea
And the reality
Between the motion
And the act
Falls the Shadow
For Thine is the Kingdom

Between the conception
And the creation
Between the emotion
And the response
Falls the Shadow
Life is very long

Between the desire
And the spasm
Between the potency
And the existence
Between the essence
And the descent
Falls the Shadow
For Thine is the Kingdom

For Thine is
Life is
For Thine is the

This is the way the world ends
This is the way the world ends
This is the way the world ends
Not with a bang but a whimper.[22]

[20] The river Acheron, which borders Hell in the *Divine Comedy;* or perhaps the Congo which cuts through Conrad's "heart of darkness."

[21] The rose which is Dante's vision of Mary and heaven in the *Divine Comedy* (*Paradiso* XXXII).

[22] A parody of the children's song, "This is the way we clap our hands," and of the *Gloria:* "Glory be to the Father, and to the Son, and to the Holy Ghost, as it was in the beginning, is now, and ever shall be, world without end."

JOURNEY OF THE MAGI

'A cold coming we had of it,
Just the worst time of the year
For a journey, and such a long journey:
The ways deep and the weather sharp,
The very dead of winter.'[23]
And the camels galled, sore-footed, refractory,
Lying down in the melting snow.
There were times we regretted
The summer palaces on slopes, the terraces,
And the silken girls bringing sherbet.
Then the camel men cursing and grumbling
And running away, and wanting their liquor and
women,
And the night-fires going out, and the lack of shelters,
And the cities hostile and the towns unfriendly
And the villages dirty and charging high prices:
A hard time we had of it.
At the end we preferred to travel all night,
Sleeping in snatches,
With the voices singing in our ears, saying
That this was all folly.

[23]The opening five lines are adapted from a nativity sermon which the seventeenth-century divine Lancelot Andrewes delivered on Christmas Day, 1622, telling of the hardships endured by the Three Wise Men. Eliot quotes the complete passage in his essay on Lancelot Andrewes.

Then at dawn we came down to a temperate valley,
Wet, below the snow line, smelling of vegetation;
With a running stream and a water-mill beating the
darkness,
And three trees on the low sky,
And an old white horse galloped away in the meadow.
Then we came to a tavern with vine-leaves over the
lintel,
Six hands at an open door dicing for pieces of silver,
And feet kicking the empty wine-skins.
But there was no information, and so we continued
And arrived at evening, not a moment too soon
Finding the place; it was (you may say) satisfactory.

All this was a long time ago, I remember,
And I would do it again, but set down
This set down
This: were we led all that way for
Birth or Death? There was a Birth, certainly,
We had evidence and no doubt. I had seen birth and
death,
But had thought they were different; this Birth was
Hard and bitter agony for us, like Death, our death.
We returned to our places, these Kingdoms,
But no longer at ease here, in the old dispensation,[24]
With an alien people clutching their gods.
I should be glad of another death.

[24]The "old dispensation" is the laws of the Old Testament, now replaced by the "new dispensation" of Christ.

Wilfred Owen (1893–1918)

Born in Shropshire, England, Wilfred Owen was educated at the Birkenhead Institute, Liverpool. Because of ill health he moved to France in 1913 where he tutored for a private family and wrote poetry, but in 1915 he felt that it was his duty to enlist in the English army. His experiences in the trenches led to a powerful change in his poetry, which had been vague and romantic. In June 1917 Owen was invalided back to England where he met the young English poet Siegfried Sassoon who would later collect Owen's poetry in a posthumous volume (1920). Against the wishes of his friends he returned to France in August 1918 and was killed one week before the Armistice. In the fragmentary preface which Owen wrote for his poems, he declared that they were concerned with "War, and the pity of War. The Poetry is in the pity. All a poet can do is warn."

STRANGE MEETING

It seemed that out of battle I escaped
Down some profound dull tunnel, long since scooped
Through granites which titanic wars had groined.

Yet also there encumbered sleepers groaned,
Too fast in thought or death to be bestirred.
Then, as I probed them, one sprang up, and stared
With piteous recognition in fixed eyes,
Lifting distressful hands, as if to bless.
And by his smile, I knew that sullen hall,—
By his dead smile I knew we stood in Hell.

With a thousand pains that vision's face was grained;
Yet no blood reached there from the upper ground,
And no guns thumped, or down the flues made moan.
'Strange friend,' I said, 'here is no cause to mourn.'
'None,' said that other, 'save the undone years,
The hopelessness. Whatever hope is yours,
Was my life also; I went hunting wild
After the wildest beauty in the world,
Which lies not calm in eyes, or braided hair,
But mocks the steady running of the hour,
And if it grieves, grieves richlier than here.
For by my glee might many men have laughed,
And of my weeping something had been left,
Which must die now. I mean the truth untold,
The pity of war, the pity war distilled.
Now men will go content with what we spoiled,
Or, discontent, boil bloody, and be spilled.
They will be swift with swiftness of the tigress.
None will break ranks, though nations trek from
progress.
Courage was mine, and I had mystery,
Wisdom was mine, and I had mastery:
To miss the march of this retreating world
Into vain citadels that are not walled.
Then, when much blood had clogged their chariot-
wheels,
I would go up and wash them from sweet wells,
Even with truths that lie too deep for taint.
I would have poured my spirit without stint
But not through wounds; not on the cess of war.
Foreheads of men have bled where no wounds were.

I am the enemy you killed, my friend.
I knew you in this dark: for so you frowned
Yesterday through me as you jabbed and killed.
I parried; but my hands were loath and cold.
Let us sleep now. . . .'

ANTHEM FOR DOOMED YOUTH

What passing-bells for these who die as cattle?
—Only the monstrous anger of the guns.
Only the stuttering rifles' rapid rattle
Can patter out their hasty orisons.
No mockeries now for them; no prayers nor bells;
Nor any voice of mourning save the choirs,—
The shrill, demented choirs of wailing shells;
And bugles calling for them from sad shires.

What candles may be held to speed them all?
Not in the hands of boys, but in their eyes
Shall shine the holy glimmers of good-byes.
The pallor of girls' brows shall be their pall;
Their flowers the tenderness of patient minds,
And each slow dusk a drawing-down of blinds.

Emily Dickinson (1830–1886)

Born in Amherst, Massachusetts, Emily Dickinson spent her entire life there except for one year at Mount Holyoke Female Seminary in nearby South Hadley, Massachusetts. She never married, and her intensely private life revolved about her garden, her friends, and her books. Inspired by the poetry of Ralph Waldo Emerson and Emily Brontë, she began to write passionate verse on the themes of death, love, and religious intimations. As her powers increased she developed a personal and idiosyncratic verse-form marked by wit, paradox, and daring technical innovations. Contemporary readers were disturbed by her slant-rhymes and staccato syntax, the very qualities that have appealed to modern poets, and she published only a handful of poems during her lifetime. Three selections from her poetry which appeared posthumously in 1890–96 gave her some reputation, but it was the collections of 1914 and afterwards that had such a profound impact on the generation of English and American poets that came to maturity after World War I. The full text of all her poems did not appear until 1955 when T. H. Johnson edited a three-volume edition with variant readings.

IF I SHOULDN'T BE ALIVE

If I shouldn't be alive
When the Robins come,
Give the one in Red Cravat,
A Memorial crumb.

If I couldn't thank you,
Being fast asleep,
You will know I'm trying
With my Granite lip!

THERE'S A CERTAIN SLANT OF LIGHT

There's a certain Slant of light,
Winter Afternoons—
That oppresses, like the Heft
Of Cathedral Tunes—

Heavenly Hurt, it gives us—
We can find no scar,
But internal difference,
Where the Meanings, are—

None may teach it—Any—
'Tis the Seal Despair—
An imperial affliction
Sent us of the Air—

When it comes, the Landscape listens—
Shadows—hold their breath—
When it goes, 'tis like the Distance
On the look of Death—

THE SOUL SELECTS HER OWN SOCIETY

The Soul selects her own Society—
Then—shuts the Door—
To her divine Majority—
Present no more—

Unmoved—she notes the Chariots—pausing—
At her low Gate—
Unmoved—an Emperor be kneeling
Upon her Mat—

I've known her—from an ample nation—
Choose One—
Then—close the Valves of her attention—
Like Stone—

AFTER GREAT PAIN

After great pain, a formal feeling comes—
The Nerves sit ceremonious, like Tombs—
The stiff Heart questions was it He, that bore,
And Yesterday, or Centuries before?

The Feet, mechanical, go round—
Of Ground, or Air, or Ought—
A Wooden way
Regardless grown,
A Quartz contentment, like a stone—

This is the Hour of Lead—
Remembered, if outlived,
As Freezing persons, recollect the Snow—
First—Chill—then Stupor—then the letting go—

BECAUSE I COULD NOT STOP FOR DEATH

Because I could not stop for Death—
He kindly stopped for me—
The Carriage held but just Ourselves—
And Immortality.

We slowly drove—He knew no haste
And I had put away

My labor and my leisure too,
For His Civility—

We passed the School, where Children strove
At Recess—in the Ring—
We passed the Fields of Gazing Grain—
We passed the Setting Sun—

Or rather—He passed Us—
The Dews drew quivering and chill—
For only Gossamer, my Gown—
My Tippet—only Tulle—

We paused before a House that seemed
A Swelling of the Ground—
The Roof was scarcely visible—
The Cornice—in the Ground—

Since then—'tis Centuries—and yet
Feels shorter than the Day
I first surmised the Horses' Heads
Were toward Eternity—

THE BUSTLE IN A HOUSE

The Bustle in a House
The Morning after Death
Is solemnest of industries
Enacted upon Earth—

The Sweeping up the Heart
And putting Love away
We shall not want to use again
Until Eternity.

Gerard Manley Hopkins (1844–1889)

Gerard Manley Hopkins was educated at Highgate School, London, and Balliol College, Oxford, where he came under the influence of John Henry (later Cardinal) Newman. Although born into the Anglican Church, Hopkins was converted to Roman Catholicism in 1866 after a period of intense spiritual turmoil. He became a Jesuit novice in 1868 and was ordained to the priesthood in 1877, serving as a parish priest and teacher in London, Oxford, Liverpool, and Glasgow. In 1884 he was appointed Professor of Greek in University College, Dublin. Hopkins burned his early poems when he entered the Jesuit order, but in 1875 he began to write again, paying tribute in a long poem to five Franciscan nuns who had perished in the wreck of the ship *Deutschland.* The poem was rejected by a Jesuit magazine and Hopkins submitted no more verse for publication during his lifetime, although he continued to write poems of daring technical innovation until his death from typhoid at the age of forty-four. His poetry was finally published in 1918 by his friend Robert Bridges and immediately had a profound impact on the younger English and American poets. His expressive rhythms, his organic use of alliteration and assonance, and his startling mixture of colloquial and formal dictions have become part of the repertory of modern poetry.

GOD'S GRANDEUR

The world is charged with the grandeur of God.
  It will flame out, like shining from shook foil;[1]
  It gathers to a greatness, like the ooze of oil
Crushed. Why do men then now not reck his rod?
Generations have trod, have trod, have trod;
  And all is seared with trade; bleared, smeared with toil;
  And wears man's smudge and shares man's smell: the soil
Is bare now, nor can foot feel, being shod.

[1] As in gold-foil or tinsel.

And for all this, nature is never spent;
There lives the dearest freshness deep down things;
And though the last lights off the black West went
Oh, morning, at the brown brink eastward, springs—
Because the Holy Ghost over the bent
World broods with warm breast and with ah! bright wings.

THE WINDHOVER:[2]

To Christ our Lord

I caught this morning morning's minion, king-
dom of daylight's dauphin, dapple-dawn-drawn Falcon, in his riding
Of the rolling level underneath him steady air, and striding
High there, how he rung upon the rein of a wimpling[3] wing
In his ecstasy! then off, off forth on swing,
As a skate's heel sweeps smooth on a bow-bend: the hurl and gliding
Rebuffed the big wind. My heart in hiding
Stirred for a bird,—the achieve of, the mastery of the thing!

Brute beauty and valour and act, oh, air, pride, plume here
Buckle! AND the fire that breaks from thee then, a billion
Times told lovelier, more dangerous, O my chevalier!

No wonder of it: shéer plód makes plough down sillion[4]
Shine, and blue-bleak embers, ah my dear,
Fall, gall themselves, and gash gold-vermilion.

[2] The kestrel, which flies head into the wind.
[3] Rippling like a folded cloth.
[4] Furrow left by a plow.

PIED BEAUTY

Glory be to God for dappled things—
For skies of couple-colour as a brinded cow;
For rose-moles all in stipple upon trout that swim;
Fresh-firecoal chestnut-falls; finches' wings;
Landscape plotted and pieced—fold, fallow, and plough;
And áll trádes, their gear and tackle and trim.

All things counter, original, spare, strange;
Whatever is fickle, freckled (who knows how?)
With swift, slow; sweet, sour; adazzle, dim;
He fathers-forth whose beauty is past change:
Praise him.

THOU ART INDEED JUST, LORD

Justus quidem tu es, Domine, si disputem tecum; verumtamen justa loquar ad te: Quare via impiorium prosperatur? &c.[5]

Thou art indeed just, Lord, if I contend
With thee; but, sir, so what I plead is just.
Why do sinners' ways prosper? and why must
Disappointment all I endeavour end?

Wert thou my enemy, O thou my friend,
How wouldst thou worse, I wonder, than thou dost
Defeat, thwart me? Oh, the sots and thralls of lust
Do in spare hours more thrive than I that spend,

Sir, life upon thy cause. See, banks and brakes
Now, leavèd how thick! lacèd they are again
With fretty chervil, look, and fresh wind shakes

Them; birds build—but not I build; no, but strain,
Time's eunuch, and not breed one work that wakes.
Mine, O thou lord of life, send my roots rain.

[5] Jeremiah 12:1. "Righteous art thou, O Lord, when I plead with thee: yet let me talk with thee of thy judgments: Wherefore doth the way of the wicked prosper?"

E. E. Cummings (1894–1962)

Born in Cambridge, Massachusetts, Edward Estlin Cummings was educated at Harvard (B.A. 1915, M.A. 1916) before volunteering for service as an ambulance driver in France in World War I. While in France he was arrested and interned for several months because of letters written to the anarchist Emma Goldman; his first book, *The Enormous Room* (1922), is an autobiographical account of life in the French internment camp. After the war Cummings spent most of his time in Greenwich Village and Paris, where he studied art. His first collection of poems, *Tulips and Chimneys* (1923), was followed by *XLI Poems* (1925) and ten other volumes of verse, all collected in the *Complete Poems* (1968). Cummings also wrote plays, criticism, and experimental prose. His early poems, such as "O sweet spontaneous," established his distinctive and idiosyncratic style in which typography and word-play are the vehicles of meaning. The complex verbal surface acts as a counterbalance to Cumming's themes, which are often merely whimsical or sentimental. In his poetry the Romantic egoism of so much American poetry finds its most naive and joyful expression.

O SWEET SPONTANEOUS

O sweet spontaneous
earth how often have
the
doting

        fingers of
prurient philosophers pinched
and
poked

thee
, has the naughty thumb
of science prodded
thy

    beauty   . how
often have religions taken
thee upon their scraggy knees
squeezing and

buffeting thee that thou mightest conceive
gods
        (but
true

to the incomparable
couch of death thy
rhythmic
lover

        thou answerest

them only with

                        spring)

I SING OF OLAF

i sing of Olaf glad and big
whose warmest heart recoiled at war:
a conscientious object-or

his wellbelovéd colonel(trig
westpointer most succinctly bred)
took erring Olaf soon in hand
but—though an host of overjoyed
noncoms(first knocking on the head
him)do through icy waters roll
that helplessness which others stroke
with brushes recently employed
anent this muddy toiletbowl,
while kindred intellects evoke
allegiance per blunt instruments—
Olaf(being to all intents
a corpse and wanting any rag
upon what God unto him gave)
responds,without getting annoyed
"I will not kiss your f.ing flag"

straightway the silver bird looked grave
(departing hurriedly to shave)

but—though all kinds of officers
(a yearning nation's blueeyed pride)
their passive prey did kick and curse
until for wear their clarion
voices and boots were much the worse,
and egged the firstclassprivates on
his rectum wickedly to tease
by means of skilfully applied
bayonets roasted hot with heat—
Olaf(upon what were once knees)
does almost ceaselessly repeat
"there is some s. I will not eat"

our president,being of which
assertions duly notified
threw the yellowsonofabitch
into a dungeon,where he died

Christ(of His mercy infinite)
i pray to see;and Olaf,too

preponderatingly because
unless statistics lie he was
more brave than me:more blond than you.

ANYONE LIVED IN A PRETTY HOW TOWN

anyone lived in a pretty how town
(with up so floating many bells down)
spring summer autumn winter
he sang his didn't he danced his did.

Women and men(both little and small)
cared for anyone not at all
they sowed their isn't they reaped their same
sun moon stars rain

children guessed(but only a few
and down they forgot as up they grew
autumn winter spring summer)
that noone loved him more by more

when by now and tree by leaf
she laughed his joy she cried his grief
bird by snow and stir by still
anyone's any was all to her

someones married their everyones
laughed their cryings and did their dance
(sleep wake hope and then)they
said their nevers they slept their dream

stars rain sun moon
(and only the snow can begin to explain
how children are apt to forget to remember
with up so floating many bells down)

one day anyone died i guess
(and noone stooped to kiss his face)
busy folk buried them side by side
little by little and was by was

all by all and deep by deep
and more by more they dream their sleep
noone and anyone earth by april
wish by spirit and if by yes.

Women and men(both dong and ding)
summer autumn winter spring
reaped their sowing and went their came
sun moon stars rain

Hart Crane (1899–1932)

Hart Crane was born in Garrettsville, Ohio, the son of a prosperous businessman. His family moved to Cleveland when he was nine and he was educated in the local schools, leaving high school before graduation. Emotional difficulties within the family left a lasting mark on Crane, and he was afflicted throughout his life by severe psychological problems. He worked at various jobs in New York and Ohio and finally settled in New York City in 1923. Crane contributed poems to the little magazines in the early 1920s so that by the time his first book, *White Buildings,* was published in 1926 he had achieved considerable fame as a young poet, gaining recognition from critics such as Allen Tate. Crane early assimilated the works of Yeats, Pound, and especially T. S. Eliot, whose *Waste Land* had a profound impact upon him. The chief accomplishment of his brief career was *The Bridge* (1930), a visionary epic of American life which took Brooklyn Bridge as its gathering symbol. On the basis of *The Bridge* Crane won a Guggenheim Fellowship and travelled to Mexico, where he hoped to write another verse epic. "The Broken Tower" was written at this time, but Crane's alcoholism and emotional turmoil prevented him from completing a longer work. While returning to New York from Mexico, he jumped into the Caribbean and was drowned.

AT MELVILLE'S TOMB[1]

Often beneath the wave, wide from this ledge
The dice of drowned men's bones he saw bequeath
An embassy. Their numbers as he watched,
Beat on the dusty shore and were obscured.

And wrecks passed without sound of bells,
The calyx of death's bounty giving back
A scattered chapter, livid hieroglyph,
The portent wound in corridors of shells.

Then in the circuit calm of one vast coil,
Its lashings charmed and malice reconciled,
Frosted eyes there were that lifted altars;
And silent answers crept across the stars.

Compass, quadrant and sextant contrive
No farther tides . . . High in the azure steeps
Monody shall not wake the mariner.
This fabulous shadow only the sea keeps.

[1] Herman Melville, the great American novelist, is buried in Woodlawn Cemetery, New York City. Before "At Melville's Tomb" was published in *Poetry: A Magazine of Verse* (October 1926) Crane wrote to the puzzled editor, Harriet Monroe, explaining the poem and his general theory of poetry. This correspondence was published with the poem and has often been reprinted (most conveniently in *Understanding Poetry,* ed. Cleanth Brooks and Robert Penn Warren).

THE BROKEN TOWER

The bell-rope that gathers God at dawn[2]
Dispatches me as though I dropped down the knell
Of a spent day—to wander the cathedral lawn
From pit to crucifix, feet chill on steps from hell.

Have you not heard, have you not seen that corps
Of shadows in the tower, whose shoulders sway
Antiphonal carillons launched before
The stars are caught and hived in the sun's ray?

[2] In the Roman Catholic Church the Angelus bell is rung three times a day, at 6 A.M., noon, and 6 P.M., in memory of the Annunciation.

The bells, I say, the bells break down their tower;
And swing I know not where. Their tongues engrave
Membrane through marrow, my long-scattered score
Of broken intervals. . . . And I, their sexton slave!

Oval encyclicals in canyons heaping
The impasse high with choir. Banked voices slain!
Pagodas, campaniles with reveilles outleaping—
O terraced echoes prostrate on the plain! . . .

And so it was I entered the broken world
To trace the visionary company of love, its voice
An instant in the wind (I know not whither hurled)
But not for long to hold each desperate choice.

My word I poured. But was it cognate, scored
Of that tribunal monarch of the air
Whose thigh embronzes earth, strikes crystal Word
In wounds pledged once to hope—cleft to despair?

The steep encroachments of my blood left me
No answer (could blood hold such a lofty tower
As flings the question true?)—or is it she
Whose sweet mortality stirs latent power?—

And through whose pulse I hear, counting the strokes
My veins recall and add, revived and sure
The angelus of wars my chest evokes:
What I hold healed, original now, and pure . . .

And builds, within, a tower that is not stone
(Not stone can jacket heaven)—but slip
Of pebbles—visible wings of silence sown
In azure circles, widening as they dip

The matrix of the heart, lift down the eye
That shrines the quiet lake and swells a tower . . .
The commodious, tall decorum of that sky
Unseals her earth, and lifts love in its shower.

Allen Tate (1899–   )

Born in Kentucky, Allen Tate entered Vanderbilt University in Nashville, Tennessee, in 1918 and soon became one of the "Fugitives," a group of conservative Southern writers who wished to defend traditional, agrarian values against the encroachment of an anonymous industrial society. He helped edit the magazine *The Fugitive* (1922–25), and contributed to the symposium volume *I'll Take My Stand* (1930) which defended the agrarian position. In 1934 he took a teaching position at Southwestern University in Memphis, Tennessee, and during his long career he has held many academic appointments, notably at Princeton University and the University of Minnesota. He has published numerous volumes of poetry, and as a critic was influential in establishing the "New Criticism," which emphasized close reading of the poetic text and promulgated T. S. Eliot's concept of the literary tradition (see Eliot's "Tradition and the Individual Talent," reprinted in the Essay section). The best of Tate's poetry and criticism may be found in *Poems* (1960) and *Essays of Four Decades* (1969). Tate has also written a brilliant novel, *The Fathers* (1938), which dramatizes his convictions about social order and tradition. "Ode to the Confederate Dead," written in the late 1920s, is the subject of Tate's essay "Narcissus as Narcissus," reprinted in the Essay section.

ODE TO THE CONFEDERATE DEAD[1]

Row after row with strict impunity
The headstones yield their names to the element,
The wind whirrs without recollection;
In the riven troughs the splayed leaves
Pile up, of nature the casual sacrament
To the seasonal eternity of death;
Then driven by the fierce scrutiny
Of heaven to their election in the vast breath,
They sough the rumour of mortality.

Autumn is desolation in the plot
Of a thousand acres where these memories grow
From the inexhaustible bodies that are not
Dead, but feed the grass row after rich row.
Think of the autumns that have come and gone!—
Ambitious November with the humors of the year,
With a particular zeal for every slab,
Staining the uncomfortable angels that rot
On the slabs, a wing chipped here, an arm there:
The brute curiosity of an angel's stare
Turns you, like them, to stone,
Transforms the heaving air
Till plunged to a heavier world below
You shift your sea-space blindly
Heaving, turning like the blind crab.

  Dazed by the wind, only the wind
  The leaves flying, plunge

You know who have waited by the wall
The twilight certainty of an animal,
Those midnight restitutions of the blood
You know—the immitigable pines, the smoky frieze
Of the sky, the sudden call: you know the rage,
The cold pool left by the mounting flood,
Of muted Zeno and Parmenides.[2]
You who have waited for the angry resolution
Of those desires that should be yours tomorrow,
You know the unimportant shrift of death
And praise the vision
And praise the arrogant circumstance
Of those who fall
Rank upon rank, hurried beyond decision—
Here by the sagging gate, stopped by the wall.

  Seeing, seeing only the leaves
  Flying, plunge and expire

Turn your eyes to the immoderate past,
Turn to the inscrutable infantry rising
Demons out of the earth—they will not last.
Stonewall, Stonewall, and the sunken fields of hemp,
Shiloh, Antietam, Malvern Hill, Bull Run.[3]
Lost in that orient of the thick-and-fast
You will curse the setting sun.

  Cursing only the leaves crying
  Like an old man in a storm

You hear the shout, the crazy hemlocks point
With troubled fingers to the silence which
Smothers you, a mummy, in time.
                                        The hound bitch
Toothless and dying, in a musty cellar
Hears the wind only.

                              Now that the salt of their blood
Stiffens the saltier oblivion of the sea,
Seals the malignant purity of the flood,
What shall we who count our days and bow
Our heads with a commemorial woe
In the ribboned coats of grim felicity,
What shall we say of the bones, unclean,
Whose verdurous anonymity will grow?
The ragged arms, the ragged heads and eyes
Lost in these acres of the insane green?
The gray lean spiders come, they come and go;
In a tangle of willows without light
The singular screech-owl's tight
Invisible lyric seeds the mind
With the furious murmur of their chivalry.

  We shall say only the leaves
  Flying, plunge and expire

We shall say only the leaves whispering
In the improbable mist of nightfall
That flies on multiple wing;
Night is the beginning and the end
And in between the ends of distraction
Waits mute speculation, the patient curse

[1] For Tate's own explanation of the poem, see his essay "Narcissus as Narcissus" in the Essay section.

[2] Parmenides and his pupil Zeno, Greek philosophers of the fifth century B.C., sought to prove the existence of the One by controverting the popular belief in the Many.

[3] "Stonewall" Jackson, the Confederate general, earned that name at the first Battle of Bull Run in 1861 where his firm stand caught the eye of General Bee, who shouted: "There is Jackson standing like a stone wall." His real name was Thomas Jonathan Jackson.
Shiloh, Antietam, Malvern Hill: the names of famous battles in the Civil War.

That stones the eyes, or like the jaguar leaps
For his own image in a jungle pool, his victim.

What shall we say who have knowledge
Carried to the heart? Shall we take the act
To the grave? Shall we, more hopeful, set up the grave
In the house? The ravenous grave?

Leave now
The shut gate and the decomposing wall:
The gentle serpent, green in the mulberry bush,
Riots with his tongue through the hush—
Sentinel of the grave who counts us all!

Langston Hughes (1902–1967)

James Langston Hughes was brought up by his grandmother and mother, his father having moved to Mexico to escape racial discrimination. He graduated from high school in Cleveland and the following summer wrote one of his best-known poems, "The Negro Speaks of Rivers." He attended Columbia University in 1921–22 and then worked his way on a freighter to Africa and Europe. While working as a busboy after returning to the United States he was "discovered" by the poet Vachel Lindsay and received a scholarship to Lincoln University in Pennsylvania from which he graduated in 1929. *The Weary Blues* (1926) was followed by nine volumes of poetry over the next forty years. Hughes was a prolific writer, producing short stories, autobiography, and juvenile fiction as well as poetry. In the 1930s he travelled to the Soviet Union and to Spain, reporting for newspapers and magazines. Hughes was the author of several books and anthologies dealing with black history and the place of the black in American society. As the temper of the times changed his art reflected the growing militancy and confidence of the black population. *The Panther and the Lash* (1967), a posthumous volume of poetry, reveals Hughes as a spokesman for the 1960s.

THE NEGRO SPEAKS OF RIVERS

I've known rivers:
I've known rivers ancient as the world and older than
    the flow of human blood in human veins.

My soul has grown deep like the rivers.

I bathed in the Euphrates when dawns were young.
I built my hut near the Congo and it lulled me to sleep.
I looked upon the Nile and raised the pyramids above
    it.
I heard the singing of the Mississippi when Abe Lincoln
    went down to New Orleans, and I've seen its
    muddy bosom turn all golden in the sunset.

I've known rivers:
Ancient, dusky rivers.

My soul has grown deep like the rivers.

DREAM DEFERRED

What happens to a dream deferred?

    Does it dry up
    like a raisin in the sun?
    Or fester like a sore—
    And then run?
    Does it stink like rotten meat?

Or crust and sugar over—
like a syrupy sweet?

Maybe it just sags
like a heavy load.

Or does it explode?

THEME FOR ENGLISH B

The instructor said,

Go home and write
a page tonight.
And let that page come out of you—
Then, it will be true.

I wonder if it's that simple?
I am twenty-two, colored, born in Winston-Salem.
I went to school there, then Durham, then here
to this college on the hill above Harlem.[1]
I am the only colored student in my class.
The steps from the hill lead down into Harlem,
through a park, then I cross St. Nicholas,
Eighth Avenue, Seventh, and I come to the Y,
the Harlem Branch Y, where I take the elevator
up to my room, sit down, and write this page:

[1] Columbia University.

It's not easy to know what is true for you or me
at twenty-two, my age. But I guess I'm what
I feel and see and hear, Harlem, I hear you:
hear you, hear me—we two—you, me, talk on this
page.
(I hear New York, too.) Me—who?

Well, I like to eat, sleep, drink, and be in love.
I like to work, read, learn, and understand life.
I like a pipe for a Christmas present,
or records—Bessie,[2] bop, or Bach.
I guess being colored doesn't make me *not* like
the same things other folks like who are other races.
So will my page be colored that I write?
Being me, it will not be white.
But it will be
a part of you, instructor.
You are white—
yet a part of me, as I am a part of you.
That's American.
Sometimes perhaps you don't want to be a part of me.
Nor do I often want to be a part of you.
But we are, that's true!
As I learn from you,
I guess you learn from me—
although you're older—and white—
and somewhat more free.

This is my page for English B.

[2] Bessie Smith, one of the greatest singers of jazz blues.

W. H. Auden (1907–1973)

The first major English poet to emerge after the generation of Pound and Eliot, Wystan Hugh Auden, the son of a doctor, was born in Yorkshire, England. He was early influenced by his father's scientific interests and by the lonely grandeur of the Yorkshire landscape, which becomes a landscape of feeling in many of his poems (see "In Praise of Limestone" where the Yorkshire of his youth is merged with the softer Italian landscape of middle age). After education at private schools, Auden entered Oxford University in 1925 where he had a strong influence on such contemporaries as Stephen Spender and C. Day Lewis. Auden was a brilliant undergraduate poet, and so powerful was his impact on others that it makes sense to speak of an "Auden Generation" in English poetry. His early poems combine schoolroom attitudes with imagery drawn from the Old English and Icelandic sagas and ideas drawn from Freud and Marx. *The Orators* (1932), a volume mixing poetry and prose, best sums up this early phase of Auden's career. During the 1930s Auden was responsive to the social pressures of the time, writing poetry and plays with a left-wing political cast, but as the decade declined Auden moved toward a more conservative position. His "reconversion" to Christianity is reflected in such works as *New Year Letter* (1941), *For the Time Being* (1944), and *The Age of Anxiety* (1947). This spiritual turning was paralleled by Auden's decision to settle in the United States: he moved to New York in 1939 and became a U.S. citizen in 1946. After the end of World War II Auden travelled easily between New York and his various residences in England and Europe. From 1956 to 1961 he was Professor of Poetry at Oxford.

Auden was an immensely prolific writer, publishing dozens of volumes of poetry, critical essays, plays, translations, and opera libretti. Some of his best criticism is available in *The Dyer's Hand* (1962). His *Collected Shorter Poems* and *Collected Longer Poems* have recently been replaced by *Collected Poems,* ed. Edward Mendelson (1976).

THE WANDERER

Doom is dark and deeper than any sea-dingle[1]
Upon what man it fall
In spring, day-wishing flowers appearing,
Avalanche sliding, white snow from rock-face,
That he should leave his house,
No cloud-soft hand can hold him, restraint by women;
But ever that man goes
Through place-keepers, through forest trees,
A stranger to strangers over undried sea,
Houses for fishes, suffocating water,
Or lonely on fell as chat,
By pot-holed becks
A bird stone-haunting, an unquiet bird.

There head falls forward, fatigued at evening,
And dreams of home,
Waving from window, spread of welcome,
Kissing of wife under single sheet;
But waking sees
Bird-flocks nameless to him, through doorway voices
Of new men making another love.

Save him from hostile capture,
From sudden tiger's spring at corner;
Protect his house,
His anxious house where days are counted
From thunderbolt protect,
From gradual ruin spreading like a stain;
Converting number from vague to certain,
Bring joy, bring day of his returning,
Lucky with day approaching, with leaning dawn.

[1] The first line is adopted from a translation of a Middle English homily: "They are so wise that they know all God's counsels, his mysteries and his judgments, which are secret and deeper than any sea-dingle." The entire poem is modeled after such Old English journey poems as *The Wanderer* and *The Seafarer,* and this Old English atmosphere is enforced by the alliteration and word order.

MUSÉE DES BEAUX ARTS[2]

About suffering they were never wrong,
The Old Masters: how well they understood
Its human position; how it takes place
While someone else is eating or opening a window or
just walking dully along;
How, when the aged are reverently, passionately
waiting
For the miraculous birth, there always must be
Children who did not specially want it to happen,
skating
On a pond at the edge of the wood:
They never forgot
That even the dreadful martyrdom must run its course
Anyhow in a corner, some untidy spot
Where the dogs go on with their doggy life and the
torturer's horse
Scratches its innocent behind on a tree.

In Brueghel's *Icarus,*[3] for instance: how everything
turns away
Quite leisurely from the disaster; the ploughman may
Have heard the splash, the forsaken cry,
But for him it was not an important failure; the sun
shone
As it had to on the white legs disappearing into the
green

[2] French for Museum of Fine Arts.

[3] Pieter Brueghel (1525–69) painted a famous *Fall of Icarus* in which the mythological disaster is almost lost in the sumptuous detail of the natural scene. See William Carlos Williams' poem on the same subject, "Landscape with the Fall of Icarus."

Water; and the expensive delicate ship that must have
seen
Something amazing, a boy falling out of the sky,
Had somewhere to get to and sailed calmly on.

IN MEMORY OF W. B. YEATS

(d. Jan. 1939)

I

He disappeared in the dead of winter:
The brooks were frozen, the airports almost deserted,
And snow disfigured the public statues;
The mercury sank in the mouth of the dying day.
What instruments we have agree
The day of his death was a dark cold day.

Far from his illness
The wolves ran on through the evergreen forests,
The peasant river was untempted by the fashionable
quays;
By mourning tongues
The death of the poet was kept from his poems.

But for him it was his last afternoon as himself,
An afternoon of nurses and rumours;
The provinces of his body revolted,
The squares of his mind were empty,
Silence invaded the suburbs,
The current of his feeling failed; he became his
admirers.

Now he is scattered among a hundred cities
And wholly given over to unfamiliar affections,
To find his happiness in another kind of wood
And be punished under a foreign code of conscience.
The words of a dead man
Are modified in the guts of the living.

But in the importance and noise of to-morrow
When the brokers are roaring like beasts on the floor
of the Bourse,[4]
And the poor have the sufferings to which they are
fairly accustomed,
And each in the cell of himself is almost convinced of
his freedom,
A few thousand will think of this day
As one thinks of a day when one did something
slightly unusual.
What instruments we have agree
The day of his death was a dark cold day.

II

You were silly like us, your gift survived it all:
The parish of rich women, physical decay,
Yourself. Mad Ireland hurt you into poetry.
Now Ireland has her madness and her weather still,
For poetry makes nothing happen: it survives
In the valley of its making where executives
Would never want to tamper, flows on south
From ranches of isolation and the busy griefs,
Raw towns that we believe and die in; it survives,
A way of happening, a mouth.

III

Earth, receive an honoured guest:
William Yeats is laid to rest.
Let the Irish vessel lie
Emptied of its poetry.

In the nightmare of the dark
All the dogs of Europe bark,
And the living nations wait,
Each sequestered in its hate;

Intellectual disgrace
Stares from every human face,
And the seas of pity lie
Locked and frozen in each eye.

Follow, poet, follow right
To the bottom of the night,
With your unconstraining voice
Still persuade us to rejoice;

With the farming of a verse
Make a vineyard of the curse,
Sing of human unsuccess
In a rapture of distress;

In the deserts of the heart
Let the healing fountain start,
In the prison of his days
Teach the free man how to praise.

[4] A European stock exchange.

IN PRAISE OF LIMESTONE

If it form the one landscape that we, the inconstant ones,
Are consistently homesick for, this is chiefly
Because it dissolves in water. Mark these rounded slopes
With their surface fragrance of thyme and, beneath,
A secret system of caves and conduits; hear the springs
That spurt out everywhere with a chuckle,
Each filling a private pool for its fish and carving
Its own little ravine whose cliffs entertain
The butterfly and the lizard; examine this region
Of short distances and definite places:
What could be more like Mother or a fitter background
For her son, the flirtatious male who lounges
Against a rock in the sunlight, never doubting
That for all his faults he is loved; whose works are but
Extensions of his power to charm? From weathered outcrop
To hill-top temple, from appearing waters to
Conspicuous fountains, from a wild to a formal vineyard,
Are ingenious but short steps that a child's wish
To receive more attention than his brothers, whether
By pleasing or teasing, can easily take.

Watch, then, the band of rivals as they climb up and down
Their steep stone gennels[5] in twos and threes, at times
Arm in arm, but never, thank God, in step; or engaged
On the shady side of a square at midday in
Voluble discourse, knowing each other too well to think
There are any important secrets, unable
To conceive a god whose temper-tantrums are moral
And not to be pacified by a clever line
Or a good lay: for, accustomed to a stone that responds,
They have never had to veil their faces in awe
Of a crater whose blazing fury could not be fixed;
Adjusted to the local needs of valleys
Where everything can be touched or reached by walking,
Their eyes have never looked into infinite space
Through the lattice-work of a nomad's comb; born lucky,
Their legs have never encountered the fungi
And insects of the jungle, the monstrous forms and lives
With which we have nothing, we like to hope, in common.
So, when one of them goes to the bad, the way his mind works
Remains comprehensible: to become a pimp
Or deal in fake jewellery or ruin a fine tenor voice
For effects that bring down the house, could happen to all
But the best and the worst of us . . .
That is why, I suppose,
The best and worst never stayed here long but sought
Immoderate soils where the beauty was not so external,
The light less public and the meaning of life
Something more than a mad camp. 'Come!' cried the granite wastes,
'How evasive is your humour, how accidental
Your kindest kiss, how permanent is death.' (Saints-to-be
Slipped away sighing.) 'Come!' purred the clays and gravels.
'On our plains there is room for armies to drill; rivers
Wait to be tamed and slaves to construct you a tomb
In the grand manner: soft as the earth is mankind and both
Need to be altered.' (Intendant Caesars rose and
Left, slamming the door.) But the really reckless were fetched
By an older colder voice, the oceanic whispers:
'I am the solitude that asks and promises nothing;
That is how I shall set you free. There is no love;
There are only the various envies, all of them sad.'

They were right, my dear, all those voices were right
And still are; this land is not the sweet home that it looks,
Nor its peace the historical calm of a site
Where something was settled once and for all: A backward
And dilapidated province, connected
To the big busy world by a tunnel, with a certain
Seedy appeal, is that all it is now? Not quite:
It has a worldly duty which in spite of itself
It does not neglect, but calls into question
All the Great Powers assume; it disturbs our rights. The poet,
Admired for his earnest habit of calling
The sun the sun, his mind Puzzle, is made uneasy

[5] A long narrow passage between houses.

By these marble statues which so obviously doubt
His antimythological myth; and these gamins,
Pursuing the scientist down the tiled colonnade
With such lively offers, rebuke his concern for Nature's
Remotest aspects: I, too, am reproached, for what
And how much you know. Not to lose time, not to get caught,
Not to be left behind, not, please! to resemble
The beasts who repeat themselves, or a thing like water
Or stone whose conduct can be predicted, these
Are our Common Prayer,[6] whose greatest comfort is music
Which can be made anywhere, is invisible,
And does not smell. In so far as we have to look forward
To death as a fact, no doubt we are right: But if
Sins can be forgiven, if bodies rise from the dead,
These modifications of matter into
Innocent athletes and gesticulating fountains,
Made solely for pleasure, make a further point:
The blessed will not care what angle they are regarded from,
Having nothing to hide. Dear, I know nothing of
Either, but when I try to imagine a faultless love
Or the life to come, what I hear is the murmur
Of underground streams, what I see is a limestone landscape.

[6] The Book of Common Prayer is the standard devotional text for the Church of England.

Theodore Roethke (1908–1963)

Theodore Roethke was born in Saginaw, Michigan, and educated at the University of Michigan where he took his M.A. in 1936. He taught at several colleges and universities and from 1947 until his death was a Professor of English at the University of Washington in Seattle. Roethke was slow to develop as a poet: his first volume of verse, *Open House,* did not appear until 1941, and much of his best poetry was written in the last years of his life. *The Waking: Poems 1933–1953* (1953) won a Pulitzer Prize, while *Words for the Wind: The Collected Verse of Theodore Roethke* (1958) brought him a National Book Award. Roethke's critical writings are collected in *On the Poet and His Craft* (1965).

MY PAPA'S WALTZ

The whiskey on your breath
Could make a small boy dizzy;
But I hung on like death:
Such waltzing was not easy.

We romped until the pans
Slid from the kitchen shelf;
My mother's countenance
Could not unfrown itself.

The hand that held my wrist
Was battered on one knuckle;
At every step you missed
My right ear scraped a buckle.

You beat time on my head
With a palm caked hard by dirt,
Then waltzed me off to bed
Still clinging to your shirt.

I KNEW A WOMAN

I knew a woman, lovely in her bones,
When small birds sighed, she would sigh back at them;
Ah, when she moved, she moved more ways than one:
The shapes a bright container can contain!
Of her choice virtues only gods should speak,
Or English poets who grew up on Greek
(I'd have them sing in chorus, cheek to cheek).

How well her wishes went! She stroked my chin,
She taught me Turn, and Counter-turn, and Stand;
She taught me Touch, that undulant white skin;
I nibbled meekly from her proffered hand;
She was the sickle; I, poor I, the rake,
Coming behind her for her pretty sake
(But what prodigious mowing we did make).

Love likes a gander, and adores a goose:
Her full lips pursed, the errant note to seize;
She played it quick, she played it light and loose;
My eyes, they dazzled at her flowing knees;
Her several parts could keep a pure repose,
Or one hip quiver with a mobile nose
(She moved in circles, and those circles moved).

Let seed be grass, and grass turn into hay:
I'm martyr to a motion not my own;
What's freedom for? To know eternity.
I swear she cast a shadow white as stone.
But who would count eternity in days?
These old bones live to learn her wanton ways:
(I measure time by how a body sways).

Robert Hayden (1913–)

Born in Detroit, Robert Hayden received his undergraduate education at Wayne State University and did graduate work at the University of Michigan, where he was a teaching fellow. In 1946 he joined the faculty of Fisk University in Nashville, Tennessee, where he taught for more than twenty years. In 1969 he returned to the University of Michigan as a Professor of English. He has received a number of awards for his poetry and was appointed Consultant in Poetry to the Library of Congress for 1976–77. Among his volumes of poetry are *A Ballad of Remembrance* (1962), *Words in the Mourning Time* (1970), *The Night-Blooming Cereus* (1972), and *Angle of Ascent* (1975, including new and selected poems).

MIDDLE PASSAGE[1]

I.

Jesús, Estrella, Esperanza, Mercy:[2]

Sails flashing to the wind like weapons,
sharks following the moans the fever and the dying;
horror the corposant[3] and compass rose.

Middle Passage:
voyage through death
to life upon these shores.

"10 April 1800—
Blacks rebellious. Crew uneasy. Our linguist says
their moaning is a prayer for death,
ours and their own. Some try to starve themselves.
Lost three this morning leaped with crazy laughter
to the waiting sharks, sang as they went under."

Desire, Adventure, Tartar, Ann:

Standing to America, bringing home
black gold, black ivory, black seed.

Deep in the festering hold thy father lies,
of his bones New England pews are made,
those are altar lights that were his eyes.[4]

[1] In the triangular trade route from New England to Africa to the Caribbean and back to New England, the Middle Passage (Africe to the West Indies) was the voyage for the transportation of slaves.

[2] The names of slave ships.

[3] Electrical discharge on the masts of ships during a storm, as in Melville's *Moby-Dick.*

[4] A parody of Ariel's song of transformation in Shakespeare's *The Tempest* (which is itself a play about the New World): "Full fathom five thy father lies, / Of his bones are coral made: / Those are pearls that were his eyes . . ."

Jesus Saviour Pilot Me
Over Life's Tempestuous Sea[5]

We pray that Thou wilt grant, O Lord,
safe passage to our vessels bringing
heathen souls unto Thy chastening.

Jesus Saviour

"8 bells. I cannot sleep, for I am sick
with fear, but writing eases fear a little
since still my eyes can see these words take shape
upon the page & so I write, as one
would turn to exorcism. 4 days scudding,
but now the sea is calm again. Misfortune
follows in our wake like sharks (our grinning
tutelary gods). Which one of us
has killed an albatross?[6] A plague among
our blacks—Ophthalmia: blindness—& we
have jettisoned the blind to no avail.
It spreads, the terrifying sickness spreads.
Its claws have scratched sight from the Capt.'s eyes
& there is blindness in the fo'c'sle
& we must sail 3 weeks before we come
to port."

What port awaits us, Davy Jones'
or home? I've heard of slavers drifting, drifting,
playthings of wind and storm and chance, their
crews
gone blind, the jungle hatred
crawling up on deck.

Thou Who Walked on Galilee

"Deponent further sayeth *The Bella J*
left the Guinea Coast
with cargo of five hundred blacks and odd
for the barracoons of Florida:

"That there was hardly room 'tween-decks for half
the sweltering cattle stowed spoon-fashion there;
that some went mad of thirst and tore their flesh
and sucked the blood:

"That Crew and Captain lusted with the comeliest
of the savage girls kept naked in the cabins;
that there was one they called The Guinea Rose
and they cast lots and fought to lie with her:

"That when the Bo's'n piped all hands, the flames
spreading from starboard already were beyond
control, the negroes howling and their chains
entangled with the flames:

"That the burning blacks could not be reached,
that the Crew abandoned ship,
leaving their shrieking negresses behind,
that the Captain perished drunken with the wenches:

"Further Deponent sayeth not."

Pilot Oh Pilot Me

II.

Aye, lad, and I have seen those factories,
Gambia, Rio Pongo, Calabar;
have watched the artful mongos[7] baiting traps
of war wherein the victor and the vanquished

Were caught as prizes for our barracoons.
Have seen the nigger kings whose vanity
and greed turned wild black hides of Fellatah,
Mandingo, Ibo, Kru[8] to gold for us.

And there was one—King Anthracite we named him—
fetish face beneath French parasols
of brass and orange velvet, impudent mouth
whose cups were carven skulls of enemies:

He'd honor us with drum and feast and conjo[9]
and palm-oil-glistening wenches deft in love,
and for tin crowns that shone with paste,
red calico and German-silver trinkets

Would have the drums talk war and send
his warriors to burn the sleeping villages
and kill the sick and old and lead the young
in coffles to our factories.

Twenty years a trader, twenty years,
for there was wealth aplenty to be harvested
from those black fields, and I'd be trading still
but for the fevers melting down my bones.

[5] Verses from a well-known hymn.
[6] The bird of good omen killed by the Ancient Mariner in Coleridge's poem *The Rime of the Ancient Mariner.*

[7] Negroes.
[8] The names of African tribes. "Barracoons" are places of confinement for slaves or convicts.
[9] A dance.

III.

Shuttles in the rocking loom of history,
the dark ships move, the dark ships move,
their bright ironical names
like jests of kindness on a murderer's mouth;
plough through thrashing glister toward
fata morgana's[10] lucent melting shore,
weave toward New World littorals that are
mirage and myth and actual shore.

Voyage through death,
voyage whose chartings are
unlove.

A charnel stench, effluvium of living death
spreads outward from the hold,
where the living and the dead, the horribly dying,
lie interlocked, lie foul with blood and excrement.

Deep in the festering hold thy father lies,
the corpse of mercy rots with him,
rats eat love's rotten gelid eyes.

But, oh, the living look at you
with human eyes whose suffering accuses you,
whose hatred reaches through the swill of dark
to strike you like a leper's claw.

You cannot stare that hatred down
or chain the fear that stalks the watches
and breathes on you its fetid scorching breath;
cannot kill the deep immortal human wish,
the timeless will.

"But for the storm that flung up barriers
of wind and wave, *The Amistad,*[11] señores,
would have reached the port of Principe in two,
three days at most; but for the storm we should
have been prepared for what befell.
Swift as the puma's leap it came. There was
that interval of moonless calm filled only
with the water's and the rigging's usual sounds,
then sudden movement, blows and snarling cries
and they had fallen on us with machete
and marlinspike. It was as though the very
air, the night itself were striking us.
Exhausted by the rigors of the storm,
we were no match for them. Our men went down
before the murderous Africans. Our loyal
Celestino ran from below with gun
and lantern and I saw, before the cane-
knife's wounding flash, Cinquez,
that surly brute who calls himself a prince,
directing, urging on the ghastly work.
He hacked the poor mulatto down, and then
he turned on me. The decks were slippery
when daylight finally came. It sickens me
to think of what I saw, of how these apes
threw overboard the butchered bodies of
our men, true Christians all, like so much jetsam.
Enough, enough. The rest is quickly told:
Cinquez was forced to spare the two of us
you see to steer the ship to Africa,
and we like phantoms doomed to rove the sea
voyaged east by day and west by night,
deceiving them, hoping for rescue,
prisoners on our own vessel, till
at length we drifted to the shores of this
your land, America, where we were freed
from our unspeakable misery. Now we
demand, good sirs, the extradition of
Cinquez and his accomplices to La
Havana. And it distresses us to know
there are so many here who seem inclined
to justify the mutiny of these blacks.
We find it paradoxical indeed
that you whose wealth, whose tree of liberty
are rooted in the labor of your slaves
should suffer the august John Quincy Adams
to speak with so much passion of the right
of chattel slaves to kill their lawful masters
and with his Roman rhetoric weave a hero's
garland for Cinquez. I tell you that
we are determined to return to Cuba
with our slaves and there see justice done.
Cinquez—
or let us say 'the Prince'—Cinquez shall die."

The deep immortal human wish,
the timeless will:

Cinquez its deathless primaveral image,
life that transfigures many lives.

Voyage through death
to life upon these shores.

[10] A mirage.

[11] The Africans of the slave ship *Armistad* mutinied off the coast of Cuba and sailed the ship into United States waters off Long Island where they sought refuge. Since the blacks had killed the captain and his slave Celestino the owners of the *Armistad* tried to have them extradited on a murder charge. They were imprisoned, but John Quincy Adams defended them before the Supreme Court in 1841 and won their freedom.

Dylan Thomas (1914–1953)

Dylan Thomas was born at Swansea, in southwest Wales, where his father was an English teacher at the local grammar school. He began to write poetry at a very early age, and many of his finest works date from his youth. His first volume of verse, *18 Poems,* was published in 1934, followed by *Twenty-five Poems* (1936). He moved to London in 1936, and *The Map of Love* (1939) and *Deaths and Entrances* (1946) consolidated his reputation as a master of the singing voice. Thomas was an immensely powerful reader of poetry, and between 1950 and 1953 he made several tours of America, reading his own poetry and that of others to university audiences. In November 1953 he died in New York City from an excess of drinking, an "insult to the brain." At the time of his death, *Collected Poems 1934–52* had given a new solidity to his reputation. Thomas also left behind him two semi-autobiographical works, *Portrait of the Artist as a Young Dog* (1940) and *Adventures in the Skin Trade* (1955). His radio play for voices, *Under Milk Wood* (1954), was presented at the Poetry Center in New York just before his death.

THE FORCE THAT THROUGH THE GREEN FUSE DRIVES THE FLOWER

The force that through the green fuse drives the flower
Drives my green age; that blasts the roots of trees
Is my destroyer.
And I am dumb to tell the crooked rose
My youth is bent by the same wintry fever.

The force that drives the water through the rocks
Drives my red blood; that dries the mouthing streams
Turns mine to wax.
And I am dumb to mouth unto my veins
How at the mountain spring the same mouth sucks.

The hand that whirls the water in the pool
Stirs the quicksand; that ropes the blowing wind
Hauls my shroud sail.
And I am dumb to tell the hanging man
How of my clay is made the hangman's lime.

The lips of time leech to the fountain head;
Love drips and gathers, but the fallen blood
Shall calm her sores.
And I am dumb to tell a weather's wind
How time has ticked a heaven round the stars.

And I am dumb to tell the lover's tomb
How at my sheet goes the same crooked worm.

A REFUSAL TO MOURN THE DEATH, BY FIRE, OF A CHILD IN LONDON

Never until the mankind making
Bird beast and flower
Fathering and all humbling darkness
Tells with silence the last light breaking
And the still hour
Is come of the sea tumbling in harness

And I must enter again the round
Zion of the water bead
And the synagogue of the ear of corn
Shall I let pray the shadow of a sound
Or sow my salt seed
In the least valley of sackcloth to mourn

The majesty and burning of the child's death.
I shall not murder
The mankind of her going with a grave truth
Nor blaspheme down the stations of the breath
With any further
Elegy of innocence and youth.

Deep with the first dead lies London's daughter,
Robed in the long friends,
The grains beyond age, the dark veins of her mother,
Secret by the unmourning water
Of the riding Thames.
After the first death, there is no other.

DO NOT GO GENTLE INTO THAT GOOD NIGHT

Do not go gentle into that good night,
Old age should burn and rave at close of day;
Rage, rage against the dying of the light.

Though wise men at their end know dark is right,
Because their words had forked no lightning they
Do not go gentle into that good night.

Good men, the last wave by, crying how bright
Their frail deeds might have danced in a green bay,
Rage, rage against the dying of the light.

Wild men who caught and sang the sun in flight,
And learn, too late, they grieved it on its way,
Do not go gentle into that good night.

Grave men, near death, who see with blinding sight
Blind eyes could blaze like meteors and be gay,
Rage, rage against the dying of the light.

And you, my father, there on the sad height,
Curse, bless, me now with your fierce tears, I pray.
Do not go gentle into that good night.
Rage, rage against the dying of the light.

John Berryman (1914–1972)

John Berryman (John Smith) was born in a small Oklahoma town and reared as a strict Roman Catholic. His father, John Smith, moved the family to Florida when his son was ten and committed suicide two years later. The mother then moved to New York where she married a banker, John Berryman, whose name the young boy adopted. Berryman was sent to private school and to Columbia College from which he graduated in 1936. After two years on a fellowship at Clare College, Cambridge (England), Berryman returned to the United States and taught for the remainder of his life at Wayne State University, Harvard, Princeton, and the University of Minnesota. *Poems* (1942) and *The Dispossessed* (1948) were followed by *Homage to Mistress Bradstreet* (1956), a long poem that honors Anne Bradstreet, America's first woman poet. *The 77 Dream Songs* (1964) were augmented by *His Toy, His Dream, His Rest* (1968) and *The Dream Songs* (1969). At the end of his life Berryman returned to the Roman Catholicism of his childhood. But he was still beset by psychological and spiritual turmoil, and in January 1972 he leaped to his death from a bridge in Minneapolis.

The Freedom of the Poet (1976) collects Berryman's best critical essays and his short stories. Another posthumous volume, *Henry's Fate and Other Poems* (1977), recalls the "Henry" of earlier poems, who was described by Berryman as "an imaginary character (not the poet, not me) named Henry, a white American in early middle age sometimes in blackface, who has suffered an irreversible loss and talks about himself sometimes in the first person, sometimes in the third, sometimes even in the second; he has a friend, never named, who addresses him as Mr. Bones and variants thereof."

WINTER LANDSCAPE

The three men coming down the winter hill
In brown, with tall poles and a pack of hounds
At heel, through the arrangement of the trees,
Past the five figures at the burning straw,
Returning cold and silent to their town,

Returning to the drifted snow, the rink
Lively with children, to the older men,
The long companions they can never reach,
The blue light, men with ladders, by the church
The sledge and shadow in the twilit street,

Are not aware that in the sandy time
To come, the evil waste of history
Outstretched, they will be seen upon the brow
Of that same hill: when all their company
Will have been irrecoverably lost,

These men, this particular three in brown
Witnessed by birds will keep the scene and say
By their configuration with the trees,
The small bridge, the red houses and the fire,
What place, what time, what morning occasion

Sent them into the wood, a pack of hounds
At heel and the tall poles upon their shoulders,
Thence to return as now we see them and
Ankle-deep in snow down the winter hill
Descend, while three birds watch and the fourth flies.

THE DREAM SONGS

14

Life, friends, is boring. We must not say so.
After all, the sky flashes, the great sea yearns,
we ourselves flash and yearn,
and moreover my mother told me as a boy
(repeatingly) 'Ever to confess you're bored
means you have no

Inner Resources.' I conclude now I have no
inner resources, because I am heavy bored.
Peoples bore me,
literature bores me, especially great literature,
Henry bores me, with his plights & gripes
as bad as achilles,

who loves people and valiant art, which bores me.
And the tranquil hills, & gin, look like a drag
and somehow a dog
has taken itself & its tail considerably away
into mountains or sea or sky, leaving
behind: me, wag.

29

There sat down, once, a thing on Henry's heart
so heavy, if he had a hundred years
& more, & weeping, sleepless, in all them time
Henry could not make good.
Starts again always in Henry's ears
the little cough somewhere, and odour, a chime.

And there is another thing he has in mind
like a grave Sienese face a thousand years
would fail to blur the still profiled reproach of. Ghastly,
with open eyes, he attends, blind.
All the bells say: too late. This is not for tears;
thinking.

But never did Henry, as he thought he did,
end anyone and hacks her body up
and hide the pieces, where they may be found.
He knows: he went over everyone, & nobody's
missing.
Often he reckons, in the dawn, them up.
Nobody is ever missing.

OF SUICIDE

Reflexions on suicide, & on my father, possess me.
I drink too much. My wife threatens separation.
She won't 'nurse' me. She feels 'inadequate'.
We don't mix together.

It's an hour later in the East.
I could call up Mother in Washington, D.C.
But could she help me?
And all this postal adulation & reproach?

A basis rock-like of love & friendship
for all this world-wide madness seems to be needed.
Epictetus is in some ways my favourite philosopher.[1]
Happy men have died earlier.

[1] Epictetus (born c. 55 A.D.) followed in his thought some of the early Stoic philosophers. "Two maxims," he said, "we must ever keep in mind—that apart from the will there is nothing good or bad, and that we must not try to anticipate or to direct events, but merely to accept them with intelligence." Man must assume that there is a God whose mind directs the universe.

I still plan to go to Mexico this summer.
The Olmec images! Chichén Itzá!
D. H. Lawrence has a wild dream of it.
Malcolm Lowry's book when it came out I taught to
    my precept at Princeton.[2]

I don't entirely resign. I may teach the Third Gospel[3]
this afternoon. I haven't made up my mind.

[2] Olmec was the first sophisticated culture in pre-Columbian Central America; the dominant motif of its artifacts was a stylized jaguar. Chichén Itzá is a ruined Mayan city in Yucatán, most famous for its tradition of human sacrifice. D. H. Lawrence wrote of Mexico's primitive heritage in his novel *The Plumed Serpent* (1926), and Malcolm Lowry's story of a disintegrating personality, *Under the Volcano* (1947), is set in Mexico.

[3] The Gospel of Luke is the most detailed of the gospels, more than half of it containing matter not found in the other gospels. Its narrative power is unmatched in the New Testament.

It seems to me sometimes that others have easier jobs
& do them worse.

Well, we must labour & dream. Gogol[4] was impotent,
somebody in Pittsburgh told me.
I said: At what age? They couldn't answer.
That is a damned serious matter.

Rembrandt was sober. There we differ. Sober.
Terrors came on him. To us too they come.
Of suicide I continually think.
Apparently he didn't. I'll teach Luke.

[4] Nikolay Gogol, nineteenth-century Russian realistic novelist, author of *Dead Souls* and "The Overcoat."

Robert Lowell (1917–1977)

A descendant of two famous New England families (James Russell Lowell was his great-great-uncle; his mother, a Winslow, was descended from one of the founders of the Plymouth Colony), Robert Lowell was born in Boston and educated at Harvard University. He was always both fascinated and repelled by his "thin Puritan heritage." During World War II Lowell refused military conscription and was sentenced to a year in the federal penitentiary, finally serving five months. His first major volume of poetry, *Lord Weary's Castle* (1946), established him as a major figure on the American literary scene. It was followed by *The Mills of the Kavanaughs* (1951) and *Life Studies* (1959), where the formality of the early poetry is replaced by a confessional note. During the 1960s Lowell's commitment to social causes was reflected in *For the Union Dead* (1964), *Near the Ocean* (1967), and *Notebook 1967–68* (1969). He also published a trilogy of plays, *The Old Glory* (1965), which reviews the progress of American history. More recent volumes of verse are *For Lizzie and Harriet* (1973) and *Selected Poems* (1976).

THE DRUNKEN FISHERMAN

Wallowing in this bloody sty,
I cast for fish that pleased my eye
(Truly Jehovah's bow suspends
No pots of gold to weight its ends);
Only the blood-mouthed rainbow trout
Rose to my bait. They flopped about
My canvas creel until the moth
Corrupted its unstable cloth.

A calendar to tell the day;
A handkerchief to wave away

The gnats; a couch unstuffed with storm
Pouching a bottle in one arm;
A whiskey bottle full of worms;
And bedroom slacks: are these fit terms
To mete the worm whose molten rage
Boils in the belly of old age?

Once fishing was a rabbit's foot—
O wind blow cold, O wind blow hot,
Let suns stay in or suns step out:
Life danced a jig on the sperm-whale's spout—
The fisher's fluent and obscene
Catches kept his conscience clean.
Children, the raging memory drools
Over the glory of past pools.

Now the hot river, ebbing, hauls
Its bloody waters into holes;
A grain of sand inside my shoe
Mimics the moon that might undo
Man and Creation too; remorse,
Stinking, has puddled up its source;
Here tantrums thrash to a whale's rage.
This is the pot-hole of old age.

Is there no way to cast my hook
Out of this dynamited brook?
The Fisher's sons must cast about
When shallow waters peter out.
I will catch Christ with a greased worm,
And when the Prince of Darkness stalks
My bloodstream to its Stygian term . . .
On water the Man-Fisher walks.

FALLING ASLEEP OVER THE AENEID

An old man in Concord forgets to go to morning service. He falls asleep, while reading Vergil, and dreams that he is Aeneas at the funeral of Pallas, an Italian prince.[1]

The sun is blue and scarlet on my page,
And *yuck-a, yuck-a, yuck-a, yuck-a,* rage
The yellowhammers mating. Yellow fire
Blankets the captives dancing on their pyre,
And the scorched lictor screams and drops his rod.
Trojans are singing to their drunken God,
Ares. Their helmets catch on fire. Their files
Clank by the body of my comrade—miles
Of filings! Now the scythe-wheeled chariot rolls
Before their lances long as vaulting poles,
And I stand up and heil the thousand men,
Who carry Pallas to the bird-priest. Then
The bird-priest groans, and as his birds foretold,
I greet the body, lip to lip. I hold
The sword that Dido[2] used. It tries to speak,
A bird with Dido's sworded breast. Its beak
Clangs and ejaculates the Punic word[3]
I hear the bird-priest chirping like a bird.
I groan a little. "Who am I, and why?"
It asks, a boy's face, though its arrow-eye
Is working from its socket. "Brother, try,
O Child of Aphrodite,[4] try to die:
To die is life." His harlots hang his bed
With feathers of his long-tailed birds. His head
Is yawning like a person. The plumes blow;
The beard and eyebrows ruffle. Face of snow,
You are the flower that country girls have caught,
A wild bee-pillaged honey-suckle brought
To the returning bridegroom—the design
Has not yet left it, and the petals shine;
The earth, its mother, has, at last, no help:
It is itself. The broken-winded yelp
Of my Phoenician hounds, that fills the brush
With snapping twigs and flying, cannot flush
The ghost of Pallas. But I take his pall,
Stiff with its gold and purple, and recall
How Dido hugged it to her, while she toiled,
Laughing—her golden threads, a serpent coiled
In cypress. Now I lay it like a sheet;
It clinks and settles down upon his feet,
The careless yellow hair that seemed to burn
Beforehand. Left foot, right foot—as they turn,
More pyres are rising: armored horses, bronze,
And gagged Italians, who must file by ones
Across the bitter river,[5] when my thumb

[1] Concord, New Hampshire, was the home of the Lowell family. Pallas was an ally of Aeneas, killed in battle by Prince Turnus (Vergil, *Aeneid,* Book X)

[2] According to Vergil, Dido was the founder of Carthage who fell in love with Aeneas and killed herself when he left her.

[3] *Punic* is an adjective referring to the character or language of ancient Carthage.

[4] Aeneas was, according to Homer, the son of the love-goddess Aphrodite.

[5] The Styx, the river of death which flows around the underworld. The Italian prisoners, part of the army responsible for the death of Pallas, are sacrificed to atone for it.

Tightens into their wind-pipes. The beaks drum;
Their headman's cow-horned death's-head bites its
tongue,
And stiffens, as it eyes the hero slung
Inside his feathered hammock on the crossed
Staves of the eagles that we winged. Our cost
Is nothing to the lovers, whoring Mars
And Venus, father's lover. Now his car's
Plumage is ready, and my marshals fetch
His squire, Acoctes, white with age, to hitch
Aethon, the hero's charger, and its ears
Prick, and it steps and steps, and stately tears
Lather its teeth; and then the harlots bring
The hero's charms and baton—but the King,
Vain-glorious Turnus, carried off the rest.
"I was myself, but Ares thought it best
The way it happened." At the end of time,
He sets his spear, as my descendants climb
The knees of Father Time, his beard of scalps,
His scythe, the arc of steel that crowns the Alps.
The elephants of Carthage hold those snows,[6]
Turms[7] of Numidian horse unsling their bows,
The flaming turkey-feathered arrows swarm
Beyond the Alps. "Pallas," I raise my arm
And shout, "Brother, eternal health. Farewell
Forever." Church is over, and its bell
Frightens the yellowhammers, as I wake
And watch the whitecaps wrinkle up the lake.
Mother's great-aunt, who died when I was eight,
Stands by our parlor sabre. "Boy, it's late.
Vergil must keep the Sabbath." Eighty years!
It all comes back. My Uncle Charles appears.
Blue-capped and bird-like. Phillips Brooks and Grant[8]
Are frowning at his coffin, and my aunt,
Hearing his colored volunteers parade
Through Concord, laughs, and tells her English maid
To clip his yellow nostril hairs, and fold
His colors on him. . . . It is I. I hold
His sword to keep from falling, for the dust
On the stuffed birds is breathless, for the bust
Of young Augustus weighs on Vergil's shelf:[9]
It scowls into my glasses at itself.

[6] A reference to Hannibal's expedition against Rome in the Second Punic War, when he crossed the Pyrenees and Alps into Italy with a military force which included elephants.

[7] Troops of horsemen.

[8] Phillips Brooks, nineteenth-century Episcopal clergyman, minister of Trinity Church, Boston; and President Ulysses S. Grant.

[9] Vergil wrote the *Aeneid* partly to celebrate the rebirth of Rome under the emperor Augustus Caesar.

FOR THE UNION DEAD

"Relinquunt Omnia Servare Rem Publicam."[10]

The old South Boston Aquarium stands
in a Sahara of snow now. Its broken windows are
boarded.
The bronze weathervane cod has lost half its scales.
The airy tanks are dry.

Once my nose crawled like a snail on the glass;
my hand tingled
to burst the bubbles
drifting from the noses of the cowed, compliant fish.

My hand draws back. I often sigh still
for the dark downward and vegetating kingdom
of the fish and reptile. One morning last March,
I pressed against the new barbed and galvanized

fence on the Boston Common. Behind their cage,
yellow dinosaur steamshovels were grunting
as they cropped up tons of mush and grass
to gouge their underworld garage.

Parking spaces luxuriate like civic
sandpiles in the heart of Boston.
A girdle of orange, Puritan-pumpkin colored girders
braces the tingling Statehouse,

shaking over the excavations, as it faces Colonel Shaw
and his bell-cheeked Negro infantry
on St. Gaudens' shaking Civil War relief,[11]
propped by a plank splint against the garage's
earthquake.

Two months after marching through Boston,
half the regiment was dead;
at the dedication,
William James[12] could almost hear the bronze Negroes
breathe.

Their monument sticks like a fishbone
in the city's throat.

[10] Latin, "They gave up all to serve the Republic."

[11] The monument by the sculptor Augustus Saint-Gaudens, which stands on Boston Common, commemorates Robert Gould Shaw, a black officer who commanded the first regiment of black troops (the 54th Massachusetts) during the Civil War. He was killed in action in 1863.

[12] The Harvard philosopher and psychologist, brother of Henry James.

Its Colonel is as lean
as a compass-needle.

He has an angry wrenlike vigilance,
a greyhound's gentle tautness;
he seems to wince at pleasure,
and suffocate for privacy.

He is out of bounds now. He rejoices in man's lovely,
peculiar power to choose life and die—
when he leads his black soldiers to death,
he cannot bend his back.

On a thousand small town New England greens,
the old white churches hold their air
of sparse, sincere rebellion; frayed flags
quilt the graveyards of the Grand Army of the
    Republic.

The stone statues of the abstract Union Soldier
grow slimmer and younger each year—
wasp-waisted, they doze over muskets
and muse through their sideburns . . .

Shaw's father wanted no monument
except the ditch,
where his son's body was thrown
and lost with his "niggers."

The ditch is nearer.
There are no statues for the last war here;
on Boylston Street, a commercial photograph
shows Hiroshima boiling

over a Mosler Safe, the "Rock of Ages"
that survived the blast. Space is nearer.
When I crouch to my television set,
the drained faces of Negro school-children rise like
    balloons.

Colonel Shaw
is riding on his bubble,
he waits
for the blessèd break.

The Aquarium is gone. Everywhere,
giant finned cars nose forward like fish;
a savage servility
slides by on grease.[13]

ARTIST'S MODEL

"If it were done, twere well it were done quickly—[14]
to quote a bromide, your vacillation
is acne." And we totter off the strewn stage,
knowing tomorrow's migraine will remind us
how drink heightened the brutal flow of
    elocution. . . .
We follow our script as timorously as actors,
divorced from making a choice by our need to act.
"If you woke and found an egg in your shoe,
would you feel you'd lost this argument?"
It's over, my clothes fly into your borrowed suitcase,
the good day is gone, the broken champagne glass
crashes in the ashcan . . . private whims, and
    illusions,
too messy for our character to survive.
I come on walking off-stage backwards.

[13] The reference is to American luxury automobiles of the late 1950s, whose rear fenders had a high, fin-like design.

[14] A contraction of the opening lines of Macbeth's famous soliloquy on murder (Act I, scene 7): "If it were done when 'tis done, then 'twere well / It were done quickly."

Philip Larkin (1922–)

Born in Coventry, England, Philip Larkin was educated at St. John's College, Oxford. His Oxford experiences provided the substance of his first novel, *Jill* (1946), which looks forward in many ways to the later fiction of Kingsley Amis and John Wain. A second novel, *A Girl in Winter,* followed in 1947. Larkin's early poetry (*The North Ship,* 1946) was much influenced by Yeats, but he soon fell under the spell of Thomas Hardy and began to write a plain, precise verse designed to express the range of ordinary experience. During the 1950s Larkin was one of the "Movement" poets, reacting against the rhetoric and grandiose claims of an older generation; his style was ideally suited to the limited world of an England much diminished by two World Wars. *The Less Deceived* (1955) and *The Whitsun Weddings* (1964), which contains "Church Going," established Larkin as the finest English poet of his generation. Since 1955 he has been the librarian of Hull University, Yorkshire. His latest volume of verse, *High Windows* (1974), adds new dimensions of lyric emotion and social satire to the dominant elegiac mode of his earlier poetry.

CHURCH GOING

Once I am sure there's nothing going on
I step inside, letting the door thud shut.
Another church: matting, seats, and stone,
And little books; sprawlings of flowers, cut
For Sunday, brownish now; some brass and stuff
Up at the holy end; the small neat organ;
And a tense, musty unignorable silence,
Brewed God knows how long. Hatless, I take off
My cycle-clips in awkward reverence,

Move forward, run my hand around the font.
From where I stand, the roof looks almost new—
Cleaned, or restored? Someone would know: I don't.
Mounting the lectern, I peruse a few
Hectoring large-scale verses, and pronounce
'Here endeth' much more loudly than I'd meant.
The echoes snigger briefly. Back at the door
I sign the book, donate an Irish sixpence,
Reflect the place was not worth stopping for.

Yet stop I did: in fact I often do,
And always end much at a loss like this,
Wondering what to look for; wondering, too,
When churches fall completely out of use
What we shall turn them into, if we shall keep
A few cathedrals chronically on show,
Their parchment, plate and pyx[1] in locked cases,
And let the rest rent-free to rain and sheep.
Shall we avoid them as unlucky places?

Or, after dark, will dubious women come
To make their children touch a particular stone;
Pick simples for a cancer; or on some
Advised night see walking a dead one?
Power of some sort or other will go on
In games, in riddles, seemingly at random;
But superstition, like belief, must die,
And what remains when disbelief has gone?
Grass, weedy pavement, brambles, buttress, sky

A shape less recognisable each week,
A purpose more obscure. I wonder who
Will be the last, the very last, to seek
This place for what it was; one of the crew
That tap and jot and know what rood-lofts were?
Some ruin-bibber, randy for antique,
Or Christmas-addict, counting on a whiff
Of gown-and-bands and organ-pipes and myrrh?
Or will he be my representative,

Bored, uninformed, knowing the ghostly silt
Dispersed, yet tending to this cross of ground
Through suburb scrub because it held unspilt
So long and equably what since is found
Only in separation—marriage, and birth,
And death, and thoughts of these—for whom was built
This special shell? For, though I've no idea
What this accoutred frowsty barn is worth,
It pleases me to stand in silence here;

A serious house on serious earth it is,
In whose blent air all our compulsions meet,
Are recognised, and robed as destinies.
And that much never can be obsolete,
Since someone will forever be surprising
A hunger in himself to be more serious,
And gravitating with it to this ground,
Which, he once heard, was proper to grow wise in,
If only that so many dead lie round.

[1] A box or vessel in which the reserved Eucharist or Host is kept.

TOADS

Why should I let the toad *work*
  Squat on my life?
Can't I use my wit as a pitchfork
  And drive the brute off?

Six days of the week it soils
  With its sickening poison—
Just for paying a few bills!
  That's out of proportion.

Lots of folk live on their wits:
  Lecturers, lispers,
Losels, loblolly-men, louts—
  They don't end as paupers;

Lots of folk live up lanes
  With fires in a bucket,
Eat windfalls and tinned sardines—
  They seem to like it.

Their nippers have got bare feet,
  Their unspeakable wives
Are skinny as whippets—and yet
  No one actually *starves*.

Ah, were I courageous enough
  To shout *Stuff your pension!*
But I know, all to well, that's the stuff
  That dreams are made on:

For something sufficiently toad-like
  Squats in me, too;
Its hunkers are heavy as hard luck,
  And cold as snow,

And will never allow me to blarney
  My way to getting
The fame and the girl and the money
  All at one sitting.

I don't say, one bodies the other
  One's spiritual truth;
But I do say it's hard to lose either,
  When you have both.

TOADS REVISITED

Walking around in the park
Should feel better than work:
The lake, the sunshine,
The grass to lie on,

Blurred playground noises
Beyond black-stockinged nurses—
Not a bad place to be.
Yet it doesn't suit me,

Being one of the men
You meet of an afternoon:
Palsied old step-takers,
Hare-eyed clerks with the jitters,

Waxed-fleshed out-patients
Still vague from accidents,
And characters in long coats
Deep in the litter-baskets—

All dodging the toad work
By being stupid or weak.
Think of being them!
Hearing the hours chime,

Watching the bread delivered,
The sun by clouds covered,
The children going home;
Think of being them,

Turning over their failures
By some bed of lobelias,
Nowhere to go but indoors,
No friends but empty chairs—

No, give me my in-tray
My loaf-haired secretary,
My shall-I-keep-the-call-in-Sir:
What else can I answer,

When the lights come on at four
At the end of another year?
Give me your arm, old toad;
Help me down Cemetery Road.

AT GRASS

The eye can hardly pick them out
From the cold shade they shelter in,
Till wind distresses tail and mane;
Then one crops grass, and moves about
—The other seeming to look on—
And stands anonymous again.

Yet fifteen years ago, perhaps
Two dozen distances sufficed
To fable them: faint afternoons
Of Cups and Stakes and Handicaps,
Whereby their names were artificed
To inlay faded, classic Junes—

Silks at the start: against the sky
Numbers and parasols: outside,
Squadrons of empty cars, and heat,
And littered grass: then the long cry
Hanging unhushed till it subside
To stop-press columns on the street.

Do memories plague their ears like flies?
They shake their heads. Dusk brims the shadows.
Summer by summer all stole away,
The starting-gates, the crowds and cries—
All but the unmolesting meadows.
Almanacked, their names live; they

Have slipped their names, and stand at ease,
Or gallop for what must be joy,
And not a fieldglass sees them home,
Or curious stop-watch prophesies:
Only the groom, and the groom's boy,
With bridles in the evening come.

A. R. Ammons (1926–)

Archie Randolph Ammons was born in Whiteville, North Carolina, and educated at Wake Forest College, Winston-Salem, North Carolina, and the University of California, Berkeley. From 1952 to 1961 he was an executive with Freidrich & Dimmock, Inc., of Millville, New Jersey, a manufacturer of biological glassware. Since 1964 he has been a teacher of creative writing at Cornell University. In 1955 he published his first volume of poetry, *Ommateum,* which was followed by several other volumes. His most recent publications are *Collected Poems, 1951–1971* (1972), which won the National Book Award for poetry, and *Sphere* (1974).

THE MISFIT

The unassimilable fact leads us on:
round the edges
   where broken shapes make poor masonry
the synthesis
fails (and succeeds) into limitation
   or extending itself too far

becomes a different synthesis:
law applies
   consistently to the molecule,
not to the ocean, unoriented, unprocessed,
it floats in, that floats in it:
   we are led on

to the boundaries
where relations loosen into chaos
   or where the nucleus fails to control,
fragments in odd shapes
expressing more and more the interstitial sea:
   we are led on

to peripheries, to the raw blocks of material,
where mortar and trowel can convert
   diversity into enlarging unity:
not the million oriented facts
but the one or two facts,
   out of place,

recalcitrant, the one observed fact
that tears us into questioning:
   what has not
joined dies into order to redeem, with
loss of singleness extends the form,
   or, unassimilable, leads us on.

CASCADILLA FALLS

I went down by Cascadilla
Falls this
evening, the
stream below the falls,
and picked up a
handsized stone
kidney-shaped, testicular, and

thought all its motions into it,
the 800 mph earth spin,
the 190-million-mile yearly
displacement around the sun,
the overriding
grand
haul

of the galaxy with the 30,000
mph of where
the sun's going:
thought all the interweaving
motions
into myself: dropped

the stone to dead rest:
the stream from other motions
broke
rushing over it:
shelterless,
I turned

to the sky and stood still:
Oh
I do
not know where I am going
that I can live my life
by this single creek.

THE CITY LIMITS

When you consider the radiance, that it does not
 withhold
itself but pours its abundance without selection into
 every
nook and cranny not overhung or hidden; when you
 consider

that birds' bones make no awful noise against the light
 but
lie low in the light as in a high testimony; when you
 consider
the radiance, that it will look into the guiltiest

swervings of the weaving heart and bear itself upon
 them,
not flinching into disguise or darkening; when you
 consider
the abundance of such resource as illuminates the
 glow-blue

bodies and gold-skeined wings of flies swarming the
 dumped
guts of a natural slaughter or the coil of shit and in no
way winces from its storms of generosity; when you
 consider

that air or vacuum, snow or shale, squid or wolf, rose
 or lichen,
each is accepted into as much light as it will take, then
the heart moves roomier, the man stands and looks
 about, the

leaf does not increase itself above the grass, and the
 dark
work of the deepest cells is of a tune with May bushes
and fear lit by the breadth of such calmly turns to
 praise.

John Ashbery (1927–   )

Born in Rochester, New York, John Ashbery received his undergraduate degree from Harvard and did graduate work at Columbia and New York University. In 1955 he was awarded a Fulbright Scholarship to France and spent most of the next ten years there. From 1960–65 he was art critic for the Paris *New York Herald Tribune;* after his return to New York in 1965 he served as executive editor of *Art News.* Since 1974 he has been Professor of English at Brooklyn College. His first book of verse, *Some Trees* (1956), was published in the Yale Younger Poets series with a preface by W. H. Auden. It was followed among other volumes by *The Tennis Fragment* (1969), *The Double Dream of Spring* (1970), *Three Poems* (1972), and *Self-Portrait in a Convex Mirror* (1975).

SOME TREES

These are amazing: each
Joining a neighbor, as though speech
Were a still performance.
Arranging by chance

To meet as far this morning
From the world as agreeing
With it, you and I
Are suddenly what the trees try

To tell us we are:
That their merely being there
Means something; that soon
We may touch, love, explain.

And glad not to have invented
Such comeliness, we are surrounded:
A silence already filled with noises,
A canvas on which emerges

A chorus of smiles, a winter morning.
Placed in a puzzling light, and moving,
Our days put on such reticence
These accents seem their own defense.

THESE LACUSTRINE CITIES[1]

These lacustrine cities grew out of loathing
Into something forgetful, although angry with history.
They are the product of an idea: that man is horrible,
for instance,
Though this is only one example.

They emerged until a tower
Controlled the sky, and with artifice dipped back
Into the past for swans and tapering branches,
Burning, until all that hate was transformed into
useless love.
Then you are left with an idea of yourself
And the feeling of ascending emptiness of the
afternoon
Which must be charged to the embarrassment of
others
Who fly by you like beacons.

The night is a sentinel.
Much of your time has been occupied by creative
games
Until now, but we have all-inclusive plans for you.

[1] Lacustrine means "of or pertaining to lakes." It can also refer to the geological strata formed by lakes, or to the prehistoric lake-dwellers of early Europe.

We had thought, for instance, of sending you to the
middle of the desert,

To a violent sea, or of having the closeness of the
others be air
To you, pressing you back into a startled dream
As sea-breezes greet a child's face.
But the past is already here, and you are nursing some
private project.

The worst is not over, yet I know
You will be happy here. Because of the logic
Of your situation, which is something no climate can
outsmart.
Tender and insouciant by turns, you see.

You have built a mountain of something,
Thoughtfully pouring all your energy into this single
monument,
Whose wind is desire starching a petal,
Whose disappointment broke into a rainbow of tears.

Thomas Kinsella (1928–)

Thomas Kinsella was reared in Dublin, where he began to write poetry under the shadow of William Butler Yeats's remembered presence. He joined the Irish Civil Service in 1946, at the age of eighteen, and worked in the department of finance for nearly twenty years. Since 1965 he has taught at Southern Illinois University (1965–70) and Temple University (1970–). He has been a director of the Dolmen Press and the Cuala Press in Dublin. His volumes of poetry include *Poems* (1956), *Another September* (1958), *Downstream* (1962), *Nightwalker and Other Poems* (1968), *Notes from the Land of the Dead* (1971), *New Poems* (1973), *Selected Poems, 1956–1968* (1973), and *One* (1974).

A COUNTRY WALK

Sick of the piercing company of women
I swung the gate shut with a furious sigh,
Rammed trembling hands in pockets and drew in
A breath of river air. A rook's wet wing
Cuffed abruptly upward through the drizzle.

On either hand dead trunks in drapes of creeper,
Strangled softly by horse-mushroom, writhed
In vanished passion, broken down like sponge.
I walked their hushed stations, passion dying,
Each slow footfall a drop of peace returning.

I clapped my gloves. Three cattle turned aside
Their fragrant bodies from a corner gate
And down the sucking chaos of a hedge
Churned land to liquid in their dreamy passage.
Briefly through the beaded grass a path
Led to the holy stillness of a well
And there in the smell of water, stone and leaf
I knelt, baring my hand, and scooped and drank,
Shivering, and inch by inch rejoiced:
Ferocity became intensity.

Or so it seemed as with a lighter step
I turned an ivied corner to confront
The littered fields where summer broke and fled.
Below me, right and left, the valley floor
Tilted in a silence full of storms;
A ruined aqueduct in delicate rigor
Clenched cat-backed, rooted to one horizon;
A vast asylum reared its potent calm
Up from the other through the sodden air,
Tall towers ochre where the gutters dripped;
A steeple; the long yielding of a railway turn

Through thorn and willow; a town endured its
place . . .

Joining the two slopes, blocking an ancient way
With crumbled barracks, castle and brewery
It took the running river, wrinkling and pouring
Into its blunt embrace. A line of roofs
Fused in veils of rain and steely light
As the dying sun struck it huge glancing blows.
A strand of idle smoke mounted until
An idler current combed it slowly west,
A hook of shadow dividing the still sky . . .
Mated, like a fall of rock, with time,
The place endured its burden: as a froth
Locked in a swirl of turbulence, a shape
That forms and fructifies and dies, a wisp
That hugs the bridge, an omphalos of scraps.

I moved, my glove-backs glistening, over flesh-
And forest-fed earth; till, skirting a marshy field
Where melancholy brambles scored the mud
By the gapped glitter of a speckled ford,
I shuddered with a visual sweet excitement.

Those murmuring shallows made a trampling place
Apt for death-combat, as the tales agree:[1]
There, the day that Christ hung dying, twin
Brothers armed in hate on either side;
The day darkened but they moved to meet
With crossed swords under a dread eclipse
And mingled their bowels at the saga's end.
There the first Normans massacred my fathers,
Then stroked their armoured horses' necks, disposed
In ceremony, sable on green sward.
Twice more the reeds grew red, the stones obscured;
When knot-necked Cromwell and his fervent sword
Despatched a convent shrieking to their Lover,
And when in peasant fear a rebel host,
Through long retreat grown half hysterical
—Methodical, ludicrous—piked in groups of three
Cromwell's puritan brood, their harmless neighbours,
Forked them half living to the sharp water
And melted into the martyred countryside,
Root eaters, strange as badgers. Pulses calmed;
The racked heroic nerved itself for peace;
Then came harsh winters, motionless waterbirds,
And generations that let welcome fail.

Road and river parted. Now my path
Lay gleaming through the greasy dusk, uphill
Into the final turn. A concrete cross
Low in the ditch grew to the memory
Of one who answered latest the phantom hag,
Tireless Rebellion, when with mouth awry
She hammered at the door, disrupting harvest.[2]
There he bled to death, his line of sight
Blocked by the corner-stone, and did not see
His town ablaze with joy, the grinning foe
Driven in heavy lorries from the field;
And he lay cold in the Hill Cemetery
When freedom burned his comrades' itchy palms,
Too much for flesh and blood, and—armed in hate—
Brother met brother in a modern light.
They turned the bloody corner, knelt and killed,
Who gather still at Easter round his grave,
Our watchful elders. Deep in his crumbled heart
He takes their soil, and chatting they return
To take their town again, that have exchanged
A trenchcoat playground for a gombeen jungle.

Around the corner, in an open square,
I came upon the sombre monuments
That bear their names: MacDonagh & McBride,
Merchants; Connolly's Commercial Arms . . .[3]
Their windows gave me back my stolid self
In attitudes of staring as I paced
Their otherworldly gloom, reflected light
Playing on lens and raincoat stonily.
I turned away. Down the sloping square
A lamp switched on above the urinal;
Across the silent handball alley, eyes
That never looked on lover measured mine
Over the Christian Brothers'[4] frosted glass
And turned away. Out of the neighbouring shades
A car plunged soundlessly and disappeared
Pitching downward steeply to the bridge.
I too descended. Naked sycamores,
Gathered dripping near the quay, stood still
And dropped from their combining arms a single
Word upon my upturned face. I trod
The river underfoot; the parapet
Above the central arch received my hands.

[1] The following passage traces in general terms the history of the "martyred countryside," from the fratricidal conflict of ancient myth and legend through the Norman invasion and the ruthless campaign against the Irish led by Cromwell in 1649 into the poverty and suffering of the nineteenth century.

[2] "Tireless Rebellion" refers to the long struggle against the English, both heroic and self-destructive, which culminated in the Easter Rebellion of 1916 and the subsequent "Troubles."

[3] An ironic play upon the ending of William Butler Yeats's "Easter 1916." Yeats's poem is essential background for all of "A Country Walk."

[4] A Roman Catholic teaching congregation founded in Ireland for the education of the poor.

Under a darkening and clearing heaven
The hastening river streamed in a slate sheen,
Its face a-swarm. Across the swollen water
(Delicate myriads vanishing in a breath)
Faint ripples winked; a thousand currents broke,
Kissing, dismembering, in threads of foam
Or poured intact over the stony bed
Glass-green and chill; their shallow, shifting world
Slid on in troubled union, forging together
Surfaces that gave and swallowed light;
And grimly the flood divided where it swept
An endless debris through the failing dusk
Under the thudding span beneath my feet.
Venit Hesperus;[5]
In green and golden light; bringing sweet trade.
The inert stirred. Heart and tongue were loosed:
'The waters hurtle through the flooded night. . . .'[6]

[5] "Hesperus [the evening star] comes," from the last line of Vergil's tenth eclogue, which opens with a reference to the sacred fount of poetry. The appearance of the star is a signal of inspiration or internal change.

[6] The first line of a new poem. The experience of "A Country Walk" has restored the poet's creative powers.

Adrienne Rich (1929–)

Adrienne Cecile Rich was born in Baltimore, Maryland, "white and middle-class," and educated at Radcliffe College-Harvard. Her first volume of poetry, *A Change of World* (1951), was published in the Yale Younger Poets series the year she graduated from college, with a preface by W. H. Auden. After study at Oxford she married in 1953 and had three sons. Her second volume of poetry, *The Diamond Cutters* (1955), was widely praised, but as the 1950s gave way to the 1960s Adrienne Rich found herself increasingly dissatisfied with her personal life and the society around her. She was deeply affected by the radical politics of the 1960s and saw a connection between political repression and her own position as a "woman poet." After *Snapshots of a Daughter-in-Law* (1962) she abandoned the technical perfection of her earlier works for a more fluid and expressive form. *Necessities of Life* (1966), *Leaflets* (1969), *The Will to Change* (1971), and *Diving into the Wreck* (1973) chart her move toward personal and artistic independence. Poems such as "Orion" (1969) and "A Valediction Forbidding Mourning" (1971) represent the power of her later verse. Her most recent collection is *Poems: Selected and New, 1950–1974* (1975). She has also written a study called *Of Woman Born: Motherhood as Experience and Institution* (1976).

ORION[1]

Far back when I went zig-zagging
through tamarack pastures
you were my genius, you
my cast-iron Viking, my helmed
lion-heart king in prison.
Years later now you're young

my fierce half-brother, staring
down from that simplified west
your breast open, your belt dragged down
by an oldfashioned thing, a sword
the last bravado you won't give over
though it weighs you down as you stride

[1] Orion, the mythical hunter, was translated into the stars after his death, where he appears as a giant with a girdle, sword, lion's skin, and club. The constellation, one of the brightest in the winter sky, is described in stanzas 2–3.

and the stars in it are dim
and maybe have stopped burning.
But you burn, and I know it;
as I throw back my head to take you in
an old transfusion happens again:
divine astronomy is nothing to it.

Indoors I bruise and blunder,
break faith, leave ill enough
alone, a dead child born in the dark.
Night cracks up over the chimney,
pieces of time, frozen geodes
come showering down in the grate.

A man reaches behind my eyes
and finds them empty
a woman's head turns away
from my head in the mirror
children are dying my death
and eating crumbs of my life.

Pity is not your forte.
Calmly you ache up there
pinned aloft in your crow's nest,
my speechless pirate!
You take it all for granted
and when I look you back

it's with a starlike eye
shooting its cold and egotistical spear
where it can do least damage.
Breathe deep! No hurt, no pardon
out here in the cold with you
you with your back to the wall.

A VALEDICTION FORBIDDING MOURNING[2]

My swirling wants. Your frozen lips.
The grammar turned and attacked me.
Themes, written under duress.
Emptiness of the notations.

They gave me a drug that slowed the healing of
wounds.

I want you to see this before I leave:
the experience of repetition as death
the failure of criticism to locate the pain
the poster in the bus that said:
my bleeding is under control.

A red plant in a cemetery of plastic wreaths.

A last attempt: the language is a dialect called
metaphor.
These images go unglossed: hair, glacier, flashlight.
When I think of a landscape I am thinking of a time.
When I talk of taking a trip I mean forever.
I could say: those mountains have a meaning
but further than that I could not say.

To do something very common, in my own way.

[2] The title is an ironic play on John Donne's famous seventeenth-century love poem, "A Valediction: forbidding Mourning."

Ted Hughes (1930–)

Born in the West Riding part of Yorkshire, England, Ted Hughes studied folklore and anthropology at Cambridge University, laying a foundation for the uses of myth and ritual in his later poetry. In 1956 he married Sylvia Plath, the young American poet who committed suicide in 1963. His first volume of poems, *The Hawk in the Rain* (1957), announced a sharp departure from the English "Movement" poets of the 1950s who had emphasized plain language and understated emotion: like his American contemporaries, Hughes did not avoid violence and personal confession. His second volume of verse, *Lupercal* (1960), was followed by

Wodwo (1967), a collection of poetry and prose which contains the story "Snow." In the "Crow" poems of the late 1960s and early 1970s, published in several small volumes, Hughes has created a personal mythology of darkness and deprivation based on traditional materials. His *Selected Poems, 1957–67* appeared in 1972.

THE HORSES

I climbed through woods in the hour-before-dawn
dark.
Evil air, a frost-making stillness,

Not a leaf, not a bird,—
A world cast in frost. I came out above the wood

Where my breath left tortuous statues in the iron light.
But the valleys were draining the darkness

Till the moorline—blackening dregs of the brightening
grey—
Halved the sky ahead. And I saw the horses:

Huge in the dense grey—ten together—
Megalith-still. They breathed, making no move,

With draped manes and tilted hind-hooves,
Making no sound.

I passed: not one snorted or jerked its head.
Grey silent fragments

Of a grey silent world.

I listened in emptiness on the moor-ridge.
The curlew's tear turned its edge on the silence.

Slowly detail leafed from the darkness. Then the sun
Orange, red, red erupted

Silently, and splitting to its core tore and flung cloud,
Shook the gulf open, showed blue,

And the big planets hanging—.
I turned

Stumbling in the fever of a dream, down towards
The dark woods, from the kindling tops,

And came to the horses.
There, still they stood,
But now steaming and glistening under the flow of
light,

Their draped stone manes, their tilted hind-hooves
Stirring under a thaw while all around them

The frost showed its fires. But still they made no
sound.
Not one snorted or stamped,

Their hung heads patient as the horizons,
High over valleys, in the red levelling rays—

In din of the crowded streets, going among the years,
the faces,
May I still meet my memory in so lonely a place

Between the streams and the red clouds, hearing
curlews,
Hearing the horizons endure.

THE THOUGHT-FOX

I imagine this midnight moment's forest:
Something else is alive
Beside the clock's loneliness
And this blank page where my fingers move.

Through the window I see no star:
Something more near
Though deeper within darkness
Is entering the loneliness:

Cold, delicately as the dark snow,
A fox's nose touches twig, leaf;
Two eyes serve a movement, that now
And again now, and now, and now

Sets neat prints into the snow
Between trees, and warily a lame
Shadow lags by stump and in hollow
Of a body that is bold to come

Across clearings, an eye,
A widening deepening greenness,
Brilliantly, concentratedly,
Coming about its own business

I, with a sudden sharp hot stink of fox
It enters the dark hole of the head.
The window is starless still; the clock ticks,
The page is printed.

A CHILDISH PRANK

Man's and woman's bodies lay without souls,
Dully gaping, foolishly staring, inert
On the flowers of Eden.
God pondered.

The problem was so great, it dragged him asleep.

Crow[1] laughed.
He bit the Worm, God's only son,
Into two writhing halves.

He stuffed into man the tail half
With the wounded end hanging out.

He stuffed the head half headfirst into woman
And it crept in deeper and up
To peer out through her eyes
Calling its tail-half to join up quickly, quickly
Because O it was painful.

Man awoke being dragged across the grass.
Woman awoke to see him coming.
Neither knew what had happened.

God went on sleeping.

Crow went on laughing.

[1] In Hughes's *Crow* poems, Crow represents the dark and irrational forces which even God cannot control.

Sylvia Plath (1932–1963)

Sylvia Plath was born in Boston. Her father, who taught German and entomology at Boston University, died in 1940, leaving her with a sense of betrayal. After graduating *summa cum laude* from Smith College she went to Cambridge University on a Fulbright Scholarship, and in 1956 she married the English poet Ted Hughes. They had two children, a girl and a boy, born in 1960 and 1962. By the end of 1962 Sylvia Plath had separated from her husband; she committed suicide in February 1963. Her early life and first breakdown are fictionally recorded in *The Bell Jar* (1963). *The Colossus* (1962) and *Ariel* (1965) contain her most important poems.

ELM

For Ruth Fainlight

I know the bottom, she says. I know it with my great
tap root:
It is what you fear.
I do not fear it: I have been there.

Is it the sea you hear in me,
Its dissatisfactions?
Or the voice of nothing, that was your madness?

Love is a shadow.
How you lie and cry after it
Listen: these are its hooves: it has gone off, like a horse.

All night I shall gallop thus, impetuously,
Till your head is a stone, your pillow a little turf,
Echoing, echoing.

Or shall I bring you the sound of poisons?
This is rain now, this big hush.
And this is the fruit of it: tin-white, like arsenic.

I have suffered the atrocity of sunsets.
Scorched to the root
My red filaments burn and stand, a hand of wires.

Now I break up in pieces that fly about like clubs.
A wind of such violence
Will tolerate no bystanding: I must shriek.

The moon, also, is merciless: she would drag me
Cruelly, being barren.
Her radiance scathes me. Or perhaps I have caught
    her.

I let her go. I let her go
Diminished and flat, as after radical surgery.
How your bad dreams possess and endow me.

I am inhabited by a cry.
Nightly it flaps out
Looking, with its hooks, for something to love.

I am terrified by this dark thing
That sleeps in me;
All day I feel its soft, feathery turnings, its malignity.

Clouds pass and disperse.
Are those the faces of love, those pale irretrievables?
Is it for such I agitate my heart?

I am incapable of more knowledge.
What is this, this face
So murderous in its strangle of branches?——

Its snaky acids kiss.
It petrifies the will. These are the isolate, slow faults
That kill, that kill, that kill.

DADDY

You do not do, you do not do
Any more, black shoe
In which I have lived like a foot
For thirty years, poor and white,
Barely daring to breathe or Achoo.

Daddy, I have had to kill you.
You died before I had time——
Marble-heavy, a bag full of God,
Ghastly statue with one grey toe
Big as a Fisco seal

And a head in the freakish Atlantic
Where it pours bean green over blue
In the waters off beautiful Nauset.
I used to pray to recover you.
Ach, du.[1]

In the German tongue, in the Polish town
Scraped flat by the roller
Of wars, wars, wars.
But the name of the town is common.
My Polack friend

Says there are a dozen or two.
So I never could tell where you
Put your foot, your root,
I never could talk to you.
The tongue stuck in my jaw.

It stuck in a barb wire snare.
Ich, ich, ich, ich,[2]
I could hardly speak.
I thought every German was you.
And the language obscene

An engine, an engine
Chuffing me off like a Jew.
A Jew to Dachau, Auschwitz, Belsen.[3]
I began to talk like a Jew.
I think I may well be a Jew.

The snows of the Tyrol, the clear beer of Vienna
Are not very pure or true.
With my gypsy ancestress and my weird luck
And my Taroc pack and my Taroc pack
I may be a bit of a Jew.

I have always been scared of *you,*
With your Luftwaffe, your gobbledygoo.
And your neat moustache
And your Aryan eye, bright blue.
Panzer-man, panzer-man, O You——

Not God but a swastika
So black no sky could squeak through.
Every woman adores a Fascist,

[1] German, "Ah, you."
[2] German, "I, I, I, I."
[3] Sites of German concentration camps where many thousands of Jews were executed.

The boot in the face, the brute
Brute heart of a brute like you.

You stand at the blackboard, daddy,
In the picture I have of you,
A cleft in your chin instead of your foot
But no less a devil for that, no not
Any less the black man who

Bit my pretty red heart in two.
I was ten when they buried you.
At twenty I tried to die
And get back, back, back to you.
I thought even the bones would do.

But they pulled me out of the sack,
And they stuck me together with glue.
And then I knew what to do.
I made a model of you,
A man in black with a Meinkampf[4] look

And a love of the rack and the screw.
And I said I do, I do.
So daddy, I'm finally through.
The black telephone's off at the root,
The voices just can't worm through.

If I've killed one man, I've killed two——
The vampire who said he was you
And drank my blood for a year,
Seven years, if you want to know.
Daddy, you can lie back now.

There's a stake in your fat black heart
And the villagers never liked you.
They are dancing and stamping on you.
They always *knew* it was you.
Daddy, daddy, you bastard, I'm through.

FEVER 103°

Pure? What does it mean?
The tongues of hell
Are dull, dull as the triple

Tongues of dull, fat Cerberus
Who wheezes at the gate. Incapable
Of licking clean

The aguey tendon, the sin, the sin.
The tinder cries.
The indelible smell

Of a snuffed candle!
Love, love, the low smokes roll
From me like Isadora's scarves, I'm in a fright

One scarf will catch and anchor in the wheel.[5]
Such yellow sullen smokes
Make their own element. They will not rise,

But trundle round the globe
Choking the aged and the meek,
The weak

Hothouse baby in its crib,
The ghastly orchid
Hanging its hanging garden in the air,

Devilish leopard!
Radiation turned it white
And killed it in an hour.

Greasing the bodies of adulterers
Like Hiroshima ash and eating in.
The sin. The sin.

Darling, all night
I have been flickering, off, on, off, on.
The sheets grow heavy as a lecher's kiss.

Three days. Three nights.
Lemon water, chicken
Water, water make me retch.

I am too pure for you or anyone.
Your body
Hurts me as the world hurts God. I am a lantern——

My head a moon
Of Japanese paper, my gold beaten skin
Infinitely delicate and infinitely expensive.

Does not my heat astound you. And my light.
All by myself I am a huge camellia
Glowing and coming and going, flush on flush.

[4] Hitler's *Mein Kampf* ("My Battle"), written in the mid-1920s, is an autobiographical work which presents his totalitarian views on race and politics.

[5] The American dancer Isadora Duncan was strangled to death in 1927 when her long scarf caught in the spoked wheel of her automobile.

I think I am going up,
I think I may rise——
The beads of hot metal fly, and I, love, I

Am a pure acetylene
Virgin
Attended by roses,

By kisses, by cherubim,
By whatever these pink things mean.
Not you, nor him

Not him, nor him
(My selves dissolving, old whore petticoats)——
To Paradise.

CRITICAL ESSAYS

One of the hallmarks of modern literature is the close relationship between literary criticism and the creative act. Ezra Pound conceived of all literary works as forms of criticism, and although most writers would reject this notion as too confining there is a sense in which it is true. Works of literature comment upon each other: T. S. Eliot's *The Waste Land* is on one level an interpretation of Conrad's *Heart of Darkness;* W. H. Auden's "In Memory of W. B. Yeats" is a profound judgment on the Yeats of the 1930s; Thomas Kinsella's "A Country Walk" reflects back on Yeats's "Easter 1916"; and the "Portrait of a Lady" poems by Williams and Pound and Eliot are indirect comments on Henry James's *The Portrait of a Lady.* In the same way, the critical essays of many modern writers may be taken as comments on their own works, even when this is not the overt subject. In this section we have included as many essays as possible by authors already represented in the anthology, while at the same time covering the major issues of literary form and language suggested by the fiction, drama, and poetry of the previous sections.

This section opens with T. S. Eliot's seminal essay of 1919, "Tradition and the Individual Talent," which is both an illuminating commentary on Eliot's poetic practice and a crucial essay for the understanding of modern literary criticism. Eliot's concept of a dynamic transaction between contemporary literature and the tradition had a profound impact on later poets and critics. W. B. Yeats's "General Introduction for My Work," written at the end of his career for a projected definitive edition of his poetry, sums up his lifelong artistic ideals and at the same time poses some of the central issues in all modern poetry. Frost's meditative monologue, "Education by Poetry," also has implications far beyond his own poetic practice. These three general essays are followed by two focused on particular works. John Berryman's essay on "Prufrock's Dilemma" and Elizabeth Hardwick's essay on Sylvia Plath combine the insights of a fellow artist with the formal methods of modern analytical criticism.

The selections from William Carlos Williams, Imamu Amiri Baraka (LeRoi Jones), and Ernest Hemingway give three characteristic views of the artist's relationship to language, and raise the general question of the connections between an individual style and our common speech. They are followed by two essays on the modern theater: Alvin Kernan provides a broad survey of the development of modern drama, while Edward Albee comments on the "theater of the absurd" and the issue of theatrical "realism" in a way that illuminates *The Zoo Story* and Pinter's *A Slight Ache.* Essays by E. M. Forster and William Gass investigate the difficult concept of "character," which is central to an understanding of modern drama and poetry as well as fiction. The section concludes with Lionel Trilling's masterful essay on the relationship between fiction and society, "Manners, Morals, and the Novel," and George Orwell's "Politics and the English Language," which eloquently defends the proposition that honesty and precision in language are essential to a healthy society.

Tradition and the Individual Talent

T. S. Eliot (1888–1965)

Thomas Stearns Eliot was born in St. Louis, Missouri, where he spent the first seventeen years of his life. He came from an old New England family (his grandfather, a graduate of Harvard Divinity School, founded Washington University in St. Louis), and some of the happiest moments of Eliot's early life occurred during summer visits to the New England coast. In 1905 he was sent East to study at Milton Academy, and the following year he entered Harvard where he eventually did graduate work in philosophy and Oriental religions. As an undergraduate Eliot first wrote poetry heavily influenced by Tennyson and the late Victorian poets, but his encounter in 1909–10 with the new French poetry (especially that of Jules Laforgue) led to a more ironic and introspective style. In 1910–11 Eliot spent a year at the Sorbonne in Paris; in 1914 he was awarded a fellowship to a German university, but the outbreak of World War I caused a change of plans and he took up residence at Merton College, Oxford (1914–15). It was at this time that he met Ezra Pound, who was so impressed by "The Love Song of J. Alfred Prufrock" that he arranged for its publication. In 1915 Eliot moved to London, and for the next ten years produced a remarkable body of influential poetry and criticism, in spite of the difficulties surrounding his marriage (in 1915) to Vivien Haigh-Wood. A collection of poems, *Prufrock and Other Observations* (1917), was followed by *Poems* (1920), in which the looser and more personal form of the early verse was replaced by the strict quatrains of the Sweeney poems. In 1922 Eliot published his long poem *The Waste Land,* a personal testament to the spiritual dryness of the contemporary world which he put into final form with the help of Ezra Pound. In these same years Eliot was writing some of his most important literary criticism. *The Sacred Wood* (1920)—which contains his famous essay on the poet's role, "Tradition and the Individual Talent," first published a year earlier—was followed in 1924 by *Homage to John Dryden.* Between 1922 and 1939 Eliot edited *The Criterion,* probably the most influential literary journal of the time.

In 1928 Eliot announced that he was a classicist in literature, a Royalist in politics (he had become a British subject in 1927), and an Anglo-Catholic in religion, thus acknowledging changes which had been evident in his life and art for some time. In 1930 he published *Ash Wednesday,* a long poem on the theme of religious conversion. In 1932 Eliot returned to the United States for the first time in nearly twenty years to lecture at Harvard and the University of Virginia, and this renewal of early experience seems to have acted as a catalyst for his poetry. Between 1935 and 1941 he published *Four Quartets,* long meditative poems on British and American landscapes which are the glory of his later career. In the 1930s he also channeled his long-standing interest in drama into the writing of plays. *Murder in the Cathedral* (1935) was followed by *The Family Reunion* (1939) and a series of "comedies" on religious themes, *The Cocktail Party* (1950), *The Confidential Clerk* (1954), and *The Elder Statesman* (1959). Eliot continued to write literary criticism until his death, but his career as a poet was concluded with *Four Quartets.* In 1948 he received the Nobel Prize for literature.

I

In English writing we seldom speak of tradition, though we occasionally apply its name in deploring its absence. We cannot refer to 'the tradition' or to 'a tradition'; at most, we employ the adjective in saying that the poetry of So-and-so is 'traditional' or even 'too traditional'. Seldom, perhaps, does the word appear except in a phrase of censure. If otherwise, it is vaguely approbative, and the implication, as to the work approved, of some pleasing archaeological reconstruction. You can hardly make the word agreeable to English ears without this comfortable reference to the reassuring science of archaeology.

Certainly the word is not likely to appear in our appreciations of living or dead writers. Every nation, every race, has not only its own creative, but its own critical turn of mind; and is even more oblivious of the shortcomings and limitations of its critical habits than of those of its creative genius. We know, or think we know, from the enormous mass of critical method or habit of the French; we only conclude (we are such unconscious people) that the French are 'more critical' than we, and sometimes even plume ourselves a little with the fact, as if the French were the less spontaneous. Perhaps they are; but we might remind ourselves that criticism is as inevitable as breathing, and that we should be none the worse for articulating what passes in our minds when we read a book and feel an emotion about it, for criticizing our own minds in their work of criticism. One of the facts that might come to light in this process is our tendency to insist, when we praise a poet, upon those aspects of his work in which he least resembles anyone else. In these aspects or parts of his work we pretend to find what is individual, what is the peculiar essence of the man. We dwell with satisfaction upon the poet's difference from his predecessors, especially his immediate predecessors; we endeavour to find something that can be isolated in order to be enjoyed. Whereas if we approach a poet without this prejudice we shall often find that not only the best, but the most individual parts of his work may be those in which the dead poets, his ancestors, assert their immortality most vigorously. And I do not mean the impressionable period of adolescence, but the period of full maturity.

Yet if the only form of tradition, of handing down, consisted in following the ways of the immediate generation before us in a blind or timid adherence to its successes, 'tradition' should positively be discouraged. We have seen many such simple currents soon lost in the sand; and novelty is better than repetition. Tradition is a matter of much wider significance. It cannot be inherited, and if you want it you must obtain it by great labour. It involves, in the first place, the historical sense, which we may call nearly indispensable to anyone who would continue to be a poet beyond his twenty-fifth year; and the historical sense involves a perception, not only of the pastness of the past, but of its presence; the historical sense compels a man to write not merely with his own generation in his bones, but with a feeling that the whole of the literature of Europe from Homer and within it the whole of the literature of his own country has a simultaneous existence and composes a simultaneous order. This historical sense, which is a sense of timeless as well as of the temporal and of the timeless and of the temporal together, is what makes a writer traditional. And it is at the same time what makes a writer most acutely conscious of his place in time, of his own contemporaneity.

No poet, no artist of any art, has his complete meaning alone. His significance, his appreciation is the appreciation of his relation to the dead poets and artists. You cannot value him alone; you must set him, for contrast and comparison, among the dead. I mean this as a principle of aesthetic, not merely historical, criticism. The necessity that he shall conform, that he shall cohere, is not onesided; what happens when a new work of art is created is something that happens simultaneously to all the works of art which preceded it. The existing monuments form an ideal order among themselves, which is modified by the introduction of the new (the really new) work of art among them. The existing order is complete before the new work arrives; for order to persist after the supervention of novelty, the *whole* existing order must be, if ever so slightly, altered; and so the relations, proportions, values of each work of art toward the whole are readjusted; and this is conformity between the old and the new. Whoever has approved this idea of order, of the form of European, of English literature will not find it preposterous that the past should be altered by the present as much as the present is directed by the past. And the poet who is aware of this will be aware of great difficulties and responsibilities.

In a peculiar sense he will be aware also that he must inevitably be judged by the standards of the past. I say judged, not amputated, by them; not judged to be as good as, or worse or better than, the dead; and certainly not judged by the canons of dead critics. It is a judgment, a comparison, in which two things are measured by each other. To conform merely would be for the new work not really to conform at all; it would not be new, and would therefore not be a work of art.

And we do not quite say that the new is more valuable because it fits in; but its fitting in is a test of its value—a test, it is true, which can only be slowly and cautiously applied, for we are none of us infallible judges of conformity. We say: it appears to conform, and is perhaps individual, or it appears individual, and may conform; but we are hardly likely to find that it is one and not the other.

To proceed to a more intelligible exposition of the relation of the poet to the past: he can neither take the past as a lump, an indiscriminate bolus, nor can he form himself wholly on one or two private admirations, nor can he form himself wholly upon one preferred period. The first course is inadmissible, the second is an important experience of youth, and the third is a pleasant and highly desirable supplement. The poet must be very conscious of the main current, which does not at all flow invariably through the most distinguished reputations. He must be quite aware of the obvious fact that art never improves, but that the material of art is never quite the same. He must be aware that the mind of Europe—the mind of his own country—a mind which he learns in time to be much more important than his own private mind—is a mind which changes, and that this change is a development which abandons nothing *en route,* which does not superannuate either Shakespeare, or Homer, or the rock drawing of the Magdalenian draughtsmen. That this development, refinement perhaps, complication certainly, is not, from the point of view of the artist, any improvement. Perhaps not even an improvement from the point of view of the psychologist or not to the extent which we imagine; perhaps only in the end based upon a complication in economics and machinery. But the difference between the present and the past is that the conscious present is an awareness of the past in a way and to an extent which the past's awareness of itself cannot show.

Someone said: 'The dead writers are remote from us because we *know* so much more than they did'. Precisely, and they are that which we know.

I am alive to a usual objection to what is clearly part of my programme for the *métier* of poetry. The objection is that the doctrine requires a ridiculous amount of erudition (pedantry), a claim which can be rejected by appeal to the lives of poets in any pantheon. It will even be affirmed that much learning deadens or perverts poetic sensibility. While, however, we persist in believing that a poet ought to know as much as will not encroach upon his necessary receptivity and necessary laziness, it is not desirable to confine knowledge to whatever can be put into a useful shape for examinations, drawing-rooms, or the still more pretentious modes of publicity. Some can absorb knowledge, the more tardy must sweat for it. Shakespeare acquired more essential history from Plutarch than most men could from the whole British Museum. What is to be insisted upon is that the poet must develop or procure the consciousness of the past and that he should continue to develop this consciousness throughout his career.

What happens is a continual surrender of himself as he is at the moment to something which is more valuable. The progress of an artist is a continual self-sacrifice, a continual extinction of personality.

There remains to define this process of depersonalization and its relation to the sense of tradition. It is in this depersonalization that art may be said to approach the condition of science. I therefore invite you to consider, as a suggestive analogy, the action which takes place when a bit of finely filiated platinum is introduced into a chamber containing oxygen and sulphur dioxide.

II

Honest criticism and sensitive appreciation is directed not upon the poet but upon the poetry. If we attend to the confused cries of the newspaper critics and the susurrus of popular repetition that follows, we shall hear the names of poets in great numbers; if we seek not Blue-book knowledge but the enjoyment of poetry, and ask for a poem, we shall seldom find it. I have tried to point out the importance of the relation of the poem to other poems by other authors, and suggested the conception of poetry as a living whole of all the poetry that has ever been written. The other aspect of this Impersonal theory of poetry is the relation of the poem to its author. And I hinted, by an analogy, that the mind of the mature poet differs from that of the immature one not precisely in any valuation of 'personality', not being necessarily more interesting, or having 'more to say', but rather by being a more finely perfected medium in which special, or very varied, feelings are at liberty to enter into new combinations.

The analogy was that of the catalyst. When the two gases previously mentioned are mixed in the presence of a filament of platinum, they form sulphurous acid. This combination takes place only if the platinum is present; nevertheless the newly formed acid contains no trace of platinum, and the platinum itself is apparently unaffected: has remained inert, neutral, and unchanged. The mind of the poet is the shred of platinum. It may partly or exclusively operate upon the experience of the man himself; but, the more perfect the artist, the more completely separate in him will be the man who suffers and the mind which creates; the more perfectly will the mind digest and transmute the passions which are its material.

The experience, you will notice, the elements which enter the presence of the transforming catalyst, are of two kinds: emotions and feelings. The effect of a work of art upon the person who enjoys it is an experience different in kind from any experience not of art. It may be formed out of one emotion, or may be a combination of several; and various feelings, inhering for the writer in particular words or phrases or images, may be added to compose the final result. Or great poetry may be made without the direct use of any emotion whatever: composed out of feelings solely. Canto XV of the *Inferno* (Brunetto Latini) is a working up of the emotion evident in the situation; but the effect, though single as that of any work of art, is obtained by considerable complexity of detail. The last quatrain gives an image, a feeling attaching to an image, which 'came', which did not develop simply out of what precedes, but which was probably in suspension in the poet's mind until the proper combination arrived for it to add itself to. The poet's mind is in fact a receptacle for seizing and storing up numberless feelings, phrases, images, which remain there until all the particles which can unite to form a new compound are present together.

If you compare several representative passages of the greatest poetry you see how great is the variety of types of combination, and also how completely any semi-ethical criterion of 'sublimity' misses the mark. For it is not the 'greatness', the intensity, of the emotions, the components, but the intensity of the artistic process, the pressure, so to speak, under which the fusion takes place, that counts. The episode of Paolo and Francesca employs a definite emotion, but the intensity of the poetry is something quite different from whatever intensity in the supposed experience it may give the impression of. It is no more intense, furthermore, than Canto XXVI, the voyage of Ulysses, which has not the direct dependence upon an emotion. Great variety is possible in the process of transmutation of emotion: the murder of Agamemnon, or the agony of Othello, gives an artistic effect apparently closer to a possible original than the scenes from Dante. In the *Agamemnon,* the artistic emotion approximates to the emotion of an actual spectator; in *Othello* to the emotion of the protagonist himself. But the difference between art and the event is always absolute; the combination which is the murder of Agamemnon is probably as complex as that which is the voyage of Ulysses. In either case there has been a fusion of elements. The ode of Keats contains a number of feelings which have nothing particular to do with the nightingale, but which the nightingale, partly perhaps because of its attractive name, and partly because of its reputation, served to bring together.

The point of view which I am struggling to attack is perhaps related to the metaphysical theory of the substantial unity of the soul: for my meaning is, that the poet has, not a 'personality' to express, but a particular medium, which is only a medium and not a personality, in which impressions and experiences combine in peculiar and unexpected ways. Impressions and experiences which are important for the man may take no place in the poetry, and those which become important in the poetry may play quite a negligible part in the man, the personality.

I will quote a passage which is unfamiliar enough to be regarded with fresh attention in the light—or darkness—of these observations:

And now methinks I could e'en chide myself
For doating on her beauty, though her death
Shall be revenged after no common action.
Does the silkworm expend her yellow labours
For thee? For thee does she undo herself?
Are lordships sold to maintain ladyships
For the poor benefit of a bewildering minute?
Why does yon fellow falsify highways,
And put his life between the judge's lips,
To refine such a thing—keeps horse and men
To beat their valours for her? . . .

In this passage (as is evident if it is taken in its context) there is a combination of positive and negative emotions: an intensely strong attraction toward beauty and an equally intense fascination by the ugliness which is contrasted with it and which destroys it. This balance of contrasted emotion is in the dramatic situation to which the speech is pertinent, but that situation alone is inadequate to it. This is, so to speak, the structural emotion, provided by the drama. But the whole effect, the dominant tone, is due to the fact that a number of floating feelings, having an affinity to this emotion by no means superficially evident, having combined with it to give us a new art emotion.

It is not in his personal emotions, the emotions provoked by particular events in his life, that the poet is in any way remarkable or interesting. His particular emotions may be simple, or crude, or flat. The emotion in his poetry will be a very complex thing, but not with the complexity of the emotions of people who have very complex or unusual emotions in life. One error, in fact, of eccentricity in poetry is to seek for new human emotions to express; and in this search for novelty in the wrong place it discovers the perverse. The business of the poet is not to find new emotions, but to use the ordinary ones and, in working them up into poetry, to express feelings which are not in actual emotions at all. And emotions which he has never experienced will serve his turn as well as those familiar to him. Consequently, we must believe that 'emotion recollected in tranquillity' is an inexact formula. For it is neither emotion, nor recollection, nor without distortion of meaning, tranquillity. It is a concentration, and a new thing resulting from the concentration, of a very great number of experiences which to the practical and active person would not seem to be experiences at all; it is a concentration which does not happen consciously or of deliberation. These experiences are not 'recollected', and they finally unite in an atmosphere which is 'tranquil' only in that it is a passive attending upon the event. Of course this is not quite the whole story. There is a great deal, in the writing of poetry, which must be conscious and deliberate. In fact, the bad poet is usually unconscious where he ought to be conscious, and conscious where he ought to be unconscious. Both errors tend to make him 'personal'. Poetry is not a turning loose of emotion, but an escape from emotion; it is not the expression of personality, but an escape from personality. But, of course, only those who have personality and emotions know what it means to want to escape from these things.

III

ὁ δὲ νοῦς ἴσως θειότερόν τι και απαθες ἐστιν.[1]

This essay proposes to halt at the frontiers of metaphysics or mysticism, and confine itself to such practical conclusions as can be applied by the responsible person interested in poetry. To divert interest from the poet to the poetry is a laudable aim: for it would conduce to a juster estimation of actual poetry, good and bad. There are many people who appreciate the expression of sincere emotion in verse, and there is a smaller number of people who can appreciate technical excellence. But very few know when there is an expression of *significant* emotion, emotion which has its life in the poem and not in the history of the poet. The emotion of art is impersonal. And the poet cannot reach this impersonality without surrendering himself wholly to the work to be done. And he is not likely to know what is to be done unless he lives in what is not merely the present, but the present moment of the past, unless he is conscious, not of what is dead, but of what is already living.

[1] "The mind is doubtless more divine and less subject to passion." (Aristotle, *De Anima*).

A General Introduction for My Work

W. B. Yeats (1865–1939)

William Butler Yeats was born in Dublin, the son of a lawyer who eventually became a well-known painter. He was descended from a long line of Anglo-Irish Protestants, and in his later work he exalted this heritage, holding up the eighteenth-century Anglo-Irish world of Jonathan Swift, Edmund Burke, and Bishop Berkeley as a model for Ireland's future. Yeats spent much of his youth in London, but his summer holidays at Sligo, in the west of Ireland, had the most profound impact on his imagination (see "The Lake Isle of Innisfree"). When Yeats was fifteen the family returned to Dublin where he entered art school and began to write lyric poetry. He early developed an interest in magic and the occult which was to become a lifelong obsession and a frequent support for his art.

Yeats's early works appeared in *The Wanderings of Oisin and Other Poems* (1889), a volume which shows his affinity with Pre-Raphaelite art. In the same year he met Maud Gonne, an Irish beauty devoted to the cause of Irish political freedom, and fell deeply in love with her. His passion for Maud Gonne dominated the next thirty years of his life, and many of his most moving poems, such as "No Second Troy," were written with her in mind. During the 1890s Yeats travelled between London and Dublin, his art vacillating between an interest in Irish legend and a fascination with the symbolic modes of the French and English "decadents." This phase of Yeats's poetic life culminated in *The Wind Among the Reeds* (1899), but even before the book appeared there was evidence of radical changes in Yeats's art. In 1897 he first visited Coole Park, the Galway home of the Irish writer and folklorist Lady Gregory (as he returned to Coole Park each summer it became an emblem of the grace and ceremony threatened by the modern world). Through Lady Gregory, Yeats became interested in popular drama and the founding of a National Theatre. As the new century opened he turned away from the *fin de siècle* mood of the 1890s and became a public figure, meanwhile seeking to infuse his art with new energy and precision. In the plays and poems of the years 1900–14 he tried to cast off the vague symbolism and langorous rhythms of his earlier work, enlarging the range of his poetry to include public affairs. The marriage of Maud Gonne to Major John MacBride in 1903 had increased his sense of personal isolation and frustration, and this was intensified by the many public controversies (such as that over John Millington Synge's *Playboy of the Western World*) which convinced Yeats that the Irish middle class could not be transfigured through national art, as he had once hoped. The poems of *Responsibilities* (1914) reflect this bitterness and discouragement, but in the years between 1914 and 1920 several events changed Yeats's life and art. The Easter Rebellion of 1916 and its tragic aftermath (see "Easter 1916") gave him a glimpse of heroic possibilities that he had thought lost to Ireland. At the same time, a revived interest in the occult led to his construction of that visionary system which gives strength and coherence to so many of the later poems, such as "Leda and the Swan" (in 1925 Yeats set forth his system for interpreting art and history in *A Vision*). Most important of all, his marriage in 1917 to George Hyde-Lees and the birth of a daughter in 1919 and a son in 1921, gave Yeats new energy and purpose. His poetry stretching from *The Wild Swans at Coole* (1917) to *The Winding Stair* (1933) is among the greatest in the language, marked by dramatic intensity and a spectacular range of verse-forms. Perhaps the most important volume is *The Tower* (1928), named after the ruined Norman tower which Yeats had renovated and made his home. Its tone is set by the opening poem, "Sailing to Byzantium," and the entire volume balances the humiliations of old age against the glories of art and philosophy.

Yeats was desperately ill in the late 1920s, and when he recovered he remade his art once again, trying to attain in some of his last poems the simple, direct truth of the ballad or the nursery rhyme. In his last years he took an apocalyptic view of the social and political violence which surrounded him, but he never lost the gaiety and historical perspective that were part of his tragic vision and which are embodied in such poems as "Lapis Lazuli." At the end of his life Yeats sought to sum up his achievement, both in poetry and prose; the "General Introduction for My Work" was designed as an introduction to the definitive edition of his poems, and in it the major themes of his life and art—the two inseparable—are brilliantly summarized. The years since Yeats's death have confirmed the judgment made in 1940 by T. S. Eliot: "the greatest poet of our time—certainly the greatest in this language, and so far as I am able to judge, in any language."

1. THE FIRST PRINCIPLE

A poet writes always of his personal life, in his finest work out of its tragedy, whatever it be, remorse, lost love, or mere loneliness; he never speaks directly as to someone at the breakfast table, there is always a phantasmagoria. Dante and Milton had mythologies, Shakespeare the characters of English history or of traditional romance; even when the poet seems most himself, when he is Raleigh and gives potentates the lie, or Shelley 'a nerve o'er which do creep the else unfelt oppressions of this earth,' or Byron when 'the soul wears out the breast' as 'the sword outwears its sheath,' he is never the bundle of accident and incoherence that sits down to breakfast; he has been reborn as an idea, something intended, complete. A novelist might describe his accidence, his incoherence, he must not; he is more type than man, more passion than type. He is Lear, Romeo, Oedipus, Tiresias; he has stepped out of a play, and even the woman he loves is Rosalind, Cleopatra, never The Dark Lady. He is part of his own phantasmagoria and we adore him because nature has grown intelligible, and by so doing a part of our creative power. 'When mind is lost in the light of the Self,' says the Prashna Upanishad, 'it dreams no more; still in the body it is lost in happiness.' 'A wise man seeks in Self,' says the Chandogya Upanishad, 'those that are alive and those that are dead and gets what the world cannot give.' The world knows nothing because it has made nothing, we know everything because we have made everything.

2. SUBJECT-MATTER

It was through the old Fenian leader John O'Leary I found my theme. His long imprisonment, his longer banishment, his magnificent head, his scholarship, his pride, his integrity, all that aristocratic dream nourished amid little shops and little farms, had drawn around him a group of young men; I was but eighteen or nineteen and had already, under the influence of *The Faerie Queene* and *The Sad Shepherd,* written a pastoral play, and under that of Shelley's *Prometheus Unbound* two plays, one staged somewhere in the Caucasus, the other in a crater of the moon; and I knew myself to be vague and incoherent. He gave me the poems of Thomas Davis, said they were not good poetry but had changed his life when a young man, spoke of other poets associated with Davis and *The Nation* newspaper, probably lent me their books. I saw even more clearly than O'Leary that they were not good poetry. I read nothing but romantic literature; hated that dry eighteenth-century rhetoric; but they had one quality I admired and admire: they were not separated individual men; they spoke or tried to speak out of a people to a people; behind them stretched the generations. I knew, though but now and then as young men know things, that I must turn from the modern literature Jonathan Swift compared to a web a spider draws out of its bowels; I hated and still hate with an ever growing hatred the literature of the point of view. I wanted, if my ignorance permitted, to get back to Homer, to those that fed at his table. I wanted to cry as all men cried, to laugh as all men laughed, and the Young Ireland poets when not writing mere politics had the same want, but they did not know that the common and its befitting language is the research of a lifetime and when found may lack popular recognition. Then somebody, not O'Leary, told me of Standish O'Grady and his interpretation of Irish legends. O'Leary had sent me to O'Curry, but his unarranged and uninterpreted history defeated my boyish indolence.

A generation before *The Nation* newspaper was founded the Royal Irish Academy had begun the study of ancient Irish literature. That study was as much a gift from the Protestant aristocracy which had created the Parliament as *The Nation* and its school, though Davis and Mitchel were Protestants; was a gift from the Catholic middle classes who were to create the Irish Free State. The Academy persuaded the English Government to finance an ordnance survey on a large scale; scholars, including that great scholar O'Donovan, were sent from village to village recording names and their legends. Perhaps it was the last moment when such work could be well done, the memory of the people was still intact, the collectors themselves had perhaps heard or seen the banshee; the Royal Irish Academy and its public with equal enthusiasm welcomed Pagan and Christian; thought the Round Towers a commemoration of Persian fire-worship. There was little orthodoxy to take alarm; the Catholics were crushed and cowed; an honoured great-uncle of mine—his portrait by some forgotten master hangs upon my bedroom wall—a Church of Ireland rector, would upon occasion boast that you could not ask a question he could not answer with a perfectly appropriate blasphemy or indecency. When several counties had been surveyed but nothing published, the Government, afraid of rousing dangerous patriotic emotion, withdrew support; large manuscript volumes remain containing much picturesque correspondence between scholars.

When modern Irish literature began, O'Grady's influence predominated. He could delight us with an extravagance we were too critical to share; a day will come, he said, when Slieve-na-mon will be more famous than Olympus, yet he was no Nationalist as we understood the word, but in rebellion, as he was fond of explaining, against the House of Commons, not against the King. His cousin, that great scholar Hayes O'Grady, would not join our non-political Irish Literary Society because he considered it a Fenian body, but boasted that although he had lived in England for forty years he had never made an English friend. He worked at the British Museum compiling their Gaelic catalogue and translating our heroic tales in an eighteenth-century frenzy; his heroine 'fractured her heart,' his hero 'ascended to the apex of the eminence' and there 'vibrated his javelin,' and afterwards took ship upon 'colossal ocean's superficies.' Both O'Gradys considered themselves as representing the old Irish land-owning aristocracy; both probably, Standish O'Grady certainly, thought that England, because decadent and democratic, had betrayed their order. It was another member of that order, Lady Gregory, who was to do for the heroic legends in *Gods and Fighting Men* and in *Cuchulain of Muirthemne* what Lady Charlotte Guest's *Mabinogion* had done with less beauty and style for those of Wales. Standish O'Grady had much modern sentiment, his style, like that of John Mitchel forty years before, shaped by Carlyle; she formed her style upon the Anglo-Irish dialect of her neighbourhood, an old vivid speech with a partly Tudor vocabulary, a syntax partly moulded by men who still thought in Gaelic.

I had heard in Sligo cottages or from pilots at Rosses Point endless stories of apparitions, whether of the recent dead or of the people of history and legend, of that Queen Maeve whose reputed cairn stands on the mountain over the bay. Then at the British Museum I read stories Irish writers of the 'forties and 'fifties had written of such apparitions, but they enraged me more than pleased because they turned the country visions into a joke. But when I went from cottage to cottage with Lady Gregory and watched her hand recording that great collection she has called *Visions and Beliefs* I escaped disfiguring humour.

Behind all Irish history hangs a great tapestry, even Christianity had to accept it and be itself pictured there. Nobody looking at its dim folds can say where Christianity begins and Druidism ends; 'There is one perfect among the birds, one perfect among the fish, and one among men that is perfect.' I can only explain by that suggestion of recent scholars—Professor Burkitt of Cambridge commended it to my attention—that St. Patrick came to Ireland not in the fifth century but towards the end of the second. The great controversies had not begun; Easter was still the first full moon after the Equinox. Upon that day the world had been created, the Ark rested upon Ararat, Moses led the Israelites out of Egypt; the umbilical cord which united Christianity to the ancient world had not yet been cut. Christ was still the half-brother of Dionysus. A man just tonsured by the Druids could learn from the nearest Christian neighbour to sign himself with the Cross without sense of incongruity, nor would his children acquire that sense. The organised clans weakened Church organisation, they could accept the monk but not the bishop.

A modern man, *The Golden Bough* and *Human Personality* in his head, finds much that is congenial in St. Patrick's Creed as recorded in his Confessions, and nothing to reject except the word 'soon' in the statement that Christ will soon judge the quick and the dead. He can repeat it, believe it even, without a thought of the historic Christ, or ancient Judea, or of anything subject to historical conjecture and shifting evidence; I repeat it and think of 'the Self' in the Upanishads. Into this tradition, oral and written, went in later years fragments of Neo-Platonism, cabbalistic words—I have heard the words 'tetragrammaton agla' in Doneraile—the floating debris of mediaeval thought, but nothing that did not please the solitary mind. Even the religious equivalent for Baroque and Rococo could not come to us as thought, perhaps because Gaelic is incapable of abstraction. It came as cruelty. That tapestry filled the scene at the birth of modern Irish literature, it is there in the Synge of *The Well of the Saints,* in James Stephens, and in Lady Gregory throughout, in all of George Russell that did not come from the Upanishads, and in all but my later poetry.

Sometimes I am told in commendation, if the newspaper is Irish, in condemnation if English, that my movement perished under the firing squads of 1916; sometimes that those firing squads made our realistic movement possible. If that statement is true, and it is only so in part, for romance was everywhere receding, it is because in the imagination of Pearse and his fellow soldiers the Sacrifice of the Mass had found the Red Branch in the tapestry; they went out to die calling upon Cuchulain:

> Fall, Hercules, from Heaven in tempests hurled
> To cleanse the beastly stable of this world.

In one sense the poets of 1916 were not of what the newspapers call my school. The Gaelic League, made timid by a modern popularisation of Catholicism sprung from the aspidistra and not from the root of Jesse, dreaded intellectual daring and stuck to dictionary and grammar. Pearse and MacDonagh and others among the executed men would have done, or attempted, in Gaelic what we did or attempted in English.

Our mythology, our legends, differ from those of other European countries because down to the end of the seventeenth century they had the attention, perhaps the unquestioned belief, of peasant and noble alike; Homer belongs to sedentary men, even to-day our ancient queens, our mediaeval soldiers and lovers, can make a pedlar shudder. I can put my own thought, despair perhaps from the study of present circumstance in the light of ancient philosophy, into the mouth of rambling poets of the seventeenth century, or even of some imagined ballad singer of to-day, and the deeper my thought the more credible, the more peasant-like, are ballad singer and rambling poet. Some modern poets contend that jazz and music-hall songs are the folk art of our time, that we should mould our art upon them; we Irish poets, modern men also, reject every folk art that does not go back to Olympus. Give me time and a little youth and I will prove that even 'Johnny, I hardly knew ye' goes back.

Mr. Arnold Toynbee in an annex to the second volume of *The Study of History* describes the birth and decay of what he calls the Far Western Christian culture; it lost at the Synod of Whitby its chance of mastering Europe, suffered final ecclesiastical defeat in the twelfth century with 'the thoroughgoing incorporation of the Irish Christendom into the Roman Church. In the political and literary spheres' it lasted unbroken till the seventeenth century. He then insists that if 'Jewish Zionism and Irish Nationalism succeed in achieving their aims, then Jewry and Irishry will each fit into its own tiny niche . . . among sixty or seventy national communities', find life somewhat easier, but cease to be 'the relic of an independent society . . . the romance of Ancient Ireland has at last come to an end . . . Modern Ireland has made up her mind, in our generation, to find her level as a willing inmate in our workaday Western world.'

If Irish literature goes on as my generation planned it, it may do something to keep the 'Irishry' living, nor will the work of the realists hinder, nor the figures they imagine, nor those described in memoirs of the revolution. These last especially, like certain great political predecessors, Parnell, Swift, Lord Edward, have stepped back into the tapestry. It may be indeed that certain characteristics of the 'Irishry' must grow in importance. When Lady Gregory asked me to annotate her *Visions and Beliefs* I began, that I might understand what she had taken down in Galway, an investigation of contemporary spiritualism. For several years I frequented those mediums who in various poor parts of London instruct artisans or their wives for a few pence upon their relations to their dead, to their employers, and to their children; then I compared what she had heard in Galway, or I in London, with the visions of Swedenborg, and, after my inadequate notes had been published, with Indian belief. If Lady Gregory had not said when we passed an old man in the woods, 'That man may know the secret of the ages,' I might never have talked with Shri Purohit Swami nor made him translate his Master's travels in Tibet, nor helped him translate the Upanishads. I think I now know why the gamekeeper at Coole heard the footsteps of a deer on the edge of the lake where no deer had passed for a hundred years, and why a certain cracked old priest said that nobody had been to hell or heaven in his time, meaning thereby that the Rath had got them all; that the dead stayed where they had lived, or near it, sought no abstract region of blessing or punishment but retreated, as it were, into the hidden character of their neighbourhood. I am convinced that in two or three generations it will become generally known that the mechanical theory has no reality, that the natural and supernatural are knit together, that to escape a dangerous fanaticism we must study a new science; at that moment Europeans may find something attractive in a Christ posed against a background not of Judaism but of Druidism, not shut off in dead history, but flowing, concrete, phenomenal.

I was born into this faith, have lived in it, and shall die in it; my Christ, a legitimate deduction from the Creed of St. Patrick as I think, is that Unity of Being Dante compared to a perfectly proportioned human body, Blake's 'Imagination,' what the Upanishads have named 'Self'; nor is this unity distant and therefore intellectually understandable, but imminent, differing from man to man and age to age, taking upon itself pain and ugliness, 'eye of newt, and toe of frog.'

Subconscious preoccupation with this theme brought me *A Vision,* its harsh geometry an incomplete interpretation. The 'Irishry' have preserved their ancient 'deposit' through wars which, during the sixteenth and seventeenth centuries, became wars of extermination; no people, Lecky said at the opening of his *Ireland in the Eighteenth Century,* have undergone greater persecution, nor did that persecution altogether cease up to our own day. No people hate as we do in whom that past is always alive, there are moments when hatred poisons my life and I accuse myself of effeminacy because I have not given it adequate expression. It is not enough to have put it into the mouth of a rambling peasant poet. Then I remind myself that though mine is the first English marriage I know of in the direct line, all my family names are English, and that I owe my soul to Shakespeare, to Spenser and to Blake, perhaps to William Morris, and to the English language in which I think, speak, and write, that everything I love has come to me through English; my hatred tortures me with love, my love with hate. I am like the Tibetan monk who dreams at his initiation that he is eater and eaten. This is Irish hatred and solitude, the hatred of human life that made Swift write *Guliver* and the epitaph upon his tomb, that can still make us wag between extremes and doubt our sanity.

Again and again I am asked why I do not write in Gaelic. Some four or five years ago I was invited to dinner by a London society and found myself among London journalists, Indian students, and foreign political refugees. An Indian paper says it was a dinner in my honour; I hope not; I have forgotten, though I have a clear memory of my own angry mind. I should have spoken as men are expected to speak at public dinners; I should have paid and been paid conventional compliments; then they would speak of the refugees; from that on all would be lively and topical, foreign tyranny would be arraigned, England seem even to those confused Indians the protector of liberty; I grew angrier and angrier; Wordsworth, that typical Englishman, had published his famous sonnet to François Dominique Toussaint, a Santo Domingo Negro:

> There's not a breathing of the common wind
> That will forget thee

in the year when Emmet conspired and died, and he remembered that rebellion as little as the half hanging and the pitch cap that preceded it by half a dozen years. That there might be no topical speeches I denounced the oppression of the people of India; being a man of letters, not a politician, I told how they had been forced to learn everything, even their own Sanskrit, through the vehicle of English till the first discoverer of wisdom had become bywords for vague abstract facility. I begged the Indian writers present to remember that no man can think or write with music and vigour except in his mother tongue. I turned a friendly audience hostile, yet when I think of that scene I am unrepentant and angry.

I could no more have written Gaelic than can those Indians write in English; Gaelic is my national language, but it is not my mother tongue.

3. STYLE AND ATTITUDE

Style is almost unconscious. I know what I have tried to do, little what I have done. Contemporary lyric poems, even those that moved me—*The Stream's Secret, Dolores*—seemed too long, but an Irish preference for a swift current might be mere indolence, yet Burns may have felt the same when he read Thomson and Cowper. The English mind is meditative, rich, deliberate; it may remember the Thames valley. I planned to write short lyrics or poetic drama where every speech would be short and concentrated, knit by dramatic tension, and I did so with more confidence because young English poets were at that time writing out of emotion at the moment of crisis, though their old slow-moving meditation returned almost at once. Then, and in this English poetry has followed my lead, I tried to make the language of poetry coincide with that of passionate, normal speech. I wanted to write in whatever language comes most naturally when we soliloquise, as I do all day long, upon the events of our own lives or of any life where we can see ourselves for the moment. I sometimes compare myself with the mad old slum women I hear denouncing and remembering; 'How dare you,' I heard one say of some imaginary suitor, 'and you without health or a home!' If I spoke my thoughts aloud they might be as angry and as wild. It was a long time before I had made a language to my liking; I began to make it when I discovered some twenty years ago that I must seek, not as Wordsworth thought, words in common use, but a powerful and passionate syntax, and a complete coincidence between period and stanza. Because I need a passionate syntax for passionate subject-matter I compel myself to accept those traditional metres that have developed with the language. Ezra Pound, Turner, Lawrence wrote admirable free verse, I could not. I would lose myself, become joyless like those mad old women. The translators of the Bible, Sir Thomas Browne, certain translators from the Greek when translators still bothered about rhythm, created a form midway between prose and verse that seems natural to impersonal meditation; but all that is personal soon rots; it must be packed in ice or salt. Once when I was in delirium from pneumonia I dictated a letter to George Moore telling him to eat salt because it was a symbol of eternity; the delirium passed, I had no memory of that letter, but I must have meant what I now mean. If I wrote of personal love or sorrow in free verse, or in any rhythm that left it unchanged, amid all its accidence, I would be full of self-contempt because of my egotism and indiscretion, and foresee the boredom of my reader. I must choose a traditional stanza, even what I alter must seem traditional. I commit my emotion to shepherds, herdsmen, camel-drivers, learned men, Milton's or Shelley's Platonist, that tower Palmer drew. Talk to me of originality and I will turn on you with rage. I am a crowd, I am a lonely man, I am nothing. Ancient salt is best packing. The heroes of Shakespeare convey to us through their looks, or through the metaphorical patterns of their speech, the sudden enlargement of their vision, their ecstasy at the approach of death: 'She should have died thereafter,' 'Of many thousand kisses, the poor last,' 'Absent thee from felicity awhile.' They have become God or Mother Goddess, the pelican, 'My baby at my breast,' but all must be cold; no actress has ever sobbed when she played Cleopatra, even the shallow brain of a producer has never thought of such a thing. The supernatural is present, cold winds blow across our hands, upon our faces, the thermometer falls, and because of that cold we are hated by journalists and groundlings. There may be in this or that detail painful tragedy, but in the whole work none. I have heard Lady Gregory say, rejecting some play in the modern manner sent to the Abbey Theatre, 'Tragedy must be a joy to the man who dies.' Nor is it any different with lyrics, songs, narrative poems; neither scholars nor the populace have sung or read anything generation after generation because of its pain. The maid of honour whose tragedy they sing must be lifted out of history with timeless pattern, she is one of the four Maries, the rhythm is old and familiar, imagination must dance, must be carried beyond feeling into the aboriginal ice. Is ice the correct word? I once boasted, copying the phrase from a letter of my father's, that I would write a poem 'cold and passionate as the dawn.'

When I wrote in blank verse I was dissatisfied; my vaguely mediaeval *Countess Cathleen* fitted the measure, but our Heroic Age went better, or so I fancied, in the ballad metre of *The Green Helmet*. There was something in what I felt about Deirdre, about Cuchulain, that rejected the Renaissance and its characteristic metres, and this was a principal reason why I created in dance plays the form that varies blank verse with lyric metres. When I speak blank verse and analyse my feelings, I stand at a moment of history when instinct, its traditional songs and dances, its general agreement, is of the past. I have been cast up out of the whale's belly though I still remember the sound and sway that came from beyond its ribs, and, like the Queen in Paul Fort's ballad, I smell of the fish of the sea. The contrapuntal structure of the verse, to employ a term adopted by Robert Bridges, combines the past and present. If I repeat the first line of *Paradise Lost* so as to emphasise its five feet I am among the folk singers—'Of mán's first dísobédience ánd the frúit,' but speak it as I should I cross it with another emphasis, that of passionate prose—'Of mán's fírst disobédience and the frúit,' or 'Of mán's fírst dísobedience and the frúit'; the folk song is still there, but a ghostly voice, an unvariable possibility, an unconscious norm. What moves me and my hearer is a vivid speech that has no laws except that it must not exorcise the ghostly voice. I am awake and asleep, at my moment of relevation, self-possessed in self-surrender; there is no rhyme, no echo of the beaten drum, the dancing foot, that would overset my balance. When I was a boy I wrote a poem upon dancing that had one good line: 'They snatch with their hands at the sleep of the skies.' If I sat down and thought for a year I would discover that but for certain syllabic limitations, a rejection or acceptance of certain elisions, I must wake or sleep.

The Countess Cathleen could speak a blank verse which I had loosened, almost put out of joint, for her need, because I thought of her as mediaeval and thereby connected her with the general European movement. For Deirdre and Cuchulain and all the other figures of Irish legend are still in the whale's belly.

4. WHITHER?

The young English poets reject dream and personal emotion; they have thought out opinions that join them to this or that political party; they employ an intricate psychology, action in character, not as in the ballads character in action, and all consider that they have a right to the same close attention that men pay to the mathematician and the metaphysician. One of the more distinguished has just explained that man has hitherto slept but must now wake. They are determined to express the factory, the metropolis, that they may be modern. Young men teaching school in some picturesque cathedral town, or settled for life in Capri or Sicily, defend their type of metaphor by saying that it comes naturally to a man who travels to his work by Tube. I am indebted to a man of this school who went through my work at my request, crossing out all conventional metaphors, but they seem to me to have rejected also those dream associations which were the whole art of Mallarmé. He had topped a previous wave. As they express not what the Upanishads call "that ancient Self" but individual intellect, they have the right to choose the man in the Tube because of his objective importance. They attempt to kill the whale, push the Renaissance higher yet, out-think Leonardo; their verse kills the folk ghost and yet would remain verse. I am joined to the 'Irishry' and I expect a counter-Renaissance. No doubt it is part of the game to push that Renaissance; I make no complaint; I am accustomed to the geometrical arrangement of history in *A Vision*, but I go deeper than 'custom' for my convictions. When I stand upon O'Connell Bridge in the half-light and notice that discordant architecture, all those electric signs, where modern heterogeneity has taken physical form, a vague hatred comes up out of my own dark and I am certain that wherever in Europe there are minds strong enough to lead others the same vague hatred rises; in four or five or in less generations this hatred will have issued in violence and imposed some kind of rule of kindred. I cannot know the nature of that rule, for its opposite fills the light; all I can do to bring it nearer is to intensify my hatred. I am no Nationalist, except in Ireland for passing reasons; State and Nation are the work of intellect, and when you consider what comes before and after them they are, as Victor Hugo said of something or other, not worth the blade of grass God gives for the nest of the linnet.

Education by Poetry

A Meditative Monologue

Robert Frost (1874–1963)

Robert Lee Frost was born in San Francisco, California, on March 26, 1874. It seems only appropriate that this master of paradoxes who became the poet-laureate of rural New England should have been born in a city a continent away and named for a Confederate general. After the death of his father (Frost was then eleven) the family settled in New England; Frost entered Dartmouth College in 1892 but stayed only a few months. For the next few years he taught school, tried his hand at farming, and wrote poetry on the side. Frost attended Harvard in 1897–99, but left without a degree and returned to farming and teaching. In 1912 he sold his farm at Derry, New Hampshire, and moved to England with his family. There he attracted the attention of other poets, notably Ezra Pound, and in 1913 his first collection of poetry, *A Boy's Will,* was published. It was followed in 1914 by *North of Boston,* and the two volumes secured Frost's reputation as a regional poet of universal appeal.

In 1915 Frost returned to the United States and became a farmer-poet, teaching frequently at Amherst, the University of Michigan, and the Bread Loaf School of English ("Education by Poetry" was delivered at Amherst College in 1930). Among his collections of poetry, *New Hampshire* (1923), *A Further Range* (1937), and *A Witness Tree* (1942) won Pulitzer Prizes. In his later years Frost became a national folk hero, creating a public image of serenity and canny wisdom which was often at variance with the darkness and isolation of his best poems. The climax to this phase of Frost's career came in 1961 when he was asked to read a poem at the inauguration of President John F. Kennedy.

I am going to urge nothing in my talk. I am not an advocate. I am going to consider a matter, and commit a description. And I am going to describe other colleges than Amherst. Or, rather say all that is good can be taken as about Amherst; all that is bad will be about other colleges.

I know whole colleges where all American poetry is barred—whole colleges. I know whole colleges where all contemporary poetry is barred.

I once heard of a minister who turned his daughter—his poetry-writing daughter—out on the street to earn a living, because he said there should be no more books written; God wrote one book, and that was enough. (My friend George Russell, "AE," has read no literature, he protests, since just before Chaucer.)

That all seems sufficiently safe, and you can say one thing for it. It takes the onus off the poetry of having to be used to teach children anything. It comes pretty hard on poetry, I sometimes think,—what it has to bear in the teaching process.

Then I know whole colleges where, though they let in older poetry, they manage to bar all that is poetical in it by treating it as something other than poetry. It is not so hard to do that. Their reason I have often hunted for. It may be that these people act from a kind of modesty. Who are professors that they should attempt to deal with a thing as high and as fine as poetry? Who are *they?* There is a certain manly modesty in that.

That is the best general way of settling the problem; treat all poetry, as if it were something else than poetry, as if it were syntax, language, science. Then you can even come down into the American and into the contemporary without any special risk.

There is another reason they have, and that is that they are, first and foremost in life, markers. They have the marking problem to consider. Now, I stand here a teacher of many years' experience and I have never complained of having had to mark. I had rather mark anyone for anything—for his looks, carriage, his ideas, his correctness, his exactness, anything you please,—I would rather give him a mark in terms of letters, A, B, C, D, than have to use adjectives on him. We are all being marked by each other all the time, classified, ranked, put in our place, and I see no escape from that. I am no sentimentalist. You have got to mark, and you have got to mark, first of all, for accuracy, for correctness. But if I am going to give a mark, that is the least part of my marking. The hard part is the part beyond that, the part where the adventure begins.

One other way to rid the curriculum of the poetry nuisance has been considered. More merciful than the others, it would neither abolish nor denature the poetry, but only turn it out to disport itself, with the plays and games—in no wise discredited, though given no credit for. Any one who liked to teach poetically could take his subject, whether English, Latin, Greek or French, out into the nowhere along with the poetry. One side of a sharp line would be left to the rigorous and righteous; the other side would be assigned to the flowery where they would know what could be expected of them. Grade marks were more easily given, of course, in the courses concentrating on correctness and exactness as the only forms of honesty recognized by plain people; a general indefinite mark of X in the courses that scatter brains over taste and opinion. On inquiry I have found no teacher willing to take position on either side of the line, either among the rigors or among the flowers. No one is willing to admit that his discipline is not partly in exactness. No one is willing to admit that his discipline is not partly in taste and enthusiasm.

How shall a man go through college without having been marked for taste and judgment? What will become of him? What will his end be? He will have to take continuation courses for college graduates. He will have to go to night schools. They are having night schools now, you know, for college graduates. Why? Because they have not been educated enough to find their way around in contemporary literature. They don't know what they may safely like in the libraries and galleries. They don't know how to judge an editorial when they see one. They don't know how to judge a political campaign. They don't know when they are being fooled by a metaphor, an analogy, a parable. And metaphor is, of course, what we are talking about. Education by poetry is education by metaphor.

Suppose we stop short of imagination, initiative, enthusiasm, inspiration and originality—dread words. Suppose we don't mark in such things at all. There are still two minimal things, that we have got to take care of, taste and judgment. Americans are supposed to have more judgment than taste, but taste is there to be dealt with. That is what poetry, the only art in the colleges of arts, is there for. I for my part would not be afraid to go in for enthusiasm. There is the enthusiasm like a blinding light, or the enthusiasm of the deafening shout, the crude enthusiasm that you get uneducated by poetry, outside of poetry. It is exemplified in what I might call "sunset raving." You look westward toward the sunset, or if you get up early enough, eastward toward the sunrise, and you rave. It is oh's and ah's with you and no more.

But the enthusiasm I mean is taken through the prism of the intellect and spread on the screen in a color, all the way from hyperbole at one end—or overstatement, at one end—to understatement at the other end. It is a long strip of dark lines and many colors. Such enthusiasm is one object of all teaching in poetry. I heard wonderful things said about Virgil yesterday, and many of them seemed to me crude enthusiasm, more like a deafening shout, many of them. But one speech and range, something of overstatement, something of statement, and something of understatement. It had all the colors of an enthusiasm passed through an idea.

I would be willing to throw away everything else but that: enthusiasm tamed by metaphor. Let me rest the case there. Enthusiasm tamed to metaphor, tamed to that much of it. I do not think anybody ever knows the discreet use of metaphor, his own and other people's, the discreet handling of metaphor, unless he has been properly educated in poetry.

Poetry begins in trivial metaphors, pretty metaphors, "grace" metaphors, and goes on to the profoundest thinking that we have. Poetry provides the one permissible way of saying one thing and meaning another. People say, "Why don't you say what you mean?" We never do that, do we, being all of us too much poets. We like to talk in parables and in hints and in indirections—whether from diffidence or some other instinct.

I have wanted in late years to go further and further in making metaphor the whole of thinking. I find some one now and then to agree with me that all thinking, except mathematical thinking, is metaphorical, or all thinking except scientific thinking. The mathematical might be difficult for me to bring in, but the scientific is easy enough.

Once on a time all the Greeks were busy telling each other what the All was—or was like unto. All was three elements, air, earth, and water (we once thought it was ninety elements; now we think it is only one). All was substance, said another. All was change, said a third. But best and most fruitful was Pythagoras' comparison of the universe with number. Number of what? Number of feet, pounds, and seconds was the answer, and we had science and all that has followed in science. The metaphor has held and held, breaking down only when it came to the spiritual and psychological or out of the way places of the physical.

The other day we had a visitor here, a noted scientist, whose latest word to the world has been that the more accurately you know where a thing is, the less accurately you are able to state how fast it is moving. You can see why that would be so, without going back to Zeno's problem of the arrow's flight. In carrying numbers into the realm of space and at the same time into the realm of time you are mixing metaphors, that is all, and you are in trouble. They won't mix. The two don't go together.

Let's take two or three more of the metaphors now in use to live by. I have just spoken of one of the new ones, a charming mixed metaphor right in the realm of higher mathematics and higher physics: that the more accurately you state where a thing is, the less accurately you will be able to tell how fast it is moving. And, of course, everything is moving. Everything is an event now. Another metaphor. A thing, they say, is an event. Do you believe it is? Not quite. I believe it is almost an event. But I like the comparison of a thing with an event.

I notice another from the same quarter. "In the neighborhood of matter space is something like curved." Isn't that a good one! It seems to me that that is simply and utterly charming—to say that space is something like curved in the neighborhood of matter. "Something like."

Another amusing one is from—what is the book?—I can't say it now; but here is the metaphor. Its aim is to restore you to your ideas of free will. It wants to give you back your freedom of will. All right, here it is on a platter. You know that you can't tell by name what persons in a certain class will be dead ten years after graduation, but you can tell actuarially how many will be dead. Now, just so this scientist says of the particles of matter flying at a screen, striking a screen; you can't tell what individual particles will come, but you can say in general that a certain number will strike in a given time. It shows, you see, that the individual particle can come freely. I asked Bohr about that particularly, and he said, "Yes, it is so. It can come when it wills and as it wills; and the action of the individual particle is unpredictable. But it is not so of the action of the mass. There you can predict." He says, "That gives the individual atom its freedom, but the mass its necessity."

Another metaphor that has interested us in our time and has done all our thinking for us is the metaphor of evolution. Never mind going into the Latin word. The metaphor is simply the metaphor of the growing plant or of the growing thing. And somebody very brilliantly, quite a while ago, said that the whole universe, the whole of everything, was like unto a growing thing. That is all. I know the metaphor will break down at some point, but it has not failed everywhere. It is a very brilliant metaphor, I acknowledge, though I myself get too tired of the kind of essay that talks about the evolution of candy, we will say, or the evolution of elevators—the evolution of this, that, and the other. Everything is evolution. I emancipate myself by simply saying that I didn't get up the metaphor and so am not much interested in it.

What I am pointing out is that unless you are at home in the metaphor, unless you have had your proper poetical education in the metaphor, you are not safe anywhere. Because you are not at ease with figurative values: you don't know the metaphor in its strength and its weakness. You don't know how far you may expect to ride it and when it may break down with you. You are not safe in science; you are not safe in history. In history, for instance—to show that it is the same in history as elsewhere—I heard somebody say yesterday that Aeneas was to be likened unto (those words, "likened unto"!) George Washington. He was that type of national hero, the middle-class man, not thinking of being a hero at all, bent on building the future, bent on his children, his descendants. A good metaphor, as far as it goes, and you must know how far. And then he added that Odysseus should be likened unto Theodore Roosevelt. I don't think that is so good. Someone visiting Gibbon at the point of death, said he was the same Gibbon as of old, still at his parallels.

Take the way we have been led into our present position morally, the world over. It is by a sort of metaphorical gradient. There is a kind of thinking—to speak metaphorically—there is a kind of thinking you might say was endemic in the brothel. It is always there. And every now and then in some mysterious way it becomes epidemic in the world. And how does it do so? By using all the good words that virtue has invented to maintain virtue. It uses honesty, first,—frankness, sincerity—those words; picks them up uses them. "In the name of honesty, let us see what we are." You know. And then it picks up the word joy. "Let us in the name of joy, which is the enemy of our ancestors, the Puritans. . . . Let us in the name of joy, which is the enemy of the kill-joy Puritan. . . ." You see. "Let us," and so on. And then, "In the name of health . . . ." Health is another good word. And that is the metaphor Freudianism trades on, mental health. And the first thing we know, it has us all in up to the top knot. I suppose we may blame the artists a good deal, because they are great people to spread by metaphor. The stage too—the stage is always a good intermediary between the two worlds, the under and the upper,—if I may say so without personal prejudice to the stage.

In all this I have only been saying that the devil can quote Scripture, which simply means that the good words you have lying around the devil can use for his purposes as well as anybody else. Never mind about my morality. I am not here to urge anything. I don't care whether the world is good or bad—not on any particular day.

Let me ask you to watch a metaphor breaking down here before you.

Somebody said to me a little while ago, "It is easy enough for me to think of the universe as a machine, as a mechanism."

I said, "You mean the universe is like a machine?"

He said, "No. I think it is one. . . . Well, it is like. . . ."

"I think you mean the universe is like a machine."

"All right. Let it go at that."

I asked him, "Did you ever see a machine without a pedal for the foot, or a lever for the hand, or a button for the finger?"

He said, "No—no."

I said, "All right. Is the universe like that?"

And he said, "No. I mean it is like a machine, only. . . ."

". . . it is different from a machine," I said.

He wanted to go just that far with that metaphor and no further. And so do we all. All metaphor breaks down somewhere. That is the beauty of it. It is touch and go with the metaphor, and until you have lived with it long enough you don't know when it is going. You don't know how much you can get out of it and when it will cease to yield. It is a very living thing. It is as life itself.

I have heard this ever since I can remember, and ever since I have taught: the teacher must teach the pupil to think. I saw a teacher once going around in a great school and snapping pupils' heads with a thumb and finger and saying, "Think." That was when thinking was becoming the fashion. The fashion hasn't yet quite gone out.

We still ask boys in college to think, as in the nineties, but we seldom tell them what thinking means; we seldom tell them it is just putting this and that together; it is just saying one thing in terms of another. To tell them is to set their feet on the first rung of a ladder the top of which sticks through the sky.

Greatest of all attempts to say one thing in terms of another is the philosophical attempt to say matter in terms of spirit, or spirit in terms of matter, to make the final unity. That is the greatest attempt that ever failed. We stop just short there. But it is the height of poetry, the height of all thinking, the height of all poetic thinking, that attempt to say matter in terms of spirit and spirit in terms of matter. It is wrong to call anybody a materialist simply because he tries to say spirit in terms of matter, as if that were a sin. Materialism is not the attempt to say all in terms of matter. The only materialist—be he poet, teacher, scientist, politician, or statesman—is the man who gets lost in his material without a gathering metaphor to throw it into shape and order. He is the lost soul.

We ask people to think, and we don't show them what thinking is. Somebody says we don't need to show them how to think; bye and bye they will think. We will give them the forms of sentences and, if they have any ideas, then they will know how to write them. But that is preposterous. All there is to writing is having ideas. To learn to write is to learn to have ideas.

The first little metaphor. . . . Take some of the trivial ones. I would rather have trivial ones of my own to live by than the big ones of other people.

I remember a boy saying, "He is the kind of person that wounds with his shield." That may be a slender one, of course. It goes a good way in character description. It has poetic grace. "He is the kind that wounds with his shield."

The shield reminds me—just to linger a minute—the shield reminds me of the inverted shield spoken of in one of the books of the *Odyssey,* the book that tells about the longest swim on record. I forget how long it lasted—several days, was it?—but at last as Odysseus came near the coast of Phoenicia, he saw it on the horizon "like an inverted shield."

There is a better metaphor in the same book. In the end Odysseus comes ashore and crawls up the beach to spend the night under a double olive tree, and it says, as in a lonely farmhouse where it is hard to get fire—I am not quoting exactly—where it is hard to start the fire again if it goes out, they cover the seeds of fire with ashes to preserve it for the night, so Odysseus covered himself with the leaves around him and went to sleep. There you have something that gives you character, something of Odysseus himself. "Seeds of fire." So Odysseus covered the seeds of fire in himself. You get the greatness of his nature.

But these are slighter metaphors than the ones we live by. They have their charm, their passing charm. They are as it were the first steps toward the great thoughts, grave thoughts, thoughts lasting to the end.

The metaphor whose manage we are best taught in poetry—that is all there is of thinking. It may not seem far for the mind to go but it is the mind's furthest. The richest accumulation of the ages is the noble metaphors we have rolled up.

I want to add one thing more that the experience of poetry is to anyone who comes close to poetry. There are two ways of coming close to poetry. One is by writing poetry. And some people think I want people to write poetry, but I don't; that is, I don't necessarily. I only want people to write poetry if they want to write poetry. I have never encouraged anybody to write poetry that did not want to write it, and I have not always encouraged those who did want to write it. That ought to be one's own funeral. It is a hard, hard life, as they say.

(I have just been to a city in the West, a city full of poets, a city they have made safe for poets. The whole city is so lovely that you do not have to write it up to make it poetry; it is ready-made for you. But, I don't know—the poetry written in that city might not seem like poetry if read outside of the city. It would be like the jokes made when you were drunk; you have to get drunk again to appreciate them.)

But as I say, there is another way to come close to poetry, fortunately, and that is in the reading of it, not as linguistics, not as history, not as anything but poetry. It is one of the hard things for a teacher to know how close a man has come in reading poetry. How do I know whether a man has come close to Keats in reading Keats? It is hard for me to know. I have lived with some boys a whole year over some of the poets and I have not felt sure whether they have come near what it is all about. One remark sometimes told me. One remark was their mark for the year; had to be—it was all I got that told me what I wanted to know. And that is enough, if it was the right remark, if it came close enough. I think a man might make twenty fool remarks if he made one good one some time in the year. His mark would depend on that good remark.

The closeness—everything depends on the closeness with which you come, and you ought to be marked for the closeness, for nothing else. And that will have to be estimated by chance remarks, not by question and answer. It is only by accident that you know some day how near a person has come.

The person who gets close enough to poetry, he is going to know more about the word *belief* than anybody else knows, even in religion nowadays. There are two or three places where we know belief outside of religion. One of them is at the age of fifteen to twenty, in our self-belief. A young man knows more about himself than he is able to prove to anyone. He has no knowledge that anybody else will accept as knowledge. In his foreknowledge he has something that is going to believe itself into fulfillment, into acceptance.

There is another belief like that, the belief in someone else, a relationship of two that is going to be believed into fulfillment. That is what we are talking about in our novels, the belief of love. And the disillusionment that the novels are full of is simply the disillusionment from disappointment in that belief. That belief can fail of course.

Then there is a literary belief. Every time a poem is written, every time a short story is written, it is written not by cunning, but by belief. The beauty, the something, the little charm of the thing to be, is more felt than known. There is a common jest, one that always annoys me, on the writers, that they write the last end first, and then work up to it; that they lay a train toward one sentence that they think is pretty nice and have all fixed up to set like a trap to close with. No, it should not be that way at all. No one who has ever come close to the arts has failed to see the difference between things written that way, with cunning and device, and the kind that are believed into existence, that begin in something more felt than known. This you can realize quite as well—not quite as well, perhaps, but nearly as well—in reading as you can in writing. I would undertake to separate short stories on that principle; stories that have been believed into existence and stories that have been cunningly devised. And I could separate the poems still more easily.

Now I think—I happen to think—that those three beliefs that I speak of, the self-belief, the love-belief, and the art-belief, are all closely related to the God-belief, that the belief in God is a relationship you enter into with Him to bring about the future.

There is a national belief like that, too. One feels it. I have been where I came near getting up and walking out on the people who thought that they had to talk against nations, against nationalism, in order to curry favor with internationalism. Their metaphors are all mixed up. They think that because a Frenchman and an American and an Englishman can all sit down on the same platform and receive honors together, it must be that there is no such thing as nations. That kind of bad thinking springs from a source we all know. I should want to say to anyone like that: "Look! First I want to be a person. And I want you to be a person, and then we can be as interpersonal as you please. We can pull each other's noses—do all sorts of things. But, first of all, you have got to have the personality. First of all, you have got to have the nations and then they can be as international as they please with each other."

I should like to use another metaphor on them. I want my palette, if I am a painter, I want my palette on my thumb or on my chair, all clean, pure, separate colors. Then I will do the mixing on the canvas. The canvas is where the work of art is, where we make the conquest. But we want the nations all separate, pure, distinct, things as separate as we can make them; and then in our thoughts, in our arts, and so on, we can do what we please about it.

But I go back. There are four beliefs that I know more about from having lived with poetry. One is the personal belief, which is a knowledge that you don't want to tell other people about because you cannot prove that you know. You are saying nothing about it till you see. The love belief, just the same, has that same shyness. It knows it cannot tell; only the outcome can tell. And the national belief we enter into socially with each other, all together, party of the first part, party of the second part, we enter into that to bring the future of the country. We cannot tell some people what it is we believe, partly because they are too stupid to understand and partly because we are too proudly vague to explain. And anyway it has got to be fulfilled, and we are not talking until we know more, until we have something to show. And then the literary one in every work of art, not of cunning and craft, mind you, but of real art; that believing the thing into existence, saying as you go more than you even hoped you were going to be able to say, and coming with surprise to an end that you foreknew only with some sort of emotion. And then finally the relationship we enter into with God to believe the future in—to believe the hereafter in.

Narcissus as Narcissus

Allen Tate (1899–)

Born in Kentucky, Allen Tate entered Vanderbilt University in Nashville, Tennessee, in 1918 and soon became one of the "Fugitives," a group of conservative Southern writers who wished to defend traditional, agrarian values against the encroachment of an anonymous industrial society. He helped edit the magazine *The Fugitive* (1922–25), and contributed to the symposium volume *I'll Take My Stand* (1930) which defended the agrarian position. In 1934 he took a teaching position at Southwestern University in Memphis, Tennessee, and during his long career he has held many academic appointments, notably at Princeton University and the University of Minnesota. He has published numerous volumes of poetry, and as a critic was influential in establishing the "New Criticism" which emphasized close reading of the poetic text and promulgated T. S. Eliot's concept of the literary tradition (see Eliot's "Tradition and the Individual Talent," reprinted in this section). The best of Tate's poetry and criticism may be found in *Poems* (1960) and *Essays of Four Decades* (1969). Tate has also written a brilliant novel, *The Fathers* (1938), which dramatizes his convictions about social order and tradition. "Ode to the Confederate Dead," written in the late 1920s, is the subject of the following essay.

On this first occasion, which will probably be the last, of my writing about my own verse, I could plead in excuse the example of Edgar Allan Poe, who wrote about himself in an essay called "The Philosophy of Composition." But in our age the appeal to authority is weak, and I am of my age. What I happen to know about the poem that I shall discuss is limited. I remember merely my intention in writing it; I do not know whether the poem is good; and I do not know its obscure origins.

How does one happen to write a poem: where does it come from? That is the question asked by the psychologists or the geneticists of poetry. Of late I have not read any of the genetic theories very attentively: years ago I read one by Mr. Conrad Aiken; another, I think, by Mr. Robert Graves; but I have forgotten them. I am not ridiculing verbal mechanisms, dreams, or repressions as origins of poetry; all three of them and more besides may have a great deal to do with it. Other psychological theories say a good deal about compensation. A poem is an indirect effort of a shaky man to justify himself to happier men, or to present a superior account of his relation to a world that allows him but little certainty, and would allow equally little to the happier men if they did not wear blinders—according to the poet. For example, a poet might be a man who could not get enough self-justification out of being an automobile salesman (whose certainty is a fixed quota of cars every month) to rest comfortably upon it. So the poet, who wants to be something that he cannot be, and is a failure in plain life, makes up fictitious versions of his predicament that are interesting even to other persons because nobody is a perfect automobile salesman. Everybody, alas, suffers a little. . . . I constantly read this kind of criticism of my own verse. According to its doctors, my one intransigent desire is to have been a Confederate general, and because I could not or would not become anything else, I set up for poet and began to invent fictions about the personal ambitions that my society has no use for.

Although a theory may not be "true," it may make certain insights available for a while; and I have deemed it proper to notice theories of the genetic variety because a poet talking about himself is often expected, as the best authority, to explain the origins of his poems. But persons interested in origins are seldom quick to use them. Poets, in their way, are practical men; they are interested in results. What is the poem, after it is written? That is the question. Not where it came from, or why. The Why and Where can never get beyond the guessing stage because, in the language of those who think it can, poetry cannot be brought to "laboratory conditions." The only real evidence that any critic may bring before his gaze is the finished poem. For some reason most critics have a hard time fixing their minds directly under their noses, and before they see the object that is there they use a telescope upon the horizon to see where it came from. They are wood cutters who do their job by finding out where the ore came from in the iron of the steel of the blade of the ax that Jack built. I do not say that this procedure is without its own contributory insights; but the insights are merely contributory and should not replace the poem, which is the object upon which they must be focused. A poem may be an instance of morality, of social conditions, of psychological history; it may instance all its qualities, but never one of them alone, nor any two or three; never less than all.

Genetic theories, I gather, have been cherished academically with detachment. Among "critics" they have been useless and not quite disinterested: I have myself found them applicable to the work of poets whom I do not like. That is the easiest way.

I say all this because it seems to me that my verse or anybody else's is merely a way of knowing something: if the poem is a real creation, it is a kind of knowledge that we did not possess before. It is not knowledge "about" something else; the poem is the fullness of that knowledge. We know the particular poem, not what it says that we can restate. In a manner of speaking, the poem is its own knower, neither poet nor reader knowing anything that the poem says apart from the words of the poem. I have expressed this view elsewhere in other terms, and it has been accused of aestheticism or art for arts sake. But let the reader recall the historic position of Catholicism: *nulla salus extra ecclesiam.* That must be religion*ism*. There is probably nothing wrong with art for art's sake if we take the phrase seriously, and not take it to mean the kind of poetry written in England forty years ago. Religion always ought to transcend any of its particular uses; and likewise the true art-for-art's-sake view can be held only by persons who are always looking for things that they can respect apart from use (though they may be useful), like poems, fly-rods, and formal gardens. . . . . These are negative postulates, and I am going to illustrate them with some commentary on a poem called "Ode to the Confederate Dead."

II

That poem is "about" solipsism, a philosophical doctrine which says that we create the world in the act of perceiving it; or about Narcissism, or any other *ism* that denotes the failure of the human personality to function objectively in nature and society. Society (and "nature" as modern society constructs it) appears to offer limited fields for the exercise of the whole man, who wastes his energy piecemeal over separate functions that ought to come under a unity of being. (Until the last generation, only certain women were whores, having been set aside as special instances of sex amid a social scheme that held the general belief that sex must be part of a whole; now the general belief is that sex must be special.) Without unity we get the remarkable self-consciousnes of our age. Everybody is talking about this evil, and a great many persons know what ought to be done to correct it. As a citizen I have my own prescription, but as a poet I am concerned with the experience of "solipsism." And an experience *of* it is not quite the same thing as a philosophical statement *about* it.

I should have trouble connecting solipsism and the Confederate dead in a rational argument; I should make a fool of myself in the discussion, because I know no more of the Confederate dead or of solipsism than hundreds of other people. (Possibly less: the dead Confederates may be presumed to have a certain privacy; and as for solipsism, I blush in the presence of philosophers, who know all about Bishop Berkeley; I use the term here in its strict etymology.) And if I call this interest in one's ego Narcissism, I make myself a logical ignoramus, and I take liberties with mythology. I use Narcissism to mean only preoccupation with self; it may be either love or hate. But a good psychiatrist knows that it means self-love only, and otherwise he can talk about it more coherently, knows more about it than I shall ever hope or desire to know. He would look at me professionally if I uttered the remark that the modern squirrel cage of our sensibility, the extreme introspection of our time, has anything whatever to do with the Confederate dead.

But when the doctor looks at literautre it is a question whether he sees it: the sea boils and pigs have wings because in poetry all things are possible—if you are man enough. They are possible because in poetry the disparate elements are not combined in logic, which can join things only under certain categories and under the law of contradiction; they are combined in poetry rather as experience, and experience has decided to ignore logic, except perhaps as another field of experience. Experience means conflict, our natures being what they are, and conflict means drama. Dramatic experience is not logical; it may be subdued to the kind of coherence that we indicate when we speak, in criticism, of form. Indeed, as experience, this conflict is always a logical contradiction, or philosophically an antinomy. Serious poetry deals with the fundamental conflicts that cannot be logically resolved: we can state the conflicts rationally, but reason does not relieve us of them. Their only final coherence is the formal recreation of art, which "freezes" the experience as permanently as a logical formula, but without, like the formula, leaving all but the logic out.

Narcissism and the Confederate dead cannot be connected logically, or even historically; even were the connection an historical fact, they would not stand connected as art, for no one experiences raw history. The proof of the connection must lie, if anywhere, in the experienced conflict which is the poem itself. Since one set of references for the conflict is the historic Confederates, the poem, if it is successful, is a certain section of history made into experience, but only on this occasion, and on these terms: even the author of the poem has no experience of his history apart from the occasion and the terms.

It will be understood that I do not claim even a partial success in the junction of the two "ideas" in the poem that I am about to discuss. I am describing an intention, and the labor of revising the poem—a labor spread over ten years—fairly exposes the lack of confidence that I have felt and still feel in it. All the tests of its success in style and versification would come in the end to a single test, an answer, yes or no, to the question: Assuming that the Confederates and Narcissus are not yoked together by mere violence, has the poet convinced the reader that, on the specific occasion of this poem, there is a necessary yet hitherto undetected relation between them? By necessary I mean dramatically relevant, a relation "discovered" in terms of the particular occasion, not historically argued or philosophically deduced. Should the question that I have just asked be answered yes, then this poem or any other with its specific problem could be said to have form: what was previously a merely felt quality of life has been raised to the level of experience—it has become specific, local, dramatic, "formal"—that is to say, *in*-formed.

III

The structure of the Ode is simple. Figure to yourself a man stopping at the gate of a Confederate graveyard on a late autumn afternoon. The leaves are falling; his first impressions bring him the "rumor of mortality"; and the desolation barely allows him, at the beginning of the second stanza, the conventionally heroic surmise that the dead will enrich the earth, "where these memories grow." From those quoted words to the end of that passage he pauses for a baroque meditation on the ravages of time, concluding with the figure of the "blind crab." This creature has mobility but no direction; energy but, from the human point of view, no purposeful world to use it in: in the entire poem there are only two explicit symbols for the locked-in ego; the crab is the first and less explicit symbol, a mere hint, a planting of the idea that will become overt in its second instance—the jaguar towards the end. The crab is the first intimation of the nature of the moral conflict upon which the drama of the poem develops: the cut-offness of the modern "intellectual man" from the world.

The next long passage or "strophe," beginning "You know who have waited by the wall," states the other term of the conflict. It is the theme of heroism, not merely moral heroism, but heroism in the grand style, elevating even death from mere physical dissolution to a formal ritual: this heroism is a formal ebullience of the human spirit in an entire society, not private, romantic illusion—something better than moral heroism, great as that may be, for moral heroism, being personal and individual, may be achieved by certain men in all ages, even ages of decadence. But the late Hart Crane's commentary, in a letter, is better than any I can make; he described the theme as the "theme of chivalry, a tradition of excess (not literally excess, rather active faith) which cannot be perpetuated in the fragmentary cosmos of today—'those desires which should be yours tomorrow,' but which, you know, will not perist nor find any way into action."

The structure then is the objective frame for the tension between the two themes, "active faith" which has decayed, and the "fragmentary cosmos" which surrounds us. (I must repeat here that this is not a philosophical thesis; it is an analytical statement of a conflict that is concrete within the poem.) In contemplating the heroic theme the man at the gate never quite commits himself to the illusion of its availability to him. The most that he can allow himself is the fancy that the blowing leaves are charging soldiers, but he rigorously returns to the refrain: "Only the wind"—or the "leaves flying." I suppose it is a commentary on our age that the man at the gate never quite achieves the illusion that the leaves are heroic men, so that he may identify himself with them, as Keats and Shelley too easily and too beautifully did with nightingales and west winds. More than this, he cautions himself, reminds himself repeatedly of his subjective prison, his solipsism, by breaking off the half-illusion and coming back to the refrain of wind and leaves—a refrain that, as Hart Crane said, is necessary to the "subjective continuity."

These two themes struggle for mastery up to the passage,

> We shall say only the leaves whispering
> In the improbable mist of nightfall—

which is near the end. It will be observed that the passage begins with a phrase taken from the wind-leaves refrain—the signal that it has won. The refrain has been fused with the main stream of the man's reflections, dominating them; and he cannot return even to an ironic vision of the heroes. There is nothing but death, the mere naturalism of death at that—spiritual extinction in the decay of the body. Autumn and the leaves are death; the men who exemplified in a grand style an 'active faith" are dead; there are only the leaves.

> Shall we then worship death . . .
>
> . . . set up the grave
> In the house? The ravenous grave . . .

that will take us before our time? The question is not answered, although as a kind of morbid romanticism it might, if answered affirmatively, provide the man with an illusory escape from his solipsism; but the he cannot accept it. Nor has he been able to live in his immediate world, the fragmentary cosmos. There is no practical solution, no solution offered for the edification of moralists. (To those who may identify the man at the gate with the author of the poem I would say: He differs from the author in not accepting a "practical solution," for the author's personal dilemma is perhaps not quite so exclusive as that of the meditating man.) The main intention of the poem has been to make dramatically visible the conflict, to concentrate it, to present it, in Mr. R. P. Blackmur's phrase, as "experienced form"—not as a logical dilemma.

The closing image, that of the serpent, is the ancient symbol of time, and I tried to give it the credibility of the commonplace by placing it in a mulberry bush—with the faint hope that the silkworm would somehow be implicit. But time is also death. If that is so, then space, or the Becoming, is life; and I believe there is not a single spatial symbol in the poem. "Sea-space" is allowed the "blind crab"; but the sea, as appears plainly in the passage beginning, "Now that the salt of their blood . . ." is life only in so far as it is the source of the lowest forms of life, the source perhaps of all life, but life undifferentiated, halfway between life and death. This passage is a contrasting inversion of the conventional

> . . . inexhaustible bodies that are not
> Dead, but feed the grass . . .

the reduction of the earlier, literary conceit to a more naturalistic figure derived from modern biological speculation. These "buried Caesars" will not bloom in the hyacinth but will only make saltier the sea.

The wind-leaves refrain was added to the poem in 1930, nearly five years after the first draft was written. I felt that the danger of adding it was small because, implicit in the long strophes of meditation, the ironic commentary on the vanished heroes was already there, giving the poem such dramatic tension as it had in the earlier version. The refrain makes the commentary more explicit, more visibly dramatic, and renders quite plain, as Hart Crane intimated, the subjective character of the imagery throughout. But there was another reason for it, besides the increased visualization that it imparts to the dramatic conflict. It "times" the poem better, offers the reader frequent pauses in the development of the two themes, allows him occasions of assimilation; and on the whole—this was my hope and intention—the refrain makes the poem seem longer than it is and thus eases the concentration of imagery—without, I hope, sacrificing a possible effect of concentration.

IV

I have been asked why I called the poem an ode. I first called it an elegy. It is an ode only in the sense in which Cowley in the seventeenth century misunderstood the real structure of the Pindaric ode. Not only are the meter and rhyme without fixed pattern, but in another feature the poem is even further removed from Pindar than Abraham Cowley was: a purely subjective meditation would not even in Cowley's age have been called an ode. I suppose in so calling it I intended an irony; the scene of the poem is not a public celebration, it is a lone man by a gate.

The dominant rhythm is "mounting," the dominant meter iambic pentameter varied with six-, four-, and three-stressed lines; but this was not planned in advance for variety. I adapted the meter to the effect desired at the moment. The model for the irregular rhyming was "Lycidas," but other models could have served. The rhymes in a given strophe I tried to adjust to the rhythm and the texture of feeling and image. For example, take this passage in the second strophe:

Autumn is desolation in the plot
Of a thousand acres where these memories grow
From the inexhaustible bodies that are not
Dead, but feed the grass row after rich row.
Think of the autumns that have come and gone!—
Ambitious November with the humors of the year,
With a particular zeal for every slab,
Staining the uncomfortable angels that rot
On the slabs, a wing chipped here, an arm there:
The brute curiosity of an angel's stare
Turns you, like them, to stone,
Transforms the heaving air
Till plunged to a heavier world below
You shift your sea-space blindly
Heaving, turning like the blind crab.

There is rhymed with *year* (to many persons, perhaps, only a half-rhyme), and I hoped the reader would unconsciously assume that he need not expect further use of that sound for some time. So when the line, "The brute curiosity of an angel's stare," comes a moment later, rhyming with *year-there,* I hoped that the violence of image would be further reinforced by the repetition of a sound that was no longer expected. I wanted the shock to be heavy; so I felt that I could not afford to hurry the reader away from it until he had received it in full. The next two lines carry on the image at a lower intensity: the rhyme, "Transforms the heaving *air,*" prolongs the moment of attention upon that passage, while at the same time it ought to begin dissipating the shock, both by the introduction of a new image and by reduction of the "meaning" to a pattern of sound, the ere-rhymes. I calculated that the third use of that sound (stare) would be a surprise, the fourth (air) a monotony. I purposely made the end words of the third from last and last lines—*below* and *crab*—delayed rhymes for *row* and *slab,* the last being an internal and half-dissonant rhyme for the sake of bewilderment and incompleteness, qualities by which the man at the gate is at the moment possessed.

This is elementary but I cannot vouch for its success. As the dramatic situation of the poem is the tension that I have already described, so the rhythm is an attempt at a series of "modulations" back and forth between a formal regularity, for the heroic emotion, and a broken rhythm, with scattering imagery, for the failure of that emotion. This is "imitative form," which Yvor Winters deems a vice worth castigation. I have pointed out that the passage, "You know who have waited by the wall," presents the heroic theme of "active faith"; it will be observed that the rhythm, increasingly after "You who have waited for the angry resolution," is almost perfectly regular iambic, with only a few initial substitutions and weak endings. The passage is meant to convey a plenary vision, the actual presence, of the exemplars of active faith: the man at the gate at that moment is nearer to realizing them than at any other in the poem; hence the formal rhythm. But the vision breaks down; the wind-leaves refrain supervenes; and the next passage, "Turn your eyes to the immoderate past," is the irony of the preceding realization. With the self-conscious historical sense he turns his eyes into the past. The next passage after this, beginning, "You hear the shout . . ." is the failure of the vision in both phases, the pure realization and the merely historical. He cannot "see" the heroic virtues; there is wind, rain, leaves. But there is sound; for a moment he deceives himself with it. It is the noise of the battles that he has evoked. Then comes the figure of the rising sun of those battles; he is "lost in that orient of the thick and fast," and he curses his own moment, "the setting sun." The "setting sun" I tried to use as a triple image, for the decline of the heroic age and for the actual scene of late afternoon, the latter being not only natural desolation but spiritual desolation as well. Again for a moment he thinks he hears the battle shout, but only for a moment; then the silence reaches him.

Corresponding to the disintegration of the vision just described, there has been a breaking down of the formal rhythm. The complete breakdown comes with the images of the "mummy" and the "hound bitch." (*Hound* bitch because the hound is a hunter, participant of a formal ritual.) The failure of the vision throws the man back upon himself, but upon himself he cannot bring to bear the force of sustained imagination. He sees himself in random images (random to him, deliberate with the author) of something lower than he ought to be: the human image is only that of preserved death; but if he is alive he is an old hunter, dying. The passages about the mummy and the bitch are deliberately brief—slight rhythmic stretches. (These are the only verses I have written for which I thought of the movement first, then cast about for the symbols.)

I believe the term "modulation" denotes in music the uninterrupted shift from one key to another: I do not know the term for change of rhythm without change of measure. I wish to describe a similar change in verse rhythm; it may be convenient to think of it as modulation of a certain kind. At the end of the passage that I have been discussing the final words are "Hears the wind only." The phrase closes the first main division of the poem. I have loosely called the longer passages strophes, and if I were hardy enough to impose the classical organization of the lyric ode upon a baroque poem, I should say that these words bring to an end the Strophe, after which must come the next main division, or Antistrophe, which was often employed to answer the matter set forth in the Strophe or to present it from another point of view. And that is precisely the significance of the next main division, beginning: "Now that the salt of their blood. . . ." But I wanted this second division of the poem to arise out of the collapse of the first. It is plain that it would not have suited my purpose to round off the first section with some sort of formal rhythm; so I ended it with an unfinished line. The next division must therefore begin by finishing that line, not merely in meter but with an integral rhythm. I will quote the passage:

The hound bitch
Toothless and dying, in a musty cellar
Hears the wind only.

Now that the salt of their blood
Stiffens the saltier oblivion of the sea,
Seals the malignant purity of the flood. . . .

The caesura, after *only,* is thus at the middle of the third foot. (I do not give a full stress to *wind,* but attribute a "hovering stress" to *wind* and the first syllable of *only.*) The reader expects the foot to be completed by the stress on the next word, *Now,* as in a sense it is; but the phrase, "Now that the salt of their blood," is also the beginning of a new movement; it is two "dactyls" continuing more broadly the fallng rhythm that has prevailed. But with the finishing off of the line with *blood,* the mounting rhythm is restored; the whole line from *Hears* to *blood* is actually an iambic pentameter with liberal inversions and substitutions that were expected to create a counter-rhythm within the line. From the caesura on, the rhythm is new; but it has—or was expected to have—an organic relation to the preceding rhythm; and it signals the rise of a new statement of the theme.

I have gone into this passage in detail—I might have chosen another—not because I think it is successful, but because I labored with it; if it is a failure, or even an uninteresting success, it ought to offer as much technical instruction to other persons as it would were it both successful and interesting. But a word more: the broader movement introduced by the new rhythm was meant to correspond, as a sort of Antistrophe, to the earlier formal movement beginning, "You know who have waited by the wall." It is a new formal movement with new feeling and new imagery. The heroic but precarious illusion of the earlier movement has broken down into the personal symbols of the mummy and the hound; the pathetic fallacy of the leaves as charging soldiers and the conventional "buried Caesar" theme have become rotten leaves and dead bodies wasting in the earth, to return after long erosion to the sea. In the midst of this naturalism, what shall the man say? What shall all humanity say in the presence of decay? The two themes, then, have been struggling for mastery; the structure of the poem thus exhibits the development of two formal passages that contrast the two themes. The two formal passages break down, the first shading into the second ("Now that the salt of their blood . . ."), the second one concluding with the figure of the jaguar, which is presented in a distracted rhythm left suspended from a weak ending—the word *victim*. This figure of the jaguar is the only explicit rendering of the Narcissus motif in the poem, but instead of a youth gazing into a pool, a predatory beast stares at a jungle stream, and leaps to devour himself.

The next passage begins:

What shall we say who have knowledge
Carried to the heart?

This is Pascal's war between heart and head, between *finesse* and *géométrie*. Should the reader care to think of these lines as the gathering up of the two themes, now fused, into a final statement, I should see no objection to calling it the Epode. But upon the meaning of the lines from here to the end there is no need for further commentary. I have talked about the structure of the poem, not its quality. One can no more find the quality of one's own verse than one can find its value, and to try to find either is like looking into a glass for the effect that one's face has upon other persons.

If anybody ever wished to know anything about this poem that he could not interpret for himself, I suspect that he is still in the dark. I cannot believe that I have illuminated the difficulties that some readers have found in the style. But then I cannot, have never been able to, see any difficulties of that order. The poem has been much revised. I still think there is much to be said for the original *barter* instead of *yield* in the second line, and for *Novembers* instead of *November* in line fifteen. The revisions were not undertaken for the convenience of the reader but for the poem's own clarity, so that, word, phrase, line, passage, the poem might at worst come near its best expression.

Prufrock's Dilemma

John Berryman (1914–1972)

John Berryman (John Smith) was born in a small Oklahoma town and reared as a strict Roman Catholic. His father, John Smith, moved the family to Florida when his son was ten and committed suicide two years later. The mother then moved to New York where she married a banker, John Berryman, whose name the young boy adopted. Berryman was sent to private school and to Columbia College from which he graduated in 1936. After two years on a fellowship at Clare College, Cambridge (England), Berryman returned to the United States and taught for the remainder of his life at Wayne State University, Harvard, Princeton, and the University of Minnesota. *Poems* (1942) and *The Dispossessed* (1948) were followed by *Homage to Mistress Bradstreet* (1956), a long poem that honors Anne Bradstreet, America's first woman poet. *The 77 Dream Songs* (1964) were augmented by *His Toy, His Dream, His Rest* (1968) and *The Dream Songs* (1969). At the end of his life Berryman returned to the Roman Catholicism of his childhood. But he was still beset by psychological and spiritual turmoil, and in January 1972 he leaped to his death from a bridge in Minneapolis. *The Freedom of the Poet* (1976), which includes "Prufrock's Dilemma," collects Berryman's best critical essays and his short stories.

To begin with Eliot's title, "The Love Song of J. Alfred Prufrock," is the second half quite what the first led us to expect? A man named J. Alfred Prufrock could hardly be expected to sing a love song; he sounds too well dressed. His name takes something away from the notion of a love song; the form of the title, that is to say, is reductive. How does he begin singing?

> Let us go then, you and I,
> When the evening is spread out against the
> sky . . .

That sounds very pretty—lyrical—he does seem, after all, in spite of his name, to be inviting her for an evening; there is a nice rhyme—it sounds like other dim romantic verse. Then comes the third line:

> Like a patient etherised upon a table . . .

With this line, modern poetry begins.

In the first place, the third line proves that the author of the first two lines did not mean them. They were a come-on, designed merely to get the reader off guard, so that he could be knocked down. The form, again, is reductive; an expectation has been created only to be diminished or destroyed. (Presently it will prove that "you" is not the woman at all, since "you" is invited to make a visit with "I" *to* her; we can hardly say yet who "you" is; an assumption has been destroyed.) And the word "then"—"Let us go *then*"—is really very unpromising; if he had only said, "Let us go," it would have sounded much more as if they were going to go; "Let us go then" sounds as if he had been giving it thought, and thought suggests hesitation. Of course he never goes at all: *the* visit, involving the "overwhelming question," the proposal of marriage, is never made. Here again we come on a reduction.

Also, the simile is not visual: it only pretends to be. No reader could possibly be assisted in seeing the evening spread out against the sky by having his attention suddenly and violently called to a patient laid out on an operating table. The device of simile is being put to a novel use, violating the ordinary logic of verse, just as the abrupt vision of a hospital violates the lyrical notion of an evening stroll.

What does the line mean? We are obliged to resort to suggestion, not to logic. The situation of a patient under ether is unenviable, risky: he is about to be cut into, soon he may be dead. This fear is basic to the poem: Prufrock finally says, in fact, "I was afraid." On the other hand, the situation of the patient can be regarded as desirable in that he *has* made a decision and now the result is out of his hands, he has no further responsibility, it is up to the surgeon to save him or not. This desire—to *have made* the proposal, and to have his fate left up to the woman—is also basic to the poem. We may think of that as quite a lot of work to get done in one line. Of course, the suggestion that Prufrock sees himself as *ill* is important also, and we will return to this.

Between the title, with its slight effect of double-take, and these opening lines, with their full effect of double-take, the poet has inserted an epigraph in Italian, six lines of it. A knowledge of Italian is of very little help. All the lines say is, "If I thought what I am going to tell you would ever get back to the world, you would hear nothing from me. But as it is," and so on. One has to know *who* is speaking in Dante's *Divine Comedy*. This is a lost soul, in Hell, damned in particular because he tried to purchase absolution *before* committing a crime. We are obliged to consider, that is, as of Prufrock with his dilemma of whether or not to propose marriage, whether the fundamental reason he does not do so—his sin—is his refusal to take the ordinary, inevitable human risks: he wants to know beforehand whether he will be accepted or not—in fact, he does *think* he knows already what will happen—but this belongs later for us.

Everything we have been saying paints a picture as different as possible from that of a writer sitting down to entertain, beguile, charm, and lull a reader or readers. Obstacles and surprise, of no pleasant kind, are this poet's stock-in-trade. The reader's expectation that *one* thing will happen is the first to be attacked. Several things are going to be happening simultaneously. One feels, even, a certain hostility on the part of the poet. The modern poet, characteristically, has *lost confidence* in his readers (this is not altogether surprising, considering the quality of most contemporary education); but so far from causing him to reduce his demands therefore, this loss of confidence has led to an *increase* in his demands. Good poetry has never been easy to read with any advanced understanding, but it has seldom been made so deliberately difficult.

Shall we connect this deliberate difficulty with the reductive devices studied earlier and suggest that the poet's impatience is based on the fact that the reader's mind is full of vague and grandiose assumptions which seem to the poet contemptible? The poet sees himself as a warning voice, like a Hebrew prophet calling on the people to repent, to understand better themselves and the world. Of course, this *is* a reduced world. In one celebrated view, we have undergone three crucial scientific revolutions. The first was the astronomical, in the sixteenth century, which taught man that so far from occupying a splendid position at the heart of the universe, he lived in a suburb, and one of no importance. He digested this unwelcome information very slowly. Then he was informed, by Darwin and others, a hundred years ago, that he was not unique but continuous with the animals whom he had always patronized. Our periods of time are getting much shorter. He had barely fifty years in which to learn to accept this biological insult, when the psychological revolution associated with the name of Freud informed man that he was not even king inside but stood at the mercy of gigantic unconscious forces within himself. All this ought to have rendered him distinctly uneasy, let us say, and has done so, depending on his degree of self-awareness; but hardly to a degree acceptable to the exceptional self-awareness of the poet. Eliot had pretty certainly not read Freud when he wrote this poem. In some ways, however, their thought is parallel, for the "you" whom Prufrock invites to go with him for the visit must be another part of his own personality, whom he vainly invites to join him in the great task before them—the instinctual part of man (as against the façade that knows itself, the I, the ego), for which Freud was to borrow the word "id" from Groddeck.

But the "you" is perhaps also the reader, addressed thus surprisingly in this dramatic monologue; and this device is French, part of the general air of elaborate sophistication adopted by Eliot in this poem. This tone is not original; it is borrowed from the French symbolist poet Jules Laforgue (1860–87), under whose influence Eliot first found his own voice. Some of the characteristic properties in "Prufrock" are Laforgue's allusions to Hamlet and the sirens. But there is influence also from Elizabethan drama, in the speech rhythms (the poem is written in what is called "free verse," which only means that the laws it obeys are different from those of traditional stanza or blank verse); and there is influence from prose works, especially the expatriate American novelist Henry James's. In any event, Laforgue could never have conceived or written the poem. He only supplied the *manner*, and anyway his music—very beautiful sometimes—is hardly Eliot's.

Eliot's manner is highly sophisticated, but perhaps we ought not to call the poem sophisticated. Let us call it primitive. The poem pretends to be a love song. It is something much more practical. It is a study—a debate by Prufrock with himself—over the *business* of proposing marriage, agreeing to lay your fate in someone else's hands, undertaking to spend your life with her, to beget and rear children, and so on. He never makes it. The first half of the poem looks forward to the proposal, the second half looks back on how it *would* have gone if it had gone at all. The poem is intensely anti-romantic, and its extremely serious subject, in a so-called Love Song, is another rebuke to the (probably romantic) reader. Primitive societies take a dim view of not marrying. Hawaiian mythology, for instance, describes a god called Nangganananaag, whose job it is to stand with an immense club on the Road to Paradise and smash off it, into nothingness, any unmarried male who, having died, tries to get by. This way of thinking is precisely Eliot's. Late in the poem Prufrock looks forward with dismay (and a certain jaunty pathos) to his endless bachelorhood—the sameness and triviality that are the lot of one who never succeeded in adopting his human responsibilities at all. It is clear that the poet sympathizes with Prufrock. It is also clear that the poet damns Prufrock. Some of the basic emotions of the poem are primitive also—fear, malice—but lust is absent, and the prevailing surface tone is one of civilized, overcivilized anxiety. Prufrock's feelings are rather abstract; he never makes the woman real at all, except in one terrible respect, which let us reserve a little. He is concerned with himself. He is mentally ill, neurotic, incapable of love. But the problem that he faces is a primitive problem.

Eliot brings to bear on Prufrock's dilemma four figures out of the spiritual history of man: Michelangelo, John the Baptist, Lazarus, and Hamlet. Prufrock identifies himself, in his imagination, with Lazarus; he says that he is *not* the Baptist or Hamlet. About the first all he says is:

> In the room the women come and go
> Talking of Michelangelo.

What are we to make of this? There is a twittering of women's voices. Their subject? A type of volcanic masculine energy—sculptor, architect, as well as painter—at the height of one of the supreme periods of human energy, the Italian Renaissance. Chit-chat. *Reduction,* we may say. Michelangelo, everything that mattered about him forgotten or not understood, has become a topic for women's voices—destructive, without even realizing it. Then Prufrock says,

> Though I have seen my head (grown slightly bald)
> brought in upon a platter,
> I am no prophet—

The situation is a visit, or the imagination of a visit, to the woman; it was *women* who got the Baptist beheaded. We might phrase the meaning as: I announce no significant time to come, I am the forerunner of (not children, not a Saviour) nothing. Then Prufrock is speculating about how it would have been, IF he had

> squeezed the universe into a ball
> To roll it toward some overwhelming question,
> To say: "I am Lazarus, come from the dead,
> Come back to tell you all, I shall tell you all"—

We have seen Prufrock already imagined as dead, the suggestion of the epigraph, and at the end of the poem he drowns. Here he thinks of himself as *come back.* Lazarus, perhaps, is the person whom one would most like to interview—another character from sacred history, not Christ's forerunner but the subject of the supreme miracles (reported, unfortunately, only in the Fourth Gospel)—the one man who would tell us . . .

what it is like. Prufrock has a message for the woman that is or ought to be of similar importance: here I am, out of my loneliness, at your feet; I am this man full of love, trust, hope; decide my fate.

Now—postponing Hamlet for a second—what Prufrock imagines the woman as saying in return for his Lazarus-communication explains his despair:

> If one, settling a pillow by her head,
> Should say: "That is not what I meant at all.
> That is not it, at all."

Here the reason for his inability to propose becomes clear. He is convinced that she will (or would) respond with the most insulting and unmanning of all attitudes: Let's be *friends;* I never thought of you as a lover or husband, only a friend. What the women's voices did to Michelangelo, her voice is here imagined as doing to him, unmanning him; the sirens' voices at the end of the poem are yet to come. This is the central image of Prufrock's fear: what he cannot face. We see better now why the image of an *operation* turned up so early in the poem, and the paranoid passages swing into focus:

> when I am formulated, sprawling on a pin,
> When I am pinned and wriggling on the wall . . .

and:

> But as if a magic lantern threw the nerves in patterns
> on a screen . . .

A reasonable study of these fears of exposure would take us not only into our well-known Anglo-Saxon fear of ridicule but into folklore and psychoanalysis.

As for Hamlet, Prufrock says he is "not Prince Hamlet." He is not even the hero, that is to say, of his own tragedy; let us have in mind again the scientific revolutions and also the hero of one of Franz Kafka's novels, *The Trial,* who suddenly says, when recounting his arrest afterward, "Oh, I've forgotten the most important person of all, myself." Prufrock is merely, he says, an extra courtier, an adviser (to himself a very bad adviser—the name "Alfred" means, ironically, good counselor, and the character in Dante who supplies the epigraph was an evil counselor). But of course he *is* Hamlet—in one view of Shakespeare's character: a man rather of reflection than of action, on whom has been laid an intolerable burden (of revenge, by the way), and who suffers from sexual nausea (owing to his mother's incest) and deserts the woman he loves.

The resort to these four analogues from artistic and sacred history suggests a man—desperate, in his ordeal—ransacking the past for help in the present, and *not finding it*—finding only ironic parallels, or real examples, of his predicament. The available tradition, the poet seems to be saying, is of no use to us. It supplies only analogies and metaphors for our pain. Needless to say, the author of this poem was not a Christian; he became one years later.

Prufrock cannot act. He can, however, reflect and feel and imagine. Here we might think of W. B. Yeats's lines in a celebrated poem called "The Second Coming":

> The best lack all conviction, while the worst
> Are full of passionate intensity.

Prufrock would be among Yeats's "best" only for sensitivity and intelligence, it is true, his human failure being otherwise complete. Let us explore a little, however, his *positive* courses of imagination; and Hamlet's desertion of Ophelia, and his "intolerable burden," as we called it, point our way.

Prufrock's not proposing to the lady (there is no suggestion that anyone else will) might be thought of as aggressive: at whatever cost to himself, he deprives her of a mate, a normal married life. For such fear and humiliation as he suffers, we should expect some sort of revenge taken. But Prufrock suffers from the inhibitions that we might imagine as accompanying a man of such crucial indecision. He has difficulty in expressing himself, for instance, and this difficulty is brought prominently into the poem. Notice particularly the lines

> And how should I begin?
> It is impossible to say just what I mean!

His incoherence is a token of his struggle, and it is hardly surprising that his resentment against the woman in the poem emerges only in malicious detail ("catty" we would call this) as—of her arms—

> in the lamplight, downed with light brown hair!

What does come forward openly is his imagination of escape from the dilemma altogether.

Prufrock's burden is that of proposing marriage when he does not know whether or not he may be ridiculed. His desire, from the outset, to have the whole thing over with, no matter how, we have seen already in the line about the "patient etherised upon a table." At the very end of the poem, in an excited and brilliant passage which might be characterized as one of negative exaltation, he imagines—like Hamlet—his death, as an escape at any rate from the dread anxiety of his ordeal. These are mermaids, sirens, the women of the poem come into the open as killers:

> I have seen them riding seaward on the waves
> Combing the white hair of the waves blown back
> When the wind blows the water white and black.

We have lingered in the chambers of the sea
By sea-girls wreathed with seaweed red and
brown
Till human voices wake us, and we drown.

This death is *desired*—like the hospital situation—as well as feared. But the basic image of escape occurs in the dead center of the poem, in a couplet, without much relation to anything apparently, *lacking* which this would be a much less impressive poem than it is. These are the lines:

I should have been a pair of ragged claws
Scuttling across the floors of silent seas.

You notice, first, that this is not much of a couplet, though it *is* a heroic couplet; the off-rhyme speaks of incongruity. As abruptly, second, as we were transferred from the prospect of a romantic evening to a hospital, are we here plunged, away from modern social life ("I have measured out my life with coffee spoons") into—into what? Man's biological past, continuous with him, but unimaginably remote, long before he emerged into the tidal areas: Prufrock sees himself, in his desire, as his own ancestor, *before this ordeal came up,* when he was sufficient unto himself, a "pair," not needing a mate. Now the whole crustacean is not imagined—only the fighting part, which is taken for the whole—the claws. But these do not seem to be in very good condition ("ragged"), and unquestionably we must take them also to be full of fear ("scuttling"), like Prufrock now. But the seas are *silent:* no woman speaks. Therefore, the situation is desirable, protected. We really need to resort to the later formulations of Freud to understand this. When a human being encounters a problem beyond his capacity to meet, Freud thought, *regression* occurs: the whole organization of the emotional and instinctual person escapes from the intolerable reality by reverting to an earlier, or ancient, stage of his individual development—paying the price of symptoms but securing partial oblivion. The antagonism toward civilization in Eliot's couplet is unmistakable. It contains, indeed, a sort of list of the penalties that civilization has exacted from man's instinctual life—having cost him: open expression of hatred, fear, remorse, intolerable responsibilities.

"I am no prophet," Prufrock says. It must be obvious, however, that this extraordinarily ambitious poem, including as it does acrid sketches not only of man's spiritual but of his biological history, is not designed as entertainment, whatever the author may say to us (Eliot has defined poetry as "a superior amusement"), and whatever his mask *inside* the poem: the sophisticate, the disillusioned, the dandy with his particular social problem in Boston, as Baudelaire had had his in Paris and Belgium and Laforgue his in Berlin. The poet has adopted the guise of light verse, but he writes as a prophet, without any trace of conciliation toward any possible audience. He does not write *directly.* He uses the mask of Prufrock—whose fate is like that of what are called the Vigliacchi in Dante. These sinners did neither good nor evil, and so they cannot be admitted even to Hell, lest the damned feel a certain superiority to them; they suffer eternally in what is called the vestibule of Hell. It is better, as Eliot says in one of his critical essays, to do evil than to do nothing. At least one exists in a relation to the moral world. Under this mask he sets up a ruinous antithesis to Victorian hope—in particular, to what must have seemed to him the vacuous optimism of the most recent master of dramatic monologue in English before him, Browning. Civilization is not condemned. The *results* of civilization are dramatized, that is all; above all, the destruction of the ability to love, and—in the well-meaning man—to be decisive. The poet speaks, in this poem, of a society sterile and suicidal.

Sylvia Plath

Elizabeth Hardwick (1916–   )

Educated at the University of Kentucky and Columbia University, Elizabeth Hardwick has taught at Barnard College. She has written two novels, *The Ghostly Lover* (1945) and *The Simple Truth* (1955), and has reviewed widely for literary journals. In 1966 she received the George Jean Nathan Award for distinguished dramatic criticism. Her essays have been collected in *A View of My Own* (1962) and *Seduction and Betrayal: Women and Literature* (1974), which contains the essay on Sylvia Plath.

In Sylvia Plath's work and in her life the elements of pathology are so deeply rooted and so little resisted that one is disinclined to hope for general principles, sure origins, applications, or lessons. Her fate and her themes are hardly separate and both are singularly terrible. Her work is brutal, like the smash of a fist; and sometimes it is also mean in its feeling. Literary comparisons are possible, echoes vibrate occasionally, but to whom can she be compared in spirit, in content, in temperament?

Certain frames for her destructiveness have been suggested by critics. Perhaps being born a woman is part of the exceptional rasp of her nature, a woman whose stack of duties was laid over the ground of genius, ambition, and grave mental instability. Or is it the 1950s, when she was going to college, growing up—is there something of that here? Perhaps; but I feel in her a special lack of national and local roots, feel it particularly in her poetry, and this I would trace to her foreign ancestors on both sides. They were given and she accepted them as a burden, not as a gift; but there they were, somehow cutting her off from what they weren't. Her father died when she was eight years old and this was serious, central. Yet this most interesting part of her history is so scorched by resentment and bitterness that it is only the special high burn of the bitterness that allows us to imagine it as a cutoff love.

For all the drama of her biography, there is a peculiar remoteness about Sylvia Plath. A destiny of such violent self-definition does not always bring the real person nearer; it tends, rather, to invite iconography, to freeze our assumptions and responses. She is spoken of as a "legend" or a "myth"—but what does that mean? Sylvia Plath was a luminous talent, self-destroyed at the age of thirty, likely to remain, it seems, one of the most interesting poets in American literature. As an *event* she stands with Hart Crane, Scott Fitzgerald, and Poe rather than with Emily Dickinson, Marianne Moore, or Elizabeth Bishop.

The outlines of her nature are odd, especially in her defiant and extensive capabilities, her sense of mastery, the craft and preparation she almost humbly and certainly industriously acquired as the foundation for an overwhelming ambition. She was born in Winthrop, Massachusetts. Her mother's parents were Austrian; her father was a German, born in Poland. He was a professor of biology, a specialist, among other interests, in bee-raising. (The ambiguous danger and sweetness of the beehive—totemic, emblematic for the daughter.) Her father died and the family moved to Wellesley, Massachusetts, to live with their grandparents. The mother became a teacher and the daughter went to public schools and later to Smith College. Sylvia Plath was a thorough success as a student and apparently was driven to try to master everything life offered—study, cooking, horseback riding, writing, being a mother, housekeeping. There seemed to have been in her character no empty patch or seam left for the slump, the incapacity, the refusal.

An early dramatic death gives one, in a literary sense, a real life, a throbbing biography. People discovered they had known a vehement, disturbing genius in their school days; mere propinquity became a challenge, and the brief life has been the subject for memories of no special usefulness. Sylvia Plath does not come closer, shine more clearly. Poems have followed her poems, making their statements and to most of these her own harsh eloquence is the proper rebuke. We do not by any means have all of her letters, and the ones she must have written during the last year haunt the mind—that is, if she had the dependent, needy relationship that can make a letter an action, a true telling of feeling. The letters—at least the excerpts we have seen thus far—tend to be minimal, flat, suppressed, impersonal, rather more an instance of her lack of genuine closeness to the recipient than of any wish to reveal herself. A. Alvarez in *The Savage God* has done the greatest credit to the live person as he knew her. He is restrained, deeply knowledgeable about Sylvia Plath's poetry, and moved by the sufferings of her last days and the moment of suicide.

Sylvia Plath went on a Fulbright to Cambridge University. She met and later married the distinguished poet Ted Hughes, and after a year or so back in America they returned to live in England. Her first book of poems, *The Colossus,* was published in 1960, the same year her daughter Frieda was born. In 1962 her son Nicholas was born—and then life began to be hard and disturbing, except that she was able to write the poems later issued under the title *Crossing the Water.* She was separated from her husband, came back to London with two small children, tried to live and work and survive alone in a bare flat during one of the coldest years in over a century. *The Bell Jar* was published under a pseudonym just before she died, in February 1963.

In the last freezing months of her life she was visited, like some waiting stigmatist, by an almost hallucinating creativity—the astonishing poems in *Ariel* and in a later volume called *Winter Trees.*

The creative visitation was not from heaven, but from the hell of rage. Yet so powerful is the art that one feels an unsettling elation as one reads the lacerating lines. The poems are about death, rage, hatred, blood, wounds, cuts, deformities, suicide attempts, stings, fevers, operations—there is no question of coming to terms with them. There is no consolation in our experience of the poems but they are alive, filled with hurt, excitement; a grinding, grating joy in the perfection of the descriptive language overcomes hesitations of the spirit.

There are also poems about children, her own, who were intensely loved. And yet "child" and "baby" as mere words are often attached to images of pain and death. Many of the poems are *tirades,* voiced at such a pitch of eloquence and passion they take your breath away. She, the poet, is frighteningly there all the time. Orestes rages, but Aeschylus lives to be almost seventy. Sylvia Plath, however, is both heroine and author; when the curtain goes down, it is her own dead body there on the stage, sacrificed to her plot.

She has the rarity of being, in her work at least, never a "nice person." There is nothing of mystical schizophrenic vagueness about her. No dreamy loss of connection, no manic slackness, impatience, and lack of poetic judgment. She is, instead, all strength, ego, drive, endurance—and yet madly concentrated somehow, perplexing. Disgust is very strong in her nature, but she faces things with a classical fierceness and never loses dignity. That is why her vision is more powerful and more pure than the loose abandon of other poets of her period.

She is capable of anything—that we know. Alvarez reminds us how typical of her nature is the scene in *The Bell Jar* in which she dashes down a ski slope without knowing how to ski; he remembers her reckless way with horses, and tells of a deliberate smashing of her own car in a suicidal burst before the final one.

It is not recklessness that makes Sylvia Plath so forbidding, but destructiveness toward herself and others. Her mother thought *The Bell Jar* represented "the basest ingratitude" and we can only wonder at her innocence in expecting anything else. For the girl in the novel, a true account of events so far as we know, the ego is disintegrating and the stifling self-enclosure is so extreme that only death—and after that fails, shock treatment—can bring any kind of relief. Persons suffering in this way simply do not have room in their heads for the anguish of others—and later many seem to survive their own torments only by an erasing detachment. But even in recollection—and *The Bell Jar* was written a decade after the happenings—Sylvia Plath does not ask the cost.

There is a taint of paranoia in her novel and also in her poetry. The person who comes through is merciless and threatening, locked in violent images. If she does not, as so many have noticed, seem to feel pity for herself, neither is she moved to self-criticism or even self-analysis. It is a sour world, a drifting, humid air of vengeance. *The Bell Jar* seems to be a realistic account of her suicide attempt during the summer before her senior year at Smith. But the novel is about madness as well, and that separates it from the poems. Death, in the poetry, is an action, a possibility, a gesture, complete in itself, unmotivated, unexamined.

The Bell Jar opens with the line, "It was a queer, sultry summer, the summer they electrocuted the Rosenbergs." The Rosenbergs are in no way a part of the story and their mention is the work of an intelligence, wondering if the sufferings of a solitary self can have general significance. Also with her uncanny recognition of connections of all kinds—sound, sensation—and her poetic ordering of material, the electrocution of the Rosenbergs and the shock treatment at the end of the book have a metaphorical if not a realistic kinship. In the end the Rosenbergs just mean death to Sylvia Plath. "I couldn't help wondering what it would be like, being burned alive, all along your nerves."

After a summer in New York, the girl goes back to Massachusetts and madness begin to close in on her. "I hadn't slept for twenty-one nights. I thought the most beautiful thing in the world must be shadow, the million moving shapes and cul de sacs of shadow. There was shadow in bureau drawers and closets and suitcases, and shadows under houses and trees and stones, and shadow at the back of people's eyes and smiles, and shadow, miles and miles of it, on the night side of the earth."

Committing suicide is desperation, demand for relief, but I don't see how we can ignore the way in which it is edged with pleasure and triumph in Sylvia Plath's work. In *The Bell Jar* she thinks of slashing her wrists in the tub and imagines the water "gaudy as poppies"—an image like those in her late poems. When she is unable to do the act, she still wants to "spill a little blood" for practice. "Then I felt a small, deep thrill, and a bright seam of red welled up at the lip of the slash. The blood gathered darkly, like fruit, and rolled down my ankle into the cup of my black patent leather shoe." These passages, and others much more brilliant in her poems, show a mind in a state of sensual distortion, seeking pain as much as death, contemplating with grisly lucidity the mutilation of the soul and the flesh. In "Daddy,"

> Every woman adores a Fascist,
> The boot in the face, the brute
> Brute heart of a brute like you.

With Sylvia Plath the submission to, the pursuit of pain are active, violent, *serious,* not at all in a Swinburnian mood of spankings and teasing degradation. Always, behind every mood, there is rage—for what reason we do not know, not even in the novel where the scene is open and explicit. In some poems the rage is directed blankly at her father, in others more obliquely, but with intensity, at her husband.

The actual suicide she attempted, and from which she was rescued only by great luck and accident, is very distressing in its details. The girl goes down into a cold, damp, cobwebbed corner of a cellar. There she hides herself behind an old log and takes fifty sleeping pills. The sense of downness, darkness, dankness, of unbearable rot and chill is savored for its ugliness and hurt. "They had to call and call / And pick the worms off me like sticky pearls" ("Lady Lazarus").

In real life there was a police search, newspaper headlines, empty pill bottle discovered; it was dramatic, unforgettable. Sylvia Plath was found, sent to the hospital, had shock treatment, and "the bell jar" in which she had been suffocating was finally lifted. The novel is not equal to the poems, but it is free of gross defects and embarrassments. The ultimate effort was not made, perhaps, but it is limited more in its intentions than in the rendering. The book has an interestingly cold, unfriendly humor. We sympathize with the heroine because of her drudging facing of it all and because of her suffering. The suffering is described more or less empirically, as if it were a natural thing, and the pity flows over you partly because she herself is so hard and glassy about her life.

This autobiographical work is written in a bare, rather collegiate 1950s style, and yet the attitude, the distance, and bitter carelessness are colored by a deep mood of affectlessness. The pleasures and sentiments of youth—wanting to be invited to the Yale prom, losing your virginity—are rather unreal in a scenario of disintegration, anger, and a perverse love of the horrible. The seduction of Esther Greenwood, as the heroine is called, is memorably grotesque and somehow bleakly suitable. The act led to a dangerous, lengthy, very unusual hemorrhaging. The blood—an obsession with the author—flows so plentifully that the girl is forced to seek medical help. She rather grimly pursues the young man with demands that he pay the doctor's bill, as if in some measure to get revenge for an action she herself cooperated with in the interest of experience.

The atrocious themes, the self-enclosure, the pain, blood, fury, infatuation with the hideous—all of that is in *The Bell Jar.* But, in a sense, softly, hesitantly. The poems in *Ariel* are much more violent. Indeed, the celebrated poem "Daddy" is as mean a portrait as one can find in literature.

Suicides are frequent enough, but the love of death, the teasing joy of it are rarely felt. Hart Crane, Virginia Woolf, many others, committed suicide. Some believe even Sappho threw herself from a rock into the sea. We think of these self-destructive actions as more or less sudden or as the culmination of an unbearable depression, one that brings with it a feeling of unworthiness and hopelessness, a despair that cannot imagine recovery.

Some of the journals Virginia Woolf wrote during the days before her death have in them the glittering contempt of a Sylvia Plath poem such as "Lesbos."

> Viciousness in the kitchen!
> The potatoes hiss.
> It is all Hollywood, windowless.

It goes on:

> You have stuck her kittens outside your window
> In a sort of cement well
> Where they crap and puke and cry and she can't
> hear.

This poem was written in the last weeks of Sylvia Plath's life and I have no clue as to whether or not it was an actual scene. The excessive violence of the language, remarkable as it is, seems to come from a mind speeding along madly and yet commanding an uncanny control of language, sound, rhythm, and metaphor that is the very opposite of madness.

In the entry of Virginia Woolf's diary there is a similar impatience. "They were powdering and painting, these common little tarts . . . Then at Fuller's. A fat, smart woman in red hunting cap, pearls, check skirt, consuming rich cakes. Her shabby dependant also stuffing. . . . Where does the money come from to feed these fat white slugs?"

Anger and contempt. And yet, when the day comes for Virginia Woolf, the pain of the illness bears down on her and she feels only apology, gratitude, and depression. Her letter to her husband reads, "Dearest, I feel certain that I am going mad again. I feel we can't go through another of those terrible times. . . . I can't fight any longer. I know I am spoiling your life, that without me you could work." She weighted her skirts and managed to drown in the river.

With Sylvia Plath suicide is a performance. "Lady Lazarus" describes it with a raging, confident pride. There is no apology or fearfulness. Suicide is an assertion of power, of the strength—not the weakness—of the personality. She is no poor animal sneaking away, giving up; instead she is strong, threatening, dangerous.

> I have done it again.
> One year in every ten
> I manage it—
>
> "Lady Lazarus"

Sometimes the performance is a reposeful one, as in "Edge":

> The woman is perfected.
> Her dead
> Body wears the smile of accomplishment,
> The illusion of a Greek necessity

Occasionally, as in the ending of "Last Words," domesticity and annihilation are mixed together:

> When the soles of my feet grow cold,
> The blue eye of my turquoise will comfort me.
> Let me have my copper cooking pots, let my rouge
> pots
> Bloom about me like night flowers, with a good
> smell.
> They will roll me up in bandages, they will store my
> heart
> Under my feet in a neat parcel. . . .

Sylvia Plath's preoccupation with the body at the moment of death reminds me of Mishima, although her concern is not to be "fit" as his apparently was, but simply to have the sensation of the corpse. With both of these suicides the action is asserted as a value, a definition, a pure leap. It is even sometimes thought of as beautiful, "pure and clean as the cry of a baby."

The circumstances of her suicide in London, the expectation that a girl would be coming in early to help with the children, the knowledge that the man in the flat below awakened early, the note with the doctor's name and phone number: these facts lead Alvarez to speculate that Sylvia Plath didn't *entirely* want to kill herself. She *risked* death—and lost.

Suicide, in that view, is thought of as a cry for help, one that cannot be uttered in the usual ways. The sheer fact of it was a tragic culmination, and yet it is not the death but the obsessions with it that are her inexplicable subject matter. Torture, mutilation, destruction are offered as interesting in themselves, without any suggestions that they are a "problem." Mishima tried to decorate his death with ideas of national policy which were, of course, ridiculous fantasies. Sylvia Plath always seems to be describing her self-destruction as an exhilarating act of contempt.

Perhaps it is important to remember that the poems are about suicide rather than about death as the waiting denouement of every life. The oddity of this is almost inexhaustible and the poems break with the universal theme of the passage of time, decay of the body, union with God, whatever death in the English poetic tradition has attached itself to. The idea of killing oneself, the sensuality of it, the drama of it, the prevision, based on other attempts, cannot fail to be a distortion, a decadence. The death wish, that limping, hanging-back companion to life, is, if it exists, an instinctual compliment to the vast and intricate efforts to survive. It is not one with a steady compulsion to jump, slit one's throat, swallow pills, turn on the gas.

The suicides are, then, a group apart, technicians, planners, plotters. Anne Sexton shares the wish, and her prose and poem about Sylvia Plath's death are strange, jaunty, casual and rather rapid, as if one were telling an anecdote in fear of interruption. She speaks of the two of them as "death-mongers," and tells with great excitement of the way they talked "their deaths in the Ritz Bar in Boston." Feel the air, imagine the scene, she says, "We talked about death with a burned-up intensity, both of us drawn to it like moths to an electric light bulb. Sucking on it!" The gaiety is profoundly saddening, the glittering eye frightens us. Anne Sexton tries, in a poem, to explain the peculiar concern for craft that dominates the suicide's imagination:

Like carpenters they want to know which tools.
They never ask why build.

Suicide is only one of the distressing themes in Sylvia Plath's work. There is fascination with hurt and damage and fury; she is a bluntly acute and rather heartless observer. There is a blind man at the table on a ship, feeling for his food. "His fingers had the noses of weasels. I couldn't stop looking." The bright reds of poppies and tulips become bloody and threatening. Gifts are not easily accepted. Slashing a finger in the kitchen is the occasion for "Cut," with its transfixed accuracy.

What a thrill—
My thumb instead of an onion.
The top quite gone
Except for a sort of hinge

Of skin,
A flap like a hat,
Dead white.
Then that red plush.

A bruise is, in like manner, painted in "Contusion."

Colour floods to the spot, dull purple.
The rest of the body is all washed out.
The colour of pearl.

Is the poem "Daddy" to be accepted as a kind of exorcism, a wild dramatic monologue of abuse screamed at a lost love?

You do not do, you do not do
Any more, black shoe
In which I have lived like a foot
For thirty years, poor and white,
Barely daring to breathe or Achoo.

Her father died of a long illness, but there is no pity for *his* lost life. Instead he is not the dead one; he is the murderer:

An engine, an engine
Chuffing me off like a Jew
A Jew to Dachau, Auschwitz, Belsen.
I began to talk like a Jew.
I think I may well be a Jew.

The association of her own pain with that of the Jews in Europe has been named very well by George Steiner, "a subtle larceny." The father did not kill anyone and "the fat black heart" is really her own. How is it possible to grieve for more than twenty years for one as evil and brutal as she asserts her father to have been? On the grounds of psychology every opposite can be made to fall neatly into place—that jagged, oddly shaped piece is truly part of a natural landscape if only you can find the spot where its cutting corners slip into the blue sky. The acrimonious family—yes, any contrary can turn up there, *logically* as it were. But even strangers, the town, are brought into the punishment of her father and this is somehow the most biting and ungenerous thought of all:

There's a stake in your fat black heart
And the villagers never liked you.
They are dancing and stamping on you.
They always knew it was you.
Daddy, daddy, you bastard, I'm through.

She insists that she is the victim—poor and white, a Jew, with a pretty red heart. But she is a dangerous and vindictive casualty: "Herr God, Herr Lucifer / Beware / Beware." "Daddy," with its hypnotic rhythms, its shameful harshness, is one of Sylvia Plath's most popular and known works. You cannot read it without shivering. It is done, completed, perfected. All the hatred in our own hearts finds its evil unforgiving music there—The Queen of the Night.

Love for her children, what about that? Isn't it mitigating? There is warmth and even joy. The boy and girl are "two roses," a child's smile is "found money," children are "the one solid the spaces lean on," the baby is a "high-riser, my little loaf." But children also appear in the images of destruction. In "Edge" the woman who is perfected by death has her dead children with her.

She has folded

Them back into her body as petals
Of a rose close when the garden

Stiffens and odours bleed
From the sweet, deep throats of the night flower.

A child's smile is a "hook." There is a poem about the deformities occasioned by thalidomide. In "Death & Co.":

He tells me how sweet
The babies look in their hospital
Icebox, a simple

Frill at the neck,
Then the flutings of their Ionian
Death gowns,
Then two little feet.

What can we make of a poet so ambitious and vengeful, so brilliant and yet so willfully vulnerable? How can we judge such a sense of personal betrayal, such rage, and such deformed passions? Her work is overwhelming; it is quite literally irresistible. The daring, the skill, the severity. It shocks and thrills. She called—in a typically awful phrase—her last burst of poetry "the blood jet."

When the time came she had earned it by all those earlier poems, slowly, carefully written, by that long ambition, burning, waiting, learning, by her A's, her Phi Beta Kappa, her driven perfectionism, her arrogance, her madness controlled to just the right degree. The loneliness which Alvarez so compellingly preserves for us, the freezing flat—without curtains—the icy early mornings, furiously writing before the children cried and before the "glassy music" of the milkman, her husband off with someone else—there we have a "modern instance" if there ever was one.

It is not a question in these last weeks of the conflict in a woman's life between the claims of the feminine and the agonized work of art. Every artist is either a man or a woman and the struggle is pretty much the same for both. All art that is not communal is, so to speak, made at home. Sylvia Plath was furious. Alvarez writes:

> I suspect that finding herself alone again now, however temporarily and voluntarily, all the anguish she had experienced at her father's death was reactivated: despite herself, she felt abandoned, injured, enraged and bereaved as purely and defenselessly as she had as a child twenty years before.

The sense of betrayal, even of hatred, did not leave her weak and complaining so much as determined and ambitious. Ambitious rage is all over *Ariel* and in the poems written at the same time and published in *Winter Trees.* "The Applicant" is a very bitter poem about the woman's part in marriage. In "For a Fatherless Son" she speaks to the child about the absence of the father that will gradually grow in the child's consciousness like a tree:

A death tree, color gone, an Australian gum tree—
Balding, gelded by lightning—an illusion,
And a sky like a pig's backside, an utter lack of
attention.

And that is what her own life was like at the end—the husband and father's "utter lack of attention."

In the explosive energy of her last months I see a determination to "win." Indeed I feel, from the evidence of her work, that it is sentimental to keep insisting that the birth of her children unlocked her poetic powers. Why should that be? The birth of children opens up the energy for taking care of them and for loving them. The common observation that one must be prepared to put off other work for a few years is strongly founded. Of course, it is foolish to generalize and it is the work itself, its hard competitiveness that glare out at every turn. When she died she was alone, exhausted from writing, miserable—but triumphant too, achieved, defined and defiant.

The suicide of a young woman with the highest gifts is inevitably a circumstance of the most moving and dramatic sort. We cannot truly separate the work from the fascination and horror of the death. It is a fact that the poems in *Ariel* were read, while Slylvia Plath was alive, with full self-control and detachment by editors, who then rejected many that have since become important additions to our literature. In the end this does not strike me as more than an astonishment and it is certain the poems would have been published. Everything, everything is published, and no matter that the claim upon our attention is more often than not unfathomable. What is more teasing to the mind and the imagination is how the poems of a dramatic suicide would read to us if the poet had held on to life, given interviews, public readings, finished a second novel, more poems.

It is interesting to make the effort to read Sylvia Plath's poems as if she were still alive. They are just as brilliant, just as much creations of genius, but they are obscured and altered. Blood, reds, the threats do not impress themselves so painfully upon us. "Cold blanks approach us: / They move in a hurry." What is that? we wonder. Unhappiness, agitation, fear? "Edge" seems to be a Greek heroine, Medea perhaps, once more. "Last Words," a profoundly well-written poem:

I do not want a plain box, I want a sarcophagus
With tigery stripes, and a face on it
Round as the moon, to stare up.

A beautiful poem in which, as the textbooks might say, the poet imagines her own death and is buried in a tomb, like an ancient Babylonian goddess of love. "The Detective," a prophetic poem about a death (or is it a murder?) that imagines us as we have become—detectives, putting the pieces together, working on the case. "Make notes," it says at the end.

Her poems have, read differently, the overcharged preoccupation with death and release found in religious poetry. For indeed she saw eternity the other night, also; she cries out "No end?" as Herbert does. But she was not religious; instead she is violently secular in her eternities, realistic about the life that slides from her side. Suicide was not a necessity to the passion and brilliance of the poems; nevertheless the act is a key, central to the overwhelming burst of achievement. She lived on her poetry during the last months of her life. Great she knew it to be; we feel that. It had to be *serious,* final. To imagine anyone's taking his life as a way of completing, fulfilling, explaining the highest work of that life may appear impudent, insulting to death. And yet is it more thoughtful to believe that love, debts, ill health, revenge are greater values to the human soul than creative, artistic powers? Artists have often been cruel to others for what they imagined to be advantages to their work. Cruelty to oneself, as the completion of creation, is far from unimaginable, especially to a spirit tempted throughout life to self-destruction.

If anything could have saved Sylvia Plath it would have been that she, in life, might have had the good fortune to know her own fulfillment, her hard, glittering achievement. In *The Review,* Douglas Dunn wrote about her: "Sylvia Plath was one of the most remarkable talents in any art of the decade, if not of the century." She has won the green cloth—no writer ever wanted it more. Or it would be more careful to say that she *earned* the green cloth and along with the first determination to be preeminent as a poet there came money and power, all by her own efforts. But it came too late, of course, and lesser spirits usurped the ground, began the sentimentalization of her own ungenerous nature and unrelenting anger.

Beyond the mesmerizing rhythms and sounds, the flow of brilliant, unforgettable images, the intensity—what does she say to her readers? Is it simple admiration for the daring, for going the whole way? To her fascination with death and pain she brings a sense of combat and brute force new in women writers. She is vulnerable, yes, to father and husband, but that is not the end of it at all. I myself do not think her work comes out of the cold war, the extermination camps, or the anxious doldrums of the Eisenhower years. If anything, she seems to have jumped ahead of her dates and to have more in common with the years we have just gone through. Her lack of conventional sentiment, her destructive contempt for her family, the failings in her marriage, the drifting, rootless rage, the peculiar homelessness, the fascination with sensation and the drug of death, the determination to try everything knowing it would not really stop the suffering—no one went as far as she did in this.

There is nothing of the social revolutionary in her, but she is whirling about in the center of an overcharged, splitting air and she especially understands everything destructive and negative. What she did not share with the youth of the present is her intense and perfect artistry, her belief in it. That religion seemed to have got from some old Prussian root memory of hard work, rigor, self-command. She is a stranger, an alien. In spite of her sea imagery—and it is not particularly local but rather psychological—she is hard to connect with Massachusetts and New England. There is nothing Yankee in her. So "crossing the water" was easy—she was as alien to nostalgia and sentiment as she was to the country itself. A basic and fundamental displacement played its part.

Sylvia Plath has extraordinary descriptive powers, it is a correctness and accuracy that combine the look of things with their fearsome powers of menace. It is not close to the magnifying-glass descriptions in Marianne Moore and Elizabeth Bishop, that sense these two writers have of undertaking a sort of decoding, startling in the newness of what is seen. When Elizabeth Bishop writes that the "donkey brays like a pump gone dry," this is a perfectly recognizable and immensely gratifying gift of the sort we often get also in Sylvia Plath. But the detail in Elizabeth Bishop's "The Fish" is of another kind:

I looked into his eyes
which were far larger than mine
but shallower, and yellowed,
the irises backed and packed
with tarnished tinfoil
seen through the lenses
of old scratched isinglass.

Marianne Moore's abstruse, peering investigations, her shining, gleaming mirror reflect—more than anything else—words. For instance, "Smooth Gnarled Crepe Myrtle" and its flowing compounds:

A brass-green bird with grass-
green throat smooth as a nut springs from
twig to twig askew, copying the
Chinese flower piece—business-like atom

in the stiff-leafed tree's blue-
pink dregs—of wine pyramids
of mathematic
circularity; one of a
pair.

In Marianne Moore and Elizabeth Bishop we are never far away from the comic spirit, from tolerance and wisdom—qualities alien to the angry illuminations of *Ariel*. But the tradition is also strong in Sylvia Plath—and taste, too, in the sense of craft utterly conquered and absorbed. Precision interests her, and she is immensely learned like the other two poets, never wishing to be a "natural" in any sense. She has also the power of the visual, part of the preference for precision over rhetoric. Perhaps this greed for particulars is the true mark of the poetry of women in our time. In the end, what is overwhelming, new, original, in Sylvia Plath is the burning singularity of temperament, the exigent spirit clothed but not calmed by the purest understanding of the English poetic tradition.

Long after I had been reading her work I came across the recording of some of her poems made in England not long before she died. I have never before learned anything from a poetry reading, unless the clothes, the beard, the girls, the poor or good condition of the poet can be considered a kind of knowledge. But I was taken aback by Sylvia Plath's reading. It was not anything like I could have imagined. Not a trace of the modest retreating, humorous Worcester, Massachusetts, of Elizabeth Bishop; nothing of the swallowed plain Pennsylvania of Marianne Moore. Instead these bitter poems—"Daddy," "Lady Lazarus," "The Applicant," "Fever 103"—were "beautifully" read, projected in full-throated, plump, diction-perfect, Englishy, mesmerizing cadences, all round and rapid, and paced and spaced. Poor recessive Massachusetts had been erased. "I have done it again!" Clearly, perfectly, staring you down. She seemed to be standing at a banquet like Timon, crying, "Uncover, dogs, and lap!"

It is a tragic story, completely original and unexpected in its scenes and its themes. Ted Hughes, her husband, has a poem about wives:

Their brief
Goes straight up to heaven and nothing more is
heard of it.

That was not true of Sylvia Plath, and since we now have no choice perhaps there is no need to weigh and to wonder whether her awful black brief was worth it.

An Essay on *Leaves of Grass*

William Carlos Williams (1883–1963)

Born in Rutherford, New Jersey, William Carlos Williams attended local schools until 1897 when his parents (who had emigrated from England and Puerto Rico) sent him to Geneva and Paris for two years of Lycée education. After returning to the United States he studied at Horace Mann High School in New York City and entered the University of Pennsylvania Medical School in 1902 where he later met Ezra Pound (then a graduate student in Romance languages). After obtaining his medical degree he was an intern in New York and spent a year in Leipzig, Germany, doing postgraduate work in pediatrics. He then returned to his native Rutherford where he pursued the double career of poet and physician for the rest of his life (except for a "sabbatical" year in Europe during the 1920s). Williams' early poems are weak and conventionally romantic, but beginning with *The Tempers* (1913) and *Al Que Quiere!* (1917) he entered the world of experimental modern poetry. Throughout his career Williams displayed an allegiance to both the European avant-garde and the native tradition in American poetry represented by Walt Whitman. The following essay on Whitman's *Leaves of Grass,* published late in Williams' career (1955), sums up his belief in a special poetic of the American language. Many of his poems, such as those of *Spring and All* (1923), reveal a strong cosmopolitan influence, yet Williams firmly rejected the international style and intellectual subject-matter of expatriate poets such as Pound and Eliot, seeking to ground his own art in the local landscape. *In the American Grain* (1925), a collection of essays on the American national character, was followed by poems which led ultimately to his five-volume epic of the Passaic valley, *Paterson* (1946–58), in which the industrial landscape of city and river becomes an archetype of modern man. In his last work on *Paterson* and in such late volumes as *The Desert Music* (1954) and *Pictures from Brueghel* (1962) Williams felt that he had discovered an expressive, musical form which could hold the natural rhythms of our speech. Throughout his life Williams was a prolific writer, stealing time from his work as a physician to produce poetry, plays, fiction, and autobiography. Just as he tried to domesticate a complex and cosmopolitan artistic vision, so he tried to make his language concrete ("No ideas but in things") while lifting concrete details to a level of general significance.

Leaves of Grass! It was a good title for a book of poems, especially for a new book of American poems. It was a challenge to the entire concept of the poetic idea, and from a new viewpoint, a rebel viewpoint, an American viewpoint. In a word and at the beginning it enunciated a shocking truth, that the common ground is of itself a poetic source. There had been inklings before this that such was the case in the works of Robert Burns and the poet Wordsworth, but in this instance the very forms of the writing had been altered: it had gone over to the style of the words as they appeared on the page. Whitman's so-called "free verse" was an assault on the very citadel of the poem itself; it constituted a direct challenge to all living poets to show cause why they should not do likewise. It is a challenge that still holds good after a century of vigorous life during which it has been practically continuously under fire but never defeated.

From the beginning Whitman realized that the matter was largely technical. It had to be free verse or nothing with him and he seldom varied from that practice—and never for more than the writing of an occasional poem. It was a sharp break, and if he was to go astray he had no one but himself to blame for it. It was a technical matter, true enough, and he would stick it out to the end, but to do any more with it than simply to write the poems was beyond him.

He had seen a great light but forgot almost at once after the first revelation everything but his "message," the idea which originally set him in motion, the idea on which he had been nurtured, the idea of democracy—and took his eye off the words themselves which should have held him.

The point is purely academic—the man had his hands full with the conduct of his life and couldn't, if they had come up, be bothered with other matters. As a result, he made no further progress as an artist but, in spite of various topical achievements, continued to write with diminishing effectiveness for the remainder of his life.

He didn't know any better. He didn't have the training to construct his verses after a conscious mold which would have given him power over them to turn them this way, then that, at will. He only knew how to give them birth and to release them to go their own way. He was preoccupied with the great ideas of the time, to which he was devoted, but, after all, poems are made out of words not ideas. He never showed any evidence of knowing this and the unresolved forms consequent upon his beginnings remained in the end just as he left them.

Verses, in English, are frequently spoken of as measures. It is a fortunate designation as it gives us, in looking at them, the idea of elapsed time. We are reminded that the origin of our verse was the dance—and even if it had not been the dance, the heart when it is stirred has its multiple beats, and verse at its most impassioned sets the heart violently beating. But as the heart picks up we also begin to count. Finally, the measure for each language and environment is accepted. In English it is predominantly the iambic pentameter, but whether that is so for the language Whitman spoke is something else again. It is a point worth considering, but apart from the briefest of notices a point not to be considered here. It may be that the essential pace of the English and the American languages is diametrically opposed each to the other and that that is an important factor in the writing of their poetry, but that is for the coming generations to discover. Certainly not only the words but the meter, the measure that governed Whitman's verses, was not English. But there were more pressing things than abstract discussions of meter to be dealt with at that time and the poet soon found himself involved in them.

Very likely the talk and the passionate talk about freedom had affected him as it had infected the French and many others earlier. It is said that, when as a young man he lived in New Orleans, he had fallen in love with a beautiful octoroon but had allowed his friends and relatives to break up the match. It is possible that the disappointment determined the pattern of his later rebellion in verse. Free verse was his great idea! *Versos sueltos* the Spanish call them. It is not an entirely new idea, but it was entirely new to the New York Yankee who was, so to speak, waiting for it with open arms and an overcharged soul and the example of Thomas Jefferson to drive him on.

But verse had always been, for Englishmen and the colonials that imitated them, a disciplined maneuver of the intelligence, as it is today, in which measure was predominant. They resented this American with his new idea, and attacked him in a characteristic way—*on moral grounds.* And he fell for it. He had no recourse but to defend himself and the fat was in the fire. How could verse be free without being immoral? There is something to it. It is the same attack, with a more modern tilt to it, that undoubtedly bothers T. S. Eliot. He is one of the best informed of our writers and would do us a great service, if free verse—mold it as he will—is not his choice, to find us an alternative. From the evidence, he has tried to come up with just that, but up to the present writing he has not brought the thing off.

The case of Mr. Eliot is in this respect interesting. He began writing at Harvard from a thoroughly well-schooled background and produced a body of verse that was immediately so successful that when his poem *The Waste Land* was published, it drove practically everyone else from the field. Ezra Pound, who had helped him arrange the poem on the page, was confessedly jealous. Other American poets had to take second place. A new era, under domination of a return to a study of the classics, was gratefully acknowledged by the universities, and Mr. Eliot, not Mr. Pound, was ultimately given the Nobel Prize. The drift was plainly away from all that was native to America, Whitman among the rest, and toward the study of the past and England.

Though no one realized it, a violent revolution had taken place in American scholarship and the interests from which it stemmed. Eliot had completely lost interest in all things American, in the very ideology of all that America stood for, including the idea of freedom itself in any of its phases. Whitman as a symbol of indiscriminate freedom was completely antipathetic to Mr. Eliot, who now won the country away from him again. The tendency toward freedom in the verse forms, which seemed to be thriving among American poets, was definitely checked and the stage was taken over for other things. I shall never forget the impression created by *The Waste Land;* it was as if the bottom had dropped out of everything. I had not known how much the spirit of Whitman animated us until it was withdrawn from us. Free verse became overnight a thing of the past. Men went about congratulating themselves as upon the disappearance of something that had disturbed their dreams; and indeed it was so—the dreams of right-thinking students of English verse had long been disturbed by the appearance among them of the horrid specter of Whitman's free verse. Now it was as if a liberator, a Saint George, had come just in the nick of time to save them. The instructors in all the secondary schools were grateful.

Meanwhile, Mr. Eliot had become a British subject and removed himself to England where he took up residence. He became a member of the Church of England. He was determined to make the break with America complete, as his fellow artist Henry James had done before him, and began to publish such poems as *Ash Wednesday* and the play *Murder in the Cathedral,* and the *Four Quartets.* Something had happened to him, something drastic, something to do, doubtless, with man's duty and his freedom in the world. It is a far cry from this to Whitman's thought of man as a free agent. The pendulum had gone the full swing.

It is inevitable for us to connect the happenings in the world generally with what takes place in the poem. When Mr. Eliot quit writing, when he quit writing poems, it looked as if he had got to a point where he had nowhere else to turn, and as if in his despair he had given up not only the poem but the world. A man as clever and well informed as he was had the whole world at his feet, but the only conclusion that he reached was that he wanted none of it. Especially did he want none of the newer freedom.

Not that he didn't in his verse try it on, for size, let us say, in his later experiments, particularly in *Four Quartets,* but even there he soon came to the end of his rope. The accented strophe he had definitely given up, as Wagner in the prelude to *Parsifal* had done the same, but to infer from that fact that he had discovered the freedom of a new measure was not true. It looked to me, at least, as if there were some profound depth to his probing beyond which he dared not go without compromising his religious faith. He did not attempt it. It is useful to record the limits of his penetration and the point at which he gave up his attempts to penetrate further. Just how far shall we go in our search for freedom and, more importantly, how shall our efforts toward a greater freedom be conditioned in our verses? All these decisions, which must be reached in deciding what to do, have implications of general value in our lives.

The young men who are students of literature today in our universities do not believe in seeking within the literary forms, the lines, the foot, the way in which to expand their efforts to know the universe, as Whitman did, but are content to follow the theologians and Mr. Eliot. In that, they are children of the times; they risk nothing, for by risking an expanded freedom you are very likely to come a cropper. What, in the words of Hjalmar Ekdahl in *The Wild Duck,* are you going to invent?

Men, offering their heads, have always come up with new proposals, and the world of events waits upon them, and who shall say whether it were better to close one's eyes or go forward like Galileo to the light or wait content in the darkness like the man in the next county? Whitman went forward to what to him seemed desirable, and so if we are to reject him entirely we must at least follow him at the start to find out what his discoveries were intended to signify and what not to signify.

Certainly, we are in our day through with such loose freedom as he employed in his verses in the blind belief that it was all going to come out right in the end. We know now that it is not. But are we, because of that, to give up freedom entirely? Merely to put down the lines as they happen to come into your head will not make a poem, and if, as happened more than once in Whitman's case, a poem result, who is going to tell what he has made? The man knew what he was doing, but he did not know all he was doing. Much still remains to discover, but that freedom in the conduct of the verses is desirable cannot be questioned.

There is a very moving picture of Whitman facing the breakers coming in on the New Jersey shore, when he heard the onomatopoeic waves talk to him direct in a Shakespearean language which might have been Lear himself talking to the storm. But it was not what it seemed; it was a new language, an unnamed language which Whitman could not identify or control.

For as the English had foreseen, this freedom of which there had been so much talk had to have limits somewhere. If not, it would lead you astray. That was the problem. And there was at about that time a whole generation of Englishmen, prominent among whom was Frank Harris, whom it did lead astray in moral grounds, just as there were Frenchmen at the time of the French Revolution who were led astray and are still being led astray under the difficult conditions that exist today. It is the reaction against such patterns of thought that moved Eliot and that part of the present generation which is not swallowed up by its fascination with the scene which draws them to Paris whenever they get the opportunity to go there. For in your search for freedom—which is desirable—you must stop somewhere, but where exactly shall you stop? Whitman could not say.

To propose that the answer to the problem should lie in the verse itself would have been to those times an impertinence—and the same would be the case even now. The Greeks had their Dionysia in the spring of the year, when morals could be forgotten, and then the control of life resumed its normal course. In other words, they departmentalized their lives, being of an orderly cast of mind, but we do not lend ourselves easily to such a solution. With us it is all or nothing, provided we are not caught at it. Either we give ourselves to a course of action or we do not give ourselves. Either we are to be free men or not free men—at least in theory. Whitman, like Tom Paine, recognized no limits and that got him into trouble.

But the waves on the Jersey shore still came tumbling in, quieting him as their secret escaped him, isolating him and leaving him lonesome—but possessed by the great mystery which won the world to his side. For he was unquestionably the child of the years. What was the wave that moved the dawning century also moved him and demanded his recognition, and it was not to be denied. All the discoveries and inventions which were to make the twentieth century exceed all others, for better or worse, were implicit in his work. He surpassed the ritualistic centuries which preceded him, just as Ehrlich and Koch and finally Einstein were to exceed Goethe. It was destined to be so, and the New World of which he was a part gave him birth. He had invented a new way of assaulting fate. "Make new!" was to him as it was to Pound much later on an imperious command which completely controlled him.

If he was to enlarge his opportunity he needed room, in verse as in everything else. But there were to be no fundamental changes in the concepts that keep our lives going at an accepted pace and within normal limits. The line was still to be the line, quite in accord with the normal contours of our accepted verse forms. It is not so much that which brought Whitman's verse into question but the freedom with which he laid it on the page. There he had abandoned all sequence and all order. It was as if a tornado had struck.

A new order had hit the world, a relative order, a new measure with which no one was familiar. The thing that no one realized, and this includes Whitman himself, is that the native which they were dealing with was no longer English but a new language akin to the New World to which its nature accorded in subtle ways that they did not recognize. That made all the difference. And not only was it new to America—it was new to the world. There was to be a new measure applied to all things, for there was to be a new order operative in the world. But it has to be insisted on that it was not disorder. Whitman's verses seemed disorderly, but ran according to an unfamiliar and a difficult measure. It was an order which was essential to the new world, not only of the poem, but to the world of chemistry and physics. In this way, the man was more of a prophet than he knew. The full significance of his innovations in the verse patterns has not yet been fully disclosed.

The change in the entire aesthetic of American art as it began to differ not only from British but from all the art of the world up to this time was due to this tremendous change in measure, a relative measure, which he was the first to feel and to embody in his works. What he was leaving behind did not seem to oppress him, but it oppressed the others and rightly so.

It is time now to look at English and American verse at the time Whitman began to write, for only by so doing can we be led to discover what he did and the course that lay before him. He had many formidable rivals to face on his way to success. But his chief opponent was, as he well knew, the great and medieval Shakespeare. And if any confirmation of Shakespeare's sacrosanct position in the language is still sought it is easily to be obtained when anything is breathed mentioning some alteration in the verse forms which he distinguished by using them. He may be imitated as Christopher Fry imitates him, but to vary or depart from him is heresy. Taken from this viewpoint, the clinical sheets of Shakespeare as a writer are never much studied. That he was the greatest word-man that ever existed in the language or out of it is taken for granted but there the inquiry ends.

Shakespeare presented Whitman with a nut hard to crack. What to do with the English language? It was all the more of a problem since the elements of it could not be presented at all or even recognized to exist. As far as the English language was concerned, there was only to use it and to use it well according to the great tradition of the masters.

And indeed it was a magnificent tradition. At the beginning of the seventeenth century it had reached an apogee which it had, to a great extent, maintained to the present day and of which it was proud and jealous. But when Shakespeare wrote, the laurels were new and had so recently been attained and had come from such distinguished achievements that the world seemed to pause for breath. It was a sort of noon and called for a halt. The man himself seemed to feel it and during an entire lifetime did no more than develop to the full his talents. It was noon sure enough for him, and he had only to stretch out in the sun and expand his mood.

Unlike Whitman, he was or represented the culmination of a historic as well as literary past whose forms were just coming to a head after the great trials which were to leave their marks on the centuries. There had been Chaucer, but the language had come of age since then as had the country. Now America had been discovered and the world could not grow much larger. Further expansion, except in a limited degree, was unlikely, so that the poet was left free to develop his world of detail but was not called upon to extend it. More was not necessary than to find something to do and develop it for the entire span of a long life. But as always with the artist, selection was an important point in the development.

For instance, as his sonnets show, Shakespeare was an accomplished rhymer, but he gave it up early. The patches of heroic couplet which he wrote for the Players in *Hamlet* are among the best examples of that form. Yet his main reliance was on blank verse—though he did, on occasion, try his hand at a triple accent which he rejected without more than a thought. The demands of the age called for other things and he was, above everything else, a practical man.

Practicing for so long a time upon the iambic pentameter, he had the opportunity to develop himself prodigiously in it. Over the years he shows a technical advance, a certain impatience with restraint in his work which makes it loose and verges more toward the conformation of prose. There is a great difference between Shakespeare's earlier and later work, the latter being freer and more natural in tone.

A feeling for prose began to be felt all through his verse. But at his death the form began to lapse rapidly into the old restrictions. It got worse and worse with the years until all the Elizabethan tenor had been stripped away, or as Milton phrased it speaking of his illustrious predecessor:

> Sweetest Shakespeare, Nature's child,
> Warbled his native woodnotes wild.

With Milton came Cromwell and the English Revolution, and Shakespeare was forgotten, together with the secrets of his versification, just as Whitman today is likely to be forgotten and the example of his verses and all that refers to him.

The interest that drove Whitman on is the same one that drove Shakespeare at the end of his life in an attempt to enlarge the scope of written verse, to find more of expression in the forms of the language employed. But the consequences of such experimentation are always drastic and amount in the end to its suppression, which in the person of a supreme genius is not easy.

From what has been said thus far, you can see why it is impossible to imitate Shakespeare; he was part of a historic process which cannot repeat itself. All imitations of the forms of the past are meaningless, empty shells, which have merely the value of decorations. So that, if anything is now to be created, it must be in a new form. Whitman, if he was to do anything of moment, could not, no matter how much he may have bowed down to the master, imitate him. It would not have had any meaning at all. And his responsibility to the new language was such that he had no alternative but to do as it bade him.

Though he may not have known it, with Whitman the whole spirit of the age itself had been brought under attack. It was a blind stab which he could not identify any more than a child. How could he, no matter how acute his instincts were, have foreseen the discoveries in chemistry, in physics, in abnormal psychology, or even the invention of the telephone or the disclosure of our subterranean wealth in petroleum? He knew only, as did those who were disturbed by his free verse, that something had occurred to the normal structure of conventional aesthetic and that he could not accept it any longer. Therefore, he acted.

We have to acknowledge at once in seeking a meaning involving the complex concerns of the world that the philosophic, the aesthetic, and the mechanical are likely to stem in their development from the same root. One may be much in advance of the other in its discoveries, but in the end a great equalizing process is involved so that the discovery of the advance in the structure of the poetic line is equated by an advance in the conception of physical facts all along the line. Man has no choice in these matters; the only question is, will he recognize the changes that are taking place in time to make the proper use of them? And when time itself is conceived of as relative, no matter how abstruse that may sound, the constructions, the right constructions, cannot be accepted with a similar interpretation. It may take time to bring this about, but when a basic change has occurred in our underlying concern it brooks no interference in the way it will work itself out.

Whitman didn't know anything about this, nor does Mr. Eliot take it into his considerations nor Father Merton either, but if they had to construct a satisfactory poetic line it had and still has to be done according to this precept. For we have learned, if we have learned anything from the past, that the principles of physics are immutable. Best, if you do not approve of what writing has become, to follow in Mr. Eliot's footsteps.

For it is important to man's fate that these matters be—if anything is important to man's fate in this modern world. At least, you cannot retrace steps that have been taken in the past. And you don't know, you simply do not know, what may come of it. No more than Whitman knew what his struggle to free verse may have implied and may still imply for us no matter how, at the moment, the world may have forsaken him. The books are not closed even though the drift in the tide of our interest may at the moment be all the other way. It cannot so soon have reversed itself. Something is still pending, though the final shape of the thing has not yet crystallized. Perhaps that is the reason for the regression. There are too many profitable leads in other associated fields of the intelligence for us to draw back now.

Where have the leads which are *not* aesthetic tended to take us in the present century? By paying attention to detail and our telescopes and microscopes and the reinterpretations of their findings, we realize that man has long since broken from the confinement of the more rigid of his taboos. It is reasonable to suppose that he will in the future, in spite of certain setbacks, continue to follow the same course.

Man finds himself on the earth whether he likes it or not, with nowhere else to go. What then is to become of him? Obviously we can't stand still or we shall be destroyed. Then if there is no room for us on the outside we shall, in spite of ourselves, have to go *in:* into the cell, the atom, the poetic line, for our discoveries. We have to break the old apart to make room for ourselves, whatever may be our tragedy and however we may fear it. By making room within the line itself for his inventions, Whitman revealed himself to be a worthy and courageous man of his age and, to boot, a farseeing one.

Expressive Language

Imamu Amiri Baraka (1934–)

Imamu Amiri Baraka (originally LeRoi Jones) was born in Newark, New Jersey. He attended Rutgers University for a year and then transferred to Howard University where he received a degree in 1953. After serving in the Strategic Air Command he did postgraduate work at Columbia University and the New School for Social Research. His books of poetry are *Preface to a Twenty Volume Suicide Note* (1960), *The Dead Lecturer* (1964), and *Black Magic* (1969). His other works include several plays on racial themes and an autobiographical novel, *The System of Dante's Hell* (1965). After a visit to Cuba in 1960 Baraka became increasingly more militant, and as the 1960s progressed he was involved in a number of movements seeking black power. At the same time he adopted his Muslim name. The following selection is from *Home: Social Essays* (1966).

Speech is the effective form of a culture. Any shape or cluster of human history still apparent in the conscious and unconscious habit of groups of people is what I mean by culture. All culture is necessarily profound. The very fact of its longevity, of its being what it is, *culture,* the epic memory of practical tradition, means that it is profound. But the inherent profundity of culture does not necessarily mean that its *uses* (and they are as various as the human condition) will be profound. German culture is profound. Generically. Its uses, however, are specific, as are all uses . . . of ideas, inventions, products of nature. And specificity, as a right and passion of human life, breeds what it breeds as a result of its context.

Context, in this instance, is most dramatically social. And the social, though it must be rooted, as are all evidences of existence, in culture, depends for its impetus for the most part on a multiplicity of influences. Other cultures, for instance. Perhaps, and this is a common occurrence, the reaction or interreaction of one culture on another can produce a social context that will extend or influence any culture in many strange directions.

Social also means *economic,* as any reader of nineteenth-century European philosophy will understand. The economic is part of the social—and in our time much more so than what we have known as the spiritual or metaphysical, because the most valuable canons of power have either been reduced or traduced into stricter economic terms. That is, there has been a shift in the actual meaning of the world since Dante lived. As if Brooks Adams were right. Money does not mean the same thing to me it must mean to a rich man. I cannot, right now, think of one meaning to name. This is not so simple to understand. Even as a simple term of the English language, *money* does not possess the same meanings for the rich man as it does for me, a lower-middle-class American, albeit of laughably "aristocratic" pretensions. What possibly can "money" mean to a poor man? And I am not talking now about those courageous products of our permissive society who walk knowledgeably into "poverty" as they would into a public toilet. I mean, The Poor.

I look in my pocket; I have seventy cents. Possibly I can buy a beer. A quart of ale, specifically. Then I will have twenty cents with which to annoy and seduce my fingers when they wearily search for gainful employment. I have no idea at this moment what that seventy cents will mean to my neighbor around the corner, a poor Puerto Rican man I have seen hopefully watching my plastic garbage can. But I am certain it cannot mean the same thing. Say to David Rockefeller, "I have money," and he will think you mean something entirely different. That is, if you also dress the part. He would not for a moment think, "Seventy cents." But then neither would many New York painters.

Speech, the way one describes the natural proposition of being alive, is much more crucial than even most artists realize. Semantic philosophers are certainly correct in their emphasis on the final dictation of words over their users. But they often neglect to point out that, after all, it is the actual importance, *power,* of the words that remains so finally crucial. Words have users, but as well, users have words. And it is the users that establish the world's realities. Realities being those fantasies that control your immediate span of life. Usually they are not your own fantasies, *i.e.,* they belong to governments, traditions, etc., which, it must be clear by now, can make for conflict with the singular human life all ways. The fantasy of America might hurt you, but it is what should be meant when one talks of "reality." Not only the things you can touch or see, but the things that make such touching or seeing "normal." Then words, like their users, have a hegemony. Socially—which is final, right now. If you are some kind of artist, you naturally might think this is not so. There is the future. But *immortality* is a kind of drug, I think—one that leads to happiness at the thought of death. Myself, I would rather live forever . . . just to make sure.

The social hegemony, one's position in society, enforces more specifically one's terms (even the vulgar have "pull"). Even to the mode of speech. But also it makes these terms an available explanation of any social hierarchy, so that the words themselves become, even informally, laws. And of course they are usually very quickly stitched together to make formal statutes only fools or the faithfully intrepid would dare to question beyond immediate necessity.

The culture of the powerful is very infectious for the sophisticated, and strongly addictive. To be any kind of "success" one must be fluent in this culture. Know the words of the users, the semantic rituals of power. This is a way into wherever it is you are not now, but wish, very desperately, to get into.

Even speech then signals a fluency in this culture. A knowledge at least. "He's an educated man," is the barest acknowledgement of such fluency . . . in any time. "He's hip," my friends might say. They connote a similar entrance.

And it is certainly the meanings of words that are most important, even if they are no longer consciously acknowledged, but merely, by their use, trip a familiar lever of social accord. To recreate instantly the understood hierarchy of social, and by doing that, cultural, importance. And cultures are thought by most people in the world to do their business merely by being hierarchies. Certainly this is true in the West, in as simple a manifestation as Xenophobia, the naïve bridegroom of anti-human feeling, or in economic terms, Colonialism. For instance, when the first Africans were brought into the New World, it was thought that it was all right for them to be slaves because "they were heathens." It is a perfectly logical assumption.

And it follows, of course, that slavery would have been an even stranger phenomenon had the Africans spoken English when they first got here. It would have complicated things. Very soon after the first generations of Afro-Amerians mastered this language, they invented white people called Abolitionists.

Words' meanings, but also the rhythm and syntax that frame and propel their concatenation, seek their culture as the final reference for what they are describing of the world. An A flat played twice on the same saxophone by two different men does not have to sound the same. If these men have different ideas of what they want this note to do, the note will not sound the same. Culture is the form, the overall structure of organized thought (as well as emotion and spiritual pretension). There are many cultures. Many ways of organizing thought, or having thought organized. That is, the form of thought's passage through the world will take on as many diverse shapes as there are diverse groups of travelers. Environment is one organizer of *groups,* at any level of its meaning. People who live in Newark, New Jersey, are organized, for whatever purpose, as Newarkers. It begins that simply. Another manifestation, at a slightly more complex level, can be the fact that blues singers from the Midwest sing through their noses. There is an explanation past the geographical, but that's the idea in tabloid. And singing through the nose does propose that the definition of singing be altered . . . even if ever so slightly. (At this point where someone's definitions must be changed, we are flitting around at the outskirts of the old city of Aesthetics. A solemn ghost town. Though some of the bones of reason can still be gathered there.)

But we still need definitions, even if there already are many. The dullest men are always satisfied that a dictionary lists everything in the world. They don't care that you may find out something *extra,* which one day might even be valuable to them. Of course, by that time it might even be in the dictionary, or at least they'd hope so, if you asked them directly.

But for every item in the world, there are a multiplicity of definitions that fit. And every word we use *could* mean something else. And at the same time. The culture fixes the use, and usage. And in "pluralistic" America, one should always listen very closely when he is being talked to. The speaker might mean something completely different from what we think we're hearing. "Where is your pot?"

I heard an old Negro street singer last week, Reverend Pearly Brown, singing, "God don't never change!" This is a precise thing he is singing. He does not mean "God does not ever change!" He means "God don't never change!" The difference, and I said it was crucial, is in the final human reference . . . the form of passage through the world. A man who is rich and famous who sings, "God don't never change," is confirming his hegemony and good fortune . . . or merely calling the bank. A blind hopeless black American is saying something very different. He is telling you about the extraordinary order of the world. But he is not telling you about his "fate." Fate is a luxury available only to those fortunate citizens with alternatives. The view from the top of the hill is not the same as that from the bottom of the hill. Nor are most viewers at either end of the hill, even certain that, in fact, there is any other place from which to look. Looking down usually eliminates the possibility of understanding what it must be like to look up. Or try to imagine yourself as not existing. It is difficult, but poets and politicians try every other day.

Being told to "speak proper," meaning that you become fluent with the jargon of power, is also a part of not "speaking proper." That is, the culture which desperately understands that it does not "speak proper," or is not fluent with the terms of social strength, also understands somewhere that its desire to gain such fluency is done at a terrifying risk. The bourgeois Negro accepts such risk as profit. But does *close-ter* (in the context of "jes a close-ter, walk wi-thee") mean the same thing as *closer?* Close-ter, in the term of its user is, believe me, exact. It means a quality of existence, of actual physical disposition perhaps . . . in its manifestation as a *tone* and *rhythm* by which people live, most often in response to common modes of thought best enforced by some factor of environmental emotion that is exact and specific. Even the picture it summons is different, and certainly the "Thee" that is used to connect the implied "Me" with, is different. The God of the damned cannot know the God of the damner, that is, cannot know he is God. As no Blues person can really believe emotionally in Pascal's God, or Wittgenstein's question, "Can the concept of God exist in a perfectly logical language?" Answer: "God don't never change."

Communication is only important because it is the broadest root of education. And all cultures communicate exactly what they have, a powerful motley of experience.

On Style

(From *Death in the Afternoon*)

Ernest Hemingway (1899 – 1961)

Born and reared in Oak Park, Illinois, a suburb of Chicago, Hemingway graduated from high school in 1917 and worked for a brief period as a reporter for the Kansas City *Star*. When the United States entered World War I he volunteered for the ambulance service and was severely wounded at the Italian front. After the armistice he became a foreign correspondent for the Toronto *Star* and soon settled into the life of an expatriate writer in Paris. His first important volume of short stories, *In Our Time* (1925), is characterized by the austerity and precision found in "Big Two-Hearted River." Hemingway's first novel, *The Sun Also Rises* (1926), based on his experiences in Paris and Spain, was followed in 1929 by his great novel of the first World War, *A Farewell to Arms.* Between 1923 and 1933 Hemingway wrote most of his important short stories. He also wrote a unique work, *Death in the Afternoon* (1932), which combines a technical description of the bullfight and meditations on the Spanish landscape with literary comment (the following selections are from that volume).

The 1930s was a difficult decade for Hemingway: essentially an aloof stylist, he did not adjust easily to the climate of political activism and social commitment. However, his experience as a reporter and partisan in the Spanish Civil War did produce a highly successful novel, *For Whom the Bell Tolls* (1940). During the later days of World War II Hemingway was a reporter and participant on the Western front, but the novel based partly on this experience, *Across the River and Into the Trees* (1950), lacks the clean objectivity of *A Farewell to Arms* and the healthy romanticism of *For Whom the Bell Tolls.* In *The Old Man and the Sea* (1952), however, Hemingway produced a fable which combines his famous gift for realistic description with a new-found interest in overt symbolism. He was awarded the Nobel Prize for Literature in 1954, but the success of *The Old Man and the Sea* was not repeated. His last years were marked by a steady physical and mental disintegration, and he committed suicide in 1961.

I was trying to write then and I found the greatest difficulty, aside from knowing truly what you really felt, rather than what you were supposed to feel, and had been taught to feel, was to put down what really happened in action; what the actual things were which produced the emotion that you experienced. In writing for a newspaper you told what happened and, with one trick and another, you communicated the emotion aided by the element of timeliness which gives a certain emotion to any account of something that has happened on that day; but the real thing, the sequence of motion and fact which made the emotion and which would be as valid in a year or in ten years or, with luck and if you stated it purely enough, always, was beyond me and I was working very hard to try to get it. The only place where you could see life and death, *i.e.,* violent death now that the wars were over, was in the bull ring and I wanted very much to go to Spain where I could study it. I was trying to learn to write, commencing with the simplest things, and one of the simplest things of all and the most fundamental is violent death. It has none of the complications of death by disease, or so-called natural death, or the death of a friend or some one you have loved or have hated, but it is death nevertheless, one of the subjects that a man may write of. I had read many books in which, when the author tried to convey it, he only produced a blur, and I decided that this was because either the author had never seen it clearly or at the moment of it, he had physically or mentally shut his eyes, as one might do if he saw a child that he could not possibly reach or aid, about to be struck by a train. In such a case I suppose he would probably be justified in shutting his eyes as the mere fact of the child being about to be struck by the train was all that he could convey, the actual striking would be an anti-climax, so that the moment before striking might be as far as he could represent. But in the case of an execution by a firing squad, or a hanging, this is not true, and if these very simple things were to be made permanent, as, say, Goya tried to make them in *Los Desastros de la Guerra,* it could not be done with any shutting of the eyes. I had seen certain things, certain simple things of this sort that I remembered, but through taking part in them, or, in other cases, having to write of them immediately after and consequently noticing the things I needed for instant recording, I had never been able to study them as a man might, for instance, study the death of his father or the hanging of some one, say, that he did not know and would not have to write of immediately after for the first edition of an afternoon newspaper.

When writing a novel a writer should create living people; people not characters. A *character* is a caricature. If a writer can make people live there may be no great characters in his book, but it is possible that his book will remain as a whole; as an entity; as a novel. If the people the writer is making talk of old masters; of music; of modern painting; of letters; or of science then they should talk of those subjects in the novel. If they do not talk of those subjects and the writer makes them talk of them he is a faker, and if he talks about them himself to show how much he knows then he is showing off. No matter how good a phrase or a simile he may have if he puts it in where it is not absolutely necessary and irreplaceable he is spoiling his work for egotism. Prose is architecture, not interior decoration, and the Baroque is over. For a writer to put his own intellectual musings, which he might sell for a low price as essays, into the mouths of artificially constructed characters which are more remunerative when issued as people in a novel is good economics, perhaps, but does not make literature. People in a novel, not skillfully constructed *characters,* must be projected from the writer's assimilated experience, from his knowledge, from his head, from his heart and from all there is of him. If he ever has luck as well as seriousness and gets them out entire they will have more than one dimension and they will last a long time. A good writer should know as near everything as possible. Naturally he will not. A great enough writer seems to be born with knowledge. But he really is not; he has only been born with the ability to learn in a quicker ratio to the passage of time than other men and without conscious application, and with an intelligence to accept or reject what is already presented as knowledge. There are some things which cannot be learned quickly and time, which is all we have, must be paid heavily for their acquiring. They are the very simplest things and because it takes a man's life to know them the little new that each man gets from life is very costly and the only heritage he has to leave. Every novel which is truly written contributes to the total of knowledge which is there at the disposal of the next writer who comes, but the next writer must pay, always, a certain nominal percentage in experience to be able to understand and assimilate what is available as his birthright and what he must, in turn, take his departure from. If a writer of prose knows enough about what he is writing about he may omit things that he knows and the reader, if the writer is writing truly enough, will have a feeling of those things as strongly as though the writer had stated them. The dignity of movement of an ice-berg is due to only one-eighth of it being above water. A writer who omits things because he does not know them only makes hollow places in his writing. A writer who appreciates the seriousness of writing so little that he is anxious to make people see he is formally educated, cultured or well-bred is merely a popinjay. And this too remember; a serious writer is not to be confounded with a solemn writer. A serious writer may be a hawk or a buzzard or even a popinjay, but a solemn writer is always a bloody owl.

The Attempted Dance: A Discussion of the Modern Theater

Alvin B. Kernan (1923–   )

Educated at Williams College, Oxford University, and Yale University, Alvin Kernan taught at Yale from 1954 until 1973. Since 1973 he has been a Professor of English at Princeton University; from 1973 until 1977 he served as Dean of the Graduate School. The General Editor of the Yale Edition of *The Plays of Ben Jonson,* Kernan has published widely on Elizabethan and modern drama. His books include *The Cankered Muse: Satire of the English Renaissance* (1959), *The Plot of Satire* (1965), and a major contribution to *The Revels History of the Drama in English, 1576–1613,* Volume Three. He has also edited *Classics of the Modern Theater, Realism and After* (1965) and *The Modern American Theater* (1967).

A great dramatic tradition impresses itself on the mind not as a series of dates or plot outlines, but as a montage of vivid scenes and arrested gestures, over which human voices hang suspended: asserting, threatening, explaining, questioning. To think of the Elizabethan theater is to see an old man standing on a bare heath in a great thunderstorm shouting at the elements, a young man at night in a walled garden below a balcony looking upward at a beautiful girl, a prince dressed in seafarer's clothing standing in a graveyard holding a skull in his hand. It is to hear such voices as "Thou art the thing itself. Unaccommodated man is no more but such a poor, bare, forked animal as thou art"—"But soft! What light through yonder window breaks? It is the east, and Juliet is the sun!"—"To what base uses we may return, Horatio! Why may not imagination trace the noble dust of Alexander till he find it stopping a bunghole?"

Such scenes as these come to define a theater because each provides a sharply focused image of man in some crucial action. The modern theater also has its great definitive scenes which sum up man as he has come to sense himself in the nineteenth and twentieth centuries—his most fundamental hopes and fears, his understanding of the shape and currents of the world, and his intuition of his stance in relation to that world. At daybreak in a dark Norwegian valley at the head of a gloomy fiord a helpless madman, who has struggled vainly through his life for light and happiness, sees the astronomically distant sun hurling bright light on the snow-covered peaks far above. He speaks flatly to a woman who a moment ago had thought that a decision to face the truth guaranteed happiness: "Mother, give me the sun."

On a bare stage in an empty Italian theater a middle-aged gentleman, who is not a person but a "character," stands trying with great effort to explain the truth of his nature to an uncomprehending director and group of actors whom he *must* persuade to stage his own personal reality in a play. As he speaks, the dreadful truth slowly overwhelms him:

> Each one of us has within him a whole world of things, each man of us his own special world. And how can we ever come to an understanding if I put in the words I utter the sense and value of things as I see them, while you who listen to me must inevitably translate them according to the conception of things each one of you has within himself. We think we understand each other, but we never really do.

A group of Russians sitting by a decayed wayside shrine in a cherry orchard, which had once been their support and justification but is now about to be sold, hear a sound like a breaking harp string, sad and faraway. They speculate aimlessly about whether they have heard the cry of some nameless bird or a lift cable snapping in some distant mineshaft. A moment of silence follows, and then they drift away, each isolated from the others and from a world they no longer understand.

High in the Swedish forests, deep with snow, an old nurse slips a strait jacket on a distraught man, a father, scientist, and one-time army officer, who had thought his authority invincible and his range unlimited, until he entered a death struggle with his wife for control of the family. The man who had once dreamed of a vast world entirely intelligible to the human intellect and manageable by reason sees his dream dissolve into the old, dark nightmare of blind struggle, containment, and death:

> So when we thought the sun should have risen for us, we found ourselves back among the ruins in the full moonlight, just as in the good old times. Our light morning sleep had only been troubled by fantastic dreams—there had been no awakening.

In Central Park, near the zoo, two men quarrel over a bench. Jerry, who speaks for all of the disorders, loneliness, and personal disasters which are censored in the official versions of our affluent society, attempts to force himself on, communicate in some manner with, Peter, a man who consistently approximates middle-class statistical norms. It is as if two half-lives, private man and public man, were coming together for a moment and attempting to join. But no communication is possible, and in the end Jerry stands impaled on the knife held defensively at arm's length by the frightened Peter.

* * *

Such gloomy images and sounds as these dominate the modern theater, though occasionally scenes of hope and the sound of laughter flash out. Bernard Shaw's supermen, the instruments of the life force, stand exposing and mocking various kinds of stupidity, cruelty, and romantic sentimentalism which threaten, but do not interrupt, the onward movement of life to its unknown goal. Thornton Wilder's less heroic, comic figures contrive somehow to escape by the skin of their teeth the traps of an apparently hostile or indifferent universe and the dangers of their own natures.

Even such a brief collection of scenes as this reveals one peculiarity of the modern theater: its international quality. The other great theaters of the West were the products of a single language and a single culture, even though that culture faced a crisis at the time it produced its great drama—fifth century Athens, the London of Elizabeth and James I, and the France of Cardinal Richelieu and Louis XIV. But the modern theater is the product of nearly all the languages of the

Western world, and its settings have ranged from the isolated country houses of the Russian upper-middle class to the fiords and forests of Scandinavia, from the arid plains of Andalusia to a bench in Central Park.

The subject matter of this theater has been as diverse as its languages and settings. Beginning as it does in the mid-nineteenth century, it has embodied at one time or another each of the major theories about the nature and destiny of man which have emerged in the last one hundred or so years. The realistic settings and the natural speech of plays by Ibsen, Chekov, and Hauptmann give solid form to the general philosophy of naturalism which is, roughly, the view that man's life is shaped entirely by his social and physical environment. Brecht's characters, struggling with the demands of earning bread and seeking shelter, constantly engaged in economic warfare, dramatize the world view of Marx. Relativism, the view that nothing, neither time nor morals, is absolute, finds its theatrical voice in the characters of Pirandello who try futilely to explain to others their personal sense of themselves, while the others interpret those explanations according to their own particular sense of things. The constant war between men and women, the grotesque sexual antagonisms, of Strindberg's plays give dramatic form to the theory of biological determinism and social Darwinism. Fabian socialism and a tempered belief in progress become the answer to the injustices and confusions of nineteenth century imperialist politics, laissez-faire economics, and Victorian morality in the plays of Shaw. The existentialist belief that man is an absurd creature loose in a universe empty of real meaning finds expression in the plays of Ionesco, Sartre, and Camus. Finally, the psychology of Freud has in the last twenty or thirty years very nearly replaced traditional theories of motivation in such plays as those of Betti, Williams, and O'Neill.

These new ideas have by no means entirely usurped the modern stage, but continue to exist in uneasy mixture or in violent opposition with older, more traditional views of man and nature. While Yeats wrote poetic plays for the Abbey Theater dealing with the ancient Gaelic legends in which ideals triumphed over vulgar reality, Sean O'Casey wrote grimly realistic plays for the same theater dealing with slum life in Dublin during the Irish Rebellion—plays which demonstrated the sham of such ideals as patriotism and duty because they destroyed life rather than fostered it. Similarly, playwrights such as Lorca, Cocteau, and Fry have continued to see in poetry ("poetry of the theater" in Cocteau's case) the power to open up new and unsuspected areas of reality, while Ionesco has devoted himself entirely to showing the emptiness of language because of its inability to communicate even the most simple facts. And while T. S. Eliot has written several verse plays that turn on the miraculous changes wrought in some lives by grace and Christian vision, Samuel Beckett's characters wait, vainly, on a nearly bare stage for some saving power whose name is uncertain and who never appears, who may have come and gone unnoticed, or who may not even exist.

The styles of modern drama are nearly as varied as the settings and the ideas which have informed the plays. A Greek tragic dramatist of the fifth century B.C. wrote in a tradition which prescribed the use of certain poetic meters, limited the number of characters who could appear on stage at one time, made obligatory the provision of odes and dances for a chorus, and directed that the plot must be drawn from heroic legend and the myths of the distant past. Modern dramatists work in no such dramatic tradition, and they have been left entirely free to choose subjects and invent new dramatic styles. The result has been a bewildering number of styles: realism, naturalism, poetic drama, symbolism, expressionism, the epic theater, the theater of the absurd, and surrealism, to name only the most prominent among them. As a result of this freedom, modern plays have taken nearly every possible shape and size, ranging from imitations of Elizabethan tragedy in blank verse to modified Japanese Noh plays; from sprawling plays which take half a day to perform and seek to encompass all of human life (Ibsen's *Emperor and Galilean,* Strindberg's *To Damascus,* O'Neill's *Mourning Becomes Electra*), to brief one-act "anti-plays" which prove the impossibility of finding any meaning in life except its meaninglessness (Ionesco's *The Chairs* or Albee's *The Sand Box*).

What is true of the dramatic form and style of the modern theater is equally true of the acting styles. The dominant mode of acting has been some modification of the Stanislavsky method (developed around the turn of the century at the Moscow Art Theater), which trains an actor, in effect, to lose his own personality while on the stage and become the character he is playing. This is the extension into the player's art of the realistic style, for just as the realistic stage is thought to become not a symbolic representation of reality but an actual place, so the Stanislavsky actor ceases to be a player representing someone else and is transformed into the character. But while this has been the dominant acting style, the reactions against it have been constant and extreme: Brecht trained the actors of his *Berliner Ensemble* to remember always that they were on stage playing a part, and actors at the Abbey Theater in Dublin, it is said, were frequently rehearsed in barrels in order to restrict their movements and to force them to concentrate on speaking their poetic lines, thus reminding them that they were no more than voices for the poetry, necessary but ultimately unimportant instruments of the author.

Attitudes toward stage designs and sets have been similarly various. One end of the range is marked by the meticulously realistic drawing-room sets of Ibsen, where the furniture, rugs, and draperies on the stage were chosen to create the illusion of rooms as real as those the audience had just left in coming to the theater. The general concern for realism led ultimately to such extremes as getting every detail on the costumes, down to the last button, historically accurate for period pieces, and the introduction of water taps that really worked, real doors, genuine gravel for walks, and television sets that showed the same program you would have seen if you hadn't come to the theater. This drive to make the stage a photographic imitation of the actual world remains in many ways the main current of the modern theater, though it has been resisted from the beginning by those who have argued that the stage is by nature a symbolic place, not an illusion of reality, and that settings and costumes should be designed with their symbolic function in mind. This view, most properly termed expressionism, has led to the construction of improbable sets in which skeletal structures represent houses, where the world is reduced to a bare stage with a single tree, where a few folding chairs stand for an automobile and household furnishings. On the expressionistic stage the world may be symbolized by a few angular pieces of abstract statuary, by a color alone, or by a few boards made into platforms of different levels; tall buildings may lean over a house to express menace, stables may flower at their peak to express hope, men may walk through mirrors to express their insubstantiality. The laws of nature and probability are suspended on the expressionistic stage, and their place is taken by the laws of poetry, which state that the writer is free to reshape the natural world in order to make his point clear.

In every area of the modern theater—language, setting, dramatic style, acting technique, theme, stage decor—we seem to find diversity, heterogeneity, and open conflict. Instead of a smoothly developing tradition, a continuing exploitation of a limited number of theatrical resources, and an ever narrowing and finer focus on a few key ethical and metaphysical questions—all the marks of the great theatrical traditions of the past—the theater of the modern age seems to jump nervously and without progression from extreme to extreme, from one bizarre experiment to its opposite, and from one explanation of human nature to its reverse. So great is this diversity that Francis Fergusson has been able to argue most persuasively that what we have is not a true "theater," which focuses "at the center of the life of the community the complementary insights of the whole culture,"[1] but only a collection of plays loosely related by the accident of having been written in the same historical period, the late nineteenth and the twentieth centuries. Fergusson explains that this is so because our age lacks any common view of life and man and history:

> Human nature seems to us a hopelessly elusive and uncandid entity, and our playwrights (like hunters with camera and flash-bulbs in the depths of the Belgian Congo) are lucky if they can fix it, at rare intervals, in one of its momentary postures, and in a single bright, exclusive angle of vision.[2]

If Fergusson is right, there is no hope of seeing modern drama as a significant whole. The best that can be done is to gather together a group of modern plays and to allow each to present its peculiar view of man and his world. Across one stage let Freudian man move in a painful attempt to exorcise his own and his family's psychic history; on another stage let Marxist man move in the search for the means of production and the socialist utopia; on still another stage let existentialist man move toward that free and irremediable act which will establish his identity. Taken at this level, the views of man which our theater has offered us are difficult if not impossible to reconcile as complementary visions of the same man and the same world. But while the characters who appear on our stage may seem so different, they stand always in the same place, in front of a common background which reflects some shared sense of the human condition. To understand this fact, we must turn to the physical arrangements of our playing houses, and a word of explanation is needed here about the view of the physical theater I am about to offer.

We know that social situations and technological ability affect the architectural style and buildings of a period, but we also know by now that a style, such as the Gothic or the Baroque—embodied in buildings such as Chartres or St. Peter's—is an index to far more than the labor available in a given time and the ability to carve stones or work in plaster. These styles and buildings are, finally, the reflection in stone and space of a people's most fundamental values: their basic sense of themselves and the world they live in. What is true of a cathedral or a palace is likely to be true of a

[1] Francis Fergusson, *The Idea of a Theater* (Princeton, 1949), p. 2.

[2] *The Idea of a Theater,* p. 1.

theater, which, at least at some times, has focused man's sense of himself and his world as finely as his churches or his civic buildings. As the drama of a great age tells us as much about that culture as its theology and its laws, so its theaters tell us as much as do its cathedrals and palaces.

Description of the physical theater (the size of the theater, the location of the stage, the costuming, machinery, and sets) has been the province of theater historians. They have tended to give us objective measurements in feet and inches and factual descriptions of the outstanding features of various theaters. Most often they have treated the change in theaters over a period of time and the development of new theatrical arrangements as evolutionary processes driven along by social events and technological advances. For example, the large indoor theaters built in the eighteenth and nineteenth centuries might be described as the result of improved engineering skill which allowed builders to span greater spaces without supporting pillars, and of an increase in the wealth and size of the middle class, which resulted in an increase in the number of people who would pay to go to the theater because they had leisure time for culture or because they wished to advertise their new prosperity in public.

As a result of the patient researches of theater historians, however, it has become apparent that each age and culture builds a particular *type* of theater, the external and decorative elements of which it may modify a great deal while leaving the basic form untouched. Consider for a moment the theater of classical Greece, where the plays of Aeschylus, Sophocles, and Euripides were performed. It was an open theater built along an axis. At one end, on seats going up the hillside, the population of the city was seated. Directly in front of them, and partly within the arms formed by the seats, was the circular orchestra or dancing floor, where the chorus of some twelve dancers chanted their odes and moved in intricate but orderly dances. This chorus was bewildered by trouble, usually incapable of direct action, and its members voiced the most conservative opinions about the actions which took place on the low stage directly before them. Here on this stage—we know little about its details—stood the two or three actors, the *doers.* Their costumes made them larger than life size, as befitted the heroes who met and challenged the mysterious powers, the will of Zeus and the other gods, which resided in the great blue sky which arched over the entire theater and formed the permanent backdrop for an Agamemnon, an Oedipus, or a Phaedra. From this mystery came curses on great houses, plagues on great cities, and frightening oracles for great men. But these terrors were met at the stage by great men who acted, suffered, and persevered until at last the mystery was clarified, the weight of ignorance was lifted, and the gods themselves, on some occasions, were forced to materialize on the stage and explain themselves. As the heroes by their pride and pain and loss gradually penetrated the mystery, the chorus behind them absorbed the new knowledge, embodied it in odes, and transmitted it by way of language and dance back to the audience which, always visible, was the human backdrop, the body of society, at the end of the theater opposite the great sky.

To move from the Greek to the modern theater is to move from a vast lighted space organized along a line to a small, isolated area located in the midst of an infinitely extended darkness. At the front of the covered auditorium, elevated above the seats, is a rectangular opening, the proscenium arch, varying in size from theater to theater. The opening in the arch is covered with a curtain while the auditorium is filling and the house lights are on. When the audience has been seated, a switch is thrown, the house lights go out, and the audience has been obliterated. There no longer is a community present, as there was in the Greek and Elizabethan theaters, where the assembled citizens were a passive but very real part of the theatrical symbolism. The curtain rises, the stage lights go on, and before us is our theater: an illuminated box with a few objects in it, floating in a darkness which extends to infinity in every direction. Out of this darkness and into the spotlights come a few actors to speak and struggle for a brief time and then retire, or be carried, back into the darkness out of which they came. The business transacted, the curtain falls and the theater empties.

In the past hundred years this basic theater has been modified in many ways. Projecting platforms have been thrown forward of the arch into the audience, the physical arch has been removed and the entire stage has been made into a circle in the center of the audience, actors have entered and excited through the auditorium in an attempt to extend the stage to the entire theater. Each of these changes has been an attempt to reach the audience, to bring the community back into the theater, but each has failed, and the actor remains isolated in the small area defined for a brief time by the stage lights. The changes do modify the symbolic values of theater in some ways: so long as the actors remain behind the proscenium arch, in that room with the fourth wall removed created by the box set, there are definite boundaries to their situation, their world is small but very solid; once they move onto a platform in the center of the audience with their acting area defined only by spotlights, their space becomes more vague, the surrounding darkness presses closer and menaces the area of light more constantly.

This theater is well known to all of us, so well known that we have lost all sense of its strangeness and ceased to wonder, as with most familiar things, about what it suggests. But here in this arrangement of light, space, and actors is focused a basic sense of the universe and man's position in it which has been shared for some time now by men who otherwise hold violently opposite views. Obviously the existentialist playwright, a Sartre or a Camus, finds himself very much at home in a theater which states by its very arrangements that man with all his "absurd" longings for meaning and validation by some transcendent power is, in fact, isolated in an empty and meaningless universe where he must carve out his own justification and even his own being by a series of acts. But can a religious playwright adjust himself to such a bleak image of time and space? Apparently he cannot if he wishes to show a world in which some certain metaphysical order exists outside man and fills that darkness beyond the narrow confines of the illuminated stage. T. S. Eliot's attempts to dramatize visions and bring spirits into the theater are a history of the awkwardness and frustration inevitable in any attempt to say in our theater what that theater seems designed to deny. But there are religious views, perhaps more common in our times than simple piety, which see the age of miracles as past and regard the life of the spirit as one of constant anxiety and a struggle to maintain a faith which flickers intermittently in a universe which never answers it unequivocally. Religious views of this kind—and by "religion" I mean here all beliefs in some metaphysical power—have found our theater well suited to their sense of the human condition. Robert Bolt in his *Man for All Seasons* and John Osborne in his *Luther* have, for example, recently presented men of powerful religious convictions, Thomas More and Martin Luther, whose sense that they were in touch with and acting in the name of some divine power derived much of its tragic intensity from the great darkness surrounding those stages where they were forced, unsupported, to defy mighty princes and great states. Whatever certainty they found came only from their own hearts. If the same theater and the basic world view it manifests can contain approaches to life as widely separated as existentialism and Christian humanism, it can without difficulty also contain Freudian psychology and conventional morality, explanations of life based on Marxian economic analysis and those based on the meaninglessness of money and possessions, and the host of other rational theories which have been advanced in plays as explanations of and solutions to the basic human condition posited by the form of our theater.

So far we have looked at only the larger dimensions of the modern theater, but we need now to take a closer look at the stage, for if this small illuminated island lost in the vastness of space is our acting ground, what is placed on this stage is of crucial importance. It will represent the substance of the world. We can begin again by a comparison with the Greek and Elizabethan stages. The Greek actor at the Theater of Dionysus in Athens acted, most frequently, in front of a stage house with pillars and portals which represented the palace of the rulers of the city or a temple of its gods. The ground in front of the stage, the dancing floor, thus became the city square, where the frightened chorus, perhaps the elders of the city, assembled to appeal to their rulers, the princes and the gods. In the center of the orchestra was an altar for sacrifices to the gods. Behind the stage house was the sky and the landscape from which the gods might appear at any time, lowered onto the stage by a machine or, less spectacularly, walking on to mingle with the actors. Thus most actions in the Greek theater took place in the context of the principal symbols, the ultimate foundations, of the Athenian world—the social and the heavenly order, the city, the palace, the temple, the abode of the mysterious gods.

Something of the same kind of symbolism was built into the Elizabethan stage. The canopy over the stage was gorgeously painted on the underside to represent the order of the heavenly bodies, a trap in the floor led to an area below the stage known as the cellarage or hell. The area at the back of the stage was splendidly decorated and could represent, with its upper balconies, the palace of a king or his throne room, the walls of a city or the house of a citizen. One writer has argued that the entire acting area was so constructed that it symbolized simultaneously "a castle, a throne, a city gate, and an altar. It was a symbol of social order and of divine order—of the real ties between man and king, between heaven and earth."[3] If this is so, no matter how much the actions and speeches of the characters might question the meaning and order of life, these solid symbols would stand to remind the audience of the unchanging social and religious order which their theater was built to affirm.

Our theater, however, has no such built-in symbols. At the back of the stage there is only a blank wall or a cyclorama. It is left to our authors and stage designers to fill the space and mark the boundaries of the stage

[3] George R. Kernodle, "The Open Stage: Elizabethan or Existentialist?" *Shakespeare Survey,* 12 (1959), 3.

in any way they wish, and they have done this in some very strange ways; indeed one might even say that each of the dramatic styles mentioned earlier—realism, expressionism, symbolism, epic theater, theater of the absurd—has given us a different kind of setting; but in general we can distinguish two major styles, again realism and expressionism, and trace a general trend in our theater from one to the other—though both have existed side by side from the beginning of the modern theater.

Realism, like all other styles, has had its excesses: real forests planted in tubs to provide the actors with living trees to climb, entire houses complete with brick chimneys constructed by carpenters and masons, and—summit of paradox!—gauzy curtains hung over the stage to provide a "realistic illusion" of such places as the forest outside Athens where the elves and fairies dance in *A Midsummer Night's Dream.* But the characteristic set of realism has been more modest and more sensible. It has been most often an interior set, such as that in Ibsen's *Ghosts* or Strindberg's *The Father,* with painted flats to suggest side walls in perspective, doors and windows that open and close, and the type of furnishings which would be found in a room of the same kind outside the theater. When the realistic set tries to reflect the outdoors, it offers, by means of paint and objects, the same sense of familiar reality. If at the edges of the realistic stage we see a most unsettling cosmic and temporal darkness, inside we see a most ordinary and familiar world of tables, chairs, rugs, bushes and trees. And the actors who move within this set increase our sense of familiarity by wearing clothes such as we wear, speaking not in blank verse but in the kind of prose we think we might hear on the street, and revealing motives very like those we expect in ordinary life.

When this realistic set first began to appear in the modern theater, around 1870, it was a great relief from the painted sets of Swiss chalets and far-away castles in Spain which had been (and still are) the staple of the popular romantic drama and opera. The exotic Bulgarian mountains and village in which *Arms and the Man* is set are a spoof of this romantic tradition, and as Shaw's play proceeds it becomes clear that the setting of moonlight and balconies is as unrealistic as are the attitudes toward life held by the figures from musical comedy with whom Shaw peoples his play. Only Bluntschli, the hard-headed Swiss soldier of fortune and hotel-keeper, is out of place in this operatic world. His solid, realistic approach to personal problems, his plain language which cuts through pretense, and his common sense belong, properly, in the new realistic sets where the realism of the stage setting signaled a realistic approach to life and a concern not with romance but with actual social problems. Even today the realistic set is thought to stand for a solid, sensible, down-to-earth treatment of life, and dramatists are praised for their "realism."

No doubt some dramatists do use realistic sets simply as appropriate places in which to locate their plays about the ordinary lives of ordinary people, but the great masters of the realistic style—Ibsen, Chekov, Strindberg, Shaw—used their sets, which appear to have been assembled at random out of the prop room to imitate day-to-day reality, as symbolic forms, carefully chosen and arranged to define the material world in which the character must live and through which they must struggle to achieve their ends. Some sense of this can be gained by noting the extreme care with which Ibsen creates and places on his stage such ordinary objects as stoves, pictures, bric-a-brac shelves, and tables. He is not merely constructing a typical Norwegian room in an upper middle-class home of the late nineteenth century—any property-room man could do this. He is arranging his set to symbolize the social and material world in which his characters are so trapped and deadened. Overstuffed chairs which swallow up the character who sits in them, heavy draperies which blot the outside light, furniture which in its very weight and richness denies the existence of the spirit, and in its cluttered placement on the stage constantly interrupts the free movement of the characters who try to stride directly and purposefully through it. The movement of Ibsen's characters has been described as an attempted dance "the opening steps of which are constantly being broken off and replaced by something else"[4] as the character encounters some solid object such as a table, a bookcase, a paper, a photograph album, an armchair, or a stove. This happens constantly in Ibsen's plays, and can be seen to advantage in *Ghosts,* where the heavy, dark rooms of the Alving house are but the most solid manifestation of the social and material facts, the realities, which everywhere impede Mrs. Alving in her "dance" toward truth and the "joy of life." Just as the furniture impedes her free physical movements on stage, so those other more sinister realities—the smoke of Oswald's pipe, his taste for liquor, Engstrand's carlessness with matches, the pressures of society for conformity, and, finally, the inherited syphilis—impede her efforts to be done with the Alving inheritance and the ghosts of old ideas and old crimes. Ibsen was fascinated with the way in which social and material realities, realized by his set, channel

[4] Daniel Haakonsen, "Ibsen the Realist," in *Discussions of Henrik Ibsen,* ed. J. W. McFarlane (Boston, 1962), p. 71.

and thwart the human spirit with what very nearly amounts to malevolence, and his realistic set is always a representation of the social and material prison in which the free spirit struggles. Chekov, another master of the realistic style, was peculiarly interested in the indifference of the material world to men and their clownish clumsiness in trying to deal with it. *The Cherry Orchard* opens in a realistic Russian room, and within the first five minutes of the play two of the characters demonstate again and again their inability to deal with the simplest facts of reality: one falls asleep over a book and fails to meet a train he had sat up purposely to meet; another enters with a vase of flowers, which he drops, and bumps into a chair—all this in new boots which he can't keep from squeaking. Throughout the play the characters show in a variety of ways their utter helplessness in dealing with the solid facts of life—with the furniture, frost, gravity, time, and death. In the end all that they have valued, all that is focused in the delicate, fragile cherry orchard, goes down before the indifferent processes of nature, just as their shins are broken by indifferent tables and their backsides by indifferent floors.

Once it is understood that the realistic set, and the realistic style in general, has been used to symbolize the solidity of the material and social worlds in which modern man is isolated, the way is clear to understand in still another way the oneness of the modern theater. While realism remains the dominant style, from the time of Ibsen to the present, there have been a great many experiments in other directions, and frequently an author will fluctuate from style to style, as Strindberg did. In general, these experiments rejected realism's basic tenet that the stage should be set to look like the familiar face of the everyday world, that the characters should speak a prose something like that spoken on the streets, and that their motives and actions should be much like those we normally think we see daily. But a large number of playwrights have constructed their plays on the premise that the function of drama, or any other art, is not to hold the mirror up to objective nature, but rather to provide an "image" of the world, to show it as it appears to our imagination rather than to our senses. For example, a realistic playwright who wished to show the inability of human beings to communicate with one another would create a group of characters moving around a conventional drawing room and talking in a normal way; but as they moved toward one another the furniture would get in their way, as they talked their speech would trail away in nervousness or ineptitude, they would be unable to find appropriate words, and they would express incredulity or fail to understand what another said. The result of their failure to communicate directly would be that the unions—love affairs, business agreements, marriages, friendships—which they had hoped to achieve would trail away into nothing, like their words and gestures.

An expressionistic playwright might go to work directly to express the same theme. He might have his characters pour out spates of nonsense, words without meaning, while at the same time they maintained grammatical form and looked as if they understood the nonsense uttered by others and expected their own to be understood. He might fill the stage with empty chairs, as Ionesco does, and have the characters babble on thinking they are talking to real people sitting in them. As a climax Ionesco has a dumb and illiterate orator deliver some "great" message to these same empty chairs. Writing of this latter kind has had many names, but it can most simply be called expressionism, the style in which the artist dispenses with probability in order to express directly his sense of life in images. Poetry is the most familiar form of expressionism, and all expressionistic drama is in some sense an extension of poetry, depending as it does on visual metaphors to establish its meaning. Man ceases to be *like* some strange monster and is actually presented as a rhinoceros or a bug; life ceases to be *like* a wearying circle and is presented as an endless bicycle race in which characters peddle faster and faster to win prizes which are never awarded.

Expressionism existed in the early years of the modern theater with the symbolic plays of Ibsen, the "dream plays" of Strindberg, and the strange subjective plays of Maeterlinck; but since about 1920 it has become much more prominent. Pirandello, Cocteau, O'Neill, and the postwar German expressionists such as Brecht were but the beginnings of a tide that has run ever more strongly down to the plays of Beckett, Albee, Ionesco, Genet, Arrabal, and many others who write for the theater of the absurd. Even the realistic drama has been strongly influenced by expressionism, and the plays of such realists as Shaw, Sartre, Miller, and Williams have been affected. Expressionism has, in fact, been so powerful that many have argued that we have not one theater but two: the theater of realism, which was dominant in the years 1870–1920, and the expressionistic or absurd theater, from about 1920 to the present. The fact that the physical theater with its symbolic arrangement of the world has not changed argues strongly against such a divison, but it can be demonstrated in another way that our expressionistic drama is but an intensified, a more openly poetic, form of the realistic drama which preceded and still acccompanies it.

Six Characters in Search of an Author is, in my opinion, the pivotal play in the modern theater. It reveals in the starkest terms possible the meaning of the realistic drama of Ibsen, Strindberg, and Chekov which leads into it and the theater of the absurd which leads out of it. The earlier realistic plays depict man as caught in an alien and hostile environment with which he struggles to achieve his peculiarly human aims with only limited success. Pirandello picked up and intensified this theme, but he perceived that the full meaning of this "human condition" could best be dramatized by showing man as trapped in the theater itself. Given the premises stated by the modern theater, that the world which appears within the illuminated box has meaning only in its own terms, that it is not backed up by metaphysical realities existing outside and beyond it, it follows that the lives of men and the events of history have a stagelike or theatrical quality. We are but actors for a brief time on the stage of the world, and our actions and creations endure for only a moment and pass on into history, just as theater sets go to property rooms and plays into anthologies or oblivion. Men are no more than characters in a play, or not even so much, since characters are at least permanently whatever they are, while real men are forever changing. Yet in this world which resembles a theater men struggle desperately to express themselves, to find for themselves a play (or a life) which will reveal their true natures adequately and give their lives a satisfactory shape, as a skillful playwright does his plot. But where the heroes of the earlier realistic drama sought to achieve some such realistic aim as to be rid of the ghosts of old ideas or to save a cherry orchard, Pirandello goes to the root of things and shows his heroes *trying to be in a play*. And where the earlier heroes found their efforts thwarted by reality, by the nature of things represented by the solid, realistic set, Pirandello's heroes find themselves thwarted by the theater of realism. If Epihodov in *The Cherry Orchard* cannot cross a room without bumping into a table, or Mrs. Alving in *Ghosts* finds herself so trammeled by the demands of society that she can act only in certain accepted ways, the characters of Pirandello's play discover that the realistic theater interferes with and finally prohibits any expression of what they conceive to be their full reality, their true nature. For the step-daughter the presence of a yellow couch in the room where she was nearly seduced is essential, and for the father it is absolutely necessary that he be given time to explain his very complex motives; but the prop room in the theater has only a green couch, and the requirement that the plot continue to move does not allow the father time to explain himself. At every turn the "realism" of the theater denies the "reality" of the characters.

Pirandello has stated in expressionistic terms the same conflict between *realism* and *reality* which Ibsen, Chekov, and Strindberg stated in realistic terms. In so doing, he clarified the meaning of the realistic plays and showed the way to a host of later expressionistic plays in which reality is presented as some bizarre form of prison with man at once a heroic and a ludicrous struggler. It may seem a very long way from a realistic play like *Ghosts* to an expressionistic play like *The Ghost Sonata,* but the strange room in Strindberg's play with its mummy, its death screen, its cook who steals all the goodness out of the broth, and the ink pot which always spills is the same place as that room where Mrs. Alving is locked with her hopelessly insane son. And the flowering hyacinth in the conservatory is but a visual expression of the same transcendent hope which drives Mrs. Alving and her son Oswald toward the light and "joy of life." The difference between the two plays is that in the expressionistic *Ghost Sonata* the situation is expressed through a variety of unusual and bizarre stage images which combine to suggest the grotesque and killing restraints society and life impose on man, while in *Ghosts* the terror of the human condition is perhaps blurred in one way and heightened in another, by being presented in the familiar surroundings of the bourgeois parlor where everything seems so normal and natural.

While each modern set may reflect reality from a particular vantage point, they all seem to say that man finds the material universe they represent to be antagonistic to his transcendent hopes and the aspirations of his spirit. In other words, where man is sustained and his social world substantiated by the great symbols of the Greek and Elizabethan stages, man on the modern stage finds himself hemmed in and opposed by the symbols of ours. The sense of entrapment in society and nature which the sets and arrangement of our theater express is, of course, a focused form of a general sense of entrapment in nature and time which has grown steadily in Western culture in the nineteenth and twentieth centuries. There is no need to recapitulate the history of thought since the Romantic revolution, but reference to a few of the leading ideas will serve to make the point that our theater stands as close to the center of our culture as the Greek and Elizabethan theaters apparently did to theirs.

Once a faith in a supernatural order weakened under the pressure of scientific rationalism, and the belief in an established hierarchical society began to break up under the attack of democratic revolutions and the doctine of absolute equality, individual man was freed to face nature, society, and himself, and to make them into what he wanted them to be. Or so it seemed. Yet each great discovery of the free, inquiring mind, while it promised control over the accidents of nature and history, turned out, paradoxically, to show more clearly the isolation of man in time and nature. Darwin's great statement on the origin, differentiation, and evolution of the species cut man adrift from his metaphysical origins and placed him in a world where survival belongs to the strong, the ruthless, and the biologically lucky; not to the moral and the just. Marx's investigations of society revealed economic man, the producer and the buyer of goods and services, who bands together with other men only for his own economic advantage and who is willy-nilly caught in a historical movement which pits the have-nots against the haves. Freud's explorations of the mind seemed to extend nature's tyranny over man inward, making him the very nearly helpless victim of unconscious drives and libidinal forces, an automaton dancing to a tune called by internal forces, or a compulsive neurotic twisting into strange shapes in the attempt to repress powers he is not even aware of repressing. Physical science broke up the familiar face of creative nature, which its traditional intimations of some regenerative force, into electrical quantities which can only be measured mathematically. The last familiar markers disappeared when the theory of relativity told us that speed and direction existed only in relation to where we stood.

All these discoveries can be viewed optimistically, of course, and were so viewed by their discoverers, as demonstrations of the power of the human mind to uncover the truth of things and thus lay the grounds for some understanding of the world and life. To believe in this way is to believe in Progress. But it is possible to believe in the necessity of knowing these hard facts and at the same time to recognize that each of them is frightening because it imprisons us in a nature which limits and denies those essential qualities which we feel to be uniquely human: in theological terms, our souls; in humanistic terms, our true natures as men. If we are no more than strugglers for survival adapting to a constantly changing environment; exploiters or exploited caught up in a predetermined class struggle for control of the means of production; walking instruments of inescapable psychological forces, chemical reactions, and social conditioning; if we are all these in a universe we cannot even see truly, where there are no absolute directions or movements, how are we to validate our consciousness, our suffering, our sense of dignity, our demand that life have meaning, our ability to look at all the forces which control us and still withdraw into some area peculiarly ourselves?

For some, these last are simply illusions, fostered by outmoded ways of thinking. For them, the sooner man accepts himself as an object moved about by an interaction of forces and natural laws, the better. But our dramatists have never shared this view. The modern theater has not denied the existence of the deterministic and morally irresponsible universe; rather it has accepted it and embodied it in the construction of its stage, in its sets, and in its plays, where the standard plot shows the entrapment of man in history, society, economics, psychology, and in some form of environment. A history of the modern drama could be written using scenes of entrapment ranging from Old Firs locked in the dying house of *The Cherry Orchard,* or the captain in *The Father* sitting still while his old nurse slips the strait jacket on him, to Mother Courage harnessed to her wagon and Blanche du Bois in *Streetcar Named Desire* trying desperately to call an unknown number for help, while Stanley Kowalski stands grinning in his red pajamas, blocking the door. But two scenes will make the point.

The first is the concluding scene of *Ghosts.* Throughout the play Mrs. Alving and her son Oswald have struggled to free themselves from the gray, dim world forced on them by society, nature, and heredity. Using the play's chief symbols, we could say they have struggled to escape from the darkness into the truth of light. But they thought, like the great rebels and formulators of truth in the nineteenth century, that light and truth would bring "joy of life." When Mrs. Alving rejects the demands of society that unpleasant truths be hidden under a cover of well-seeming, and tells her son that his sickness and the drunken debauchery of his father were the results of heredity and an unfavorable environment, not of moral failing, she breaks into the world of truth. But the truth proves unendurable. Oswald, who is in the last stages of syphilis, goes insane before her eyes, his fear unassuaged and his madness no less terrible for being not his own fault. The son and mother stand at last in the full light of truth, and as the sun rises, shining on the icy peaks far above the dark valley in which they live, the insane son's cry, "Mother, give me the sun," distills modern man's sense of isolation and helplessness in the midst of alien nature. Clarity of vision reveals only the desperateness of the situation in which we long like children for light and heat which originate ninety million miles away to send only the dimmest emanations into our homes.

The other scene is from Lorca's *Blood Wedding,* in which the violent, uncontrollable power of blood and passion, represented by the horse, has destroyed an entire family and wasted a country. Her husband and son dead, a mother sits wondering how it can be that so small a thing as a knife, a mere piece of steel, can destroy so great a thing as a man:

> Neighbors: with a knife,
> with a little knife,
> on their appointed day, between two and three,
> these two men killed each other for love.
> With a knife,
> with a tiny knife
> that barely fits the hand,
> but that slides in clear
> through the astonished flesh
> and stops at the place
> where trembles, enmeshed,
> the dark root of a scream.

There is no question in our theater that life is subject to objects so small as a knife in such strange places as "between two and three," but the peasant mother's astonishment that this is so is an astonishment that has kept our theater alive.

When William Butler Yeats first saw a performance of *Ghosts,* he remarked:

> All the characters seemed to be less than life-size; the stage, though it was but the little Royalty stage, seemed larger than I had ever seen it. Little whimpering puppets moved here and there in the middle of that great abyss. Why did they not speak with louder voices or move with freer gestures? What was it that weighed upon their souls perpetually? Certainly they were all in prison, and yet there was no prison.[5]

Yeats is being disingenuous here, for he knew the prison very well—his poetry is a record of a heroic struggle with it—and he knew that it is as real as the stage says it is. But he was right in one way about the figures in this prison: they are small and ineffective. It is a commonplace of criticism that our dramatic heroes are but shadows of those of previous days. The figures of Greek tragedy were demigods, titans, founders of kingdoms, and rulers of great cities. When they, or the kings and queens of Elizabethan drama, rose or fell, kingdoms rose or fell with them, and all mankind shared in their fortunes. But the heroes of modern tragedy are neither so great nor so powerful in the scheme of things. They are likely to be a group of ineffective, middle-class Russians in some isolated country house, a salesman who tries to sell himself in a territory where no one wants to buy, two tramps waiting on a bare stage, an old woman trying to pull a battered wagon about, or two old people who think they have something of importance to say to the world but don't really know what it is they have to say. Where the fate of kingdoms turned on the actions of earlier heroes, much less is involved in the actions of our heroes: they try to save a cherry orchard, pay for a house and raise their children, wait for someone who will probably never come, or just find someone who will be kind to them.

As their statures and their aims are diminished, so are their voices. Playwrights are frequently exhorted by modern critics to give their characters poetry, and some of our dramatists have tried, without much success. A type of realistic prose, a heightened version of the speech of everyday life, seems to be the most congenial form of speech for our heroes. One of the principal themes of modern drama has been the inability of language to convey the full meanings desired by the speakers, and this theme has been carried in large part by the characters' struggle with the flat, realistic prose they most often speak. I am not arguing that Ibsen or Chekov could have written poetry of a quality equal to Shakespeare's had they wished to do so; rather I am suggesting that these and other dramatists of our theater were led away from attempting dramatic poetry of the older variety by the nature of their theme, the isolation of man in a universe where all his environment, including the very language he speaks, thwarts his efforts to express what he feels to be his essential self. Behind the mumbling, inarticulate dying voices of Chekov's characters there are hints of passion and depth of feeling something like Romeo's or Hamlet's, but these feelings are first qualified and lose their force in the mind and are then finally dissipated in the awkward, flat phrases which are the only language available to modern man. The failure of language to express the fullness of self which is implicit in the realistic drama becomes explicit in the expressionistic drama— *The Chairs, Zoo Story*—where we are shown characters who cannot convey any sense of their own reality by words, who babble on in long speeches which sound very serious but mean nothing, who spout open nonsense, or who stand mutely on stage.

But with all the limitations which are imposed on him on the modern stage, man has not given up the struggle on that stage and accepted the role of a machine moved in a predictable manner by a variety of unchanging forces, which his world tries to force on him. No matter how close the darkness may creep toward him—and it has come very close in the most recent plays—he continues to occupy a place in the center of the stage and at least one light still shines on him. His desires remain spacious. Unsupported by any visible metaphysical order, thwarted by society, at odds with external nature and his own being, he still

[5] W. B. Yeats, "The Irish Dramatic Movement," in *Plays and Controversies* (New York, 1924), p. 122.

continues to act and to try to tear from the world those things without which he feels he cannot live as a human being: his freedom, his dignity, his reality. In this persistent effort he becomes one with the great strugglers of the older drama who moved toward these same goals, but his chances of success are greatly diminished. Not only is his environment more hostile, but the fact that he is a salesman or a tattered tramp, whose voice no longer fills the theater and batters at the world which denies him, suggests that his chances of success are far less than those of older heroes, and that his success or failure will not disturb the order of things greatly.

Our theater does not underestimate the dangers of the universe in which man lives, but it has not lost faith in man either. When pressed to the extremes, in the bleak place where almost everything has lost its meaning, man on the modern stage at least still waits:

> What are we doing here, *that* is the question. And we are blessed in this, that we happen to know the answer. Yes, in this immense confusion one thing alone is clear. We are waiting for Godot to come—

This waiting is as likely to be the height of foolishness as the absolute of virtue: an ambiguity which haunts most actions on the modern stage. But man, no matter how tattered and inarticulate, is still *there;* he has not yet walked off and left the stage to darkness.

Which Theater Is the Absurd One?

Edward Albee (1928–)

Abandoned at an early age by his natural parents, Edward Albee was adopted by Reed A. Albee, the wealthy owner of the Keith-Albee chain of vaudeville theaters. He attended the Lawrenceville School, Valley Forge Military Academy, and the Choate School, graduating from the latter in 1946. He then attended Trinity College, Hartford, for two years. After leaving college he worked at a number of jobs for ten years, among them office boy for an advertising firm, record salesman at Bloomingdale's, counterman at a luncheonette, and Western Union messenger. He had begun to write fiction while at Choate, and in 1953 Thornton Wilder encouraged him to try his hand at drama. His first play, *The Zoo Story* (1959), was followed among others by *The Sandbox* (1959), *The American Dream* (1961), *Who's Afraid of Virginia Woolf?* (1961), *Tiny Alice* (1964), *A Delicate Balance* (1966), which won the Pulitzer Prize, *All Over* (1971), and *Seascape* (1975).

A theater person of my acquaintance—a man whose judgment must be respected, though more for the infallibility of his intuition than for his reasoning—remarked just the other week, "The Theater of the Absurd has had it; it's on its way out; it's through."

Now this, on the surface of it, seems to be a pretty funny attitude to be taking toward a theater movement which has, only in the past couple of years, been impressing itself on the American public consciousness. Or is it? Must we judge that a theater of such plays as Samuel Beckett's *Krapp's Last Tape,* Jean Genet's *The Balcony* (both long, long runners off-Broadway) and Eugène Ionesco's *Rhinoceros*—which, albeit in a hoked-up production, had a substantial season *on* Broadway—has been judged by the theater public and found wanting?

And shall we have to assume that The Theatre of the Absurd Repertory Company, currently [in 1962] playing at New York's Off-Broadway Cherry Lane

Theatre—presenting works by Beckett, Ionesco, Genet, Arrabal, Jack Richardson, Kenneth Koch, and myself—being the first such collective representation of the movement in the United States, is also a kind of farewell to the movement? For that matter, just what *is* The Theater of the Absurd?

Well, let me come at it obliquely. When I was told, about a year ago, that I was considered a member in good standing of The Theater of the Absurd I was deeply offended. I was deeply offended because I had never heard the term before and I immediately assumed that it applied to the theater uptown—Broadway.

What (I was reasoning to myself) could be more absurd than a theater in which the esthetic criterion is something like this: A "good" play is one which makes money; a "bad" play (in the sense of "Naughty! Naughty!" I guess) is one which does not; a theater in which performers have plays rewritten to correspond to the public relations image of themselves; a theater in which playwrights are encouraged (what a funny word!) to think of themselves as little cogs in a great big wheel; a theater in which imitation has given way to imitation of imitation; a theater in which London "hits" are, willy-nilly, in a kind of reverse of chauvinism, greeted in a manner not unlike a colony's obeisance to the Crown; a theater in which real-estate owners and theater-party managements predetermine the success of unknown quantities; a theater in which everybody scratches and bites for billing as though it meant access to the last bomb shelter on earth; a theater in which, in a given season, there was not a single performance of a play by Beckett, Brecht, Chekhov, Genet, Ibsen, O'Casey, Pirandello, Shaw, Strindberg—or Shakespeare? What, indeed, I thought, could be more absurd than that? (My conclusions . . . obviously.)

For it emerged that The Theater of the Absurd, aside from being the title of an excellent book by Martin Esslin on what is loosely called the avant-garde theater, was a somewhat less than fortunate catch-all phrase to describe the philosophical attitudes and theater methods of a number of Europe's finest and most adventurous playwrights and their followers.

I was less offended, but still a little dubious. Simply: I don't like labels; they can be facile and can lead to non-think on the part of the public. And unless it is understood that the playwrights of The Theater of the Absurd represent a group only in the sense that they seem to be doing something of the same thing in vaguely similar ways at approximately the same time—unless this is understood, then the labeling itself will be more absurd than the label.

Playwrights, by nature, are grouchy, withdrawn, envious, greedy, suspicious and, in general, quite nice people—and the majority of them wouldn't be caught dead in a colloquy remotely resembling the following:

> *Ionesco. (At a Left Bank café table, spying Beckett and Genet strolling past in animated conversation.)* Hey! Sam! Jean!
>
> *Genet.* Hey, it's Eugene! Sam, it's Eugene!
>
> *Beckett.* Well, I'll be damned. Hi there, Eugene boy.
>
> *Ionesco.* Sit down, kids.
>
> *Genet.* Sure thing.
>
> *Ionesco. (Rubbing his hands together.)* Well, what's new in The Theater of the Absurd?
>
> *Beckett.* Oh, less than a lot of people think. *(They all laugh.)*

Etc. No. Not very likely. Get a playwright alone sometime, get a few drinks in him, and maybe he'll be persuaded to sound off about his "intention" and the like—and hate himself for it the next day. But put a group of playwrights together in a room, and the conversation—if there is any—will, more likely than not, concern itself with sex, restaurants, and the movies.

Very briefly, then—and reluctantly, because I am a playwright and would much rather talk about sex, restaurants, and the movies—and stumblingly, because I do not pretend to understand it entirely, I will try to define The Theater of the Absurd. As I get it, The Theater of the Absurd is an absorption-in-art of certain existentialist and post-existentialist philosophical concepts having to do, in the main, with man's attempts to make sense for himself out of his senseless position in a world which makes no sense—which makes no sense because the moral, religious, political, and social structures man has erected to "illusion" himself have collapsed.

Albert Camus put it this way: "A world that can be explained by reasoning, however faulty, is a familiar world. But in a universe that is suddenly deprived of illusions and of light, man feels a stranger. His is an irremediable exile, because he is deprived of memories of a lost homeland as much as he lacks the hope of a promised land to come. This divorce between man and his life, the actor and his setting, truly constitutes the feeling of Absurdity."

And Eugène Ionesco says this: "Absurd is that which is devoid of purpose. . . . Cut off from his religious, metaphysical, and transcendental roots, man is lost; all his actions become senseless, absurd, useless."

And to sum up the movement, Martin Esslin writes, in his book *The Theatre of the Absurd:* "Ultimately, a phenomenon like The Theatre of the Absurd does not reflect despair or a return to dark irrational forces but expresses modern man's endeavor to come to terms with the world in which he lives. It attempts to make him face up to the human condition as it really is, to free him from illusions that are bound to cause constant maladjustment and disappointment. . . . For the dignity of man lies in his ability to face reality in all its senselessness; to accept it freely, without fear, without illusions—and to laugh at it."

Amen.

(And while we're on the subject of Amen, one wearies of the complaint that The Theater of the Absurd playwrights alone are having at God these days. The notion that God is dead, indifferent, or insane—a notion blasphemous, premature, or academic depending on your persuasion—while surely a tenet of some of the playwrights under discussion, is, it seems to me, of a piece with Mr. Tennessee Williams' description of the Deity, in *The Night of the Iguana,* as "a senile delinquent.")

So much for the attempt to define terms. Now, what of this theater? What of this theater in which, for example, a legless old couple live out their lives in twin ashcans, surfacing occasionally for food or conversation (Samuel Beckett's *Endgame*); in which a man is seduced, and rather easily, by a girl with three well-formed and functioning noses (Eugène Ionesco's *Jack, or The Submission*); in which, on the same stage, one group of Negro actors is playing at pretending to be Negro (Jean Genet's *The Blacks*)?

What of this theater? Is it, as it has been accused of being, obscure, sordid, destructive, anti-theater, perverse, and absurd (in the sense of foolish)? Or is it merely, as I have so often heard it put, that, "This sort of stuff is too depressing, too . . . too mixed-up; I go to the theater to relax and have a good time."

I would submit that it is this latter attitude—that the theater is a place to relax and have a good time—in conflict with the purpose of The Theater of the Absurd—which is to make a man face up to the human condition as it really is—that has produced all the brouhaha and the dissent. I would submit that The Theater of the Absurd, in the sense that it is truly the contemporary theater, facing as it does man's condition as it is, is the Realistic theater of our time; and that the supposed Realistic theater—the term used here to mean most of what is done on Broadway—in the sense that it panders to the public need for self-congratulation and reassurance and presents a false picture of ourselves to ourselves, is, with an occasional very lovely exception, really and truly The Theater of the Absurd.

And I would submit further that the health of a nation, a society, can be determined by the art it demands. We have insisted of television and our movies that they not have anything to do with anything, that they be our never-never land; and if we demand this same function of our live theater, what will be left of the visual-auditory arts—save the dance (in which nobody talks) and music (to which nobody listens)?

It has been my fortune, the past two or three years, to travel around a good deal, in pursuit of my career—Berlin, London, Buenos Aires, for example; and I have discovered a couple of interesting things. I have discovered that audiences in these and other major cities demand of their commercial theater—and get—a season of plays in which the froth and junk are the exception and not the rule. To take a case: in Berlin, in 1959, Adamov, Genet, Beckett, and Brecht (naturally) were playing the big houses; this past fall, Beckett again, Genet again, Pinter twice, etc. To take another case: in Buenos Aires there are over a hundred experimental theaters.

These plays cannot be put on in Berlin over the head of a protesting or an indifferent audience; these experimental theaters cannot exist in Buenos Aires without subscription. In the end—and it must always come down to this, no matter what other failings a theater may have—in the end a public will get what it deserves, and no better.

I have also discovered, in my wanderings, that young people throng to what is new and fresh in the theater. Happily, this holds true in the United States as well. At the various colleges I have gone to to speak I have found an eager, friendly, and knowledgeable audience; an audience which is as dismayed by the Broadway scene as any proselytizer for the avant-garde. I have found among young people an audience which is not so preconditioned by pap as to have cut off half its responses. (It is interesting to note, by the way, that if an Off-Broadway play has a substantial run, its audiences will begin young and grow older; as the run goes on, cloth coats give way to furs, walkers and subway riders to taxi-takers. Exactly the opposite is true on Broadway.)

The young, of course, are always questioning values, knocking the status quo about, considering shibboleths to see if they are pronounceable. In time, it is to be regretted, most of them—the kids—will settle down to their own version of the easy, the standard; but in the meanwhile . . . in the meanwhile they are a wonderful, alert, alive, accepting audience.

And I would go so far as to say that it is the responsibility of everyone who pretends any interest at all in the theater to get up off their six-ninety seats and find out what the theater is *really* about. For it is a lazy public which produces a slothful and irresponsible theater.

Now, I would suspect that my theater-friend with the infallible intuition is probably right when he suggests that The Theater of the Absurd (or the avant-garde theater, or whatever you want to call it) as it now stands is on its way out. Or at least is undergoing change. All living organisms undergo constant change. And while it is certain that the nature of this theater will remain constant, its forms, its methods—its devices, if you will—most necessarily will undergo mutation.

This theater has no intention of running downhill; and the younger playwrights will make use of the immediate past and mold it to their own needs. (Harold Pinter, for example, could not have written *The Caretaker* had Samuel Beckett not existed, but Pinter is, nonetheless, moving in his own direction.) And it is my guess that the theater in the United States will always hew more closely to the post-Ibsen/Chekhov tradition than does the theater in France, let us say. It is our nature as a country, a society. But we will experiment, and we will expect your attention.

For just as it is true that our response to color and form was forever altered once the impressionist painters put their minds to canvas, it is just as true that the playwrights of The Theater of the Absurd have forever altered our response to the theater.

And one more point: The avant-garde theater is fun; it is free-swinging, bold, iconoclastic, and often wildly, wildly funny. If you will approach it with childlike innocence—putting your standard responses aside, for they do not apply—if you will approach it on its own terms, I think you will be in for a liberating surprise. I think you may no longer be content with plays that you can't remember halfway down the block. You will not only be doing yourself some good, but you will be having a great time, to boot. And even though it occurs to me that such a fine combination must be sinful, I still recommend it.

Flat and Round Characters

E. M. Forster (1879–1970)

Edward Morgan Forster, the son of an architect, was born in London. His father died when he was young, and he was reared by his mother and paternal aunts. He was sent as a day boy to Tonbridge School, Kent, and afterwards to King's College, Cambridge. After leaving Cambridge Forster soon took up residence in Italy where he drafted his first two novels, *Where Angels Fear to Tread* (1905) and *A Room with A View* (1908). These novels have an Italian background, but in *The Longest Journey* (published in 1907, the year he returned to England) Forster dealt with his English experiences at Tonbridge and Cambridge. His first important success, *Howard's End,* appeared in 1910, providing a compelling image of contemporary threats to the nineteenth-century liberal imagination.

Forster had been writing short stories for some years, and *The Celestial Omnibus* (1911) collected the best of his early work. During the first World War Forster spent three years in Alexandria, while in 1912 and 1921 he visited India. These experiences led to his most famous novel, *A Passage to India* (1924), where the liberal imagination is found almost incapable of handling an alien culture. After *A Passage to India* Forster published no more major fiction; an early novel with a homosexual theme, *Maurice,* appeared posthumously in 1971. In 1927 Forster delivered the Clark Lectures at King's College, Cambridge, on the subject of the art of fiction. They were published the same year as *Aspects of the Novel* (the following selection is from that volume). In 1946 King's made Forster an honorary fellow, and he spent his remaining years in Cambridge. The work of his later years was composed mainly of lectures and essays.

We now in turn from transplantation to acclimatization. We have discussed whether people could be taken out of life and put into a book, and conversely whether they could come out of books and sit down in this room. The answer suggested was in the negative and led to a more vital question: can we, in daily life, understand each other? Today our problems are more academic. We are concerned with the characters in their relation to other aspects of the novel; to a plot, a moral, their fellow characters, atmosphere, etc. They will have to adapt themselves to other requirements of their creator.

It follows that we shall no longer expect them to coincide as a whole with daily life, only to parallel it. When we say that a character in Jane Austen, Miss Bates for instance, is "so like life" we mean that each bit of her coincides with a bit of life, but that she as a whole only parallels the chatty spinster we met at tea. Miss Bates is bound by a hundred threads to Highbury. We cannot tear her away without bringing her mother too, and Jane Fairfax and Frank Churchill, and the whole of Box Hill; whereas we could tear Moll Flanders away, at least for the purposes of experiment. A Jane Austen novel is more complicated than a Defoe, because the characters are inter-dependent, and there is the additional complication of a plot. The plot in *Emma* is not prominent and Miss Bates contributes little. Still it is there, she is connected with the principals, and the result is a closely woven fabric from which nothing can be removed. Miss Bates and Emma herself are like bushes in a shrubbery—not isolated trees like Moll—and anyone who has tried to thin out a shrubbery knows how wretched the bushes look if they are transplanted elsewhere, and how wretched is the look of the bushes that remain. In most books the characters cannot spread themselves. They must exercise a mutual restraint.

The novelist, we are beginning to see, has a very mixed lot of ingredients to handle. There is the story, with its time-sequence of "and then . . . and then . . ."; there are ninepins about whom he might tell the story, and tell a rattling good one, but no, he prefers to tell his story about human beings; he takes over the life by values as well as the life in time. The characters arrive when evoked, but full of the spirit of mutiny. For they have these numerous parallels with people like ourselves, they try to live their own lives and are consequently often engaged in treason against the main scheme of the book. They "run away," they "get out of hand": they are creations inside a creation, and often inharmonious towards it; if they are given complete freedom they kick the book to pieces, and if they are kept too sternly in check, they revenge themselves by dying, and destroy it by intestinal decay.

These trials beset the dramatist also, and he has yet another set of ingredients to cope with—the actors and actresses—and they appear to side sometimes with the characters they represent, sometimes with the play as a whole, and more often to be the mortal enemies of both. The weight they throw is incalculable, and how any work of art survives their arrival I do not understand. Concerned with a lower form of art, we need not worry—but, in passing, is it not extraordinary that plays on the stage are often better than they are in the study, and that the introduction of a bunch of rather ambitious and nervous men and women should add anything to our understanding of Shakespeare and Chekov?

No, the novelist has difficulties enough, and today we shall examine two of his devices for solving them—instinctive devices, for his methods when working are seldom the same as the methods we use when examining his work. The first device is the use of different kinds of characters. The second is connected with the point of view.

We may divide characters into flat and round. Flat characters were called "humorous" in the seventeenth century, and are sometimes called types, and sometimes caricatures. In their purest form, they are constructed round a single idea or quality: when there is more than one factor in them, we get the beginning of the curve towards the round. The really flat character can be expressed in one sentence such as "I never will desert Mr. Micawber." There is Mrs. Micawber—she says she won't desert Mr. Micawber, she doesn't, and there she is. Or: "I must conceal, even by subterfuges, the poverty of my master's house." There is Caleb Balderstone in *The Bride of Lammermoor.* He does not use the actual phrase, but it completely describes him; he has no existence outside it, no pleasures, none of the private lusts and aches that must complicate the most consistent of servitors. Whatever he does, wherever he goes, whatever lies he tells or plates he breaks, it is to conceal the poverty of his master's house. It is not his *idée fixe,* because there is nothing in him into which the idea can be fixed. He is the idea, and such life as he possesses radiates from its edges and from the scintillations it strikes when other elements in the novel impinge. Or take Proust. There are numerous flat characters in Proust, such as the Princess of Parma, or Legrandin. Each can be expressed in a single sentence, the Princess's sentence being, "I must be particularly careful to be kind." She does nothing except to be particularly careful, and those of the other characters who are more complex than herself easily see through the kindness, since it is only a by-product of the carefulness.

One great advantage of flat characters is that they are easily recognized whenever they come in—recognized by the reader's emotional eye, not by the visual eye, which merely notes the recurrence of a proper name. In Russian novels, where they so seldom occur, they would be a decided help. It is a convenience for an author when he can strike with his full force at once, and flat characters are very useful to him, since they never need reintroducing, never run away, have not to be watched for development, and provide their own atmosphere—little luminous disks of a pre-arranged size, pushed hither and thither like counters across the void or between the stars; most satisfactory.

A second advantage is that they are easily remembered by the reader afterwards. They remain in his mind as unalterable for the reason that they were not changed by circumstances; they moved through circumstances, which gives them in retrospect a comforting quality, and preserves them when the book that produced them may decay. The Countess in *Evan Harrington* furnishes a good little example here. Let us compare our memories of her with our memories of Becky Sharp. We do not remember what the Countess did or what she passed through. What is clear is her figure and the formula that surrounds it, namely, "Proud as we are of dear papa, we must conceal his memory." All her rich humour proceeds from this. She is a flat character. Becky is round. She, too, is on the make, but she cannot be summed up in a single phrase, and we remember her in connection with the great scenes through which she passed and as modified by those scenes—that is to say, we do not remember her so easily because she waxes and wanes and has facets like a human being. All of us, even the sophisticated, yearn for permanence, and to the unsophisticated permanence is the chief excuse for a work of art. We all want books to endure, to be refuges, and their inhabitants to be always the same, and flat characters tend to justify themselves on this account.

All the same, critics who have their eyes fixed severely upon daily life—as were our eyes last week—have very little patience with such renderings of human nature. Queen Victoria, they argue, cannot be summed up in a single sentence, so what excuse remains for Mrs. Micawber? One of our foremost writers, Mr. Norman Douglas, is a critic of this type, and the passage from him which I will quote puts the case against flat characters in a forcible fashion. The passage occurs in an open letter to D. H. Lawrence, with whom he is quarrelling: a doughty pair of combatants, the hardness of whose hitting makes the rest of us feel like a lot of ladies up in a pavilion. He complains that Lawrence, in a biography, has falsified the picture by employing "the novelist's touch," and he goes on to define what this is:

> It consists, I should say, in a failure to realize the complexities of the ordinary human mind; it selects for literary purposes two or three facets of a man or woman, generally the most spectacular, and therefore useful ingredients of their character and disregards all the others. Whatever fails to fit in with these specially chosen traits is eliminated—must be eliminated, for otherwise the description would not hold water. Such and such are the data: everything incompatible with those data has to go by the board. It follows that the novelist's touch argues, often logically, from a wrong premise: it takes what it likes and leaves the rest. The facets may be correct as far as they go but there are too few of them: what the author says may be true and yet by no means the truth. That is the novelist's touch. It falsifies life.

Well, the novelist's touch as thus defined is, of course, bad in biography, for no human being is simple. But in a novel it has its place: a novel that is at all complex often requires flat people as well as round, and the outcome of their collisions parallels life more accurately than Mr. Douglas implies. The case of Dickens is significant. Dickens' people are nearly all flat (Pip and David Copperfield attempt roundness, but so diffidently that they seem more like bubbles than solids). Nearly every one can be summed up in a sentence, and yet there is this wonderful feeling of human depth. Probably the immense vitality of Dickens causes his characters to vibrate a little, so that they borrow his life and appear to lead one of their own. It is a conjuring trick; at any moment we may look at Mr. Pickwick edgeways and find him no thicker than a gramophone record. But we never get the sideway view. Mr. Pickwick is far too adroit and well-trained. He always has the air of weighing something, and when he is put into the cupboard of the young ladies' school he seems as heavy as Falstaff in the buck-basket at Windsor. Part of the genius of Dickens is that he does use types and caricatures, people whom we recognize the instant they re-enter, and yet achieves effects that are not mechanical and a vision of humanity that is not shallow. Those who dislike Dickens have an excellent case. He ought to be bad. He is actually one of our big writers, and his immense success with types suggests that there may be more in flatness than the severer critics admit.

Or take H. G. Wells. With the possible exceptions of Kipps and the aunt in *Tono Bungay,* all Wells' characters are as flat as a photograph. But the photographs are agitated with such vigour that we forget their complexities lie on the surface and would disappear if it were scratched or curled up. A Wells character cannot indeed be summed up in a single phrase; he is tethered much more to observation, he does not create types. Nevertheless his people seldom pulsate by their own strength. It is the deft and powerful hands of their maker that shake them and trick the reader into a sense of depth. Good but imperfect novelists, like Wells and Dickens, are very clever at transmitting force. The part of their novel that is alive galvanizes the part that is not, and causes the characters to jump about and speak in a convincing way. They are quite different from the perfect novelist who touches all his material directly, who seems to pass the creative finger down every sentence and into every word. Richardson, Defoe, Jane Austen, are perfect in this particular way; their work may not be great but their hands are always upon it; there is not the tiny interval between the touching of the button and the sound of the bell which occurs in novels where the characters are not under direct control.

For we must admit that flat people are not in themselves as big achievements as round ones, and also that they are best when they are comic. A serious or tragic flat character is apt to be a bore. Each time he enters crying "Revenge!" or "My heart bleeds for humanity!" or whatever his formula is, our hearts sink. One of the romances of a popular contemporary writer is constructed round a Sussex farmer who says, "I'll plough up that bit of gorse." There is the farmer, there is the gorse; he says he'll plough it up, he does plough it up, but it is not like saying "I'll never desert Mr. Micawber," because we are so bored by his consistency that we do not care whether he succeeds with the gorse or fails. If his formula were analysed and connected up with the rest of human outfit, we should not be bored any longer, the formula would cease to be the man and become an obsession in the man; that is to say he would have turned from a flat farmer into a round one. It is only round people who are fit to perform tragically for any length of time and can move us to any feelings except humour and appropriateness.

So now let us desert these two-dimensional people, and by way of transition to the round, let us go to *Mansfield Park,* and look at Lady Bertram, sitting on her sofa with pug. Pug is flat, like most animals in fiction. He is once represented as straying into a rosebed in a cardboard kind of way, but that is all, and during most of the book his mistress seems to be cut out of the same simple material as her dog. Lady Bertram's formula is, "I am kindly, but must not be fatigued," and she functions out of it. But at the end there is a catastrophe. Her two daughters come to grief—to the worst grief known to Miss Austen's universe, far worse than the Napoleonic wars. Julia elopes; Maria, who is unhappily married, runs off with a lover. What is Lady Bertram's reaction? The sentence describing it is significant: "Lady Bertram did not think deeply, but, guided by Sir Thomas, she thought justly on all important points, and she saw therefore in all its enormity, what had happened, and neither endeavoured herself, nor required Fanny to advise her, to think little of guilt and infamy." These are strong words, and they used to worry me because I thought Jane Austen's moral sense was getting out of hand. She may, and of course does, deprecate guilt and infamy herself, and she duly causes all possible distress in the minds of Edmund and Fanny, but has she any right to agitate calm, consistent Lady Bertram? Is not it like giving pug three faces and setting him to guard the gates of Hell? Ought not her ladyship to remain on the sofa saying, "This is a dreadful and sadly exhausting business about Julia and Maria, but where is Fanny gone? I have dropped another stitch"?

I used to think this, through misunderstanding Jane Austen's method—exactly as Scott misunderstood it when he congratulated her for painting on a square of ivory. She is a miniaturist, but never two-dimensional. All her characters are round, or capable of rotundity. Even Miss Bates has a mind, even Elizabeth Eliot a heart, and Lady Bertram's moral fervour ceases to vex us when we realize this: the disk has suddenly extended and become a little globe. When the novel is closed, Lady Bertram goes back to the flat, it is true; the dominant impression she leaves can be summed up in a formula. But that is not how Jane Austen conceived her, and the freshness of her reappearances are due to this. Why do the characters in Jane Austen give us a slightly new pleasure each time they come in, as opposed to the merely repetitive pleasure that is caused by a character in Dickens? Why do they combine so well in a conversation, and draw one another out without seeming to do so, and never perform? The answer to this question can be put in several ways: that, unlike Dickens, she was a real artist, that she never stooped to caricature, etc. But the best reply is that her characters though smaller than his are more highly organized. They function all round, and even if her plot made greater demands on them than it does, they would still be adequate. Suppose that Louisa Musgrove had broken her neck on the Cobb. The description of her death would have been feeble and ladylike—physical violence is quite beyond Miss Austen's powers—but the survivors would have reacted properly as soon as the corpse was carried away, they would have brought into view new sides of their character, and though *Persuasion* would have been spoiled as a book, we should know more than we do about Captain Wentworth and Anne. All the Jane Austen characters are ready for an extended life, for a life which the scheme of her books seldom requires them to lead, and that is why they lead their actual lives so satisfactorily. Let us return to Lady Bertram and the crucial sentence. See how subtly it modulates from her formula into an area where the formula does not work. "Lady Bertram did not think deeply." Exactly: as per formula. "But guided by Sir Thomas she thought justly on all important points." Sir Thomas' guidance, which is part of the formula, remains, but it pushes her ladyship towards an independent and undesired morality. "She saw therefore in all its enormity what had happened." This is the moral fortissimo—very strong but carefully introduced. And then follows a most artful decrescendo, by means of negatives. "She neither endeavoured herself, nor required Fanny to advise her, to think little of guilt or infamy." The formula is reappearing, because as a rule she does try to minimize trouble, and does require Fanny to advise her how to do this; indeed Fanny has done nothing else for the last ten years. The words, though they are negatived, remind us of this, her normal state is again in view, and she has in a single sentence been inflated into a round character and collapsed back into a flat one. How Jane Austen can write! In a few words she has extended Lady Bertram, and by so doing she has increased the probability of the elopements of Maria and Julia. I say probability because the elopements belong to the domain of violent physical action, and here, as already indicated, Jane Austen is feeble and ladylike. Except in her school-girl novels, she cannot stage a crash. Everything violent has to take place "off"—Louisa's accident and Marianne Dashwood's putrid throat are the nearest exceptions—and consequently all the comments on the elopement must be sincere and convincing, otherwise we should doubt whether it occurred. Lady Bertram helps us to believe that her daughters have run away, and they have to run away, or there would be no apotheosis for Fanny. It is a little point, and a little sentence, yet it shows us how delicately a great novelist can modulate into the round.

All through her works we find these characters, apparently so simple and flat, never needing reintroduction and yet never out of their depth—Henry Tilney, Mr. Woodhouse, Charlotte Lucas. She may label her characters "Sense," "Pride," "Sensibility," "Prejudice," but they are not tethered to those qualities.

As for the round characters proper, they have already been defined by implication and no more need be said. All I need do is to give some examples of people in books who seem to me round so that the definition can be tested afterwards:

All the principal characters in *War and Peace,* all the Dostoevsky characters, and some of the Proust—for example, the old family servant, the Duchess of Guermantes, M. de Charlus, and Saint Loup; Madame Bovary—who, like Moll Flanders, has her book to herself, and can expand and secrete unchecked; some people in Thackery—for instance, Becky and Beatrix; some in Fielding—Parson Adams, Tom Jones; and some in Charlotte Brontë, most particularly Lucy Snowe. (And many more—this is not a catalogue). The test of a round character is whether it is capable of surprising in a convincing way. If it never surprises, it is flat. If it does not convince, it is a flat pretending to be round. It has the incalculability of life about it—life within the pages of a book. And by using it sometimes alone, more often in combination with the other kind, the novelist achieves his task of acclimatization and harmonizes the human race with the other aspects of his work.

The Concept of Character in Fiction

William Gass (1924–   )

William Gass did his undergraduate work at Kenyon College and received a Ph.D. from Cornell in 1954. He has taught philosophy and literature at several institutions, most recently at Washington University in St. Louis. His novel *Omensetter's Luck* (1966) was followed by a collection of stories, *In the Heart of the Heart of the Country* (1968). The following selection is from his critical study, *Fiction and the Figures of Life* (1970).

I have never found a handbook on the art of fiction or the stage, nor can I imagine finding one, that did not contain a chapter on the creation of character, a skill whose mastery, the author of each manual insists, secures for one the inner secrets of these arts: not, mind you, an easy thing: rather as difficult as the whole art itself, since, in a way, it *is* the whole art: to fasten in the memory of the reader, like a living presence, some bright human image. All well and good to paint a landscape, evoke a feeling, set a tempest loose, but not quite good enough to nail an author to his immortality if scheming Clarence, fat, foul-trousered Harry, or sweetly terraced Priss do not emerge from the land they huff and rage and eat in fully furnished out by Being; enough alive, indeed, to eat and huff in ours—dear God, more alive than that!—sufficiently enlarged by genius that they threaten to eat up and huff down everything in sight.

Talk about literature, when it is truly talk about something going on in the pages, if it is not about ideas, is generally about the people in it, and ranges from those cries of wonder, horror, pleasure, or surprise, so readily drawn from the innocently minded, to the annotated stammers of the most erudite and nervous critics. But it is all the same. Great character is the most obvious single mark of great literature. The rude, the vulgar, may see in Alyosha nothing more than the image of a modest, God-loving youth; the scholar may perceive through this demeanor a symbolic form; but the Alyosha of the untutored is somehow more real and present to him than the youth on his street whom he's known since childhood, loving of his God and modest too, equally tried, fully as patient; for in some way Alyosha's visionary figure will take lodging in him, make a model for him, so to reach, without the scholar's inflationary gifts, general form and universal height; whereas the neighbor may merely move away, take cold, and forget to write. Even the most careful student will admit that fiction's fruit survives its handling and continues growing off the tree. A great character has an endless interest; its fascination never wanes. Indeed it is a commonplace to say so. Hamlet. Ahab. Julien Sorel. Madame Bovary. There is no end to their tragedy. Great literature is great because its characters are great, and characters are great when they are memorable. A simple formula. The Danish ghost cries to remember him, and obediently—for we are gullible and superstitious clots—we do.

It hasn't always been a commonplace. Aristotle regarded character as a servant of dramatic action, and there have been an endless succession of opinions about the value and function of characters since—all dreary—but the important thing to be noted about nearly every one of them is that whatever else profound and wonderful these theories have to say about the world and its personalities, characters are clearly conceived as living outside language. Just as the movie star deserts herself to put on some press agent's more alluring fictional persona, the hero of a story sets out from his own landscape for the same land of romance the star reached by stepping there from life. These people—Huckleberry Finn, the Snopeses, Prince Myshkin, Pickwick, Molly Bloom—seem to have come to the words of their novels like a visitor to town . . . and later they leave on the arm of the reader, bound, I suspect, for a shabbier hotel, and dubious entertainments.

However, Aristotle's remark was a recommendation. Characters ought to exist for the sake of the action, he thought, though he knew they often did not, and those who nowadays say that given a sufficiently powerful and significant plot the characters will be dominated by it are simply answered by asking them to imagine the plot of *Moby Dick* in the hands of Henry James, or that of *Sanctuary* done into Austen. And if you can persuade them to try (you will have no success), you may then ask how the heroes and the heroines come out. The same disastrous exercise can be given those who believe that traits make character like definitions do a dictionary. Take any set of traits you like and let Balzac or Joyce, Stendhal or Beckett, loose in a single paragraph to use them. Give your fictional creatures qualities, psychologies, actions, manners, moods; present them from without or from within; let economics matter, breeding, custom, history; let spirit wet them like a hose: all methods work, and none do. The nature of the novel will not be understood at all until this is: *from any given body of fictional text, nothing necessarily follows, and anything plausibly may.* Authors are gods—a little tinny sometimes but omnipotent no matter what, and plausible on top of that, if they can manage it.

Though the handbooks try to tell us how to create characters, they carefully never tell us we are making images, illusions, imitations. Gatsby is not an imitation, for there is nothing he imitates. Actually, if he were a copy, an illusion, sort of shade or shadow, he would not be called a character at all. He must be unique, entirely himself, as if he had a self to be. He is required, in fact, to act *in character,* like a cat in a sack. No, theories of character are not absurd in the way representational theories are; they are absurd in a grander way, for the belief in Hamlet (which audiences often seem to have) is like the belief in God—incomprehensible to reason—and one is inclined to seek a motive: some deep fear or emotional need.

There are too many motives. We pay heed so easily. We are so pathetically eager for this other life, for the sounds of distant cities and the sea; we long, apparently, to pit ourselves against some trying wind, to follow the fortunes of a ship hard beset, to face up to murder and fornication, and the somber results of anger and love; oh, yes, to face up—*in books*—when on our own we scarcely breathe. The tragic view of life, for instance, in Shakespeare or in Schopenhauer, Unamuno, Sartre, or Sophocles, is not one jot as pure and penetratingly tragic as a pillow stuffed with Jewish hair, and if we want to touch life where it burns, though life is what we are even now awash with—futilely, stupidly drawing in—we ought not to back off from these other artifacts (wars, pogroms, poverty: men make them, too). But of course we do, and queue up patiently instead to see Prince Hamlet moon, watch him thrust his sword through a curtain, fold it once again into Polonius, that foolish old garrulous proper noun. The so-called life one finds in novels, the worst and best of them, is nothing like actual life at all, and cannot be; it is not more real, or thrilling, or authentic; it is not truer, more complex, or pure, and its people have less spontaneity, are less intricate, less free, less full.

It is not a single cowardice that drives us into fiction's fantasies. We often fear that literature is a game we can't afford to play—the product of idleness and immoral ease. In the grip of that feeling it isn't life we pursue, but the point and purpose of life—its facility, its use. So Sorel is either a man it is amusing to gossip about, to see in our friends, to puppet around in our dreams, to serve as our more able and more interesting surrogate in further fanciful adventures; or Sorel is a theoretical type, scientifically profound, representing a deep human strain, and the writing of *The Red and the Black* constitutes an advance in the science of—what would you like? sociology?

Before reciting a few helpless arguments, let me suggest, in concluding this polemical section, just how absurd these views are which think of fiction as a mirror or a window onto life—as actually creative of living creatures—for really one's only weapon against Tertullians is ridicule.

There is a painting by Picasso which depicts a pitcher, candle, blue enamel pot. They are sitting, unadorned, upon the barest table. Would we wonder what was cooking in that pot? Is it beans, perhaps, or carrots, a marmite? The orange of the carrot is a perfect complement to the blue of the pot, and the genius of Picasso, neglecting nothing, has surely placed, behind that blue, invisible disks of dusky orange, which, in addition, subtly enrich the table's velvet brown. Doesn't that seem reasonable? Now I see that it must be beans, for above the pot—you can barely see them—are quaking lines of steam, just the lines we associate with boiling beans . . . or is it blanching pods? Scholarly research, supported by a great foundation, will discover that exactly such a pot was used to cook cassoulet in the kitchens of Charles the Fat . . . or was it Charles the Bald? There's a dissertation in that. And this explains the dripping candle standing by the pot.

(Is it dripping? no? a pity. Let's go on.) For isn't Charles the Fat himself that candle? Oh no, some say, he's not! Blows are struck. Reputations made and ruined. Someone will see eventually that the pot is standing on a table, not a stove. But the pot has just come from the stove, it will be pointed out. Has not Picasso caught that vital moment of transition: The pot is too hot. The brown is burning. Oh, not *this* table, which has been coated with resistant plastic. Singular genius—blessed man—he thinks of everything.

Here you have half the history of our criticism in the novel. Entire books have been written about the characters in Dickens, Trollope, Tolstoi, Faulkner. But why not? Entire books have been written about God, his cohorts, and the fallen angels.

2

Descartes, examining a piece of beeswax fresh from the hive, brought it near a flame and observed all of its sensible qualities change. He wondered why he should believe that wax remained. His sensations lent him nothing he could fasten his judgment firmly to. Couldn't he give that puddle in his hand another name? He might have added that the sleights of the mountebanks did not bewilder him. Somehow he knew milady's hanky didn't disappear in a fist to emerge as a rose. It occurred to Descartes then that perhaps his imagination was the unifying faculty. But the wax was capable of an infinite number of spills, reaching every stage of relaxation, and he was unable, he writes in what is now a brilliant phrase, "to compass this infinity by imagination." How then? Some higher, finer capacity was required. His knowledge of the wax, soft or hard, sweet or flat, became an intuition of the mind.

Like so many philosophical arguments, this one was erected upside down, and consequently is a bit unsteady on its head. How, I'd rather ask, from the idea of wax, can we predict and picture just this sticky mess? What do we see when we peer through a glass of words?

If we ask this question of Hume, he will give us, as usual, a brilliantly reasonable, and entirely wrong answer—out of the habit empiricists have, I suppose, of never inspecting their experience. Nothing is more free than the imagination of man, he says; "it can feign a train of events with all the appearance of reality . . ." *With all the appearance of reality* . . . Then we might suppose that it's my imagination which allows me to descend from a writer's words, like a god through the clouds, and basket down on sweet Belinda's belly at the moment of her maximum response (or less excitingly, to picture upon the palm in my mind a slowly sprawling blob of molten wax).

To imagine so vividly is either to be drunk, asleep, or mad. Such images are out of our control and often terrifying. If we could feign with *every* appearance of reality, we would not wish to feign *Nostromo,* or even *Pride and Prejudice.* Of course, the imagination cannot give us every appearance of reality, and just as well, but perhaps it can give us every appearance of a *faded* reality: the shadow of Belinda's body on the bed (so far has this theory fallen through the space of a sentence!), an image seen the way I see this print and paper now, though with the mind's disocular eye. Or, as Gilbert Ryle writes:

> Sometimes, when someone mentions a blacksmith's forge, I find myself instantaneously back in my childhood, visiting a local smithy. I can vividly "see" the glowing red horseshoe on the anvil, fairly vividly "hear" the hammer ringing on the shoe and less vividly "smell" the singed hoof. How should we describe this "smelling in the mind's nose"?[1]

Certainly not by explaining that there is a smell in me, a shadow of a smell, a picture of a smell, an image, and putting to my noseless spirit the task of smelling it. Not as a bruise to its blow, as Ryle says, are our imaginings related to our experience. Yet Hume sometimes supposes that imagination works like madness. If it can give to fiction all the appearance of reality, how is one to know what to believe when an author's words, stirring in us like life, managing our minds with the efficiency of reality, throw Anna Karenina under the train's wheels before our eyes?

Here is the whole thing in a single passage:

> The imagination has the command over all its ideas and can join and mix and vary them in all the ways possible. It may conceive fictitious objects with all the circumstances of place and time. It may set them in a manner before our eyes, in their true colors, just as they might have existed. But as it is impossible that this faculty of imagination can ever, of itself, reach belief, it is evident that belief consists not in the peculiar nature or order of ideas, but in the manner of their conception and in their feeling to the mind.[2]

[1] In *The Concept of Mind* (New York: Barnes & Noble, 1950).

[2] Hume, *An Enquiry Concerning Human Understanding* (New York: Oxford University Press). There is reason to suppose that Hume thinks the imagination plays with ideas only after they have lost all vivifying power. Then, however, their arrangement could satisfy only our conceptions of things, not our perceptions of them.

The name of this feeing is belief, and I am given it by the greater intensity and steadiness with which actual impressions occupy me—a narrow difference, one only of degree. Don't mystery stories make us lock our doors?

But I should suppose that "seeing things" through novels did not involve succumbing to a drunken frenzy, finding animals in walls or naked ladies draped on desert rocks like some long celibate Saint Anthony.

We do visualize, I suppose. Where did I leave my gloves? And then I ransack a room in my mind until I find them. But the room I ransack is abstract—a simple schema. I leave out the drapes and the carpet, and I think of the room as a set of likely glove locations. The proportion of words which we can visualize is small, but quite apart from that, another barrier to the belief that vivid imagining is the secret of a character's power is the fact that when we watch the pictures which a writer's words have directed us to make, we miss their meaning, for the point is *never* the picture. It also takes concentration, visualization does—takes slowing down; and this alone is enough to rule it out of novels, which are never waiting, always flowing on.

> Instantly Hugh's shack began to take form in her mind. But it was not a shack—it was a home! It stood, on wide-girthed strong legs of pine, between the forest of pine and high, high waving alders and tall slim birches, and the sea. There was the narrow path that wound down through the forest from the shore, with salmonberries and thimbleberries and wild blackberry bushes that on bright winter nights of frost reflected a million moons; behind the house was a dogwood tree that bloomed twice in the year with white stars. Daffodils and snowdrops grew in the little garden.[3]

And so forth. Do you have all that? the salmonberries and the thimbleberries? I'm afraid you'll be all day about it. One reason is that our imaginings are mostly imprecise. They are vague and general. Even when colored, they're gray.

> A hare vaguely perceived is nevertheless a specific hare. But a hare which is the object of a vague image is a vague hare.[4]

Consequently, writing which carefully defines its object, however visual its terms, sets the visual successfully aside. It does, that is, if what we see inside us are misty visual schema. But

> Suppose that I have an image of a head that is nonspecific about baldness, is this not rather queer? For presumably this head must be neither bald nor not bald nor even a half-way house with just a few hairs.[5]

Enter Mr. Cashmore, who is a character in *The Awkward Age*.

> Mr. Cashmore, who would have been very redheaded if he had not been very bald, showed a single eyeglass and a long upper lip; he was large and jaunty, with little petulant movements and intense ejaculations that were not in the line of his type.

We can imagine any number of other sentences about Mr. Cashmore added to this one. Now the question is: what is Mr. Cashmore? Here is the answer I shall give: Mr. Cashmore is (1) a noise, (2) a proper name, (3) a complex system of ideas, (4) a controlling conception, (5) an instrument of verbal organization, (6) a pretended mode of referring, and (7) a source of verbal energy.[6] But Mr. Cashmore is not a person. He is not an object of perception, and nothing whatever that is appropriate to persons can be correctly said of him. There is no path from idea to sense (this is Descartes' argument in reverse), and no amount of careful elaboration of Mr. Cashmore's single eyeglass, his upper lip or jauntiness is going to enable us to *see* him. How many little petulant movements are there? Certainly as many as the shapes which may be taken by soft wax. If we follow Hume, we think we picture things through language because we substitute, on cue, particular visual memories of our own, and the more precisely language defines its object, the less likely we are to find a snapshot in our book to fit it. Our visualizations interfere with Mr. Cashmore's development, for if we think of him as someone we have met, we must give him qualities his author hasn't yet, and we may stubbornly, or through simple lack of attention, retain these later, though they've been explic-

[3] Malcolm Lowry, *Under the Volcano* (New York: Reynal and Hitchcock, 1947).

[4] Sartre, *Psychology of Imagination* (New York: Citadel, 1961).

[5] J. M. Shorter, "Imagination," in *Mind,* LXI.

[6] (1) He is always a "mister," and his name functions musically much of the time. "He was an odd compound, Mr. Cashmore, and the air of personal good health, the untarnished bloom which sometimes lent a monstrous serenity to his mention of the barely mentionable, was on occasion balanced or matched by his playful application of extravagant terms to matters of much less moment." What a large mouthful, that sentence. His name (2) locates him, but since he exists nowhere but on the page (6), it simply serves to draw other words toward him (3), or actualize others, as in conversation (7), when they seem to proceed from him, or remind us of all that he is an emblem of (4), and richly interact with other, similarly formed and similarly functioning verbal emblem centers (5).

itly debarred. "On your imaginary forces work," *Henry V's* Prologuer begs. "Piece out our imperfections with your thoughts . . . Think, when we talk of horses, that you see them / Printing their proud hoofs i' th' receiving earth," and then the audience (and the similarly situated novel reader) is praised for having done so; but this is worse than the self-congratulating pap which periodically flows from the bosom of the "creative" critic, because these generous additions destroy the work as certainly as "touching up" and "painting over." The unspoken word is often eloquent.

Well, I finally met Mr. Mulholland.
Oh, what's he like?
He has large thumbs.

Characters in fiction are mostly empty canvas. I have known many who have passed through their stories without noses, or heads to hold them; others have lacked bodies altogether, exercised no natural functions, possessed some thoughts, a few emotions, but no psychologies, and apparently made love without the necessary organs. The true principle is direct enough: Mr. Cashmore has what he's been given; he also *has* what he *hasn't,* just as strongly. Mr. Cashmore, in fact, has been cruelly scalped.

Now, is there a nose to this Mr. Cashmore? Let's suppose it—but then, of what sort? We're not told. He is an eyeglass without eyes, he has no neck or chin, his ears are unexplored. "Large"—how indefinite a word. But would it have been better to have written "sixteen stone"? Not at all, nor do we know how this weight is disposed. If it is impossible to picture Mr. Cashmore, however carefully we draw him, will it be easier to limn his soul? Or perhaps we may imagine that this sentence describes not Mr. Cashmore, out or in, but his impression—what sort of dent he makes in his surroundings. He gives the impression of a man who would have been redheaded if he hadn't been bald. Very well. What impression, exactly, is that? Will it do to think of Mr. Cashmore as a man with red eyebrows and a red fringe above his ears, but otherwise without hair? That would rephrase Mr. Cashmore, and rephrase him badly. The description of Mr. Cashmore stands as James wrote it, even if Mr. Cashmore hasn't a hair on his body. As a set of sensations Mr. Cashmore is simply impossible; as an idea he is admirably pungent and precise.

Similarly, it is not at all correct to infer that because Mr. Mulholland has thumbs, he has hands, arms, torso, self. That inference destroys the metaphor (a pure synecdoche), since his thumbs are all he seems to be. Mr. Mulholland is monumentally clumsy, but if you fill him in behind his thumbs, clumsiness will not ensue.

So sometimes, then, we are required to take away what we've been given, as in the case of Mr. Cashmore's red hair; sometimes it's important to hold fast to what we've got and resist any inclination we may have to elaborate, as in the case of Mr. Mulholland, who I said had thumbs; and sometimes we must put our minds to the stretch, bridging the distances between concepts with other concepts, as in the two examples which follow; or we may be called upon to do all these things at once, as in what I promise will be my final misuse of poor Mulholland.[7]

Well, I finally met Mr. Mulholland.
Oh, what's he like?
A silver thimble.

I saw Mr. Mulholland today.
Oh, what was he doing?
Walking his thumbs.

Mr. Mulholland's face had
a watchful look. Although
its features had not arrived,
they were momentarily expected.

To summarize, so far:

1. Only a few of the words which a writer normally uses to create a character can be "imaged" in any sense.
2. To the extent these images are faded sensations which we've once had, they fill in, particularize, and falsify the author's account.
3. To the degree these images are as vivid and lively as reality is, they will very often be unpleasant, and certainly can't be "feigned." Then words would act like a mind-expanding drug.
4. To the degree these images are general schema, indistinct and vague, the great reality characters are supposed to have becomes less plausible, and precise writing (so often admired) will interfere with their formation.
5. Constructing images of any kind takes time, slows the flow of the work; nor can imagining keep up, in complexity, with the incredibly intricate conceptual

[7] The entire matter is far more complicated than I have indicated. Not only is there a linear order of apprehension (the reader is first told Mr. Mulholland has been seen, then that he was walking his thumbs), but also an order, in depth, of implications. Analysis, in searching out these implications, frequently upsets this order, bringing the bottom to the top. Meanings, uncovered, must be put back as they were found. It is a delicate operation.

systems which may be spun like a spiderweb in a single sentence.

6. We tend to pay attention to our pictures, and lose sight of the meaning. The novelist's words are not notes which he is begging the reader to play, as if his novel needed something more done to it in order to leap into existence.

Words in daily life are signposts, handles, keys. They express, instruct, command, inform, exhort—in short, they serve; and it is difficult to think of our servants as kings. But among real things words win the gold medals for Being. Ortega y Gasset asks us to imagine we are looking through a window at a garden.

> The clearer the glass is, the less (of the glass) we will see. But then making an effort we may withdraw attention from the garden; and by retracing the ocular ray, we may fixate it upon the glass. Then the garden will disappear in our eyes and we will see instead only some confused masses of color which seem to stick to the glass. Consequently to see the garden and to see the glass in the windowpane are two incompatible operations. . . . Likewise he who in the work of art aims to be moved by the fate of John and Mary, or of Tristan and Iseult, and readjusts to them his spiritual perception will not be able to see the work of art. . . . Now the majority of people are unable to adjust their attention to the glass and the transparency which is the work of art; instead they penetrate through it to passionately wallow in the human reality which the work of art refers to. If they are invited to let loose their prey and fix their attention upon the work of art itself, they will say they see nothing in it, because, indeed, they see no human realities there, but only artistic transparencies, pure essences.[8]

Ortega seems to believe, however, that words are windows through which something can be seen, and I have argued that words are opaque, as opaque as my garden gloves and trowel, objects which, nevertheless, may vividly remind me of spring, earth, and roses. Or Uncle Harry, Africa, the tsetse fly, and lovesick elephants.

On the other side of a novel lies the void. Think, for instance, of a striding statue; imagine the purposeful inclination of the torso, the alert and penetrating gaze of the head and its eyes, the outstretched arm and pointing finger; everything would appear to direct us toward some goal in front of it. Yet our eye travels only to the finger's end, and not beyond. Though pointing, the finger bids us stay instead, and we journey slowly back along the tension of the arm. In our hearts we know what actually surrounds the statue. The same surrounds every other work of art: empty space and silence.

[8] Ortega y Gasset, *The Dehumanization of Art* (New York: Anchor Books, 1956).

3

A character, first of all, is the noise of his name, and all the sounds and rhythms that proceed from him. We pass most things in novels as we pass things on a train. The words flow by like the scenery. All is change. But there are some points in a narrative which remain relatively fixed; we may depart from them, but soon we return, as music returns to its theme. Characters are those primary substances to which everything else is attached. Hotels, dresses, conversations, sausage, feelings, gestures, snowy evenings, faces—each may fade as fast as we read of them. Yet the language of the novel will eddy about a certain incident or name, as Melville's always circles back to Ahab and his wedding with the white whale. Mountains are characters in Malcolm Lowry's *Under the Volcano,* so is a ravine, a movie, mescal, or a boxing poster. A symbol like the cross can be a character. An idea or a situation (the anarchist in *The Secret Agent,* bomb ready in his pocket), or a particular event, an obsessive thought, a decision (Zeno's, for instance, to quit smoking), a passion, a memory, the weather, Gogol's overcoat—anything, indeed, which serves as a fixed point, like a stone in a stream or that soap in Bloom's pocket, functions as a character. Character, in this sense, is a matter of degree, for the language of the novel may loop back seldom, often, or incessantly. But the idea that characters are like primary substances has to be taken in a double way, because if any thing becomes a character simply to the degree the words of the novel qualify it, it also loses some of its substance, some of its primacy, to the extent that it, in turn, qualifies something else. In a perfectly organized novel, every word would ultimately qualify one thing, like the God of the metaphysician, at once the subject and the body of the whole.[9] Normally, characters are fictional human beings, and thus are given proper names. In such cases, to create a character is to give meaning to an unknown X; it is *absolutely* to *define;* and since nothing in life corresponds to these Xs, their reality is borne by their name. They *are,* where it *is.*

[9] There is no reason why every novel should be organized in this way. This method constructs a world according to the principles of Absolute Idealism.

Most of the words the novelist uses have their meanings already formed. Proper names do not, except in a tangential way. It's true that Mr. Mulholland could not be Mr. Mull, and Mr. Cashmore must bear, as best he can, the curse of his wealth forever, along with his desire for gain. Character has a special excitement for a writer (apart from its organizing value) because it offers him a chance to give fresh meaning to new words. A proper name begins as a blank, like a wall or a canvas, upon which one might paint a meaning, perhaps as turbulent and mysterious, as treacherous and vast, as Moby Dick's, perhaps as delicate, scrupulous, and sensitive as that of Fleda Vetch.

I cannot pause here over the subject of rhythm and sound, though they are the heartbeat of writing, of prose no less than poetry.

> Their friend, Mr. Grant-Jackson, a highly preponderant pushing person, great in discussion and arrangement, abrupt in overture, unexpected, if not perverse, in attitude, and almost equally acclaimed and objected to in the wide midland region to which he had taught, as the phrase was, the size of his foot—their friend had launched his bolt quite out of the blue and had thereby so shaken them as to make them fear almost more than hope.[10]

Mr. Grant-Jackson is a preponderant pushing person because he's been made by *p's,* and the rhythm and phrasing of James's writing here prepares and perfectly presents him to us. Certainly we cannot think of Molly Bloom apart from her music, or the gay and rapid Anna Livia apart from hers.

If one examines the texture of a fiction carefully, one will soon see that some words appear to gravitate toward their subject like flies settle on sugar, while others seem to emerge from it. In many works this logical movement is easily discernible and very strong. When a character speaks, the words seem to issue from him and to be acts of his. Description first forms a *nature,* then allows that nature to *perform.* We must be careful, however, not to judge by externals. Barkis says that Barkis is willing, but the expression *functions* descriptively to qualify Barkis, and it is Dickens' habit to treat speech as if it were an attribute of character, like tallness or honesty, and not an act. On the other hand, qualities, in the right context, can be transformed into verbs. Later in the book don't we perceive the whiteness of the whale as a design, an intention of Moby Dick's, like a twist of his flukes or the smashing of a small boat?

[10] Henry James, "The Birthplace."

Whether Mr. Cashmore was once real and sat by James at someone's dinner table, or was instead the fabrication of James's imagination, as long as he came into being from the world's direction he once existed outside language. The task of getting him in I shall call the problem of rendering. But it must be stressed (it cannot be stressed too severely) that Mr. Cashmore may never have had a model, and may never have been imagined either, but may have come to be in order to serve some high conception (a Mr. Moneybags) and represent a type, not just himself, in which case he is not a reality *rendered,* but a universal *embodied.* Again, Mr. Cashmore might have had still other parents. Meanings in the stream of words before his appearance might have suggested him, dramatic requirements may have called him forth, or he may have been the spawn of music, taking his substance from rhythm and alliteration. Perhaps it was all of these. In well-regulated fictions, most things are *overdetermined.*

So far I have been talking about the function of a character in the direct stream of language, but there are these two other dimensions, the rendered and the embodied, and I should like to discuss each briefly.

If we observe one of J. F. Powers' worldly priests sharpening his eye for the pin by putting through his clerical collar, the humor, with all *its* sharpness, lives in the situation, and quite incidentally in the words. One can indeed imagine Powers thinking it up independently of any verbal formula. Once Powers had decided that it would be funny to show a priest playing honeymoon bridge with his housekeeper, then his problem becomes the technical one of how best to accomplish it. What the writer must do, of course, is not only render the scene, but render the scene inseparable from its language, so that if the idea (the chaste priest caught in the clichés of marriage) is taken from the situation, like a heart from its body, both die. Far easier to render a real cornfield in front of you, because once that rendering has reached its page, the cornfield will no longer exist for literary purposes, no one will be able to see it by peering through your language, and consequently there will be nothing to abstract from your description. But with a "thought up" scene or situation, this is not the case. It comes under the curse of story. The notion, however amusing, is not literary, for it might be painted, filmed, or played. If we inquire further and ask why Powers wanted such a scene in the first place, we should find, I think, that he wanted it in order to embody a controlling "idea"—at one level of abstraction, the worldliness of the church, for instance. If he had nuns around a kitchen table counting the Sunday take and listening to the Cubs, *that* would do it. Father Burner beautifully embodies just such a controlling idea in Powers' celebrated story "The Prince of Darkness." Both rendering and embodying involve great risks because they require working into a scientific order of words what was not originally there. Any painter knows that a contour may only more or less enclose his model, while a free line simply and completely is. Many of the model's contours may be esthetically irrelevant, so it would be unwise to follow them. The free line is subject to no such temptations. Its relevance can be total. As Valéry wrote: There are no details in execution.

Often novelists mimic our ordinary use of language. We report upon ourselves; we gossip. Normally we are not lying; and our language, built to refer, actually does. When these selfsame words appear in fiction, and when they follow the forms of daily use, they create, quite readily, that dangerous feeling that a real Tietjens, a real Nickleby, lives just beyond the page; that through that thin partition we can hear a world of love. But the writer must not let the reader out; the sculptor must not let the eye fall from the end of his statue's finger; the musician must not let the listener dream. Of course, he will; but let the blame be on himself. High tricks are possible: to run the eye rapidly along that outstretched arm to the fingertip, only to draw it up before it falls away in space; to carry the reader to the very edge of every word so that it seems he must be compelled to react as though to truth as told in life, and then to the clear and brilliant world of concept, to the realm of order, proportion, and dazzling construction . . . to fiction, where characters, unlike ourselves, freed from existence can shine like essence, and purely Be.

Manners, Morals, and the Novel

Lionel Trilling (1905–1975)

Born in New York City, Lionel Trilling remained a New Yorker while becoming a cosmopolitan literary critic. Educated at Columbia University, he published pioneering studies of Matthew Arnold (1939) and E. M. Forster (1943). His influential essays on literature as a social act were collected in *The Liberal Imagination* (1950), *The Opposing Self* (1955), and *Beyond Culture* (1965). His novel *The Middle of the Journey* (1947) and his superb short story "Of This Time, Of That Place" display an ability to locate individual characters in a social context. Trilling's last major work was a series of essays called *Sincerity and Authenticity* (1972). The following essay was written in 1947.

The invitation that was made to me to address you this evening was couched in somewhat uncertain terms. Time, place, and cordiality were perfectly clear, but when it came to the subject our hosts were not able to specify just what they wanted me to talk about. They wanted me to consider literature in its relation to manners—by which, as they relied on me to understand, they did not really mean *manners*. They did not mean, that is, the rules of personal intercourse in our culture; and yet such rules were by no means irrelevant to what they did mean. Nor did they quite mean manners in the sense of *mores*, customs, although, again, these did bear upon the subject they had in mind.

I understood them perfectly, as I would not have understood them had they been more definite. For they were talking about a nearly indefinable subject.

Somewhere below all the explicit statements that a people makes through its art, religion, architecture, legislation, there is a dim mental region of intention of which it is very difficult to become aware. We now and then get a strong sense of its existence when we deal with the past, not by reason of its presence in the past but by reason of its absence. As we read the great formulated monuments of the past, we notice that we are reading them without the accompaniment of something that always goes along with the formulated monuments of the present. The voice of multifarious intention and activity is stilled, all the buzz of implication which always surrounds us in the present, coming to us from what never gets fully stated, coming in the tone of greetings and the tone of quarrels, in slang and humor and popular songs, in the way children play, in the gesture the waiter makes when he puts down the plate, in the nature of the very food we prefer.

Some of the charm of the past consists of the quiet—the great distracting buzz of implication has stopped and we are left only with what has been fully phrased and precisely stated. And part of the melancholy of the past comes from our knowledge that the huge, unrecorded hum of implication was once there and left no trace—we feel that because it is evanescent it is especially human. We feel, too, that the truth of the great preserved monuments of the past does not fully appear without it. From letters and diaries, from the remote, unconscious corners of the great works themselves, we try to guess what the sound of the multifarious implication was and what it meant.

Or when we read the conclusions that are drawn about our own culture by some gifted foreign critic—or by some stupid native one—who is equipped only with a knowledge of our books, when we try in vain to say what is wrong, when in despair we say that he has read the books "out of context," then we are aware of the matter I have been asked to speak about tonight.

What I understand by manners, then, is a culture's hum and buzz of implication. I mean the whole evanescent context in which its explicit statements are made. It is that part of a culture which is made up of half-uttered or unuttered or unutterable expressions of value. They are hinted at by small actions, sometimes by the arts of dress or decoration, sometimes by tone, gesture, emphasis, or rhythm, sometimes by the words that are used with a special frequency or a special meaning. They are the things that for good or bad draw the people of a culture together and that separate them from the people of another culture. They make the part of a culture which is not art, or religion, or morals, or politics, and yet it relates to all these highly formulated departments of culture. It is modified by them; it modifies them; it is generated by them; it generates them. In this part of culture assumption rules, which is often so much stronger than reason.

The right way to begin to deal with such a subject is to gather together as much of its detail as we possibly can. Only by doing so will we become fully aware of what the gifted foreign critic or the stupid native one is not aware of, that in any complex culture there is not a single system of manners but a conflicting variety of manners, and that one of the jobs of a culture is the adjustment of this conflict.

But the nature of our present occasion does not permit this accumulation of detail and so I shall instead try to drive toward a generalization and an hypothesis which, however wrong they turn out to be, may at least permit us to circumscribe the subject. I shall try to generalize the subject of American manners by talking about the attitude of Americans toward the subject of manners itself. And since in a complex culture there are, as I say, many different systems of manners and since I cannot talk about them all, I shall select the manners and the attitude toward manners of the literate, reading, responsible middle class of people who are ourselves. I specify that they be reading people because I shall draw my conclusions from the novels they read. The hypothesis I propose is that our attitude toward manners is the expression of a particular conception of reality.

All literature tends to be concerned with the question of reality—I mean quite simply the old opposition between reality and appearance, between what really is and what merely seems. "Don't you *see?*" is the question we want to shout at Oedipus as he stands before us and before fate in the pride of his rationalism. And at the end of *Oedipus Rex* he demonstrates in a particularly direct way that he now sees what he did not see before. "Don't you *see?*" we want to shout again at Lear and Gloucester, the two deceived, self-deceiving fathers: blindness again, resistance to the clear claims of reality, the seduction by mere appearance. The same with Othello—reality is right under your stupid nose, how *dare* you be such a gull? So with Molière's Oregon—my good man, my honest citizen, merely *look* at Tartuffe and you will know what's what. So with Milton's Eve—"Woman, watch out! Don't you see—anyone can see—that's a *snake!*"

The problem of reality is central, and in a special way, to the great forefather of the novel, the great book of Cervantes, whose four-hundredth birthday was celebrated in 1947. There are two movements of thought in *Don Quixote,* two different and opposed notions of reality. One is the movement which leads toward saying that the world of ordinary practicality *is* reality in its fullness. It is the reality of the present moment in all its powerful immediacy of hunger, cold, and pain, making the past and the future, and all ideas, of no account. When the conceptual, the ideal, and the fanciful come into conflict with this, bringing their notions of the past and the future, then disaster results. For one thing, the ordinary proper ways of life are upset—the chained prisoners are understood to be good men and are released, the whore is taken for a lady. There is general confusion. As for the ideal, the conceptual, the fanciful, or romantic—whatever you want to call it—it fares even worse: it is shown to be ridiculous.

Thus one movement of the novel. But Cervantes changed horses in midstream and found that he was riding Rosinante. Perhaps at first not quite consciously—although the new view is latent in the old from the very beginning—Cervantes begins to show that the world of tangible reality is not the real reality after all. The real reality is rather the wildly conceiving, the madly fantasying mind of the Don: people change, practical reality changes, when they come into its presence.

In any genre it may happen that the first great example contains the whole potentiality of the genre. It has been said that all philosophy is a footnote to Plato. It can be said that all prose fiction is a variation on the theme of *Don Quixote*. Cervantes sets for the novel the problem of appearance and reality: the shifting and conflict of social classes becomes the field of the problem of knowledge, of how we know and of how reliable our knowledge is, which at that very moment of history is vexing the philosophers and scientists. And the poverty of the Don suggests that the novel is born with the appearance of money as a social element—money, the great solvent of the solid fabric of the old society, the great generator of illusion. Or, which is to say much the same thing, the novel is born in response to snobbery.

Snobbery is not the same thing as pride of class. Pride of class may not please us but we must at least grant that it reflects a social function. A man who exhibited class pride—in the day when it was possible to do so—may have been puffed up about what he *was,* but this ultimately depended on what he *did.* Thus, aristocratic pride was based ultimately on the ability to fight and administer. No pride is without fault, but pride of class may be thought of as today we think of pride of profession, toward which we are likely to be lenient.

Snobbery is pride in status without pride in function. And it is an uneasy pride of status. It always asks, "Do I belong—do I really belong? And does he belong? And if I am observed talking to him, will it make me seem to belong or not to belong?" It is the peculiar vice not of aristocratic societies which have their own appropriate vices, but of bourgeois democratic societies. For us the legendary strongholds of snobbery are the Hollywood studios, where two thousand dollars a week dare not talk to three hundred dollars a week for fear he be taken for nothing more than fifteen hundred dollars a week. The dominant emotions of snobbery are uneasiness, self-consciousness, self-defensiveness, the sense that one is not quite real but can in some way acquire reality.

Money is the medium that, for good or bad, makes for a fluent society. It does not make for an equal society but for one in which there is a constant shifting of classes, a frequent change in the personnel of the dominant class. In a shifting society great emphasis is put on appearance—I am using the word now in the common meaning, as when people say that "a good appearance is very important in getting a job." To appear to be established is one of the ways of becoming established. The old notion of the solid merchant who owns far more than he shows increasingly gives way to the ideal of signalizing status by appearance, by showing more than you have: status in a democratic society is presumed to come not with power but with the tokens of power. Hence the development of what Tocqueville saw as a mark of democratic culture, what he called the "hypocrisy of luxury"—instead of the well-made peasant article and the well-made middle-class article, we have the effort of all articles to appear as the articles of the very wealthy.

And a shifting society is bound to generate an interest in appearance in the philosophical sense. When Shakespeare lightly touched on the matter that so largely preoccupies the novelist—that is, the movement from one class to another—and created Malvolio, he immediately involved the question of social standing with the problem of appearance and reality. Malvolio's daydreams of bettering his position present themselves to him as reality, and in revenge his enemies conspire to convince him that he is literally mad and that the world is not as he sees it. The predicament of the characters in *A Midsummer Night's Dream* and of Christopher Sly seems to imply that the meeting of social extremes and the establishment of a person of low class in the privileges of a high class always suggested to Shakespeare's mind some radical instability of the senses and the reason.

The characteristic work of the novel is to record the illusion that snobbery generates and to try to penetrate to the truth which, as the novel assumes, lies hidden beneath all the false appearances. Money, snobbery, the ideal of status, these become in themselves the objects of fantasy, the support of the fantasies of love, freedom, charm, power, as in *Madame Bovary,* whose heroine is the sister, at a three-centuries' remove, of Don Quixote. The greatness of *Great Expectations* begins in its title: modern society bases itself on great expectations which, if ever they are realized, are found to exist by reason of a sordid, hidden reality. The real thing is not the gentility of Pip's life but the hulks and the murder and the rats and decay in the cellarage of the novel.

An English writer, recognizing the novel's central concern with snobbery, recently cried out half-ironically against it. "Who cares whether Pamela finally exasperates Mr. B. into marriage, whether Mr. Elton is more or less than moderately genteel, whether it is sinful for Pendennis nearly to kiss the porter's daughter, whether young men from Boston can ever be as truly refined as middle-aged women in Paris, whether the District Officer's fiancée ought to see so much of Dr. Aziz, whether Lady Chatterley ought to be made love to by the gamekeeper, even if he was an officer during the war? Who cares?"

The novel, of course, tells us much more about life than this. It tells us about the look and feel of things, how things are done and what things are worth and what they cost and what the odds are. If the English novel in its special concern with class does not, as the same writer says, explore the deeper layers of personality, then the French novel in exploring these layers must start and end in class, and the Russian novel, exploring the ultimate possibilities of spirit, does the same—every situation in Dostoevski, no matter how spiritual, starts with a point of social pride and a certain number of rubles. The great novelists knew that manners indicate the largest intentions of men's souls as well as the smallest and they are perpetually concerned to catch the meaning of every dim implicit hint.

The novel, then, is a perpetual quest for reality, the field of its research being always the social world, the material of its analysis being always manners as the indication of the direction of man's soul. When we understand this we can understand the pride of profession that moved D. H. Lawrence to say, "Being a novelist, I consider myself superior to the saint, the scientist, the philosopher and the poet. The novel is the one bright book of life."

Now the novel as I have described it has never really established itself in America. Not that we have not had very great novels but that the novel in America diverges from its classic intention, which, as I have said, is the investigation of the problem of reality beginning in the social field. The fact is that American writers of genius have not turned their minds to society. Poe and Melville were quite apart from it; the reality they sought was only tangential to society. Hawthorne was acute when he insisted that he did not write novels but romances—he thus expressed his awareness of the lack of social texture in his work. Howells never fulfilled himself because, although he saw the social subject clearly, he would never take it with full seriousness. In America in the nineteenth century, Henry James was alone in knowing that to scale the moral and aesthetic heights in the novel one had to use the ladder of social observation.

There is a famous passage in James's life of Hawthorne in which James enumerates the things which are lacking to give the American novel the thick social texture of the English novel—no state; barely a specific national name; no sovereign; no court; no aristocracy; no church; no clergy; no army; no diplomatic service; no country gentlemen; no palaces; no castles; no manors; no old country houses; no parsonages; no thatched cottages; no ivied ruins; no cathedrals; no great universities; no public schools; no political society; no sporting class—no Epsom no Ascot! That is, no sufficiency of means for the display of a variety of manners, no opportunity for the novelist to do his job of searching out reality, not enough complication of appearance to make the job interesting. Another great American novelist of very different temperament had said much the same thing some decades before: James Fenimore Cooper found that American manners were too simple and dull to nourish the novelist.

This is cogent but it does not explain the condition of the American novel at the present moment. For life in America has increasingly thickened since the nineteenth century. It has not, to be sure, thickened so much as to permit our undergraduates to understand the characters of Balzac, to understand, that is, life in a crowded country where the competitive pressures are great, forcing intense passions to express themselves fiercely and yet within the limitations set by a strong and complicated tradition of manners. Still, life here has become more complex and more pressing. And even so we do not have the novel that touches significantly on society, on manners. Whatever the virtues of Dreiser may be, he could not report the social fact with the kind of accuracy it needs. Sinclair Lewis is shrewd, but no one, however charmed with him as a social satirist, can believe that he does more than a limited job of social understanding. John Dos Passos sees much, sees it often in the great way of Flaubert, but can never use social fact as more than either backdrop or "condition." Of our novelists today perhaps only William Faulkner deals with society as the field of tragic reality and he has the disadvantage of being limited to a provincial scene.

It would seem that Americans have a kind of resistance to looking closely at society. They appear to believe that to touch accurately on the matter of class, to take full note of snobbery, is somehow to demean themselves. It is as if we felt that one cannot touch pitch without being defiled—which, of course, may possibly be the case. Americans will not deny that we have classes and snobbery, but they seem to hold it to be indelicate to take precise cognizance of these phenomena. Consider that Henry James is, among a large part of our reading public, still held to be at fault for noticing society as much as he did. Consider the conversation that has, for some interesting reason, become a part of our literary folklore. Scott Fitzgerald said to Ernest Hemingway, "The very rich are different from us." Hemingway replied, "Yes, they have more money." I have seen the exchange quoted many times and always with the intention of suggesting that Fitzgerald was infatuated by wealth and had received a salutary rebuke from his democratic friend. But the truth is that after a certain point quantity of money does indeed change into quality of personality: in an important sense the very rich *are* different from us. So are the very powerful, the very gifted, the very poor. Fitzgerald was right, and almost for that remark alone he must surely have been received in Balzac's bosom in the heaven of novelists.

It is of course by no means true that the American reading class has no interest in society. Its interest fails only before society as it used to be represented by the novel. And if we look at the commercially successful serious novels of the last decade, we see that almost all of them have been written from an intense social awareness—it might be said that our present definition of a serious book is one which holds before us some image of society to consider and condemn. What is the situation of the dispossessed Oklahoma farmer and whose fault it is, what situation the Jew finds himself in, what it means to be a Negro, how one gets a bell for Adano, what is the advertising business really like, what it means to be insane and how society takes care of you or fails to do so—these are the matters which are believed to be most fertile for the novelist, and certainly they are the subjects most favored by our reading class.

The public is probably not deceived about the quality of most of these books. If the question of quality is brought up, the answer is likely to be: no, they are not great, they are not imaginative, they are not "literature." But there is an unexpressed addendum: and perhaps they are all the better for not being imaginative, for not being literature—they are not literature, they are reality, and *in a time like this* what we need is reality in large doses.

When, generations from now, the historian of our times undertakes to describe the assumptions of our culture, he will surely discover that the word *reality* is of central importance in his understanding of us. He will observe that for some of our philosophers the meaning of the word was a good deal in doubt, but that for our political writers, for many of our literary critics, and for most of our reading public, the word did not open discussion but, rather, closed it. Reality, as conceived by us, is whatever is external and hard, gross, unpleasant. Involved in its meaning is the idea of power conceived in a particular way. Some time ago I had occasion to remark how, in the critical estimates of Theodore Dreiser, it is always being said that Dreiser has many faults but that it cannot be denied that he has great power. No one ever says "a kind of power." Power is assumed to be always "brute" power, crude, ugly, and undiscriminating, the way an elephant appears to be. It is seldom understood to be the way an elephant actually is, precise and discriminating; or the way electricity is, swift and absolute and scarcely embodied.

The word *reality* is an honorific word and the future historian will naturally try to discover our notion of its pejorative opposite, appearance, mere appearance. He will find it in our feeling about the internal; whenever we detect evidences of style and thought we suspect that reality is being a little betrayed, that "mere subjectivity" is creeping in. There follows from this our feeling about complication, modulation, personal idiosyncrasy, and about social forms, both the great and the small.

Having gone so far, our historian is then likely to discover a puzzling contradiction. For we claim that the great advantage of reality is its hard, bedrock, concrete quality, yet everything we say about it tends toward the abstract and it almost seems that what we want to find in reality is abstraction itself. Thus we believe that one of the unpleasant bedrock facts is social class, but we become extremely impatient if ever we are told that social class is indeed so real that it produces actual differences of personality. The very people who talk most about class and its evils think that Fitzgerald was bedazzled and Hemingway right. Or again, it might be observed that in the degree that we speak in praise of the "individual" we have contrived that our literature should have no individuals in it—no people, that is, who are shaped by our liking for the interesting and memorable and special and precious.

Here, then, is our generalization: that in proportion as we have committed ourselves to our particular idea of reality we have lost our interest in manners. For the novel this is a definitive condition because it is inescapably true that in the novel manners make men. It does not matter in what sense the word manners is taken—it is equally true of the sense which so much interested Proust or of the sense which interested Dickens or, indeed, of the sense which interested Homer. The Duchesse de Guermantes unable to delay departure for the dinner party to receive properly from her friend Swann the news that he is dying but able to delay to change the black slippers her husband objects to; Mr. Pickwick and Sam Weller; Priam and Achilles—they exist by reason of their observed manners.

So true is this, indeed, so creative is the novelist's awareness of manners, that we may say that it is a function of his love. It is some sort of love that Fielding has for Squire Western that allows him to note the great, gross details which bring the insensitive sentient man into existence for us. If that is true, we are forced to certain conclusions about our literature and about the particular definition of reality which has shaped it. The reality we admire tells us that the observation of manners is trivial and even malicious, that there are things much more important for the novel to consider. As a consequence our social sympathies have indeed broadened, but in proportion as they have done so we have lost something of our power of love, for our novels can never create characters who truly exist. We make public demands for love, for we know that broad social feeling should be infused with warmth, and we receive a kind of public product which we try to believe is not cold potatoes. The reviewers of Helen Howe's novel of a few years ago, *We Happy Few,* thought that its satiric first part, an excellent comment on the manners of a small but significant segment of society, was ill-natured and unsatisfactory, but they approved the second part, which is the record of the heroine's self-accusing effort to come into communication with the great soul of America. Yet it should have been clear that the satire had its source in a kind of affection, in a real community of feeling, and told the truth, while the second part, said to be so "warm," was mere abstraction, one more example of our public idea of ourselves and our national life. John Steinbeck is generally praised both for his reality and his warmheartedness, but in *The Wayward Bus* the lower-class characters receive a doctrinaire affection in proportion to the suffering and sexuality which define their existence, while the ill-observed middle-class characters are made to submit not only to moral judgment but to the withdrawal of all fellow-feeling, being mocked for their very misfortunes and almost for their susceptibility to death. Only a little thought or even less feeling is required to perceive that the basis of his creation is the coldest response to abstract ideas.

Two novelists of the older sort had a prevision of our present situation. In Henry James's *The Princess Casamassima* there is a scene in which the heroine is told about the existence of a conspiratorial group of revolutionaries pledged to the destruction of all existing society. She has for some time been drawn by a desire for social responsibility; she has wanted to help "the people," she has longed to discover just such a group as she now hears about, and she exclaims in joy, "Then it's real, it's solid!" We are intended to hear the Princess's glad cry with the knowledge that she is a woman who despises herself, "that in the darkest hour of her life she sold herself for a title and a fortune. She regards her doing so as such a terrible piece of frivolity that she can never for the rest of her days be serious enough to make up for it." She seeks out poverty, suffering, sacrifice, and death because she believes that these things alone are real; she comes to believe that art is contemptible; she withdraws her awareness and love from the one person of her acquaintance who most deserves them, and she increasingly scorns whatever suggests variety and modulation, and is more and more dissatisfied with the humanity of the present in her longing for the more perfect humanity of the future. It is one of the great points that the novel makes that with each passionate step that she takes toward what she calls the real, the solid, she in fact moves further away from the life-giving reality.

In E. M. Forster's *The Longest Journey* there is a young man named Stephen Wonham who, although a gentleman born, has been carelessly brought up and has no real notion of the responsibilities of his class. He has a friend, a country laborer, a shepherd, and on two occasions he outrages the feelings of certain intelligent, liberal, democratic people in the book by his treatment of this friend. Once, when the shepherd reneges on a bargain, Stephen quarrels with him and knocks him down; and in the matter of the loan of a few shillings he insists that the money be paid back to the last farthing. The intelligent, liberal, democratic people know that this is not the way to act to the poor. But Stephen cannot think of the shepherd as the poor nor, although he is a country laborer, as an object of research by J. L. and Barbara Hammond; he is rather a reciprocating subject in a relationship of affection—as we say, a friend—and therefore liable to anger and required to pay his debts. But this view is held to be deficient in intelligence, liberalism, and democracy.

In these two incidents we have the premonition of our present cultural and social situation, the passionate self-reproachful addiction to a "strong" reality which must limit its purview to maintain its strength, the replacement by abstraction of natural, direct human feeling. It is worth noting, by the way, how clear is the line by which the two novels descend from *Don Quixote*—how their young heroes come into life from *large preconceived ideas and are knocked about in consequence; how both are concerned with the problem of appearance and reality, The Longest Journey* quite explicitly, *The Princess Casamassima* by indirection; how both evoke the question of the nature of reality by contriving a meeting and conflict of diverse social classes and take scrupulous note of the differences of manners. Both have as their leading characters people who are specifically and passionately concerned with social injustice and both agree in saying that to act against social injustice is right and noble but that to choose to act so does not settle all moral problems but on the contrary generates new ones of an especially difficult sort.

I have elsewhere given the name of moral realism to the perception of the dangers of the moral life itself. Perhaps at no other time has the enterprise of moral realism ever been so much needed, for at no other time have so many people committed themselves to moral righteousness. We have the books that point out the bad conditions, that praise us for taking progressive attitudes. We have no books that raise questions in our minds not only about conditions but about ourselves, that lead us to refine our motives and ask what might lie behind our good impulses.

There is nothing so very terrible in discovering that something does lie behind. Nor does it need a Freud to make the discovery. Here is a publicity release sent out by one of our oldest and most respectable publishing houses. Under the heading "What Makes Books Sell?" it reads, "Blank & Company reports that the current interest in horror stories has attracted a great number of readers to John Dash's novel . . . because of its depiction of Nazi brutality. Critics and readers alike have commented on the stark realism of Dash's handling of the torture scenes in the book. The publishers originally envisaged a woman's market because of the love story, now find men reading the book because of the other angle." This does not suggest a more than usual depravity in the male reader, for "the other angle" has always had a fascination, no doubt a bad one, even for those who would not themselves commit or actually witness an act of torture. I cite the extreme example only to suggest that something may indeed lie behind our sober intelligent interest in moral politics. In this instance the pleasure in the cruelty is protected and licensed by moral indignation. In other instances moral indignation, which has been said to be the favorite emotion of the middle class, may be in itself an exquisite pleasure. To understand this does not invalidate moral indignation but only sets up the conditions on which it ought to be entertained, only says when it is legitimate and when not.

But, the answer comes, however important it may be for moral realism to raise questions in our minds about our motives, is it not at best a matter of secondary importance? Is it not of the first importance that we be given a direct and immediate report on the reality that is daily being brought to dreadful birth? The novels that have done this have effected much practical good, bringing to consciousness the latent feelings of many people, making it harder for them to be unaware or indifferent, creating an atmosphere in which injustice finds it harder to thrive. To speak of moral realism is all very well. But it is an elaborate, even fancy, phrase and it is to be suspected of having the intention of sophisticating the simple reality that is easily to be conceived. Life presses us so hard, time is so short, the suffering of the world is so huge, simple, unendurable—anything that complicates our moral fervor in dealing with reality as we immediately see it and wish to drive headlong upon it must be regarded with some impatience.

True enough: and therefore any defense of what I have called moral realism must be made not in the name of some highflown fineness of feeling but in the name of simple social practicality. And there is indeed a simple social fact to which moral realism has a simple practical relevance, but it is a fact very difficult for us nowadays to perceive. It is that the moral passions are even more willful and imperious and impatient than the self-seeking passions. All history is at one in telling us that their tendency is to be not only liberating but also restrictive.

It is probable that at this time we are about to make great changes in our social system. The world is ripe for such changes and if they are not made in the direction of greater social liberality, the direction forward, they will almost of necessity be made in the direction backward, of a terrible social niggardliness. We all know which of those directions we want. But it is not enough to want it, not even enough to work for it—we must want it and work for it with intelligence. Which means that we must be aware of the dangers which lie in our most generous wishes. Some paradox of our natures leads us, when once we have made our fellow men the objects of our enlightened interest, to go on to make them the objects of our pity, then of our wisdom, ultimately of our coercion. It is to prevent this corruption, the most ironic and tragic that man knows, that we stand in need of the moral realism which is the product of the free play of the moral imagination.

For our time the most effective agent of the moral

imagination has been the novel of the last two hundred years. It was never, either aesthetically or morally, a perfect form and its faults and failures can be quickly enumerated. But its greatness and its practical usefulness lay in its unremitting work of involving the reader himself in the moral life, inviting him to put his own motives under examination, suggesting that reality is not as his conventional education has led him to see it. It taught us, as no other genre ever did, the extent of human variety and the value of this variety. It was the literary form to which the emotions of understanding and forgiveness were indigenous, as if by the definition of the form itself. At the moment its impulse does not seem strong, for there never was a time when the virtues of its greatness were so likely to be thought of as weaknesses. Yet there never was a time when its particular activity was so much needed, was of so much practical, political, and social use—so much so that if its impulse does not respond to the need, we shall have reason to be sad not only over a waning form of art but also over our waning freedom.

Politics and the English Language

George Orwell (1903–1950)

Eric Arthur Blair (the penname "George Orwell" was adopted when he published his first book) was born in Bengal, India, the son of a minor British civil servant. At the age of eight he was sent to an English preparatory school where his poverty and awkwardness made him intensely unhappy (see his autobiographical essay *Such, Such Were the Joys*). From preparatory school Orwell went to Eton where one of his masters was Aldous Huxley. After leaving Eton he served for some time as a civil servant in Burma, a period later recalled in his novel *Burmese Days* (1934) and his superb essay on the burdens of Imperialism, "Shooting an Elephant." In 1927 Orwell left the Imperial Police and began his career as a writer. His experiences as an impoverished worker in Paris and London led to his first book, *Down and Out in Paris and London* (1933). Orwell wrote two novels in the mid-1930s, but his most interesting work was a Socialist critique of English society, *The Road to Wigan Pier* (1937). During the Spanish Civil War he joined the Republican militia and was seriously wounded. His experiences in Spain, recorded in *Homage to Catalonia* (1938), led to his later political ambivalence, a hatred for reactionary politics being matched by a dislike for Communist hypocrisy. During World War II Orwell worked for the Indian service of the British Broadcasting Corporation and wrote a great deal of perceptive journalism, which was informed by an equal distaste for left-wing and right-wing fanaticism. His satire on the Russian revolution and its doctrine of unequal equality, *Animal Farm* (1945), was followed by *Nineteen Eighty-Four* (1949), a chilling fantasy of a totalitarian future in which language is corrupted in order to stifle personal freedom. His essay "Politics and the English Language," like most of his best works, equates a healthy language with a healthy society.

Most people who bother with the matter at all would admit that the English language is in a bad way, but it is generally assumed that we cannot by conscious action do anything about it. Our civilization is decadent and our language—so the argument runs—must inevitably share in the general collapse. It follows that any struggle against the abuse of language is a sentimental archaism, like preferring candles to electric light or hansom cabs to aeroplanes. Underneath this lies the half-conscious belief that language is a natural growth and not an instrument which we shape for our own purposes.

Now, it is clear that the decline of a language must ultimately have political and economic causes: it is not due simply to the bad influence of this or that individual writer. But an effect can become a cause, reinforcing the original cause and producing the same effect in an intensified form, and so on indefinitely. A man may take to drink because he feels himself to be a failure, and than fail all the more completely because he drinks. It is rather the same thing that is happening to the English language. It becomes ugly and inaccurate because our thoughts are foolish, but the slovenliness of our language makes it easier for us to have foolish thoughts. The point is that the process is reversible. Modern English, especially written English, is full of bad habits which spread by imitation and which can be avoided if one is willing to take the necessary trouble. If one gets rid of these habits one can think more clearly, and to think clearly is a necessary first step toward political regeneration: so that the fight against bad English is not frivolous and is not the exclusive concern of professional writers. I will come back to this presently, and I hope that by that time the meaning of what I have said here will have become clearer. Meanwhile, here are five specimens of the English language as it is now habitually written.

These five passages have not been picked out because they are especially bad—I could have quoted far worse if I had chosen—but because they illustrate various of the mental vices from which we now suffer. They are a little below the average, but are fairly representative samples. I number them so that I can refer back to them when necessary:

(1) I am not, indeed, sure whether it is not true to say that the Milton who once seemed not unlike a seventeenth-century Shelley had not become, out of an experience ever more bitter in each year, more alien [*sic*] to the founder of that Jesuit sect which nothing could induce him to tolerate.

Professor Harold Laski
(Essay in *Freedom of Expression*)

(2) Above all, we cannot play ducks and drakes with a native battery of idioms which prescribes such egregious collocations of vocables as the Basic *put up with* for *tolerate* or *put at a loss* for *bewilder*.

Professor Lancelot Hogben (*Interglossa*)

(3) On the one side we have the free personality: by definition it is not neurotic, for it has neither conflict nor dream. Its desires, such as they are, are transparent, for they are just what institutional approval keeps in the forefront of consciousness; another institutional pattern would alter their number and intensity; there is little in them that is natural, irreducible, or culturally dangerous. But *on the other side,* the social bond itself is nothing but the mutual reflection of these self-secure integrities. Recall the definition of love. Is not this the very picture of a small academic? Where is there a place in this hall of mirrors for either personality or fraternity?

Essay on psychology in *Politics* (New York)

(4) All the "best people" from the gentlemen's clubs, and all the frantic fascist captains, united in common hatred of Socialism and bestial horror of the rising tide of the mass revolutionary movement, have turned to acts of provocation, to foul incendiarism, to medieval legends of poisoned wells, to legalize their own destruction of proletarian organizations, and rouse the agitated petty-bourgeoisie to chauvinistic fervor on behalf of the fight against the revolutionary way out of the crisis.

Communist pamphlet

(5) If a new spirit *is* to be infused into this old country, there is one thorny and contentious reform which must be tackled, and that is the humanization and galvanization of the B.B.C. Timidity here will bespeak canker and atrophy of the soul. The heart of Britain may be sound and of strong beat, for instance, but the British lion's roar at present is like that of Bottom in Shakespeare's *Midsummer Night's Dream*—as gentle as any sucking dove. A virile new Britain cannot continue indefinitely to be traduced in the eyes or rather ears, of the world by the effete languors of Langham Place, brazenly masquerading as "standard English." When the Voice of Britain is heard at nine o'clock, better far and infinitely less ludicrous to hear aitches honestly dropped than the present priggish, or inhibited, school-ma'amish arch braying of blameless bashful mewing maidens!

Letter in *Tribune*

Each of these passages has faults of its own, but, quite apart from avoidable ugliness, two qualities are common to all of them. The first is staleness of imagery: the other is lack of precision. The writer either has a meaning and cannot express it, or he inadvertently says something else, or he is almost indifferent as to whether his words mean anything or not. This mixture of vagueness and sheer incompetence is the most marked characteristic of modern English prose, and especially of any kind of political writing. As soon as certain topics are raised, the concrete melts into the abstract and no one seems able to think of turns of speech that are not hackneyed: prose consists less and less of *words* chosen for the sake of their meaning, and more and more of *phrases* tacked together like the sections of a prefabricated henhouse. I list below, with notes and examples, various of the tricks by means of which the work of prose-construction is habitually dodged:

Dying metaphors. A newly invented metaphor assists thought by evoking a visual image, while on the other hand a metaphor which is technically "dead" (e.g. *iron resolution*) has in effect reverted to being an ordinary word and can generally be used without loss of vividness. But in between these two classes there is a huge dump of worn-out metaphors which have lost all evocative power and are merely used because they save people the trouble of inventing phrases for themselves. Examples are: *Ring the changes on, take up the cudgels for, toe the line, ride roughshod over, stand shoulder to shoulder with, play into the hands of, no axe to grind, grist to the mill, fishing in troubled waters, on the order of the day, Achilles' heel, swan song, hotbed.* Many of these used without knowledge of their meaning (what is a "rift," for instance?), and incompatible metaphors are frequently mixed, a sure sign that the writer is not interested in what he is saying. Some metaphors now current have been twisted out of their original meaning without those who use them even being aware of the fact. For example, *toe the line* is sometimes written *tow the line.* Another example is *the hammer and the anvil,* now always used with the implication that the anvil gets the worst of it. In real life it is always the anvil that breaks the hammer, never the other way about: a writer who stopped to think what he was saying would be aware of this, and would avoid perverting the original phrase.

Operators or *verbal false limbs.* These save the trouble of picking out appropriate verbs and nouns, and at the same time pad each sentence with extra syllables which give it an appearance of symmetry. Characteristic phrases are: *render inoperative, militate against, make contact with, be subjected to, give rise to, give grounds for, have the effect of, playing a leading part (role) in, make itself felt, take effect, exhibit a tendency to, serve the purpose of, etc., etc.* The keynote is the elimination of simple verbs. Instead of being a single word, such as *break, stop, spoil, mend, kill,* a verb becomes a *phrase,* made up of a noun or adjective tacked on to some general-purpose verb such as *prove, serve, form, play, render.* In addition, the passive voice is wherever possible used in preference to the active, and noun constructions are used instead of gerunds (*by examination of* instead of *by examining*). The range of verbs is further cut down by means of the *ize* and *de-* formations, and the banal statements are given an appearance of profundity by means of the *not un-* formation. Simple conjunctions and prepositions are replaced by such phrases as *with respect to, having regard to, the fact that, by dint of, in view of, in the interests of, on the hypothesis that;* and the ends of sentences are saved from anticlimax by such resounding commonplaces as *greatly to be desired, cannot be left out of account, a development to be expected in the near future, deserving of serious consideration, brought to a satisfactory conclusion,* and so on and so forth.

Pretentious diction. Words like *phenomenon, element, individual* (as noun), *objective, categorical, effective, virtual, basic, primary, promote, constitute, exhibit, exploit, utilize, eliminate, liquidate,* are used to dress up simple statement and give an air of scientific impartiality to biased judgments. Adjectives like *epoch-making, epic, historic, unforgettable, triumphant, age-old, inevitable, inexorable, veritable,* are used to dignify the sordid processes of international politics, while writing that aims at glorifying war usually takes on an archaic color, its characteristic words being: *realm, throne, chariot, mailed fist, trident, sword, shield, buckler, banner, jackboot, clarion.* Foreign words and expressions such as *cul de sac, ancien régime, deus ex machina, mutatis mutandis, status quo, gleichshaltung, weltanschauung,* are used to give an air of culture and elegance. Except for the useful abbreviations *i.e., e.g.,* and *etc.,* there is no real need for any of the hundreds of foreign phrases now current in English. Bad writers, and especially scientific, political, and sociological writers, are nearly always haunted by the notion that Latin or Greek words are grander than Saxon ones, and unnecessary words like *expedite, ameliorate, predict, extraneous, deracinated, clandestine, subaqueous,* and hundreds of others constantly gain ground from their Anglo-Saxon opposite numbers.[1] The jargon peculiar to Marxist writing (*hyena, hang-*

[1] An interesting illustration of this is the way in which the English flower names which were in use till very recently are being ousted by Greek ones, *snapdragon* becoming *antirrhinum, forget-me-not* becoming *myosotis,* etc. It is hard to see any practical reason for this change of fashion: it is probably due to an instinctive turning away from the more homely word and a vague feeling that the Greek word is scientific.

man, cannibal, petty bourgeois, these gentry, lackey, flunkey, mad dog, White Guard, etc.) consists largely of words and phrases translated from Russian, German, or French; but the normal way of coining a new word is to use a Latin or Greek root with the appropriate affix and, where necessary, the -ize formation. It is often easier to make up words of this kind (*deregionalize, impermissible, extramarital, non-fragmentatory,* and so forth) than to think up the English words that will cover one's meaning. The result, in general, is an increase in slovenliness and vagueness.

Meaningless words. In certain kinds of writing, particularly in art criticism and literary criticism, it is normal to come across long passages which are almost completely lacking in meaning.[2] Words like *romantic, plastic, values, human, dead, sentimental, natural, vitality,* as used in art criticism, are strictly meaningless, in the sense that they not only do not point to any discoverable object, but are hardly ever expected to do so by the reader. When one critic writes, "The outstanding feature of Mr. X's work is its living quality," while another writes, "The immediately striking thing about Mr. X's work is its peculiar deadness," the reader accepts this as a simple difference of opinion. If words like *black* and *white* were involved, instead of the jargon words *dead* and *living,* he would see at once that language was being used in an improper way. Many political words are similarly abused. The word *Fascism* has now no meaning except in so far as it signifies "something not desirable." The words *democracy, socialism, freedom, patriotic, realistic, justice,* have each of them several different meanings which cannot be reconciled with one another. In the case of a word like *democracy,* not only is there no agreed definition, but the attempt to make one is resisted from all sides. It is almost universally felt that when we call a country democratic we are praising it: consequently the defenders of every kind of régime claim that it is a democracy, and fear that they might have to stop using the word if it were tied down to any one meaning. Words of this kind are often used in a consciously dishonest way. That is, the person who uses them has his own private definition, but allows his hearer to think he means something quite different. Statements like *Marshal Pétain was a true patriot, The Soviet press is the freest in the world, The Catholic Church is opposed to persecution,* are almost always made with intent to deceive. Other words used in variable meanings, in most cases more or less dishonestly, are: *class, totalitarian, science, progressive, reactionary, bourgeois, equality.*

Now that I have made this catalogue of swindles and perversions, let me give another example of the kind of writing that they lead to. This time it must of its nature be an imaginary one. I am going to translate a passage of good English into modern English of the worst sort. Here is a well-known verse from *Ecclesiastes:*

> I returned and saw under the sun, that the race is not to the swift, nor the battle to the strong, neither yet bread to the wise, nor yet riches to men of understanding, nor yet favour to men of skill; but time and chance happeneth to them all.

Here it is in modern English:

> Objective considerations of contemporary phenomena compels the conclusion that success or failure in competitive activities exhibits no tendency to be commensurate with innate capacity, but that a considerable element of the unpredictable must invariably be taken into account.

This is a parody, but not a very gross one. Exhibit (3), above, for instance, contains several patches of the same kind of English. It will be seen that I have not made a full translation. The beginning and ending of the sentence follow the original meaning fairly closely, but in the middle the concrete illustrations—race, battle, bread—dissolve into the vague phrase "success or failure in competitive activities." This had to be so, because no modern writer of the kind I am discussing—no one capable of using phrases like "objective consideration of contemporary phenomena"—would ever tabulate his thoughts in that precise and detailed way. The whole tendency of modern prose is away from concreteness. Now analyze these two sentences a little more closely. The first contains forty-nine words but only sixty syllables, and all its words are those of everyday life. The second contains thirty-eight words of ninety syllables: eighteen of its words are from Latin roots, and one from Greek. The first sentence contains six vivid images, and only one phrase ("time and chance") that could be called vague. The second contains not a single fresh, arresting phrase, and in spite of its ninety syllables it gives only a shortened version of the meaning contained in the first. Yet without a doubt it is the second kind of sentence that is gaining ground in modern English. I do not want to exaggerate. This

[2] Example: "Comfort's catholicity of perception and image, strangely Whitmanesque in range, almost the exact opposite in aesthetic compulsion, continues to evoke that trembling atmospheric accumulative hinting at a cruel, an inexorably serene timelessness. . . . Wrey Gardiner scores by aiming at simple bull's-eyes with precision. Only they are not so simple, and through this contented sadness runs more than the surface bittersweet of resignation." (*Poetry Quarterly.*)

kind of writing is not yet universal, and outcrops of simplicity will occur here and there in the worst-written page. Still, if you or I were told to write a few lines on the uncertainty of human fortunes, we should probably come much nearer to my imaginary sentence than to the one from *Ecclesiastes.*

As I have tried to show, modern writing at its worst does not consist in picking out words for the sake of their meaning and inventing images in order to make the meaning clearer. It consists in gumming together long strips of words which have already been set in order by someone else, and making the results presentable by sheer humbug. The attraction of this way of writing is that it is easy. It is easier—even quicker, once you have the habit—to say *In my opinion it is a not unjustifiable assumption that* than to say *I think.* If you use ready-made phrases, you not only don't have to hunt about for words; you also don't have to bother with the rhythms of your sentences, since these phrases are generally so arranged as to be more or less euphonious. When you are composing in a hurry—when you are dictating to a stenographer, for instance, or making a public speech—it is natural to fall into a pretentious, Latinized style. Tags like *a consideration which we should do well to bear in mind* or *a conclusion to which all of us would readily assent* will save many a sentence from coming down with a bump. By using stale metaphors, similes, and idioms, you save much mental effort, at the cost of leaving your meaning vague, not only for your reader but for yourself. This is the significance of mixed metaphors. The sole aim of a metaphor is to call up a visual image. When these images clash—as in *The Fascist octopus has sung its swan song, the jackboot is thrown into the melting pot*—it can be taken as certain that the writer is not seeing a mental image of the objects he is naming; in other words he is not really thinking. Look again at the examples I gave at the beginning of this essay. Professor Laski (1) uses five negatives in fifty-three words. One of these is superfluous, making nonsense of the whole passage, and in addition there is the slip—*alien* for akin—making further nonsense, and several avoidable pieces of clumsiness which increase the general vagueness. Professor Hogben (2) plays ducks and drakes with a battery which is able to write prescriptions, and, while disapproving of the everyday phrase *put up with,* is unwilling to look *egregious* up in the dictionary and see what it means; (3), if one takes an uncharitable attitude towards it, is simply meaningless: probably one could work out its intended meaning by reading the whole of the article in which it occurs. In (4), the writer knows more or less what he wants to say, but an accumulation of stale phrases chokes him like tea leaves blocking a sink. In (5), words and meaning have almost parted company. People who write in this manner usually have a general emotional meaning—they dislike one thing and want to express solidarity with another—but they are not interested in the detail of what they are saying. A scrupulous writer, in every sentence that he writes, will ask himself at least four questions, thus: What am I trying to say? What words will express it? What image or idiom will make it clearer? Is this image fresh enough to have an effect? And he will probably ask himself two more: Could I put it more shortly? Have I said anything that is avoidably ugly? But you are not obliged to go to all this trouble. You can shirk it by simply throwing your mind open and letting the ready-made phrases come crowding in. They will construct your sentences for you—even think your thoughts for you, to a certain extent—and at need they will perform the important service of partially concealing your meaning even from yourself. It is at this point that the special connection between politics and the debasement of language becomes clear.

In our time it is broadly true that political writing is bad writing. Where it is not true, it will generally be found that the writer is some kind of rebel, expressing his private opinions and not a "party line." Orthodoxy, of whatever color, seems to demand a lifeless, imitative style. The political dialects to be found in pamphlets, leading articles, manifestoes, White Papers and the speeches of undersecretaries do, of course, vary from party to party, but they are all alike in that one almost never finds in them a fresh, vivid, homemade turn of speech. When one watches some tired hack on the platform mechanically repeating the familiar phrases—*bestial atrocities, iron heel, bloodstained tyranny, free peoples of the world, stand shoulder to shoulder*—one often has a curious feeling that one is not watching a live human being but some kind of dummy: a feeling which suddenly becomes stronger at moments when the light catches the speaker's spectacles and turns them into blank discs which seem to have no eyes behind them. And this is not altogether fanciful. A speaker who uses that kind of phraseology has gone some distance toward turning himself into a machine. The appropriate noises are coming out of his larynx, but his brain is not involved as it would be if he were choosing his words for himself. If the speech he is making is one that he is accustomed to make over and over again, he may be almost unconscious of what he is saying, as one is when one utters the responses in church. And this reduced state of consciousness, if not indispensable, is at any rate favorable to political conformity.

In our time, political speech and writing are largely the defense of the indefensible. Things like the continuance of British rule in India, the Russian purges and deportations, the dropping of the atom bombs on Japan, can indeed be defended, but only by arguments which are too brutal for most people to face, and which do not square with the professed aims of political parties. Thus political language has to consist largely of euphemism, question-begging and sheer cloudy vagueness. Defenseless villages are bombarded from the air, the inhabitants driven out into the countryside, the cattle machine-gunned, the huts set on fire with incendiary bullets: this is called *pacification*. Millions of peasants are robbed of their farms and sent trudging along the roads with no more than they can carry: this is called *transfer of population* or *rectification of frontiers*. People are imprisoned for years without trial, or shot in the back of the neck or sent to die of scurvy in Arctic lumber camps: this is called *elimination of unreliable elements*. Such phraseology is needed if one wants to name things without calling up mental pictures of them. Consider for instance some comfortable English professor defending Russian totalitarianism. He cannot say outright, "I believe in killing off your opponents when you can get good results by doing so." Probably, therefore, he will say something like this:

"While freely conceding that the Soviet régime exhibits certain features which the humanitarian may be inclined to deplore, we must, I think, agree that a certain curtailment of the right to political opposition is an unavoidable concomitant of transitional periods, and that the rigors which the Russian people have been called upon to undergo have been amply justified in the sphere of concrete achievement."

The inflated style is itself a kind of euphemism. A mass of Latin words falls upon the facts like soft snow, blurring the outlines and covering up all the details. The great enemy of clear language is insincerity. When there is a gap between one's real and one's declared aims, one turns as it were instinctively to long words and exhausted idioms, like a cuttlefish squirting out ink. In our age there is no such thing as "keeping out of politics." All issues are political issues, and politics itself is a mass of lies, evasions, folly, hatred, and schizophrenia. When the general atmosphere is bad, language must suffer. I should expect to find—this is a guess which I have not sufficient knowledge to verify—that the German, Russian and Italian languages have all deteriorated in the last ten or fifteen years, as a result of dictatorship.

But if thought corrupts language, language can also corrupt thought. A bad usage can spread by tradition and imitation, even among people who should and do know better. The debased language that I have been discussing is in some ways very convenient. Phrases like *a not unjustifiable assumption, leaves much to be desired, would serve no good purpose, a consideration which we should do well to bear in mind,* are a continuous temptation, a packet of aspirins always at one's elbow. Look back through this essay, and for certain you will find that I have again and again committed the very faults I am protesting against. By this morning's post I have received a pamphlet dealing with conditions in Germany. The author tells me that he "felt impelled" to write it. I open it at random, and here is almost the first sentence that I see: "[The Allies] have an opportunity not only of achieving a radical transformation of Germany's social and political structure in such a way as to avoid a nationalistic reaction in Germany itself, but at the same time of laying the foundations of a co-operative and unified Europe." You see, he "feels impelled" to write—feels, presumably, that he has something new to say—and yet his words, like cavalry horses answering the bugle, group themselves automatically into the familiar dreary pattern. This invasion of one's mind by ready-made phrases (*lay the foundations, achieve a radical transformation*) can only be prevented if one is constantly on guard against them, and every such phrase anaesthetizes a portion of one's brain.

I said earlier that the decadence of our language is probably curable. Those who deny this would argue, if they produced an argument at all, that language merely reflects existing social conditions, and that we cannot influence its development by any direct tinkering with words and constructions. So far as the general tone or spirit of a language goes, this may be true, but it is not true in detail. Silly words and expressions have often disappeared, not through any evolutionary process but owing to the conscious action of a minority. Two recent examples were *explore every avenue* and *leave no stone unturned,* which were killed by the jeers of a few journalists. There is a long list of flyblown metaphors which could similarly be got rid of if enough people would interest themselves in the job; and it should also be possible to laugh the *not un-* formation out of existence,[3] to reduce the amount of Latin and Greek in the average sentence, to drive out foreign phrases and strayed scientific words, and, in general, to make pretentiousness unfashionable. But all these are minor points. The defense of the English language

[3] One can cure oneself of the *not un-* formation by memorizing this sentence: *A not unblack dog was chasing a not unsmall rabbit across a not ungreen field.*

implies more than this, and perhaps it is best to start by saying what it does *not* imply.

To begin with it has nothing to do with archaism, with the salvaging of obsolete words and turns of speech, or with the setting up of a "standard English" which must never be departed from. On the contrary, it is especially concerned with the scrapping of every word or idiom which has outworn its usefulness. It has nothing to do with correct grammar and syntax, which are of no importance so long as one makes one's meaning clear, or with the avoidance of Americanisms, or with having what is called a "good prose style." On the other hand it is not concerned with fake simplicity and the attempt to make written English colloquial. Nor does it even imply in every case preferring the Saxon word to the Latin one, though it does imply using the fewest and shortest words that will cover one's meaning. What is above all needed is to let the meaning choose the word, and not the other way about. In prose, the worst thing one can do with words is to surrender to them. When you think of a concrete object, you think wordlessly, and then, if you want to describe the thing you have been visualizing you probably hunt about till you find the exact words that seem to fit it. When you think of something abstract you are more inclined to use words from the start, and unless you make a conscious effort to prevent it, the existing dialect will come rushing in and do the job for you, at the expense of blurring or even changing your meaning. Probably it is better to put off using words as long as possible and get one's meaning as clear as one can through pictures or sensations. Afterward one can choose—not simply *accept*—the phrases that will best cover the meaning, and then switch round and decide what impression one's words are likely to make on another person. This last effort of the mind cuts out all stale or mixed images, all prefabricated phrases, needless repetitions, and humbug and vagueness generally. But one can often be in doubt about the effect of a word or a phrase, and one needs rules that one can rely on when instinct fails. I think the following rules will cover most cases:

(i) Never use a metaphor, simile, or other figure of speech which you are used to seeing in print.

(ii) Never use a long word where a short one will do.

(iii) If it is possible to cut a word out, always cut it out.

(iv) Never use the passive where you can use the active.

(v) Never use a foreign phrase, a scientific word, or a jargon word if you can think of an everyday English equivalent.

(vi) Break any of these rules sooner than say anything outright barbarous.

These rules sound elementary, and so they are, but they demand a deep change of attitude in anyone who has grown used to writing in the style now fashionable. One could keep all of them and still write bad English, but one could not write the kind of stuff that I quoted in those five specimens at the beginning of this article.

I have not here been considering the literary use of language, but merely language as an instrument for expressing and not for concealing or preventing thought. Stuart Chase and others have come near to claiming that all abstract words are meaningless, and have used this as a pretext for advocating a kind of political quietism. Since you don't know what Fascism is, how can you struggle against Fascism? One need not swallow such absurdities as this, but one ought to recognize that the present political chaos is connected with the decay of language, and that one can probably bring about some improvement by starting at the verbal end. If you simplify your English, you are freed from the worst follies of orthodoxy. You cannot speak any of the necessary dialects, and when you make a stupid remark its stupidity will be obvious, even to yourself. Political language—and with variations this is true of all political parties, from Conservatives to Anarchists—is designed to make lies sound truthful and murder respectable, and to give an appearance of solidity to pure wind. One cannot change this all in a moment, but one can at least change one's own habits, and from time to time one can even, if one jeers loudly enough, send some worn-out and useless phrase—some *jackboot, Achilles' heel, hotbed, melting pot, acid test, veritable inferno,* or other lump of verbal refuse—into the dustbin where it belongs.

Glossary of Critical Terms

accent (stress): a vocal emphasis given to certain syllables in a word or passage. *See* foot, meter.

allegory: a fictional narrative capable of simultaneous literal and symbolic interpretations.

alliteration: the repetition of similar consonant sounds, especially at the beginnings of words, for poetic effect. In the opening lines of Hart Crane's "At Melville's Tomb," for instance, note the recurrence of the "b," "d," "s," and "w" sounds:

> Often beneath the wave, wide from this ledge
> The dice of drowned men's bones he saw bequeath
> An embassy.

allusion: a literary reference either to another literary work or to information drawn from some other field, such as myth, history, biography, science, or current affairs. A literary allusion may be explicit, like Berryman's references to D. H. Lawrence and Malcolm Lowry's works ("Of Suicide"): or implicit, like the title of Lowell's "For the Union Dead," which recalls Allen Tate's "Ode to the Confederate Dead." Historical and biographical allusions are represented in Auden's references to Yeats's career ("In Memory of W. B. Yeats") and Sylvia Plath's reference to Isadora Duncan's accidental death ("Isadora's scarves," in "Fever 103°").

ambiguity: the use of a word or phrase having, in context, two or more distinct meanings. In Yeats's "Easter 1916," the word "bewildered" ("And what if excess of love / Bewildered them till they died?") can be taken to mean either "confused" (the standard meaning) or "made wild" (suggested by etymology and context). By forcing the reader to entertain alternative interpretations, such ambiguities may enrich the response to the passage.

assonance: the repetition of similar vowel sounds for poetic effect. In the opening lines of Robert Lowell's "For the Union Dead," note the recurrence of "o" sounds: "The old South Boston Aquarium stands / in a Sahara of snow now. Its broken windows are boarded."

blank verse: unrhymed iambic pentameter. Frost's "Mending Wall" and "Directive" are predominantly in blank verse.

caesura: a pause or break in the rhythm of a line of verse in accordance with sense, grammar, or punctuation. An example would be the opening line of W. B. Yeats's "Leda and the Swan": "A sudden blow: the great wings beating still . . ."

central consciousness (or **center of consciousness):** the character in a narrative work whose thoughts and reactions are most fully described, or through whose mind the action is refracted.

character: a personage in a literary work, especially one identified by name and portrayed realistically rather than symbolically; the distinctive nature and attributes of such a personage.

conceit: an unusual or elaborate comparison; a metaphor in which defined and defining terms have several points of comparison. In Eliot's "Love Song of J. Alfred Prufrock," for instance, the movement of the fog and smoke is described as a series of feline actions:

> The yellow fog that rubs its back upon the window-panes,
> The yellow smoke that rubs its muzzle on the window-panes,
> Licked its tongue into the corners of the evening,
> Lingered upon the pools that stand in drains,
> Let fall upon its back the soot that falls from chimneys,
> Slipped by the terrace, made a sudden leap,
> And seeing that it was a soft October night,
> Curled once about the house, and fell asleep.

connotation: a subjective meaning of a term, as opposed to its objective or "dictionary" meaning. In Eliot's "Sweeney Among the Nightingales," the word "vertebrate" ("the silent vertebrate in brown") connotes the qualities of a subhuman animal. Strictly speaking, of course, any human being is a vertebrate.

context: the totality of elements within a work that qualify the meaning of a particular passage; also, the totality of elements, especially historical and cultural, surrounding the creation of a work.

convention: any customary practice, especially one pertaining to a particular literary form, mode, or theme. That soliloquies and asides are to be regarded as sincere is a convention of the drama; the division of a sonnet into eight-line and six-line rhyming sequences is one of the conventions of that verse form. By refusing to capitalize the initial letters of verse-lines and proper names, E. E. Cummings calls attention to conventions of typography.

denotation: the objective or "dictionary" meaning of a term, as opposed to possible subjective meanings. *See* connotation.

denouement: the point in a narrative where complications of plot and misunderstandings between characters are resolved.

diction: an author's choice of words, considered as an element of style.

dramatic monologue: a poem consisting of an extended speech by a single character, addressed either to the reader or to a hypothetical listener, that reveals the nature of the speaker. Eliot's "Love Song of J. Alfred Prufrock" and Robert Lowell's "Falling Asleep over the Aeneid" are examples of dramatic monologues.

elision: the elimination for metrical purposes of a syllable or a natural pause between words. In the following line from Yeats's "Among School Children," note the elision of "the" and "other": "I look upon one child or t'other there."

end-stopped line: a line of verse concluding with a caesura or rhythmic break. *See* enjambed (run-on) line.

enjambed (run-on) line: a line of verse not concluded with a caesura or rhythmic break. In the opening lines of Frost's "After Apple Picking," lines 1, 3 and 4 are enjambed or run-on, lines 2 and 5 end-stopped:

> My long two-pointed ladder's sticking through a tree
> Toward heaven still,
> And there's a barrel that I didn't fill
> Beside it, and there may be two or three
> Apples I didn't pick upon some bough.

feminine line: a line of verse in which the next-to-last syllable is stressed and the last syllable is unstressed; a line of verse concluded with a trochaic foot. *See* masculine line.

feminine rhyme: a pair of rhyme words accented on the next-to-last syllables. In the following stanza from Theodore Roethke's "My Papa's Waltz," the second and fourth lines have feminine rhyme, the first and third masculine rhyme:

> The hand that held my wrist
> Was battered on one knuckle;
> At every step you missed
> My right ear scraped a buckle.

See masculine rhyme.

foot: a portion of verse, either two or three syllables in length, forming a standard metrical pattern; hence, the basic metrical unit in verse. The most common types of metrical feet are:

iamb: a two-syllable unit composed of one unaccented syllable followed by an accented one ("about").

trochee: a two-syllable unit composed of one accented syllable followed by an unaccented one ("never").

dactyl: a three-syllable unit composed of one accented syllable followed by two unaccented ones ("suffering").

anapest: a three-syllable unit composed of two unaccented syllables followed by an accented one ("understood").

spondee: a metrical foot composed exclusively of accented syllables; hence, inevitably a variation from the prevailing metrical pattern in a poem. In the following line from Wilfred Owen's "Anthem for Doomed Youth," note how the third metrical foot breaks the iambic pattern: "The pallor of girls' brows shall be their pall."

frame narrative: a fictional work in which the main narrator of the story and the occasion for his telling it are introduced at the beginning of the work. The opening chapters of Conrad's *Heart of Darkness,* for instance, establish the circumstances in which Marlow decides to relate the events that form the core of the novel.

free verse: poetry lacking a consistent metrical pattern, line length, or rhyme-scheme. Adrienne Rich's "A Valediction Forbidding Mourning" is in free verse.

genre: a class of works linked by similar conventions of style, theme, structure, and mode of presentation; especially, a class traditionally recognized as such. Allen Tate's "Ode to the Confederate Dead," for instance, belongs to the genre of the ode, as well as to the sub-genre of the funeral ode.

image: a pictorial idea or impression, especially one created by figurative language. In "The Love Song of J. Alfred Prufrock," Eliot uses the image of a lobster as a metaphor or symbol for Prufrock's sense of isolation: "I should have been a pair of ragged claws / Scuttling across the floors of silent seas."

irony: a tone which an author or speaker adopts to signal a discrepancy between his statements and his meaning; also, a sequence of events in which actions have results radically different from those that were intended or anticipated. In "i sing of Olaf glad and big," E. E. Cummings ironically adopts the dubious values of "erring Olaf's" colonel. In Auden's "Musée des Beaux Arts," an important event evokes an incongruous lack of response in the observers.

lyric: a poem, particularly one that is short or song-like, expressing the subjective emotions of the speaker or author.

masculine line: a line of verse in which the last syllable is accented. *See* feminine line.

masculine rhyme: a rhyme in which the last syllables of the rhyme words are stressed. *See* feminine rhyme.

metaphor: a figure of speech comparing basically dissimilar objects, particularly one that suggests an identity (rather than simply a likeness) between them. In Yeats's "Sailing to Byzantium," an "aged man" is identified with "A tattered coat upon a stick."

meter: the pattern of accented and unaccented syllables in a line of verse. The common meters in English verse are the iambic ("I found a dimpled spider, fat and white") and trochaic ("Earth, receive an honoured guest"). *See* foot.

motif: a recurrent image or symbol in a literary work. In "Among School Children," for example, Yeats invokes the myth of Leda and the Swan several times, helping to unify the poem thematically and structurally.

myth: a tale that symbolically reflects themes and patterns of behavior (especially unconscious ones) considered universal to human culture. Yeats uses the myth of Leda's rape by Jove in the form of a swan to express (among other things) man's yearning for knowledge and experience of the divine.

narrator: the character or personage who relates the events of a fictional work. A limited or unreliable narrator is one whose account of events is restricted by his incomplete knowledge or understanding of them. By contrast, an omniscient author has a knowledge of events and psychological states that would not realistically be available to an observer of the action.

near-rhyme: the repetition of similar, but not identical, sounds at the ends of lines of verse. In the opening stanza of Theodore Roethke's "My Papa's Waltz," the second and fourth lines have near-rhyme, the first and third perfect rhyme:

> The whiskey on your breath
> Could make a small boy dizzy;
> But I hung on like death:
> Such waltzing was not easy.

In Wilfred Owen's "Strange Meeting," all the lines have "slant" or near-rhyme.

pathetic fallacy: the attribution of human feelings to nonhuman or inanimate objects. In "Orion," Adrienne Rich describes a constellation as if it had human emotions:

> Pity is not your forte.
> Calmly you ache up there
> pinned aloft in your crow's nest,
> my speechless pirate!

persona: the narrator or speaker in a literary work, regarded as distinct from the author or as a projection of the author's personality.

personification: the attribution of human traits and behavior to abstract or inanimate objects. In "Ode to the Confederate Dead," Allen Tate describes the month of November as "Ambitious"; in his poem "In Memory of W. B. Yeats," Auden describes Ireland as "Mad."

plot: the story line or sequence of events in a narrative work.

point of view: a narrator's perspective on his subject, especially as regards his knowledge and understanding of events and characters. *See* narrator.

rhyme-scheme: the sequence of rhymes within a stanza or poem.

rhythm: accentual cadence in a passage of prose or verse; collectively, the kind of meter and the number of feet in a line of verse. Iambic pentameter, the most popular rhythm in English verse, has five iambic feet to a line; trochaic tetrameter has four trochaic feet per line. *See* foot, meter.

scansion: an analysis of the metrical characteristics of a line of verse or a poem.

sensibility: an author's or character's distinctive mode of perceiving and responding to his environment.

setting: the physical and spatial context in which an action occurs.

simile: a figure of speech explicitly comparing (with the word "like" or "as") basically dissimilar objects. In "Middle Passage," Robert Hayden describes "Sails flashing to the wind like weapons."

soliloquy: an extended speech, directed to the audience or reader rather than another character, and representing by convention the real thoughts of the speaker.

sonnet: in its standard form, a rhymed poem in iambic pentameter having fourteen lines. The sonnet usually has two separate rhyming sequences of eight lines and six lines each (octet and sestet), as exemplified in Frost's "Design" and "The Oven Bird" and Wilfred Owen's "Anthem for Doomed Youth." There are many variations within the fourteen-line form, such as Yeats's "Leda and the Swan" or Gerard Manley Hopkins's "The Windhover," and Hopkins's "Pied Beauty" is a "curtailed" sonnet of 10½ lines which preserves the basic proportions.

stanza: a group of lines, considered as a formal unit, that comprises a part of a poem. Typically, all the stanzas in a given poem will have the same number of lines, meter, and rhyme scheme. A two-line stanza is called a couplet or distich; a three-line stanza a tercet; a four-line stanza a quatrain.

stream of consciousness: a method of narration that uses "free association" rather than discursive reasoning as its model for representing the succession of ideas in the mind of the narrator or central consciousness. In "Snow," Ted Hughes may be said to employ "stream of consciousness" narration.

style: the characteristic manner of expression of an author or a work.

symbol: an image that signifies, by context or convention, a complex idea or set of ideas. In Yeats's "Sailing to Byzantium," the city of Byzantium symbolizes (variously and simultaneously) the fulfillment of man's desires for aesthetic perfection and mystical transcendence of the changing world.

synecdoche: a metaphor in which a part of some object represents the whole. In Auden's "In Memory of W. B. Yeats," the word "verse" ("With the farming of a verse / Make a vineyard of the curse") seems to mean not a single line of verse but a whole poem or poetry in general.

theme: the subject matter or central idea in a literary work; also, any significant idea or concern in a literary work. Thus, Wilfred Owen's poems take war (and the pity of war) as their theme. More specifically, one theme of "Strange Meeting" is the lost potential for friendship between soldiers of opposite sides.

tone: an author's attitude toward his subject matter or his reader, reflected in the details of structure and language.

(continued from page iv)

Saul Bellow, "Looking for Mr. Green." From *Seize the Day* by Saul Bellow. Copyright 1951 by Saul Bellow. Reprinted by permission of The Viking Press.

Flannery O'Connor, "Revelation." Reprinted with the permission of Farrar, Straus & Giroux, Inc. from *Everything That Rises Must Converge* by Mary Flannery O'Connor, Copyright © 1964, 1965 by the Estate of Mary Flannery O'Connor.

James Baldwin, "Sonny's Blues" excerpted from *Going to Meet the Man* by James Baldwin. Copyright © 1957 by James Baldwin. Originally published in *Partisan Review*. Reprinted by permission of The Dial Press.

Ted Hughes, "Snow" from *WODWO* (1967) by Ted Hughes. Copyright © 1962 by Ted Hughes. Reprinted by permission of Harper & Row, Publishers, Inc.

Donald Barthelme, "See the Moon?" Reprinted with the permission of Farrar, Straus & Giroux, Inc. from *Unspeakable Practices, Unnatural Acts* by Donald Barthelme, copyright © 1966, 1968 by Donald Barthelme. "See the Moon?" appeared originally in *The New Yorker*.

NOVELS

The Great Gatsby by F. Scott Fitzgerald is reprinted by permission of Charles Scribner's Sons. Copyright 1925 by Charles Scribner's Sons.

The Old Man and the Sea by Ernest Hemingway is reprinted by permission of Charles Scribner's Sons. Copyright 1952 by Ernest Hemingway.

DRAMA

Pygmalion by Bernard Shaw. Copyright 1913, 1914, 1916, 1930, 1941, 1944, George Bernard Shaw. Copyright 1957, The Public Trustee as Executor of the Estate of George Bernard Shaw. Reprinted by permission of Dodd, Mead & Company, Inc. and The Society of Authors for the Estate of George Bernard Shaw.

Eugene O'Neill, "Desire Under the Elms." Copyright 1924 and renewed 1952 by Eugene O'Neill. Reprinted from *Selected Plays of Eugene O'Neill,* by permission of Random House, Inc.

Tennessee Williams. From *The Glass Menagerie,* by Tennessee Williams. Copyright 1945 by Tennessee Williams and Edwina D. Williams and renewed 1973 by Tennessee Williams. Reprinted by permission of Random House, Inc.

Edward Albee, *The Zoo Story.* Reprinted by permission of Coward, McCann & Geoghegan, Inc. from *The Zoo Story* by Edward Albee. Copyright © 1960 by Edward Albee. *The Zoo Story* is the sole property of the author and is fully protected by copyright. It may not be acted either by professionals or amateurs without written consent. Public readings, radio and television broadcasts likewise are forbidden. All enquiries concerning these rights should be addressed to the William Morris Agency, 1350 Avenue of the Americas, NYC 10019.

Harold Pinter, *A Slight Ache.* Reprinted by permission of Grove Press, Inc. Copyright 1961 by Harold Pinter.

POETRY

Thomas Hardy. All poems reprinted with permission of Macmillan Publishing Co., Inc. from *Collected Poems* by Thomas Hardy. "The Darkling Thrush," "Channel Firing," "The Voice," "In Time of 'The Breaking of Nations,' " copyright 1925 by Macmillan Publishing Co., Inc. "Snow in the Suburbs," copyright 1925 by Macmillan Publishing Co., Inc., renewed 1953 by Lloyds Bank Ltd.

A. E. Housman. "Loveliest of Trees," "When I was One-and Twenty," "To an Athlete Dying Young," "With Rue My Heart Is Laden," from "A Shropshire Lad"—Authorised Edition—from *The Collected Poems of A. E. Housman.* Copyright 1939, 1940, © 1965 by Holt, Rinehart and Winston. Copyright © 1967, 1968 by Robert E. Symons. "The chestnut casts his flambeaux" from *The Collected Poems of A. E. Housman.* Copyright 1922 by Holt, Rinehart and Winston. Copyright 1950 by Barclays Bank Ltd. Reprinted by permission of Holt, Rinehart and Winston, Publishers.

W. B. Yeats. All poems reprinted with permission of Macmillan Publishing Co., Inc. from *Collected Poems* by William Butler Yeats. "The Lake Isle of Innisfree" and "The Sorrow of Love," copyright 1906 by Macmillan Publishing Co., Inc., renewed 1934 by William Butler Yeats. "No Second Troy," copyright 1912 by Macmillan Publishing Co., Inc., renewed 1940 by Bertha Georgie Yeats. "The Wild Swans at Coole," copyright 1919 by Macmillan Publishing Co., Inc., renewed 1947 by Bertha Georgie Yeats. "Easter 1916," "Leda and the Swan," "Sailing to Byzantium" and "Among School Children," copyright 1928 by Macmillan Publishing Co., Inc., renewed 1956 by Georgie Yeats. "Lapis Lazuli," copyright 1940 by Georgie Yeats, renewed 1968 by Bertha Georgie Yeats, Michael Butler Yeats and Anne Yeats.

Edwin Arlington Robinson. "Miniver Cheevy" (copyright 1907 Charles Scribner's Sons) is reprinted by permission of Charles Scribner's Sons from *The Town Down the River* by Edwin Arlington Robinson. "Mr. Flood's Party" reprinted with permission of Macmillan Publishing Co., Inc. from *Collected Poems* by Edwin Arlington Robinson. Copyright 1921 by Edwin Arlington Robinson, renewed 1949 by Ruth Nivison.

Robert Frost. "After Apple-Picking," "Mending Wall," "The Oven Bird," "Stopping by Woods on a Snowy Evening," "Acquainted with the Night," "Design," "Directive." From *The Poetry of Robert Frost* edited by Edward Connery Lathem. Copyright 1916, 1923, 1928, 1930, 1939, 1947, © 1969 by Holt, Rinehart and Winston. Copyright 1936, 1944, 1951, © 1956, 1958 by Robert Frost. Copyright © 1964, 1967, 1975 by Lesley Frost Ballantine. Reprinted by permission of Holt, Rinehart and Winston, Publishers.

Wallace Stevens. "Sunday Morning," Copyright 1923 and renewed 1951 by Wallace Stevens. "Thirteen Ways of Looking at a Blackbird," Copyright 1923 and renewed 1951 by Wallace Stevens. "To an Old Philosopher in Rome," Copyright 1952 by Wallace Stevens. "The Idea of Order at Key West," Copyright 1936 and renewed 1951 by Wallace Stevens. "The Emperor of Ice-Cream," Copyright 1923 and renewed 1951 by Wallace Stevens. All reprinted from *The Collected Poems of Wallace Stevens,* by permission of Alfred A. Knopf, Inc. "The Course of a Particular," Copyright © 1957 by Elsie Stevens and Holly Stevens. Reprinted from *Opus Posthumous,* edited with an introduction by Samuel French Morse, by permission of Alfred A. Knopf, Inc.

William Carlos Williams. "Portrait of a Lady," "Queen-Ann's-Lace," "The Red Wheelbarrow," "The Yachts," "Proletarian Portrait," from William Carlos Williams, *Collected Earlier Poems.* Copyright 1938 by New Directions Publishing Corporation. Reprinted by permission of New Directions Publishing Corporation. "Landscape with the Fall of Icarus," William Carlos Williams, *Pictures from Brueghel and Other*

Poems. Copyright © 1960 by William Carlos Williams. Reprinted by permission of New Directions Publishing Corporation.

Ezra Pound. "Portrait d'une Femme," "In a Station of the Metro," "The River Merchant's Wife: A Letter," "Medallion," from Ezra Pound, *Personae.* Copyright 1926 by Ezra Pound. Reprinted by permission of New Directions Publishing Corporation.

D. H. Lawrence, "Love on the Farm," "Piano," "Snake," "Bavarian Gentians." From *The Complete Poems of D. H. Lawrence,* edited by Vivian de Sola Pinto and F. Warren Roberts. Copyright © 1964, 1971 by Angelo Ravagli and C. M. Weekley, Executors of The Estate of Frieda Lawrence Ravagli. Reprinted by permission of The Viking Press.

T. S. Eliot. "The Love Song of J. Alfred Prufrock," "Portrait of a Lady," "Sweeney Among the Nightingales," "The Hollow Men," "Journey of the Magi." From *Complete Poems 1909–1962* by T. S. Eliot, copyright, 1936, by Harcourt Brace Jovanovich, Inc.; copyright © 1963, 1964, by T. S. Eliot. Reprinted by permission of the publisher.

Wilfred Owen. "Anthem for Doomed Youth," "Strange Meeting." Wilfred Owen, *Collected Poems.* Copyright Chatto & Windus Ltd. 1946, 1963. Reprinted by permission of New Directions Publishing Corporation.

Emily Dickinson, "If I Shouldn't Be Alive," "There's a Certain Slant of Light," "The Soul Selects Her Own Society," "Because I Could Not Stop for Death," "The Bustle in a House." Reprinted by permission of the publishers and the Trustees of Amherst College from *The Poems of Emily Dickinson,* edited by Thomas H. Johnson, Cambridge, Mass.: The Belknap Press of Harvard University Press, Copyright © 1951, 1955 by the President and Fellows of Harvard College. "After Great Pain," from *The Complete Poems of Emily Dickinson,* edited by Thomas H. Johnson, by permission of Little, Brown and Co.

Gerard Manley Hopkins, "God's Grandeur," "The Windhover," "Pied Beauty," "Thou Art Indeed Just, Lord," from *The Poems of Gerard Manley Hopkins,* 4th ed. (1967), edited by W. H. Gardner and N. H. MacKenzie, published by arrangement with the Society of Jesus. By permission of Oxford University Press.

E. E. Cummings. "O sweet spontaneous," Copyright, 1923, 1951, by E. E. Cummings. "i sing of Olaf," Copyright, 1931, 1959, by E. E. Cummings. "anyone lived in a pretty how town," Copyright, 1940, by E. E. Cummings; copyright, 1968, by Marion Morehouse Cummings. Reprinted from his volume *Complete Poems 1913–62* by E. E. Cummings by permission of Harcourt Brace Jovanovich, Inc.

Hart Crane. "At Melville's Tomb," "The Broken Tower." Reprinted from *The Complete Poems and Selected Letters and Prose of Hart Crane,* edited by Brom Weber. By permission of Liveright Publishing Corporation. Copyright 1933, © 1958, 1966 by Liveright Publishing Corporation.

Allen Tate. Reprinted with permission of Farrar, Straus & Giroux, Inc., "Ode to the Confederate Dead," by Allen Tate, copyright 1927 by The Macaulay Company, copyright renewed 1955 by Allen Tate.

Langston Hughes. "The Negro Speaks of Rivers," Copyright 1926 by Alfred A. Knopf, Inc. and renewed 1954 by Langston Hughes. Reprinted from *Selected Poems,* by Langston Hughes, by permission of Alfred A. Knopf, Inc. "A Dream Deferred," Copyright 1951 by Langston Hughes. Reprinted from *The Panther and the Lash: Poems of Our Times,* by Langston Hughes, by permission of Alfred A. Knopf, Inc. and by permission of Harold Ober Associates Incorporated. "Theme for English B," from *Montage of a Dream Deferred.* Reprinted by permission of Harold Ober Associates Incorporated. Copyright 1951 by Langston Hughes.

W. H. Auden. "The Wanderer," Copyright 1934 and renewed 1962 by W. H. Auden. "Musée des Beaux Arts," and "In Memory of W. B. Yeats," Copyright 1940 and renewed 1968 by W. H. Auden. "In Praise of Limestone," Copyright 1951 by W. H. Auden. All reprinted from *Collected Poems,* by W. H. Auden, edited by Edward Mendelson, by permission of Random House, Inc.

Theodore Roethke. "My Papa's Waltz," copyright 1942 by Hearst Magazines, Inc., and "I Knew A Woman," copyright 1954 by Theodore Roethke from the book *The Collected Poems of Theodore Roethke.* Reprinted by permission of Doubleday & Company, Inc.

Robert Hayden. "Middle Passage." Reprinted from *Angle of Ascent, New and Selected Poems,* by Robert Hayden. By permission of Liveright Publishing Corporation. Copyright © 1975, 1972, 1970, 1966, by Robert Hayden.

Dylan Thomas, "The force that through the green fuse drives the flower," "A Refusal to Mourn the Death, by Fire, of a Child in London," "Do Not Go Gentle into That Good Night," from *The Poems of Dylan Thomas.* Copyright 1939 by New Directions Publishing Corporation, copyright 1945 by the Trustees for the Copyrights of Dylan Thomas. Copyright 1952 by Dylan Thomas. Reprinted by permission of New Directions Publishing Corporation.

John Berryman. All poems reprinted with the permission of Farrar, Straus & Giroux, Inc. "Winter Landscape" by John Berryman, copyright 1940 by John Berryman, copyright renewed 1968 by John Berryman. "Dream Song 14" and "Dream Song 29" from *77 Dream Songs* by John Berryman, copyright © 1959, 1962, 1963, 1964 by John Berryman. "Of Suicide" reprinted with permission of Farrar, Straus & Giroux, Inc. from *Love and Fame* by John Berryman. Copyright © 1970 by John Berryman.

Robert Lowell. "The Drunken Fisherman" from *Lord Weary's Castle,* copyright, 1946, 1974, by Robert Lowell. Reprinted by permission of Harcourt Brace Jovanovich, Inc. "Falling Asleep Over the Aeneid," Copyright, 1948, 1976, by Robert Lowell. Reprinted from his volume *The Mills of the Kavanaughs* by permission of Harcourt Brace Jovanovich, Inc. Reprinted by permission of Farrar, Straus & Giroux, Inc.: "For the Union Dead" from *For the Union Dead* by Robert Lowell, copyright © 1960, 1964 by Robert Lowell; "Artist's Model" from *The Dolphin* by Robert Lowell, copyright © 1973 by Robert Lowell.

Philip Larkin. "Church Going," "Toads," and "At Grass" by Philip Larkin are reprinted from *The Less Deceived* by permission of The Marvell Press, England. "Toads Revisited" reprinted by permission of Faber and Faber Ltd from *The Whitsun Weddings* by Philip Larkin.

A. R. Ammons. "The Misfit," "Cascadilla Falls," "The City Limits" reprinted from *Collected Poems, 1951–1971,* by A. R. Ammons. By permission of W. W. Norton & Company, Inc. Copyright © 1972 by A. R. Ammons.

John Ashbery. "Some Trees" from *Some Trees* by John Ashbery, published by Ecco Press. "These Lacustrine Cities" from *Rivers and Mountains,* by John Ashbery, published by Ecco Press. Reprinted by permission of Georges Borchardt, Inc.

Thomas Kinsella. "A Country Walk," Copyright © 1967, 1968 by Thomas Kinsella. Reprinted from *Nightwalker and Other Poems,* by Thomas Kinsella, by permission of Alfred A. Knopf, Inc.

Adrienne Rich. "Orion," reprinted from *Leaflets, Poems, 1965–1968,* by Adrienne Rich. Copyright © 1969 by W. W. Norton & Company, Inc. "A Valediction Forbidding Mourning," reprinted from *The Will to Change, Poems, 1968–1970,* by Adrienne Rich. Copyright © 1971 by W. W. Norton & Company, Inc. Reprinted by permission of W. W. Norton & Company, Inc.

Ted Hughes. "The Horses" and "The Thought-Fox," Copyright © 1957 by Ted Hughes. From *Selected Poems* (1974) by Ted Hughes. "A Childish Prank" from *Crow* (1971) by Ted Hughes. Copyright © 1971 by Ted Hughes. Reprinted by permission of Harper & Row, Publishers, Inc.

Sylvia Plath. "Elm," "Daddy," "Fever 103°." From *Ariel* (1966) by Sylvia Plath. Copyright © 1965 by Ted Hughes. "Elm" originally appeared in *The New Yorker.* Reprinted by permission of Harper & Row, Publishers, Inc.

CRITICAL ESSAYS

T. S. Eliot, "Tradition and the Individual Talent." From *Selected Essays,* New Edition, by T. S. Eliot, copyright, 1932, 1936, 1950, by Harcourt Brace Jovanovich, Inc.; copyright, 1960, 1964, by T. S. Eliot. Reprinted by permission of the publisher.

William Butler Yeats, "A General Introduction for My Work." Reprinted with permission of Macmillan Publishing Co., Inc. from *Essays and Introductions* by W. B. Yeats. © Mrs. W. B. Yeats, 1961.

Robert Frost, "Education by Poetry." From *Selected Prose of Robert Frost* edited by Hyde Cox and Edward Connery Lathem. Copyright 1939, 1954, © 1966, 1967 by Holt, Rinehart and Winston. Copyright 1946, © 1959 by Robert Frost. Reprinted by permission of Holt, Rinehart and Winston, Publishers.

Allen Tate, "Narcissus as Narcissus." Reprinted from *Essays of Four Decades* © by Allen Tate by permission of The Swallow Press, Inc., Chicago.

John Berryman. Reprinted by permission of Farrar, Straus & Giroux, Inc., "Prufrock's Dilemma," revised form, from *The Freedom of the Poet* by John Berryman, copyright © 1976 by Kate Berryman.

Elizabeth Hardwick, "Sylvia Plath." From *Seduction and Betrayal: Women and Literature,* by Elizabeth Hardwick. Copyright © 1970, 1971, 1972, 1973, 1974 by Elizabeth Hardwick Lowell. Reprinted by permission of Random House Inc. Poetry excerpts: from *Ariel* by Sylvia Plath. Copyright © 1965 by Ted Hughes; from "Last Words" from *Crossing the Water* by Sylvia Plath. Copyright © 1971 by Ted Hughes; from "For A Fatherless Son" from *Winter Trees* by Sylvia Plath. Copyright © 1972 by Ted Hughes. Reprinted by permission of Harper & Row, Publishers, Inc.

William Carlos Williams. "An Essay on Leaves of Grass," copyright 1955 by Florence H. Williams. Reprinted by permission of New Directions Publishing Corporation.

Imamu Amiri Baraka (Leroi Jones), "Expressive Language." Reprinted by permission of William Morrow & Co., Inc. Copyright © 1963, 1966 by Leroi Jones.

Ernest Hemingway. Reprinted by permission of Charles Scribner's Sons from *Death in the Afternoon* by Ernest Hemingway. Copyright 1932 Charles Scribner's Sons.

Alvin Kernan, "The Attempted Dance: A Discussion of the Modern Theatre." From *Classics of the Modern Theatre* edited by Alvin B. Kernan, © 1965 by Harcourt Brace Jovanovich, Inc. and reprinted with their permission.

Edward Albee, "Which Theater is the Absurd One?" Reprinted by permission of William Morris Agency, Inc. Copyright © 1962 by Edward Albee. Orginally printed in the *New York Times.*

E. M. Forster, "Flat and Round Characters." From *Aspects of the Novel* by E. M. Forster, copyright, 1927, by Harcourt Brace Jovanovich, Inc.; copyright, 1955, by E. M. Forster. Reprinted by permission of the publisher.

William H. Gass, "The Concept of Character in Fiction." Copyright © 1970 by William H. Gass. Reprinted from *Fiction and the Figures of Life,* by William H. Gass, by permission of Alfred A. Knopf, Inc., and by permission of International Creative Management.

Lionel Trilling. "Manners, Morals, and the Novel" is reprinted by permission of Charles Scribner's Sons from *The Liberal Imagination* by Lionel Trilling. Copyright © 1976 Diana Trilling.

George Orwell, "Politics and the English Language." From *Shooting an Elephant and Other Essays* by George Orwell, copyright, 1945, 1946, 1949, 1950, by Sonia Brownell Orwell; copyright, 1973, 1974, by Sonia Orwell. Reprinted by permission of Harcourt Brace Jovanovich, Inc.

Index